This is Volume 20 of WEST'S NEW YORK PRACTICE SERIES

West's New York Practice Series

Vol. 1	Walker, et al., New York Limited Liability Companies and Partnerships: A Guide to Law and Practice
Vols. 2-4	Haig, et al., Commercial Litigation in New York State Courts
Vol. 5	Barker and Alexander, Evidence in New York State and Federal Courts
Vol. 6	Greenberg, Marcus, et al., New York Criminal Law
Vol. 7	Marks, et al., New York Pretrial Criminal Procedure
Vol. 8	Davies, Stecich, Gold, et al., New York Civil Appellate Practice
Vol. 9	Ginsberg, Weinberg, et al., Environmental Law and Regulation in New York
Vol. 10	Sobie, et al., New York Family Court Practice
Vols. 11-12	Scheinkman, et al., New York Law of Domestic Relations

Vol. 13	Taber, et al., Employment Litigation in New York
Vols. 14-16	Kreindler, Rodriguez, et al., New York Law of Torts
Vols. 17-19	Field, Moskin, et al., New York and Delaware Business Organizations: Choice, Formation, Operation, Financing and Acquisitions
Vols. 20-25	Ostertag, Benson, et al., General Practice in New York
Vol. 26	Borchers, Markell, et al., New York State Administrative Procedure and Practice
Vol. A	Borges, et al., Enforcing Judgments and Collecting Debts in New York
Vols. B-C	Bensel, Frank, McKeon, et al., Personal Injury Practice in New York
Vols. D-E	Preminger, et al., Trusts and Estates Practice in New York
Vols. F-G	Finkelstein and Ferrara, Landlord and Tenant Practice in New York

COORDINATED RESEARCH IN NEW YORK FROM WEST

New York Practice 2d
David D. Siegel

Handling the DWI Case in New York
Peter Gerstenzang

New York Elder Law Practice
Vincent J. Russo and Marvin Rachlin

WEST'S McKINNEY'S FORMS

Civil Practice Law and Rules

Uniform Commercial Code

Business Corporation Law

Matrimonial and Family Law

Real Property Practice

Estates and Surrogate Practice

Criminal Procedure Law

Not-For-Profit Corporation Law

Tax Practice and Procedure

Local Government Forms

Selected Consolidated Law Forms

McKinney's Consolidated Laws of New York Annotated

West's New York Legal Update

New York Digest

New York Law Finder

PAMPHLETS

New York Civil Practice Law and Rules

New York Sentence Charts

WESTLAW®

COORDINATED RESEARCH FROM WEST

WEST*Check*® and WESTMATE®

West CD–ROM Libraries™

To order any of these New York practice tools, call your West Representative or 1–800–328–9352.

> **NEED RESEARCH HELP?**
>
> **If you have research questions concerning WESTLAW or West Publications, call West's Reference Attorneys at 1–800–733–2889.**

GENERAL PRACTICE IN NEW YORK

By

ROBERT L. OSTERTAG
HON. JAMES D. BENSON

Sections 1.1 to 6.188

ST. PAUL, MINN.
WEST GROUP
1998

GENERAL PRACTICE IN NEW YORK
FORMS ON DISK™

The **Forms on Disk**™ which accompany these volumes provide instant access to WordPerfect 5.1/5.2 versions of the forms included in *General Practice in New York*. These electronic forms will save you hours of time drafting legal documents. The electronic forms can be loaded into your word processing software and formatted to match the document style of your law firm. These electronic forms become templates for you to use over and over without having to retype them each time.

The forms in Volumes 20, 21, 22, 23, 24 and 25 that are included on the accompanying disks are marked with the following disk icon for easy identification.

COPYRIGHT © 1998 By WEST GROUP
610 Opperman Drive
P.O. Box 64526
St. Paul, MN 55164–0526
1–800–328–9352

All rights reserved
Printed in the United States of America
ISBN 0–314–23141–2

TEXT IS PRINTED ON 10% POST CONSUMER RECYCLED PAPER

FOREWORD

The thirty-nine chapters contained in these six volumes are the work of a team of authors, all of whom are among the leading experts in their fields. Each of them has contributed to this work hundreds of hours of time, effort and expertise in order to provide practitioners with the latest and most authoritative substantive and practical information available on subjects extending alphabetically from adoption to zoning. Each chapter provides the reader with a statement of the substantive law on the subject, a discussion of practical approaches to particular but commonly appearing problems, practical hints and guidelines, and useful forms from which the practitioner may meaningfully address his or her client's problems and obtain effective solutions. It is the authors' generosity in sharing their knowledge and expertise that has made this one-of-a-kind New York treatise possible. We thank them all for the quality of their work, their commitment to excellence and their willingness to give so generously of their time—most of it at the expense of their own personal and professional lives.

A decade or so ago, the general practice of law was thought to be something of an anachronism. Clearly, general practice had become a far more demanding exercise than theretofore, brought about primarily by a number of factors, not the least of which was specialization. The increasing complexity of the law and the seemingly constant precedential and legislative changes affecting so many areas of practice made it increasingly difficult to maintain expertise in more than a small handful of substantive areas. That has not changed. Yet, three out of every four private practitioners in this state, indeed in the nation, are or consider themselves to be general practitioners, and that applies to those in large firm settings as well as in solo and small firm offices. Meantime, of course, the specialist has found it increasingly difficult to maintain his or her own particular expertise for similar reasons. For both the general practitioner and the specialist, therefore, useful and authoritative sources of information are the *sine qua non,* indeed the very life blood, of their professional existence.

The information to be found in these volumes, the practice pointers, the many citations, and the many and useful suggested forms and practice hints, all of which will regularly be updated, are meant to address the burdens of the practitioner in satisfying his or her need to know the law, to understand it within the context of his or her clients' needs, to be able to apply it, and to be satisfied in the final analysis that what he or she has accomplished for the client has met the client's needs and constitutes a quality effort that has brought about a quality result. We believe you will find these volumes a particularly useful and valuable addition to your research library.

FOREWORD

We have been privileged to serve as co-editors of this impressive work. Our efforts have involved the investment of additional hundreds of hours of time reading, cite checking, suggesting material revisions here and there (although our distinguished authors brought that part of the effort to a minimum), rereading, rechecking, reforming and occasionally updating. But the reward has been a priceless education in many areas of the law with which we were not as familiar as we might have been, or as to which we inexplicably thought we pretty much knew it all, only to learn we didn't. Thanks so much to our authors.

Finally, we would like to acknowledge the contributions of Marilyn K. Minzer, Manager of New York Practice Products for West Group, and her very able assistant, Terry Yard. They have provided us with a particularly unique insight into West Group's highly competent and professional product development program. Thanks so much.

ROBERT L. OSTERTAG
HON. JAMES D. BENSON

January 1998

ABOUT THE CO-EDITORS-IN-CHIEF

Robert L. Ostertag has practiced privately in a small upstate urban setting for thirty-seven years. Prior to that, he served as a United States Air Force Judge Advocate and as a Staff Attorney for the Internal Revenue Service at its Washington, D.C., headquarters. He is a graduate of Fordham University, where he obtained his Bachelor of Arts Degree, St. John's University School of Law, where he obtained his law degree, and of the Georgetown University Law Center, where he acquired a Masters in Law degree in Taxation and Estate Planning. He practices primarily in the areas of estate planning and administration, corporate law and litigation.

Mr. Ostertag served for fifteen years as an adjunct Professor of Paralegal Studies at Marist College in Poughkeepsie, New York, and currently is an Adjunct Professor of Law at the Fordham University School of Law.

Mr. Ostertag has been actively involved in organized bar activities for many years, primarily on behalf of solo and small firm practitioners. He has served as President of the New York State Bar Association and the Dutchess County Bar Association and is a many-year-long member of both the New York State's and the American Bar Association's Houses of Delegates. He is also a Director of the New York Bar Foundation.

He was instrumental in forming the New York State Bar Association's General Practice Section and served as its charter chairman. He also created the ABA General Practice Section's Conference of State Bar General Practice Leaders (now GP Link), an entity designed to provide a free flow of information among general practice sections and committees and their constituencies throughout the nation. He successfully led the debate within the New York State Bar Association's House of Delegates in support of a mandatory plan of continuing legal education in New York (a plan ultimately adopted by the Administrative Board of the Courts), and he successfully initiated a recent State Bar effort to permit the sale of law practices in New York, a current rule of primary significance to solo and small firm general practitioners. He presently is engaged on behalf of the American Bar Association's Senior Lawyers Division in encouraging the adoption of similar legislation or rules throughout the nation.

Mr. Ostertag has been the author of charters and administrative codes for at least five counties throughout the State of New York, and of ethics codes for several municipalities, and he has been the recipient of awards in recognition of his service to both the profession and his community. He continues to offer his time and services to the organized bar,

ABOUT THE CO-EDITORS–IN–CHIEF

and at present he chairs a State Bar Association's Special Committee on the Future of the Profession.

The Honorable James D. Benson is admitted to practice in the State of New York as well as to practice in the United States District Court for the Southern District of New York, the Circuit Court of Appeals for the Second Circuit, the United States Supreme Court and the Tax Court of the United States.

James D. Benson has practiced law in New York State in partnership and as a sole practitioner. He has served as a confidential law secretary to a Justice of the New York State Supreme Court, as the County Attorney of Dutchess County, New York, as the County Executive of Dutchess County, New York. He was the Surrogate of Dutchess County, New York and an Acting Justice of the New York State Supreme Court from 1983 until 1992.

He was the Coordinator of Court Facilities for the Ninth Judicial District of New York from 1987 until 1989 and has been a member of the New York State Bar Association's Committee on Court Facilities from 1987 until the present time. During his term as Surrogate of Dutchess County he served as the New York State Surrogates' delegate to the New York State Judicial Conference. He now serves as a Judicial Hearing Officer in the Ninth Judicial District and the Third Judicial District of the State of New York in the counties of Westchester, Putnam, Rockland, Orange, Columbia, Ulster, Greene and Albany.

He is of counsel to the law firm of Van DeWater and Van DeWater of Poughkeepsie, New York where he has practiced law since June, 1992.

Judge Benson is a member of the Executive Committee of the Dutchess County Environmental Management Counsel and Chairman of the Long Range Planning Committee of the New York YMCA, Holiday Hills Branch. He is a trustee of the Sharon Corporation.

He conducted a seminar in conjunction with Charles Groppe at the New York State Judicial Seminar in Rochester, New York on the Prudent Man Rule and has addressed seminars on estate planning and estate management for the Dutchess County and New York State Bar Associations.

ABOUT THE CONTRIBUTING AUTHORS

Miriam R. Adelman (*Chapter 22, Guardianship*) earned a B.A., *cum laude,* from Brooklyn College, City University of New York, and a J.D. from Brooklyn Law School. She was admitted to the New York Bar in 1967, the Supreme Court of the United States in 1974, and the Eastern and Southern Districts of New York in 1979. She was for many years a writer, editor and manager at Matthew Bender & Co., Inc. She is currently in private practice concentrating in wills and estates and has written extensively about Surrogate's Court practice for publications such as Warren's Heaton on Surrogate's Courts and Cox, Arenson, Medina, NYCP-Surrogate's Court Procedure Act (Matthew Bender). She is the author of "Surrogate Decision Making in the Absence of Advance Directives," *Elder Law Advisory,* May 1997 and contributor to *Planning Issues for Older New Yorkers,* New York State Bar Association, Committee on Women in the Law (New York State Bar Association, 1996).

She is a member of the Association of the Bar of the City of New York, Committee on the Legal Problems of the Aging, NAELA, and the New York State Bar Association, Trusts and Estates and Elder Law Sections and the Committee on Women in the Law.

Norman B. Arnoff (*Chapter 28, Legal Malpractice*), a member of the New York City firm of Capuder & Arnoff, P.C., has been in private practice for over twenty years with a focus on professional liability of lawyers, accountants and securities brokers, having practiced extensively in both federal and state courts, before federal regulatory agencies and in securities arbitrations. His career also includes government service with the SEC, the Department of Justice and the FDIC. After successfully defending a lawyer falsely accused of fraud and malpractice, he argued the first Rule 11 sanctions case in the United States Supreme Court, *Pavilic & Leflore v. The Marvel Entertainment Group,* which led directly to the 1993 amendments to Federal Rule of Civil Procedure 11, to provide for the sanctioning of law firms for their lawyers' frivolous conduct. Since 1991 he has co-authored a regular column for the *New York Law Journal* on lawyers' and accountants' liability matters, and in 1992-1995 he served as the Chairperson of the Lawyers Professional Liability Committee of the New York County Lawyers' Association. He is a periodic contributor to CCH's Business Strategies and Andrews Professional Liability Reporter and has been a frequent presenter of courses, seminars and papers for the ABA, PLI, chapters of the N.Y.S. Society of CPA's, New York County Lawyers' Association and numerous other groups. He holds B.A. (*Phi Beta Kappa*) and J.D. degrees from New York University.

Ralph W. Bandel (*Chapter 3, Municipal Law*) is a member of the law firm of O'Connell and Aronowitz in its Albany, New York office. He

ABOUT THE CONTRIBUTING AUTHORS

has had more than 20 years experience in all aspects of municipal law. Following graduation from law school in 1973, Mr. Bandel served for 13 years in the Municipal Law Bureau of the State Comptroller's Office which has responsibility for audit and oversight of all municipalities and school districts in the state. While with that office, he was primarily responsible for the preparation of more than 1,500 published advisory legal opinions and he regularly counseled municipalities and school districts on a wide range of legal issues affecting their day-to-day activities.

Since entering private practice in 1988, Mr. Bandel has served as bond counsel for municipalities, school districts and public authorities on numerous financings. He also has represented various municipalities as special counsel in connection with solid waste matters, industrial development projects, the creation of special improvement districts and other special projects. He is a member of the Executive Committee of the Municipal Law Section of the New York State Bar Association and Chairman of the Section's Legislative Committee and also a member of the National Association of Bond Lawyers.

Suzanne M. Berger (*Chapter 11, Mortgage Foreclosure*) is special counsel at Robinson Silverman Pearce Aronsohn & Berman LLP. Her areas of speciality include litigation affecting problem loans, with particular emphasis on real estate mortgage foreclosures and related litigation. She is a graduate of Fordham University School of Law where she was an Associate Editor of the *Fordham Law Review*. Ms. Berger is a member of the Bars of the State of New York, the United States District Courts for the Southern and Eastern Districts of New York, the Second Circuit Court of Appeals and the United States Supreme Court. She received a B.A. from Barnard College, Columbia University (1978) and a J.D. from Fordham University School of Law (1984).

Patrick J. Borchers (*Chapter 4, New York Administrative Law*) is a Professor of Law and Associate Dean at Albany Law School of Union University. After graduation from law school, he served as a law clerk to the Hon. Anthony M. Kennedy—then of the Ninth Circuit Court of Appeals—and practiced law with a Sacramento, California law firm. He is the author of West's ***New York State Administrative Procedure and Practice*** and several articles on constitutional and administrative law topics and has taught administrative law since arriving at Albany Law School in 1990. He is a member of the California (inactive status) and New York Bars.

Martin H. Brownstein (*Chapter 37, Civil Appellate Practice Before the Appellate Division and Other Intermediate Appellate Courts, Chapter 38, Criminal Appellate Practice Before the Appellate Division and Other Intermediate Appellate Courts, Chapter 39, Civil and Criminal Appeals to the Court of Appeals*) has been the Clerk of the Appellate Division, Second Judicial Department, since 1986. He has been with the court since

ABOUT THE CONTRIBUTING AUTHORS

1970 serving as a staff lawyer, supervisor of the Decision Department and Deputy Clerk. He has lectured on appellate practice for the New York State Bar Association and many local Bar associations. In 1993 he was the recipient of the Brooklyn Bar Association's Nathan R. Sobel award for distinguished service to the legal community. He and his wife Susan have two children and live in Rockland County.

Abraham M. Buchman (*Chapter 36, Alcoholic Beverage Control Law*), the founding partner of Buchman & O'Brien, received his Bachelor of Law degree, *cum laude,* from St. Lawrence University in 1938 and his Doctor of Judicial Science degree, *summa cum laude,* from St. Lawrence University in 1939. Mr. Buchman is a member of the bar in New York and is admitted to practice before the U.S. District Court, Southern District of New York, the U.S. Court of Appeals and the U.S. Supreme Court. He is also admitted to practice before the U.S. Interstate Commerce Commission. Mr. Buchman is a member of the American Bar Association, the Federal Bar Association, the Association of Interstate Commerce Commission Practitioners, the Federal Bar Council and the International Bar Association. Although Mr. Buchman's legal career has focused on alcoholic beverage control, his practice includes all areas of administrative law, with appearances before the Bureau of Alcohol, Tobacco & Firearms, Securities and Exchange Commission, Interstate Commerce Commission, Internal Revenue Service, New York State Liquor Authority, New York State Department of Taxation and Finance, as well as other federal and state agencies. He has served as counsel to the American Wine Association, the Vermouth Institute, and the American Beverage International Alcohol Association.

Prior to practicing law, Mr. Buchman was employed as a plant manager and controller of Athan Import and Export Corp., a producer of domestic wines and importer and distributor of foreign wines. With sixty-six years of experience in the alcoholic beverage industry, as both an industry member and as an attorney, Mr. Buchman is truly an elder statesman in this field. At 81 years of age, Mr. Buchman still actively practices law and frequently speaks before regional and national gatherings of both the National Conference of State Liquor Administrators and the National Alcohol Beverage Association on various topics relating to alcoholic beverage control.

Joseph R. Carrieri (*Chapter 20, Adoptions*) is a member of the firm of Carrieri & Carrieri, P.C., Mineola, New York and specializes in family law, particularly foster care and adoptions. He holds a B.S. from Fordham University 1958 and an L.L.B. from Fordham University School of Law 1961. He has written extensively on the field of foster care and adoptions having authored the book, *Child Custody: Foster Care and Adoptions* (Lexington Press); he has written numerous books for the Practising Law Institute on the subject of child abuse, neglect and the foster care system and has chaired the Practising Law Institute's Semi-

ABOUT THE CONTRIBUTING AUTHORS

nar on foster care and adoption for the past 20 years. He is the commentator for *McKinney's Social Services Law* and *Vehicle and Traffic Laws* and has written extensively for the *New York Law Journal* on the subject of foster care and adoptions. He has lectured at seminars sponsored by the Nassau County Bar Association, Suffolk Social Services Administration, Administration for Child Services, City of New York and for various child care agencies. Mr. Carrieri represents St. Christopher-Ottilie and Little Flower Children's Services, two of the largest voluntary child care agencies in New York State.

Stuart M. Cohen (*Chapter 37, Civil Appellate Practice Before the Appellate Division and Other Intermediate Appellate Courts, Chapter 38, Criminal Appellate Practice Before the Appellate Division and Other Intermediate Appellate Courts, Chapter 39, Civil and Criminal Appeals to the Court of Appeals*) is Clerk of the New York Court of Appeals, which he served as Deputy Clerk for nine years before assuming his present position. Mr. Cohen has also served as law clerk to a Chief Judge and an Associate Judge of the Court of Appeals, and as a law assistant to the Justices of the Supreme Court, Appellate Division, Second Department. A frequent lecturer and author on Court of Appeals and New York appellate practice, Mr. Cohen also has teaching and private practice experience. He received his Bachelor's degree from Connecticut College and his Juris Doctor degree from New York University School of Law.

Jayne E. Daly (*Chapter 16, Land Use Law*) is the Co-Director of the Land Use Law Center at Pace University School of Law. The Land Use Law Center works with government and not-for-profit organizations throughout the state and region to promote cost-effective land uses and development patterns. Recently, the Law Center received a federal grant to create the Community Leadership Alliance, a program to train local leaders in land use policies that foster watershed protection.

In addition to her work with the Law Center, Ms. Daly is the Ciba Research Professor, a professorship endowed at Pace Law School by Ciba-Geigy in recognition of the need to strengthen and coordinate land development and conservation law and policy. In that capacity, she works with students on environmental issues in the corporate context and teaches in the areas of environmental law and land use. Professor Daly received her J.D. *magna cum laude* from Pace Law School with a Certificate in Environmental Law and a B.A. in History from Marymount College *summa cum laude*. She is admitted to practice law in the states of New York and New Jersey.

Warren A. Estis (*Chapter 13, Landlord-Tenant Law*) is a founding partner of Rosenberg & Estis, P.C., a New York City law firm specializing in commercial and real estate litigation and transactions. He is the firm's lead trial attorney and supervises and trains litigators in preparing for trial. He has litigated cases on such diverse issues as commercial

ABOUT THE CONTRIBUTING AUTHORS

and transactional disputes, partnership disputes, brokerage commissions, mortgage foreclosures, residential and commercial landlord/tenant disputes—rent strikes, summary non-payment and holdover proceedings, co-op and condo disputes, loft litigation, declaratory judgments and actions for injunctive relief.

Mr. Estis is the editor and co-author of the Landlord/Tenant Law Column in the *New York Law Journal*. He is a member of the Housing Advisory Council of the Civil Court of the City of New York and serves on the Committee on Civil Courts of the Association of the Bar of the City of New York. He is also a member of the Housing Court Task Force of the Association of the Bar of the City of New York, a member of the Civil Court Practice Section of the New York County Lawyers' Association and the Real Property Division of the American Bar Association.

Mr. Estis received his undergraduate degree from Long Island University, C.W. Post College, and his law degree from Brooklyn Law School. He would like to acknowledge the work of Mary Ann Hallenborg, Esq. in the preparation of his chapter.

Myrna Felder (*Chapter 21, Domestic Relations*) is a matrimonial lawyer who practices in both the trial and appellate levels. A contributor of chapters to Lindey, *Separation Agreements and Antenuptial Contracts;* and *New York Appellate Practice* published by Matthew Bender, she authors a bi-monthly column on Family Law for the *New York Law Journal*. A popular lecturer for all the major bar associations on domestic relations topics, Ms. Felder has also been an instructor for the New York State Judicial Seminar, Supreme Court Law Secretarys and New York City Civil Court Judges. A member of the New York State Office of Court Administration's Civil Practice Advisory Committee, Ms. Felder chairs its Subcommittee on Matrimonial Procedures. She would like to acknowledge the work of Susan Weisenfeld, Esq. in the preparation of her chapter.

James B. Fishman (*Chapter 7, Consumer Law*) is a member of Fishman & Neil. His practice involves all areas of consumer law on behalf of consumers, including automobile Lemon Law, automobile fraud cases, consumer credit, deceptive business practices cases, credit reporting matters and illegal debt collection claims. Mr. Fishman is a graduate of Bard College (1976) and New York Law School (1979). He is admitted to the Bar of the State of New York as well as the bars of the United States Supreme Court, the United States Court of Appeals for the Second Circuit and the Southern and Eastern District of New York. He is a charter member of the National Association of Consumer Advocates. Mr. Fishman served as an Assistant Attorney General in the Bureau of Consumer Frauds and Protection of the New York State Department of Law and as a Senior Staff Attorney with the Civil Division of The Legal Aid Society. Mr. Fishman's publications include Lemon Law pleadings from

ABOUT THE CONTRIBUTING AUTHORS

Walker v. General Motors, published by Bender's Forms, CPLR Art. 75, 1994 edition; "Applying Consumer Protection Laws in Landlord-Tenant Disputes" New York State Bar Association Continuing Legal Education Committee, October, 1994; "Purchase of New and Used 'Lemons'," *Caveat Venditor,* Julius Blumberg, Inc., New York, New York, 1994; "New York Needs A Private Right Of Action For Debt Collection Abuses," *New York Law Journal,* p. 1, June 23, 1983.

Mary Beth Forshaw *(Chapter 31, Insurance)* is a graduate of Barnard College and the Yale Law School. She is a partner at the law firm of Simpson Thacher & Bartlett in New York City. She has worked in the firm's Litigation Department throughout her tenure. Her areas of practice include insurance coverage, reinsurance, franchise law, bankruptcy, securities fraud and general commercial litigation.

Robert M. Freedman *(Chapter 23, Elder Law)* is a partner in the law firm of Freedman and Fish. He practices in the areas of Elder Law and Trusts and Estates. Mr. Freedman is a Founder and past Chair of the Elder Law Section of the New York State Bar Association and he has chaired the New York State Bar Association Continuing Legal Education Programs on Elder Law for the past ten years. Mr. Freedman is also a Fellow, a Founder and a former member of the Board of Directors of the National Academy of Elder Law Attorneys. Prior to the founding of the firm of Freedman and Fish, Mr. Freedman was an Assistant Clinical Professor at the Benjamin N. Cardozo School of Law, a staff attorney at Legal Services for the Elderly and a staff attorney at the Institute of Law and Rights of Older Adults at the Brookdale Center on Aging of Hunter College. Mr. Freedman is a graduate of Tufts University and New York University School of Law.

The Honorable Bertram R. Gelfand *(Chapter 25, Probate and Estate Administration)* received a B.A. from New York University in 1951 and a LL.B. from New York University School of Law in 1952. He was admitted to the New York Bar in 1953. After graduation, Judge Gelfand served in the Adjutant General Corps of the United States Army and as an Assistant District Attorney and City Councilman. In 1972, he was elected Surrogate, Bronx County, a position he held until 1987. As Surrogate, Judge Gelfand authored several opinions which led to major statutory amendments. Judge Gelfand served as Special Counsel to the New York City Commissioner of Housing Preservation and Development from 1988 to 1990 and is currently in private practice specializing in trusts and estates.

He is the author of numerous articles. Judge Gelfand is a recipient of the Emilio Nunez Award from the Puerto Rican Bar Association for Service to the Hispanic Community and has been honored by the Metropolitan Women's Bar Association and the Black Bar Association of Bronx County.

ABOUT THE CONTRIBUTING AUTHORS

Peter Gerstenzang (*Chapter 33, Local Criminal Court Practice*) is the senior partner in the Albany, New York law firm of Gerstenzang, O'Hern, Hickey & Gerstenzang. He is a well known criminal defense lawyer with a practice that ranges from Long Island to Buffalo, and throughout upstate New York. The author of West's ***Handling the DWI Case in New York***, he specializes in the defense of driving while intoxicated cases and vehicular crimes.

Mr. Gerstenzang commenced his legal career as a prosecutor for the United States Army in the Republic of Vietnam. From 1972 to 1975, he was an Assistant District Attorney for the County of Albany. For 12 years, he taught at the New York State Police Academy in their DWI Breathalyzer training program and was certified as a Breathalyzer operator.

In addition to trying DWI and vehicular crimes cases, he serves on the faculty of the Office of Court Administration Judges Training Program, and lectures for the New York State Bar Association, as well as numerous defense and law enforcement organizations. He is Co-Chairman of the New York State Bar Association's Committee on Traffic Safety.

Lee S. Goldsmith (*Chapter 29, Medical Malpractice*) is a member of the firm of Goldsmith & Richman.

Dr. Goldsmith is a graduate of New York University School of Medicine and its School of Law. He has served as President of the American College of Legal Medicine and as President of the Association of Trial Lawyers-New Jersey. He has taught the course of Law and Medicine at the Fordham University School of Law. He is currently Co-Chairman of the joint committee between the Bergen County Medical Society and the Bergen County Bar Association in New Jersey. His practice in both the States of New York and New Jersey has covered all of the areas of law and medicine with a special emphasis on the problems associated with medical malpractice litigation. Dr. Goldsmith has edited and written multiple books and articles including the seven volume set entitled *Medical Malpractice, Guide to Medical Issues*. He is a member of the American Medical Association, a Fellow of the New York Academy of Medicine, a member of the Association of the Bar of the City of New York and the New York State Trial Lawyers' Association.

Norman S. Goldsmith (*Chapter 30, Damages*) specializes in general civil litigation in the state and federal courts. Prior to establishing his own practice, he was a partner in the firm of Jones, Hirsch, Connors and Bull.

He received his J.D. from Yale Law School where he was an Associate Editor of the *Yale Law Journal*. Among his works while on the Law Journal were publications on "Deportable Aliens and Physical Persecu-

ABOUT THE CONTRIBUTING AUTHORS

tion" and "The Use of the Sherman Antitrust Act to Eliminate Discrimination in Housing."

Mr. Goldsmith is an Adjunct Professor of Law at the Jacob D. Fuchsberg Law Center at Touro College where he teaches New York practice and insurance law. He recently replaced Professor David Siegel, who returned to Albany Law School, at the "Court Careers" Review Course, and lectures on the CPLR to New York State Court Clerks in the New York Court System.

Mr. Goldsmith is a member of the American Association of Trial Lawyers, New York State Trial Lawyers' Association, New York State Bar Association, the Association of the Bar of the City of New York and the New York County Lawyers' Association, and has lectured extensively at Bar Association programs on a variety of topics including "Estoppel and the Statute of Limitations" and "Reargument, Renewal and Reconsideration."

Sandra D. Grannum (*Chapter 28, Legal Malpractice*) is an Associate General Counsel for PaineWebber. She was previously associated with Tenzer Greenblatt LLP in New York City and has handled professional liability matters for securities broker/dealers before federal and state courts, arbitration panels, regulatory agencies and disciplinary boards. Prior to that she was associated with Cravath, Swaine & Moore. Her experience includes all phases of commercial and securities litigation, trials and appeals; stock exchange investigations; and handling Minority Business Certification Appeals before New York State. She has served on seminar panels for New York County Lawyers' Association on such topics as lawyers' professional liability defenses and amendments to Federal Rule 11, and for the Association of the Bar of the City of New York she serves on Committees on Courts of Superior Jurisdiction and Women in the Profession. She holds a B.A. from New York University and a J.D. from Harvard Law School.

Ronald David Greenberg (*Chapter 1, Business Organizations: Corporations*) has taught business law and taxation at Columbia University (1970-94) and is working on a textbook on international business law and taxation. He was counsel to Delson & Gordon (1973-87) and continues to practice law as a solo practitioner, dividing his time between corporate and individual clients. His corporate practice includes experience with both small close corporations and large multinationals. He has been a Visiting Professor at Stanford University (1978) and Harvard University (1981), has chaired the Committees on Corporations, Banking and Business Law and on Taxation (American Bar Association, General Practice Section) and the Committees on Business Law and on Tax Law (New York State Bar Association, General Practice Section), and is chair of the Editorial Advisory Board of the *New York International Law Review*. He has a Bachelor of Science degree from the University of Texas

ABOUT THE CONTRIBUTING AUTHORS

(physics and engineering), an M.B.A. from Harvard Business School, and J.D. from Harvard Law School. He is the author of, and has reviewed, publications on business law and taxation, with his articles appearing in such journals as the *Business Lawyer, California Law Review,* and *Urban Lawyer.* He has been a lecturer and consultant in training programs for commercial banks, investment banks, and other organizations.

David Grunblatt (*Chapter 19, Immigration and Nationality Law: Permanent Residence Applications*) is a partner in Wildes & Weinberg, a New York City law firm specializing in immigration and nationality law. He serves as Chair of the New York Chapter of the American Immigration Lawyers' Association and was formerly Chair of that association's National Committee on Ethics and Professional Responsibility. He was Chair of the Committee on Immigration and Nationality Law at the New York County Lawyers' Association, and directed its Continuing Legal Education Program on Immigration and Nationality Law and the Pro Bono Immigration Defense Project. He lectures and writes extensively on the subject of immigration and nationality law. Mr. Grunblatt received his undergraduate degree from Brooklyn College and his law degree and LL.M. in Taxation from New York University School of Law.

John H. Haley (*Chapter 28, Legal Malpractice*), a member of the New York City firm Harrington Haley LLP, has engaged in an insurance/reinsurance practice in New York City for over twenty years, with a specialty in professional liability, including that of attorneys, accountants, directors and officers, actuaries, bank fiduciary services, employee benefit consultants, insurance brokers, reinsurance intermediaries, real estate brokers, and public officials. He has also practiced extensively in the areas of reinsurance and insurer insolvency, in 1990 having won a leading reinsurance case at the New York Court of Appeals, *Sumitomo Marine & Fire Ins. Co. v. Cologne Reinsurance Co.* In addition to long experience defending insureds, he has extensive expertise in coverage litigation, policy drafting, arbitration and serving as an expert witness. Mr. Haley is the author of the chapter "Directors and Officers Liability Insurance" in Matthew Bender & Co.'s multi-volume legal treatise, *New York Insurance Law.* He has been a frequent seminar speaker on professional liability matters for such groups as The Wyatt Company's D&O Liability Symposiums, Institutional Investor's Corporate Financial Executive Roundtable, Risk and Insurance Management Society, and others. He currently chairs the Lawyers' Professional Liability Committee of the New York County Lawyers' Association. Mr. Haley is a graduate of Fordham University School of Law.

Lawrence Kaplan (*Chapter 5, Commercial Sales Contracts*) received a B.S. from the City College of New York in 1968 and a J.D. from St. John's University School of Law in 1974. He was admitted to practice before the New York Bar in 1974. For more than twenty years, Mr. Kaplan was a writer, editor, manager and director at Matthew Bender &

ABOUT THE CONTRIBUTING AUTHORS

Co., Inc. He has been associated, in one capacity or another, with the publication of many hundreds of titles in areas ranging from New York and federal practice to corporate law and taxation. He assisted in the creation of Bender's New York Practice Guide Series, and has contributed to such publications as *Weinstein, Korn and Miller: New York Civil Practice, Moore's Federal Practice* and *Business Organizations with Tax Planning*. He has also authored several articles for *ALR Federal*: "What Constitutes 'Trade Secrets and Commercial or Financial Information Obtained From a Person and Privileged or Confidential,' Exempt From Disclosure under the Freedom of Information Act"; and "Propriety and Prejudicial Effect in Civil Trial of Federal Judge's Disparaging Remarks Concerning Party, Witness or Attorney." For many years, Mr. Kaplan also represented indigent criminal defendants in appeals before the Appellate Division, under the Bar Association's Plan for Providing Counsel for Indigent Defendants in New York City. Mr. Kaplan is currently working as a legal researcher and writer.

Carolyn A. Kubitschek (*Chapter 34, Social Security Disability Cases*) is an attorney in private practice with the law firm of Lansner & Kubitschek in New York City, where she specializes in Social Security and federal practice. She has litigated Social Security cases at administrative hearings, Appeals Council reviews, in federal district courts, and in the Second Circuit Court of Appeals. Her cases include *Cruz v. Sullivan*, 912 F.2d 8 (2d Cir.1990).

Ms. Kubitschek started one of the first Social Security disability projects in a federally-funded legal services program and has been an Assistant Clinical Professor of Law at Hofstra University. She has also lectured and written extensively on the subject of Social Security disability law and practice.

Ms. Kubitschek is the author of *Social Security Disability Law and Procedure in Federal Court,* published by Clark Boardman Callaghan in 1994. Her writings have also appeared in the *New York Law Journal, Pittsburgh Law Review, The Arizona Law Review* and *Am. Jur. Trials*. Ms. Kubitschek graduated from Oberlin College and the University of Chicago Law School.

Roxanne H. Levine (*Chapter 19, Immigration and Nationality Law: Permanent Residence Applications*) is an associate with the law firm of Wildes & Weinberg in New York City. Admitted to the New York Bar in 1985, she received her J.D. degree (1984) from The Touro School of Law. Ms. Levine earned a Master of Science degree in History (1981) and a Bachelor of Arts degree (1978) from Yeshiva University. She is a member of the American Immigration Lawyers Association.

David L. Markell (*Chapter 4, Administrative Law*) is Associate Professor of Law at Albany Law School of Union University. Before joining the law school's faculty, Professor Markell served as Director of the New

ABOUT THE CONTRIBUTING AUTHORS

York Department of Environmental Conservation's Division of Environmental Enforcement. Professor Markell also spent several years practicing law with the federal government and in private practice in Washington, D.C. He serves on the Executive Committee of the New York State Bar Association's Environmental Law Section, is the co-author of West's *New York State Administrative Procedure and Practice* and author of several articles on administrative law and environmental law topics, and has testified on such topics before Congress and the New York State Legislature. He is a member of the New York and District of Columbia (inactive status) bars.

Martin Minkowitz (*Chapter 32, Workers' Compensation*) is a partner in the law firm of Stroock & Stroock & Lavan. He was Deputy Superintendent and General Counsel of the New York State Insurance Department for seven years; prior to that he was General Counsel of the New York State Workers' Compensation Board for five years. Before appointment to public service, he was a senior partner in a New York City law firm for twelve years. He has a Master of Laws degree.

Mr. Minkowitz writes the Commentaries to *McKinney's New York Workers' Compensation Law,* he has written extensively on a broad range of topics, and his articles have appeared in several American Bar Association, Practising Law Institute and New York State Bar Association publications, and other professional magazines and journals. He is also the co-author of several legal texts. He is on the Editorial Board of the University of Rochester Medical Center, "Journal of Occupational Rehabilitation."

He is an Adjunct Professor of Law at New York Law School. He is a member of the Advisory Board of the College of Insurance. He is a frequent lecturer on a variety of topics for the American Bar Association, Continuing Legal Education Program of the New York State Bar Association; the Practising Law Institute; New York Chamber of Commerce Workshop Programs, College of Insurance, and numerous professional, labor and industry organizations.

Mr. Minkowitz is the Chair of the General Practice Section Committee on Workers' Compensation of the New York State Bar Association. He served as the Chair of the Committee on Professional Discipline and is presently a member. He is also a member of the Committee on Judicial Selection of the New York State Bar Association. He is a member of the Board of Directors of the New York County Lawyers' Association.

Arthur M. Neiss (*Chapter 8, Enforcement of Money Judgments*), a 1985 graduate of Fordham University School of Law, practices with the firm of Greene & Zinner, P.C. in White Plains, New York. Specializing in commercial litigation, his practice includes bankruptcy litigation, construction law, insurance law and creditors' rights. Mr. Neiss is the instructor of the Enforcement of Money Judgments course in the Continu-

ABOUT THE CONTRIBUTING AUTHORS

ing Legal Education Department of Fordham University School of Law, in New York City. He is a member of the Bars of New York, New Jersey and various federal courts; the Banking/Creditors' Rights Committee of the Commercial and Federal Litigation Section of the New York State Bar Association; the American Bar Association; the Association of the Bar of the City of New York and the New York County Lawyers' Association.

John R. Nolon (*Chapter 16, Land Use Law*) is a tenured Professor of Law at Pace University School of Law, where he teaches property, land use and environmental law and is the Director of the law school's Land Use Law Center. Professor Nolon received a Fulbright Scholarship to develop a framework law for sustainable development in Argentina where he worked during 1994 through 1996; he also conducted research and wrote on the subjects of regulatory takings and land use planning law under a Research Professorship Award in 1991.

Professor Nolon received his J.D. degree from the University of Michigan where he was a member of the Barrister's Academic Honor Society and received his undergraduate degree from the University of Nebraska, where he was President of the Senior Honor Society. He has served as a consultant to both President Carter's Council on Development Choices for the 1980's and President Clinton's Council on Sustainable Development.

Professor Nolon's writings include over a dozen law review articles and a book published by McGraw Hill. He is a frequent guest speaker at national, state, and local conferences in his areas of expertise.

E. Vincent O'Brien (*Chapter 36, Alcoholic Beverage Control Law*) is a senior partner in the New York office of Buchman & O'Brien. He was born in 1937 in Jersey City, New Jersey. He is a *magna cum laude* graduate of Fordham University (B.S.–valedictorian), a *summa cum laude* graduate of New York University Graduate School of Business (M.B.A.–valedictorian), a *cum laude* graduate of Fordham University School of Law (J.D.–salutarian) and a graduate of New York University Graduate School of Law (LL.M. in Taxation).

Mr. O'Brien has practiced beverage alcohol law since 1963, when he joined the Wall Street law firm of White & Case and was assigned to its Seagram account. Five years later Mr. O'Brien joined Seagram as Assistant General Counsel and was subsequently elected General Counsel, Vice President and Director, and was elevated to Executive Vice President while maintaining his roles as General Counsel and Director.

In 1979, Mr. O'Brien joined forces with Abe Buchman to found the beverage alcohol specialty firm of Buchman & O'Brien. Mr. O'Brien represents beverage alcohol clients in all aspects of the beer, wine and spirits industries in all parts of the world. He has maintained his interna-

ABOUT THE CONTRIBUTING AUTHORS

tional expertise while continuing as member and past Chairman of the United States delegation to the International Federation of Wines & Spirits (the world's largest association of international wine and spirits producers).

Mr. O'Brien has served as Executive Vice President and Executive Committee member of The Distilled Spirits Council of the United States, as a Director and Executive Committee member of The National Association of Beverage Importers, as a member of the United States delegation to the *Office International de la Vigne et du Vin* ("OIV") (the international association of wine regulators), and as a BATF and Wine Institute representative on the Wine Law, Regulations and Controls and Appellations of Origin working groups. He also has made presentations at The World Intellectual Property Organization and at several OIV sponsored international wine symposia. He represents several United States trade associations including Wine Institute, President's Forum of the Beverage Alcohol Industry, and American Brandy Association.

A charter member of the International Wine Lawyers Association, Mr. O'Brien has been a frequent guest lecturer at major international wine and spirits conferences, festivals and trade shows such as the annual Impact seminars, VinItaly, VinExpo (France), Intervittis (Germany), Pacific Rim Wine Festival (Australia) and the 100th anniversary of the St. Emillion Wine Association.

Barry R. Ostrager (*Chapter 31, Insurance*) is a senior litigation partner at the law firm of Simpson Thacher & Bartlett in New York City where he supervises the firm's insurance and reinsurance practices. Mr. Ostrager and his firm frequently serve as national coordinating counsel for various insurers with respect to insurance and reinsurance issues. He has been lead trial counsel in many major insurance coverage cases, including *Shell Oil Co. v. Winterthur Swiss Insurance Co.*, a multi-billion dollar environmental insurance coverage dispute in which the jury returned a verdict for the insurers after a 16-month trial. Mr. Ostrager has also been lead counsel in major reinsurance coverage cases, including *North River Insurance Co. v. CIGNA Reinsurance Corp.* in which the United States Court of Appeals for the Third Circuit definitively clarified the law concerning the "follow the fortunes" doctrine.

Mr. Ostrager is co-author of the *Handbook on Insurance Coverage Disputes* (Aspen Law & Business 1995), a widely used reference now in its eighth edition. The *Handbook* has been cited by dozens of appellate courts, including the United States Supreme Court, the New York Court of Appeals and the United States Courts of Appeal for the First, Second, Third, Fourth, Sixth, Seventh, Ninth, Tenth and Eleventh Circuits. He is also co-author of the recently published treatise entitled *Modern Reinsurance Law and Practice* (Glasser Legal Works 1995). Mr. Ostrager lectures extensively on insurance and reinsurance issues and has Co-

ABOUT THE CONTRIBUTING AUTHORS

Chaired the Practising Law Institute's program *Insurance, Excess and Reinsurance Coverage Disputes* for the past fourteen years.

Mr. Ostrager has been prominently involved in many high-profile non-insurance cases. For example, Mr. Ostrager successfully represented Manufacturers Hanover Trust Company in a securities fraud action against Arthur Andersen & Co., obtaining a $24 million jury award which was affirmed on appeal. In 1993, Mr. Ostrager was lead trial and appellate counsel for Paramount Communications in the widely publicized *QVC v. Paramount* tender offer litigation. Recently, Mr. Ostrager successfully argued before the United States Supreme Court the closely followed *Epstein v. Matsushita* case.

Wayne N. Outten (*Chapter 17, Employment Law*) is a member of Lankenau Kovner Kurtz & Outten, LLP, New York, New York. He specializes in representing individual employees in all areas of employment law and in civil litigation. Mr. Outten was a founding member of the Executive Board of the National Employment Lawyers Association and is the founder and president of the New York affiliate of that organization. In addition, he is a Co-Chair of the Committee on Employee Rights and Responsibilities of the Section on Labor and Employment Law of the American Bar Association and is an active member of the New York State Bar Association's Labor & Employment Law Section. Mr. Outten has lectured extensively on employment law, especially on negotiation and mediation of employment disputes and on privacy issues. He received his B.S. from Drexel University in 1970 and received his J.D. from New York University School of Law in 1974, where he was an Arthur Garfield Hays Civil Liberties Fellow. He was a law clerk for United States District Court Judge Gus J. Solomon, District of Oregon, 1974-76. His writings include *The Rights of Employees and Union Members* (S. Ill. Univ. Press, 2d edition 1994) and the "Privacy in the Employment Relationship" chapter in *Privacy Law and Practice* (Matthew Bender 1987). He is a member of the Board of Directors of the New York Civil Liberties Union (and its Nassau Chapter) and is its Secretary.

Frances M. Pantaleo (*Chapter 23, Elder Law*) is associated with the firm of Keane and Beane in White Plains, New York. She is a member of the Executive Committee of the New York State Bar Association Elder Law Section as Liaison with Law School Professors and Teachers. She was formerly an Adjunct Professor of Law at Pace University School of Law where she taught Legal Problems of the Elderly and an Associate Clinical Professor of Law at Benjamin N. Cardozo School of Law where she also served as Assistant Director of the Bet Tzedek Legal Services Clinic which represents elderly and disabled individuals. She has been a Lecturer at New York University School of Social Work and a Staff Attorney with the Civil Division of the Legal Aid Society in New York City and Brooklyn Office for the Aging. She often writes and speaks on elder law topics for lawyers, law students, social workers and lay people. She

ABOUT THE CONTRIBUTING AUTHORS

was a presenter at the 3rd Annual Symposium on Elder Law of the National Academy of Elder Law Attorneys. Professor Pantaleo is a 1979 graduate of New York University School of Law.

Mark S. Pelersi (*Chapter 6, Buying and Selling a Small Business*) is an attorney and Certified Public Accountant who has been actively engaged in the practice of law and accounting for over twenty years. He received his Bachelor of Business Administration in Accounting from Siena College, Loudonville, New York and his Juris Doctor from Albany Law School of Union University, Schenectady, New York. In addition to practicing law, he has served as an Adjunct Business Law Professor at SUNY Albany, New York. Mr. Pelersi is also a frequent lecturer and panel faculty member at seminars on such topics as "Drafting Corporate Documents for the Close Corporation," "Limited Liability Companies: The Entity of Choice in New York," "Forming and Advising a New Business Entity" and "Tax Deferred Exchanges Under I.R.C. Section 1031" sponsored by several organizations including the New York State Bar Association, The National Business Institute, Dean Witter Reynolds Inc.

Mr. Pelersi is admitted to practice in the United States Supreme Court, United States Tax Court, the United States District Courts for the Northern and Western Districts of New York as well as all New York State Courts.

He maintains an office in Albany, New York.

Jack A. Raisner (*Chapter 17, Employment Law*) is Associate Professor of Law, St. John's University, College of Business Administration. He practices law with the Manhattan firm Lankenau Kovner Kurtz & Outten, LLP, representing plaintiffs in employment disputes. He serves as Co-Chair of the Drug and Alcohol Abuse in the Workplace Subcommittee of the Committee on Employee Rights and Responsibilities (Section on Labor and Employment Law) of the American Bar Association, and chairs the Employment and Labor Section of the Academy of Legal Studies in Business. Mr. Raisner co-authored *New York Employment Complaints and Answers\FAST* (West), chapters in *Employment Litigation in New York* (West), *Employee Rights Litigation: Pleading & Practice* (Matthew Bender Co.), and *Disability Discrimination in the Workplace* (Callaghan), and has contributed articles to many journals, and other publications, including "Employment Discrimination in the Second Circuit District Courts 1993-1994," 14 *Quinnipiac Law Review* 707 (1994). Mr. Raisner received his B.S. from Boston University (1978) and J.D. from Benjamin N. Cardozo School of Law (1983).

John J. Rapisardi (*Chapter 9, Bankruptcy*) is a member of Weil, Gotshal & Manges, LLP, a law firm with domestic and international offices. Mr. Rapisardi represents various multi-debtor corporations and individuals in chapter 11 and numerous creditors in in-court and out-of-court proceedings. Mr. Rapisardi is an Adjunct Professor at Pace Univer-

ABOUT THE CONTRIBUTING AUTHORS

sity School of Law, teaching a Creditors" Rights and Bankruptcy Course. He is the Bankruptcy Practice columnist for the *New York Law Journal*, authoring articles on recent cases of interest. Mr. Rapisardi holds a B.S. in accounting from Fordham University (1979–*Beta Gamma Sigma*), a J.D. from Pace University School of Law (where he was a member of the law review) (1982) and an LL.M. in commercial and corporate law from New York University School of Law (1986). Mr. Rapisardi is presently a member of the American Bankruptcy Institute, American and New York Bar Associations, and has lectured frequently in the field of debtors' and creditors' rights. Mr. Rapisardi is also a mediator for the Bankruptcy Court in the Southern District of New York.

James E. Reid (*Chapter 26, Personal Injury*) is a partner of Greene and Reid of Syracuse, where he limits his practice to personal injury litigation. He is a member and former Chair of the New York State Bar Association's General Practice Section and is a former Chair of that Section's Insurance Negligence, Compensation and Litigation Committee. He is also a member of the New York State Bar Association's Trial Lawyers Section Committee of Certification and Specialization. In addition, Mr. Reid is a member of ATLA, NYSTLA, the Onondaga County Bar Association and president of the Upstate Trial Lawyers Association. Mr. Reid has authored several publications, including *Service of Process Manual for the Attorney* and "Handling the Plaintiff's Personal Injury Case" in the *New York Lawyer's Deskbook and Formbook* (NYSBA, 1994). He is a life member of the Board of Visitors of Syracuse University College of Law and is listed in Who's Who in American Law, Fourth Edition.

Patricia Youngblood Reyhan (*Chapter 14, Eminent Domain*) is a Professor at Albany Law School of Union University, where she has taught for 17 years. Professor Reyhan has written numerous articles and co-authored a number of books in the fields of real property and international law. Professor Reyhan received her B.A. from Washington State University, her J.D. from Willamette University College of Law and her LL.M. from Harvard Law School.

Bernard M. Rifkin (*Chapter 12, Purchase and Sale of Real Estate*) is chief counsel emeritus for the Title Guarantee Company in New York. He received his LL.B. from Columbia Law School, his LL.M. from New York University School of Law and was admitted to practice in New York in 1949. Mr. Rifkin is a member of the American Bar Association and the Association of the Bar of the City of New York. He is also a member of the New York State Bar Association and is active in its Real Property Law Section. He has written articles on real property law for the *New York Law Journal, New York State Bar Journal,* and other publications. Mr. Rifkin is a past Chairman of the Real Property Law Section of the New York State Bar Association and a former Adjunct Professor of Law at New York University School of Law.

ABOUT THE CONTRIBUTING AUTHORS

Mr. Rifkin has lectured for Continuing Legal Education programs for the Practising Law Institute, the Association of the Bar of the City of New York, the New York County Lawyers' Association, the New York State Bar Association and the Real Property Section of the New York State Bar Association.

William J. Robbins (*Chapter 13, Landlord–Tenant Law*) is a partner in Rosenberg & Estis, P.C., a New York City law firm specializing in commercial and real estate litigation and transactions. He concentrates in commercial landlord/tenant litigation in Supreme Court and Civil Court. Mr. Robbins is presently, and has been since 1993, co-author of the Landlord/Tenant Law Column in the *New York Law Journal*.

He is a Harvard Law School graduate (1976), and received his undergraduate degree from Yale University. He would like to acknowledge the work of Mary Ann Hallenborg, Esq. in the preparation of his chapter.

Francisco J. Rodriguez (*Chapter 29, Medical Malpractice*) is an associate with the offices of Goldsmith & Richman, a law firm specializing in medical malpractice, health care law and Federal Tort Claims Act matters, with offices in New York City and Englewood Cliffs, New Jersey.

Mr. Rodriguez concentrates on plaintiff's medical malpractice and is a member of the New York and New Jersey Bars. He has previously written on "Using the Internet to Win Your Next Medical Negligence Case" with Howard S. Richman, published in the September 1996 issue of the *ATLA Professional Negligence Law Reporter*.

Mr. Rodriguez received his undergraduate degree from Rutgers College and his law degree from New York University School of Law, where he was the Executive Editor of the *Review of Law and Social Change*.

The Honorable Albert M. Rosenblatt (*Chapter 37, Civil Appellate Practice Before the Appellate Division and Other Intermediate Appellate Courts, Chapter 38, Criminal Appellate Practice Before the Appellate Division and Other Intermediate Appellate Courts, Chapter 39, Civil and Criminal Appeals to the Court of Appeals*) is a Justice of the Supreme Court, Appellate Division Second Department, where he has served since 1989. From 1987 to 1989 he was the Chief Administrative Judge of the State of New York. His trial experience includes terms as Supreme Court Justice in the Ninth Judicial District, County Judge of Dutchess County and District Attorney of Dutchess County. He is a member of the Board of Editors of the *New York State Bar Journal*, and has written numerous legal and popular articles for publications including the *New York State Bar Journal*, the *New York Law Journal*, *The New York Times*, *Harper's Magazine*, *The Baker Street Journal*, and *Ski Magazine*. He has lectured widely, and has written works on New York appellate practice. He is a

ABOUT THE CONTRIBUTING AUTHORS

graduate of the University of Pennsylvania and Harvard Law School, where he has served as Judge of the Ames Moot Court Competition.

Gideon Rothschild (*Chapter 24, Estate Planning*) is a partner with the New York City law firm of Siller Wilk LLP, specializing in estate planning and asset protection planning. He is on the Board of Advisors for the Journal of Asset Protection and The Practical Accountant. He has authored numerous articles for publications including the *New York Law Journal, Journal of Asset Protection* and *Estate Planning*. Mr. Rothschild is a member of the American Bar Association, the Offshore Institute, the Estate Planning Council of New York and the National Academy of Elder Law Attorneys. He has lectured frequently on asset protection and estate planning to professional groups including the New York University Federal Tax Institute, the New York State Bar Association, the American Bar Association (program chair) and the American Institute of Certified Public Accountants. Mr. Rothschild holds a B.B.A. from Baruch College (1973) and J.D. from New York Law School (1980) and is also licensed as a Certified Public Accountant.

Steven Russo (*Chapter 15, Environmental Law*) practices environmental law at Sive, Paget & Riesel, P.C. in New York City. Mr. Russo represents clients in a wide array of environmental matters, including environmental litigation under the federal Clean Water Act, the Resource Conservation and Recovery Act, Superfund, the New York State Environmental Quality Review Act and state tidal and freshwater wetlands laws. From 1992-1995, Mr. Russo served as an Assistant Corporation Counsel in the Environmental Law Division of the New York City Corporation Counsel's office, and was Deputy Assistant Chief of that division from 1994 to 1995. He graduated from Columbia Law School, where he was Head Articles Editor of the *Columbia Journal of Environmental Law* and a Harlan Fiske Stone Scholar.

Michele A. Santucci (*Chapter 6, Buying and Selling a Small Business*) is a principal of the Troy, New York law firm of Pattison, Sampson, Ginsberg and Griffin, P.C. She is a graduate of Manhattanville College and the George Mason University School of Law, and is admitted to practice in New York State and the District of Columbia. Ms. Santucci serves clients in the areas of business organization law, not-for-profit corporations, taxation and related matters including business-based immigration. She lectures frequently in these areas for the New York State Bar Association (Continuing Legal Education Program) and for other professional organizations, including the National Business Institute. Ms. Santucci sits on numerous not-for-profit boards and currently serves as the Rensselaer County Coordinator for the New York State Bar's Mock Trial Program.

Stuart A. Schlesinger (*Chapter 27, Products Liability*) is a partner in Julien & Schlesinger, P.C., New York, New York. He has a broad

ABOUT THE CONTRIBUTING AUTHORS

based litigation background with a specialty in products liability, medical malpractice, personal injury and commercial matters. Mr. Schlesinger is a graduate of the University of Wisconsin and Fordham University School of Law. He is an Adjunct Professor at New York Law School where he teaches a Medical/Legal Trial Workshop. New York Law School honored him with the John Marshall Harlan Award in 1994.

Mr. Schlesinger is a sustaining member and has served as an officer in numerous bar associations including the Association of Trial Lawyers of America and the New York State Trial Lawyers' Association.

Together with his partner, David B. Turret, he co-authors a regular column on Products Liability Law for the *New York Law Journal*.

David Schmudde (*Chapter 35, Income Tax*) is an Associate Professor of Law at Fordham University School of Law, where he teaches income tax, corporate tax, partnership tax, tax procedure, property and real estate finance. He is also an Adjunct Professor at the Fordham Graduate School of Business where he teaches tax procedure. He is a member of the Bars of New York and Florida, and is admitted to practice in the United States Tax Court and various federal courts. He serves as a mediator in the United States District Court, Southern District of New York. He is a member of the Committee on Taxation of the American Bar Association. Professor Schmudde has previously served as a legislative attorney for the Office of Chief Counsel to the Internal Revenue Service in Washington, D.C. and had been a Senior Trial Attorney for the Internal Revenue Service in New York. He is a graduate of University of Florida College of Law. Professor Schmudde is a contributing editor of the *Real Estate Tax Digest* and has published numerous articles on taxation.

Jacqueline B. Stuart (*Chapter 9, Bankruptcy*) is a member of the Business Finance and Restructuring Department of Weil, Gotshal & Manges, a law firm with domestic and international offices. Ms. Stuart is a graduate of Barnard College, Columbia University (A.B., 1963) and Columbia University (M.A., 1967). She earned a J.D. *cum laude* from Benjamin N. Cardozo School of Law (1990), where she was Supervising Editor of Law Review and received the Benjamin N. Cardozo Award for Best Law Review Note. Since joining Weil, Gotshal & Manges in 1990, Ms. Stuart has represented both debtors and creditors in out-of-court restructurings and cases under the Bankruptcy Code. She is the Managing Editor and a frequent contributor to the firm's monthly newsletter, *Bankruptcy Bulletin*, and also is author or co-author of articles that have appeared in the *Journal of Commercial Lending* and the *New York Law Journal*.

Marilyn Trautfield Sugarman (*Chapter 18, Civil Rights Law*) is a court attorney in the Law Department of the Supreme Court of the State of New York, New York County. Formerly, Ms. Sugarman was an Assis-

ABOUT THE CONTRIBUTING AUTHORS

tant Attorney General in the New York State Attorney General's office, where she represented state agencies and employees in civil rights and employment discrimination actions. She received her undergraduate degree from Cornell University in 1981 and her law degree from Brooklyn Law School in 1984, where she was an editor of the *Journal of International Law* and received the Brooklyn Journal of International Law Writing Award for Best Note. After law school graduation, Ms. Sugarman was a *pro se* law clerk in the United States District Court for the Southern District of New York. Ms. Sugarman is the draft author of the chapter on Rule 25 of the Federal Rules of Civil Procedure for the third edition of *Moore's Federal Practice* (published by Matthew Bender & Co. 1997).

Jeffrey L. Tanenbaum (*Chapter 9, Bankruptcy*) is a member of Weil, Gotshal & Manges, LLP, a law firm with domestic and international offices. A *cum laude*, Phi Beta Kappa graduate of the State University of New York at Binghamton (B.A.–1973) and graduate with honors from, and a member of the law review at, the State University of New York at Buffalo School of Law (J.D.–1976), Mr. Tanenbaum has extensive experience in all aspects of debtors' and creditors' rights, as well as in real-estate workouts and bankruptcies. He joined Weil, Gotshal & Manges' Business Finance and Restructuring Department in 1978 and has represented borrowers, lenders and investors in out-of-court restructurings and chapter 11 cases both in the Southern District of New York and throughout the United States. He is a Business Watch Columnist for the *National Law Journal*, authoring articles on major bankruptcy decisions emanating from the Supreme and Circuit Courts. He is presently a member of the American Bankruptcy Institute, American and New York Bar Associations, and has lectured extensively in the field of debtors' and creditors' rights.

Laurence S. Tauber (*Chapter 10, Mechanic's Liens*) is with the firm of Gratch Jacobs & Brozman, P.C., where his practice concentrates on securities, mergers and acquisitions and real estate law. He has written extensively and has contributed to the following legal treatises and publications: *White on New York Corporations, Powell on Real Property, Real Estate Financing, Business Organizations with Tax Planning, Benders Forms for the Civil Practice,* and *Weinstein, Korn & Miller, CPLR Manual*. Mr. Tauber graduated *magna cum laude* from Brooklyn College of the City University of New York and received his law degree from New York University School of Law.

David B. Turret (*Chapter 27, Products Liability*) is a partner in Julien & Schlesinger, P.C., New York, New York. He specializes in federal and state litigation, including products liability, medical malpractice, personal injury and commercial matters. Mr. Turret is a graduate of New York University and Fordham University School of Law. Following

ABOUT THE CONTRIBUTING AUTHORS

law school, Mr. Turret served as law secretary to the Honorable Arthur Markewich of the Appellate Division, First Department.

Since January 1995, Mr. Turret has been a member of the faculty at the New York University Institute of Paralegal Studies where he teaches courses in litigation and basic and advanced research and writing.

Together with his partner, Stuart A. Schlesinger, he co-authors a regular column on Products Liability Law for the *New York Law Journal*.

Karon S. Walker (*Chapter 2, Non-Corporate Entities: Limited Liability Companies and Partnerships*) is a partner in the New York City law firm of Christy & Viener, where she is a member of the Corporate and Financial Services group. She is lead author and editor of *New York Limited Liability Companies and Partnerships, a Guide to Law and Practice*, published by West Publishing Company in 1995 and the author of several other pieces on New York LLCs and partnerships, including *New York and Delaware Business Entities: Choice, Formation, Operation, Financing and Acquisitions* published by West Group in 1997. Ms. Walker is a graduate of Williams College and received her law degree from Columbia University in 1984. She is a Rhodes Scholar.

Robert A. Wolf (*Chapter 11, Mortgage Foreclosure*) Mr.Wolf is a litigation partner at Robinson Silverman Pearce Aronsohn & Berman LLP. His areas of specialty include litigation affecting problem loans, with particular emphasis on real estate mortgage foreclosures, foreclosures on Uniform Commercial Code interests involving cooperatives, the law regarding guarantees and the negotiation of workout agreements. Mr.Wolf chaired the Practising Law Institute's annual program on "How to Handle Your First Foreclosure" from 1991 through 1994. He also co-chaired the New York State Bar Association's 1995 program on Mortgage Foreclosures and Workouts and is a member of the New York State Bar Association Task Force to Reform the Mortgage Foreclosure Laws. Mr. Wolf received a B.A. from Princeton University (1973) and a J.D. from New York University School of Law (1976).

Mr. Wolf and Suzanne M. Berger, the co-authors of the within chapter on Mortgage Foreclosure, wish to dedicate the chapter to the memory of Saul Pearce, Esq., a founding partner of Robinson Silverman Pearce Aronsohn & Berman LLP, and their beloved mentor, who helped guide them through the complex maze of New York's foreclosure process and who with his unique style, instilled within them the knowledge and interest that made the writing of the chapter possible. Thank you, Saul.

*

WESTLAW® ELECTRONIC RESEARCH GUIDE

Coordinating Legal Research with WESTLAW

The *New York Practice Series* is an essential aid to legal research. WESTLAW provides a vast, online library of over 8000 collections of documents and services that can supplement research begun in this publication, encompassing:

- Federal and state primary law (statutes, regulations, rules, and case law), including West's editorial enhancements, such as headnotes, Key Number classifications, annotations

- Secondary law resources (texts and treatises published by West Group and by other publishers, as well as law reviews)

- Legal news

- Directories of attorneys and experts

- Court records and filings

- Citators

Specialized topical subsets of these resources have been created for more than thirty areas of practice.

In addition to legal information, there are general news and reference databases and a broad array of specialized materials frequently useful in connection with legal matters, covering accounting, business, environment, ethics, finance, medicine, social and physical sciences.

This guide will focus on a few aspects of WESTLAW use to supplement research begun in this publication, and will direct you to additional sources of assistance.

Databases

A database is a collection of documents with some features in common. It may contain statutes, court decisions, administrative materials, commentaries, news or other information. Each database has a unique identifier, used in many WESTLAW commands to select a database of interest. For example, the database containing New York cases has the identifier NY-CS.

The WESTLAW Directory is a comprehensive list of databases with information about each database, including the types of documents each

WESTLAW ELECTRONIC RESEARCH GUIDE

contains. The first page of a standard or customized WESTLAW Directory is displayed upon signing on to WESTLAW, except when prior, saved research is resumed. To access the WESTLAW Directory at any time, enter DB.

Databases of potential interest in connection with your research include:

NY-AG	New York Attorney General Opinions
NYETH-EO	New York Ethics Opinions
NYETH-CS	Legal Ethics & Professional Responsibility - New York Cases
WLD-NY	West's Legal Directory - New York
LAWPRAC	The Legal Practice Database

For information as to currentness and search tips regarding any WESTLAW database, enter the SCOPE command SC followed by the database identifier (e.g., SC NY-CS). It is not necessary to include the identifier to obtain scope information about the currently selected database.

WESTLAW Highlights

Use of this publication may be supplemented through the WESTLAW Bulletin (WLB), the WESTLAW New York State Bulletin (WSB-NY) and various Topical Highlights. Highlights databases contain summaries of significant judicial, legislative and administrative developments and are updated daily; they are searchable both from an automatic list of recent documents and using general WESTLAW search methods for documents accumulated over time. The full text of any judicial decision may be retrieved by entering FIND.

Consult the WESTLAW Directory (enter DB) for a complete, current listing of highlights databases.

Retrieving a Specific Case

The FIND command can be used to quickly retrieve a case whose citation is known. For example:

FI 616 A.2d 1336

Updating Case Law Research

There are a variety of citator services on WESTLAW for use in updating research.

Insta-Cite® may be used to verify citations, find parallel citations, ascertain the history of a case, and see whether it remains valid law. References are also provided to secondary sources, such as Corpus Juris Secundum®, that cite the case. To view the Insta-Cite history of a displayed case, simply enter the command IC. To view the Insta-Cite history of a selected case, enter a command in this form:

IC 574 A.2d 502

Shepard's® Citations provides a comprehensive list of cases and publications that have cited a particular case, with explanatory analysis to indicate how the citing cases have treated the case, e.g., "followed," "explained." To view the Shepard's Citations about a displayed case, enter the command SH. Add a case citation, if necessary, as in the prior Insta-Cite example.

For the latest citing references, not yet incorporated in Shepard's Citations, use Shepard's PreView® (SP command) and QuickCite™ (QC command), in the same way.

To see a complete list of publications covered by any of the citator services, enter its service abbreviation (IC, SH, SP or QC) followed by PUBS. To ascertain the scope of coverage for any of the services, enter the SCOPE command (SC) followed by the appropriate service abbreviation. For the complete list of commands available in a citator service, enter its service abbreviation (IC, SH, SP or QC) followed by CMDS.

Retrieving Statutes, Court Rules and Regulations

Annotated and unannotated versions of the New York statutes are searchable on WESTLAW (identifiers NY-ST-ANN and NY-ST), as are New York court rules (NY-RULES) and New York Administrative Code (NY-ADC).

The United States Code and United States Code - Annotated are searchable databases on WESTLAW (identifiers USC and USCA, respectively), as are federal court rules (US-RULES) and regulations (CFR).

In addition, the FIND command may be used to retrieve specific provisions by citation, obviating the need for database selection or search. To FIND a desired document, enter FI, followed by the citation of the desired document, using the full name of the publication, or one of the abbreviated styles recognized by WESTLAW.

If WESTLAW does not recognize the style you enter, you may enter one of the following, using US, NY, or any other state code in place of XX:

FI XX-ST	Displays templates for codified statutes
FI XX-LEGIS	Displays templates for legislation
FI XX-RULES	Displays templates for rules
FI XX-ORDERS	Displays templates for court orders

Alternatively, entering FI followed by the publication's full name or an accepted abbreviation will normally display templates, useful jump

WESTLAW ELECTRONIC RESEARCH GUIDE

possibilities, or helpful information necessary to complete the FIND process. For example:

FI USCA	Displays templates for United States Code - Annotated
FI FRAP	Displays templates for Federal Rules of Appellate Procedure
FI FRCP	Displays templates for Federal Rules of Civil Procedure
FI FRCRP	Displays templates for Federal Rules of Criminal Procedure
FI FRE	Displays templates for Federal Rules of Evidence
FI CFR	Displays templates for Code of Federal Regulations
FI FR	Displays templates for Federal Register

To view the complete list of FINDable documents and associated prescribed forms, enter FI PUBS.

Updating Research in re Statutes, Rules and Regulations

When viewing a statute, rule or regulation on WESTLAW after a search or FIND command, it is easy to update your research. A message will appear on the screen if relevant amendments, repeals or other new material are available through the UPDATE feature. Entering the UPDATE command will display such material.

Documents used to update New York statutes are also searchable in New York Legislative Service (NY-LEGIS). Those used to update rules are searchable in New York Orders (NY-ORDERS).

Documents used to update federal statutes, rules, and regulations are searchable in the United States Public Laws (US-PL), Federal Orders (US-ORDERS) and Federal Register (FR) databases, respectively.

When documents citing a statute, rule or regulation are of interest, Shepard's Citations on WESTLAW may be of assistance. That service covers federal constitutional provisions, statutes and administrative provisions, and corresponding materials from many states. The command SH PUBS displays a directory of publications which may be Shepardized on WESTLAW. Consult the WESTLAW manual for more information about citator services.

Using WESTLAW as a Citator

For research beyond the coverage of any citator service, go directly to the databases (cases, for example) containing citing documents and use standard WESTLAW search techniques to retrieve documents citing specific constitutional provisions, statutes, standard jury instructions or other authorities.

Fortunately, the specific portion of a citation is often reasonably distinctive, such as 22:636.1, 301.65, 401(k), 12-21-5, 12052. When it is, a search on that specific portion alone may retrieve applicable documents without any substantial number of inapplicable ones (unless the number happens to be coincidentally popular in another context).

Similarly, if the citation involves more than one number, such as 42 U.S.C.A. §1201, a search containing both numbers (e.g., 42 +5 1201) is likely to produce mostly desired information, even though the component numbers are common.

If necessary, the search may be limited in several ways:

A. Switch from a general database to one containing mostly cases within the subject area of the cite being researched;

B. Use a connector (&, /S, /P, etc.) to narrow the search to documents including terms which are highly likely to accompany the correct citation in the context of the issue being researched;

C. Include other citation information in the query. Because of the variety of citation formats used in documents, this option should be used primarily where other options prove insufficient. Below are illustrative queries for any database containing New York cases:

N.Y.Const.! Const.! Constitution /s 6 VI +3 3

will retrieve cases citing the New York State Constitution, Art. 6, §3; and

"Criminal Procedure Law" CPL /s 30.30

will retrieve cases citing Criminal Procedure Law §30.30.

Alternative Retrieval Methods

WIN® (WESTLAW Is Natural™) allows you to frame your issue in plain English to retrieve documents:

Does new trial motion extend (toll) the time for filing (taking) appeal?

Alternatively, retrieval may be focused by use of the Terms and Connectors method:

TO(30) /P DI(NEW +1 TRIAL /P EXTEND!
EXTENSION TOLL! /P APPEAL)

In databases with Key Numbers, either of the above examples will identify Appeal and Error ⟴345.1 as a Key Number collecting headnotes relevant to this issue if there are pertinent cases.

Since the Key Numbers are affixed to points of law by trained specialists based on conceptual understanding of the case, relevant cases that were not retrieved by either of the language-dependent methods will often be found at a Key Number.

WESTLAW ELECTRONIC RESEARCH GUIDE

Similarly, citations in retrieved documents (to cases, statutes, rules, etc.) may suggest additional, fruitful research using other WESTLAW databases (e.g., annotated statutes, rules) or services (e.g., citator services).

Key Number Search

Frequently, case law research rapidly converges on a few topics, headings and Key Numbers within West's Key Number System that are likely to contain relevant cases. These may be discovered from known, relevant reported cases from any jurisdiction; Library References in West publications; browsing in a digest; or browsing the Key Number System on WESTLAW using the JUMP feature or the KEY command.

Once discovered, topics, subheadings or Key Numbers are useful as search terms (in databases containing reported cases) alone or with other search terms, to focus the search within a narrow range of potentially relevant material.

For example, to retrieve cases with at least one headnote classified to Appeal and Error ⇨345.1, sign on to a caselaw database and enter

    30k345.1 [use with other search terms, if desired]

The topic name (Appeal and Error) is replaced by its numerical equivalent (30) and the ⇨ by the letter k. A list of topics and their numerical equivalents is in the WESTLAW Reference Manual and is displayed in WESTLAW when the KEY command is entered.

Using JUMP

WESTLAW's JUMP feature allows you to move from one document to another or from one part of a document to another, then easily return to your original place, without losing your original result. Opportunities to move in this manner are marked in the text with a JUMP symbol (▶). Whenever you see the JUMP symbol, you may move to the place designated by the adjacent reference by using the Tab, arrow keys or mouse click to position the cursor on the JUMP symbol, then pressing Enter or clicking again with the mouse.

Within the text of a court opinion, JUMP arrows are adjacent to case cites and federal statute cites, and adjacent to parenthesized numbers marking discussions corresponding to headnotes.

On a screen containing the text of a headnote, the JUMP arrows allow movement to the corresponding discussion in the text of the opinion,

    ▶ (3)

WESTLAW ELECTRONIC RESEARCH GUIDE

and allow browsing West's Key Number System beginning at various heading levels:

- ▶ 30   APPEAL AND ERROR
- ▶ 30VII   Transfer of Cause
- ▶ 30VII(A)   Time of Taking Proceedings
- ▶ 30k343   Commencement of Period of Limitation
- ▶ 30k345.1 k.   Motion for new trial.

To return from a JUMP, enter GB (except for JUMPs between a headnote and the corresponding discussion in opinion, for which there is a matching number in parenthesis in both headnote and opinion). Returns from successive JUMPs (e.g., from case to cited case to case cited by cited case) without intervening returns may be accomplished by repeated entry of GB or by using the MAP command.

General Information

The information provided above illustrates some of the ways WESTLAW can complement research using this publication. However, this brief overview illustrates only some of the power of WESTLAW. The full range of WESTLAW search techniques is available to support your research.

Please consult the WESTLAW Reference Manual for additional information or assistance or call West's Reference Attorneys at 1-800-REF-ATTY (1-800-733-2889).

For information about subscribing to WESTLAW, please call 1-800-328-9352.

*

SUMMARY OF CONTENTS

Page

Volume 20

Chapter
1. Business Organizations: Corporations — 2
2. Non-corporate Entities: Limited Liability Companies and Partnerships — 253
3. Municipal Law — 403
4. Administrative Law — 468
5. Commercial Sales Contracts — 594
6. Buying and Selling a Small Business — 670

Volume 21

7. Consumer Law — 2
8. Enforcement of Money Judgments — 181
9. Bankruptcy — 253
10. Mechanic's Liens — 541
11. Mortgage Foreclosure — 683
12. Purchase and Sale of Real Estate — 792

Volume 22

13. Landlord–Tenant Law — 2
14. Eminent Domain — 108
15. Environmental Law — 212
16. New York Land Use Law — 296
17. New York Employment Law — 467
18. Civil Rights Law — 609
19. Immigration and Nationality Law—Permanent Residence Applications — 733
20. Adoptions — 857

Volume 23

21. Domestic Relations — 2
22. Guardianship — 162
23. Elder Law — 329
24. Estate Planning — 448
25. Probate and Estate Administration — 545
26. Personal Injury — 638

XLI

SUMMARY OF CONTENTS

Chapter | Page
27. Products Liability | 722

Volume 24

28. Legal Malpractice | 2
29. Medical Malpractice | 92
30. Damages | 166
31. Insurance | 251
32. Workers' Compensation | 315
33. Local Criminal Court Practice | 382
34. Social Security Disability Cases | 452
35. Income Tax | 551
36. Alcoholic Beverage Control Law | 653
37. Civil Appellate Practice Before the Appellate Division and Other Intermediate Appellate Courts | 738

Volume 25

38. Criminal Appellate Practice Before the Appellate Division and Other Intermediate Appelllate Courts | 2
39. Civil and Criminal Appeals to the Court of Appeals | 145

Table of Jury Instructions | 235
Table of Forms | 236
Table of Statutes | iii
Table of Rules | iii
Table of Cases | iii
Index | iii

TABLE OF CONTENTS

Volume 20

CHAPTER 1. BUSINESS ORGANIZATIONS: CORPORATIONS

Sec.
- 1.1 Scope Note.
- 1.2 Strategy.
- 1.3 Strategy Checklist.
- 1.4 Overview.
- 1.5 Definitions.
- 1.6 Formation of Corporations.
- 1.7 ___ Certificates; Notices.
- 1.8 ___ Corporate Seal.
- 1.9 ___ Corporate Purposes.
- 1.10 ___ ___ Upholding and Disregarding the Corporate Entity.
- 1.11 ___ ___ General Powers.
- 1.12 ___ ___ Defense of *Ultra Vires*.
- 1.13 ___ Corporate Name.
- 1.14 ___ ___ Reservation of Name.
- 1.15 ___ Service of Process.
- 1.16 ___ ___ Records and Certificates of Department of State.
- 1.17 ___ ___ Statutory Designation of Secretary of State as Agent for Service of Process.
- 1.18 ___ ___ Registered Agent for Service of Process.
- 1.19 ___ ___ Upon Unauthorized Foreign Corporation.
- 1.20 ___ Incorporators and Promoters.
- 1.21 ___ Certificate of Incorporation.
- 1.22 ___ Bylaws.
- 1.23 ___ Organization Meeting; Biennial Statement; Franchise Tax.
- 1.24 ___ Formation of Corporations Summary.
- 1.25 ___ Formation of Corporations Checklist.
- 1.26 Capital Structure.
- 1.27 ___ Authorized Shares.
- 1.28 ___ Preferred Shares in Series.
- 1.29 ___ Subscription for Shares.
- 1.30 ___ Consideration and Payment for Shares.
- 1.31 ___ Rights to Purchase Shares.
- 1.32 ___ Stated Capital.
- 1.33 ___ Corporate Bonds; Convertible Securities.
- 1.34 ___ Federal Income Taxation Aspects.
- 1.35 ___ Capital Structure Summary.
- 1.36 ___ Capital Structure Checklist.
- 1.37 Distributions.
- 1.38 ___ Dividends; Share Distributions and Changes.
- 1.39 ___ Purchase or Redemption of Shares.

TABLE OF CONTENTS

Sec.	
1.40	___ Federal Income Tax Aspects.
1.41	___ Distributions Summary.
1.42	___ Distributions Checklist.
1.43	Shareholders' Meetings and Agreements—Generally.
1.44	___ Notice Requirements.
1.45	___ Voting.
1.46	___ Quorum Requirements.
1.47	___ Agreements; Voting Trusts.
1.48	___ Action Without a Meeting.
1.49	Shareholders' Meetings and Agreements Summary.
1.50	Shareholders' Meetings and Agreements Checklist.
1.51	Shareholders' Rights.
1.52	___ Preemptive Rights.
1.53	___ Inspection of Books and Records.
1.54	___ Shareholders' Rights Summary.
1.55	___ Shareholders' Rights Checklist.
1.56	Shareholders' Liabilities.
1.57	___ Shareholders' Liabilities Summary.
1.58	___ Shareholders' Liabilities Checklist.
1.59	Directors.
1.60	___ Vacancies; New Directorships.
1.61	___ Removal.
1.62	___ Meetings.
1.63	___ ___ Quorum and Voting Requirements.
1.64	___ Executive Committee; Other Committees.
1.65	___ Fiduciary Duties.
1.66	___ Liabilities.
1.67	___ Directors Summary.
1.68	___ Directors Checklist.
1.69	Officers.
1.70	___ Officers Summary.
1.71	___ Officers Checklist.
1.72	Amendment of Certificate of Incorporation.
1.73	___ Procedure.
1.74	___ Class Vote.
1.75	___ Certificate of Amendment.
1.76	___ Certificate of Change.
1.77	___ Restated Certificate of Incorporation.
1.78	___ Reorganization Under Act of Congress.
1.79	Amendment of Certificate of Incorporation Summary.
1.80	Amendment of Certificate of Incorporation Checklist.
1.81	Business Combinations.
1.82	___ Mergers and Consolidations.
1.83	___ ___ Procedures.
1.84	___ ___ Effect.
1.85	___ Sale, Lease, Exchange, or Other Disposition of Assets.
1.86	___ ___ Mortgage or Security Interest in Assets.
1.87	___ ___ Guarantee Authorized by Shareholders.
1.88	___ Share Exchanges.
1.89	___ Takeover Bids.

TABLE OF CONTENTS

Sec.	
1.90	——— Right of Shareholder to Receive Payment for Shares.
1.91	——— Federal Income Taxation Aspects.
1.92	Business Combinations Summary.
1.93	Business Combinations Checklist.
1.94	Dissolution.
1.95	——— Non-judicial Dissolution.
1.96	——— ——— Authorization.
1.97	——— ——— Certificate of Dissolution.
1.98	——— ——— Notice to Creditors.
1.99	——— Judicial Dissolution.
1.100	——— ——— Attorney General's Action.
1.101	——— ——— Directors' Petition.
1.102	——— ——— Shareholders' Petition.
1.103	——— ——— Petition Upon Deadlock Among Directors or Shareholders and in Other Circumstances.
1.104	——— ——— Procedures.
1.105	——— ——— Preservation of Assets; Appointment of Receiver.
1.106	——— ——— Certain Transfers and Judgments Void; Injunction.
1.107	——— Liquidation Distributions.
1.108	——— ——— Federal Income Tax Aspects.
1.109	——— Dissolution Summary.
1.110	——— Dissolution Checklist.
1.111	Receivership.
1.112	Receivership—Summary.
1.113	——— Checklist.
1.114	Foreign Corporations.
1.115	——— Authorization to Do Business in New York.
1.116	——— Application for Authority.
1.117	——— ——— Effect of Filing.
1.118	——— Surrender of Authority.
1.119	——— Termination of Existence.
1.120	Foreign Corporations Summary.
1.121	Foreign Corporations Checklist.
1.122	Professional Service Corporations.
1.123	Professional Service Corporations Summary.
1.124	Professional Service Corporations Checklist.
1.125	Foreign Professional Service Corporations.
1.126	Foreign Professional Service Corporations Summary.
1.127	Foreign Professional Service Corporations Checklist.
1.128	Transactional Checklist—Generally.
1.129	——— Formation ("Birth").
1.130	——— Operation ("Growth").
1.131	——— Business Combinations ("Marriage").
1.132	——— Spin-offs and Split-offs ("Children" and "Divorce").
1.133	——— Repurchase of Shares ("Redemption").
1.134	——— Dissolution; Liquidation ("Death").
1.135	Procedural Checklist—Generally.
1.136	——— Notices.
1.137	——— Reservation of Corporate Name.
1.138	——— ——— Foreign Corporations.

TABLE OF CONTENTS

Sec.
1.139 —— Mandatory and Permissive Provisions in Certificate of Incorporation.
1.140 —— Incorporation.
1.141 —— Filing Certificate of Incorporation.
1.142 —— Bylaws.
1.143 —— Organization Meetings.
1.144 —— Share Certificate.
1.145 —— Shareholder Approval Requirements.
1.146 —— Shareholder's Right to Receive Payment for Shares.
1.147 —— Close Corporations.
1.148 —— Foreign Corporations.
1.149 Drafting Checklist.
1.150 Form—Application to Reserve Corporate Name. 💾
1.151 —— Certificate of Incorporation. 💾
1.152 —— Bylaws. 💾
1.153 —— Subscription Agreement. 💾
1.154 —— Certificate of Amendment. 💾
1.155 —— Certificate of Dissolution. 💾

CHAPTER 2. NON-CORPORATE ENTITIES: LIMITED LIABILTY COMPANIES AND PARTNERSHIPS

2.1 Scope Note.
2.2 Strategy—Choice of Entity.
2.3 Tax Classification.
2.4 —— Eagerly–Awaited Simplification.
2.5 —— Former Corporate Characteristics Test.
2.6 —— —— Limited Liability.
2.7 —— —— Continuity of Life.
2.8 —— —— Free Transferability of Interests.
2.9 —— —— Centralized Management.
2.10 Partnership vs. LLC.
2.11 —— Tax Implications.
2.12 —— Liability.
2.13 —— Flexibility.
2.14 Limited Liability Companies.
2.15 —— Governing Law.
2.16 —— Formation.
2.17 —— —— Articles of Organization.
2.18 —— —— Publication.
2.19 —— —— Operating Agreement.
2.20 —— —— Other Issues.
2.21 —— Members.
2.22 —— —— Admission of New Members.
2.23 —— —— Liability.
2.24 —— —— One-member LLCs.
2.25 —— Management.
2.26 —— —— Members vs. Managers.
2.27 —— —— Voting: Members.
2.28 —— —— Voting: Managers.

XLVI

TABLE OF CONTENTS

Sec.
2.29 ____ ____ Non-waivable Requirements.
2.30 ____ ____ Delegation of Responsibility.
2.31 ____ ____ Standard of Care.
2.32 ____ ____ Agency Authority.
2.33 ____ Assignment of Interests.
2.34 ____ ____ Default Rules.
2.35 ____ ____ Vote Required to Admit Assignee as Member.
2.36 ____ Dissolution.
2.37 ____ ____ Events.
2.38 ____ ____ Continuation of Business after Dissolution Event.
2.39 ____ ____ Winding Up.
2.40 ____ Conversions/Mergers.
2.41 ____ ____ Procedures.
2.42 ____ ____ Dissenters' Rights.
2.43 ____ PLLCs.
2.44 General Partnerships.
2.45 ____ Governing Law.
2.46 ____ Formation.
2.47 ____ ____ Agreement.
2.48 ____ ____ Business Certificate.
2.49 ____ ____ Publication.
2.50 ____ ____ Other Issues.
2.51 ____ Partners.
2.52 ____ ____ Admission of New Partners.
2.53 ____ ____ Liability.
2.54 ____ ____ Contribution Issues.
2.55 ____ Management.
2.56 ____ ____ Voting.
2.57 ____ ____ Non-waivable Requirements.
2.58 ____ ____ Delegation of Responsibility.
2.59 ____ ____ Standard of Care.
2.60 ____ ____ Agency Authority.
2.61 ____ Assignment of Interests.
2.62 ____ ____ Default Rules.
2.63 ____ ____ Vote Required to Admit New Partner.
2.64 ____ Dissolution.
2.65 ____ ____ Events.
2.66 ____ ____ Continuation of Business after Dissolution Event.
2.67 ____ ____ Winding Up.
2.68 ____ Conversions/Mergers.
2.69 ____ ____ Procedures.
2.70 ____ ____ Dissenters' Rights.
2.71 ____ Professional Organizations.
2.72 Limited Liability Partnerships.
2.73 ____ Governing Law.
2.74 ____ Comparison with General Partnerships.
2.75 ____ Formation/Registration.
2.76 ____ Other Issues.
2.77 Limited Partnerships.
2.78 ____ Governing Law.

TABLE OF CONTENTS

Sec.
2.79 ___ Formation.
2.80 ___ ___ Certificate of Limited Partnership.
2.81 ___ ___ Publication.
2.82 ___ ___ Agreement.
2.83 ___ ___ Other Issues.
2.84 ___ Partners.
2.85 ___ ___ Admission of New Partners.
2.86 ___ ___ Liability.
2.87 ___ Contribution Issues.
2.88 ___ Management.
2.89 ___ ___ Voting: General Partners.
2.90 ___ ___ Voting: Limited Partners.
2.91 ___ ___ Delegation of Responsibility.
2.92 ___ ___ Standard of Care.
2.93 ___ ___ Agency Authority.
2.94 ___ Assignment of Interests.
2.95 ___ ___ Default Rules.
2.96 ___ ___ Vote Required to Admit New Partner.
2.97 ___ Dissolution.
2.98 ___ ___ Events.
2.99 ___ ___ Continuation of Business after Dissolution Event.
2.100 ___ ___ Winding Up.
2.101 ___ Conversions/Mergers.
2.102 ___ ___ Procedures.
2.103 ___ ___ Dissenters' Rights.
2.104 ___ Professional Organizations.
2.105 Due Diligence Issues.
2.106 Securities Laws Issues.
2.107 Summary.
2.108 Chart Comparing New York Entities.
2.109 Drafting Checklist.
2.110 Forms.
2.111 ___ LLC Articles of Organization. 💾
2.112 ___ Operating Agreement: Member–Managed LLC. 💾
2.113 ___ Registration as LLP. 💾
2.114 ___ Certificate of Limited Partnership. 💾
2.115 ___ Limited Partnership Agreement. 💾

CHAPTER 3. MUNICIPAL LAW

3.1 Scope Note.
3.2 Strategy.
3.3 Municipal Corporations.
3.4 ___ Creation.
3.5 ___ Consolidation, Annexation and Dissolution.
3.6 ___ ___ Annexation Checklist.
3.7 Powers of Municipal Corporations.
3.8 ___ Governmental v. Proprietary Powers.
3.9 ___ Police Powers.
3.10 Legislative Enactments.

TABLE OF CONTENTS

Sec.
3.11 ____ Resolutions.
3.12 ____ Ordinances.
3.13 ____ Rules and Regulations.
3.14 ____ Local Laws.
3.15 ____ Referendum Requirements.
3.16 Acquisition and Disposition of Property.
3.17 Officers and Employees.
3.18 ____ Qualifications.
3.19 ____ Terms.
3.20 ____ Removal.
3.21 ____ Collective Bargaining.
3.22 ____ Conflicts of Interest.
3.23 ____ ____ Checklist.
3.24 Contracts.
3.25 ____ Competitive Bidding.
3.26 Municipal Finance.
3.27 ____ Municipal Borrowing.
3.28 Public Meetings.
3.29 Access to Records.
3.30 Tort Claims Against Municipalities.
3.31 ____ Checklist.
3.32 Challenges to Governmental Determinations.
3.33 Special Purpose Units of Government.
3.34 ____ Industrial Development Agencies.
3.35 ____ Public Authorities.
3.36 Forms.
3.37 ____ Notice of Claim. 💾
3.38 ____ Verified Complaint in Tort Action. 💾

CHAPTER 4. ADMINISTRATIVE LAW

4.1 Scope Note.
4.2 Strategy.
4.3 ____ Checklist.
4.4 Procedural Due Process.
4.5 ____ Individualized State Action.
4.6 ____ Protected Interests.
4.7 ____ The Process Due.
4.8 ____ Summary.
4.9 ____ Checklist.
4.10 Adjudicatory Proceedings.
4.11 ____ Definition of an Adjudicatory Proceeding.
4.12 ____ Notice.
4.13 ____ Discovery.
4.14 ____ Right to Counsel.
4.15 ____ Evidence.
4.16 ____ Cross-Examination and Witness Attendance.
4.17 ____ Official Notice.
4.18 ____ Statement of Decision and Decisional Record.
4.19 ____ Burden of Proof.

TABLE OF CONTENTS

Sec.
4.20	____ Intervention.
4.21	____ Unreasonable Agency Delay.
4.22	____ Agency Duty to Decide Consistently.
4.23	____ Intra-agency Review.
4.24	____ Checking Agency Bias.
4.25	____ *Res Judicata* and Collateral Estoppel Effect.
4.26	____ Special Rules Applicable to Licensing Matters.
4.27	____ Special Issues in Handling Licensing Matters.
4.28	____ ____ Basic License Information.
4.29	____ ____ The Role of SAPA and SEQRA in the Licensing Process.
4.30	____ ____ Accuracy and Completeness in Applications.
4.31	____ ____ Opportunities to Expedite the Process.
4.32	____ ____ Opportunities for Variances from Standard Approaches.
4.33	____ ____ Renewal, Suspension and Revocation Issues.
4.34	____ Special Issues in Handling Enforcement Matters.
4.35	____ ____ Strategies to Minimize Violations.
4.36	____ ____ Agency Fact–Finding in the Pre-enforcement Phase.
4.37	____ ____ Agency Enforcement Options.
4.38	____ ____ The Settlement Process.
4.39	____ ____ The Hearing Process.
4.40	____ ____ Post–Hearing Issues.
4.41	____ Summary.
4.42	____ Checklist.
4.43	Administrative Rulemaking.
4.44	____ Rulemaking Compared With Other Agency Action.
4.45	____ Rulemaking Notice.
4.46	____ Comments and Agency Assessment of Comments.
4.47	____ Agency Duty to Reveal Underlying Information.
4.48	____ Notice of Adoption and Effective Date of Rules.
4.49	____ Ancillary Documentation and the Role of GORR.
4.50	____ Rule Filing and Publication.
4.51	____ Declaratory Rulings Regarding Rules.
4.52	____ Overlapping State and Federal Rules.
4.53	____ Special Strategic Considerations in Handling Administrative Rulemaking Matters.
4.54	____ ____ Basic Sources of Information on Rulemaking.
4.55	____ ____ Participating in the Rulemaking Process.
4.56	____ ____ Special Issues in Negotiated Rulemakings.
4.57	____ ____ Special Issues in Emergency Rulemakings.
4.58	____ ____ Agency Guidance Documents.
4.59	____ Summary.
4.60	____ Checklist.
4.61	Agency Information–Gathering.
4.62	____ Administrative Searches.
4.63	____ Administrative Subpoenas.
4.64	____ Reporting and Recordkeeping Requirements.
4.65	____ Summary.
4.66	____ Checklist.
4.67	Judicial Review.
4.68	____ Delegation of Authority to Agencies.

TABLE OF CONTENTS

Sec.
4.69	____ Standing to Seek Judicial Review.
4.70	____ Ripeness.
4.71	____ Final Order and Relief in the Nature of Prohibition.
4.72	____ Exhaustion of Administrative Remedies.
4.73	____ Primary Jurisdiction.
4.74	____ Statutory Preclusion of Judicial Review.
4.75	____ Article 78 and the Consolidation of the Common Law Prerogative Writs.
4.76	____ Standards of Review.
4.77	____ ____ Review of Agency Determinations of Law.
4.78	____ ____ Review of Agency Determinations of Fact Under the Substantial Evidence Test.
4.79	____ ____ Review of Agency Determinations of Fact Under the Arbitrary and Capricious Test.
4.80	____ ____ Review of Administrative Rules.
4.81	____ ____ Review of Administrative Discretion.
4.82	____ Statutes of Limitation Applicable to Judicial Review of Agency Action.
4.83	____ Venue in Article 78 Proceedings.
4.84	____ Subject Matter Jurisdiction in Article 78 Proceedings.
4.85	____ Summary.
4.86	____ Checklist.
4.87	Forms.
4.88	____ Notice of Appearance in Licensing or Permitting Matter.
4.89	____ Notice for Discovery and Inspection in an Administrative Proceeding.
4.90	____ Notice of Deposition in an Administrative Proceeding.
4.91	____ Notice to Permit Entry Upon Real Property.

CHAPTER 5. COMMERCIAL SALES CONTRACTS

5.1	Scope Note.
5.2	Strategy.
5.3	Transactional Checklist—Breach of Contract.
5.4	Defining a Contract.
5.5	Governing Law.
5.6	____ Freedom to Contract—Generally.
5.7	____ ____ Presumption of Legality.
5.8	____ ____ ____ Burden of Proof.
5.9	____ ____ ____ Determining the Contract's Validity.
5.10	____ ____ ____ Not All Illegal Contracts Are Unenforceable.
5.11	____ Public Policy Issues.
5.12	____ Unconscionability.
5.13	____ ____ Elements.
5.14	____ ____ Codification in UCC.
5.15	____ Duty of Good Faith—Generally.
5.16	____ ____ Codification in UCC.
5.17	The Written Contract—Statute of Frauds.
5.18	____ ____ General Rules.
5.19	____ ____ Formal Requirements.

TABLE OF CONTENTS

Sec.
5.20 ___ ___ Nature of the Writing.
5.21 ___ Parol or Extrinsic Evidence.
5.22 ___ Offer.
5.23 ___ Acceptance.
5.24 ___ ___ Additional Terms.
5.25 ___ Indefiniteness.
5.26 ___ Use of Open Terms.
5.27 Warranties.
5.28 ___ Warranty of Title Against Infringement.
5.29 ___ Express Warranty.
5.30 ___ Implied Warranty of Merchantability.
5.31 ___ Implied Warranty of Fitness for a Particular Purpose.
5.32 Assumption of the Risk of Loss.
5.33 ___ In the Absence of Breach.
5.34 ___ In the Event of a Breach.
5.35 Performance.
5.36 ___ Buyer's Response to Tender of Delivery.
5.37 ___ ___ Acceptance.
5.38 ___ ___ Rejection.
5.39 ___ ___ Revocation of Acceptance.
5.40 Breach of Contract.
5.41 ___ Seller's Remedies.
5.42 ___ ___ Action for the Price.
5.43 ___ ___ Withholding the Goods and Stopping Delivery.
5.44 ___ ___ Recovery of Goods Delivered.
5.45 ___ ___ Resale.
5.46 ___ ___ Damages for Non-acceptance or Repudiation.
5.47 ___ Buyer's Remedies.
5.48 ___ ___ Cover.
5.49 ___ ___ Damages for Non-delivery.
5.50 ___ ___ Damages for Breach Regarding Accepted Goods.
5.51 ___ ___ Specific Performance or Replevin.
5.52 ___ Liquidated Damages.
5.53 ___ Mitigation of Damages.
5.54 Third-Party Interests.
5.55 ___ Subsequent Buyers.
5.56 ___ Other Creditors.
5.57 Drafting Checklists—Order of Goods for Resale by Buyer.
5.58 ___ Verified Complaint On Account Stated for Goods, Services and Wares Delivered.
5.59 ___ Plaintiff's Notice of Motion for Summary Judgment in Contract Action.
5.60 ___ Affidavit of Officer of Plaintiff Company in Support of Summary Judgment Motion in Contract Action.
5.61 ___ Notice of Petition for Order Staying Arbitration in Dispute Over Contract for Sale of Goods.
5.62 ___ Petition for Order Staying Arbitration in Dispute Over Contract for Sale of Goods.
5.63 ___ Affidavit in Opposition to Petition for Order Staying Arbitration in Dispute Over Contract for Sale of Goods.

TABLE OF CONTENTS

Sec.
- 5.64 ___ Answer to Petition for Order Staying Arbitration in Dispute Over Contract for Sale of Goods.
- 5.65 Forms—Order of Goods for Resale by Buyer. 💾
- 5.66 ___ Verified Complaint On Account Stated for Goods, Services and Wares Delivered. 💾
- 5.67 ___ Plaintiff's Notice of Motion for Summary Judgment in Contract Action. 💾
- 5.68 ___ Affidavit of Vice President of Plaintiff Purchaser in Support of Summary Judgment Motion in Contract Action. 💾
- 5.69 ___ Notice of Petition for Order Staying Arbitration in Dispute Over Contract for Sale of Goods. 💾
- 5.70 ___ Petition for Order Staying Arbitration in Dispute Over Contract for Sale of Goods. 💾
- 5.71 ___ Affidavit in Opposition to Petition for Order Staying Arbitration in Dispute Over Contract for Sale of Goods. 💾
- 5.72 ___ Answer to Petition for Order Staying Arbitration in Dispute Over Contract for Sale of Goods. 💾

CHAPTER 6. BUYING AND SELLING A SMALL BUSINESS

- 6.1 Scope Note.
- 6.2 Strategy: Representing the Buyer—Introduction.
- 6.3 ___ The Attorney's Role.
- 6.4 ___ Different Considerations Depending on the Type of Transaction.
- 6.5 ___ General Stages of the Transaction.
- 6.6 Representing the Buyer—Investigating the Business.
- 6.7 ___ Nature and Operation of Business.
- 6.8 ___ Geographic Location.
- 6.9 ___ The Negotiating Team.
- 6.10 ___ The Letter of Intent.
- 6.11 ___ Confidentiality Agreements.
- 6.12 ___ Drafting the Agreement.
- 6.13 Due Diligence Investigation.
- 6.14 ___ Legal Issues.
- 6.15 ___ ___ Organizational Documents.
- 6.16 ___ ___ Ownership Documents.
- 6.17 ___ ___ Existing Contracts.
- 6.18 ___ ___ Liens and Security Interests.
- 6.19 ___ ___ Corporate and Trade Names.
- 6.20 ___ ___ Real Estate.
- 6.21 ___ ___ Compliance With Law.
- 6.22 ___ ___ Litigation Investigation.
- 6.23 ___ Financial Issues—General Considerations.
- 6.24 ___ ___ Seller's Records From the Buyer's Position.
- 6.25 ___ ___ Buyer's Records From the Seller's Position.
- 6.26 ___ ___ Public Records.
- 6.27 ___ ___ Financial Statements.
- 6.28 ___ ___ The Need for Other Professionals.
- 6.29 ___ ___ Valuation of the Business.

TABLE OF CONTENTS

Sec.
6.30 ———— Tax Returns.
6.31 Tax Issues for Buyer.
6.32 ——— Asset Purchase.
6.33 ———— Allocation of Purchase Price.
6.34 ———— Depreciation of Assets.
6.35 ———— Land.
6.36 ———— Good Will and Covenants Not to Compete.
6.37 ———— Inventory.
6.38 ———— Cash.
6.39 ———— Supplies.
6.40 ———— Patents, Franchises, Trademarks, Trade Names.
6.41 ——— Stock Purchase.
6.42 ———— Basis of Stock.
6.43 ———— Basis of Corporate Assets.
6.44 ———— Election to Treat Stock Purchase as Asset Purchase.
6.45 ——— Mergers, Consolidations, and Exchanges.
6.46 Structuring the Buyer's Transaction.
6.47 ——— Type of Payment.
6.48 ——— Assumption of Seller's Liabilities.
6.49 ——— Security to Seller.
6.50 ——— Notes.
6.51 ——— Escrow Arrangements and Agreements.
6.52 Drafting the Buyer's Asset Purchase Agreement.
6.53 ——— Identification of the Parties.
6.54 ——— Recitals.
6.55 ——— Assets and Property to Be Conveyed.
6.56 ——— Retained Assets of Seller.
6.57 ——— Purchase Price and Method of Payment.
6.58 ——— Closing.
6.59 ——— Representations, Warranties and Covenants of Seller.
6.60 ——— Representations, Warranties and Covenants of Buyer.
6.61 ——— Conduct of Business Prior to Closing.
6.62 ——— Indemnifications.
6.63 ——— Corporate or Other Name.
6.64 ———— Notice to Customers and Suppliers.
6.65 ———— UCC Bulk Sale Notices or Escrow Agreement in Lieu of UCC Bulk Sale Notice.
6.66 ———— NYS Sales Tax and Bulk Sale Notification.
6.67 ———— Covenant Not to Compete.
6.68 ——— Matters Respecting Real Property.
6.69 ——— Conditions Precedent to Purchaser's Obligations.
6.70 ——— Conditions Precedent to Seller's Obligations.
6.71 ——— Nature and Survival of Representations and Warranties.
6.72 ——— Non-disclosure Provisions.
6.73 ——— Miscellaneous Agreements Between Buyer and Seller.
6.74 ——— Documents to Be Delivered to Purchaser at Closing.
6.75 ——— Documents to Be Delivered to Seller at Closing.
6.76 ——— Notices, Severability and Other General Provisions.
6.77 ——— Documents to Be Prepared or Reviewed Prior to Closing.
6.78 Drafting the Buyer's Stock Purchase Agreement.

TABLE OF CONTENTS

Sec.
6.79	___ Identification of the Parties.
6.80	___ Recitals.
6.81	___ Sale of Shares.
6.82	___ Purchase Price and Method of Payment.
6.83	___ Closing.
6.84	___ Representations, Warranties and Covenants of Seller.
6.85	___ Representations, Warranties and Covenants of Buyer.
6.86	___ Conduct of Business Prior to Closing.
6.87	___ Indemnifications.
6.88	___ Covenant Not to Compete.
6.89	___ Matters Respecting Real Property.
6.90	___ Nondisclosure Provisions.
6.91	___ Conditions Precedent to Purchaser's Obligations.
6.92	___ Conditions Precedent to Seller's Obligations.
6.93	___ Nature and Survival of Representations and Warranties.
6.94	___ Documents to Be Delivered to Purchaser at Closing.
6.95	___ Documents to Be Delivered to Seller at Closing.
6.96	___ Notices, Severability and Other General Provisions.
6.97	___ Documents to Be Prepared or Reviewed Prior to Closing.
6.98	Post–Contract and Pre-closing.
6.99	___ Bulk Sales Act—UCC Article 6.
6.100	___ NYS Sales Tax and Bulk Sale Notification.
6.101	___ Plant Closing Notice.
6.102	___ Environmental Searches and Testing.
6.103	___ Certificate of Good Standing.
6.104	___ Real Property Transfer Gains Tax.
6.105	Closing and Post–Closing.
6.106	Strategy: Representing the Seller—Introduction.
6.107	___ The Attorney's Role.
6.108	___ Different Considerations Depending on the Type of Transaction.
6.109	___ General Stages of the Transaction.
6.110	Representing the Seller—General Investigation.
6.111	___ Investigating the Buyer.
6.112	___ The Negotiating Team.
6.113	___ The Letter of Intent.
6.114	___ Confidentiality Agreements.
6.115	___ Drafting the Agreement.
6.116	Tax Issues for the Seller—General Overview.
6.117	___ Asset Sale.
6.118	___ ___ Allocation of Purchase Price.
6.119	___ ___ Depreciation Recapture.
6.120	___ ___ Capital Gains or Losses.
6.121	___ ___ Ordinary Income.
6.122	___ ___ Income to Corporation.
6.123	___ ___ Real Property Transfer Gains Tax.
6.124	___ ___ Covenant Not to Compete and Consulting Agreements.
6.125	___ Stock Sale—General Advantages.
6.126	___ ___ Capital Gain or Loss.
6.127	___ ___ No Concern for Income to a Corporate Entity.

TABLE OF CONTENTS

Sec.
6.128 ___ ___ Real Property Transfer Gains Tax.
6.129 ___ ___ Consulting and Non-compete Agreements.
6.130 ___ ___ I.R.C. § 1244 Stock and Qualified Small Business Stock.
6.131 ___ ___ Stock Transfer Tax.
6.132 ___ ___ Collapsible Corporation.
6.133 ___ ___ Mergers, Consolidations and Exchanges.
6.134 Structuring the Seller's Transaction—General Overview.
6.135 ___ Purchase Price and Payment Terms.
6.136 ___ Security to Seller.
6.137 ___ Notes.
6.138 ___ Escrow Arrangements.
6.139 Drafting the Seller's Asset Sale Agreement.
6.140 ___ Identification of the Parties.
6.141 ___ Recitals.
6.142 ___ Assets and Property to Be Conveyed.
6.143 ___ Assets Retained by Seller.
6.144 ___ Sale Price and Method of Payment.
6.145 ___ Closing.
6.146 ___ Representations, Warranties and Covenants of Buyer.
6.147 ___ Representations, Warranties and Covenants of Seller.
6.148 ___ Conduct of Business Prior to Closing.
6.149 ___ Indemnifications.
6.150 ___ Matters Respecting Real Property.
6.151 ___ Notice to Customers and Suppliers.
6.152 ___ Covenant Not to Compete and Consulting Agreements.
6.153 ___ UCC Bulk Sale Notices or Escrow Agreements in Lieu of UCC Bulk Sale Notice.
6.154 ___ New York State Sales Tax and Bulk Sale Notification.
6.155 ___ Nature and Survival of Representations and Warranties.
6.156 ___ Non-disclosure Provisions.
6.157 ___ Conditions Precedent to Seller's Obligations.
6.158 ___ Conditions Precedent to Buyer's Obligations.
6.159 ___ Documents to Be Delivered to Seller at Closing.
6.160 ___ Documents to Be Delivered to Buyer at Closing.
6.161 ___ Notices, Severability and Other General Provisions.
6.162 ___ Documents to Be Prepared or Reviewed Prior to Closing.
6.163 Drafting the Seller's Stock Sale Agreement.
6.164 ___ Identification of the Parties.
6.165 ___ Recitals.
6.166 ___ Sale of Shares.
6.167 ___ Sale Price and Method of Payment.
6.168 ___ Closing.
6.169 ___ Representations, Warranties and Covenants of Buyer.
6.170 ___ Representations, Warranties and Covenants of Seller.
6.171 ___ Conduct of Business Prior to Closing.
6.172 ___ Indemnifications.
6.173 ___ Matters Respecting Real Property.
6.174 ___ Non-disclosure Provisions.
6.175 ___ Covenants Not to Compete and Consulting Agreements.
6.176 ___ Notice to Customers and Suppliers.

TABLE OF CONTENTS

Sec.
6.177	____ Conditions Precedent to Seller's Obligations.
6.178	____ Conditions Precedent to Buyer's Obligations.
6.179	____ Nature and Survival of Representations and Warranties.
6.180	____ Documents to Be Delivered to Seller at Closing.
6.181	____ Documents to Be Delivered to Buyer at Closing.
6.182	____ Notices, Severability and Other General Provisions.
6.183	____ Documents to Be Prepared or Reviewed Prior to Closing.
6.184	Post–contract and Pre-closing.
6.185	Closing and Post–Closing.
6.186	Forms.
6.187	____ Asset Purchase and Sale Agreement. 💾
6.188	____ Agreement of Purchase and Sale of Stock. 💾

Volume 21

CHAPTER 7. CONSUMER LAW

7.1	Scope Note.
7.2	Strategy—Generally.
7.3	____ Automobile Sales Cases.
7.4	____ Automobile Leasing Cases.
7.5	____ Credit Reporting.
7.6	____ Debt Collection.
7.7	____ Deceptive Business Practices.
7.8	____ Information to Obtain at Outset of Case.
7.9	Lemon Laws.
7.10	____ New Cars.
7.11	____ Used Cars.
7.12	____ Arbitration or Plenary Action?
7.13	____ Arbitration Procedure.
7.14	____ ____ Preparation for the Hearing.
7.15	____ ____ The Hearing.
7.16	____ ____ Appeals and Confirmation Proceedings.
7.17	____ ____ Scope of Review.
7.18	____ Source Materials.
7.19	Automobile Leasing—Overview.
7.20	____ Statutory Protection Overview.
7.21	____ The Consumer Leasing Act.
7.22	____ The Motor Vehicle Retail Leasing Act.
7.23	Motor Vehicle Installment Sales.
7.24	Repossession—Overview.
7.25	____ Prevention and Avoidance.
7.26	____ Defending Deficiency Claims.
7.27	Automobile Repairs.
7.28	Automobile Repair Shop Liens—Overview.
7.29	____ Statutory Challenges.
7.30	Credit Reporting—Overview.
7.31	____ Consumer Rights.
7.32	____ Non-litigation Strategies.
7.33	____ Litigating Credit Reporting Matters.

TABLE OF CONTENTS

Sec.
7.34 Debt Collection—History and Overview.
7.35 ___ Claims for Intentional Infliction of Emotional Distress.
7.36 ___ Statutory Overview.
7.37 ___ FDCPA—Contacts With Third Parties.
7.38 ___ ___Contacts With a Debtor.
7.39 ___ ___ Prohibited Tactics.
7.40 ___ ___ Improper Omissions and Disclosures.
7.41 ___ ___ Harassment or Abuse.
7.42 ___ ___ Improper Demands.
7.43 ___ ___ Judicial Enforcement.
7.44 ___ State Law.
7.45 Deceptive Practices Act—Overview.
7.46 ___ Elements of the Claim.
7.47 ___ Types of Recovery Available.
7.48 Drafting Checklist—List of Essential Allegations.
7.49 Forms—Lemon Law Document Request Pursuant to 13 NYCRR § 300.9(a).
7.50 ___ Notice of Petition to Vacate Lemon Law Arbitration Award Pursuant to CPLR Article 75.
7.51 ___ Petition to Vacate Lemon Law Arbitration Award Pursuant to CPLR Article 75.
7.52 ___ Complaint for Fraud, Breach of Warranties, Deceptive Business Practices, Used Car Lemon Law, Rescission and Revocation of Acceptance for Fraudulent Leasing Practices.
7.53 ___ Answer and Third-party Complaint Alleging Fraud, Deceptive Practices, Breach of Warranty, and Federal Odometer Law Claims in Fraudulent Automobile Lease Case.
7.54 ___ Answer to Complaint by Automobile Leasing Company for Deficiency Following Repossession, Alleging Commercially Unreasonable Resale and Deceptive Business Practices.
7.55 ___ Affirmation in Opposition to Lessor's Motion for Summary Judgment and in Support of Lessee's Cross-motion for Summary Judgment Alleging Commercially Unreasonable Resale.
7.56 ___ Notice of Rescission And/or Revocation of Acceptance and Demand for Restitution Pursuant to UCC 2–601 and 2–608.
7.57 ___ Order to Show Cause in Proceeding under Lien Law § 201–a to Vacate Garageman's Lien.
7.58 ___ Verified Petition in Proceeding under Lien Law § 201–a to Vacate Garageman's Lien.
7.59 ___ Affirmation in Support of Petition in Proceeding under Lien Law § 201–a to Vacate Garageman's Lien.
7.60 ___ Complaint Against Credit Reporting Agency Alleging Violations of the Fair Credit Reporting Act and the New York State Fair Credit Reporting Act and Deceptive Business Practices.
7.61 ___ Stipulation of Settlement of Plaintiff's Lemon Law Claims Providing for Cancellation of Lease and Deletion of Any Derogatory Credit Information.

TABLE OF CONTENTS

Sec.

7.62 ___ Complaint Alleging Violations of the Fair Debt Collection Practices Act and the Deceptive Practices Act. 💾
7.63 ___ Order to Show Cause with Temporary Restraining Order, Seeking Preliminary Injunction in Action Alleging Fraud, Deceptive Business Practices and Breach of Warranties. 💾
7.64 ___ Affirmation in Support of Temporary Restraining Order and Preliminary Injunction in Action Alleging Fraud, Deceptive Business Practices and Breach of Warranties. 💾
7.65 ___ Complaint in Action Alleging Fraud, Deceptive Business Practices and Breach of Warranties. 💾

CHAPTER 8. ENFORCEMENT OF MONEY JUDGMENTS

8.1 Scope Note.
8.2 Strategy.
8.3 Judgments—Generally.
8.4 ___ Methods to Obtain.
8.5 Form of Judgment—Judgment–Roll.
8.6 ___ Interest.
8.7 ___ Fees, Costs and Disbursements.
8.8 ___ Entry.
8.9 ___ Transcript of Judgment.
8.10 Matters Affecting Judgment—Vacatur.
8.11 ___ Satisfaction By Payment or Otherwise.
8.12 ___ Assignment.
8.13 ___ Death of Judgment Debtor.
8.14 ___ Amendment or Correction.
8.15 Actions on Judgments.
8.16 Entry of a Foreign Judgment—Sister–State Judgments.
8.17 ___ Federal Court Judgments.
8.18 ___ Foreign Country Judgments.
8.19 Judgment Enforcement Against Property—Definition of Property.
8.20 ___ Exemptions.
8.21 ___ Property in the Possession of Others.
8.22 ___ Disclosure of Property.
8.23 ___ ___ Subpoenas.
8.24 Article 52 Enforcement Devices—Introduction.
8.25 ___ Restraining Notices—Nature and Use.
8.26 ___ ___ Formal Requirements.
8.27 ___ ___ Service and Punishment for Disobedience.
8.28 ___ Execution.
8.29 ___ ___ Property Execution With Regard to Personal Property.
8.30 ___ ___ ___ Sale, Distribution and Priority In Proceeds.
8.31 ___ ___ Property Execution With Regard to Real Property.
8.32 ___ ___ ___ Notice and Sale of Real Property.
8.33 ___ ___ ___ Distribution of Proceeds of Sale and Conveyance of Title.
8.34 ___ Income Execution.
8.35 ___ Installment Payment Order—Nature and Purpose.
8.36 ___ ___ Form of Application and Service.

LIX

TABLE OF CONTENTS

Sec.	
8.37	___ Receiver.
8.38	___ ___ Application, Appointment and Extension.
8.39	___ Turnover Orders For Property or Debts.
8.40	___ ___ Turnover Against the Judgment Debtor.
8.41	___ ___ Turnover Against A Garnishee.
8.42	___ Contempt.
8.43	___ Arrest of the Judgment Debtor.
8.44	Protective Orders.
8.45	Proceeding To Determine Adverse Claims.
8.46	Forms.
8.47	___ Statement For Judgment (Default Judgment), Affidavit of Facts Constituting the Claim, the Default and the Amount Due.
8.48	___ Affidavit of Confession of Judgment and Judgment by Confession.
8.49	___ Notice to Judgment Debtor [or Obligor].
8.50	___ Subpoena (*Duces Tecum*) To Take Deposition of Judgment Debtor With Restraining Notice.
8.51	___ Subpoena (*Duces Tecum*) To Take Deposition of Witness With Restraining Notice.
8.52	___ Information Subpoena.
8.53	___ Restraining Notice to Judgment Debtor.
8.54	___ Execution.
8.55	___ Income Execution.
8.56	___ Affirmation and Order To Show Cause To Punish Judgment Debtor—Witness For Contempt. 💾

CHAPTER 9. BANKRUPTCY

9.1	Scope Note.
9.2	Strategy.
9.3	___ Checklist for Representing a Debtor.
9.4	___ Checklist for Representing a Creditor.
9.5	Governing Law.
9.6	Nature of Cases Under Each Chapter of the Bankruptcy Code.
9.7	Eligibility to File.
9.8	Commencement of a Case—Voluntary Cases.
9.9	___ Involuntary Cases.
9.10	___ ___ Procedure.
9.11	___ Additional Requirements.
9.12	___ First–Day Orders.
9.13	Joint Administration.
9.14	Substantive Consolidation.
9.15	Types of Proceedings in Cases Under the Bankruptcy Code.
9.16	___ Adversary Proceedings.
9.17	___ Contested Matters.
9.18	Jurisdiction of the Bankruptcy Court.
9.19	___ Types of Jurisdiction.
9.20	___ Case Ancillary to Foreign Proceedings.
9.21	Venue.
9.22	Withdrawal of Reference.

TABLE OF CONTENTS

Sec.
9.23 Abstention.
9.24 Removal.
9.25 Appeals—To District Court and Bankruptcy Appellate Panel From Bankruptcy Court.
9.26 ____ To Court of Appeals From District Court.
9.27 The Debtor in Possession.
9.28 ____ Rights, Powers and Duties.
9.29 Employment of Professionals.
9.30 ____ Compensation.
9.31 ____ ____ Fee Applications.
9.32 U.S. Trustee.
9.33 ____ Duties Owed by Debtors and Trustees.
9.34 Bankruptcy Trustee.
9.35 Mediators.
9.36 Creditors.
9.37 ____ Meeting of Creditors.
9.38 ____ ____ Scope of Examination.
9.39 Examinations Under Bankruptcy Rule 2004.
9.40 ____ Notice Requirements.
9.41 ____ Subpoena.
9.42 Right of Parties in Interest to Be Heard.
9.43 Statutory Committees.
9.44 ____ Function and Duties.
9.45 ____ Right to Bring Litigation.
9.46 ____ Fiduciary Duty.
9.47 ____ Removal of Members.
9.48 ____ Organizational Meeting.
9.49 Property of the Estate.
9.50 Automatic Stay.
9.51 ____ Exceptions.
9.52 ____ Obtaining Relief.
9.53 ____ ____ Strategy.
9.54 ____ ____ Hearing.
9.55 ____ ____ Single Asset Real Estate Debtor.
9.56 Adequate Protection.
9.57 ____ Types.
9.58 ____ Strategy.
9.59 ____ Objections and Hearing.
9.60 Use, Sale, or Lease of Property.
9.61 ____ Ordinary Course of Business.
9.62 ____ Outside Ordinary Course of Business.
9.63 ____ Sales Free and Clear of Liens.
9.64 ____ Appeals from Order Authorizing Sale.
9.65 Cash Collateral.
9.66 ____ Strategy.
9.67 ____ Hearing.
9.68 ____ Postpetition Proceeds.
9.69 ____ ____ Security Interests in Rents and Hotel Revenues.
9.70 Abandonment of Property.
9.71 Postpetition Financing.

TABLE OF CONTENTS

Sec.	
9.72	____ Hearing.
9.73	____ Appeals From Order Authorizing.
9.74	Executory Contracts and Unexpired Leases.
9.75	____ Strategy.
9.76	____ Time for Assumption or Rejection.
9.77	____ Nonresidential Real Property Leases.
9.78	____ Assumption by the Debtor.
9.79	____ Assumption and Assignment.
9.80	____ Exceptions to Assumption and Assignment.
9.81	____ Rejection by Debtor.
9.82	____ Damages Arising From Rejection: Debtor as Tenant/Lessee.
9.83	____ Calculation of Allowed Real Property Lease Rejection Damages.
9.84	____ Debtor as Landlord/Lessor.
9.85	____ Unexpired Personal Property Leases.
9.86	Collective Bargaining Agreements.
9.87	Retired Employees' Insurance Benefits.
9.88	____ Procedure for Modifying.
9.89	Utility Services.
9.90	Claims Procedures.
9.91	____ Filing Proofs of Claim or Interest.
9.92	____ ____ Bar Dates.
9.93	____ Late–Filed Proofs of Claim.
9.94	____ Amendment of Proofs of Claim or Interest.
9.95	____ Withdrawal of Claims.
9.96	____ Allowance of, and Objections to, Claims or Interests.
9.97	____ Compromise and Settlement of Claims.
9.98	____ Allowance of Administrative Expense Claims.
9.99	____ Secured Claims.
9.100	____ ____ Bifurcation of Claims.
9.101	____ ____ Avoidance of Liens.
9.102	____ Interest on Claims and Charges Against Secured Claims.
9.103	____ Valuation of Collateral.
9.104	____ ____ Methods of Valuation.
9.105	____ Reclamation Claims.
9.106	Priorities.
9.107	Subordination.
9.108	____ Strategy.
9.109	Setoff.
9.110	____ Strategy.
9.111	____ Characteristics of Claims.
9.112	Recoupment.
9.113	The Avoiding Powers.
9.114	____ Strategy.
9.115	____ Strong Arm Powers.
9.116	____ Avoidance of Certain Statutory Liens.
9.117	____ Preferences.
9.118	____ Exceptions to the Avoidance of Preferential Transfers.
9.119	____ Fraudulent Conveyances.
9.120	____ Liability of Transferee of Avoided Transfer.

TABLE OF CONTENTS

Sec.
9.121 ____ Statute of Limitations and Standing.
9.122 ____ Relation–Back Provision.
9.123 ____ Reclamation.
9.124 Return of Goods by Debtor.
9.125 Exemptions.
9.126 ____ Procedure.
9.127 ____ Objections.
9.128 ____ Lien Avoidance.
9.129 ____ Liens on Exempt Property.
9.130 Reaffirmation of Debts.
9.131 ____ Strategy.
9.132 Protection Against Discriminatory Treatment.
9.133 Tax Considerations.
9.134 Conversion and Dismissal of Cases Under Title 11.
9.135 Effect of Conversion.
9.136 Effect of Dismissal.
9.137 Closing and Reopening Cases.
9.138 Chapter 11—Appointment of a Trustee.
9.139 ____ Duties of a Trustee.
9.140 ____ Appointment of an Examiner.
9.141 ____ Duties of an Examiner.
9.142 ____ Exclusivity—Right to File a Plan.
9.143 ____ ____ Small Businesses.
9.144 ____ ____ Strategy: Representing a Debtor.
9.145 ____ ____ Strategy: Representing a Creditor.
9.146 ____ ____ Appealability of Orders.
9.147 ____ Plan.
9.148 ____ ____ Mandatory Provisions.
9.149 ____ ____ Discretionary Provisions.
9.150 ____ ____ Exemption from Securities Registration.
9.151 ____ ____ Retention of Jurisdiction by the Court.
9.152 ____ Classification of Claims.
9.153 ____ ____ Effect on Voting.
9.154 ____ ____ Substantially Similar Claims.
9.155 ____ ____ Convenience Class.
9.156 ____ Recourse and Nonrecourse Claims: The § 1111(b) Election.
9.157 ____ ____ Strategy.
9.158 ____ Impairment of Claims or Interests.
9.159 ____ ____ Rights Are Altered.
9.160 ____ ____ Defaults Are Not Cured.
9.161 ____ Disclosure and Solicitation.
9.162 ____ Acceptance of a Plan.
9.163 ____ Prepackaged and Prenegotiated Plans.
9.164 ____ Modification of a Plan.
9.165 ____ Confirmation.
9.166 ____ Cramdown.
9.167 ____ Effect of Confirmation.
9.168 ____ Discharge.
9.169 ____ ____ Limitations.
9.170 ____ ____ Release of Nondebtor.

TABLE OF CONTENTS

Sec.
9.171 ____ Channelling Injunctions: Asbestos–Related Cases.
9.172 ____ Plan Implementation.
9.173 ____ Small Business Reorganizations.
9.174 ____ Conversion or Dismissal of Cases.
9.175 ____ ____ Procedure.
9.176 ____ Closing and Reopening Cases.
9.177 Chapter 7—Overview.
9.178 ____ Commencement of a Case.
9.179 ____ Fees.
9.180 ____ Appointment of an Interim Trustee.
9.181 ____ Election of a Permanent Trustee.
9.182 ____ Duties of a Trustee.
9.183 ____ Employment of Professionals.
9.184 ____ Creditors' Committee.
9.185 ____ Protection Against Discriminatory Treatment.
9.186 ____ The Debtor's Statement of Intention.
9.187 ____ Exemptions.
9.188 ____ Redemption of Property.
9.189 ____ ____ Procedure.
9.190 ____ Reaffirmation of Debts.
9.191 ____ Abandonment of Property.
9.192 ____ Debtor's Surrender of Property and Records.
9.193 ____ Trustee's Turnover Powers.
9.194 ____ Liability of General Partners.
9.195 ____ Trustee's Operation of the Business.
9.196 ____ Executory Contracts.
9.197 ____ Adversary Proceedings to Avoid Liens and Transfers.
9.198 ____ ____ Statute of Limitations.
9.199 ____ Treatment of Certain Liens.
9.200 ____ Trustee's Sale of Assets.
9.201 ____ Disposition of Property Subject to the Interest of Another.
9.202 ____ Priorities.
9.203 ____ Special Tax Provisions.
9.204 ____ Discharge.
9.205 ____ ____ Exceptions to General Discharge of the Debtor.
9.206 ____ ____ Procedure for Objections to General Discharge of the Debtor.
9.207 ____ ____ Exceptions to Discharge of Particular Debts.
9.208 ____ ____ Procedure for Objections to Discharge of Particular Debts.
9.209 ____ Conversion or Dismissal of Cases.
9.210 ____ ____ Procedure.
9.211 ____ Closing and Reopening Cases.
9.212 Chapter 12—Overview.
9.213 ____ Rights and Powers of Debtor.
9.214 ____ Appointment of a Trustee.
9.215 ____ Duties of a Trustee.
9.216 ____ Automatic Stay.
9.217 ____ Property of the Estate.
9.218 ____ Sales Free of Interests.

TABLE OF CONTENTS

Sec.	
9.219	____ Adequate Protection.
9.220	____ Exclusivity—Right to File a Plan.
9.221	____ Plan.
9.222	____ ____ Mandatory Provisions.
9.223	____ ____ Discretionary Provisions.
9.224	____ ____ Modification.
9.225	____ ____ Confirmation.
9.226	____ ____ Confirmation: Objections.
9.227	____ Disbursements.
9.228	____ Effect of Confirmation.
9.229	____ Discharge.
9.230	____ Modification after Confirmation.
9.231	____ Special Tax Provisions.
9.232	____ Revocation of Confirmation Order.
9.233	____ Conversion or Dismissal of Cases.
9.234	____ ____ Procedure.
9.235	____ Closing and Reopening Cases.
9.236	Chapter 13—Overview.
9.237	____ Eligibility.
9.238	____ Rights and Powers of Debtor.
9.239	____ Appointment of a Trustee.
9.240	____ Duties of a Trustee.
9.241	____ Automatic Stay.
9.242	____ ____ Relief.
9.243	____ Property of the Estate.
9.244	____ ____ Use, Sale, or Lease.
9.245	____ Exclusivity—Right to File a Plan.
9.246	____ Plan.
9.247	____ ____ Mandatory Provisions.
9.248	____ ____ Discretionary Provisions.
9.249	____ ____ Discretionary Provisions: Debtor's Principal Residence.
9.250	____ ____ Modification.
9.251	____ ____ Confirmation.
9.252	____ ____ Confirmation: Objections.
9.253	____ ____ Confirmation: Effect.
9.254	____ Payments.
9.255	____ Discharge.
9.256	____ ____ Exceptions.
9.257	____ ____ Objections.
9.258	____ ____ Revocation.
9.259	____ Postconfirmation Modification of a Plan.
9.260	____ Revocation of Confirmation Order.
9.261	____ Conversion or Dismissal of Cases.
9.262	____ ____ Procedure.
9.263	____ Closing and Reopening Cases.
9.264	Procedural Checklist—Commencing a Voluntary Case.
9.265	____ Lists and Schedules to be Filed at the Commencement of a Case Under Chapter 7, 11, 12, or 13.
9.266	____ Commencing an Adversary Proceeding.
9.267	____ Commencing a Contested Matter.

TABLE OF CONTENTS

Sec.

9.268 ___ Appeal from an Interlocutory Judgment, Order, or Decree of a Bankruptcy Judge.
9.269 ___ Creditor's Motion to Request Relief from the Automatic Stay.
9.270 ___ Creditor's Motion to Obtain Adequate Protection.
9.271 ___ Debtor's Motion to Use, Sell, or Lease Property of the Estate.
9.272 ___ Debtor's Motion to Request Use of Cash Collateral.
9.273 ___ Cash Collateral Stipulation.
9.274 ___ Debtor's Motion to Obtain Postpetition Financing.
9.275 ___ Request to Assume, Reject, or Assign an Executory Contract or Unexpired Nonresidential Real Property Lease.
9.276 ___ Debtor's Motion to Reject or Modify a Collective Bargaining Agreement.
9.277 ___ Debtor's Motion to Obtain Approval of a Compromise and Settlement of a Claim.
9.278 ___ Claiming Exemptions.
9.279 ___ Debtor's Motion to Avoid a Judicial Lien or a Nonpossessory, Nonpurchase–Money Security Interest that Impairs Exempt Property.
9.280 ___ Debtor's Motion to Obtain Court Approval of a Reaffirmation Agreement.
9.281 ___ Debtor's Motion to Request an Extension of Exclusivity.
9.282 ___ Filing a Chapter 11 Plan and Disclosure Statement.
9.283 ___ Soliciting Acceptance of a Chapter 11 Plan.
9.284 ___ Filing a Chapter 12 or 13 Plan of Debt Adjustment.
9.285 ___ Objection to a Chapter 12 or 13 Plan.
9.286 ___ Debtor's Motion to Request Modification of a Chapter 12 or 13 Plan after Confirmation
9.287 Drafting Checklist—General Rules for all Motions, Applications, and Complaints.
9.288 ___ Complaint in an Adversary Proceeding.
9.289 ___ Motion for Leave to Appeal From an Interlocutory Judgment, Order, or Decree of a Bankruptcy Judge.
9.290 ___ Motion for a Stay of a Bankruptcy Court Judgment or Order Pending Appeal.
9.291 ___ Application of Debtor or Statutory Committee to Retain Professionals.
9.292 ___ Creditor's Motion to Request Relief From the Automatic Stay.
9.293 ___ Creditor's Motion to Obtain Adequate Protection.
9.294 ___ Debtor's Motion to Use, Sell, or Lease Property of the Estate.
9.295 ___ Debtor's Motion to Request Use of Cash Collateral.
9.296 ___ Cash Collateral Stipulation.
9.297 ___ Debtor's Motion to Obtain Postpetition Financing.
9.298 ___ Motion to Assume or Reject an Executory Contract or Unexpired Non-residential Real Property Lease.
9.299 ___ Debtor's Motion to Reject or Modify a Collective Bargaining Agreement (CBA).
9.300 ___ Debtor's Motion to Obtain Approval of a Compromise and Settlement of a Claim.

TABLE OF CONTENTS

Sec.
9.301 ____ Debtor's Motion to Avoid a Judicial Lien or a Nonpossessory, Nonpurchase–Money Security Interest that Impairs Exempt Property.
9.302 ____ Reaffirmation Agreement.
9.303 ____ Debtor's Motion for Approval of a Reaffirmation Agreement.
9.304 ____ Debtor's Motion to Request an Extension of Exclusivity.
9.305 Forms—Notice of Appearance and Demand for Service of Documents. 💾
9.306 ____ Contested Matter—Motion. 💾
9.307 ____ ____ Notice of Motion. 💾
9.308 ____ ____ Proposed Order. 💾
9.309 ____ Adversary Proceeding—Complaint. 💾
9.310 ____ Retention of Professionals—Application. 💾
9.311 ____ ____ Affidavit. 💾
9.312 ____ Plan Provision for Retention of Jurisdiction. 💾

CHAPTER 10. MECHANIC'S LIENS

10.1 Scope Note.
10.2 Strategy.
10.3 Nature of Mechanic's Lien.
10.4 Creation of Mechanic's Lien—Elements.
10.5 ____ ____ Protected Class.
10.6 ____ ____ Improvements to Real Property.
10.7 ____ ____ Consent or Request of Owner.
10.8 Extent of Lien—Ownership Interest at Time of Filing.
10.9 ____ Sale of Property.
10.10 ____ Insurance Proceeds.
10.11 ____ Amount.
10.12 ____ Loss of Profits.
10.13 Subcontractors and Materialmen—Derivative Rights.
10.14 ____ ____ Statutory Protections.
10.15 Procedure—Notice of Lien.
10.16 ____ ____ Contents.
10.17 ____ ____ Filing.
10.18 ____ ____ Service.
10.19 Amendment of Notice of Lien.
10.20 Lien for Private Improvements—Checklist.
10.21 Liens Under Contract for Public Improvements—Extent of Lien.
10.22 ____ Notice of Lien.
10.23 ____ Filing of Notice of Lien.
10.24 ____ Notice of Completion and Acceptance.
10.25 ____ Checklist.
10.26 Lien Priorities—Private Improvements—Parity of Mechanic's Liens.
10.27 ____ ____ Assignments of Contract Rights.
10.28 ____ ____ Building Loan Mortgages.
10.29 ____ ____ Contracts of Sale.
10.30 ____ ____ Seller's Mortgage.
10.31 ____ ____ Deeds.

TABLE OF CONTENTS

Sec.

10.32	____ Contracts for Public Improvements.
10.33	Assignment of Liens.
10.34	Assignments of Contracts for Private Improvements and Orders to be Filed—Filing of Notice of Assignment.
10.35	____ Contents of Notice of Assignment.
10.36	____ Extension of Term of Notice of Assignment.
10.37	Assignment of Contracts and Orders for Public Improvements.
10.38	Duration of Lien for Private Improvements—Notice of Pendency.
10.39	____ Extensions.
10.40	Duration of Lien Under Contract for a Public Improvement—Notice of Pendency.
10.41	____ Extension of Lien.
10.42	Discharge of Lien for Private Improvement—Satisfaction of Lien.
10.43	____ Expiration of Term.
10.44	____ Termination of Notice of Pendency.
10.45	____ Failure to Prosecute.
10.46	____ Undertaking.
10.47	____ Judgment.
10.48	____ Defective Lien.
10.49	____ Deposit of Money with County Clerk or Court.
10.50	Discharge of Lien for Public Improvement—Satisfaction of Lien.
10.51	____ Expiration of Lien.
10.52	____ Satisfaction of Judgment.
10.53	____ Deposit of Money.
10.54	____ Undertaking.
10.55	____ Retention of Credit.
10.56	____ Invalidity of Lien.
10.57	____ Failure to Prosecute.
10.58	____ Procedures.
10.59	Building Loan Contracts—Filing Requirements.
10.60	____ Checklist.
10.61	Subordination of Liens—Agreement with Owner.
10.62	____ ____ Postponement of Judgments.
10.63	Subordination of Liens to Subsequent Mortgage.
10.64	Subordination of Notices of *Lis Pendens*.
10.65	Discharge of Liens on Sale of Real Property.
10.66	Limitations on Waiver of Mechanic's Lien.
10.67	Effect of Filing of Notice of Lien on Right of Arbitration.
10.68	Bond to Discharge Liens—Effect of Bond.
10.69	____ Requirements of Bond.
10.70	____ Claim Against Bond.
10.71	____ Notice of Claim.
10.72	____ Action on Bond.
10.73	____ Discharge of Liens and Notices of Claims.
10.74	Protecting the Owner—Itemized Statement.
10.75	____ Lien Wilfully Exaggerated.
10.76	Repossession of Materials Not Used.
10.77	Enforcement of Mechanic's Liens—Courts.
10.78	____ Courts of Record—Procedures.
10.79	____ ____ Necessary Parties.

TABLE OF CONTENTS

Sec.
10.80 _____ Actions in a Court Not of Record—Summons and Complaint.
10.81 _____ _____ Proceedings Upon Return of Summons.
10.82 _____ _____ Judgments and Transcripts.
10.83 _____ Costs and Disbursements.
10.84 _____ Effect of Failure to Establish Lien.
10.85 _____ Deposit of Money or Securities to Discharge Lien—Procedures.
10.86 _____ _____ Effect of Order.
10.87 _____ _____ Preference Over Contractors.
10.88 _____ _____ Delivery of Property in Lieu of Money.
10.89 _____ Deficiency Judgment.
10.90 _____ Vacating of Mechanic's Lien, Cancellation of Bond or Return of Deposit.
10.91 _____ Public Improvements.
10.92 _____ New Parties.
10.93 _____ Service of Answer on State or Public Corporation.
10.94 Trust Funds—Purpose.
10.95 _____ Creation.
10.96 _____ Contractors and Subcontractors.
10.97 _____ Beneficiaries.
10.98 Diversion of Trust Assets.
10.99 Notice of Lending.
10.100 Record Keeping Obligations.
10.101 Right of Beneficiaries to Examine Books or Records.
10.102 Action to Enforce Trust—Standing and Procedure.
10.103 _____ Remedies.
10.104 _____ Preferences.
10.105 Relief After Judgment on Obligation Constituting Trust Claim; Effect on Mechanic's Liens.
10.106 Misappropriation of Trust Funds.
10.107 Procedural Checklist.
10.108 Forms.
10.109 _____ Notice of Mechanic's Lien—General Form.
10.110 _____ Notice of Lien for Public Improvement.
10.111 _____ Form For Demand for Terms of Contract.
10.112 _____ Demand for Notice of Completion and Acceptance of Public Improvement.
10.113 _____ Petition to Amend Notice of Mechanic's Lien—Correct Name of Owner of Property.
10.114 _____ Assignment of Lien for Public Improvement.
10.115 _____ Assignment of Mechanic's Lien.
10.116 _____ Assignment of Moneys Due or to Become Due Under Public Improvement Contract.
10.117 _____ Affidavit for Continuance of Mechanic's Lien.
10.118 _____ Affidavit for Continuance of Lien for Public Improvement.
10.119 _____ Petition to Discharge Mechanic's Lien Where Notice of Lien Defective.
10.120 _____ Petition for Order Discharging Mechanic's Lien Upon Filing of Undertaking.

TABLE OF CONTENTS

Sec.
10.121 ____ Undertaking to Discharge Mechanic's Lien.
10.122 ____ Petition for Order Fixing Amount of Undertaking to Discharge Mechanic's Lien.
10.123 ____ Approval by Lienors of Subordination of Mechanic's Liens to Trust Bond or Note and Mortgage.
10.124 ____ Affidavit for Order Fixing Amount of Bond to Discharge All Mechanic's Liens.
10.125 ____ Petition for Order Requiring Itemized Statement.
10.126 ____ Notice of Application for Order Requiring Itemized Statement.
10.127 ____ Demand for Itemized Statement.
10.128 ____ Affidavit in Support of Application to Cancel Mechanic's Lien for Failure to Furnish Itemized Statement.
10.129 ____ Notice Requiring Lienor to Commence Action to Enforce Mechanic's Lien.
10.130 ____ Affidavit in Support of Application to Cancel Notice of Mechanic's Lien for Failure to Commence Action.
10.131 ____ Notice Requiring Lienor to Commence Action to Enforce Lien for Public Improvement.
10.132 ____ Affidavit in Support of Application to Cancel Notice of Lien for Public Improvement for Failure to Commence Action.
10.133 ____ Complaint for Foreclosure of Lien for Public Improvement.
10.134 ____ Complaint for Foreclosure of Mechanic's Lien—Contractor.
10.135 ____ Defense and Counterclaim Based on Wilful Exaggeration of Mechanic's Lien.
10.136 ____ Affidavit in Support of Motion to Consolidate Actions for Foreclosure of Mechanic's Liens.
10.137 ____ Notice of Motion to Consolidate Actions to Foreclose Mechanic's Liens.
10.138 ____ Acceptance of Offer to Pay Money Into Court in Discharge of Mechanic's Lien.
10.139 ____ Offer to Pay Money Into Court in Discharge of Mechanic's Lien.
10.140 ____ Judgment of Foreclosure and Sale—Mechanic's Lien.
10.141 ____ Judgment of Foreclosure—Lien for Public Improvement—Where Lien Discharged and Fund Retained for Payment.
10.142 ____ Affidavit in Support of Motion for Summary Judgment—Foreclosure of Lien for Public Improvement.
10.143 ____ Demand for Verified Statement from Trustee.
10.144 ____ Petition for Verified Statement from Trustee of Trust Funds.
10.145 ____ Complaint by Subcontractor to Enforce Trust Against Funds Received by Contractor or Assignee of Contractor.
10.146 ____ Complaint by Surety to Have Parties Declared Trustees of Subcontract Moneys and for Accounting.
10.147 ____ Affidavit in Support of Motion to Determine if Class Action Can be Maintained—Action to Impress and Enforce Trust.

TABLE OF CONTENTS

CHAPTER 11. MORTGAGE FORECLOSURE

Sec.
- 11.1 Scope Note.
- 11.2 Strategy—Initial Client Interview.
- 11.3 ___ First Review of Loan Documents.
- 11.4 ___ Foreclosure Title Certificate.
- 11.5 New York Mortgage Foreclosure Law.
- 11.6 ___ Choice of Remedies: Foreclosure Action or Money Action.
- 11.7 ___ Partial Foreclosure Action.
- 11.8 ___ Non-Judicial Foreclosure.
- 11.9 Representing Subordinate Lienors.
- 11.10 Pre-commencement Procedure.
- 11.11 ___ Notice of Default.
- 11.12 ___ Notice of Acceleration.
- 11.13 ___ Foreclosure Title Certificate.
- 11.14 Determining the Necessary Defendants.
- 11.15 ___ The United States As a Necessary Defendant.
- 11.16 Starting the Foreclosure Action.
- 11.17 ___ Notice of Pendency of Action.
- 11.18 Summons.
- 11.19 ___ Venue.
- 11.20 Complaint.
- 11.21 ___ Allegations Regarding Parties.
- 11.22 ___ Allegations Regarding Loan, Note and Mortgage.
- 11.23 ___ References to Pertinent Terms of Note and Mortgage.
- 11.24 ___ Asserting Default(s).
- 11.25 ___ Reserving Right to Add Advances Made by Plaintiff to Indebtedness Secured by Mortgage.
- 11.26 ___ Allegation Regarding Subordinate Interest of Defendant(s).
- 11.27 ___ Whether There Has Been or is Pending Another Action Regarding the Mortgage Debt.
- 11.28 ___ Amendments.
- 11.29 Receivers.
- 11.30 ___ Considerations in Determining Whether to Seek Appointment of Receiver.
- 11.31 ___ *Ex Parte* Motion for Appointment of Receiver.
- 11.32 ___ Compensation.
- 11.33 ___ Opposing Appointment of Receiver.
- 11.34 ___ Discharging Receiver.
- 11.35 Defendant's Response.
- 11.36 ___ Motion to Dismiss Complaint.
- 11.37 ___ Answer and Defenses.
- 11.38 ___ Notice of Appearance and Waiver.
- 11.39 Obtaining Judgment.
- 11.40 ___ Motion for Judgment.
- 11.41 ___ Opposing Motion for Judgment.
- 11.42 Reference to Compute.
- 11.43 ___ Hearing Before Referee to Compute.
- 11.44 ___ Report of Referee to Compute.
- 11.45 ___ Motion to Confirm Referee's Computation Report and for Judgment of Foreclosure and Sale.

TABLE OF CONTENTS

Sec.
11.46 Judgment of Foreclosure and Sale.
11.47 Foreclosure Sale.
11.48 ____ Noticing and Advertising the Sale.
11.49 ____ Conducting the Sale.
11.50 ____ Vacating the Sale.
11.51 Referee's Deed, Other Closing Documents and Referee's Report of Sale.
11.52 Deficiency Judgment.
11.53 Surplus Money Proceedings.
11.54 Eviction of Tenants and Other Occupants After Foreclosure Sale.
11.55 Drafting Checklists.
11.56 ____ Notice of Default.
11.57 ____ Notice of Acceleration.
11.58 ____ Notice of Pendency of Action.
11.59 ____ Summons.
11.60 ____ Complaint.
11.61 ____ Order Appointing Receiver.
11.62 ____ Affidavit in Support of *Ex Parte* Application for Receiver.
11.63 ____ Notice of Motion for Summary Judgment and Related Relief.
11.64 ____ Affidavit of Regularity and in Support of Plaintiff's Motion for Summary Judgment and Related Relief.
11.65 ____ Judgment of Foreclosure and Sale.
11.66 ____ Notice of Sale.
11.67 ____ Terms and Memorandum of Sale.
11.68 Forms.
11.69 ____ Notice of Default. 💾
11.70 ____ Notice of Acceleration. 💾
11.71 ____ Notice of Pendency of Action. 💾
11.72 ____ Summons. 💾
11.73 ____ Verified Complaint for Foreclosure of Mortgage Affecting Single Family Residence. 💾
11.74 ____ Verified Complaint for Foreclosure of Mortgage Affecting Commercial, Multi–Unit Residential or Mixed Property. 💾
11.75 ____ Order Appointing Receiver. 💾
11.76 ____ Affidavit in Support of Motion for Appointment of Receiver. 💾
11.77 ____ Notice of Motion for Summary Judgment and Related Relief. 💾
11.78 ____ Affidavit of Regularity and in Support of Motion for Summary Judgment. 💾
11.79 ____ Judgment of Foreclosure and Sale. 💾
11.80 ____ Notice of Sale. 💾
11.81 ____ Terms and Memorandum of Sale. 💾

CHAPTER 12. PURCHASE AND SALE OF REAL ESTATE

12.1 Scope Note.
12.2 Strategy.
12.3 ____ Pre-contract Checklist.
12.4 Contract of Sale.

TABLE OF CONTENTS

Sec.
12.5	____ Preparation and Delivery
12.6	____ Recordation.
12.7	Residential Contract of Sale.
12.8	____ Parties.
12.9	____ Premises.
12.10	____ Personal Property.
12.11	____ Purchase Price and Method of Payment.
12.12	____ ____ Down Payment.
12.13	____ ____ Assumption of Existing Mortgage.
12.14	____ ____ Purchase Money Mortgage.
12.15	____ ____ Mortgage Contingency.
12.16	____ ____ Acceptable Funds.
12.17	____ Permitted Exceptions.
12.18	____ Governmental Violations and Orders.
12.19	____ Seller's Representations.
12.20	____ Condition of Property.
12.21	____ Insurable and Marketable Title.
12.22	____ Closing, Deed and Title.
12.23	____ Closing Date and Place.
12.24	____ Conditions to Closing.
12.25	____ Deed Transfer and Recording Taxes.
12.26	____ Apportionments.
12.27	____ Allowance for Unpaid Taxes.
12.28	____ Title Examination; Seller's Inability to Convey; Limitation of Liability.
12.29	____ Defaults and Remedies.
12.30	____ Assignment.
12.31	____ Broker.
12.32	____ Risk of Loss.
12.33	Condominium Contract of Sale.
12.34	____ Comparisons to the Residential Contract of Sale.
12.35	____ Homeowner's Associations.
12.36	Contract of Sale for Office, Commercial and Multi-family Residential Premises.
12.37	Contract of Sale for Cooperative Apartment
12.38	____ Standard Form.
12.39	Contract of Sale for New Construction.
12.40	Title Insurance.
12.41	____ The Buyer's Obligation.
12.42	____ Role of the Title Insurer.
12.43	____ Duration and Cost.
12.44	____ Basic and Extended Coverage.
12.45	Title Insurance Policy.
12.46	____ Loan Policy Coverage.
12.47	____ New York Modifications of Loan Policy.
12.48	____ Owner's Policy Coverage.
12.49	____ New York Modifications of Owner's Policy.
12.50	____ Standard Exceptions.
12.51	____ Endorsements.
12.52	____ Exclusions.

TABLE OF CONTENTS

Sec.

12.53	Title Examination: Recording Title and the Torrens System.
12.54	___ Objections to Be Disposed of Prior to Closing.
12.55	___ ___ Checklist.
12.56	The Survey Map.
12.57	___ What it May Disclose.
12.58	___ Effect on Marketability of Title.
12.59	___ ___ Where Contract Is Silent on the Matter of Survey.
12.60	___ ___ Where Contract Subject to Any State of Facts an Accurate Survey May Show.
12.61	___ ___ Where Contract Subject to Any State of Facts an Accurate Survey May Show Provided Same Does Not Render Title Unmarketable.
12.62	___ ___ Where Contract Subject to Specific Encroachments or to Facts Shown on a Specific Survey.
12.63	___ ___ Suggested Clause.
12.64	Marketability of Title.
12.65	___ What Renders Title Unmarketable.
12.66	___ ___ Encroachments Due to Adverse Possession.
12.67	___ ___ Party Walls.
12.68	___ Driveway Easements.
12.69	___ Other Covenants and Restrictions.
12.70	___ Reservations for Public Utilities.
12.71	___ Land Abutting Bodies of Water and the Federal Navigational Servitude.
12.72	Closing of Title.
12.73	___ Checklist.
12.74	___ Recording Fees and Filings.
12.75	___ Disclosure and Other Requirements.
12.76	___ ___ Foreign Investors Real Property Tax.
12.77	___ ___ Form 1099-S Federal Requirement for One to Four Family Residence.
12.78	___ ___ Form 1099-S Federal Requirement for One to Four Family Residence—Checklist.
12.79	___ ___ Cash Payments Received by Businesses in Excess of $10,000.
12.80	___ ___ Lead Paint Hazards.
12.81	___ ___ Agricultural Foreign Investment Disclosure Act.
12.82	___ Payment of Taxes.
12.83	___ ___ New York State Real Estate Transfer Tax and Mansion Tax.
12.84	___ ___ Article 31-B—Real Property Transfer Gains Tax.
12.85	___ ___ New York City Real Property Transfer Tax.
12.86	___ ___ Cities of Mount Vernon and Yonkers.
12.87	___ ___ Real Estate Investment Trusts.
12.88	___ ___ Mortgage Recording Tax Outside New York City.
12.89	___ ___ Mortgage Recording Tax Rate in New York City.
12.90	___ Method of Payment.
12.91	___ Other Required Forms and Information.
12.92	Forms.
12.93	___ Residential Contract of Sale.

TABLE OF CONTENTS

Sec.
12.94	____ Contract of Sale—Condominium Unit.
12.95	____ ____ Office, Commercial and Multi–Family Residential Premises.
12.96	____ ____ Cooperative Apartment.
12.97	____ Durable General Power of Attorney. 💾
12.98	____ Power of Attorney to Take Effect at a Later Time. 💾

Volume 22

CHAPTER 13. LANDLORD–TENANT LAW

13.1	Scope Note.
13.2	Strategy.
13.3	____ Checklists.
13.4	Summary Proceedings.
13.5	____ Venue and Jurisdiction.
13.6	____ Service of Process.
13.7	____ ____ Personal Delivery.
13.8	____ ____ Substituted Service.
13.9	____ ____ Conspicuous Place Service.
13.10	____ ____ New York City Civil Court "Postcard Requirement."
13.11	Non-payment Proceedings.
13.12	____ Rent Demands.
13.13	____ Notice of Petition.
13.14	____ ____ Form of Notice.
13.15	____ ____ Content of Notice.
13.16	____ ____ Defects in the Notice.
13.17	____ The Petition.
13.18	____ ____ Defects in the Petition.
13.19	____ ____ Verification.
13.20	____ ____ Defects in the Verification.
13.21	Responding to the Non-payment Petition.
13.22	____ The Answer.
13.23	____ The Motion to Dismiss.
13.24	____ The RPAPL § 755 Motion to Stay.
13.25	Tenant Defenses to the Non-payment Proceeding.
13.26	____ No Landlord Tenant Relationship.
13.27	____ Tenant Out of Possession.
13.28	____ Statutory Noncompliance.
13.29	____ Illegal Rent.
13.30	____ Actual Eviction.
13.31	____ Constructive Eviction.
13.32	____ Warranty of Habitability.
13.33	____ Laches.
13.34	____ Payment.
13.35	Holdover Proceedings.
13.36	____ Predicate Notices.
13.37	____ ____ Month-to-Month Tenants.
13.38	____ ____ Illegal Use.
13.39	____ ____ Rent–Controlled Tenants.

TABLE OF CONTENTS

Sec.
13.40 ___ ___ Rent–Stabilized Tenants.
13.41 ___ The Notice of Petition.
13.42 ___ ___ Defects in the Notice.
13.43 ___ Holdover Petition—Form and Content.
13.44 ___ ___ Defects in the Petition.
13.45 ___ ___ Verification and Verification Defects.
13.46 Responding to the Holdover Petition.
13.47 ___ The Answer.
13.48 ___ The Motion to Dismiss.
13.49 Tenant Defenses to the Holdover Proceeding.
13.50 ___ Acceptance of Rent After Expiration or Termination of Tenancy.
13.51 ___ Defective Predicate Notice.
13.52 ___ ___ Rent–Regulated Apartments.
13.53 ___ Waiver.
13.54 ___ Equitable Estoppel.
13.55 ___ Succession Rights to Rent–Regulated Apartments.
13.56 Counterclaims.
13.57 Bill of Particulars.
13.58 Discovery.
13.59 ___ Notice to Admit.
13.60 ___ Freedom of Information Law.
13.61 The Trial—Adjournments.
13.62 ___Amending Petition and Burden of Proof.
13.63 Stipulations—Overview.
13.64 ___ Non-payment Proceedings.
13.65 ___ Holdover Proceedings.
13.66 ___ Enforcement and Vacatur.
13.67 The Judgment and Warrant.
13.68 ___ Staying the Warrant in Non-payment Proceedings.
13.69 ___ Staying the Warrant in New York City Residential Holdover Proceedings.
13.70 Yellowstone Actions.
13.71 ___ Obtaining the Injunction.
13.72 Article 7–A Proceedings.
13.73 Rent Regulatory Proceedings.
13.74 ___ Rent Overcharge.
13.75 ___ Service Reduction.
13.76 ___ Major Capital Improvement Rent Increase.
13.77 Checklist of Essential Allegations.
13.78 ___ Petition Non-payment.
13.79 ___ Holdover Petition.
13.80 ___ Stipulation Settling Non-payment Proceeding.
13.81 ___ Stipulation Settling Holdover Proceeding.
13.82 Forms.
13.83 ___ Petition Non-payment.
13.84 ___ Petition Holdover.
13.85 ___ Individual Verification.
13.86 ___ Corporate Officer Verification.
13.87 ___ Partnership Verification.

TABLE OF CONTENTS

Sec.
13.88 ____ Attorney Verification.
13.89 ____ Stipulations.
13.90 ____ ____ Settling Non-payment Proceeding.
13.91 ____ ____ Settling Non-payment Proceeding With Final Judgment in Favor of Petitioner.
13.92 ____ ____ Settling Holdover Proceeding Where Tenant Agrees to Cure Lease Violation.
13.93 ____ ____ Settling Holdover Proceeding Where Tenant–Respondent Agrees to Vacate Premises.

CHAPTER 14. EMINENT DOMAIN

14.1 Scope Note.
14.2 Strategies for Condemnors and Condemnees.
14.3 Exercise of the Power of Eminent Domain.
14.4 ____ The State as Condemnor.
14.5 ____ Other Public Entities as Condemnor.
14.6 ____ Private Entities.
14.7 Property Rights Subject to Acquisition.
14.8 ____ Real Property.
14.9 ____ Easements.
14.10 ____ Leases.
14.11 ____ Personal Property.
14.12 ____ Public Property/Priority of Taking.
14.13 ____ Excess Property.
14.14 *De Facto* Taking.
14.15 Public Use, Benefit or Purpose.
14.16 ____ Particular Uses.
14.17 ____ Incidental Private Benefit.
14.18 Just Compensation.
14.19 Summary.
14.20 The First Stage: The Condemnation Phase.
14.21 Public Hearing.
14.22 Exemptions From the Public Hearing Requirement.
14.23 ____ Overlap with Other Governmental Requirements.
14.24 ____ Overlap with Issuance of a Certificate of Environmental Compatibility and Public Need.
14.25 ____ Alternate Public Hearing.
14.26 ____ *De Minimis* Acquisition or Emergency Situation.
14.27 ____ Section 41.34 of the Mental Hygiene Law.
14.28 Notice.
14.29 Conduct of the Public Hearing and Requirement of a Record.
14.30 Determination and Findings.
14.31 ____ Publication of Synopsis.
14.32 ____ Interplay with SEQRA.
14.33 ____ Amendments for Field Conditions.
14.34 Judicial Review of Determination and Findings.
14.35 ____ Prerequisite Determination.
14.36 ____ Persons Entitled to Review.
14.37 ____ 30–Day Statute of Limitations.

TABLE OF CONTENTS

Sec.
14.38 ____ Scope of Review.
14.39 Summary.
14.40 The Second Stage—The "Offer and Negotiation" Phase.
14.41 ____ Pretaking Appraisals.
14.42 ____ Pretaking Discovery.
14.43 ____ Offer as Payment in Full.
14.44 ____ Advance Payment.
14.45 Use and Occupancy by Condemnee After Taking.
14.46 Summary.
14.47 The Third Stage—The Acquisition Phase.
14.48 ____ Court of Claims v. Supreme Court Jurisdiction.
14.49 ____ Statute of Limitations for Bringing an Acquisition Proceeding.
14.50 ____ ____ Acquisition in Stages.
14.51 ____ Acquisition Map.
14.52 Acquisition of Property—Court of Claims Jurisdiction.
14.53 ____ Condemnors Subject to Court of Claims Jurisdiction.
14.54 ____ Filing and Notice Requirements.
14.55 ____ Vesting of Title.
14.56 Acquisition of Property—Supreme Court Jurisdiction.
14.57 ____ Notice of Pendency.
14.58 ____ Petition in Condemnation.
14.59 ____ ____ Content.
14.60 ____ ____ Additional Content Rules for Certain Non-governmental Condemnors.
14.61 ____ Notice.
14.62 ____ ____ Certification of Names of Reputed Condemnees.
14.63 ____ Answer by Condemnee.
14.64 ____ ____ Defenses.
14.65 ____ Vesting of Title and Order of Condemnation.
14.66 Notice of Acquisition.
14.67 Immediate Entry.
14.68 Summary.
14.69 The Fourth Stage—The Compensation Phase.
14.70 ____ Court of Claims.
14.71 ____ ____ Time to File Claim.
14.72 ____ ____ Service.
14.73 ____ Supreme Court.
14.74 ____ ____ Time to File Claim.
14.75 ____ ____ Service.
14.76 Content of Claim.
14.77 Scope of Just Compensation.
14.78 ____ "Highest and Best Use."
14.79 ____ Total Taking.
14.80 ____ ____ Direct Damages.
14.81 ____ ____ Improvements.
14.82 ____ Partial Taking.
14.83 ____ Temporary Taking.
14.84 ____ ____ Easements.
14.85 Methods of Valuation to Determine Compensation.

TABLE OF CONTENTS

Sec.
14.86 ____ Market Approach to Value.
14.87 ____ Income Approach to Value.
14.88 ____ Cost Approach to Value.
14.89 Specialty Property.
14.90 Effect of Environmental Contamination on Property Value.
14.91 Fixtures.
14.92 ____ Compensable Fixtures.
14.93 ____ Valuation of Fixtures.
14.94 Leasehold Interests.
14.95 ____ Valuation and Compensation.
14.96 Loss of Business and Goodwill.
14.97 Going Concern Value.
14.98 Moving and Relocation Expenses.
14.99 Conflicting Claims by Condemnees.
14.100 ____ Conflicting Claims to the Condemnor's Offer.
14.101 ____ Conflicting Claims to the Award.
14.102 The Trial on Compensation.
14.103 ____ Preference.
14.104 ____ Filing and Exchange of Appraisals.
14.105 ____ Expert Testimony.
14.106 ____ Viewing of the Property.
14.107 ____ Joint or Consolidated Trials.
14.108 ____ Interest.
14.109 Setoff for Indirect Benefit.
14.110 Incidental Expenses and Proration of Taxes.
14.111 Abandonment of Procedure by Condemnor.
14.112 Finding that Condemnor is Not Legally Authorized to Acquire the Property.
14.113 Finding Contrary to Claim by Condemnor That it Did Not Take Property.
14.114 Decision By the Court and Entry of Judgment.
14.115 Additional Allowances for Costs and Expenses.
14.116 Payment Pending Appeal.
14.117 Small Claims Proceedings.
14.118 Summary.
14.119 Procedural Checklist.
14.120 Forms—Demand on Condemnor to File Copy of Proceedings to Determine Need and Location of Public Project with Appellate Division for Purpose of Judicial Review.
14.121 ____ Petition for Review of Determination and Finding that Public Use, Benefit or Purpose Will be Served by Proposed Acquisition.
14.122 ____ Judgment of Appellate Division Rejecting the Determination and Finding that Public Use, Benefit or Purpose Will be Served by Proposed Acquisition.
14.123 ____ Complaint by Condemnee to Establish Fair and Reasonable Value for Temporary Use and Occupancy After Acquisition by Eminent Domain.

TABLE OF CONTENTS

Sec.

14.124 ____ Notice of Pendency of Proceeding in Supreme Court to Acquire Property by Eminent Domain and File Acquisition Map.

14.125 ____ Notice of Petition in Proceeding in Supreme Court to Acquire Property by Eminent Domain and File Acquisition Map.

14.126 ____ Petition in Proceeding in Supreme Court to Acquire Property by Eminent Domain and File Acquisition Map.

14.127 ____ Petition in Proceeding in Supreme Court to Acquire Property by Eminent Domain and File Acquisition Map—Petitioner Exempt from Compliance with Eminent Domain Procedure Law Article 2.

14.128 ____ Answer to Petition in Proceeding in Supreme Court to Acquire Property by Eminent Domain and File Acquisition Map.

14.129 ____ Order to Show Cause Why Condemnor Should Not be Permitted to Enter Immediately upon Real Property and Devote It Temporarily to Public Use Specified in Petition Upon Deposit of a Fixed Sum with the Court.

14.130 ____ Order to Show Cause Why Condemnor Should Not be Permitted to File Acquisition Maps or Enter upon Real Property.

14.131 ____ Order in Proceeding in Supreme Court to Acquire Property by Eminent Domain and File Acquisition Map.

14.132 ____ Notice of Acquisition by Eminent Domain Where Supreme Court Has Jurisdiction.

14.133 ____ Claim for Damages Arising from Acquisition by Eminent Domain—General Form.

14.134 ____ Judgment Awarding Compensation in Claim for Acquisition of Property by Eminent Domain.

14.135 ____ Notice of Motion for Additional Allowance to Condemnee for Expert Witnesses.

14.136 ____ Affidavit in Support of Motion for Additional Allowance to Condemnee for Expert Witnesses.

14.137 ____ Order Granting Additional Allowance to Condemnee for Expert Witnesses.

CHAPTER 15. ENVIRONMENTAL LAW

15.1 Scope Note.
15.2 Strategy.
15.3 State Environmental Quality Review Act.
15.4 ____ Determination of Significance.
15.5 ____ The Environmental Impact Statement and Findings Statement.
15.6 ____ Judicial Review.
15.7 ____ Checklist.
15.8 Water Pollution Control.
15.9 ____ SPDES Permit Program.
15.10 ____ Stormwater Discharges and Oil Spills.
15.11 ____ Enforcement.

TABLE OF CONTENTS

Sec.
15.12 ___ Strategy: Clean Water Act Citizen Suit Checklist.
15.13 Wetlands Protection.
15.14 ___ Strategy: Checklist.
15.15 ___ The Federal Scheme.
15.16 ___ New York Tidal and Freshwater Wetlands Law.
15.17 ___ Permit Procedure and Criteria.
15.18 ___ Penalties.
15.19 Air Pollution Control.
15.20 ___ The 1990 CAA Amendments.
15.21 ___ New York State Requirements.
15.22 ___ Enforcement.
15.23 Regulation of Solid and Hazardous Waste.
15.24 ___ New York Hazardous Waste Regulation.
15.25 ___ Enforcement.
15.26 Regulation of Underground Storage Tanks and Petroleum Storage Tanks—Federal Law.
15.27 ___ New York Law.
15.28 Regulation of Inactive Hazardous Waste Sites—CERCLA.
15.29 ___ CERCLA Section 107(a).
15.30 ___ Lender Liability, Contribution and Indemnification Under CERCLA.
15.31 ___ New York Law.
15.32 Relevant Common Law Doctrines—Nuisance.
15.33 Common Law Doctrines—Trespass.
15.34 Regulatory Takings.
15.35 Drafting Checklist—Clean Water Act Citizen Suit Notice Letter.
15.36 ___ Clean Water Act and Resource Conservation and Recovery Act Citizen Suit Notice Letter.
15.37 ___ Clean Water Act Complaint.
15.38 ___ Nuisance and Trespass Complaint.
15.39 ___ Oil Spill Complaint.
15.40 Forms—Clean Water Act Citizen Suit Notice Letter.
15.41 ___ Clean Water Act and Resource Conservation and Recovery Act Citizen Suit Notice Letter.
15.42 ___ Clean Water Act Complaint.
15.43 ___ Nuisance and Trespass Complaint.
15.44 ___ Oil Spill Complaint.

CHAPTER 16. LAND USE LAW

16.1 Scope Note.
16.2 Strategy.
16.3 Local Land Use Law.
16.4 ___ Delegated Authority.
16.5 ___ Enabling Acts.
16.6 ___ ___ New York City.
16.7 ___ Home Rule Authority.
16.8 ___ ___ Flexibility.
16.9 ___ ___ Floating Zone.
16.10 ___ Summary.

TABLE OF CONTENTS

Sec.
16.11 Comprehensive Plan.
16.12 ____ Judicial Definition.
16.13 ____ Statutory Definition.
16.14 ____ Preparation and Adoption.
16.15 ____ Protects Zoning Against Challenge.
16.16 ____ Summary.
16.17 Substantive Limits—Illustrative Case.
16.18 ____ Substantive Due Process.
16.19 ____ Procedural Due Process.
16.20 ____ Equal Protection.
16.21 ____ *Ultra Vires*.
16.22 ____ Regulatory Takings.
16.23 ____ Vested Rights.
16.24 ____ Preemption.
16.25 ____ First Amendment.
16.26 ____ Summary.
16.27 Local Process.
16.28 ____ Structure of Local Regulations.
16.29 ____ Adoption.
16.30 ____ Amendment.
16.31 ____ Other Regulations/Official Map.
16.32 ____ Building Regulations and Permits.
16.33 ____ Summary.
16.34 Local Boards and Practices.
16.35 ____ Local Legislature.
16.36 ____ Planning Board.
16.37 ____ Zoning Board of Appeals.
16.38 ____ Freedom of Information.
16.39 ____ Open Meetings.
16.40 ____ Conflict of Interests.
16.41 ____ Summary.
16.42 Judicial Review.
16.43 ____ Procedures.
16.44 ____ Standards.
16.45 ____ ____ Local Legislature.
16.46 ____ ____ Zoning Board of Appeals.
16.47 ____ ____ Planning Board.
16.48 ____ Standing.
16.49 ____ Exhaustion.
16.50 ____ Remedies.
16.51 ____ Summary.
16.52 Local Environmental Review.
16.53 ____ Actions Subject to SEQRA.
16.54 ____ ____ Building Permits.
16.55 ____ ____ Variances.
16.56 ____ ____ Subdivisions.
16.57 ____ ____ Site Plans.
16.58 ____ ____ Rezoning.
16.59 ____ Summary.
16.60 Zoning Law—In General.

TABLE OF CONTENTS

Sec.
16.61 As of Right Use.
16.62 Nonconforming Use—Definition and Application.
16.63 ___ Changes.
16.64 ___ Reconstruction and Restoration.
16.65 ___ Enlargement, Alteration or Extension.
16.66 ___ Changes to Another Nonconforming Use.
16.67 ___ Termination.
16.68 ___ Abandonment.
16.69 ___ Amortization.
16.70 ___ Transfer of Ownership.
16.71 ___ Procedures.
16.72 ___ Summary.
16.73 Use Variance.
16.74 ___ Statutory Standard.
16.75 ___ ___ Reasonable Return.
16.76 ___ ___ Unique Hardship.
16.77 ___ ___ Protect Essential Neighborhood Character.
16.78 ___ ___ Self-Created Hardship.
16.79 ___ Minimum Variance Needed.
16.80 ___ Procedure.
16.81 ___ Summary.
16.82 Area Variance.
16.83 ___ Statutory Balancing Test.
16.84 ___ ___ Guiding Principles from Case Law.
16.85 ___ ___ Balancing Factors.
16.86 ___ Minimum Variance Needed.
16.87 ___ Procedure.
16.88 ___ Summary.
16.89 Conditions Imposed on Use and Area Variances.
16.90 Special Use Permits.
16.91 ___ Imposition and Use of Standards.
16.92 ___ Findings and Determination of Board.
16.93 ___ Limitation on Imposition of Conditions.
16.94 ___ Procedure.
16.95 ___ Summary.
16.96 Subdivision Approval.
16.97 ___ Procedure.
16.98 ___ ___ How Affected By SEQRA.
16.99 ___ Provision of Essential Services.
16.100 ___ Parkland.
16.101 ___ Decisions and Conditions.
16.102 ___ Summary.
16.103 Site Plans.
16.104 ___ Responsible Agency.
16.105 ___ ___ Procedure.
16.106 ___ ___ Standards for Review.
16.107 ___ ___ Conditions Imposed.
16.108 ___ Summary.
16.109 Particularized Actions.
16.110 ___ Spot Zoning.

TABLE OF CONTENTS

Sec.
- 16.111 ____ ____ Challenge Dismissed.
- 16.112 ____ ____ Challenge Successful.
- 16.113 ____ Rezoning.
- 16.114 ____ ____ Conditions.
- 16.115 ____ ____ Contract Zoning.
- 16.116 ____ ____ Development Agreements.
- 16.117 ____ Summary.
- 16.118 Special Regulations.
- 16.119 ____ Accessory Uses.
- 16.120 ____ Accessory Apartments.
- 16.121 ____ Home Offices.
- 16.122 ____ Definition of Family.
- 16.123 ____ Affordable Housing.
- 16.124 ____ Mobile Homes.
- 16.125 ____ Aesthetics.
- 16.126 ____ ____ Architectural Review.
- 16.127 ____ ____ Historic Preservation.
- 16.128 ____ Public Uses.
- 16.129 ____ ____ Public Utilities.
- 16.130 ____ ____ Cellular Transmission Facilities.
- 16.131 ____ ____ Religious Uses.
- 16.132 ____ Summary.
- 16.133 Forms—Environmental Assessment—Short Form. 💾
- 16.134 ____ Environmental Assessment—Long Form. 💾

CHAPTER 17. EMPLOYMENT LAW

- 17.1 Scope Note.
- 17.2 Strategy.
- 17.3 ____ Plaintiff's Counsel's Investigation.
- 17.4 ____ Defendant's Counsel's Investigation.
- 17.5 ____ Pre-litigation Settlement Process.
- 17.6 ____ Negotiating With Opposing Counsel.
- 17.7 ____ Alternative Dispute Resolution ("ADR").
- 17.8 ____ ____ Mediation.
- 17.9 ____ ____ Arbitration.
- 17.10 ____ Settlement and Severance Agreements.
- 17.11 ____ ____ Older Workers Benefit Protection Act ("OWBPA").
- 17.12 ____ ____ COBRA.
- 17.13 ____ ____ Pay.
- 17.14 ____ ____ Income Taxes.
- 17.15 ____ ____ Benefits.
- 17.16 ____ Other Severance Issues.
- 17.17 ____ Independent Contractor vs. Employee.
- 17.18 ____ Checklist: Initial Considerations for Plaintiff.
- 17.19 ____ Checklist: Terminating an Employee.
- 17.20 Causes of Action.
- 17.21 ____ Tort–Assault.
- 17.22 ____ ____ Battery.
- 17.23 ____ ____ Conspiracy.

TABLE OF CONTENTS

Sec.
- 17.24 ___ ___ Conversion.
- 17.25 ___ ___ Defamation.
- 17.26 ___ ___ False Imprisonment; Malicious Prosecution.
- 17.27 ___ ___ Fraud, Negligent Misrepresentation and Fraudulent Inducement.
- 17.28 ___ ___ Intentional Infliction of Emotional Distress.
- 17.29 ___ ___ Interference with Business Relations.
- 17.30 ___ ___ Negligence.
- 17.31 ___ ___ *Prima Facie* Tort.
- 17.32 ___ ___ Wrongful Discharge.
- 17.33 ___ Contract.
- 17.34 ___ ___ Express Promises.
- 17.35 ___ ___ Implied Promises.
- 17.36 ___ ___ Estoppel.
- 17.37 Statutory Causes of Action—Age Discrimination.
- 17.38 ___ Anti-reprisal Provisions of Various Statutes.
- 17.39 ___ Arrest Records.
- 17.40 ___ Bankruptcy.
- 17.41 ___ Convictions.
- 17.42 ___ Credit Information.
- 17.43 ___ Disability.
- 17.44 ___ Equal Pay.
- 17.45 ___ Family and Medical Leave Act (FMLA).
- 17.46 ___ Health Plan Coverage (COBRA).
- 17.47 ___ Legal Off Duty Activities.
- 17.48 ___ Marital Status Discrimination.
- 17.49 ___ Discrimination on the Basis of Race, Color or National Origin.
- 17.50 ___ Pension Plans.
- 17.51 ___ Plant Closing, Mass Layoffs.
- 17.52 ___ Polygraphs.
- 17.53 ___ Public Employees.
- 17.54 ___ Pregnancy.
- 17.55 ___ Privacy.
- 17.56 ___ Religious Discrimination.
- 17.57 ___ Sex Discrimination, Harassment.
- 17.58 ___ Sexual Orientation Discrimination.
- 17.59 ___ Title VII, Burdens of Proof.
- 17.60 ___ Unemployment Insurance.
- 17.61 ___ Unionization, Rights Within Unions.
- 17.62 ___ Unsafe Workplace.
- 17.63 ___ Wages; Unpaid Compensation; Overtime.
- 17.64 ___ Whistleblowing/*Qui Tam*.
- 17.65 ___ Workers' Compensation.
- 17.66 Procedure—Anti-discrimination Agency Practice.
- 17.67 ___ Filing and Responding to Administrative Charges.
- 17.68 ___ Election of Remedies.
- 17.69 ___ Statutes of Limitations and Prerequisites to Private Lawsuits.
- 17.70 Private Lawsuits.

TABLE OF CONTENTS

Sec.
17.71 ____ Discovery—General Considerations.
17.72 ____ ____ Plaintiff's Strategy.
17.73 ____ Summary Judgment.
17.74 ____ Trial.
17.75 ____ Fee Application.
17.76 ____ Post–Trial Motions and Appeal.
17.77 ____ Checklist: Statutes of Limitations.
17.78 ____ Checklist: Commencement of New York State Actions.
17.79 ____ Checklist: Commencement of Federal Court Actions.
17.80 Miscellaneous Practice Issues—OFCCP/Glass Ceiling Audits.
17.81 ____ Employment Policies and Handbooks.
17.82 Drafting the Complaint.
17.83 Drafting Checklist—Complaint.
17.84 Drafting the Answer.
17.85 Drafting Checklist—Answer
17.86 Forms—Client (Plaintiff) Intake Questionnaire.
17.87 ____ Severance/Release Agreement.
17.88 ____ Letter to EEOC Requesting "Mohasco" Waiver of State Processing.
17.89 ____ Charge of Discrimination—New York State Division of Human Rights (Official Form).
17.90 ____ Information Sheet—New York State Division of Human Rights (Official Form).
17.91 ____ SDHR Information Sheet.
17.92 ____ Charge of Discrimination—Equal Employment Opportunity Commission (Official Form).
17.93 ____ Affidavit for a Charge of Discrimination—Equal Employment Opportunity Commission (Official Form).
17.94 ____ EEOC Filing Cover Letter Requesting EEOC Processing of Dual–filed Charge.
17.95 ____ Letter Requesting Administrative Convenience Dismissal from State or City Administrative Agency.
17.96 ____ Pleadings—New York State Complaint.
17.97 ____ ____ New York State Answer.
17.98 ____ ____ Federal Complaint.
17.99 ____ ____ Federal Answer.

CHAPTER 18. CIVIL RIGHTS

18.1 Scope Note.
18.2 Strategy.
18.3 ____ Checklist.
18.4 Overview of New York and Federal Civil Rights Provisions.
18.5 Jurisdiction over Civil Rights Actions.
18.6 New York Bill of Rights.
18.7 ____ Overview.
18.8 ____ Comparison With Federal Bill of Rights.
18.9 ____ Search and Seizure.
18.10 ____ ____ Civil Liability.
18.11 ____ ____ Return of Seized Property.

TABLE OF CONTENTS

Sec.
- 18.12 ____ Rights of Persons Accused of Crimes.
- 18.13 ____ ____ Public Trial/Closure of Courtroom.
- 18.14 ____ ____ Exclusion of Public or Press.
- 18.15 ____ Rights of Jurors.
- 18.16 General Federal Civil Rights Provisions.
- 18.17 ____ 42 U.S.C.A. § 1981.
- 18.18 ____ 42 U.S.C.A. § 1983.
- 18.19 ____ Other Federal Civil Rights Provisions.
- 18.20 Police and Prosecutorial Misconduct.
- 18.21 ____ Excessive Force.
- 18.22 ____ False Arrest.
- 18.23 ____ False Imprisonment.
- 18.24 ____ Search and Seizure.
- 18.25 ____ Malicious Prosecution.
- 18.26 First Amendment.
- 18.27 ____ Freedom of Speech.
- 18.28 ____ Freedom of Religion.
- 18.29 Rights of Prisoners.
- 18.30 Defenses to Federal Actions.
- 18.31 ____ Absolute Immunity.
- 18.32 ____ Qualified Immunity.
- 18.33 ____ Eleventh Amendment.
- 18.34 ____ *Monell* and Its Progeny.
- 18.35 ____ *Respondeat Superior*.
- 18.36 ____ Abstention.
- 18.37 ____ *Res Judicata* and Collateral Estoppel.
- 18.38 ____ Statute of Limitations.
- 18.39 Housing.
- 18.40 ____ Prohibition Against Discrimination in Publicly Assisted Housing.
- 18.41 ____ ____ Owners and Lessors.
- 18.42 ____ ____ Real Estate Agents and Brokers.
- 18.43 ____ ____ Remedies for Discrimination.
- 18.44 ____ Prohibition Against Discrimination in Private Housing.
- 18.45 ____ ____ Owners and Lessors.
- 18.46 ____ ____ Real Estate Agents and Brokers.
- 18.47 ____ ____ Cooperatives.
- 18.48 ____ ____ Remedies for Discrimination.
- 18.49 ____ ____ ____ Administrative Proceedings.
- 18.50 ____ ____ ____ Actions in State and Federal Court.
- 18.51 ____ *Prima Facie* Case and Burden of Proof.
- 18.52 ____ Summary of Procedure for Filing an Administrative Claim and Challenging an SDHR Order.
- 18.53 Education.
- 18.54 Equal Rights in Places of Public Accommodation and Amusement.
- 18.55 ____ General Provisions.
- 18.56 ____ Private Clubs.
- 18.57 ____ Persons With Disabilities Accompanied by a Guide Dog, Hearing Dog or Service Dog.
- 18.58 ____ Remedies for Discrimination.

TABLE OF CONTENTS

Sec.
18.59 Employment Discrimination Provisions Exclusive to the New York Civil Rights Law.
18.60 ___ In General.
18.61 ___ Persons With Disabilities.
18.62 ___ Persons With Genetic Disorders.
18.63 Right of Privacy.
18.64 ___ Generally.
18.65 ___ Police Officers, Corrections Officers and Firefighters.
18.66 ___ Victims of Sex Offenses.
18.67 Changing One's Name.
18.68 ___ Procedure for Petition to Change Name.
18.69 ___ ___ Contents of Petition.
18.70 ___ ___ Special Procedures for Infants.
18.71 ___ Factors to Be Considered by the Court.
18.72 ___ Publication Requirement.
18.73 ___ Checklist.
18.74 Heart Balm Statute.
18.75 ___ Penalty for Bringing Action.
18.76 ___ Action for Return of Gifts Made in Contemplation of Marriage.
18.77 ___ ___ Procedure.
18.78 Miscellaneous Rights and Immunities.
18.79 ___ Frivolous Litigation.
18.80 ___ ___ Protection from SLAPP Suits.
18.81 ___ Libel and Slander.
18.82 ___ ___ Defenses.
18.83 ___ Breast Feeding.
18.84 ___ Suspension of Rights Due to Imprisonment.
18.85 ___ Shield Law.
18.86 ___ Performing Abortion.
18.87 ___ "Good Samaritan" Law Provisions.
18.88 Drafting Checklists.
18.89 ___ Framing the Federal Court § 1983 Complaint.
18.90 ___ Petition to Change One's Name.
18.91 Forms.
18.92 ___ Complaint for False Arrest, False Imprisonment and Malicious Prosecution.
18.93 ___ Complaint for Excessive Force.
18.94 ___ Complaint for Return of Seized Property.
18.95 ___ Complaint Against Landlord for Housing Discrimination.
18.96 ___ Complaint Against Cooperative for Discrimination.
18.97 ___ Notice of Commencement of Action for Discrimination.
18.98 ___ Complaint for Discrimination in Place of Public Accommodation.
18.99 ___ Petition to Change Name.

CHAPTER 19. IMMIGRATION AND NATIONALITY LAW —PERMANENT RESIDENCE APPLICATIONS

19.1 Scope Note.

TABLE OF CONTENTS

Sec.
19.2	Strategy.
19.3	____ Flowchart.
19.4	Overview of the U.S. Immigration System.
19.5	____ Numerical Limitations on Immigrant Selection.
19.6	____ Implementation: Foreign State Chargeability and Quota Allocation.
19.7	Family–Based Immigration.
19.8	____ Immediate Relative Categories.
19.9	____ Family Preference Categories.
19.10	____ Qualifying as a Relation.
19.11	____ ____ "Child" and "Parent" Issues.
19.12	____ ____ "Marriage" Issues.
19.13	____ Petitioning Procedures and Documentation.
19.14	____ ____ I–130 Petition.
19.15	____ Orphans and Amerasians.
19.16	____ Abused Spouse and Children.
19.17	Employment–Based Immigration.
19.18	____ First Employment Preference Applicants (Priority Workers).
19.19	____ ____ Extraordinary Ability Aliens.
19.20	____ ____ Outstanding Professors and Researchers.
19.21	____ ____ Managerial or Executive Intracompany Transferees.
19.22	____ Second Employment Preference Applicants.
19.23	____ ____ Exceptional Ability Aliens.
19.24	____ ____ Advanced Degree Professionals.
19.25	____ ____ The Role of "National Interest."
19.26	____ Third Employment Preference Applicants.
19.27	____ ____ Professional and Skilled Workers.
19.28	____ ____ Unskilled Workers.
19.29	____ I–140 Petition, Procedures and Documentation.
19.30	____ ____ Checklist.
19.31	____ Labor Certification.
19.32	____ ____ Procedures.
19.33	____ ____ Legal Issues.
19.34	____ ____ Job Description.
19.35	____ ____ Business Necessity.
19.36	____ ____ Recruitment.
19.37	____ ____ Approvals.
19.38	____ ____ Notices of Findings.
19.39	____ ____ Denials and Administrative Appeal.
19.40	____ Fourth Employment Preference Applicants.
19.41	____ ____ Religious Workers and Ministers.
19.42	____ Fifth Employment Preference Applicants (Immigrant Investors).
19.43	____ Petition Procedures and Requirements.
19.44	____ ____ Special Immigrant Investor Programs.
19.45	Special Categories.
19.46	____ The Diversity (Lottery) Program.
19.47	____ Registry.
19.48	____ Cancellation of Removal.
19.49	____ Legislatively Created Programs.

TABLE OF CONTENTS

Sec.
19.50 ____ Asylum and Refugee Status.
19.51 Applying for Permanent Residence.
19.52 ____ Exclusionary Grounds.
19.53 ____ Immigrant Visa Processing.
19.54 ____ ____ Framework of the Immigrant Visa Processing System.
19.55 ____ ____ Special Requirements, Public Law No. 103–317.
19.56 ____ ____ Checklist of Required Documents.
19.57 ____ Adjustment of Status.
19.58 ____ ____ General Requirements.
19.59 ____ ____ Special Provisions of Section 245(i).
19.60 ____ ____ Discretionary Factors.
19.61 ____ ____ Application Process.
19.62 ____ ____ Concurrent Filing of Petition and Adjustment of Status.
19.63 ____ ____ Completion of the Process.
19.64 ____ ____ Administrative and Judicial Review.
19.65 ____ ____ Checklist.
19.66 ____ Tactical Considerations.
19.67 ____ ____ Nonimmigrant Status as a Factor.
19.68 ____ ____ Immigrant Visa Processing Versus Adjustment of Status.
19.69 ____ ____ Flowchart.
19.70 The Green Card and its Limitations.
19.71 ____ Conditional Residence.
19.72 ____ ____ Marriage Cases, Removal of Condition.
19.73 ____ ____ Immigrant Investors, Removal of Condition.
19.74 ____ Unconditional Permanent Residence.
19.75 Forms.
19.76 ____ Form I–130.
19.77 ____ Form I–140.
19.78 ____ Form I–485.
19.79 ____ Form OF–230.

CHAPTER 20. ADOPTIONS

20.1 Scope Note.
20.2 Strategy.
20.3 ____ Checklist: Pre-adoption—Counsel for Parents.
20.4 ____ Checklist: Interview With Birth Mother.
20.5 Adoptions—Generally.
20.6 ____ Defined.
20.7 ____ Rationale.
20.8 ____ Judicial Construction of Statutes.
20.9 ____ Concurrent Jurisdiction.
20.10 ____ ____ Where to File Adoption Proceedings.
20.11 ____ Choice of Venue.
20.12 ____ Types.
20.13 ____ Effect of Adoption.
20.14 ____ Who May Adopt—Statutory Mandates.
20.15 ____ ____ Separated Persons.

TABLE OF CONTENTS

Sec.
- 20.16 ____ ____ Foster Parents: Preference to Adopt.
- 20.17 ____ ____ Second Parent Adoptions.
- 20.18 ____ ____ Unwed Putative Fathers.
- 20.19 ____ ____ Citizens and Aliens.
- 20.20 ____ ____ Age as a Factor.
- 20.21 ____ ____ Extended Family as Factor.
- 20.22 ____ ____ Adult Unmarried Person.
- 20.23 ____ Who May Be Adopted—In General.
- 20.24 ____ ____ Adult Adoptions.
- 20.25 ____ ____ Aliens.
- 20.26 ____ ____ Non-marital Children.
- 20.27 ____ ____ Interracial Adoptions.
- 20.28 ____ ____ Religion as a Factor.
- 20.29 ____ Consents Required—Statutory Mandate.
- 20.30 ____ ____ Rights of Unwed Fathers.
- 20.31 ____ ____ When Consent Not Required.
- 20.32 ____ ____ Notice of a Proposed Adoption.
- 20.33 ____ ____ Checklist of Fathers to Receive Notice of Adoption.
- 20.34 ____ Persons Excluded from Notice.
- 20.35 ____ Purpose of Notice.
- 20.36 ____ Procedure.
- 20.37 Private Placement Adoptions—In General.
- 20.38 ____ Terminating Parental Rights Based Upon Abandonment.
- 20.39 ____ Terminating Parental Rights Based Upon Mental Retardation.
- 20.40 ____ Dual Representation Prohibited.
- 20.41 ____ Independent Counsel.
- 20.42 ____ Permissible Dual Representation.
- 20.43 ____ Independent Representation of the Child.
- 20.44 ____ The Attorney's Fee.
- 20.45 ____ Locating an Infant for Adoption—The Attorney's Responsibility.
- 20.46 ____ Illegal Sale of Babies.
- 20.47 ____ Advertisement.
- 20.48 ____ Foreign Infants.
- 20.49 ____ Readoption of Foreign Infants.
- 20.50 ____ Native American Children.
- 20.51 ____ Residency Requirements.
- 20.52 ____ Permissible Payments by Adoptive Parents.
- 20.53 ____ Interstate Compact on the Placement of Children.
- 20.54 ____ Pre-certification of Adoptive Parents—In General.
- 20.55 ____ ____ Requirement of Pre-certification.
- 20.56 ____ ____ Procedure.
- 20.57 ____ ____ Checklist of Documents Needed for Certification.
- 20.58 ____ Hospital Procedures—Physical Transfer of Custody of the Infant to the Adoptive Parents.
- 20.59 ____ ____ Certification Procedures.
- 20.60 ____ Petition for Temporary Guardianship—Legislative Background.
- 20.61 ____ ____ Impact of Pre-placement Certification.

TABLE OF CONTENTS

Sec.

20.62	___ Procedure Upon Filing Petition for Temporary Guardianship.
20.63	___ Consent of Birth Parents.
20.64	___ ___ Extra-Judicial Consent.
20.65	___ ___ Judicial Consents.
20.66	___ ___ Personal Appearances Required.
20.67	___ ___ Step-Parent Adoptions.
20.68	___ Foreign Born Children.
20.69	___ Petition for Adoption.
20.70	___ The Agreement of Adoption.
20.71	___ Affidavit of Attorney Representing Adoptive Parents.
20.72	___ Confidential Affidavit.
20.73	___ Attorney's Affidavit of Financial Disclosure.
20.74	___ Notification of Order of Adoption; Report of Adoption.
20.75	___ Order of Adoption.
20.76	___ Birth Mother's Affidavit Regarding Putative Father.
20.77	___ Affidavit of Intermediary.
20.78	___ Attorney's Affidavit Regarding Legal Fees.
20.79	___ Affidavit of Explanation of Criminal Activity.
20.80	___ Investigation by Disinterested Person.
20.81	___ The Hearing.
20.82	___ Certificate of Adoption.
20.83	___ The New Birth Certificate.
20.84	___ Checklist of Documents Required for Private Placement Adoption.
20.85	Agency Adoptions—Defined.
20.86	___ Definition of "Authorized Agency."
20.87	___ Venue.
20.88	___ Child's Entry into the System.
20.89	___ ___ Voluntary Transfer of Legal Custody of Children to the Authorized Agency.
20.90	___ ___ Judicial Surrender.
20.91	___ ___ Extra-Judicial Surrender.
20.92	___ ___ Court Approval of Extra-Judicial Surrender.
20.93	___ ___ Assigned Counsel.
20.94	___ ___ Required Notice of Application.
20.95	___ ___ Notification to Court.
20.96	___ ___ Court Order.
20.97	___ ___ Conditional Surrender.
20.98	___ ___ Recording a Surrender.
20.99	___ ___ Revocation of Surrender.
20.100	___ ___ Proceedings Subsequent to Execution of Extra-Judicial Surrender.
20.101	___ ___ Court Ordered Transfer of Children to Authorized Agency.
20.102	___ Procedures.
20.103	___ The Petition.
20.104	___ The Agreement of Adoption.
20.105	___ Verified Schedule.
20.106	___ Affidavit of Financial Disclosure.
20.107	___ Confidential Affidavit.

TABLE OF CONTENTS

Sec.

20.108	___	Marital Affidavit.
20.109	___	Child's Medical History.
20.110	___	Supplemental Affidavit.
20.111	___	Notification of Order of Adoption; Report of Adoption.
20.112	___	Doctor's Certificate of Health.
20.113	___	Authorization and Approval for Subsidized Adoption.
20.114	___	Adoption Homestudy.
20.115	___	Affidavit Identifying Party.
20.116	___	Order of Adoption.
20.117	___	Certificate of Adoption.
20.118	___	Abuse Clearance Form.
20.119	___	Unavailability of Abuse Clearance Form and Criminal Conviction Check.
20.120	___	Attorney's Affidavit of Legal Fees.
20.121	___	Checklist of Other Required Supporting Documentation.
20.122	___	The Adoption Hearing.
20.123		Post-adoption Issues—The Open Adoption.
20.124	___	Visitation With Siblings.
20.125	___	Sealing Adoption Records.
20.126	___ ___	Constitutionality of Laws Relating to Sealing Records.
20.127	___ ___	Good Cause for Unsealing Records.
20.128	___ ___ ___	Criminal Investigation and Probation Department.
20.129	___ ___ ___	Requirement of Medical Information.
20.130	___ ___ ___	Religion.
20.131	___	Abrogation of Order.
20.132		Checklist of Facts and Allegations to be Included in the Petition for a Private Placement Adoption.
20.133		Forms—Private Placement Adoptions—Petition for Certification as a Qualified Adoptive Parent. 💾
20.134	___ ___	Petition for Temporary Guardianship. 💾
20.135	___ ___	Judicial Consent of Natural Parent. 💾
20.136	___ ___	Extra-Judicial Consent of Natural Parent. 💾
20.137	___ ___	Petition for Adoption. 💾
20.138	___ ___	Order of Adoption (Private Placement). 💾
20.139	___	Agency Adoptions—Petition for Adoption. 💾
20.140	___ ___	Verified Schedule. 💾
20.141	___ ___	Marital Affidavit. 💾
20.142	___ ___	Marital Affidavit Dispensing With Consent of Spouse After Three Year Separation. 💾
20.143	___ ___	Confidential Affidavit. 💾
20.144	___ ___	Affidavit Pursuant to Section 111-a of the Domestic Relations Law. 💾
20.145	___ ___	Agreement of Adoption and Consent. 💾
20.146	___ ___	Affidavit Identifying Party. 💾
20.147	___ ___	Affidavit of Financial Disclosure by Parents. 💾
20.148	___ ___	Order of Adoption. 💾

Volume 23

CHAPTER 21. DOMESTIC RELATIONS

21.1   Scope Note.

TABLE OF CONTENTS

Sec.
21.2 Strategy.
21.3 Jurisdiction.
21.4 ⎯⎯ Residence Requirements.
21.5 ⎯⎯ Uniform Child Custody Jurisdiction Act.
21.6 Competency of the Court to Grant Relief.
21.7 ⎯⎯ Equitable Distribution.
21.8 ⎯⎯ Support.
21.9 ⎯⎯ Custody and Visitation.
21.10 Jurisdiction Over the Defendant's Person or Property.
21.11 ⎯⎯ Personal Jurisdiction.
21.12 ⎯⎯ Long Arm Jurisdiction.
21.13 ⎯⎯ *In Rem* Jurisdiction.
21.14 *Quasi in Rem* Jurisdiction.
21.15 Venue.
21.16 ⎯⎯ Changing Venue.
21.17 Joinder, Consolidation and Joint Trials.
21.18 Grounds for Divorce.
21.19 ⎯⎯ No Official No–Fault Ground.
21.20 ⎯⎯ Cruel and Inhuman Treatment.
21.21 ⎯⎯ ⎯⎯ Defenses.
21.22 ⎯⎯ Abandonment.
21.23 ⎯⎯ ⎯⎯ Defenses.
21.24 ⎯⎯ ⎯⎯ Effect of Separation Agreement.
21.25 ⎯⎯ Imprisonment.
21.26 ⎯⎯ Adultery.
21.27 ⎯⎯ ⎯⎯ Defenses.
21.28 ⎯⎯ ⎯⎯ Effect of Separation Agreement.
21.29 ⎯⎯ Divorce Action Based Upon Living Apart Pursuant to Separation Decree or Judgment.
21.30 ⎯⎯ Divorce Action Based Upon Living Apart Pursuant to Separation Agreement.
21.31 ⎯⎯ Dual Divorce.
21.32 Effect of Sister State Divorce Judgment.
21.33 Equitable Distribution.
21.34 ⎯⎯ When Available.
21.35 ⎯⎯ Identification of Property.
21.36 ⎯⎯ Characterization of Property.
21.37 ⎯⎯ ⎯⎯ Marital Property.
21.38 ⎯⎯ ⎯⎯ ⎯⎯ Pensions.
21.39 ⎯⎯ ⎯⎯ ⎯⎯ Professional Practices, Licenses, Degrees and Careers.
21.40 ⎯⎯ ⎯⎯ Separate Property.
21.41 ⎯⎯ ⎯⎯ ⎯⎯ Increase in Value of Separate Property.
21.42 ⎯⎯ Valuation Dates.
21.43 ⎯⎯ Valuation Methods.
21.44 ⎯⎯ Distribution Factors.
21.45 ⎯⎯ Tax Considerations.
21.46 Maintenance.
21.47 ⎯⎯ Legislative Factors.
21.48 ⎯⎯ Effect of Fault.

TABLE OF CONTENTS

Sec.
21.49 ____ Current Trends.
21.50 ____ Payments Fixed by Agreement.
21.51 ____ Tax Consequences.
21.52 Child Support.
21.53 ____ Child Support Standards Act.
21.54 ____ ____ Where Statutory Percentages Are Unfair or Inappropriate.
21.55 ____ ____ Recent Trends.
21.56 ____ Effect of Agreement or Stipulation.
21.57 Health and Life Insurance.
21.58 Custody.
21.59 ____ Visitation.
21.60 ____ Relocation of Custodial Parent With the Child.
21.61 ____ Joint Custody.
21.62 ____ Proceedings in Which Custody Dispositions Are Available.
21.63 Financial Disclosure.
21.64 Disclosure on Matters Going to the Merits of the Case.
21.65 Net Worth Statement.
21.66 Statement of Proposed Disposition.
21.67 Findings of Fact and Conclusions of Law; Judgments.
21.68 Modification.
21.69 ____ Maintenance.
21.70 ____ Child Support.
21.71 ____ Custody.
21.72 Enforcement.
21.73 ____ Plenary Action to Enforce Agreement.
21.74 ____ Defenses.
21.75 Practice Considerations.
21.76 ____ Procedure for Attorneys in Domestic Relations Matters.
21.77 ____ Disciplinary Rules.
21.78 ____ Fee Arbitration Rules.
21.79 ____ Rules Regarding Case Management.
21.80 Procedural Checklist—Calendar Control.
21.81 Drafting Checklist—Retainer Agreements.
21.82 _____ Complaint in Action for Divorce.
21.83 _____ Statement of Proposed Disposition.
21.84 Forms.
21.85 ____ Retainer Agreement.
21.86 ____ Complaint for Divorce.
21.87 ____ Statement of Net Worth.
21.88 ____ Statement of Proposed Disposition.
21.89 ____ Findings of Fact and Conclusions of Law.
21.90 ____ Matrimonial Judgments.
21.91 ____ Referee's Report on Findings of Fact and Conclusions of Law.
21.92 ____ Matrimonial Judgment Entered Upon Referee's Report.

CHAPTER 22. GUARDIANSHIP

22.1 Scope Note.

XCV

TABLE OF CONTENTS

Sec.
22.2 Strategy.
22.3 Checklists.
22.4 Prior Law—Generally.
22.5 ―――― Role of Committees and Conservators.
22.6 ―――― Problems Encountered.
22.7 ―――― Impact of *Matter of Grinker (Rose)*.
22.8 Legislative Purpose of Mental Hygiene Law Article 81.
22.9 Definitions.
22.10 Summary.
22.11 Power to Appoint Guardian—Generally.
22.12 ―――― Elements.
22.13 ―――― Incapacity.
22.14 ―――― Primary Considerations.
22.15 ―――― Jurisdiction.
22.16 ―――― Venue.
22.17 ―――― Standing to Commence Proceeding.
22.18 ―――― Summary.
22.19 Proceeding to Appoint Guardian.
22.20 ―――― Time and Method of Service of Notice.
22.21 ―――― Persons Entitled to Notice.
22.22 ―――― Notice Requirements.
22.23 ―――― Petition.
22.24 ―――― Summary.
22.25 Court Evaluator—Persons Eligible for Appointment.
22.26 ―――― Duties.
22.27 ―――― Compensation.
22.28 ―――― Appointment of Counsel for the Alleged Incapacitated Person.
22.29 ―――― Summary.
22.30 Hearing and Order—An Overview.
22.31 ―――― Procedure.
22.32 ―――― Presence of Person Alleged to be Incapacitated.
22.33 ―――― Evidence.
22.34 ―――― Findings of the Court.
22.35 ―――― ―――― Voluntary Appointment.
22.36 ―――― ―――― Personal Needs.
22.37 ―――― ―――― Property Management.
22.38 ―――― Dispositional Alternatives.
22.39 ―――― Award of Counsel Fees to Petitioner.
22.40 ―――― Person to be Appointed Guardian.
22.41 ―――― Priority and Criteria for Appointment.
22.42 ―――― Requirement of Bond.
22.43 ―――― Designation of Clerk and Issuance of Commission.
22.44 ―――― Summary.
22.45 Role of Guardian—Overview.
22.46 ―――― Duties.
22.47 ―――― Powers; Property Management.
22.48 ―――― Substituted Judgment.
22.49 ―――― Petition for Authorization to Transfer Property.
22.50 ―――― ―――― Notice of Application.

TABLE OF CONTENTS

Sec.
22.51 ____ ____ Considerations of Court.
22.52 ____ ____ Granting Petition.
22.53 ____ ____ Powers; Personal Needs.
22.54 ____ Effect of Appointment on Incapacitated Person.
22.55 ____ Summary.
22.56 Provisional Remedies.
22.57 ____ Temporary Guardian.
22.58 ____ Injunction and Temporary Restraining Orders.
22.59 ____ Notice of Pendency.
22.60 ____ Summary.
22.61 Compensation of Guardian.
22.62 Reports by Guardian.
22.63 ____ Initial Report.
22.64 ____ Annual Report.
22.65 ____ Examination; Court Examiners.
22.66 ____ Intermediate and Final Reports.
22.67 ____ Decree Upon Approving Accounts.
22.68 ____ Summary.
22.69 Removal, Discharge and Resignation of Guardian—Removal.
22.70 ____ Discharge or Modification of Powers.
22.71 ____ Resignation or Suspension of Powers.
22.72 ____ Vacancy in Office; Appointment of Interim and Successor Guardians.
22.73 ____ Standby Guardian.
22.74 ____ Summary.
22.75 Education Requirements—Generally.
22.76 ____ Guardian Training.
22.77 ____ Court Evaluator Training.
22.78 ____ Court Examiner Training.
22.79 ____ Compliance.
22.80 ____ Summary.
22.81 Proceedings to Discover Property Withheld.
22.82 ____ Petition and Supporting Papers.
22.83 ____ Grounds For Inquiry.
22.84 ____ Answer.
22.85 ____ Trial.
22.86 ____ Decree.
22.87 ____ Summary.
22.88 Drafting Checklists.
22.89 ____ Order to Show Cause.
22.90 ____ Petition.
22.91 ____ Court Evaluator's Report.
22.92 ____ Order and Judgment.
22.93 ____ Initial Report of the Guardian.
22.94 ____ Annual Report.
22.95 ____ Decree Approving Accounts.
22.96 ____ Petition on Proceeding to Discover Property Withheld.
22.97 Forms.
22.98 ____ Order to Show Cause. 💾
22.99 ____ Petition. 💾

TABLE OF CONTENTS

Sec.
22.100 —— Court Evaluator's Report.
22.101 —— Order and Judgment Appointing Guardian of the Person and Property.
22.102 —— Oath and Designation of Guardian.
22.103 —— Commission of Guardian.
22.104 —— Initial Report of Guardian.
22.105 —— Annual Report and Inventory of Guardian.
22.106 —— Decree Upon Approving Accounts.
22.107 —— Petition on Proceeding to Discover Property Withheld.

CHAPTER 23. ELDER LAW

23.1 Scope Note.
23.2 Strategy.
23.3 Ethical Considerations.
23.4 —— Identifying the Client.
23.5 —— Confidentiality.
23.6 —— Diminished Capacity.
23.7 Social Security Benefits.
23.8 —— Quarters of Coverage.
23.9 —— Insured Status.
23.10 —— Calculation of Benefits.
23.11 —— Retirement Benefits.
23.12 —— Benefits for Spouses, Survivors and Dependents.
23.13 —— Reduction in Benefits Due to Earned Income.
23.14 —— Overpayments and Underpayments.
23.15 —— Administrative and Judicial Appeals.
23.16 —— Representation by Attorneys.
23.17 Supplemental Security Income for the Elderly.
23.18 —— Categorical Eligibility.
23.19 —— Financial Eligibility.
23.20 —— Benefit Calculation.
23.21 —— Underpayments and Overpayments.
23.22 —— Administrative and Judicial Appeals.
23.23 —— Representation by Attorneys.
23.24 Retirement Income from Qualified Plans.
23.25 —— Eligibility, Vesting and Accrual.
23.26 —— Contribution Limitations.
23.27 —— Payment of Benefits.
23.28 —— Alienation and Assignment.
23.29 —— Spousal Rights.
23.30 —— Qualified Domestic Relations Orders.
23.31 —— Waiver of Spousal Rights.
23.32 —— Taxation of Contributions.
23.33 —— Distributions.
23.34 —— Termination or Merger.
23.35 —— Appeals.
23.36 Railroad Retirement Benefits.
23.37 Benefits for Federal Employees.
23.38 —— Federal Employees Retirement System ("FERS").

TABLE OF CONTENTS

Sec.	
23.39	____ Civil Service Retirement Act ("CSRA").
23.40	____ Appeals.
23.41	Veterans' Benefits.
23.42	Medicare.
23.43	____ Eligibility and Enrollment.
23.44	____ Part A Benefits.
23.45	____ ____ Hospital Services.
23.46	____ ____ Skilled Nursing Facilities.
23.47	____ ____ Home Health Care.
23.48	____ ____ Hospice Care.
23.49	____ Part B Supplementary Medical Insurance.
23.50	____ ____ Deductibles and Coinsurance.
23.51	____ ____ Assignment of Claims/Participating Physicians.
23.52	____ ____ Limitations on Balance Billing.
23.53	____ Administrative and Judicial Appeals.
23.54	____ ____ Eligibility for Benefits.
23.55	____ ____ Part A Fiscal Intermediary Decisions.
23.56	____ ____ Part A Peer Review Organization Decisions.
23.57	____ ____ Part B Determinations.
23.58	Supplemental Medical Insurance (Medigap Plans).
23.59	____ Gaps in Medicare Coverage.
23.60	____ Federal and State Regulation of the Industry.
23.61	____ Ten Standard Plans.
23.62	____ Criteria for Choosing the Right Plan.
23.63	Long Term Care Insurance.
23.64	____ Regulation Under New York Law.
23.65	____ Relationship to Medicaid Eligibility.
23.66	____ The Partnership For Long Term Care/Robert Wood Johnson Program.
23.67	____ Choosing a Policy.
23.68	____ Tax Issues.
23.69	Medicaid.
23.70	____ Covered Services.
23.71	____ Basic Eligibility Requirements.
23.72	____ Surplus Income Program for the "Medically Needy."
23.73	____ Income.
23.74	____ Resources.
23.75	____ Exempt Resources.
23.76	____ Transfer of Resources.
23.77	____ Treatment of Trusts.
23.78	____ ____ Self Settled Trusts.
23.79	____ ____ Third Party Trusts.
23.80	____ Spousal Budgeting: Protection of Resources and Income for the Community Spouse.
23.81	____ Recoveries Against Estates.
23.82	____ Liens.
23.83	____ Administrative and Judicial Appeals.
23.84	Home Care Coverage.
23.85	____ Medicare.
23.86	____ Medicaid.

TABLE OF CONTENTS

Sec.
23.87 ____ Expanded In–Home Services for the Elderly Program ("EISEP").
23.88 ____ Private Insurance.
23.89 Hospital Patients Rights.
23.90 ____ Bill of Rights.
23.91 ____ Discharge Planning.
23.92 Nursing Home Resident Rights.
23.93 ____ Admission to a Facility.
23.94 ____ Bill of Rights.
23.95 ____ Financial Rights.
23.96 ____ Transfer and Discharge.
23.97 ____ Bed Hold Policy.
23.98 ____ Remedies for Violation of Rights or Improper Treatment.
23.99 Housing Issues.
23.100 ____ Real Property Tax Exemption.
23.101 ____ Real Property Tax Credit.
23.102 ____ Tax Assistance Loans.
23.103 ____ Home Repair Assistance.
23.104 ____ Reverse Mortgages and Home Equity Loans.
23.105 ____ Home Energy Assistance Program ("HEAP").
23.106 ____ Tenant Protections.
23.107 ____ Life Care Retirement Communities.
23.108 ____ Community Based Services.
23.109 Health Care Decision Making.
23.110 ____ Health Care Proxy.
23.111 ____ The Living Will.
23.112 ____ Do Not Resuscitate Orders.
23.113 ____ Physician Assisted Suicide.
23.114 Tax Issues.
23.115 ____ Additional Standard Deduction for the Aged and Blind.
23.116 ____ Incapacity.
23.117 ____ Sale of a Principal Residence.
23.118 ____ Medical Deductions.
23.119 Miscellaneous Programs.
23.120 ____ Elderly Pharmaceutical Insurance Coverage ("EPIC").
23.121 ____ Life Line Telephone Service.
23.122 Forms.
23.123 ____ Documentation Letter.
23.124 ____ Consultation Letter.
23.125 ____ Health Care Proxy Statutory Form.
23.126 ____ Sample Living Will.

CHAPTER 24. ESTATE PLANNING

24.1 Scope Note.
24.2 Strategy.
24.3 Wills.
24.4 ____ Execution Requirements.
24.5 ____ ____ Signature.
24.6 ____ ____ Publication.

TABLE OF CONTENTS

Sec.	
24.7	_____ _____ Witnesses.
24.8	_____ _____ Self Proving Affidavit.
24.9	_____ Provisions—Personal Property Dispositions.
24.10	_____ _____ Debts and Taxes.
24.11	_____ _____ Real Property.
24.12	_____ _____ Residuary Estate.
24.13	_____ _____ Dispositions in Trust.
24.14	_____ _____ Guardianships.
24.15	_____ _____ Appointment of Executors and Trustees.
24.16	_____ _____ Fiduciary Powers.
24.17	_____ _____ Miscellaneous.
24.18	Federal Estate and Gift Taxes.
24.19	_____ Rates.
24.20	New York State Estate and Gift Tax.
24.21	Estate Tax Planning—Utilizing the Unified Credit.
24.22	_____ Utilizing the Marital Deduction.
24.23	_____ Formula Clauses.
24.24	Generation Skipping Transfer Tax.
24.25	_____ Taxable Termination.
24.26	_____ Direct Skip.
24.27	_____ Taxable Distribution.
24.28	_____ Generation Assignment.
24.29	_____ Multiple Skips.
24.30	_____ Exemption.
24.31	_____ "Reverse QTIP."
24.32	Charitable Bequests.
24.33	Planning With Certain Assets.
24.34	_____ Life Insurance.
24.35	_____ _____ Life Insurance Trusts.
24.36	_____ _____ _____ "Crummey Powers."
24.37	_____ Retirement Benefits.
24.38	_____ Closely Held Business Interests.
24.39	_____ _____ Buy-Sell Agreements.
24.40	_____ _____ Liquidity Issues.
24.41	_____ _____ Minority Discounts.
24.42	_____ Farms and Business Real Property.
24.43	_____ Installment Obligations.
24.44	Lifetime Planning.
24.45	_____ Valuation of Gifts.
24.46	_____ _____ Grantor Retained Trusts.
24.47	_____ _____ Residence Trusts.
24.48	_____ _____ _____ Income Tax Considerations.
24.49	_____ Annual Gift Tax Exclusion.
24.50	_____ _____ Section 2503(c) Trusts.
24.51	_____ _____ Uniform Transfers to Minor's Act Accounts.
24.52	_____ _____ Crummey Trusts.
24.53	_____ _____ Family Limited Partnerships.
24.54	_____ Charitable Remainder Trusts.
24.55	_____ Charitable Lead Trusts.
24.56	Planning in Special Situations—Terminally Ill.

TABLE OF CONTENTS

Sec.
24.57 __ __ Self-Canceling Installment Notes.
24.58 __ Non-citizen Spouses.
24.59 __ Multiple Marriages.
24.60 __ __ Spousal Rights.
24.61 __ __ __ Joint Wills and Contracts to Make Wills.
24.62 __ __ Long Term Care.
24.63 __ Separation.
24.64 __ Divorce.
24.65 __ __ Death During Divorce Proceeding.
24.66 __ Unmarried Couples.
24.67 Postmortem Planning.
24.68 __ Disclaimers.
24.69 __ __ Disclaimer Trusts.
24.70 __ __ Creditor Avoidance.
24.71 __ __ New York Statutory Requirements.
24.72 __ Partial QTIP Election.
24.73 __ Electing Alternate Valuation Date.
24.74 __ Allocation of Income and Expenses.
24.75 __ __ U.S. Savings Bonds.
24.76 __ __ Expenses.
24.77 __ Choosing the Fiscal Year of the Estate.
24.78 __ Electing to File Joint Return with Decedent's Spouse.
24.79 __ Waiving Commissions.
24.80 Probate Avoidance.
24.81 __ Revocable Trusts.
24.82 __ Totten Trusts.
24.83 __ Jointly Held Assets.
24.84 Asset Protection.
24.85 __ Statutory Exemptions.
24.86 __ Family Partnerships.
24.87 __ Domestic Trusts.
24.88 __ Foreign Trusts.
24.89 Powers of Attorney.
24.90 Advance Directives.
24.91 __ Health Care Proxy.
24.92 __ Living Will.
24.93 Ethical Considerations in Estate Planning.
24.94 __ Multiple Clients.
24.95 __ Attorney/Draftsman as Fiduciary or Beneficiary.
24.96 Forms
24.97 __ Estate Planner's Checklist.
24.98 __ Sample Information Request Letter.
24.99 __ Client Questionnaire.
24.100 __ "Durable" Power of Attorney Form.
24.101 __ Crummey Notice.
24.102 __ Spousal Conflicts Letter.

CHAPTER 25. PROBATE AND ESTATE ADMINISTRATION

25.1 Scope Note.

TABLE OF CONTENTS

Sec.

25.2 Explanation of Basic Legal Terms in Estate Practice.
25.3 Strategy.
25.4 Who May Commence the Estate of a Person Who Dies Without a Will.
25.5 Who Is Entitled to Letters of Administration.
25.6 Who May Commence the Estate of a Person Who Dies With a Will.
25.7 Documents Required on Application for Letters of Administration.
25.8 Who Must Be Cited on an Application for Letters of Administration.
25.9 When a Guardian *Ad Litem* Must be Appointed.
25.10 Denial or Revocation of Letters of Administration.
25.11 Letters of Temporary Administration.
25.12 Venue.
25.13 Duty of the Fiduciary to Expeditiously Seek Probate.
25.14 When a Beneficiary Should Petition for Probate.
25.15 When a Creditor Should Petition for Probate.
25.16 When a Person in Litigation with an Estate Should Petition for Probate.
25.17 Information to Be Gathered by Attorney.
25.18 Contents of Petition for Probate.
25.19 Documents Required to Accompany Probate Petition.
25.20 What to Do If Your Client Cannot Produce the Original Will.
25.21 Requirements and Procedure for Proving a Will Where the Original Is Lost.
25.22 How to Get a Will Admitted to Probate If None of the Witnesses to the Will are Available.
25.23 When a Court Must Appoint a Guardian *Ad Litem* in a Probate Proceeding.
25.24 Who May Oppose the Admission to Probate of a Will By Filing Objections.
25.25 When Objections Must Be Filed.
25.26 How to Start an Estate Administration Where There Will Be a Delay in Getting a Will Admitted to Probate.
25.27 Form of Objections to Probate.
25.28 Burden of Proof
25.29 Requirement of a Notice of Objections to Complete Jurisdiction in a Contested Probate.
25.30 Right to a Trial by Jury.
25.31 Right to Discovery in a Probate, Administration or Accounting Proceeding.
25.32 Who Is Entitled to Letters of Administration When a Person Dies Without a Will.
25.33 Procedures to Follow in Administering the Estate.
25.34 How to Force an Estate Administration to Be Completed—Compelling an Accounting.
25.35 Concluding an Estate Administration Without an Accounting Proceeding.
25.36 Obtaining a Decree Concluding the Estate Based on Filed Receipts and Releases.
25.37 Concluding an Estate by a Formal Judicial Accounting.

TABLE OF CONTENTS

Sec.
25.38 Objections to an Account.
25.39 Prosecuting Objections to an Account.
25.40 Claims Against an Estate by a Creditor.
25.41 Representing a Claimant Against an Estate.
25.42 Obtaining Information About Estate Assets and Recovering Estate Property.
25.43 How to Proceed When Your Client Has a Claim Against an Estate.
25.44 A Special Provision for an Estate Beneficiary Obtaining Funds for Education.
25.45 Who Is Entitled to Assets When Two or More Fiduciaries Are in Dispute.
25.46 Compensation of Executor and Administrator, When Payable.
25.47 Attorney's Fees.
25.48 Declining to Serve as an Executor or Trustee.
25.49 Renouncing an Inheritance.
25.50 Construction of a Will.
25.51 Forms.
25.52 ____ Probate Petition.
25.53 ____ Affidavit Proving Correct Copy of Will.
25.54 ____ Citation in Probate.
25.55 ____ Affidavit of Service of Citation.
25.56 ____ Affidavit of Mailing Notice of Application for Letters of Administration.
25.57 ____ Waiver and Consent.
25.58 ____ Notice of Probate.
25.59 ____ Deposition Affidavit of Subscribing Witness.
25.60 ____ Objections to Probate.
25.61 ____ Decree Granting Probate.
25.62 ____ Receipt and Release Agreement Concluding an Estate Without an Accounting Proceeding.
25.63 ____ Receipt and Release (Legacy).
25.64 ____ Petition to Judicially Settle Executor's Account.
25.65 ____ Citation to Executor to Show Cause Why Judicially Executor Should Not Account.
25.66 ____ Accounting Form.
25.67 ____ Petition for Letters of Administration or Limited Letters of Administration or Temporary Administration.
25.68 ____ Decree Appointing Administrator.
25.69 ____ Affidavit Asking Court to Fix Amount of Administrator's Bond.
25.70 ____ Waiver of Citation, Renunciation of Signer's Claim to Letters and Consent to Appointment of Administrator.
25.71 ____ Notice of Application for Letters of Administration.
25.72 ____ Citation That Can Be Adopted for Use in Any Proceeding.

CHAPTER 26. PERSONAL INJURY

26.1 Scope Note.
26.2 Strategy.

TABLE OF CONTENTS

Sec.	
26.3	____ Client Interview.
26.4	____ Valuing the Case.
26.5	____ Skills and Ethics.
26.6	____ Retainer.
26.7	____ ____ Retainer Statement.
26.8	____ Expenses.
26.9	Investigation.
26.10	____ Premises Liability.
26.11	____ Medical Malpractice.
26.12	____ ____ Hospital.
26.13	____ ____ Dental and Podiatric Malpractice.
26.14	____ Products Liability.
26.15	____ Dog Bites.
26.16	____ Chemical Exposure.
26.17	____ Automobile Accidents.
26.18	____ ____ Police Report.
26.19	____ ____ Witness Statements.
26.20	____ ____ MV104.
26.21	____ ____ Application of No–Fault.
26.22	____ ____ Medical Records.
26.23	____ ____ Photographs.
26.24	____ ____ Insurance Policies and Coverage.
26.25	Claims Procedure for Automobile Accidents.
26.26	____ Filing Notice of Claim With the Motor Vehicle Accident Indemnity Corporation.
26.27	____ ____ Procedure for Cases in Which There Is No Insurance.
26.28	____ ____ Procedure for Cases in Which There Is No Insurance and the Identity of the Wrongdoer Is Not Ascertainable (Hit and Run).
26.29	____ ____ Procedure for Cases in Which Insurance Initially Is Believed to Exist, But There Is No Insurance After Later Disclaimer.
26.30	____ ____ Late Claims.
26.31	Theories of Liability.
26.32	Filing the Action.
26.33	____ When.
26.34	____ Where.
26.35	____ Potential Defendants.
26.36	The Summons and the Complaint.
26.37	The Answer.
26.38	Actions Against Municipal Corporations.
26.39	____ Notice of Claim.
26.40	____ ____ Content.
26.41	Actions Against the State.
26.42	Discovery—Generally.
26.43	____ Depositions.
26.44	____ Interrogatories.
26.45	____ Document Discovery and Inspection.
26.46	____ Bills of Particulars.
26.47	____ Demand for a Bill of Particulars.

TABLE OF CONTENTS

Sec.
26.48 Settlement.
26.49 Liens.
26.50 Alternative Dispute Resolution.
26.51 Trial Preparation: Introductory Note.
26.52 Trial.
26.53 ____ Subpoenas.
26.54 ____ Exhibits.
26.55 ____ *Voir Dire*.
26.56 Disbursement of Proceeds of Settlement or Recovery.
26.57 Drafting Checklists.
26.58 ____ Complaint.
26.59 ____ Answer.
26.60 ____ Demand for Bill of Particulars.
26.61 ____ Responses to Demand for Bill of Particulars.
26.62 Forms—Client's Retainer Agreement.
26.63 ____ Retainer Statement.
26.64 ____ Department of Motor Vehicles MV104 Form.
26.65 ____ Summons and Complaint.
26.66 ____ Amended Answer, Counterclaim and Cross Claim.
26.67 ____ Defendant's Demand for a Verified Bill of Particulars.
26.68 ____ Defendant's CPLR 3101 Demands.
26.69 ____ Plaintiff's Demand for a Verified Bill of Particulars.
26.70 ____ Plaintiff's CPLR 3101 Demands.
26.71 ____ Closing Statement.

CHAPTER 27. PRODUCTS LIABILITY

27.1 Scope Note.
27.2 Strategy.
27.3 Historical Overview.
27.4 Bases of a Products Liability Claim.
27.5 Theories of Liability.
27.6 ____ Manufacturing Defect or Mistake in the Manufacturing Process.
27.7 ____ Defective Design.
27.8 ____ ____ Burden of Proof.
27.9 ____ ____ Defense.
27.10 ____ Failure to Warn or Inadequate Warnings.
27.11 ____ ____ Burden of Proof.
27.12 ____ ____ Duty to Warn.
27.13 ____ ____ Adequacy of Warning.
27.14 ____ ____ Jury Question.
27.15 ____ ____ Informed Intermediary Defense.
27.16 ____ ____ Duty to Warn the Unusually Sensitive.
27.17 ____ ____ Non-Commercial Cases.
27.18 ____ Failure to Test.
27.19 ____ ____ FDA Approval.
27.20 ____ ____ Jury Question.
27.21 ____ ____ Preemption Defense.
27.22 Distributors' or Sellers' Liability.

CVI

TABLE OF CONTENTS

Sec.
27.23 ____ Sale Must Be Part of Ordinary Business.
27.24 ____ Service v. Sales.
27.25 ____ Medical Care Providers.
27.26 Successor Liability.
27.27 ____ Burden of Proof.
27.28 ____ Punitive Damages.
27.29 Liability of the Manufacturer of Component Parts.
27.30 Liability of the Manufacturer of the Complete Product.
27.31 Introducing Evidence of Post Accident Modification or Repairs.
27.32 Introducing Evidence of Other Incidents.
27.33 Effect of Destruction of the Product Upon Plaintiff's Ability to Prove a Defect.
27.34 Proof of Causation.
27.35 ____ Question for the Jury or Question for the Judge.
27.36 Foreseeability of Harm.
27.37 Discovery Issues.
27.38 ____ Confidentiality Orders or Stipulations.
27.39 Statute of Limitations.
27.40 Intervening Acts of Negligence—Plaintiff's Misuse of the Product.
27.41 ____ Alteration of the Product After it Has Left the Hands of the Manufacturer.
27.42 Preemption of Private Claims.
27.43 ____ Old Rule.
27.44 ____ New Rule.
27.45 ____ National Traffic & Motor Vehicle Safety Act and Its Savings Clause.
27.46 ____ Public Health Cigarette Labeling & Advertising Act of 1965 and the Public Health Cigarette Smoking Act of 1969—The *Cipollone* Decision.
27.47 ____ Federal Insecticide, Fungicide and Rodenticide Act (FIFRA) and Its Impact on Labeling Requirements.
27.48 ____ Medical Device Amendments to FDA Regulations.
27.49 ____ Limits on Preemption and Statutory Defenses.
27.50 ____ Validity of the Safety Standard or Regulatory Statute.
27.51 ____ Checklist.
27.52 Imposing Liability when the Manufacturer of a Fungible or Generic Product Is Unknown (Concert of Action/Market Share Liability).
27.53 Collateral Estoppel in Products Liability Cases.
27.54 Proof of Allegations Checklist.
27.55 Drafting Checklist—Complaint.
27.56 ____ Answer.
27.57 Forms—Products Liability Complaint.
27.58 ____ Products Liability Answer.

Volume 24

CHAPTER 28. LEGAL MALPRACTICE

28.1 Scope Note.

TABLE OF CONTENTS

Sec.	
28.2	Strategy.
28.3	The Duty of Care.
28.4	____ Specific Acts—Erroneous Advice.
28.5	____ ____ Incompetent Tax Advice.
28.6	____ ____ Proper Withdrawal.
28.7	____ ____ Detecting Fraud.
28.8	____ Causation.
28.9	____ ____ The Doctrine of Compelled Settlement.
28.10	____ Damages.
28.11	____ Defenses—The Privity Rule.
28.12	____ ____ Lawyer's Judgment Rule.
28.13	____ ____ Statute of Limitations.
28.14	____ ____ Continuous Representation Tolling Doctrine.
28.15	____ ____ Extension by Estoppel.
28.16	____ ____ Standard Negligence Defenses of Lack of Foreseeability and Supervening Act.
28.17	____ ____ Concealment of Malpractice Not a Separate Cause of Action.
28.18	____ ____ Need for Consistent Positions.
28.19	The Duty of Loyalty.
28.20	____ Conflict of Interest.
28.21	____ Disqualification.
28.22	____ Misappropriation of Client Funds.
28.23	Liability for Negligence of Independent Contractors.
28.24	Statutory Liability Under Judiciary Law § 487.
28.25	Vicarious Liability for Partner's Misdeeds.
28.26	Liability for Indemnity and Contribution.
28.27	Fee Disputes.
28.28	____ Alternative Dispute Resolution.
28.29	____ ____ Retainer Agreements Given Strict Scrutiny.
28.30	____ ____ Arbitration Clause in Retainer Agreement May Waive Other Client Rights.
28.31	____ Statutory Limitations.
28.32	____ Account Stated.
28.33	____ A Standard of Reasonableness.
28.34	Limited Liability Companies and Limited Liability Partnerships.
28.35	Lawyers Professional Liability Insurance.
28.36	____ Extended Reporting Period.
28.37	____ What Is a "Claim" and When Is It "Made"?
28.38	____ Professional Capacity and Typical Exclusions.
28.39	____ Limits, Deductibles and Defense.
28.40	____ Notice of Claim and Notice of Occurrence.
28.41	____ Cancellation.
28.42	____ Innocent Partner Coverage.
28.43	____ Application for Coverage and Rescission of Policy.
28.44	____ Bad Faith.
28.45	____ Cautions for Dissolving Law Firms.
28.46	Conclusion.
28.47	Drafting Checklist—Retainer Agreement.
28.48	____ Malpractice Complaint Against Attorney.

TABLE OF CONTENTS

Sec.
28.49 ____ Answer to Malpractice Complaint on Behalf of Attorney.
28.50 Forms—Retainer Agreement With ADR Clause. 💾
28.51 ____ Retainer Agreement Without ADR Clause. 💾
28.52 ____ Complaint for Malpractice: Commercial Transaction. 💾
28.53 ____ Complaint for Malpractice: Personal Injury Action. 💾
28.54 ____ Answer: Commercial Transaction. 💾
28.55 ____ Answer: Personal Injury Action. 💾

CHAPTER 29. MEDICAL MALPRACTICE

29.1 Scope Note.
29.2 Strategy.
29.3 ____ Determining the Presence or Absence of Medical Malpractice.
29.4 ____ The Nature and Degree of Damages.
29.5 ____ Interviewing the Client.
29.6 ____ ____ History of the Current Condition.
29.7 ____ ____ Past Medical Conditions.
29.8 ____ ____ Current Medical Condition.
29.9 ____ ____ Miscellaneous Issues.
29.10 The Common Law Standards.
29.11 ____ The Standard of Care.
29.12 ____ ____ Hospitals' *Respondeat-Superior* Liability.
29.13 ____ ____ Hospitals' Direct Liability.
29.14 ____ Informed Consent.
29.15 ____ Health Maintenance Organizations.
29.16 ____ Expert Witnesses.
29.17 ____ Defenses in Medical Malpractice Cases.
29.18 Regulatory Standards.
29.19 ____ Qualifications of Nurse Midwives.
29.20 ____ Clinical Laboratories.
29.21 ____ Blood Banks.
29.22 ____ Testing for Phenylketonuria and Other Diseases and Conditions/Early Intervention Program.
29.23 ____ Hospitals.
29.24 Damages.
29.25 Procedure.
29.26 ____ Statutes of Limitation.
29.27 ____ Steps for Filing an Action.
29.28 ____ ____ Certificate of Merit.
29.29 ____ ____ Notice of Medical Malpractice Action.
29.30 ____ ____ Pre-calendar Conferences.
29.31 ____ Periodic Payment of Large Verdicts.
29.32 Hospital Operations and Medical Negligence—Credentialling of Physicians.
29.33 ____ Quality Assurance and Risk Management.
29.34 ____ Departmentalization of Services—Departmental Chairs.
29.35 Training and Education of Physicians.
29.36 ____ Medical School.
29.37 ____ PGY–1 (Internship).
29.38 ____ Residency.

TABLE OF CONTENTS

Sec.	
29.39	____ Fellowships.
29.40	____ Board Certification & Re-certification.
29.41	____ Associations, Societies, and Continuing Medical Education.
29.42	____ National Practitioner Data Bank.
29.43	Medical Literature.
29.44	____ Obtaining Medical Literature.
29.45	____ Sources.
29.46	____ Using Medical Literature to Evaluate a Case.
29.47	____ Preparing for Depositions.
29.48	____ Preparing for Trial.
29.49	____ Use of Treatises in State Court.
29.50	____ Use of Treatises in Federal Court.
29.51	Evaluating and Understanding Medical Records—Physician's Records.
29.52	____ Hospital Records.
29.53	____ ____ Informed Consent Forms.
29.54	____ ____ Progress Notes.
29.55	____ ____ Order Sheets.
29.56	____ ____ Consultation Records.
29.57	____ ____ Operative Records.
29.58	____ ____ Medication Records.
29.59	____ ____ Intake and Output Records.
29.60	____ ____ Radiographic Records.
29.61	____ ____ Obstetrical Records.
29.62	____ ____ ICU/CCU Records.
29.63	____ ____ Nurses' Notes.
29.64	Discovery.
29.65	____ Obtaining and Identifying Relevant Records.
29.66	____ ____ Physician's Records.
29.67	____ ____ Hospital Records.
29.68	____ ____ Billing Records.
29.69	____ ____ Pharmacy Records.
29.70	____ ____ Allied Health Provider Records.
29.71	____ ____ Workers' Compensation Claims File.
29.72	____ ____ Autopsy Report.
29.73	____ ____ Workers' Compensation Actions.
29.74	____ ____ Medical Malpractice Actions.
29.75	Trial Preparation.
29.76	Drafting Checklists.
29.77	____ Order to Show Cause to Obtain Medical Records.
29.78	____ Affirmation in Support of Order to Show Cause.
29.79	____ Certificate of Merit.
29.80	Forms
29.81	____ Order to Show Cause to Obtain Medical Records. 💾
29.82	____ Affirmation in Support of Order to Show Cause. 💾
29.83	____ Certificate of Merit. 💾

CHAPTER 30. DAMAGES

30.1	Scope Note.

TABLE OF CONTENTS

Sec.
- 30.2 Strategy.
- 30.3 ___ Pretrial Stage.
- 30.4 ___ Trial Stage.
- 30.5 The Nature of Damages.
- 30.6 Compensatory Damages.
- 30.7 ___ Personal Injury.
- 30.8 ___ ___ Physical Pain and Suffering.
- 30.9 ___ ___ Mental or Emotional Pain and Suffering.
- 30.10 ___ ___ Loss of Earnings and Impairment of Future Earning Ability.
- 30.11 ___ ___ Aggravation of Pre-existing Injuries.
- 30.12 ___ Wrongful Death.
- 30.13 ___ ___ Damages Sustained Before Death.
- 30.14 ___ ___ Damages Sustained After Death.
- 30.15 ___ Loss of Consortium.
- 30.16 ___ Property Damage.
- 30.17 ___ ___ Real Property.
- 30.18 ___ Personal Property.
- 30.19 ___ Breach of Contract.
- 30.20 ___ ___ Contract Price and Actual Loss.
- 30.21 ___ ___ Delay in Performance.
- 30.22 ___ ___ Defective Performance.
- 30.23 ___ ___ Anticipatory Breach.
- 30.24 ___ ___ Damages Within the Contemplation of the Parties, and Loss of Profits.
- 30.25 ___ ___ Building and Construction.
- 30.26 ___ Minimizing and Mitigating Damages.
- 30.27 ___ ___ Contracts.
- 30.28 ___ ___ Personal Injury.
- 30.29 ___ Excessive or Inadequate Damages.
- 30.30 ___ ___ Specific Awards.
- 30.31 Punitive Damages.
- 30.32 ___ Intentional Torts.
- 30.33 ___ Negligence.
- 30.34 ___ Contract.
- 30.35 ___ Awards.
- 30.36 ___ Mitigation.
- 30.37 Nominal Damages.
- 30.38 Statutory Damages.
- 30.39 Liquidated Damages and Penalties.
- 30.40 Interest.
- 30.41 Attorney Fees.
- 30.42 ___ Statutory.
- 30.43 ___ Agreements and Miscellaneous.
- 30.44 Periodic Payment of Judgments.
- 30.45 Forms.
- 30.46 ___ *Ad Damnum* Clause in Ordinary Complaint. 💾
- 30.47 ___ *Ad Damnum* Clause in Complaint in Medical or Dental Malpractice Action or in Action Against Municipal Government (Supreme Court). 💾

TABLE OF CONTENTS

Sec.
30.48 ____ Clauses in Complaint in Action Involving Automobile Accident. 💾
30.49 ____ Request for Supplemental Demand for Relief in Medical or Dental Malpractice Action or Action Against Municipal Corporation. 💾
30.50 ____ Defense of Culpable Conduct in Answer. 💾
30.51 ____ Defense of Failure to Use Seat Belt Contained in Answer. 💾
30.52 ____ Defense of Indemnification From Collateral Sources. 💾
30.53 ____ Partial Defense; Mitigation of Damages. 💾
30.54 ____ Partial Defense; Mitigation of Damages in Libel Action. 💾
30.55 ____ Partial Defense; Inability to Convey Property. 💾
30.56 ____ Notice of Motion to Amend Verdict (or Judgment) to Add Interest. 💾
30.57 ____ Affidavit in Support of Motion to Amend Verdict (or Judgment) to Add Interest. 💾
30.58 ____ Notice of Motion to Fix Date From Which Interest is to Be Computed. 💾
30.59 ____ Affidavit in Support of Motion to Fix Date From Which Interest is to Be Computed. 💾
30.60 Pattern Jury Instructions.
30.61 ____ Personal Injury—Subsequent Injury, Accident.
30.62 ____ ____ Loss of Earnings.
30.63 ____ Damages—Personal Injury—Shock and Fright and Physical Consequences.
30.64 ____ ____ Aggravation of Injury.
30.65 ____ Payment of Income Taxes on Damages for Personal Injury.
30.66 ____ Reduction to Present Value.
30.67 ____ Wrongful Death—Conscious Pain and Suffering.
30.68 ____ Personal Injury—Collateral Sources—Itemized Verdict (CPLR 4111).
30.69 ____ Damages—Property Without Market Value.
30.70 ____ Damages—Property With Market Value.
30.71 ____ Contracts—Damages—Generally.
30.72 ____ ____ Damages—Employment Contract.

CHAPTER 31. INSURANCE

31.1 Scope Note.
31.2 Strategy.
31.3 ____ Checklist.
31.4 Sources of New York Insurance Law.
31.5 Third Parties Involved in the Placement and Administration of the Insurance Contract.
31.6 ____ Insurance Brokers.
31.7 ____ Insurance Agents.
31.8 Nature of Insurance.
31.9 Interpreting an Insurance Policy.
31.10 Notice.
31.11 The Cooperation Clause.

TABLE OF CONTENTS

Sec.
31.12	The Insurer's Duty to Defend.
31.13	_____ Responding to a Request for a Defense.
31.14	_____ Damages for Breach of the Duty.
31.15	Reservations of Rights By an Insurer.
31.16	Disclaiming/Denying Coverage.
31.17	The Insurer's Duty of Good Faith and Fair Dealing.
31.18	Rescission of Insurance Policies.
31.19	Reformation.
31.20	Lost Policies.
31.21	Nature of Relief.
31.22	Service of Process.
31.23	Pre-answer Security.
31.24	Arbitration Clauses.
31.25	Choice of Law.
31.26	Statutes of Limitation.
31.27	Burden of Proof.
31.28	Insolvent Insurers.
31.29	Subrogation.
31.30	Allocation of Losses Between Co-insurers.
31.31	Checklist of Essential Allegations.
31.32	Forms—Complaint By Policyholder for Declaratory Relief and Breach of Contract. 💾
31.33	_____ Complaint By Insurer for Declaratory Relief. 💾
31.34	_____ Complaint By Insurer for Rescission. 💾
31.35	_____ Affirmative Defenses Asserted By Insurer in a Coverage Action. 💾

CHAPTER 32. WORKERS' COMPENSATION

32.1	Scope Note.
32.2	Strategy.
32.3	_____ Employer's Counsel's Checklist.
32.4	_____ Employee's Counsel's Checklist.
32.5	Introduction to The Workers' Compensation Law.
32.6	_____ History and Theory.
32.7	_____ _____ Workmen's Compensation Law of 1910.
32.8	_____ _____ Constitutional Amendment.
32.9	_____ _____ Workmen's Compensation Law of 1914.
32.10	_____ _____ Statutory Changes.
32.11	Workers' Compensation Board.
32.12	Employer's Obligations and Methods of Coverage.
32.13	Compensable Injury.
32.14	Exclusive Remedy Doctrine.
32.15	_____ Exceptions.
32.16	Pre-hearing Conference.
32.17	Hearings.
32.18	_____ Statute of Limitations.
32.19	_____ Burden of Proof, Presumptions and Defenses.
32.20	_____ Conciliation Process.
32.21	Benefits.

TABLE OF CONTENTS

Sec.
32.22	——	Classification of Disability.
32.23	——	Wage Replacement.
32.24	—— ——	Schedule vs. Non-schedule Awards.
32.25	—— ——	Rehabilitation.
32.26	—— ——	Industrially Disabled.
32.27	—— ——	Special Disability Fund.
32.28	——	Medical Benefits.
32.29	——	Facial Disfigurement.
32.30	——	Death Awards.
32.31	—— ——	Funeral Expenses.
32.32	——	Assignments, Liens and Lump-sum Settlements.
32.33		Board Review of Decisions, Orders and Awards.
32.34		Appeal to Court.
32.35		Reopening Closed Claims.
32.36		Discrimination.
32.37		Licensed Representative.
32.38		Attorney's Fees.
32.39		Posted Notice of Coverage.
32.40		Uninsured Employers' Fund.
32.41		Insurance Policy for Workers' Compensation.
32.42		State Insurance Fund.
32.43		Federal Workers' Compensation Laws and Benefits.
32.44		Disability Benefits Law.
32.45	——	Employer's Obligations.
32.46	——	Exempt Employees.
32.47	——	Benefits and Employee Contribution.
32.48	——	Special Fund.
32.49	——	Employee Eligibility.
32.50	——	Claim Filing.
32.51	——	Pregnancy.
32.52	——	End Note.
32.53		Forms.
32.54	——	Workers' Compensation Board Employee's Claim For Compensation. (C–3 7–97)
32.55	——	Workers' Compensation Board Employer's Report of Work-Related Accident/Occupational Disease. (C–2 10–97)
32.56	——	Workers' Compensation Board Attending Doctor's Report and Carrier/Employer Billing. (C–4 3–97)
32.57	——	Workers' Compensation Board Notice that Right to Compensation is Controverted. (C–7 2–97)
32.58	——	Workers' Compensation Board Notice that Payment of Compensation for Disability has Been Stopped or Modified. (C–8/8.6 4–97)
32.59	——	Notice and Proof of Claim for Disability Benefits. (DB–450 3–97)
32.60	——	Notice of Total or Partial Rejection of Claim for Disability Benefits. (DB–451 3–97)

CHAPTER 33. LOCAL CRIMINAL COURT PRACTICE

33.1 Scope Note.

TABLE OF CONTENTS

Sec.
33.2 Strategy.
33.3 Overview of Local Criminal Court Process.
33.4 Police/Citizen Encounters.
33.5 ___ Vehicle Stops.
33.6 ___ The Parked Car.
33.7 ___ Arrest Without Warrant.
33.8 Accusatory Instruments.
33.9 ___ Information.
33.10 ___ Simplified Information.
33.11 ___ Prosecutor's Information.
33.12 ___ Misdemeanor and Felony Complaints.
33.13 ___ Supporting Depositions.
33.14 ___ ___ Procedure.
33.15 ___ ___ When Must They Be Provided?
33.16 ___ ___ Who Must Be Served?
33.17 ___ ___ Service of Request Must be Timely.
33.18 ___ ___ Request By Attorney Requires Service on Counsel.
33.19 ___ ___ Dismissal For Failure to Serve.
33.20 ___ ___ Motion Must Be In Writing.
33.21 ___ ___ Motion to Dismiss Must Be Timely.
33.22 ___ ___ Factual Insufficiency Not Jurisdictional: Plea Waives Defect.
33.23 ___ ___ Superseding Information Disallowed.
33.24 ___ ___ People May File New Information Upon Dismissal of Supporting Deposition.
33.25 ___ ___ Failure to Serve Not An Amendable Defect.
33.26 ___ ___ Verification.
33.27 Probable Cause Hearing.
33.28 Plea Bargaining.
33.29 ___ Plea Bargain Can Be Conditioned Upon Waiver of Right to Appeal.
33.30 ___ Plea Bargaining—No Penalty for Asserting Right to Trial.
33.31 Pretrial Discovery.
33.32 ___ Applicable to Simplified Informations.
33.33 ___ Applicable to Traffic Infractions.
33.34 ___ Subpoenas.
33.35 ___ Demands to Produce/Bills of Particulars.
33.36 ___ ___ Must Be Filed Within 30 Days.
33.37 ___ ___ Response Within 15 Days.
33.38 ___ ___ People's Failure to Comply With Time Limits.
33.39 ___ *Brady* Material.
33.40 ___ ___ Prosecutor Need Not Be Aware of Evidence.
33.41 ___ ___ Timely Disclosure.
33.42 Evidence.
33.43 ___ Motions to Suppress.
33.44 ___ *Sandoval* Issues—Prior Convictions.
33.45 ___ ___ Procedure.
33.46 ___ ___ *Sandoval* Criteria.
33.47 ___ ___ Defendant's Presence at *Sandoval* Hearing.
33.48 ___ *Miranda*.

TABLE OF CONTENTS

Sec.	
33.49	__ __ Applicable to Misdemeanor Traffic Offenses.
33.50	__ __ Stop and Frisk Does Not Constitute Custodial Interrogation.
33.51	__ __ Sobriety Checkpoint Stops Are Non-custodial.
33.52	__ __ Interrogation Defined.
33.53	__ __ Public Safety Exception.
33.54	__ __ Pedigree Exception.
33.55	__ __ Waiver Following Assertion of Right to Remain Silent.
33.56	__ __ Waiver Following Request for Counsel.
33.57	__ Involuntary Statements.
33.58	__ __ May Not Be Used to Impeach.
33.59	__ __ Applicability of Harmless Error Doctrine.
33.60	__ The Use of Defendant's Pre-arrest Silence.
33.61	__ Corroboration of Admission or Confession Required.
33.62	Trial.
33.63	__ Modes of Trial.
33.64	__ Order of Jury Trial Proceedings.
33.65	__ Order of Bench Trial Proceedings.
33.66	__ Trial of Speeding Tickets.
33.67	__ __ Discovery.
33.68	__ __ People's *Prima Facie* Case.
33.69	__ __ When Not to Request a Supporting Deposition.
33.70	__ __ Speeding Trial Summary.
33.71	Speedy Trial Pursuant to CPL § 30.20.
33.72	__ Application to Traffic Infractions.
33.73	__ Criteria.
33.74	CPL § 30.30.
33.75	__ Vehicle and Traffic Law Violations Generally Excluded.
33.76	__ __ Unless Combined With Felony, Misdemeanor or Violation.
33.77	__ People's Readiness Rule.
33.78	__ Requirements for An Assertion of Readiness.
33.79	__ __ Actual Readiness for Trial.
33.80	__ Guilty Plea Waives CPL § 30.30 Motion.
33.81	__ Burden of Proof.
33.82	__ Commencement of Criminal Action—Appearance Tickets.
33.83	__ Uniform Traffic Tickets.
33.84	__ Excludable Time.
33.85	__ __ Motions.
33.86	__ __ Defective Accusatory Instrument.
33.87	__ __ Adjournments.
33.88	__ __ Delays by the Court.
33.89	__ __ Effect of Defendant's Unavailability.
33.90	__ Post Readiness Delay.
33.91	Procedural Checklists.
33.92	__ Notice of Motion to Dismiss For Failure to Serve a Timely Supporting Deposition/Attorney Affirmation in Support of Motion.
33.93	__ Demand to Produce: Speeding Ticket.
33.94	Drafting Checklists.

TABLE OF CONTENTS

Sec.
33.95 ___ Notice of Motion to Dismiss For Failure to Serve a Timely Supporting Deposition.
33.96 ___ Attorney Affirmation in Support of Motion to Dismiss For Failure to Serve a Timely Supporting Deposition.
33.97 ___ Demand to Produce: Speeding Ticket.
33.98 Forms.
33.99 ___ Notice of Motion to Dismiss For Failure to Serve a Timely Supporting Deposition. 💾
33.100 ___ Attorney Affirmation in Support of Motion to Dismiss For Failure to Serve a Timely Supporting Deposition. 💾
33.101 ___ Demand to Produce: Speeding Ticket. 💾

CHAPTER 34. SOCIAL SECURITY DISABILITY CASES

34.1 Scope Note.
34.2 Strategy.
34.3 The Law of Disability.
34.4 ___ Statutory Definition of Disability.
34.5 ___ Judicial Definitions.
34.6 ___ Durational Requirements.
34.7 ___ Comparison to Workers' Compensation.
34.8 ___ Assessing Disability: The Sequential Evaluation.
34.9 ___ ___ Substantial Gainful Activity.
34.10 ___ ___ Severity.
34.11 ___ ___ Listings of Impairments.
34.12 ___ ___ Ability to Do Past Relevant Work.
34.13 ___ ___ Ability to Do Other Work.
34.14 ___ ___ Dispensing With Individualized Assessment.
34.15 Financial Consideration of The Two Federal Programs: Social Security Disability Insurance Benefits and Supplemental Security Income.
34.16 ___ Income.
34.17 ___ Assets.
34.18 ___ Amount of Benefits.
34.19 ___ SSI: Based on Financial Need.
34.20 ___ SSDIB: Based on FICA Withholding.
34.21 ___ Eligibility for Both SSI and SSDIB.
34.22 ___ Retroactivity of Benefits.
34.23 Administrative Procedure.
34.24 ___ Application.
34.25 ___ Reconsideration.
34.26 ___ Termination of Benefits.
34.27 ___ Administrative Hearing.
34.28 ___ Appeals Council.
34.29 ___ Federal District Court.
34.30 ___ Court of Appeals, Second Circuit.
34.31 Handling the Case—Generally.
34.32 ___ Initial Interview.
34.33 ___ Retainer Agreements.
34.34 ___ Social Security Administration's Records.

TABLE OF CONTENTS

Sec.
- 34.35 ____ Medical Evidence.
- 34.36 ____ ____ Hospital Records.
- 34.37 ____ ____ Reports from Treating Physicians.
- 34.38 ____ Other Evidence.
- 34.39 ____ ____ Former Co-workers and Employers.
- 34.40 ____ ____ Family Members.
- 34.41 ____ Preparing for the Hearing.
- 34.42 ____ ____ Preparing the Claimant.
- 34.43 ____ ____ Other Witnesses or Documents.
- 34.44 ____ Conducting the Hearing.
- 34.45 ____ ____ Testimony of the Claimant.
- 34.46 ____ ____ Medical Advisors.
- 34.47 ____ ____ Vocational Experts.
- 34.48 ____ Post-hearing Evidence and Memoranda.
- 34.49 Implementing Favorable Decisions.
- 34.50 ____ Collecting SSDIB Benefits.
- 34.51 ____ Collecting SSI Benefits.
- 34.52 ____ Collecting Fees.
- 34.53 ____ ____ Fee Applications.
- 34.54 ____ ____ Fee Agreements.
- 34.55 Appealing Unfavorable Decisions.
- 34.56 ____ Strategic Considerations Regarding Unfavorable Decisions.
- 34.57 ____ Strategic Considerations Regarding Partially Favorable Decisions.
- 34.58 Reopening Prior Applications.
- 34.59 ____ Reopening SSDIB.
- 34.60 ____ Reopening SSI.
- 34.61 ____ Review of Grants of Reopening.
- 34.62 ____ Review of Denials of Reopening.
- 34.63 ____ Court Decisions Requiring Reopening.
- 34.64 ____ Statutes and Regulations Requiring Reopening.
- 34.65 Procedural Checklist.
- 34.66 Checklists of Allegations—Medical Claims.
- 34.67 ____ Psychiatric Claims.
- 34.68 Forms—Claimant Questionnaire.
- 34.69 ____ Retainer Agreement.
- 34.70 ____ Retainer Agreement: Concurrent Benefits.
- 34.71 ____ Fee Agreement: Maximum Fee.
- 34.72 ____ Request for Medical Records.
- 34.73 ____ Medical Release.
- 34.74 ____ Medical Questionnaire for Treating Physician.
- 34.75 ____ Psychiatric Questionnaire.
- 34.76 ____ Cover Letter to Treating Physician.
- 34.77 ____ Thank-you Letter to Treating Physician.
- 34.78 ____ Request for Appeals Council Review.

CHAPTER 35. INCOME TAX

- 35.1 Scope Note.
- 35.2 Strategy.

TABLE OF CONTENTS

Sec.
- 35.3 ___ Checklist.
- 35.4 Personal Income Tax.
- 35.5 ___ Computing Federal Adjusted Gross Income.
- 35.6 ___ Computing Federal Taxable Income.
- 35.7 ___ Definition of New York Taxable Income.
- 35.8 ___ Computing New York Adjusted Gross Income.
- 35.9 ___ Computing New York Taxable Income.
- 35.10 ___ New York Personal Exemptions.
- 35.11 ___ Itemized Deductions for Married Couple.
- 35.12 ___ Exclusion of Pension and Disability Distributions From New York Income.
- 35.13 ___ New York Minimum Tax.
- 35.14 ___ Definition of Residency.
- 35.15 ___ Burden of Proving Non-residency.
- 35.16 ___ Domicile and Change of Domicile.
- 35.17 ___ New York Income Tax on Non-resident Individuals.
- 35.18 ___ Checklist.
- 35.19 New York Corporate Franchise Tax.
- 35.20 ___ Comparison With Federal Taxation.
- 35.21 ___ Initial Tax on Corporate Capital Structure.
- 35.22 ___ Foreign Corporations.
- 35.23 ___ Corporations Subject to Tax.
- 35.24 ___ Corporations Exempt From Tax.
- 35.25 ___ Necessary Level of Activity.
- 35.26 ___ Calculation.
- 35.27 ___ Tax on Net Income Base.
- 35.28 ___ ___ Subtractions From Federal Taxable Income.
- 35.29 ___ Items From Subsidiaries.
- 35.30 ___ Tax on Capital Base.
- 35.31 ___ ___ Definition of Capital Base.
- 35.32 ___ ___ Exemption for Small Businesses.
- 35.33 ___ Minimum Taxable Income Base.
- 35.34 ___ Fixed Dollar Minimum Tax.
- 35.35 ___ Apportionment of Tax Bases to New York.
- 35.36 ___ ___ Business Allocation Percentage.
- 35.37 ___ ___ Investment Allocation Percentage.
- 35.38 ___ Definition of Subsidiary Capital.
- 35.39 ___ Franchise Tax Checklist.
- 35.40 Department of Taxation and Finance.
- 35.41 ___ Role of Office of the Counsel.
- 35.42 ___ Taxpayer Services Division.
- 35.43 ___ Office of Revenue and Information Management.
- 35.44 ___ Office of Tax Operations.
- 35.45 ___ ___ Audit Division.
- 35.46 ___ ___ Tax Compliance Division.
- 35.47 ___ ___ Revenue Opportunity Division.
- 35.48 ___ ___ Office of Tax Enforcement.
- 35.49 ___ ___ Division of Tax Appeals.
- 35.50 ___ Summary.
- 35.51 Filing Returns.

TABLE OF CONTENTS

Sec.
35.52	___	Where to File.
35.53	___	Keeping Records of Returns.
35.54	___	Extensions of Time for Filing.
35.55	___	Obtaining New York Tax Forms.
35.56	___	Filing Claims for Refund.
35.57	___	Time Limitations.
35.58	___	Where to File.
35.59	___	Special Refund Authority.
35.60	___	Claim Based on Federal Changes.
35.61	___	Petitions for Refund.
35.62	___	Judicial Review of Denied Refund Claims.
35.63	___	Checklist.
35.64	Statutes of Limitation.	
35.65	___	General Statutes for Income Tax Assessment.
35.66	___	Effect.
35.67	___	Exceptions.
35.68	___	Request for Prompt Assessment.
35.69	___	Waiver.
35.70	Penalties.	
35.71	___	Late Filing.
35.72	___	Late Payment.
35.73	___	Reasonable Cause.
35.74	___	Negligence.
35.75	___	Substantial Understatement.
35.76	___	Underpayment of Estimated Taxes.
35.77	___ ___	Exceptions.
35.78	___	Fraud.
35.79	___ ___	Elements.
35.80	___ ___	Specific Determination Methods.
35.81	___ ___	Common Cases.
35.82	___ ___	Creative Methods of Proof.
35.83	___	Interest on Underpayment or Overpayment.
35.84	___	Checklist.
35.85	Audits and Appeals.	
35.86	___	Audit Methods.
35.87	___	Taxpayer Bill of Rights.
35.88	___	Representation of Taxpayer.
35.89	___	Audit Results.
35.90	___	Bureau of Conciliation and Mediation Services.
35.91	___ ___	Requesting a Conciliation Conference.
35.92	___ ___	Conferences.
35.93	___ ___	Conference Orders.
35.94	___	Petition to Division of Tax Appeals.
35.95	___ ___	Referral to Bureau of Conciliation and Mediation Services.
35.96	___ ___	Small Claims Hearings.
35.97	___	Summary.
35.98	___	Checklist.
35.99	Judicial Actions.	
35.100	___	Appeal by Article 78 Proceeding.

TABLE OF CONTENTS

Sec.
- 35.101 __ __ Payment of Taxes.
- 35.102 __ __ Initiation.
- 35.103 __ __ Burden of Proof.
- 35.104 __ Declaratory Judgment Actions.
- 35.105 __ Appeal to New York Court of Appeals.
- 35.106 __ Summary.
- 35.107 __ Checklist.
- 35.108 Assessment and Collection of Tax.
- 35.109 __ Summary Assessment.
- 35.110 __ Deficiency Assessment.
- 35.111 __ Statute of Limitations.
- 35.112 __ Jeopardy Assessment.
- 35.113 __ Collection of Tax.
- 35.114 __ __ Lien.
- 35.115 __ __ Duration of Lien.
- 35.116 __ Collection by Levy or Warrant.
- 35.117 __ Installment Payment Agreements.
- 35.118 __ Offer in Compromise.
- 35.119 __ Bankruptcy as an Option.
- 35.120 __ Checklist.
- 35.121 Criminal Tax Provisions.
- 35.122 __ Failure to File Return.
- 35.123 __ False or Fraudulent Return.
- 35.124 __ Aiding or Assisting in False Return or Statement.
- 35.125 __ Failure to Pay Tax.
- 35.126 __ Failure to Properly Withhold Taxes.
- 35.127 Forms.
- 35.128 __ Power of Attorney to Represent an Individual.
- 35.129 __ Application for Automatic Extension of Time for Filing Return.
- 35.130 __ Application For Additional Extension of Time to File for Individuals.
- 35.131 __ Notice of Exception to Tax Tribunal.
- 35.132 __ Petition to Division of Tax Appeals.
- 35.133 __ Petition for Advisory Opinion.
- 35.134 __ Statement of Financial Condition.
- 35.135 __ Petition for Declaratory Ruling.
- 35.136 __ Request for Conciliation Conference.
- 35.137 __ Offer in Compromise.

CHAPTER 36. ALCOHOLIC BEVERAGE CONTROL LAW

- 36.1 Scope Note.
- 36.2 Strategy.
- 36.3 __ Checklist.
- 36.4 Historical Background of State and Federal Regulations.
- 36.5 Jurisdiction.
- 36.6 New York State Liquor Authority.
- 36.7 Licenses.
- 36.8 __ Retail Licenses.

TABLE OF CONTENTS

Sec.
- 36.9 ____ ____ On-Premises Licenses.
- 36.10 ____ ____ Off-Premises Licenses.
- 36.11 ____ Wholesale Licenses.
- 36.12 ____ Manufacturing Licenses.
- 36.13 ____ General Application Requirements.
- 36.14 ____ Special Qualifications for Licensees.
- 36.15 Permits.
- 36.16 ____ Temporary Permits.
- 36.17 ____ Other Permits.
- 36.18 Brand and/or Label Registration.
- 36.19 Penal and Tax Bonds.
- 36.20 Application Form (Retail) Reviewed.
- 36.21 ____ Lease Information.
- 36.22 ____ Applicant Information.
- 36.23 ____ Information Regarding Premises.
- 36.24 ____ Financial Information and Criminal Background.
- 36.25 ____ Community Notification.
- 36.26 ____ Landlord Information.
- 36.27 ____ Additional Requirements for On–Premises Consumption Licenses.
- 36.28 ____ ____ Neighborhood.
- 36.29 ____ ____ Premises Exterior.
- 36.30 ____ ____ Premises Interior.
- 36.31 ____ ____ Bars.
- 36.32 ____ ____ Kitchen.
- 36.33 ____ ____ Permits.
- 36.34 ____ ____ Hotel.
- 36.35 ____ Proposed Method of Operation.
- 36.36 ____ Additional Requirements for Off–Premises Liquor Store Applicants.
- 36.37 ____ Additional Requirements for Grocery Store Applicants.
- 36.38 ____ Liquidators Permit.
- 36.39 ____ Affidavit Requirements.
- 36.40 ____ Personal Questionnaire.
- 36.41 ____ On–Premises Liquor Applications 500 Foot Verification.
- 36.42 ____ Miscellaneous Requirements.
- 36.43 ____ Checklist.
- 36.44 Record–Keeping Requirements.
- 36.45 Reporting Changes.
- 36.46 ____ Application for Endorsement Certificate.
- 36.47 ____ Application for Approval of Corporate Change.
- 36.48 ____ Alteration of Premises.
- 36.49 ____ Removal of Premises.
- 36.50 ____ Financing and Method of Operation.
- 36.51 Renewals.
- 36.52 Trade Practices.
- 36.53 Enforcement.
- 36.54 Penalties.
- 36.55 ____ Revocation Order.
- 36.56 ____ Cancellation Order.

TABLE OF CONTENTS

Sec.
36.57	⎯⎯ Suspension Order.
36.58	⎯⎯ ⎯⎯ Forthwith.
36.59	⎯⎯ ⎯⎯ Deferred.
36.60	⎯⎯ ⎯⎯ Combined Forthwith and Deferred Suspension.
36.61	⎯⎯ Letters of Warning.
36.62	⎯⎯ Suspension Proceedings.
36.63	⎯⎯ Revocation Notice of Pleading.
36.64	Pleadings and Procedure.
36.65	⎯⎯ Hearings.
36.66	⎯⎯ Judicial Review.
36.67	Forms.
36.68	⎯⎯ Application for Alcoholic Beverage Control Retail License.
36.69	⎯⎯ Application for Endorsement Certificate.
36.70	⎯⎯ Application for Approval of Corporate Change.
36.71	⎯⎯ Application for Permission to Make Alterations.
36.72	⎯⎯ Application for Wholesale License.
36.73	⎯⎯ Retail License and Filing Fee Schedule.

CHAPTER 37. CIVIL APPELLATE PRACTICE BEFORE THE APPELLATE DIVISION AND OTHER INTERMEDIATE APPELLATE COURTS

37.1	Scope Note.
37.2	Strategy.
37.3	Judiciary Structure.
37.4	Administration of the Appellate Division.
37.5	Administrative Powers of the Appellate Division.
37.6	⎯⎯ Admission, Removal and Disciplinary Jurisdiction.
37.7	⎯⎯ Administration of the Courts.
37.8	⎯⎯ Law Guardian Program.
37.9	⎯⎯ Mental Hygiene Legal Service Oversight.
37.10	⎯⎯ Assigned Counsel.
37.11	⎯⎯ Powers Relating to Appellate Term.
37.12	⎯⎯ Marshals.
37.13	An Overview of the Statutory Framework of the Appellate System and the Rules of the Court.
37.14	Appeals to the Appellate Division.
37.15	⎯⎯ Courts of Original Jurisdiction From Which Appeals Lie.
37.16	⎯⎯ ⎯⎯ Supreme Court and County Court.
37.17	⎯⎯ ⎯⎯ Court of Claims.
37.18	⎯⎯ ⎯⎯ Surrogate's Court.
37.19	⎯⎯ ⎯⎯ Family Court.
37.20	⎯⎯ Appeals From Other Appellate Courts.
37.21	⎯⎯ Who May Appeal.
37.22	⎯⎯ ⎯⎯ Aggrieved Parties.
37.23	⎯⎯ ⎯⎯ ⎯⎯ Defaulters; Orders or Judgments on Consent.
37.24	⎯⎯ ⎯⎯ ⎯⎯ Intervenors.
37.25	⎯⎯ ⎯⎯ ⎯⎯ Substitution of Parties.
37.26	⎯⎯ ⎯⎯ ⎯⎯ Third Party Defendants.
37.27	⎯⎯ Scope of Review.

TABLE OF CONTENTS

Sec.
37.28 ___ ___ Questions of Law.
37.29 ___ ___ Questions of Fact and the Exercise of Discretion.
37.30 ___ ___ Limitations in Notice of Appeal or Brief.
37.31 ___ ___ Mootness.
37.32 ___ ___ Change in Law While Case Is Pending.
37.33 ___ Appeals as of Right.
37.34 ___ ___ Appeals From Final and Interlocutory Judgments.
37.35 ___ ___ Appeals From Orders.
37.36 ___ Appeals by Permission.
37.37 ___ Non-appealable Matters.
37.38 ___ Appealable Paper.
37.39 ___ Time for Taking the Appeal.
37.40 ___ ___ Appeal as of Right.
37.41 ___ ___ Appeal by Permission.
37.42 ___ ___ Cross-Appeal.
37.43 ___ ___ Extensions; Omissions.
37.44 ___ ___ Other Statutory Provisions.
37.45 ___ Notice of Appeal—Form and Content.
37.46 ___ ___ Service and Filing Requirements.
37.47 ___ Reargument; Subsequent Orders.
37.48 ___ Assignment of Counsel.
37.49 ___ Perfecting the Appeal.
37.50 ___ ___ Time.
37.51 ___ ___ Methods of Perfection.
37.52 ___ ___ Briefs.
37.53 ___ ___ Consolidation.
37.54 ___ What to File; Number of Copies.
37.55 ___ ___ First Department.
37.56 ___ ___ Second Department.
37.57 ___ ___ Third Department.
37.58 ___ ___ Fourth Department.
37.59 ___ Location; Transfer Plan.
37.60 ___ Calendars.
37.61 ___ Preferences.
37.62 ___ Oral Arguments.
37.63 ___ Disposition of the Appeal.
37.64 ___ ___ Affirmance.
37.65 ___ ___ Reversal or Modification.
37.66 ___ ___ Dismissal.
37.67 ___ ___ Costs and Disbursements; Attorneys' Fees.
37.68 ___ Post-disposition Proceedings.
37.69 ___ ___ Reargument.
37.70 ___ ___ Leave to Appeal to the Court of Appeals.
37.71 ___ ___ Enforcement.
37.72 ___ ___ Resettlement or Clarification.
37.73 ___ ___ *Certiorari* to the U.S. Supreme Court.
37.74 ___ Motion Practice—Generally.
37.75 ___ ___ First Department.
37.76 ___ ___ Second Department.
37.77 ___ ___ Third Department.

TABLE OF CONTENTS

Sec.
37.78	____ ____	Fourth Department.
37.79	____ ____	Interim Relief.
37.80	____ ____	Stays.
37.81	____ ____	*Amicus Curiae*.
37.82	____ ____	Miscellaneous Motions.
37.83	____	Sanctions.
37.84	____	Preargument Conferences.
37.85	____	Unperfected Appeals.
37.86		Other Proceedings in the Appellate Division.
37.87	____	CPLR Article 78 Proceedings.
37.88	____	Writs of *Habeas Corpus*.
37.89	____	CPLR 5704 *Ex Parte* Order Review.
37.90	____	Miscellaneous Proceedings.
37.91		Appeals to Other Intermediate Courts.
37.92	____	Appeals from Justice Courts.
37.93	____ ____	Courts to Which Appeals Are Taken.
37.94	____ ____	Applicability of CPLR Article 55.
37.95	____ ____	Appeals as of Right and by Permission.
37.96	____ ____	Taking the Appeal: Settlement of Case and Return on Appeal.
37.97	____ ____	Perfection of Appeal.
37.98	____ ____	Costs on Appeal.
37.99	____ ____	Small Claims Review.
37.100	____ ____	Rule Governance by Administrative Board.
37.101	____	Appeals From City Courts.
37.102	____ ____	Courts to Which Appeals Are Taken.
37.103	____ ____	Applicability of CPLR Article 55.
37.104	____ ____	Appeals as of Right and by Permission.
37.105	____ ____	Taking the Appeal: Settlement of Case and Return on Appeal; Variations from CPLR.
37.106	____ ____	Perfection of Appeal.
37.107	____ ____	Costs on Appeal.
37.108	____ ____	Small Claims Review.
37.109	____	Appeals From District Courts.
37.110	____ ____	Court to Which Appeals Are Taken.
37.111	____ ____	Applicability of CPLR Article 55
37.112	____ ____	Appeals as of Right and by Permission.
37.113	____ ____	Taking the Appeal: Settlement of Case and Return on Appeal.
37.114	____ ____	Perfecting the Appeal.
37.115	____ ____	Costs on Appeal.
37.116	____ ____	Small Claims Review.
37.117	____	Appeals from the Civil Court of the City of New York.
37.118	____ ____	Courts to Which Appeals Are Taken.
37.119	____ ____	Applicability of CPLR Article 55.
37.120	____ ____	Appeals as of Right and by Permission.
37.121	____ ____	Appeals to the Court of Appeals.
37.122	____ ____	Taking the Appeal: Settlement of Case and Return on Appeal; Variations From CPLR.
37.123	____ ____	Perfecting the Appeal.

TABLE OF CONTENTS

Sec.
- 37.124 __ __ Costs on Appeal.
- 37.125 __ __ Small Claims Review.
- 37.126 __ Appeals from County Courts.
- 37.127 Procedural Checklist.
- 37.128 Forms.
- 37.129 __ Notice of Appeal. 💾
- 37.130 __ Notice of Motion for a Stay of Proceedings. 💾
- 37.131 __ Order to Show Cause for a Stay of Proceedings. 💾
- 37.132 __ Affirmation in Support of Motion or Order To Show Cause for a Stay of Proceedings. 💾
- 37.133 __ Notice of Motion for a Preference to Expedite the Appeal. 💾
- 37.134 __ Affirmation in Support of Motion for a Preference to Expedite the Appeal. 💾
- 37.135 __ Notice of Motion to Enlarge Time for (Appellant to Perfect Appeal)(Respondent To File Brief). 💾
- 37.136 __ Affirmation in Support of Motion to Enlarge Time for (Appellant to Perfect Appeal) (Respondent to File Brief). 💾
- 37.137 __ Notice of Motion to Strike Matter *Dehors* the Record (Appendix)(Brief). 💾
- 37.138 __ Affirmation in Support of Motion to Strike Matter *Dehors* the Record(Appendix)(Brief). 💾
- 37.139 __ Notice of Motion for Reargument or Leave to Appeal to the Court of Appeals. 💾
- 37.140 __ Affirmation in Support of Motion for Reargument or Leave to Appeal to the Court of Appeals. 💾

Volume 25

CHAPTER 38. CRIMINAL APPELLATE PRACTICE BEFORE THE APPELLATE DIVISION AND OTHER INTERMEDIATE APPELLATE COURTS

- 38.1 Scope Note.
- 38.2 Strategy.
- 38.3 Appeals to the Appellate Division—General Principles.
- 38.4 __ Courts of Original Jurisdiction From Which Appeals Lie.
- 38.5 __ Who May Appeal.
- 38.6 __ __ Status as Aggrieved by "Adverse" Determination.
- 38.7 __ __ Appeals by the Defendant From Superior Courts.
- 38.8 __ __ __ As of Right.
- 38.9 __ __ __ Appeals by Permission.
- 38.10 __ __ Appeals by the People.
- 38.11 __ __ Appeals from Orders Accepting or Sealing Grand Jury Reports; Appeals by Prosecutors; Appeals by Public Servants.
- 38.12 __ Appeal Process—Appeals as of Right.
- 38.13 __ __ Appeals by Permission: Certificate Granting Leave.
- 38.14 __ __ Extensions of Time.
- 38.15 __ __ Stay of Judgment or Order.
- 38.16 __ __ Poor Person Relief and Assignment of Counsel.

TABLE OF CONTENTS

Sec.
38.17 _____ _____ Perfecting and Calendaring the Appeal.
38.18 _____ Scope of Review.
38.19 _____ _____ Questions of Law.
38.20 _____ _____ Questions of Fact; Weight of Evidence.
38.21 _____ _____ Interest of Justice/Discretion.
38.22 _____ _____ Change in Law While Case Pending.
38.23 _____ Disposition of Appeal.
38.24 _____ _____ Affirmance.
38.25 _____ _____ Modification.
38.26 _____ _____ Reversal.
38.27 _____ _____ Character of Order of Reversal or Modification: On the Law, On the Facts, in the Interest of Justice.
38.28 _____ _____ Corrective Action.
38.29 _____ Post-disposition Proceedings.
38.30 _____ _____ Responsibilities of Counsel.
38.31 _____ _____ Reargument.
38.32 _____ _____ Leave to Appeal.
38.33 _____ _____ *Certiorari* to U.S. Supreme Court.
38.34 _____ _____ *Coram Nobis*—Ineffective Assistance of Appellate Counsel.
38.35 _____ _____ Clarification/Resettlement.
38.36 _____ Motions in Connection With Appeals—Generally.
38.37 _____ _____ *Pro Se* Supplemental Brief.
38.38 _____ _____ *Anders* Brief.
38.39 _____ _____ Dismissal.
38.40 _____ _____ Reconstruction Hearing; Summary Reversal.
38.41 _____ _____ Death or Absence of a Defendant.
38.42 _____ _____ Assignment of New Counsel.
38.43 _____ _____ Expanding the Judgment Roll.
38.44 _____ _____ Briefs.
38.45 _____ _____ Withdrawal of Appeal.
38.46 Appeals to Intermediate Appellate Courts Other Than the Appellate Division.
38.47 _____ Appeals From Village Courts, Town Courts, City Courts and District Courts.
38.48 _____ Appeals From Criminal Court of the City of New York.
38.49 _____ _____ New York and Bronx County Branches.
38.50 _____ _____ Kings, Queens, Richmond County Branches.
38.51 _____ Orders, Sentences and Judgments Appealable.
38.52 _____ Taking the Appeal—Appeal as of Right.
38.53 _____ _____ Appeals by Permission.
38.54 _____ Stays Pending Appeal.
38.55 _____ Perfecting the Appeal.
38.56 _____ Determination of the Appeal.
38.57 Governance of the Appellate Term.
38.58 Original Application to County Court for Change of Venue.
38.59 Procedural Checklist for Appeals to Appellate Division.
38.60 Forms—Notice of Motion for a Stay of Execution of Judgment. 💾

TABLE OF CONTENTS

Sec.
38.61 ____ Affirmation in Support of Motion for a Stay of Execution of Judgment. 💾
38.62 ____ Notice of Motion for an Extension of Time to Take an Appeal. 💾
38.63 ____ Affirmation in Support of Motion for an Extension of Time to Take an Appeal. 💾
38.64 Chart.

CHAPTER 39. CIVIL AND CRIMINAL APPEALS TO THE COURT OF APPEALS

39.1 Scope Note.
39.2 Strategy.
39.3 Civil Appeals.
39.4 ____ Finality.
39.5 ____ Non-appealable Orders.
39.6 ____ Appealable Paper.
39.7 ____ Scope of Review.
39.8 ____ Appeal as of Right.
39.9 ____ ____ Appellate Division Orders or Judgments.
39.10 ____ ____ Final Judgment of Court of Original Instance.
39.11 ____ ____ Judgment of Court of Original Instance to Review Prior Non-final Determination of the Appellate Division.
39.12 ____ Appeals by Permission of the Appellate Division or the Court of Appeals.
39.13 ____ ____ Judgment of Court of Original Instance to Review Prior Non-final Determination of the Appellate Division.
39.14 ____ ____ Final Order of the Appellate Division Determining the Action.
39.15 ____ ____ Non-final Appellate Division Orders in Proceedings by or Against Public Officers or Others.
39.16 ____ Appeals by Permission of the Appellate Division.
39.17 ____ Form, Content and Service of Motions for Leave to Appeal.
39.18 ____ ____ Motions Filed in the Appellate Division.
39.19 ____ ____ Motions Filed in the Court of Appeals.
39.20 ____ Time for Taking the Appeal or Moving for Leave to Appeal—Appeals as of Right.
39.21 ____ ____ Motions for Leave to Appeal.
39.22 ____ ____ Cross Appeals.
39.23 ____ ____ Extensions of Time.
39.24 ____ ____ Omissions.
39.25 ____ Notice of Appeal—Form and Content.
39.26 ____ The Jurisdictional Statement.
39.27 ____ Jurisdictional Inquiry.
39.28 ____ Perfecting and Readying the Appeal.
39.29 ____ ____ Full Briefing and Oral Argument.
39.30 ____ ____ *Sua Sponte* Merits Consideration ("SSM").
39.31 ____ Determination of the Appeal—*Remittitur*.
39.32 ____ Motion Practice.
39.33 ____ ____ Motion for a Stay.

TABLE OF CONTENTS

Sec.

39.77 Forms—Notice of Appeal to Court of Appeals From Order of Appellate Division Finally Determining Action With Two Dissents on Question of Law.

39.78 ____ Notice of Appeal to Court of Appeals From Order of Appellate Division Finally Determining Action Where Construction of Constitution is Directly Involved.

39.79 ____ Notice of Appeal to Court of Appeals From Judgment of Supreme Court Where Constitutionality of Statute is Directly Involved.

39.80 ____ Notice of Appeal to Court of Appeals From Appellate Division Order of Reversal Granting New Trial With Stipulation for Judgment Absolute.

39.81 ____ Notice of Appeal to Court of Appeals From Judgment of Supreme Court to Review Prior Non-final Determination of Appellate Division.

39.82 ____ Rule 500.2 Jurisdictional Statement.

39.83 ____ Notice of Motion in Court of Appeals for Leave to Appeal to Court of Appeals From Order of Appellate Division.

39.84 ____ Affidavit in Support of Motion in Court of Appeals for Leave to Appeal to Court of Appeals From Order of Appellate Division.

39.85 ____ Notice of Motion in Court of Appeals for Reargument of Motion for Leave to Appeal.

39.86 ____ Notice of Motion in Court of Appeals for Leave to Appear *Amicus Curiae.*

39.87 ____ Notice of Motion to Dismiss Appeal as Untimely Taken.

39.88 ____ Affidavit in Support of Motion to Dismiss Appeal as Untimely Taken.

39.89 ____ CPLR 5531 Statement.

39.90 ____ Letter Seeking Leave to Appeal in Criminal Case.

	Page
Table of Jury Instructions	235
Table of Forms	236
Table of Statutes	iii
Table of Rules	iii
Table of Cases	iii
Index	iii

TABLE OF CONTENTS

Sec.
- 39.34 ___ ___ Motion to File an *Amicus* Brief.
- 39.35 ___ ___ Motion for Poor Person Relief.
- 39.36 ___ ___ Motion for Reconsideration.
- 39.37 Criminal Appeals.
- 39.38 ___ Definition of Criminal Case.
- 39.39 ___ Orders and Judgments From Which Appeals May Be Taken.
- 39.40 ___ By the Defendant in Death Penalty Cases.
- 39.41 ___ By the Prosecution in Death Penalty Cases.
- 39.42 ___ Intermediate Appellate Courts.
- 39.43 ___ Additional Limitations on Appealability.
- 39.44 ___ Appeals by Permission.
- 39.45 ___ ___ Obligation of Intermediate Appellate Court Counsel.
- 39.46 ___ ___ Who May Grant Leave to Appeal.
- 39.47 ___ ___ Criminal Leave Application ("CLA") Practice.
- 39.48 ___ ___ Stays and Continuation of Bail.
- 39.49 ___ Appeals Practice.
- 39.50 ___ Scope of Review.
- 39.51 ___ Disposition of Appeal.
- 39.52 ___ Motion Practice.
- 39.53 ___ ___ Poor Person Relief and Assignment of Counsel.
- 39.54 ___ ___ Extension of Time to Seek Leave to Appeal.
- 39.55 ___ ___ Dismissal of Appeal.
- 39.56 ___ ___ Withdrawal of Appeal.
- 39.57 ___ ___ Reargument.
- 39.58 Other Proceedings in the Court of Appeals.
- 39.59 ___ Review of Determinations of the Commission on Judicial Conduct.
- 39.60 ___ Certified Questions From Other Courts.
- 39.61 ___ Matters Regarding Admission of Attorneys and Licensing of Foreign Legal Consultants.
- 39.62 *Certiorari* to the Supreme Court of the United States.
- 39.63 Procedural Checklists.
- 39.64 ___ Civil Appeals as of Right.
- 39.65 ___ Civil Appeals by Permission of Court of Appeals.
- 39.66 ___ Criminal Appeals by Leave of a Court of Appeals Judge.
- 39.67 ___ Civil Appeals by Leave of the Appellate Division and Criminal Appeals by Leave of an Appellate Division Justice.
- 39.68 ___ Appeals Selected for Expedited Review Pursuant to Rule 500.4
- 39.69 ___ Appeals Tracked to Full Briefing and Oral Argument.
- 39.70 Drafting Checklists.
- 39.71 ___ Notice of Appeal.
- 39.72 ___ Rule 500.2 Jurisdictional Statement.
- 39.73 ___ Motion for Leave to Appeal to Court of Appeals Filed in Court of Appeals.
- 39.74 ___ Application for Leave to Appeal in Criminal Case Filed in Court of Appeals.
- 39.75 ___ Appellant's Brief on the Merits.
- 39.76 ___ Respondent's Brief on the Merits.

WEST'S NEW YORK PRACTICE SERIES

GENERAL PRACTICE IN NEW YORK

Volume 20

Chapter 1

BUSINESS ORGANIZATIONS: CORPORATIONS

by
Ronald David Greenberg[*]

Table of Sections

1.1	Scope Note.
1.2	Strategy.
1.3	Strategy Checklist.
1.4	Overview.
1.5	Definitions.
1.6	Formation of Corporations.
1.7	___ Certificates; Notices.
1.8	___ Corporate Seal.
1.9	___ Corporate Purposes.
1.10	___ ___ Upholding and Disregarding the Corporate Entity.
1.11	___ ___ General Powers.
1.12	___ ___ Defense of *Ultra Vires*.
1.13	___ Corporate Name.
1.14	___ ___ Reservation of Name.
1.15	___ Service of Process.
1.16	___ ___ Records and Certificates of Department of State.
1.17	___ ___ Statutory Designation of Secretary of State as Agent for Service of Process.
1.18	___ ___ Registered Agent for Service of Process.
1.19	___ ___ Upon Unauthorized Foreign Corporation.
1.20	___ Incorporators and Promoters.
1.21	___ Certificate of Incorporation.
1.22	___ Bylaws.
1.23	___ Organization Meeting; Biennial Statement; Franchise Tax.
1.24	___ Formation of Corporations Summary.
1.25	___ Formation of Corporations Checklist.
1.26	Capital Structure.
1.27	___ Authorized Shares.
1.28	___ Preferred Shares in Series.
1.29	___ Subscription for Shares.
1.30	___ Consideration and Payment for Shares.
1.31	___ Rights to Purchase Shares.
1.32	___ Stated Capital.

[*] Professor Greenberg is grateful for the assistance of C. Golis.

Ch. 1 BUSINESS ORGANIZATIONS: CORPORATIONS

1.33 ___ Corporate Bonds; Convertible Securities.
1.34 ___ Federal Income Taxation Aspects.
1.35 ___ Capital Structure Summary.
1.36 ___ Capital Structure Checklist.
1.37 Distributions.
1.38 ___ Dividends; Share Distributions and Changes.
1.39 ___ Purchase or Redemption of Shares.
1.40 ___ Federal Income Tax Aspects.
1.41 ___ Distributions Summary.
1.42 ___ Distributions Checklist.
1.43 Shareholders' Meetings and Agreements—Generally.
1.44 ___ Notice Requirements.
1.45 ___ Voting.
1.46 ___ Quorum Requirements.
1.47 ___ Agreements; Voting Trusts.
1.48 ___ Action Without a Meeting.
1.49 Shareholders' Meetings and Agreements Summary.
1.50 Shareholders' Meetings and Agreements Checklist.
1.51 Shareholders' Rights.
1.52 ___ Preemptive Rights.
1.53 ___ Inspection of Books and Records.
1.54 ___ Shareholders' Rights Summary.
1.55 ___ Shareholders' Rights Checklist.
1.56 Shareholders' Liabilities.
1.57 ___ Shareholders' Liabilities Summary.
1.58 ___ Shareholders' Liabilities Checklist.
1.59 Directors.
1.60 ___ Vacancies; New Directorships.
1.61 ___ Removal.
1.62 ___ Meetings.
1.63 ___ ___ Quorum and Voting Requirements.
1.64 ___ Executive Committee; Other Committees.
1.65 ___ Fiduciary Duties.
1.66 ___ Liabilities.
1.67 ___ Directors Summary.
1.68 ___ Directors Checklist.
1.69 Officers.
1.70 ___ Officers Summary.
1.71 ___ Officers Checklist.
1.72 Amendment of Certificate of Incorporation.
1.73 ___ Procedure.
1.74 ___ Class Vote.
1.75 ___ Certificate of Amendment.
1.76 ___ Certificate of Change.
1.77 ___ Restated Certificate of Incorporation.
1.78 ___ Reorganization Under Act of Congress.
1.79 Amendment of Certificate of Incorporation Summary.
1.80 Amendment of Certificate of Incorporation Checklist.
1.81 Business Combinations.
1.82 ___ Mergers and Consolidations.
1.83 ___ ___ Procedures.

BUSINESS ORGANIZATIONS: CORPORATIONS Ch. 1

1.84	__ __ Effect.
1.85	__ Sale, Lease, Exchange, or Other Disposition of Assets.
1.86	__ __ Mortgage or Security Interest in Assets.
1.87	__ __ Guarantee Authorized by Shareholders.
1.88	__ Share Exchanges.
1.89	__ Takeover Bids.
1.90	__ Right of Shareholder to Receive Payment for Shares.
1.91	__ Federal Income Taxation Aspects.
1.92	Business Combinations Summary.
1.93	Business Combinations Checklist.
1.94	Dissolution.
1.95	__ Non-judicial Dissolution.
1.96	__ __ Authorization.
1.97	__ __ Certificate of Dissolution.
1.98	__ __ Notice to Creditors.
1.99	__ Judicial Dissolution.
1.100	__ __ Attorney General's Action.
1.101	__ __ Directors' Petition.
1.102	__ __ Shareholders' Petition.
1.103	__ __ Petition Upon Deadlock Among Directors or Shareholders and in Other Circumstances.
1.104	__ __ Procedures.
1.105	__ __ Preservation of Assets; Appointment of Receiver.
1.106	__ __ Certain Transfers and Judgments Void; Injunction.
1.107	__ Liquidation Distributions.
1.108	__ __ Federal Income Tax Aspects.
1.109	__ Dissolution Summary.
1.110	__ Dissolution Checklist.
1.111	Receivership.
1.112	Receivership—Summary.
1.113	__ Checklist.
1.114	Foreign Corporations.
1.115	__ Authorization to Do Business in New York.
1.116	__ Application for Authority.
1.117	__ __ Effect of Filing.
1.118	__ Surrender of Authority.
1.119	__ Termination of Existence.
1.120	Foreign Corporations Summary.
1.121	Foreign Corporations Checklist.
1.122	Professional Service Corporations.
1.123	Professional Service Corporations Summary.
1.124	Professional Service Corporations Checklist.
1.125	Foreign Professional Service Corporations.
1.126	Foreign Professional Service Corporations Summary.
1.127	Foreign Professional Service Corporations Checklist.
1.128	Transactional Checklist—Generally.
1.129	__ Formation ("Birth").
1.130	__ Operation ("Growth").
1.131	__ Business Combinations ("Marriage").
1.132	__ Spin-offs and Split-offs ("Children" and "Divorce").
1.133	__ Repurchase of Shares ("Redemption").

Ch. 1 SCOPE NOTE § 1.1

1.134 ____ Dissolution; Liquidation ("Death").
1.135 Procedural Checklist—Generally.
1.136 ____ Notices.
1.137 ____ Reservation of Corporate Name.
1.138 ____ ____ Foreign Corporations.
1.139 ____ Mandatory and Permissive Provisions in Certificate of Incorporation.
1.140 ____ Incorporation.
1.141 ____ Filing Certificate of Incorporation.
1.142 ____ Bylaws.
1.143 ____ Organization Meetings.
1.144 ____ Share Certificate.
1.145 ____ Shareholder Approval Requirements.
1.146 ____ Shareholder's Right to Receive Payment for Shares.
1.147 ____ Close Corporations.
1.148 ____ Foreign Corporations.
1.149 Drafting Checklist.
1.150 Form—Application to Reserve Corporate Name.
1.151 ____ Certificate of Incorporation.
1.152 ____ Bylaws.
1.153 ____ Subscription Agreement.
1.154 ____ Certificate of Amendment.
1.155 ____ Certificate of Dissolution.

WESTLAW Electronic Research

See WESTLAW Electronic Research Guide preceding the Summary of Contents.

---

§ 1.1 Scope Note

This chapter introduces the basic provisions and associated cross-references, decisions, and other materials related to New York corporate law that may be of interest to the general practitioner.[1] It also provides a practice tool covering the most common types of corporate transactions and questions likely to be encountered by an attorney.

§ 1.1

1. The attorney is responsible for thoroughly investigating the facts and circumstances pertaining to each client's matter and, perhaps in some cases with the help of a corporations or securities regulation expert, adapt these generalizations to the client's case. Because of unique facts and circumstances attending each case that an attorney handles, he or she should consider the need for further research in the New York Business Corporation Law ("NYBCL") and its annotations (e.g., commentary, cross-references to other statutory provisions, law review articles, relevant judicial and administrative decisions, procedures, and forms) and "Shepardizing" citations provided in this chapter. See also, Field and Moskin, New York and Delaware Business Entities: Choice, Formation, Operation, Financing and Acquisitions (West 1997); H. Henn and J. Alexander, Laws of Corporations and Other Business Enterprises (1983) ("Henn and Alexander")(which is cited in the NYBCL among the annotations following each section); Revised Model Business Corporation Act ("RMBCA"); D. Herwitz, Business Planning, Materials on the Planning of Corporate Transactions (Temporary 2d ed. 1984) ("Herwitz").

5

§ 1.1 BUSINESS ORGANIZATIONS: CORPORATIONS Ch. 1

The chapter begins in Sections 1.2–1.4 with a discussion of the strategic questions that an attorney should ask to formulate a coherent business plan for a client's corporation over its life cycle, particularly the issues for an initial meeting with the client. Section 1.5 contains a list of definitions used throughout the chapter. Section 1.6 continues with a general discussion of the formation of a business corporation, including further treatment of the topics the attorney will want to discuss with a client. Sections 1.7–1.25 contain a more detailed discussion of corporate purposes, the defense of *ultra vires* and shareholder liability, reservation of the corporation's name, service of process on the corporation, and the corporation's certificate of incorporation, bylaws, incorporators, and organizational meeting.[2]

Sections 1.26–1.36 cover corporate finance as it pertains to the issuance of shares of common and preferred stock, the consideration and payment for shares, the issuance of debt obligations, and related federal income and state tax questions. Federal and state securities laws are mentioned. Sections 1.37–1.42 consider corporate distributions in various forms such as dividends and redemptions compared with the payment of interest, salaries, and rent among others; how these transactions relate to corporate restructurings is discussed.

Sections 1.43–1.71 treat operational issues affecting a corporation, including shareholders' meetings, agreements, and rights; directors' meetings and duties; officers' duties; and indemnification of directors and officers. Sections 1.72–1.80 cover the procedure required for amending the corporation's certificate of incorporation to change a corporation's name, office, or registered agent; the rights and preferences of its shares; and the rights of shareholders, directors, and officers, among other modifications.

The chapter continues in Sections 1.81–1.93 with a discussion of various business combinations, including mergers and acquisitions, share exchanges, major sales and purchases of assets, mortgage of assets, the Security Takeover Disclosure Act, and the right of dissenting shareholders to payment of the fair value of their shares in certain mergers and acquisitions. Federal income tax aspects of various business combinations are also outlined.

Sections 1.94–1.113 cover dissolution, liquidation, and receivership, and Sections 1.114–1.127 examine foreign corporations, professional service corporations, and foreign professional service corporations.

The chapter concludes in Sections 1.128–1.155 with transactional, procedural, and drafting checklists. It includes some basic forms, with references to additional forms.

---

2. For discussion about choice of organizational form and other business entities besides the corporation (such as general partnerships, limited partnerships, limited liability companies, and limited liability partnerships), *see* Chapter 2 "Non–Corporate Entities: Limited Liability Companies and Partnerships," *infra. See also, e.g.*, W. Klein and J. Coffee, *Business Organization and Finance* 1–10, 48, 97 (4th ed. 1990).

§ 1.2 Strategy

When first meeting with a client interested in either establishing a corporation or in seeking assistance for an existing corporation, the attorney should help the client in strategic business planning.[1] What is the *desirability* from the client's viewpoint of various alternatives, what is the *feasibility* of each alternative, and what are the *consequences* to the client of implementing a particular alternative?[2]

The desirability of a course of action will depend on the client's wants and needs with respect to such factors as what *risk*[3] the client is willing to accept in the business activity involved, what *income*[4] or return the client demands on his or her investment, what management *control*[5] the client wants to exercise, and what *tax* implications are associated with each alternative. In interviewing the client the attorney will gather the facts necessary to determine a desirable business plan for the enterprise.

The question of which is the desirable choice among alternative business organizational forms (*i.e.*, proprietorship, general partnership, limited partnership, "C" corporation, "S" corporation, or limited liabili-

---

§ 1.2

1. *See, e.g.*, Herwitz, *supra* § 1.1, note 1, iii-iv; R. Weise, *Representing the Corporate Client: Designs for Quality* (1991) (re corporate legal departments primarily but useful for any attorney that represents corporate clients).

2. *See, e.g.*, Chapter 3, R. Greenberg, "Tax Implications of Forming a Corporation" in *New York Lawyer's Deskbook* (7th ed. 1995) p. 3–1 (hereinafter "Greenberg, Corporate Tax").

3. *See, e.g.*, P. Hunt, C. Williams, and G. Donaldson, *Basic Business Finance* (1958) pp. 449–453; Henn and Alexander, *supra* § 1.1, note 1, p. 396. For risk of corporate illiquidity *see infra*, § 1.26. For risk to investors *see infra*, §§ 1.10 and 1.56 (limited liability protection lost), 1.26–1.27 (liquidation preferences in capital structure), 1.107 (diminished return of capital in liquidation distribution). For risk to directors and officers *see infra*, §§ 1.65–1.66, 1.69. These risks arise at various stages of a corporation's life cycle. *See infra*, § 1.4.

4. *See, e.g.*, P. Hunt, C. Williams, and G. Donaldson, *Basic Business Finance* (1958) pp. 453–456. *See infra*, §§ 1.10, 1.26 (rate of return; tax implications; treatment of income (loss) in a separate entity (as opposed to pass-through conduit treatment) depends on upholding desired organizational corporate form), 1.31 (shareholder value realized in options and other rights to purchase shares), 1.38 (dividends), 1.39 (shareholder value realized in redemption of shares), 1.33 (interest income on bonds), 1.34 (tax implications), 1.81–1.90 (shareholder value realized in mergers and acquisitions and other business combinations), 1.91 (tax implications). These issues arise at various stages of a corporation's life cycle. *See infra*, § 1.4.

5. *See, e.g.*, P. Hunt, C. Williams, and G. Donaldson, *Basic Business Finance* (1958) pp. 456–459. *See infra*, §§ 1.43–1.55 (shareholder voting rights and other means of control of corporate affairs), 1.59 and 1.61 (shareholder election and removal of directors), 1.69 (director election or appointment and removal of officers), 1.64 (centralized management by executive committee of board of directors), 1.10 (continuity of control by upholding continuity of corporate entity), 1.21, 1.26–1.31, 1.47–1.48, 1.51–1.52 (transferability of shares and restrictions thereon). These issues arise at various stages of a corporation's life cycle. *See infra*, § 1.4.

CAVEAT: For a corporation formed outside the United States that is controlled by U.S. shareholders, a so-called controlled foreign corporation (or CFC), *see infra*, § 1.34, notes 27 and 30.

§ 1.2 BUSINESS ORGANIZATIONS: CORPORATIONS Ch. 1

ty company)[6] should be considered at the outset by the attorney. The *alternatives*[7] to a corporation must be considered because one of them may serve the interests of the client better (*e.g.*, a partnership (general or limited) may provide greater flexibility to allocate financial interests). Accordingly, the attorney must describe the *advantages* and *disadvantages*[8] of each type of organization to his or her client.[9]

Several advantages redound to the corporate entity that should be mentioned briefly here because they are important to formulating a coherent business strategy. The principle of *continuity*[10] of life generally permits a corporation to continue business operations notwithstanding the death, insanity, bankruptcy, retirement, resignation, or expulsion of any owner or member of the organization. *Centralized management*[11] is found in the board of directors (or the executive committee of the board) of the corporation. The corporation is recognized as a separate legal entity with *limited liability*,[12] which means that the owners' (shareholders') liability is generally limited to the amount of their investment in the corporation. Each shareholder has free *transferability*[13] of his or her ownership interest in the corporation, meaning that the shareholder has the power, without the consent of the other shareholders, to transfer that interest (or a portion thereof) to another shareholder or to an outsider, unless the shareholders agree otherwise. Because of these characteristics, a corporation generally has easier access to capital than other types of organizations.

One important disadvantage of the corporate form is double taxation of earnings—taxes are incurred by the corporate entity as a separate taxpayer and again by the shareholders when dividends are distributed to them. This disadvantage can be lessened by various means, depending on what the business scenario is expected to be. The attorney should consider the following possibilities.

When a corporation distributes all its earnings as dividends (a rare case), electing to be taxed as an "S" corporation is advantageous because the earnings are taxed once, not twice.[14] The "S" corporation, like the

---

6. For discussion of limited liability companies and partnerships and choice of entity, see Chapter 2 "Non–Corporate Entities: Limited Liability Companies and Partnerships," *infra*.

7. Greenberg, Corporate Tax, *supra* note 2, pp. 15–16.

8. *Id.*

9. *Id.*

10. Treas. Reg. § 301.7701–2(b). See Chapter 2 "Non–Corporate Entities: Limited Liability Companies and Partnerships," *infra*.

11. Treas. Reg. § 301.7701–2(c). See Chapter 2 "Non–Corporate Entities: Limited Liability Companies and Partnerships," *infra*.

12. Treas. Reg. § 301.7701–2(d). See Chapter 2 "Non–Corporate Entities: Limited Liability Companies and Partnerships," *infra*.

13. Treas. Reg. § 301.7701–2(e). See Chapter 2 "Non–Corporate Entities: Limited Liability Companies and Partnerships," *infra*.

14. *See* Chapter 2 "Non–Corporate Entities: Limited Liability Companies and Partnerships," *infra*. *Cf.* Herwitz, *supra* § 1.1, note 1, p. 213. If the investors expect the business to incur losses in its early

partnership, is desirable when the individual's (shareholder's) tax rate is lower than the corporate tax rate for the taxable income involved. In that event the choice to elect "S" corporation status is clear because it has pass-through taxation (*i.e.,* is not taxed) though it remains a corporate entity under the NYBCL for purposes of limited liability.

In a more common case, the shareholders withdraw most of the corporate profits as salaries, rent, and interest (all such expenses being deductible from the corporation's income under I.R.C. §§ 162 and 163) so that little corporate income tax will be owed by the "C" corporation, undercutting the disadvantage of double taxation. A corporation's electing "S" corporation status would eliminate disputes with the IRS over the reasonableness or other requirements for deduction of the expenses because "S" corporations are not taxed on income and thus do not deduct expenses for tax purposes.

In perhaps the most common case, where the corporation accumulates a substantial portion of its operating income to meet future business needs rather than distribute it as dividends to its shareholders, decreasing the client's double taxation burden depends upon the applicable tax arithmetic or accounting. For example, if the corporate tax rate is less than the shareholders' individual tax rates (*e.g.,* where corporate taxable income is $75,000 or less), a "C" corporation realizes tax savings because the corporate earnings are taxed only once (because the earnings are accumulated, not distributed) and at a corporate tax rate that is lower than the applicable individual tax rate.[15] In that situation a "C" corporation incurs a lower tax burden (and is the desirable organizational form) because it pays the income tax instead of the shareholder.[16]

The *feasibility* of meeting the client's needs must also be analyzed (*i.e.,* can the attorney formulate a plan that meets the relevant legal requirements)[17] as well as the *consequences* of forming a corporation.[18]

For example, a client, one of perhaps several founders of a business, might strongly want to be protected from risk of liability, and thus the limited liability of shareholders in a corporation would be desirable.[19] If

---

years, the "S" corporation is advantageous because the losses can be passed through to the shareholders *pro rata* as if they incurred the losses.

15. See I.R.C. §§ 1 and 11.

16. **CAVEAT:** An attorney should be alert to the accumulated earnings tax in cases where a corporation is formed for the *purpose* of avoiding the income tax on shareholders by accumulating rather than distributing its earnings. Accumulations beyond the reasonable needs of the business are proof of the forbidden purpose unless the corporation proves to the contrary by a preponderance of the evidence. See I.R.C. §§ 531–533, 537; Treas. Reg. §§ 1.532–1(a)(1); 1.533–1(a)(1). The reasonable needs of a business are discussed in Treas. Reg. § 1.537–1(a), (b) (specific, definite, and feasible plans to use accumulation within a reasonable time).

17. Greenberg, Corporate Tax, *supra* note 2, pp. 15–16.

18. *Id.*

19. **PRACTICE POINTER:** In negotiating what the capital structure of the organization will be, each of the founders should be represented by counsel to protect their respective contributions to the business.

CAVEAT: Each founder should be alert to certain tax consequences of forming a

§ 1.2 BUSINESS ORGANIZATIONS: CORPORATIONS Ch. 1

the business being incorporated is in its incipiency, losses during its early years may be expected. The founders thus would favor a pass-through entity (partnership or "S" corporation) during this stage of the business when it is incurring losses so that they can offset these losses against their income.

Assuming that the business becomes profitable, the desirable organizational form will depend on the expected scenario.[20] A limited partnership might be preferable if, *e.g.*, the number of investors exceeds the 35 shareholder limit of an "S" corporation.[21] The founders might insist on having control of business operations initially as well as later when, say, an issue of shares to outside investors is planned.[22] The feasibility of achieving both pass-through of loss or profit and limited liability will depend on whether the corporation formed under the NYBCL (which will assure limited liability for the founders) is eligible to elect to be taxed as an "S" corporation (which will achieve the pass-through feature).[23] The control objective can be assured by issuing voting stock to the founders on the formation of the corporation and perhaps issuing limited-voting or non-voting shares to outside investors later.[24]

Limited liability and pass-through of losses (or profits) are two desired consequences of subchapter "S" status.[25] However, other consequences, perhaps less appealing, will also obtain. For example, an "S" corporation may not have more than one class of stock,[26] though it will not be treated as having more than one class of stock merely because of differences in voting rights among shares of common stock.[27] The investors' receiving non-voting shares will not disqualify the "S" corporation. Preferred shares (with respect to dividends or to liquidation proceeds) would disqualify the "S" corporation.

If the corporate form is deemed to be appropriate for the business in question, the attorney must consider the impact of various issues that arise from time to time during the life cycle of the corporation.[28] Issues

corporation. *See infra*, § 1.34. Each should also be aware of securities regulatory restraints on raising capital. *See infra*, § 1.26.

20. *See supra*, § 1.2, notes 14–16 and accompanying text.

21. *See* I.R.C. § 1361. *See also*, Chapter 2 "Non–Corporate Entities: Limited Liability Companies and Partnerships," *infra*.

22. A limited partnership or limited liability company may permit the founders greater flexibility in maintaining control than the "S" corporation given the limitation on one class of stock applicable to "S" corporations. *See supra*, § 1.2, note 19.

23. *See, e.g.*, 1997 CCH U.S. Master Tax Guide ¶¶ 301–321 (1996)("Master Tax Guide").

24. For other means of maintaining control of the corporation, *see infra*, § 1.3. If the number of outside investors causes the "S" corporation to be disqualified, then a limited partnership format might be appropriate with a (or the) general partner being a "C" corporation and the founders its shareholders (with unlimited liability for the corporate-general partner and limited liability for its shareholders). *See infra*, § 1.10. If the "C" corporation qualifies to elect to be taxed as an "S" corporation, then pass-through of losses can be achieved.

25. *See supra*, § 1.2, notes 19–22 and accompanying text.

26. *See* I.R.C. § 1361(b)(1)(D).

27. *See* I.R.C. § 1361(c)(4).

28. *See infra*, § 1.4.

that arise on the formation of the corporation should be considered as a preliminary matter.[29] The attorney should investigate whether or not licenses and approvals from local, state, or federal government are required to operate the business. The federal, state,[30] and local income tax implications must be considered. The attorney should also determine if compliance with laws pertaining to securities, environmental protection, labor, patent, trademarks, copyright, and other specialized laws, or laws unique to the business, are applicable. Violations of these laws can be very costly for an enterprise, and the strategy developed by the attorney should take account of them, if applicable.

§ 1.3 Strategy Checklist

1. Alternative business organizational forms in light of client's objectives. (*See* § 1.2)
2. Compare advantages and disadvantages of each alternative. (*See* § 1.2)
3. Risk of liability, client's willingness to assume under each alternative, such as corporate general partner in limited partnership versus "S" corporation. (*See* §§ 1.2, note 24; 1.10)
4. Risk of loss of investment, client's willingness to assume under each alternative. (*See* §§ 1.2, 1.10, 1.107, 1.111)
   - Limited liability protection lost. (*See* §§ 1.10, 1.56)
   - Liquidation preferences in capital structure. (*See* §§ 1.26–1.27)
   - Return of capital in liquidation distribution. (*See* § 1.107)
5. Risk to directors and officers. (*See* §§ 1.65–1.66, 1.69)
6. Return on investment, type desired by client, such as senior security versus common stock. (*See* §§ 1.26–1.36)
   - Rate of return; treatment of income (loss) in a separate entity (as opposed to pass-through conduit treatment) depends on desired organizational corporate form. (*See* §§ 1.10, 1.26)
   - Shareholder value realized in options and other rights to purchase shares. (*See* § 1.31)
   - Dividends. (*See* § 1.38)
   - Shareholder value realized in redemption of shares. (*See* § 1.39)
   - Interest income on bonds. (*See* § 1.33)
   - Shareholder value realized in mergers and acquisitions and other business combinations. (*See* §§ 1.81–1.90)

---

29. *See infra,* § 1.4.

30. *See* Chapter 35 "Income Tax," *infra,* §§ 35.19–35.39.

§ 1.3 BUSINESS ORGANIZATIONS: CORPORATIONS Ch. 1

- Tax implications. (*See* §§ 1.34, 1.91)

7. Control desired by client over investment for each alternative. (*See* §§ 1.2, 1.45–1.47, 1.59–1.61)

    - Shareholder voting rights, non-voting shares, supermajority voting provisions, supermajority quorum provisions, eliminating consent without meeting provision, cumulative voting, voting agreements, voting trust agreements, preemptive rights, share transfer restrictions, options and rights to purchase shares ("poison pills"), convertible shares and bonds, additional issuance of shares to friendly or neutral purchasers, shareholder list analysis, and other means of control of corporate affairs. (*See* §§ 1.31, 1.33, 1.43–1.55)

    - Shareholder election and removal of directors. (*See* §§ 1.59, 1.61)

    - Classification of directors; staggered board. (*See* § 1.59)

    - Director election or appointment and removal of officers. (*See* § 1.69)

    - Centralized management by executive committee of board of directors. (*See* §§ 1.59, 1.64)

    - Certain takeover defenses and disclosure protection; "greenmail" protection (*See* §§ 1.27, 1.31, 1.39, 1.81, 1.89); applicability of securities laws.

    - Purchase by corporation of its own shares subject to securities law regulation (federal and New York) and directors' fiduciary duty. (*See* §§ 1.26, 1.39, 1.65)

    - Continuity of control. (*See* § 1.10)

    - Restrictions on transferability of shares. (*See* §§ 1.21, 1.26–1.31, 1.47–1.48, 1.51–1.52)

    - Employment contract. (*See* § 1.69)

    - Multiple corporations. (*See* § 1.81)

    - Corporate pyramiding. (*See* § 1.81)

8. Tax treatment of each alternative, such as tax free exchange, carryover of basis to shares, holding period for capital gain. (*See* §§ 1.2, 1.34, 1.40, 1.91, 1.108)

9. Feasibility of attaining client's desired ends under each alternative; check that legal requirements of NYBCL, tax, securities, and other relevant laws (*e.g.*, securities (federal and New York/other Blue Sky), antitrust (federal and New York), environmental, intellectual property, labor), licenses to do business (federal, state, and local) can be met assuming the alternative is financially feasible. (*See* § 1.2)

§ 1.4 Overview

Each corporation has stages in its life cycle: choice of organizational form ("prenatal"), formation of the corporation ("birth"),[1] operations ("growth"),[2] mergers, acquisitions, and other business combinations ("marriage"),[3] spin-offs ("children"),[4] split-offs ("divorce"),[5] share repurchases ("redemption"),[6] and dissolution and liquidation ("death").[7]

§ 1.5 Definitions

The following terms and their meanings are used in this chapter:[1]

(1) "Bonds" includes secured and unsecured bonds, debentures, and notes.[2]

(2) "Certificate of incorporation" includes (a) the original certificate of incorporation or any other instrument filed or issued under any statute to form a domestic or foreign corporation, as amended, supplemented, or restated by certificates of amendment, merger, or consolidation or other certificates or instruments filed or issued under any statute or (b) a special act or charter creating a domestic or foreign corporation, as amended, supplemented, or restated.[3]

(3) "Corporation" or "domestic corporation" means a corporation for profit formed under the NYBCL but not a corporation that may be formed under the cooperative corporations law. Profit is an essential element of a New York stock corporation.[4]

---

§ 1.4

1. *See infra*, §§ 1.6, 1.26, and 1.34. For questions on the choice of organizational form and business organizations other than the corporation, *see* Chapter 2 "Non–Corporate Entities: Limited Liability Companies and Partnerships," *infra. See also*, W. Klein and J. Coffee, *Business Organization and Finance* (4th ed. 1990) pp. 5, 48, and 97. Assuming that a corporate form is selected, a preliminary question is choice of jurisdiction of incorporation. *See, e.g.*, Henn and Alexander, *supra* § 1.1, note 1, pp. 176–235 (contains 110 factors to consider generally plus specific comparisons of advantages and disadvantages of Delaware, New York, California, and jurisdictions following the MBCA (not updated to the RMBCA)); H. Guthmann and H. Dougall, *Corporate Financial Policy* (3d ed. 1955) pp. 46–51. *See also*, NYBCL Appendix 2, Henn and Alexander, Advantages and Disadvantages of New York Incorporation (Checklist 1); Henn and Alexander, *supra* § 1.1, note 1, pp. 267–272 (checklist of typical steps in incorporation procedures).

2. *See infra*, §§ 1.37, 1.43, 1.51, 1.56, 1.59, and 1.69.

3. *See infra*, § 1.81.

4. *See infra*, §§ 1.37, 1.40, and 1.81.

5. *See infra*, §§ 1.37, 1.40, and 1.81.

6. *See infra*, §§ 1.37, 1.39, 1.40, and 1.81.

7. *See infra*, §§ 1.94, 1.107, and 1.108.

§ 1.5

1. *See* NYBCL § 102. *See also*, NYBCL § 103 (applicability to domestic and foreign corporations; not applicable to corporations formed under Banking Law, Insurance Law, Railroad Law, Transportation Corporations Law, and certain other laws).

2. NYBCL § 102(a)(1). *See infra*, § 1.33.

3. NYBCL § 102(a)(2). *See infra*, § 1.21. The term "articles of incorporation" is used in corporation statutes of most states and in the RMBCA.

4. NYBCL § 102(a)(3). *See* Kittinger v. Churchill, 161 Misc. 3, 292, N.Y.S. 35 (Sup. Ct., Erie County, 1936), aff'd 249 App.Div. 703, 292 N.Y.S. 51 (4th Dep't 1936).

(4) "Director" means any member of the governing board of a corporation, whether designated as director, trustee, manager, governor, or by any other title. The term "board" means "board of directors."[5]

(5) "Foreign corporation" means a business corporation formed under the laws of a state other than New York; "authorized" with respect to a foreign corporation means having authority under NYBCL Article 13.[6]

(6) "Insolvent" means a corporation's inability to pay its debts as they become due in the usual course of the corporation's business.[7]

(7) "Net assets" means the amount by which a corporation's total assets exceed its total liabilities. Stated capital and surplus are not liabilities.[8]

(8) "Office of a corporation" means the office location stated in the certificate of incorporation of a domestic corporation or in the application for authority of a foreign corporation to do business in New York or an amendment thereof. The office need not be a place where business activities are conducted by the corporation.[9]

(9) "Process" means judicial process and all orders, demands, notices, or other papers required or permitted by law to be personally served on a domestic or foreign corporation for the purpose of acquiring jurisdiction over the corporation in any action or proceeding, civil or criminal, whether judicial, administrative, arbitrative, or other, in New York or in the federal courts sitting in or for New York.[10]

(10) "Stated capital" means the sum of (a) the par value of all shares with par value that have been issued by the corporation, (b) the amount of the consideration received for all shares without par value that have been issued by the corporation, except the part of the consideration legally allocated to surplus, and (c) the amounts that have been transferred to the corporation's stated capital, whether upon the distribution of its shares or other transaction, minus all reductions from that sum as have been effected in a manner permitted by law.[11]

---

5. NYBCL § 102(a)(4). See infra, § 1.59.

6. NYBCL § 102(a)(5). See infra, § 1.114.

7. NYBCL § 102(a)(6). See infra, § 1.38. See also, 11 U.S.C.A. § 101 ("insolvent" defined).

8. NYBCL § 102(a)(7). See infra, § 1.32. See also, Chapter 45, R. Greenberg, "Accounting and the Law" in J. Burton, R. Palmer, R. Kay, Handbook of Accounting and Auditing (1981) p. 45–24 (hereinafter "Greenberg, Accounting Law").

9. NYBCL § 102(a)(8). See infra, §§ 1.16 and 1.19.

10. NYBCL § 102(a)(9). See infra, §§ 1.15–1.19.

11. NYBCL § 102(a)(10). See infra, § 1.32. See also, Greenberg, Accounting Law, supra note 8, pp. 45–23 to 45–24.

(11) "Surplus" means the excess of net assets over the stated capital of the corporation.[12]

(12) "Treasury shares" means shares that have been issued, have been subsequently acquired, and are retained uncancelled by the corporation. Treasury shares are issued, but not outstanding, shares and are not assets of the corporation.[13]

§ 1.6 Formation of Corporations

A preliminary issue in forming a corporation is that of determining the corporate name and reserving it within New York and possibly other jurisdictions as well.[1] Basic financial relationships must be fixed, such as: the relative ownership interests of the initial shareholders, the type of ownership interest (*e.g.*, common stock versus preferred stock or bonds), the voting power of various classes of stock, and the business purpose of the enterprise.[2] The tax consequences of the formation of the corporation to the shareholders and to the corporation should be determined.[3]

§ 1.7 Formation of Corporations—Certificates; Notices

Certificates or other instruments filed by the New York Department of State relating to either a domestic or a foreign corporation and containing statements of fact required or permitted by law to be contained in the certificate are admissible in all courts, public offices, and official bodies as *prima facie* evidence of the stated facts and of the execution of the instruments.[1] Whenever by the laws of any jurisdiction other than New York certificates of (or copies of instruments certified or exemplified by) officers in that jurisdiction may be received as *prima facie* evidence of the incorporation, existence, or capacity of any foreign corporation incorporated in that jurisdiction (or claiming to be), the certificates or instruments (or copies) when exemplified are admissible in all courts and public offices of New York as *prima facie* evidence with the same force as in the foreign jurisdiction.[2] The certificates or certified copies are admissible without being exemplified if they are certified by the Secretary of State (or by an official performing the equivalent function) in the foreign jurisdiction.[3]

Procedure. The NYBCL prescribes general requirements for the

---

12. NYBCL § 102(a)(11). *See infra,* §§ 1.32, 1.38, and 1.39. *See also,* Greenberg, Accounting Law, *supra* note 8, pp. 45–23.

13. NYBCL § 102(a)(12). *See infra,* § 1.39. *See also,* Greenberg, Accounting Law, *supra* note 8, p. 45–24.

§ 1.6

1. *See infra,* §§ 1.13–1.14. If the corporate form is deemed to be desirable, the jurisdiction of incorporation must be selected. *See supra,* § 1.4, note 1.

2. *See infra,* §§ 1.9 and 1.10.

3. *See infra,* § 1.34.

§ 1.7

1. NYBCL § 106(a).
2. NYBCL § 106(b).
3. *Id.*

§ 1.7   BUSINESS ORGANIZATIONS: CORPORATIONS   Ch. 1

contents, signing, filing, effectiveness, and other aspects of certificates.[4] A certificate may be signed either (1) by the holders of all outstanding shares entitled to vote, (2) by the chairman/person of the board, the president, or a vice president, and by the secretary or an assistant secretary, (3) if no such officers exist, by a majority of the directors, or those designated by a majority of directors, in office, (4) if no directors exist, by the holders (or those designated by the holders) of record of a majority of the votes of shares entitled to vote, (5) if no shareholders of record exist, by a subscriber for shares whose subscription has been accepted or by a successor in interest, or (6) if no subscription for shares has been accepted, by an incorporator or anyone acting in the incorporator's stead under NYBCL § 615(c).[5] The signer's name and the capacity in which the certificate was signed must be stated beneath or opposite the signature.[6] Certificates of correction are permitted to be filed to correct certain errors in a certificate or other instrument.[7] The Department of State files and indexes instruments whose form complies with requirements of law.[8] If the consent or approval of a public official is required, the instrument must have attached to it evidence of the consent or approval; if a filing fee or tax is required, the fee or tax must have been paid.[9] No certificate of authentication or other proof is required for any verification, oath, or acknowledgment of instruments delivered to the Department of State if the verification, oath, or acknowledgment purports to be made before a notary public (or person performing an equivalent function) of one of the States (or a subdivision of a State) of the United States or the District of Columbia.[10]

Notwithstanding NYBCL § 403 that corporate existence begins on the filing of the certificate of incorporation, and that the certificate is conclusive evidence that all conditions precedent have occurred for the corporation's formation, the filing and indexing of the certificate of incorporation do not amount to a finding that the certificate conforms to law, do not constitute an approval by the Department of State of the

---

4. NYBCL § 104.
5. NYBCL § 104(d).
6. NYBCL § 104.

PRACTICE POINTER: This requirement is important not only in signing certificates but is a good practice to follow on contracts and other documents signed on behalf of the corporation to avoid any question that the signer is acting in his or her own behalf rather than that of the corporation. *See infra*, § 1.10.

CAVEAT: In lieu of being signed and verified or acknowledged, a certificate may be subscribed and affirmed as true under penalties of perjury. NYBCL § 104(d). Whenever an instrument is required to set forth the date of filing of the certificate of incorporation, the original certificate of incorporation is meant. NYBCL § 104(c).

This requirement is satisfied, in the case of a corporation created by special act, by setting forth the chapter number and year of passage of the act. *Id. See supra*, § 1.21, note 1. *See also*, NYBCL § 104(a), (b), and (e) (English language, addresses, consent of public official attached).

7. NYBCL § 105 (re any informality or error apparent on the face of the instrument, incorrect statement or defect in execution thereof, including the deletion of any matter not permitted to be stated therein). *See infra*, § 1.20, note 1.

8. NYBCL § 104(e).
9. *Id.*
10. *Id.*

corporation's name or the contents of the certificate, and do not prevent any person from contesting the legality of the certificate.[11] Unless otherwise provided by the NYBCL, instruments become effective upon their filing by the Department of State.[12] The Department must make, certify, and transmit a copy of the instrument to the clerk of the county in which the office of the domestic or foreign corporation is or is to be located; the county clerk must file and index the copy of the instrument.[13]

Fees. The Department of State collects stipulated fees for filing various instruments.[14] For service of process on the Secretary of State pursuant to NYBCL § 306 or 307, the Department of State collects a stipulated fee, but no fee is collected for process served on behalf of a county, city, town, village, or other subdivision of New York.[15]

Notices. Whenever under the NYBCL, the certificate of incorporation or bylaws, or by the terms of any agreement or instrument, a corporation (or the board or any committee thereof) is authorized to take any action after notice to any person or after the lapse of a prescribed period of time, the action may be taken without notice and without the lapse of the period of time, if at any time (either before or after the action is completed) the person entitled to the notice (or entitled to participate in the action to be taken), or in the case of a shareholder, his or her attorney-in-fact, submits a signed waiver of notice of such requirements.[16] Whenever (1) any notice or communication is required to be given to any person by the NYBCL, the certificate of incorporation or bylaws, or by the terms of any agreement or instrument, or as a condition precedent to taking any corporate action and (2) communication with the person is unlawful under any statute of New York or of the United States (or any regulation, proclamation, or order issued thereunder), then the notice or communication is not required to be given to such person and no duty is imposed to apply for license or other permission to do so.[17] Whenever any notice or communication is required or permitted by the NYBCL to be given by mail, it must, except as otherwise expressly provided in the NYBCL, be mailed to the person to whom it is directed at the address designated by the person for that purpose or, if none is designated, at the person's last known address.[18]

11. *Id.*
12. NYBCL § 104(f).
13. NYBCL § 104(g). *See also,* Arts and Cultural Affairs Law § 57.07.
14. NYBCL § 104–A.
15. NYBCL § 104–A(c).
16. NYBCL § 108(a).
17. NYBCL § 108(b). Any affidavit, certificate, or other instrument that is required to be made or filed as proof of the giving of any notice or communication required under the NYBCL must, if such notice or communication to any person is dispensed with under NYBCL § 108(b), include a statement that the notice or communication was not given to any person with whom communication is unlawful. *Id.* The affidavit, certificate, or other instrument is as effective for all purposes as though personally given to such person. *Id.*

18. NYBCL § 108(c). Notice must be by first class mail except where otherwise required by the NYBCL. *Id.* Notice is given when so deposited, with postage thereon

§ 1.8 Formation of Corporations—Corporate Seal

The presence of the corporate seal on a written instrument purporting to be executed by authority of a domestic or a foreign corporation is *prima facie* evidence that the instrument was duly executed.[1] The seal is *prima facie* proof that it was affixed by the proper authority, and any party objecting to the instrument's execution has the burden of establishing that the seal was affixed improperly.[2]

Library References:

West's Key No. Digests, Corporations ⚖51.

§ 1.9 Formation of Corporations—Corporate Purposes

A corporation may be formed under the NYBCL for any lawful business purpose.[1] Certain purposes may not be included in a certificate of incorporation without evidence of the approval of certain New York agencies.[2] Any corporation formed as a cooperative or for the purpose of

---

§ 1.8

1. NYBCL § 107.
2. Quackenboss v. Globe & Rutgers Fire Ins. Co., 177 N.Y. 71, 69 N.E. 223 (1903).

§ 1.9

1. NYBCL § 201(a). A business denotes activity engaged in for profit or as a livelihood. Investment in property might not be a business even though the property is held for the production of income. A similar distinction is drawn in the federal income tax law. See, e.g., I.R.C. §§ 1231 (property used in a business) and 1221 (property (capital asset) held whether or not connected with a business excluding, among others, property held primarily for sale to customers in the ordinary course of a business (inventory) and property used in a business); 162 (trade or business expenses) and 212 (expenses for the production of income (*i.e.*, investment expenses)); 167 (depreciation allowed on property used in a business and on property held for the production of income). Investment incident to a business (*e.g.*, investment of funds not currently employed in business operations) would be permitted. But see, e.g., I.R.C. §§ 533(a) (accumulations beyond the reasonable needs of a business); 533(b) (the fact that a corporation is a mere holding or investment company is *prima facie* evidence of a purpose to avoid the income tax with respect to shareholders). For purposes of foreign corporations, see NYBCL § 1301.

CAVEAT: An exception to this general rule is applicable when the client wishes to do in New York any business for which formation is permitted under any other New York statute unless that statute permits formation under the NYBCL. NYBCL § 201(a). Purposes unlawful for business corporations are prescribed by various statutes. See, e.g., Penal Law § 280 and Education Law §§ 6513, 6612(4)(d), 7009, 7209, and 7307. NYBCL § 402(a)(2) requires that the certificate of incorporation set forth the purpose or purposes for which the corporation is to be formed. See infra, § 1.21.

2. NYBCL § 201(d)(re establishment or operation of a day care center for children, approval of the Commissioner of Social Services); NYBCL § 201(e)(re establishment or maintenance of a hospital or health care facility (for a definition of these terms, see Public Health Law Article 28), approval of Public Health Council). See infra, § 1.21. See also, infra, §§ 1.122 and 1.125. The approval of the Industrial Board of Appeals is required to file any certificate of incorporation, certificate of merger or consolidation, or application of a foreign corporation for authority to do business in New York

banking, insurance, railroad activities, or transportation is subject to the New York Cooperative Corporations Law, Banking Law, Insurance Law, Railroad Law, or Transportation Corporations Law respectively.[3] Professional service corporations require approval of the applicable New York licensing authority.[4]

The general powers that a corporation may exercise are quite broad.[5] Corporations must do business in New York under the name appearing in the certificate of incorporation unless the corporation complies with the filing requirements for conducting business under an assumed name.[6]

Library References:

West's Key No. Digests, Corporations ⚖14.

§ 1.10 Formation of Corporations—Corporate Purposes and Powers—Upholding and Disregarding the Corporate Entity

One of the important reasons to incorporate is to limit the liability of the owners of the business (*i.e.*, the shareholders) to their investment in the corporation.[1] As a general rule, assets that shareholders do not invest in the corporation are shielded from the claims of the corpora-

that states as a purpose either (1) the formation of an organization of groups of workers or (2) the performance, rendition, or sale of services as labor consultants or advisors on labor-management relations or as arbitrators or negotiators in labor-management disputes. NYBCL § 201(b). In time of war or other national emergency, a corporation may do any lawful business in aid of the emergency (notwithstanding the purposes in its certificate of incorporation) at the request or direction of any competent governmental authority. NYBCL § 201(c). This provision in effect broadens the corporation's purposes during these emergencies when amendment of the certificate of incorporation might be difficult.

3. NYBCL § 201, Legislative Studies and Reports, Comment.

4. See *infra*, §§ 1.122 and 1.125.

5. NYBCL § 202(a). See *infra*, §§ 1.10, 1.11, 1.20, and 1.21.

6. NYBCL § 202(b). See General Business Law § 130. See *infra*, §§ 1.13, notes 16–20 and accompanying text; 1.115.

§ 1.10

1. Clients could attempt to protect themselves against this risk of liability through various liability insurance policies. The wisdom of how much, if any, insurance coverage should be acquired will depend on each client's circumstances. *See* Chapter 31 "Insurance," *infra*.

CAVEAT: Even if the client obtains insurance coverage, in whatever amount is deemed reasonable, the risk remains that a loss could befall the business that exceeds the upper limit of the insurance benefits (*e.g.*, a judgment in a product liability or environmental liability suit). The owner of an unincorporated business would be liable for the difference. *See* Chapter 15 "Environmental Law" and Chapter 27 "Products Liability," *infra*. Insurance coverage is a valuable protection to reduce the out-of-pocket loss to the business, and insurance will help keep a business solvent (unless the loss and other liabilities of the business exceed the insurance proceeds for the loss plus the other assets of the business). The shareholders may decide to increase their investment in the business to keep it afloat, augmenting their investment through compromise, composition, or other contractual means, or even pursuant to bankruptcy or other insolvency proceedings. *See* Chapter 5 "Commercial Sales Contracts" and Chapter 9 "Bankruptcy," *infra*.

§ 1.10   BUSINESS ORGANIZATIONS: CORPORATIONS   Ch. 1

tion's creditors.[2] In other words, shareholders might invest in a corporation, and be willing to put at risk, only a small portion of their capital, with the remainder invested otherwise. The importance of the limited liability of shareholders is apparent, for example, in product liability suits[3] against a corporation where substantial compensatory damages and possibly punitive damages are sought. If the plaintiffs are successful, the corporation's liabilities (including the plaintiffs' judgment) might exceed its assets, bringing it to a state of insolvency[4] and raising the possibility of its liquidation.[5] Under such circumstances the shareholders could lose their investments in the corporation, but their other assets generally would not be at risk.

A corporation is generally considered to be a separate person, or legal entity, for liability purposes and is distinct from its shareholders.[6] This general rule is subject to exceptions. These exceptions apply in instances where the corporate form is used to defraud creditors, to evade existing obligations, or otherwise for fraudulent or illegal purposes, or contrary to public policy.[7] Disregarding the corporate entity under such circumstances is also referred to as piercing the corporate veil.[8] The party seeking to pierce a corporate veil has the burden of establishing one or more grounds for doing so.[9]

Corporate veils have been pierced to impose liability upon shareholders (1) where parent and subsidiary corporations were found not to have

---

2. *But see*, NYBCL § 630 (liability of ten largest shareholders for wages due employees).

3. *See* Chapter 27 "Products Liability," *infra*.

4. In NYBCL § 102(a)(8) insolvency is defined as being unable to pay debts as they become due in the usual course of business, which is framed in the equity sense. *See supra*, § 1.5(6). Insolvency in the bankruptcy (or balance sheet) sense occurs when a corporation's liabilities exceed its assets. 11 U.S.C.A. § 101(32). *See, e.g.*, Henn and Alexander, *supra* § 1.1, note 1, p. 1157. *See also*, Chapter 8 "Enforcement of Judgments" and Chapter 9 "Bankruptcy," *infra*. *See infra*, §§ 1.94, 1.101, 1.102, and 1.111.

5. Liquidation (and dissolution) should be distinguished from insolvency. *See, e.g., infra*, §§ 1.94–1.95, 1.97, and 1.107. *See also, e.g.*, Henn and Alexander, *supra* § 1.1, note 1, pp. 1147–1159 (non-bankruptcy liquidation; bankruptcy liquidation); D. Epstein, *Bankruptcy and Other Debtor–Creditor Laws* (5th ed. 1995) pp. 5–7.

6. It is also a separate person, or taxpayer, for tax purposes, whose income is subject to double taxation (*i.e.*, the corporation is taxed on its earnings, and the shareholders are taxed on those earnings to the extent distributed to them by the corporation) unless it elects to be treated as a so-called "S" corporation, in which case it is treated, generally speaking, for *tax purposes* as a pass-through entity. *See* Chapter 2 "Non–Corporate Entities: Limited Liability Companies and Partnerships," *infra*. An "S" corporation is a separate entity for *liability purposes* (*i.e.*, shareholders have limited liability) even though for tax purposes profits and losses are treated as earned or incurred by the shareholders (*i.e.*, passed through to the shareholders).

7. Alfred P. Sloan Foundation, Inc. v. Atlas, 42 Misc.2d 603, 248 N.Y.S.2d 524 (Sup.Ct., Nassau County, 1964), aff'd 23 A.D.2d 820, 258 N.Y.S.2d 807 (2d Dep't 1965).

8. **CAVEAT**: The client should be advised of the pitfalls of neglecting to abide by the formalities and other considerations in establishing and operating the corporation to avoid losing the limited liability protection that shareholders enjoy as a general rule. The corporation may be disregarded for tax purposes. *See infra*, § 1.34.

9. Katz v. N.Y. Tint Taxi Corp., 213 A.D.2d 599, 624 N.Y.S.2d 65 (2d Dep't 1995).

dealt with each other at arms' length;[10] (2) where a bank's subsidiary was found to have been a "mere instrumentality" of the bank, with overlapping personnel, officers, and directors;[11] (3) where an intent to perpetrate fraud upon creditors was found;[12] (4) where an individual was found to have exercised complete dominion and control over a corporate entity that was his mere alter ego, the corporation had no assets, liabilities, or income and had never transacted any business other than entering into the subject lease, and the individual had used that control to commit an alleged wrong;[13] (5) where a parent corporation masterminded a scheme to strip its subsidiary of its assets to render it unable to honor its obligations under a guarantee;[14] (6) where a parent corporation exercised control over the daily operations of its subsidiary and acted as the prime mover behind its subsidiary's action;[15] (7) where the sole shareholder operated corporations as dummies to conduct the shareholder's personal business;[16] (8) where a foreign subsidiary was treated by its parent corporation as a department of the parent rather than as an independent corporate subsidiary;[17] and (9) where shareholders used the corporation merely as a conduit to conduct their personal business in order to shield themselves from personal liability.[18] Even when corporate veils have not been pierced, the courts' analyses are instructive.[19]

10. Weinreich v. Sandhaus, 850 F.Supp. 1169 (S.D.N.Y.1994), opinion amended in part 156 F.R.D. 60 (S.D.N.Y.1994).

11. Citicorp Intern. Trading Co., Inc. v. Western Oil & Refining Co., Inc., 790 F.Supp. 428 (S.D.N.Y.1992).

12. In re Shailam, 144 B.R. 626 (N.D.N.Y.1992).

13. Fern, Inc. v. Adjmi, 197 A.D.2d 444, 602 N.Y.S.2d 615 (1st Dep't 1993).

14. Chase Manhattan Bank (Nat. Assn.) v. 264 Water Street Associates, 174 A.D.2d 504, 571 N.Y.S.2d 281 (1st Dep't 1991).

15. Pritchard Services (NY) Inc. v. First Winthrop Properties, Inc., 172 A.D.2d 394, 568 N.Y.S.2d 775 (1st Dep't 1991).

16. Wade v. Citibank, N.A., 118 A.D.2d 648, 122 A.D.2d 625, 500 N.Y.S.2d 7 (2d Dep't 1986), appeal denied, stay dismissed 68 N.Y.2d 607, 506 N.Y.S.2d 1031, 498 N.E.2d 433.

17. Tesoro Petroleum Corp. v. Holborn Oil Co., Ltd., 118 A.D.2d 506, 500 N.Y.S.2d 118 (1st Dep't 1986).

18. Perez v. One Clark Street Housing Corp., 108 A.D.2d 844, 485 N.Y.S.2d 346 (2d Dep't 1985).

19. *See also,* Porter v. LSB Industries, Inc., 192 A.D.2d 205, 600 N.Y.S.2d 867 (4th Dep't 1993) (subsidiary neither undercapitalized nor misused either to perpetrate a fraud or to inflict injury); In re Golden Distributors, Ltd., 134 B.R. 770 (S.D.N.Y. 1991) (complete disregard of corporate formalities in operation of corporation: employee supervisor (who was not an officer or a shareholder) authorized to sign checks); 29/35 Realty Associates v. 35th Street New York Yarn Center, Inc., 181 A.D.2d 540, 581 N.Y.S.2d 43 (1st Dep't 1992) (corporation was mere instrumentality and alter ego of owner; unjust and inequitable loss would result if corporation were not disregarded; owner used corporation for purely personal ends); Lorkowski v. J.C. Pitman Co., Inc., 177 A.D.2d 1021, 578 N.Y.S.2d 40 (4th Dep't 1991) (parent did not involve itself in management, or dominate, its wholly-owned subsidiary); Bowles v. Errico, 163 A.D.2d 771, 558 N.Y.S.2d 734 (3d Dep't 1990) (no evidence corporation was a sham); Pebble Cove Homeowners' Ass'n, Inc. v. Fidelity New York FSB, 153 A.D.2d 843, 545 N.Y.S.2d 362 (2d Dep't 1989) (corporate veil not pierced where complaint fails to allege the means by which parent corporation totally controlled everyday operation of subsidiary); Jeras v. East Mfg. Corp., 168 A.D.2d 889, 566 N.Y.S.2d 418 (4th Dep't 1990), appeal granted 77 N.Y.2d 807, 569 N.Y.S.2d 611, 572 N.E.2d 52, motion to dismiss appeal denied 77 N.Y.2d 935, 569 N.Y.S.2d 606, 572 N.E.2d 47, appeal withdrawn 78 N.Y.2d 953, 573 N.Y.S.2d 648, 578 N.E.2d 446 (1991) (par-

§ 1.11 Formation of Corporations—Corporate Purposes and Powers—General Powers

A corporation has very broad general powers, including the ability to sue and be sued, purchase and sell property, create mortgages and other security interests in its property, make contracts, give guarantees, incur liabilities, lend money, and do business.[1] It also has all powers necessary and convenient to effect any of the purposes for which it is formed.[2] The powers conferred are liberally construed, and substantial compliance with the law's conditions in accordance with its spirit and intent is all that is required.[3]

Library References:
West's Key No. Digests, Corporations ⚖370.

§ 1.12 Formation of Corporations—Corporate Purposes and Powers—Defense of *Ultra Vires*

Contracts are *ultra vires* where they involve transactions outside of the scope of powers given to corporations by their charters.[1] However, the defense of *ultra vires* is limited in New York[2] A corporation's incapacity or lack of power to act may be asserted only: (1) in an action by a shareholder against the corporation to enjoin the act,[3] (2) in an action by or in the right of the corporation to procure a judgment in its

---

ent corporation not liable for death of subsidiary's worker where plaintiff failed to prove complete dominion and control of subsidiary by parent; no proof that parent's control or misuse caused injury); McMullin v. Pelham Bay Riding, Inc., 190 A.D.2d 529, 593 N.Y.S.2d 27 (1st Dep't 1993) (genuine issue of fact (precluding summary judgment for president and sole shareholder of corporation defendant) whether corporation was "dummy" for individual to carry on business in personal capacity in absence of any external indicia of separate corporate identity).

CAVEAT: *Cf.* Patterson v. Comm., 25 T.C.M. (CCH) 1230 (1966) (corporate entity disregarded for tax purposes by IRS if corporation is a sham or a dummy). On lack of corporate formalities, inadequate initial capital, fraud, dominion and control, and other rationales that courts invoke to disregard the corporate entity in corporate, tax, contract, tort, and other contexts, *see also*, *e.g.*, Henn and Alexander, *supra* § 1.1, note 1, pp. 344–375; R. Hamilton, *Law of Corporations* (2d ed. 1987) pp. 81–99.

§ 1.11
1. NYBCL § 202(a).
2. *Id.*
3. *See* Lord v. Yonkers Fuel Gas Co., 99 N.Y. 547, 2 N.E. 909 (1885). *See also*, NYBCL § 202, Notes of Decisions (particular powers outlined, such as borrowing money; lending money; bylaws; compensation and employment of officers, employees, or agents; contracts; donations; guarantees and liabilities; internal affairs; leases; liabilities; necessity of borrowing and lending money; acquisition of other corporations' stock; acquisition of corporation's own shares; partnerships or joint ventures; real property).

§ 1.12
1. Jemison v. Citizens' Sav. Bank, 122 N.Y. 135, 25 N.E. 264 (1890). *See also*, Bath Gaslight Co. v. Claffy, 151 N.Y. 24, 45 N.E. 390 (1896); Leslie v. Lorillard, 110 N.Y. 519, 18 N.E. 363, 1 L.R.A. 456 (1888).
2. NYBCL § 203(a).
3. NYBCL § 203(a)(1).

favor against incumbent or former officers or directors for loss or damage due to their unauthorized acts,[4] or (3) in an action or special proceeding by the Attorney General to annul or dissolve the corporation or to enjoin it from the doing of unauthorized business.[5] NYBCL § 203 thus changes New York case law by sustaining *ultra vires* contracts wholly executory on both sides, eliminating the defense of *ultra vires* in those circumstances.[6] Actions by shareholders under NYBCL § 203 are subject to existing equitable or other limitations that apply to the actions.[7] Acts of a corporation that are not *per se* illegal, but that are *ultra vires* and affect only the interests of the shareholders, may be ratified by them so that third parties that deal in good faith with the corporation will be protected in reliance upon those acts.[8] Shareholders may not ratify a corporation's illegal acts.[9]

Library References:

West's Key No. Digests, Corporations ⚘487.

§ 1.13 Formation of Corporations—Corporate Name

The name of a domestic or a foreign corporation must contain the word (or an abbreviation of) "corporation," "incorporated," or "limited."[1] The name may not be the same as the name of any other corporation (or the fictitious name of an authorized foreign corporation)

4. NYBCL § 203(a)(2).

5. NYBCL § 203(a)(3). *See also*, NYBCL § 109 (other actions and special proceedings by Attorney General; jury trial; certain of foreign corporation's acts constitute appointment of Secretary of State as its agent for service of process).

6. *See* NYBCL § 203, Legislative Studies and Reports, Comment (second sentence) (cites Jemison v. Citizens' Sav. Bk. of Jefferson, 122 N.Y. 135, 25 N.E. 264 (1890)).

7. NYBCL § 203, Legislative Studies and Reports, Comment (third sentence).

8. Kent v. Quicksilver Min. Co., 78 N.Y. 159 (1879). *See also*, Skinner v. Smith, 134 N.Y. 240, 31 N.E. 911 (1892); Nadel v. Brillo Mfg. Co., 123 Misc. 952, 206 N.Y.S. 631 (App.Term, 1st Dep't, 1924).

9. Runcie v. Corn Exchange Bank Trust Co., 6 N.Y.S.2d 616 (Sup.Ct., Nassau County, 1938). *See also*, Runcie v. Central Hanover Bank & Trust Co., 6 N.Y.S.2d 625 (Sup. Ct., Nassau County, 1938). The doctrine of *ultra vires* applies to the corporation's contracts but not to its torts. Massa v. Wanamaker Academy of Beauty Culture, 80 N.Y.S.2d 923 (N.Y. City Ct., N.Y. County, 1948).

PRACTICE POINTER: If the business conducted by agents (or employees) of a corporation is authorized by the board (or officers), under agency principles (or *respondeat superior* doctrine) the corporation should be liable for the torts of its agents (or employees) committed within the scope of their authority (or course of their employment) even though the agents (or employees) were engaged in business outside that authorized in the corporation's charter. *See, e.g.,* H. Ballantine, *On Corporations* (1946) pp. 272–274; R. Steffen, *Agency-Partnership* (1977) pp. 72–80.

§ 1.13

1. NYBCL § 301(a)(1). *See* NYBCL § 302 (corporate name; certain exceptions). A foreign corporation whose name is not acceptable for authorization pursuant to NYBCL §§ 301 and 302 may submit in its application for authority to do business pursuant to NYBCL § 1304 a fictitious name under which it will do business in New York. NYBCL § 1301(d). *See* General Business Law §§ 135, 138, and 139; Education Law §§ 224, 7209, and 7302; 18 U.S.C.A. § 706; 36 U.S.C.A. §§ 27, 48, and 67-p. *See also*, Henn and Alexander, *supra* § 1.1, note 1, pp. 268–270.

on file with the Department of State, Division of Corporations ("corporate name index"), or a name reserved by the Secretary of State, or a name so similar to these names as to tend to confuse or deceive third parties.[2] The name may not contain any word, phrase, abbreviation, or derivative whose use is prohibited or restricted by any other statute of New York except upon compliance with any restrictions.[3] Nor may the name imply that the corporation is formed (or, if a foreign corporation, is authorized) for any purpose, or is possessed in New York of any power, other than that for which the corporation may be and is formed (or the foreign corporation is authorized).[4]

Certain phrases[5] and words related to banking, finance, insurance, lawyers, or doctors;[6] labor-management;[7] blind or handicapped;[8] or an

2. NYBCL § 301(a)(2). *See, e.g.*, People ex rel. United States Grand Lodge of Order of Brith Abraham, 161 N.Y. 229, 55 N.E. 849 (1900); Jervis Corp. v. Secretary of State, 43 Misc.2d 185, 250 N.Y.S.2d 544 (Sup.Ct., Nassau County, 1964).

3. NYBCL § 301(a)(3).

4. NYBCL § 301(a)(4).

5. NYBCL § 301(a)(5)(A). The corporate name must not contain any of the following phrases (or any abbreviation or derivative thereof): board of trade, state police, urban development, chamber of commerce, state trooper, urban relocation, community renewal, or tenant relocation. *Id.*

6. *See* NYBCL § 301(a)(5)(B). The following words (or any abbreviation or derivative thereof) must not be used unless evidence of the approval of the Superintendent of Banks or the Superintendent of Insurance, as appropriate, is attached to the certificate of incorporation or application for authority, or amendment thereof: acceptance, annuity, assurance, bank, benefit, bond, casualty, endowment, fidelity, finance, guaranty, indemnity, insurance, investment, loan, mortgage, savings, surety, title, trust, or underwriter. NYBCL § 301(a)(5)(B). The word "doctor" or "lawyer" (or an abbreviation or derivation thereof) must not be used in the name of a university faculty practice corporation formed pursuant to the Not-for-Profit Corporation Law § 1412, or a professional service corporation formed pursuant to NYBCL Article 15, or a foreign professional service corporation authorized to do business in New York pursuant to NYBCL Article 15–A, unless the members or shareholders of such corporation are composed exclusively of doctors or lawyers, respectively, or the word is used in a context that clearly denotes a purpose other than the practice of law or medicine. NYBCL § 301(a)(5)(B).

7. *See* NYBCL § 301(a)(6). Unless evidence of the approval of presumably both the Commissioner of Labor and the Industrial Board of Appeals is attached to the certificate of incorporation or application for authority, or amendment thereof, a corporate name must not contain the words or phrases "union" or "labor" or "council" or "industrial organization" (or any abbreviation or derivative thereof) in a context that indicates or implies that the domestic corporation is formed, or the foreign corporation is authorized, as an organization of working men or women or wage earners or for the performance, rendition, or sale of services as a labor or management consultant, an adviser, or a specialist, or as a negotiator or an arbitrator in labor-management disputes. *Id. See* L. 1975, Ch. 756, § 21, eff. Aug. 9, 1975, as amended, transferring all functions, powers, and duties of the State Board of Standards and Appeals, whose approval was required prior to Aug. 9, 1975, to the Commissioner of Labor and the Industrial Board of Appeals.

8. NYBCL § 301(a)(7). A corporate name must not contain the word "blind" or "handicapped" unless evidence of the approval of the State Department of Social Services is attached to the certificate of incorporation or application for authority, or amendment thereof. *Id.* The approval is granted by the State Department of Social Services if in its opinion the word "blind" or "handicapped" as used in the corporate name proposed will not tend to mislead or confuse the public into believing that the corporation is organized for charitable or non-profit purposes related to the blind or the handicapped. *Id.*

exchange[9] are prohibited from being used unless the requisite approval is received.[10] A corporate name must not contain any words or phrases (or abbreviations or derivations) in a context that will tend to mislead the public into believing that the corporation is an agency or instrumentality of the United States or the State of New York (or a subdivision thereof) or is a public corporation.[11] A corporate name also must not contain words or phrases (or abbreviations or derivations) that, separately or in context, are indecent or obscene, or ridicule or degrade any person, group, belief, business, or agency of government, or indicate or imply any unlawful activity.[12]

The word "company" may be considered colloquially as meaning "corporation" yet does not have that meaning in law, as "company" is frequently used both by individuals and partnerships.[13] NYBCL § 301 prevents corporations from using names within New York that might lead persons dealing with them to believe that they are not corporations and that personal liability for corporate obligations exists on the part of the members of the organization or the individual whose name is used by the corporation.[14] No hard and fast rule on this subject appears to have been formed.[15]

Fictitious and Assumed Names; Individual's Own Name. The fact that a domestic corporation has in good faith incorporated in New York does not prevent a foreign corporation having a substantially similar name from doing business in New York, regardless of whether the name is generic or descriptive and regardless of whether actual competition or damage is shown. In granting a corporate franchise, New York merely sanctions the use of a name, if the use is lawful under the NYBCL, and does not adjudicate the legality of the name chosen for other purposes.[16]

---

9. NYBCL § 301(a)(10). Unless evidence of the approval of the Attorney General is attached to the certificate of incorporation or application for authority, or amendment thereof, a corporate name must not contain the word "exchange" or any abbreviation or derivative thereof. *Id.* The approval will not be granted if in the Attorney General's opinion the use of the word "exchange" in the proposed corporate name would falsely imply that the corporation conducts its business at a place where trade is carried on in securities or commodities by brokers, dealers, or merchants. *Id.*

10. *See supra*, § 1.13, notes 6–9. *See also*, Notes of Decisions to NYBCL § 301 for decisions on various words (*e.g.*, "limited" and "company").

11. NYBCL § 301(a)(8).

12. NYBCL § 301(a)(9).

13. In re American Cigar Lighter Co., 77 Misc. 643, 138 N.Y.S. 455 (Sup.Ct., N.Y. County, 1912).

14. *See* Op. Atty. Gen. 9 (1912). In these situations, the Secretary of State would appear to have discretion to refuse to file a certificate of incorporation or an application for authority to do business in New York. *See, e.g.*, Guenther Pub. Corp. v. Lomenzo, 29 A.D.2d 708, 286 N.Y.S.2d 497 (3d Dep't 1968); Jervis Corp. v. Secretary of State, 43 Misc.2d 185, 250 N.Y.S.2d 544 (Sup.Ct., Nassau County, 1964).

15. *See* Op. Atty. Gen. 9 (1912).

16. Sterling Products Corp. v. Sterling Products, 43 F.Supp. 548 (S.D.N.Y.1942).

CAVEAT: Accordingly, conflicting claims to the same or similar corporate names may arise. The Secretary of State is vested with discretion in the matter of whether to permit a corporation to amend its name. Frank

§ 1.13   BUSINESS ORGANIZATIONS: CORPORATIONS   Ch. 1

Corporations conducting a business under an assumed name must file with the appropriate county clerk an assumed name certificate and display it in every office it has in New York.[17] NYBCL § 301 does not apply to an *individual* doing business under an assumed name.[18] The law protects the right of persons to use their own names in their own businesses, even if the use is injurious to another who has established a prior business of the same kind using the same name and who has gained a reputation that goes with the name. The courts, however, require that a name be honestly used, without deceit designed to mislead the public and palm off the business as that of the person who first established it.[19] Persons have the right not only to use their family name in their proprietorship businesses but to have it used as part of the corporate name of a corporation in which the individual is a shareholder.[20]

Library References:

West's Key No. Digests, Corporations ⇐43–50.

§ 1.14   Formation of Corporations—Corporate Name— Reservation of Name

A corporate name may be reserved by (1) any person intending to form a domestic corporation, (2) any domestic corporation intending to change its name, (3) any foreign corporation intending to apply for authority to do business in New York, (4) any authorized foreign corporation intending to change its name, and (5) any person intending to incorporate a foreign corporation and to have it apply for authority to do business in New York.[1] A fictitious name may be reserved by (1) any foreign corporation intending to apply for authority to do business in New York,[2] (2) any authorized foreign corporation intending to change its fictitious name under which it does business in New York, and (3) any authorized foreign corporation that has changed its corporate name in its jurisdiction and the new corporate name is not available in New York.[3]

Procedure. An application to reserve a corporate name must be delivered to the Department of State, and it must set forth the name and address of the applicant, the name to be reserved, and a statement of the

Boufford Co. v. Lomenzo, 38 A.D.2d 986, 329 N.Y.S.2d 644 (3d Dep't 1972).

17. General Business Law § 130(1)(b). *See* General Business Law § 130(5)(b) (filing fee plus county clerk's fee for each county where corporation does or intends to do business); CPLR 8021(b)(2).

18. Op. Atty. Gen., 48 St. Dep't 460 (1933).

19. Chas. S. Higgins Co. v. Higgins Soap Co., 144 N.Y. 462, 39 N.E. 490 (1895).

20. Romeike v. Romeike, 179 App.Div. 712, 167 N.Y.S. 235 (1st Dep't 1917), affirmed by 227 N.Y. 561, 124 N.E. 898 (1917). *See also*, Romeike v. Romeike, 251 Fed. 273, 163 C.C.A. 429 (C.C.A. 1918).

§ 1.14

1. NYBCL § 303(a).

2. NYBCL § 1301(d). *See infra*, §§ 1.114–1.116.

3. NYBCL § 303(b).

basis under NYBCL § 303(a) or (b) for the application.[4] The Secretary of State may require that the application include a statement of the nature of the business to be conducted by the corporation.[5] If the name is available for corporate use, the Department of State will reserve the name for the use of the applicant for a period of sixty days and issue a certificate of reservation.[6]

The restrictions and qualifications set forth in NYBCL § 301(a) are not waived by the issuance of a certificate of reservation.[7] The certificate of reservation must include the name of the applicant, the name reserved, and the date of the reservation.[8] The certificate of reservation (or in lieu thereof, an affidavit by the applicant or by the applicant's agent or attorney that the certificate of reservation has been lost or destroyed) must accompany the certificate of incorporation or the application for authority when either is delivered to the Department of State.[9]

The Secretary of State may extend the reservation for additional periods of not more than sixty days each upon the written request of the applicant, its attorney or agent delivered to the Department of State.[10] The request must be filed before the expiration of the reservation period then in effect and must have attached to it the certificate of reservation of name.[11] More than two extensions are not permitted.[12] An applicant may request before the reserved period expires that the Department of State cancel the reservation.[13]

Library References:

West's Key No. Digests, Corporations ⚖49.

§ 1.15 Formation of Corporations—Service of Process

The manner of serving process on domestic corporations and foreign corporations is specified in the NYBCL.[1] Certain records of service of process must be kept by the Secretary of State.[2]

4. NYBCL § 303(c).

PRACTICE POINTER: Some attorneys use the services of an agent (*e.g.*, Prentice-Hall Corporate Services (now CSC Networks), CT Corporation System, Julius Blumberg, Inc., or Blackstone) to reserve the corporate name because they are unable to do the necessary paperwork as expeditiously as an experienced agent. These corporate services can be useful in other steps of incorporation. See *infra*, §§ 1.21 and 1.23.

5. NYBCL § 303(c). See *infra*, § 1.150 Form—Application to Reserve Corporate Name.

6. NYBCL § 303(c).

7. *Id.*

8. *Id.*

9. *Id.*

10. NYBCL § 303(d).

11. *Id.*

12. *Id.*

13. NYBCL § 303(e). The request must be signed by the applicant or by the applicant's attorney or agent. NYBCL § 303(f).

§ 1.15

1. NYBCL §§ 304–307. See *infra*, §§ 1.17–1.19.

2. NYBCL § 308. See *infra*, § 1.16.

§ 1.15   BUSINESS ORGANIZATIONS: CORPORATIONS   Ch. 1

Library References:

West's Key No. Digests, Corporations ⊕507.

§ 1.16   Formation of Corporations—Service of Process—Records and Certificates of Department of State

The Department of State maintains a record of each process served upon the Secretary of State under the NYBCL, including the date of service.[1] The Secretary must, upon request made within ten years after service, issue a certificate under the Department's seal certifying (1) the date and place process was received by an authorized person and (2) that the statutory fee was received.[2] Records of process served upon the Secretary of State under the NYBCL are destroyed after ten years.[3]

Library References:

West's Key No. Digests, Corporations ⊕507(12).

§ 1.17   Formation of Corporations—Service of Process—Statutory Designation of Secretary of State as Agent for Service of Process

The Secretary of State is the agent of every domestic corporation and every authorized foreign corporation upon whom process against the corporation may be served.[1] Neither a domestic corporation nor a foreign corporation may be formed or authorized to do business in New York unless in its certificate of incorporation or application for authority it designates the Secretary of State as its agent for service of process purposes.[2]

Library References:

West's Key No. Digests, Corporations ⊕507(12).

§ 1.18   Formation of Corporations—Service of Process—Registered Agent for Service of Process

In addition to the designation of the Secretary of State, every domestic corporation or authorized foreign corporation may designate a

§ 1.16
1. NYBCL § 308.
2. Id.
3. Id.

§ 1.17
1. NYBCL § 304(a).

2. NYBCL § 304(b). See NYBCL § 109(a)(6), (c) (actions and proceedings by Attorney General against foreign corporations; Secretary of State not designated as agent for service of process).

registered agent in New York upon whom process against the corporation may be served.[1] The agent may be a natural person who is a resident of, or has a business address in, New York, or the agent may be a domestic corporation or foreign corporation of any type or kind formed or authorized to do business in New York under the NYBCL or under any other New York statute.[2] The designation of a registered agent may be made, revoked, or changed.[3] A registered agent may resign upon written notice given to the agent's principal.[4]

Procedure. If a corporation is to have a registered agent, the designation may be made in the certificate of incorporation[5] or, for a foreign corporation, in its application for authority to do business.[6] The designation may be changed by amendment to the certificate of incorporation.[7] The designation may also be made, revoked, or changed by filing a certificate of change authorized by the board.[8]

If the agent resigns, a certificate entitled "Certificate of resignation of registered agent of [name of designating corporation] under section 305 of the Business Corporation Law" must be signed, verified by the registered agent, and delivered to the Department of State.[9] It must set forth: (1) that the agent resigns as registered agent for the corporation, (2) the date on which the corporation's certificate of incorporation or application for authority to do business in New York was filed by the Department of State, and (3) that the agent has sent a copy of the certificate of resignation by registered mail to the corporation at the post office address on file in the Department of State specified for the mailing of process or, if that address is the address of the registered agent, to the office of the corporation in the jurisdiction of its formation or incorporation.[10] The designation of a registered agent terminates thirty days after the filing by the Department of State of the certificate of resignation or a certificate containing a revocation or change of designation, whichever is filed earlier.[11] A certificate designating a new registered agent may be delivered to the Department of State by the corporation anytime after such filing.[12]

Library References:

West's Key No. Digests, Corporations ⇨507(5).

§ 1.18

1. *See also*, CPLR 318. For service upon corporations or governmental subdivisions, see CPLR 311.
2. NYBCL § 305(a).
3. NYBCL § 305(b).
4. NYBCL § 305(c).
5. NYBCL § 402(a)(8). *See infra*, § 1.21.
6. NYBCL § 1304(a)(7). *See infra*, §§ 1.115 and 1.116.
7. NYBCL § 805. *See infra*, §§ 1.72–75.
8. NYBCL § 805-A. *See infra*, § 1.76.
9. NYBCL § 305(c).
10. *Id.*
11. NYBCL § 305(d).
12. *Id.*

§ 1.19 Formation of Corporations—Service of Process—Upon Unauthorized Foreign Corporation

In cases where non-domiciliaries of New York would be subject to the personal or other jurisdiction of the courts of New York under CPLR Article 3,[1] foreign corporations not authorized to do business in New York are subject to like jurisdiction.[2] Process against the foreign corporation may be served upon the Secretary of State as its agent.[3] The process may issue in any court in New York having subject matter jurisdiction.[4] This method of service of process has the same force and validity as personal service made within New York.[5]

Procedure. Service of process upon the Secretary of State is made by personally delivering to and leaving with the Secretary, a deputy, or other person authorized to receive the service, at the office of the Department of State in Albany, a copy of the process together with the statutory fee, which is a taxable disbursement.[6] Service is sufficient if notice of service upon the Secretary of State and a copy of the process are: (1) delivered personally outside New York to the foreign corporation and in the manner authorized by the law of the jurisdiction in which service is made or (2) transmitted to the foreign corporation by registered mail, return receipt requested, at the post office address filed at the Department of State in its jurisdiction (or if no address is there specified, to its registered or other office specified or, if none, to its last known address).[7] Where service of a copy of process is effected by personal service, proof of service must be by affidavit of compliance with NYBCL § 307 filed, together with the process, within 30 days after the service, with the clerk of the court in which the action or special proceeding is pending.[8] Service of process is complete ten days after the papers are filed with the clerk of the court.[9]

Where service of a copy of process is effected by mailing, proof of service must be by affidavit of compliance with NYBCL § 307 filed, together with the process, within 30 days after receipt of the return receipt signed by the foreign corporation (or other official proof of delivery or of the original envelope mailed).[10] If a copy of the process is mailed in accordance with NYBCL § 307, the affidavit of compliance

---

§ 1.19

1. For acts subjecting a non-domiciliary to personal jurisdiction, *see, e.g.,* CPLR 302.
2. NYBCL § 307(a).
3. *Id.*
4. *Id.*
5. NYBCL § 307(d).
6. NYBCL § 307(b). A party to whom costs are awarded in an action or appeal is permitted to tax (*i.e.,* charge and recover from) the losing party for certain expenses, CPLR 8301(a), including reasonable and necessary expenses specified by express provision of law, such as NYBCL § 307(b). CPLR 8301(a)(12). *Cf.* Fed. Rules of Civ. Proc. 54(d)(1).
7. NYBCL § 307(b)(2).
8. NYBCL § 307(c)(1).
9. *Id.*
10. NYBCL § 307(c)(2).

must be filed with either (1) the return receipt signed by the foreign corporation or other official proof of delivery or (2) the original envelope with a notation by the postal authorities that acceptance was refused by the foreign corporation.[11]

If acceptance of service is refused, a copy of the notice and process, together with the notice of mailing by registered mail and the refusal to accept, must promptly be sent to the foreign corporation at the same address by ordinary mail, and the affidavit of compliance must so state.[12] Service of process is complete ten days after the papers are filed with the clerk of the court.[13] The refusal to accept delivery of the registered mail or to sign the return receipt does not affect the validity of service, and the foreign corporation is charged with knowledge of the mail's contents.[14]

Library References:

West's Key No. Digests, Corporations ⚖668.

§ 1.20 Formation of Corporations—Incorporators and Promoters

One or more natural persons of the age of 18 years or over may act as incorporators of a corporation to be formed under the NYBCL.[1] A

11. *Id.*
12. *Id.*
13. *Id.*
14. *Id.*

§ 1.20

1. NYBCL § 401.

PRACTICE POINTER: Corporations are frequently formed by a sole incorporator. As a matter of convenience to the principals of the enterprise (who may wish to avoid many of the details of corporate formation), incorporators are usually the nominees of the principals or promoters (*e.g.,* counsel (or employees in counsel's law office) or a corporate service company). Aside from their obligation to hold, after the corporate existence begins, an organization meeting (or to act without a meeting), each incorporator is required to sign the certificate of incorporation. NYBCL §§ 402(a) and 404. *Cf.* RMBCA § 2.01, Official Comment. *See infra*, §§ 1.21 and 1.23. The signatures must be acknowledged (or in lieu thereof, the certificate may be subscribed and affirmed by an incorporator under penalties of perjury). NYBCL § 104(d).

CAVEAT: The certificate of incorporation might, on occasion, contain a false statement. Where the error involves, *e.g.,* a misspelled corporate name or the failure to express a corporate purpose the incorporators intended, filing a certificate of correction would correct the error but does not affect any *right* or *liability* accrued or incurred before the certificate of correction was filed. NYBCL § 105. In other cases, a certificate of amendment would be required (*e.g.,* to change the corporate purposes or name). NYBCL § 801. The extent of any right or liability (*i.e.,* to whom the right accrues and against whom the liability is incurred), and damages, might depend on whether the error was trivial or serious and whether any injury caused the corporation, its investors, or others by the error was the result of, *e.g.,* willful misconduct, negligence, or simply an innocent mistake despite the exercise of due care. *See, e.g.,* N. Lattin, *The Law of Corporations* (1959) pp. 158–159; H. Ballantine, *Corporations* (1946) p. 104; RMBCA §§ 1.24 (incorrect statement); 1.29 (penalty for false statement). *Cf.*, R. Hamilton, *The Law of Corporations* (2d ed. 1987) p. 33 (general belief is that an incorporator has no risk of liability for actions taken). If an incorporator also acted as a promoter, then liability might be premised upon a breach of the promoter's fiduciary duties owed the corporation and investors in it, such as a failure to provide full disclosure to the investors. *See, e.g.,* Henn and Alexander, *supra* § 1.1, note 7, pp. 239

corporation may not be an incorporator.[2]

Promoters of new corporate enterprises engage in activities that will vary depending on the business being formed. They usually find or create a business opportunity for the enterprise, evaluate the enterprise's prospects (such as the desirability of its product or service and the feasibility of entering the market), gather the required resources (capital and human) to establish the new enterprise,[3] and enter into various preincorporation offers, agreements, and contracts.[4] Preincorporation subscriptions for shares are not enforceable unless in writing and signed by the subscriber.[5]

Library References:

West's Key No. Digests, Corporations ⟐30.

§ 1.21 Formation of Corporations—Certificate of Incorporation

Procedure. The certificate must be entitled "Certificate of incorporation of [name of corporation] under section 402 of the Business Corporation Law" and must be signed by the incorporators, with their names and addresses stated beneath or opposite their signatures, ac-

and 303, note 14; Note, *Corporations: Use of Accommodation Incorporators, Directors, Officers: Potential Liability of Accommodation Personnel*, Cornell L. J. 443 (1962) p. 47. A person's merely signing a certificate of incorporation does not make the person a promoter, even though the formation of a corporation is a small part of promotion. H. Ballantine, *Corporations* (1946) p. 101.

2. NYBCL § 401, Legislative Studies and Reports, Comment 2.

3. *See, e.g.*, Henn and Alexander, pp. 786–811 (compliance with federal and state securities law); General Business Law §§ 352–359–h (Martin Act). *See supra*, § 1.6. *See also, infra*, § 1.26, note 2.

4. PRACTICE POINTER: If any uncertainty exists about effecting the corporate formation or, upon its coming into existence, the corporation's acceptance, adoption, or ratification of these preincorporation offers, agreements, or contracts, the promoters should condition the agreements on the formation of the corporation and its acceptance, adoption, or ratification of them. *See* Henn and Alexander, *supra* § 1.1, note 7, pp. 246–264. If the promoters arrange for the corporation to be formed before taking any steps in promoting the enterprise, these contractual problems are largely avoided.

5. NYBCL § 503(b). *See infra*, § 1.29.

CAVEAT: Promoters in attempting to raise capital for the enterprise should be advised of federal and New York securities regulations. For example, if the promoters/incorporators are creating an enterprise in which the *public* will invest (unlikely until some sort of financial record has been established by the enterprise but possible inasmuch as a public offering is very broadly defined under the federal and New York securities laws), a securities lawyer should be consulted at the earliest stage of the capital raising activities (*i.e.*, *before* soliciting offers to buy shares or other securities in the new corporation, even if overtures are made to only a few offerees). If, in contrast, a New York parent corporation is forming a wholly-owned subsidiary, or an individual with adequate capital is launching a new enterprise alone, the only subscriber and purchaser of the new corporation's securities is the parent corporation or the individual, and no securities regulation issues normally arise. If clients' plans fall anywhere between these two examples, they must be advised how to avoid running afoul of the securities laws.

knowledged and delivered to the Department of State.[1] Filing fees are specified in the NYBCL.[2] An organization tax on authorized shares must be paid.[3] The contents of a certificate of incorporation are specified by statute.[4]

Mandatory Provisions. The certificate must set forth: (1) the name of the corporation;[5] (2) the purposes for which it is formed;[6] (3) the county within New York where the office of the corporation is to be located;[7] (4) the aggregate number of shares authorized to be issued;[8] (5) if the shares are to be divided into classes, the designation of each class and a statement of the relative rights, preferences, and limitations of the shares of each class;[9] (6) if the shares of any preferred class are to be issued in series, the designation of each series, a statement of the variations in the relative rights, preferences, and limitations between two (or among three or more) series insofar as these variations are to be fixed in the certificate of incorporation, and a statement of any authority to be vested in the board to establish and designate the series and to fix the variations in the relative rights, preferences, and limitations between

§ 1.21

1. NYBCL § 402(a). *See supra,* § 1.20. For a form of certificate of incorporation, *see infra,* § 1.151. Corporations may be created by special act for municipal purposes only, except in cases where, in the judgment of the legislature, the objects of the corporation cannot be attained under general laws. N.Y. Constitution Art. X, § 1. *See also, supra,* § 1.7, note 6.

2. NYBCL § 104–A(d). The filing fee is $125.

3. Tax Law § 180. *See infra,* § 1.30, note 22.

4. NYBCL § 402(a). For a checklist of mandatory and permissive provisions with indications of provisions authorized (1) in the certificate of incorporation *or* the by-laws and (2) in the certificate of incorporation *or* specific provisions of the bylaws adopted by the shareholders, *see infra,* § 1.140. *See also,* NYBCL, Appendix 2; Henn and Alexander, *supra* § 1.1, note 1, Certificate of Incorporation (checklist 3).

5. NYBCL § 402(a)(1). *See also,* NYBCL §§ 102(a)(10), 104, 201(a), 202, 301–306, 501, 502, 512, 612(a), 613, 617, 622, 906, 909. *See* Scarsdale Pub. Co.-The Colonial Press v. Carter, 63 Misc. 271, 116 N.Y.S. 731 (App.Term, 1909).

6. NYBCL § 402(a)(2). The certificate is sufficient if it states, either alone or with other purposes, that the purpose of the corporation is to engage in any lawful act or activity for which corporations may be organized under the NYBCL. *Id.* By including this statement, corporate purposes are subject only to express limitations in the certificate or in the NYBCL. *Id.* It must also state that the corporation is not formed to engage in any act or activity requiring the consent or approval of any state official, department, board, agency, or other body without such consent or approval first being obtained. *Id. See supra,* § 1.9.

7. NYBCL § 402(a)(3).

8. If the corporation's shares are to consist of one class only, the certificate must state the par value of the shares or state which shares, if any, are without par value. NYBCL § 402(a)(4).

9. NYBCL § 402(a)(2). The Secretary of State is not required to file a certificate of incorporation unless the statement of the relative rights, preferences, and limitations of the shares of each class is definite and complete; the rights, preferences, and limitations so defined must not be subject to subsequent action on the part of the corporation. People ex rel. Siegel v. Lyons, 201 App.Div. 530, 194 N.Y.S. 484 (1st Dep't 1922) (The Secretary of State is not required to file certificate designating preferred stock with a liquidation preference to payment at par entitled only to such dividends, if any, as will be provided by the bylaws of the corporation.). If the shares are to be divided into classes, the certificate must set forth the number of shares of each class and the par value of the shares having par value and state which shares, if any, are without par value. NYBCL § 402(a)(4).

two (or among three or more) series, and a statement of any limit on the authority of the board to change the number of shares of any series of preferred shares as provided in NYBCL § 502(e) (issue of any class of preferred shares in series);[10] (7) a designation of the Secretary of State as agent of the corporation for service of process against the corporation and the post office address within or without New York to which the Secretary of State must mail a copy of any process;[11] (8) if the corporation has a registered agent, the agent's name and New York address and a statement that the registered agent is to be the agent of the corporation for service of process;[12] and (9) the duration of the corporation, if other than perpetual.[13]

Permissive Provisions. The certificate of incorporation may set forth any provision not inconsistent with the NYBCL or any other New York statute relating to the business of the corporation, its affairs, rights, or powers, or the rights or powers of its shareholders, directors, or officers, including any provision relating to matters that under the NYBCL are either required or permitted to be in the bylaws.[14] The certificate of incorporation may contain provisions eliminating or limiting the personal liability of any director to the corporation or its shareholders for damages for any breach of the director's duty.[15] These provisions do not eliminate or limit the liability of directors if a final adjudication establishes that (1) their acts or omissions were in bad faith or involved intentional misconduct or a knowing violation of law, (2) they personally gained a financial profit or other advantage to which they were not legally entitled, or (3) their acts violated NYBCL § 719 by authorizing an improper distribution or loan.[16] The certificate of incorporation need not set forth any of the powers of a corporation enumerated in the NYBCL.[17]

Approvals and Consents.[18] Certificates of incorporation that include among the corporation's purposes the establishment or operation

10. NYBCL § 402(a)(6).
11. NYBCL § 402(a)(7).
12. NYBCL § 402(a)(8).
13. NYBCL § 402(a)(9).

CAVEAT: To effect a valid incorporation, the certificate should be complete in all its essential particulars at the time the incorporators affix their signatures to it. *See, e.g.,* In re New York, etc., R. Co., 35 Hun 220 (1885). On whether or not the incorporators may delegate to someone else the authority to complete the instrument by inserting the missing information, *see* Dutchess, etc., County R. Co. v. Mabbett, 58 N.Y. 397 (1874). *See supra,* § 1.20.

14. NYBCL § 402(c). The provisions specified in NYBCL § 402(a) are mandatory. Permissive provisions are indicated in NYBCL § 402(b) and (c). *See infra,* § 1.139.

15. NYBCL § 402(b).

16. NYBCL § 402(b)(2) adds that the certificate may not contain a provision that will eliminate or limit the liability of any director for any act or omission occurring prior to the adoption of a provision authorized by NYBCL § 402(b)(1).

17. NYBCL § 402(c). *See* NYBCL § 202. *See supra,* § 1.11.

18. **CAVEAT:** On approvals of certain corporate purposes, *see* NYBCL §§ 201(b) (Industrial Board of Appeals), 201(d) (Commissioner of Social Services), and 201(e) (Public Health Council). *See supra,* § 1.9. On approvals of certain corporate names, *see* NYBCL §§ 301(a)(5)(B) (Superinten-

of (1) a children's day care center must so state and have the approval of the New York State Department of Social Services,[19] (2) an alcoholism or alcohol abuse services program must have the approval of the Director of the New York State Division of Alcoholism and Alcohol Abuse,[20] and (3) a substance abuse program must have the consent of the Director of the Division of Substance Abuse Services.[21] A certificate of incorporation that includes among the corporation's purposes the establishment or operation of a hospital or health services facility must so state and have the approval of the Public Health Council.[22]

Transfer Restrictions. Reasonable restrictions upon the transfer of the stock of a corporation may be imposed by the certificate of incorporation[23] and are enforceable if notice thereof is stamped or otherwise indicated on the stock certificates.[24] Share transfer restrictions can also be set forth in the bylaws or in a shareholders' agreement.[25]

Corporate Existence; De Facto Corporation. The corporate existence begins upon the filing of the certificate of incorporation by the

dent of Banks or of Insurance), 301(a)(6) (Commissioner of Labor; Industrial Board of Appeals), 301(a)(7) (Department of Social Services), and 301(a)(10) (Attorney General). See supra, § 1.13.

19. NYBCL § 405. See NYBCL § 201(d). See supra, § 1.9.

20. NYBCL § 406.

21. NYBCL § 407. The approval or consent must be endorsed on, or evidence thereof annexed to, the certificate of incorporation. NYBCL §§ 405, 406, and 407.

22. NYBCL § 201(e). The approval must be annexed to (not endorsed on) the certificate of incorporation. *Id. See also,* Public Health Law Art. 28 (definitions).

23. *See, e.g.,* Bloomingdale v. Bloomingdale, 107 Misc. 646, 177 N.Y.S. 873 (Sup. Ct., N.Y. County, 1919). *See also, e.g.,* Henn and Alexander, *supra* § 1.1, note 7, pp. 756–771.

PRACTICE POINTER: A reasonable restriction would be one prohibiting transferability of the shares except in compliance with the federal securities laws. The client should be advised to have an appropriate legend placed on stock certificates representing the shares until such time as the transferability of the shares is no longer restricted under the securities laws. *See supra,* § 1.20, notes 4 and 5 and accompanying text. Restrictions on transfer would also be proper to maintain the shareholders' proportionate interests and to keep outsiders from buying shares. The question of restrictions on transferability of shares raises a broader question about the choice of business organizational form. If the owners desire to keep ownership of shares in the enterprise restricted to a particular group of investors, they should consider forming instead, *e.g.,* a partnership (general or limited) or a limited liability company (LLC) as the business format to be used where greater leeway is available to place restrictions on transferability of ownership interests. *See* Chapter 2 "Non–Corporate Entities: Limited Liability Companies and Partnerships," *infra.* A clause in the certificate of incorporation providing that shares of stock in the corporation are not transferable without the written consent of the board of directors is illegal and void as against public policy. *See, e.g.,* Op. Atty. Gen. 404 (1910); In the Matter of the Application by Bon Neuve Realty Corp., 196 A.D.2d 694, 601 N.Y.S.2d 491 (1st Dep't 1993).

24. *See* UCC 8–204 (a restriction on transfer of a security, even if otherwise lawful, is ineffective against any person without actual knowledge of it unless the security is certificated and the restriction is noted conspicuously on the security or the security is not certificated and a notation of the restriction is contained in the initial transaction statement sent to that person or the registered owner or pledgee).

25. *See infra,* §§ 1.22, 1.47, and 1.51. *See also, e.g.,* R. Hamilton, *The Law of Corporations* (1987) pp. 203–216.

Department of State.[26] A corporation has been deemed to exist as a *de facto* corporation where an attempt was made in good faith to comply with requirements of law on filing a certificate of incorporation, a certificate was filed with the Secretary of State, and the corporation had used its name.[27] Where no certificate of incorporation is ever prepared or acknowledged, no *de facto* corporation exists.[28]

Library References:

West's Key No. Digests, Corporations ⚷18.

§ 1.22 Formation of Corporations—Bylaws

The initial bylaws of a corporation are adopted by its incorporator or incorporators at the organization meeting.[1] Thereafter, subject to limitations on the right to vote under NYBCL § 613, bylaws may be adopted, amended, or repealed by a majority of the votes of the shares entitled to vote for the election of directors.[2] When provided in the certificate of incorporation or a bylaw adopted by the shareholders, bylaws may also be adopted, amended, or repealed by the board by the vote specified in the bylaw, which may be greater than the vote otherwise prescribed by the NYBCL, but any bylaw adopted by the board may be amended or

26. NYBCL § 403. The certificate of incorporation is conclusive evidence that all conditions precedent have been fulfilled and that the corporation has been formed under the NYBCL except in an action or special proceeding brought by the Attorney General of New York. *Id.* A certificate of incorporation may set forth a date subsequent to filing, not to exceed ninety days after filing, upon which date the corporate existence begins. *Id.*

CAVEAT: *See infra,* § 1.23 on the requirement of filing, and on the penalties of failing to file, certain statements biennially after the corporation comes into existence.

PRACTICE POINTER: The date that a corporation begins business for tax purposes is a question of fact that must be determined in each case in light of all the circumstances of the particular case. Treas. Reg. § 1.248–1(a)(3). Ordinarily, a corporation begins business when it starts the business operations for which it is organized (*e.g.*, acquisition of operating assets), whereas it comes into existence on the date that it is incorporated. Treas. Reg. § 1.248–1(a)(3). These dates are important for tax purposes because start-up expenditures are amortized over a prescribed period of no shorter than sixty months (I.R.C. § 195(a)), whereas expenses paid or incurred in a trade or business are deductible currently (I.R.C. § 162(a)). Organizational expenditures are capitalized. I.R.C. § 248(a). *See infra,* § 1.34.

27. *See, e.g.*, Bankers Trust Co. of Western New York v. Zecher, 103 Misc.2d 777, 426 N.Y.S.2d 960 (Sup.Ct., Monroe County, 1980); Lamming v. Galusha, 81 Hun 247, 30 N.Y.S. 767 (1894), aff'd 151 N.Y. 648, 45 N.E. 1132 (1896).

28. Conway v. Samet, 59 Misc.2d 666, 300 N.Y.S.2d 243 (Sup.Ct., Nassau County, 1969).

CAVEAT: Incorporators, promoters, and others active in the formation of the corporation could be subject to *personal liability* if they enter into transactions prior to the filing of the certificate of incorporation (or if the certificate of incorporation is not filed after the transactions occur). *See, e.g.*, Stevens v. Episcopal Church History, 140 App. Div. 570, 125 N.Y.S. 573 (1st Dep't 1910). The risk of personal liability for preincorporation activity seems unwarranted when incorporation is reasonably simple and inexpensive to accomplish. A strong argument can be made that only full compliance with the NYBCL § 402 requirements should result in limited liability protection of the investors in the enterprise. *See* RMBCA § 2.04, Official Comment.

§ 1.22

1. NYBCL § 601(a).

2. *Id.*

repealed by the shareholders entitled to vote.[3] The bylaws may contain any provision relating to the business of the corporation, the conduct of its affairs, its rights or powers, or the rights or powers of its shareholders, directors, or officers, not inconsistent with the NYBCL, any other New York statute, or the certificate of incorporation.[4]

Library References:
West's Key No. Digests, Corporations ⚖53–58.

§ 1.23 Formation of Corporations—Organization Meeting; Biennial Statement; Franchise Taxes

After the corporation's existence begins, an organization meeting of the incorporators must be held for the purpose of adopting bylaws, electing directors to hold office until the first annual meeting of shareholders, and the transaction of other business that may come before the meeting.[1] The meeting may be held either within or without New York.[2] The meeting should be held within a reasonable time after the certificate of incorporation is filed, inasmuch as a corporation is to be managed under the direction of its board of directors[3] and not operated indefinitely by its incorporators.[4]

Procedure. If two or more incorporators are used, the meeting may be held at the call of any incorporator, who must give at least five days' notice of the meeting by mail to the other incorporators, setting forth the time and place of the meeting.[5] Notice need not be given to any incorporator who attends the meeting or submits a signed waiver of notice before or after the meeting.[6] If more than two incorporators are used, a majority constitutes a quorum, and the act of a majority of the incorporators present at a meeting at which a quorum is present is the act of the incorporators.[7] An incorporator may act in person or by proxy signed by the incorporator or an attorney-in-fact.[8] Any action permitted to be taken at the organization meeting may be taken without a meeting

---

3. *Id.*
4. NYBCL § 601(b).

§ 1.23

1. NYBCL § 404(a). *See also, supra,* § 1.20. If the election is for a staggered board, the directors' terms of office expire in successive annual meetings. NYBCL § 704(a) and (b). *See* Henn and Alexander, *supra* § 1.1, note 1, pp. 318–320 (organization meeting agenda); NYBCL, Appendix 2, Checklist 5 Organization Meeting(s).
2. NYBCL § 404(a).
3. *See infra,* § 1.59.
4. Concrete Const. Systems, Inc. v. Jensen, 65 A.D.2d 918, 410 N.Y.S.2d 460 (4th Dep't 1978).

5. NYBCL § 404(a).

PRACTICE POINTER: The attorney should prepare in advance of this meeting the notices of the meeting, the proposed incorporation documents (*e.g.*, bylaws, certificate of incorporation, organizational meeting minutes), and the arrangements for various filings with the Secretary of State and other officials, as required. Some attorneys use corporate services firms to help them prepare for this meeting. *See supra,* § 1.14, note 4. *See also,* Henn and Alexander, *supra* § 1.1, note 1, pp. 316–320 (meeting agenda).

6. NYBCL § 404(a).
7. *Id.*
8. *Id.*

§ 1.23 BUSINESS ORGANIZATIONS: CORPORATIONS Ch. 1

if the incorporators or their attorneys-in-fact sign an instrument setting forth the action taken.[9] If an incorporator dies or is for any reason unable to act, any person for whom the incorporator was acting as agent may act in the incorporator's stead, or if such person also dies or is unable to act, that person's legal representative may act.[10]

Biennial Statement. Each domestic corporation, and each foreign corporation authorized to do business in New York, must file biennially a statement setting forth: (a) the name and business address of the chairman/person of the board of directors, (b) the street address of its principal executive office, and (c) the post office address within or without New York to which the Secretary of State must mail a copy of service of process.[11] The post office address supersedes any previous address on file for this purpose with the Department of State.[12]

Biennial Statement Procedure. The biennial statement must (1) be made on forms prescribed by the Secretary of State, (2) contain information current as of the date of the execution of the statement, (3) include only information required under NYBCL § 408(1), and (4) be signed, verified, and delivered to the Department of State.[13] For purposes of NYBCL § 408(1), the filing must be made in the calendar month during which its original certificate of incorporation or application for authority was filed (or the later effective date, if stated).[14] The applicable biennial filing period starts on April 1 and ends on March 31 of the following year.[15] Thirty days after a corporation has failed to file its statement within the time required by NYBCL § 408, it is shown to be "past due" on the records of the Department of State.[16]

Penalty for Failure to File. A corporation that has failed to file its statement for two years is shown to be "delinquent" on the records of the Department of State starting 60 days after a notice of delinquency

9. NYBCL § 404(b).

10. NYBCL § 404(c). *See also,* NYBCL § 615(c).

11. NYBCL § 408(1). When an instrument is required to set forth an address, it must include the street and number or other particular description; this requirement does not apply where a post office address is specified to be set forth. NYBCL § 104(b).

12. NYBCL § 408(1)(c). The provisions of Executive Law § 96(11) (fee for special handling (within 24 hours) of requests made to Bureau of Corporations of the Department of State for certain certificates to be filed or issued under official seal) and NYBCL § 104(g) (Department of State to make, certify, and transmit a copy of certain instruments to the clerk of the county in which the office of the domestic corporation or foreign corporation is and is to be located) are not applicable to these filings. NYBCL § 408(4). Nor do the provisions of NYBCL §§ 408 (filing of biennial statement) and 409 (penalties for failure to file biennial statement) apply to a farm corporation. NYBCL § 408(5). For the purposes of NYBCL § 408(5), the term "farm corporation" means any domestic corporation or foreign corporation authorized to do business in New York under the NYBCL engaged in the production of crops, livestock, and livestock products on land used in agricultural production, as defined in Agriculture and Markets Law § 301. *Id.*

13. NYBCL § 408(2).

14. NYBCL § 408(3).

15. *Id.*

16. NYBCL § 409(1).

has been mailed to the last known address of the corporation.[17] The corporation is removed from the Department of State's delinquency records upon the filing of the current statement required by NYBCL § 408 and the payment of a $250 fine.[18] The notice of delinquency must state the cure and fine for the delinquency and the period during which the delinquency will be forborne without the imposition of the fine.[19]

Franchise taxes. A franchise tax is imposed on domestic and foreign corporations.[20]

Library References:

West's Key No. Digests, Corporations ⊃1–30(6).

§ 1.24 Formation of Corporations Summary

Preliminary issues to be determined before forming a corporation are choosing the state of incorporation, determining the corporation's name, and reserving the name within New York and other jurisdictions, if necessary. In addition to the designation of the Secretary of State as agent for service of process, consideration should be given to whether or not a registered agent for that purpose is desirable. Incorporators and promoters must take the necessary steps to form the organization, including filing the certificate of incorporation, arranging preincorporation contracts, raising capital (for small enterprises, via subscription agreements; for large enterprises, by private placement or perhaps public offering). The allocation of ownership interests (senior securities versus common shares) must be determined. State taxes and filing fees must be paid, and the incorporators must hold an organization meeting to adopt bylaws, elect directors, and transact other business. Corporations must file biennial statements with the Department of State.

Library References:

West's Key No. Digests, Corporations ⊃1–30(6).

§ 1.25 Formation of Corporations Checklist

1. Selecting the state of incorporation. (*See* § 1.4, note 1)

---

17. NYBCL § 409(2).
18. *Id.*
19. NYBCL § 409(3).
20. Tax Law §§ 209 and 210. *See, e.g.,* Forms CT–3–P (general business corporation) and CT–3–S–P (S corporation). For New York City general corporation tax returns, *see, e.g.,* Forms NYC–4S (short form), NYC–3L (long form), and NYC–3A combined form (*i.e.*, combined group of corporations). *See* N.Y. City Administrative Code 11–602.1. An "S" Corporation is subject to the N.Y. City general corporation tax and must file either Form NYC–4S or NYC–4L, whichever is applicable. *See also,* Chapter 35 "State Income Tax," *infra,* §§ 35.20–35.41. *See generally,* state and local tax reports published by Commerce Clearing House, Prentice–Hall, or Matthew Bender. *See also,* P. Comeau, S. Heckelman, and R. Helm, *New York Tax Analysis* (1996) §§ 20.20 (overview of corporate franchise tax), 21.20 (domestic (New York) corporations), 21.40 (foreign corporations), 32.20 (S corporations), 142.20 (New York City general corporation tax).

§ 1.25 BUSINESS ORGANIZATIONS: CORPORATIONS Ch. 1

- Tax burden (filing fee, annual franchise tax, state income tax).
- Desirable features and undesirable restrictions of corporate and other laws (*e.g.*, qualifications of incorporators and directors, place of corporate meetings, shareholder voting and subscription rights, ease of amendment of certificate of incorporation or charter, powers of directors to amend charter and otherwise act for the corporation).
- How well developed corporate law of jurisdiction is.

2. Formalities of organizing a corporation.
    - Application to reserve corporation's name. (See § 1.14; for form, *see* § 1.150)
    - Certificate designating or changing registered agent; certificate of resignation of registered agent (*see* § 1.18); service of process on unauthorized foreign corporation. (See § 1.19)
    - Certificate of incorporation. (*See* § 1.21; for form, *see* § 1.151); consents and approvals from officials (*see* §§ 1.9, 1.13, 1.21); filing and indexing of certificate of incorporation (*see* § 1.7); delivery of certificate of incorporation to Department of State with filing fee and organization tax on shares (*see* §§ 1.7 and 1.30); biennial statement by domestic and foreign corporations filed with Secretary of State. (*See* § 1.23)
    - Organization meetings (*see* § 1.23): incorporators (adopt bylaws, elect initial directors; other business); first meeting of directors (approval of bylaws, corporate seal, share certificate form; acceptance of share subscriptions; authorize issuance of shares; adoption of any preincorporation agreements, election of officers, adoption of certain employment agreements with founders,[1] resolution to file to obtain federal employer identification number from IRS; resolution to establish bank account of corporation; resolution to obtain insurance on corporate property and key employees). (*See* §§ 1.20, 1.22, 1.26–1.34)

Library References:

West's Key No. Digests, Corporations ⟐1–30(6).

§ 1.25 (2d ed. 1969) pp. 80–81, 85–86 and 97–98.
1. *See, e.g.*, Herwitz, *supra*, § 1.1, note 1, pp. 68–69; C. Israels, *Corporate Practice*

§ 1.26 Capital Structure

The initial sources of capital for a new corporation are investors[1] who receive securities for their contribution of cash or other property to the corporation.[2] Its capital structure[3] will typically be equity and long-term debt.[4] The particular capital structure that emerges for a corpora-

---

§ 1.26

1. The initial investors in a new enterprise are usually the founders, their relatives, and close associates, though some funds might be provided by bank credit. See, e.g., H. Guthmann and H. Dougall, *Corporate Financial Policy* (3d ed. 1955) pp. 201–203 (initial sources of long-term financing for small and medium-sized, and even some large, promotions of new corporations); Henn and Alexander, *supra*, § 1.1, note 1, pp. 377 (sources of funds), 695 (some large corporations are privately-held, even closely-held; vast majority of business corporations are closely-held); D. Logue, *Handbook of Modern Finance* (1984) p. 27–8 (the amount of debt at various stages of the corporate life cycle).

2. **PRACTICE POINTER:** A new corporation might raise funds through a private placement of its securities. The investors who might be interested in the corporation's securities would depend on the circumstances, some of which are outlined as follows. For a new enterprise, the only feasible sources of funds, other than the founders themselves, might be limited to those investors close to the founders or management (e.g., friends, associates, and employees) or perhaps those interested in cementing future relations with the corporation (e.g., creditors, suppliers, and customers). After its initial years of operations (during which period a corporation might incur losses), it can begin to establish an earnings record that may be attractive enough to permit it to raise funds in a privately-negotiated placement of its securities with one or more institutional investors (e.g., savings banks, trust companies, mortgage banks, investment companies, insurance companies, commercial banks, and pension funds). If a going concern is incorporated, the new corporation's financial record may be strong enough for a private placement with institutional investors soon after incorporation. See, e.g., J. Bogen, *Financial Handbook* (4th ed. 1968) 9.6; D. Logue, *Handbook of Modern Finance* (1984) pp. 4–12 to 4–13; H. Guthmann and H. Dougall, *Corporate Financial Policy* (3d ed. 1955) pp. 201–203, 291, and 310–313; Henn and Alexander, p. 377. Assuming that a corporation is willing to incur the time and expense (and to subject itself to the disclosure and other regulatory obligations associated with) going public, its access to the capital markets through a public offering of its securities usually awaits, among other factors or conditions, its establishing a strong enough record of earnings and growth potential to induce investment bankers to sell the corporation's securities to the public. For a general discussion of public corporations and the regulatory regime (securities and antitrust regulation; self regulation) in which they operate, along with references to leading authorities on securities law, see, e.g., Henn and Alexander, *supra*, § 1.1, note 1, pp. 784–867; J. Bogen, *Financial Handbook* (4th ed. 1968) 9.2–9–4. See also, *supra*, § 1.20, notes 3 and 5.

3. See, e.g., H. Guthmann and H. Dougall, *Corporate Financial Policy* (3d ed. 1955) p. 76 (capital structure includes bonds, long-term loans, and shareholders' equity); R. Brealey and S. Myers, *Principles of Corporate Finance* (1991) pp. 330 (capital structure; debt-to-equity ratio), 397, 422–424, and 922 (capital structure, debt, tax factors, and value of firm). Working capital, sometimes referred to as net working capital, is usually defined as the excess of current assets over current liabilities (i.e., net current assets). See, e.g., H. Guthmann and H. Dougall, *Corporate Financial Policy* (3d ed. 1955) p. 387; R. Brealey and S. Myers, *Principles of Corporate Finance* (1991) p. 724; J. Bogen, *Financial Handbook* (4th ed. 1968) 16.1–16.2.

4. See, e.g., W. Klein and J. Coffee, *Business Organization and Finance* (4th ed. 1990) pp. 297–301, 306; Henn and Alexander, *supra*, § 1.1, note 1, pp. 385–395 (debt securities); H. Ballantine, *On Corporations* (1946) §§ 210–211; D. Logue, *Handbook of Modern Finance* (1984) Chapters 9–2 to 9–13 (equity), 7–8 to 7–9 (debt), 27–1 to 27–4 (capital structure); W. Fruhan, W. Kester, S. Mason, T. Piper, R. Ruback, *Case Problems in Finance* (1992) pp. 9–10, 125; R.

§ 1.26   BUSINESS ORGANIZATIONS: CORPORATIONS   Ch. 1

tion will depend on various ingredients, such as the bargaining strength of each investor, the value of the property and services investors contribute to the enterprise,[5] the risk to investors of the new venture, the type of return they desire, what control they want over the enterprise, and the tax implications associated with the various securities to be issued.[6] The corporation's sources of funds will grow beyond its initial capital as the corporation operates and grows.[7] These sources will include, among others, accounts payable[8] and other short-term credit, retained earnings,

---

Brealey and S. Myers, *Principles of Corporate Finance* (1991) pp. 315–335; J. Bogen, *Financial Handbook* (4th ed. 1968) §§ 13 (equity), 14 (debt), 16 (working capital).

PRACTICE POINTER: The debt-to-equity ratio should be analyzed to assure that the corporation is not thinly capitalized, a condition that risks characterizing the debt as equity for tax purposes. *See, e.g.*, I.R.C. 385; Master Tax Guide ¶ 733A; 1997 CCH Std. Fed. Tax Rep. ¶ 17,340 (1995). Other issues scrutinized by the IRS are, *e.g.*, debt instruments of unreasonably long maturity and interest payments (and deductions) by the corporation on purported debt.

CAVEAT: Capital structure may have an effect on whether the corporation will be disregarded as an entity for purposes of limited liability of shareholders. *See supra*, § 1.10. The issuance of securities requires compliance with federal and state securities laws. *See supra*, §§ 1.20, notes 3 and 5; 1.26, note 2.

 5. *See, e.g.*, Herwitz, *supra*, § 1.1, note 1, pp. 1–57 (valuation of existing enterprises (closely-held and publicly-held); new enterprises); J. Bogen, *Financial Handbook* (4th ed. 1968) 20.25–20.27.

 6. *See, e.g.*, D. Logue, *Handbook of Modern Finance* (1984) pp. 27–1 to 27–4; W. Fruhan, W. Kester, S. Mason, T. Piper, R. Ruback, *Case Problems in Finance* (1992) pp. 9–10, 125–130; R. Brealey and S. Myers, *Principles of Corporate Finance* (1991) pp. 330–334, 447–448; Ballantine, *On Corporations* (1946) pp. 499–501.

 7. *See, e.g.*, Henn and Alexander, *supra*, § 1.1, note 1, pp. 377–378.

 8. PRACTICE POINTER: An increase in accounts payable, such as trade debt on open account, like *any other debt or borrowing*, is a source of funds and reduces the amount of funds to be raised from other sources. *See, e.g.*, Henn and Alexander, *supra*, § 1.1, note 1, pp. 377–378 (trade credits (accounts payable) as a source of funds); A. Conard, R. Knauss, and S. Siegel, *Enterprise Organization* (2d ed. 1977) pp. 666–668 (sources of funds include, among others, stocks, bonds, loans, trade debt, and other liabilities); W. Klein and J. Coffee, *Business Organization and Finance* (4th ed. 1990) p. 6; R. Brealey and S. Myers, *Principles of Corporate Finance* (4th ed. 1991) pp. 727–729 (an increase in accounts payable represents, in effect, additional borrowing from suppliers—a *source* of funds; an increase in accounts receivable represents, in effect, additional lending to customers—a *use* of funds); H. Guthmann and H. Dougall, *Corporate Financial Policy* (3d ed. 1955) pp. 414–417 (short-term sources of current assets include, among other creditors, trade creditors and commercial banks (short-term loans (notes payable))). Accounts receivable *financing*, where a corporation's accounts receivable, either *pledged* as collateral for a loan or *sold* outright to a factor, can provide another source of funds. *See, e.g.*, J. Bogen, *Financial Handbook* (4th ed. 1968) 16.14–16.15; H. Guthmann and H. Dougall, *Corporate Financial Policy* (3d ed. 1955) pp. 445–450; W. Fruhan, W. Kester, S. Mason, T. Piper, R. Ruback, *Case Problems in Finance* (1992) pp. 42–43. The collection of accounts receivable is another source. D. Logue, *Handbook of Modern Finance* (1984) p. 21–5 (collection of accounts receivable is a source of funds; *payment* of accounts payable is a use of funds); H. Guthmann and H. Dougall, *Corporate Financial Policy* (3d ed. 1955) p. 395 (receivables are a source of cash only as they are collected).

CAVEAT: A focus on changes in *working capital* (current assets minus current liabilities) instead of *cash* may mask short-term liquidity problems of the business (*e.g.*, business operations may be a net provider (source) of working capital, but most of the increase in working capital might have resulted from a buildup of receivables and inventory (both current assets), in which case business operations would be a net user, rather than a provider, of cash—the cash is tied up (invested) in receivables and inventory and not available for necessary

and additional offerings of equity and long-term debt.[9]

§ 1.27 Capital Structure—Authorized Shares

A corporation has the power to create and issue the number of shares stated in its certificate of incorporation.[1] The shares may be all of one class or may be divided into two or more classes, and each class must consist of either shares with par value or shares without par value, having the designation and relative voting, dividend, liquidation, and other rights, preferences, and limitations consistent with the NYBCL, as stated in the certificate of incorporation.[2] If the shares are divided into two or more classes, the shares of each class must be designated to distinguish them from the shares of all other classes.[3] Subject to the designations, relative rights, preferences, and limitations applicable to separate series,[4] each share is equal to every other share of the same class.[5] Authorized shares must be distinguished from shares that are

cash outlays of the business). Funds (cash) flow analysis may thus help in uncovering an important operational (financing) risk. *See, e.g.,* D. Logue, *Handbook of Modern Finance,* pp. 15–24 to 15–25 (1984); R. Kay and D. Searfoss, *Handbook of Accounting and Auditing* (2d ed. 1989) pp. 3–24 to 3–29. On risk generally, *see, supra,* § 1.2, note 3 and accompanying text.

9. *See, e.g.,* Henn and Alexander, *supra,* § 1.1, note 1, pp. 377–378; W. Fruhan, W. Kester, S. Mason, T. Piper, R. Ruback, *Case Problems in Finance* (1992) pp. 9–10, 125–130.

PRACTICE POINTER: Caution should be counselled about business growth that is too rapid in light of the corporation's total resources available (overall capacity—human and capital—for expansion) including sources of funds to finance the business expansion. The ratio of debt to equity should not be so large that a strain is placed on the corporation's ability to meet its obligations and thereby risk default on them.

CAVEAT: A corporation's issuance of securities must be in compliance with federal and New York securities laws. *See* Henn and Alexander, *supra,* § 1.1, note 1, pp. 786–811, 844–850; General Business Law §§ 352–359-h ("Martin Act"). *See supra,* § 1.20, notes 3 and 5.

§ 1.27

1. NYBCL § 501(a).

2. *Id.*

CAVEAT: The certificate of incorporation may deny, limit, or otherwise define the voting rights and may limit or otherwise define the dividend or liquidation rights of shares of any class, but no such denial, limitation, or definition of voting rights is effective unless at the time one or more classes of outstanding shares or bonds, singly or in the aggregate, are entitled to full voting rights, and no such limitation or definition of dividend or liquidation rights shall be effective unless at the time one or more classes of outstanding shares, singly or in the aggregate, are entitled to unlimited dividend and liquidation rights. *Id. See* Mitchell, *The Puzzling Paradox of Preferred Stock (And Why We Should Care About It),* 51 Business Lawyer 443 (1996).

3. NYBCL § 501(b).

CAVEAT: Shares that are entitled to preference in the distribution of dividends or of assets may not be designated as common shares. Shares that are not entitled to preference in the distribution of dividends or of assets must be common shares, even if identified by a class or other designation, and may not be designated as preferred shares. *Id.*

4. Except as otherwise permitted by NYBCL § 505(a)(2).

5. NYBCL § 501(c). *See also,* Beaumont v. American Can Co., 160 A.D.2d 174, 553 N.Y.S.2d 145 (1st Dep't 1990) (unequal treatment in corporate merger); *but see* Beaumont v. American Can Co., 215 A.D.2d 249, 626 N.Y.S.2d 201 (1st Dep't 1995) (director-shareholder denied equal treatment); Bank of New York Co., Inc. v. Irving Bank Corp., 142 Misc.2d 145, 536 N.Y.S.2d 923 (Sup.Ct., N.Y. County, 1988) (discriminato-

§ 1.27 BUSINESS ORGANIZATIONS: CORPORATIONS Ch. 1

issued and outstanding as well as from treasury shares.[6]

Library References:

West's Key No. Digests, Corporations ⚖=60–68.

§ 1.28 Capital Structure—Preferred Shares in Series

If the certificate of incorporation so provides, a corporation may issue any class of preferred shares in series, and shares of each series when issued must be designated to distinguish them from shares of other series.[1] The number of shares included in the series of any classes of preferred shares and the designations, relative rights, preferences, and limitations of series may be fixed in the certificate of incorporation subject to certain limitations.[2] If these parameters are not fixed in the certificate of incorporation, the board may fix them to the extent

---

ry bargain price "flip in"); Cawley v. SCM Corp., 72 N.Y.2d 465, 534 N.Y.S.2d 344, 530 N.E.2d 1264 (1988) (sharing of tax deductions).

CAVEAT: With respect to corporations owning or leasing residential premises and operating them as cooperatives, if (1) liquidation or other distribution rights are substantially equal per share, (2) changes in maintenance charges and general assessments pursuant to a proprietary lease are equal per share or per room or are an equal percentage of the maintenance charges, and (3) voting rights are substantially equal per share or the certificate of incorporation provides that the shareholders holding the shares allocated to each apartment or dwelling unit owned by the corporation is entitled to one vote in the aggregate regardless of the number of shares allocated to the apartment or dwelling unit or the number of shareholders holding such shares, then shares of the same class are not considered unequal because of variations in fees or charges payable to the corporation upon sale or transfer of shares and appurtenant proprietary leases, as long as those fees or charges are provided for in proprietary leases, occupancy agreements, or offering plans, or properly approved amendments thereto. NYBCL § 501(c). See, e.g., Lowy v. Bay Terrace Co-op, Section VIII, Inc., 698 F.Supp. 1058 (E.D.N.Y.1988), aff'd 869 F.2d 173 (2d Cir.1989) (dual resale policies); Fe Bland v. Two Trees Management Co., 66 N.Y.2d 556, 498 N.Y.S.2d 336, 489 N.E.2d 223 (1985) (flip tax variations); Cohen v. 120 Owners Corp., 205 A.D.2d 394, 613 N.Y.S.2d 615 (1st Dep't 1994) (special maintenance surcharge); Amer v. Bay Terrace Co-op. Section II, Inc., 142 A.D.2d 704, 531 N.Y.S.2d 33 (2d Dep't 1988); McCabe v. Hoffman, 138 A.D.2d 287, 526 N.Y.S.2d 93.(1st Dep't 1988) (maintenance surcharge); Meichsner v. Valentine Gardens Co-op., Inc., 137 A.D.2d 797, 525 N.Y.S.2d 345 (2d Dep't 1988) (waiver of option fee); de Mello v. 79th Street Tenants Corp., 136 Misc.2d 73, 517 N.Y.S.2d 892 (Civ.Ct., N.Y. County, 1987) (transfer fee); Mullins v. 510 East 86th Street Owners, Inc., 126 Misc.2d 758, 483 N.Y.S.2d 631 (Civ.Ct., N.Y. County, 1984) (different transfer fees); Fe Bland v. Two Trees Management Co., 125 Misc.2d 111, 479 N.Y.S.2d 123 (Sup.Ct., N.Y. County, 1984), aff'd 109 A.D.2d 1110, 487 N.Y.S.2d 453 (1st Dep't 1985), appeal granted 110 A.D.2d 1093, 489 N.Y.S.2d 449, affirmed, 66 N.Y.2d 556, 498 N.Y.S.2d 336, 489 N.E.2d 223 (1985) (different transfer fees).

6. See supra, § 1.5(14) (definition of treasury shares). See infra, §§ 1.32 and 1.39.

§ 1.28

1. NYBCL § 502(a).

2. NYBCL § 502(b). This provision is subject to the limitation that, unless the certificate of incorporation provides otherwise, if the stated dividends and amounts payable on liquidation are not paid in full, the shares of all series of the same class will share ratably (1) in dividends including accumulations, if any, in accordance with the amounts payable on such shares if all dividends were declared and paid in full and (2) in any liquidation distribution in accordance with the amounts payable on such distribution if paid in full. Id.

authorized by the certificate of incorporation.[3]

Procedure. Before the corporation's issuance of any shares of a series established by the board, a certificate of amendment under NYBCL § 805 must be delivered to the Department of State.[4] The certificate must set forth: (1) the name of the corporation and, if the name has been changed, the name under which the corporation was formed, (2) the date the certificate of incorporation was filed by the Department of State, (3) that the certificate of incorporation is thereby amended by the addition of a provision stating the number, designation, relative rights, preferences, and limitations of the shares of the series as fixed by the board, and (4) the text of the provision in full.[5]

Library References:

West's Key No. Digests, Corporations ⟬156.

§ 1.29 Capital Structure—Subscriptions for Shares

Unless otherwise provided by the subscription agreement, a subscription for shares of a corporation to be formed is irrevocable, except with the consent to the contrary of all other subscribers or the corporation, for a period of three months from its date.[1] A subscription, whether made before or after the formation of a corporation, is not enforceable unless in writing and signed by the subscriber.[2] Subscriptions for shares must be paid in full at the time, or in installments and at the times, determined by the board, unless otherwise provided by the subscription

---

3. NYBCL § 502(c). Unless otherwise provided in the certificate of incorporation, the number of preferred shares of any series so fixed by the board may be increased (but not above the total number of authorized shares of the class) or decreased (but not below the number of shares thereof then outstanding) by the board. *Id.* In case the number of such shares is decreased, the number of shares by which the series is decreased must, unless eliminated pursuant to NYBCL § 502(e), resume the status that they had prior to being designated as part of a series of preferred shares. *Id.* Action by the board to increase or decrease the number of preferred shares of any series pursuant to NYBCL § 502(c) becomes effective by delivering to the Department of State a certificate of amendment under NYBCL § 805. NYBCL § 502(e). *See infra,* § 1.75. The certificate of amendment must set forth: (1) the name of the corporation and, if it has been changed, the name under which it was formed; (2) the date its certificate of incorporation was filed with the Department of State; (3) that the certificate of incorporation is thereby amended to increase or decrease, as the case may be, the number of preferred shares of any series so fixed by the board, setting forth the specific terms of the amendment and the number of shares so authorized following the effectiveness of the amendment. NYBCL § 502(e). When no shares of any such series are outstanding, either because none were issued or because no issued shares of any such series remain outstanding, the certificate of amendment under NYBCL § 805 may also set forth a statement that none of the authorized shares of such series is outstanding and that none will be issued subject to the certificate of incorporation. NYBCL § 502(e). The certificate of amendment's acceptance for filing effects an elimination from the certificate of incorporation of all matters set forth therein on such series of preferred shares. NYBCL § 502(e).

4. NYBCL § 502(d).

5. *Id.*

§ 1.29

1. NYBCL § 503(a).
2. NYBCL § 503(b).

agreement.[3] In the event of a default in payment of any installment or call when due, the corporation may proceed to collect the amount due in the same manner as any debt due the corporation, or the board may declare a forfeiture of the subscription in default.[4] The subscription agreement may prescribe other penalties, not amounting to forfeiture, for failure to pay installments or calls that may become due.[5] No forfeiture of the subscription will be declared against any subscriber unless the amount due remains unpaid for a period of at least 30 days after written demand has been made by the corporation.[6]

Procedure. If mailed by the corporation, the written demand is deemed to be made when deposited in the United States mail in a sealed envelope, postage prepaid, addressed to the subscriber at his or her last post office address known to the corporation.[7] Upon forfeiture of the subscription, if at least fifty percent of the subscription price has been paid, the shares subscribed for must be offered for sale for cash, or a binding obligation to pay cash, at a price at least sufficient to pay the full balance owed by the delinquent subscriber plus the expenses incidental to the sale.[8] Any excess of net proceeds realized over the amount owed on the shares must be paid to the delinquent subscriber (or to his or her legal representative). If no prospective purchaser offers cash sufficient to pay the full balance owed plus expenses incidental to the sale, or if less than fifty percent of the subscription price has been paid, the shares subscribed for must be cancelled and restored to the status of authorized but unissued shares, and all previous payments are forfeited to the corporation and transferred to its surplus.[9]

Library References:

West's Key No. Digests, Corporations ⟲69–93.

§ 1.30 Capital Structure—Consideration and Payment for Shares

Consideration for the issue of shares may consist of money, other tangible or intangible property, labor or services actually received by or performed for the corporation or for its benefit or in its formation or

---

3. NYBCL § 503(c). Any call made by the board for payment on subscriptions must be uniform for all shares of the same class or of the same series. *Id.* If a receiver of the corporation has been appointed, all unpaid subscriptions must be paid at the times and in the installments that the receiver or the court may direct. *Id. See also,* Chapter 9 "Bankruptcy," *infra.*

4. NYBCL § 503(d). On the liability of subscriber for payment for shares, *see* NYBCL § 628.

5. NYBCL § 503(d).

6. *Id.*

7. *Id.*

8. *Id.*

9. *Id.*

CAVEAT: Notwithstanding the provisions of NYBCL § 503(d), in the event of default in payment or other performance under the instrument evidencing a subscriber's binding obligation to pay a portion of the subscription price or to perform services, the corporation may pursue such remedies as are provided in the instrument, or a related agreement, or under law. NYBCL § 503(e).

Ch. 1 CONSIDERATION AND PAYMENT FOR SHARES § 1.30

reorganization, a binding obligation to pay the purchase price or the subscription price in cash or other property, a binding obligation to perform services having an agreed value, or any combination thereof.[1] In the absence of fraud in the transaction, the judgment of the board or of the shareholders, as the case may be, regarding the value of the consideration received for shares is conclusive.[2] The obligation of the subscriber for future services does not constitute payment or part payment for shares of a corporation.[3] Shares with par value may be issued for the consideration, not less than the par value, fixed from time to time by the board.[4] Shares without par value may be issued for the consideration fixed from time to time by the board, unless the certificate of incorporation reserves to the shareholders the right to fix it.[5] If the right is reserved to the shareholders, they must by vote either fix the consideration to be received for the shares or authorize the board to fix the consideration.[6] Treasury shares may be disposed of by a corporation on the terms and conditions fixed from time to time by the board.[7]

Upon the distribution of authorized but unissued shares to shareholders (*i.e.*, a stock dividend), that part of the surplus of a corporation concurrently transferred to stated capital must be the consideration for the issue of the shares.[8] In the event of a conversion of either bonds into shares or shares into other shares, or an exchange of bonds for shares or of shares for other shares (with or without par value), the consideration for the shares issued in conversion or exchange is the sum of (1) either the principal of (and accrued interest on) the bonds exchanged or converted or the stated capital represented by the shares exchanged or converted, (2) additional consideration paid to the corporation for the new shares, (3) stated capital allocated to the new shares, and (4) surplus transferred to stated capital and allocated to the new shares.[9]

Certificates for shares may not be issued until the amount of the consideration for the shares, determined to be stated capital pursuant to NYBCL § 506 (determination of stated capital), has been paid in the form of cash, services rendered, personal or real property, or a combination thereof, and consideration for the balance (if any) complying with

§ 1.30

1. NYBCL § 504(a). *See* Herwitz, *supra*, § 1.1, note 1, pp. 94–97 (argues that bar against issue of stock for future services is particularly unwarranted in the case of a close corporation). *Cf.*, RMBCA § 6.21(b), (e); Delaware General Corporations Law §§ 152, 153, and 156.

2. NYBCL § 504(a).

3. NYBCL § 504(b). They could constitute consideration for interests in limited liability company (LLC). *See* NYLLCL § 501. *See also*, Chapter 2 "Non–Corporate Entities: Limited Liability Companies and Partnerships," *infra*. Shares received by a shareholder in return for past services rendered (or also future services to be rendered, in the case of an LLC) would constitute taxable income to the shareholder (or LLC member) who had rendered the services. I.R.C. §§ 61 and 83. *See also*, *infra*, § 1.34, note 28 and accompanying text.

4. NYBCL § 504(c).

5. NYBCL § 504(d).

6. *Id.*

7. NYBCL § 504(e).

8. NYBCL § 504(f).

9. NYBCL § 504(g).

NYBCL § 504(a) has been provided, except as provided in NYBCL §§ 505(e) and (f) regarding the issue to directors, officers, and employees of rights and options to purchase shares.[10] When the consideration for shares has been provided in compliance with NYBCL § 504(h), the subscriber is entitled to all the rights and privileges of a holder of shares and to a certificate representing the shares; the shares are then fully paid and nonassessable.[11]

Fractional Shares and Scrip. A corporation may, but is not obliged to, issue fractions of a share (either represented by a certificate or uncertificated).[12] As an alternative, a corporation may pay in cash the fair value of fractional shares to holders thereof.[13] A corporation also may issue scrip in registered or bearer form over the manual or facsimile signature of an officer of the corporation (or its agent) that is exchangeable for full shares, but the scrip does not entitle the holder to any rights of a shareholder except as otherwise provided therein.[14] Scrip may be issued subject to the condition that it will become void if not exchanged for full shares before a specified date, or subject to the condition that the shares for which scrip is exchangeable may be sold by the corporation and the proceeds distributed to the holders of the scrip, or subject to any other conditions that the board may determine.[15] A corporation may provide a reasonable opportunity for persons entitled to fractional shares or scrip to sell it or to purchase additional fractions of a share or scrip as necessary to acquire a full share.[16]

Certificates Representing Shares; Uncertificated Shares. The NYBCL sets forth various requirements with respect to certificates representing shares, including (1) signatures of the chair or vice-chair of

---

10. NYBCL § 504(h). *See infra*, § 1.31.
11. NYBCL § 504(i).

CAVEAT: Notwithstanding that such shares may be fully paid and non-assesable, the corporation may place in escrow shares issued for a binding obligation to pay cash or other property or to perform future services, or make other arrangements to restrict the transfer of the shares, and may credit distributions on the shares against the obligation, until the obligation is performed. NYBCL § 504(j). If the obligation is not performed, in whole or in part, the corporation may pursue such remedies as are provided in the instrument evidencing the obligation, or a related agreement, or under law. *Id.* The reasonable expenses of formation or reorganization of a corporation, and the reasonable expenses of the sale or underwriting of its shares, may be paid by the corporation out of the consideration received by it in payment for its shares without thereby impairing the fully paid and nonassessable status of the shares. NYBCL § 507. For federal income tax purposes, organization expenses are amortizable over a prescribed period no shorter than 60 months. I.R.C. § 248. *See infra*, § 1.34.

12. NYBCL § 509(a).
13. NYBCL § 509(b).
14. NYBCL § 509(c).
15. NYBCL § 509(c).
16. NYBCL § 509(d).

CAVEAT: NYBCL § 509(a) and (b) present a two-edged sword: a shareholder may risk being "frozen out" if a corporation has the power through a reverse stock split (or other transaction with similar effect) to buy out a shareholder who ends up with only a fraction of a share after the transaction; from the corporation's viewpoint, NYBCL § 509(a) and (b) provide a means by which it may be able to eliminate dissident shareholders by forcing them to accept cash for their fractional shares. Thus, the reverse stock split might be, for public corporations, a method of going private. *See infra*, §§ 1.38, note 30; 1.51, note 22; 1.81, note 1.

Ch. 1   CONSIDERATION AND PAYMENT FOR SHARES   § 1.30

the board or the president or vice-president and the secretary or an assistant secretary or treasurer or an assistant treasurer,[17] (2) statements of relative rights, preferences, and limitations of classes of shares and other information, (3) manner of transfer, (4) corporate seal, and (5) lost or destroyed certificates.[18]

Each share certificate must state upon its face (1) that the corporation is formed under the laws of New York, (2) the name of the person(s) to whom issued, and (3) the number and class of shares, and the designation of the series, if any, that the certificate represents.[19]

Unless otherwise provided in the certificate of incorporation or bylaws, the board may by resolution permit uncertificated shares, as long as the resolution does not apply to shares represented by certificates until those certificates are surrendered to the corporation.[20] Except as otherwise provided by law, the rights and obligations of the holders of uncertificated shares and holders of certificates representing shares of the same class and series are identical.[21]

Organization Tax; Stock Transfer Tax. An organization tax is imposed on authorized shares, but no original issue tax is imposed on shares issued by the corporation to its shareholders.[22] A stock transfer tax is imposed, with a claim for rebate of tax permitted.[23]

Library References:

West's Key No. Digests, Corporations ⟹88, 99.

17. NYBCL § 508. For requirements related to facsimile signatures on, and countersigning of, certificates, *see* NYBCL § 508(a).

18. NYBCL § 508.

19. NYBCL § 508(c).

20. NYBCL § 508(f).

21. NYBCL § 508(f). *See, e.g.*, UCC article 8 (contains rules for certificated shares, such as that they can be lost, destroyed, or stolen (UCC 8–405; NYBCL § 508(e)), transferred in bearer form or registered in the name of the transferee (UCC 8–107), negotiable instruments (UCC 8–105), and required to have restrictions on transferability noted conspicuously on them (UCC 8–204); uncertificated securities are not subject to these rules). *Procedure.* Within a reasonable time after the issuance of uncertificated shares, the corporation must send the registered owner of the shares a written notice containing the information required to be set forth or stated on the face or back of a stock certificate. NYBCL § 508(f). *See* NYBCL § 508(b) and (c).

22. Tax Law § 180 (the tax is at the rate of one-twentieth of one per cent upon the amount of the par value of all the authorized shares with a par value and a tax of five cents on each authorized share without a par value; the minimum tax is $10). The fee for filing the certificate of incorporation is $125 (*see* NYBCL § 104–A(d)), which is paid along with the organization tax at the time of filing. Tax Law § 180 also imposes a tax on changes of capital. *See infra*, § 1.72

23. Tax Law § 270 (where the shares or certificates are sold, the tax is at the rate of: (1) one and one-quarter cents for each share where the selling price is less than five dollars per share, (2) two and one-half cents for each share where the selling price is five dollars or more per share and less than ten dollars per share, (3) three and three-quarters cents for each share where the selling price is ten dollars or more per share and less than $20 per share, and (4) five cents for each share where the selling price is $20 or more per share; for transfers without a sale, the tax imposed is two and one-half cents for each share). *But see*, Tax Law § 280–a (rebate of stock transfer tax; filing of claim for rebate with the State Tax Commission). The maximum tax is $350. Tax Law § 270–e.

§ 1.31 Capital Structure—Rights to Purchase Shares

Except as otherwise provided in NYBCL § 505 or in the certificate of incorporation, a corporation may create and issue, in connection with the issue and sale of its shares or bonds or otherwise, rights or options entitling the holders thereof to purchase from the corporation, upon the consideration, terms, and conditions fixed by the board, shares of any class or series (whether authorized but unissued shares, treasury shares, or shares to be acquired) or assets of the corporation.[1] The consideration for shares to be purchased under any right or option must comply with the requirements of NYBCL § 504 (consideration and payment for shares).[2] The terms and conditions of rights or options, including when and at what price they may be exercised and any limitations upon transferability, must be set forth, or incorporated by reference, in instruments evidencing the rights or options.[3] In the absence of fraud in the transaction, the judgment of the board is conclusive regarding the adequacy of the consideration (tangible or intangible) received or to be received by the corporation for the issuance of the rights or options.[4]

Rights or Options to Directors, Officers, or Employees. The issuance of rights or options to directors, officers, or employees of a corporation (or a subsidiary or an affiliate), or to a trustee on their behalf, as an incentive to their service, must be (1) authorized by a majority of the votes cast at a meeting of shareholders by the holders of shares entitled to vote or (2) authorized by and consistent with a plan so

---

§ 1.31

1. NYBCL § 505(a)(1). In the case of a domestic corporation that has a class of voting stock registered with the Securities and Exchange Commission pursuant to the Exchange Act § 12 (15 U.S.C.A. § 78*l*), the terms and conditions of the rights or options may include restrictions or conditions on the receipt, exercise, or transfer of the rights or options (or even void the rights or options held) by interested shareholders or their transferees—a species of "poison pill" defense. NYBCL § 505(a)(2)(i). For the purpose of NYBCL § 505(a)(2)(i) the terms "voting stock," "Exchange Act," and "interested shareholder" have the same meanings as set forth in NYBCL § 912 (requirements relating to certain business combinations). *Cf.* NYBCL § 912 (d) (certain business combinations are not subject to NYBCL § 912 regulation (*e.g.*, a business combination of a domestic corporation having no class of voting stock registered with the S.E.C. under the Exchange Act § 12 unless the certificate of incorporation provides otherwise)). Determinations of the board to impose, enforce, waive, or otherwise render ineffective the restrictions or conditions permitted by NYBCL § 505(a)(2)(i) are subject to judicial review in an appropriate proceeding where the standard is whether the board acted in the best interests (long-term and short-term) of the corporation and its shareholders. NYBCL § 505(a)(2)(ii). The courts consider such factors as the corporation's prospects for potential growth, development, productivity, and profitability in connection with the board's action and its effects. *Id.* For other takeover defenses, *see, e.g.*, D. Logue, *Handbook of Modern Finance* (1984) pp. 29–44 to 29–51. *See infra*, § 1.81.

2. NYBCL § 505(b). *See supra*, § 1.30.

PRACTICE POINTER: If shareholders approve the issuance of rights or options, the approval may authorize the board to increase, by certificate of amendment under NYBCL § 805 (*see infra*, § 1.75), the authorized shares of any class or series to the number sufficient, when added to the previously authorized but unissued shares of the class or series, for the holders of the rights or options to purchase from the corporation authorized but unissued shares of that class or series. NYBCL § 505(g).

3. NYBCL § 505(c).

4. NYBCL § 505(h).

adopted by the shareholders.[5] A plan adopted by the shareholders must include the material terms and conditions of issuances thereunder.[6] Material terms and conditions include, but are not limited to, any restrictions on the aggregate number of shares that eligible individuals may have the right or option to purchase, the method of administering the plan, the terms and conditions of payment for shares in full or in installments, the issuance of certificates for shares to be paid for in installments, any limitations upon the transferability of the shares, and the voting and dividend rights to which the holders of the shares may be entitled, though full payment for the shares has not been made.[7] If shareholders approve the issuance of rights or options to individuals other than under an approved plan pursuant to NYBCL § 505(e), the grantees of the rights or options may not be granted voting or dividend rights until the shares to which they are entitled are fully paid.[8] If under the certificate of incorporation shareholders have preemptive rights to purchase any of the shares to be subject to rights or options, the issuance or plan must also be approved by the vote or written consent of the holders of a majority of the shares entitled to exercise the preemptive rights.[9] Upon such approval, the preemptive rights in question are extinguished.[10]

Library References:

West's Key No. Digests, Corporations ⚖︎74.

§ 1.32 Capital Structure—Stated Capital

The consideration received by a corporation upon the issuance of its shares constitutes stated capital to the extent of the par value of the shares.[1] For shares issued without par value, the entire consideration received constitutes stated capital unless the board within a period of

---

5. NYBCL § 505(d).

6. NYBCL § 505(e). *See also, supra,* § 1.31, note 3 and accompanying text.

7. NYBCL § 505(e). No certificate for shares may be delivered to a shareholder prior to full payment for the shares, unless the fact that the shares are partly paid is noted conspicuously on the face or back of the certificate. NYBCL § 505(e).

8. NYBCL § 505(f).

9. NYBCL § 505(d).

10. *Id.* In the absence of preemptive rights, nothing in NYBCL § 505(d) requires shareholder approval for the issuance of rights or options to purchase shares of the corporation in substitution for, or upon the assumption of, rights or options issued by another corporation, if the substitution or assumption is in connection with the other corporation's merger or consolidation with (or the acquisition of the other corporation's shares or assets by) the corporation or its subsidiary. *Id.* The provisions of NYBCL § 505 are inapplicable to the holders of convertible shares or bonds who have the right to acquire shares upon conversion under NYBCL § 519. NYBCL § 505(i).

§ 1.32

1. NYBCL § 506(a). *See supra,* § 1.5(10).

PRACTICE POINTER: The term "capital stock" is sometimes used in reference to a corporation's aggregate *outstanding* shares, both common and preferred, excluding surplus. *See, e.g.,* J. Bogen, *Financial Handbook* (4th ed. 1968) 8.21; Delaware General Corporations Law § 154. The term is, however, susceptible to other uses. *See, e.g.,* R. Hamilton, *The Law of Corporations* (2d ed. 1987) p. 446 (another term for common shares, often used when the corporation has only one class of shares outstanding); H. Ballantine, *On Corporations* (1946)

sixty days after issue allocates to surplus a portion, but not all, of the consideration.[2] For preferred shares without par value having a preference in the assets of the corporation upon involuntary liquidation, only the consideration, if any, in excess of the preference upon involuntary liquidation may be allocated to surplus.[3] None of the consideration for the issuance of shares without par value that is fixed by the shareholders pursuant to a right reserved in the certificate of incorporation may be allocated to surplus unless the allocation is authorized by vote of the shareholders.[4] The stated capital of a corporation may be increased from time to time by resolution of the board transferring all or part of the surplus of the corporation to stated capital, and the board may direct that the amount so transferred reflect the stated capital of any designated class or series of shares.[5]

Library References:
West's Key No. Digests, Corporations ⚖16.

§ 1.33 Capital Structure—Corporate Bonds; Convertible Securities

A corporation may issue bonds only for money, other tangible or intangible property, or labor or services actually received by or per-

pp. 478, 480, 584 and 625 (unfortunate ambiguity of term "capital stock" with varied meanings, encircled with confusion). *Cf.* RMBCA §§ 6.01 (authorized shares), 6.03 (issued and outstanding shares), 6.21 (issuance of shares), Official Comments. *See also, e.g.*, Wixon, Kell, and Bedford, *Accountants' Handbook* (5th ed. 1970) §§ 21.21–21.24 (trend away from the use of the term "capital stock"). The current use of the term in corporate annual reports also varies.

2. NYBCL § 506(b).

3. *Id.* Preferred stock is defined in NYBCL § 501(b), which provides that shares "entitled to preference in the distribution of dividends *or* assets" must not be designated as common shares (emphasis supplied). *See also,* NYBCL §§ 501(a) and 502(b). *Cf.* J. Bogen, *Financial Handbook* (4th ed. 1968) 13.19 (preferred shares have preference over dividends, may be preferred also as regards distribution of assets upon dissolution, and have other privileges not enjoyed by the common shareholders, but the dividend preference feature is the most important, and absent further stipulations, preferred shares will in other respects have all the rights of common shares); H. Guthmann and H. Dougall, *Corporate Financial Policy* (3d ed. 1955) p. 83 (preferred stock is granted a prior right to a stipulated dividend and usually a prior right to assets on liquidation); R. Wixon, W. Kell, and N. Bedford, *Accountants' Handbook* (5th ed. 1970) §§ 21.10–21.11 (most common claim of preferred stock is a prior claim on corporate earnings; significant provisions, among others, customarily included in preferred stock are cumulation of dividend priority and preferences to assets and dividends of corporate dissolution); R. Kay and D. Searfoss, *Handbook of Accounting and Auditing* (2d ed. 1989) pp. 20-2 to 20-3 (preferred stock rights usually consist of a preference in the distribution of earnings (dividends) and a preference in the distribution of assets upon liquidation); E. Faris, *Accounting and Law* (1984) pp. 238–40 (summarizes preferences possible).

4. NYBCL § 506(b).

5. NYBCL § 506(c). *See also,* NYBCL § 802 (reduction of stated capital by amendment); NYBCL § 516 (reduction of stated capital in certain cases); NYBCL § 102 (definition of stated capital); NYBCL § 806 (amount of stated capital in certificate of amendment).

PRACTICE POINTER: Stated capital is affected by various transactions: *e.g.*, on share distributions and changes (*see* NYBCL § 511(f) and (g). *See infra*, §§ 1.38, 1.39, and 1.72.

formed for the corporation (or for its benefit, or in its formation or reorganization), or a binding obligation to pay the purchase price thereof in cash or other property, or a binding obligation to perform services having an agreed value, or a combination thereof.[1] In the absence of fraud in the transaction, the judgment of the board with respect to the value of the consideration received is conclusive.[2] If a corporation distributes its own bonds to holders of any class or series of its outstanding shares, an amount of surplus equal to the principal amount of (and any accrued interest on) the bonds must be transferred concurrently to the liabilities of the corporation.[3] The amount of the surplus transferred reflects the consideration for the issue of bonds.[4] A corporation may, in its certificate of incorporation, confer upon the holders of any bonds issued or to be issued by the corporation rights to inspect the corporate books and records and to vote in the election of directors and on any other matters on which shareholders of the corporation may vote.[5]

Unless otherwise provided in the certificate of incorporation, and subject to the restrictions in NYBCL §§ 513 and 519(c) and (d), a corporation may issue shares or bonds convertible into or exchangeable for, at the option of the holder, the corporation, or another person, or upon the happening of a specified event, shares of any class, or shares of any series of any class, or cash, other property, indebtedness, or other securities of the same or another corporation.[6] If shareholders approve the issuance of convertible or exchangeable bonds or shares, they may permit the board, by certificate of amendment under NYBCL § 805, to increase the number of authorized shares of any class or series as necessary for the issuance of shares upon conversion or exchange of the bonds or shares.[7]

Convertible or exchangeable bonds or shares may be issued only if a sufficient number of authorized but unissued shares, or treasury shares, of the appropriate class or series have been reserved by the board to be available for issuance upon conversion or exchange of the bonds shares.[8] The aggregate conversion rights[9] of convertible or exchangeable bonds or

---

§ 1.33

1. NYBCL § 518(a).
2. Id.
3. NYBCL § 518(b).
4. Id.
5. NYBCL § 518(c). Recognizing that bondholders might become concerned about the management of the corporation, NYBCL § 518(c) empowers a corporation to give bondholders voting rights and inspection rights, which are usually made conditional upon default. See also, NYBCL § 501(a) (denial or limitation of voting rights of any class of shares not effective unless at the time other shares or bonds are entitled to full voting rights).

6. NYBCL § 519(a).
7. NYBCL § 519(b). See infra, §§ 1.73 and 1.75.
8. NYBCL § 519(c)(1). For a comparison of conversion features, warrants, and stock rights, see, e.g., D. Logue, Handbook of Modern Finance (1984) pp. 9–8 to 9–13. See supra, § 1.31.
9. **PRACTICE POINTER:** Convertible securities often are convertible only before or after a certain date, or during a limited number of years, after issuance, though some are convertible at any time during the life of the security. The "conversion right" is sometimes referred to as "conversion feature" or "conversion privilege." See, e.g., V.

shares may not exceed the aggregate number of shares reserved under NYBCL § 519(c)(1) plus any additional shares that may be authorized by the board under NYBCL § 519(b).[10] In the case of the conversion or exchange of shares of common stock *other than* into other shares of common stock, then a class or series of common stock not subject to conversion or exchange other than into other shares of common stock must remain outstanding.[11] Upon conversion or exchange of any shares or bonds, the corporation must receive at least the minimum consideration required to be received upon the issuance of new such shares.[12] NYBCL § 504(g) specifies how the consideration for shares issued upon conversion is to be allocated in the corporation's capital accounts.[13] Converted or exchanged shares must be cancelled.[14] When bonds have been converted or exchanged, they must be cancelled and not reissued except upon compliance with the provisions governing the issuance of convertible or exchangeable bonds.[15]

Library References:

West's Key No. Digests, Corporations ⊚63.1, 468.

§ 1.34 Capital Structure—Federal Income Taxation Aspects[1]

Organizational Expenditures. The organizational expenditures of a corporation may, at the election of the corporation, be treated as deferred expenses (*i.e.*, capitalized). In computing the corporation's taxable income, deferred expenses are allowed as a deduction ratably over a period not shorter than 60 months, as selected by the corporation, commencing with the month in which the corporation *begins business*.[2] The election must be made for any taxable year no later than the time prescribed by law (including any extension thereof) for filing the corpo-

---

Brudney and M. Chirelstein, *Cases and Materials on Corporate Finance* (3d ed. 1987) p. 223 ("conversion privilege—the right of the stockholder to convert the preferred stock into common stock"); J. Bogen, *Financial Handbook* (4th ed. 1968) §§ 14.30–14.33; D. Logue, *Handbook of Modern Finance* (1984) pp. 9–8 to 9–9; H. Guthmann and H. Dougall, *Corporate Financial Policy* (3d ed. 1955) pp. 85–86, 229 (convertible preferred stock), 146–148 (convertible bonds; bonds with warrants).

10. NYBCL § 519(c)(2).

11. NYBCL § 519(c)(3). This requirement does not apply to corporations of the type described in the exceptions to the provisions of NYBCL § 512(b) (redeemable shares). NYBCL § 519(c)(3). See *infra*, § 1.39, notes 16–18 and accompanying text.

12. NYBCL § 519(d).

13. *Id. See supra*, § 1.30.

14. NYBCL § 519(e).

15. *Id. See supra*, § 1.33, notes 6–10 and accompanying text.

§ 1.34

1. For a more detailed discussion of the tax issues outlined in this and other sections of this chapter, *see, e.g.*, B. Bittker and J. Eustice, *Federal Income Taxation of Corporations and Shareholders* (6th ed. 1994); M. Rose and J. Chommie, *Federal Income Taxation* (3d ed. 1988); J. Pratt and W. Kulsrud, *Corporate, Partnership, Estate, and Gift Taxation* (latest annual edition); S. Leimberg et al., *Stanley & Kilcullen's Federal Income Tax Law* (1994); M. Scholes and M. Wolfson, *Taxes and Business Strategy, A Planning Approach* (1992); CCH Std. Fed. Tax Rep. (annual edition).

2. I.R.C. § 248(a).

rate return for the taxable year; the period elected applies for computation of the taxable income of the corporation in the taxable year for which the election is made and in all subsequent taxable years.[3]

The term "organizational expenditure" means any amount paid or incurred that is (1) incident to the creation of the corporation, (2) chargeable to its capital account, and (3) of a character that, if expended incident to the creation of a corporation having a limited life, would be amortizable over that life.[4] Examples of organizational expenditures are amounts paid or incurred for (1) attorneys' fees for legal services related to the organization of the corporation, such as drafting the corporate charter, bylaws, minutes of organizational meetings, and terms of original stock issuances, (2) necessary accounting services, (3) expenses of temporary directors and of organizational meetings of directors and shareholders, and (4) fees imposed by the jurisdiction of incorporation (*e.g.*, filing fees paid to the Secretary of State).[5] Expenditures that are not organizational expenditures within the meaning of I.R.C. § 248 include expenditures related to (1) issuing or selling shares of stock or other securities of the corporation, such as commissions, professional fees, and printing costs, (2) transferring property to the corporation, and (3) reorganizing the corporation unless directly incident to the creation of a corporation.[6]

The date that a corporation begins business is a question of fact to be determined in each case in light of all the circumstances. For example, the acquisition of operating assets that are necessary to the conduct of the type of business contemplated may indicate the beginning of business.[7] When a corporation *begins business* is not the same as when a corporation *begins its existence*. Ordinarily, a corporation begins business when it starts the operations for which it is organized; it comes into existence on the date that it is incorporated.[8]

Start-up Expenditures. As a general rule, no deduction is allowed for start-up expenditures.[9] Start-up expenditures may, at the election of the taxpayer (here, the corporation), be treated as deferred expenses (*i.e.*, capitalized) to be allowed as a deduction prorated (amortized) in equal installments over a period not shorter than 60 months, as selected by the taxpayer, starting with the month in which the trade or business begins.[10] Where a taxpayer disposes of an entire trade or business before the end of the selected period, any deferred expenses that were not

---

3. I.R.C. § 248(c).
4. I.R.C. § 248(b).
5. Treas. Reg. § 1.248–1(b)(2). See supra, §§ 1.6–1.23.
6. Treas. Reg. § 1.248–1(b).
7. Treas. Reg. § 1.248–1(a)(3).
8. Id.
9. I.R.C. § 195(a).

10. I.R.C. § 195(b). As with organizational expenses, the period selected applies to computations of taxable income in the taxable year for which the election is made and in all subsequent taxable years. I.R.C. § 195(d)(2). The election must be made no later than the time prescribed for filing the return (including extensions thereof) for the taxable year in which the trade or business begins. I.R.C. § 195(d)(1).

allowed as a deduction by reason of I.R.C. § 195 may be deducted as losses to the extent allowable under I.R.C. § 165.[11]

The term "start-up expenditure" means any amount paid or incurred for (1) investigating the creation or acquisition of an active trade or business, (2) creating an active trade or business, or (3) any activity engaged in for profit and for the production of income before the date on which the active trade or business begins in anticipation of the activity becoming an active trade or business.[12] Start-up expenditures are those that, if paid or incurred in the operation of an existing trade or business in the same field, would be allowable as a deduction for the taxable year in which paid or incurred.[13] They do not include any amount allowed as a deduction under I.R.C. §§ 163(a) for interest expense, 164 for certain state and local taxes, or 174 for research and experimental expenditures.[14] The determination of when an active trade or business begins for purposes of start-up expenditures is made in accordance with regulations prescribed by the Secretary of the Treasury.[15] However, an acquired trade or business is treated as beginning when the taxpayer acquires it.[16]

Disregard of the Corporation for Income Tax Purposes. Occasionally, even though a taxpayer organizes in corporate form, the Internal Revenue Service does not recognize that form for tax purposes. The Commissioner has reclassified corporations as other organizations, or realigned certain corporate transactions, for tax purposes on the following grounds, although the entities remain corporations for other purposes:[17] (1) sham corporation (*i.e.*, the corporate form is sufficiently similar in substance to other business organizations (*e.g.*, partnership or proprietorship) to be taxed in the same way (substance over form));[18] (2) nominee and dummy corporations (*i.e*, the real party in interest is the shareholder, and the corporation is merely the shareholder's agent);[19] (3) income has been assigned (*i.e.*, the real earner of the income should pay the income tax);[20] (4) income should be reallocated (*i.e.*, if two or more

---

11. I.R.C. § 195(b)(2).
12. I.R.C. § 195(c)(1)(A).
13. I.R.C. § 195(c)(1)(B).
14. I.R.C. § 195(c)(1).
15. I.R.C. § 195(c)(2)(A). No regulations have been promulgated, but the position of the IRS has been that the standard for determining when a business begins for purposes of I.R.C. § 195 is different from the standard applicable for purposes of I.R.C. §§ 248 (organizational expenses for corporations) and 709 (organizational expenses for partnerships) even though the legislative history applicable to I.R.C. § 195 indicates that the determination of "when a business begins is to be made in reference to the existing provisions for the amortization of organizational expenditures" under I.R.C. §§ 248 and 709. Committee Report on P.L. 96–605 (Miscellaneous Revenue Act of 1980) reproduced at 1997 CCH Std. Fed. Tax Rep. ¶ 12,370.30.

16. I.R.C. § 195(c)(2)(B).

17. In some of these circumstances a court might also "pierce the corporate veil" for purposes of finding a corporation's shareholders liable for its debts. See supra, § 1.10.

18. *See, e.g.*, Patterson v. Comm., 25 T.C.M. 1230 (1966).

19. *See, e.g.*, Factor v. Comm., 281 F.2d 100 (9th Cir.1960).

20. *See, e.g.*, Lucas v. Earl, 281 U.S. 111, 50 S.Ct. 241, 74 L.Ed. 731 (1930); Helvering v. Horst, 311 U.S. 112, 61 S.Ct. 144, 85 L.Ed. 75 (1940); Frederick H. Fogle-

controlled business organizations, trades, or businesses have been chosen to evade taxes or do not clearly reflect income, the Commissioner may reallocate the income and deductions among them);[21] (5) personal service corporation used for tax avoidance or evasion purposes[22] (*i.e.*, where substantially all of the services of the personal service corporation are performed for (or on behalf of) *one* other corporation, partnership, or other entity and the *principal purpose* of forming (or availing) the corporation is tax avoidance or evasion by any employee-owner, the Commissioner may reallocate income and deductions between the personal service corporation[23] and its employee-owners[24] either to prevent tax evasion or to reflect income clearly.[25]

De Facto Corporations. If state corporate law recognizes as a corporation an organization that attempted but failed to comply with the requirements of incorporation, the IRS and the courts have also classified the organization as a corporation for tax purposes.[26]

Transfers of Property to a Controlled Corporation. Because Congress did not want the general tax rules applicable to exchanges under the Internal Revenue Code to discourage the formation of corporations,[27] it provided for an exception for the transfer of property to a corporation in exchange for the corporation's shares under certain circumstances, if the transfer is a mere change in the form of the transferor's investment. I.R.C. § 351(a) provides that no gain *or loss* is recognized or reported by a transferor or transferors of *property*[28] to a

---

song Co., T.C. Memo. 1976-294, 1976 WL 3474, 35 T.C.M. (CCH) 1309, 76,294 P–H Memo (TC) (1976), reversed and remanded by 621 F.2d 865 (7th Cir.1980), on remand to 77 T.C. 1102 (1981), reversed by 691 F.2d 848 (7th Cir. 1982)(cases discuss assignment of income and other principles used by Commissioner to disregard corporate form for tax purposes).

21. I.R.C. § 482.

PRACTICE POINTER: If a corporation deals with its controlling shareholder as shareholder-investor (and, *e.g.*, not as a shareholder-proprietor business), I.R.C. § 482 would not apply. *See, e.g.*, B. Bittker and J. Eustice, *Federal Income Taxation of Corporations and Shareholders* (6th ed. 1994) ¶ 13.20(2)(a).

22. I.R.C. § 269A(b)(1). *See infra*, §§ 1.122, note 5, 1.125, note 5.

23. *Id.*

24. I.R.C. § 269A(b)(2).

25. I.R.C. § 269A(a).

PRACTICE POINTER: I.R.C. § 269A(a) would not apply to corporations rendering services to more than one customer.

26. *See, e.g.*, Dennis M. O'Bryan, 62 T.C.M. (CCH) 1347 (1991). *See supra*, § 1.21, notes 26–28 and accompanying text.

27. I.R.C. §§ 61(a)(3) (gains from dealings in property are included in income) and 1001(a)-(c) (the gain realized from the sale or other disposition of property is the excess of the amount realized therefrom by the transferor over the transferor's adjusted basis of the property transferred; gain realized is recognized, except as otherwise provided in the I.R.C.). The transfer of property to a corporation in exchange for stock issued to the transferor fits within these statutory templates as "dealing in" and "disposition of" property, and thus the transaction would be taxable under these general rules absent an applicable exception (such as I.R.C. § 351). For transfers to a corporation in an international context, *see, e.g.*, B. Bittker and J. Eustice, *Federal Income Taxation of Corporations and Shareholders* ¶ 15.80 (6th ed. 1994). *See also, infra*, § 1.34, note 30.

28. **CAVEAT:** A transferor must contribute property, not services, for the stock issued in consideration therefor to be counted for control purposes. A person who has

§ 1.34 BUSINESS ORGANIZATIONS: CORPORATIONS Ch. 1

corporation if the property is transferred solely in exchange for the corporation's stock and, immediately after the exchange, the transferors of property have *control*[29] of the corporation.[30] Section 351 applies to

contributed, contributes, or will contribute services and receives stock from the corporation as compensation for the services rendered is taxed on the value of the stock received for the services. I.R.C. §§ 61(a)(1), 83 and 351(d).

PRACTICE POINTER: If a shareholder has provided, provides, or will provide services to the corporation and also transfers enough property to the corporation to be treated as a transferor of property, the transferor's stock will be counted for 80% control purposes although the value of the stock and securities received for the services contributed will be taxed as ordinary income. Treas. Reg. § 1.351–1(a)(2). Stock and securities issued to the transferor for property that is of relatively small value compared to the value of the stock and securities already owned (or to be received for services) by the transferor will not be treated as having been exchanged for property if the primary purpose is to qualify the transfer under I.R.C. § 351. Treas. Reg. § 1.351–1(a)(1)(ii). The property transferred is *not* considered to be of relatively small value if its fair market value is equal to, or in excess of, 10% of the fair market value of the stock or securities, or both, received by the transferor for *services* (*i.e.*, 1/11 of the fair market value of *all* the stock and securities received for services *and* the property). Rev. Proc. 77–37, 1977–2 C.B. 568.

CAVEAT: If the transferor does (or transferors of property as a group, if more than one transferor is involved, do) not have 80% control of the corporation, then the transfer (or each transfer) of property will not qualify under I.R.C. § 351 and the transferor (or each of the transferors) will have to recognize gain or loss on the transfer. I.R.C. §§ 61 and 1001(c). The corporation recognizes no gain on the transaction in any event. I.R.C. § 1032.

29. I.R.C. § 368(c) defines control as 80% of the voting shares and 80% of all other classes of shares.

30. The term "stock" includes shares of stock, whether common shares or preferred shares. I.R.C. § 368(c). Stock rights and stock warrants do not qualify as "stock." Treas. Reg. § 1.351–1 (a)(1).

PRACTICE POINTER: Qualifying for a tax-deferred exchange depends on whether or not the transferor is (or transferors of property are) in "control" of the corporation immediately after the exchange. The "immediately after" criterion does not necessarily require simultaneous exchanges by the transferors but comprehends a situation where the rights of the parties (transferor(s) and corporation) have been "previously defined" and the execution of the agreement proceeds with an "expedition consistent with orderly procedure." Treas. Reg. § 1.351–1(a)(1). Transitory control is not sufficient if the transferors agreed before the exchange to transfer enough of their stock to lose "control" or if the later transfer is an integral part of the plan of incorporation. *See, e.g.*, Rev. Rul. 70–140, 1970–13 I.R.B. 11; Rev. Rul. 79–522, 1970–41 I.R.B. 13; Manhattan Bldg. Co., 27 T.C. 1032 (1957) (step transaction doctrine). These factors may be given less weight in gift cases where the transferor and the transferor's donees control the corporation, as opposed to commercial arms' length transactions. *See, e.g.*, Stanton v. United States, 512 F.2d 13 (3d Cir.1975) (upon incorporation, transferor received 51% of stock and his wife 49%, held that transferor had control immediately after the exchange because he had the absolute right to designate who would receive stock).

With respect to a corporation formed outside the United States that is controlled by U.S. shareholders, a so-called controlled foreign corporation (or CFC), *see, e.g.*, Horwood and Hechtman, *Global Warning: Review the Subpart F Rules Before Going Abroad*, 21 J. of Corp. Taxation 366 (1995); Internal Revenue Service, Publication 953 International Tax Information for Business 2 (Rev. 1994); P. Postlewaite and T. Frantzen, *International Taxation, Corporate and Individual* §§ 10.02–10.06 (2d ed. 1995); M. Moore and E. Outslay, *U.S. Tax Aspects of Doing Business Abroad* (3rd ed. rev. 1991); M. Mulroney, *Foreign Income, Subpart F—Background, Basic Concepts and Terminology (Tax Management Portfolio (Bureau of National Affairs)* 1986, latest update); T. Bissell, *Controlled Foreign Corporations—Section 956* (1986, latest update); B. Bittker and L. Lokken, *Federal Taxation of Income, Estates and Gifts* Ch. 65.1, 66, 68, and 70 (1997); R. Doernberg, *International Taxation* Ch. 2, 9 (1993); J. Isenbergh, *Interna-*

transfers to corporations already controlled by the transferors as well as to newly-formed corporations controlled by the transferors.[31] In determining control, the fact that a *corporate* transferor distributes any of the stock received in the exchange to its shareholders is not taken into account.[32]

An exception to I.R.C. § 351(a) applies to each transferor who, in addition to receiving stock from the corporation, also receives money or other property (called boot) from the corporation.[33] Under this exception, gain *realized* (if any) by a transferor is *recognized* or reported by each transferor who receives boot, but the gain recognized may not exceed (1) the amount of money received by the transferor plus (2) the fair market value of other property received by the transferor.[34] The gain recognized by the transferor due to the boot received cannot exceed the gain realized on the transfer.[35] If, as additional consideration to the transferor, the corporation either assumes a liability of the transferor or acquires the property subject to a liability, then, as a general rule, these liabilities will not be treated as boot received by the transferor.[36] If, however, the transferor's principal purpose in incurring the liability was tax avoidance, or was not a *bona fide* business purpose (*e.g.*, the transferor borrows on the eve of the transfer without a business purpose), then the *total* amount of liabilities assumed (or subject to which property is taken) by the corporation (not merely the "tainted" liability) is treated as money (boot) received by the transferor on the exchange.[37]

The transferor's *basis* in the stock received in the exchange is (1) the same as the basis of the transferred property, (2) decreased by any boot received by the transferor (typically the amount of money and the

---

tional Taxation, U.S. Taxation of Foreign Taxpayers and Foreign Income Ch. 24, 25–29, and 32 (1990); B. Bittker and J. Eustice, *Federal Income Taxation of Corporations and Shareholders* ¶¶ 15.60 and 15.80 (6th ed. 1994); R. Rhodes and M. Langer, *U.S. International Taxation and Tax Treaties* (1997); J. Kuntz and R. Peroni, *U.S. International Taxation* (1992; Suppl. 1994); R. Lawrence, *International Tax and Estate Planning* (3rd ed. 1996); J. Pratt and W. Kulsrud, *Corporate, Partnership, Estate and Gift Taxation* 9–26 to 9–32 (1994 ed.). *See also, generally*, I.R.C. §§ 951–958; Treas. Reg. §§ 1.951–1, 1.952–1, 1.954–1, 1.954–2, 1.954–4, 1.957–1, 1.958–1, 1.958–2, 4.954–1. For other foreign corporations (such as foreign personal holding companies and passive foreign investment companies) and foreign source income, *see, e.g.*, B. Bittker and J. Eustice, *Federal Income Taxation of Corporations and Shareholders* ¶¶ 15.02, 15.20–15.24, 15.40–15.46 (6th ed. 1994).

31. *See, e.g.*, B. Bittker and J. Eustice, *Federal Income Taxation of Corporations and Shareholders* (6th ed. 1994) ¶ 3.01.

32. I.R.C. § 351(c).

33. I.R.C. § 351(b).

34. *Id.*

35. *Id.*

36. I.R.C. § 357(a).

37. I.R.C. § 357(b).

CAVEAT: If the aggregate liabilities assumed by the corporation, or to which the property is subject, (trade payables for cash method taxpayers not included) exceed the aggregate adjusted basis of the property transferred to the corporation, then the amount by which the liabilities on the property exceed the property's basis must be treated by the transferor as gain from the sale or exchange of property. I.R.C. § 357(c). This gain may be capital gain if the property transferred was a capital asset in the transferor's hands.

fair market value of other property received by a transferor, including any liability of the transferor either assumed by the corporation or to which the property transferred to the corporation was subject),[38] and (3) increased by the amount of gain recognized and any dividends received by the transferor on the exchange.[39] The basis of any other property (except money) received by transferor in consideration for the exchange is its fair market value.[40]

The general rule is that no gain or loss is recognized by a corporation on its receipt of money or other property in exchange for its stock.[41] This rule applies whether or not the *transferors* recognize gain on the transfer to the corporation either in a "tax-free" (*i.e.*, tax-deferred) I.R.C. § 351 transaction (because boot is received by the transferors) or in a fully-taxable transaction under I.R.C. § 1001(c).[42] If property is received by a corporation on a transaction to which I.R.C. § 351 applies (as paid-in surplus or as a contribution to capital), then the corporation's basis in the property received is (1) the same as the property's basis in the hands of the transferor (carryover basis) and (2) increased by the amount of gain recognized by the *transferor* on the transfer.[43]

Bargain Purchases. If an investor purchases a corporation's shares at less than fair market value, the bargain element might be considered income for tax purposes.[44]

---

38. I.R.C. §§ 358(a)(1)(A)(i)-(ii) and 358(d) (liabilities are treated as money received for purposes of determining *basis*).

39. I.R.C. § 358(a)(1)(B).

40. I.R.C. § 358(a)(2). Important for distinguishing short-term capital gain from long-term capital gain is the holding period of the shares. I.R.C. § 1223(1) provides that if the *basis* of the stock in the hands of the transferor (in whole or in part) is the same as the *basis* of the property transferred to the corporation, the transferor's *holding period* of the property transferred is added (tacked on) to the holding period of the stock received by the transferor from the corporation. This tacking-on rule applies only if the property transferred to the corporation was in the transferor's hands as either a capital asset under I.R.C. § 1221 or as so-called business-use property under I.R.C. § 1231. If the property transferred by the transferor was neither a capital asset nor I.R.C. § 1231 property in the transferor's hands, the holding period of the stock received by the transferor dates from the time of the exchange. If the property transferred to the corporation consists of any mixture of capital assets, I.R.C. § 1231 (business-use) property, and other (ordinary) assets, the stock will have varying holding periods, determined by some method of allocation. No single method of allocation appears to have been designated by the courts as appropriate. *See, e.g.*, Runkle v. Comm., 39 B.T.A. 458 (1939).

41. I.R.C. § 1032.

42. *Id.*

43. I.R.C. § 362. I.R.C. § 1223(2) provides that if the basis of the property received by the corporation is (in whole or in part) the same as the basis the property had in the hands of the transferor, the *corporation's* holding period for the property received by the corporation includes (tacks on) the period that the *transferor* held the property. I.R.C. § 1223(2) provides that the period the transferor held the property is tacked on to the corporation's holding period, regardless of the character of the property transferred to the corporation.

44. *See, e.g.*, Herwitz, *supra*, § 1.1, note 1, p. 99; 1997 U. S. Master Tax Guide ¶ 789 (1996).

PRACTICE POINTER: If investors pay the same price (equal to fair market value) per share, no bargain purchases would occur. In some cases, however, certain investors might pay a lower price per share than other investors.

CAVEAT: These cases are a trap for the unwary because the transaction could be

Tax Strategies on Transfers to Controlled Corporations. Where property to be transferred to a corporation has a basis that exceeds the property's value, transferors would realize a *loss* on the exchange. In such a case, a tax-deferred exchange under I.R.C. § 351 might be undesirable because the transferors might be able to offset a capital loss against their realized capital gains. Nevertheless, a taxable exchange resulting in the transferors' recognition of loss and consequent reduction of the corporation's basis in the property[45] may not be desirable *unless* the tax savings on recognition of the loss to the transferors outweigh the present value of the future tax savings to the corporation from the depreciation on the higher carryover basis[46] in a tax-deferred exchange. If, however, the property transferred to the corporation is not depreciable, a tax-deferred exchange may have no reason to be considered because a taxable exchange would permit the transferors to recognize the capital loss in that tax year. And if the stock is expected to be realigned by the IRS *as if* shares had first been received by the investors in proportion to the value of each of their contributions, then transferred to those who contributed proportionately less capital, with the transfer(s) characterized, depending on the circumstances, as a gift or as a payment to satisfy obligations of the transferor (*e.g.*, for compensation, rent, or interest owed). Treas. Reg. § 1.351–1(b)(1). Assume, as a fairly simple example, that investors A, B, C, and D form a corporation with capital contributions in exchange for equal shares in the corporation as follows: A, $50,000; B and C, each $25,000; and D, future services (because D can not contribute more than a nominal amount of cash to the enterprise). If the four founders agree to equal shares (to satisfy D's desire to have a significant proprietary stake in the enterprise (*i.e.*, in the future profits of the business and an equal voice in its affairs), each of them has a claim to 25% of the corporation's $100,000 initial capital). After their capital contributions to the corporation, an immediate transfer of an equity interest of $25,000 is, in effect, made by A, B, and C to D, with a proportionate dilution in the interests of A, B, and C. The bargain element transferred to D might be characterized, *e.g.*, as a gift (A is D's mother) or as compensation paid (A owes D for services rendered), depending on the circumstances. To avoid the implied transfer associated with an all common stock capital structure, senior securities could be issued (such as bonds and preferred stock) to investors contributing the bulk of the capital (A, B, and C). Voting common stock could be issued to *all* the investors in proportion to the amount paid for their common shares (equal shares here but in other proportions if they so agree, or they could agree to other control devices (*e.g.*, two classes of stock (one class issued to D, the other to A, B, and C) with each class having the right to elect a specified number of directors; or cumulative voting (*see supra*, §§ 1.3(6) and (7)). A, B, C, and D each would pay a nominal amount, say $1 per share, for a fourth of 400 common shares outstanding. They appear to have purchased their shares for an amount equal to the value of the common shares ($1), assuming that liquidation value is an appropriate method of valuing this *new* enterprise immediately after it is formed (*i.e.*, A, B, and C would have the right to receive in liquidation the first $100,000 of the corporation's assets in respect of their senior securities; A, B, C, and D as common shareholders would share the remaining $400 equally). No bargain element would seem to exist, and D as a result would have no compensation income. For a more detailed discussion of the corporate, tax, and valuation issues in close corporation settings (*i.e.*, incorporation of a new enterprise or of a going business), *see, e.g.*, Herwitz, *supra*, § 1.1, note 1, pp. 7–12, 94–105. *See also*, NYBCL § 504(a) (a corporation's shares may be issued for money, other property, and services rendered but not for services *to be* rendered). *See supra*, § 1.30. *See also*, *infra*, § 1.40 (disguised dividends and other payments).

45. I.R.C. § 1012 (corporation's basis: cost). The property's fair market value would be the corporation's cost.

46. I.R.C. § 362(a)(1).

held either a long time (so that the present value of the tax effects is negligible) or until the transferor's death, the tax advantage to the transferor of being able to deduct a loss on the exchange could be lost through a nontaxable exchange (because under I.R.C. § 1014 the basis of the stock received from a decedent is, as a general rule, the fair market value of the stock on the date of death; assuming that the decedent's *basis* in the property still exceeds the stock's value on that date, the recipients cannot deduct the difference if they eventually sell the stock because their basis was *stepped down* to fair market value at the date of death).

Similarly, when a transferor's property has a value that exceeds its basis, the transferor would realize a *gain* on the exchange. In this case, a tax-free transfer might be desirable for the transferors, but if gain were recognized by them, the corporation's basis in the property, as transferee, would be stepped up to the value of the property at the time of the exchange,[47] resulting in higher corporate depreciation deductions. The present value of the benefits to the corporation of the depreciation deductions could outweigh the transferors' present tax burden of their immediately recognizing gain in a taxable exchange.[48] Thus, the corporation's earnings against which depreciation could be deducted, as well as the transferors' capital gains and losses, together with the character of the property in the corporation's hands, should be considered in deciding whether either a tax-deferred or a taxable exchange will ultimately yield better results for the owners of the corporation.

If the transferors determine that a taxable transfer of property to the corporation is desirable, one possible way to effect such a transfer is for the transferors to fail the I.R.C. § 351 control test (*i.e.*, to have more than twenty percent of the stock issued in the transaction issued to someone who contributes only *services* (or services plus an insignificant amount of property)).[49] Another approach that may be feasible is for the transferors to sell the property to a third party, rather than contribute it to the corporation; the transferors could then transfer the cash from the sale in exchange for the corporation's stock.

Worthless Securities. Securities (*i.e.*, shares, rights to shares, and bonds and other evidences of corporate indebtedness)[50] that become worthless are treated by their holders as losses from the sale or exchange of a capital asset.[51] Special rules apply to gains and losses on so-called

---

47. I.R.C. § 1012 (corporation's basis: cost). *Cf.* I.R.C. § 362(a)(1), which applies to a tax-free exchange under I.R.C. § 351 (corporation's basis: carryover of transferor's basis plus gain, if any, recognized in the exchange by the transferor).

48. *See, e.g.*, Gus Russell v. Comm., 36 T.C. 965 (1961).

49. Only transferors of property are counted for purposes of the control test. I.R.C. § 351(a). *See supra*, § 1.34, note 28. The services would constitute "services actually received or performed for the corporation" for purposes of NYBCL § 504(a). *See supra*, § 1.30.

50. I.R.C. § 165(g)(2).

51. I.R.C. § 165(g).

small business stock, the effect of which is to give the shareholder a "heads I win (capital gain); tails the IRS loses (ordinary loss)" position.[52]

Pass-through of Income or Loss. In cases where a corporation qualifies for and elects "S" corporation status,[53] it will be able to pass through its income and losses to its owners for tax purposes. This possibility may be an important business planning consideration because it permits *double taxation* to be avoided while limited liability for the shareholders is retained. If a client would be better served by a non-corporate structure, how such an organization is classified for tax purposes has depended on an analysis of several characteristics that are associated with a corporation:[54] continuity of the business organization's life (*i.e.*, corporate existence continues even though shareholders sell their shares or die),[55] centralization of the organization's management (*i.e.*, authority to manage the business is concentrated in the corporate board of directors),[56] limited liability of the organization's owners (*i.e.*, shareholders' risk is limited to their investment),[57] and free transferability of the organization's ownership interests (*i.e.*, corporation's shareholders generally have this freedom of transferability).[58] If the alternative organization has a majority of corporate characteristics, it will be treated as an association for tax purposes and taxed as if it were a corporation[59] (even though the organization is a partnership or an LLC under New York law), which means that the pass-through feature will be lost for tax purposes and the client's objectives on this issue will be frustrated.[60]

---

52. I.R.C. §§ 1244 (losses on qualified small business stock deductible as ordinary loss, not as capital loss, up to $50,000 ($100,000 on a joint return)); 1202(a) (a noncorporate shareholder may exclude 50% of any gain (up to $10,000,000 or ten times the shareholder's basis in the stock) on the sale or exchange of qualified small business stock held for more than five years).

53. I.R.C. §§ 1361–1363.

54. Treas. Reg. § 301.7701–2(a).

CAVEAT: *But see, infra,* § 1.34, note 60, for new regulations effective Jan. 1, 1997.

55. Treas. Reg. § 301.7701–2(b).

56. Treas. Reg. § 301.7701–2(c).

57. Treas. Reg. § 301.7701–2(d).

58. Treas. Reg. § 301.7701–2(e).

PRACTICE POINTER: If desired restrictions on transferability of interests are likely to be considered unreasonable (*e.g.*, board consent is required for share transfers (*see supra*, § 1.21)), the corporate form (with or without an "S" corporation election for tax purposes) may not be feasible. Even with shareholder approval of such severe restrictions, they would probably be an invitation to litigation, and an alternative business form (*e.g.*, partnership) might have to be used.

59. Treas. Reg. § 301.7701–2(a).

60. The IRS has proposed a simplified elective system for classification of unincorporated organizations. Notice 95–14 (1995–14 I.R.B. 7). This system (the so-called "check-the-box" rules) became effective Jan. 1, 1997. Treas.Reg. §§ 301.7701–1 to 7701–3. *See also,* Stack, *Recent Developments Concerning Limited Liability Companies,* 67 N.Y. State Bar J. 50 (Sept./Oct. 1995). *See* Chapter 2 "Non–Corporate Entities: Limited Liability Companies and Partnerships," *infra.*

PRACTICE POINTER: A corporate general partner in a limited partnership might elect to be an "S" corporation to pass through partnership income and loss to its shareholders. However, under the prior system the corporate general partner must have had an adequate net worth to lack limited liability for current tax classification purposes. Treas. Reg. § 301.7701–2(d)(1). Personal liability of a corporate general partner of the limited partnership existed (and thus the *limited partnership* did not have the corporate characteristic of limited liability) when the corporate general partner had substantial assets, other than its

§ 1.34 BUSINESS ORGANIZATIONS: CORPORATIONS Ch. 1

Stock Options. Options might be granted to corporate directors, officers, and other employees in connection with the performance of services.[61] These options fall into two categories: nonqualified options[62] and qualified options.[63]

In a nonqualified option, if the *option* to purchase stock (as opposed to the underlying stock) has a readily ascertainable fair market value when granted, the grantee is taxed in the tax year in which the grant occurred, and the measure of the income to the grantee (reportable as ordinary income) is the difference between the fair market value of the option on that date and the amount, if any, paid by the grantee for the option.[64] If the option when granted has no readily ascertainable fair market value, the grantee will recognize ordinary income only upon the *exercise* of the option, equal to the spread between the fair market value of the *stock* on the date that the option is exercised and the amount the grantee paid for the stock (and the option, if anything).[65]

If the *stock* received upon the exercise of the option (1) is subject to a risk of forfeiture *and* (2) is not transferable, ordinary income will be recognized by the grantee when *either* the risk of forfeiture or the transfer restriction ends.[66] The grantee's basis in the stock will be equal to the amount, if any, paid for the option plus the amount of gain recognized either on the grant of the option, *or* on the exercise of the option, *or* when either the risk of forfeiture or the transfer restriction on

interest in the partnership. Treas. Reg. § 301.7701–2(d)(2); Rev. Proc. 89–12, 1989–7, I.R.B. 22, 1989–1 C.B. 798, amplified by 91–13, supplemented by 92–33, modified by 92–87, amplified by 94–46, modified by 95–10. Even if the corporate general partner was inadequately capitalized, and the limited partnership had the corporate characteristic of limited liability, it still might have been classified as a limited partnership for tax purposes because it did not have *three* or more corporate characteristics, and the pass-through feature would be preserved.

CAVEAT: The desirability and feasibility of retaining the limited liability of (and pass through (for tax purposes) of income and loss to) the owners are important issues to consider if other than a corporate form of business organization is used. The lack of limited liability of general partners in a general partnership (or general partner(s) in a limited partnership) or the loss of this protection in an LLC in some cases (*e.g.,* business operations in a jurisdiction that does not recognize the validity of LLCs) should be considered. The use of a *corporate* general partner in a partnership bestows limited liability on the *shareholders* of the corporate general partner, assuming that no reason exists for piercing the corporate veil (*e.g.,* even if the corporation is adequately capitalized for this determination (which may be different from adequate capital for tax classification purposes), other reasons for disregarding corporateness must not be present). The corporate general partner would have unlimited liability, and the shareholders would risk losing their investment in the corporation but no more, as a general rule. See supra, § 1.10.

61. For rights to buy stock distributed in a noncompensatory context, *see, e.g.,* I.R.C. §§ 305(a),(d). *Cf.* Comm. v. Lo Bue, 351 U.S. 243, 76 S.Ct. 800, 100 L.Ed. 1142 (1956); Hunley v. Comm., T.C. Memo. 1966-066, 1966 WL 1307, 25 T.C.M. (CCH) 355, ¶ 66,066 P–H Memo. TC (1966) (re noncompensatory bargain purchase of shares). See also, supra, § 1.34, note 44.

62. Treas. Reg. § 1.83–7(a).

63. I.R.C. § 422. See also, Master Tax Guide ¶¶ 1922–1934A.

64. I.R.C. § 83; Treas. Reg. §§ 1.83–1(a), 1.83–7(a). See also, Master Tax Guide ¶ 1923.

65. I.R.C. § 83; Treas. Reg. § 1.83–7(a). See also, Master Tax Guide ¶ 1924.

66. Treas. Reg. §§ 1.83–1 to 1.83–7.

the stock acquired upon the exercise of the option lapses, as the case may be.[67] The grantee is taxed at ordinary income rates at only *one* of these times. Further gain or loss will be reported as capital gain or loss, assuming that the relevant requirements for such treatment have been fulfilled, when the stock is either sold or exchanged in a taxable transaction.[68] The corporation is entitled to deduct the amount the grantee includes in his or her income in the same year that the grantee recognizes the income.[69]

In the case of a qualified option (also called statutory options or incentive stock options ("ISO's")), an employee will not recognize any gross income upon grant or exercise. Any gain realized upon the *sale* of the stock acquired upon exercise of the option is capital gain.[70] The corporation is not entitled to any deduction.[71]

Corporate Bonds. When a bondholder *pays* a *premium* to buy a bond, the bondholder may either (1) amortize the premium over the life of the bond and reduce the bond's basis by the amortized amount or (2) treat the premium as part of the bond's basis.[72] When a corporate borrower *receives* a *premium* on the issuance of its bonds, the corporation should include the premium in gross income prorated over the life of the bonds.[73] When a bondholder *buys* a bond at a *discount*, the bondholder must include the original issue discount in gross income over the life of the bond.[74] When a corporate borrower *receives* a *discounted* amount

67. CAVEAT: The basis of the stock includes the amount of gain recognized because the grantee includes the gain in gross income, and, having included the gain once in income, the grantee should not include it twice at some later time if the stock is sold. Double counting of the gain would occur if the basis of the stock were merely the amount paid for the stock and the option, since if the stock is sold later, the understated basis when subtracted from the amount realized on the sale would result in a gain realized that is overstated by the amount of gain recognized earlier.

68. The employee may elect to recognize income upon the exercise of the option, measured by the difference between the fair market value of the stock and the amount the employee paid for the stock (and the option, if anything). I.R.C. § 83(b).

PRACTICE POINTER: If the employee believes that the stock's value will increase substantially during the period the stock is subject to the forfeiture risk or transfer restriction, the employee might decide to elect to report the ordinary income on *exercise* of the option, rather than wait until either the forfeiture risk or restriction *lapsed* (and report a much larger amount of ordinary income, particularly if the stock poses some downside risk thereafter). Any appreciation (or decline) in the stock's value after the election would be taxed as capital gain (or loss) on the employee's sale of the stock later.

69. I.R.C. § 83(h).

70. I.R.C. § 422. *See also*, Master Tax Guide ¶¶ 1929–1930 (re restrictions on incentive stock options and statutory or qualified stock options).

71. Temp. Treas. Reg. § 14a.422A–1, Q & A–1.

72. I.R.C. § 171. *See also*, Treas. Reg. § 1.171–1; Master Tax Guide ¶ 1967. For special rules for bonds and other debt instruments, *see* IRC §§ 1271–1288. For convertible bonds, *see* I.R.C. §§ 171(b)(1) (amortization of premium paid for conversion feature disallowed); 249 (limited corporate deduction for premium paid to repurchase bond).

73. Treas. Reg. § 1.61–12(c)(2).

74. I.R.C. § 1272; Treas. Reg. § 1.1272–1. *See also*, Master Tax Guide ¶¶ 1950, 1952, 1956, 1958, 1961.

§ 1.34 BUSINESS ORGANIZATIONS: CORPORATIONS

for the bonds it issues, it may deduct the discount over the life of the bonds.[75]

§ 1.35 Capital Structure Summary

The capital structure of a corporation includes its equity and long-term debt securities. How stated capital and surplus are determined, and the circumstances under which stated capital is or may be reduced, are specified in the NYBCL. Corporations are authorized to issue common and preferred shares, as specified in the certificate of incorporation. Preferred shares may be issued in series, the terms of which may be fixed by the certificate of incorporation or by the board to the extent authorized by the certificate of incorporation. A corporation may issue bonds as well as convertible shares and convertible bonds. The NYBCL establishes rules for the irrevocability, enforceability, and other aspects of subscriptions for shares. The consideration acceptable as payment for shares is also specified. Corporations may issue rights and options to purchase shares; options and rights also may be issued to directors, officers, and employees of the corporation. The NYBCL dictates the form and content of certificates that represent shares and has specific rules on shares without certificates (uncertificated shares) and fractional shares.

Library References:

West's Key No. Digests, Corporations ⚖60–169.

§ 1.36 Capital Structure Checklist

1. Sources of capital. (*See* § 1.26)
2. Authorized shares. (*See* § 1.27)
    - Number
    - Par value or without par value?
    - More than one class?
    - Non-voting common shares?
    - Transfer restrictions? (*See* § 1.21)
    - Voting arrangements? (*See* §§ 1.45–1.47)
3. Preferred shares in series. (*See* § 1.28)
    - Dividend preference?
    - Liquidation preference?
    - Cumulative dividend? What rate? Any limit placed thereon?
    - Conversion rights? Conversion rate? Conversion period? Warrants v. conversion rights? Warrant exercise price?
    - Voting rights?

---

75. Treas. Reg. § 1.163–37(b).

Ch. 1   CAPITAL STRUCTURE CHECKLIST   § 1.36

- Sinking fund?
- Call feature?

4. Subscriptions for shares. (*See* § 1.29)
   - Irrevocable? How long?
   - Payment terms?
   - Penalties for default in payment for shares?

5. Consideration acceptable as payment for shares. (*See* § 1.30)
   - Money, other property, tangible or intangible, labor or services done?
   - Partly paid shares.
   - Allocation to surplus. (*See* § 1.32)

6. Rights and options to purchase shares. (*See* § 1.31)
   - Terms? When exercised? At what price?
   - Transfer restrictions?
   - Issuance to employees? Officers? Directors?

7. Stated capital. (*See* § 1.32)
   - Allocation to surplus on issuance of shares without par value?
   - Increases by transfer of surplus?
   - Reduction?
       (i) By amendment? Authorized by board? By shareholders?
       (ii) By board if permitted by certificate of incorporation?
       (iii) Disclosure requirements.

8. Certificated shares? Uncertificated shares? (*See* § 1.30)

9. Fractional shares? Scrip? Cash payment? (*See* § 1.30)

10. Corporate bonds. (*See* § 1.33)
    - Permissible consideration: money? Other property, tangible or intangible? Labor or services done?
    - Maturity date?
    - Right to inspect corporate books and records? Right to vote?
    - Convertible? Conversion period? Warrants attached?
    - Subordinated? Secured? Covenants acceptable to corporation?

11. Federal income tax implications; state organization tax. (*See* § 1.34)

§ 1.36 BUSINESS ORGANIZATIONS: CORPORATIONS   Ch. 1

Library References:

West's Key No. Digests, Corporations ⚙︎60–169.

§ 1.37 Distributions

A corporation may make distributions to its shareholders in a variety of transactions. For example, the board may declare a cash dividend to be paid by the corporation on its outstanding common and preferred shares.[1] A corporation may repurchase or reacquire its shares for cash in a redemption.[2] Distributions also may be made in connection with other corporate transactions such as recapitalizations,[3] mergers,[4] share exchanges,[5] the acquisition of assets or shares of another corporation,[6] or liquidations.[7]

§ 1.38 Distributions—Dividends; Share Distributions and Changes

Distribution of Dividends in Cash or Other Property. A corporation may declare and pay dividends or make other distributions in respect of its outstanding shares in cash, its bonds or property, including the shares or bonds of other corporations, except when the corporation is insolvent or would thereby be made insolvent, or when the declaration, payment, or distribution would be contrary to any restrictions contained in the certificate of incorporation.[1] Dividends may be declared or paid, and other distributions may be made, out of[2] surplus[3] only, so that the

---

§ 1.37

1. See *infra*, § 1.38.
2. See *infra*, § 1.39.
3. See *infra*, § 1.38, notes 15–36 and accompanying text.

PRACTICE POINTER: Very broadly speaking, recapitalizations involve a reshuffling of a corporation's capital structure. These transactions take different shapes, and the financial parlance has not uniformly described them. Distinctions among different terms for "recapitalization" and how it is accomplished are not sharply drawn. Some of the synonyms for recapitalization include: reclassification, readjustment, rearrangement, revision, stock dividend, stock split, reverse stock split, par value change, capital reduction, or debt readjustment. See, e.g., J. Bogen, *Financial Handbook* (4th ed. 1968) §§ 21.1–21.18.

4. See *infra*, §§ 1.81 and 1.82.
5. See *infra*, § 1.88.
6. See *infra*, §§ 1.81, 1.88 and 1.89.
7. See *infra*, § 1.107.

§ 1.38

1. NYBCL § 510(a).

2. *I.e.*, if (and to the extent) the measure of surplus permits the dividend payment.

3. See *supra*, § 1.5(11). See NYBCL § 517 for rules applicable to determining the amount or availability of surplus.

CAVEAT: NYBCL § 510 uses the phrase "*out of* surplus" (emphasis supplied) in the sense of an accounting *measuring rod*. The dividend is paid "with" or "in" cash (or "out of" the cash account). Statements of funds flow or of uses and sources of funds are helpful accounting tools, and surplus (*i.e.*, generally speaking, retained earnings (analogous to a part of surplus termed earned surplus) plus additional paid-in capital (analogous to a part of surplus termed capital surplus)) is, and describes, a source of funds in this accounting sense. But the corporation must distribute funds (*e.g.*, cash and other *assets*), not surplus, to its shareholders. The cash or other assets distributed do not come *out of* surplus in any physical sense; the corporation must have cash on hand (*e.g.*, reflected in the *cash* account, not in the surplus account, on its balance sheet). The permissible amount of cash to be distributed is *measured* by the

§ 1.38 DISTRIBUTIONS—DIVIDENDS

net assets[4] of the corporation remaining after the declaration, payment, or distribution equal at least the amount of its stated capital.[5] A dividend may be declared if the *value* of the corporate assets remaining after the dividend is paid is equal to or greater than the excess of the corporation's net assets over stated capital.[6] To determine whether a surplus

surplus account, but the surplus account should not be viewed as containing cash or other assets out of which dividends are paid. For example, a corporation could have cash but no surplus, in which case no dividend would be permitted. Or it could have a surplus but no cash, in which case a dividend would be permitted if it could raise enough cash (*e.g.*, by borrowing the cash needed in exchange for a promissory note issued (payable) to the lender). *See supra*, §§ 1.5(7) and 1.5(11).

4. *See supra*, § 1.5(7).

CAVEAT: The value of its net assets must be determined by the board. *See infra*, § 1.38, note 6.

5. *See supra*, § 1.5(10). A corporation engaged in the exploitation of natural resources or other wasting assets, including patents, or formed primarily for the liquidation of specific assets, may declare and pay dividends or make other distributions in excess of its surplus, computed after taking due account of depletion and amortization, to the extent that the cost of the wasting or specific assets has been recovered by depletion reserves, amortization, or sale, if the net assets remaining after such dividends or distributions are sufficient to cover the liquidation preferences of shares having such preferences in involuntary liquidation. NYBCL § 510(b).

6. The excess of net assets over stated capital equals surplus. *See supra*, §§ 1.5(7)(net assets); 1.5(10)(stated capital); 1.5(11)(surplus). The value of the corporation's net assets may include increases resulting from a revaluation of its assets, but the directors must account for all assets at actual value (not book value), must consider unrealized depreciation and unrealized appreciation, and must determine the value of the corporation's assets at each dividend declaration. *See, e.g.*, Randall v. Bailey, 23 N.Y.S.2d 173 (Sup.Ct., N.Y. County, 1940), aff'd 262 App.Div. 844, 29 N.Y.S.2d 512 (1st Dep't 1941), motion denied, 262 App.Div. 994, 30 N.Y.S.2d 808; appeal granted 287 N.Y. 857, 39 N.E.2d 309, aff'd 288 N.Y. 280, 43 N.E.2d 43 (1942); Vowteras v. Argo Compressor Service Corp., 83 A.D.2d 834, 441 N.Y.S.2d 562 (2d Dep't 1981); appeal denied 55 N.Y.2d 605, 447 N.Y.S.2d 1028, 432 N.E.2d 603 (1982). *Cf.* Henn and Alexander, *supra*, § 1.1, note 1, pp. 894–897, notes 38, 57, 58, 60, and 61. *But see*, C. Israels, *Corporate Practice* (2d ed. 1969) pp. 340–348 (*Randall* and unrealized appreciation discussed); J. Cox, *Financial Information, Accounting, and the Law: Cases and Materials* (1980) pp. 257 (*Randall* and unrealized appreciation discussed) 703; Herwitz, *supra*, § 1.1, note 1, 230–240 (*Randall* and unrealized appreciation discussed); the term "value of assets" in the predecessor to NYBCL § 510 not included in NYBCL § 510, but former NYBCL § 102(a)(6) (earned surplus) stated that unrealized appreciation of assets is not included in earned surplus, leaving inference that such appreciation is permitted to be included in capital surplus, and available for dividends, subject to the notice requirement in NYBCL § 510(c)); J. Bogen, *Financial Handbook* (4th ed. 1968) §§ 18.18–18.23 (NYBCL § 510 and other state's dividend provisions discussed). On revaluation of plant, *see, e.g.*, Wixon, Kell and Bedford, *Accountant's Handbook* (5th ed. 1970) §§ 18.1–18.49 (various valuation methods used in appraisals are discussed, such as: replacement cost, reproduction cost, income capitalization, market data or comparative approach, fair market value, and fair value); 22.30–22.32 (revaluation increases for dividend purposes discussed).

CAVEAT: Although NYBCL § 510 would appear to permit unrealized appreciation to be included in surplus for dividend purposes, caution must be the standard, given the liability of directors for improper dividends. NYBCL § 719(a)(1). *See infra*, § 1.66. Although directors are permitted under NYBCL § 717 to rely on information, opinions, reports, or statements, including financial statements and other financial data presented by public accountants and certain other persons, directors should be conservative in this regard to avoid an overstatement of revaluation surplus and, hence, surplus.

§ 1.38   BUSINESS ORGANIZATIONS: CORPORATIONS   Ch. 1

exists, assets cannot be valued on a mere expectation of profits.[7] Even if a surplus does not exist as cash on hand, a corporation may incur debt to pay the dividend if the corporation has a surplus[8] and capital is unimpaired.[9]

Dividend Policy. Apart from whether a corporation meets the tests for dividend payments under the NYBCL,[10] whether and to what extent a corporation should pay dividends depends upon the status of its affairs, financial condition, problems, and prospects.[11] Whether or not a distribution should be made is exclusively a matter of business judgment for the corporation's board of directors, and though the directors have wide discretion, they must exercise it within legal limits.[12] Courts will not ordinarily interfere with the internal affairs and management of a corporation by its board of directors so long as its discretion is not abused.[13] The board's action regarding dividends is conclusive in the absence of bad faith, private advantage, or other breach of duty.[14]

Share Distributions (Stock Dividends). A corporation may make *pro rata* distributions of its authorized but unissued shares to holders of any class or series of its outstanding shares.[15] If shares are distributed, they must be issued at not less than their par value (or stated value), and an amount of surplus equal to the aggregate par value of (or stated value represented by) the shares must be transferred to stated capital at the time of the distribution.[16] If a distribution of shares without par value is made, the amount of stated capital to be represented by each such share must be fixed by the board, unless the certificate of incorporation reserves to the shareholders the right to fix the consideration for

---

7. Hutchinson v. Curtiss, 45 Misc. 484, 92 N.Y.S. 70 (Sup.Ct., N.Y. County, 1904) (corporate contracts for future deliveries of its product not yet produced from raw material not yet purchased cannot be taken into account).

8. Cox v. Leahy, 209 App.Div. 313, 204 N.Y.S. 741 (3d Dep't 1924). *See also*, Frank Gilbert Paper Co. v. Prankard, 195 N.Y.S. 638 (Sup.Ct., Schenectady County, 1922), affirmed by 204 A.D. 83, 198 N.Y.S. 25 (3d Dep't 1923).

9. Weinberger v. Semenenko, 36 N.Y.S.2d 396 (Sup.Ct., N.Y. County, 1942).

10. The two tests are that the corporation (1) is not currently insolvent and will not be rendered insolvent by the distribution and (2) has a surplus. NYBCL § 510(a) and (b).

11. *See, e.g.*, Gordon v. Elliman, 280 App.Div. 655, 116 N.Y.S.2d 671 (1st Dep't 1952), appeal granted 281 App.Div. 745, 118 N.Y.S.2d 733, aff'd 306 N.Y. 456, 119 N.E.2d 331 (1954). *See also*, J. Bogen, *Financial Handbook* (4th ed. 1968) §§ 18.16–18.18; H. Guthmann and H. Dougall, *Corporate Financial Policy* (3d ed. 1955) pp. 512–529.

12. *See, e.g.*, Swinton v. W.J. Bush & Co., 199 Misc. 321, 102 N.Y.S.2d 994 (Sup. Ct., N.Y. County, 1951), aff'd 278 App.Div. 754, 103 N.Y.S.2d 1019; appeal denied 278 App.Div. 823, 105 N.Y.S.2d 408 (1st Dep't 1951); Kamin v. American Exp. Co., 86 Misc.2d 809, 383 N.Y.S.2d 807 (Sup.Ct., N.Y. County, 1976), aff'd 54 A.D.2d 654, 387 N.Y.S.2d 993 (1st Dep't 1976).

13. *See, e.g.*, Lockley v. Robie, 276 App. Div. 291, 94 N.Y.S.2d 335 (4th Dep't 1950), modified on other grounds 301 N.Y. 371, 93 N.E.2d 895 (1950), reargument denied 301 N.Y. 731, 95 N.E.2d 409 (1950).

14. Lippman v. New York Water Service Corp., 25 Misc.2d 267, 205 N.Y.S.2d 541 (Sup.Ct., N.Y. County, 1960); appeal conditionally dismissed 12 A.D.2d 611, 214 N.Y.S.2d 715 (1st Dep't 1960).

15. NYBCL § 511(a).

16. NYBCL § 511(a)(1).

the issue of the shares.[17] A distribution of shares of a certain class or series may be made to holders of that or any other class or series of shares, unless the certificate of incorporation provides otherwise.[18] A corporation making a *pro rata* distribution of authorized but unissued shares to the holders of any class or series of outstanding shares may at its option make an equivalent distribution upon treasury shares of the same class or series, and the shares distributed must be treasury shares.[19]

No transfer from surplus to stated capital need be made on a distribution of treasury shares to holders of any class of outstanding shares, or on a stock split or division of issued shares of any class into a greater number of shares of the same class, or on the combination of issued shares of any class into a lesser number of shares of the same class, if no increase results in the aggregate stated capital represented by the shares.[20] A corporation may make other transfers from surplus to stated capital in connection with share distributions or other transactions.[21]

Procedure. Any distribution to shareholders of certificates representing a share distribution or a change of shares that affects stated capital or surplus must be accompanied by a written notice to the shareholders (1) disclosing the amounts by which the distribution or change affects stated capital and surplus or (2) if the amounts cannot be determined at the time of the notice, disclosing the approximate effect of the distribution or change on the corporation's stated capital and surplus, and stating that the amounts are not yet determinable.[22]

Changes in Issued Shares. A change in a corporation's issued shares of any class that increases the stated capital represented by those shares[23] may be made if the surplus of the corporation is sufficient to

---

17. NYBCL § 511(a)(2).

18. NYBCL § 511(a)(3). A distribution of any class or series of shares is subject to the preemptive rights, if any, applicable to such shares pursuant to the NYBCL. NYBCL § 511(a)(4). *See infra*, § 1.52.

CAVEAT: In the case of a corporation incorporated prior to the effective date of NYBCL § 511(a)(4), a distribution of shares of any class or series of shares of such corporation, so long as any shares of such class remain outstanding, may be made only to holders of the same class or series of shares unless the certificate of incorporation permits distribution to holders of another class or series or unless the distribution is approved by the affirmative vote or the written consent of the holders of a majority of the outstanding shares of the class or series to be distributed. NYBCL § 511(a)(3).

19. NYBCL § 511(b).

20. NYBCL § 511(d).

21. NYBCL § 511(e).

22. NYBCL § 511(f).

CAVEAT: Failure to comply with the notice requirement of NYBCL § 511(f) makes the corporation liable for damages sustained by any shareholder in consequence of such failure. NYBCL § 520.

23. For example, recapitalizations or reclassifications work changes from par shares to no-par shares of higher stated value, changes from no-par shares to par shares, increases in per share par or stated value, or increases in the number of shares without changing par or stated value per share.

PRACTICE POINTER: Recapitalizations are undertaken for various reasons. A

permit the amount of the increase to be transferred from surplus to stated capital and if the transfer is concurrently made.[24] When issued shares are changed in any manner that affects the corporation's capital accounts (stated capital or surplus), and no distribution to shareholders of certificates representing any shares resulting from the change is made,[25] the corporation must disclose the effect of the change upon its capital accounts to shareholders.[26]

Procedure. A change in issued shares is accomplished by an amendment to the certificate of incorporation authorized by board resolution and followed by shareholder approval and, in some instances, a class vote.[27] Disclosure must be made in the next financial statement covering the period in which the change occurs furnished to shareholders of the class or series affected, or, if practicable, in the first notice of dividend, share distribution, or change that is furnished to the shareholders between the date of the change and the next financial statement, or, in any event, within six months after the date of the change.[28]

Reduction of Capital. Unless the certificate of incorporation otherwise provides, the board may at any time reduce a corporation's stated capital by eliminating from stated capital any portion of amounts previously transferred from surplus and not allocated to any designated class or series of shares.[29] Stated capital can also be reduced by reducing or eliminating any amount represented by issued shares having a par value that exceeds the aggregate par value of the shares,[30] by reducing the

---

common practice is to reduce the stated capital account through a recapitalization because the reduction in stated capital is transferred to surplus and thus augments the measuring rod by which the amount of permissible cash dividends is determined. Stock splits, which increase the number of shares, commonly are effected to reduce the stock's price to broaden the market for the corporation's shares and to reduce the earnings per share. Corporations effect reverse splits to narrow the market for the corporation's shares, to increase the earnings per share, or to freeze out a minority interest. *See supra*, § 1.30, note 16. *See infra*, §§ 1.51, 1.81, note 1. Other changes in capital structure commonly provide opportunities for an improvement in a corporation's financial or strategic position (*e.g.*, increase surplus after incurring large operating deficits, reduce voting stock outstanding, simplify the capital structure, eliminate noncallable and high dividend preferred shares, and eliminate dividend arrearages on cumulative preferred shares). *See, e.g.*, J. Bogen, *Financial Handbook* (4th ed. 1968) §§ 21.1–21.14; Henn and Alexander, pp. 285–294, 402–408, 975–979.

24. NYBCL § 511(c).

25. PRACTICE POINTER: Some recapitalizations or reclassifications work a change in a corporation's capital structure by, *e.g.*, changing with respect to any class the (1) number of shares authorized or issued, (2) par value or stated value, or (3) designation, rights, preferences, and limitations of any series. *See, e.g.*, NYBCL §§ 801(b)(7)–(12), 802(a), and 806(b). Newly authorized shares can be exchanged for old shares, which are cancelled.

26. NYBCL § 511(g).

CAVEAT: Failure to comply with the disclosure requirement of NYBCL § 511(g) makes the corporation liable for damages sustained by any shareholder in consequence of such failure. NYBCL § 520.

27. *See infra*, §§ 1.73 and 1.74.

28. NYBCL § 511(g).

29. NYBCL § 516(a).

30. This excess presumably refers to the amounts transferred to stated capital, whether upon the distribution of shares or other transaction. NYBCL § 102(a)(12)(C). The directors would appear to have the power to capitalize an amount of surplus in excess of the par value of the shares distrib-

amount of stated capital represented by issued shares without par value, or by applying to an otherwise authorized purchase, redemption, conversion, or exchange of outstanding shares some or all of either (1) the stated capital represented by the shares being purchased, redeemed, converted, or exchanged or (2) any stated capital that has not been allocated to any particular shares, or both.[31] After the reduction, stated capital must exceed (1) the amounts payable upon involuntary liquidation in respect of all issued shares having preferential rights in assets plus (2) the par value of all other issued shares with par value.[32] Disclosure of the amount of reduction of capital must be made.[33]

Procedure. A reduction of capital may be effected by the board[34] or by amendment of the certificate of incorporation authorized by the board, followed by shareholder approval.[35] Disclosure of a reduction of capital must be made in the next financial statement covering the period in which the reduction occurs (and that is furnished to all its shareholders) or, if practicable, in the first notice of dividend or share distribution that the corporation furnishes shareholders between the date of the reduction and the next financial statement, and, in any event, to all its shareholders within six months after the date of the reduction.[36]

Library References:

West's Key No. Digests, Corporations ⇔152–157.

uted (*e.g.*, equal to the market value less the par value of the shares distributed where the number of additional shares is small enough not to affect the market price). *See, e.g.*, Wixon, Kell, and Bedford, *Accountant's Handbook* (5th ed. 1970) §§ 21.42–21.45. *See supra*, §§ 1.5(10), 1.32 and 1.38, notes 23–29 and accompanying text.

31. NYBCL § 516(a). However, notwithstanding these permitted ways to reduce capital by the board, if the consideration for the issue of shares without par value was fixed by the shareholders under NYBCL § 504, the board may not reduce the stated capital represented by the shares except to the extent, if any, that the board was authorized by the shareholders to allocate any portion of the consideration to surplus. *Id.*

PRACTICE POINTER: One purpose of a reduction of capital is to increase surplus, which is the measuring rod for the payment of dividends. *See also, supra*, § 1.38, note 30.

32. NYBCL § 516(b).

33. NYBCL § 516(c).

34. NYBCL § 516(a). A reduction of capital may also be achieved by the corporation's repurchasing its shares at less than the amount representing the shares in the corporation's capital accounts. *See supra*, § 1.38, notes 30 and 38 and accompanying text. *See infra*, § 1.39, notes 22–26 and accompanying text.

35. NYBCL §§ 802 and 803. *See also*, NYBCL § 806(b)(1) and (b)(3). *See infra*, §§ 1.72–1.73.

36. NYBCL § 516(c).

CAVEAT: Failure to comply with the disclosure requirement of NYBCL § 516(c) makes the corporation liable for damages

§ 1.39 Distributions—Purchase or Redemption of Shares

Shares may be purchased or redeemed only out of surplus.[1] Notwithstanding any authority contained in the certificate of incorporation, the shares of a corporation may not be purchased by the corporation (or, if the shares are redeemable, convertible, or exchangeable, may not be redeemed, converted, or exchanged) in each case for or into cash, other property, indebtedness, or other securities of the corporation (other than shares of the corporation and rights to acquire such shares) when the corporation is then insolvent or would be rendered insolvent by the redemption, conversion, or exchange.[2] When the corporation purchases its redeemable,[3] convertible, or exchangeable shares within the period during which such shares may be redeemed, converted, or exchanged at the option of the corporation, the purchase price thereof may not exceed the applicable redemption, conversion, or exchange price stated in the certificate of incorporation.[4] Upon a redemption, conversion, or exchange, the amount payable by the corporation for shares having a cumulative preference on dividends may include the stated redemption, conversion, or exchange price plus accrued dividends to the next dividend date following the date of redemption, conversion, or exchange of such shares.[5] A corporation may create sinking funds for the redemption or purchase of, and certain other transactions with respect to, its shares.[6]

An agreement by a corporation to purchase its own shares from a shareholder is enforceable to the extent it is permitted at the time of purchase by NYBCL § 513.[7] That a corporation may not be able to purchase its shares under NYBCL § 513 is not a ground for denying to either party specific performance of the agreement if at the time for performance the corporation can purchase all or part of the shares under NYBCL § 513.[8] A domestic corporation that is subject to the provisions of NYBCL § 912[9] may not purchase or agree to purchase, in connection with certain business combinations,[10] more than ten percent of its stock[11] from a shareholder for more than the stock's market value[12] unless the

sustained by any shareholder in consequence of such failure. NYBCL § 520.

§ 1.39

1. *I.e.*, if a surplus exists or to the extent of (or measured by) surplus.

CAVEAT: NYBCL § 513(a) uses the phrase "purchase ... or redeem ... *out of surplus*" (emphasis supplied) in the sense of an accounting *measuring rod*. But the corporation must use (distribute) funds (*e.g.*, cash and other assets), not surplus, to acquire its shares. This limitation is similar to the one that applies to dividends. *See supra*, § 1.38, notes 2 and 3.

2. NYBCL § 513(a).

3. Redeemable shares are commonly termed callable.

4. NYBCL § 513(b).

5. *Id.*

6. NYBCL § 512(d). *See also*, NYBCL § 513.

7. NYBCL § 514(a). *See supra*, § 1.39, note 1 and accompanying text.

8. NYBCL § 514(b). *See supra*, § 1.39, note 1 and accompanying text.

9. *See infra*, §§ 1.81, 1.82, 1.85, 1.88, and 1.89.

10. *See infra*, §§ 1.81 and 1.89.

11. As defined in NYBCL § 912.

12. As defined in NYBCL § 912.

purchase or agreement to purchase is approved by the board of directors, and a majority of the votes of all outstanding shares entitled to vote (unless the certificate of incorporation requires a greater percentage of the votes of the outstanding shares for approval).[13]

Redeemable Shares. Subject to the restrictions contained in NYBCL § 513 (purchase, redemption, and certain other transactions by a corporation with respect to its own shares) and NYBCL § 512(b), a corporation may provide in its certificate of incorporation for one or more classes or series of shares that are redeemable,[14] in whole or in part, at the option of the corporation, the holder, or another person, or upon the happening of a specified event.[15] No redeemable common shares (other than shares of an investment company,[16] a member corporation of a national securities exchange registered under a statute of the United States such as the Securities Exchange Act of 1934,[17] or a corporation described in NYBCL § 512) may be issued or redeemed *unless* the corporation at the time has outstanding a class of common shares that is not subject to redemption.[18] When a corporation purchases its redeemable, convertible, or exchangeable shares within the redemption period, during which such shares may be redeemed, converted, or exchanged at the option of the corporation,[19] the purchase price may not exceed the price specified in the certificate of incorporation.[20] Upon a redemption, conversion, or exchange, the amount payable by the corporation for shares having a cumulative preference on dividends may include the specified redemption price plus accrued dividends to the next dividend

---

13. NYBCL § 513(c). The provisions of NYBCL § 513(c), which prohibit "greenmail," do not apply when the domestic corporation offers to purchase shares from all holders of stock or shares of stock that the holder has been the beneficial owner of (as defined in NYBCL § 912) for more than two years. NYBCL § 513(c).

14. Redeemable shares are commonly termed callable.

15. NYBCL § 512(a).

16. As defined in the Investment Company Act of 1940 (15 U.S.C.A. §§ 80a–1 *et seq.*), as amended. NYBCL § 512(b).

17. 15 U.S.C.A. §§ 78 *et seq.*

18. NYBCL § 512(b). Any common shares of a corporation that directly (or through a subsidiary) has a license or franchise to conduct a business that is conditioned upon some or all of the holders of the corporation's common shares possessing prescribed qualifications may be made subject to redemption to the extent necessary to prevent the loss of, or to reinstate, the license or franchise. *Id. See infra*, §§ 1.122 and 1.125.

19. **PRACTICE POINTER:** Although redeemable preferred shares have no maturity date, some provision is frequently made for periodic retirement at a specified price on certain advance notice. The call price for preferred shares is normally set at an amount equal to par plus a premium of, say, the annual dividend (to compensate the holder for termination of the investment). Sometimes a sinking fund is used to retire shares according to a set schedule. *See, e.g.,* R. Brealey and S. Myers, *Principles of Corporate Finance* (4th ed. 1991) pp. 320–321; D. Logue, *Handbook of Modern Finance* (1984) p. 9–5; H. Guthmann and H. Dougall, *Corporate Financial Policy* (3d ed. 1955) p. 90; J. Bogen, *Financial Handbook* (4th ed. 1968) §§ 13.21–13.22.

20. NYBCL § 513(b). Shares of any class or series that may be made redeemable under NYBCL § 512 may be redeemed for cash, other property, indebtedness, or other securities of the corporation, or another corporation, at such time or times, price or prices, or rate or rates, and with such adjustments, as is stated in the certificate of incorporation. NYBCL § 512(c).

date following the date of redemption, conversion, or exchange of such shares.[21]

Reacquired Shares. Issued shares that have been purchased, redeemed, or otherwise reacquired by a corporation must be cancelled if they are reacquired out of stated capital, if they are converted shares, or if the certificate of incorporation requires that such shares be cancelled upon reacquisition.[22] Any shares reacquired by the corporation and not required to be cancelled may be either retained as treasury shares or cancelled by the board at the time of reacquisition or at any time thereafter.[23] Neither the retention of reacquired shares as treasury shares, nor their subsequent distribution to shareholders or disposition for consideration, changes stated capital.[24] Cancelled shares are restored to the status of authorized but unissued shares.[25] However, if the certificate of incorporation prohibits the reissue of any shares required or permitted to be cancelled under NYBCL § 515(e), the board must, by certificate of amendment under NYBCL § 805, reduce the number of authorized shares accordingly.[26]

Library References:

West's Key No. Digests, Corporations ⋘82.

§ 1.40 Distributions—Federal Income Tax Aspects

Distributions of Cash and Other Property. For tax purposes, distributions of cash or other property are treated as *dividends* and included in the *income* of the *shareholders* to the extent of the corporation's earnings and profits.[1] Amounts, if any, distributed in excess of corporate earnings and profits are treated as a return of each shareholder's basis in the shares.[2] To the extent that the distribution exceeds both the corporation's earnings and profits and each shareholder's basis, it is treated as a gain to the shareholder from the sale or exchange of property.[3] As a general rule, distributions of corporate shares (and rights to acquire shares) are not included in the income of shareholders.[4]

---

21. *Id. See also,* NYBCL § 515.
22. NYBCL § 515(a).
23. NYBCL § 515(b).
24. NYBCL § 515(c). When treasury shares are disposed of, the surplus is increased by the full amount of the consideration received. *Id.*
25. NYBCL § 515(d).
26. *Id. See supra,* §§ 1.32, note 5 and 1.38, notes 29–36 and accompanying text.

§ 1.40
1. I.R.C. §§ 301(c)(1) and 316(a).

2. I.R.C. § 301(c)(2).
3. I.R.C. § 301(c)(3).
4. I.R.C. § 305(a).

CAVEAT: An exception to the general rule applies to certain distributions specified in I.R.C. § 305(b) (re distributions of shares in lieu of money, disproportionate distributions, distributions of common and preferred shares, preferred share distributions, and distributions of convertible preferred stock).

A *corporation* does not recognize gain or loss on any distribution of property or its shares (or rights to acquire its shares), in respect of its outstanding shares.[5] However, distributions of appreciated property are treated as if the corporation had sold the property to the shareholder.[6]

Dividends and other distributions in respect of a corporation's shares are not deductible by a corporation, whereas interest paid or accrued by a corporation on its indebtedness is deductible.[7] Whether or not the corporation's indebtedness is treated for tax purposes as equity depends on the facts.[8]

Stock and Stock Rights Distributed. As a general rule, a shareholder does not recognize income on the value of stock or rights to acquire stock ("new stock") received.[9] The shareholder's basis in nontaxable new stock (or the basis of stock acquired on the exercise of nontaxable rights) is determined by allocating the basis of the stock on which the stock or rights are distributed ("old stock") to both the old stock and the new stock in proportion to their fair market values on the date of the distribution of the new stock.[10]

Redemptions. As a general rule, a corporation's redemption of its shares is treated by the shareholder as a distribution in part or full payment in *exchange* for the shares.[11] If the redemption does *not* qualify as an exchange under I.R.C. § 302(b), the redemption constitutes a

5. I.R.C. § 311(a).
6. I.R.C. § 311(b).
7. I.R.C. § 163(a). *See* I.R.C. §§ 163(d) (limitation on investment interest) and 163(e) (original issue discount).
8. I.R.C. § 385(b). Various factors are taken into account to determine whether a debtor-creditor relationship or a corporation-shareholder relationship exists, such as, the corporation's debt-to-equity ratio, whether the purported indebtedness (or equity) is subordinated to (or has a preference over) any indebtedness of the corporation, and whether the interest in question is convertible into stock of the corporation. I.R.C. § 305(b). *See also*, B. Bittker and J. Eustice, *Federal Income Taxation of Corporations and Shareholders* (6th ed. 1994) ¶¶ 4.02–4.04 and 4.20–4.21 (retirement of debt versus redemption of stock); M. Rose and J. Chommie, *Federal Income Taxation* (1988) § 10.05. *See supra*, § 1.26.

PRACTICE POINTER: Care must be exercised to avoid "thin capitalization" (*e.g.*, high debt-to-equity ratio) or a reliance on hybrid securities (*e.g.*, convertible debentures or subordinated debentures) because the IRS may attempt, for tax purposes, to recharacterize purported debt as equity, or purported equity as debt, depending on the circumstances. *See supra*, § 1.26, note 4.

9. I.R.C. § 305; Treas. Reg. §§ 1.305–1 to 1.305–8. *See also*, Master Tax Guide ¶¶ 738 and 1907. I.R.C. § 301 may, however, apply to certain share distributions. *See, e.g.*, I.R.C. § 305(c); Treas. Reg. §§ 1.305–4(b), Examples; 1.305–5(d), Examples; 1.305–7(a). *See supra*, § 1.40, notes 1–4.

10. I.R.C. § 307; Treas. Reg. §§ 1.307–1 and 1.307–2. *See also*, Master Tax Guide ¶ 1907. For an example of this allocation, *see* Treas. Reg. § 1.307–1(b), Example. This allocation is required to be made by the distributee if the value of the rights is 15% or more of the value of the old stock; if the fair market value of the rights is less than 15% of the value of the old stock, the distributee may elect to allocate the old stock's basis in proportion to the fair market values of such stock and the rights. If the distributee elects not to allocate basis in that way, the basis of the rights is zero, and the basis of the underlying stock is not changed. *See* Master Tax Guide ¶ 1907.

11. I.R.C. § 302(a). *See* I.R.C. §§ 302(c)(2) and 318(a) (constructive ownership of shares). *See also*, I.R.C. §§ 303(a) (redemptions of shares to pay death taxes), 304(a) (redemptions using related corporations), and 306(a) (distributions of preferred stock).

distribution to the shareholder under I.R.C. § 301.[12] Four safe harbors qualify a redemption for exchange treatment: (1) the redemption is not essentially equivalent to a dividend,[13] (2) the redemption is substantially disproportionate,[14] (3) the redemption terminates a shareholder's interest, and (4) the redemption is of a noncorporate shareholder's stock in partial liquidation of the corporation.[15]

Bargain purchases. No gain or loss is recognized by a *corporation* upon the receipt of money or other property in exchange for its shares, whether issued at a premium or a discount.[16] As a general rule, a *shareholder* (or anybody) who buys shares (or anything else) at a discount from market value (bargain purchase) does not have income. However, if a shareholder buys shares from a corporation at a bargain, the bargain element to the shareholder may in effect be a disguised dividend,[17] salary (payment by the corporation for services rendered),[18] rent (on property leased by the shareholder to the corporation), royalties (on intellectual property of the shareholder licensed to the corporation), interest (on money lent by the shareholder to the corporation); if so, the shareholder would recognize the bargain element as income.[19]

§ 1.41 Distributions Summary

A corporation may pay dividends to shareholders in cash or other property, except when the corporation is insolvent or would be rendered insolvent by the payment. A corporation may also make *pro rata* distributions of its shares under certain conditions. It may purchase or redeem its shares except when it is insolvent or would be rendered insolvent by the transaction. It may make agreements to purchase its

---

12. I.R.C. § 302(d). *See also*, Treas.Reg. § 1.305(c). *See supra*, § 1.40, notes 1–3 and accompanying text.

13. Treas. Reg. § 1.302–2(b).

14. For an illustration of a disproportionate redemption, *see* Treas. Reg. § 1.302–3(b), Example.

15. I.R.C. § 302(b).

PRACTICE POINTER: Each of these safe harbors has different requirements. To qualify a redemption as not essentially equivalent to a dividend for tax purposes is probably open to more uncertainty than satisfying the tests for a substantially disproportionate redemption. The tests for qualifying as a redemption terminating a shareholder's interest and a redemption of a noncorporate shareholder's stock in partial liquidation of the corporation also may be easier to meet than trying to come within the rubric of a redemption that is not essentially equivalent to a dividend. *See, e.g.*, B. Bittker and J. Eustice, *Federal Income Taxation of Corporations and Shareholders* (6th ed. 1994) ¶¶ 9.03–9.07.

16. I.R.C. § 1032(a).

17. Treas. Reg. § 1.301–1(j).

18. **PRACTICE POINTER:** If the payment is reasonable compensation to the shareholder-employee, the corporation may deduct the payment as a business expense. I.R.C. § 162(a)(1). To the extent that the payment represents unreasonable salary, no deduction is allowed the corporation. I.R.C. § 162(a)(1). Deductible compensation, however, may be more attractive to the corporation than a non-deductible distribution.

19. *See, e.g.*, Treas. Reg. § 1.61–2; Master Tax Guide ¶ 789.

PRACTICE POINTER: A similar issue arises when the corporation pays more than an arm's length price for property purchased from a shareholder, because the excess could be a disguised distribution. *See supra*, § 1.34, note 44 and accompanying text.

shares. Shares reacquired by a corporation may be retained as treasury shares or cancelled, except in cases where the NYBCL requires reacquired shares to be cancelled. A corporation is liable in damages sustained by shareholders as a consequence of the corporation's failure to make the disclosures required in connection with dividends or other distributions in cash or other property, share distributions and changes, reacquired shares, certain reductions of stated capital, and conversions of convertible shares.

§ 1.42 Distributions Checklist

1. Declaration and payment of dividend by corporation; distribution of dividends in cash or other property. (*See* § 1.38, notes 1–21 and accompanying text)

    - Declared by board. (*See* § 1.38, notes 1–16 and accompanying text)
    - Insolvency and surplus tests. (*See* § 1.38, notes 1–9 and accompanying text)

2. Distribution of corporation's shares. (*See* § 1.38, notes 22–28 and accompanying text)

    - Capitalization of surplus. (*See* § 1.38, note 23 and accompanying text)
    - Disclosure required. (*See* § 1.38, note 29 and accompanying text)

3. Changes in shares. (*See* § 1.38, notes 30–33 and accompanying text)

    - Capital accounts affected. (*See* § 1.38, notes 30–33 and accompanying text)
    - Board and shareholder approval. (*See* § 1.38, note 34 and accompanying text)
    - Disclosure required. (*See* § 1.38, note 35 and accompanying text)

4. Reduction of capital. (*See* § 1.38, notes 36–40 and accompanying text)

    - Liquidation preferences protection. (*See* § 1.38, note 39 and accompanying text)
    - Board and shareholder approval. (*See* § 1.38, notes 41–42 and accompanying text)
    - Disclosure required. (*See* § 1.38, note 43 and accompanying text)

5. Distribution by purchase of shares by corporation; redemption of redeemable shares by corporation. (*See* § 1.39)

§ 1.42 BUSINESS ORGANIZATIONS: CORPORATIONS Ch. 1

- Insolvency and surplus tests. (*See* § 1.39, notes 1–6 and accompanying text)
- Sinking fund. (*See* § 1.39, note 7 and accompanying text)
- Board and shareholder approval of agreements by corporation to purchase shares; "greenmail." (*See* § 1.39, notes 8–14 and accompanying text)
- Redeemable shares; call price; sinking fund. (*See* § 1.39, notes 15–22 and accompanying text)
- Reacquired shares. (*See* § 1.39, notes 23–29 and accompanying text)

6. Conversion of convertible bonds or shares. (*See* § 1.33)
7. Disclosure required. (*See* § 1.38, notes 29, 33, and 40 and accompanying text)
8. Liability for failure to disclose. (*See* § 1.38, notes 29, 33 and 40 and accompanying text)
9. Tax consequences. (*See* § 1.40)
    - Dividends. (*See* § 1.40, notes 1–8 and accompanying text)
    - Stock rights and options. (*See* § 1.40, notes 9–10 and accompanying text)
    - Redemptions. (*See* § 1.40, notes 11–15 and accompanying text)
    - Bargain purchases. (*See* § 1.40, notes 16–19 and accompanying text)

§ 1.43 Shareholders' Meetings and Agreements—Generally

Meetings of shareholders may be held at any place, within or without New York, as may be fixed in or pursuant to the corporate bylaws.[1] If the place (or how it is determined) is not fixed in the bylaws, then the place of the meeting is at the New York office of the corporation.[2] A meeting of shareholders must be held annually for the election of directors and the transaction of other business on a date fixed in the bylaws.[3] Special meetings of the shareholders may be called by the board or other persons authorized by the certificate of incorporation or the bylaws.[4] At any special meeting, only business that is related to the

---

§ 1.43
1. NYBCL § 602(a).
2. *Id.*
3. NYBCL § 602(b). A failure to hold the annual meeting on the date fixed or to elect a sufficient number of directors to conduct the business of the corporation does not work a forfeiture or give cause for dissolution of the corporation, except as provided in NYBCL § 1104(c) (petition in case of deadlock among directors or shareholders). *See infra*, § 1.103.
4. NYBCL § 602(c).

Ch. 1 SHAREHOLDERS' MEETINGS & AGREEMENTS § 1.43

purposes set forth in the notice required by NYBCL § 605 may be transacted.[5]

Special Meeting for the Election of Directors. If the shareholders after a certain grace period[6] fail to elect a sufficient number of directors to conduct the business of the corporation, the board must call a special meeting for the election of directors.[7] If the special meeting is not called by the board within two weeks after the expiration of the grace period, or if it is called and directors are not elected for two months more, the holders of at least ten percent of the votes of the shares entitled to vote in an election of directors may, in writing, demand the call of a special meeting to elect directors, specifying the meeting date, which must not be fewer than 60 nor more than 90 days after the date of the written demand.[8] The secretary of the corporation, upon receiving the written demand, must promptly give notice of the meeting to the shareholders, or, if the secretary fails to do so within five business days, any shareholder signing the demand may give the notice.[9] The meeting must be held at the place fixed in the bylaws or, if not fixed in the bylaws, at the office of the corporation.[10] At the special meeting, notwithstanding normal shareholder quorum requirements,[11] the shareholders attending, in person or by proxy, and entitled to vote in an election of directors, constitute a quorum for the purpose of electing directors but not for the transaction of any other business.[12]

---

5. *Id.* Except as otherwise required by the NYBCL, the bylaws may designate reasonable procedures for the calling and conduct of a shareholders' meeting, including but not limited to specifying: (1) who may call and who may conduct the meeting, (2) the means by which the order of business to be conducted is established, (3) the procedures and requirements for the nomination of directors, (4) the procedures with respect to the making of shareholder proposals, and (5) the procedures to be established for the adjournment of any shareholders' meeting. NYBCL § 602(d). No amendment of the bylaws pertaining to the election of directors or the procedures for the calling and conduct of a shareholders' meeting affects the election of directors or the procedures for the calling or conduct of any shareholders' meeting unless adequate notice thereof is given to the shareholders in a manner reasonably calculated to provide shareholders with sufficient time to respond thereto prior to the meeting. *Id.*

6. For a period of one month after the date fixed in the bylaws for the annual shareholders' meeting or, if no date has been fixed, for a period of thirteen months after the formation of the corporation or the last meeting. NYBCL § 603(a).

7. NYBCL § 603(a).

8. *Id.*

9. *Id.*

CAVEAT: NYBCL § 603(a) does not specify who bears the expense of the notice. The amount of expense could range from insignificant (in the case of a closely-held corporation) to substantial (in the case of a widely-held public corporation). *Cf., e.g.,* NYBCL § 626(d) (court may determine which one or more of the parties to a derivative action shall bear the expense of giving of notice of its discontinuance, compromise, or settlement). Alternatives to a shareholder's giving notice of the special meeting might be considered. *See, e.g.,* NYBCL § 1104(a)(2) (petition for dissolution where shareholders are so divided that the votes required for the election of directors cannot be obtained). *See also, infra,* §§ 1.51 and 1.103.

10. NYBCL § 603(a). *Cf.* NYBCL § 602(a) specifying that if the meeting place is not fixed by or in the bylaws, it is at the office of the corporation in New York.

11. NYBCL § 608. *See infra,* § 1.46.

12. NYBCL § 603(b).

§ 1.43 BUSINESS ORGANIZATIONS: CORPORATIONS   Ch. 1

Record Date. Absent a provision in the bylaws for fixing a record date, the board may fix, in advance, a date for the purpose of determining the shareholders entitled (1) to notice of, or to vote at, any meeting of shareholders or any adjournment thereof, (2) to express consent to, or dissent from, any proposal without a meeting, (3) to receive payment of any dividend or the allotment of any rights, or (4) for any other purpose.[13] The record date may not be more than 50 nor fewer than ten days before the date of the meeting, nor more than 50 days prior to any other action.[14] If no record date is fixed, the record date is: (1) for determining the shareholders entitled to notice of, or to vote at, a meeting of shareholders, the close of business on the day next preceding the day on which notice is given, or, if no notice is given, the day on which the meeting is held,[15] or (2) for determining the shareholders of record for any other purpose, the close of business on the day on which the board resolution relating thereto is adopted.[16] The record date to determine the shareholders entitled to notice of, or to vote at, any meeting of shareholders, applies to any adjournment of the meeting, unless the board fixes a new record date for the adjourned meeting.[17]

Shareholder Aggrieved by an Election. Any shareholder aggrieved by an election may petition the supreme court at a special term held within the judicial district where the office of the corporation is located to hear forthwith the proofs and allegations of the parties and to confirm the election, order a new election, or take other action that justice may require.[18] Notice must be given to the corporation, to the

---

13. NYBCL § 604(a).
14. Id.
15. NYBCL § 604(b).
16. Id.
17. NYBCL § 604(c).
18. NYBCL § 619.

CAVEAT: Care must be taken that the proceeding is commenced before a defense of laches may be interposed. *See, e.g.,* Scheeler v. Buffalo Wire Works Co., 50 Misc.2d 158, 269 N.Y.S.2d 897 (Sup.Ct., Erie County, 1966) (minority shareholder who waited eight months after corporate meeting before going to court to challenge actions taken at the meeting waived his objections). *Cf.* Wyatt v. Armstrong, 186 Misc. 216, 59 N.Y.S.2d 502 (Sup.Ct., N.Y. County, 1945) (proceeding not barred by failure to act more promptly in absence of showing that directors elected were injured by such delay); Christ v. Lake Erie Distributors, Inc., 51 Misc.2d 811, 273 N.Y.S.2d 878 (Sup.Ct., Erie County, 1966), aff'd 28 A.D.2d 817, 282 N.Y.S.2d 728, aff'd 28 A.D.2d 825, 282 N.Y.S.2d 728 (4th Dep't 1967) (four-month rule under CPLR 217 is applicable). **Procedure.** Without limiting the manner in which a shareholder may authorize another person or persons to act for him or her as proxy pursuant to NYBCL § 609(a), a shareholder may grant such authority in writing executed by the shareholder or the shareholder's authorized officer, director, employee, or agent signing such writing or causing his or her signature to be affixed to such writing by any reasonable means including, but not limited to, by facsimile signature. NYBCL § 609(i). A shareholder may authorize another person or persons to act for the shareholder as proxy by transmitting or authorizing the transmission of a telegram, cablegram, or other means of electronic transmission to the person who will be the holder of the proxy or to a proxy solicitation firm, proxy support service organization, or like agent duly authorized by the person who will be the holder of the proxy to receive such transmission, provided that the transmission either set forth or be submitted with information from which a determination can be reasonably made that the transmission was authorized by the shareholder. *Id.* If a transmission is determined to be valid, the inspectors (or, if no inspectors are appersons declared elected at the contested election, and to other persons as the court may specify.[19] The scope of review is limited to issues pertinent to the election of directors and officers.[20] Among the grounds for relief are: ballot tampering,[21] cumulative voting violations,[22] failure to give proper notice,[23] proxy violations,[24] material misstatements,[25] breach of shareholder agreement,[26] greater number of directors than certificate of incorporation permitted,[27] and votes improperly excluded had material effect on election.[28]

§ 1.44 Shareholders' Meetings and Agreements—Notice Requirements

Written notice of the place, date, and hour of a shareholders' meeting must be given to shareholders and, unless it is the annual meeting, indicate that the notice is being sent by or at the direction of the persons calling the meeting.[1] Notice of a special meeting must also

pointed, such other persons making that determination) must specify the nature of the information upon which they relied. *Id.* Any copy, facsimile telecommunication, or other reliable reproduction of the writing or transmission created pursuant to NYBCL § 609(i) may be substituted or used in lieu of the original writing or transmission for any and all purposes for which the original writing or transmission could be used, provided that such reproduction is of the entire original writing or transmission. NYBCL § 609(j).

19. NYBCL § 619.

20. *See, e.g.,* Matter of Schmidt, 97 A.D.2d 244, 468 N.Y.S.2d 663 (2d Dep't 1983).

21. In re Societa Mutuo Soccorso San Rocco Fra I Cittadini De Palo Colle Bari, 255 App.Div. 815, 7 N.Y.S.2d 337 (2d Dep't 1938).

22. *See, e.g.,* In re American Fibre Chair Seat Corp., 241 App.Div. 532, 272 N.Y.S. 206 (2d Dep't 1934), aff'd 265 N.Y. 416, 193 N.E. 253, reargument denied 266 N.Y. 500, 195 N.E. 171 (1934).

23. *See, e.g.,* In re Green Bus Lines, 166 Misc. 800, 2 N.Y.S.2d 556 (Sup.Ct., N.Y. Couunty, 1937); Application of Vallone 92 A.D.2d 799, 460 N.Y.S.2d 44 (1st Dep't 1983).

CAVEAT: This prohibition does not apply to votes, proxies, or consents given by preferred shareholders in connection with a proxy or consent solicitation made on identical terms to all holders of shares of the same class or series and remaining open for acceptance for at least twenty business days. *Id.*

24. *See, e.g.,* In re Ideal Mut. Ins. Co., 9 A.D.2d 60, 190 N.Y.S.2d 895 (1st Dep't 1959), appeal denied 7 N.Y.2d 706, 193 N.Y.S.2d 1027, 162 N.E.2d 754; Wyatt v. Armstrong, 186 Misc. 216, 59 N.Y.S.2d 502 (Sup.Ct., N.Y. County, 1945).

25. *See, e.g.,* In re R. Hoe & Co., 14 Misc.2d 500, 137 N.Y.S.2d 142 (Sup.Ct., Bronx County, 1954), aff'd 285 App.Div. 927, 139 N.Y.S.2d 883 (1st Dep't 1955), aff'd 309 N.Y. 719, 128 N.E.2d 420 (1955), reargument denied 309 N.Y. 802, 130 N.E.2d 603; Application of Morrison, 7 A.D.2d 42, 180 N.Y.S.2d 760 (1st Dep't 1958).

26. Matter of Katz, 2 Misc.2d 325, 143 N.Y.S.2d 282 (Sup.Ct., N.Y. County, 1955), aff'd 1 A.D.2d 657, 147 N.Y.S.2d 10 (1st Dep't 1955), aff'd 1 A.D.2d 658, 147 N.Y.S.2d 11 (1st Dep't 1955).

27. *See, e.g.,* Mitchell v. Forest City Printing Co., 107 Misc. 709 (Sup. Ct., Tompkins County, 1916), affirmed 107 Misc. 709, 187 App.Div. 743, 176 N.Y.S. 157 (3d Dep't 1919).

28. *See, e.g.,* In re Workmen's Benefit Fund of U.S., 265 App.Div. 176, 38 N.Y.S.2d 429 (1st Dep't 1942), appeal denied 265 App.Div. 991, 39 N.Y.S.2d 990 (1st Dep't 1943). *Cf.* Matter of Schmidt, 97 A.D.2d 244, 468 N.Y.S.2d 663 (2d Dep't 1983).

§ 1.44

1. NYBCL § 605(a).

state the purposes for which the meeting is called.[2] If, at any meeting, action is proposed to be taken that would, if taken, entitle shareholders fulfilling the requirements of NYBCL § 623 to receive payment for their shares,[3] the notice of the meeting must include a statement to that effect and must be accompanied by a copy of NYBCL § 623 or an outline of its material terms.[4]

A copy of the notice of any meeting must be given, personally or by first class mail, no fewer than ten nor more than 50 days before the date of the meeting, to each shareholder entitled to vote at the meeting.[5] A copy of the notice may be given by third class mail no fewer than twenty-four nor more than 50 days before the date of the meeting.[6] If mailed, the notice is deemed given when deposited in the United States mail, postage prepaid, directed to the shareholder's address appearing on the record of shareholders, or, if the shareholder has filed with the secretary of the corporation a written request that notices be mailed to some other address, then the notice must be directed to the other address.[7] An affidavit of the corporation's secretary (or its transfer agent or other person giving the notice) that the notice has been given is, in the absence of fraud, *prima facie* evidence of the facts stated in the affidavit.[8]

When a meeting is adjourned to another time or place, notice of the adjourned meeting is not necessary, unless the bylaws require otherwise, if the time and place to which the meeting is adjourned are announced at the meeting at which the adjournment is taken.[9] At the adjourned meeting, any business may be transacted that might have been transacted on the original date of the meeting.[10] However, if after the adjournment the board fixes a new record date for the adjourned meeting, notice of the adjourned meeting must be given to each shareholder of record on the new record date.[11]

Notice of a meeting need not be given to any shareholder who submits a signed waiver of notice, in person or by proxy, whether before or after the meeting.[12] The attendance of any shareholder at a meeting, in person or by proxy, without protesting prior to the conclusion of the meeting the lack of notice of the meeting, constitutes the shareholder's waiver of notice.[13]

2. *Id.*

3. *See* NYBCL §§ 513 (redemption of shares), 806 (amendments or changes to certificate of incorporation), 808 (reorganization under Act of Congress), 910 (merger, consolidation, or extraordinary sale, lease, exchange, or other disposition), 1005 (dissolution). *Cf.* NYBCL § 1118 (petitioning shareholders' shares purchased by other shareholders or corporation at fair value). *See also, supra* § 1.39 and *infra* §§ 1.72, 1.78, 1.81, 1.95, and 1.103.

4. NYBCL § 605(a).

5. *Id.*
6. *Id.*
7. *Id.*
8. *Id.*
9. NYBCL § 605(b).
10. *Id.*
11. *Id.*
12. NYBCL § 606.
13. *Id.*

§ 1.45 Shareholders' Meetings and Agreements—Voting

As a general rule, a shareholder of record is entitled to one vote for every share standing in the shareholder's name on the record of shareholders, unless otherwise provided in the certificate of incorporation.[1] However, limitations on the right to vote in respect of any class of authorized shares may be contained in the certificate of incorporation.[2] Greater than normal (supermajority) voting requirements are permitted.[3] Treasury shares are not entitled to vote or to be counted in determining the total number of a corporation's outstanding shares, nor are its shares held by any other corporation (domestic or foreign corporation of any type or kind) if it holds a majority of the other corporation's shares entitled to vote in the election of directors of the other corporation.[4]

Class voting. The certificate of incorporation may require that any class or series of shares vote as a class in connection with the transaction of any business or any specified item of business at a meeting of shareholders, including amendments to the certificate of incorporation.[5] The affirmative vote required for a class to take action is the proportionate vote prescribed in the certificate of incorporation.[6] If none is prescribed, a plurality of the votes cast by the class is required to elect

---

§ 1.45

1. NYBCL § 612(a).

PRACTICE POINTER: The vote of a particular class of shares, in addition to other voting requirements, may permit the holders of that class to exercise control over certain decisions. For example, the certificate of incorporation could provide that particular board action (*e.g.*, approval of certain contracts) or other corporate action requiring shareholder approval (*e.g.*, a merger) could not be approved without the affirmative vote of both a majority of all shareholders and a majority of the particular class (*e.g.*, preferred shareholders).

2. NYBCL § 613. These limitations must be consistent with NYBCL § 501, which requires that at least one class of outstanding shares be entitled to full voting rights.

PRACTICE POINTER: Investors who want to control corporate operations could be issued voting shares, and other investors (who may not be interested in taking an active role in the corporation's affairs) could receive non-voting shares. (Non-voting shares are no longer barred from listing on the New York Stock Exchange.) Cumulative voting and class voting can also be used to achieve a degree of control for a particular group. *See infra*, § 1.45 (class voting; cumulative voting).

3. NYBCL § 616(a)(2). *See* NYBCL § 616(c) (conspicuous notation on certificate required).

CAVEAT: supermajority voting requirements risk being held invalid. *See* Benintendi v. Kenton Hotel, Inc., 294 N.Y. 112, 60 N.E.2d 829 (1945) (invalidating bylaws in a close corporation requiring unanimous vote of all shareholders for shareholder action and to elect the three-director board). *See also, e.g.,* Henn and Alexander, *supra*, § 1.1, note 1, pp. 719–722.

4. NYBCL § 612(b). *See also*, RMBCA § 7.21(b), Official Comment 3 (on circular holdings, *i.e.*, the shares of one corporation held by a second corporation where the first corporation owns a majority of the voting shares of the second corporation—the second corporation is a majority-owned subsidiary of the first).

5. NYBCL § 617(a).

6. NYBCL § 617(b).

directors, and a majority of the votes cast by the class is required for any other corporate action.[7]

Shares Held by Fiduciaries, Receivers, or Pledgees. Shares held by an administrator, executor, guardian, conservator, committee, or other fiduciary, except a trustee, may be voted, either in person or by proxy, without transfer of the shares into the fiduciary's name on the corporate stock records.[8] Shares held by a trustee may be voted, either in person or by proxy, only after the shares have been transferred into the trustee's name as trustee or into the name of a nominee.[9] Shares held by or under the control of a receiver may be voted by the receiver although the shares have not been transferred into the receiver's name if authority to do so is contained in the court order appointing the receiver.[10] A shareholder whose shares are pledged is entitled to vote the shares until the shares have been transferred into the name of the pledgee or a nominee of the pledgee.[11]

Redeemable shares. Redeemable shares that have been called for redemption are not deemed to be outstanding shares for the purpose of voting or determining the total number of shares entitled to vote on any matter on and after the date on which written notice of redemption has been sent to holders of the shares, if a sum sufficient to redeem the shares has been deposited with a bank or trust company with irrevocable instructions and authority to pay the redemption price upon the surrender of certificates evidencing the shares.[12]

Shares Standing in the Name of Another Corporation. Shares recorded in the name of another domestic or foreign corporation may be voted by the officer, agent, or proxy of that corporation as its bylaws may provide, or, in the absence of a provision, as the board of that corporation may determine.[13]

Shares Recorded in the Names of Two or More Persons. Shares registered in the names of two or more persons (such as fiduciaries, partners, joint tenants, tenants in common, tenants by the entirety, or assignees), or where two or more persons have the same fiduciary relationship respecting the same shares, must be voted in accordance with NYBCL § 612(h), unless the secretary of the corporation is given *written* notice to the contrary and is furnished with a copy of the

---

7. *Id. See also, supra*, § 1.45, note 1.

PRACTICE POINTER: Class voting provides a means of allocating voting power to effect the control desired by a client. For example, the corporation could have several classes of stock with *each* class having the right to elect a specified number of directors (irrespective of the number of shares in a class). Dividend and liquidation rights could, however, be in proportion to the number of shares of each class. Alternative means of allocating voting power to gain a measure of desired control are by nonvoting shares and cumulative voting. *See supra*, § 1.45, note 2 (non-voting shares). *See infra*, § 1.45, notes 30–33 (cumulative voting).

8. NYBCL § 612(c).
9. *Id.*
10. NYBCL § 612(d).
11. NYBCL § 612(e).
12. NYBCL § 612(f).
13. NYBCL § 612(g).

instrument or order so providing.[14] NYBCL § 612(h) provides that (1) if only one of the registered owners votes, the vote must be accepted by the corporation as the vote of all such owners; (2) if more than one vote, the act of the majority so voting must be accepted by the corporation as the vote of all; (3) if more than one vote, but the vote is equally divided on any particular matter, the vote must be accepted by the corporation as a proportionate vote of the shares, unless the corporation has evidence, on the record of shareholders or in other respects, that the shares are held in a fiduciary capacity; (4) when two or more fiduciaries in whose name shares are registered are equally divided in their votes, any court having jurisdiction may, upon petition by any of the fiduciaries or by any party in interest, direct the voting of the shares for the best interest of the beneficiaries, unless the instrument or the court order appointing the fiduciaries otherwise directs how the shares are to be voted; and (5) if the instrument or court order furnished to the secretary of a corporation shows that multiple registered owners hold unequal interests, a majority (or equal division) for the purposes of NYBCL § 612(h) is a majority (or equal division) in interest.[15] NYBCL § 612(h) does not alter the requirements of other applicable law (including EPTL § 10–10.7) that the exercise of fiduciary powers be by act of a majority.[16] A corporation is entitled to treat the persons in whose names shares stand on the record of shareholders as the owners of the shares for all purposes.[17]

Proxies. Shareholders may also act through proxies.[18] Every proxy must be signed by the shareholder (or the shareholder's attorney-in-fact) and is valid for 11 months from the date of the proxy, unless otherwise provided therein.[19] Every proxy is revocable at the pleasure of the shareholder executing it, except as otherwise provided in NYBCL § 609.[20] The incompetence or death of the shareholder who executed the proxy does not revoke the proxy unless, before the proxy is exercised, written notice of an adjudication of the incompetence or death is received by the corporate officer responsible for maintaining the list of shareholders.[21] Except as authorized in NYBCL §§ 609 and 620,[22] shareholders may not sell their right to vote or issue a proxy for value.[23]

A proxy can be made irrevocable, but it must be entitled "irrevocable proxy" and state that it is irrevocable, and it must be limited to the following persons or their nominees: (1) pledgees; (2) persons who

14. NYBCL § 612(h).
15. *Id.*
16. NYBCL § 612(h)(3).
17. NYBCL § 612(i).
18. NYBCL § 609(a).
19. NYBCL § 609(b).
20. *Id.*
21. NYBCL § 609(c). *See* NYBCL § 609(f). *See also, infra*, § 1.45, note 24 and accompanying text. Unless otherwise agreed in writing, the record holder of shares held by a pledgee or otherwise as security (or owned by another person) must grant the pledgor (or the owner of the shares) a proxy to vote or take other action, upon demand and payment of necessary expenses by the pledgor (or owner). NYBCL § 609(d).
22. *See infra*, § 1.47.
23. NYBCL § 609(e).

purchased, or who have agreed, to purchase the shares; (3) creditors of the corporation who extend or continue credit in consideration of the proxy if the proxy states that it was given in consideration of the extension or continuation of credit, the amount, and the name of the creditor; (4) persons employed as officers of the corporation, if a proxy is required by the employment contract and if the proxy states the employee's name, the period of employment, and that it was given in consideration of the employment; and (5) persons designated by a shareholders' agreement.[24] The proxy becomes revocable once the pledge is redeemed, the debt is paid, the employment period terminates, or the shareholders' agreement terminates.[25] Proxies granted to creditors and employees pursuant to NYBCL § 609(f) become revocable three years after their date or at the end of the period, if any, specified in the proxy, whichever period is shorter, unless the period of irrevocability is renewed from time to time by the execution of a new irrevocable proxy.[26] A proxy may also be revoked, notwithstanding a provision making it irrevocable, by a purchaser of shares without knowledge of the provision, unless the existence of the proxy and its irrevocability are noted conspicuously on the certificate representing the shares.[27]

Vote of Shareholders. Unless otherwise required by the NYBCL, by the certificate of incorporation as permitted by the NYBCL, or by the specific provision of a bylaw adopted by the shareholders, whenever any corporate action (other than the election of directors) is to be taken by vote of the shareholders, the action must be authorized by a majority of the votes cast in favor of such action at the meeting by the holders of shares entitled to vote.[28] Directors are elected by a *plurality* of the votes, except as otherwise required by the NYBCL or by the certificate of

24. NYBCL § 609(f). See also, e.g., H. Ballantine, *On Corporations* (1946) pp. 409, 424–425 (a shareholder may revoke the proxy (agency) at any time, even if it is expressly agreed to be irrevocable, unless it is coupled with an interest; which interests are so coupled is a somewhat unsettled question; as a matter of policy, the irrevocable power of voting even if coupled with an interest or otherwise created by contract by the owner of the shares has not been favored, citing, among other examples, the predecessor to NYBCL § 609(f)); R. Hamilton, *The Law of Corporations* (2d ed. 1987) pp. 190–193 (cites NYBCL § 609(f) as defining five proxies "coupled with an interest" but presenting the danger that a reasonable irrevocable proxy not fitting within these categories might be invalidated). A distinction has been drawn between the case of a principal (shareholder) who may revoke the power of the agent (proxy) but who may not revoke a contract with the agent without incurring liability in damages for breach. See, e.g., Henn and Alexander, supra, § 1.1, note 1, p. 520; R. Steffen, *Agency—Partnership* (1977) pp. 42–45. Cf. RMBCA § 7.22(d) (describes several accepted forms of relationship as examples, not as an exhaustive listing, of "proxies coupled with an interest"). See NYBCL § 620(a) (shareholder agreements) and 621(a) (voting trusts). See infra, § 1.47.

25. NYBCL § 609(g).

26. *Id.* The duration of a proxy under NYBCL § 609(b) is not affected by NYBCL § 609(g). *Id. See supra,* § 1.45, notes 19 and 20 and accompanying text.

27. NYBCL § 609(h).

28. NYBCL § 614(b). Except as otherwise provided in the certificate of incorporation or the specific provision of a bylaw adopted by the shareholders, an abstention does not constitute a vote cast. *Id.*

incorporation as permitted by the NYBCL.[29]

Cumulative Voting. The purpose of cumulative voting, as opposed to straight voting,[30] is to enable minority shareholders to have the opportunity to be represented on the board.[31] In this regard, the certificate of incorporation may provide that in elections of directors the number of votes to which each shareholder is entitled is equal to the number of shares held, multiplied by the number of directors to be elected.[32] Shareholders may cast *all* of their votes for a single director or may distribute their votes among the candidates as they desire.[33]

29. NYBCL § 614(a).

30. Straight voting means that each shareholder has one vote for each share owned. For example, if the majority shareholder held 60 shares out of a total of 100 shares outstanding in a corporation with a board of three directors, under straight voting, the majority shareholder could elect all of the majority's candidates to the board whether the directors are elected by a plurality of votes or by a majority of votes cast. The majority shareholder would cast 60 votes for its three candidates, the minority shareholder would cast 40 votes for its three candidates, and all three of the majority shareholder's candidates would be elected. See, e.g., R. Hamilton, *The Law of Corporations* (2d ed. 1987) pp. 182–183.

31. PRACTICE POINTER: The extent to which a shareholder takes advantage of this opportunity depends on various voting strategies, which can be tricky and complex, and whether other devices limit the effectiveness of cumulative voting (*e.g.*, staggered board, reduced size of board, voting trusts, voting agreements, nonvoting shares, inconvenient meeting times or places, board delegation of certain matters to committees controlled by majority, and informal director discussion in advance of board meetings). *See, e.g.*, R. Hamilton, *The Law of Corporations* (2d ed. 1987) pp. 182–190.

32. NYBCL § 618.

33. *Id.*

PRACTICE POINTER: To assure minority shareholders a seat on the board of directors, the minimum number of shares required to be owned by the minority is determined by the following formula:

$$n = (Nd \div (D+1)) + 1$$

where: n = minimum number of shares required to elect number of directors desired

N = total number of outstanding shares entitled to vote

d = desired number of directors

D = total number of directors to be elected.

If minority shareholders are able, in negotiations when acquiring their shares, to acquire the minimum number of shares necessary to elect one director to the board, the minority is assured of representation at board meetings. If the certificate of incorporation provides that certain board action requires a unanimous vote, then the minority director has veto power over that action. An example illustrating the use of the formula may be helpful. If the total number of outstanding shares is 6,000, and minority shareholders would like to elect one director to a board consisting of five directors, then the minority must own at least 1,001 shares. The 1,001 shares could all be cast for the *sixth* of six or more candidates, which would limit the majority's holding of 4,999 shares to be cast to elect no more than four directors because the *fifth* candidate would receive only 4,999 votes (with the *first four* receiving 4,999 each, the minority's candidate receiving 5,005, and the "+1" in the formula being the difference).

CAVEAT: Careless casting of the majority shareholder's votes in a cumulative voting system could allow the minority to gain control. For example, if 100 shares are outstanding, a majority shareholder owns 60 shares, and five directors are to be elected, if the majority shareholder evenly casts 300 (=60×5) cumulative votes for each candidate (*i.e.*, 60 votes for each candidate), the minority could cumulate its votes (40×5=200) and cast them 66, 67, and 67 and elect three of the five directors to be elected, capturing control of the board.

PRACTICE POINTER: The best strategy in cumulative voting is to be wary of simply voting straight (evenly) for each candidate without cumulating votes as may be deemed desirable in the particular election lest the cumulative voting feature not be

§ 1.45   BUSINESS ORGANIZATIONS: CORPORATIONS   Ch. 1

Shareholders' List. A list of shareholders of record, certified by the corporate officer responsible for its preparation (or by the corporation's transfer agent), must be produced at any shareholders' meeting upon a shareholder's request made at, or prior to, the meeting.[34] All persons who appear from the list to be shareholders entitled to vote may vote at the meeting.[35] If the right to vote at any meeting is challenged, the list of shareholders of record must be produced as evidence of the right to vote.[36]

Inspectors of Election. The board of directors must appoint one or more inspectors to act at (or any adjournment of) the meeting and to make a written report thereof.[37] The duties of inspectors at shareholders' meetings include determining the number of shares outstanding and the voting power of each, the shares represented at the meeting, the existence of a quorum, and the validity and effect of proxies.[38] They also receive votes, ballots, or consents, hear and determine all challenges and questions arising in connection with the right to vote, count and tabulate all votes, ballots, or consents, determine the result, and otherwise conduct the election or vote with fairness to all shareholders.[39] Before discharging their duties, inspectors must sign an oath to execute their duties faithfully with strict impartiality and according to the best of

---

utilized to best advantage. A desirable strategy is to determine the proportion of the total number of shares (N) expected to be voted at the election necessary to elect the desired number of directors; the client should then cumulatively vote the shares held for that proportion of the number of directors to be elected. In the second example above, the 300 cumulative shares (representing 60% of the 500 total) should be cast for three candidates (60% of the candidates), a strategy that would assure the majority of three candidates being elected. The minority would cast 200 votes for its candidates, but in this case the majority's voting will have limited the minority to two directors. For a discussion of voting strategies, *see, e.g.*, R. Hamilton, *The Law of Corporations* (2d ed. 1987) pp. 182–190; H. Ballantine, *On Corporations* (1946) pp. 404–406. For other means available to the minority to effect a measure of control in the election of directors and perhaps other matters, *see supra*, § 1.45 (nonvoting shares; class voting) and *infra*, §§ 1.46 (higher-than-normal shareholder quorum requirement), 1.63 (higher-than-normal director quorum requirement). *Cf. infra*, §§ 1.47 (shareholder agreements; voting trusts), 1.61 (removal of directors), 1.59 (staggered board) and *supra* 1.21 (share transfer restrictions).

34. NYBCL § 607.

35. *Id.*

36. *Id.*

37. NYBCL § 610(a). The board of directors may designate one or more persons as alternate inspectors to replace any inspector who fails to act. *Id.* If no inspector or alternate has been appointed, or if appointed is unable to act at a meeting of shareholders, the person presiding at the meeting must appoint one or more inspectors to act at the meeting. *Id.* Unless otherwise provided in the certificate of incorporation or bylaws, NYBCL § 610(a) is inapplicable to a corporation that does not have a class of voting stock listed on a national securities exchange or authorized for quotation on an interdealer quotation system of a registered national securities association. NYBCL § 610(b). However, any corporation may take these actions even though not required to do so under NYBCL § 610(a). *Id.*

PRACTICE POINTER: Appointment of a small number of inspectors facilitates decision; an odd number avoids stalemate, and the usual number of inspectors is one or three. *See* Henn and Alexander, pp. 508–509 (in close corporations, use of inspectors is burdensome formality usually disregarded in practice).

38. NYBCL § 611(a).

39. *Id.*

their ability.[40] On request of the person presiding, or any shareholder entitled to vote thereat, the inspectors must report in writing any challenge, question, or other matter determined, and execute a certificate of any fact found by them.[41] Any report or certificate made by an inspector is *prima facie* evidence of the facts stated and of the vote as certified by them.[42]

In determining the validity and counting of proxies, ballots, and consents, the inspectors are limited to an examination of the proxies, any envelopes submitted with those proxies and consents, any information provided in accordance with NYBCL § 609 (proxies), ballots, and the regular books and records of the corporation, except that the inspectors may consider other reliable information for the limited purpose of reconciling proxies, ballots, and consents submitted by or on behalf of banks, brokers, their nominees, or similar persons that represent more votes than the holder of a proxy is authorized by the record owner to cast or more votes than the stockholder holds of record.[43] If the inspectors consider other reliable information for the limited purpose permitted by NYBCL § 611(b), at the time they make their certification pursuant to NYBCL § 611(a) they must specify the precise information considered by them including the person or persons from whom they obtained the information, when the information was obtained, the means by which the information was obtained, and the basis for their belief that such information is reliable.[44]

The date and time (which need not be a particular time of day) of the opening and the closing of the polls for each matter upon which the shareholders will vote at a meeting must be announced by the person presiding at the meeting at the beginning of the meeting, and, if no date and time is so announced, the polls must close at the end of the meeting, including any adjournment thereof.[45] No ballots, proxies, or consents, nor any revocation thereof or changes thereto, may be accepted by the inspectors after the closing of polls in accordance with NYBCL § 605 (notice of meetings of shareholders) unless the supreme court at a special term held within the judicial district where the office of the corporation is located upon application by a shareholder determines otherwise.[46] Unless otherwise provided in the certificate of incorporation or bylaws, NYBCL §§ 611(a) and (c) do not apply to a corporation that does not have a class of voting stock that is listed on a national securities exchange or authorized for quotation on an interdealer quotation system of a registered national securities association; however, any corporation may take the actions set forth in NYBCL §§ 611(a) and (c).[47]

---

40. NYBCL § 610(a).
41. NYBCL § 611(a).
42. *Id.*
43. NYBCL § 611(b).
44. *Id.*
45. NYBCL § 611(c).
46. *Id.*
47. NYBCL § 611(d).

§ 1.46 Shareholders' Meetings and Agreements—Quorum Requirements

The holders of a majority of the votes of shares entitled to vote constitute a quorum at a meeting of shareholders for the transaction of any business, provided that when a specified item of business is required to be voted on by a class or series, voting as a class, the holders of a majority of the shares of the class or series constitute a quorum for that purpose.[1] The certificate of incorporation or the bylaws may provide for any lesser quorum, but not less than one-third of the votes of shares entitled to vote,[2] and the certificate of incorporation may provide for a greater quorum.[3] When a quorum is once present at a meeting, it is not broken by the subsequent withdrawal of any shareholders.[4] The shareholders present may adjourn the meeting despite the absence of a quorum.[5]

Library References:

West's Key No. Digests, Corporations ⚖︎195.

§ 1.47 Shareholders' Meetings and Agreements—Agreements; Voting Trusts

Shareholder Voting Agreements. Shareholders' agreements, if in writing and signed by the parties, may provide that their shares are to

§ 1.46

1. NYBCL § 608(a).
2. NYBCL § 608(b).
3. See NYBCL § 616 (certificate of incorporation may contain provisions specifying a greater quorum requirement than otherwise prescribed by the NYBCL). An amendment of the certificate of incorporation that changes or strikes out a provision permitted by NYBCL § 616 must be authorized at a meeting of shareholders by at least two-thirds of the votes of all outstanding shares entitled to vote, or of the greater proportion of votes of shares, or of a particular class or series of shares, provided specifically in the certificate of incorporation. NYBCL § 616(b).

CAVEAT: If the certificate of incorporation contains a provision authorized by NYBCL § 616, the existence of the provision must be noted conspicuously on the face or back of every certificate for shares issued by the corporation, except for any class of equity security registered pursuant to Securities Exchange Act § 12, as amended (15 U.S.C.A. § 78l). NYBCL § 616(c).

PRACTICE POINTER: A measure of control (*e.g.*, veto power) on matters requiring shareholder action or director action may be achieved by greater than normal voting and quorum requirements.

CAVEAT: But these means are not without risks (*e.g.*, invalidity; shareholders' or directors' deadlock). See, *e.g.*, Herwitz, *supra*, § 1.1, note 1, pp. 64–67 (greater than normal shareholder quorum/voting requirements) and 69–72 (greater than normal director quorum/voting requirements); Henn and Alexander, *supra*, § 1.1, note 1, §§ 266 (greater than normal shareholder quorum/voting requirements) and 274 (greater than normal director quorum/voting requirements). See *supra*, §§ 1.45, note 3 and accompanying text, and *infra* 1.47, note 3 and accompanying text.

4. NYBCL § 608(c).
5. NYBCL § 608(d).

Ch. 1 VOTING TRUSTS § 1.47

be voted in accordance with the agreement.[1]

Provision in Certificate of Incorporation Restricting Board. A provision in the certificate of incorporation that improperly restricts the board in its management of the business of the corporation or improperly transfers to shareholders (or to others selected by them) the management otherwise within the authority of the board is generally prohibited.[2] However, it will be valid if (1) all the incorporators or holders of record of all outstanding shares (whether or not having voting power) have authorized the provision in the certificate of incorporation and (2) subsequent to the adoption of the provision, shares are transferred or issued only to persons who had knowledge or notice of (or consented in writing to) the provision.[3] This provision is valid only so long as no shares of the corporation are listed on a national securities exchange or regularly quoted in an over-the-counter market.[4] An amendment to strike out the provision must be authorized by the shareholders.[5] Alternatively, if the provision ceases to be valid, the board may

§ 1.47

1. NYBCL § 620(a).

2. *See, e.g.,* R. Hamilton, *The Law of Corporations* (2d ed. 1987) pp. 159–174.

3. NYBCL § 620(b).

PRACTICE POINTER: The certificate of incorporation constitutes a contract between the shareholders and the corporation. NYBCL § 620(b), which authorizes the embodiment in the certificate of incorporation of shareholders' agreements affecting directors' functions, is limited, as a practical matter, to close corporations. It expands the ruling of Clark v. Dodge, 269 N.Y. 410, 199 N.E. 641 (1936) (unanimous shareholders' agreement affecting directors' functions upheld because, among other reasons, all shareholders were parties to the agreement and the agreement damaged nobody) and to the extent therein provided overrules Long Park, Inc. v. Trenton–New Brunswick Theatres Co., 297 N.Y. 174, 77 N.E.2d 633 (1948) (unanimous shareholder agreement on corporate management held invalid as an infringement of statutory duty of board to manage corporation); McQuade v. Stoneham, 263 N.Y. 323, 189 N.E. 234 (1934) (shareholders' agreement (not unanimous) on such matters as officer salaries, selection of officers, and corporate policy held invalid as impermissible restraint on directors discretion); Manson v. Curtis, 223 N.Y. 313, 119 N.E. 559 (1918) (shareholders' agreement (not unanimous) on management matters held invalid impingement on directors' duty to manage corporation). Shareholder agreements not otherwise prohibited by law would appear to be valid even if not embodied in the certificate of incorporation; the agreement's provisions affecting directors' functions should be made subject to the discretion of the board, and provisions in respect of officers' tenure should contain a qualification that the officers remain faithful, efficient, and competent. *See, e.g.*, Henn and Alexander, *supra*, § 1.1, note 1, pp. 723–735 (shareholders' agreements) and 744–746 (directors' agreements); C. Israels, *Corporate Practice* (2d ed. 1969) pp. 108–116; H. Ballantine, *On Corporations* pp. 419–424; N. Lattin, *On Corporations* (1959) pp. 331–336; R. Hamilton, *The Law of Corporations* (2d ed. 1987) pp. 167–173; RMBCA § 8.01(b). *Cf.* Delaware General Corporations Law §§ 141(a), 342, 350, and 354. *See infra*, §§ 1.59 and 1.69. *See also*, NYBCL §§ 701 (business of the corporation to be managed under the direction of its board); 715(b) (certificate of incorporation provision permitting officers to be elected by shareholders); and 716 (officers elected by shareholders may be removed (with or without cause) by shareholder vote, but the board may suspend the officers for cause).

4. NYBCL § 620(c).

5. NYBCL § 620(d). ***Procedure***. Except as provided in NYBCL § 620(e), the amendment must be authorized at a meeting of shareholders by (1) for any corporation in existence *on* the effective date of NYBCL § 620(d)(2), at least *two-thirds* of the votes of all outstanding shares entitled to vote and (2) for any corporation in existence *on* the effective date of NYBCL § 620(d)(1)(A)(ii) whose certificate of incor-

authorize a certificate of amendment[6] striking out the provision.[7] The effect of the provision is to relieve the directors and impose upon the shareholders liability for managerial acts or omissions otherwise imposed on directors by the NYBCL as long as the discretion or powers of the board are controlled by the provision.[8] If the certificate of incorporation contains such a provision, its existence must be noted conspicuously on the face or back of every certificate for shares issued by the corporation.[9]

Voting Trusts. Shareholders may transfer their shares to a trustee to vote them for a period not exceeding ten years in accordance with the terms and conditions of a written agreement.[10] The certificates representing the transferred shares must be surrendered by the shareholders, cancelled, and new certificates must be issued in the name of the voting trustee, as trustee.[11] The new certificates must state that they are issued under the voting trust agreement; the corporation must note these facts in its records.[12] The shareholders may receive voting trust certificates representing their interests in the shares.[13] The trustee must keep available for inspection by holders of voting trust certificates correct and complete books and records of account relating to the trust and a record containing the names and addresses of all holders of voting trust certificates, the number and class of shares represented by the certificates, and when they became owners of the certificates.[14] The holder of a voting trust certificate is regarded as a shareholder for the purpose of,

poration expressly provides such (and for any corporation incorporated *after* the effective date of NYBCL § 620(d)(2)), a *majority* of the votes of all outstanding shares entitled to vote (or, in either case, by such greater proportion of votes of shares as may be required by the certificate of incorporation for that purpose). NYBCL § 620(d)(1). The effective date of both NYBCL §§ 620(d)(1)(A)(ii) and (d)(2) is the one hundred eightieth day after the act amending the NYBCL became law (*see* 1997 NY S.B. 476 (SN) § 71; 1997 NY S.B. 5680 (SN) § 7); S.B. 476 was enacted on Aug. 26, 1997, and its effective date is Feb. 22, 1998. A corporation may adopt an amendment of the certificate of incorporation in accordance with NYBCL § 620(d)(1) to provide that any further amendment of the certificate of incorporation that strikes out the provision must be authorized at a shareholders' meeting by a specified proportion of votes of outstanding shares, or votes of a class or series of shares, entitled to vote, provided that such proportion may not be less than a majority. NYBCL § 620(d)(2).

6. NYBCL § 805. *See infra*, §§ 1.72–1.75.

7. NYBCL § 620(e). The certificate must set forth the event resulting in the provision to cease to be valid. *Id.*

8. NYBCL § 620(f).

9. NYBCL § 620(g).

10. NYBCL § 621(a).

11. *Id.*

12. *Id.*

13. NYBCL § 621(b).

14. *Id.* The record may be in written form or any other form capable of being converted into written form within a reasonable time. *Id.* The books and records must be available at the trustee's office, at a place designated in the agreement, or at a place of which the holders of voting trust certificates have been notified in writing. *Id.* A duplicate of the voting trust agreement must be filed in the corporation's office, and it and the record of voting trust certificate holders are subject to the same right of inspection by a shareholder of record or a holder of a voting trust certificate (in person or by agent or attorney) as are the records of the corporation under NYBCL § 624 (books and records; right of inspection; *prima facie* evidence). NYBCL § 621(c).

and entitled to the remedies provided in, NYBCL § 624.[15]

At any time within six months before the expiration of a voting trust agreement (as originally fixed or as extended one or more times), the holders of voting trust certificates may, by written agreement, extend the duration of the voting trust agreement, nominating the same or substitute trustees, for an additional period not exceeding ten years.[16] The extension agreement does not affect the rights or obligations of persons not parties to it, and it must in every respect comply with all the provisions of NYBCL § 621 applicable to the original voting trust agreement.[17]

Library References:

West's Key No. Digests, Corporations ⚖188–190.

§ 1.48 Shareholders' Meetings and Agreements—Action Without a Meeting

Whenever under the NYBCL shareholders are required or permitted to take any action by vote, they may act without a meeting, on their written consent, setting forth the action taken and signed by the holders of all outstanding shares entitled to vote or, if the certificate of incorporation so permits, signed by the holders of outstanding shares having not less than the minimum number of votes that would be necessary to authorize or take such action at a meeting at which all shares entitled to vote were present and voted.[1] When no shareholders of record exist, the written consent may be signed by a majority in interest of the subscribers for shares whose subscriptions have been accepted (or their successors in interest) or, if no subscription has been accepted, by the incorporator or a majority of the incorporators.[2] Where the requirement is in a

---

15. NYBCL § 621(c). *See infra*, § 1.53.
16. NYBCL § 621(d).
17. *Id.*

§ 1.48

1. NYBCL § 615(a). ***Procedure***. No written consent is effective to take the corporate action referred to therein unless, within 60 days of the earliest dated consent delivered in the manner required by NYBCL § 615(b) to the corporation, written consents signed by a sufficient number of holders to take action are delivered to the corporation by delivery to its registered office in New York, its principal place of business, or an officer or agent of the corporation having custody of the book in which proceedings of meetings of shareholders are recorded. NYBCL § 615(b). Delivery made to a corporation's registered office must be by hand or by certified or registered mail, return receipt requested. *Id.* Prompt notice of the taking of the corporate action without a meeting by less than unanimous written consent must be given to those shareholders who have not consented in writing. NYBCL § 615(c). Written consent thus given by the holders of such number of shares as is required under NYBCL § 615(b) has the same effect as a valid vote of holders of such number of shares, and any certificate with respect to the authorization or taking of any such action that is to be delivered to the Department of State must recite that written consent has been given in accordance with, and that written notice has been given as and to the extent required by, NYBCL § 615. NYBCL § 615(d).

2. NYBCL § 615(e). When two or more incorporators exist, if any of them dies or is for any reason unable to act, the other or others may act. *Id.* If no incorporator is able to act, any person for whom an incorporator was acting as agent may act in the

provision of the certificate of incorporation, it may provide, to the extent it is not inconsistent with the NYBCL, that the written consent of the holders of less than all outstanding shares is sufficient to take corporate action.[3]

Library References:
West's Key No. Digests, Corporations ⚷191.

§ 1.49 Shareholders' Meetings and Agreements Summary

Meetings of shareholders may be held at any place, within or without New York, as fixed in the bylaws (or, if not fixed in the bylaws, then at the corporation's New York office). A meeting of shareholders must be held annually for the election of directors and the transaction of other business on a date fixed in or pursuant to the bylaws. Special meetings of the shareholders may be called by the board or by other persons authorized by the certificate of incorporation or the bylaws. If the shareholders after a certain grace period fail to elect a sufficient number of directors to conduct the business of the corporation, the board must call a special meeting for the election of directors, and if the required number of directors is not elected within a prescribed period, holders of at least ten percent of the voting shares may demand the call of a special meeting for the election of directors.

Shareholders must be given written notice of the place, date, and hour of a shareholders' meeting. Notice of a special meeting must also state the purpose(s) for which the meeting is called. If action is proposed to be taken at the meeting that, if taken, would entitle shareholders to enforce their right to receive payment for their shares under NYBCL § 623, the notice must include a statement to that effect and must be accompanied by a copy of NYBCL § 623 or an outline of its material terms.

As a general rule, shareholders of record are entitled to one vote for every share standing in their name on the record of shareholders, unless otherwise provided in the certificate of incorporation. However, the certificate of incorporation may contain limitations on the right to vote, and nonvoting shares may be issued. The NYBCL prescribes the manner in which shares held by fiduciaries, receivers, or pledgees, and shares registered in the name of two or more persons are to be voted. Treasury shares and redeemable shares called for redemption are not deemed to be outstanding shares for voting purposes, nor are shares owned by a

incorporator's stead, or if the other person also dies or is for any reason unable to act, the incorporator's legal representative may act. *Id.*

3. NYBCL § 615(a). *See, e.g.*, NYBCL § 511(a)(3) (certain share distributions of any class or series may be approved by the affirmative vote, or the written consent, of the holders of a majority of the class or series to be distributed). *Cf.* Delaware General Corporations Law § 228.

majority-owned subsidiary of the corporation. Shares standing in the name of another domestic or foreign corporation may be voted as its bylaws provide or board may determine. Shareholders may also act through proxies. A proxy is revocable unless made irrevocable under specific rules in the NYBCL.

Most corporate action (other than the election of directors) required to be taken by the shareholders must be taken by majority vote. Directors, however, are elected by a plurality of the votes cast at a meeting of shareholders, except as otherwise required by the NYBCL or by the certificate of incorporation. Normally, a majority of the shares constitutes a quorum at shareholders' meetings, but greater than normal quorum requirements are permitted if specified in the certificate of incorporation. The certificate of incorporation may permit cumulative voting. A shareholders' list must be available at shareholders' meetings. The NYBCL prescribes rules for the appointment and duties of inspectors of election and for shareholders' agreements and voting trust agreements. Shareholder action by consent without a meeting is permitted but must be unanimous unless the certificate of incorporation or the NYBCL specifies otherwise.

Library References:

West's Key No. Digests, Corporations ⚖=191–201.

§ 1.50 Shareholders' Meetings and Agreements Checklist

1. Annual meetings. (*See* § 1.43)
2. Special meetings. (*See* § 1.43)
   - Called by board or others authorized in certificate of incorporation or bylaws. (*See* § 1.43)
   - Called by board on failure to elect directors. (*See* § 1.43)
   - Called on demand of shareholders. (*See* § 1.43)
3. Record date. (*See* § 1.43)
4. Shareholders aggrieved by election. (*See* § 1.43)
5. Notice requirements. (*See* § 1.44)
6. Voting. (*See* § 1.45)
   - Shareholders of record. (*See* § 1.45)
   - Limitations on the right to vote. (*See* § 1.45)
   - Nonvoting shares. (*See* § 1.45)
   - Class voting. (*See* § 1.45)
   - Shares held by fiduciaries, receivers, and pledgees. (*See* § 1.45)

§ 1.50 BUSINESS ORGANIZATIONS: CORPORATIONS Ch. 1

- Redeemable shares. (*See* § 1.45)
- Shares standing in the name of another corporation. (*See* § 1.45)
- Shares recorded in the name of two or more persons. (*See* § 1.45)
- Proxies. (*See* § 1.45)
- Vote of shareholders. (*See* § 1.45)
- Cumulative voting. (*See* § 1.45)
- Shareholders' list. (*See* § 1.45)
- Inspectors of election. (*See* § 1.45)

7. Quorum requirements. (*See* § 1.46)
   - Normal rule. (*See* § 1.46)
   - Lesser quorum. (*See* § 1.46)
   - Greater quorum. (*See* § 1.46)
8. Shareholder voting agreements. (*See* § 1.47)
9. Certificate of incorporation provision restricting board. (*See* § 1.47)
10. Voting trust agreements. (*See* § 1.47)
11. Shareholder action (consent) without a meeting. (*See* § 1.48)

Library References:

West's Key No. Digests, Corporations ⟝191–201.

§ 1.51 Shareholders' Rights

Shareholders have a bundle of rights.[1] Three basic investment criteria—income, control, and risk[2]—are reflected in shareholders' fundamental rights: the right to income in the form of dividends when

---

§ 1.51

1. *See supra*, §§ 1.2 and 1.4.

PRACTICE POINTER: In negotiations among the founders upon formation of the corporation, whether the client should bargain for a senior interest in addition to, or as an alternative to, common stock will depend on what the client's aims are. If the client is one of the largest investors in the enterprise, senior securities (bonds or preferred stock) may be indicated to lessen the *risk* of not recovering the client's investment upon liquidation of the corporation's assets. The client may also be interested in *control* over the corporation's affairs, in *income* from corporate earnings distributed as shareholder dividends, and in possible appreciation in the value of the shares. Accordingly, a controlling percentage of the voting common stock would be desirable for the client. These various aims may or may not be feasible, depending on the client's bargaining power and the limitations imposed by applicable corporate, securities, tax, and antitrust laws. *See supra*, § 1.34. *See also*, NYBCL § 625 re rights (including the right to disaffirm) and capacity to vote and receive distributions of infant shareholders and bondholders; written notice that holder is an infant to officer (or transfer agent) maintaining shareholder list (or for bonds, the treasurer or other paying officer). For the definition of "infant," *see* NYBCL § 102(7–a).

2. *See supra*, § 1.2.

declared by the board,[3] the right to vote at shareholders' meetings,[4] and the right to share in the proceeds of dissolution and liquidation.[5] Examples of other shareholders' rights[6] include the right to transfer ownership of their shares,[7] inspect the corporation's records,[8] vote by proxy,[9] act by written consent without a meeting,[10] contest a corporate election,[11] bring a derivative action,[12] receive payment for shares,[13] vote on the desirability of a share exchange,[14] merger,[15] sale of substantially all the corporation's assets,[16] or nonjudicial dissolution of the corporation,[17] dissent from certain corporate action,[18] and petition for judicial dissolution of the corporation.[19]

Shareholders' Right to Dissent and to Receive Payment for Their Shares. Shareholders have the right to dissent from certain fundamental corporate changes and thereby receive payment for their shares.[20] This right serves to resolve the tension between majority shareholders, who have almost unlimited power to change the character and shape of the business (subject to their fiduciary duties to minority shareholders and the corporation under New York law),[21] and dissenting shareholders, who are able to escape the disagreeable business policies or

---

3. NYBCL §§ 501 and 510. *See supra*, § 1.38.

4. NYBCL §§ 501 and 614. *See also*, NYBCL § 617. *See supra*, § 1.45.

5. NYBCL § 501(a), (b) (regarding limited and unlimited liquidation rights). *See infra*, §§ 1.94 and 1.107.

6. The existence of some rights depends on their being granted in the certificate of incorporation (*e.g.*, cumulative voting (NYBCL § 618) or voting by class (NYBCL § 617)); others exist unless otherwise provided in or limited by the certificate of incorporation (*e.g.*, preemptive rights (NYBCL § 622) or voting rights (NYBCL §§ 501 and 613)). *See supra*, §§ 1.21, 1.26–1.31, 1.47–48 and *infra* § 1.52.

7. *See also*, NYBCL §§ 607, 628, and 629. *See supra*, § 1.21 (transfer restrictions) and *infra*, § 1.56 (transferor liability on unpaid balance of subscription).

8. NYBCL § 624. *See infra*, § 1.53.

9. NYBCL § 609(a). *See supra*, § 1.45.

10. NYBCL § 615(a). *See supra*, § 1.48.

11. NYBCL § 619.

12. NYBCL § 626(a). *See infra*, § 1.51, notes 86–96 and accompanying text.

13. NYBCL § 623. *See infra*, §§ 1.51, notes 20–85 and accompanying text; 1.90.

14. NYBCL § 913(c). *See infra*, §§ 1.81 and 1.88. *Cf. infra*, § 1.89.

15. NYBCL § 903(a)(2). *See infra*, § 1.83.

16. NYBCL § 909(a)(1). *See infra*, § 1.85.

17. NYBCL § 1001. *See infra*, § 1.96.

18. *See, e.g.*, NYBCL §§ 623 (election to dissent), 806 (certain amendments and changes), 910 (merger or other extraordinary disposition), 1005 (certain sales in dissolution).

19. NYBCL §§ 1103 and 1104. *See infra*, §§ 1.102 and 1.103.

20. NYBCL § 623(a). *See* NYBCL § 513 (corporate right to purchase its shares under NYBCL § 513(b)(3) stated capital (rather than surplus) measure if purchase is for purpose of paying dissenter's right to receive payment), 806(b)(6) (dissenter's right to receive payment upon amendment to certificate of incorporation that alters or abolishes any preemptive right), 910(a) (dissenter's right to receive payment upon merger and other disposition of assets), 1005 (dissenter's right to receive payment upon liquidation distribution that is not wholly in cash). *See also*, RMBCA § 13.02(a).

21. *See* NYBCL § 623, Notes of Decisions. *See also*, *supra*, § 1.47 and *infra*, § 1.103. *See also, e.g.*, R. Hamilton, *The Law of Corporations* (1987) pp. 255–266, 303; Henn and Alexander, *supra*, § 1.1, note 1, pp. 651, 653–661.

practices imposed by the majority and receive the fair market value of their investment.[22]

Payment for Shares: Pre-judicial Procedure. Shareholders intending to enforce their dissenting rights if a proposed corporate action is taken must file written objection to the action with the corporation, either before the shareholders' meeting at which the action is submitted to a vote or at the meeting, but before the vote.[23] The objection must include a notice of an election to dissent, the shareholder's name and residence address, the number and classes of shares to which the dissent relates,[24] and a demand for payment of the fair value of the shares if the action is authorized.[25]

An objection is not required from shareholders to whom the corporation did not give notice of the meeting in accordance with the NYBCL or where the proposed action is authorized by written consent of shareholders without a meeting.[26] Within ten days after the shareholders' authorization date,[27] the corporation must give written notice thereof by registered mail to shareholders who filed a written objection, or from whom a written objection was not required, but not to shareholders who voted for or consented in writing to the proposed action and who are therefore deemed to have elected not to enforce their dissenters' rights.[28]

Within 20 days after the corporation's notice to shareholders, any shareholder not required to make written objection and who elects to dissent must file with the corporation a written notice of election, stating the shareholder's name and residence address, the number and classes of shares to which the dissent relates, and a demand for payment of the fair value of the shares.[29] Any shareholder who elects to dissent from the merger of a subsidiary corporation into its parent under NYBCL § 905, the merger or consolidation of domestic and foreign corporations under

---

22. *See* RMBCA, Chapter 13, Introductory Comment.

PRACTICE POINTER: Dissenters' rights are a shield assuring that fair value is paid for the minority's shares, but they may also be used as a sword by the corporation in certain transactions (*e.g.*, mergers or share exchanges) to force minority interests out of the shareholder ranks upon payment for their shares. *See supra*, § 1.30, note 16. *See infra*, § 1.81, note 1.

23. NYBCL § 623(a). This section does not apply to foreign corporations except as provided in NYBCL § 907(e)(2) regarding merger or consolidation of domestic and foreign corporations. NYBCL § 623(m).

24. *See* NYBCL §§ 801(b)(12) and 806(b)(6) (amendments and changes that adversely affect rights, preferences, and limitations regarding certain classes or series of shares of a holder). *See also*, RMBCA 13.02(a)(4), Official Comment 1(4). *See infra*, § 1.72.

25. NYBCL § 623(a).

26. *Id.* Except as otherwise expressly provided in NYBCL § 623, any notice to be given by a corporation to shareholders must be given in the manner provided in NYBCL § 605 for notice of shareholders' meetings. NYBCL § 623(*l*).

27. The term "shareholders' authorization date" is used in NYBCL § 623 and means the date on which the shareholders' vote authorizing the action was taken or the date on which consent without a meeting was obtained from the requisite shareholders. NYBCL § 623(b).

28. NYBCL § 623(b).

29. NYBCL § 623(c). *See also*, *supra*, § 1.51, notes 23–25 and accompanying text.

NYBCL § 907(c), or a share exchange under NYBCL § 913(g) must file a written notice of election to dissent within twenty days after the shareholder has been given a copy of the plan of merger or exchange (or an outline of the plan's material features) under NYBCL §§ 905 or 913.[30]

Within one month after filing the notice of election to dissent, the shareholder must submit shares represented by certificates to the corporation or its transfer agent, which must forthwith note conspicuously on the certificates that such a notice of election has been filed.[31] The corporation or its transfer agent must thereafter return the certificates to the shareholder or other person who submitted them on the shareholder's behalf.[32] Shareholders who fail to submit certificates for the required notation lose their dissenters' rights at the option of the corporation.[33] Upon transfer of a certificate bearing the notation, each new certificate issued therefor must bear a similar notation together with the name of the original dissenting holder of the shares.[34] A transferee acquires no rights other than those the original dissenting shareholder had at the time of transfer.[35]

Shareholders may not dissent with respect to fewer than all the shares for which they have a right to dissent and which they hold of record and own beneficially.[36] A nominee or fiduciary may not dissent with respect to fewer than all the shares for which he or she has a right to dissent and holds of record.[37]

Upon consummation of the corporate action in question, a dissenting shareholder ceases to have any of the rights of a shareholder, except the right to be paid the fair value of the shares[38] and any other rights under NYBCL § 623.[39] A notice of election may be withdrawn by a shareholder at any time prior to acceptance in writing of an offer by the corporation pursuant to NYBCL § 623(g)[40] but in no case later than 60 days after the corporate action is consummated.[41] If the corporation fails to make a timely offer pursuant to NYBCL § 623(g), the time for withdrawing a notice of election must be extended until 60 days after the offer is made.[42] After that time, withdrawal of a notice of election requires the corporation's written consent.[43] In order to be effective, a

---

30. NYBCL § 623(c).
31. NYBCL § 623(f).
32. *Id.*
33. *Id.* The corporation must exercise its option to cancel the dissenters' rights by written notice to the shareholder within forty-five days after the filing of the notice of election to dissent, unless a court, for good cause shown, otherwise directs. *Id.*
   CAVEAT: Special care must be exercised to make sure that the certificates are submitted for the required notation rather than risk losing dissenters' rights.
34. NYBCL § 623(f).
35. *Id.*
36. NYBCL § 623(d).
37. *Id.*
38. See *infra*, § 1.51, notes 49–77 and accompanying text.
39. NYBCL § 623(e).
40. See *infra*, § 1.51, notes 49–59 and accompanying text.
41. NYBCL § 623(e).
42. *Id.*
43. *Id.*

withdrawal must be accompanied by the return of any advance payment made by the corporation to the shareholder in respect of his or her rights.[44]

Shareholders do not have the right to receive payment for their shares if a notice of election is withdrawn, the corporate action is rescinded, a court determines that the shareholder is not entitled to receive the payment, or the shareholder otherwise loses his or her dissenter's rights.[45] In these cases, shareholders reacquire all the rights held by non-dissenting shareholders as of the consummation of the corporate action, including any intervening preemptive rights and the right to payment of any intervening dividend or other distribution.[46] If any of these rights have expired, or any noncash dividend or distribution has been completed, in lieu thereof, at the election of the corporation, the corporation may pay the shareholder the fair value thereof, in cash, as determined by the board as of the date the rights expired, but without prejudice otherwise to any corporate proceedings[47] that may have been taken in the interim.[48]

Payment for Shares: Pre-judicial Procedure—Purchase Offer by Corporation. Within 15 days after the expiration of the period within which shareholders may file their notices of election to dissent, or within 15 days after the proposed corporate action is consummated, whichever is later (but in no case later than 90 days after the shareholders' authorization date), the corporation or, in the case of a merger or consolidation, the surviving or new corporation, must make a written offer by registered mail to dissenting shareholders to pay what the corporation considers to be the fair value of their shares.[49] The offer must be accompanied by a statement setting forth the aggregate number of shares for which dissent notices have been received and the aggregate number of holders of the shares.[50] If the corporate action has been consummated, the offer must also be accompanied by (1) to shareholders who have submitted the certificates representing their shares, an advance payment equal to eighty percent of the offered amount and (2) to shareholders who have not submitted certificates, a statement that an advance payment equal to eighty percent of the amount offered will be made to them by the corporation promptly following submission of the certificates.[51] If the corporate action has not been consummated at the time the offer is made, the advance payment (or statement that an

44. Id.
45. Id.
46. Id.
47. Such as proceedings in equity on grounds that the corporate action is unlawful or fraudulent. See NYBCL § 623, Notes of Decisions (various cases cited). See also, RMBCA § 13.02, Official Comment 2 (exclusivity of dissenters' rights).
48. NYBCL § 623(e).
49. NYBCL § 623(g).
50. Id.
51. Id.

advance payment will be made) must be sent forthwith upon consummation.[52]

Every advance payment (or statement that an advance payment will be made) must include advice to the shareholder to the effect that acceptance of the payment does not constitute a waiver of any dissenters' rights.[53] If the corporate action has not been consummated within ninety days after the shareholders' authorization date, the corporation's offer may be conditioned upon the consummation of the action.[54] The offered price per share must be the same for all dissenting shareholders of the same class or series, and the offer must be accompanied by the latest available balance sheet[55] of the corporation and profit and loss statements for not shorter than the 12-month period ended on the date of the balance sheet.[56] The corporation is not required to furnish a balance sheet or profit and loss statements to shareholders to whom these financial statements were previously furnished[57] or to whom the corporation furnished a proxy statement or an information statement that included financial statements pursuant to Regulation 14A or Regulation 14C of the United States Securities and Exchange Commission in obtaining the shareholders' authorization for or consent to the proposed corporate action.[58] If, within 30 days after making the offer, the corporation and any shareholder agree upon the price to be paid for the shareholder's shares, full payment of the price must be made within 60 days after either the offer or the consummation of the proposed corporate action, whichever is later, and upon the surrender of the certificates for shares.[59]

Payment for Shares: Procedure for Judicial Determination (Appraisal). If the corporation fails to make an offer within 15 days after the expiration of time within which shareholders may file their notices of election to dissent, or if it makes the offer and any dissenting shareholders fail to accept it within 30 days, a judicial determination of the rights of dissenting shareholders and the value of their shares will be made as follows:[60]

(1) Within 20 days after the expiration of the 15-day period (within which the corporation failed to make an offer) or the 30-day period (within which any dissenting shareholders failed to accept an offer made), the corporation must institute a special proceeding in the supreme court in the judicial district in which the office of the corporation

---

52. *Id.*

53. *Id.*

54. *Id.*

55. The balance sheet must not be dated earlier than twelve months before the making of the offer. NYBCL § 623(g).

56. NYBCL § 623(g). If the corporation was not in existence throughout the twelve-month period, the profit and loss statements must be for the portion of the twelve-month period during which it was in existence. *Id.*

57. NYBCL § 623(g).

58. *Id.*

59. *Id.*

60. NYBCL § 623(h).

is located to determine the rights of dissenting shareholders and to fix the fair value of their shares.[61] If, in the case of merger or consolidation, the surviving or new corporation is a foreign corporation without an office in New York, the proceeding must be brought in the county where the office of the domestic corporation, whose shares are to be valued, was located.[62]

(2) If the corporation fails to institute the proceeding within the 20-day period, any dissenting shareholder may institute the proceeding for the same purpose not later than 30 days after the expiration of the 20-day period.[63] If the proceeding is not instituted within the 30-day period, all dissenters' rights are lost unless the supreme court, for good cause shown, otherwise directs.[64]

(3) All dissenting shareholders, except those who have agreed with the corporation upon the price to be paid for their shares, must be made parties to the proceeding, which has the effect of an action *quasi in rem* against their shares.[65] The corporation must serve a copy of the petition in the proceeding upon each dissenting shareholder who is a resident of New York in the manner provided by law for the service of a summons and upon each nonresident dissenting shareholder either by registered mail and publication or in any other manner permitted by law.[66] The jurisdiction of the court is plenary and exclusive.[67]

(4) As to each dissenting shareholder for whom the court is requested to make a determination, the court shall first determine whether the shareholder is entitled to receive payment, and if a shareholder is so entitled, the court must fix the fair value of the shareholder's shares as of the close of business on the day prior to the shareholders' authorization date.[68] To fix the fair value of the shares, the court considers the nature of the transaction giving rise to the dissenter's right to payment and its effects on the corporation and its shareholders, the concepts and methods then customary in the relevant securities and financial markets for determining fair value of shares of a corporation engaging in a similar transaction under comparable circumstances, and all other relevant factors.[69] Fair value is fixed without a jury and without referral to an appraiser or referee.[70]

---

61. NYBCL § 623(h)(1).
62. *Id.*
63. NYBCL § 623(h)(2).
64. *Id.*
  CAVEAT: The procedure must be followed meticulously to avoid losing the right to payment.
65. NYBCL § 623(h)(3).
66. *Id.*
67. *Id.*
68. NYBCL § 623(h)(4).
69. *Id.*
70. *Id.* Upon application by the corporation or any shareholder party to the proceeding, the court may, in its discretion, permit pretrial disclosure, including, but not limited to, disclosure of any expert's reports relating to the fair value of the shares, whether or not intended for use at the trial in the proceeding and notwithstanding CPLR 3101(d). *Id.*

(5) A final order in the proceeding must be entered against the corporation in favor of each dissenting shareholder who is party to the proceeding and who was determined to be entitled to the fair value of his or her shares.[71] The final order must include an allowance for interest, at the rate the court finds to be equitable, from the date the corporate action was consummated to the date of payment in full of fair value.[72] If the court finds that any shareholder's refusal to accept the corporation's offer was arbitrary, vexatious, or otherwise not in good faith, no interest is allowed that shareholder.[73]

(6) Each party to the proceeding must bear its own costs and expenses, including the fees and expenses of its counsel and of any experts employed by it.[74] The court may, however, apportion and assess all or any part of the costs, expenses, and fees incurred by the corporation against any or all of the dissenting shareholders party to the proceeding, including those who withdraw their notices of election, if it finds that their refusal to accept the corporate offer was arbitrary, vexatious, or otherwise not in good faith.[75] The court may also apportion and assess against the corporation all or any part of the costs, expenses, and fees incurred by any or all of the dissenting shareholders party to the proceeding if it finds that the fair value of the shares materially exceeds the amount that the corporation offered to pay, that no offer or required advance payment was made by the corporation, that the corporation failed to institute the special proceeding within the period specified, or that any action of the corporation in connection with its obligations under NYBCL § 623 was arbitrary, vexatious, or otherwise not in good faith.[76]

(7) Within 60 days after the court's final determinations, the corporation must pay to each dissenting shareholder the amount found to be due, upon surrender of the certificates representing the dissenter's shares.[77]

No payment may be made to dissenting shareholders at a time when the corporation is insolvent or when the payment would render it insolvent.[78] In that event, dissenting shareholders have two options. They may withdraw their notice of election, which is deemed withdrawn with the written consent of the corporation.[79] Or they may retain their status as claimants against the corporation, and if the corporation is

---

71. NYBCL § 623(h)(5).
72. NYBCL § 623(h)(6). In determining the rate of interest, the court must consider all relevant factors, including the rate of interest that the corporation would have had to pay to borrow money during the pendency of the proceeding. *Id.*
73. NYBCL § 623(h)(6).
74. NYBCL § 623(h)(7).
75. *Id.*
76. *Id.* In making any determination whether the fair value materially exceeded the amount offered by the corporation, the court may consider the dollar amount or the percentage, or both, by which the fair value of the shares exceeds the corporate offer. *Id.*
77. NYBCL § 623(h)(8).
78. NYBCL § 623(j).
79. *Id.*

liquidated, they are subordinated to the rights of its creditors but have rights superior to the non-dissenting shareholders.[80] If the corporation is not liquidated, they retain their rights to be paid for their shares, and the corporation is obliged to satisfy these rights when it is not insolvent or when the payment would not render it insolvent.[81] Dissenting shareholders must exercise either option by written notice filed with the corporation within 30 days after the corporation has given them written notice that payment for their shares cannot be made because of these restrictions on payment.[82] If a dissenting shareholder fails to exercise either option within the 30-day period, the corporation must do so by written notice given to the shareholder within 20 days after the expiration of the 30-day period.[83]

Dissenters' shares acquired by the corporation upon payment, as agreed or as determined by the court, become treasury shares or are cancelled as provided in NYBCL § 515, except that, in the case of a merger or consolidation, the shares may be held and disposed of as the plan of merger or consolidation may otherwise provide.[84] Dissenters' rights under NYBCL § 623 are exclusive of other remedies available to shareholders unless the transaction in question is unlawful or fraudulent.[85]

Shareholders' Derivative Action. Any shareholder, record holder of voting trust certificates, or holder of a beneficial interest in such shares or certificates has the right to bring an action on behalf of a domestic or a foreign corporation to enforce the corporation's right to procure a judgment in its favor.[86] The action is derivative because the shareholders sue not in their own right, but in the right of the corporation, for wrongs against the corporation and because the corporation failed to bring suit on its own behalf.[87] The shareholders bringing the action must have owned their shares at the time of the transaction of which they complain.[88]

The complaint must set forth with particularity the efforts of the plaintiff to have the board initiate the action or the plaintiff's reasons for not making that effort.[89] A good faith demand upon the corporation to institute the suit is ordinarily a prerequisite to bringing the action,

---

80. Id.
81. Id.
82. Id.
83. Id.
84. Id.
85. NYBCL § 623(k).
86. NYBCL § 626(a).
87. *See, e.g.,* Alexander v. Donohoe, 143 N.Y. 203, 38 N.E. 263 (1894).
88. NYBCL § 626(b). The shareholder may bring the action if the shares or interest in the shares devolved upon the shareholder by operation of law. Id. *See, e.g.,* Salter v. Columbia Concerts, 191 Misc. 479, 77 N.Y.S.2d 703 (Sup.Ct., N.Y. County, 1948); Albert v. Salzman, 41 A.D.2d 501, 344 N.Y.S.2d 457 (1st Dep't 1973). *Cf.* RMBCA § 7.40 (person may bring action if became a shareholder through transfer by operation of law from a contemporaneous holder, *i.e.,* from a person who was a shareholder at the time that the transaction complained of occurred).
89. NYBCL § 626(c).

unless the demand would be futile.[90] The action must not be discontinued, compromised, or settled without the approval of the court having jurisdiction of the action.[91] If the court determines that the interests of shareholders will be substantially affected by the action's discontinuance, compromise, or settlement, the court may direct that notice, by publication or other means, be given to shareholders whose interest it determines will be affected.[92] If the court directs that notice be given, it may determine which parties to the action shall bear the expense of giving notice.[93]

If the derivative action is successful (in whole or in part, or if anything was received by the plaintiffs or claimants as the result of a judgment, compromise, or settlement), the court may award them reasonable expenses, including reasonable attorneys' fees, and direct them to account to the corporation for the remainder of the proceeds received by them (but not for any judgment rendered for the benefit of injured shareholders only and limited to a recovery of the loss or damage sustained by them).[94]

Unless the plaintiffs either hold five percent or more of any class of outstanding shares (or voting trust certificates, or a beneficial interest in shares, representing five percent or more of any such class) *or* their shares, voting trust certificates, and beneficial interest have an aggregate fair value in excess of 50 thousand dollars, the corporation is entitled to security for expenses, including attorneys' fees, that may be incurred by it (and by any other defendants).[95] The amount of the security may from time to time be increased or decreased in the discretion of the court upon showing that the security provided has or may become inadequate or excessive.[96]

§ 1.52 Shareholders' Rights—Preemptive Rights

Preemptive rights are granted to protect shareholders from dilution of their interest in the corporation.[1] These rights enable shareholders to

---

90. *See, e.g.*, Marx v. Akers, 88 N.Y.2d 189, 644 N.Y.S.2d 121, 666 N.E.2d 1034 (1996) (futility of demand discussed). *See also*, cases cited at NYBCL § 626, Notes of Decisions 40 (demand ordinarily a condition precedent to action), 41 (failure or refusal of board to act), and 42 (futility of demand).

91. NYBCL § 626(d).

92. *Id.*

93. *Id.* The court may also determine the amount of expense that is reasonable in the circumstances; expenses are awarded as special costs of the action and recoverable in the same manner as statutory taxable costs. *Id. See supra*, § 1.19, note 6.

94. NYBCL § 626(e).

95. NYBCL § 627. *Cf.* RMBCA 7.40(d) and Official Comment 1.h.

96. NYBCL § 627. The corporation is entitled at any stage of the proceedings before final judgment to require the plaintiffs to give security for the reasonable expenses, to which the corporation has recourse in whatever amount, if any, that the court determines upon the termination of the action. *Id.*

§ 1.52

1. *See supra*, § 1.2. *See also*, NYBCL §§ 505(d) (option to purchase shares subject to preemptive rights), 511 (share distributions subject to preemptive rights), 806 (amendment affecting preemptive rights).

§ 1.52 BUSINESS ORGANIZATIONS: CORPORATIONS Ch. 1

maintain their proportionate interest in (1) their voting power in the corporation, (2) the corporation's earnings, and (3) the corporation's assets.[2]

Shareholders do not have preemptive rights unless otherwise provided in the certificate of incorporation.[3] Shareholders with preemptive rights are entitled to purchase shares (or other securities convertible into shares) in a proposed offering at prices no less favorable than the prices at which they are proposed to be offered for sale to others (without deduction of reasonable expenses of the sale, underwriting, or purchase of the shares or other securities by underwriters or dealers).[4]

If all of the shares entitling the holders to preemptive rights do not each confer the same unlimited dividend rights or voting rights, the board must apportion the shares (or other securities to be offered or optioned for sale) among the shareholders having preemptive rights to purchase the shares (or other securities) so as to preserve as far as practicable the relative unlimited dividend rights and voting rights of the holders at the time of the proposed offering.[5] The apportionment made by the board, absent fraud or bad faith, is binding on all shareholders.[6]

Except as *otherwise* provided in the certificate of incorporation, and except as provided in NYBCL § 622, no holder of any shares *qua* holder has any preemptive right to purchase any other shares or securities that at any time may be sold or offered for sale by the corporation.[7] Unless otherwise provided in the certificate of incorporation, shares or other securities, including rights or options to purchase shares, of the corpora-

PRACTICE POINTER: When preemptive rights are limited or not granted to the shareholders in the certificate of incorporation (*see* NYBCL § 622(b)), the corporation may, by action of the board alone or at the request of shareholders, grant them the right to subscribe to a particular new issue of its shares even though it would not be obligated to do so.

2. NYBCL § 622(d).
3. NYBCL §§ 620(b) and (c).

CAVEAT: With respect to corporations incorporated *prior*, and to holders of *voting* shares of any class having any preemptive right under NYBCL § 622(c) on the date immediately *prior*, to the effective date of NYBCL § 622(b)(2), except as *otherwise* provided in the certificate of incorporation, and except as provided in NYBCL § 622, if a proposed issuance of any voting or other equity shares, or the proposed grant of rights or options to purchase any voting or other equity shares (or any shares or other securities convertible into or carrying rights or options to purchase any of its voting or other equity shares) would adversely affect the unlimited dividend rights or voting rights of the holders of voting or other equity shares, those holders have the right, during a reasonable time and on reasonable conditions fixed by the board, to purchase the proposed to be issued shares, options, or other securities in proportions determined under NYBCL § 622. NYBCL §§ 622(b)(2) and (c). With respect to corporations incorporated *on or after* the effective date of NYBCL § 622(b)(2), the holders of such shares do *not* have any preemptive right, except as otherwise expressly provided in the certificate of incorporation. NYBCL § 622(b)(2). The effective date of NYBCL § 622(b)(2) is the one hundred eightieth day after the act amending the NYBCL became law (*see* 1997 NY S.B. 476 (SN) § 71; 1997 NY S.B. 5680 (SN) § 7); S.B. 476 was enacted on Aug. 26, 1997, and its effective date is Feb. 22, 1998. *See* NYBCL § 622(a) (definitions of terms).

4. NYBCL § 622(d).
5. *Id.*
6. *Id.*
7. NYBCL § 622(i).

tion offered for sale are not subject to preemptive rights under NYBCL §§ 622(b) or (c) if they: (1) are authorized by the board to be issued to effect a merger or consolidation or are offered for consideration other than cash; (2) are to be issued under NYBCL § 505(d); (3) are to be issued to satisfy conversion or option rights earlier granted by the corporation; (4) are treasury shares; (5) are a portion of the shares or other securities of the corporation authorized in its original certificate of incorporation and are issued, sold, or granted within two years from the date of filing the certificate; or (6) are to be issued under a plan of reorganization approved in a federal proceeding for reorganization of corporations.[8]

Shareholders entitled to preemptive rights are determined on the record date fixed by the board under NYBCL § 604 or, if no record date is fixed, then on the record date determined under NYBCL § 604.[9] The board must give each shareholder entitled to preemptive rights a notice personally or by mail at least 15 days prior to the expiration of the period during which the shareholder has the right to purchase.[10] The notice must set forth the time within which, and the terms and conditions upon which, the shareholder may purchase the shares or other securities; it must also set forth any apportionment of the right to purchase among the shareholders entitled to preemptive rights.[11] All shareholders entitled to preemptive rights to whom due notice is given are deemed conclusively to have had a reasonable time in which to exercise their preemptive rights.[12]

If shareholders with preemptive rights have not exercised their rights within the time fixed by the board, the shares or other securities offered to the shareholders may be issued, sold, or granted to other persons during a period not exceeding one year following the expiration of the time fixed and at a price not less than that at which they were offered to those shareholders (without deduction for reasonable expenses of the sale, underwriting, or purchase of the shares by underwriters or dealers).[13] Any shares or other securities not issued, sold, or granted to others during the one-year period are thereafter subject again to preemptive rights.[14] Unless otherwise provided in the certificate of incorporation, holders of bonds on which voting rights are conferred under NYBCL § 518 have no preemptive rights.[15]

Library References:

West's Key No. Digests, Corporations ⟐ 170–190.

8. NYBCL § 622(e).
9. NYBCL § 622(f).
10. NYBCL § 622(g). Except as provided in NYBCL § 622(g), the notice must be given in the manner provided in NYBCL § 605. *Id.*
11. NYBCL § 622(g).
12. *Id.*
13. NYBCL § 622(h).
14. *Id.*
15. NYBCL § 622(i).

§ 1.53 Shareholders' Rights—Inspection of Books and Records

A corporation must keep correct and complete books and records of account plus minutes of the proceedings of its shareholders, board, and executive committee, if any.[1] It must also keep at its New York office, or at the office of its transfer agent or registrar in New York, a record of the names and addresses of shareholders, the number and class of shares held by each, and the dates when they became owners of record.[2]

Any persons who have been a shareholder of record are entitled to inspect and copy certain corporate records if they give the corporation at least five days' written notice of their demand to inspect for any purpose reasonably related to such person's interest as a shareholder.[3] They have the right to examine in person (or by agent or attorney) the minutes of shareholder proceedings and the record of shareholders and to make extracts of these materials during the corporation's usual business hours.[4] Any such agent or attorney must be authorized in a writing that satisfies the requirements of a writing under NYBCL § 609(b) (proxies).[5] A corporation requested to provide information pursuant to NYBCL § 624(b) must make the information available in written form and in any other format in which the information is maintained by the corporation; it is not required to provide the information in any other format.[6]

An inspection may be denied if those demanding it fail to furnish the corporation (or its transfer agent or registrar) their affidavit that the inspection is *not* desired for a purpose that is in the interest of a

---

§ 1.53

1. NYBCL § 624(a). Any of the corporation's books, minutes, or records may be in written form or in any other form capable of being converted into written form within a reasonable time. *Id.*

2. NYBCL § 624(a).

3. NYBCL § 624(b). Holders of voting trust certificates representing shares of the corporation are regarded as shareholders for inspection purposes. *Id. See also,* NYBCL § 621(c) (voting trust certificate holders entitled to remedies provided in NYBCL § 624). *See supra,* § 1.47. For others having rights of inspection, *see* NYBCL §§ 518(c) (bondholders) and 630(a) (employees). *See also,* RMBCA §§ 7.23, Official Comment (shares held by nominees; beneficial owner of shares that are registered in name of a nominee is recognized by the corporation as the shareholder (*i.e.,* shares are registered in the "street name" of broker-dealers or other financial institutions who deposit securities with a depository (or clearing corporation defined in UCC § 8-102(3)) who become the registered owners of the shares); the depository being the registered owner for the account of the financial institution that in turn holds the shares for the account of the beneficial owner) and 1.40(22) (shareholder means a person in whose name shares are registered in the records of the corporation or the beneficial owner of shares to the extent of the rights granted by a nominee certificate on file with the corporation (*e.g.,* the right to receive notice of, and vote at, a shareholders' meeting)); Henn and Alexander, *supra,* § 1.1, note 1, p. 490.

4. NYBCL § 624(b).

5. *Id.*

6. *Id.* If the request includes a request to furnish information regarding beneficial owners, the corporation must make available such information in its possession regarding beneficial owners as is provided to the corporation by a registered broker or dealer or a bank, an association, or other entity that exercises fiduciary powers in connection with the forwarding of information to such owners. *Id.* The corporation is not required to obtain information about beneficial owners not in its possession. *Id.*

business or object *other than* the business of the corporation and that they have not within five years sold or offered for sale any list of corporate shareholders or aided or abetted any other person in procuring any record of shareholders for that purpose.[7] Upon the corporation's refusal to permit the inspection, the persons demanding the inspection may apply to the supreme court in the judicial district where the office of the corporation is located, upon notice as directed by the court, for an order directing the corporation, its officer, or agent to show cause why an order should not be granted permitting the inspection by the applicant.[8]

Upon the written request of any shareholder, the corporation must give or mail to that shareholder an annual balance sheet and profit and loss statement for the preceding fiscal year and, if any interim balance sheet or profit and loss statement has been distributed to shareholders or otherwise made available to the public, the most recent interim balance sheet or profit and loss statement.[9] The corporation is allowed a reasonable time to prepare the annual balance sheet and profit and loss statement.[10]

Nothing contained in NYBCL § 624 impairs a court's power to compel the production for examination of the books and records of a corporation.[11] The books and records constitute *prima facie* evidence of the facts therein stated in favor of the plaintiff in any action or special proceeding against the corporation or any of its officers, directors, or shareholders.[12]

Library References:

West's Key No. Digests, Corporations ⟐181.

§ 1.54 Shareholders' Rights Summary

Shareholders have a bundle of rights, three of which are basic: the right to income in the form of dividends when declared by the board, the right to vote at shareholders' meetings, and the right to share in the proceeds of the dissolution and liquidation of a corporation. Shareholders do not have preemptive rights unless (with exceptions) otherwise provided in the certificate of incorporation. Shareholders have the right to dissent from certain fundamental corporate changes and receive pay-

---

7. NYBCL § 624(c). *Cf.* RMBCA § 16.02(c) (shareholders may inspect and copy specified records only if their demand is made in good faith and for a "proper purpose," they describe with reasonable particularity the purpose and the records desired to be inspected, and the records are directly connected to that purpose); Delaware General Corporations Law § 220(c).

8. NYBCL § 624(d). Upon the return day of the order to show cause, the court must hear the parties summarily (by affidavit or other means), and if the court finds that the applicants are qualified and entitled to the inspection, the court grants an order compelling the inspection and awarding whatever further relief that to the court may seem just and proper. *Id.*

9. NYBCL § 624(e).

10. *Id.*

11. NYBCL § 624(f).

12. NYBCL § 624(g). *See supra*, § 1.51.

ment for their shares, but the NYBCL specifies in detail the procedure dissenting shareholders must follow to obtain the payment. If they fail to follow the procedure precisely, they lose their right to payment.

Shareholders have the right to bring a derivative action on behalf of a corporation to enforce its rights when the board of directors has not done so. Demand by the shareholders upon the board to bring the action is ordinarily a prerequisite, unless the demand would be futile. The shareholders bringing the action must have owned their shares at the time of the transaction of which they complain, or their shares or interest in the shares must have devolved upon them by operation of law. If the derivative action (or claim) against the corporation is successful, a court may award the plaintiffs (or claimants) reasonable expenses, including reasonable attorneys' fees, and direct them to account to the corporation for the remainder of the proceeds received.

Corporations must keep correct and complete books and records of account plus minutes of the proceedings of its shareholders, board, and executive committee, if any. Shareholders are entitled to inspect and copy certain corporate records if they give the corporation at least five days' written notice of a demand to inspect. They must furnish the corporation with an affidavit that their inspection is not desired for a purpose that is in the interest of a business or object other than the business of the corporation and that they have not in the past five years aided any person in procuring any record of shareholders for that purpose.

Library References:

West's Key No. Digests, Corporations ⌾170–190.

§ 1.55 Shareholders' Rights Checklist

1. Fundamental rights to income, vote, and share assets in liquidation. (*See* § 1.51)
2. Right to dissent and to receive payment for their shares. (*See* § 1.51)
    - Pre-judicial procedure. (*See* § 1.51)
        (i) Written objection.
        (ii) Written notice of election.
        (iii) Submission of share certificates to corporation.
        (iv) Withdrawal of notice of election.
    - Judicial procedure. (*See* § 1.51)
        (i) Corporation's failure to make offer.
        (ii) Special proceeding (to determine dissenting shareholders' rights to payment and to fix fair value of their shares).

Ch. 1　　　SHAREHOLDERS' LIABILITIES　　　§ 1.56

(iii) Costs and expenses.

(iv) Insolvency of corporation.

3. Derivative action. (*See* § 1.51)
4. Preemptive rights. (*See* § 1.52)
5. Rights to inspection of books and records. (*See* § 1.53)
   - Books and records of account. (*See* § 1.53)
   - Minutes of the proceedings of its shareholders, board, and executive committee, if any. (*See* § 1.53)
   - Voting trust certificate holders, bondholders, and employees. (*See* § 1.53)
   - Absence of improper purpose of inspection; affidavit. (*See* § 1.53)

Library References:

West's Key No. Digests, Corporations ⇨170–190.

§ 1.56　Shareholders' Liabilities

The liability of shareholders, as a general rule, is limited to their investment in the corporation, but the courts have, in certain circumstances, disregarded the corporate entity—pierced the corporate veil—to impose liability on shareholders.[1] In addition, a shareholder's liability for corporate obligations is, in some cases, predicated upon particular statutory provisions and, in other cases, on contract, tort, and other principles.[2]

Liability for Unpaid Balance of Subscription. The NYBCL provides that holders of, or subscribers for, shares are under no obligation to the corporation other than to pay the unpaid portion of their subscription.[3] In no event may the total payment be less than the amount of the consideration for which the shares could be issued lawfully.[4] Any assignee or transferee of shares (or of a subscription for shares) in good faith and without notice that the full consideration for the shares has not been paid is not personally liable for the unpaid portion.[5] The transferor remains liable for the unpaid balance.[6] A person holding shares in any corporation as collateral security is not personally liable as a shareholder; the pledgor is considered the holder of the shares for purposes of shareholder liability.[7] Executors, administrators, guard-

§ 1.56

1. *See supra*, § 1.10.
2. *See, e.g.*, Henn and Alexander, *supra*, § 1.1, note 1, pp. 546–550.
3. NYBCL § 628(a).
4. *Id.*
5. NYBCL § 628(b).
6. *Id.*
7. NYBCL § 628(c).

CAVEAT: Although NYBCL § 628 relates to the obligation of shareholders to pay the unpaid portion of their subscriptions but no less than the minimum consideration required by NYBCL § 504, NYBCL § 628(c) applies to any liability as a share-

ians, trustees, or other fiduciaries are not personally liable as shareholders, but the estate and funds in their hands are subject to shareholder liability.[8] The transfer or assignment of shares (or of a subscriber's interest in the corporation) does not relieve the transferor or assignor of any liability as a shareholder or subscriber *if* at the time of the transfer or assignment, the aggregate fair value of the corporation's property (exclusive of any property that it may have conveyed, transferred, concealed, removed with intent to defraud, hinder, or delay its creditors) is, or may imminently become, insufficient in amount to pay the corporation's debts.[9]

Liability for Wages Due Employees. The ten largest shareholders, as determined by the fair value of their beneficial interests as of the beginning of the period during which the unpaid services are performed, of every corporation[10] whose shares are not listed on a national securities exchange or regularly quoted in an over-the-counter market (by one or more members of a national or an affiliated securities association), are jointly and severally personally liable for all debts, wages, or salaries owed employees for services they perform for the corporation.[11] Unpaid employees must give the shareholders notice in writing that they intend to hold the shareholders liable.[12] The notice must be given within 180 days after the termination of the employee's services, except that if, within that period, the employee demands an examination of the record of shareholders under NYBCL § 624(b), the notice may be given within 60 days after the record has been made available.[13] An action to enforce the shareholders' liability under NYBCL § 630 must be commenced within 90 days after the return of an execution unsatisfied upon a judgment recovered against the corporation for services rendered.[14] For the purposes of NYBCL § 630, wages or salaries mean all compensation and benefits payable by an employer to or for the account of the employee for personal services rendered by the employee.[15] Under NYBCL § 630(b), compensation and benefits specifically include but are not limited to salaries, overtime, vacation, holiday, and severance pay, employer contributions to or payments of insurance or welfare benefits, employer contributions to pension or annuity funds, and any other moneys properly due or payable for services rendered by the employee.[16]

holder. NYBCL § 628(c), Legislative Studies and Reports (comment on paragraph (c)). *See infra*, § 1.56, notes 22–30 and accompanying text.

8. NYBCL § 628(c).

9. NYBCL § 629.

10. Excluded are investment companies registered under the Investment Company Act of 1940. 15 U.S.C.A. § 80a–1 *et seq.*

11. NYBCL § 630(a). The term "employees" does not, for these purposes, include directors, officers, or other executive personnel. *See, e.g.*, Harris v. Lederfine, 196 Misc. 410, 92 N.Y.S.2d 645 (Sup.Ct., Bronx County, 1949).

12. NYBCL § 630(a).

13. *Id.*

14. *Id.*

15. NYBCL § 630(b).

16. *Id.*

Commissions and any other form of compensation for services rendered by the employee would be included.[17]

Shareholders who have paid more than their *pro rata* share of the liability for wages under NYBCL § 630 are entitled to contribution *pro rata* from the other shareholders liable with respect to the excess amount paid and may sue the other shareholders, jointly or severally, to recover the amount due from them.[18] The recovery may be had in a separate action.[19] Before a shareholder may claim contribution, he/she must give the other shareholders notice in writing that he/she intends to hold them so liable (unless the other shareholders already have been given notice by employees under NYBCL § 630(a)).[20] The notice of intent to seek contribution must be given within 20 days after the shareholder was given notice under NYBCL § 630(a) by an employee.[21]

Liability for Control of Directors. Liability for managerial acts or omissions that is normally otherwise imposed on directors by the NYBCL is imposed upon shareholders authorizing, or consenting to, a provision in the certificate of incorporation that permits the shareholders to control the board in its direction of the management of the business.[22] Liability is imposed on the shareholders, and the directors are relieved of liability, to the extent that, and so long as, pursuant to the provision, shareholders control the discretion or powers of the board in its direction of the management of corporate affairs.[23]

Other Liability. Shareholders may be personally liable in other cases,[24] such as those involving (1) seriously defective incorporation,[25] (2) personal guarantees or other contractual obligations incurred by shareholders,[26] (3) their tortious conduct,[27] (4) improper distributions,[28] (5) violation of securities laws,[29] or (6) piercing the corporate veil.[30]

---

17. *Id.*

18. NYBCL § 630(c). For contribution purposes, *"pro rata"* means in proportion to beneficial share interest. *Id.*

19. NYBCL § 630(c).

20. *Id.*

21. *Id.*

22. NYBCL § 620(b). See *supra*, § 1.47. See *infra*, § 1.66.

23. NYBCL § 620(f).

24. *See generally, e.g.,* Henn and Alexander, *supra*, § 1.1, note 1, pp. 546–550; RMBCA § 6.22(b); H. Ballantine, *On Corporations* (1946) pp. 781–823.

25. *See, e.g.,* Henn and Alexander, *supra*, § 1.1, note 1, pp. 342–344. *See supra*, § 1.21.

26. *See, e.g.,* Henn and Alexander, p. 547; RMBCA § 6.22(b) (a shareholder is not liable for acts or debts of a corporation but may become personally liable by reason of the shareholder's own acts or conduct (*e.g.,* assumed voluntarily)). This liability arises as a matter of contract, not as an incident of shareholder status.

27. *See, e.g.,* Henn and Alexander, *supra*, § 1.1, note 1, p. 547.

28. NYBCL § 719(d)(1)

29. Such as liability for insider trading on non-public information or for short-swing profits. *See, e.g.,* Henn and Alexander, *supra*, § 1.1, note 1, pp. 823–836.

30. *See supra,* § 1.10.

§ 1.57 Shareholders' Liabilities Summary

Shareholders, as a general rule, enjoy limited liability, unless the corporate veil is pierced. In certain other cases, they can incur personal liability for corporate obligations.

The NYBCL imposes liability on holders of or subscribers for shares, and in some cases, assignees or transferees of shares, pledgees, executors, administrators, guardians, trustees, and other fiduciaries, to pay the unpaid balance due on shares. Any transfer or assignment of shares by shareholders (or the interest in the corporation by a subscriber for shares) does not relieve the transferor or assignor of this liability if the corporation's property is not sufficient to pay its debts.

The ten largest shareholders of a privately-held corporation are jointly and severally personally liable for its employees' salaries if the employees give the shareholders notice in writing of their intention to hold the shareholders liable. Shareholders have the right to contribution *pro rata* from the other shareholders liable for the amount of salaries paid in excess of their shares and may sue the other shareholders jointly or severally to recover the amount due.

As long as shareholders control, under a provision in the certificate of incorporation, the discretion or powers of the board in its direction of the management of corporate affairs, the shareholders may be liable as though they were directors. Shareholders may be personally liable in certain other cases such as those involving (1) seriously defective incorporation, (2) personal guarantees or other contractual obligations incurred by shareholders, (3) tortious conduct of shareholders, (4) improper distributions, (5) violation of securities laws, or (6) piercing the corporate veil.

Library References:

West's Key No. Digests, Corporations ⬅170–190.

§ 1.58 Shareholders' Liabilities Checklist

1. Holders of or subscribers for shares liable for unpaid balance of subscription, which must be no less than the amount of consideration for which shares may be lawfully issued. (*See* §§ 1.30 and 1.56)

    - Assignees or transferees of shares in good faith and without knowledge that full consideration not paid are not liable; pledgors, executors, administrators, guardians, trustees, or other fiduciaries are not liable, but transferors, pledgors, or estates/funds in hands of fiduciaries are subject to liability. (*See* § 1.56)

    - Any transfer by shareholders of their shares, or by subscribers for shares of their interest in the corporation, does not relieve them of any liability as shareholders or subscribers if at the time of the transfer, the aggregate fair value of the corporation's property is, or may imminently become, insufficient to pay the corporation's debts. (*See* § 1.56)

2. Ten largest shareholders of private corporation jointly and severally personally liable for employees' salaries. (*See* § 1.56)

   • Employees must give shareholders notice in writing. (*See* § 1.56)

   • Shareholders' right to contribution. (*See* § 1.56)

3. Liability of shareholders by reason of provision in certificate of incorporation, unanimously authorized by shareholders, restricting board of directors' management of business or transferring to any shareholder(s) authority to manage business. (*See* §§ 1.47 and 1.56)

4. Other liability. (*See* § 1.56)

   • Seriously defective incorporation. (*See* § 1.56)

   • Personal guarantees or other contractual obligations incurred by shareholders. (*See* § 1.56)

   • Tortious conduct of shareholders. (*See* § 1.56)

   • Improper distributions. (*See* § 1.56)

   • Violation of securities laws. (*See* § 1.56)

   • Piercing the corporate veil. (*See* §§ 1.10 and 1.56)

Library References:

West's Key No. Digests, Corporations ⟾170–190.

§ 1.59 Directors

Subject to any provision in the certificate of incorporation authorized by NYBCL § 620(b) (shareholder control of directors)[1] or by NYBCL § 715(b) (shareholder election of officers),[2] the business of a corporation is managed by its board of directors.[3] Each director must be at least 18 years of age, and the certificate of incorporation or the bylaws may prescribe additional qualifications.[4]

---

§ 1.59

1. *See supra*, § 1.47. *See also*, *e.g.*, Henn and Alexander, *supra*, § 1.1, note 1, pp. 534–536, 576–577, 723–735, 744–746, and 778–781 (discussion of agreements that completely restrict the discretion of the directors though nominally shareholder agreements are in effect director agreements, which are ordinarily invalid, absent a permissive statutory provision).

2. *See infra*, § 1.69.

3. NYBCL § 701.

4. *Id.* These qualifications might include age (maximum or retirement), residence, employment (inside or outside corporation;

The board of directors must consist of one or more members.[5] Subject to this minimum, the number of directors may be fixed in the bylaws, by action of the shareholders, or by action of the board under the specific provisions of a bylaw adopted by the shareholders.[6] If not otherwise fixed pursuant to NYBCL § 702(a), the number of directors is one.[7] The number of directors may be increased or decreased by amendment of the bylaws, by action of the shareholders, or by action of the board under the specific provisions of a bylaw adopted by the shareholders, subject to the following limitations: (1) if the board is authorized by the bylaws to change the number of directors, whether by amending the bylaws or by taking action as permitted under a specific bylaw, the amendment or action requires the vote of a majority of the entire board and (2) no decrease may shorten the term of any incumbent director.[8]

Election of Directors. At each annual meeting of shareholders, directors are elected to hold office until the next annual meeting, except as authorized by NYBCL § 704 (classification of directors).[9] Each director holds office until the expiration of the term for which elected and until a successor has been elected and qualified.[10]

Classification of Directors. The certificate of incorporation may provide for the election of one or more directors by the holders of the shares of any class or series (or by the holders of bonds entitled to vote in the election of directors pursuant to NYBCL § 518), voting as a class.[11] The certificate of incorporation or the specific provisions of a bylaw adopted by the shareholders may provide that the directors be divided into either two, three, or four classes.[12] All classes must be as nearly equal in number as possible.[13] Upon initial classification the term of the first class expires at the next annual meeting of shareholders, the second class at the second succeeding annual meeting, the third class, if any, at the third succeeding annual meeting, and the fourth class, if any, at the fourth succeeding annual meeting.[14] At each annual meeting after the initial classification, directors to replace those whose terms expire at the annual meeting are elected to hold office until the second (or third or fourth) succeeding annual meeting, if two (or if three or four) classes

management or independent), professional, public interest, and others.

5. NYBCL § 702(a). As used in NYBCL Article 7, "entire board" means the total number of directors that the corporation would have if no vacancies on the board exist. NYBCL § 702(a).

6. NYBCL § 702(a).

7. *Id.*

8. NYBCL § 702(b).

9. NYBCL § 703(a).

10. NYBCL § 703(b). Vacancies occurring for any reason such as death, resignation, or disqualification may be filled by vote of the board but not for (1) removal with cause, unless the certificate of incorporation or specific bylaw provision adopted by the shareholders (or if elected by cumulative voting or by class vote, the certificate of incorporation) permits such removal by the board, and (2) removal without cause. NYBCL §§ 705(a) and 706(a).

11. NYBCL § 703(a).

12. NYBCL § 704(a).

13. *Id.*

14. *Id.*

exist.[15] If directors are classified and the number (changed: (1) any newly created directorships, or ; number of directorships, must be apportioned be among the three or four) classes to make all classe number as possible and (2) when the number of d and any newly created directorships are filled, by the ᴜᴏᴀ.ᴜ, _ tion of the additional directors is permitted until the next annual meeting of shareholders.[16]

Inspection of List of Directors and Officers. If a shareholder makes a written demand to inspect a current list of its directors, the corporation must, within two business days after receiving the demand, and for a period of one week thereafter, make the list available for inspection at its office during usual business hours.[17] If the corporation refuses to make the list available, the person making the demand may apply, *ex parte*, to the supreme court at a special term held within the judicial district where the office of the corporation is located, for an order directing the corporation to do so.[18]

§ 1.60 Directors—Vacancies and New Directorships

Newly-created directorships resulting from an increase in the number of directors, and vacancies occurring in the board for any reason other than the removal of directors without cause, may be filled by the board.[1] If the number of directors then in office is less than a quorum, the newly-created directorships and vacancies may be filled by vote of a majority of the directors then in office.[2] Unless the certificate of incorporation or the specific provision of a bylaw adopted by the shareholders provides that the board may fill vacancies occurring by reason of the removal of directors without cause, those vacancies may be filled only by vote of the shareholders.[3] Directors elected to fill vacancies, unless elected by the shareholders, hold office until the next meeting of shareholders at which the election of directors is in the regular order of business and until their successors are elected and qualified.[4] Unless otherwise provided in the certificate of incorporation or bylaws, notwithstanding the provisions of NYBCL § 705(a) and (b), whenever the

---

15. NYBCL § 704(b).
16. NYBCL § 704(c).
17. NYBCL § 718(a). The demand may be made in person or by an attorney or agent, or a representative of the District Attorney, Secretary of State, Attorney General, or other state official. *Id.*
18. NYBCL § 718(b). The court may also take other action that it deems just and proper. *Id.*

§ 1.60
1. NYBCL § 705(a).
2. NYBCL § 705(a). Nothing in NYBCL § 705(a) affects any provision of the certificate of incorporation *or* the bylaws that mandates that newly created directorships or vacancies be filled by vote of the shareholders or any provision of the certificate of incorporation that requires a greater quorum or vote of directors, as permitted by NYBCL § 709. *Id.*
3. NYBCL § 705(b).
4. NYBCL § 705(c).

olders of any class or classes of shares or series thereof are entitled to elect one or more directors by the certificate of incorporation, any vacancy that may be filled by the board or a majority of the directors then in office, as the case may be, must be filled by a majority of the directors elected by such class or classes or series thereof then in office or, if no such director is in office, then as provided in NYBCL § 705(a) or (b), as the case may be.[5]

Library References:

West's Key No. Digests, Corporations ⚖=295.

§ 1.61 Directors—Removal

Directors may be removed for cause by vote of the shareholders.[1] The certificate of incorporation or the specific provisions of a bylaw adopted by the shareholders may provide for removal for cause by action of the board or, in the case directors elected by cumulative voting, by the holders of the shares of any class or series (or holders of bonds) voting as a class.[2] If the certificate of incorporation or the bylaws permit, directors may be removed without cause by vote of the shareholders.[3]

The removal of directors, with or without cause, is subject to the following limitations: (1) in the case of a corporation having cumulative voting, directors may not be removed if the votes cast against their removal would be sufficient to elect them if voted cumulatively at an election at which the same total number of votes were cast and the entire board, or the entire class of directors of which they are a member, were then being elected; (2) when by the certificate of incorporation the holders of the shares of any class or series (or holders of bonds) voting as a class are entitled to elect one or more directors, the directors that they elected may be removed only by their applicable vote.[4]

An action to obtain a judgment removing a director for cause may be brought by the Attorney General or by the holders of at least ten percent of the outstanding shares, whether or not entitled to vote.[5] The court may bar (for a period fixed by the court) the re-election of the directors removed.[6]

Library References:

West's Key No. Digests, Corporations ⚖=294.

§ 1.62 Directors—Meetings

Unless otherwise provided in the NYBCL, any reference in the NYBCL to corporate action to be taken by the board means such action

5. NYBCL § 705(d).

§ 1.61
1. NYBCL § 706(a).
2. Id.
3. NYBCL § 706(b).
4. NYBCL § 706(c).
5. NYBCL § 706(d).
6. Id.

at a meeting of the board.[1] The vote of a majority of the directors present at the time of the vote, if a quorum is present at the time, is the act of the board, unless otherwise provided in the NYBCL.[2] Unless otherwise restricted by the certificate of incorporation or the bylaws, any action required or permitted to be taken by the board or its committees may be taken without a meeting if all members of the board or the committee consent in writing to adopt a resolution authorizing the action.[3] Unless otherwise restricted by the certificate of incorporation or the bylaws, members of the board or its committees may participate in a meeting by means of a conference telephone or similar communications equipment allowing all persons participating in the meeting to hear each other at the same time.[4] Participation by such means constitutes presence in person at a meeting.[5]

Regular and special meetings of the board may be held at any place within or without New York, unless otherwise provided by the certificate of incorporation or the bylaws.[6] The time and place of meetings may be fixed by or under the bylaws or, if not so fixed, by the board.[7] Unless otherwise provided by the bylaws, regular meetings of the board may be held without notice if the time and place of the meetings are fixed by the bylaws or the board.[8] Special meetings of the board must be held upon notice to the directors.[9]

The bylaws may prescribe what constitutes notice of a meeting of the board. A notice, or waiver of notice, need not specify the purpose of any meeting (regular or special), unless required by the bylaws.[10] Notice of a meeting need not be given to directors who submit a signed waiver of notice (whether before or after the meeting) or who attend the meeting without protesting (prior to or at its commencement) the lack of notice to them.[11]

A majority of the directors present, whether or not a quorum is present, may adjourn any meeting to another time and place.[12] If the bylaws so provide, notice of any adjournment of a meeting must be given

§ 1.62

1. NYBCL § 708(a).

2. NYBCL § 708(d). See NYBCL § 709(a)(2).

3. NYBCL § 708(b). The resolution and the written consents must be filed with the minutes of the proceedings of the board or committee. *Id.*

4. NYBCL § 708(c).

5. *Id.* The emphasis on directors' acting either by meeting, written consent without a meeting, or conference communication underlines the importance of their fiduciary duty of care. The policy underlying the rule is to imbue them with the responsibility of having the corporation managed under their direction as a board, not as individual directors. The law, accordingly, requires that directors reach decisions in the crucible of a meeting (or its substantial equivalent) with the opportunity for the discussion and recording of their views. *See, e.g.,* H. Ballantine, *On Corporations*, pp. 123–124. See *infra*, § 1.65.

6. NYBCL § 710.

7. *Id.*

8. NYBCL § 711(a).

9. *Id.*

10. NYBCL § 711(b).

11. NYBCL § 711(c).

12. NYBCL § 711(d).

§ 1.62 BUSINESS ORGANIZATIONS: CORPORATIONS Ch. 1

to the directors who were not present at the time of the adjournment and, unless the time and place of the adjourned meeting are announced at the meeting, to the other directors as well.[13]

Library References:

West's Key No. Digests, Corporations ⟲298.

§ 1.63 Directors—Meetings—Quorum and Voting Requirements

A majority of the *entire* board constitutes a quorum for the transaction of business, unless a greater quorum is required by the certificate of incorporation.[1] The certificate of incorporation or the bylaws may fix the quorum at less than a majority (but not less than one-third) of the entire board.[2] Except as otherwise provided in the NYBCL, the vote of a majority of the directors present at the time of the vote, if a quorum is present at the time, is the act of the board;[3] the certificate of incorporation may require a greater vote.[4]

An amendment of the certificate of incorporation that changes any director quorum or voting provision permitted by NYBCL § 709(a) must be authorized by the shareholders.[5]

---

13. *Id.*

§ 1.63

1. NYBCL § 707. The certificate of incorporation may require a greater quorum. NYBCL § 709(a)(1).

2. NYBCL § 707.

3. NYBCL § 708(d).

4. NYBCL § 709(a)(2).

PRACTICE POINTER: Allocation of control over designated operations of the enterprise may be accomplished by various techniques, among which is requiring greater than normal (supermajority) *vote* or *quorum*, or both, at board meetings.

CAVEAT: In effect, this technique may be used to give a veto power to a director of a corporation and might be held invalid. *See Benintendi v. Kenton Hotel, Inc.*, 294 N.Y. 112, 60 N.E.2d 829 (1945) (invalidated bylaw of close corporation requiring unanimous vote of all directors for board action). *Cf. Weber v. Weber*, 213 A.D.2d 1021, 624 N.Y.S.2d 323 (4th Dep't 1995) (certificate of incorporation requirement of unanimous director approval of operating budget did not apply to raising rental revenue, where approval by majority of directors was sufficient). *See supra*, § 1.59, note 1 and accompanying text. *See also, supra,* §§ 1.45, note 3 (supermajority shareholder vote), 1.46, note 3 (shareholder quorum requirements), and 1.47, note 2 and accompanying text (shareholders' agreements restricting board).

5. NYBCL § 709(b). *Procedure.* The amendment must be authorized at a meeting of shareholders by (1) for any corporation in existence *on* the effective date of NYBCL § 709(b)(2), at least *two-thirds* of the votes of all outstanding shares entitled to vote and (2) for any corporation in existence *on* the effective date of NYBCL § 709(b)(1) whose certificate of incorporation expressly provides such and for any corporation incorporated *after* the effective date of NYBCL § 709(b)(2), a *majority* of the votes of all outstanding shares entitled to vote, or, in either case, such greater proportion of votes of shares, or votes of a class or series of shares, as may be provided specifically in the certificate of incorporation for changing or striking out a provision permitted by NYBCL § 709(b). NYBCL § 709(b)(1). The effective date of both NYBCL § 709(b)(1) and (2) is the one hundred eightieth day after the act amending the NYBCL became law (*see* 1997 NY S.B. 476 (SN) § 71; 1997 NY S.B. 5680 (SN) § 7); S.B. 476 was enacted on Aug. 26, 1997, and its effective date is Feb. 22, 1998. A corporation may adopt an amendment of

§ 1.64 Directors—Executive Committee; Other Committees

If the certificate of incorporation or the bylaws so provide, the board, by resolution adopted by a majority of the *entire* board, may designate from among its members an executive committee and other committees, each consisting of one or more directors.[1] To the extent provided in the resolution, certificate of incorporation, or bylaws, each committee has all the authority of the board, except that no committee has authority to (1) submit to the shareholders any action that requires shareholders' approval under the NYBCL; (2) fill vacancies in the board or in its committees; (3) fix compensation of the directors for serving on the board or any committee; (4) amend or repeal the bylaws or adopt new bylaws; (5) amend or repeal any board resolution that by its terms is not amendable or repealable.[2] The board may designate directors as alternate members of any committee, to replace any absent or disqualified member or members at any meeting of that committee.[3] Each committee serves at the pleasure of the board.[4] The board's designation of a committee, its delegation of authority to the committee, or action by the committee pursuant to that authority does not alone constitute performance by any noncommittee board member of that director's duty to the corporation under NYBCL § 717.[5]

Library References:

West's Key No. Digests, Corporations ⇐299.

§ 1.65 Directors—Fiduciary Duties

Duty of Care. A director must perform his or her duties as a director and as a member of any committee in good faith and with that

§ 1.64

1. NYBCL § 712(a).

2. *Id.* This section works a major change in the common law by authorizing the delegation of policy-making power to the certificate of incorporation in accordance with any applicable clause or subclause of NYBCL § 709(b)(1) to provide that any further amendment of the certificate of incorporation that changes or strikes out a provision permitted by NYBCL § 709 must be authorized at a meeting of the shareholders by vote of a specified proportion of the holders of outstanding shares, or class or series of shares, entitled to vote, provided that such proportion may not be less than a majority. NYBCL § 709(b)(2).

committees. NYBCL § 712, Legislative Studies and Reports (Comment).

3. NYBCL § 712(b).

4. NYBCL § 712(c).

5. *Id.* This provision makes clear the board's (including the directors who are not members of the committee in question) continuing duty of supervision, and consequent responsibility, in important areas of corporate policy despite its delegation of policy-making power to a committee. It is not intended to connote that board members should be responsible for mistakes made in execution of corporate policies by committees acting in the period between board meetings. NYBCL § 712(c), Legislative Studies and Reports (Comment). *Cf.* RMBCA § 8.25(f), Official Comment.

degree of care that an ordinarily prudent person in a like position would use under similar circumstances.[1] In performing their duties, directors are entitled to rely on information, opinions, reports, or statements (including financial statements and other financial data) prepared or presented by (1) officers or employees of the corporation (or any other corporation, of which at least fifty percent of the outstanding shares of stock entitling the holders thereof to vote for the election of directors is owned, directly or indirectly, by the corporation) that the director believes to be reliable and competent in the matters presented, (2) counsel, public accountants, or other persons on matters that the director believes to be within that person's professional or expert competence, or (3) a committee of the board upon which the director does not serve, duly designated in accordance with a provision of the certificate of incorporation or the bylaws, on matters within its designated authority, which committee the director believes to merit confidence, so long as in so relying the director is acting in good faith and with the requisite degree of care.[2] Persons who so perform their duties have no liability by reason of being or having been a director of the corporation.[3]

In taking action, including any action that may relate to a change in the control[4] of the corporation, a director is entitled to consider such matters as (1) the long-term and short-term interests of the corporation and its shareholders and (2) the effects that its actions may have in the short term or in the long term upon any of the following: (a) its prospects for potential growth, development, productivity, and profitability; (b) its current employees; (c) its retired employees and other beneficiaries receiving or entitled to receive retirement, welfare, or similar benefits pursuant to any plan sponsored, or agreement entered into, by the corporation; (d) its customers and creditors; and (e) its ability to provide, as a going concern, goods, services, employment opportunities and benefits, and otherwise to contribute to the communities in which it does business.[5] Nothing in NYBCL § 717(b) imposes any duties on directors to consider or to accord any particular weight to any of the foregoing interests and effects; nor does NYBCL § 717(b) abrogate any

§ 1.65

1. NYBCL § 717(a). See also, e.g., I. Millstein, *The Professional Board*, 50 Business Lawyer 1427 (1995); J. Tobin, *The Squeeze on Directors—Inside and Out*, 49 Business Lawyer 1707 (1994).

2. NYBCL § 717(a). Directors are not considered to be acting in good faith if they have knowledge concerning the matter in question that would cause their reliance to be unwarranted. *Id.*

3. NYBCL § 717(a). *See infra*, § 1.66.

4. For purposes of NYBCL § 717(b), "control" means the possession, directly or indirectly, of the power to direct or cause the direction of the management and policies of the corporation, whether through the ownership of voting stock, by contract, or by other means.

5. NYBCL § 717(b). See also, e.g., L. Johnson and D. Millon, *The Case Beyond Time*, 45 Business Lawyer 2105 (1990) (re duty of directors to consider corporation's short-term and long-term interests and to maximize shareholder value in context of takeover bids).

duties of directors created by statute or recognized by common law or in court decisions.[6]

Duty of Loyalty. Directors, as fiduciaries, have a duty of loyalty to the corporation.[7] A case of a director's divided loyalty is presented when his or her interest conflicts with that of the corporation in the context of a corporate transaction.[8] In such a case, a contract or other transaction between a corporation and one or more of its directors (or an entity in which the director is interested)[9] is neither void nor voidable for this reason alone or because the interested directors are present at the meeting of the board (or committee) that approves the transaction, even if their votes are counted for that purpose, *if* the material facts of the director's interest are disclosed in good faith or are known (1) to the board (or committee) and it approves the transaction without counting the vote of the interested directors or, if the disinterested directors' votes are insufficient to constitute an act of the board,[10] by unanimous vote of the disinterested directors or (2) to the shareholders entitled to vote and they approve the transaction.[11] If a contract or other transaction between a corporation and one or more of its directors, or between a corporation and any other corporation, firm, association, or other entity in which one or more of its directors are directors or officers, or have a substantial financial interest, is not approved in accordance with NYBCL § 713(a), the corporation may avoid the transaction unless the party or parties thereto establish affirmatively that it was fair and reasonable to the corporation at the time it was approved.[12] Notwithstanding these general rules, the certificate of incorporation may contain additional restrictions on transactions with interested directors and may provide that contracts or transactions in violation of these restrictions are void or voidable by the corporation.[13]

Loans to directors also present a conflict of interest proscribed by the NYBCL.[14] A corporation may not lend money to or guarantee the

6. NYBCL § 717(b). *See* cases cited at NYBCL § 717, Notes and Decisions (Note 8 (Degree of Care)).

7. *See, e.g.*, Henn and Alexander, *supra*, § 1.1, note 1, pp. 628–656 (re duty of loyalty and usurpation of corporate opportunity, conflicting interest, insider trading (state and federal aspects), oppression of minority shareholders (comparing directors' and controlling shareholders' duties), disposition of control, excessive compensation, and self-dealing); D. Ruder, *Duty of Loyalty—A Law Professor's Report*, 40 Business Lawyer 1383–1402 (1985) (citing New York and Delaware cases); E. Veasey, *Duty of Loyalty: The Criticality of the Counselor's Role*, 45 Business Lawyer 2065–2081 (1990); *The Role of Disinterested Directors in "Conflict" Transactions: The ALI Corporate Governance Project and Existing Law*, Business Lawyer 2083–2103 (1990).

8. NYBCL § 713. *Cf.* RMBCA 8.31, Official Comment.

9. *I.e.*, between a corporation and any other firm in which its directors are directors or officers or have a substantial financial interest. NYBCL § 713(a).

10. NYBCL § 708(d).

11. NYBCL § 713(a).

12. *Id.* Common or interested directors may be counted in determining the presence of a quorum at a meeting of the board or of a committee that approves the contract or transaction. NYBCL § 713(c).

13. NYBCL § 713(d).

14. NYBCL § 714.

§ 1.65   BUSINESS ORGANIZATIONS: CORPORATIONS   Ch. 1

obligation of a director of the corporation unless the loan or guarantee is approved by the shareholders, with the holders of a majority of the shares entitled to vote constituting a quorum, but shares held of record or beneficially by directors who are benefitted by such loan or guarantee are not entitled to vote or to be included in the determination of a quorum.[15] A loan or guarantee made in violation of NYBCL § 714 does not affect the borrower's liability on the loan.[16] Moreover in setting their own compensation, directors could face a conflict of interest.[17] However, unless otherwise provided in the certificate of incorporation or the bylaws, the board has authority to fix the compensation of directors for services in any capacity.[18]

Library References:

West's Key No. Digests, Corporations ⚎307–324.

§ 1.66 Directors—Liabilities

Subject to certain exceptions,[1] directors who vote for or concur in the following corporate action are jointly and severally liable to the corporation for the benefit of its creditors or shareholders to the extent of any injury they suffer as a result of the action:[2] (1) the declaration of any dividend or other distribution to the extent that it is contrary to the provisions of NYBCL § 510(a) and (b);[3] (2) the purchase of shares of the corporation to the extent that it is contrary to the provisions of NYBCL § 513;[4] (3) the distribution of assets to shareholders after dissolution of the corporation without paying or adequately providing for all known liabilities of the corporation;[5] and (4) making any loan to a director

---

15. NYBCL § 714(a)(1). With respect to any corporation in existence *on* the effective date of NYBCL § 714(a)(2) whose certificate of incorporation expressly provides such and with respect to any corporation incorporated *after* the effective date of NYBCL § 714(a)(2), the board must determine that the loan or guarantee benefits the corporation and either approves the specific loan or guarantee or a general plan authorizing loans and guarantees. NYBCL § 714(a)(2). The effective date of BCL § 714(a)(2) is the one hundred eightieth day after the act amending the NYBCL became law (*see* 1997 NY S.B. 476 (SN) § 71; 1997 NY S.B. 5680 (SN) § 7); S.B. 476 was enacted on Aug. 26, 1997, and its effective date is Feb. 22, 1998.

16. NYBCL § 714(b).

17. *E.g.*, compensation that is excessive and involves self-dealing. *See* cases cited at NYBCL § 713, Notes and Decisions (Notes 24 (re, *e.g.*, directors who are also officers) and 25 (excessive compensation)).

18. NYBCL § 713(e).

§ 1.66

1. *See infra*, § 1.66, notes 12–14 and accompanying text.

2. NYBCL § 719(a). On directors' civil and criminal liabilities generally, *see, e.g.*, Henn and Alexander, *supra*, § 1.1, note 1, pp. 234, 582–585, 611–67 and 902–903; D. Webb, S. Molo, and J. Hurst, *Understanding and Avoiding Executive Criminal Liability*, 49 Business Lawyer 617–668 (1994) (re taxation, securities, purchasing and sales, government contracts, campaign contributions, and international transaction); R. Gruner, *Clarifying Corporate Criminal Liability*, Business Law Today 52–54 (July/Aug. 1994).

3. NYBCL § 719(a)(1).

4. NYBCL § 719(a)(2).

5. NYBCL § 719(a)(3). Such liabilities include claims filed by creditors within the time limit set in a notice given to creditors as required under NYBCL Articles 10 (nonjudicial dissolution) and 11 (judicial dissolution). *Id. See infra*, §§ 1.95 and 1.99.

contrary to NYBCL § 714.[6]

Director's Right to Dissent. Directors who are present at a meeting of the board (or committee) when action is taken are presumed to have concurred in the action unless (1) their dissent is entered in the minutes of the meeting, (2) they submit their written dissent to the person acting as the secretary of the meeting before adjournment, or (3) they deliver or send by registered mail their dissent to the secretary of the corporation promptly after the adjournment of the meeting.[7] A director who voted in favor of an action has no such right to dissent.[8] Directors absent from a meeting of the board, or any of its committees, when action is taken are presumed to have concurred in the action unless they deliver or send by registered mail their dissent to the secretary of the corporation or cause their dissent to be filed with the minutes of the proceedings of the board or committee within a reasonable time after learning of the action.[9]

Right of Contribution. Any director against whom a claim is successfully asserted under NYBCL § 719 is entitled to contribution from the other directors who voted for or concurred in the action upon which the claim is based.[10] Directors against whom a claim is successfully asserted under NYBCL § 719 are entitled, to the extent of the amounts paid by them to the corporation as a result of the claims, to: (1) be subrogated to the rights of the corporation against shareholders who received an improper dividend or distribution knowing that it was not authorized under NYBCL § 510; (2) have the corporation rescind an improper purchase and recover the purchase price from sellers who sold shares to the corporation knowing that the purchase was not authorized under NYBCL § 513; (3) be subrogated to the rights of the corporation against shareholders who received an improper distribution of assets in violation of NYBCL § 719(a)(3); and (4) be subrogated to the rights of the corporation against the director who received the improper loan.[11]

Due Care; Business Judgment Rule. Directors are not liable under NYBCL § 719 if, in the circumstances, they performed their duties in accordance with the standards of care and good faith prescribed by NYBCL § 717(a)[12] or they did not vote for or concur in any of the

---

6. NYBCL § 719(a)(4).
7. NYBCL § 719(b).
8. Id.
9. Id.
10. NYBCL § 719(c).
11. NYBCL § 719(d).
12. NYBCL § 719(e). The elements of the business judgment rule and the circumstances for its application are continuing to be developed by the courts. See RMBCA § 8.30, Official Comment 1. Cf. Henn and Alexander, supra, § 1.1, note 1, pp. 661–663 (business judgment rule sustains corporate transactions and immunizes management from liability where the transaction is within the powers of the corporation and authority of management and involves the exercise of due care and compliance with applicable fiduciary duties). See also, e.g., D. Block, N. Barton, and S. Radin, *The Business Judgment Rule: Fiduciary Duties of Corporate Directors* (4th ed. 1993) reviewed in Siegel, 49 Business Lawyer 1977 (1994); D. Block, S. Radin, and J. Rosenzweig, *The Role of the Business Judgment Rule in Shareholder Litigation at the Turn of the Decade*, 45 Business Lawyer 469–510

§ 1.66   BUSINESS ORGANIZATIONS: CORPORATIONS   Ch. 1

corporate actions specified in NYBCL § 719(a).[13] Liabilities otherwise imposed by law upon any director are not affected by NYBCL § 719.[14]

Action Against Directors and Officers for Misconduct. An action may be brought by a corporation (or its receiver, trustee in bankruptcy, officer, director, or judgment creditor) for the relief provided in NYBCL §§ 719(a) and 720(a) or in a derivative action by a shareholder, voting trust certificate holder, or the owner of a beneficial interest in shares of the corporation as set forth in NYBCL § 626.[15] An action under NYBCL § 720 may be brought against directors or officers of a corporation, subject to any provision of the certificate of incorporation authorized pursuant to NYBCL § 402(b), to compel them to account for the violation of their duties (1) in the management and disposition of corporate assets committed to their charge or (2) in the acquisition by themselves, transfer to others, or loss or waste of corporate assets.[16] The action may also be brought to set aside an unlawful transfer of corporate assets where the transferee knew of its unlawfulness[17] and to enjoin a proposed unlawful transfer of corporate assets where sufficient evidence exists that it will be made.[18]

Indemnification: Other Than by Court Award. A corporation may indemnify directors and officers against judgments, fines, amounts paid in settlement, and reasonable expenses (including attorneys' fees) incurred in actions (whether civil or criminal, but other than a derivative action) if they acted in good faith for a purpose that they reasonably believed to be in (or, in the case of service for any other corporation or enterprise, not opposed to) the best interests of the corporation and if, in

(1990) (re derivative actions: demand on the board, demand refused, and futile demands; Auerbach v. Bennett, 47 N.Y.2d 619, 419 N.Y.S.2d 920, 393 N.E.2d 994 (1979); Syracuse Television, Inc. v. Channel 9, Syracuse, Inc., 51 Misc.2d 188, 273 N.Y.S.2d 16 (Sup. Ct.1966)); C. Hansen, *The Duty of Care, the Business Judgment Rule, and the American Law Institute Corporate Governance Project*, 48 Business Lawyer 1355–1376 (1993) (board action not protected by rule if the action is illegal, citing Abrams v. Allen, 297 N.Y. 52, 74 N.E.2d 305 (1947), *ultra vires*, not independent (*i.e.*, dominated by controlling person), or involves fraud, abuse, or corporate waste; compares reasonable diligence, citing Casey v. Woodruff, 49 N.Y.S.2d 625, 643 (Sup.Ct., N.Y. County, 1944) with decision *process*, citing Smith v. Van Gorkom, 488 A.2d 858 (Del.1985)). *Cf.* RMBCA § 8.30(a) (requisite care, good faith, and belief are not necessarily elements of business judgment rule); R. Balotti and J. Hanks, *Rejudging the Business Judgment Rule*, 48 Business Lawyer 1337–1353 (1993) (the rule as a presumption, defense, or safe harbor).

13.   NYBCL § 719(a).

PRACTICE POINTER: Directors who do not vote for or concur in a corporate action specified in NYBCL § 719(a) that is approved at a meeting should have their dissent recorded in the minutes of that meeting.

14.   NYBCL § 719(f). *See, e.g.*, Henn and Alexander, *supra*, § 1.1, note 1, pp. 621–625, 661–663.

15.   NYBCL § 720(b).

16.   NYBCL § 720(a)(1). *E.g.*, self-dealing, conflict of interest, abuse of corporate opportunities, conversion or misappropriation of corporate funds, fraud, negligence, bad faith, or waste of corporate assets. *See* cases cited at NYBCL § 720, Notes of Decisions.

17.   NYBCL § 720(a)(2). *See supra*, § 1.66, note 16.

18.   NYBCL § 720(a)(3). *See supra*, § 1.66, note 16.

addition, in criminal actions or proceedings, they had no reasonable cause to believe that their conduct was unlawful.[19] The termination of any civil or criminal action or proceeding by judgment, settlement, or conviction (or upon a plea of *nolo contendere* or its equivalent) does not in itself create a presumption that directors or officers did not so act in good faith or that they had reasonable cause to believe that their conduct was unlawful.[20]

In the case of actions brought (or threatened to be brought) by or in the right of the corporation, a corporation may indemnify directors and officers against amounts paid in settlement and reasonable expenses (including attorneys' fees) necessarily incurred by them if they acted in good faith for a purpose that they reasonably believed to be in (or, in the case of service for any other corporation or other enterprise, not opposed to the best interests) of the corporation.[21] No director or officer who is adjudged liable to the corporation may be indemnified, unless the court in which the action was brought (or, if no action was brought, any court of competent jurisdiction) determines that the director or officer is fairly and reasonably entitled to indemnity for such portion of the settlement amount and expenses as the court deems proper.[22]

Under NYBCL § 723(a), the board may authorize indemnification of a person who has been successful (on the merits or otherwise) in the defense of a civil or criminal action or proceeding of the character described in NYBCL § 722.[23] Except for indemnification under NYBCL

---

19. NYBCL § 722(a). Any indemnification and advancement of expenses granted are not to be deemed exclusive of any other rights to which directors or officers may be entitled, whether contained in the certificate of incorporation or the bylaws (or, when authorized by the certificate of incorporation or bylaws, a resolution of shareholders or of directors or an agreement providing for such indemnification), but no indemnification may be made to any directors or officers if a judgment or other final adjudication adverse to them establishes that their acts were committed in bad faith or were the result of active and deliberate dishonesty and were material to the cause of action adjudicated or that they personally gained a financial profit or other advantage to which they were not legally entitled. NYBCL § 721. Rights to indemnification to which corporate personnel other than directors and officers may be entitled by contract or otherwise under law are not affected by NYBCL Article 7. *Id. See also*, RMBCA § 8.58, Official Comment (provision treating the indemnification of directors by the corporation in articles of incorporation, bylaws, shareholders' or directors' resolution, or in a contract or other document, is valid only if and to the extent it is consistent with RMBCA provisions on indemnification; the phrase "is valid only if and to the extent it is consistent with" is not synonymous with "exclusive" and is thought to be more accurate than the term "nonexclusive"; nonstatutory indemnification provisions protecting against the consequences of bad faith or willful misconduct are not consistent with the RMBCA provisions and would be invalid).

20. NYBCL § 722(b).

21. NYBCL § 722(c). *Cf.* RMBCA § 8.51(e), Official Comments 1 and 5 (in actions by or in the right of a corporation, indemnification is limited to expenses incurred to avoid circularity involved if a corporation indemnified a director or officer for amounts paid to the corporation to settle or satisfy substantive claims).

22. NYBCL § 722(c). *See also*, NYBCL § 722(d) (employee benefit plans).

23. *See supra*, § 1.66, notes 19–21 and accompanying text.

PRACTICE POINTER: The relationship between the degree of success and the amount of indemnification is not clear, though a literal reading of NYBCL § 723(a) would permit indemnification for cases set-

§ 723(a) for such a successful defense, indemnification under NYBCL § 722[24] (or otherwise permitted by reason of the nonexclusivity of the NYBCL indemnification provisions,[25] unless ordered by a court)[26] may be made by the corporation if authorized (1) by the board, acting by a quorum consisting of directors who are not parties to the action or proceeding, upon a finding that the director or officer has met the requisite standard of conduct or (2) if a quorum of disinterested directors directs, either (a) by the board upon the written opinion of independent counsel that indemnification is proper in the circumstances because the director or officer has met the applicable standard of conduct or (b) by the shareholders upon a finding that the director or officer has met the applicable standard of conduct.[27]

Indemnification: by Court Award. Notwithstanding the failure of a corporation to provide indemnification, and despite any contrary resolution of the board or of the shareholders in the specific case under NYBCL § 723 (indemnification other than by court award),[28] indemnification may be awarded by a court to the extent authorized under NYBCL § 722 (authorization for corporation to indemnify directors and officers)[29] and NYBCL § 723(a).[30] Application for indemnification may be made either: (1) in the civil action or proceeding in which the expenses were incurred or other amounts were paid[31] or (2) to the supreme court in a separate proceeding, in which case the application must set forth the disposition of any previous application made to any court for the same or similar relief and the reasonable cause for the failure to make application for such relief in the action or proceeding in which the expenses were incurred or other amounts were paid.[32] The application must be made in such manner and form as may be required by the applicable rules of court or, in the absence thereof, by direction of a court to which it is made.[33] It must also be upon notice to the corporation,[34] and the court may direct that notice be given, at the expense of the corporation, to shareholders and such other persons as designated in such manner as the court may require.[35] Where indemnification is sought by judicial action, the court may allow a person such reasonable expenses, including attorneys' fees, during the pendency of the litigation as are necessary in

tled for, presumably, any amount less than the amount demanded by the person bringing (or threatening to bring) the action. *Cf.* RMBCA § 8.52 ("wholly successful" standard).

24. Authorization of corporation to indemnify directors and officers if they meet requisite standards of conduct. *See supra,* § 1.66, notes 19–22 and accompanying text.

25. NYBCL § 721. *See supra,* § 1.66, note 19.

26. NYBCL § 724. *See infra,* § 66, notes 28–36 and accompanying text.

27. NYBCL § 723(b). *See also, generally,* RMBCA §§ 8.50–8.56.

28. *See supra,* § 1.66, notes 19–27 and accompanying text.

29. *See supra,* § 1.66, notes 19–22 and accompanying text.

30. NYBCL § 724(a).

31. NYBCL § 724(a)(1).

32. NYBCL § 724(a)(2).

33. NYBCL § 724(b).

34. *Id.*

35. *Id.*

connection with his or her defense therein, if the court shall find that the defendant has by his or her pleadings or during the course of the litigation raised genuine issues of fact or law.[36]

Indemnification: Corporate Advances and Court Allowances; Limitations. Expenses incurred in defending a civil or criminal action or proceeding may be paid by the corporation in advance of the final disposition of the action or proceeding upon receipt of an undertaking by the director or officer to repay the amount as required by NYBCL § 725(a).[37] All expenses incurred in defending a civil or criminal action or proceeding that are advanced by the corporation under NYBCL § 723(c)[38] or allowed by a court under NYBCL § 724(c)[39] must be repaid if the recipient is ultimately found, under the procedure set forth in NYBCL Article 7, not to be entitled to indemnification or, where indemnification is granted, to the extent the expenses so advanced or allowed exceed the indemnification to which the recipient is entitled.[40] No indemnification, advancement, or allowance may be made under NYBCL Article 7 in any circumstance where the indemnification would appear to be: (1) inconsistent with the law of the jurisdiction of incorporation of a foreign corporation prohibiting or otherwise limiting the indemnification; (2) inconsistent with a provision of the certificate of incorporation, a bylaw, a resolution of the board or of the shareholders, an agreement, or other proper corporate action, in effect at the time of the accrual of the alleged cause of action asserted in the threatened or pending action or proceeding in which the expenses were incurred or other amounts were paid, prohibiting, or otherwise limiting indemnification; or (3) if a settlement has been approved by the court, inconsistent with any condition expressly imposed by the court in its order.[41]

Indemnification: Procedure. If any indemnification is paid other than by court order or action by the shareholders, the corporation must, not later than the next annual meeting of shareholders (unless the meeting is held within three months from the date of the payment) and, in any event, within 15 months after the payment, mail to its shareholders of record at the time entitled to vote for the election of directors a statement specifying the persons and amounts paid and the nature and status of the litigation or threatened litigation at the time of the payment.[42] If any action with respect to indemnification of directors or officers is taken by amendment of the bylaws, resolution of directors, or agreement, the corporation must, not later than the next annual meeting

---

36. NYBCL § 724(c).

37. NYBCL § 723(c). *Cf.* RMBCA § 8.53. *See also,* NYBCL §§ 724 (indemnification awarded by a court); 725 (other provisions affecting indemnification of directors and officers; notification to be mailed to shareholders).

38. Payment of indemnification other than by court award.

39. Indemnification of directors and officers by court award.

40. NYBCL § 725(a).

41. NYBCL § 725(b).

42. NYBCL § 725(c). *See infra,* § 1.66, note 43.

§ 1.66   BUSINESS ORGANIZATIONS: CORPORATIONS   Ch. 1

of shareholders (unless the meeting is held within three months from the date of the action) and, in any event, within 15 months after the action, mail to its shareholders of record at the time entitled to vote for the election of directors a statement describing the action taken.[43]

Indemnification Insurance. A corporation may purchase and maintain insurance to indemnify: (1) the corporation for any obligation to indemnify directors or officers under the provisions of NYBCL Article 7, (2) directors or officers in instances in which they may be indemnified by the corporation under the provisions of NYBCL Article 7, and (3) directors or officers in instances in which they may not otherwise be indemnified by the corporation under the provisions of NYBCL Article 7, if the contract of insurance covering such directors or officers provides, in a manner acceptable to the Superintendent of Insurance, for a retention amount and for co-insurance.[44] However, no insurance may provide for any payment, other than cost of defense, to or on behalf of any director or officer: (1) if a judgment or other final adjudication adverse to the insured director or officer establishes that his or her acts were active and deliberate dishonesty and were material to the cause of action so adjudicated or that he or she personally gained in fact a financial profit or other advantage to which he or she was not legally entitled or (2) in relation to any risk the insurance of which is prohibited under the Insurance Law.[45]

Indemnification Insurance: Procedure. The corporation must, within the time limits and to the persons provided in NYBCL § 725(c),[46] mail a statement in respect of any indemnification insurance it has purchased or renewed, specifying the insurance carrier, date and cost of the contract, the corporate positions insured, and an explanation of all payments made under any indemnification insurance contract not previously reported in a statement to shareholders.[47]

Indemnification and Insurance: Public Policy; Foreign Corporations. The public policy of New York is to spread the risk of corporate management, notwithstanding any other general or special law of New York, or of any other jurisdiction, including the federal government.[48] The provisions of NYBCL Article 7 relating to indemnification of directors and officers and insurance therefor apply to domestic corporations and foreign corporations doing business in New York, except as

---

43. NYBCL § 725(d). Any notification required to be made pursuant to NYBCL § 725 (c) or (d) by any domestic mutual insurer must be satisfied by compliance with the corresponding provisions of Insurance Law § 1216. NYBCL § 725(e).

44. NYBCL § 726(a). *See, e.g.*, S. Weiss, *Doing D & O Insurance Right*, Business Law Today 50–54 (Nov./Dec. 1994).

45. NYBCL § 726(b). Insurance may be included in a single contract or supplement thereto. NYBCL § 726(c). Retrospective rated contracts are prohibited. *Id.*

46. *See supra*, § 1.66, note 42 and accompanying text.

47. NYBCL § 726(d).

48. NYBCL § 726(e).

provided in NYBCL § 1320 (exemption from certain provisions).[49]

Library References:
West's Key No. Digests, Corporations ⚷325–369.

§ 1.67 Directors Summary

Subject to any provision in the certificate of incorporation authorizing shareholder control of directors or to shareholder election of officers, the business of a corporation is managed under the direction of its board of directors, each of whom must be at least 18 years of age and have the other qualifications required by the certificate of incorporation or the bylaws. The entire board must consist of one or more members. At each annual meeting of shareholders, directors are elected to hold office until the next annual meeting except when the directors are divided into classes.

The corporation must make a current list of its directors and officers available for inspection by certain persons at its office during usual business hours. The NYBCL prescribes rules for filling vacancies in the board that occur for any reason, including vacancies resulting from removal with or without cause.

Action at a meeting of the board constitutes corporate action unless otherwise provided in the NYBCL. The vote of a majority of the directors present at a meeting at which a quorum is present, at the time of the vote, is the act of the board, unless otherwise required by the NYBCL. A majority of the entire board constitutes a quorum for the transaction of business, unless a greater quorum is required by the certificate of incorporation or a lesser quorum (but not less than one-third of the entire board) is fixed in the certificate of incorporation or bylaws. Unless otherwise restricted by the certificate of incorporation or the bylaws, action may be taken without a meeting if all members of the board or a committee consent in writing. Regular and special meetings of the board may be held at any place within or without New York, unless otherwise provided by the certificate of incorporation or the bylaws.

If the certificate of incorporation or the bylaws so provide, the board, by resolution adopted by a majority of the entire board, may designate an executive committee and any other committee, each consisting of one or more directors. To the extent so provided in the resolution, certificate of incorporation, or bylaws, each committee has all the authority of the board, with certain exceptions.

Directors must perform their duties in good faith and with that degree of care that an ordinarily prudent person in a like position would use under similar circumstances. Directors are entitled to rely on information, opinions, reports, or statements (including financial statements

---

49. NYBCL § 725(f). *But see, supra,* § 1.66, note 41 and accompanying text.

and other financial data) prepared or presented by certain persons designated in the NYBCL, including corporate officers and employees believed to be reliable and competent in the matters presented, counsel, public accountants, and other persons on matters believed to be within that person's professional or expert competence, and any committee of the board upon which the director does not serve.

Directors are fiduciaries of the corporation and have a duty of loyalty to it. The ability to undertake transactions that may give rise to a conflict of interest for any director is proscribed by the NYBCL.

Directors of a corporation who vote for or concur in certain corporate actions are jointly and severally (personally) liable to the corporation for the benefit of its creditors or shareholders to the extent of any injury suffered by them as a result of any such action. The actions that give rise to personal liability on the part of a director are (1) the declaration of improper dividends or other distributions, (2) improper purchases of the corporation's shares, (3) improper distributions of assets to shareholders after dissolution, and (4) improper loans to directors. Directors who are present at a meeting of the board (or committee) when the action is taken are presumed to have concurred in the action unless they duly register their dissent. A director who voted in favor of the action does not have such right to dissent. Directors absent from a meeting when the action is taken are presumed to have concurred in the action unless they register their dissent within a reasonable time after learning of the action. Any director against whom a claim is successfully asserted is entitled to contribution from the other directors who voted for or concurred in the action. Directors are not liable for board action if, in the circumstances, they performed their duties to the corporation in accordance with the standards of care and good faith prescribed by the NYBCL.

The NYBCL provisions on indemnification of directors are not exclusive of other rights to which directors may be entitled. A corporation may indemnify directors and officers against judgments, fines, amounts paid in settlement, and reasonable expenses (including attorneys' fees) incurred in actions (whether civil or criminal, but other than derivative actions) if they acted in good faith for a purpose that they reasonably believed to be in the best interests of the corporation (and in criminal actions or proceedings, in addition, had no reasonable cause to believe that their conduct was unlawful). Similarly, in derivative actions the NYBCL permits a corporation to indemnify directors against amounts paid in settlement and reasonable expenses (including attorneys' fees). In certain cases, indemnification may be awarded by a court. In any event, the corporation must notify shareholders within specified time limits of indemnification or other action taken.

A corporation may purchase and maintain insurance to indemnify the corporation for any obligation that it incurs as a result of its indemnification of its directors. It must notify shareholders of certain information regarding the insurance.

Library References:
West's Key No. Digests, Corporations ⊙=281–369.

§ 1.68 Directors Checklist

1. Business of a corporation is managed under the direction of its board of directors. (*See* § 1.59)

2. Number of directors; minimum number; increasing board size. (*See* § 1.59)

3. Election of directors. (*See* § 1.59)

4. Classification of directors. (*See* § 1.59)

5. Inspection of directors and officers list. (*See* § 1.59)

6. Vacancies and new directorships. (*See* § 1.60)

7. Removal of directors for cause and without cause; limitations; action by Attorney General. (*See* § 1.61)

8. Regular and special meetings of the board. (*See* § 1.62)

9. Meeting via conference telephone or similar communications equipment. (*See* § 1.62)

10. Time and place of regular, and special, board meetings; notice of meeting; adjournment of meetings; notice of adjournment. (*See* § 1.62)

11. Meetings' quorum and voting requirements; majority of the entire board constitutes a quorum; greater quorum fixed by certificate of incorporation; lesser quorum fixed by certificate of incorporation or bylaws, but not less than one-third of entire board. (*See* § 1.63)

12. Majority vote of directors, if a quorum present, is the act of the board, unless certificate of incorporation provides for a greater vote. (*See* § 1.63)

13. Amendment of certificate of incorporation that changes or deletes a quorum or voting provision. (*See* § 1.63)

14. Executive committee and other committees; each committee has all the authority of the board; exceptions. (*See* § 1.64)

15. Directors' fiduciary duties. (*See* § 1.65)

    • Duty of care and good faith. (*See* § 1.65)

    (i) May rely on information, opinions, reports, or statements (including financial statements) prepared or presented by certain persons. (*See* § 1.65)

§ 1.68 BUSINESS ORGANIZATIONS: CORPORATIONS Ch. 1

(ii) May rely on officers or employees of the corporation (or certain other corporations) believed to be reliable and competent in the matters presented. (*See* § 1.65)

(iii) May rely on counsel, public accountants, or other persons on matters believed to be within person's competence. (*See* § 1.65)

(iv) May rely on board committee upon which director does not serve on matters within its designated authority, believed, in good faith upon exercise of requisite care, to merit confidence, unless knowledge on matter makes reliance unwarranted. (*See* § 1.65)

(v) On action regarding a change in control of corporation, may consider its and its shareholders' long-term and short-term interests and the short-term or long-term effects of its actions upon its prospects and constituencies. (*See* § 1.65)

- Duty of loyalty. (*See* § 1.65)

(i) Director's conflict of interest in transaction. (*See* § 1.65)

(ii) Corporation may avoid transaction unless the party(ies) to it establish affirmatively that it was fair and reasonable to corporation at the time it was approved. (*See* § 1.65)

(iii) Certificate of incorporation restrictions on transactions between the corporation and its directors that render transactions in violation of restrictions void or voidable by corporation. (*See* § 1.65)

(iv) Corporate loans to directors not permitted unless authorized by shareholders. (*See* § 1.65)

16. Directors' joint and several liability for *improper* distributions, share repurchases, liquidation distributions, and loans to directors. (*See* § 1.66)

17. Directors' right to dissent. (*See* § 1.66)

18. Directors' right to contribution and subrogation. (*See* § 1.66)

19. Directors not liable if duties performed in accordance with the requisite standards of care and good faith. (*See* § 1.66)

20. Indemnification of directors permitted by other than court award and by court award; shareholder notification. (*See* § 1.66)

21. Indemnification insurance; shareholder notification. (*See* § 1.66)

Library References:

West's Key No. Digests, Corporations ⇌281–369.

§ 1.69 Officers

The board may elect or appoint a president, one or more vice-presidents, a secretary, a treasurer, and other officers, as it may determine or as may be provided in the bylaws.[1] The certificate of incorporation may provide that all officers or that specified officers be elected by the shareholders instead of by the board.[2] Unless otherwise provided in the certificate of incorporation or the bylaws, all officers are elected or appointed to hold office until the meeting of the board following the next annual meeting of shareholders or, in the case of officers elected by the shareholders, until the next annual meeting of shareholders.[3] Officers hold office for the term for which they are elected or appointed and until their successors have been elected or appointed and qualified.[4] Any two or more offices may be held by the same person.[5] When all of the issued and outstanding stock of the corporation is owned by one person, that person may hold all or any combination of offices.[6]

Authority. All officers, as between themselves and the corporation, have the authority and perform the duties in the management of the corporation as set forth in the bylaws or, to the extent not so provided, by the board.[7] Officers must perform their duties in good faith and with that degree of care that an ordinarily prudent person in a like position would use under similar circumstances.[8] They are entitled to rely on information, opinions, reports, or statements including financial statements and other financial data, prepared or presented by certain persons,[9] including (1) other officers or employees of the corporation (or of any other corporation of which the corporation owns, directly or indirectly, at least fifty percent of the outstanding shares of voting stock) that the officer believes to be reliable and competent in the matters presented and (2) counsel, public accountants, and other persons on matters that the officer believes to be within the person's professional or expert competence, so long as in so relying the officer acts in good faith and with the requisite degree of care.[10] Officers are not considered to be acting in good faith if they have knowledge concerning the matter in

---

§ 1.69

1. NYBCL § 715(a).

PRACTICE POINTER: This list of officers is permissive, not mandatory. *See, e.g.,* RMBCA § 8.40, Official Comment (permissive (permits every corporation to designate the officers it wants); corporation has officers described in its bylaws or appointed by the board in accordance with its bylaws). *Cf.* Delaware General Corporations Law § 142. *See also, e.g.,* Henn and Alexander, *supra,* § 1.1, note 1, p. 387 (gives examples of states having mandatory provisions and those having permissive provisions).

2. NYBCL § 715(b).
3. NYBCL § 715(c).
4. NYBCL § 715(d).
5. NYBCL § 715(e).
6. *Id.*
7. NYBCL § 715(g). *See* NYBCL § 715(g), Notes of Decisions (cases cited at part II, Authority and Duties). *See also, e.g.,* Henn and Alexander, *supra,* § 1.1, note 1, pp. 593–605 (re actual authority (express and implied), apparent authority, and estoppel).
8. NYBCL § 715(h). *See also, e.g.,* Henn and Alexander, *supra,* § 1.1, note 1, pp. 625–651 (fiduciary duties of officers).
9. NYBCL § 715(h).
10. *Id.*

question that would cause their reliance to be unwarranted.[11] Officers who so perform their duties have no liability by reason of being or having been an officer of the corporation.[12] The board may require any officer to give security for the faithful performance of his or her duties.[13]

Removal. Officers elected or appointed by the board may be removed by the board with or without cause.[14] Officers elected by the shareholders may be removed, with or without cause, only by vote of the shareholders, but their authority to act as officers may be suspended by the board for cause.[15] The removal of an officer without cause does not prejudice the officer's contract rights, if any,[16] but the election or appointment of an officer does not of itself create any such contract rights.[17] An action to remove an officer for cause may be brought by the Attorney General or by the holders of at least ten percent of the votes of outstanding shares, whether or not entitled to vote.[18] The court may bar from re-election or reappointment for a period fixed by the court any officer so removed.[19]

Indemnification; Insurance. A corporation may indemnify its officers.[20] A corporation may purchase and maintain insurance to cover any obligation to indemnify its officers.[21]

§ 1.70 Officers Summary

The board *may* elect or appoint a president, one or more vice-presidents, a secretary, a treasurer, and other officers, as it may determine or as may be provided in the bylaws. The certificate of incorporation may provide that all officers or that specified officers be elected by the shareholders instead of by the board. Any two or more offices may be held by the same person. All officers as between themselves and the corporation have the authority and perform the duties in the management of the corporation as may be provided in the bylaws or, to the extent not so provided, by the board. Officers must perform their duties in good faith and with that degree of care that an ordinarily prudent person in a like position would use under similar circumstances. Officers are entitled to rely on information, opinions, reports, or statements including financial statements and other financial data, prepared or presented by certain persons. Officers elected or appointed by the board may be removed by the board with or without cause; those elected by the shareholders may be removed, with or without cause, only by vote of the

---

11. Id.
12. Id.
13. NYBCL § 715(f).
14. NYBCL § 716(a).
15. Id.
16. NYBCL § 716(b).
17. Id.
18. NYBCL § 716(c).
19. Id.
20. NYBCL §§ 721–725. *See supra,* § 1.66, notes 19–27 and accompanying text.
21. NYBCL § 726. *See supra,* § 1.66, notes 44–45 and accompanying text.

shareholders. A corporation may indemnify its officers and may purchase and maintain indemnification insurance for officers.

Library References:
West's Key No. Digests, Corporations ⇌281–369.

§ 1.71 Officers Checklist

1. Board elects or appoints officers, as it may determine or as may be provided in the bylaws. (*See* § 1.69)
2. Certificate of incorporation may provide that all officers or specified officers be elected by shareholders instead of by board. (*See* § 1.69)
3. Tenure of officers. (*See* § 1.69)
4. Officers' authority. (*See* § 1.69)
5. Officers' duties of good faith and due care. (*See* § 1.69)
6. Officers entitled to rely on certain information and opinions prepared or presented by certain persons. (*See* § 1.69)
7. Board may require any officer to give security for faithful performance of duties. (*See* § 1.69)
8. Officers elected or appointed by board removable by board with or without cause. (*See* § 1.69)
9. Officers elected by shareholders removable with or without cause, only by vote of the shareholders, but authority to act as officer may be suspended by board for cause. (*See* § 1.69)
10. Corporation may indemnify officers and purchase and maintain indemnification insurance for this purpose. (*See* § 1.69)

Library References:
West's Key No. Digests, Corporations ⇌281–369.

§ 1.72 Amendment of Certificate of Incorporation

A corporation may amend its certificate of incorporation, from time to time, in any and as many respects as may be desired, to include any provision that might be lawfully contained in an original certificate of incorporation at the time the amendment is made.[1] In particular (but without limiting the general power to amend),[2] a corporation may amend its certificate of incorporation to: (1) change its name; (2) enlarge, limit, or otherwise change its corporate purposes; (3) specify or change the

---

§ 1.72

1. NYBCL § 801(a). A corporation created by special act may accomplish the amendments permitted (and in the manner and subject to the conditions provided) in NYBCL Article 8. NYBCL § 801(c). *See also, supra,* § 1.7, note 6 and § 1.21, note 1.

2. A change in a mandatory provision in the certificate of incorporation requires an amendment to the certificate of incorporation, as does a change in a permissive provision that was included in the certificate of incorporation. *See supra,* § 1.21.

location of its office; (4) specify or change the post office address to which the Secretary of State must mail a copy of any process against the corporation served upon the Secretary; (5) make, revoke, or change the designation of a registered agent or specify or change the agent's address; (6) extend the duration of the corporation or, if it has ceased to exist because the duration specified in its certificate of incorporation has expired, revive its existence; (7) increase or decrease the aggregate number of shares, or shares of any class or series, with or without par value, that the corporation has authority to issue; (8) remove from authorized shares any class of shares, or any shares of any class, whether issued or unissued; (9) increase or reduce the par value of any authorized shares of any class with par value, whether issued or unissued; (10) change any authorized shares, with or without par value, whether issued or unissued, into a different number of shares of the same class or into the same or a different number of shares of any one or more classes or any series thereof, either with or without par value; (11) fix, change or abolish the designation of any authorized class or any series thereof or any of the relative rights, preferences, and limitations of any shares of any authorized class or any series thereof, whether issued or unissued, including provisions in respect of any undeclared dividends (whether or not cumulative or accrued), the redemption of any shares, any sinking fund for the redemption or purchase of any shares, or any preemptive right to acquire shares or other securities; (12) grant authority to the board or change or revoke the board's authority to establish and designate series and fix the number of shares and the relative rights, preferences, and limitations as between series in respect of the shares of any preferred class then or theretofore authorized that may be issued in series; or (13) strike out, change, or add any provision, not inconsistent with the NYBCL or any other statute, relating to the business of the corporation, its affairs, its rights or powers, or the rights or powers of its shareholders, directors, or officers, including any provision that under the NYBCL is required or permitted to be set forth in the bylaws.[3] A corporation may reduce its stated capital by an amendment to its certificate of incorporation under NYBCL § 801 that: (1) reduces the par value of any issued shares with par value, (2) changes issued shares under NYBCL § 801(b)(11) (change number of authorized shares) and results in a reduction of stated capital, or (3) removes reacquired and cancelled shares from authorized shares.[4]

Certain amendments and changes may affect stated capital and the

---

[3]. NYBCL § 801(b). A certificate of amendment may not be filed to reduce the duration of the corporation. *Id.* For taxation of recapitalizations, *see infra*, §§ 1.74, note 2; 1.91.

[4]. NYBCL § 802(a). A corporation is not prevented by NYBCL § 802 from reducing its stated capital in any other manner permitted by the NYBCL. NYBCL § 802(b). *See supra*, §§ 1.32, note 5 and accompanying text; 1.38, notes 34 and 35 and accompanying text; and 1.39, notes 22–26 and accompanying text.

rights of shareholders.[5] In these cases, the following rules apply.[6] The stated capital of shares without par value resulting from a change of issued shares is the amount of stated capital of the shares changed (or, if stated capital is reduced by the amendment, the reduced amount stated in the certificate of amendment).[7] A corporation may not change issued shares into both shares with par value and shares without par value unless the stated capital of the shares changed (or, if stated capital is reduced by the amendment, the reduced amount of stated capital stated in the certificate of amendment) *exceeds* the par value of the shares with par value resulting from the change; the excess is the stated capital of the shares without par value resulting from the change.[8] A corporation may not increase the aggregate par value of its issued shares with par value unless, after giving effect to the increase, the stated capital is at least equal to the amount required by NYBCL § 102(a)(12).[9] Stated capital may not be reduced by amendment unless, after the reduction, the stated capital exceeds the aggregate preferential amount payable upon involuntary liquidation in respect of all issued shares having preferential rights in assets plus the par value of all other issued shares with par value.[10] Any change in the relative rights, preferences, and limitations of authorized shares of any class by a certificate of amendment that does not eliminate them from authorized shares or change them into shares of another class does not effect an issue of a new class of shares.[11]

No amendment or change will affect any existing cause of action in favor of or against the corporation, any pending suit to which it is a party, or the existing rights of persons other than shareholders.[12] If the corporate name is changed, no suit brought by or against the corporation under its former name abates for that reason.[13]

Adversely Affected Rights. A holder of adversely affected shares who does not vote for or consent in writing to an amendment or change has, subject to and by complying with the provisions of NYBCL § 623,[14] the right to dissent and to receive payment for the shares if the amendment: (1) alters or abolishes any preferential right of the shares;

---

5. NYBCL § 806(b)(1).

6. Except cases under NYBCL § 808 (reorganization under act of Congress). *See infra*, § 1.78.

7. NYBCL § 806(b)(1). *See infra*, § 1.75.

8. NYBCL § 806(b)(1). *See infra*, § 1.75.

9. NYBCL § 806(b)(2). *See supra*, § 1.5. *See infra*, § 1.75.

10. NYBCL § 806(b)(3). A corporation may reduce its stated capital by an amendment of its certificate of incorporation under NYBCL § 801 that: (1) reduces the par value of any issued shares with par value; (2) changes issued shares under NYBCL § 801(b)(11) that results in a reduction of stated capital; (3) removes from authorized shares, shares that have been issued, reacquired, and cancelled by the corporation. NYBCL § 802(a). A corporation may reduce its stated capital in any other manner that the NYBCL permits. NYBCL § 802(b).

11. NYBCL § 806(b)(4).

12. NYBCL § 806(b)(5).

13. *Id.*

14. *See supra*, § 1.51.

(2) creates, alters, or abolishes any provision or right in respect of the redemption of the shares or any sinking fund for the redemption or purchase of the shares; (3) alters or abolishes any preemptive right of the holder to acquire shares or other securities; or (4) excludes or limits the right of the holder to vote on any matter, except as the right may be limited by the voting rights given new shares then being authorized of any existing or new class.[15]

§ 1.73 Amendment of Certificate of Incorporation—Procedure

Procedure. Amendment of the certificate of incorporation may be authorized by vote of the board, followed by vote of the holders of a majority of all outstanding shares entitled to vote, provided, however, that whenever the certificate of incorporation requires action by the board of directors, by the holders of any class or series of shares, or by the holders of any other securities having voting power, by the vote of a greater number or proportion than is required by any section of the NYBCL Article 8, the provision of the certificate of incorporation requiring such greater vote may not be altered, amended, or repealed except by such greater vote.[1] Certain changes or specifications may be authorized by the board alone (*i.e.*, without shareholder approval being required).[2] An amendment of the certificate of incorporation of a corporation that has no shareholders of record, no subscribers for shares whose subscriptions have been accepted, and no directors may be authorized by the sole incorporator or a majority of the incorporators.[3]

Library References:

West's Key No. Digests, Corporations ⟶40.

§ 1.74 Amendment of Certificate of Incorporation—Class Vote

A class vote is required on certain amendments, whether or not the class is otherwise entitled to vote.[1] Notwithstanding any provision in the certificate of incorporation, the holders of shares of a class are entitled to vote and to vote as a class upon the authorization of an amendment, and, in addition to the authorization of the amendment by a majority of the votes of all outstanding shares entitled to vote, the amendment must be authorized by a majority of the votes of all outstanding shares of the

---

15. NYBCL § 806(b)(6).

§ 1.73

1. NYBCL § 803(a).

CAVEAT: This section does not alter the vote required under any other section of the NYBCL for the authorization of a specific amendment, nor does it alter the authority of the board to authorize amendments under any other section of the NYBCL. NYBCL § 803(c).

2. *See infra*, § 1.76.

3. NYBCL § 803(d).

§ 1.74

1. NYBCL § 804(a).

class when a proposed amendment would: (1) exclude or limit their right to vote on any matter, except as the right may be limited by voting rights given to new shares then being authorized of any existing or new class or series; (2) subordinate their rights by authorizing shares having preferences in any respect superior to their rights; or (3) change their shares under NYBCL §§ 801(b)(10) (reduction in par value of any class), 801(b)(11) (change number of authorized shares), or 801(b)(12) (fix or change the designation, or the relative rights, preferences, or limitations, of a class), provide that their shares may be converted into shares of any other class or into shares of any other series of the same class, alter the terms or conditions upon which their shares are convertible, or change the shares issuable upon conversion of their shares, if the action would adversely affect the holders.[2] If the proposed amendment would adversely affect the rights of the holders of shares of only one or more series of any class, but not the entire class, then only the holders of those series whose rights would be affected are considered a separate class for voting purposes.[3]

Library References:

West's Key No. Digests, Corporations ⚖40.

§ 1.75 Amendment of Certificate of Incorporation—Certificate of Amendment

The contents of a certificate of amendment are specified in NYBCL § 805(a).[1] Any number of amendments or changes may be included in a

---

2. *Id. See also*, I.R.C. § 368(a)(1)(E) (recapitalizations treated as tax-free exchanges); Treas. Reg. § 1.368–2(e) (gives five examples of recapitalizations: old bonds for new preferred shares, old preferred shares for new common shares, old common shares for new preferred shares, old preferred shares with certain dividend and liquidation preferences for new common shares without any preferences, and old preferred shares with dividend arrearages for other shares). *Cf.* I.R.C. § 305(c) (share distributions and recapitalization having effect of a distribution under I.R.C. § 301 (*see supra*, § 1.38, notes 1–3 and accompanying text)); Treas. Reg. § 1.305–7(c) (recapitalizations that increase a shareholder's proportionate interest treated as a distribution under I.R.C. § 301). *See, e.g.*, Henn and Alexander, pp. 974–977 (cites New York cases on amendments of certificate of incorporation involving recapitalizations). *See* Tax Law § 180 (tax on change of (1) shares with par value into shares without par value, (2) shares without par value into shares with par value, (3) shares without par value into shares without par value, (4) shares with par value into both shares with par value and shares without par value, (5) shares without par value into both shares with par value and shares without par value). *See infra*, § 1.91.

3. NYBCL § 804(b).

§ 1.75

1. NYBCL § 805(a). ***Procedure***. To accomplish any amendment, a certificate of amendment, entitled "Certificate of amendment of the certificate of incorporation of _____ (name of corporation) under section 805 of the Business Corporation Law," must be signed, verified, and delivered to the Department of State. NYBCL § 805(a). The certificate must set forth: (1) the name of the corporation and, if it has been changed, the name under which it was formed; (2) the date its certificate of incorporation was filed by the Department of State; (3) each amendment effected thereby, with the subject matter of each provision of the certificate of incorporation that is to be amended or eliminated and the full text of the provision or provisions, if any, that are

certificate,[2] provided that any additional statements required by any other applicable NYBCL sections are also included.[3] Except as otherwise provided in the NYBCL, the certificate becomes effective upon filing by the Department of State.[4] Where a change in shares is made by amendment, the resulting shares are deemed substituted for the former shares upon the filing of the certificate of amendment.[5]

The Department of State may not file a certificate of amendment reviving the existence of a corporation without the consent of the State Tax Commission.[6] If the name of the corporation being revived is not available for use under NYBCL § 301, the certificate of amendment must change the name to one that is available.[7]

Library References:

West's Key No. Digests, Corporations ⇐40.

§ 1.76 Amendment of Certificate of Incorporation— Certificate of Change

The board is authorized, without shareholder approval being required, to: (1) change or specify the location of the corporation's office; (2) change or specify the post office address to which the Secretary of State must mail a copy of any process against the corporation served upon the Secretary; or (3) make, revoke, or change the designation of a registered agent or change or specify the registered agent's address.[1] These changes may be accomplished by filing a certificate of change.[2]

to be substituted or added; (4) if an amendment provides for a change of shares, then (a) the number, par value, and class of issued shares changed, (b) the number, par value, and class of issued shares resulting from such change, (c) the number, par value, and class of unissued shares changed, (d) the number, par value, and class of unissued shares resulting from such change, and (e) the terms of each such change, and if an amendment makes two or more such changes, a like statement must be included for each change; (5) if any amendment reduces stated capital, then a statement of the manner in which the same is effected and the amounts from which and to which stated capital is reduced; (6) the manner in which the amendment of the certificate of incorporation was authorized (and if the amendment was authorized under NYBCL § 803(d), then a statement that the corporation does not have any shareholders of record, subscribers for shares whose subscriptions have been accepted, and directors. NYBCL § 805(a)).

2. NYBCL § 805(b).

3. Id.

4. NYBCL § 104(f). See supra, § 1.7.

5. NYBCL § 805(c).

6. NYBCL § 806(a).

7. Id.

§ 1.76

1. NYBCL § 803(b).

2. NYBCL § 805–A(a). *Procedure*. The certificate of change must be entitled "Certificate of change of _____ (name of corporation) under section 805–A of the Business Corporation Law" and must be signed, verified, and delivered to the Department of State. The certificate must set forth: (1) the name of the corporation, and if it has been changed, the name under which it was formed; (2) the date its certificate of incorporation was filed by the Department of State; (3) each change effected; (4) the manner in which the change was authorized. NYBCL § 805–A(a). A certificate of change that changes only the post office address of the corporate agent for service of process may be signed, verified, and delivered to the Department of State by the agent. NYBCL § 805–A(b). It must set forth the state-

§ 1.77 Amendment of Certificate of Incorporation—Restated Certificate of Incorporation

If a certificate of incorporation has been amended from time to time, a corporation may want to incorporate all of the prior amendments and changes into one document. When authorized by the board, the text of a corporation's certificate of incorporation may be restated in a single certificate without thereby making any amendment or change.[1] It may include amendments or changes authorized by the board without a vote of shareholders;[2] alternatively, it may restate its certificate of incorporation as amended to effect any amendments or changes permitted by the NYBCL, when authorized by the required vote of the shareholders.[3] A restated certificate need not name the incorporators, the original subscribers for shares, or the first directors.[4]

Even if the corporation was required by statute to secure a public official's consent or approval to the filing of its certificate of incorporation or a certificate of amendment, the consent or approval is not

Library References:
West's Key No. Digests, Corporations ⟶40.

---

ments required under NYBCL § 805-A(a)(1), (2), and (3); it must also state that a notice of the proposed change was mailed to the corporation by the party signing the certificate no fewer than thirty days prior to the date of delivery to the Department, that the corporation has not objected to the change, and that the party signing the certificate is the agent of the corporation to whose address the Secretary of State is required to mail copies of process or the registered agent, if such be the case. *Id.*

§ 1.77

1. NYBCL § 807(a). ***Procedure***. A restated certificate of incorporation, entitled "Restated certificate of incorporation of _____ (name of corporation) under section 807 of the Business Corporation Law," must be signed, verified, and delivered to the Department of State. NYBCL § 807(b). The certificate shall set forth: (1) the name of the corporation and, if it has been changed, the name under which it was formed; (2) the date its certificate of incorporation was filed by the Department of State; (3) if the restated certificate restates the text of the certificate of incorporation without making any amendment or change, then a statement that the text of the certificate of incorporation is thereby restated without amendment or change to read as therein set forth in full; (4) if the restated certificate restates the text of the certificate of incorporation as amended or changed thereby, then a statement that the certificate of incorporation is amended or changed to effect one or more of the amendments or changes authorized by the NYBCL, specifying each amendment or change and that the text of the certificate of incorporation is thereby restated as amended or changed to read as therein set forth in full; (5) if an amendment, effected by the restated certificate, provides for a change of issued shares, then the number and kind of shares changed, the number and kind of shares resulting from such change, and the terms of change, and if any amendment makes two or more such changes, a like statement must be included for each such change; (6) if the restated certificate contains an amendment that effects a reduction of stated capital, then a statement of the manner in which the capital reduction is effected and the amounts from which and to which stated capital is reduced; (7) the manner in which the restatement of the certificate of incorporation was authorized. NYBCL § 807(b).

2. NYBCL § 807(a).

3. *Id.* See *supra*, § 1.77, note 1 (procedure re restated certificate of incorporation).

4. NYBCL § 807(c). This paragraph removes the need to include outdated statements regarding original founders. *Id.*, Legislative Studies and Reports (Comment).

required for a restated certificate if the certificate makes no further amendment and if all previously required consents and approvals have been obtained.[5] Upon filing by the Department, the original certificate of incorporation is superseded and the restated certificate of incorporation (including any amendments and changes made thereby) becomes the current certificate of incorporation of the corporation.[6]

Library References:
West's Key No. Digests, Corporations ⊕40.

§ 1.78 Amendment of Certificate of Incorporation—Reorganization Under Act of Congress

Whenever a plan of corporate reorganization has been confirmed by a decree or order of a court in proceedings under an applicable act of Congress, the corporation has authority, *without* shareholder or board action, to effectuate the plan and take any action for which provision is made in any statute governing the corporation or for which provision is, or might be, made in its certificate of incorporation or bylaws.[1] The corporate action may be taken as directed by the decree or order or by the trustees of the corporation appointed in the reorganization proceedings with like effect as if taken by unanimous action of the board and shareholders of the corporation.[2]

If the decree or order provides for the formation of a new domestic corporation or for the authorization of a new foreign corporation to do business in New York under a name the same as or similar to that of the corporation being reorganized, the certificate of incorporation of the new

---

5. NYBCL § 807(e). *See also,* NYBCL § 807(d).

6. NYBCL § 807(f).

§ 1.78

1. NYBCL § 808(a). The corporate reorganizations to which NYBCL § 808 applies are proceedings under the Bankruptcy Act (11 U.S.C.A. §§ 101 *et seq.*) and perhaps other federal laws (*e.g.*, Public Utility Holding Company Act 15 U.S.C.A. §§ 79 *et seq.*). For reorganizations as defined for tax purposes in I.R.C. § 368, *see infra*, § 1.91. Reorganizations under I.R.C. § 368 correspond basically to, and are usually known by the terms, mergers and acquisitions described in NYBCL §§ 901, 905, 909, and 913.

2. NYBCL § 808(b). ***Procedure.*** Any certificate, required or permitted by law to be filed or recorded to accomplish any corporate purpose, must be signed, and verified or acknowledged, under the decree or order, by the trustees and must certify that provision for the certificate is contained in the plan of reorganization or in a decree or order of the court and that the plan has been confirmed as provided in an applicable act of Congress specified in the certificate, with the title and venue of the proceeding and the date when the decree or order confirming the plan was made, and the certificate must be delivered to the Department of State. NYBCL § 808(c). If after the certificate is filed by the Department of State, the decree or order of confirmation of the plan of reorganization is reversed or vacated or the plan is modified, additional certificates must be executed and delivered to the Department of State conforming to the plan of reorganization as finally confirmed or to the decree or order as finally made. NYBCL § 808(f). Except as otherwise provided in NYBCL § 808, no certificate filed by the Department of State confers on a corporation powers other than those permitted to be conferred on a corporation formed under the NYBCL. NYBCL § 808(g).

domestic corporation or the application of the new foreign corporation must set forth that it is being delivered pursuant to the decree or order and must be endorsed with the consent of the court having jurisdiction of the proceeding.[3] After the new domestic corporation's certificate of incorporation, or the new foreign corporation's application, has been filed, the corporation being reorganized may not continue the use of its name except in connection with the reorganization proceeding and as may be necessary to adjust and wind up its affairs.[4]

Library References:

West's Key No. Digests, Corporations ⚖=40.

§ 1.79 Amendment of Certificate of Incorporation Summary

A corporation may amend its certificate of incorporation, from time to time, in as many respects desired, to include any provision that might be lawfully contained in an original certificate of incorporation at the time the amendment is made. Amendments are permitted for a variety of purposes related to such matters as corporate name, purposes, office location, address for service of process, registered agents, duration (extension, not reduction), authorized shares (*e.g.*, number of shares, par value (with or without), and relative rights, preferences, and limitations), redemption of shares, and preemptive rights. Amendment of the certificate of incorporation may be authorized by the board, followed by vote of a majority of shareholders. The board may authorize, without shareholder authorization, certain changes in connection with the location of the corporation's office, the post office address for service of process, or the designation and address of registered agents.

Regardless of any provision in the certificate of incorporation, a class vote is required on certain amendments, whether or not the class is otherwise entitled to vote, if a proposed amendment would limit or

---

3. NYBCL § 808(h). Shareholders of the corporation have no right to receive payment for their shares but have only the rights, if any, provided in the plan of reorganization. NYBCL § 808(d). Notwithstanding the requirements of NYBCL § 504 on consideration and payment for shares, a corporation may, after the confirmation of the plan, issue its shares, bonds, and other securities for the consideration specified in the plan of reorganization and may issue warrants or other rights or options for the purchase of shares upon terms and conditions set forth in the plan. NYBCL § 808(e). *See also*, I.R.C. § 368(a)(1)(G) (transfer by a corporation to another corporation in a Title 11 or similar case). *See infra*, § 1.91.

4. NYBCL § 808(h). Thirty days after such filing, the reorganized domestic corporation is automatically dissolved or the authority of the reorganized foreign corporation to transact business in New York ceases. *Id.* To the extent that the adjustment and winding up of the affairs of the dissolved corporation are not accomplished as a part of the proceeding or prescribed by the decree or order, it must proceed in accordance with the provisions of NYBCL Article 10 pertaining to non-judicial dissolution. *Id. See infra*, § 1.95.

CAVEAT: NYBCL § 808 does not relieve any corporation from obtaining from a public official or agency any consent or approval required by statute. NYBCL § 808(i).

exclude the voting rights of the class or would adversely affect the class by classifying or reclassifying shares.

The contents of a certificate of amendment are specified in the NYBCL. Any number of amendments or changes may be included in the certificate.

Certain rules apply to amendments and changes that may affect stated capital and the rights of shareholders. Holders of any adversely affected shares who do not vote for or consent in writing to the amendment or change have the right to dissent and to receive payment for their shares if the amendment alters or abolishes preferential rights, redemption rights or any redemption sinking fund, preemptive rights, or voting rights (except voting rights given new shares of any existing or new class then being authorized). Changes that may be authorized by the board, without shareholder authorization, may be accomplished by filing a certificate of change.

A corporation may incorporate into one document all prior amendments and changes to its certificate of incorporation. Upon the filing of a restated certificate of incorporation by the Department of State, it becomes the effective certificate of incorporation of the corporation. In corporate reorganizations under federal law, the corporation has authority, *without* action of its shareholders or board, to effectuate the plan and take any action for which provision is made in any statute governing the corporation or for which provision is, or might be, made in its certificate of incorporation or bylaws.

Library References:
    West's Key No. Digests, Corporations ⚖40.

§ 1.80 Amendment of Certificate of Incorporation Checklist

1. Amendment of certificate of incorporation permitted, from time to time, in as many respects desired, and may include any provision lawfully contained in an original certificate of incorporation when amendment made. (*See* § 1.72)

2. Amendment or change of the certificate of incorporation may be authorized by vote of the board, followed by majority vote of shareholders. (*See* § 1.73)

3. Certain changes may be authorized by the board without shareholder approval. (*See* §§ 1.73, 1.76)

4. Class vote required on certain amendments whether or not class otherwise entitled to vote when proposed amendment adversely affects the class. (*See* § 1.74)

5. Contents of certificate of amendment. (*See* § 1.75)

6. Consent of State Tax Commission. (*See* § 1.75)

7. Amendments and changes that affect stated capital; rights of shareholders in these cases. (*See* § 1.75)

8. Holders of adversely affected shares given right to dissent to amendment or change and to receive payment for their shares. (*See* § 1.75)

9. Changes authorized by board alone. (*See* § 1.76)

   - Change or specify the location of the corporation's office.
   - Change or specify the post office address to which the Secretary of State must mail a copy of any process against the corporation served upon the Secretary.
   - Make, revoke, or change the designation of a registered agent or change or specify the registered agent's address.

10. Certificate of change that changes only the post office address of agent of corporation for service of process. (*See* § 1.76)

11. Restated certificate of incorporation. (*See* § 1.77)

12. In corporate reorganizations under federal law, corporation has authority, *without* action of its shareholders or board, to take any action for which provision is, or might be, made in its certificate of incorporation or bylaws. (*See* § 1.78)

Library References:

West's Key No. Digests, Corporations ⇔40.

§ 1.81 Business Combinations

Business combinations through mergers and acquisitions may enhance shareholder value, both for the acquiring corporation's shareholders and for the acquired (or target) corporation's shareholders.[1] Three

---

§ 1.81

1. *See, e.g.*, D. Logue, *Handbook of Modern Finance* (1984) pp. 29–1 to 29; R. Gilson, *The Law and Finance of Corporate Acquisitions* (1986) pp. 257, 341, 445–460.

PRACTICE POINTER: Business combinations offer a means of maintaining control through corporate pyramiding. *See, e.g.*, N. Lattin, *The Law of Corporations* (1959) pp. 341–344; H. Guthmann and H. Dougall, *Corporate Financial Policy* (3d ed. 1955) pp. 589–590. Pyramiding is subject to, *e.g.*, certain antitrust constraints, tax limitations, and risk of collapse. *See, e.g.*, W. Klein and J. Coffee, *Business Organization and Finance* pp. 301–303 (4th ed. 1990). Controlling operations and limiting risk by means of multiple corporations might also be feasible, but this method also risks antitrust violation and is subject to certain tax limitations. *See, e.g.*, B. Bittker and J. Eustice, *Federal Income Taxation of Corporations and Shareholders* (6th ed. 1994) ¶¶ 13.01–13.02 (certain tax benefits (*e.g.*, each corporation's enjoying the lowest tax rates under I.R.C. § 11(b)) are limited by I.R.C. §§ 1561 and 269); Henn and Alexander, *supra*, § 1.1, note 1, pp. 109, 851–861 (federal and state antitrust regulation). Going private transactions (*e.g.*, as a corporate repurchase (self tender) of shares held publicly or by a recalcitrant minority; in a reverse triangular merger format paying cash, not exchanging shares of parent, to target's shareholders) whether or not structured as leveraged or management buyouts, provide another means of attaining or maintaining control. *See, e.g.*, Henn and Alexander, *supra*, § 1.1, note 1, pp. 651–656 and 986–988 (protection of minority shareholders in cash out mergers); N. Wallner

§ 1.81   BUSINESS ORGANIZATIONS: CORPORATIONS   Ch. 1

basic methods of combining corporations are typically used and may be tax free or taxable to certain of the parties: (1) the merger of a corporation into another corporation, (2) the acquisition by a corporation of substantially all of the *assets* of another corporation, or (3) the acquisition by a corporation of the *shares* (e.g., a controlling interest) of another corporation.[2] Spin-offs and split-offs, within or without a divisive reorganization,[3] whether tax free or taxable, may also be useful methods to realize shareholder value.[4] Other species of business combinations include consolidations, recapitalizations, reclassifications, and certain other transactions.[5]

§ 1.82 Business Combinations—Mergers and Consolidations

Business combinations may be effected through mergers and consolidations, which follow similar procedures under the NYBCL.[1] These combinations, as well as certain asset acquisitions and share acquisitions, can have similar practical effects on the parties (constituent corporations and their shareholders) under the NYBCL, but important distinctions, with attendant advantages and disadvantages, exist in practice.[2]

and J. Greve, *How To Do A Leveraged Buyout or Acquisition* (1982) pp. 119–238; W. Klein and J. Coffee, *Business Organization and Finance* (4th ed. 1990) pp. 166–168. See supra, §§ 1.30, note 16; 1.38, note 30; 1.51, note 22.

2. *See, e.g.*, Herwitz, *supra*, § 1.1, note 1, pp. 623–624; Report, *Committee on Negotiated Acquisitions, Purchasing the Stock of a Privately Held Company: The Legal Effect of an Acquisition Review*, 51 Business Lawyer 479 (1996); Schulman and Schenk, *Shareholders' Voting and Appraisal Rights in Corporate Acquisition Transactions* (1983) p. 1529.

CAVEAT: Thought must be given to other laws that may affect the planned transaction (e.g., tax, securities, accounting antitrust, contract, labor, successor liability, and environmental laws). *See, e.g.*, Kury, *Acquisition Checklist*, 36 Business Lawyer 207 (1981); R. Gilson, *The Law and Finance of Corporate Acquisitions* (1986) pp. 933–934, 1079, and 1144; Darrell, *The Use of Reorganization Techniques in Corporate Acquisitions* (1957) pp. 1183–1206. See NYBCL § 912(a)(5). *See infra*, §§ 1.82, 1.85, 1.88, 1.89, and 1.91.

3. See *infra*, § 1.91, note 4.

4. Very generally: in a spin-off, a parent corporation distributes to its shareholders shares of its subsidiary (either preexisting or newly created). A split-off is identical to a spin-off, except that the parent's shareholders exchange their shares in the parent for shares of the subsidiary. In a split-up, the parent distributes the shares of two or more of its subsidiaries (either preexisting or newly created) to its shareholders in complete liquidation of the subsidiaries. See *infra*, § 1.91.

5. See *infra*, § 1.91.

CAVEAT: NYBCL § 912(a)(5) broadly defines "business combination" to include certain transactions between a domestic corporation and an "interested shareholder" (i.e., a shareholder owning twenty percent or more of a domestic corporation's voting stock). *See infra*, §§ 1.82, 1.85, 1.88 and 1.89. *See also, e.g.*, J. Bogen, *Financial Handbook* (4th ed. 1968) 20.4, 20.31–20.34, and 20.46–20.48 (combination by lease, long-term sales contract, or joint venture). *See supra*, § 1.81, note 1.

§ 1.82

1. See NYBCL §§ 901–905, 909, and 913. See *infra*, §§ 1.83 and 1.88.

2. *See, e.g.*, Herwitz, *supra*, § 1.1, note 1, pp. 623–624 (compares three basic combinations: (1) in a *merger*, the surviving corporation takes title to the assets (and assumes the obligations) of the transferor

§ 1.83 Business Combinations—Mergers and Consolidations—Procedures

The NYBCL provides that two or more domestic corporations may merge into one of the corporations participating in the merger.[1] They may instead consolidate into a single new corporation to be formed corporation, the transferor disappears, and the transferor's shareholders receive shares of the surviving corporation (and, similarly, in a consolidation two or more corporations consolidate (in effect merge) into a new corporation, with the disappearing corporations' shareholders receiving shares of the new corporation); (2) in an *asset acquisition*, if a corporation acquires all of the assets of another corporation in exchange for the acquirer's shares, and if the acquirer assumes the transferor's obligations and the transferor distributes the acquirer's shares to the transferor's shareholders in dissolution and liquidation, the parties end up in the same position as under a merger; (3) in a *share acquisition*, if a corporation acquires all of the shares of another corporation in exchange for the acquirer's shares, the acquired corporation's shareholders become shareholders of the acquirer, and the acquired corporation becomes a wholly-owned subsidiary of the acquirer (with little practical difference to the acquirer between operating the acquired corporation's business as either a division or a subsidiary), but if the acquirer (parent) exchanges the subsidiary's shares for the subsidiary's assets in liquidation and dissolution of the subsidiary, the parties end up in the same position as under a merger). See *infra*, §§ 1.84, 1.85, and 1.88.

PRACTICE POINTER: Mergers and consolidations permit greater cash leeway than asset acquisitions or share acquisitions without disqualifying the transaction's tax-free treatment. Upon filing the certificate of merger or consolidation, title to the disappearing corporation's assets are automatically transferred to the surviving or consolidated corporation, whereas in an asset acquisition title to the acquired corporation's properties (including contract rights) must be transferred by various instruments of conveyance, assignment, or other documents. In an asset acquisition, the acquirer undertakes to pay the agreed consideration, including all, or only part, of the transferor's obligations, whereas in a merger or consolidation, the surviving or new consolidated corporation assumes all the liabilities of the constituent corporations. Mergers and consolidations require the approval of the constituent corporations' shareholders, whereas the acquisition of substantially all of the assets, or *all* of the outstanding shares of one or more classes, of an acquired corporation by an acquirer, requires only the acquired corporation's shareholders' approval of the transaction. See *infra*, §§ 1.85 (disposition of substantially all assets) and 1.88 (binding share exchange). See also, e.g., J. Bogen, *Financial Handbook* (4th. ed. 1968) 20–8 to 20–23, and 20–34 to 20–39 (advantages and disadvantages of different combinations); Herwitz, *supra*, § 1.1, note 1, pp. 624–635 (re, *e.g.*, continuing minority interests in acquired corporation, creation of substantial voting block in acquirer, nonassignable contracts and franchises, preservation of acquired corporation's charter, unknown and contingent liabilities, and transferee liability).

§ 1.83

1. NYBCL § 901(a)(1). The following definitions are used in NYBCL Article 9: "merger" means a procedure by which two or more domestic corporations merge into a single corporation, which is one of the constituent corporations (NYBCL § 901(a)(1) and (b)(1)); "consolidation" means a procedure by which two or more domestic corporations consolidate into a single new corporation to be formed pursuant to the consolidation (NYBCL § 901(a)(2) and (b)(2)); "constituent corporation" means an existing corporation that is participating in the merger or consolidation with one or more other corporations; "surviving corporation" means the constituent corporation into which one or more other constituent corporations are merged; "consolidated corporation" means the new corporation into which two or more constituent corporations are consolidated. NYBCL § 901(b).

CAVEAT: See NYBCL § 912(a)(5)(A). See *infra*, § 1.89, notes 11–14.

§ 1.83   BUSINESS ORGANIZATIONS: CORPORATIONS   Ch. 1

pursuant to the plan of consolidation.[2]

Procedure. The board of each corporation proposing to participate in a merger or consolidation must adopt a plan of merger or consolidation, setting forth: (1) the name of each constituent corporation (and, if the name of any of them has been changed, the name under which it was formed) and the name of the surviving, or consolidated, corporation; (2) for each constituent corporation, the designation and number of outstanding shares of each class and series, specifying the classes and series entitled to vote as well as each class and series, if any, entitled to vote as a class and, if the number of any shares is subject to change prior to the effective date of the merger or consolidation, the manner in which the change may occur; (3) the terms and conditions of the proposed merger or consolidation, including the manner and basis of converting the shares of the constituent corporations into shares, bonds, or other securities of the surviving or consolidated corporation, or the cash or other consideration (or any combination of consideration) to be paid in exchange for shares of the constituent corporations; (4) for a merger, the amendments or changes in the certificate of incorporation of the surviving corporation to be effected by the merger; for a consolidation, the statements required to be included in a certificate of incorporation for a corporation formed under NYBCL (other than facts not available at the time the plan is adopted by the board); and (5) such other provisions with respect to the proposed merger or consolidation as the board considers necessary or desirable.[3]

Shareholder Authorization. Upon adopting the plan of merger or consolidation, the board of each constituent corporation must submit it to a vote of shareholders, as follows.[4] Notice of a meeting must be given to each shareholder of record, whether or not entitled to vote, and a copy of the plan or an outline of its material features must accompany the notice.[5] The plan must be adopted by vote of the holders of at least *two-thirds* of all outstanding shares entitled to vote thereon.[6] Notwithstand-

2. NYBCL § 901(a)(2).
3. NYBCL § 902(a).
4. NYBCL § 903(a).
5. *Id.*
6. NYBCL § 903(a)(2).

CAVEAT: The requisite vote is (1) for corporations in existence *on* the effective date of NYBCL § 903(a)(2) whose certificate of incorporation expressly provides such or corporations incorporated *after* the effective date of NYBCL § 903(a)(2)(A), the holders of a *majority* of all outstanding shares entitled to vote or (2) for other corporations in existence *on* the effective date of NYBCL § 903(a)(2)(A), at least *two-thirds* of the votes of all outstanding shares entitled to vote. NYBCL § 903(a)(2). The effective date of NYBCL § 903(a)(2)(A) is the one hundred eightieth day after the act amending the NYBCL became law (*see* 1997 NY S.B. 476 (SN) § 71; 1997 NY S.B. 5680 (SN) § 7); S.B. 476 was enacted on Aug. 26, 1997, and its effective date is Feb. 22, 1998. Notwithstanding any provision in the certificate of incorporation, the holders of shares of a class or series of a class are entitled to vote together and to vote as a separate class if both of the following conditions are satisfied: (1) such shares will remain outstanding after the merger or consolidation or will be converted into the right to receive shares of stock of the surviving or consolidated corporation or another corporation and (2) the certificate or articles of incorporation of the surviving or consolidated corporation or

ing any provision in the certificate of incorporation, the holders of shares of a class or series are entitled to vote and to vote as a class if the plan of merger or consolidation contains any provision that, if contained in an amendment to the certificate of incorporation, would entitle such holders to vote and to vote as a class.[7] In that case, in addition to authorization by vote of the holders of at least two-thirds of all outstanding shares entitled to vote thereon, the merger or consolidation must be authorized by the holders of a majority of all outstanding shares of each such class or series.[8] Notwithstanding shareholder authorization and at any time prior to the filing of the certificate of merger or consolidation, the plan may be abandoned pursuant to a provision for abandonment, if any, contained in the plan.[9] After the adoption of the plan by the board *and* the shareholders of each constituent corporation, a certificate of merger or consolidation must be filed.[10]

Short-form Merger. A domestic corporation owning at least ninety percent of the outstanding shares of each class of one or more other domestic corporations may—in a so-called short, or short-form, merger—either merge the other corporations into itself without the authorization of the shareholders of the other corporations or merge itself and one or more of the other corporations into one of the other corporations with the authorization of the parent corporation's shareholders in accordance

of such other corporation immediately after the effectiveness of the merger or consolidation would contain any provision that is not contained in the certificate of incorporation of the corporation and that, if contained in an amendment to the certificate of incorporation, would entitle the holders of shares of such class or such one or more series to vote and to vote as a separate class pursuant to NYBCL § 804 (class voting on amendment). The merger or consolidation must also be authorized by a majority of the votes of all outstanding shares of the class entitled to vote as a separate class. *Id.* If any provision referred to in NYBCL § 903(a)(2)(B) would affect the rights of the holders of shares of only one or more series of any class but not the entire class, then only the holders of those series whose rights would be affected are together considered a separate class for purposes of NYBCL § 903. *Id.*

7. *Id.*
8. *Id.*
9. NYBCL § 903(b).
10. NYBCL § 904(a). ***Procedure.*** The certificate, entitled "Certificate of merger (or consolidation) of _____ and _____ into _____ (names of corporations) under section 904 of the Business Corporation Law," must be signed and verified on behalf of each constituent corporation and delivered to the Department of State. *Id.* It must set forth: (1) the statements required by NYBCL § 902(a)(1), (2), and (4) to be in the plan of merger or consolidation; (2) the effective date of the merger or consolidation if other than the date of filing of the certificate of merger or consolidation by the Department of State; (3) for a consolidation, any statement required to be included in a certificate of incorporation for a corporation formed under the NYBCL but that was omitted under NYBCL § 902(a)(4); (4) the date when the certificate of incorporation of each constituent corporation was filed by the Department of State; (5) the manner in which the merger or consolidation was authorized for each constituent corporation. *Id.* The surviving or consolidated corporation must file a copy of the certificate, certified by the Department of State, in the office of the clerk of each county in which the office of a constituent corporation (other than the surviving corporation) is located and in the office of the official who is the recording officer of each county in New York in which real property of a constituent corporation (other than the surviving corporation) is situated. NYBCL § 904(b).

with NYBCL § 903(a).[11] In addition, a certificate of merger must be filed.[12] Notwithstanding shareholder authorization, and at any time prior to the filing of the certificate of merger, the plan of merger may be abandoned pursuant to a provision for abandonment, if any, contained in the plan.[13]

Combination of Domestic and Foreign Corporations. One or more foreign corporations and one or more domestic corporations may be merged or consolidated into a corporation organized in New York or in another jurisdiction, if the merger or consolidation is permitted by the laws of the jurisdiction under which each foreign corporation is incorporated.[14] Each domestic corporation must comply with the provisions of the NYBCL relating to merger or consolidation of domestic corporations, including shareholder authorization, and each foreign corporation must comply with the applicable provisions of the law of the jurisdiction under

---

11. NYBCL § 905(a). *See* NYBCL § 905(f) (other merger rights). *Procedure.* In either case, the board of the parent corporation must adopt a plan of merger, setting forth: (1) the name of each corporation to be merged and the name of the surviving corporation, and if the name of any of them has been changed, the name under which it was formed; (2) the designation and number of outstanding shares of each class of each corporation to be merged and the number of the shares of each class, if any, owned by the surviving corporation, and if the number of any of the shares is subject to change prior to the effective date of the merger, the manner in which the change may occur; (3) the terms and conditions of the proposed merger, including the manner and basis of converting shares of non-surviving subsidiary corporations not owned by the parent into shares, bonds, or other securities of the surviving corporation, cash or other consideration, or any combination of consideration; (4) if the parent is not the surviving corporation, provision for the *pro rata* issuance of shares of the surviving corporation to the shareholders of the parent upon surrender of certificates therefor; (5) if the parent is not the surviving corporation, a statement of any amendments or changes in the certificate of incorporation of the surviving corporation to be effected by the merger; (6) other provisions with respect to the proposed merger that the board considers necessary or desirable. NYBCL § 905(a). If the surviving corporation is the parent, a copy of the plan of merger or an outline of its material features must be given, personally or by mail, to all holders (other than the parent) of shares of each subsidiary corporation to be merged, unless those holders have waived such requirement. NYBCL § 905(b).

12. NYBCL § 905(c). *Procedure.* The certificate must be signed, verified, and delivered to the Department of State by the surviving corporation. NYBCL § 905(c). It is entitled "Certificate of merger of _____ into _____ (names of corporations) under section 905 of the Business Corporation Law" and must set forth the information specified in NYBCL § 905(c)(1)-(6). *Id.*

CAVEAT: If the surviving corporation is the parent corporation and it does not own *all* shares of each subsidiary to be merged, the certificate must be delivered no fewer than thirty days after the copy or outline of the material features of the plan of merger has been delivered to the shareholders (other than the parent) of each subsidiary corporation or any time after all such holders have waived the requirement. *Id.* The surviving corporation must thereafter file a copy of the certificate, certified by the Department of State, in the office of the clerk of each county in which the office of a constituent corporation (other than the surviving corporation) is located and in the office of the official who is the recording officer of each county in New York in which real property of a constituent corporation (other than the surviving corporation) is situated. NYBCL § 905(d).

13. NYBCL §§ 905(e) and 903(b).

14. NYBCL § 907(a). References in NYBCL § 901 to a "corporation" include both domestic and foreign corporations, unless the context otherwise requires. NYBCL § 907(a).

which it is incorporated.[15] The short-form merger procedure under NYBCL § 905 is available where either a subsidiary corporation or the corporation owning at least ninety percent of the outstanding shares of each class of a subsidiary is a foreign corporation and the merger is permitted by the laws of the jurisdiction under which such foreign corporation is incorporated.[16] If the surviving or consolidated corporation is, or is to be, a domestic corporation, it must comply with specific procedures pertaining to the filing of a certificate of merger.[17] If the surviving or consolidated corporation is, or is to be, formed under the law of any jurisdiction other than New York, it must comply with the provisions of the NYBCL relating to foreign corporations if it is to do business in New York.[18]

---

15. NYBCL § 907(b).

16. NYBCL § 907(c).

17. NYBCL § 907(d). **Procedure.** A certificate of merger or consolidation must be signed, verified, and delivered to the Department of State as provided in NYBCL § 904 (mergers and consolidations) or § 905 (short-form mergers), as the case may be. *Id. See supra,* § 1.83, notes 10 and 12. In addition, the certificate must set forth for each constituent foreign corporation the jurisdiction and date of its incorporation, the date when its application for authority to do business in New York was filed by the Department of State, and its fictitious name used in New York pursuant to NYBCL Article 13, if applicable, or, if no application for authority has been filed, a statement to that effect. NYBCL § 907(d).

18. NYBCL § 907(e)(1). **Procedure.** It must deliver to the Department of State a certificate, entitled "Certificate of merger (or consolidation) of _____ and _____ into _____ (names of corporations) under section 907 of the Business Corporation Law," that must be signed and verified on behalf of each constituent domestic and foreign corporation. NYBCL § 907(e)(2). If the combination was effected in compliance with NYBCL § 902 (plan of merger or consolidation) and § 903 (authorization by shareholders), the certificate must contain: (i) the statements required by NYBCL § 902(a)(1) and (2); (ii) the effective date of the combination (if other than the filing date); and (iii) the manner in which the combination was authorized by each constituent domestic corporation and that the combination is permitted by the laws of the jurisdiction of each constituent foreign corporation and is in compliance therewith. *Id.* If the combination was effected in compliance with NYBCL § 905 (short merger), the certificate must contain: (i) the statements required by § 905(a)(1), (2), (4), and (5); (ii) the effective date of the combination (if other than the filing date); (iii) if the surviving foreign corporation is the parent corporation and that corporation does not own all the shares of a subsidiary domestic corporation being merged, then either the date of the delivery of a copy of the plan of merger or an outline of its material features to the shareholders (other than the parent) of each subsidiary, or a statement that such requirement has been waived; (iv) that the combination is permitted by the laws of the jurisdiction of each constituent foreign corporation and is in compliance therewith; and (v) if the parent domestic corporation is not the surviving corporation, then a statement that the proposed combination has been approved by the shareholders of the parent domestic corporation in accordance with NYBCL § 903(a). *Id.* All certificates must include (A) the jurisdiction and date of incorporation of the surviving or consolidated foreign corporation, the date when its application for authority to do business in New York was filed, and its fictitious name used in New York, if applicable, or, if no application for authority has been filed, a statement to that effect and that the surviving corporation will not do business in New York until an application for authority has been filed; (B) the date when the certificate of incorporation of each constituent domestic corporation was filed and the jurisdiction and date of incorporation of each constituent foreign corporation (other than the surviving or consolidated foreign corporation) and, in the case of each such corporation authorized to do business in New York, the date when its application for authority was filed; (C) an agreement that the surviving or consolidated foreign corporation may be served with process in New York in any proceeding to enforce any obligation of any

§ 1.84 Business Combinations—Mergers and Consolidations—Effect

Upon the filing of the certificate of merger or consolidation by the Department of State (or on a date not to exceed 30 days[1] thereafter, as set forth in the certificate), the merger or consolidation is effected.[2] When a merger or consolidation is effected: (1) the surviving or consolidated corporation thereafter (consistent with its certificate of incorporation, as altered (established) by the certificate of merger (consolidation)) possesses all the rights, privileges, immunities, powers, and purposes of each of the constituent corporations;[3] (2) all the property, real and personal, including subscriptions to shares, causes of action, and every other asset of each of the constituent corporations, vests in the surviving or consolidated corporation without further act or deed;[4] (3) the surviving or consolidated corporation assumes, and is liable for, all the liabilities, obligations, and penalties of each of the constituent corporations;[5] and (4) for a merger, the certificate of incorporation of domestic corporation or of any foreign corporation, previously amenable to suit in New York, that is a constituent corporation and to enforce against the surviving or consolidated corporation the rights of dissenting shareholders of any constituent domestic corporation to receive payment for their shares; (D) an agreement that, subject to the provisions of NYBCL § 623, the surviving or consolidated foreign corporation shall promptly pay to the dissenting shareholders the amount, if any, to which they are entitled as payment for their shares; (E) a designation of the Secretary of State of the State of New York as the surviving corporation's agent upon whom process against it may be served and a post office address to which the Secretary of State shall mail a copy of any such process served upon the Secretary, that post office address to supersede any prior address designated as the address to which process must be mailed; and (F) a certification that all fees and taxes (including penalties and interest) administered by the Department of Taxation and Finance then due and payable by each constituent domestic corporation have been paid and that a cessation franchise tax report (estimated or final) through the anticipated date of the merger or consolidation (which report, if estimated, is subject to amendment) has been filed by each constituent domestic corporation and an agreement that the surviving or consolidated foreign corporation will within 30 days after the filing of the certificate of merger or consolidation file the cessation franchise tax report, if an estimated report was previously filed, and promptly pay to the Department of Taxation and Finance all fees and taxes (including penalties and interest), if any, due that Department by each constituent domestic corporation. NYBCL § 907(e)(2). The surviving or consolidated domestic or foreign corporation must file a copy of the certificate, certified by the Department of State, in the office of the clerk of each county in which the office of a constituent corporation (other than the surviving corporation) is located and in the office of the official who is the recording officer of each county in New York in which real property of a constituent corporation (other than the surviving corporation) is situated. NYBCL § 907(h).

§ 1.84

1. Or, in the case of a combination of domestic and foreign corporations, ninety days. NYBCL § 907(f).
2. NYBCL § 906(a).
3. NYBCL § 906(b)(1).
4. NYBCL § 906(b)(2).
5. NYBCL § 906(b)(3). No obligations of, or claims against, the corporations, or any of their shareholders, officers, or di-

the surviving corporation is automatically amended to the extent, if any, that amendments thereto are set forth in the plan (and certificate) of merger; for a consolidation, the statements set forth in the certificate of consolidation constitute its certificate of incorporation.[6]

Where foreign and domestic corporations are merged or consolidated, if the surviving or consolidated corporation is, or is to be, formed under the law of New York, the effect of the merger or consolidation is the same as in the case of the combination of domestic corporations under NYBCL § 906.[7] If the surviving or consolidated corporation is, or is to be, incorporated under the law of a foreign jurisdiction, the effect of the combination is the same as for a combination of domestic corporations, except where the law of the other jurisdiction provides otherwise.[8]

Library References:
West's Key No. Digests, Corporations ⚖︎586–591.

§ 1.85 Business Combinations—Sale, Lease, Exchange, or Other Disposition of Assets

Procedure. A sale, lease, exchange, or other disposition of all or substantially all the assets of a corporation, if not made in the usual or regular course of the business actually conducted by the corporation, is duly authorized only if (1) the board has approved the disposition and directed its submission to a vote of shareholders; (2) notice of the meeting at which the disposition is to be considered is given to each shareholder of record, whether or not entitled to vote; and (3) the shareholders have approved, by a majority vote[1] of all outstanding shares entitled to vote,[2] the disposition and have fixed (or have authorized the

rectors, are released or impaired by the merger or consolidation. *Id.* No action or proceeding, whether civil or criminal, then pending by or against any constituent corporation, or any shareholder, officer, or director thereof, abates or is discontinued by the merger or consolidation and may be enforced, prosecuted, settled, or compromised as if the merger or consolidation had not occurred, or the surviving or consolidated corporation may be substituted in the action or special proceeding in place of any constituent corporation. *Id.*

6. NYBCL § 906(b)(4).
7. NYBCL § 907(h).
8. *Id.*

§ 1.85

1. CAVEAT: The requisite vote is (1) for corporations in existence *on* the effective date of NYBCL § 903(a)(3) whose certificate of incorporation expressly provides such or corporations incorporated *after* the effective date of NYBCL § 903(a)(3), a *majority* of the votes of all outstanding shares entitled to vote or (2) for other corporations in existence *on* the effective date of NYBCL § 903(a)(3), at least *two-thirds* of the votes of all outstanding shares entitled to vote. NYBCL § 903(a)(3). The effective date of NYBCL § 903(a)(3) is the one hundred eightieth day after the act amending the NYBCL became law (*see* 1997 NY S.B. 476 (SN) § 71; 1997 NY S.B. 5680 (SN) § 7); S.B. 476 was enacted on Aug. 26, 1997, and its effective date is Feb. 22, 1998.

2. NYBCL § 909(a). A recital in a deed, lease, or other instrument of conveyance executed by a corporation that the property described in the instrument does not constitute all or substantially all the assets of the corporation, or that the disposition of the property was made in the usual or regular course of business of the corporation, or that the shareholders have duly authorized

§ 1.85 BUSINESS ORGANIZATIONS: CORPORATIONS Ch. 1

board to fix) the terms and conditions thereof, including the consideration to be received by the corporation therefor.[3] Notwithstanding shareholder approval, the board may abandon the proposed sale, lease, exchange, or other disposition without further action by the shareholders, subject to the rights, if any, of third parties under any contract relating to the disposition.[4] Whenever a corporation transfers, leases, or otherwise disposes of substantially all its assets, *including* its name, to a new corporation formed under the same name as the existing corporation, then 30 days after the filing of the certificate of incorporation of the new corporation (with evidence of the consent of the New York State Tax Commission attached), the existing corporation is automatically dissolved, unless, before the end of the 30-day period, that corporation has changed its name.[5]

Library References:

West's Key No. Digests, Corporations ⇔434–446.

§ 1.86 Business Combinations—Sale, Lease, Exchange, or Other Disposition of Assets—Mortgage or Security Interest in Assets

The board may authorize any mortgage or pledge of, or the creation of a security interest in, all or any part of the corporate property, or any interest therein, wherever situated.[1] Unless the certificate of incorporation provides otherwise, no vote or consent of shareholders is required to approve such action by the board.[2]

Library References:

West's Key No. Digests, Corporations ⇔475.

the disposition, is presumptive evidence of the fact recited. NYBCL § 909(b).

CAVEAT: An action to set aside a deed, lease, or other instrument of conveyance executed by a corporation affecting real property or real and personal property may not be maintained for failure to comply with the requirements of NYBCL § 909(a) unless the action is commenced and a notice of pendency of action is filed within one year after the conveyance, lease, or other instrument is recorded. NYBCL § 909(c).

3. NYBCL § 909(a). The consideration may consist in whole or in part of cash or other property, real or personal, including shares, bonds, or other securities of any other domestic or foreign corporation. NYBCL § 909(a)(3).

4. NYBCL § 909(f).

5. NYBCL § 909(d).

CAVEAT: The adjustment and winding up of the affairs of the dissolved corporation must proceed in accordance with the provisions of NYBCL Article 10 for non-judicial dissolution. NYBCL § 909(d). *Procedure*. The certificate of incorporation of the new corporation must set forth the name of the existing corporation, the date when its certificate of incorporation was filed, and that its shareholders have authorized the sale, lease, exchange, or other disposition of all or substantially all the assets of that corporation, including its name, to the new corporation to be formed under the same name as the existing corporation. NYBCL § 909(e). *See* NYBCL § 912(a)(5)(B). See *infra*, § 1.89, notes 11–14.

§ 1.86

1. NYBCL § 911.
2. *Id.*

§ 1.87 Business Combinations—Sale, Lease, Exchange, or Other Disposition of Assets—Guarantee Authorized by Shareholders

A guarantee may be given by a corporation, although not in furtherance of its corporate purposes, when authorized by at least two-thirds of the votes of all outstanding shares entitled to vote.[1] If authorized by a like vote, the guarantee may be secured by a mortgage or pledge of, or the creation of a security interest in, all or any part of the corporate property.[2]

Library References:

West's Key No. Digests, Corporations ⚖484(3).

§ 1.88 Business Combinations—Share Exchanges

Two New York corporations may agree that one of them shall acquire *all* the outstanding shares of one or more classes of the other corporation in a binding share exchange.[1] The board of the acquiring corporation and the board of the subject corporation must adopt a plan of exchange.[2] Except as provided in NYBCL § 913(g), the board of the

§ 1.87
1. NYBCL § 908.
2. Id.

§ 1.88
1. NYBCL § 913(a)(1). An "acquiring corporation" is a corporation that is acquiring *all* the outstanding shares of one or more classes of a subject corporation. NYBCL § 913(a)(2)(A). A "subject corporation" is a corporation all of whose outstanding shares of one or more classes are being acquired by an acquiring corporation. NYBCL § 913(a)(2)(B). If the subject corporation has more than one class of outstanding shares, the acquiring corporation must, arguably, acquire all the shares of each class. *Cf., e.g.,* I.R.C. § 368(c) (control means 80% of *each* class of shares outstanding). *Cf. also,* I.R.C. § 1504 (re consolidated returns). *See* Bittker and Eustice, ¶ ¶ 3.07(3) and 13.41(2). But the policy underlying NYBCL § 912 is to regulate tender offers and the ability of a tender offeror to consummate a business combination with a domestic corporation. If more than one class is outstanding and the standard under NYBCL § 913(a)(2) is the acquisition of all the shares of *any* class of outstanding shares, then NYBCL § 912 setting preconditions to the consummation of certain business combinations is applicable under NYBCL § 913(i) upon the acquisition of all the outstanding shares of merely one, rather than each, class—an interpretation that, presumably, is more in harmony with the intended purposes of NYBCL §§ 912 and 913 than one requiring the acquisition of all the shares of each class.

CAVEAT: A binding share exchange under NYBCL § 913 constitutes a "business combination" under NYBCL § 912 if the subject corporation is a domestic corporation and the acquiring corporation is an "interested shareholder" of the subject corporation, as these terms are defined in NYBCL § 912. NYBCL § 913(i)(1).

PRACTICE POINTER: NYBCL § 913 does not limit the power of a domestic or foreign corporation to acquire all *or part* of the shares of one or more classes of another domestic or foreign corporation by means of a voluntary exchange or by other means. NYBCL § 913(h). *See also, e.g.,* Henn and Alexander, *supra,* § 1.1, note 1, pp. 469 and 473–474 (power to acquire shares), 852–862 (federal and state antitrust regulation of business combinations), and 819–822 (federal regulation of tender offers). *See infra,* §§ 1.89 and 1.91. *See supra,* § 1.81.

2. NYBCL § 913(b). *Procedure.* The plan of exchange must set forth: (1) the names of the acquiring corporation and the subject corporation, and, if the name of either of them has been changed, the name under which it was formed; (2) the designation and number of outstanding shares of

subject corporation, upon adopting the plan, must submit it to a vote of shareholders.[3] After adoption of the plan as so required, unless the exchange is abandoned in accordance with NYBCL § 913(c), a certificate of exchange must be signed and verified on behalf of each corporation and delivered to the Department of State.[4] Upon the filing of the each class and series of the acquiring corporation and the subject corporation, specifying the classes and series entitled to vote and each class and series, if any, entitled to vote as a class; (3) if the number of any such shares is subject to change prior to the effective date of the exchange, the manner in which such change may occur; (4) the terms and conditions of the proposed exchange, including the manner and basis of exchanging the shares to be acquired for shares, bonds, or other securities of the acquiring corporation, cash, or other consideration, or a combination thereof; and (5) other provisions with respect to the proposed exchange that the board considers necessary or desirable. NYBCL § 913(b).

3. NYBCL § 913(c). *Procedure.* Notice of the meeting must be given to each shareholder of record, whether or not entitled to vote, and a copy of the plan or an outline of its material features must accompany the notice. NYBCL § 913(c)(1). The plan must be adopted by (1) for any corporation in existence *on* the effective date of NYBCL § 913(c)(2)(A)(ii), at least *two-thirds* of the votes of all outstanding shares entitled to vote and (2) for any corporation in existence *on* the effective date of NYBCL § 913(c)(2)(A)(ii) whose certificate of incorporation expressly provides such and for any corporation incorporated *after* the effective date of NYBCL § 913(c)(2)(A)(ii), a *majority* of the votes of all outstanding shares entitled to vote. NYBCL § 913(c)(2)(A). The effective date of NYBCL § 913(c)(2)(A)(ii) is the one hundred eightieth day after the act amending the NYBCL became law (*see* 1997 NY S.B. 476 (SN) § 71; 1997 NY S.B. 5680 (SN) § 7); S.B. 476 was enacted on Aug. 26, 1997, and its effective date is Feb. 22, 1998.

Notwithstanding any provision in the certificate of incorporation, the holders of shares of a class or series of a class are entitled to vote together and to vote as a separate class if both of the following conditions are satisfied: (1) such shares will be converted into shares of the acquiring corporation and (2) the certificate or articles of incorporation of the acquiring corporation immediately after the share exchange would contain any provision that is not contained in the certificate of incorporation of the subject corporation and that, if contained in an amendment to the certificate of incorporation of the subject corporation, would entitle the holders of shares of such class or such one or more series to vote and to vote as a separate class pursuant to NYBCL § 804 (class voting on amendment). In such case, in addition to the authorization of the exchange by the proportion of votes indicated above of all outstanding shares entitled to vote, the exchange must be authorized by a majority of the votes of all outstanding shares of the class entitled to vote as a separate class. *Id.* If any provision referred to in NYBCL § 913(c)(2)(A)(ii) would affect the rights of the holders of shares of only one or more series of any class but not the entire class, then only the holders of those series whose rights would be affected shall together be considered a separate class for purposes of NYBCL § 913. *Id.*

Notwithstanding shareholder authorization and at any time prior to the filing of the certificate of exchange, the plan may be abandoned pursuant to a provision for abandonment, if any, contained in the plan. NYBCL § 913(c)(2)(A). Any corporation may adopt an amendment of the certificate of incorporation that provides that such plan of exchange must be adopted at a meeting of the shareholders by vote of a specified proportion of the holders of outstanding shares, or class or series of shares, entitled to vote, provided that such proportion may not be less than a majority and subject to NYBCL § 913(c)(2)(A)(second sentence). NYBCL § 913(c)(2)(B).

4. NYBCL § 913(d). *Procedure.* The certificate of exchange is entitled "Certificate of exchange of shares of _____, subject corporation, for shares of _____, acquiring corporation, or other consideration, under section 913 of the Business Corporation Law" and must set forth: (1) the statements required by NYBCL § 913(b)(1) and (2); (2) the effective date of the exchange if other than the date of filing of the certificate of exchange; (3) the date when the certificate of incorporation of each corporation was filed; (4) the designation of the shares to be acquired by the acquiring corporation and a statement of the consideration for the shares; and (5) the manner in which the exchange was authorized with respect to each corporation. *Id.*

certificate (or on the date subsequent thereto, not to exceed thirty days, set forth in the certificate) the exchange is effected.[5]

When the exchange has been effected, ownership of the shares of the subject corporation vests in the acquiring corporation, whether or not the certificates for such shares have been surrendered for exchange, and the acquiring corporation is entitled to have new certificates registered in its name or at its direction.[6] Shareholders whose shares have been acquired become entitled to the shares, bonds, or other securities of the acquiring corporation, or the other consideration, required to be paid or delivered in exchange pursuant to the plan.[7] Subject to any terms of the plan, the certificates representing acquired shares evidence only the right to receive the consideration required to be paid or delivered in exchange therefor pursuant to the plan or, in the case of dissenting shareholders, their rights under NYBCL §§ 910 and 623.[8] With respect to convertible securities and other securities evidencing a right to acquire shares of a subject corporation, a binding share exchange pursuant to NYBCL § 913 has the same effect on the rights of the holders of such securities as would a merger in which the subject corporation is the surviving corporation.[9]

Foreign and Domestic Corporations. A foreign corporation and a domestic corporation may participate in a share exchange but, if the subject corporation is a foreign corporation, only if the exchange is permitted by the laws of the jurisdiction under which the foreign corporation is incorporated.[10] If the subject corporation is a foreign corporation, the certificate of exchange must set forth certain additional information.[11]

Ninety Percent Subsidiaries. Any corporation owning at least ninety percent of the outstanding common shares, having full voting

---

5. NYBCL § 913(e).
6. *Id.*
7. *Id.*
8. *Id.*
9. NYBCL § 913(i)(2). A binding share exchange pursuant to NYBCL § 913 that is effectuated on or after September 1, 1991, is intended to have the same effect as a "merger" in which the subject corporation is the surviving corporation, within the meaning of any provision of its certificate of incorporation or bylaws, or a contract or other instrument, by which the subject corporation was bound on September 1, 1986, unless these documents indicate that the term "merger" was not intended to include a binding share exchange. NYBCL § 913(i)(3).
10. NYBCL § 913(f)(1). Any reference in NYBCL § 913(a)(2) to a corporation, unless the context otherwise requires, includes both domestic and foreign corporations, and the provisions of NYBCL § 913(b), (c), (d), and (e) apply, except to the extent otherwise provided in NYBCL § 913(f). *Id.* **Procedure**. A domestic corporation must comply with the provisions of the NYBCL relating to share exchanges (including the requirement of shareholder authorization) in which domestic corporations are participating, and a foreign corporation must comply with the applicable provisions of the law of the jurisdiction under which it is incorporated. NYBCL § 913(f)(2).
11. NYBCL § 913(f)(3). **Procedure**. In addition to the matters specified in NYBCL § 913(d), the certificate must set forth the jurisdiction and date of incorporation of the corporation and a statement that the exchange is permitted by the laws of that jurisdiction and complies with them. *Id.*

§ 1.88 BUSINESS ORGANIZATIONS: CORPORATIONS Ch. 1

rights, of another corporation may acquire by exchange the remainder of the outstanding common shares, without the authorization of the shareholders of the subject corporation and with the effect provided for in NYBCL § 913(e).[12] The board of the acquiring corporation must adopt a plan of exchange, and file a certificate of exchange, complying with the NYBCL.[13] A corporation's right to exchange shares under NYBCL § 913(g) does not preclude it from exercising any other right of exchange under the NYBCL.[14]

§ 1.89 Business Combinations—Takeover Bids

Disclosure. The NYBCL provisions governing takeover bids—designated as the Security Takeover Disclosure Act[1]—apply to takeover bids[2]

12. NYBCL § 913(g)(1). *See supra,* § 1.88, notes 5–8 and accompanying text.

13. NYBCL § 913(g)(1). *Procedure.* The plan must set forth the matters specified in NYBCL § 913(b), and a copy of the plan or an outline of its material features must be given, personally or by mail, to all holders of shares of the subject corporation other than the acquiring corporation, unless this requirement has been waived by such holders. *Id.* The certificate of exchange, entitled "Certificate of exchange of shares of _____, subject corporation, for shares of _____, acquiring corporation, or other consideration, under paragraph (g) of section 913 of the Business Corporation Law" and complying with the provisions of NYBCL § 913(d) and, if applicable, NYBCL § 913(f)(3), must be signed, verified, and delivered to the Department of State by the acquiring corporation no fewer than thirty days after delivery of a copy, or outline of the material features, of the plan, or at any time after waiver thereof. NYBCL § 913(g)(2). This procedure for the exchange of shares is also available (1) where either the subject corporation or the acquiring corporation is a foreign corporation and (2) if the subject corporation is a foreign corporation, where the exchange is permitted by the laws of the jurisdiction under which it is incorporated. NYBCL § 913(g)(4).

14. NYBCL § 913(g)(3).

§ 1.89

1. NYBCL Art. 16. Various defenses to takeovers (and methods of maintaining control) of a corporation include such pre-offer devices as shark repellent amendments (*e.g.*, staggered board, supermajority shareholder vote requirement, and fair price provision), poison pills, and takeover statutes and post-offer devices as antitrust challenge, target's own offer for bidder's stock ("Pac-man" defense), white knight, scorched earth, and standstill agreements. For details on these an other defensive tactics, *see, e.g.*, R. Gilson and Black, *The Law and Finance of Corporate Acquisitions* (1986 and 1991 supplement) pp. 631–696, 746–751; D. Logue, *Handbook of Modern Finance* (1984) pp. 29–44 to 29–51; W. Klein and J. Coffee, *Business Organization and Finance* (4th ed. 1990) pp. 169–172; Sroufe and Gelband, *Business Combination Statutes: A "Meaningful Opportunity" for Success?*, 45 Business Lawyer 891–899 (1990); Helman and Junewicz, *Fresh Look at Poison Pills*, 42 Business Lawyer 771 (1987). See also, *supra,* §§ 1.21 (share transfer restrictions), 1.45 (non-voting shares; class voting), 1.46 (higher-than-normal quorum requirement), 1.47 (shareholder agreements; voting trusts), 1.59 (staggered board), 1.61 (removal of directors), and 1.63 (higher-than-normal quorum requirement).

2. NYBCL § 1601(a). A "takeover bid" is defined as the acquisition of, or offer to acquire, pursuant to a tender offer or request or invitation for tenders, any equity security of a target company, if after the acquisition the offeror would, directly or indirectly, be a beneficial owner of more than five percent of any class of the outstanding equity securities of the target company. *Id.* The term "bid" in the definition of "takeover bid" appears to be used not in the sense of "offer" but in a broader sense of "effort" or "attempt." For offers not within the definition of takeover bid, *see* NYBCL § 1601(a)(1)-(a)(4). *See also*, NYBCL § 1610 (exclusions). An "offeror" is a person who makes, or in any way participates or aids in making, a takeover bid, and includes persons acting jointly or in concert, for an equity security[3] of a target company.[4] No takeover bid may be made unless, as soon as practicable on the date the takeover bid commences, the offeror files with the Attorney General at its New York City office and delivers to the target company at its principal executive offices,[5] a registration statement containing certain information.[6] The

or who intend to exercise jointly or in concert any voting rights attached to the securities for which the takeover bid is made. NYBCL § 1601(b). An offeror includes an issuer of securities whose securities are, or are to be, the subject of a takeover bid (*i.e*, self-tender) whether or not the issuer, upon acquisition, will become the beneficial owner of the securities. *Id*. An offeror does not include any bank or broker-dealer in securities lending funds to the offeror in the ordinary course of the business of the bank or broker-dealer in securities and not otherwise participating in the takeover bid, or any bank, broker-dealer in securities, attorney, accountant, or consultant furnishing information or advice to an offeror and not otherwise participating in the takeover bid. *Id*. An "offeree" is the beneficial owner, residing in New York, of securities that an offeror acquires or offers to acquire in connection with a takeover bid. NYBCL § 1601(c). For tender offer regulation (federal and state), *see, e.g.*, Henn and Alexander, *supra*, § 1.1, note 1, pp. 819–823; V. Brudney and M. Chirelstein, *Corporate Finance* (3d ed. 1987) pp. 825–987.

CAVEAT: Tender offers (whether from the point of view of the offeror, offeree, or target company) involve securities law issues that require the services of an experienced securities attorney.

3. NYBCL § 1601(e). An "equity security" means any stock, bond, or other obligation of a target company, the holder of which has the right to vote for the election of members of its board of directors (or an equivalent body exercising a similar function, if the target company is not a corporation) and also includes any security convertible into an equity security and any right, option, or warrant to purchase an equity security. *Id*.

4. NYBCL § 1601(d). A "target company" means a corporation, organized under the laws of New York and having its principal executive offices or significant business operations located within New York. *Id*. *See* NYBCL §§ 1606 (administration of takeover bid regulation; filing fees); 1607 (prosecutions and immunity); 1608 (re nonresident offerors (except foreign corporations that have appointed and keep a resident agent in New York); designation of Secretary of State for service of process; method of service).

5. NYBCL § 1602(a).

6. NYBCL § 1602(b). *Procedure*. The registration statement must include: (1) copies of all prospectuses, brochures, advertisements, circulars, letters, or other matter by means of which the offeror proposes to disclose to offerees all information material to a decision to accept or reject the offer; (2) the identity and background of all persons on whose behalf the acquisition of any equity security of the target company has been or is to be effected; (3) the exact title and number of shares outstanding of the class of equity securities being sought, the number of securities being sought, and the consideration being offered; (4) the source and amount of funds or other consideration used or to be used in acquiring any equity security, including a statement describing any securities, other than the existing capital stock or long-term debt of the offeror, that are being offered in exchange for the equity securities of the target company, including copies of all loan or credit agreements and letters of commitment used or to be used to secure financing for the acquisition of any equity security of the target company; (5) a statement of any plans or proposals that the offeror, upon gaining control, may have to liquidate the target company, sell its assets, effect a merger or consolidation of it, or make any other major change in its business, corporate structure, management personnel, or policies of employment; (6) the number of shares of any equity security of the target company of which each offeror is beneficial or record owner or has a right to acquire, directly or indirectly, together with the name and address of each offeror; (7) particulars on contracts, arrangements, or understandings to which an offeror is party with respect to any equity security of the target company, such as, transfers of any equity security, joint ventures, loans or option arrangements, puts and calls, guarantees of loan, guarantees against loss, guarantees of profits, division of losses or profits, or the giving or

registration statement must provide offerees full and fair disclosure of material information.[7] No solicitation or recommendation to the offerees to accept or reject a takeover bid may be made by or on behalf of an offeror or a target company unless, at the time copies of the solicitation or recommendation are first published, sent, or given to the offerees, the person making the solicitation or recommendation has filed copies of it with the Attorney General at its New York City office.[8] If the takeover bid is not subject to the requirements of the Securities Exchange Act of

withholding of proxies, naming the persons with whom the contracts, arrangements, or understandings have been entered into; (8) complete information on the organization and operations of the offeror, including without limitation the year of organization, form of organization, jurisdiction in which it is organized, a description of each class of the offeror's capital stock and of its long-term debt, financial statements for the current period and for the three most recent annual accounting periods, a description of pending legal proceedings other than routine litigation to which the offeror or any of its subsidiaries is a party or of which any of their property is the subject, a brief description of the business done and projected by the offeror and its subsidiaries and the general development of the business over the past five years, the names of all directors and executive officers together with their biographical summaries for the preceding three years to date; (9) a statement on the potential impact, if any, of the offeror's plans or proposals on the residents of New York, including any material change in the location of the target company's offices or business activities within New York; any plant or facility relocation; any plant or facility closings; any significant reduction in the work force at an individual plant or facility; any other material change in the number, job classification, compensation, or other terms and conditions of employment of persons employed by the target company in New York; any material change in the relationships of the target company with suppliers or customers within New York, or any other material changes in the target company's business, corporate structure, management, personnel, or activities that would have a substantial impact on residents of New York; (10) particulars on pension plans, profit sharing plans, savings plans, educational opportunities, relocation adjustments, labor relations records (including violations of the federal National Labor Relations Act (29 U.S.C.A. §§ 141 et seq.), Occupational Safety and Health Act of 1970 (29 U.S.C.A. §§ 651 et seq.), Fair Labor Standards Act (29 U.S.C.A. §§ 201 et seq.), or Employee Retirement and Income Security Act (29 U.S.C.A. §§ 1001 et seq.) as amended, finally adjudicated, or settled within five years of the commencement of the takeover bid); earnings and dividend growth; community activities; and charitable, cultural, educational, and civic contributions of the offeror; (11) if the offeror is a natural person, information concerning his or her identity and background, including without limitation financial statements for the current and three preceding years, a description of the offeror's business activities and affiliations during that time period, and a description of any pending legal or administrative proceedings, other than routine and immaterial litigation, to which the offeror is a party or of which any of his or her property is the subject; and (12) if debt securities or preferred stock are either offered in the takeover bid or used as a source of funds in making the takeover bid, the investment rating, if any, by a generally recognized rating service of the debt security or preferred stock. NYBCL § 1603(a).

CAVEAT: If any material change occurs in the facts set forth in the registration statement required by NYBCL § 1602(a), the offeror must promptly notify the Attorney General and the target company of such change in writing (or by telephone confirmed in writing) and must promptly amend the registration statement to reflect such change but not later than the date notice of such change is first published, sent, or given to offerees. NYBCL § 1603(b). The Attorney General may permit the omission of any information required by NYBCL § 1603(a) if the Attorney General determines that the information is immaterial or otherwise unnecessary for the protection of offerees. NYBCL § 1603(c).

7. NYBCL § 1602(b).
8. NYBCL § 1602(c).

1934 § 14(d),[9] additional requirements apply.[10]

Preconditions to Consummation of Certain Business Combinations. If an offeror is an interested shareholder[11] and the target corporation is a domestic corporation,[12] NYBCL § 912 prohibits the offeror from effecting a business combination with the domestic corporation[13] *unless* the transaction is approved in advance by the target's

---

9. 15 U.S.C.A. § 78n(d).

10. NYBCL § 1612. ***Procedure***. The additional requirements are: (a) the takeover bid must be made on the same terms to all offerees holding the same class or series of securities; (b) the period of time within which equity securities may be deposited pursuant to a takeover bid must not be less than thirty business days; (c) equity securities deposited pursuant to a takeover bid may be withdrawn at any time (i) up to the date thirty business days after the commencement of the takeover bid, and at any time (ii) after the sixty-five day period following commencement of the takeover bid, if the shares have not been purchased, and (iii) until ten business days following the date of commencement of another offeror's takeover bid for the same equity securities if the shares have not been purchased and if the bidder has received notice or otherwise has knowledge of the commencement of the takeover bid; (d) where a takeover bid is made for less than all the outstanding equity securities of a class and where a greater number of such securities is deposited than the offeror is bound or willing to take up and pay for, the offeror must take up and pay for such securities as nearly *pro rata* as possible; (e) where an offeror increases the consideration offered in a takeover bid, the offeror must pay the increased consideration for all equity securities accepted, whether accepted before or after the increase; (f) within ten days after the filing of the registration statement, the Attorney General may schedule public hearings or conduct investigations for the purpose of determining compliance with the requirements of NYBCL Article 16, provided the hearing or investigation is declared by order of the Attorney General and commences within twenty days after the filing of the registration statement; (g) if the Attorney General schedules a public hearing or otherwise conducts an investigation, the Attorney General may also, in his or her discretion, issue an order staying the offeror from purchasing or paying for any shares tendered; (h) if the Attorney General issues such a stay, the Attorney General must, no later than thirty days after the issuance of the stay payment order, issue findings of fact and conclusions of law; (i) any stay payment order automatically expires sixty days after its issuance, unless the Attorney General's findings of fact and conclusions of law condition the purchase and payment for shares tendered upon changes or modifications in the registration statement, in which event any stay payment order must be vacated by the Attorney General after being satisfied that the changes or modifications have been publicly disseminated to offerees; (j) the Attorney General may apply, on notice to the offeror and the target company, to a court of competent jurisdiction, and the court may grant an application, for good cause, to extend any of the time periods set forth in NYBCL § 1612 if an extension is necessary for the protection of offerees. *Id.*

Article 16 does not apply when (1) the offeror *or* the target company is a federally regulated public utility or public utility holding company, a bank or a bank holding company, or a savings and loan holding company and the takeover bid is subject to approval by the appropriate federal agency or (2) the offeror *and* the target company are banks and the offer is part of a merger transaction subject to approval by appropriate federal or state supervisory authorities. NYBCL § 1610.

11. Defined as (1) a beneficial owner of twenty percent or more of a domestic corporation's voting stock or (2) an affiliate or associate of the domestic corporation that at any time within a five-year period immediately preceding the date in question beneficially owned twenty percent or more of its voting stock. NYBCL § 912(a)(10)(A). For the definition of "affiliate," "associate," and "beneficial owner," *see* NYBCL § 912(a)(1), (3), and (4).

12. The business combination provisions of NYBCL §§ 912 and 913 apply to all New York corporations. Reference to a "resident domestic corporation" has been deleted. *See* L. 1996, Ch. 404.

13. Broadly defined to include certain transactions between a domestic corpora-

§ 1.89 BUSINESS ORGANIZATIONS: CORPORATIONS Ch. 1

board, the interested shareholder pays a fair price for the target's securities that meets specific conditions set forth in NYBCL § 912(c)(3), or the interested shareholder waits five years to obtain the approval of a majority of a target's disinterested shareholders (*i.e.*, excluding the interested shareholder).[14]

Fraud; Insider Trading. Fraudulent, deceptive, or manipulative practices are the subject of takeover bid regulation.[15] A person must not make any untrue statement of a material fact or omit to state any material fact necessary in order to make any statements made, in the light of the circumstances under which they are made, not misleading, nor may the person engage in any fraudulent, deceptive, or manipulative acts or practices, in connection with any takeover bid or any solicita-

tion and an interested shareholder involving (1) merger or consolidation, (2) sale, lease, exchange, mortgage, pledge, transfer, or other disposition by a domestic corporation to an interested shareholder, (3) the issuance or transfer by a domestic corporation (or any subsidiary) of any stock of the domestic corporation (or any subsidiary) to an interested shareholder, (4) liquidation or dissolution of a domestic corporation, (5) reclassification of securities (such as stock split, stock dividend, or reverse stock split) or recapitalization by a domestic corporation, (6) loans, advances, guarantees, pledges, other financial assistance, or tax advantages to an interested shareholder. NYBCL § 912(a)(5). *See also,* NYBCL § 513(e). *See supra,* 1.39, notes 9–13 and accompanying text.

14. NYBCL § 912(b) and (c).

CAVEAT: NYBCL § 912 does not apply to any business combination of a domestic corporation (1) that does not have a class of voting stock registered with the Securities and Exchange Commission pursuant to the Securities Exchange Act § 12 (15 U.S.C.A. §§ 78a *et seq.*), unless the certificate of incorporation provides otherwise; (2) that has amended its certificate of incorporation to provide that it shall be subject to NYBCL § 912, even though it did not have a class of voting stock so registered with the Securities and Exchange Commission on the effective date of the amendment, but the business combination is with an interested shareholder whose stock acquisition date (*i.e.*, the date on which a person becomes an interested shareholder) is prior to the effective date of the amendment; (3) that (i) has included in its original certificate of incorporation a provision expressly electing not to be governed by NYBCL § 912, or (ii) has adopted an amendment to its bylaws prior to March 31, 1986, expressly electing not to be governed by NYBCL § 912, or (iii) adopts an amendment to its bylaws, approved by the affirmative vote of a majority of votes of its outstanding voting stock (excluding the voting stock of interested shareholders and their affiliates and associates) expressly electing not to be governed by NYBCL § 912, provided that the amendment to the bylaws shall not be effective until eighteen months after such vote and shall not apply to any business combination of it with an interested shareholder whose stock acquisition date is on or prior to the effective date of the amendment; or (4) with an interested shareholder that inadvertently attained that status, if the interested shareholder (i) as soon as practicable, divests itself of a sufficient amount of the domestic corporation's voting stock so that the interested shareholder no longer is the beneficial owner, directly or indirectly, of twenty percent or more of the outstanding voting stock of the domestic corporation and (ii) would not, at any time within the five-year period preceding the announcement date of the final (and definitive) proposal for the business combination, have been an interested shareholder but for the inadvertent acquisition. NYBCL § 912(d). The NYBCL also does not apply to any business combination with an interested shareholder who was the beneficial owner, directly or indirectly, of five percent or more of the outstanding voting stock of a domestic corporation on October 30, 1985, and remained so up to the interested shareholder's stock acquisition date. *Id.*

15. NYBCL § 1609(a).

CAVEAT: Fraudulent, deceptive, or manipulative acts or practices include those acts and practices proscribed by rules and regulations of the Attorney General. NYBCL § 1609(c).

of offerees in opposition to or in favor of any such takeover bid.[16] Insider trading constitutes a violation of this regulation.[17]

Enforcement. The enforcement of regulatory requirements for takeover bids is the responsibility of the Attorney General, who may conduct investigations concerning any takeover bid to determine compliance with the requirements of the NYBCL.[18] If the Attorney General determines that any person is violating or about to violate any provision of NYBCL Article 16, or any order, rule, or regulation issued pursuant thereto, the Attorney General may seek, in a court of competent jurisdiction, an injunction temporarily or permanently barring that person from making, taking part in, or continuing a takeover bid or from taking up or paying for shares tendered by offerees pursuant to a takeover bid.[19] The court may grant the relief applied for or so much thereof as it may deem proper.[20]

A private right of action is accorded offerees who have been injured by any violation of NYBCL Article 16.[21] They may bring the action in

---

16. NYBCL § 1609(a).

17. NYBCL § 1609(b).

CAVEAT: A person violates the insider trading prohibition when, in possession of material information relating to any takeover bid (whether the information was acquired before or after the commencement of the takeover bid) that such person knows or has reason to know is nonpublic or has been acquired directly or indirectly from an offeror, a target company, or any officer, director, partner, employee, or any other person acting on behalf of the offeror or target company, the person *purchases or sells*, or causes to be purchased or sold, within or from New York, any securities sought or to be sought in the takeover bid or any securities convertible into or exchangeable for the securities or any option or right to obtain or to dispose of any of the securities. NYBCL § 1609(b). On federal insider trading laws, *see, e.g.*, Henn and Alexander, *supra*, § 1.1, note 1, pp. 823–836; R. Jennings and H. Marsh, *Securities Regulation* (6th ed. 1987) pp. xx, 1391–1393; W. Klein and J. Coffee, *Business Organization and Finance* (4th ed. 1990) pp. 144–152. *See also, e.g.*, CCH Securities Regulation Reporter; L. Loss, *Securities Regulation* (latest edition); L. Soderquist, *Securities Regulation* (3d ed. 1994).

18. NYBCL § 1604(a). As part of any investigation, the Attorney General may require persons to file statements in writing and under oath at its office, subpoena witnesses, compel their attendance, examine them under oath, and require the production of books, records, documents, and papers. *Id. See supra*, § 1.89, notes 6 and 10.

19. NYBCL § 1604(b).

20. *Id.*

CAVEAT: Every person who willfully violates any provision of NYBCL Article 16 is guilty of a class E felony; every person who willfully violates any order, rule, or regulation issued pursuant thereto is guilty of a class A misdemeanor. NYBCL § 1605(a). A violation of any provision of NYBCL Article 16 constitutes a fraudulent practice within the meaning of General Business Law Article 23. NYBCL § 1605(b). Every individual is subject to a civil penalty of one thousand dollars per violation; every corporation is subject to a fine of ten thousand dollars per violation. NYBCL § 1605(c). When the violation is the failure to file a registration statement as required by NYBCL § 1602(a), the failure to file a solicitation or recommendation as required by NYBCL § 1602(a), or the failure to amend the registration statement as required by NYBCL § 1603(b), each business day during which the failure continues constitutes a separate violation. NYBCL § 1605(c). The penalty imposed by NYBCL § 1605(c) is cumulative, and more than one penalty is recoverable in the same action in any court of competent jurisdiction. NYBCL § 1605(c).

21. NYBCL § 1613.

their own names to enjoin the unlawful act or practice and to recover actual damages, if successful, with reasonable attorneys' fees.[22]

§ 1.90 Business Combinations—Right of Shareholder to Receive Payment for Shares

Subject to their complying with NYBCL § 623, shareholders of a domestic corporation involved in a business combination have the right to dissent from the transaction and receive payment of the fair value of their shares in certain cases.[1] A plan of merger or consolidation to which the corporation is a party gives rise to dissenters' rights, except that shareholders of the parent corporation in a short merger authorized by NYBCL § 905 or a merger or consolidation of domestic and foreign corporations authorized by NYBCL § 907(c) are not entitled to payment for their shares.[2] Dissenting shareholders of the surviving corporation in a merger are not entitled to such payment rights unless the merger effects one or more of the changes specified in NYBCL § 806(b)(6) with respect to their rights.[3] A right to payment is afforded dissenters to any sale, lease, exchange, or other disposition of all or substantially all of the assets of a corporation that requires shareholder approval under NYBCL § 909 (other than a transaction wholly for cash where the shareholders' approval thereof is conditioned upon the dissolution of the corporation and the distribution of substantially all of its net assets to the shareholders in accordance with their respective interests within one year after the date of the transaction).[4] Also yielding dissenters' rights is any share exchange authorized by NYBCL § 913 in which the corporation is participating as a subject corporation, except that the right to receive payment of the fair value of their shares is not available to shareholders whose shares have not been acquired in the exchange.[5] A right to payment is granted dissenting shareholders of the subsidiary corporation in a short-form merger authorized by NYBCL §§ 905 or 907(c) or in a share exchange with a ninety percent subsidiary authorized by NYBCL § 913(g) if they file with the corporation a written notice of election to dissent as provided in NYBCL § 623(c).[6] A right to payment is granted to any shareholder, not entitled to vote with respect to a plan of merger or consolidation to which the corporation is a party, whose shares will be

---

22. Id.

§ 1.90

1. NYBCL § 910. See supra, § 1.51.

2. NYBCL § 910(a)(1)(A)(i).

3. NYBCL § 910(a)(1)(A)(ii). See supra, § 1.72, notes 14 and 15 and accompanying text. The right to receive payment is not available to a shareholder for shares of any class or series (or depository receipts in respect thereof) that at the record date fixed to determine the shareholders entitled to receive notice of the shareholders' meeting to vote upon the plan of merger or consolidation were listed on a national securities exchange or designated as a national market system security on an interdealer quotation system by the National Association of Securities Dealers, Inc. NYBCL § 910(a)(1)(A)(iii).

4. NYBCL § 910(a)(1)(B). See supra, § 1.85.

5. NYBCL § 910(a)(1)(C). See supra, § 1.88.

6. NYBCL § 910(a)(2).

cancelled or exchanged in the merger or consolidation for cash or other consideration other than shares of the surviving or consolidated corporation or another corporation.[7]

Library References:

West's Key No. Digests, Corporations ⚖182.4, 584.

§ 1.91 Business Combinations—Federal Income Tax Aspects

Business combinations may be either tax free or taxable to the parties (*i.e.*, to the constituent corporations and to the shareholders of the target company). The various tax-free types are called Type A (merger or consolidation),[1] Type B (exchange of shares of acquiring corporation for shares of target corporation's shareholders),[2] Type C

---

7. NYBCL § 910(a)(3).

§ 1.91

1. I.R.C. § 368(a)(1)(A). The Type A reorganization, which in its basic mode as well as in its variations is tax free to the parties to it, derives its name from the subparagraph bearing the capital letter in I.R.C. § 368(a)(1)(A). The other basic tax-free reorganizations (Types "B" and "C") are similarly designated. For the basic Type "A" transaction (defined in I.R.C. § 368(a)(1)(A) as a "statutory merger or consolidation", where the term "statutory" means relevant *state* statute) to be tax free to the disappearing corporation in the case of a merger (and to the two or more disappearing corporations in the case of a consolidation) and to its (or their) shareholders, the transaction must be a merger (or consolidation) effected under the NYBCL. *Id.* One variation of the Type "A" is a forward triangular Type "A" merger, which is in many respects identical to the basic Type "A" except that stock of the *parent* of the subsidiary-acquiring corporation is used in the transaction and involves the merger of the target corporation (which disappears) *into* the subsidiary-acquiring corporation. I.R.C. § 368(a)(2)(D). A second variation, a reverse triangular Type "A" merger, involves similar geometry to that of the forward triangular Type "A" except that the subsidiary merges (and disappears) into the target, with the parent's stock required to be received by the target's shareholders in exchange for their stock (*i.e.*, the parent ends up with control of the target). I.R.C. § 368(a)(2)(E). A third variation permits all or part of the target's assets acquired by the acquiring corporation in a basic Type "A" to be transferred ("dropped down") to a controlled subsidiary of the acquiring corporation. I.R.C. § 368(a)(2)(C).

PRACTICE POINTER: The Type "A" reorganization allows greater leeway in the permissible cash consideration than do Types "B" and "C". The reverse triangular merger is also a useful technique in certain cases (for example, when the parties want the target corporation to be the surviving corporation). The reverse triangular pattern can be effected using cash, rather than the parent's shares, in the acquisition. Although the transaction will be taxable, dilution of the parent's equity is avoided. This method is commonly used in a two-step takeover technique (an offer, as step one, for a certain percentage of the target's shares that will be sufficient to consummate, as the second step, a merger of the acquiring subsidiary into the target). For other requirements and details applicable to the Type "A" reorganization and its variations, *see* B. Bittker and J. Eustice, *Federal Income Taxation of Corporations and Shareholders* (6th ed. 1994) ¶¶ 12.02–12.04, 12.20–12.22, 12.25, 12.40–12.46, 15.80. *See also, supra,* § 1.82.

2. I.R.C. § 368(a)(1)(B). The Type "B" reorganization involves the acquisition by one corporation, in exchange solely for all or a part of its voting stock, of the stock of another corporation if, immediately after the acquisition, the acquiring corporation has control of the other corporation (whether or not the acquiring corporation had control immediately before the acquisition). Control is the ownership of at least eighty percent of the total combined voting power of all classes of stock entitled to vote, and of the total number of shares of all other

§ 1.91   BUSINESS ORGANIZATIONS: CORPORATIONS   Ch. 1

(exchange of acquiring corporation's shares for all or substantially all of acquired (target) corporation's property),[3] Type D (divisive and nondivisive),[4] Type E (recapitalizations),[5] Type F,[6] and Type G.[7]

classes of stock, of the acquired corporation. I.R.C. § 368(c). One tax-free variation, a triangular Type "B" reorganization, is identical to the basic Type "B" except that the acquiring corporation uses the voting stock of its parent. *Id.* A second tax-free variation of the basic Type "B" permits all or part of the stock acquired by the acquiring corporation to be transferred ("dropped down") to a subsidiary controlled by the acquiring corporation. I.R.C. § 368(a)(2)(C).

PRACTICE POINTER: Although control may be achieved in steps (creeping acquisitions or control), the only consideration permitted, for the exchange to be tax free to the shareholders of the acquired corporation, is voting stock (except to pay for fractional shares). For other requirements and details applicable to the Type "B" reorganization and its variations, *see* B. Bittker and J. Eustice, *Federal Income Taxation of Corporations and Shareholders* ¶ ¶ 12.02–12.04, 12.20–12.21, 12.23 (6th ed. 1994). *See also, supra,* §§ 1.88 and 1.89.

3. I.R.C. § 368(a)(1)(C). The basic tax-free Type "C" reorganization involves the acquisition by one corporation, in exchange solely for its voting stock, of substantially all the properties of another corporation. *Id.* In determining whether the exchange is solely for stock, the assumption by the acquiring corporation of a liability of the transferor, or that property is acquired subject to a liability, is disregarded. *Id.* One tax-free variation, a triangular Type "C", is identical to the basic Type "C" except that the acquiring corporation uses the voting stock of its parent. Another tax-free variation permits all or part of the target's assets acquired by the acquiring corporation in a basic Type "C" to be transferred ("dropped down") to a subsidiary controlled by the acquiring corporation. I.R.C. § 368(a)(2)(C).

PRACTICE POINTER: If, for example, all the target's properties are acquired, up to twenty percent of the fair market value of the property may be acquired for consideration other than voting stock. I.R.C. § 368(a)(2)(B).

CAVEAT: Since at least *eighty* percent of the fair market value of all the properties *must* be acquired for voting stock (I.R.C. § 368(a)(2)(B)(iii)), care must be exercised in calculating the value of the properties. For an example of this calculation, *see* B.

Bittker and J. Eustice, *Federal Income Taxation of Corporations and Shareholders* (6th ed. 1994) ¶ 12.24(3)(d). For other requirements and details applicable to the Type "B" reorganization and its variations, *see id.* ¶ ¶ 12.02–12.04, 12.20–12.21, 12.24, 12.40–12.46 (6th ed. 1994). *See also, supra,* § 1.85.

4. I.R.C. § 368(a)(1)(D) (a transfer by a corporation of all or part of its assets to another corporation if immediately after the transfer, the transferor or one or more of its shareholders, or any combination thereof, is in control of the transferee corporation, but only if, pursuant to a plan of reorganization, stock or securities are distributed in a transaction that qualifies under I.R.C. §§ 354, 355, or 356). *See* B. Bittker and J. Eustice, *Federal Income Taxation of Corporations and Shareholders* (6th ed. 1994) ¶ ¶ 12.26, 12.40–12.46. *See also, supra,* § 1.81. The principal transactions that qualify as tax-free nondivisive or divisive Type "D" reorganizations fit the following patterns: A *nondivisive* reorganization involves the transfer by one corporation of *substantially all* its assets to a *fifty-percent* controlled corporation, followed by a distribution to its shareholders of the subsidiary's shares in *complete liquidation* of the parent. A *divisive* reorganization involves the transfer by one corporation of *part* (less than substantially all) of its assets to an *eighty-percent* controlled corporation, followed by a distribution of the subsidiary's (or subsidiaries') shares in a *spin-off, split-off,* or *split-up.* I.R.C. § 368(a)(1)(D). *See also, e.g.,* B. Bittker and J. Eustice, *Federal Income Taxation of Corporations and Shareholders* (6th ed. 1994) 12–90 to 12–101.

PRACTICE POINTER: Because a Type "D" reorganization involves the *transfer* of assets to a controlled corporation *and* a *distribution* of the transferee's shares to the transferor's shareholders, if the assets are *already* held by the subsidiary-transferee (or subsidiaries, if a split-up is involved), then the distribution occurs without a Type "D" reorganization but can be tax free if the requirements of I.R.C. § 355 are met. To qualify a spin-off, split-off, or split-up for tax-free treatment under I.R.C. § 355, certain statutory criteria must be met (*viz.,*

5.–7. See footnotes 5 through 7 on p. 171.

170

§ 1.92 Business Combinations Summary

Business combinations through mergers and acquisitions may enhance shareholder value, both for the acquiring corporation's shareholders as well as the shareholders of the acquired (or target) corporation. Three basic methods of combining two or more businesses are: (1) the merger of one corporation into another, (2) the acquisition by one corporation of substantially all the *assets* of another, and (3) the acquisition by one corporation of a controlling block of *shares* of another. The advantages and disadvantages (tax, cost, procedural, and other) of each method should be analyzed. For example, in the sale of substantially all or all of a corporation's assets, various transfer documents might be necessary to transfer title to its assets to the transferee, a process that can be expensive. However, in a merger, title to the assets and contract rights of the transferor (disappearing) corporation is automatically transferred to the surviving (transferee) corporation upon the filing of the certificate of merger. Certain share exchanges and takeover bids are subject to NYBCL rules. These and other share exchanges result in the acquisition of a subsidiary without the assumption of its liabilities by the acquiring corporation.

Mergers and consolidations require, for each constituent corporation, adoption of a plan of merger by the board and approval thereof by vote of shareholders (with exceptions). The short-form merger of at least a ninety percent owned subsidiary into a parent corporation may be approved by the parent's board alone. The sale, lease, or other disposition of substantially all a corporation's assets requires adoption by its board and approval by a majority vote of its shareholders (with exceptions). A binding share exchange requires that the boards of both the acquiring and subject corporations adopt a plan of exchange for approval by a majority vote of shareholders of the subject corporation (with exceptions). In the case of a parent that owns at least ninety percent of a subsidiary's common shares, the parent's board alone may adopt a plan of exchange to acquire the remainder of such shares.

but very generally (with certain additional qualifications), the parent must control the subsidiary (or subsidiaries) immediately before the distribution, both the parent and the subsidiary (or each subsidiary) must have been engaged in an active business for at least five years, the parent must distribute to its shareholders a controlling number of shares, and the transaction must not be a device for the distribution of the parent's earnings). I.R.C. § 355. *See also, e.g.,* Master Tax Guide ¶ 2201; Henn and Alexander, *supra*, § 1.1, note 1, pp. 1014–1016; Bittker and Eustice, *Federal Income Taxation of Corporations and Shareholders* (6th ed. 1994) ¶¶ 11–5 to 11–6 and 11–10 to 11–14. *See supra,* § 1.81.

5. I.R.C. § 368(a)(1)(E) (recapitalization). *See* B. Bittker and J. Eustice, *Federal Income Taxation of Corporations and Shareholders* (6th ed. 1994) ¶ 12.27. *See also, supra,* §§ 1.38 and 1.72.

6. I.R.C. § 368(a)(1)(F) (change in identity, form, or place of organization of one corporation, however effected). *See* B. Bittker and J. Eustice, *Federal Income Taxation of Corporations and Shareholders* (6th ed. 1994) ¶¶ 12.28, 12.40–12.46.

7. I.R.C. § 368(a)(1)(G) (insolvency reorganizations). *See* B. Bittker and J. Eustice, *Federal Income Taxation of Corporations and Shareholders* (6th ed. 1994) ¶¶ 12.30, 12.40–12.46. *See supra,* § 1.78.

§ 1.92 BUSINESS ORGANIZATIONS: CORPORATIONS   Ch. 1

Guarantees (secured or unsecured) may be given by a corporation if authorized by at least a two-thirds' vote of its shareholders. Unless the certificate provides otherwise, the board may authorize the mortgage or other security interest in corporate property without shareholder authorization.

Library References:

West's Key No. Digests, Corporations ⇔581–591.

§ 1.93 Business Combinations Checklist

1. Mergers and consolidations. (See § 1.83)
    - Domestic corporations. (See § 1.83)
    - Short-form merger. (See § 1.83)
    - Domestic and foreign corporations. (See § 1.83)
2. Sale, lease, exchange, or other disposition of all or substantially all corporate assets not made in the usual or regular course of business . (See § 1.85)
3. Share exchanges. (See § 1.88)
    - Generally. (See § 1.88)
    - Subsidiary at least ninety percent owned. (See § 1.88)
    - Foreign and domestic corporations. (See § 1.88)
4. Takeover bids. (See § 1.89)
    - Disclosure to offerees. (See § 1.89)
    - Preconditions to effect certain business combinations. (See § 1.89)
    - Fraud; insider trading. (See § 1.89)
    - Enforcement. (See § 1.89)
5. Mortgage or security interest in corporate property. (See § 1.86)
6. Corporate guarantee. (See § 1.87)
7. Dissenting shareholders' right to payment. (See § 1.90)
8. Federal income tax aspects. (See § 1.91)

Library References:

West's Key No. Digests, Corporations ⇔581–591.

§ 1.94 Dissolution

A corporation may be dissolved by authorization of the corporation's shareholders without judicial intervention.[1] In some cases, a corporation may be dissolved by order of a court in an action brought by the

§ 1.94
1. NYBCL § 1001.

Attorney General[2] or in a special proceeding brought by the corporation's directors[3] or by its shareholders.[4] The dissolution procedures prescribed in the NYBCL are for the protection of the public,[5] the corporation's creditors,[6] and its shareholders.[7]

§ 1.95 Dissolution—Non-judicial Dissolution

In a voluntary (as opposed to a judicial) dissolution, a corporation is dissolved when a certificate of dissolution is filed.[1] It then winds up its affairs[2] and gives notice of its dissolution to its creditors.[3]

Petition to Annul or Suspend Dissolution. At any time after filing the certificate of dissolution, however, a special proceeding may be instituted upon the petition of the corporation[4] to suspend or annul the dissolution or continue the liquidation of the corporation under the supervision of the court.[5] These special proceedings are brought in the supreme court in the judicial district where the office of the corporation was located at the date of its dissolution, and the court may make any order it deems proper in all matters in connection with the dissolution or the winding up of the affairs of the corporation.[6]

---

2. NYBCL § 109(a)(1), (a)(2), and (a)(5); NYBCL § 1101.

3. NYBCL § 1102.

4. NYBCL § 1103. A corporation may also be dissolved by expiration of its period of duration. NYBCL § 1109. Corporations delinquent for two years in the payment of franchise taxes may be declared, by proclamation of the Secretary of State, dissolved. Tax Law § 203–a; NYBCL § 1109. *See supra,* § 1.23. A constituent corporation that merges into a surviving corporation (or consolidated corporation) is in effect dissolved. NYBCL § 906.

5. *See, e.g.,* NYBCL §§ 1004, 1111(b)(1).

6. *See, e.g.,* NYBCL §§ 1005(a)(3), 1113, 1210, 1211.

7. NYBCL § 1111(b)(2).

§ 1.95

1. NYBCL § 1004. The Department of State will not file a certificate of dissolution unless evidence of the consent of the State Tax Commission to the dissolution is attached to the certificate. *Id.*

2. *See infra,* § 1.97.

3. *See infra,* § 1.98.

4. If approved by the court, additional petitioners permitted are creditors, claimants, directors, officers, shareholders, subscribers for shares, incorporators, or the Attorney General. NYBCL § 1008(a).

5. NYBCL § 1008(a).

6. *Id. See* NYBCL § 1008(a)(1)-(a)(11) (nonexhaustive list of court orders re, *e.g.,* validity of corporate authorization of dissolution; adequacy of notice; validity (and barring) of claims; liability of directors, officers, shareholders, or corporation; payment and compromise of claims; corporate records; receivers; injunctions; distributions to shareholders; assets distributable to unknown creditors or shareholders to be paid to New York Comptroller as abandoned property). ***Procedure.*** Orders may be entered *ex parte,* except that if the special proceeding was not instituted upon petition of the corporation, notice must be given to the corporation in such manner as the court may direct. NYBCL § 1008(b). Notice must be given of any hearings and of the entry of any orders on such matters, and in such manner and to such other persons interested, as the court may deem proper. *Id.* All such orders are binding upon the Attorney General, the corporation, its officers, directors, shareholders, subscribers for shares, incorporators, creditors, and claimants. *Id.* Simultaneously with the institution of the special proceeding, the petitioner must apply to the Department of State to reserve the corporation name. NYBCL § 1008(c)(1). If such name is not available, the petitioner, upon being notified thereof, must apply forthwith for the reservation of another and available name. *Id.* Any judgment or order of annulment made in the proceeding shall direct the petitioner to exe-

§ 1.96 Dissolution—Non-judicial Dissolution—Authorization

Procedure. The voluntary dissolution of a corporation must be authorized by a majority of the votes of all outstanding shares entitled to vote, except as otherwise provided in the certificate of incorporation.[1] If the certificate of incorporation contains a provision that any shareholder, or the holders of any specified number or proportion of shares or votes of shares (or of any class or series), may require the dissolution of the corporation at will or upon the occurrence of a specified event, a certificate of dissolution may be filed as authorized by such person(s).[2] An amendment of the certificate of incorporation that adds such a provision, or that changes or strikes out such a provision, must be authorized by vote of the holders of all outstanding shares, whether or not otherwise entitled to vote on any amendment, or of a lesser proportion of shares, or of a class or series of shares, but not less than a majority of all outstanding shares entitled to vote on any amendment, as may be provided specifically in the certificate of incorporation for adding, changing, or striking out such a provision.[3]

cute a certificate of change of the corporate name to the other name. *Id.* The clerk of the court, or such other person as the court may direct, must transmit a certified copy of the judgment or order of annulment (together with the certificate of change of corporate name, in the appropriate case) to the Department of State and to the clerk of the county in which the office of the corporation was located on the date of the dissolution. NYBCL § 1008(c)(2). Upon filing by the Department of State, the annulment of dissolution is effected. *Id.*

§ 1.96

1. NYBCL §§ 1001, 1002(a).

CAVEAT: The requisite vote is: (1) for corporations whose certificate of incorporation expressly provides such or corporations incorporated *after* the effective date of NYBCL § 1001(b), a *majority* of the votes of all outstanding shares entitled to vote or (2) for other corporations, at least *two-thirds* of the votes of all outstanding shares entitled to vote, except, in either case, as otherwise provided under NYBCL § 1002 (dissolution under provision in certificate of incorporation). NYBCL § 1001(a). The effective date of NYBCL § 1001(b) is the one hundred eightieth day after the act amending the NYBCL became law (*see* 1997 NY S.B. 476 (SN) § 71; 1997 NY S.B. 5680 (SN) § 7); S.B. 476 was enacted on Aug. 26, 1997, and its effective date is Feb. 22, 1998. A corporation may adopt an amendment of the certificate of incorporation providing that such dissolution must be authorized at a meeting of shareholders by a specified proportion of votes of all outstanding shares entitled to vote, provided that such proportion may not be less than a majority. NYBCL § 1001(b).

2. NYBCL § 1002(a). *Procedure.* A certificate of dissolution under NYBCL § 1003 (*see infra*, § 1.97) may be signed, verified, and delivered to the Department of State as provided in NYBCL § 104 when authorized by a holder or holders of the number or proportion of shares or votes of shares specified in the certificate of incorporation, with authorization given in the manner specified (or if no manner is specified, when authorized on written consent signed by the holder or holders); or the certificate may be signed, verified, and delivered to the Department by the holder or holders or by any of such holders as are designated by them. *Id.*

3. NYBCL § 1002(b). If the certificate of incorporation contains a provision authorized by NYBCL § 1002, the existence of the provision must be noted conspicuously on the face or back of every certificate for

§ 1.97 Dissolution—Non-judicial Dissolution—Certificate of Dissolution

Upon the filing of the certificate of dissolution,[1] the corporation is dissolved.[2] After dissolution, the corporation may not carry on any business except for the purpose of winding up its affairs.[3]

Winding Up Corporation's Affairs. Upon dissolution, the corporation must proceed to wind up its affairs.[4] In that connection, it continues to have power to fulfill or discharge its contracts, collect its assets and sell them at public or private sale, discharge or pay its liabilities, and do all other acts appropriate to liquidate its business.[5] After paying, or adequately providing for the payment of, its liabilities, the corporation, if authorized by a majority of the votes of all outstanding shares entitled to vote, may sell all or part of its remaining assets and distribute the proceeds among the shareholders according to their respective rights.[6] Whether or not it has made any sale, the corporation may distribute any remaining assets, in cash or in kind, among its shareholders according to their respective rights.[7]

Library References:
West's Key No. Digests, Corporations ⚖=610(1).

§ 1.97

1. NYBCL § 1004. *Procedure*. A certificate of dissolution entitled "Certificate of dissolution of ...... (name of corporation) under section 1003 of the Business Corporation Law" must be signed, verified, and delivered to the Department of State. NYBCL § 1003. The certificate must set forth: (1) the name of the corporation and, if its name has been changed, the name under which it was formed; (2) the date its certificate of incorporation was filed; (3) the name and address of each of its officers and directors; (4) that the corporation elects to dissolve; and (5) the manner in which the dissolution was authorized. NYBCL § 1003(a). The Department of State may not file a certificate of dissolution unless evidence of the consent of the State Tax Commission to the dissolution is attached to the certificate. NYBCL § 1004.

2. NYBCL § 1004.

3. NYBCL § 1005(a)(1).

4. NYBCL § 1005(a)(2).

5. *Id.*

6. NYBCL § 1005(a)(3)(A).

shares issued by the corporation. NYBCL § 1002(c).

CAVEAT: In the case of a sale under NYBCL § 1005(a)(3)(A) where the consideration is, in whole or in part, other than cash, shareholders entitled to vote who do not vote for or consent in writing to the sale have the right to receive payment for their shares upon compliance with NYBCL § 623. *Id.* NYBCL § 909 (on the sale, lease, exchange, or other disposition of assets) is not applicable to this type of sale of assets. *Id. See supra*, § 1.51.

7. NYBCL § 1005(a)(3)(B).

CAVEAT: When no shareholders exist, upon dissolution all subscriptions for shares are cancelled and all obligations of the corporation to issue shares or of the subscribers to pay their subscriptions terminate, except for payments required to enable the corporation to pay its liabilities. NYBCL § 1005(b). Upon the winding up of the affairs of the corporation, any assets distributable to a creditor or shareholder who is unknown or cannot be found, or who is under disability and for whom no legal representative exists, must be paid to the New York State Comptroller as abandoned property within six months from the date fixed for the payment of the final liquidating distribution and be subject to the provisions of the abandoned property law. NYBCL § 1005(c).

Corporate Continuity During Winding Up. A dissolved corporation, its directors, officers, and shareholders may continue to function for the purpose of winding up the affairs of the corporation in the same manner as if the dissolution had not taken place, except as otherwise provided in the NYBCL or by court order.[8] The directors of a dissolved corporation are not deemed to be trustees of its assets; title to the assets does not vest in them but remains in the corporation until transferred by it in its corporate name.[9] Dissolution does not change quorum or voting requirements for the board or shareholders, or provisions regarding election, appointment, resignation or removal of, or filling vacancies among, directors or officers, or provisions regarding amendment or repeal of bylaws or adoption of new bylaws.[10] Shares may be transferred and determinations of shareholders of record for any purpose may be made until the time, if any, that the record is closed either by the board or the shareholders.[11] The corporation may sue or be sued in all courts and participate in actions and proceedings in its corporate name, and process may be served by or upon it.[12] Dissolution does not affect any remedy available to or against the corporation, its directors, officers, or shareholders for any right or claim existing, or any liability incurred, before dissolution, except as provided in NYBCL § 1007 (notice to creditors; filing or barring claims) or NYBCL § 1008 (jurisdiction of the supreme court to supervise dissolution and liquidation).[13]

Library References:

West's Key No. Digests, Corporations ⚖610(1).

§ 1.98 Dissolution—Non-judicial Dissolution—Notice to Creditors

Procedure. At any time after dissolution, a corporation may give notice to its creditors and claimants, including those with unliquidated or contingent claims and those with whom the corporation has unfulfilled contracts, to present their claims.[1] Such claims must be presented in detail in writing at a specified place and by a specified day at least six months after first publication of the notice.[2] The notice must be publish-

---

8. NYBCL § 1006(a).
9. NYBCL § 1006(a)(1).
10. NYBCL § 1006(a)(2).
11. NYBCL § 1006(a)(3).
12. NYBCL § 1006(a)(4).
13. NYBCL § 1006(b).

§ 1.98

1. NYBCL § 1007(a).
2. *Id.*

PRACTICE POINTER: Although no other contents of a notice are specified by the NYBCL, the notice must be adequate. *See* NYBCL § 1008(a)(2) (adequacy of notice; further notice requirement if original notice inadequate). Under this standard, and in the interest of the corporation's learning of the parameters of a claim at the outset, sound practice would appear to require that the notice also state that, in addition to the claimant's name, address, and telephone number (and facsimile number and e-mail address, if any), the claim be described in complete detail (its amount, a description of the transaction or other circumstances out of which the claim arose (including relevant dates and places), the names of persons involved, together with

ed at least once a week for two successive weeks in a newspaper of general circulation in the county in which the office of the corporation was located at the date of dissolution.[3] On or before the date of first publication, the corporation must mail a copy of the notice to persons believed to be creditors of, or claimants against, it, whose names and addresses are known to, or can with due diligence be ascertained by, the corporation.[4]

The giving of the notice does not constitute an admission by the corporation that any person is a proper creditor or claimant.[5] Neither does it revive, validate, or operate as a waiver of any defense or counterclaim in respect of any claim against the corporation, its assets, directors, officers, or shareholders that is barred by any statute of limitations, invalid for any reason, or in respect of which the corporation, its directors, officers, or shareholders, has any defense or counterclaim.[6]

Claims filed as provided in the notice but disputed by the corporation may be submitted to the supreme court for determination under NYBCL § 1008.[7] Claims barred by any Statute of Limitations and all other claims that are not timely filed as provided in the notice (except claims that are the subject of litigation on the date of first publication of the notice and claims that are filed but disallowed by the court under NYBCL § 1008[8]) may not be pursued against the corporation, its assets, directors, officers, and shareholders, except to the extent, if any, that the court allows claims against any remaining assets of the corporation for creditors who show satisfactory reason for their failure to file within the time permitted.[9]

Tax claims and other claims of New York and of the United States are not required to be filed under NYBCL §§ 1007 and 1008, nor are these claims barred because they have not been so filed.[10] Distribution of the assets of the corporation may be deferred until determination of

---

all other relevant information necessary, and provided in the detail sufficient, to constitute a *complete*, *exclusive*, and *final* statement of the claim).

3. NYBCL § 1007(a).

4. *Id.*

5. *Id.*

6. *Id.* Any person whose claim is, at the date of the first publication of the notice, barred by any statute of limitations is not a creditor or claimant entitled to notice under NYBCL §§ 1007 or 1008. NYBCL § 1007(b). A claim filed by the trustee or paying agent for the holders of bonds or coupons has the same effect as if filed by the holder of the bond or coupon. *Id.*

7. NYBCL § 1007(b).

8. The court may determine the validity and amount, or the invalidity, of any claims against the corporation. NYBCL § 1008(a)(3).

9. NYBCL § 1007(b). The court may, if it determines that the original notice was inadequate, require a further notice under NYBCL § 1008(a)(2); thereafter, any reference to "notice" in NYBCL § 1007 (to the extent that the court so orders) means the further notice. *Id.* A claim that has been filed in accordance with a notice under NYBCL § 1007 need not be refiled under the further notice. *Id.*

10. NYBCL § 1007(c).

these claims.[11] Laborers' wages are preferred claims that are entitled to payment, before any other unsecured creditors,[12] out of the assets of the corporation in excess of the amount of valid prior liens or encumbrances.[13]

Library References:

West's Key No. Digests, Corporations ⚖610(4).

§ 1.99 Dissolution—Judicial Dissolution

The Attorney General may bring an action for dissolution of a corporation;[1] directors[2] or shareholders[3] may also petition for judicial dissolution. Upon presentation of the petition, the court issues an order requiring the corporation and all persons interested in it to show cause why the corporation should not be dissolved.[4] At any stage of the action or proceeding, the court may appoint a receiver to preserve the corporation's property.[5] The court may also void certain transfers of the corporation's property; it may grant an injunction during the pendency of the action or proceeding.[6]

Library References:

West's Key No. Digests, Corporations ⚖611.

§ 1.100 Dissolution—Judicial Dissolution—Attorney General's Action

The Attorney General may bring an action for the dissolution of a corporation on the grounds that it: (1) procured its formation through fraudulent misrepresentation or concealment of a material fact,[1] (2) has exceeded the authority conferred upon it by law, (3) has violated any law and, as a result, forfeited its charter, (4) has conducted its business in a persistently fraudulent or illegal manner, or (5) has abused its powers, contrary to the public policy of New York.[2] The action is triable by jury

---

11. *Id.*

12. *Cf.* Bankruptcy Reform Act, 11 U.S.C.A § 507 (priorities of unsecured claims (higher third priority of unsecured claims for employees' wages (up to $4,000) over eighth priority of unsecured claims of governmental units)).

13. NYBCL § 1007(d). *See, e.g.,* Bankruptcy Reform Act, 11 U.S.C.A. § 506 (determination of secured status; secured claims (*e.g.,* federal and state tax liens)).

§ 1.99

1. *See infra,* § 1.100.
2. *See infra,* § 1.101.
3. *See infra,* §§ 1.102 and 103.
4. *See infra,* § 1.104.

5. *See infra,* §§ 1.105 and 1.111.
6. *See infra,* § 1.106.

§ 1.100

1. NYBCL § 1101(a)(1).

2. NYBCL § 1101(a)(2). The Attorney General or other state officials are not precluded from bringing actions or special proceedings for the annulment or dissolution of a corporation for other causes provided in the NYBCL or in any other New York statute. NYBCL § 1101(c). *See, e.g.,* NYBCL § 109 (Attorney General proceeding against a corporation that has not been duly formed or has acted beyond its capacity or power) and Tax Law §§ 203 (Attorney General proceeding against a corporation that has in-

as a matter of right.[3]

Library References:

West's Key No. Digests, Corporations ⚛613.

§ 1.101 Dissolution—Judicial Dissolution—Directors' Petition

Directors of a corporation may petition for judicial dissolution if a majority of the board adopts a resolution finding that the corporation's assets are insufficient to discharge its liabilities or that a dissolution will be beneficial to the shareholders.[1] In this way, an insolvent corporation may petition for dissolution based on the good faith judgment of its board alone.[2]

Library References:

West's Key No. Digests, Corporations ⚛614.

§ 1.102 Dissolution—Judicial Dissolution—Shareholders' Petition

Shareholders may present a petition for judicial dissolution if they find that the corporation's assets are not sufficient to discharge its liabilities or that a dissolution would be beneficial to the shareholders.[1] A shareholders' meeting to consider such a resolution may be called by the holders of at least ten percent of the votes of all outstanding shares entitled to vote (or by a lesser proportion if the certificate of incorpo-

tentionally failed to file a report or pay taxes); 203–a (Secretary of State proclamation against corporations that fail to file reports or pay taxes for two years).

3. NYBCL § 1101(b).

§ 1.101

1. NYBCL § 1102.

2. *See, e.g.*, Leibert v. Clapp, 13 N.Y.2d 313, 247 N.Y.S.2d 102, 196 N.E.2d 540 (1963).

PRACTICE POINTER: The directors, charged with fiduciary duties, should consider desirable alternatives, if any, to dissolution, such as settling out of court with creditors (*e.g.*, by extension, composition, depositing the corporation's shares with a creditors' committee under a voting trust, making an assignment for benefit of creditors, finding a financially strong partner (proverbial "White Knight") with whom the corporation can join forces, or filing for bankruptcy). *See* Debtor and Creditor Law § 3 (requisites of general assignment for benefit of creditors). The board should take into consideration which alternative is likely, *e.g.*, to be the most efficient and to involve the least time, expense, waste, publicity, and harm to the corporation's (or its owners') reputation. In a dissolution, if the corporate assets are insufficient, in winding up, to pay the creditors in full, the creditors may not look to the shareholders for payment, unless a reason to pierce the corporate veil (or some other reason for shareholder liability) exists. *See supra*, §§ 1.10 and 1.56. *See also*, § 1.66 (directors' liability under NYBCL § 719(a)(3) for improper liquidating distribution to shareholders). *Cf.* RMBCA § 14.30(3) (grounds for judicial dissolution include corporate insolvency; federal bankruptcy proceeding mentioned as an alternative to dissolution). *See* Chapter 9 "Bankruptcy," *infra*. *See also*, Ayer, *How to Think about Bankruptcy Ethics*, 60 Am. Bankr. L. J. 355, 377–378 (1986) (bankruptcy should be regarded as a remedy for a debtor's unanticipated misfortune, not as a business planning device).

§ 1.102

1. NYBCL § 1103(a).

ration so authorizes) but may not be called more often than once in any 12 consecutive months.[2] The resolution may be adopted by a majority of the votes of all outstanding shares entitled to vote (or, if the certificate of incorporation requires, by a greater proportion).[3]

Library References:
West's Key No. Digests, Corporations ⚖=614.

§ 1.103 Dissolution—Judicial Dissolution—Petition Upon Deadlock Among Directors or Shareholders and in Other Circumstances

Deadlock. Except as otherwise provided in the certificate of incorporation,[1] the holders of at least one-half of all outstanding shares of a corporation entitled to vote in an election of directors may present a petition for dissolution on one or more of the following grounds: (1) the board of directors is so divided on the management of the corporation's affairs that the votes required for its action cannot be obtained; (2) the shareholders are so divided that the votes required to elect directors cannot be obtained; or (3) internal dissension between different factions of shareholders has so divided them that dissolution would be beneficial to them.[2] When the shareholders are so divided that they have failed for at least two consecutive annual meetings (or meeting dates, if no meetings were held) to elect successors to directors whose terms have expired, or would have expired upon the election and qualification of their successors, the hopelessness of the deadlock is clear, and *any* holder (*i.e.*, one shareholder) of shares entitled to vote at an election of directors of a corporation may present a petition for its dissolution.[3]

Other Circumstances. When the directors or those in control of the corporation have been guilty of illegal, fraudulent, or oppressive[4] actions toward the complaining shareholders, or when the property of the corporation is being looted, wasted, or diverted for non-corporate purposes by its directors, officers, or those in control of the corporation, the holders of twenty percent or more of the votes of all outstanding shares entitled to vote in an election of directors may present a petition for dissolution[5] of a corporation[6] whose shares are not regularly traded.[7]

2. NYBCL § 1103(b).

3. NYBCL § 1103(c).

§ 1.103

1. See NYBCL §§ 501 and 613.

2. NYBCL § 1104(a). If the certificate of incorporation provides that the vote required for action by the board, or the vote of shareholders required for election of directors, is greater than that otherwise required by the NYBCL, the petition may be presented by the holders of more than one-third of the votes of all outstanding shares entitled to vote on non-judicial dissolution under NYBCL § 1001. NYBCL § 1104(b).

3. NYBCL § 1104(c).

4. See, e.g., R. Thompson, *The Shareholder's Cause of Action for Oppression*, 48 Business Lawyer 699–745 (1993).

5. NYBCL § 1104–a(a).

6. Other than a corporation registered as an investment company under the Investment Company Act of 1940 (15 U.S.C.A. §§ 80a–1 et seq.). NYBCL § 1104–a.

7. That is, no shares of which are listed on a national securities exchange or regu-

Ch. 1   PETITION: DEADLOCK AMONG DIRECTORS   § 1.103

The granting of the petition is a matter of the court's discretion.[8] Within 30 days after the filing of the petition, in addition to all other disclosure requirements,[9] the directors or those in control of the corporation must make the corporate financial books and records for the past three years available for inspection and copying by the petitioners.[10]

Because dissolution is a drastic remedy, petitioners are accorded, under NYBCL § 1118, an alternative means of receiving a fair return on their investment. Under NYBCL § 1118, any non-petitioning shareholders *or* the corporation may elect to purchase the petitioners' shares at any time within ninety days after the filing of a petition for dissolution under NYBCL § 1104–a (or later, if the court in its discretion allows).[11] Any purchase of the shares must be at fair value and upon terms and conditions approved by the court.[12] The election is irrevocable unless the court deems otherwise.[13] If either the shareholders or the corporation elect to purchase the shares and are unable to agree with the petitioners upon the fair value of the shares, the court, upon the application of the prospective purchasers or the petitioners, may stay the proceedings and determine the fair value.[14] If the election is made more than ninety days after the filing of the petition and the court allows the petition, the court may award the petitioners reasonable expenses incurred in the proceeding prior to the election, including reasonable attorneys' fees.[15] The court may also require, at any time prior to the actual purchase of the

---

larly quoted in an over-the-counter market by one or more members of a national or an affiliated securities association. NYBCL § 1104–a(a).

8. *See, e.g.*, Matter of Kemp & Beatley, Inc., 64 N.Y.2d 63, 484 N.Y.S.2d 799, 473 N.E.2d 1173 (1984). In determining whether to proceed with an involuntary dissolution, the court must take into account whether liquidation of the corporation is the only feasible means by which the petitioners may reasonably *expect* to obtain a fair return on their investment and whether the liquidation is reasonably necessary for the protection of the rights and interests of any substantial number of shareholders or the petitioners. NYBCL § 1104–a(b). The standard in NYBCL § 1104–a(b) appears to be the value of the *chance* to obtain a fair return. The court, under this standard, must compare the expected values (or if the time value of money is relevant because of delay, the expected present values) of various alternatives to dissolution. Upon a finding of willful or reckless dissipation or transfer of corporate property without just or adequate compensation, the court may order that valuations of shares be adjusted and provide for a surcharge upon the directors or those in control of the corporation. NYBCL § 1104–a(d).

9. Presumably, the requirements under NYBCL § 624 (right of inspection).

10. NYBCL § 1104–a(c).

11. NYBCL § 1118(a).

PRACTICE POINTER: Minority shareholders may attempt to have their shares purchased under NYBCL §§ 1104–a and 1118 rather than pursuant to a shareholders' agreement that sets the price and other terms at which the minority may sell its shares. A disparity between fair value under NYBCL § 1118 and the price set in the shareholders' agreement is likely to exist. *See, e.g.*, Banks, *The Unresolved Tension Between the 1979 Amendments to the BCL and Shareholder Agreements in Close Corporations*, 67 N.Y.S.B.J. 16 (Feb. 1995).

12. NYBCL § 1118(a).

13. *Id.*

14. NYBCL § 1118(b). In determining fair value, the court may award interest from the date the petition is filed to the date of payment for the petitioners' shares. *Id.*

15. NYBCL § 1118(c)(1).

petitioners' shares, the posting of a bond or other acceptable security in an amount sufficient to secure the petitioners' receiving fair value for their shares.[16]

Library References:
West's Key No. Digests, Corporations ⚖=614.

§ 1.104 Dissolution—Judicial Dissolution—Procedures

Procedure—Petition for Dissolution. A petition for dissolution must specify the section or sections of the NYBCL under which it is authorized and state the reasons why the corporation should be dissolved.[1] It must be verified by the one of the petitioners.[2]

Order to Show Cause. Upon presentation of a petition, the court must issue an order requiring the corporation and all persons interested in the corporation to show cause no sooner than four weeks after the issuance of the order why the corporation should not be dissolved.[3] The court may order the corporation, its officers, and directors to furnish a schedule of pertinent information, including a statement of corporate assets and liabilities and the names and addresses of each shareholder and of each creditor and claimant, including claimants with unliquidated or contingent claims, as well as claimants with whom the corporation has unfulfilled contracts.[4] A copy of the order to show cause must be published at least once a week in each of the three weeks before the hearing date, in one or more newspapers specified in the order and generally circulated in the county in which the office of the corporation is located on the date of the order.[5]

The order to show cause must be served upon the New York State Tax Commission, the corporation, and each person named in the petition (or in any schedule of information furnished to the court) as a shareholder, creditor, or claimant.[6] Service must be made personally, at least ten

---

16. NYBCL § 1118(c)(2).

§ 1.104

1. NYBCL § 1105. At any stage before a final order is issued, the court may grant an order amending the petition or any other paper filed. NYBCL § 1107. Subject to the provisions of NYBCL Article 11, the provisions of NYBCL §§ 1005 (procedure after dissolution), 1006 (corporate action and survival of remedies after dissolution), 1007 (notice to creditors; filing or barring claims), and 1008 (jurisdiction of supreme court to supervise dissolution and liquidation) apply to a corporation dissolved under NYBCL Article 11. NYBCL § 1117(a). Orders provided for in NYBCL § 1008 may be made at any stage of an action or a special proceeding, and if the corporation is dissolved, the court may retain jurisdiction for the purpose of making the orders, after the dissolution, in the action or special proceeding. NYBCL § 1117(b). The court may also make the orders in separate special proceedings as provided in section 1008. Id. Notice to creditors and claimants provided for in NYBCL § 1007 may also be given, by order of the court, at any stage of an action or special proceeding under NYBCL Article 11. NYBCL § 1117(c).

2. NYBCL § 1105.
3. NYBCL § 1106(a).
4. Id.
5. NYBCL § 1106(b).
6. NYBCL § 1106(c). A person whose address is stated to be unknown and cannot with due diligence be ascertained by the corporation need not be served. Id.

days before the time appointed for the hearing, or by mailing a copy of the order, postage prepaid, at least 20 days before the hearing date, addressed to the persons to be served at their last known addresses.[7] Within ten days after the order is entered, a copy of the order to show cause and the petition must be filed with the clerk of the county where the office of the corporation is located on the date of the order.[8] A copy of each schedule furnished to the court must, within ten days thereafter, be filed with the clerk.[9] Publication, service, and filing must be effected by the corporation or such other persons as the court may order.[10]

Referee. At the time and place specified in the order to show cause, or at any other time and place to which the hearing is adjourned, the court or the referee[11] must hear the allegations and proofs of the parties and determine the facts.[12] The decision of the court or the report of the referee must be made and filed with the clerk of the court with all convenient speed.[13]

Hearing; Application for Final Order. When the hearing is before a referee, a motion for a final order must be made to the court upon notice to each party who has appeared.[14] The notice of motion may be served as prescribed for the service of papers upon an attorney in an action in that court.[15] When the hearing is before the court, a motion for a final order may be made at the hearing or at such time and upon such notice as the court prescribes.[16]

Judgment or Final Order of Dissolution. If the court determines, in its discretion, that a corporation should be dissolved, it makes a judgment or final order dissolving the corporation.[17] In making its decision, the court must take into consideration the following: (1) in an action brought by the Attorney General, the paramount importance of the public interest and (2) in a special proceeding brought by directors or shareholders, the paramount importance of the benefit to the shareholders of the dissolution.[18] In a special proceeding brought under NYBCL § 1104 (petition in case of deadlock among directors or shareholders) or NYBCL § 1104–a (petition by holders of twenty percent or more of the outstanding shares), dissolution is not to be denied merely because the

7. NYBCL § 1106(c).
8. NYBCL § 1106(d).
9. *Id.*
10. NYBCL § 1106(e).
11. If a referee was not designated in the order to show cause, the court in its discretion may appoint a referee when or after the order is returnable. NYBCL § 1108. The court may at any time appoint a successor referee. *Id.*
12. NYBCL § 1109.
13. *Id.*
14. NYBCL § 1110.
15. *Id.*
16. *Id.*
17. NYBCL § 1111(a). The clerk of the court transmits certified copies of the judgment or final order of dissolution to the Department of State and to the clerk of the county in which the office of the corporation was located on the date of the judgment or order. NYBCL § 1111(d).
18. NYBCL § 1111(b).

corporate business has been or could be conducted at a profit.[19] If the judgment or final order provides for dissolution, the court may also provide for the distribution of the corporation's property to those entitled thereto in accordance with their respective rights.[20] Upon filing of the judgment or final order by the Department of State, the corporation is dissolved,[21] after which the corporation must promptly transmit a certified copy of the judgment or final order to the clerk of each other county in which its certificate of incorporation was filed.[22]

Venue. An action or special proceeding for dissolution must be brought in the supreme court in the judicial district in which the office of the corporation is located at the time of the (1) service on the corporation of a summons in the action or (2) presentation to the court of the petition in the special proceeding.[23]

Discontinuance. An action or special proceeding for the dissolution of a corporation may be discontinued at any stage if the court determines that adduced facts establish that cause for dissolution did not exist or no longer exists.[24] In that event, the court must dismiss the action or special proceeding and direct any receiver to redeliver to the corporation all its remaining property.[25]

Library References:
West's Key No. Digests, Corporations ⊙613, 614.

§ 1.105 Dissolution—Judicial Dissolution—Preservation of Assets; Appointment of Receiver

At any stage of an action or special proceeding, the court may, in its discretion, make such orders as it deems proper in connection with preserving the property, and carrying on the business, of the corporation, including the appointment and removal of a receiver under NYBCL Article 12 (receivership).[1] The receiver may be a director, officer, or shareholder of the corporation.[2]

Library References:
West's Key No. Digests, Corporations ⊙621, 622.

§ 1.106 Dissolution—Judicial Dissolution—Certain Transfers and Judgments Void; Injunction

After service upon the corporation of a summons in an action, or an order to show cause in a special proceeding, a sale, mortgage, convey-

---

19. Id.
20. NYBCL § 1111(c).
21. NYBCL § 1111(d).
22. NYBCL § 1111(e). See NYBCL § 104(g) (Department of State transmits various certificates to, and for filing by, the clerk of the county in which the corporate office is, and is to be, located). See also, supra, § 1.7.
23. NYBCL § 1112.
24. NYBCL § 1116.
25. Id.

§ 1.105

1. NYBCL § 1113. See infra, § 1.111.
2. NYBCL § 1113.

ance, or other transfer of any of its property for any consideration or in payment of, or as security for, an *existing* or *prior* debt, made without the prior approval of the court, is void as against such persons, and to the extent the court determines.[1] At any stage of an action or special proceeding, the court may, in its discretion, grant an injunction, effective during the pendency of the proceeding (or such shorter period as the court may specify) for one or more of the following purposes: (1) to restrain the corporation and its directors and officers from transacting any unauthorized business or exercising any corporate powers, except by permission of the court;[2] (2) to restrain the corporation and its directors and officers from collecting or receiving any debt owed to, or other property of, the corporation, or from paying out or otherwise transferring or delivering any property of the corporation, except by permission of the court;[3] (3) to restrain the creditors of the corporation from beginning any action against the corporation, or from taking further action in proceedings already commenced, except by permission of the court.[4]

§ 1.107 Dissolution—Liquidation Distributions

After dissolution, a corporation winds up its affairs and liquidates its business.[1] After paying its creditors, it may sell remaining assets and distribute the proceeds to its shareholders according to their respective rights in liquidation.[2]

§ 1.108 Dissolution—Liquidation Distributions—Federal Income Tax Aspects

Distributions to shareholders in complete liquidation of a corporation are, for tax purposes, treated by the shareholders as though the distributions were received by them in exchange for their shares (and not as a dividend thereon).[1] The corporation, as a general rule, recognizes gain or loss as if the property distributed had been sold to the distributee-shareholders at fair market value.[2] No gain or loss is recog-

§ 1.106

1. NYBCL § 1114. Also void is a judgment rendered against the corporation by confession or upon the acceptance of any offer. Id.

2. NYBCL § 1115(a)(1).

3. NYBCL § 1115(a)(2).

4. NYBCL § 1115(a)(3).

§ 1.107

1. NYBCL §§ 1005(a)(1), (2). *See supra,* § 1.97.

2. NYBCL §§ 1005(a)(3), (c). *See supra,* § 1.97.

§ 1.108

1. I.R.C. § 331. *See* I.R.C. §§ 1001(a), (c) (general rules), 1222(11) (net capital gain), and 1(h) (maximum tax rate on capital gains). For losses, *see, e.g.,* I.R.C. §§ 1222(10) (net capital loss), 165(f) (limitations), and 165(g) (worthless securities). The basis of property received by the distributee (shareholder) is the fair market value of the property received. *See* I.R.C. § 334(a). For liquidations in an international context, *see, e.g.,* B. Bittker and J. Eustice, *Federal Income Taxation of Corporations and Shareholders* ¶ 15.80 (6th ed. 1994).

2. I.R.C. § 336(a).

nized on the receipt by a parent corporation of property distributed in complete liquidation of a subsidiary in which the parent owns at least eighty percent of the subsidiary's shares[3] (measured by voting power and by total value of the shares),[4] and no gain or loss is recognized by the subsidiary on the distribution.[5]

§ 1.109 Dissolution Summary

Except as otherwise provided in the certificate of incorporation, corporations may be dissolved under the NYBCL by a majority vote of shareholders (with exceptions). After dissolution, the corporation carries on no business except for the winding up of its affairs. The corporation, its directors, officers, and shareholders may continue to function as if no dissolution had occurred for purposes of paying corporate debts, making liquidating distribution, and conducting actions and proceedings in which the corporation may be involved. The NYBCL requires notice of dissolution to a corporation's creditors. Creditors' claims that are disputed by the corporation may be submitted for determination to the supreme court in the judicial district where the corporation's office was located at the date of its dissolution. A receiver may be appointed by the court at any stage of the proceedings for the purpose of preservation of corporate assets.

Library References:

West's Key No. Digests, Corporations ⛬592–630(6).

§ 1.110 Dissolution Checklist

1. Non-judicial (voluntary) dissolution. (*See* § 1.95)
    - Certificate of dissolution. (*See* § 1.95)
    - Authorization by shareholders. (*See* § 1.96)
    - Certificate of incorporation provision. (*See* § 1.96)
    - Petition to suspend or annul the dissolution. (*See* § 1.95)
    - Certificate of dissolution contents. (*See* § 1.97)
    - Winding up. (*See* § 1.97)
    - Corporate continuity during winding up. (*See* § 1.97)
    - Discharge of corporate liabilities. (*See* § 1.97)
    - Sale of remaining corporate assets. (*See* § 1.97)
    - Notice to creditors. (*See* § 1.98)
2. Judicial (involuntary) dissolution. (*See* § 1.99)

3. I.R.C. § 332.
4. I.R.C. § 1504(a)(2).
5. I.R.C. § 337. For the basis of property received by the distributee (parent corporation), see I.R.C. § 334(b) (carryover basis as a general rule).

- Attorney General's action. (*See* § 1.100)
- Directors' petition. (*See* § 1.101)
- Shareholders' petition. (*See* § 1.102)
- Shareholders' petition on deadlock of directors or shareholders. (*See* § 1.103)
- Shareholders' petition for circumstances of illegal, fraudulent, or oppressive action against petitioning shareholders or of corporate assets being looted, wasted, or diverted. (*See* § 1.103)
- Petition for judicial dissolution; contents. (*See* § 1.104)
- Order to show cause. (*See* § 1.104)
- Referee; hearing. (*See* § 1.104)
- Application for final order. (*See* § 1.104)
- Judgment or final order of dissolution. (*See* § 1.104)
- Venue. (*See* § 1.104)
- Discontinuance of action or proceeding. (*See* § 1.104)
- Preservation of assets; receiver. (*See* § 1.105)
- Injunction. (*See* § 1.106)
- Voidable transfers. (*See* § 1.106)

3. Liquidation distributions; federal income tax aspects. (*See* §§ 1.107, 108)

Library References:

West's Key No. Digests, Corporations ⚖ 592–630(6).

§ 1.111 Receivership

Appointment. A receiver of property of a domestic or foreign corporation may be appointed by a court in the following cases: (1) an action or special proceeding brought for non-judicial dissolution[1] or judicial dissolution;[2] (2) an action by a judgment creditor for sequestration;[3] (3) an action brought by the Attorney General or by a shareholder to preserve the assets of a corporation that has no officer within New York qualified to administer them;[4] or (4) an action to preserve any assets (tangible or intangible) located in New York of a foreign corporation that has been dissolved or nationalized or has its authority or existence otherwise terminated in the jurisdiction of its incorporation or

§ 1.111

1. NYBCL § 1202(a)(1). *See supra*, § 1.95.
2. NYBCL § 1202(a)(1). *See supra*, § 1.99.
3. NYBCL § 1202(a)(2). *See* NYBCL § 1201.
4. NYBCL § 1202(a)(3).

that has ceased to do business, if brought by a creditor or shareholder of the corporation or by one on whose behalf an order of attachment against such corporate property has been issued.[5]

Notice of an application for the appointment of a receiver must be given to the Attorney General and to other persons as the court directs.[6] A court's determination that a receiver, or an attorney for a receiver, should be appointed, and the allowance of expenses, commissions, or compensation to the receiver or the receiver's attorney, is subject to review on appeal.[7] A permanent receiver is a receiver appointed by, or a temporary receiver who is continued by, the final judgment or order.[8] The court may confer upon temporary receivers the powers, and subject them to the duties, of permanent receivers.[9]

Oath; Compensation. Before entering upon their duties, receivers must take and subscribe an oath that they will faithfully, honestly, and impartially discharge the trust committed to them.[10] A receiver must also obtain and file a bond in an amount fixed by the court to secure, and to be conditioned on, the faithful discharge of the receiver's duties.[11] The compensation of receivers is prescribed in the NYBCL.[12]

Designation of Depositories by Court. All orders appointing a receiver of a corporation must designate one or more places of deposit for all corporate funds not needed for immediate disbursement; no other deposits (and no investment) of the funds may be made except upon order of the court.[13]

Powers of Permanent Receiver. A permanent receiver, upon qualifying on oath and security, is vested with title to all the property of a domestic corporation wherever situated (or the property of a foreign corporation located in New York against which an action or special proceeding has been brought under NYBCL § 1202(a)(4)) for the benefit

---

5. NYBCL § 1202(a)(4).
6. NYBCL § 1203(a).
7. *Id.*
8. NYBCL § 1203(b).
9. *Id.*
10. NYBCL § 1204(a)(1). **Procedure.** The oath must be filed with the clerk of the court in which the action or special proceeding is pending. *Id.*
11. NYBCL § 1204(a)(2). The bond, payable to the people of New York, must have at least two sufficient sureties or be executed by any fidelity or surety company authorized by the laws of New York to transact business. *Id.* The court may, at any time, direct a receiver to give a new bond with new sureties and with like condition. *Id.*
12. NYBCL § 1217. A receiver, in addition to necessary expenses incurred, is entitled to such commissions upon the amounts received and disbursed, as may be allowed by the court, as follows: (1) on the first $20,000, not exceeding five percent; on the next $80,000, not exceeding two and one-half percent; and on the remainder, not exceeding one percent. NYBCL § 1217(a). If the commissions so computed do not amount to $100, the court in its discretion may allow an amount not exceeding $100 as shall be reasonable. NYBCL § 1217(b). When more than one receiver is appointed, they divide the compensation specified in NYBCL § 1217(a), as the court directs. NYBCL § 1217(c).
13. NYBCL § 1205.

of its creditors and shareholders.[14] Permanent receivers have the power to sue in their own name to recover the corporation's property and debts owed to, and causes of action of, the corporation.[15] They also have the power to sell at public or private sale all the property vested in them,[16] to examine on oath to be administered by them any person concerning any matter pertaining to the receivership,[17] and to settle or compound[18] any demands by or against the receivership.[19]

Duties of Receivers. Receivers must give immediate notice of their appointment by publication once a week for two successive weeks in two newspapers of general circulation in the county where the office of the corporation is located (or in the case of a foreign corporation against which an action has been brought under NYBCL § 1202(a)(4), in a newspaper of general circulation as directed by the court).[20] The receiver in the notice is obliged to require (1) debtors of the corporation to account for their debts owed the corporation and to pay the debts to the receiver;[21] (2) persons in possession of any property of the corporation to deliver it to the receiver;[22] and (3) creditors and claimants, including any with unliquidated or contingent claims and any with whom the corporation has unfulfilled contracts, to present their claims to the receiver in detail in writing not less than six months after the first publication of the notice.[23] The notice must stipulate that payment to the receiver be at a specified place and by a specified date.[24] Persons having possession of property belonging to the corporation who wrongfully retain the property after the day specified in the notice forfeit double the value of the property, which amount may be recovered in an action by the receiver.[25]

Receivers must call a general meeting of creditors of the corporation within four months after their appointment.[26] The call must be by notice published in the same manner as the notice of appointment and must set forth the time and place of the meeting.[27] The meeting date must be sometime between one and two months after the first publication of the notice.[28] At the meeting the receivers present a statement of all accounts and demands for and against the corporation, its subsisting contracts,

14. NYBCL § 1206(a).

15. NYBCL § 1206(b)(1). No set-off or counterclaim is allowed by the defendant in the action unless it was owing by the corporation to the defendant before the commencement of the action or special proceeding in which the receiver was appointed or unless it has been incurred by the receiver subsequent to being appointed. *Id.*

16. NYBCL § 1206(b)(2).

17. NYBCL § 1206(b)(3).

18. That is, to compromise or to effect a composition with a creditor.

19. NYBCL § 1206(b)(4).

20. NYBCL § 1207(a)(1).

21. NYBCL § 1207(a)(1)(A).

22. NYBCL § 1207(a)(1)(B).

23. NYBCL § 1207(a)(1)(C). Whenever a receiver is appointed in a non-judicial dissolution (NYBCL Article 10) or a judicial dissolution (NYBCL Article 11), NYBCL § 1007 controls the giving of notice to creditors and claimants and the filing and barring of claims. *Id.*

24. NYBCL § 1207(a)(1).

25. NYBCL § 1208.

26. NYBCL § 1207(a)(2).

27. *Id.*

28. *Id.*

and the money and other assets in their hands.[29] The order of payment to claimants against the corporation is set forth in the NYBCL.[30]

Receivers must keep true books of account of all moneys received and expended by them as receivers; the books must be open for inspection at reasonable times by creditors or other interested persons.[31] On or before the first day of February in each year, receivers must file with the clerk of the court by which they were appointed a verified statement for the preceding calendar year showing the assets received, their disposition, money on hand, all payments made (specifying payees and why paid), the amount necessary to be retained to meet necessary expenses of, and claims against, the receiver, and the distributive share in the remaining funds of each person interested in the funds.[32] A copy of the statement must be served by the receiver upon the Attorney General within five days after filing.[33]

Disposition of Funds; Final Accounting. Other matters set forth in the NYBCL pertaining to receivers' duties are final distribution by the receiver,[34] disposition of funds retained,[35] and a final accounting.[36]

Powers. Receivers have the power by verified petition to seek an order to enjoin or restrain the transfer of assets of the corporation that they believe are being wrongfully concealed, disposed of, or withheld.[37]

Omissions and Defaults. Upon notice to the Attorney General and upon such notice to creditors or others interested as the court shall direct, the court may, in the furtherance of justice, relieve a receiver from any omission or default, on such conditions as may be imposed and, upon compliance therewith, confirm the receiver's action.[38]

Removal; Vacancies. The Attorney General may move for an order (1) removing a receiver, (2) compelling the receiver to account, or (3) otherwise facilitating the closing of the receivership.[39] The NYBCL prescribes a procedure for resignation of a receiver and for filling any vacancy resulting from resignation, removal, death, or other cause.[40]

Foreign Corporations. Provisions relating to actions or special proceedings against foreign corporations are set forth in the NYBCL.[41]

§ 1.112 Receivership—Summary

The NYBCL deals with the various phases of receivership. Receivers may be imposed in actions or special proceedings brought for voluntary (non-judicial) and involuntary (judicial) dissolutions, actions by judgment

29. Id.
30. NYBCL § 1210.
31. NYBCL § 1207(a)(3).
32. Id.
33. Id.
34. NYBCL § 1211.
35. NYBCL § 1212.
36. NYBCL § 1216.
37. NYBCL § 1209.
38. NYBCL § 1213.
39. NYBCL § 1214.
40. NYBCL § 1215.
41. NYBCL § 1218.

creditors for sequestration, actions brought by the Attorney General or by shareholders to preserve the assets of a corporation that has no officer within New York, and actions brought by creditors or shareholders to preserve assets in New York of a foreign corporation that has been dissolved, nationalized, or otherwise terminated in its jurisdiction of incorporation.

A permanent receiver, upon qualifying on oath and security, is vested with title to all the property of a domestic corporation wherever situated (or the property located in New York of a foreign corporation against which an action or special proceeding has been brought) for the benefit of its creditors and shareholders. Permanent receivers have the power, among other powers, to sue in their own name to recover the corporation's property, to examine on oath to be administered by them any person concerning any matter pertaining to the receivership, to settle any demands by or against the receivership, and to seek, by verified petition, an order to enjoin or restrain assets of the corporation that they believe are being wrongfully concealed, disposed of, or withheld.

Library References:

West's Key No. Digests, Corporations ⚖621, 622.

§ 1.113 Receivership—Checklist

1. Sequestration action. (*See* § 1.111.)
2. Appointment of temporary and permanent receivers. (*See id.*)
3. Oath; security; depositories. (*See id.*)
4. Powers; duties. (*See id.*)
5. Penalties for concealing property from receiver. (*See id.*)
6. Recovery of assets. (*See id.*)
7. Order of payment of claims. (*See id.*)
8. Final distribution. (*See id.*)
9. Disposition of funds retained. (*See id.*)
10. Omissions and defaults of receiver. (*See id.*)
11. Removal of receiver; closing of receivership. (*See id.*)
12. Resignation; vacancies. (*See id.*)
13. Final accounting; notice; duty of Attorney General. (*See id.*)
14. Foreign corporations, proceedings against. (*See id.*)

Library References:

West's Key No. Digests, Corporations ⚖621, 622.

§ 1.114 Foreign Corporations

Foreign corporations are not permitted to do business in New York until they have been authorized to do so.[1] They may apply for authority to do business in New York by filing an application for authority with the Department of State.[2] After receiving authority to do business, they may also surrender it.[3] Dissolution in their home jurisdiction has the same effect in New York as a surrender of authority to do business in New York.[4] Foreign corporations authorized to do business in New York may sue,[5] and be sued,[6] within certain limits, in the state, but if they are not so authorized, they may not bring a suit in New York until all fees, penalties, and franchise taxes owed to New York have been paid.[7]

Foreign corporations must maintain in New York a record of shareholders subject to examination by qualified New York resident shareholders.[8] If a voting trust has been created, voting trust records must also be made available in New York for examination.[9] Directors and officers of foreign corporations are subject to liability under NYBCL §§ 719 (directors' liability) and 720 (action against directors and officers for misconduct) to the same extent as are directors and officers of domestic corporations.[10] Foreign corporations have an obligation, and are liable for the failure, to disclose information related to certain transactions in the same manner as domestic corporations.[11] Certain NYBCL provisions (in addition to those in NYBCL Article 13) apply to foreign corporations doing business in New York and their directors, officers and shareholders;[12] foreign corporations and their directors, officers, and

---

§ 1.114

1. *See infra*, § 1.115.
2. *See infra*, § 1.116.
3. *See infra*, § 1.118.
4. *See infra*, § 1.119.
5. NYBCL § 1313.
6. NYBCL § 1314. *See* NYBCL § 109(a)(6) and (c) (actions and special proceedings by Attorney General related to foreign corporations). *See also*, NYBCL § 109(b) (jury trial in actions; immunity; temporary restraining order; temporary receiver; attachment; subpoena).
7. NYBCL § 1312.
8. NYBCL § 1315(a). *See supra* § 1.53; *see also*, NYBCL §§ 1315(b) (denial of examination for refusal to furnish affidavit on purpose of examination and prior sale of record of shareholders) and 1315(c) (application to supreme court, upon denial of examination, to permit examination of record of shareholders).
9. NYBCL § 1316(a). *See also*, NYBCL §§ 1316(b) (deposit of voting trust agreement at foreign corporation's, or its transfer agent's, New York office); 1316(c) (right of examination); 1316(d) (application to supreme court, upon denial of examination, to permit examination of record of shareholders); 1316(e) (voting trust agreement is an express trust where the foreign corporation's principal business operations, or greater part of its property, is located within New York).
10. NYBCL § 1317. *See supra*, §§ 1.66 and 1.69.
11. NYBCL § 1318. *See supra*, §§ 1.38 and 1.39.
12. NYBCL § 1319 (NYBCL Articles 1 (definitions; application; certificates; miscellaneous) and 3 (corporate name; service of process); NYBCL §§ 623 (shareholder's right to payment), 626 (shareholders' derivative action), 627 (security for expenses), 721–727 (indemnification; insurance), 808 (reorganization under federal act), and 907 (short-form merger)).

shareholders are exempt from certain NYBCL provisions.[13]

§ 1.115 Foreign Corporations—Authorization to Do Business in New York

A foreign corporation may be authorized to do in New York any business that may be done lawfully by a domestic corporation, to the extent that the foreign corporation is authorized to do that business in the jurisdiction of its incorporation.[1] It may do no other business.[2]

A foreign corporation is not considered to be doing business in New York if it carries on any one or more of the following activities in New York: (1) maintaining, defending, or settling any action or proceeding (or settling other claims or disputes); (2) holding meetings of its directors or shareholders; (3) maintaining bank accounts; and (4) maintaining offices or agencies only for the transfer, exchange and registration of its securities, or appointing and maintaining trustees or depositaries with relation to its securities.[3] These activities do not establish a standard that subjects foreign corporations to service of process under the NYBCL or any other statute of New York.[4]

---

13. NYBCL § 1320 (NYBCL §§ 1316(e) (certain voting trusts), 1317(a)(1) (liabilities of directors and officers of foreign corporations), 1318 (disclosure obligations), 1319(a)(4) (indemnification; insurance)).

§ 1.115

1. NYBCL § 1301(a).

2. *Id.*

3. NYBCL § 1301(b).

PRACTICE POINTER: Doing business within New York requires a regular and continuous course of conduct, above a certain threshold, within New York; isolated or occasional transactions within the state are not enough. What does, and does not, constitute doing business is not always separated by a clear line. In close cases, thorough research of the relevant decisions must be undertaken. See NYBCL § 1301, Notes of Decisions, subd. II (doing business in state) (*e.g.*, not doing business: isolated instances in New York of advertising, bank accounts, brokerage accounts, consignments, investments, lawsuits, negotiations of contracts, or solicitation of business; doing business: long-continued practice, within New York, of purchasing or selling or of maintaining offices, salesrooms, officers' residences, or certain buying or selling agents' offices). *Cf.* RMBCA § 15.01 (activities within a state, among others, that do not constitute transacting business there: selling through independent contractors, soliciting orders that are accepted outside the state, owning (without more) real or personal property, an isolated transaction completed within thirty days, or transacting interstate (no intrastate) business). What constitutes doing business for purposes of requiring a foreign corporation to qualify to do business within New York (*see infra*, § 1.116) should be distinguished from the threshold of activity in New York that subjects a foreign corporation to process, taxation, or regulation. *See, e.g.*, NYBCL §§ 1301, Notes of Decisions, subd. I (generally) (regulation and taxation) and 1312(b); Henn and Alexander, pp. 201–235. Investment in real estate is not doing business within the meaning of the predecessor of NYBCL § 1312 (proceedings by unauthorized foreign corporations), unless the corporation is organized for that purpose. Singer Mfg. Co. v. Granite Spring Water Co., 66 Misc. 595, 123 N.Y.S. 1088 (Sup.Ct., N.Y. County, 1910). Although owning and operating rental realty would be doing business, query whether merely owning, without operating, the property (or owning unimproved property) would constitute doing business. *See infra*, § 1.115, note 4.

4. NYBCL § 1301(c).

CAVEAT: The corporation's owning real property in New York would subject the corporation to *in personam* jurisdiction under NYCPLR 302.

§ 1.115 BUSINESS ORGANIZATIONS: CORPORATIONS — Ch. 1

Fictitious Name. A foreign corporation whose corporate name is not acceptable for authorization pursuant to NYBCL §§ 301 and 302[5] may submit in its application for authority a fictitious name under which it will do business in New York.[6] A fictitious name submitted is subject to the provisions of NYBCL §§ 301(a)(2)-(a)(9)[7] and 302[8] on corporate names.[9]

Violations; Attorney General Action. The Attorney General may bring an action to restrain a foreign corporation from doing business in New York without authority, including any business not set forth in its application for authority, as amended.[10] For other violations, the Attorney General may bring actions or special proceedings to annul a foreign corporation's authority to do business in New York.[11] The Attorney General must deliver a certified copy of the order of annulment to the Department of State for filing.[12] Upon the filing of the order of annulment, the authority of the foreign corporation to do business in New York is annulled.[13] The Secretary of State continues as agent upon whom process may be served in any action or special proceeding based upon any liability or obligation incurred by the foreign corporation within New York *prior to* the filing of the order of annulment.[14]

Library References:
West's Key No. Digests, Corporations ⌦657(7).

§ 1.116 Foreign Corporations—Application for Authority

For a foreign corporation to qualify to do business within New York, it must file an application for authority with the Department of State.[1]

5. NYBCL § 1301(c). *See supra*, § 1.13.
6. NYBCL § 1301(d).
7. These subsections relate to fictitious, distinguishing, prohibited, misleading, and degrading names as well as names subject to approval of a regulatory authority.
8. This section contains exceptions to NYBCL § 301. *See, e.g.*, NYBCL § 302(b)(3) (foreign corporation with similar name to, but not in same business as, that of another corporation, where the public is unlikely to be deceived or confused).
9. NYBCL § 1301(d). A foreign corporation authorized to do business in New York under a fictitious name may use the fictitious name in all its dealings with the Secretary of State and in the conduct of its business in New York. *Id.*
CAVEAT: General Business Law § 130 (assumed names) does not apply to any fictitious name filed by a foreign corporation pursuant to NYBCL § 1301, and a filing under General Business Law § 130 does not constitute the adoption of a fictitious name. *Id. See supra*, § 1.13.

10. NYBCL § 1303.
11. NYBCL § 1303 (violations specified).
12. NYBCL § 1303.
13. *Id.*
14. *Id.*

§ 1.116

1. NYBCL §§ 1304 and 1305. ***Procedure.*** An application, entitled "Application for authority of .... (name of corporation) under section 1304 of the Business Corporation Law," must be signed and verified by an officer of or attorney-in-fact for the corporation and delivered to the Department of State. NYBCL § 1304(a). It must set forth: (1) the name of the foreign corporation; (2) the fictitious name, if any, the corporation agrees to use in New York

Library References:
West's Key No. Digests, Corporations ⊜657(7).

§ 1.117 Foreign Corporations—Application for Authority—Effect of Filing

Upon the filing of an application for authority by the Department of State, a foreign corporation is authorized to do in New York any business set forth in the application.[1] The authority continues so long as the foreign corporation has authority to do that business in the jurisdiction of its incorporation and its authority to do business in New York has not been surrendered, suspended, or annulled.[2] An authorized foreign corporation has the powers permitted by the laws of the jurisdiction of its incorporation but no greater powers than those of a domestic corporation formed for the business set forth in the application for authority.[3]

Amendments to Application for Authority. If an authorized foreign corporation has changed its name in the jurisdiction of its incorporation, or has changed its jurisdiction of incorporation, it must deliver to the New York Department of State within 20 days after the change became effective in that jurisdiction a certificate of amendment under NYBCL § 1309(a).[4] If it fails to deliver the certificate within the

pursuant to NYBCL § 1301, if applicable; (3) the jurisdiction and date of its incorporation; (4) the purposes for which it is formed, being sufficient to state, either alone or with other purposes, that the purpose of the corporation is to engage in any lawful act or activity for which corporations may be organized under the NYBCL, provided that it also state that it is not formed to engage in any act or activity requiring the consent or approval of any New York official, department, board, agency, or other body without the consent or approval first being obtained (by which statement all lawful acts and activities are within the purposes of the corporation, except for express limitations therein or in the NYBCL, if any); (5) the county within New York in which its office is to be located; (6) a designation of the Secretary of State as its agent upon whom process against it may be served and the post office address within or without New York to which the Secretary of State must mail a copy of the service of process; (7) if it is to have a registered agent, the agent's name and address within New York and a statement that the registered agent is to be its agent upon whom process against it may be served; (8) a statement that the foreign corporation has not since its incorporation or since the date its authority to do business in New York was last surrendered, engaged in any activity in New York, except as set forth in NYBCL § 1301(b), or in lieu thereof the consent of the New York State Tax Commission to the filing of the application, evidence of which consent must be attached. *Id.* A certificate by an authorized officer of the jurisdiction of its incorporation that the foreign corporation is an existing corporation must be attached to the application for authority. NYBCL § 1304(b). If the certificate is in a foreign language, a translation under oath of the translator must be attached. *Id.*

§ 1.117

1. NYBCL § 1305.

2. *Id.*

3. NYBCL § 1306. A foreign corporation may acquire and hold real property in New York in furtherance of its corporate purposes and may convey the property by deed or other means in the same manner as a domestic corporation. NYBCL § 1307.

4. NYBCL § 1309(c). *Cf.* RMBCA § 15.04 (foreign corporation must amend certificate of authority if it changes its name, its duration, or the jurisdiction of its incorporation).

20 days, its authority to do business in New York is suspended.[5] If a certificate of amendment is filed with the Department of State within 120 days after the effective date of the change of name or jurisdiction, the suspension is annulled, and the foreign corporation's authority to do business in New York is restored and continues as if no suspension had occurred.[6]

An authorized foreign corporation may amend or change its application for authority from time to time to do any and as many of the following as may be desired:[7] (1) change its corporate name, if the change has been effected under the laws of the jurisdiction of its incorporation; (2) change its fictitious name to another fictitious name, if its true corporate name is not available for use in New York; (3) delete its fictitious name, if its true corporate name is available for use in New York; (4) adopt a fictitious name, when its corporate name is changed and is not available in New York; (5) enlarge, limit, or otherwise change the business that it proposes to do in New York; (6) change the location of its office in New York; (7) specify or change the post office address to which the Secretary of State is to mail a copy of service of process; (8) make, revoke, or change the designation of a registered agent or to specify or change the agent's address; and (9) change the jurisdiction of its incorporation if the change has been effected under laws permitting the change.[8]

---

5. NYBCL § 1309(c).

6. *Id.*

7. NYBCL § 1308. The amendments must include only provisions that would be lawfully contained in an application for authority at the time of making the amendment. *Id.*

8. NYBCL § 1308. *Procedure*. A certificate, entitled "Certificate of amendment of application for authority of .... (name of corporation) under section 1309 of the Business Corporation Law," must be signed and verified by an officer of or attorney-in-fact for the foreign corporation and delivered to the Department of State. It must set forth: (1) the name of the foreign corporation (as it appears on the index of names of corporations in the Department of State, Division of Corporations) and the fictitious name, if any, the corporation has agreed to use in New York pursuant to NYBCL § 1301(d); (2) the jurisdiction of its incorporation, and if the jurisdiction of its incorporation has been changed, a statement that the change has been effected under laws permitting the change to occur, citing the laws, and including the date the change was effected and a statement that annexed to the certificate of amendment of application for authority is the certificate required by NYBCL § 1309(b); (3) the date it was authorized to do business in New York; (4) each amendment effected; (5) if the true corporate name of the foreign corporation is to be changed, a statement that the change of name has been effected under the laws of the jurisdiction of its incorporation and the date of the change; (6) if the business it proposes to do in New York is to be enlarged, limited, or otherwise changed, a statement that it is authorized to do in the jurisdiction of its incorporation the business that it proposes to do in New York. NYBCL § 1309(a). If the jurisdiction of its incorporation has been changed, a certificate by an authorized officer of the new jurisdiction that the foreign corporation is an existing corporation domiciled in that jurisdiction must be annexed to the certificate of amendment of application for authority. NYBCL § 1309(b). If the annexed certificate is not in the English language, a translation into English under oath of the translator must be attached. *Id.* The Secretary of State continues as agent for service of process in the manner set forth in NYBCL § 306(b) in any action or special proceeding based upon liabilities incurred by the foreign corporation within New York before the filing of the certificate of amendment. NYBCL § 1309(c).

Changes in Application for Authority. In lieu of a certificate of amendment, an authorized foreign corporation may make the following *changes* in its application for authority: (1) a change of location of its office in New York; (2) a change (or designation) of the post office address to which the Secretary of State must mail a copy of service of process; (3) the designation, revocation, or change of the designation of a registered agent or a change (or designation) of the agent's address.[9] A certificate of change of application for authority that changes only the post office address to which the Secretary of State must mail a copy of service of process or changes the address of its registered agent may be undertaken by the agent.[10]

Library References:

West's Key No. Digests, Corporations ⊗=657(7).

§ 1.118 Foreign Corporations—Surrender of Authority

An authorized foreign corporation may surrender its authority to do business in New York.[1] The authority of the foreign corporation to do

---

9. NYBCL § 1309–A(a). *Procedure.* A certificate entitled "Certificate of change of application for authority of .... (name of corporation) under section 1309–A of the Business Corporation Law" must be signed and verified by an officer or attorney-in-fact for the foreign corporation and delivered to the Department of State. It must set forth: (1) the name of the foreign corporation (as it appears on the index of names of corporations in the Department of State, Division of Corporations) and the fictitious name, if any, the corporation has agreed to use in New York pursuant to NYBCL § 1301(d); (2) the jurisdiction of its incorporation; (3) the date it was authorized to do business in New York; and (4) each change effected by the certificate of change. NYBCL § 1309–A(b).

10. NYBCL § 1309–A(c). The post office address must be that of the agent whose address is to be changed. *Id. Procedure.* The certificate may be signed, verified, and delivered to the Department of State by the agent. *Id.* The certificate of change of application for authority must set forth the statements required by NYBCL § 1309–A(b), that a notice of the proposed change was mailed by the signatory of the certificate to the authorized foreign corporation not less than thirty days before delivery to the Department of State, that the corporation has not objected to the change, and that the signatory is the agent of the foreign corporation to whose address the Secretary of State is required to mail copies of process or the registered agent, if such be the case. *Id.* A certificate signed, verified, and delivered under NYBCL § 1309–A does not effect a change of location of the office of the foreign corporation. *Id.*

§ 1.118

1. NYBCL § 1310(a). *Procedure.* A certificate, entitled "Certificate of surrender of authority of .... (name of corporation) under section 1310 of the Business Corporation Law," must be signed, verified by an officer of or attorney-in-fact for the foreign corporation or by a trustee, receiver, or other liquidator of the corporation, and delivered to the Department of State. NYBCL § 1310(a). It must set forth: (1) the name of the foreign corporation (as it appears on the index of names of corporations in the Department of State, Division of Corporations) and the fictitious name, if any, the corporation has agreed to use in New York pursuant to NYBCL § 1301(d); (2) the jurisdiction of its incorporation; (3) the date it was authorized to do business in New York; (4) that it surrenders its authority to do business in New York; (5) that it revokes the authority of its registered agent, if any, previously designated and consents that process against it in any action or special proceeding based upon any liability or obligation incurred by it within New York before the filing of the certificate of surrender may be served on the Secretary of State after the filing of the certificate in the manner set forth in NYBCL § 306(b); and (6) a post office ad-

§ 1.118 BUSINESS ORGANIZATIONS: CORPORATIONS   Ch. 1

business in New York terminates on the filing by the Department of State of the certificate of surrender of authority.[2] The post office address set forth in the certificate of surrender of authority to which the Secretary of State must mail a copy of any service of process against the foreign corporation may be changed.[3]

Library References:
West's Key No. Digests, Corporations ⚖=657(7).

§ 1.119 Foreign Corporations—Termination of Existence

An authorized foreign corporation's authority to do business in New York terminates when it is (1) dissolved or its authority or existence is otherwise terminated or cancelled in the jurisdiction of its incorporation or (2) merged into or consolidated with another foreign corporation.[1]

§ 1.120 Foreign Corporations Summary

Foreign corporations are not permitted to do business in New York until they have been authorized to do so. They may apply for authority to do business in New York by filing an application for authority with the Department of State. They may also surrender their authority, and

---

dress within or without New York to which the Secretary of State must mail a copy of any service of process against the foreign corporation. NYBCL § 1310(a). The Department of State may not file the certificate unless evidence of the consent of the New York State Tax Commission to the surrender of authority is attached. NYBCL § 1310(b).

2. NYBCL § 1310(c).

3. NYBCL § 1310(d). *Procedure*. A certificate, entitled "Certificate of amendment of certificate of surrender of authority of .... (name of corporation) under section 1310 of the Business Corporation Law," must be signed, verified as provided in NYBCL § 1310(a), and delivered to the Department of State. *Id.* It must set forth: (1) the name of the foreign corporation; (2) the jurisdiction of its incorporation; (3) the date its certificate of surrender of authority was filed by the Department of State; and (4) the changed post office address, within or without New York, to which the Secretary of State must mail a copy of any service of process against the foreign corporation. *Id.*

§ 1.119

1. NYBCL § 1311. *Procedure*. A certificate of the Secretary of State of the jurisdiction of incorporation of the foreign corporation attesting to the occurrence of any of these events must be delivered to the Department of State. *Id.* If any such event was effected by order of a court of the jurisdiction directing the dissolution, termination, or cancellation, a certified copy of the order must be delivered to the Department of State. *Id.* The filing of the certificate or order has the same effect as the filing of a certificate of surrender of authority. *Id.* The Secretary of State continues as agent of the foreign corporation upon whom process against the foreign corporation may be served in the manner set forth in NYBCL § 306(b) in any action or special proceeding based upon any liability or obligation incurred by the foreign corporation within New York prior to the filing of the certificate or order. *Id.* The Secretary of State must promptly cause a copy of the process to be mailed by registered mail, return receipt requested, to the foreign corporation at the post office address on file in the Secretary of State's office. *Id.* The post office address may be changed by signing, verifying, and delivering to the Department of State a certificate of change setting forth the statements required under NYBCL § 1309–A to effect a change in the post office address under NYBCL § 1308(a)(7). *Id.*

dissolution in their jurisdiction has the same effect in New York as a surrender of their authority. Even if a foreign corporation is not authorized to do business in New York, it may be sued in New York, within certain limits, but it may not bring a suit in New York until all fees, penalties, and franchise taxes owed the state have been paid. The NYBCL sets standards, which are similar to those applicable to domestic corporations, for the liability of directors and officers and for disclosure obligations with respect to certain transactions. The NYBCL also requires that a foreign corporation maintain within New York a record of shareholders (and a record of voting trust certificate holders, if a voting trust exists) subject to the right of examination similar to that accorded the holders of such interests in domestic corporations.

Library References:

West's Key No. Digests, Corporations ⚖=631–691.

§ 1.121 Foreign Corporations Checklist

1. Authorization to do business; fictitious name; violations. (*See* § 1.115)

2. Application for authority; contents; effect. (*See* §§ 1.116, 1.117)

    • Certificate of amendment; contents. (*See* § 1.117)

    • Certificate of change; contents. (*See id.*)

3. Powers of authorized foreign corporations. (*See id.*)

4. Holding real property in New York. (*See id.*)

5. Amendments to application for authority; changes. (*See id.*)

6. Surrender of authority. (*See* § 1.118)

    • Certificate of surrender of authority; contents. (*See id.*)

    • Certificate of amendment of certificate of surrender of authority; contents. (*See id.*)

7. Termination of existence; certificate of. (*See* § 1.119)

8. Proceedings by and against foreign corporations. (*See* § 1.114)

9. Record of shareholders; voting trust records. (*See id.*)

10. Liabilities of directors and officers of foreign corporations. (*See id.*)

11. Disclosure obligations of foreign corporations. (*See id.*)

12. NYBCL applicability and exemptions. (*See id.*)

Library References:

West's Key No. Digests, Corporations ⚖=631–691.

§ 1.122 Professional Service Corporations

Organization; Certificate of Incorporation. Individuals duly authorized by law to render professional services within New York may organize a professional service corporation for pecuniary profit under NYBCL Article 15 to render that professional service.[1] Individuals duly authorized by law to practice professional engineering, architecture, landscape architecture, or land surveying within New York may organize a professional service corporation to render such professional services as the individuals are authorized to practice.[2]

The certificate of incorporation of a professional service corporation must (1) meet the requirements of the NYBCL, (2) state the profession or professions to be practiced by the corporation and the names and residence addresses of all individuals who are to be the original shareholders, directors, and officers of the corporation, and (3) have attached certificates issued by the licensing authority certifying that each of the proposed shareholders, directors, and officers is authorized by law to practice the (or each) profession that the corporation is being organized to practice.[3]

Licensing Authorities' Continued Jurisdiction. A professional service corporation (other than one authorized to practice law) is under the supervision of the regents of the University of the State of New York and is subject to disciplinary proceedings and penalties, and its certificate of incorporation is subject to suspension, revocation, or annulment for cause, in the same manner and to the same extent as is provided with respect to individuals and their licenses, certificates, and registrations in NYEDUC Title VIII relating to the applicable profession.[4]

§ 1.122

1. NYBCL § 1503(a). As used in NYBCL Article 15, unless the context otherwise requires, the term: (a) "licensing authority" means the regents of the University of the State of New York or the State Education Department, as the case may be, in the case of all professions licensed under Education Law Title VIII, and the appropriate appellate division of the supreme court, in the case of the profession of law; (b) "profession" includes any practice as an attorney or a counselor-at-law, as a licensed physician, and as a practitioner in those occupations designated in Education Law Title 8; (c) "professional service" means any type of service to the public that may be lawfully rendered by members of a profession within the purview of their profession; (d) "professional service corporation" means a corporation organized under NYBCL Article 15; (e) "officer" does not include the secretary or an assistant secretary of a corporation having only one shareholder. NYBCL § 1501.

2. NYBCL § 1503(a).

3. NYBCL § 1503(b). ***Procedure.*** A certified copy of the certificate of incorporation and of each amendment thereto must be filed by the corporation with the appropriate licensing authority within 30 days after filing with the Department of State. NYBCL § 1503(c).

4. NYBCL § 1503(d). A professional service corporation authorized to practice medicine is subject to the prehearing and hearing procedures provided with respect to individual physicians and their licenses in the Public Health Law Article 2, Title II–A. *Id.* A corporation authorized to practice law is subject to the regulation and control of, and its certificate of incorporation subject to suspension, revocation, or annulment for cause by, the appellate division of the supreme court and the Court of Appeals in the same manner and to the same extent provided in the Judiciary Law with respect to individual attorneys and counsellors-at-law; the corporation need not qualify for

§ 1.122   Rendering of Professional Services; Professional Relationships and Liabilities

Rendering of Professional Services; Professional Relationships and Liabilities. Professional service corporations may render professional services only through individuals authorized by law to render the professional services.[5] The documents issued by professional service corporations (*e.g.*, architectural plans, engineering reports, medical diagnoses, shorthand transcripts, accounting records, or legal opinions) must be signed by the professional in responsible charge (or in the case of accountants, responsible).[6]

Shareholders, employees, or agents of a professional service corporation are personally and fully liable and accountable for any negligent or wrongful act or misconduct committed by them or by any person under their direct supervision and control while rendering professional services on behalf of the corporation.[7] That individual professionals are shareholders, directors, officers, employees, or agents of a professional service corporation does not modify or diminish the jurisdiction over them of the licensing authority and, in the case of attorneys and counsellors-at-law,

any certification under the Judiciary Law § 464, take an oath of office under the Judiciary Law § 466, or register under the Judiciary Law § 467. NYBCL § 1503(e).

5. NYBCL § 1504(a).

CAVEAT: A professional service corporation is susceptible to being taxed as a personal holding company for federal income tax purposes. I.R.C. §§ 541–547. The tax on personal holding companies, in addition to the regular tax on corporations, is 39.6 percent on undistributed personal holding company income. I.R.C. § 541. This undistributed income includes investment income such as dividends, interest, royalties, and rents. I.R.C. § 543(a). It also includes certain compensation paid to shareholders owning twenty-five percent or more of the corporation who are also under personal services contracts (*i.e.*, income received by the corporation from contracts for personal services that give some person *other than* the corporation the right to designate (or in which the contract designates) the individual to perform the services and the designated individual owns at least twenty-five percent of the corporation's stock at *some* time during the year). I.R.C. § 543(a)(7). Although this tax was intended to cover such activities as incorporated pocketbooks (corporation holds investment securities) and incorporated talent (highly compensated actor or other individual works for corporation at relatively modest salary while corporation contracts out the individual's services at the much higher market value), it is applicable to professional service corporations.

CAVEAT: For the risk of a professional service corporation being classified by the IRS as a personal service corporation with reallocation by the IRS of income, deductions, and other allowances of the corporation, *see* § 1.34, notes 22–25 and accompanying text.

PRACTICE POINTER: If the *corporation* (rather than the person seeking to obtain the services) designates who is to perform the services, the corporation would appear to be clear of the risk of being treated as a personal holding company. If the contract also requires the services by other persons who are important and essential, only the income allocable to the twenty-five percent shareholder is personal holding company income. Treas. Reg. § 1.543–1(b)(8)(ii). *See also*, I.R.C. § 543(a)(6) (compensation received by corporation from twenty-five percent or more shareholder for use of corporate property by that shareholder).

6. NYBCL § 1504(b)-(f). In addition, documents prepared by a corporation that under the rules, regulations, laws, or customs of the applicable profession are required to bear the signature of individuals in responsible charge of the document must be signed by those individuals. NYBCL § 1504(g).

7. NYBCL § 1505(a). *See, e.g.*, We're Associates Co. v. Cohen, Stracher & Bloom, P.C., 65 N.Y.2d 148, 490 N.Y.S.2d 743, 480 N.E.2d 357 (1985).

the courts of New York.[8] A professional service corporation may not engage in any business other than the rendering of the professional services for which it was incorporated; the corporation may, however, invest its funds in real estate, mortgages, stocks, bonds, or other investments.[9]

Issuance of Shares. A professional service corporation may issue shares only to individuals who are authorized by law to practice in New York a profession that the corporation is authorized to practice and who are or have been engaged in the practice of the profession in the corporation or its predecessor or who will engage in the practice of the profession in the corporation within 30 days after the date the shares are issued.[10] Shareholders of a professional service corporation may not enter into a voting trust agreement, proxy or any other type agreement vesting in other persons (except other shareholders or persons who would be eligible to become shareholders if employed by the corporation) the authority to exercise voting power of their shares.[11] All shares issued, agreements made or proxies granted in violation of this rule are void.[12]

Shareholders, Directors, Officers, and Employees; Qualification and Disqualification. Individuals may not be directors or officers of a professional service corporation unless they are authorized by law to practice in New York a profession that the corporation is authorized to practice and are either shareholders of the corporation or engaged in the practice of their profession in the corporation.[13] Shareholders, directors, officers, or employees of the corporation who become disqualified to practice their profession in New York must sever all employment with, and financial interests (other than as a creditor) in, the corporation forthwith or as otherwise provided in NYBCL § 1510.[14] Their legal disqualification to practice their profession within New York is deemed to constitute an irrevocable offer by the disqualified shareholders to sell their shares to the corporation pursuant to the provisions of NYBCL § 1510[15] or of the certificate of incorporation, bylaws or agreement among the corporation and all shareholders, whichever is applicable.[16] Compliance with the terms of the offer are specifically enforceable in the courts of New York.[17] A professional service corporation's failure to enforce compliance with the offer's terms constitutes a ground for forfeiture of its certificate of incorporation and its dissolution.[18]

8. NYBCL § 1505(b).
9. NYBCL § 1506.
10. NYBCL § 1507.
11. *Id.*
12. *Id.*
13. NYBCL § 1508.
14. NYBCL § 1509. Section 1509 also incorporates other provisions of law regulating the rendering of professional services by shareholders, directors, officers and employees of a professional corporation who are elected or appointed to public office.

15. *See infra,* § 1.122, notes 19–23 and accompanying text.
16. NYBCL § 1509.
17. *Id.*
18. *Id.*

Death or Disqualification of Shareholders; Corporate Purchase of Shares. When a shareholder dies or is disqualified, a professional service corporation must purchase or redeem the shareholder's shares within six months after the appointment of the executor or other legal representative of the shareholder's estate or the shareholder's disqualification, as the case may be.[19] Unless otherwise determined by the certificate of incorporation, the bylaws, or an agreement among the corporation and *all* shareholders, the purchase or redemption price must be equal to the book value of the shares at the end of the month immediately preceding the death or disqualification as determined from the corporation's books and records in accordance with its regular method of accounting.[20] The certificate of incorporation, bylaws or such agreement may set a different payment period.[21] If the corporation fails to purchase or redeem the shares within the required period, a successful plaintiff in an action to recover the purchase price of the shares shall be awarded reasonable attorneys' fees and costs.[22] The corporation is not required to purchase or redeem the shares of a deceased or disqualified shareholder if the shares, within the six month time limits prescribed, are sold or transferred to another professional.[23]

Transfer of Shares. Shareholders of a professional service corporation may sell or transfer their shares only to individuals who are eligible to have shares issued to them by the corporation (or issued in trust to individuals who would be eligible to receive shares if they were employed by the corporation).[24] Shares may be transferred by operation of law or by court decree,[25] but the transferees may not vote the shares for any purpose except with respect to corporate action under NYBCL §§ 909 (on the sale or other disposition of all or substantially all of a corporation's assets) and 1001 (on authorization of dissolution).[26] This restriction does not apply, however, where the transferees would be eligible to have shares issued to them if they were employees of the corporation and, if the corporation has other shareholders, a majority of the other shareholders fail to redeem the shares transferred (pursuant to NYBCL § 1510) within 60 days after receiving written notice of the transfer.[27]

19. NYBCL § 1510(a).

20. *Id.*

21. *Id.* Nothing in NYBCL § 1510 prevents a corporation from paying, or continuing to pay, pension benefits or other deferred compensation to or on behalf of a former or deceased officer, director, or employee as otherwise permitted by law. *Id.*

22. NYBCL § 1510(a).

CAVEAT: Limitations on the purchase or redemption of shares set forth in NYBCL § 513 do not apply to the purchase or redemption of shares pursuant to NYBCL § 1510. *Id.* The corporation is not required to purchase the shares of disqualified shareholders where the period of disqualification is for less than six months and they again are eligible to practice their profession within six months after the date of disqualification. *Id.*

23. NYBCL § 1510(b). See NYBCL § 1511.

24. NYBCL § 1511.

25. *Id.*

26. *Id.*

27. *Id.*

Any sale or transfer of shares (except by operation of law or court decree and except for a corporation having only one shareholder) may be made only after the sale or transfer has been approved by the board of directors or at a special shareholders' meeting called for that purpose by at least a majority of the outstanding shares, as may be provided in the certificate of incorporation or the bylaws of the professional service corporation.[28] At the shareholders' meeting the shares held by the shareholder proposing to sell or transfer the shares may not be voted or counted for any purpose, unless all shareholders consent.[29] In cases where shares are proposed to be transferred, the certificate of incorporation or the bylaws, or the professional service corporation and the shareholders by agreement, may require the corporation to redeem or purchase the shares on specified terms.[30] The existence of the restrictions on the sale or transfer of shares (under the provisions of NYBCL Article 15 or, if applicable, in the certificate of incorporation, bylaws, or shareholders' agreement) must be noted conspicuously on the face or back of every certificate of the corporation's issued shares, and any sale or transfer in violation of the restrictions is void.[31]

Corporate Name. The name of a professional service corporation may contain any word that, at the time of incorporation, could be used in the name of a partnership practicing a profession that the corporation is authorized to practice.[32] The name of the corporation may not contain the name of a deceased person unless the person's name was part of (1) the corporate name at the time of the person's death or (2) the name of an existing partnership and at least two-thirds of the partnership's partners become shareholders of the corporation.[33] The corporate name must end with the words "Professional Corporation" or the abbreviation "P.C."[34]

Business Corporation Law Applicable. The NYBCL is applicable to professional service corporations, except for NYBCL Article 13 (foreign corporations) and NYBCL Article 15–A (foreign professional service corporations) and except to the extent that NYBCL provisions conflict with NYBCL Article 15 (professional service corporations).[35]

Corporate Mergers, Consolidations, and Other Reorganizations. Pursuant to the provisions of NYBCL Article 9 on mergers and consolidations, a professional service corporation may be merged or consolidated with a domestic corporation or with a foreign corporation,

28. Id.
29. Id.
30. Id.
31. Id.
32. NYBCL § 1512(a).
33. Id.
34. NYBCL § 1512(b).

CAVEAT: NYBCL § 301(a)(1) (requirement that corporate name contain "corporation," "incorporated," or "limited," or an abbreviation thereof) does not apply to a professional service corporation. Id.

35. NYBCL § 1513.

or may be otherwise reorganized.[36] However, the corporation that survives (or is formed in a consolidation) must be a professional service corporation or a foreign professional service corporation authorized to practice its profession in New York or its state of incorporation.[37] Restrictions on the issuance, transfer or sale of shares are suspended for a period not to exceed 30 days with respect to any issuance, transfer or sale of shares made pursuant to the merger, consolidation or reorganization, during which period only eligible shareholders may vote their shares of, or receive distributions from, the corporation.[38] The professional service corporation that survives (or is created) is subject to all the provisions of NYBCL Article 15, and its shares may be held only by eligible persons.[39] Despite the NYBCL provisions permitting mergers, consolidations or reorganizations of professional service corporations with other corporations, a corporation may provide professional services in New York through qualified individuals only if it is incorporated under NYBCL Article 15, authorized to do business in New York under NYBCL Article 15–A, or authorized and registered to practice a profession under Education Law Article 145.[40]

Limited Liability Companies and Limited Liability Partnerships. A professional service corporation may be a member of a professional service limited liability company, a foreign professional service limited liability company, a registered limited liability partnership or a foreign limited liability partnership.[41] It may be a member, however, only if all the professions practiced by the limited liability company or limited liability partnership could be practiced by a single corporation organized under NYBCL Article 15.[42]

36. For the purposes of NYBCL § 1516, other reorganizations are limited to those reorganizations defined in I.R.C. § 368(a)(1). NYBCL § 1516.

37. NYBCL § 1516. If one of the original corporations is authorized to practice engineering, land surveying, or architecture, the corporation that survives (or is formed in a consolidation) must be a corporation authorized and registered to practice the same profession pursuant to the applicable law on engineers, land surveyors, or architects. *Id.* A professional service corporation may consolidate or merge with another domestic professional service corporation, with a foreign professional service corporation authorized to do business in New York, or with a corporation authorized and registered to practice engineering and land surveying or architecture in New York, provided, however, that all of the professions practiced by the corporations could be practiced by a single corporation organized under NYBCL Article 15. NYBCL § 1513. *See* Education Law §§ 7209(6) (engineers and land surveyors) and 7307(4) (architects).

38. NYBCL § 1516.

39. *Id.*

40. *Id.*

41. NYBCL § 1513. *See* Chapter 2 "Non–Corporate Entities: Limited Liability Companies and Partnerships," *infra. See also,* Walker, *New York Limited Liability Companies and Partnerships: A Guide to Law and Practice* (West 1995) pp. 283, 324–325 (1995); Banoff, *Alphabet Soup: A Navigator's Guide*, Business Law Today 10, 12, 14–16 (vol. 4, number 4 March/April 1995); Lurie, *A Closer Look, How LLPs and LLCs Have Changed the Pension World*, N.Y. State Bar News 9–11 (vol. 37, number 7 Nov./Dec. 1995); Reuben, *Law Practice, Added Protection—Law Firms are Discovering That Limited Liability Business Structures Can Shield Them From Devastating Malpractice Awards and Double Taxation,* A.B.A.J. 54–57 (vol. 80, Sept. 1994).

42. NYBCL § 1513.

Triennial Statement. Every three years, on or before the first day of July, a professional service corporation must furnish a statement to the applicable licensing authority listing the names and residence addresses of its shareholders, directors and officers and certifying that they are authorized by law in New York to practice a profession that the corporation is authorized to practice.[43] The statement must be signed by the president or any vice-president of the corporation and attested to by the secretary or any assistant secretary of the corporation.[44]

§ 1.123 Professional Service Corporations Summary

Individuals duly authorized by law to render professional services within New York may organize a professional service corporation for the purpose of rendering the same professional service. The certificate of incorporation of a professional service corporation must meet the requirements of the NYBCL and state the profession(s) to be practiced by the corporation and the names and residence addresses of all individuals who are to be the corporation's original shareholders, directors and officers. It must have attached certificates issued by the licensing authority certifying that each of the proposed shareholders, directors and officers is authorized by law to practice the (or each) profession that the corporation is being organized to practice. A certified copy of the certificate of incorporation and of each amendment to it must be filed by the corporation with the licensing authority within 30 days after the filing of the certificate or amendment with the Department of State. Licensing authorities continue their jurisdiction over the practice of the profession by the corporation.

Shareholders, employees or agents of a professional service corporation are personally and fully liable for any negligence or misconduct committed by them or by any person under their direct supervision and control while rendering professional services on behalf of the corporation. The corporation may issue shares only to individuals who are authorized by law to practice in New York a profession that the corporation is authorized to practice. Individuals may not be directors or officers of the corporation unless they are similarly authorized to practice and are either shareholders of the corporation or engaged in the practice of their profession in the corporation. Shareholders, directors, officers or employees of a professional service corporation who become disqualified to practice in New York must sever all employment with and financial interests (other than as a creditor) in the corporation.

When shareholders die or are disqualified, the corporation must purchase or redeem their shares within six months after the appointment of the executor or other legal representative of the estate of a deceased shareholder or after the shareholder's disqualification, as the

---

43. NYBCL § 1514.

44. *Id.*

case may be, unless certain other permitted terms under the NYBCL for the purchase are set forth in the certificate of incorporation, bylaws or shareholders' agreement. Shareholders may sell or transfer their shares only to individuals who are eligible to have shares issued to them by the corporation (or issued in trust to individuals who would be eligible to receive shares if they were employed by the corporation).

The corporation's name may contain any word that at the time of incorporation could be used in the name of a partnership practicing a profession that the corporation is authorized to practice. A professional service corporation may be merged or consolidated with a domestic corporation or with a foreign corporation, or may be otherwise reorganized if the corporation that survives (or is formed in a consolidation) is a professional service corporation authorized to practice in New York or a foreign professional service corporation authorized to practice in its jurisdiction.

A professional service corporation may be a member of a professional service limited liability company, a foreign professional service limited liability company, a registered limited liability partnership, or a foreign limited liability partnership. It may be a member, however, only if all the professions practiced by the limited liability companies or limited liability partnerships could be practiced by a single professional service corporation.

Every three years on or before the first day of July, a professional service corporation must furnish a statement to its licensing authority. The statement must list the names and residence addresses of its shareholders, directors, and officers and certify that they are authorized by law in New York to practice a profession that the corporation is authorized to practice.

Library References:
West's Key No. Digests, Corporations ⚖︎377.5.

§ 1.124 Professional Service Corporations Checklist

1. Organization of professional service corporation. (*See* § 1.122)
2. Certificate of incorporation; amendments. (*See id.*)
3. Licensing authority's jurisdiction. (*See id.*)
4. Rendering of professional service. (*See id.*)
    - Documents issued.
    - Professional relationships.
    - Liabilities.
    - Investments permitted.
5. Issuance of shares. (*See id.*)

§ 1.124 BUSINESS ORGANIZATIONS: CORPORATIONS   Ch. 1

6. Shareholders, directors, officers, and employees. (*See id.*)
   - Qualification.
   - Disqualification.
        (i) Irrevocable offer to sell shares to corporation.
        (ii) Offer specifically enforceable in New York courts.
        (iii) Failure to comply with offer; forfeiture; dissolution.
   - Death.
   - Corporate purchase of shares; death or disqualification.
7. Transfer of shares. (*See id.*)
8. Corporate name. (*See id.*)
9. NYBCL applicability. (*See id.*)
10. Corporate mergers and other reorganizations. (*See id.*)
11. LLCs and LLPs. (*See id.*)
12. Triennial statement. (*See id.*)

Library References:

West's Key No. Digests, Corporations ⋘377.5.

§ 1.125 Foreign Professional Service Corporations

Rendering of Professional Service. Foreign professional service corporations[1] may render professional services in New York only through individuals authorized by law to render those professional services as individuals in New York.[2] Documents (*e.g.*, architectural plans, engineering reports, medical diagnoses, shorthand transcripts, accounting records

§ 1.125

1. Unless the context otherwise requires, the term: (a) "foreign professional service corporation" means a professional service corporation, whether or not denominated as such, organized under the laws of a jurisdiction other than New York, all of the shareholders, directors and officers of which are authorized and licensed to practice the profession for which the corporation is licensed to do business (but all shareholders, directors, and officers of a foreign professional service corporation that provides health services in New York must be licensed in New York); (b) "licensing authority" means the regents of the University of the State of New York or the New York State Education Department, as the case may be, in the case of all professions licensed under Education Law Title VIII, and the appropriate appellate division of the supreme court in the case of the profession of law; (c) "profession" includes any practice as an attorney and counsellor-at-law, or as a licensed physician, and those professions designated in Education Law Title VIII; (d) "professional service" means any type of service to the public that may be lawfully rendered by a member of a profession within the purview of his or her profession; (e) "officer" does not include the secretary or an assistant secretary of a corporation having only one shareholder. NYBCL § 1525.

2. NYBCL § 1525. This restriction is emphasized in NYBCL § 1533, which states that officers, directors, shareholders or employees of foreign professional service corporations are prohibited from practicing their profession in New York unless they are duly licensed to practice in New York. NYBCL § 1533.

or legal opinions) issued by foreign professional service corporations must be signed by the professional in responsible charge.[3] In addition, documents prepared by a foreign professional corporation that under the rules, regulations, laws, or customs of the applicable profession are required to bear the signature of individuals in responsible charge of the document must be signed by the individuals licensed to practice in New York.[4] A foreign professional service corporation must not engage in any business in New York other than the rendering of the professional services for which it is incorporated and is authorized to do in New York, but the corporation may invest its funds in real estate, mortgages, stocks, bonds or other investments.[5]

Professional Relationships and Liabilities. Shareholders, employees, or agents of a foreign professional service corporation who perform professional services in New York on behalf of the corporation are personally and fully liable and accountable for any negligent or wrongful act or misconduct committed by them (or by any person under their direct supervision and control) while rendering the professional services.[6] They bear professional responsibility for the corporation's compliance with all laws, rules, and regulations governing the practice of its profession in New York.[7] Applicable licensing authorities continue to have jurisdiction over the individuals rendering professional services in New York for a foreign professional service corporation.[8]

Business Corporation Law Applicable. Except for the provisions of NYBCL §§ 1303 (violations), 1304 (application for authority), 1316 (voting trust records), 1317 (liabilities of directors and officers), and 1320 (exemptions), the NYBCL is applicable to foreign professional service corporations unless its provisions conflict with NYBCL Article 15–A (foreign professional service corporations).[9] A foreign professional service corporation may practice in New York, may consolidate or merge with another corporation, or may be a member of a professional service limited liability company, a foreign professional service limited liability company, a registered limited liability partnership, or foreign limited liability partnership, *only if* all of the professions practiced by the corporation, limited liability company, or limited liability partnership could be practiced by a single professional service corporation organized in New York[10] and *if* the foreign professional service corporation is domiciled in a state or territory of the United States whose laws, at the

3. NYBCL § 1526(b)-(f).
4. NYBCL § 1526(g).
5. NYBCL § 1528.

CAVEAT: Beware of the personal holding company tax. *See supra*, § 1.122, note 5. For the risk of professional service corporation being classified by the IRS as a personal service corporation with reallocation by the IRS of income, deductions and other allowances of the corporation, *see supra*, § 1.34, notes 22–25 and accompanying text.

6. NYBCL § 1527(a).
7. *Id.*
8. *Id.* For definitions, *see supra*, § 1.125, note 1.
9. NYBCL § 1529.
10. *Id.*

time of application by the corporation under NYBCL § 1530, contain a reciprocal provision under which professional service corporations domiciled in New York may similarly apply for the privilege of doing business in that state or territory.[11]

Application for Authority to Do Business in New York; Annual Statement. A foreign professional service corporation may apply for authority to do business in New York.[12] On or before the first day of July of each year, each foreign professional service corporation must furnish a statement to the applicable New York licensing authority.[13]

---

11. *Id.* A foreign professional service corporation practicing professional engineering, land surveying, architecture or landscape architecture, or any combination of these professions, may not be a member or partner of a professional service limited liability company, a foreign professional service limited liability company, a registered limited liability partnership, or a foreign limited liability partnership unless all of the shareholders, directors, and officers of the foreign professional service corporation are licensed to practice one or more of these professions in New York. *Id.*

12. NYBCL § 1530(a). *Procedure.* The application is entitled "Application for Authority of .... (name of corporation) under Section fifteen hundred thirty of the Business Corporation Law." *Id.* It must be signed and verified by an officer of or attorney-in-fact for the corporation and delivered to the Department of State. It must set forth: (1) the name of the foreign professional service corporation, and if the name does not end with the words "Professional Corporation" or the abbreviation "P.C.," it must add the words "Professional Corporation" or the abbreviation "P.C." to its name to be used in New York; (2) the jurisdiction and date of its incorporation; (3) a statement of the profession or professions to be practiced in New York and a statement that the foreign professional service corporation is authorized to practice the profession or professions in the jurisdiction of its incorporation; (4) the name, address, and license number of each person within the foreign professional service corporation who is licensed to practice the profession or professions in New York; (5) the city, incorporated village, or town and the county within New York in which its office is to be located; (6) a designation of the Secretary of State as its agent upon whom process against it may be served and the post office address within or without New York to which the Secretary of State must mail a copy of service of process against the corporation; (7) if it is to have a registered agent, the agent's name and address within New York and a statement that the registered agent is to be its agent upon whom process against the corporation may be served; (8) a statement that the foreign professional service corporation has not since its incorporation or since the date its authority to do business in New York was last surrendered, engaged in any activity in New York (or in lieu of the statement, the consent of the New York State Tax Commission to the filing of the application, with evidence of the consent attached). *Id.* The application must have the following attached to it: (1) a certificate by an authorized officer of the jurisdiction of its incorporation that the foreign professional service corporation is an existing corporation; (2) certificate(s) issued by the licensing authority that each individual within the corporation intending to practice the profession or professions in New York is licensed to practice the profession or professions in New York (and to obtain the certificates, a copy of the certificate of incorporation must be furnished to the licensing authority); and (3) certificate(s) issued by the licensing authority in the case of a foreign professional service corporation providing health services that each shareholder, officer, and director of the foreign professional service corporation is licensed to practice that profession in New York. NYBCL § 1530(b). The fee for filing the application for authority is $200, payable to the Department of State, and the fee is $50 for a certificate of authority issued by the New York State Education Department. NYBCL § 1530(c).

13. NYBCL § 1531. *Procedure.* The statement must list the name and residence address of each shareholder, director, officer, and corporate employee licensed by that licensing authority and certifying that the individuals intending to practice a profession that the corporation is authorized to practice in New York are licensed to prac-

Licensing Authority Regulation of Professions. NYBCL Article 15–A on foreign professional service corporations does not repeal, modify or restrict provisions of the Education Law or the Judiciary Law or any rules or regulations adopted thereunder except to the extent those laws conflict with NYBCL Article 15–A.[14] A foreign professional service corporation, other than one authorized to practice law, is under the supervision of the regents of the University of the State of New York and is subject to disciplinary proceedings and penalties, and its authority to do business subject to suspension, revocation, or annulment for cause, in the same manner and to the same extent provided with respect to individuals and their licenses, certificates, and registrations of Education Law title VIII relating to the applicable profession.[15] A foreign professional service corporation authorized to practice medicine is subject to the prehearing and hearing procedures regarding individual physicians and their licenses in Public Health Law Article 2, Title II–A.[16] A foreign professional service corporation authorized to practice law is subject to the regulation and control of, and its authority to do business is subject to, the Judiciary Law as though it were an individual attorney and counsellor-at-law; however, it need not qualify for any certification under Judiciary Law § 464, take an oath of office under Judiciary Law § 466, or register under Judiciary Law § 467.[17]

§ 1.126 Foreign Professional Service Corporations Summary

Foreign professional service corporations may render professional services in New York only through individuals authorized by law to render the professional services as individuals in New York. Documents issued by the corporations must be signed by the professional in responsible charge. Shareholders, employees, or agents of the corporation who perform professional services in New York on its behalf are personally and fully liable for any negligence or misconduct committed by them (or by any person under their direct supervision and control) while rendering professional services and bear professional responsibility for the corporation's compliance with all laws, rules, and regulations governing the practice of the profession in New York. Except for certain NYBCL provisions, the NYBCL is applicable to foreign professional service corporations unless in conflict with NYBCL Article 15–A (foreign professional service corporations).

---

tice the profession in New York. *Id.* In the case of a foreign professional service corporation providing health services, the statement must also certify that each shareholder, officer, and director of the corporation is licensed to practice the profession in New York. *Id.* The statement must be signed by the president or any vice-president, and attested to by a secretary or any assistant secretary, of the corporation. *Id.*

14. NYBCL § 1532(a).
15. NYBCL § 1532(b).
16. *Id.*
17. NYBCL § 1532(c).

§ 1.126 BUSINESS ORGANIZATIONS: CORPORATIONS Ch. 1

A foreign professional service corporation may apply for authority to do business in New York through an application for authority. The application must be signed and verified by an officer of or attorney-in-fact for the corporation and delivered to the Department of State. It must set forth substantially the same information required of a domestic professional service corporation in its certificate of incorporation and a foreign corporation in its application for authority, except for certain differences applicable to foreign professional service corporations. The fee for filing the application for authority is $200, payable to the Department of State, and the fee is $50 for a certificate of authority issued by the New York State Education Department.

§ 1.127 Foreign Professional Service Corporations Checklist

1. Rendering professional services. (*See* § 1.125)
2. Professional relationships and liabilities. (*See id.*)
3. NYBCL applicability. (*See id.*)
4. Application for authority; filing requirements and contents. (*See id.*)
5. Annual statement. (*See id.*)
6. Licensing authority's regulation. (*See id.*)

§ 1.128 Transactional Checklist—Generally

1. Choice of organizational form. (*See* § 1.4, note 1)
2. Choice of jurisdiction of incorporation. (*See id.*)
3. Choice of financing (*e.g.*, private placement versus public offering). (*See* § 1.26, notes 2 and 4)
4. Tax factors in business decisions (*e.g.*, when (taxable versus tax-deferred), how (ordinary income versus capital gain), who (income splitting among taxpayers through use of "C" corporations, "S" corporations, limited partnerships, trusts, and other organizations)). (*See* §§ 1.34, 1.40, 1.91, 1.108)
5. Ease of formation of business organization.
6. Control desired as owners (*e.g.*, use of voting and non-voting shares to maximize control with minimum investment). (*See* §§ 1.2, 1.3)
7. Liability owners willing to accept. (*See* § 1.3)
8. Income return desired by owners. (*See* § 1.3)
9. Liquidation rights desired by owners; vary risk assumed (*e.g.*, corporation issues senior securities to the most risk-averse investors, issues common shares to the least risk-averse investors, and divides its shares into classes for interests in between). (*See* § 1.3)

Ch. 1   OPERATION ("GROWTH")   § 1.130

10. Leverage desired in financing business. (*See* § 1.26, notes 1 and 4)

§ 1.129   Transactional Checklist—Formation ("Birth")

1. Preincorporation agreements or contracts by promoters or incorporators. (*See* §§ 1.20, 1.153)

2. Subscription for shares. (*See* §§ 1.29, 1.153)

3. Shares issued for organizational services and expenses. (*See* §§ 1.29, 1.30, 1.153)

4. Transfer of property to corporation for shares and other securities. (*See* §§ 1.30, 1.153)

5. Rendering of services to corporation for shares and other securities.
   - Consideration permitted under corporate law. (*See* § 1.30)
   - Consideration permitted under federal income tax law to qualify for tax-free transfer to corporation. (*See* § 1.34)

6. Rights and options to purchase shares. (*See* §§ 1.31, 1.34)

7. Rental of property to corporation by shareholder; intellectual property of shareholder used by corporation. (*See* § 1.34)

8. Issuance of shares; effect on stated capital. (*See* §§ 1.32, 1.38)

9. Issuance of fractional shares, cash, or scrip to effect share transfers, share distributions, reclassifications, mergers, consolidations, or reorganizations. (*See* § 1.30)

10. Issuance of bonds. (*See* § 1.33)

11. Issuance of convertible shares and bonds. (*See* § 1.33)

12. Issuance of shares and other securities to public. (*See* § 1.20, notes 3 and 5; § 1.26, note 2)

13. Issuance of shares and other securities privately or in other transaction exempt from securities laws. (*See id.*)

14. Transfer of shares; reasonable restrictions on transfer; shareholder liabilities survive. (*See* § 1.21, notes 23–25)

15. Conversion of shares and other securities. (*See* § 1.33)

Library References:

West's Key No. Digests, Corporations ⟐1–30(6).

§ 1.130   Transactional Checklist—Operation ("Growth")

1. Declaration of cash dividends. (*See* § 1.38)

2. Declaration of share dividends. (*See id.*)

3. Reclassifications of shares. (*See id.*)
4. Corporate purchase of shares and redemption (call) of redeemable shares. (*See* § 1.39)
5. Agreement by corporation to purchase its shares. (*See id.*)
6. Shareholders' voting agreements. (*See* § 1.47)
7. Shareholders' agreement (or provision in certificate of incorporation) to control board. (*See id.*)
8. Shareholders' voting trust agreements. (*See id.*)
9. Corporate contracts and interested directors. (*See* § 1.65)
10. Loans to directors. (*See id.*)

§ 1.131 Transactional Checklist—Business Combinations ("Marriage")

1. Mergers. (*See* § 1.82)
2. Consolidations. (*See id.*)
3. Sale, lease, exchange, or other disposition of all or substantially all of corporation's assets. (*See* § 1.85)
4. Mortgage of or security interest in corporate property. (*See* § 1.86)
5. Guarantee by corporation, secured or unsecured. (*See* § 1.87)
6. Share exchanges. (*See* § 1.88)
7. Takeover bids (tender offers); directors' duty of care; interested shareholders. (*See* §§ 1.65, 1.89)
8. Share acquisitions of less than all but at least eighty percent of target corporation's shares. (*See* § 1.81)

§ 1.132 Transactional Checklist—Spin-offs and Split-offs ("Children" and "Divorce")

1. Spin-offs. (*See* § 1.81)
2. Split-offs. (*See id.*)
3. Divisive reorganizations. (*See id.*)
4. Nondivisive reorganizations. (*See id.*)

§ 1.133 Transactional Checklist—Repurchase of Shares ("Redemption")

1. Purchase of shares. (*See* § 1.39)
2. Redemption of redeemable (callable) shares. (*See id.*)

§ 1.134 Transactional Checklist—Dissolution; Liquidation ("Death")

1. Distributions in liquidation. (*See* § 1.107)
2. Certain corporate transfers void in actions or petitions for dissolution. (*See* § 1.106)

Library References:

West's Key No. Digests, Corporations ⟻592–630(6).

§ 1.135 Procedural Checklist—Generally

If a section in this chapter contains materials on procedure under the NYBCL, each treatment of these matters is introduced by its own italicized subheading—"*Procedure*"—whether the treatment is in the text or footnotes.[1]

§ 1.136 Procedural Checklist—Notices

Generally

1. Proof of giving notice when notice not required; certificates, affidavits, or other instruments include statement that notice not given when unlawful to deliver notice to or to communicate with persons required to be given notice.[1] (*See* § 1.7)
2. Mailing notice.[2] (*See id.*)
3. Bylaws: action to be taken after notice; notice waived.[3] (*See id.*)
4. Certificate of incorporation: action to be taken after notice; notice waived.[4] (*See id.*)

Formation and Capital Structure

1. Notice of organization meeting.[5] (*See* § 1.23)
2. Notice of: partly paid shares conspicuously on certificate; information re uncertificated shares.[6] (*See* §§ 1.30, 1.31, note 7)

§ 1.135

1. At the end of each main section of this chapter, a broad overview of that section is provided in brief narrative form (*i.e.*, Summary) as well as in outline form (*i.e.*, Checklist) for an attorney who needs an answer in an instant (*e.g.*, client is in the waiting room). The topics included in each checklist mirror, to a large degree, the italicized subheadings within the chapter section to which the checklist relates, to facilitate an attorney's finding the topic mentioned in that checklist.

§ 1.136

1. *See* NYBCL § 108.
2. *See* NYBCL § 108.
3. *See* NYBCL § 108.
4. *See* NYBCL § 108.
5. *See* NYBCL § 404.
6. *See* NYBCL §§ 505(e), 508(f).

§ 1.136 BUSINESS ORGANIZATIONS: CORPORATIONS   Ch. 1

Distributions (Income)

1. Preemptive rights: notice of right to purchase.[7] (*See* § 1.52)

2. Notice of: dividend payment from source other than surplus; share distributions; change in issued shares affecting capital accounts; reduction of capital; application of surplus to eliminate deficits; conversion of shares.[8] (*See* § 1.38)

3. Penalties for failure to comply with notice or disclosure requirements.[9] (*See* § 1.38)

Management and Shareholders (Control)

1. Shareholders' meetings, notice of: meeting; adjournment; directors' election; fixing record date; special meeting; place; greater than normal quorum or vote requirement[10] (*see* § 1.44) and waiver of notice.[11] (*See id.*)

2. Directors' meetings: notice; waiver of notice.[12] (*See* § 1.62)

3. Certificate of incorporation: greater than normal quorum or vote requirement for directors or for shareholders noted conspicuously on share certificate.[13] (*See* §§ 1.45, 1.46, 1.63)

4. Notation conspicuously on share certificate of provisions controlling board or of irrevocable proxy.[14] (*See* §§ 1.45 and 1.47)

5. Notice of application for order to produce for examination voting trust records of foreign corporation.[15] (*See* § 1.114)

6. Notice to corporation of application for indemnification.[16] (*See* § 1.66)

7. Notice to shareholders of various information on indemnification paid.[17] (*See id.*)

8. Notice to: corporation of infant shareholder; shareholders for wages due.[18] (*See* §§ 1.51, note 1; 1.56)

Extraordinary Matters (Business Combinations; Amendments)

1. Shareholder's notice of election to dissent; corporate notice to cancel dissenters' rights.[19] (*See* §§ 1.51 and 1.90)

2. Notice of: mergers, consolidations, substantial dispositions, share

7. *See* NYBCL § 622.
8. *See* NYBCL §§ 510, 511, 515, 516, 517, 519, and 520.
9. *See* NYBCL § 520.
10. *See* NYBCL §§ 601–605, and 616.
11. *See* NYBCL § 606.
12. *See* NYBCL § 711.
13. *See* NYBCL §§ 616 and 709.
14. *See* NYBCL §§ 609(h) and 620.
15. *See* NYBCL § 1316.
16. *See* NYBCL § 724.
17. *See* NYBCL § 725.
18. *See* NYBCL §§ 625 and 630.
19. *See* NYBCL § 623.

exchanges, and takeover bids; amendments.[20] (*See* §§ 1.73, 1.83, 1.85, 1.88, and 1.89)

Dissolution and Liquidation

1. Notice of application (motion) for final order of court for dissolution.[21] (*See* § 1.104)

2. Notice of order to show cause why corporation should not be dissolved.[22] (*See id.*)

3. Notice to creditors and claimants after dissolution; notice of court supervision, hearings, and entry of orders[23] (*see* § 1.98); adequacy of notice.[24] (*See id.*)

4. Receivership notices: application; foreign corporation; appointment; calling general meeting of creditors; extension of time to settle accounts; relief by court; to District Attorney; resignation; final distribution; final accounting.[25] (*See* § 1.111)

§ 1.137 Procedural Checklist—Reservation of Corporate Name

1. Application to set forth:

    • Name and address of applicant. (*See* § 1.14)

    • Basis of application under NYBCL § 303(a) or (b). (*See id.*)

    • May be required to set forth nature of business to be conducted by corporation. (*See id.*)

2. Application to reserve name to be filed with Department of State. (*See id.*)

3. Available names reserved for 60 days; certificate of reservation. (*See id.*)

Library References:

West's Key No. Digests, Corporations ⇌43–50.

§ 1.138 Procedural Checklist—Reservation of Corporate Name—Foreign Corporations

1. Corporate name may be reserved by foreign corporation:

    • Intending to apply for authority to do business in New York.[1] (*See* § 1.14)

---

20. *See* NYBCL §§ 903, 909, 913, 1602, 1603, and 1608.
21. *See* NYBCL § 1110.
22. *See* NYBCL § 1106.
23. *See* NYBCL §§ 1007 and 1008.
24. *See* NYBCL § 1008.
25. *See* NYBCL §§ 1203, 1207, 1209, 1211, and 1213–1216.

§ 1.138

1. *See* NYBCL § 303(a)(3).

§ 1.138 BUSINESS ORGANIZATIONS: CORPORATIONS Ch. 1

- Intending to change its name.[2] (*See id.*)

2. Corporate name may be reserved by person intending to incorporate a foreign corporation and have it apply for authority to do business in New York.[3] (*See id.*)

3. Fictitious name may be reserved by foreign corporation:

    - Intending to apply for authority to do business in New York. (included in application for authority).[4] (*See id.*)

    - Intending to change its fictitious name under which it does business in New York.[5] (*See id.*)

    - That has changed its corporate name in its jurisdiction and new corporate name not available in New York.[6] (*See id.*)

§ 1.139 Procedural Checklist—Mandatory and Permissive Provisions in Certificate of Incorporation

Mandatory Provisions[1]

1. Name of corporation. (*See* § 1.21)

2. Purposes for which corporation is formed. (*See id.*)

3. County within New York where office of corporation is to be located. (*See id.*)

4. Aggregate number of shares authorized to be issued. (*See id.*)

5. If shares to be divided into classes, designation of each class and a statement of the relative rights, preferences, and limitations of shares of each class. (*See id.*)

6. If shares of any preferred class to be issued in series, designation of each series, statement of variations in relative rights, preferences, and limitations insofar as variations to be fixed in the certificate of incorporation, and statement of any authority to be vested in board to establish and designate series and to fix variations in relative rights, preferences, and limitations. (*See id.*)

7. Designation of the Secretary of State as agent of the corporation for service of process against the corporation and the post office address within or without New York to which the Secretary of State must mail a copy of the process. (*See id.*)

---

2. *See* NYBCL § 303(a)(4).
3. *See* NYBCL § 303(a)(5).
4. *See* NYBCL §§ 303(b)(1) and 1301(d);
5. *See* NYBCL §§ 303(b)(2) and 1301.
6. *See* NYBCL §§ 303(b)(3) and 1301.

§ 1.139

1. *See also*, NYBCL, Appendix 2, Henn and Alexander, *supra*, § 1.1, note 1, Certificate of Incorporation (Checklist 3).

Ch. 1   INCORPORATION   **§ 1.140**

8. If the corporation is to have a registered agent, agent's name and New York address and statement that registered agent to be the agent of corporation for service of process. (*See id.*)

9. Duration of the corporation if other than perpetual. (*See id.*)

10. If the corporation is to be managed by shareholders, a provision to that effect. (*See* § 1.47)

Permissive Provisions[2]

1. Provisions eliminating or limiting the personal liability of any director to the corporation or its shareholders for damages for any breach of the director's duty. (*See* § 1.21)

2. Provisions not inconsistent with the NYBCL or any other New York statute relating to the business of the corporation, its affairs, its rights or powers, or the rights or powers of its shareholders, directors, or officers including any provision relating to matters that under the NYBCL are either required or permitted to be in the bylaws. (*See id.*)

3. Powers of a corporation enumerated in the NYBCL. (*See id.*)

Library References:

West's Key No. Digests, Corporations ⟐18.

§ 1.140   Procedural Checklist—Incorporation[1]

1. Corporation, definition of. (*See* § 1.5)

2. Permissible purposes. (*See* § 1.9)

3. Selection and reservation of corporate name. (*See* §§ 1.13, 1.14)

4. Preincorporation share subscriptions. (*See* § 1.29)

5. Other preincorporation agreements. (*See* § 1.20)

6. Certificate of incorporation provisions. (*See* § 1.21)

7. Official consents or approvals. (*See* §§ 1.9, 1.13, 1.21)

8. Certificate of incorporation execution by incorporators. (*See* § 1.20)

9. Certificate of incorporation delivered to (filed with) Department of State; filing fee and organization tax. (*See* §§ 1.7, 1.20, 1.21 and 1.30)

10. Corporate existence begins. (*See* §§ 1.7, 1.21, 1.34)

---

2. *See also*, NYBCL, Appendix 2, Henn and Alexander, *supra*, § 1.1, note 1, Certificate of Incorporation (Checklist 3).

§ 1.140

1. *See also*, NYBCL, Appendix 2, Henn and Alexander, *supra*, § 1.1, note 1, Incorporation Procedure (Checklist 2).

§ 1.140 BUSINESS ORGANIZATIONS: CORPORATIONS Ch. 1

11. Certified copy of certificate of incorporation sent by Department of State to, and filed and indexed by, county clerk of the county in which the corporate office is, or is to be, located. (*See* § 1.7)

12. Bylaws. (*See* § 1.22)

13. Corporate outfit (*e.g.*, minutes book; corporate seal; certificate book; stock transfer ledger (share register)). (*See* § 1.14)

14. Organization meeting or signed instrument in lieu of meeting. (*See* § 1.23)

15. Check applicability of federal securities laws and New York's (and other states') Blue Sky laws to the issuance and sale of shares and other securities. (*See* § 1.20, notes 3 and 5; § 1.26, note 2)

16. Share subscriptions; payment for and issuance of shares. (*See* §§ 1.29, 1.30)

17. Assumed name certificate filed with Secretary of State; display certificate in every corporate office in New York; filing fee plus county clerks' fees. (*See* § 1.13)

18. Filing stock transfer tax certificate and claim for rebate. (*See* § 1.30)

19. "S" corporation election. (*See* § 1.2)

Library References:

West's Key No. Digests, Corporations ⚖1–30(6).

§ 1.141 Procedural Checklist—Filing Certificate of Incorporation

1. Title of certificate. (*See* § 1.21)

2. Signed by incorporators. (*See id.*)

3. Incorporators' names and addresses. (*See id.*)

4. Acknowledged and delivered to Department of State; filing fees. (*See id.*)

Library References:

West's Key No. Digests, Corporations ⚖22.

§ 1.142 Procedural Checklist—Bylaws[1]

1. Amendment or repeal by vote of shareholders entitled to vote in election of directors. (*See* § 1.22)

§ 1.142

1. *See also*, NYBCL, Appendix 2, Henn and Alexander, *supra*, § 1.1, note 1, Bylaws (Checklist 4) (contains list of NYBCL sections referring to bylaws indicating those authorized in certificate of incorporation or specific provisions of bylaws adopted by shareholders).

Ch. 1   ORGANIZATION MEETINGS   **§ 1.143**

2. When provided in certificate of incorporation or bylaw adopted by shareholders, bylaws to be adopted, amended, or repealed by board by vote specified in bylaw, which may be greater than normal vote, but bylaw adopted by board to be amended or repealed by the shareholders entitled to vote. (*See id.*)

3. If bylaw regulating impending election of directors adopted, amended, or repealed by board, the notice of next shareholders' meeting for election of directors to set forth bylaw adopted, amended, or repealed together with a concise statement of changes made. (*See id.*)

4. Bylaws may contain provisions on business of corporation, the conduct of its affairs, its rights or powers, or rights or powers of its shareholders, directors, or officers, not inconsistent with the NYBCL, any other New York statute, or the certificate of incorporation. (*See id.*)

5. Provisions on matters required or permitted in bylaws are permitted in certificate of incorporation. (*See* §§ 1.21, 1.22)

Library References:

West's Key No. Digests, Corporations ⚖=53–58.

§ 1.143 Procedural Checklist—Organization Meetings[1]

1. Organization meeting of incorporators to adopt bylaws, elect directors to hold office until first annual meeting of shareholders, and transact other business that may come before the meeting. (*See* §§ 1.22, 1.23)

2. Meeting may be held either within or without New York. (*See* § 1.23)

3. If two or more incorporators, the meeting held at call of any incorporator on at least five days' notice by mail to other incorporators, setting forth time and place of meeting. (*See id.*)

4. Notice need not be given to any incorporator who attends the meeting or submits a signed waiver of notice before or after the meeting. (*See id.*)

5. If more than two incorporators, majority constitutes quorum, and act of majority of incorporators present at meeting at which quorum present is act of incorporators. (*See id.*)

6. Incorporator acting in person or by proxy signed by the incorporator or an attorney-in-fact. (*See id.*)

---

§ 1.143

1. *See also*, NYBCL, Appendix 2, Henn and Alexander, *supra*, § 1.1, note 1, Organization Meeting (Checklist 5).

§ 1.143 BUSINESS ORGANIZATIONS: CORPORATIONS   Ch. 1

7. Action permitted to be taken at organization meeting may be taken without a meeting if incorporators or their attorneys-in-fact sign an instrument setting forth action taken. (*See id.*)

8. If incorporator dies or unable to act for any reason, action may be taken by written consent of incorporators without a meeting. (*See id.*)

§ 1.144 Procedural Checklist—Share Certificate[1]

1. Signatures (chairman (or a vice-chairman) of the board or president (or a vice-president) and secretary (or an assistant secretary) or treasurer (or an assistant treasurer)); facsimile and countersigned.[2] (*See* § 1.30)

2. Statement of relative rights, preferences, and limitations of the shares of each class and other information. (*See id.*)

3. Manner of transfer. (*See id.*)

4. Lost or destroyed certificates. (*See id.*)

5. Statement on face of each share certificate. (*See id.*)

    • Corporation formed under laws of New York.

    • Name of person(s) to whom issued.

    • Number and class of shares, and designation of series, if any, that certificate represents.

6. Within reasonable time after issuance of uncertificated shares, corporation must send registered owner of shares written notice containing information required on face or back of certificate representing shares. (*See id.*)

7. Seal. (*See id.*)

8. Statement on face or back that corporation will furnish shareholder or set forth designation, relative rights, preferences, and limitations of each class of shares (and similarly for classes of preferred in series).[3] (*See id.*)

9. Legends.

    • Shares partly paid noted conspicuously on face or back.[4] (*See* § 1.31)

    • Agreement for purchase by corporation of its own shares.[5] (*See* § 1.39)

---

§ 1.144

1. *See also*, NYBCL, Appendix 2, Henn and Alexander, *supra*, § 1.1, note 1, Share Certificate (Checklist 6).
2. *See* NYBCL § 508(a).
3. *See* NYBCL § 508(b).
4. *See* NYBCL §§ 504(h) and 505(e).
5. *See* NYBCL § 514.

Ch. 1   SHAREHOLDER APPROVAL REQUIREMENTS   § 1.145

- Existence of proxy; irrevocability.[6] (*See* § 1.45)
- Greater than normal quorum or voting of shareholders.[7] (*See* §§ 1.45, 1.46)
- Certificate of incorporation provision restrictive of board's discretion.[8] (*See* § 1.47)
- Statement that certificates issued under voting trust agreement.[9] (*See id.*)
- Notice of election to dissent by shareholder.[10] (*See* § 1.51)
- Greater than normal quorum or voting of directors.[11] (*See* § 1.63)
- Dissolution at will of shareholder(s) or on occurrence of certain event.[12] (*See* § 1.96)
- Transfer restrictions on shares of professional service corporation.[13] (*See* § 1.122)
- Transfer restrictions on shares of corporation.[14] (*See* § 1.21)

Library References:
West's Key No. Digests, Corporations ⚖94–110.

§ 1.145   Procedural Checklist—Shareholder Approval Requirements[1]

1. Shareholders' voting rights. (*See* § 1.45)
2. Other voting rights: bondholders; infants. (*See* §§ 1.45, 1.51)
3. Limited or no voting rights; treasury shares. (*See* § 1.45)
4. Record date. (*See id.*)
5. Notice of meetings. (*See* §§ 1.44, 1.136)
6. Quorum of shareholders. (*See* § 1.46)
7. Corporate action by vote of shareholders for election of directors; cumulative voting; class voting. (*See* § 1.45)
8. Other corporate action: class voting and fixing share consideration; domestic corporation purchase of more than ten percent of corporation's shares; amending, repealing, or adopting bylaws; fixing number of directors; filling new directorships and vacancies; removal of

---

6. *See* NYBCL § 609(h).
7. *See* NYBCL § 616(c).
8. *See* NYBCL § 620(b) and 620(g).
9. *See* NYBCL § 621(a).
10. *See* NYBCL § 623(f).
11. *See* NYBCL § 709(c).
12. *See* NYBCL § 1002(c).
13. *See* NYBCL § 1511.
14. *See* UCC § 8–204.

§ 1.145

1. *See also*, NYBCL, Appendix 2, Henn and Alexander, *supra*, § 1.1, note 1, Shareholder Approval Requirements (Checklist 7).

directors (with and without cause); contract involving interested director; director loans; removal of officer elected by shareholders; electing specified officers; indemnification. (*See* §§ 1.22, 1.39, 1.45, 1.59, 1.60, 1.65, 1.66, 1.69)

9. Written shareholder consent without meeting. (*See* § 1.48)

10. Greater than normal shareholder vote. (*See* § 1.45)

11. Extraordinary corporate action: options and rights issued to directors, officers, and employees (*see* § 1.31); distribution of shares of one class or series to another class or series[2]; amendment or change of certificate of incorporation (*see* §§ 1.75, 1.76); other amendments; business combinations; guarantee; mortgage; voluntary dissolution; judicial dissolution; shareholder voting agreements; executive committee and other committees; reorganization under act of Congress. (*See* §§ 1.47, 1.64, 1.77, 1.78, 1.83, 1.86, 1.87, 1.96, 1.102, 1.103)

§ 1.146 Procedural Checklist—Shareholder's Right to Receive Payment for Shares[1]

1. Available regarding: amendment of certificate of incorporation (*see* § 1.72); business combinations (*see* §§ 1.83, 1.85, 1.88, 1.89, 1.90); dissolved corporation's sale of remaining assets.[2] (*See* § 1.97)

2. Pre-judicial procedure. (*See* § 1.51)

3. Procedure for judicial determination (appraisal). (*See id.*)

Library References:

West's Key No. Digests, Corporations ⚖=182.4, 584.

§ 1.147 Procedural Checklist—Close Corporations[1]

1. Incorporators; qualifications.[2] (*See* § 1.20)

2. Certificate of incorporation.[3] (*See* §§ 1.139–1.141)

3. Bylaws.[4] (*See* § 1.142)

4. Organization meeting.[5] (*See* § 1.143)

2. See NYBCL § 511(a)(3).

§ 1.146

1. *See also*, NYBCL, Appendix 2, Henn and Alexander, *supra*, § 1.1, note 1, Right of Shareholders to Receive Payment for Shares (Checklist 8).

2. See NYBCL § 1005(a)(3)(A).

§ 1.147

1. *See also*, NYBCL, Appendix 2, Henn and Alexander, *supra*, § 1.1, note 1, Closely Held Corporations (Checklist 9).

2. See NYBCL § 401.
3. See NYBCL § 402.
4. See NYBCL § 601.
5. See NYBCL § 404.

Ch. 1 FOREIGN CORPORATIONS § 1.148

5. Shareholder action: quorum; vote; without meeting; class voting; cumulative voting.[6] (*See* § 1.45)

6. Directors: number; qualification; classified boards; shareholder removal; judicial removal.[7] (*See* §§ 1.59, 1.61)

7. Officers: shareholder election; shareholder removal; judicial removal; multiple officer positions.[8] (*See* § 1.69)

8. Shareholder voting agreements; proxies; voting trusts.[9] (*See* §§ 1.45, 1.47)

9. Agreement by corporation to purchase its shares.[10] (*See* § 1.39)

10. Directors' action: quorum; vote, without a meeting; by telephone; executive committee and other committees.[11] (*See* §§ 1.59, 1.62, 1.64)

11. Provisions applicable to corporations with unlisted shares: provision restrictive of board discretion; shareholder liability for wages; shareholder petition for dissolution under certain circumstances.[12] (*See* §§ 1.47, 1.56, 1.102, 1.103)

12. Dissolution: non-judicial (generally; under shareholder agreement; under certificate of incorporation provision);[13] judicial (generally; directors' petition; shareholders' petition; on deadlock of directors or shareholders; under special circumstances and with purchase of petitioner's shares).[14] (*See* §§ 1.94, 1.95, 1.99)

13. Share transfer restrictions; securities law requirement.[15] (*See* § 1.21)

14. Share certificate. (*See* § 1.144)

Library References:

West's Key No. Digests, Corporations ⚖3.

§ 1.148 Procedural Checklist—Foreign Corporations[1]

1. Application for authority. (*See* §§ 1.115, 1.116)

2. Fictitious name. (*See* § 1.115)

3. Violations. (*See id.*)

6. *See* NYBCL §§ 608(a) and 614–618.
7. *See* NYBCL §§ 617, 701, 702(a), 704, and 706.
8. *See* NYBCL §§ 715 and 716.
9. *See* NYBCL §§ 609, 620, and 621.
10. *See* NYBCL §§ 513 and 514.
11. *See* NYBCL §§ 702, 707–709, and 712.
12. *See* NYBCL §§ 539, 616, 620(b), 630, 701, 1104–a, and 1118.
13. *See* NYBCL §§ 1002, 1001, and 620(a).
14. *See* NYBCL §§ 1102–1104, 1104–a, 1118, and 1111.
15. *See* UCC § 8–204.

§ 1.148

1. *See also*, NYBCL, Appendix 2, Henn and Alexander, *supra*, § 1.1, note 1, Foreign Corporations (Checklists 10 and 11).

§ 1.148 BUSINESS ORGANIZATIONS: CORPORATIONS   Ch. 1

4. Surrender of authority. (See § 1.118)
5. Termination of existence. (See § 1.119)

Library References:
West's Key No. Digests, Corporations ⚖=631–691.

§ 1.149 Drafting Checklist[1]

Preincorporation Planning

1. Choice of business organizational form. (See § 1.4)
2. Choice of jurisdiction of incorporation. (See id.)
3. Selection of corporate name with second and third choices in case name unavailable. (See §§ 1.13, 1.14)
4. Names and addresses of expected incorporators, shareholders, directors, and officers. (See §§ 1.20–1.23)
5. Investors' desires regarding risk, income, and control; classification of shares or directors, or both. (See §§ 1.2–1.4, 1.26, 1.45, 1.59)[2]
6. Incorporators' and promoters' agreements or contracts contingent on corporation's existence. (See §§ 1.4, 1.20)
7. Organization meeting. (See § 1.23)[3]

Formation and Capital Structure

1. Business purpose(s) of corporation. (See § 1.9)[4]
2. Office location(s) of corporation. (See § 1.21)[5]
3. Registered agent of corporation? If so, name and address. (See id.)[6]
4. Duration of corporation if not to be perpetual. (See id.)
5. Share certificate; other securities. (See § 1.144)
6. Investors who will render services to corporation, or to other investors, for shares? (See §§ 1.2–1.4, 1.30, 1.34)

§ 1.149

1. For basic forms, see infra, §§ 1.150–1.155. References to related forms are given at the beginning of each of these sections. For references to other forms, see infra, §§ 1.149, notes 2–14. Additional references to forms are given in the annotations to the NYBCL. For drafting techniques, see Henn and Alexander, supra, § 1.1, note 1, pp. 272–306 (certificate of incorporation) and 761–783 (for closely-held corporations: share transfer restrictions, preincorporation agreements, certificate of incorporation, bylaws, shareholder agreements, voting trusts, irrevocable proxies, employment contracts, share certificate legends, and notifications for uncertificated shares).

2. See West's McKinney's Forms (hereinafter "West's BCL Forms") §§ 7:41–7:42 (shareholders' agreement restricting transfer of shares).

3. See West's BCL Forms §§ 3:36–3:39 (banking resolutions).

4. See West's BCL Forms § 9:09 (certificate of amendment of corporate purposes).

5. See West's BCL Forms § 9:10 (change of office of corporation).

6. See West's BCL Forms §§ 3:115 (resignation of registered agent); 3:113 (revocation of designation).

7. Investors who will contribute a going business? Valuation of business? Liabilities assumed (or assets taken subject to liabilities) by corporation? Related tax questions. (*See* §§ 1.2–1.4, 1.30, 1.34)

8. Cash or other property contributions? If disproportionate compared to other investors, consider senior securities? Control, risk, income, and tax-related questions; payment for shares in installments; shares divided into classes regarding voting rights? Income? Liquidation? Options to purchase additional shares? (*See* §§ 1.2–1.4, 1.26, 1.27, 1.30, 1.31, 1.33, and 1.34)

9. Financing sources beyond small group of investor-entrepreneurs? Securities law applicable; restrict transfer of stock? (*See* § 1.20, notes 3 and 5; § 1.26, notes 2 and 4; § 1.30)

10. Additional capital needed in future? From whom? Preemptive rights to founders? (*See* § 1.20, note 5; § 1.26, notes 2 and 4; §§ 1.30, 1.56)

11. Retirement plans? Insurance? Liquidation preferences? (*See* §§ 1.107, 1.108)

Distributions (Income)

1. All common share capital structure with proportionate dividend rights? shares divided into classes? (*See* §§ 1.2–1.4, 1.26, 1.28, 1.33, 1.34)[7]

2. Options to purchase additional shares? To whom? Executives? Other employees? (*See* § 1.31)

3. Character of distribution: Dividend? In redemption? Corporate purchase of its shares? Leverage buyout? Salary expense? Interest on corporate debt? Rent expense? Other? Tax-related questions (disguised dividends)? (*See* § 1.34)

Management (Control)

1. Which investors, if any, want to be active in management of corporation? Non-voting or limited voting shares to certain investors? Senior securities? Preferred shares? Bonds? (*See* §§ 1.2–1.4, 1.26, 1.33, 1.34, 1.45)

2. Shareholders' meetings: Method of notice? Greater than normal quorum and voting requirements? (*See* §§ 1.45, 1.46)[8]

---

[7]. *See* West's BCL Forms §§ 6:02 (resolution for declaration of dividends); 6:20 (notice of dividend from other than earned surplus).

[8]. *See infra*, § 1.151. *See also*, West's BCL Forms §§ 4:23–4:24 (notice of annual meeting of shareholders); 4:02 (agenda for meeting); 4:04 (minutes of regular meeting); 4:10 (demand for special meeting to elect directors); 4:36 (waiver of notice of meeting by shareholder); 4:21 (certified list of shareholders); 4:74–4:76 (proxy for shareholders' meeting); 4:80 (irrevocable proxy); 4:41–4:42 (inspectors of election oath); 5:08 (ballot for election of directors); 8:02–8:07 (complaint in shareholders' derivative action). For various forms for petitions or orders to show cause related to

3. Shareholders' voting agreement? Voting trust? (*See* § 1.47)[9]
4. Covenants not to compete? Nondisclosure (secrecy) agreements? (*See* §§ 1.34, 1.81)
5. Veto power in minority shareholder(s)? Greater than normal quorum or voting requirements? Classification of shares and directors? Cumulative voting? Allocation of managerial responsibilities to different corporate divisions or subsidiaries? (*See* §§ 1.43–1.47, 1.51)
6. Standards for removal of directors? Officers? Employees? Legal, ethical, and general business practices and customs. (*See* §§ 1.61, 1.69)[10]
7. Directors' meetings: Frequency? Where? When? Length of notice? Means of notice? Executive committee? Other committees? Consent without meeting? (*See* §§ 1.62, 1.64)[11]
8. Extraordinary matters defined: Business combinations? Other? Greater than normal vote required? (*See* §§ 1.45, 1.46, and 1.81–1.89)[12]
9. Fiduciary duties and interested directors. (*See* § 1.65)[13]
10. Indemnification of officers and directors? (*See* § 1.66)
11. Authority and responsibility of officers: Board resolutions? Bylaws? Employment contracts? (*See* § 1.69)
12. Options to purchase additional shares. (*See* §§ 1.31, 1.34)

Business Combinations

1. Defensive measures? preventive? reactive? shareholder value enhancement versus management entrenchment? duty of care documentation? (*See* §§ 1.81, 1.89)
2. Acquisitions by corporation? different capital structures to accomplish efficiently? Sale of substantially all of corporation's assets? Leverage buyout? (*See* §§ 1.26, 1.81)[14]

---

setting aside elections, *see, e.g.*, West's BCL Forms 4:45–4:49, 4:50–4:54.

9. *See* West's BCL Forms §§ 7:08–7:09, 7:11–7:13 (shareholder voting agreements); 4:82–4:87 (voting trust agreements); 4:88 (voting trust certificate).

10. *See* West's BCL Forms § 5:74 (removal of officers by resolution of directors).

11. *See* West's BCL Forms §§ 5:23 (notice of regular meeting of board); 5:22 (notice of special meeting of board); 3:33 (waiver of notice of meeting); 5:34 (consent without a meeting).

12. *See* West's BCL Forms §§ 4:114 (notice of shareholder's election to dissent); 4:132 (withdrawal of election to dissent);

4:117 (offer to pay for shares of dissenting shareholder).

13. *See* West's BCL Forms §§ 5:53–5:57 (complaint for breach of fiduciary duties).

14. *See* West's BCL Forms §§ 10:03 (resolution of board approving plan of merger); 10:04 (plan of merger); 10:05 (notice of special meeting for authorization of merger); 10:07 (shareholder resolution authorizing merger); 10:11 (certificate of merger); 10:14 (resolution of directors on merger of subsidiary corporation); 10:16 (certificate of merger of subsidiary corporation); 10:40 (directors' resolution authorizing sale of assets); 10:41 (directors' resolution authorizing purchase of assets); 10:38–

3. Spin-offs and split-offs (and other similar techniques) to enhance shareholder value? Transfers to controlled subsidiaries? Allocation of control of operations affected? Liquidation preferences affected? Income rights affected? Distributions to (or exchanges with) shareholders? Taxable? Tax-deferred? (*See* § 1.81)

Dissolution and Liquidation

1. Liquidation preferences? (*See* §§ 1.26, 1.27, 1.33, 1.34, 1.94, 1.07, 1.108)
2. Formula offer price to purchase minority shareholder's shares. (*See* § 1.103)
3. Increased likelihood of dissolution because of deadlock of shareholders or board with greater than normal quorum or voting requirements? Voting agreements? Allocation of managerial control? (*See* §§ 1.45, 1.46, 1.62, 1.63, 1.101–1.103)

§ 1.150 Form—Application to Reserve Corporate Name[1]

APPLICATION TO RESERVE CORPORATE NAME

The undersigned, _____, does hereby apply pursuant to section 303 of the Business Corporation Law of the State of New York, for the reservation of a corporate name for a period of sixty days and for that purpose does hereby set forth:

(1) The name of the applicant is _____.

(2) The address of the applicant is No. _____ Street, City of _____, County of _____, State of _____.

(3) The corporate name to be reserved is _____.

(4) The basis for this application under paragraph (a) of section 303 of the Business Corporation Law of the State of New York is that the applicant is a person intending to form a domestic corporation [or] a domestic corporation intending to change its name [or] a foreign corporation intending to apply for authority to do business in the State of New York [or] an authorized foreign corporation intending to change its name [or] a person intending to incorporate a foreign corporation and to have it apply for authority to do business in the State of New York.

Dated: _____, 19__

Name & Address of Applicant

By (Signature)

Name and Capacity

10:39 (shareholders' resolution authorizing sale of substantially all of corporation's assets); 10:44 (agreement for sale of assets); 10:33 (resolution of directors' authorizing mortgage).

§ 1.150

1. *See also* West's BCL Forms §§ 2:24 to 2:26 (complaint for injunction and damages for wrongful use of name).

[or]

Name & Address of Applicant

By (Signature)

Name & Address of Attorney or Agent

Library References:

West's Key No. Digests, Corporations ⟺43–50.

§ 1.151 Form—Certificate of Incorporation[1]

CERTIFICATE OF INCORPORATION

OF

[name of corporation]

UNDER SECTION 402 OF THE BUSINESS CORPORATION LAW

The undersigned, for the purpose of forming a corporation pursuant to section 402 of the Business Corporation Law of the State of New York, do hereby certify:

(1) The name of this corporation is _____.

[First alternative purpose clause: all-purpose statement pursuant to NYBCL 402(a)(2).]

(2) The purpose of the corporation is to engage in any lawful act or activity for which corporations may be organized under the Business Corporation Law of the State of New York. The corporation is not formed to engage in any act or activity requiring the consent or approval of any state official, department, board, agency, or other body without the consent or approval first being obtained.[2]

[Second alternative purpose clause: statement of specific purpose plus all-purpose statement pursuant to NYBCL 402(a)(2).]

(2) The purposes of the corporation are to carry on the business of _____ and further to engage in any lawful act or activity for which corporations may be organized under the Business Corporation Law of the State of New York. The corporation is not formed to engage in any act or activity requiring the consent or approval of any state official,

---

§ 1.151

1. *See* West's BCL Forms § 3:03 (certificate of incorporation, short form). *See also*, West's BCL Forms § 3:111 (chart I of provisions valid only if contained in the certificate of incorporation; chart II of provisions valid if contained in certificate of incorporation or the bylaws). For designation of a registered agent, *see* West's BCL Forms § 3:110. For notice of organization meeting, *see* West's BCL Forms § 3:324. For minutes of organization meeting, *see* West's BCL Forms § 3:330.

2. *See supra*, §§ 1.9, 1.13, and 1.21.

department, board, agency, or other body without the consent or approval first being obtained.

(3) The office of this corporation is to be located in the County of _____, State of New York.

[Use the following par. (4) if shares are to be of one class only.]

(4) The corporation shall have authority to issue an aggregate of _____ (_____) shares, which shall be of one class only and which shall [have a par value of _____ dollars ($_____) per share] [be without par value].

[Use the following par. (4), with par. (5), if shares are to be divided into classes.]

(4) The corporation shall have authority to issue an aggregate of _____ (_____) shares, which shall be divided into classes bearing the designations specified in paragraph (5) of this certificate of incorporation.

The first designated class shall consist of _____ (_____) authorized shares [that shall have a par value of _____ dollars ($_____) per share] [that shall be without par value].

The second designated class shall consist of _____ (_____) authorized shares [that shall have a par value of _____ dollars ($_____) per share] [that shall be without par value].

[Continue as needed for additional classes, if any.]

[Use the following with second alternative par. (4) if shares are to be divided into classes.]

(5) The designations of classes of shares, and their relative rights, preferences, and limitations, are as follows:

The first designated class of shares referred to in paragraph (4) of this certificate of incorporation shall be designated as [class designation] shares and shall have the following relative rights, preferences, and limitations:[3]

The second designated class of shares referred to in paragraph (4) of this certificate of incorporation shall be designated as [class designation] shares and shall have the following relative rights, preferences, and limitations:

---

3. *See* West's BCL Forms § 6:51 (liquidation preference).

§ 1.151 BUSINESS ORGANIZATIONS: CORPORATIONS Ch. 1

[Continue as needed for additional classes, if any.]

[Use the following paragraph if shares of any preferred class are to be issued in series and if variations in the relative rights, preferences, and limitations as between series are to be fixed in the certificate of incorporation.]

(6) Preferred shares in the class designated as [class designation] shares shall be issued in series. The designation of each series, and the variations in the relative rights, preferences, and limitations as between series, are as follows:

_____ (_____) preferred shares in the class designated as [class designation] shares shall be designated as [class designation] shares, [series designation] series. The variations in the relative rights, preferences, and limitations as between series with respect to the shares of the series shall be as follows:[4]

_____ (_____) preferred shares in the class designated as [class designation] shares shall be designated as [class designation] shares, [series designation] series. The variations in the relative rights, preferences, and limitations as between series with respect to the shares of the series shall be as follows:

[Continue as needed for additional series, if any.]

[Use the following paragraph if authority is to be vested in the board of directors to establish and designate series respecting shares of any preferred class and to fix the variations in relative rights, preferences, and limitations as between series.]

(6) Preferred shares in the [class designation] class may be issued in series. The board of directors shall have authority to establish and designate the series and to fix the variations in the relative rights, preferences, and limitations as between series.

(7) The Secretary of State of the State of New York is hereby designated the agent of this corporation upon whom process against this corporation may be served. The post office address to which the Secretary of State shall mail a copy of any process against this corporation served upon the Secretary as agent of this corporation is No. _____ _____ Street, City of _____, County of _____, State of _____, [zip code].

(8) [If the corporation is to have a registered agent for service of process, insert a provision designating either a natural person or a domestic or authorized foreign corporation as such agent.][5]

4. See West's BCL Forms § 6:46 (preferred shares issued in series).

5. See West's BCL Forms § 3:109 (designation of registered agent for service of process).

Ch. 1   CERTIFICATE OF INCORPORATION   § 1.151

[If the duration of the corporation is other than perpetual, add:]

(9) The duration of this corporation shall be _____.

[The following provision is optional.]

(10) The personal liability of directors to the corporation or its shareholders for damages for any breach of duty in the capacity of a director shall be limited to _____ dollars ($_____) [or No director shall be personally liable to the corporation or its shareholders for damages for any breach of duty in such capacity], except that this provision shall neither eliminate nor limit the liability of any director if a judgment or any other final adjudication adverse to the director establishes that the director's acts or omissions were in bad faith or involved intentional misconduct or a knowing violation of law or that the director personally gained in fact a financial profit or other advantage to which the director was not legally entitled or that the director's acts violated section 719 of the Business Corporation Law, nor shall this provision eliminate or limit the liability of any director for any act or omission prior to the adoption of this provision.

IN WITNESS WHEREOF, the undersigned [have signed and acknowledged this certificate or have signed this certificate and caused it to be acknowledged or has subscribed this certificate and hereby affirms it as true under the penalties of perjury or have subscribed this certificate and hereby affirm it as true under the penalties of perjury] this _____ day of _____, 19___.

[Signature]
_____

[Name of incorporator]
[Address]

[Signature]
_____

[Name of Incorporator]
[Address]
[Continue as needed with
signatures and addresses of
incorporators.]

[Acknowledgment, unless affirmed above]

Library References:

West's Key No. Digests, Corporations ⚖18.

§ 1.152 Form—Bylaws[1]

BYLAWS

[name of corporation]

ARTICLE I
LOCATION OF OFFICES

SECTION 1. Office. The office of the corporation shall be located in the County of _____, State of New York.

SECTION 2. Additional Offices. The corporation may also have offices at such other places within or without the State of New York as the board of directors may from time to time appoint or the business of the corporation may require.

ARTICLE II
SHAREHOLDERS

SECTION 1. Place of Meeting. Meetings of shareholders shall be held at the office of the corporation at No. _____ Street, City of _____, County of _____, State of _____.

SECTION 2. Annual Meetings. Commencing with the _____ day of _____, 19__, a meeting of shareholders shall be held annually for the election of directors and the transaction of other business on the first [insert day of week, *e.g.*, Tuesday] in the month of _____ in every year at _____ o'clock A.M. [P.M.], local time, if not a Saturday, Sunday, or legal holiday in the place of meeting, and if a Saturday, Sunday, or legal holiday, then on the next business day following not a Saturday, Sunday, or legal holiday at _____ o'clock A.M. [P.M.].

SECTION 3. Notice of Meetings. Written notice of the annual meeting stating the place, date, and hour shall be given personally or by mail not less than ten nor more than fifty days before the date of the meeting to each shareholder entitled to vote at such meeting. Written notice of a special meeting stating the place, date, and hour, and indicating that it is being issued by or at the direction of the person or persons calling the meeting, and stating the purpose or purposes for which the meeting is called, shall be given, personally or by mail, not less than ten nor more than fifty days before the date of the meeting to each shareholder entitled to vote at such meeting. If at any meeting, action is proposed to be taken that would entitle the shareholders to receive payment for their shares, pursuant to section 623 of the Business Corporation Law of the State of New York (hereinafter "Business Corporation Law"), the notice of meeting shall include a statement of

---

§ 1.152

1. *See* West's BCL Forms § 3:45 for an outline of the contents of the bylaws with references to the NYBCL.

that purpose and to that effect and shall be accompanied by a copy of section 623 of the Business Corporation Law or an outline of its material terms. If any bylaw regulating an impending election of directors is adopted, amended, or repealed by the board, the notice of the next meeting of shareholders for the election of directors shall set forth the bylaws so adopted, amended, or repealed, together with a concise statement of the change made.

SECTION 4. Notices and Waivers thereof. Whenever communication with any shareholder or director is unlawful under any statute of this state or of the United States or any regulation, proclamation, or order issued under said statutes, then the giving of such notice or communication to such person shall not be required, and the corporation shall have no duty to apply for license or other permission to do so. Notice of meeting need not be given to any shareholder who submits a signed waiver of notice, in person or by proxy, whether before or after the meeting. The attendance of any shareholder at a meeting, in person or by proxy, without protesting prior to the conclusion of the meeting the lack of notice of such meeting, shall constitute a waiver of notice by the shareholder. Notice of a meeting need not be given to any director who submits a signed waiver of notice whether before or after the meeting, or who attends the meeting without protesting, prior thereto or at its commencement, the lack of notice to the director. Waiver of notice need not specify the purpose of any regular or special meeting of the board.

SECTION 5. Quorum. (a) Except as provided in section 5, paragraph (b) hereof, the holders of a majority of the shares entitled to vote thereat shall constitute a quorum at a meeting of shareholders for the transaction of any business, provided that when a specified item of business is required to be voted on by a class or series, voting as a class, the holders of a majority of the shares of the class or series shall constitute a quorum for the transaction of the specified item of business.

(b) At any special meeting called on demand of shareholders pursuant to section 603(a) of the Business Corporation Law for the election of directors, the shareholders attending, in person or by proxy, and entitled to vote in an election of directors shall constitute a quorum for the purpose of electing directors but not for the transaction of any other business.

(c) When a quorum is once present to organize a meeting, it is not broken by the subsequent withdrawal of any shareholders.

(d) The shareholders present may adjourn the meeting despite the absence of a quorum.

SECTION 6. Voting. (a) Every shareholder of record shall be entitled at every meeting of shareholders to one vote for every share standing in his or her name on the record of shareholders, unless otherwise provided in the certificate of incorporation.

(b) Directors shall, except as otherwise required by the Business Corporation Law, or by the certificate of incorporation as permitted by the aforementioned law, be elected by a plurality of the votes cast at a meeting of shareholders by the holders of shares entitled to vote in the election.

(c) Whenever any corporate action, other than the election of directors, is to be taken under the Business Corporation Law by vote of the shareholders, it shall, except as otherwise required by the aforementioned law or by the certificate of incorporation as permitted by the aforementioned law, be authorized by a majority of the votes cast at a meeting of shareholders by the holders of shares entitled to vote thereon.

SECTION 7. Proxies. Every shareholder entitled to vote at a meeting of shareholders or to express consent or dissent without a meeting may authorize another person or persons to act for him or her by proxy. Proxies must be in writing and signed by the shareholder or the shareholder's attorney-in-fact. No proxy shall be valid after the expiration of eleven months from the date thereof unless otherwise provided in the proxy. Every proxy shall be revocable at the pleasure of the shareholder executing it, except as otherwise provided by law.

SECTION 8. Inspectors at Shareholders' Meetings. The board of directors, in advance of any shareholders' meeting, may appoint one or more inspectors to act at the meeting or any adjournment thereof. If inspectors are not so appointed, the person presiding at a shareholders' meeting may, and on the request of any shareholder entitled to vote thereat shall, appoint one or more inspectors. In case any person appointed fails to appear or act, the vacancy may be filled by appointment made by the board in advance of the meeting or at the meeting by the person presiding thereat. Each inspector, before entering upon the discharge of his or her duties, shall take and sign an oath faithfully to execute the duties of inspector at the meeting with strict impartiality and according to the best of his or her ability. The inspectors shall determine the number of shares outstanding and the voting power of each, the shares represented at the meeting, the existence of a quorum, and the validity and effect of proxies. The inspectors shall receive votes, ballots, or consents, hear and determine all challenges and questions arising in connection with the right to vote, count, and tabulate all votes, ballots, or consents, determine the result, and do such acts as are proper to conduct the election or vote with fairness to all shareholders. On request of the person presiding at the meeting or any shareholder entitled to vote thereat, the inspectors shall make a report in writing of any challenge, question, or matter determined by them and execute a certificate of any fact found by them. Any report or certificate made by them shall be *prima facie* evidence of the facts stated and of the vote as certified by them.

[Alternative clause]

SECTION 8. Inspectors of Election. The board of directors, in advance of any shareholders' meeting, may appoint [number] inspectors of election to act at the meeting or any adjournment thereof and to serve as inspectors only for such meeting, and in the event any person appointed fails to appear or refuses to act, the vacancy may be filled by appointment made by the board in advance of the meeting or at the meeting by the person presiding thereat.

SECTION 9. Agenda. The order of business at the annual meeting of shareholders shall be as follows:

(a) Calling the meeting to order.

(b) Proof of notice of meeting or waiver thereof.

(c) Reading of minutes of last annual meeting.

(d) Reports of officers.

(e) Reports of committees.

(f) Election of directors.

(g) Transaction of other business.

SECTION 10. Written Consent of Shareholders. Whenever under the Business Corporation Law shareholders are required or permitted to take any action by vote, the action may be taken without a meeting on written consent, setting forth the action so taken, signed by the holders of all outstanding shares entitled to vote thereon. However, this section shall not be construed to alter or modify any provision of law [or of the certificate of incorporation] under which the written consent of the holders of less than all outstanding shares is sufficient for corporate action.

SECTION 11. List of Shareholders at Meeting. A list of shareholders as of the record date, certified by [specify corporate officer responsible] or by the transfer agent, shall be produced at any meeting of shareholders upon the request thereat or prior thereto of any shareholder. If the right to vote at any meeting is challenged, the inspectors of election, or person presiding thereat, shall require the list of shareholders to be produced as evidence of the right of the persons challenged to vote at the meeting, and all persons who appear from the list to be shareholders entitled to vote thereat may vote at the meeting.

SECTION 12. Adjourned Meetings. The shareholders present may adjourn a meeting despite the absence of a quorum. When a determination of shareholders of record entitled to notice of or to vote at any meeting of shareholders has been made, the determination shall apply to any adjournment thereof unless the board of directors fixes a new record date for the adjourned meeting. When a meeting is adjourned to another time or place, no notice of the adjourned meeting is necessary if the time and place to which the meeting is adjourned are announced at the meeting at which the adjournment is taken, and at the adjourned meeting any business may be transacted that might have been transacted on the original date of the meeting. However, if after the adjournment the board of directors fixes a new record date for the adjourned meeting, a notice of the adjourned meeting shall be given to each shareholder of record on the new record date entitled to notice.

SECTION 13. Special Meetings. Special meetings of the shareholders, for any purpose or purposes, may be called by the president or the board of directors and shall be called by the president or the secretary at the request in writing by shareholders owning _____ per cent of the shares of the corporation issued and outstanding and entitled to vote. The notice for special meetings shall state the purpose or purposes thereof.

ARTICLE III
BOARD OF DIRECTORS

SECTION 1. Board of Directors. The business of this corporation shall be managed under the direction of its board of directors.

SECTION 2. Number of Directors. The number of directors constituting the entire board shall be _____. The number of directors may be increased or decreased by action of a majority of the entire board subject to the limitation that no decrease shall shorten the term of any incumbent director.

SECTION 3. Qualifications of Directors. Each director shall be at least eighteen years of age.

SECTION 4. Election and Term of Directors. At each annual meeting of shareholders, directors shall be elected to hold office until the expiration of the term for which they are elected and until their successors have been elected and qualified.

[Election by holders of shares of a class]

[Number] directors shall be elected by ballot by a plurality of the votes cast at the meeting by the holders of [class] shares, and [number] directors shall be elected by ballot by a plurality of the votes cast at the meeting by the holders of [class] shares.

[Classification of Directors]

The directors of the corporation shall be divided into _____ classes, hereby designated class _____. [number] directors shall be in each class. The term of office of the initial class _____ directors shall expire at the next annual meeting of shareholders, the term of office of the initial class _____ directors shall expire at the second succeeding annual meeting, the term of office of the initial class _____ directors shall expire at the third succeeding annual meeting. At each annual meeting after the initial classification of directors, directors to replace those whose terms expire at such annual meeting shall be elected to hold office until the third succeeding annual meeting.

SECTION 5. Meetings of the Board. The first meeting of each newly elected board of directors shall be held at the office of the corporation at No. _____ _____ Street, City of _____, County of _____, State of _____ on the first business day following the annual meeting of shareholders at _____ o'clock A.M. [P.M.], local time of that day. Regular meetings of the board of directors may be held without notice at such time and place as fixed by the board of directors. Special meetings of the board of directors shall be held upon notice to the directors. A majority of the directors present, whether or not a quorum is present, may adjourn any meeting to another time and place.

SECTION 6. Notice of Meetings of the Board. The first meeting of each newly elected board of directors may be held without notice. Regular meetings may also be held without notice to the directors. Special meetings shall be held upon written notice to the directors at the call of [specify persons authorized to call meeting]. The notice of a special meeting shall state the place, date, and hour of the meeting, indicate that it is being issued by or at the direction of a person or persons calling the meeting, and specify the purpose thereof. The notice shall be given personally or by mail, not less than _____ nor more than _____ days before the date of the meeting to each director. The notice shall be deemed to be given when deposited in the United States mail, with postage thereon prepaid, directed to the directors at their address or, if a director has filed with the secretary of the corporation a written request that notices be mailed to some other address, then directed to that director at the other address. Notice of any adjourned meeting of the board, specifying the time and place of the next meeting, shall be given to the directors who were not present at the time of the adjournment and, unless the time and place are announced at the meeting, to the other directors.

SECTION 7. Quorum and Vote of Directors. [Specify proportion, which may be a majority or less than a majority, but not less than one third] of the entire board shall constitute a quorum for the transaction of business or of any specified item of business. Except as otherwise provided in the Business Corporation Law, the vote of a majority of the directors present at the time of the vote, if a quorum is present at such time, shall be the act of the board.

SECTION 8. Removal of Directors. Any or all of the directors may be removed for cause, or without cause, by vote of the shareholders, and for cause by action of the board, provided that (a) no director may be removed when the votes cast against the director's removal would be sufficient to elect the director if voted cumulatively at an election of directors at which the same total number of votes were cast and the entire board, or the entire class of directors of which the director is a member, were then being elected and (b) when the holders of the shares of any class or series, or holders of bonds, voting as a class, are entitled to elect one or more directors, any director so elected may be removed only by the applicable vote of the holders of the shares of that class or series or of the holders of such bonds, voting as a class.

SECTION 9. Newly Created Directorships and Vacancies. Newly created directorships resulting from an increase in the number of directors and vacancies occurring in the board of directors for any reason except the removal of directors without cause may be filled by vote of a majority of the directors then in office, although less than a quorum exists. Vacancies occurring in the board by reason of the removal of directors without cause may be filled only by vote of the shareholders. A director elected to fill a vacancy shall be elected to hold office for the unexpired term of the director's predecessor and until his or her successor has been elected and qualified.

SECTION 10. Resignation of Directors. Any director may resign at any time. The resignation shall be made in writing; it shall take effect at the time specified therein or, if no time is specified, at the time of its receipt by the President or Secretary. The acceptance of a resignation shall not be necessary to make it effective, but no resignation shall discharge any accrued obligation or duty of a director.

SECTION 11. Dividends. The board of directors may but shall not be required to declare, and the corporation may pay, dividends in cash or its bonds or its property, including the shares or bonds of other corporations, on its outstanding shares. The dividends may be declared or paid out of surplus only and upon the terms and conditions provided by the certificate of incorporation or bylaws. Before the declaration and payment of any dividend, the directors, from time to time, in their absolute discretion, may set aside out of the surplus available for dividends the sum or sums as they think proper, as a reserve fund to meet contingencies, or for equalizing dividends, or for repairing or maintaining any property of the corporation, or for such other purposes as the directors shall think conducive to the interests of the corporation.

SECTION 12. Compensation of Directors. Directors, as such, shall not receive any salary for their services as directors, but by resolution of the board of directors, a fixed sum and expenses of attendance, if any, may be allowed for attendance at each regular or special meeting of the board and of any committee of the board of directors, provided, however, that nothing herein contained shall be construed to preclude any director from serving the corporation in any other capacity and receiving compensation therefor.

SECTION 13. Committees of the Board. The board of directors, by resolution adopted by a majority of the entire board, may designate from among its members an executive committee and other committees, each consisting of three or more directors, and each of which, to the extent provided in the resolution, shall have all the authority of the board, except on the following matters: (1) the submission to shareholders of any action that needs shareholders' approval under the Business Corporation Law; (2) the filling of vacancies in the board of directors or in any committee; (3) the fixing of compensation of any director for serving on the board or on any committee; (4) the amendment or repeal of the bylaws or the adoption of new bylaws; (5) the amendment or repeal of any resolution of the board that by its terms shall not be so amendable or repealable. The board may designate one or more directors as alternate members of any committee, who may replace any absent member or members at any meeting of a committee. Each committee shall serve at the pleasure of the board of directors.

SECTION 14. Indemnification. [To prohibit indemnification:] The indemnification of directors and officers that otherwise would be permissible under article seven of the New York Business Corporation Law is hereby prohibited. [To limit indemnification:] The indemnification of directors and officers that otherwise would be permissible under article seven of the New York Business Corporation Law shall be limited [in any one year or in any one action or proceeding] as follows:

(1) Indemnification of the Chairman of the Board shall be so limited to _____ times his or her annual salary from the corporation in effect at the time the indemnification is duly authorized.

(2) Indemnification of any director other than the Chairman of the Board shall be so limited to _____ times the director's annual salary from the corporation in effect at the time the indemnification is duly authorized.

(3) Indemnification of the President shall be so limited to _____ times the officer's annual salary from the corporation in effect at the time the indemnification is duly authorized.

(4) Indemnification of any Vice–President shall be so limited to _____ times the annual salary of the Vice–President from the corporation in effect at the time the indemnification is duly authorized.

(5) Indemnification of the Secretary shall be so limited to _____ times the Secretary's annual salary from the corporation in effect at the time the indemnification is duly authorized.

(6) Indemnification of the Treasurer shall be so limited to _____ times the Treasurer's annual salary from the corporation in effect at the time the indemnification is duly authorized.

SECTION 15. Contracts or Other Transactions. Inasmuch as the directors of this corporation are likely to be persons of large and diversified business interests and to be connected with other corporations with which, from time to time, this corporation may have business dealings:

§ 1.152 BUSINESS ORGANIZATIONS: CORPORATIONS Ch. 1

(a) No contract or other transaction between a corporation and one or more of its directors, or between a corporation and any other corporation, firm, association, or other entity in which one or more of its directors are directors or officers, or have a substantial financial interest, shall be either void or voidable for this reason alone or by reason alone that the interested director or directors are present at the meeting of the board, or of a committee thereof, that approves the contract or transaction, or that his or her or their votes are counted for that purpose:

(1) if the material facts concerning the director's interest in the contract or transaction and any common directorship, officership, or financial interest are disclosed in good faith or are known to the board or committee, and the board or committee approves the contract or transaction by a vote sufficient for such purpose without counting the vote of the interested director or, if the votes of the disinterested directors are insufficient to constitute an act of the board as defined in section 708 of the Business Corporation Law (action by the board), by unanimous vote of the disinterested directors; or

(2) if the material facts concerning the director's interest in the contract or transaction and any common directorship, officership, or financial interest are disclosed in good faith or are known to the shareholders entitled to vote thereon, and the contract or transaction is approved by vote of such shareholders.

(b) If good faith disclosure of the material facts concerning the director's interest in the contract or transaction and any common directorship, officership, or financial interest is made known to the directors or shareholders, or is known to the board or committee or shareholders approving the contract or transaction, as provided in Section 15 paragraph (a) herein, the contract or transaction may not be avoided by the corporation for the reasons set forth in said paragraph (a). If no such disclosure was made or knowledge existed, or if the vote of the interested director was necessary for the approval of the contract or transaction at a meeting of the board or committee at which it was approved, the corporation may avoid the contract or transaction unless the party or parties thereto shall establish affirmatively that the contract or transaction was fair and reasonable to the corporation at the time the contract or transaction was approved by the board, a committee, or the shareholders.

(c) Common or interested directors may be counted in determining the presence of a quorum at a meeting of the board or of a committee that approves such contract or transaction.

SECTION 16. Director and Committee Action by Conference Telephone. Any one or more members of the board of directors, or of any committee thereof, may participate in a meeting of the board or committee by means of a conference telephone or similar equipment that allows all persons participating in the meeting to hear each other at the same time. Participation by such means shall constitute presence in person at such a meeting.

SECTION 17. Action by Board of Directors Without a Meeting. Any action required or permitted to be taken by the Board or any Committee thereof may be taken without a meeting if all the members of the Board or the Committee consent in writing to the adoption of a resolution authorizing the action.

ARTICLE IV
OFFICERS

SECTION 1. Number. The officers of this corporation shall be a president, one or more vice-presidents, a secretary, a treasurer, and [specify other officers], each of whom shall be elected [or appointed] by the board of directors. Any two or more offices may be held by the same person, except the offices of president and secretary.

SECTION 2. Selection and Term of Office. All officers shall be elected or appointed by the board to hold office for the term of _____, and each shall hold office for such term and until his or her successor has been elected or appointed and qualified.

SECTION 3. President. The president shall preside at all meetings of shareholders and [, in the absence of the chairman of the board of directors,] at all meetings of the directors. The president shall be an *ex officio* member of all standing committees and shall, in general, supervise, manage, and control all of the business and affairs of the corporation, subject to the control of the board of directors. The president shall have power to sign certificates representing shares of this corporation and to sign and execute all contracts and instruments of conveyance in the name of the corporation, to sign checks, drafts, notes, and orders for the payment of money, and to appoint and discharge agents and employees, subject to the approval of the board of directors. The president shall perform all the duties usually incident to the office of president.

SECTION 4. Vice–President(s). The vice-presidents shall be as follows:

> [Set forth the titles and responsibilities of the various vice-presidents, such as executive vice-president, marketing vice-president, production vice-president, engineering vice-president, and research vice-president.]

SECTION 5. Secretary. The secretary shall keep the minutes of all meetings of the board of directors, the minutes of all meetings of the shareholders, and also, unless otherwise directed, the minutes of all meetings of committees in books provided for that purpose. The secretary shall give, or cause to be given, notice of all meetings of shareholders and directors, and all other notices required by law or by these bylaws; in case of his or her absence or refusal so to give notice, the notice may be given by any person thereunto directed by the president or by the directors or shareholders upon whose requisition the meeting is called. The secretary shall have charge of the corporate books and records. The secretary shall have the custody of the seal of the corporation and affix the same to all instruments requiring it when authorized by the directors or the president, and he or she shall attest the same. The secretary shall file all written requests that notices be mailed to shareholders at an address other than that appearing on the record of shareholders. The secretary shall sign with [the chairman or vice-chairman of the board or] the president or vice-president all certificates representing shares of the corporation. And he or she shall, in general, perform all the duties incident to the office of secretary.

SECTION 6. Treasurer. The treasurer shall have custody of all funds, securities, evidences of indebtedness, and other valuable documents of the corporation; when necessary or proper he or she shall indorse on behalf of the corporation for collection checks, notes, and other obligations and shall deposit the same to the credit of the corporation in such bank or banks or depositary as the board of directors [or the finance committee] may designate. The treasurer shall receive and give or cause to be given receipts and acquittances for moneys paid in on account of the corporation and shall pay out of the funds on hand all just debts of the corporation of whatever nature upon maturity of the same; the treasurer shall enter or cause to be entered in books of the corporation to be kept for that purpose full and accurate accounts of all moneys received and paid out on account of the corporation, and whenever required by the president or the directors [or the finance committee], the treasurer shall render a statement of his or her accounts. The treasurer shall keep or cause to be kept such other books as will show a true record of the expenses, losses, gains, assets, and liabilities of the corporation; the treasurer shall at all reasonable times exhibit his or her books and accounts to any director of the corporation upon application at the office of the corporation during business hours; the treasurer shall sign with [the chairman or vice-chairman of the board or] the president or a vice-president certificates representing shares of the corporation; he or she shall perform all other duties and acts incident to the office of treasurer. The treasurer shall give the corporation security for the faithful performance of his or her duties in such sum and with such surety as the board of directors may require.

SECTION 7. Assistant Secretaries and Assistant Treasurers. The assistant secretaries and the assistant treasurers may sign with [the chairman or vice-chairman of the board or] the president or vice-president, certificates representing shares of the corporation. The assistant secretaries and the assistant treasurers shall have such other powers and shall perform such other duties as may be assigned to them by the board of directors, the president, the secretary, or the treasurer, respectively. In the absence or disability of the secretary or the treasurer, the assistant secretary or the assistant treasurer, respectively, shall perform all their duties and exercise all their powers. The assistant treasurer may be required to give security for the faithful performance of his or her duties in such sum and with such surety as the board of directors may require.

SECTION 8. Signing of Obligations. All checks, drafts, notes or other obligations of the corporation shall be signed by the president [or such of the officers of the corporation or by such other person or persons as may be authorized by the board of directors or the finance committee].

SECTION 9. Removal of Officers. Any officer elected or appointed by the board of directors may be removed by the board of directors with or without cause. [Or: An officer elected by the shareholders may be removed, with or without cause, only by vote of the shareholders, but the officer's authority to act may be suspended by the board of directors for cause.]

SECTION 10. Vacancies. If the office of any officer becomes vacant, the directors may appoint any qualified person to fill the vacancy, who shall hold office for the unexpired term of his or her predecessor and until a successor is elected or appointed and qualified.

SECTION 11. Compensation of Officers. The officers shall receive such salary or compensation as may be determined by the board of directors. No officer shall be precluded from receiving any compensation by reason of the fact that he or she is also a director of the corporation.

ARTICLE V
SHARES

SECTION 1. Certificate Representing Shares. The shares of the corporation shall be represented by certificates in such form as shall be prepared or be approved by the board of directors and shall be numbered consecutively. The certificates shall be signed by [the chairman or a vice-chairman of the board or] the president or a vice-president and the secretary or an assistant secretary or the treasurer or an assistant treasurer of the corporation and may be sealed with the seal of the corporation or a facsimile thereof. The signatures of the officers upon a certificate may be facsimiles if the certificate is countersigned by a transfer agent or registered by a registrar other than the corporation itself or its employee. In case any officer who has signed or whose facsimile signature has been placed upon a certificate shall have ceased to be an officer before the certificate is issued, it may be issued by the corporation with the same effect as if he or she were the officer at the date of issue. Each certificate shall state upon the face thereof: (1) the corporation is formed under the laws of New York, (2) the name of the person or persons to whom the shares were issued, and (3) the number and class of shares and the designation of the series, if any, that the certificate represents. [If the corporation is authorized to issue shares of more than one class, add: Each certificate representing shares shall set forth upon the face or back of the certificate or shall state that the corporation will furnish to any shareholder upon request and without charge, a full statement of the designation, relative rights, preferences, and limitations of the shares of each class authorized to be issued and, if the corporation is authorized to issue any class of preferred shares in series, the designation, relative rights, preferences and limitations of each such series so far as the same have been fixed and the authority of the board to designate and fix the relative rights, preferences, and limitations of other series.]

SECTION 2. Transfer of Shares. The certificated shares of the corporation shall be transferable only upon its books by the holders thereof in person or by their duly authorized attorneys or legal representatives, and upon the transfer the old certificates duly endorsed or accompanied by evidence of succession, assignment or authority to transfer shall be surrendered to the company by the delivery thereof to the person in charge of the list of shareholders and the transfer books and ledgers, or the transfer agent, or to such other person as the directors may designate, by whom the old certificates shall be cancelled and new certificates shall thereupon be issued. A record shall be made of each transfer, and whenever a transfer shall be made for collateral security, and not absolutely, it shall be so expressed in the entry of the transfer on the record of shareholders of the corporation.

SECTION 3. Record of Shareholders. The corporation shall keep at its office in this state or at the office of its transfer agent or registrar in this state, a record containing the names and addresses of all shareholders, the number and class of shares held by each, and the dates when they respectively became the owners of record thereof. The record shall be in written form or in any other form capable of being converted into written form within a reasonable time. The corporation shall be protected in treating the persons in whose names shares stand on the record of shareholders as the owners thereof for all purposes.

SECTION 4. Fixing Record Date. For the purpose of determining the shareholders entitled to notice of or to vote at any meeting of shareholders or any adjournment thereof, or to express consent to or dissent from any proposal without a meeting, or for the purpose of determining shareholders entitled to receive payment of any dividend or the allotment of any rights, or for the purpose of any other action, the board of directors may fix, in advance, a date as the record date for any such determination of shareholders. The date shall not be more than fifty nor less than ten days before the date of the meeting nor more than fifty days prior to any other action.

SECTION 5. Lost, Destroyed, and Stolen Share Certificates. Any person claiming a certificate representing shares to be lost, apparently destroyed, or wrongfully taken shall make an affidavit or affirmation of that fact and advertise the same in such manner as the board of directors may require and shall give the corporation an indemnity bond in such form and with one or more sureties satisfactory to the board, in such amount as the board may determine, that shall be at least double the par value of the shares represented by said certificate, to protect the corporation or any person injured by the issue of the new certificate from any liability or expense that the corporation or that person may incur by reason of the original certificate remaining outstanding, whereupon a new certificate may be issued of the same tenor and for the same number of shares as the one alleged to be lost, destroyed, or wrongfully taken if the claimant so requests prior to notice to this corporation that the lost, apparently destroyed, or wrongfully taken certificate has been acquired by a bona fide purchaser.

SECTION 6. Annual Statement. The board of directors shall publish and submit to the shareholders at least _____ days before the annual meeting of the shareholders, a statement of the physical and financial condition of the corporation, including a consolidated balance sheet showing the assets and liabilities of the corporation and a profit and loss statement covering the preceding fiscal year, certified by independent public accountants.

ARTICLE VI
MISCELLANEOUS PROVISIONS

SECTION 1. Fiscal Year. The fiscal year of the corporation shall begin on the first day of _____ and terminate on the _____ day of _____ in each calendar year. [Or: The fiscal year of the corporation shall be fixed by the board of directors.]

SECTION 2. Seal of Corporation. The seal of the corporation shall be circular in form and have inscribed thereon the name of the corporation, the year of its organization, and the words "Corporate Seal" and "New York." The seal shall be in the charge of the secretary. If and when so directed by the board of directors [the executive committee] or the president, a duplicate of the seal may be kept and used by the secretary, assistant secretary, treasurer, or assistant treasurer. The seal may be used by causing it or a facsimile to be affixed or impressed or reproduced in any other manner.

§ 1.152 BUSINESS ORGANIZATIONS: CORPORATIONS   Ch. 1

SECTION 3. Interested Shareholders and Business Combinations. The corporation hereby expressly elects not to be governed by section 912 of the Business Corporation Law.

SECTION 4. Amendment and Repeal. Bylaws may be amended, repealed, or adopted by the board of directors, but any bylaw adopted by the board of directors may be amended or repealed by the holders of shares at the time entitled to vote in the election of any directors.

Library References:

West's Key No. Digests, Corporations ⚖ 53–58.

§ 1.153 Form—Subscription Agreement[1]

SUBSCRIPTION AGREEMENT

We [or I], the undersigned, do hereby subscribe for the number of shares of [name of corporation] of the class set opposite each of our names [my name] and do hereby agree to pay the at least the par value [stated value] in cash as follows: _____ percent of the amount subscribed on the signing of this subscription, and the remaining _____ percent in _____ equal installments on the _____ day of each month thereafter until at least the full par value [stated value] is paid, at which time certificates for said shares shall be issued to each subscriber [me] for the number of shares subscribed.

Name: _____ Address: _____ Shares: _____ [Class _____]

_____

[Signature]
Dated, _____, 19___.

Name: _____ Address: _____ Shares: _____ [Class _____]

_____

[Signature]
Dated, _____, 19___.

Name: _____ Address: _____ Shares: _____ [Class _____]

_____

[Signature]
Dated, _____, 19___.

Library References:

West's Key No. Digests, Corporations ⚖ 75.

§ 1.153

1. *See also,* West's BCL Forms §§ 2:15 (agreement with sole proprietor to form corporation); 2:16 (agreement among partners to form corporation); 6:65–6:66, 2:07–

§ 1.154 Form—Certificate of Amendment[1]

CERTIFICATE OF AMENDMENT
OF THE
CERTIFICATE OF INCORPORATION
OF
[Name of Corporation]
UNDER SECTION 805 OF THE BUSINESS CORPORATION LAW

The undersigned, being [specify persons entitled to sign pursuant to NYBCL 104(d)], do[does] hereby certify and set forth:

(1) The name of the corporation is _____. [If name has been changed, add: The name under which the corporation was formed is _____.]

(2) The certificate of incorporation of [name of corporation] was filed by the Department of State on the _____ day of _____, 19___.

(3) Paragraph _____ of the certificate of incorporation of [name of corporation], which sets forth [indicate subject matter of provision to be amended], is hereby amended to read as follows: [set forth text of provision in its amended form].

[or]

(3) The certificate of incorporation of [name of corporation] is hereby amended by eliminating paragraph _____ thereof, which sets forth [indicate subject matter of provision being eliminated].

[or]

(3) The certificate of incorporation of [name of corporation] is hereby amended by adding the following provision: [set forth text of provision to be added].

[or, if multiple amendments in one certificate]

(3) The certificate of incorporation of [name of corporation] is hereby amended in the following respects:

(a) Paragraph _____ of the certificate of incorporation, which sets forth [indicate subject matter of provision to be amended], is hereby amended to read as follows: [set forth text of provision in its amended form].

§ 1.154

1. *See also*, West's BCL Forms §§ 7:21 (greater than normal requirements on quorum and vote of directors); 7:19 (greater than normal requirements on voting of shareholders); 7:18 (greater than normal requirements on quorum of shareholders). For a form of certificate of change, *see* West's Forms § 9:21 (by board).

2:10 (preincorporation subscription for shares).

(b) Paragraph _____ of the certificate of incorporation, which sets forth [indicate subject matter of provision to be eliminated], is hereby eliminated.

(c) A new paragraph _____ is hereby added to the certificate of incorporation as follows: [set forth text of provision to be added].

[If an amendment provides for a change of shares, include the following in connection with the statement relating to the amendment:]

This amendment provides for the following change of shares:

Issued Shares: The amendment provides for a change of [number] issued [class] shares of the par value of _____ ($_____) dollars per share. Resulting from the change are [number] issued [class] shares of the par value of _____ ($_____) dollars per share. The terms of the change are as follows: _____.

Unissued Shares: The amendment provides for a change of [number] unissued [class] shares of the par value of _____ ($_____) dollars per share. Resulting from the change are [number] unissued [class] shares of the par value of _____ ($_____) dollars per share. The terms of the change are as follows: _____.

[If an amendment reduces stated capital, include the following in connection with the statement relating to the amendment:]

This amendment reduces the stated capital of the corporation by [set forth manner in which stated capital is reduced, *e.g.*, removal from authorized shares of shares reacquired and cancelled by the corporation, indicating the number, class, and par value of the shares]. The stated capital is thereby reduced from _____ ($_____) dollars to _____ ($_____) dollars, a reduction of _____ ($_____) dollars, which amount represents [*e.g.*, the aggregate par value of the cancelled reacquired shares removed from authorized status] and which amount is transferred from stated capital to capital surplus.

(4) This amendment to the certificate of incorporation of [name of corporation] was authorized by [specify manner of authorization, which will depend on the nature of the amendment and other factors; *see* forms at West's Forms §§ 9:07A–1 to 9:07A–12 for clauses illustrating authorization under a variety of circumstances.]

IN WITNESS WHEREOF, the undersigned have (has) executed and signed this certificate this _____ day of _____, 19___.

[Signature]

_____
(Name and Capacity)

Ch. 1   FORM—CERTIFICATE OF DISSOLUTION   § 1.155

[Signature]

_____

(Name and Capacity)
[Verification]

§ 1.155 Form—Certificate of Dissolution[1]

CERTIFICATE OF DISSOLUTION
OF
[Name of Corporation]
UNDER SECTION 1003 OF THE BUSINESS CORPORATION LAW

The undersigned, _____ and _____, being, respectively, the president and the secretary of [name of corporation] [or, the holders of all outstanding shares of [name of corporation] entitled to vote on dissolution of the corporation], do hereby certify and set forth:

(1) The name of the corporation is _____. [If name has been changed, add: The name under which the corporation was formed is _____.]

(2) The certificate of incorporation was filed by the Department of State on the _____ day of _____, 19___.

(3) The name and address of each of the officers and directors are as follows:

Officers
Name: Office: Address:
_____   _____   _____
_____   _____   _____

Directors
Name: Address:
_____   _____
_____   _____
_____   _____

(4) The [name of corporation] hereby elects to dissolve.

(5) The dissolution of [name of corporation] was authorized at a meeting of shareholders by vote of the holders of at least two-thirds of all the outstanding shares entitled to vote thereon.

[Alternative clause]

(5) The dissolution of [name of corporation] was authorized by unanimous written consent, setting forth the action so taken, signed by

---

§ 1.155

1. See West's BCL Forms §§ 11:04 (directors' resolution); 11:05 (notice of special meeting of shareholders); 11:06 (shareholders' resolution); 11:07 (certificate of consent by shareholders); 11:14 (notice to creditors after dissolution); 11:25B (shareholders' petition); 11:24–11:29 (petition on division of directors); 11:26–11:27, 11:31 (petition on division and dissension among shareholders); 11:32 (petition under special circumstances); 11:34–11:35 (order to show cause why corporation should not be dissolved); 11:41 (notice of motion for final order of dissolution).

§ 1.155 BUSINESS ORGANIZATIONS: CORPORATIONS Ch. 1

the holders of all outstanding shares entitled to vote thereon, without a meeting.

[Alternative clause]

(5) The dissolution was authorized pursuant to a provision in the certificate of incorporation. That provision reads: [set forth full text of provision]. In accordance with the foregoing provision, the dissolution was authorized in the following manner: [state actual authorization action taken pursuant to the quoted provision].

IN WITNESS WHEREOF, the undersigned have signed this certificate this _____ day of _____, 19___.

[Signature]
_____
[Name and Capacity]
and
[Signature]
_____
[Name and Capacity]
[or]
[Signature of Shareholder]
_____
[Name and Capacity]

[Signature of Shareholder]
_____
[Name and Capacity]

[Verification]

Library References:

West's Key No. Digests, Corporations ⚖︎592–630(6).

Chapter 2

NON-CORPORATE ENTITIES: LIMITED LIABILITY COMPANIES AND PARTNERSHIPS

by
Karon S. Walker

Table of Sections

2.1	Scope Note.
2.2	Strategy—Choice of Entity.
2.3	Tax Classification.
2.4	____ Eagerly–Awaited Simplification.
2.5	____ Former Corporate Characteristics Test.
2.6	____ ____ Limited Liability.
2.7	____ ____ Continuity of Life.
2.8	____ ____ Free Transferability of Interests.
2.9	____ ____ Centralized Management.
2.10	Partnership vs. LLC.
2.11	____ Tax Implications.
2.12	____ Liability.
2.13	____ Flexibility.
2.14	Limited Liability Companies.
2.15	____ Governing Law.
2.16	____ Formation.
2.17	____ ____ Articles of Organization.
2.18	____ ____ Publication.
2.19	____ ____ Operating Agreement.
2.20	____ ____ Other Issues.
2.21	____ Members.
2.22	____ ____ Admission of New Members.
2.23	____ ____ Liability.
2.24	____ ____ One-member LLCs.
2.25	____ Management.
2.26	____ ____ Members vs. Managers.
2.27	____ ____ Voting: Members.
2.28	____ ____ Voting: Managers.
2.29	____ ____ Non-waivable Requirements.
2.30	____ ____ Delegation of Responsibility.
2.31	____ ____ Standard of Care.
2.32	____ ____ Agency Authority.
2.33	____ Assignment of Interests.

2.34	__ __ Default Rules.
2.35	__ __ Vote Required to Admit Assignee as Member.
2.36	__ Dissolution.
2.37	__ __ Events.
2.38	__ __ Continuation of Business after Dissolution Event.
2.39	__ __ Winding Up.
2.40	__ Conversions/Mergers.
2.41	__ __ Procedures.
2.42	__ __ Dissenters' Rights.
2.43	__ PLLCs.
2.44	General Partnerships.
2.45	__ Governing Law.
2.46	__ Formation.
2.47	__ __ Agreement.
2.48	__ __ Business Certificate.
2.49	__ __ Publication.
2.50	__ __ Other Issues.
2.51	__ Partners.
2.52	__ __ Admission of New Partners.
2.53	__ __ Liability.
2.54	__ __ Contribution Issues.
2.55	__ Management.
2.56	__ __ Voting.
2.57	__ __ Non-waivable Requirements.
2.58	__ __ Delegation of Responsibility.
2.59	__ __ Standard of Care.
2.60	__ __ Agency Authority.
2.61	__ Assignment of Interests.
2.62	__ __ Default Rules.
2.63	__ __ Vote Required to Admit New Partner.
2.64	__ Dissolution.
2.65	__ __ Events.
2.66	__ __ Continuation of Business after Dissolution Event.
2.67	__ __ Winding Up.
2.68	__ Conversions/Mergers.
2.69	__ __ Procedures.
2.70	__ __ Dissenters' Rights.
2.71	__ Professional Organizations.
2.72	Limited Liability Partnerships.
2.73	__ Governing Law.
2.74	__ Comparison with General Partnerships.
2.75	__ Formation/Registration.
2.76	__ Other Issues.
2.77	Limited Partnerships.
2.78	__ Governing Law.
2.79	__ Formation.
2.80	__ __ Certificate of Limited Partnership.
2.81	__ __ Publication.
2.82	__ __ Agreement.
2.83	__ __ Other Issues.
2.84	__ Partners.

2.85 ____ ____ Admission of New Partners.
2.86 ____ ____ Liability.
2.87 ____ Contribution Issues.
2.88 ____ Management.
2.89 ____ ____ Voting: General Partners.
2.90 ____ ____ Voting: Limited Partners.
2.91 ____ ____ Delegation of Responsibility.
2.92 ____ ____ Standard of Care.
2.93 ____ ____ Agency Authority.
2.94 ____ Assignment of Interests.
2.95 ____ ____ Default Rules.
2.96 ____ ____ Vote Required to Admit New Partner.
2.97 ____ Dissolution.
2.98 ____ ____ Events.
2.99 ____ ____ Continuation of Business after Dissolution Event.
2.100 ____ ____ Winding Up.
2.101 ____ Conversions/Mergers.
2.102 ____ ____ Procedures.
2.103 ____ ____ Dissenters' Rights.
2.104 ____ Professional Organizations.
2.105 Due Diligence Issues.
2.106 Securities Laws Issues.
2.107 Summary.
2.108 Chart Comparing New York Entities.
2.109 Drafting Checklist.
2.110 Forms.
2.111 ____ LLC Articles of Organization.
2.112 ____ Operating Agreement: Member–Managed LLC.
2.113 ____ Registration as LLP.
2.114 ____ Certificate of Limited Partnership.
2.115 ____ Limited Partnership Agreement.

WESTLAW Electronic Research

See WESTLAW Electronic Research Guide preceding the Summary of Contents.

§ 2.1 Scope Note

This chapter identifies many of the issues that affect a client's choice of entity for his business.[1] Because the decision to organize as a non-corporate entity usually depends on whether it will receive pass-through tax treatment, this chapter also discusses recently enacted regulations that have simplified federal tax classification and, for historic context, summarizes the now-obsolete "corporate characteristics" classification test.[2]

§ 2.1
1. *See infra*, § 2.2.

2. *See infra*, §§ 2.3–2.9.

§ 2.1 NON-CORPORATE ENTITIES

After a brief comparison of the various significant forms of non-corporate entities,[3] this chapter describes the formation, ownership, management and operation of limited liability companies ("LLCs"),[4] general partnerships,[5] limited liability partnerships (a special form of general partnership)[6] and limited partnerships under New York law.[7] A chart comparing the basic New York business organizational forms follows.[8] The chart may be used for quick reference when questions arise about the relative characteristics and tax treatment of LLCs and different types of corporations and partnerships. A checklist of issues to discuss with clients before drafting a partnership or operating agreement is also included.[9] Forms of Articles of Organization of an LLC, Registration as a Limited Liability Partnership, Certificate of Limited Partnership, member-managed LLC Operating Agreement and Limited Partnership Agreement conclude the chapter.

§ 2.2 Strategy—Choice of Entity

New York enterprises are lucky to enjoy a full menu of alternatives for the form in which they will conduct business. An attorney must be familiar with the nature and operation of all those alternatives, as well as their tax implications, to advise commercial clients on the type of entity appropriate for them.[1] For example, if an enterprise expects to incur losses that could shelter its owners' other income, or if it will borrow relatively large sums, but make significant distributions to its members, the members may best be served by a non-corporate entity taxed as a partnership. Investors who prefer to remain uninvolved in the management of their entity, as long as they have limited personal liability therefor, and expect to realize their return largely upon the resale of their interests (as opposed to ongoing distributions) might logically choose the corporate form. Furthermore, as the number of owners increases, governance and continuity of an LLC or partnership structure may become unwieldy, depending upon its management structure, indicating that a corporate form is more appropriate.

Entrepreneurial clients are generally familiar with corporate organizations, including their operation, management and tax implications. Such clients frequently choose to organize high-risk enterprises as corporations, with the main goal of limiting their personal liability for the debts and obligations of the business. Except in rare circumstances where the "corporate veil" is pierced, and under Section 630 of the New York Business Corporation Law (the "NYBCL"), shareholders are not

---

3. *See infra*, §§ 2.10–2.13.
4. *See infra*, §§ 2.14–2.43.
5. *See infra*, §§ 2.44–2.71.
6. *See infra*, §§ 2.72–2.76.
7. *See infra*, §§ 2.77–2.104.
8. *See infra*, §§ 2.108.

9. *See infra*, § 2.109.

§ 2.2

1. *See* chart at § 2.108, *infra*. *See also, infra*, § 2.43, for a discussion of additional considerations for professionals choosing their organizational entity.

liable for a corporation's obligations merely by virtue of being shareholders. They are, instead, at risk only for their investments.

Clients also understand inherently the roles of shareholder and director in a corporation. Shareholders elect the company's board of directors to represent their interests, and are protected by procedural safeguards like the notice provisions of the NYBCL and the annual meeting requirement.[2] By-laws describing meetings and responsibilities of directors and the election and duties of officers typically follow familiar precedents. It is also generally known that, absent an agreement among shareholders to the contrary, and subject to applicable securities laws, interests in a corporation are transferable without restriction (although there may be no ready market for them). A corporate entity generally has continuity of life, regardless of the fate of individual shareholders. And, unless the shareholders of a corporation make an election under Subchapter S of the Internal Revenue Code (the "Code"), distributions to them in respect of their ownership interests will have been taxed twice: once at the corporate level, as corporate income, and again at the shareholder level, as income to the shareholder.

As a result, owners of small corporations who meet its strict requirements often make an election under Subchapter S of the Code. In a Subchapter S corporation (an "S corporation"), all items of income, loss, deduction and credit are passed through to its shareholders for federal tax purposes.[3] To obtain this more favorable tax treatment, however, shareholders of a Subchapter S corporation forfeit a considerable amount of flexibility to address other issues affecting their ownership rights.

For example, any type of person or entity may be a shareholder of a regular, Subchapter C corporation (a "C corporation"). On the other hand, an S corporation may have as shareholders only individuals who are United States citizens or residents and certain types of trusts.[4] Accordingly, if a corporation, partnership, foreign individual or trust other than those permitted under the Code wishes to own an equity interest in a corporation, that corporation will not be able to elect Subchapter S status. Moreover, the transfer of shares of an S corporation to an ineligible owner will automatically terminate the company's Subchapter S status.

---

2. Although centralized, representative management is the rule, § 620 of the NYBCL permits the shareholders of certain qualifying New York corporations to manage the business and affairs of a corporation in their capacity as shareholders, rather than electing directors to do so. See supra, § 1.47.

3. CAVEAT: New York State and New York City, however, impose taxes at the corporate level on S corporations. Under certain circumstances, a corporate level federal tax can be imposed if the S corporation had previously been a C corporation. For a more complete comparison of the tax treatment of various forms of New York entities, see David G. Levere, Ch. 4, "Tax Considerations in Choice of Entity," in Walker, *Limited Liability Companies and Partnerships: A Guide to Law and Practice* (West 1995).

4. See I.R.C. §§ 1361(b)(2), (d).

§ 2.2   NON-CORPORATE ENTITIES

While a C corporation may have as many shareholders as it desires, an S corporation is theoretically limited to 75 shareholders.[5] Furthermore, aside from differences in voting rights, an S corporation may not create different classes of stock. All shareholders of an S corporation must have the same rights to distributions (based on their relative ownership), both during the life of the corporation and upon liquidation. Unlike C corporations, S corporations may not have preferred stock or preferential returns, nor may their shareholders have percentage interests in profits and losses that shift over time.

If both flexibility and pass-through tax treatment are important to business owners, they may opt instead to organize as a partnership. As in S corporations, items of income, loss, deduction and credit pass through partnerships, and entities treated as partnerships for tax purposes, to their owners, avoiding an entity-level tax. Any type of individual or entity may be a partner of a partnership, and the range of financial and other arrangements between partners is limited only by their imagination and the "substantial economic effect" test imposed by the Code.[6] There is no restriction on the number of partners a partnership may have, but, practically, they should not exceed 500, since the publicly traded partnership rules under Section 7704 of the I.R.C. would require such a large partnership to be taxed as a corporation.

As noted in Section 2.4, *infra*, regulations considerably simplifying entity classification rules became effective on January 1, 1997, permitting taxpayers to elect to treat their unincorporated business organization as either a partnership or corporation for tax purposes without regard to the "corporate characteristics" test described briefly in Sections 2.5 through 2.9, *infra*. Accordingly, pass-through tax treatment now requires little sacrifice other than, perhaps, familiarity with the form of entity. Like all choices, however, organizing as a partnership rather than a corporation may involve other trade-offs. For example, under the New York Partnership Law (the "NYPL"), general partners are jointly liable for the contractual debts and obligations of the partnership (unless the contract otherwise provides), and jointly and severally liable for torts committed in the course of the partnership's business (in each case, after the assets of the partnership have been exhausted).[7] Highly risky ventures, therefore, are unlikely to be structured as general partnerships, unless existing corporations can become their partners without undue expense. Even a limited partnership organized under the New York Revised Limited Partnership Act (the "NYRLPA") (Article 8A

---

5. *See* I.R.C. § 1361(b)(1)(A). The Internal Revenue Service (the "IRS") has previously indicated, however, that a series of S corporations, each with at most 35 shareholders, could form a partnership in order to circumvent the 35-shareholder restriction that was effective prior to the liberalization of Subchapter S that took place in 1996. *See* Revenue Ruling ("Rev. Rul.") 94–43, 1994–27 I.R.B. 8.

6. Treasury Regulation ("Treas. Reg.") § 1.704–1(b). *See infra*, discussion at § 2.13.

7. NYPL § 26.

of the NYPL) is required to have at least one general partner that will be personally responsible for all of the partnership's debts and obligations.[8] Limited partners are personally liable to a limited partnership only to the extent of their contributions made or agreed to be made, and, under certain circumstances, for wrongful distributions by the partnership. Nonetheless, limited partners may lose their protection and become liable as general partners if they are deemed to be "control persons" by virtue of the role they play in partnership management.[9]

A general partnership may register as a limited liability partnership ("LLP") under the NYPL, thereby limiting its partners' personal liability for the contractual debts and obligations of the partnership as though they were limited partners.[10] LLPs, however, may be formed only by professionals, and each professional partner nevertheless remains personally responsible for his own negligent acts and those committed by others under his "direct supervision and control."[11]

Since October 1994, when the New York Limited Liability Company Law (the "NYLLCL") took effect, New York businesses have also been able to organize as LLCs. LLCs would seem to be the ideal structure for many businesses, since LLC owners, or members, may have their preferred tax treatment and limited liability, too. As a result, some describe LLCs as limited partnerships without general partners, or S corporations with flexibility, but, in fact, LLCs are hybrid creatures whose nature is not wholly captured by either description.

Virtually all of the provisions of the NYLLCL are permissive. Members of an LLC may rely on the NYLLCL to provide "default" rules to govern their relationships and the operation of the LLC, or they may implement particular business arrangements. Accordingly, LLCs may pick and choose among those characteristics they wish to avoid in a manner not always possible under New York partnership laws. For example, an LLC may opt, by a provision in its operating agreement, for automatic continuity of life, notwithstanding the withdrawal of any of its members—something a limited partnership may ultimately be able to achieve with clever drafting of its partnership agreement, but not as easily as an LLC. By statute, members of LLCs have even greater protection from personal liability for the LLC's obligations than do shareholders of corporations, if the members so desire.[12] They may, on

8. NYPL §§ 121–101(h), 121–303(a). In the past, if the general partner was not adequately capitalized, the partnership was deemed to possess limited liability (one of the four corporate characteristics) for federal tax classification purposes.

9. NYPL § 121–303(a). A limited partner may, of course, be an employee of a limited partnership and have certain voting rights without risking characterization as a control person. See NYPL §§ 121–303(b), (c), (d), (e) and § 2.86, infra.

10. NYPL § 26. See infra, discussion at §§ 2.72–76.

11. NYPL § 26(c).

12. **PRACTICE POINTER**: Protection for LLC members is greater because the NYLLCL does not contain any provision similar to NYBCL § 630, the operation of which exposes those with the ten largest

§ 2.2 NON-CORPORATE ENTITIES Ch. 2

the other hand, elect to assume liability for any or all obligations of the LLC.[13] The members of an LLC thus have the freedom of contract to structure their financial relationships, and the management of their business, exactly as they wish within the parameters of New York law.

Until January 1, 1997, when the "check the box" federal tax classification scheme went into effect, the operating agreement of an LLC, like a partnership agreement, had to be drafted with care. The unwary draftsman could have fallen into traps that would have prevented the LLC from being classified as a partnership for tax purposes—precisely the most likely reason for choosing an LLC structure in the first place. In general, the operation of the default provisions of the NYLLCL (other than the provision limiting members' liability) was intended to qualify a New York LLC as a partnership for federal tax purposes under the corporate characteristics test, but those default rules might not actually have had that result.[14] Fortunately, the inconsistencies between state and federal law are no longer of any moment for entities organized post-simplification. If non-corporate entities organized before "check the box" had a "reasonable basis" to believe that taxation as a partnership was warranted, the IRS will respect that position hereafter.[15]

§ 2.3 Tax Classification

Federal income tax law distinguishes between two types of business entities: corporations and partnerships. A partnership is not itself subject to tax. The Code provides, in essence, that a partnership's items of income, expense and credit are passed through to its partners, who report those items on their own tax returns. Partners thus pay tax on a partnership's profits at their own marginal rates, and report its losses (subject to certain limitations) on their individual returns, where it can offset their other income.

Assuming that a Subchapter S election has not been made, a corporation, in contrast, is itself generally subject to tax. A C corporation generally must pay tax at the entity-level rate on all of its profits. If it has a net loss, the loss may be used to offset income only at the corporate level, in the form of a net operating loss carryback or carryforward. If a C corporation distributes after-tax income to its shareholders, they will generally incur income tax in respect thereof at their individual rates. A C corporation's income thus can be subjected to tax both at the corporation level and then at the shareholder level.

---

shareholdings in a privately-held New York corporation to personal liability for the unpaid wages, salaries and commissions of its employees.

13. NYLLCL § 609(b).
14. *See, e.g., infra,* §§ 2.7, 2.8.
15. *See infra,* § 2.4.

§ 2.4 Tax Classification—Eagerly-Awaited Simplification

Classification of an entity for tax purposes depended historically upon the application of the corporate characteristics test summarized below at Sections 2.5 through 2.9, *infra*. At the end of March 1995, however, the IRS issued Notice 95–14, proposing to simplify existing entity classification rules to allow taxpayers to elect to treat an unincorporated organization as either a partnership or a corporation for tax purposes. The Notice explained, in pertinent part:

> The existing classification regulations are based on the historical differences under local law between partnerships and corporations. However, many states recently have revised their statutes to provide that partnerships and other unincorporated organizations may possess characteristics that have traditionally been associated with corporations, thereby narrowing considerably the traditional distinctions between corporations and partnerships. For example, some partnership statutes have been modified to provide that no partner is unconditionally liable for all of the debts of the partnership. Similarly, almost all states have enacted statutes allowing the formation of limited liability companies. These entities are designed to provide liability protection to all members and to otherwise resemble corporations, while generally qualifying as partnerships for federal tax purposes. *See, e.g.*, Rev. Rul. 88–76, 1988–2 C.B. 360.
>
> One consequence of the narrowing of the differences under local law between corporations and partnerships is that taxpayers can achieve partnership tax classification for a non-publicly traded organization that, in all meaningful respects, is virtually indistinguishable from a corporation. Taxpayers and the Service, however, continue to expend considerable resources in determining the proper classification of domestic unincorporated business organizations.

In order to reduce the amount of resources so expended, as well as the uncertainty heretofore inherent in an entity's tax classification, the IRS issued a Notice of Proposed Rulemaking and Hearing (PS–43–95, 1996–24 I.R.B. 20) on Simplification of Entity Classification Rules on May 13, 1996, and held a public hearing on its proposed rules on August 21, 1996. The new regulations replaced Treas. Reg. §§ 301.7701–1,–2 and–3, effective January 1, 1997.

Under the new "check the box" regulations, unincorporated organizations with at least two "associates" and an objective to carry on a business and divide the gains therefrom may choose, prospectively, whether they will be treated as a partnership or an association (corporation) for tax purposes, unless their taxation is determined under another

§ 2.4 NON-CORPORATE ENTITIES Ch. 2

Code provision.[1] A non-corporate business entity with a single member (and accordingly, not a "partnership") may elect to be classified as a corporation, or it will be disregarded as an entity separate from its owner.[2] Elections are to be executed by all members of the organization at the time made, and bind future members, but an entity satisfied with its default classification under the regulations is not required to make any filing. The default rule for all new non-corporate business entities (other than trusts) having at least two associates is to treat them as partnerships for tax purposes; a non-corporate entity with a single member will be disregarded for federal tax purposes unless it elects to be treated as a corporation.[3]

Changes in an election are treated the same way a change in classification was previously treated: an entity presently taxed as a corporation, upon election to be taxed as a partnership, would be deemed to have liquidated and a new partnership formed. In addition, the regulations generally prevent an eligible entity that has previously elected its classification from electing a different classification within 60 months after the effective date of the prior election.[4]

In order to qualify for default classification under the simplification rules, a pre-existing entity must have claimed the same classification based on the classification tests in place before the new rules went into effect. The IRS will not challenge the classification of an existing entity during any period before the "check the box" rules were in effect if (a) the entity had a reasonable basis (within the meaning of Code § 6662) for its claimed classification, (b) the entity has not claimed any other classification, and (c) neither the entity nor any member thereof was notified in writing prior to May 8, 1996, that the entity's classification was under examination.[5]

Whether an entity was treated as a partnership for tax purposes prior to January 1, 1997, was determined by the application of the corporate characteristics regulations previously promulgated under Code § 7701, Treas. Reg. § 301.7701–2. Accordingly, if a preexisting non-corporate entity, like an LLC or a partnership, had a "reasonable basis" for believing that it qualified for pass-through federal tax treatment

---

§ 2.4

1. As an example, a publicly-traded partnership under I.R.C. § 7704 will continue to be taxed as a corporation thereunder. In addition, under the new rules, certain enumerated foreign business entities are automatically classified as corporations for U.S. tax purposes.

2. Treas. Reg. §§ 301.7701–2(a),–3(b). Accordingly, the owner alone would be taxed (as though he were a partner).

3. Treas. Reg. § 301.7701–3(b). Note that the regulations do not affect the ability of an organization taxed as a partnership to elect to be excluded from subchapter K if it qualifies under Treas.Reg. § 1.761–2.

4. Treas. Reg. § 301.7701–3(c)(1)(iv). Note that this restriction applies only to a change in classification by *election*, not to an entity that elects out of a default classification. Nor does it apply if the organization's business is transferred to another entity. *Id.*

5. Treas. Reg. § 301.7701–3(f)(2).

under those rules, its continued treatment as such generally will not be challenged.

§ 2.5 Tax Classification—Former Corporate Characteristics Test

Corporations have six basic characteristics, according to former Treas. Reg. § 301.7701–2: (1) associates, (2) an objective to carry on business and divide the gain therefrom, (3) continuity of life, (4) centralized management, (5) the owners' liability for corporate debts limited to corporate property, and (6) free transferability of ownership interests. Because the first two characteristics are common to corporations and partnerships, partnerships were distinguished from corporations for tax purposes by reference to the other four characteristics. Prior to January 1, 1997, an entity had to lack at least two of those four corporate characteristics in order for it to be treated as a partnership for tax purposes.

§ 2.6 Tax Classification—Former Corporate Characteristics Test—Limited Liability

The corporate characteristic of limited liability existed if:

(1) . . . . under local law there is no member who is personally liable for the debts of or claims against the organization. Personal liability means that a creditor of an organization may seek personal satisfaction from a member of the organization to the extent that the assets of such organization are insufficient to satisfy the creditor's claim. . . . [I]n the case of a limited partnership subject to a statute corresponding to the Uniform Limited Partnership Act, personal liability exists with respect to each general partner, except as provided in subparagraph (2) of this paragraph.

(2) In the case of an organization formed as a limited partnership, personal liability does not exist, for purposes of this paragraph, with respect to a general partner when he has no substantial assets (other than his interest in the partnership) which could be reached by a creditor of the organization and when he is merely a "dummy" acting as the agent of the limited partners.[1]

The provisions of Revenue Procedure ("Rev. Proc.") 92–88[2] determined whether the general partner of a limited partnership had "substantial assets."

General partners, by law, are personally liable for the debts and obligations of a general partnership, and, accordingly, a general partnership lacked limited liability.[3] LLPs, on the other hand, possess limited

§ 2.6
1. Former Treas. Reg. § 301.7701–2(d).
2. 1992 C.B. 496 (1992).
3. NYPL § 26(a).

liability, notwithstanding that individual partners remain personally responsible for their own malpractice and that committed under their direct supervision and control.[4] By statute, contractual claims and other non-tort obligations against an LLP may be satisfied only out of the LLP's assets,[5] so the partners of an LLP were deemed to enjoy limited liability for tax purposes.[6]

Typically, an LLC, as its name implies, possesses the corporate characteristic of limited liability. The NYLLCL provides that no member of an LLC will be liable for any debts of the LLC unless its Articles of Organization, the document filed with the Secretary of State to establish the LLC, provide otherwise.[7]

Under Section 5.04 of Rev. Proc. 95–10,[8] an LLC lacked limited liability if at least one member meeting certain criteria[9] validly assumed personal liability for all, but not less than all, of the LLC's obligations. The member could not so assume liability via contractual agreement alone.[10] The NYLLCL expressly authorizes one or more members to assume liability for any or all of the LLC's obligations.[11] If (a) the Articles of Organization provided that a member would have unlimited liability, (b) that member met the criteria set forth in Rev. Proc. 95–10, and (c) the consent requirements of the statute were satisfied, the LLC did not have limited liability for federal tax purposes.[12]

Rev. Proc. 95–10 generally required the assuming members to have an aggregate net worth equal to at least 10% of the total contributions to the LLC, which net worth was to continue throughout the life of the LLC. If the assuming members did not satisfy this 10% safe harbor, then the LLC must have been able to demonstrate that the assuming members collectively had substantial assets, other than their interests in the LLC, that could be reached by creditors of the LLC. The guidelines established by Rev. Proc. 92–88 were to be applied to LLC members to determine if they had "substantial assets."

4. NYPL § 26(c).

5. NYPL § 26(b).

6. A person's unlimited liability for professional malpractice alone did not create unlimited liability under former Treas. Reg. § 301.7701–2(a).

7. NYLLCL §§ 609(b), 206(a)(7).

CAVEAT: Note, however, that members of a professional LLC (a "PLLC") remain personally liable for their own professional negligence and that committed by those under their direct supervision and control. NYLLCL § 1205(a); see infra, § 2.43. See also, infra, §§ 2.16–2.20, for a discussion of the formation of an LLC.

8. 1995–3 I.R.B. 20 (1995).

9. The assuming member or members were generally required to own at least a combined 1% interest in the LLC and make at least 1% of the total capital contributions to the LLC.

10. See Richlands Medical Association v. C.I.R., 60 T.C.M. 1572, 1584 (1990), aff'd 953 F.2d 639 (4th Cir.1992) (former Treas. Reg. § 301.7701–2(d) required liability for the debts of an organization to arise under local law, not by contract).

11. NYLLCL § 609(a).

12. PRACTICE POINTER: NYLLCL § 609(b) requires any member liable for any of the LLC's debts to (a) specifically consent in writing (i) to the adoption of the provision in the Articles of Organization or (ii) to be bound by such provision or (b) specifically vote for the adoption of the provision.

§ 2.7 Tax Classification—Former Corporate Characteristics Test—Continuity of Life

Former Treas. Reg. § 301.7701–2(b)(1) set out the elements of the corporate characteristic of continuity of life:

> An organization has continuity of life if the death, insanity, bankruptcy, retirement, resignation, or expulsion of a member will not cause a dissolution of the organization. On the other hand, if the death, insanity, bankruptcy, retirement, resignation, or expulsion of any member will cause a dissolution of the organization, continuity of life does not exist. If the death, insanity, bankruptcy, retirement, resignation, expulsion, or other event of withdrawal of a general partner of a limited partnership causes the dissolution of the partnership, continuity of life does not exist; furthermore, continuity of life does not exist notwithstanding the fact that a dissolution of the limited partnership may be avoided, upon such an event of withdrawal of a general partner, by the remaining general partners agreeing to continue the partnership or by at least a majority in interest of the remaining partners agreeing to continue the partnership.

Continuity of life does not mean perpetual life. Even if its organizational documents set a specified date for its termination, an organization would have had continuity of life unless the bankruptcy, etc. of its members or partners caused the organization to dissolve.[1] Conversely, an entity could lack continuity even if its term was perpetual, as long as those events would cause its dissolution.[2]

For tax purposes, "dissolution" means "an alteration of the identity of an organization by reason of a change in the relationship between its members as determined under local laws."[3] As an example, because a partner's resignation from a general partnership destroys the mutual agency between the withdrawing partner and his partners, thereby altering the personal relation between them, the resignation of a partner dissolves the partnership.[4] Dissolution does not necessarily require a partnership to cease its business operations.

Former Treas. Reg. § 301.7701–2(b)(3) provided a safe harbor for partnerships organized under a statute corresponding to the Uniform Partnership Act or the Uniform Limited Partnership Act. New York general and limited partnerships formed under applicable New York law were organized under a statute so corresponding; they did not possess continuity of life for purposes of the corporate characteristics test. An

---

§ 2.7

1. See former Treas. Reg. § 301.7701–2(b)(3); Rev. Rul. 93–38, 1993–1 C.B. 233; Hynes v. C.I.R., 74 T.C. 1266, 1281–82 (1980) (trust possessed continuity of life notwithstanding specific 20-year term).

2. See, e.g., Rev. Rul. 93–5, 1993–1 C.B. 227.

3. Former Treas. Reg. § 301.7701–2(b)(2).

4. Id.

LLP formed under NYPL § 121–1500 was not subject to a statute that corresponds to the UPA for purposes of the regulations.[5] However, Section 60 of the NYPL, which governs both general partnerships and LLPs, provides that an LLP or a general partnership is dissolved:

(1) without violation of the agreement between the parties, by the express will of any partner when no definite term or particular undertaking is specified or

(2) in contravention of the agreement between the partners, when the circumstances do not permit a dissolution under [NYPL § 62], by the express will of any partner at any time.

Accordingly, an LLP lacked continuity of life as well.

The NYLLCL does not, however, "correspond" to either the Uniform Partnership Act or the Uniform Limited Partnership Act, so a pre-existing New York LLC could not rely on this safe harbor.[6] The NYLLCL's default rule provides that an LLC will be dissolved upon the bankruptcy, death, dissolution, expulsion, incapacity or withdrawal of any member, or of only the members specified in the operating agreement, unless within 180 days after such event the LLC is continued by the vote or written consent of a majority in interest of all of the remaining members.[7] The default provision, however, can be varied by the operating agreement, which could, for example, provide that an LLC will continue automatically regardless of any specified event of bankruptcy, etc., or upon the approval of less than a majority in interest of all members or of a designated group of members or managers only. In theory, an operating agreement could also provide that, except for one specified dissolution event with respect to one specified member, dissolution would not occur.

Rev. Proc. 95–10, however, stated that if dissolution was keyed to less than all the events listed in the tax regulations, the taxpayer had to be able to establish clearly that the designated event or events provided a meaningful possibility of dissolution in order to avoid having continuity of life.[8] As to which members, if not all, to whom dissolution events would apply, Section 5.01(2) of Rev. Proc. 95–10 stated that, for an LLC that did not designate or elect one or more members as managers,[9] the IRS would rule that continuity of life was lacking only if all members

---

5. Rev. Rul. 95–55, *supra*.

6. Tax Decision 8475, 1993–1 C.B. 236, the preamble to the 1993 amendment to former Treas. Reg. § 301.7701–2(b)(1), rejected a request that the amended regulation expressly include LLCs.

7. NYLLCL § 701(d). NYLLCL § 102(*o*) defines "majority in interest of the members" as the members owning interests representing, in the aggregate, more than half of the interests in current profits (unless the operating agreement provides otherwise). Dissolution of an LLC can also take place upon the date or events (if any) specified in the Articles of Organization or operating agreement, by vote of the members, or by judicial decree. NYLLCL §§ 701(a), (b), (c), (e).

8. Rev. Proc. 95–10, *supra*, § 2.6, note 8, § 5.01(4).

9. For a discussion of member-management and manager-management of LLCs, *see infra*, §§ 2.25–2.28.

were subject to dissolution events. If the LLC named one or more members as managers, then all of the member-managers had to be subject to the dissolution events.[10] The IRS had previously held that events with respect to only the sole member-manager of an LLC would prevent continuity from existing.[11]

Although the NYLLCL allows an operating agreement to require consent to continue business after a dissolution event from less than a majority in interest of members, or from only a certain class or group of members, such a provision would have risked a finding of continuity of life.[12] Furthermore, differences between the way "majority in interest" was defined for tax purposes and the way it is defined in the NYLLCL had the potential, prior to "check the box," to create a trap for the unwary.

§ 2.8 Tax Classification—Former Corporate Characteristics Test—Free Transferability of Interests

Free transferability of interests existed in an entity:

if each of its members or those members owning substantially all of the interests in the organization have the power, without the consent of other members, to substitute for themselves in the same organization a person who is not a member of the organization. In order for this power of substitution to exist in the corporate sense, the member must be able, without the consent of other members, to confer upon his substitute all the attributes of his interest in the organization. Thus, the characteristic of free transferability of interests does not exist in a case in which each member can, without the consent of other members, assign only his right to share in profits but cannot so assign his rights to participate in the management of the organization.[1]

A member's or partner's ability to assign freely only the economic attributes of his interest, *i.e.*, the right to receive distributions and allocations of profit and loss, did not constitute free transferability. Free

---

10. Rev. Proc. 95–10, *supra*, § 2.6, note 8, § 5.01(1) also required member-managers to satisfy certain capital contribution and profit and loss interest requirements.

11. *See* PLR 9210019 (December 6, 1991) (Texas). For a discussion of the difficulties in applying the standards of Rev. Proc. 95–10 to New York LLCs to determine whether they lacked continuity of life, *see* D.G. Levere, "Tax Classification of a Limited Liability Company," § 2.2 in Walker, *Limited Liability Companies and Partnerships: A Guide to Law and Practice* (West 1995).

12. PRACTICE POINTER: The NYLLCL, unlike New York's partnership statutes, permits an operating agreement to provide for automatic continuation of the LLC's business after a dissolution event. As a result, it is easier for an LLC to take advantage of the IRS' new flexibility than for a partnership.

§ 2.8

1. Former Treas. Reg. § 301.7701–2(e)(1).

transferability required, in addition, the ability to assign the right to participate in the management of the entity.

In general, free transferability did not exist if the transfer of interests representing more than 20% of all interests in partnership capital, income, gain, loss, deduction and credit was restricted.[2] Therefore, slightly less than 80% of the interests in a partnership or LLC could be freely transferable without creating the corporate characteristic of free transferability, and the operating or partnership agreement could so provide. Where the members' or partners' respective interests varied over time, restrictions on transferability had to be carefully drafted so that they would always apply to more than the 20% minimum.[3]

The tax regulations also implied that a partnership or LLC would lack free transferability even where there was no restriction on transfers between members or partners. Consistent with this, one private ruling specifically held that an LLC lacked free transferability where the statute permitted the free transfer of LLC interests to other members.[4]

Section 5.02(4) of Rev. Proc. 95-10 provided that the IRS would not rule that free transferability was lacking in an LLC unless the power to withhold consent to the transfer constituted a meaningful restriction. A restriction without meaning is one where, for example, consent could not be unreasonably withheld.[5]

NYLLCL § 603(1) provides, as a statutory default, that an interest in an LLC may be freely assigned, but Sections 603(2) and (3) track the language of the former tax regulations. They provide that, unless otherwise permitted in the operating agreement, an assignee is not entitled to participate in the management and affairs of the LLC or to become or to exercise any rights or powers of a member, and that the only effect of the assignment is to entitle the assignee to receive distributions and allocations of profits and loss.[6] These default provisions allow maximum flexibility to assign economic interests.[7]

NYLLCL §§ 604(a) and 102(o) provide that assignees can become members, having all of the management participation rights associated therewith, upon the vote or written consent of at least a majority of the

---

2. Rev. Proc. 92-33, 1992-1 C.B. 782.

3. A two-member entity, formed under the limited liability company law of a foreign country, that restricted the transfer of one member's interest but not the other's, lacked free transferability of interests where the freely transferable interest would always be less than 80% of capital, income, gain, loss, deduction or credit "throughout the life of the partnership." PLR 9306008 (November 10, 1992).

4. PLR 9350013 (Sept. 15, 1993).

5. *See also,* Larson v. Commissioner, 66 T.C. 159 (1976).

6. The assignee will also succeed to the capital account of its assignor.

7. **CAVEAT**: For an LLC whose operating documents provide for participation in management by all members, an assignment of an economic interest only would result in some owners of economic interests having management powers (the original members) and other owners of economic interests having no management powers (the assignees), effectively creating two classes of owners.

current profits interest of members other than the assignor (unless the operating agreement otherwise provides).[8] NYLLCL § 603(a)(4) provides, further, that a member ceases to be a member, and to have the power to exercise any rights or powers of a member, upon assignment of all of its membership interest. This provision presumably is designed to prevent a member from assigning the economic component of its interest (which does not require consent), and also assigning its voting and management rights, in effect, by entering into a contract (such as a proxy) with its assignee to exercise those rights as the assignee may direct.[9]

The NYLLCL default rule (a majority of the current profits interests of the members other than the transferring member must consent to transfer) might not have met the requirements of prior tax law, however. Sections 5.02(2) and (3) of Rev. Proc. 95–10 indicated that free transferability would not exist if a "majority" of all members approved the transfer and admission of the transferee as a member, defining majority as any of (i) a majority of both capital and profits interests, within the meaning of Rev. Proc. 94–46, (ii) a majority determined on a *per capita* basis, or (iii) a majority of either the capital or profits interests. Profits interest within the meaning of Rev. Proc. 94–46 is not necessarily the same as interests in current profits, but is based on both current and future allocations if they may shift. If profits interest for purposes of test (iii) is similarly defined, then the NYLLCL statutory default is not on all fours with the prior IRS guidelines.

The IRS has also ruled privately that an LLC or a partnership would lack free transferability even though involuntary transfers upon the death, dissolution, liquidation, or bankruptcy of a member were not subject to transfer restrictions.[10] Assignments of interests to creditors, pursuant to pledges or otherwise, likely do not qualify as involuntary transfers for this purpose. However, under the NYLLCL, creditors

---

8. The NYLLCL does not provide that members can withhold their consent in their sole discretion.

9. PRACTICE POINTER: The problem with this provision, from a drafting perspective, is that a member may thus assign part of its economic interest and, because it is still a member, retain, and have the ability by contract to assign, its voting and management rights as well. An operating agreement probably should include a provision preventing this scenario.

10. PLR 9210019 (March 6, 1992). *See also*, PLR 9253013 (September 30, 1992) (limited partnership; transfer without restriction pursuant to will does not create free transferability). *But see* G.C.M. 38,012 (July 13, 1979) (ability of a corporate partner to transfer partnership interest through a merger into another corporation qualifies as free transferability).

PRACTICE POINTER: Under NYLLCL § 608, the estate of a deceased or incompetent member, as well as the legal representative or successor of a dissolved or terminated corporation, trust or other entity member, has all the powers of the member for purposes of settling his or her estate or administering his or her property. That Section also states that if a member is a corporation, trust or other entity and is dissolved or terminated, "the powers of that member may be exercised by its legal representative or successor." This latter provision arguably is inconsistent with the general rule of NYLLCL § 603(a) that assignees are not entitled to exercise any rights or powers of members.

acquire by assignment or pledge only the economic attributes of a member's interest in an LLC.[11]

A more difficult question concerned transfers to related persons, such as family members of, or entities affiliated with, an LLC member, or other limited groups of permitted transferees. It would seem that a right of transfer, without consent, limited to such transferees would not be a "free" right of transfer and thus could safely have been incorporated into an operating agreement prior to January 1, 1997 (at which time it clearly became permissible without any effect on tax classification issues). Several respected commentators, however, expressed concern that this transferability, even though limited, could create the corporate characteristic of free transferability.[12] The tax regulations clearly indicated that an agreement allowing a member to transfer its interest after first offering it to other members, *i.e.*, a right of first refusal, without other restrictions, would also give rise to free transferability.[13]

Section 40(7) of the NYPL, applicable to both New York general partnerships and LLPs, provides that no person may become a member of a partnership without the consent of all the partners. Accordingly, those entities formed before January 1, 1997, did not have freely transferable interests. Sections 121–702 and 121–704 of the NYRLPA are virtually identical to their counterparts under the NYLLCL. As a result, New York limited partnerships may have had freely transferable interests or not, as their organizers chose, subject to all of the factors discussed above with respect to restrictions imposed by the IRS.

§ 2.9 Tax Classification—Former Corporate Characteristics Test—Centralized Management

An organization had centralized management if "any person (or any group of persons which does not include all the members) has continuing exclusive authority to make the management decisions" necessary to the conduct of the organization's business.[1] The persons who are vested with such management authority "resemble in power and function the directors of corporations."[2] Centralized management did not exist "when

---

11. NYLLCL § 607 provides that creditor assignees acquire only the economic attributes of an LLC interest, not voting and management rights. The operating agreement may not vary this treatment.

12. See McKee, Nelson & Whitmire, *Federal Taxation of Partnerships and Partners* (2d ed. 1990) (hereafter, "McKee") ¶ 3.06(4)(d); Brannan, *Lingering Partnership Classification Issues*, 1 Fla. Tax Rev. 197, 222 (1993). Neil Auerbach, IRS Branch Chief, Office of Associate Chief Counsel (International), stated on June 7, 1994, that in his view the potential for unrestricted transfers to affiliates or family members should create the corporate characteristic of free transferability of interests. Tax Notes International (July 25, 1994).

13. Former Treas. Reg. § 301.7701-2(e)(2).

§ 2.9

1. Former Treas. Reg. § 301.7701-2(c)(1).

2. *Id.*

the centralized authority is merely to perform ministerial acts as an agent at the direction of a principal."[3]

The regulations provided that a limited partnership organized under a statute corresponding to the Uniform Limited Partnership Act generally did not have centralized management, but that it would have this corporate characteristic if "substantially all" the interests in the partnership were owned by the limited partners.[4] The reasoning behind the "substantially all" rule was that a general partner always acts in a representative capacity, but when it has a meaningful interest, *i.e.*, the limited partners do not own substantially all of the partnership, the general partner acts on its own behalf as well.[5] The regulations did not define "substantially all," but they provided an example where 94.3% was "substantially all."

Even if subject to a state law corresponding to the Uniform Limited Partnership Act, a limited partnership might also have possessed centralized management where "all or a specified group of the limited partners may remove a general partner."[6] The rationale behind this rule was that an unrestricted right of removal indicated that the general partner was managing in a representative capacity rather than on its own behalf.[7] However, "[a] substantially restricted right of the limited partners to remove the general partner (*e.g.*, in the event of the general partner's gross negligence, self-dealing, or embezzlement) [would] not itself cause the partnership to possess centralized management."[8]

Section 20 of the NYPL, applicable to both general partnerships and LLPs, provides that every partner is an agent of the partnership for the purpose of its business, and the act of every partner, including the execution in the partnership name of any instrument, for apparently carrying on business in the usual way binds the partnership. Because of this mutual agency, the IRS ruled that a general partnership or an LLP could not effectively concentrate management powers and, therefore, would not have centralized management.

Under NYLLCL § 206(a)(6), the Articles of Organization of an LLC must state whether the LLC is to be managed by its members or by one or more managers.[9] NYLLCL Section 412(a) further provides that, unless the Articles of Organization vest management power in a manager,

---

3. Former Treas. Reg. § 301.7701-2(c)(3).
4. Former Treas. Reg. § 301.7701-2(c)(4).
5. *See* Glensder Textile Co., 46 B.T.A. 176, 185 (1942).
6. Former Treas. Reg. § 301.7701-2(c)(4).
7. *See* T.D. 7889, 1983–1 C.B. 362, 363.
8. Former Treas. Reg. § 301.7701-2(c)(4).

9. This provision would indicate that there is no statutory default rule governing an LLC's management. NYLLCL § 401(a) however, states that unless the Articles of Organization provide for management by a manager or managers, then management of an LLC shall be vested in its members. This statutory provision could be argued to provide a statutory default of member management, notwithstanding NYLLCL § 206(a)(6).

every member is an agent of the limited liability company for the purpose of its business, and the act of every member, including the execution in the name of the limited liability company of any instrument, for apparently carrying on in the usual way the business of the limited liability company, binds the limited liability company, unless (i) the member so acting has in fact no authority to act for the limited liability company in the particular matter and (ii) the person with whom he or she is dealing has knowledge of the fact that the member has no such authority.

If the Articles of Organization do vest management powers in a manager, NYLLCL § 412(b)(1) puts the world on notice that members who are not designated as managers do not have authority to bind the LLC.

The operating agreement, like a partnership agreement, can also limit management powers to only certain members, or classes or groups of members.[10] If such limitations are contained only in the operating agreement and not in the Articles of Organization, third parties presumably are not on notice that members without management powers do not have authority to bind the LLC, and, accordingly, even those members would bind the LLC vis-a-vis third parties.[11]

If an LLC had no managers, but was managed by all of its members exclusively in their capacity as members, Section 5.03(1) of Rev. Proc. 95–10 stated that the LLC would lack centralized management. While not expressly mentioned in the NYLLCL, an LLC may appoint individuals to perform the roles, and have the titles, of officers of corporations, *e.g.*, president, vice president, secretary and treasurer.[12]

§ 2.10 Partnership vs. LLC

Once the decision to organize as a non-corporate entity is made, clients will have to choose among the various forms of partnerships and LLCs. Unless they are professionals, the LLP will not be an alternative. General and limited partnerships have the advantages of familiarity and predictability over LLCs. LLCs, however, ultimately may prove the most flexible structure and the most protective of all of their owners' personal liability. The costs of organizing a limited partnership and an LLC under the New York law will probably be equivalent, although upkeep of an LLC might be slightly more expensive (due to the per-member annual fee—*see infra*, Section 2.11). Because a general partnership requires neither a centralized filing with the state (although it does require

---

10. NYLLCL § 417(a)(iii). The operating agreement can also limit the voting rights of specified members. *See* NYLLCL § 418(a).

11. *See* NYLLCL § 412(a). Such members without the right to bind the LLC would presumably be liable to the LLC and the other members for damages resulting from their actions in breach of the operating agreement.

12. PRACTICE POINTER: Appointment of "officers," so long as they are not formally designated "managers," would not change the statutory default that all members continue to have agency power to bind the LLC.

county filings) nor a written agreement, it may be the cheapest of all to organize, but the real cost of a general partnership is the risk to which its partners' personal assets are exposed.

§ 2.11 Partnership vs. LLC—Tax Implications

Assuming they do not elect to be classified other than as pass-through entities, LLCs and their owners probably will be treated much the same way that partnerships and their partners are treated for most tax purposes.[1] Certain concepts that rely on the distinction between general and limited partners, however, may require further elucidation from the IRS before their application to LLCs is clear.[2]

A partnership, or an LLC taxable as a partnership, does not pay any "entity" level tax for federal, New York City or New York State purposes other than the 4% New York City unincorporated business tax imposed on most business activities in the City. An LLC treated as a partnership for federal tax purposes is treated as a partnership for all purposes of New York State and New York City tax laws, including income, sales and other taxes.[3] Corporate taxes like the accumulated earnings tax and the personal holding company tax do not apply to an entity taxed as a partnership.

Unlike a limited or general partnership, an LLC (and an LLP) is subject to a yearly per-member fee of $50 imposed by the State, and authorized to be imposed (although not yet imposed) by New York City. This fee is levied only if the LLC or LLP has New York source income, *i.e.*, income from the ownership of any interest in real or tangible personal property located in New York, or the conduct of a business, trade or profession in New York (City or State).[4] The minimum annual fee is $325; the maximum, $10,000, which, of course, would double for New York City LLCs and LLPs if the City fee were to become effective.

Members of both partnerships and LLCs are treated the same way when they contribute property in return for their ownership interests.[5] A member or partner generally recognizes no gain on contributions of appreciated property to an LLC or partnership.[6] If the liabilities to which the property is subject exceed the property's basis, a contributor will not necessarily recognize gain equal to such excess. Instead, gain will be recognized only to the extent the owner is deemed to have received a

§ 2.11

1. For a full treatment of partnership taxation, *see supra*, McKee, § 2.8, note 13.

2. *See generally* D.G. Levere, Ch. 9, "Special Tax Issues," in Walker, *Limited Liability Companies and Partnerships: A Guide to Law and Practice* (West 1995) for a discussion of the application of non-classification tax concepts to LLCs.

3. TSB–M–94 (October 25, 1994).

4. Tax Law § 631(b).

5. For a comparison of the treatment of corporations and entities taxable as partnerships in this context, *see* D.G. Levere, Ch. 4, "Tax Considerations in Choice of Entity," § 4.4, in Walker, *Limited Liability Companies and Partnerships: A Guide to Law and Practice* (West 1995).

6. I.R.C. § 721.

"distribution," by virtue of having been "relieved" of net liabilities, that exceeds the basis of the contributed property.[7] Accordingly, a contributor will recognize gain in this case only to the extent that the total liabilities allocable to other members or partners exceeds his basis in the contributed property.[8]

Debt incurred by both LLCs and partnerships is included in the bases of their owners' interests under Code §§ 722 and 752.[9] This enhances a member's or partner's ability to deduct his share of losses, which is limited by the basis of his interest in the entity. In addition, cash distributions to an owner that exceed his basis result in his recognition of income, so this characteristic of entities treated as partnerships can be very attractive.

Distributions of property by LLCs and partnerships receive the same treatment, and both LLCs and partnerships will terminate for tax purposes if 50% or more of the capital and profits interests therein (including the sale or exchange of economic interests only) are transferred within a twelve-month period.[10]

§ 2.12 Partnership vs. LLC—Liability

As discussed in Section 2.6, *supra*, members of LLCs are not, in the absence of an election otherwise, personally liable for the debts and obligations of the LLC merely by reason of their being members. They are liable to the LLC for their contributions to its capital, and for the performance of their obligations to make contributions. They may also be liable to return to the LLC distributions that rendered the LLC insolvent and which they knew at the time to have been wrongful.[1] It is conceivable that courts might apply to LLCs the "veil piercing" concept infrequently used to hold shareholders personally responsible for the obligations of a corporation,[2] but on what theories the "LLC veil" might be pierced can only be imagined. Since the LLC structure is now recognized in all fifty states and the District of Columbia, fears about how a state without an LLC law would treat a foreign LLC have now receded.

Under the NYPL, as noted in Section 2.6, *supra*, partners of a general partnership are jointly and severally liable for the torts of their partners committed in the course of the partnership's business, and jointly liable for partnership contractual obligations, unless otherwise

---

7. *See* I.R.C. § 752(b).

8. *See supra*, D.G. Levere, Ch. 4, "Tax Considerations in Choice of Entity," § 4.4, in Walker, *Limited Liability Companies and Partnerships: A Guide to Law and Practice* (West 1995); Treas. Reg. § 1.752-3(a)(2).

9. **PRACTICE POINTER**: This treatment is a significant advantage over S corporations. Unless a shareholder lends to an S corporation, its debt has no bearing on the shareholder's basis, even if the debt is personally guaranteed by them.

10. I.R.C. § 708(b)(1)(B).

§ 2.12

1. NYLLCL § 508.

2. *See infra*, § 2.23, note 19.

provided in the contract. Although the assets of the partnership must first be marshaled for the payment of any of its obligations, the partners' personal assets are at risk for obligations that exceed partnership assets.[3] The same is true for general partners of limited partnerships. To minimize the general partner's exposure, many limited partnerships establish a corporate general partner, preserving pass-through tax status by electing Subchapter S status for it if available. Of course, a corporate general partner may be costly to organize and maintain.

Limited partners, like members of LLCs, generally are liable to a limited partnership for their capital contributions made or agreed to be made, and, under certain circumstances, for distributions that render the partnership insolvent.[4] Partners of both LLPs and members of professional LLCs ("PLLCs"), as discussed in Section 2.6, *supra*, are not liable for any of the contractual debts and obligations of their entities, but they do remain at personal risk for their own negligence and that of other professionals working under their direct supervision and control.

Library References:
West's Key No. Digests, Partnership ⚖125–223.

§ 2.13 Partnership vs. LLC—Flexibility

Particularly now that their tax classification as pass-through entities has become automatic under the check the box regulations, partnerships and LLCs are certainly the most flexible business entities available. Any type of entity may own an interest in a partnership or an LLC (although only professionals or entities comprising professionals may own an interest in a PLLC or an LLP), and what may be owned by LLCs and partnerships generally, including interests in entities other than S corporations, is not restricted. There are few procedural formalities imposed on either partnerships or LLCs. Governing documents usually may address management and the owners' financial relationships in any way agreed by the parties.

All manner of special allocations and other financial interests may be created in partnerships and LLCs as long as they have "substantial economic effect."[1] Substantial economic effect is lacking if allocations are inconsistent with economic sharing arrangements among the participants, or if they achieve tax savings without corresponding economic benefit or detriment.[2]

An LLC may actually be a more flexible entity than a partnership, limited or general, and may therefore more easily avail itself of the opportunities presented by the check the box regulations. For example,

3. See Helmsley v. Cohen, 56 A.D.2d 519, 391 N.Y.S.2d 522 (1st Dep't 1977).
4. NYPL §§ 121-303(a), 121-502, 121-607(b).

§ 2.13
1. Treas. Reg. § 1.704–1(b)(2).
2. Id.

an LLC may elect to have continuity of life by placing an appropriate provision in its operating agreement, creating a corporate-like structure that will appeal to investors and lenders alike. While a limited partnership agreement might be carefully drafted to have more or less the same effect, the New York partnership laws are not nearly as straightforward as the NYLLCL.

Another shortcoming of a limited partnership is that a limited partner risks losing his limited liability if he exercises "control" over the partnership.[3] All members of an LLC may participate in its management if this is desired. Generally, all partners of a general partnership are charged with its management, unless the partnership agreement otherwise provides.[4] In any case, all members of a general partnership may bind the partnership vis-a-vis third parties.

§ 2.14 Limited Liability Companies

The LLC is perhaps the least familiar and most unpredictable business structure available to New York entrepreneurs, although its potential utility has made it immediately popular. For many types of new enterprises, including real estate investments and closely-held businesses, it has become the organization of choice because of its unique combination of flexibility, limited liability and pass-through tax treatment.

§ 2.15 Limited Liability Companies—Governing Law

Since Utah adopted the first LLC statute in 1977, the remainder of the country and the District of Columbia have authorized the creation of LLCs. New York first began to consider LLC legislation in the early 1990s, when a Joint Drafting Committee of The Association of the Bar of The City of New York and The New York State Bar Association prepared a draft of the NYLLCL. The Committee's goal was to produce a cohesive, flexible statute that would permit businesspeople to tailor a New York LLC to their specific needs. The Committee drew heavily from the NYRLPA, and, in places, the NYBCL, for the NYLLCL's provisions, which were intended both to reflect normal business expectations and to ensure tax treatment as a partnership for federal and New York State purposes under the then-applicable corporate characteristics test. Since the NYLLCL became effective in October 1994, thousands of New York LLCs have been formed.

Unlike the LLC statutes adopted in most other jurisdictions, the NYLLCL addresses a wide range of organizational, procedural, management and liability issues, in addition to the default provisions discussed above. Accordingly, although most of its provisions may be altered by agreement, the NYLLCL offers guidance for the operation of New York

---

3. *See* NYPL § 121–303; § 2.86, *infra*. 4. NYPL § 40.

LLCs that is not available to LLCs organized under other statutes. To the extent the provisions of the NYLLCL clearly derive from either the NYRLPA or the NYBCL, such laws might supply precedents for the interpretation of the NYLLCL, perhaps making its application less unpredictable.

§ 2.16 Limited Liability Companies—Formation

New York LLCs may be formed for any lawful business purpose, except they may not do any business in New York that must, by law, be pursued in another form.[1] "Business" means "every trade, occupation, profession or commercial activity."[2] Although the use of the phrase "business purpose" may imply that LLCs must be for-profit enterprises, the NYLLCL does not specifically require LLCs to be established for pecuniary profit.[3]

The name of an LLC must contain words or an abbreviation giving notice of its status as a limited liability company, and may not contain words, like "partnership," that might mislead people about the LLC's essential nature.[4] LLC names may be reserved prior to organization pursuant to NYLLCL § 205.

A New York LLC has broad powers comparable to those granted to a New York business corporation, unless the LLC's Articles of Organization provide otherwise.[5] These powers include the power to sue or be sued, to purchase, sell or lease real or personal property, to conduct business and maintain offices in any state, foreign country or other jurisdiction and to have and exercise all powers necessary or convenient to effect any of the purposes for which the LLC was formed.[6] The NYLLCL imposes certain limitations upon an LLC's ability to enter guaranty contracts.[7] Such limitations may, however, be removed by the operating agreement.[8]

An LLC is formed when its Articles of Organization are filed with the Secretary of State of the State of New York, or on such later date (not more than 60 days after filing) as specified in the Articles.[9] One or more persons or entities may act as the organizer or organizers of a New

§ 2.16

1. NYLLCL § 201. Insurance underwriting, for example, may not be conducted by LLCs, but "investment" LLCs may now be formed.

2. NYLLCL § 102(e).

3. NYLLCL § 1203(a), on the other hand, specifically requires PLLCs to be established for pecuniary profit.

PRACTICE POINTER: Care must be taken, however, to ensure that other state LLC statutes will permit foreign LLCs to engage in not-for-profit activities if a New York not-for-profit LLC expects to "do business" extra-territorially.

4. NYLLCL § 204.

5. NYLLCL § 201.

6. NYLLCL § 202. Note that the NYLLCL grants an LLC the power to indemnify a broader class of individuals than those who may be indemnified by a New York business corporation. Cf. NYLLCL § 420 and NYBCL § 202(a)(10).

7. NYLLCL § 202(e).

8. Id.

9. NYLLCL § 203(d).

York LLC.[10] An organizer may, but need not, be a member of the LLC being formed.[11] However, since an LLC must have at least one member at the time of formation, it is advisable that the organizer(s) include at least one such member, or that a non-member organizer have clear instructions from a member to file the Articles of Organization.[12]

§ 2.17 Limited Liability Companies—Formation—Articles of Organization

The Articles of Organization of a New York LLC must contain the following information:

(i) the name of the LLC, which must include either the words "Limited Liability Company" or the abbreviation "L.L.C." or "LLC";[1]

(ii) the county within New York State in which the office (or principal office, if the LLC has more than one New York office) of the LLC is to be located;

(iii) if the LLC is to have a specific date of dissolution, the latest date on which the LLC is to dissolve;

(iv) a designation of the Secretary of State as agent of the LLC upon whom process against the LLC may be served, and the post office address within or without the State of New York to which the Secretary of State shall mail a copy of any process against the LLC served upon the Secretary;

(v) if the LLC is to have a registered agent, its name and address within New York and a statement that the registered agent is to be the agent of the LLC upon whom process against the LLC must be served;

(vi) a statement as to whether the LLC is to be managed by one or more members or a class or classes of members, or by one or more managers or a class or classes of managers;

(vii) if all or specified members are to be liable in their capacity as members for all or specified debts, obligations or liabilities of the LLC, a statement to such effect; and

(viii) any other provisions, not inconsistent with law, that the members of the LLC elect to include in the Articles for the regulation of the "internal" affairs of the LLC, including, but not limited to, the business purpose for which the LLC is formed, a statement as to whether there are limitations on the authority of members or

---

10. NYLLCL § 203(a).
11. NYLLCL § 203(b).
12. *See* discussion of one-member LLCs at § 2.24, *infra*.

§ 2.17
1. NYLLCL § 204(a).

managers to bind the LLC and any provisions that are required or permitted to be included in the operating agreement of the LLC.[2]

Under the NYLLCL's default provisions, each member may bind the LLC in the usual course of the LLC's business, unless such member lacks authority to act for the LLC in the particular matter and the person with whom he is dealing knows that the member has no authority.[3] A member's ability to bind the LLC *vis-a-vis* third parties can be limited only if the Articles of Organization so provide (by indicating that managers, not members, will manage the company). If the LLC's operating agreement alone limits management authority to a group less than all members, the other members and the LLC may have an action against a member acting without authorization, but third parties without knowledge may nevertheless enforce against the LLC obligations entered by an unauthorized member.

The managers' performance of their duties for the LLC is governed by a prudent person standard.[4] However, the Articles of Organization or operating agreement of an LLC may eliminate or limit the managers' personal liability to the LLC or its members for damages resulting from a breach of duty in any capacity, with limited exceptions, including where a final judgment establishes that the manager has acted in bad faith or intentionally engaged in acts of misconduct.[5]

Other specific provisions included in the Articles pursuant to (viii) above may limit the flexibility of the operations of an LLC, or require frequent, and perhaps costly, amendment of the Articles. For example, a narrow definition of business purpose will limit the business activities as to which the managers of an LLC may bind it in the ordinary course, but if the business of the LLC changes or expands, the Articles must be amended. Likewise, a specific term for the existence of the LLC may be included in its Articles of Organization, perhaps in connection with defining members' rights to withdraw from the LLC during an initial period. (There would appear to be no other reason to include such a provision in the Articles.) If, for some reason, the members forget that such a provision exists, and the Articles are not amended, the LLC will terminate on that date, with possibly dire consequences.[6]

The Department of State charges a $200 fee for filing an LLC's Articles of Organization.[7] When its Articles of Organization are filed, an

---

2. NYLLCL § 206. See *infra*, § 2.111, for a simple form of Articles of Organization.

3. NYLLCL § 412(a).

4. "A manager shall perform his or her duties as a manager in good faith and with that degree of care that an ordinarily prudent person in a like position would use under similar circumstances." NYLLCL § 409(a). See *infra*, discussion at § 2.31.

5. NYLLCL §§ 202(k), 417(a), 420. See *infra*, discussion at § 2.31.

6. PRACTICE POINTER: The inconvenience of having to amend the Articles can be avoided by addressing dissolution in the operating agreement either with or without reference to a specific term.

7. NYLLCL § 1101(f).

LLC should also apply for an employer identification number ("EIN") from the IRS. The EIN is obtained by filing Form SS-4 with the IRS, or on an expedited basis by telephoning the IRS.

An LLC in certain cases must, and otherwise may, amend its Articles of Organization by preparing and filing with the Secretary of State a Certificate of Amendment under Section 211 of the NYLLCL. The Certificate of Amendment must be signed by at least one member, manager or authorized person of the LLC.[8] Except as otherwise provided in the operating agreement of the LLC, an amendment to the Articles must be authorized by at least a majority in interest of the members entitled to vote thereon.[9] However, a Certificate of Amendment making only certain administrative changes, such as a change of the name or address of the registered agent, may be authorized by only a majority of the managers of the LLC, if any.[10] The Certificate of Amendment is effective upon filing.[11]

If a publicly-filed document relating to an LLC, including its Articles of Organization, Certificate of Amendment or other certificate filed under the NYLLCL, contains a materially false statement, anyone who reasonably relies on that statement may recover damages for a resulting loss from (a) any person who executed the document, or caused another to execute it on his or her behalf, and knew the statement to be false in any material respect at the time, and (b) any manager who knew of the filing and who knew, or, with the exercise of reasonable care and diligence, should have known, the statement to be false in any material respect at the time the document was executed.[12] In addition, any person suffering such a loss may recover damages from any manager who thereafter knows of the filing of such document and who knows or should know with the exercise of reasonable care and diligence that any arrangement or other fact described therein has changed, making the statement false in any material respect.[13] If, however, an amendment or other corrective document is filed within 90 days after the time a person knew or should have known that a statement was false in any material respect, that person will not be liable.[14]

§ 2.18 Limited Liability Companies—Formation—Publication

In addition to filing its Articles of Organization with the Department of State, an LLC is required to publish notice of its formation.

---

8. NYLLCL § 211(a).

9. NYLLCL § 213(a). "Majority in interest" is defined by the Act as members holding a majority of the aggregate shares of the LLC's current profits. *See* NYLLCL § 102(*o*).

10. NYLLCL § 213(b). Of course, the operating agreement may require other authorization.

11. NYLLCL § 211(e).
12. NYLLCL § 210(a)(1).
13. NYLLCL § 210(a)(2).
14. NYLLCL § 210(b).

Within 120 days after filing, an LLC's Articles, or a notice containing the substance thereof, must be published once a week for six consecutive weeks in two newspapers designated by the county clerk in the county where the principal office of the LLC is located. One of the designated newspapers must be published in the town where the LLC's office is located.[1] If there is no such newspaper, the county clerk will designate the "nearest" such newspaper.[2] An affidavit of the printer or publisher of each such newspaper is evidence of publication and must be filed with the Department of State.[3]

If the Articles themselves are not reproduced, the notice must provide certain information, including: (a) the name of the LLC; (b) the date of filing of the Articles of Organization with the Secretary of State; (c) the county within New York in which the office of the LLC is to be located; (d) a statement that the Secretary of State has been designated as the agent of the LLC upon whom process against it may be served; (e) the name and address of the registered agent of the LLC, if any; (f) the dissolution date of the LLC, if any; and (g) the character or purpose of the business of the LLC.[4] However, the notice does not require a statement as to whether the LLC is member or manager-managed or whether there is a waiver of any limitation of liability, nor is the substance of amendments to the Articles required to be published. It is hard to see how the publication requirements of the NYLLCL in fact provide much actual notice.

Failure to file proof of publication within 120 days after the effective date of the Articles of Organization will prevent an LLC from maintaining an action in New York unless and until it files such proof. However, the failure to file proof of publication does not impair the validity of any contract or act of the LLC or the right of any other party to maintain any action thereon.[5]

§ 2.19 Limited Liability Companies—Formation—Operating Agreement

The NYLLCL requires an LLC to adopt a written operating agreement, analogous to corporate by-laws or a partnership agreement, within

---

§ 2.18

1. NYLLCL § 206(c). The contents of a foreign LLC's Certificate of Authority must likewise be published. *See* NYLLCL § 802(b).

2. NYLLCL § 206(c).

3. *Id.* Cost of publication is substantially as follows, but can be lowered by attention to the form of notice and if corporate service intermediaries are eliminated: New York County $600–$1600; Kings County $800–$1500; Queens County $800–$1800; Westchester County $400–$800; Nassau County $300–$700; Suffolk County $300–$700; and Rockland County $400–$800. Amendments to NYLLCL § 206(c) have been introduced that would limit the required publication to one week—not six.

4. NYLLCL § 206(c).

5. *Id.*

90 days following formation.[1] The operating agreement should deal, in sufficient detail, with the management and operation of the LLC, the members' financial arrangements, issues pertaining to withdrawal, the dissolution of the LLC and other nuances of the parties' relationship. The drafting of an operating agreement no longer requires close attention to historic tax classification requirements, discussed in Sections 2.6 through 2.9, *supra,* and indeed, an LLC may adopt all the "corporate" desired characteristics, including centralized management, continuity of life and free transferability of interests.[2] To the extent certain issues are not addressed, the default provisions of the NYLLCL will govern.[3] An operating agreement may, in addition, contain any other provisions not inconsistent with law or the LLC's Articles of Organization.[4] An operating agreement is not a matter of public record, but its contents may well be disclosed to potential investors, lenders and others interested in dealing with the LLC.

An operating agreement should be adopted by the members of an LLC as of the date of its formation. If such an agreement is in place before Articles of Organization are filed, it may have created a general partnership of the parties thereto. If adopted as of a date afterwards, the default provisions of the NYLLCL probably will govern the members' relations during the period between filing and adoption.

An operating agreement may be amended from time to time as provided therein.[5] If amendments are not addressed in the agreement, the vote or consent of a majority in interest of members is required to change the agreement.[6]

§ 2.20 Limited Liability Companies—Formation—Other Issues

Each domestic LLC must maintain certain records, including the names and addresses of each member and manager (if any); the contribution and share of profits and losses of each member, or information from which such share can be "readily derived;" a copy of the Articles of

---

§ 2.19

1. NYLLCL § 417(a), (c).
2. An LLC is probably least likely to adopt free transferability of interests, since LLCs are most common among—and useful to—closely-held businesses, which usually desire control over who becomes an investor.
3. *See infra,* § 2.112, for a simple form of operating agreement.
4. **PRACTICE POINTER:** Presumably, members could adopt as their written operating agreement the LLC's Articles and leave to the default provisions of the NYLLCL the issues not addressed by the Articles. This approach is not recommended. If the Articles are detailed enough to be of practical guidance in the management of an LLC, those details become a matter of public record (and the Articles must be amended every time they change). If the Articles are brief, to avoid public disclosure of private business arrangements, it will be inconvenient, at best, to consult the NYLLCL whenever an action needs to be taken, especially if the members are not fully familiar with the statute's default rules.
5. NYLLCL § 417(b).
6. NYLLCL §§ 402(c)(3), 407(a).

Organization and all amendments thereto; a copy of the operating agreement and any amendments thereto, and a copy of the LLC's federal, state and local income tax returns.[1] These records may, but need not, be kept in New York.[2]

The NYLLCL also requires each LLC formed or authorized to conduct business under the NYLLCL to file a biennial statement on forms prescribed by the Secretary of State.[3]

§ 2.21 Limited Liability Companies—Members

Any person or entity, including associations, corporations, trusts, partnerships, LLCs, individuals and nominees, domestic or foreign, may own an interest in an LLC.[1] Subject to the terms and conditions of the members' business arrangements, a membership interest entitles its owner to share in the profits and losses of the LLC, receive distributions and participate in its management, by vote or otherwise.[2] It is the aggregate of a member's financial rights, together with his right to vote or otherwise exercise management rights, that comprises a "membership interest."[3]

An LLC membership interest is personal property,[4] like shares of stock and limited partnership interests; in fact, an LLC may issue certificates representing interests in the LLC.[5] A member's interest may therefore be either a certificated security[6] or uncertificated security[7] within the meaning of New York Uniform Commercial Code (the "UCC") § 8–102, or not a security at all (see infra, Section 2.106). If the requirements of UCC § 8–102 are not met, the membership interest is deemed a general intangible asset.[8] These designations determine how an LLC interest will be treated for various commercial law purposes, including creation and perfection of security interests and their priority.

Unlike a shareholder of a corporation, an LLC member may contribute not only cash, property or services rendered in return for his

§ 2.20

1. NYLLCL § 1102(a). Members of an LLC are permitted, subject to any reasonable standards set forth in the operating agreement, to inspect and copy such records. Presumably, assignees of members (including creditors) are not afforded such rights. NYLLCL § 1102(b).

2. NYLLCL § 1102(a).

3. NYLLCL § 301(e).

§ 2.21

1. NYLLCL § 102(q), (w).

2. NYLLCL § 102(r).

3. Id. A member may strip his financial rights from his membership interest and transfer them apart from management rights, see infra, § 2.34, but the membership interest itself is not thereby transferred. NYLLCL § 603(a).

4. NYLLCL § 601.

5. NYLLCL § 603(b).

6. A certificated security is an instrument which is issued in bearer or registered form, is commonly dealt with on a security exchange, is one of a class of instruments and evidences a share or participation. New York Uniform Commercial Code (the "UCC") § 8–102(1)(a).

7. An uncertificated security is not represented by an instrument and can only be issued in registered form. UCC § 8–102(b).

8. NYLLCL § 603(b).

interest, but also a promissory note or other obligation to contribute cash or property or render services in the future.[9] An obligation to so contribute may be enforced by the LLC, notwithstanding a member's death or disability.[10]

Members share in profits and losses, and are entitled to receive distributions, as set forth in the operating agreement. If, however, the operating agreement neglects to address these issues, profits and losses are allocated, and rights to distributions determined, based on the relative value of each member's contribution to the LLC, to the extent the contribution has been received or promised (but not including obligations in default).[11] Participants in an LLC would do well to insist that the operating agreement address allocations and distributions specifically, as the relative value of the members' contributions from time to time may not accurately reflect what they understand their shares of profits to be.

A member may transact business with an LLC without restriction, as though he were an unaffiliated party.[12] Transactions between an LLC and a manager, or an entity in which a manager has an interest, however, are subject to certain restrictions, including disclosure requirements, imposed by the NYLLCL.[13]

A member may withdraw from an LLC upon the occurrence of any event, or at a time, specified in the operating agreement.[14] If the operating agreement is silent on these issues, a member may withdraw upon the written consent of at least two-thirds in interest of the remaining members.[15] If the members do not consent, or if withdrawal is not addressed in the operating agreement, a member may nonetheless withdraw upon six months' prior written notice to the LLC.[16]

An operating agreement may prohibit a member's voluntary withdrawal at any time before the dissolution and winding up of an LLC.[17] While such a provision may not be specifically enforceable, the operating agreement may further provide that withdrawal in breach thereof will require payment of substantial damages.[18] A withdrawing member is

---

9. NYLLCL § 501. The valuation of contributions other than in cash, and the tax consequences of contributions of future services, must be carefully considered before they are made.
10. NYLLCL § 502(a).
11. NYLLCL §§ 503, 504.
12. NYLLCL § 611.
13. NYLLCL § 411.
14. NYLLCL § 606.
15. Id.
16. Id. The same time period is specified for withdrawal of limited partners in NYPL § 121–603. Because a withdrawn member is entitled to receive "fair value" for his interest (see below), he may realize some liquidity for what otherwise could be an illiquid investment, but this default might also undermine a member's ability to claim the highest estate and gift tax valuation discounts for lack of marketability in connection with gifts of interests.
17. Id.
18. NYLLCL § 606.

entitled to receive, upon withdrawal, distributions as provided in the operating agreement[19] and, if the operating agreement does not otherwise provide, he is also entitled to receive the fair value of his membership interest as of the date of withdrawal within a reasonable time thereafter.[20] If the member withdraws in violation of the operating agreement, the LLC may offset its damages (as specified in the operating agreement or as otherwise determined) against any distributions due the wrongfully withdrawing member.[21] The operating agreement may also place conditions, including non-competition by the withdrawn member or continued services to the LLC, upon any payments to be made. If the operating agreement so provides, payment in respect of a withdrawn member's interest may be made only upon dissolution of the LLC, and the member may, or may not, be permitted to receive distributions in respect thereof until then. Since payments to a withdrawing member could create a cash flow problem for an LLC, its operating agreement should address the amount and terms of any required payout.[22] Under the default provisions of the NYLLCL, the withdrawal of a member will result in the dissolution of the LLC, unless its business is continued by vote of the remaining members.[23]

A judgment creditor, upon petition to the appropriate court, may charge the membership interest of a member with the unsatisfied amount of a judgment, plus interest,[24] but the creditor will have only the rights of an assignee of a membership interest, *i.e.*, rights to the member's share of profits, losses and distributions, but no right to vote or otherwise participate in management.[25] A creditor has no right in law or equity with respect to the property of the LLC.[26] However, a creditor may have rights against an LLC that makes a wrongful distribution to a member as set forth in Section 508(a) of the NYLLCL, and against the member under Section 508(b).

A deceased or incompetent member's legal representative may exercise all of that member's rights under the LLC's operating agreement, but only for the purpose of settling the member's estate or administering

19. *Id.*
20. NYLLCL § 509. The term "fair value" is not defined in the NYLLCL but is used in NYBCL §§ 623(a), 1118(a).

CAVEAT: The NYLLCL also does not indicate what constitutes a "reasonable time." Depending on the type of business and the amount to be paid, a reasonable time might be as little as a few months or as much as a year. Because the statutory term is undefined, the operating agreement should address these issues specifically.

21. NYLLCL § 606.
22. **PRACTICE POINTER**: The operating agreement could include a method of determining fair value or any other means of valuing and paying for a member's interest. As noted above, the opportunity to withdraw from an LLC and receive fair value for his interest might provide a measure of liquidity to a member if transfers of interests to third parties are otherwise restricted.

23. NYLLCL § 701(d). *See infra*, § 2.38.
24. NYLLCL § 607. *See* NYPL § 121-703 for a similar provision.
25. *See* NYLLCL §§ 603, 604. NYPL § 121-703 is similar.
26. *Id.*

his affairs.[27] If a member corporation, trust or other entity is dissolved or terminated, its legal representative or successor may exercise the same powers as the member.[28]

A member of an LLC cannot be either a plaintiff or defendant in an action brought against or on behalf of an LLC, except to enforce the member's right against, or liability to, the LLC.[29]

§ 2.22 Limited Liability Companies—Members—Admission of New Members

One becomes a member of a New York LLC on the date its Articles of Organization become effective or the date specified in the operating agreement, whichever is later.[1] If it is not possible to ascertain a date from the operating agreement, it is as stated in the records of the LLC.[2] Each of NYLLCL §§ 602(a) and 203(c) assumes that at least one member exists at the time the LLC is formed. However, the initial member or members are not required to sign the Articles of Organization.[3]

Once an LLC has been established, a person may be admitted as a member either upon the vote or written consent of a majority in interest of the members[4] or otherwise as required by the operating agreement.[5] If a person acquires his interest from a member and thereafter becomes a member himself, he may inherit the obligations of his predecessor to make capital contributions. Admission of an assignee of a member as a member of the LLC is discussed in Section 2.35, *infra*.

§ 2.23 Limited Liability Companies—Members—Liability

As noted above, an LLC protects its members from unlimited personal liability in much the same way that a corporate structure

---

27. NYLLCL § 608. *See* NYPL § 121-706 for a similar provision. If the operating agreement is silent on the conditions for succession by a legal representative, the provisions of the NYLLCL must be satisfied.

28. *Id.*

29. NYLLCL § 610.

PRACTICE POINTER: If an action is brought by a non-member assignee to enforce a member's rights, the question may arise whether the assignor or assignee may maintain such action or whether anybody has the right to bring such an action. The concepts of record and beneficial holder under New York corporate law might provide guidance in these cases.

§ 2.22

1. NYLLCL § 602(a)(1), (2).
2. NYLLCL § 602(a)(2).
3. NYLLCL §§ 203(a), 203(b), 207(a). These Sections would allow an attorney to establish an LLC for a client without the client's signature. This practice is similar to that permitted under the NYBCL § 401.
4. NYLLCL § 102(*o*) defines "majority in interest of the members" as the members whose aggregate share of current profits constitute more than one-half the aggregate of such shares of all members, unless otherwise provided in the operating agreement.
5. NYLLCL § 602(b)(1).

shields its shareholders.[1] Accordingly, a member is not personally responsible for the debts, obligations and liabilities of the LLC, whether arising in tort or otherwise, by virtue of his ownership or participation in the management of the LLC.[2]

This, of course, does not mean that a member, manager or agent may not be liable to the LLC or to third parties under certain circumstances. Generally, a member, manager or agent will be personally liable if he commits a tort in his individual capacity,[3] if he individually guarantees any debt of the LLC[4] or if he individually, and without disclosing he is acting on behalf of an LLC, enters into a contract with a third party.[5] A member who acts on behalf of a defectively formed LLC is probably liable in his individual capacity.[6] Likewise, members who operate before the LLC is established will probably be liable as partners or in their individual capacity.

If a member receives a distribution that renders the LLC insolvent, he is liable to repay it to the LLC or its creditors if he knew at the time of the distribution that it violated Section 508(a) of the NYLLCL.[7] However, a member is not liable to the LLC or to creditors after three years from the date of the distribution.[8] An LLC member may also be liable for self-employment taxes.[9]

A member who fails to perform a promise to make a capital contribution to, or perform services for, an LLC, is liable to the LLC for

§ 2.23

1. NYLLCL § 609(a). *But see* § 2.2, note 14, *supra*.

2. NYLLCL § 609(a).

3. **CAVEAT**: A member is not liable generally for a tort committed by an employee of the LLC. *Id.* However, a tort committed by a member in his individual capacity will not be shielded by the limitation on liability contained in NYLLCL § 609(a). That Section limits protection to acts performed (or omitted) in the course of the conduct of the LLC's business.

4. NYLLCL § 611 authorizes a member to act as a guarantor or surety. Liability arises from such a contractual obligation.

5. *Restatement (Second) of Agency* § 322 (1958) addresses the liability of the agent of an undisclosed principal.

6. NYLLCL § 212. Both corporate law and limited partnership law produce the same result.

7. The test requires a determination of the net worth of the LLC after the distribution. The fair market value of the assets of the LLC must exceed its debts to all creditors, not counting liabilities to members on account of their membership interests and liabilities to creditors that have recourse to specific assets of the LLC. NYLLCL § 508(a).

8. *Id.* This Section of the Act creates a new Statute of Limitations which probably cannot be modified as to third parties by the operating agreement.

9. In general, a partner must pay self-employment tax under I.R.C. § 1401 on his distributive share of income if the partnership is involved in a trade or business. I.R.C. § 1402(a) and Treas. Reg. § 1.1402(a)–1(a)(2). Until the enactment of I.R.C. § 1402(a)(13), it was generally believed that even a limited partner's distributive share of income from a limited partnership engaged in a trade or business was subject to self-employment tax. *See* Estate of Ellsasser v. C.I.R., 61 T.C. 241 (1973).

CAVEAT: Therefore, it is possible that a member will be subject to self-employment tax on his share of LLC income from a trade or business.

such performance.[10] The LLC may require the member (or his estate) to make the delinquent contribution in cash, regardless of any previous agreement, or the LLC may obtain specific performance.[11] Third-party creditors may enforce a member's promise to make a capital contribution even if the LLC's members have compromised that obligation.[12]

A member who is a "responsible person" within the meaning of I.R.C. § 6672, or a person who is "under a duty to perform an act" under Tax Law § 685 is personally responsible for the payment of federal and New York State withholding taxes.[13] It is to be expected that the LLC shield will not protect a member[14] from such liability, since shareholders of corporations and limited partners of limited partnerships are not protected if they come within such definitions. The New York State sales tax law has been amended to make it possible to impose personal liability for sales tax on an employee or manager of an LLC.[15]

The NYLLCL also allows members to waive their limited liability protection for specific debts, obligations or liabilities of an LLC under certain circumstances.[16] A member is not bound by such a waiver unless the waiver is contained in the LLC's Articles and that member specifically consents in writing to the adoption of the provision or to be bound by such provision, or specifically voted for the adoption of the provision.

In addition, a member or manager might be liable for false statements contained in filed documents under certain circumstances.[17]

If reference is made to corporate law to determine additional circumstances under which a member of an LLC may be personally liable for the LLC's debts, a theory similar to "piercing the corporate veil" might be applied to LLCs.[18]

---

10. NYLLCL § 502(a). This liability survives death, disability, or any other reason for non-payment. *Id.*

11. *Id.*

12. Compromise requires the consent of all members. A creditor's right to enforce a compromised capital contribution obligation requires that the creditor show that (1) he relied upon the capital contribution to extend credit; (2) the member agreed in writing to make the capital contribution; and (3) the creditor extended credit before the compromise. NYLLCL § 502(b).

13. Liability under I.R.C. § 6672 and Tax Law § 685 is limited to the trust fund portion of the withholding taxes that the employer did not pay to the IRS or New York State. It does not include interest or penalties charged at the entity level. I.R.C. § 6672(a) and Tax Law § 685(g). The general test to determine if a person is a responsible person is whether he had the power to determine which creditors would be paid. *See generally* Hochstein v. United States, 900 F.2d 543 (2d Cir.1990). Liability under Tax Law § 1131 is likewise limited to the amount of sales tax due and does not include interest and penalties. Laks v. Division of Taxation of Dept. of Taxation & Finance of State, 183 A.D.2d 316, 590 N.Y.S.2d 958 (4th Dep't 1992). Generally the same standards that are applied for withholding taxes are applied for sales taxes. *See* Vogel v. NYS Dept. of Taxation & Finance, 98 Misc.2d 222, 413 N.Y.S.2d 862 (Sup.Ct., N.Y. County, 1979).

14. Tax Law § 685(n) includes a member as a person responsible to act.

15. Tax Law § 1131(*l*).

16. NYLLCL § 609(b).

17. *See supra*, § 2.17.

18. The corporate veil has been pierced in New York where (1) the original investment in the corporation is small compared to the risk, Walkovszky v. Carlton, 18

§ 2.24 Limited Liability Companies—Members—One-Member LLCs

Unlike most LLC statutes, which require an LLC to have at least two members from their beginning, the NYLLCL permits an LLC to have one member, both at formation and at any time thereafter.[1] Under the new tax classification regime, a one-member LLC will receive pass-through tax treatment for federal purposes, not as a partnership, but because it will be disregarded as an entity apart from its member.[2] A one-member LLC will also be taxed as a pass-through entity for New York State tax purposes.

§ 2.25 Limited Liability Companies—Management

How an LLC will be managed is a matter of contract, tempered by practical considerations. At one end of the spectrum, a single person or entity, whether or not a member, may manage an LLC, as is the case with many limited partnerships. At the other end, more like a general partnership, management power and authority may be dispersed throughout an LLC's membership, *per capita* or based on any other criteria.

§ 2.26 Limited Liability Companies—Management—Members vs. Managers

Unless its Articles provide that an LLC will be managed by one or more managers, the LLC will be deemed to be managed by its members, in their capacity as members.[1] Each member of a member-managed LLC will have the power to bind the LLC *vis-a-vis* third parties.[2] Managers are non-members, or fewer than all members, elected or appointed by the members to manage the LLC.[3] When fewer than all members, or anyone other than each and every member, are intended to have the power to bind the company *vis-a-vis* third parties, the LLC's Articles must indicate that it will be managed by one or more managers.

N.Y.2d 414, 276 N.Y.S.2d 585, 223 N.E.2d 6 (1966); (2) a single business was divided into several different corporations to avoid liabilities, Mangan v. Terminal Transportation System, 157 Misc. 627, 284 N.Y.S. 183 (Sup.Ct., N.Y. County, 1935), aff'd 247 App. Div. 853, 286 N.Y.S. 666 (3d Dep't 1936); (3) a corporation was used to further an individual's goals, not those of the corporation, Berkey v. Third Ave. Ry. Co., 244 N.Y. 84, 155 N.E. 58 (1926); (4) necessary to prevent fraud or to achieve equity, International Aircraft Trading Co. v. Manufacturers Trust Co., 297 N.Y. 285, 292, 79 N.E.2d 249, 252 (1948); and (5) corporate (or other) formalities have not been observed, Planned Consumer Marketing, Inc. v. Coats & Clark, Inc., 127 A.D.2d 355, 513 N.Y.S.2d 417 (1st Dep't 1987), aff'd 71 N.Y.2d 442, 527 N.Y.S.2d 185, 522 N.E.2d 30 (1988).

§ 2.24

1. NYLLCL § 203(c).

2. *See supra*, § 2.4.

§ 2.26

1. NYLLCL § 401(a).

2. *See infra*, § 2.32, with respect to matters of agency authority.

3. NYLLCL §§ 401(a), 409(a).

A member exercising management powers is deemed to be a manager for purposes of applying the provisions of the NYLLCL.[4] Accordingly, the sections of the statute governing managers (like the default standard of care set forth in Section 409) also apply to members when they exercise management powers. They do not confer formal manager status on the members.

§ 2.27 Limited Liability Companies—Management—Voting: Members

Unless altered by the operating agreement, members are required to meet at least annually to act on matters within the scope of their authority, as defined in the operating agreement or otherwise.[1] Written notice of the place, date, hour and, if a special meeting, purpose of members' meetings must be given, unless the operating agreement abrogates that requirement.[2] In the absence of any contrary provision in the operating agreement, the NYLLCL sets a quorum at a majority in interest of the members entitled to vote.[3] In no event may a quorum be less than "one-third in interest of the members entitled to vote."[4]

As a default rule, members take action by vote of a majority in interest of the members' votes cast at a meeting where a quorum is present.[5] The NYLLCL specifically provides that, unless the operating agreement requires a different vote, and whether or not the LLC is member-managed or managed by managers, the vote or consent of a majority in interest of the members entitled to vote thereon shall be necessary to (1) admit new members, (2) incur debt other than in the ordinary course and (3) subject to additional restrictions imposed by NYLLCL §§ 402(e) and 417(b), amend the Articles or the operating agreement.[6]

As discussed in Section 2.7, note 7, *supra*, the default calculation of a majority in interest under the NYLLCL is based on the members' aggregate shares of current profits of the company. If the operating agreement does not address members' shares of current profits or how they are determined, Section 503 of the NYLLCL operates to divide current profits among members based on the relative value of their

4. NYLLCL § 401(b)(i).

§ 2.27
1. NYLLCL § 403.
2. NYLLCL § 405(a).
3. NYLLCL § 404(a).
4. NYLLCL § 404(b).

CAVEAT: Note the potential problem that this non-waivable requirement creates: an operating agreement may define majority in interest on the basis of capital, on a *per capita* basis, or otherwise. It is conceivable that a quorum in accordance with the operating agreement might not meet the Act's unchangeable minimum requirement, which is at least one-third in interest based on members' shares of current profits.

5. NYLLCL § 402(f).

6. NYLLCL § 402(c). *See* D. Adair, Ch. 6, "Management," § 6.3.2 in Walker, *Limited Liability Companies and Partnerships: A Guide to Law and Practice* (West 1995) for a thorough discussion of member voting issues.

contributions actually made or promised to the company and not in default.[7]

Members may also act by written consent if the consent is executed by the number of members whose affirmative vote would have been necessary to take such action at a meeting of all members.[8] Section 402(b) permits any member to vote in person or by proxy at a meeting, but does not prescribe the form or other requirements for proxies. This Section effectively permits a member to delegate his management responsibilities to another, even in a member-managed LLC.

It should be noted that all of the member voting provisions of the NYLLCL apply to members acting in their capacities both as members and as managers of the LLC. Accordingly, statutory provisions governing the election, removal and voting of managers, discussed in Section 2.28, *infra*, apply only to managers of manager-managed LLCs.

The NYLLCL permits members extraordinary flexibility to create different classes of equity owners of an LLC.[9] The rights, powers, preferences and limitations of those classes may be defined by their relative voting, or management rights in the company; they may also depend on the members' different financial interests.

§ 2.28 Limited Liability Companies—Management—Voting: Managers

Anyone may be a manager of an LLC, as the operating agreement may permit.[1] In the absence of provisions in the operating agreement to the contrary, managers are to be elected or appointed annually by the members; they hold their offices, with such responsibilities as the members delegate, for the specified term (which may be unlimited), until their successors are elected or until the managers earlier resign or are removed.[2]

Unlike member meetings, for which the NYLLCL provides some default guidance, the timing, location, notice and other aspects of managers' meetings are left entirely to the operating agreement.[3] Unless

---

7. Other statutes impose a *per capita* voting default.
PRACTICE POINTER: There may be many situations where such a *per capita* vote, or a basis other than shares of current profits, is appropriate. An operating agreement should address such situations.
8. NYLLCL § 407(a). In contrast, the NYBCL permits action by written consent only if all stockholders entitled to vote thereon execute the consent. See NYBCL § 615(a).
9. NYLLCL § 418(a).

PRACTICE POINTER: Although the NYLLCL does not expressly authorize the creation of member committees, presumably the ability to denominate classes with specific "duties" permits the establishment of such committees.

§ 2.28
1. NYLLCL § 410.
2. NYLLCL § 413.
3. NYLLCL § 419(b).

otherwise provided in the operating agreement, managers take action by affirmative vote of a majority thereof.[4]

The NYLLCL permits any number of approaches to manager voting, flexibility that would be unfamiliar to those who usually operate through corporate boards of directors.[5] The statute does not address specifically quorum requirements, action by written consent, or a manager's ability to vote by proxy, but rather invites members to create their own standards, if any, in the operating agreement.[6] Under the NYLLCL, the operating agreement may "grant to all or to one or more classes of managers the right to vote upon any matter on a *per capita*, class or other basis."[7] In addition, classes of managers may be distinguished on the basis of relative rights, duties, responsibilities and preferences. There is no limitation on the number of managers whose written consent may be required to take action without a meeting.[8] And, of course, the ability to exercise management rights by proxy, as noted above, has no counterpart in New York's corporate law.

If certain criteria are met, transactions between an LLC and a manager or an entity in which a manager has an interest will not be void or voidable merely by virtue of the relationship, or because the interested manager was present or voted at the meeting at which the transaction was approved. As long as the material facts of the manager's interest are disclosed in good faith or are otherwise known and either the disinterested managers or the members approve the transaction, it may not be avoided.[9] Even if there was no such disclosure or knowledge, or appropriate approval was not obtained, the transaction may not be avoided if the parties thereto establish that it was fair and reasonable to the LLC at the time.[10] The operating agreement may contain additional restrictions, but may not abrogate these requirements.

Managers may resign by giving written notice to that effect, but the LLC may recover damages if resignation violates any contractual agreement.[11] Unless the operating agreement restricts their ability, the members may remove any manager with or without cause by vote of a majority in interest of the members.[12] If vacancies occur among the managers for any reason, they may be filled by vote of a majority in interest of the members or in any other manner prescribed by the operating agreement.[13]

4. NYLLCL § 408(b).
5. Compare, for example, a manager's ability to manage by proxy against the NYBCL's requirement that a participating director exercise independent judgment.
6. NYLLCL § 408(b).
7. NYLLCL § 419(a).
8. NYLLCL § 408(c).
9. NYLLCL § 411(a), (b).
10. NYLLCL § 411(b).
11. NYLLCL § 415.
12. NYLLCL § 414.
13. NYLLCL § 416.

§ 2.29 Limited Liability Companies—Management—Non-waivable Requirements

Few provisions of the NYLLCL may not be waived or altered in the operating agreement. However, once voting rights are granted, they cannot be eliminated or changed without the consent of those to whom they were granted, as required by the Articles or the operating agreement.[1] In addition, an agreement to merge or consolidate with or into another entity must be approved by at least a majority in interest of an LLC's members.[2]

§ 2.30 Limited Liability Companies—Management—Delegation of Responsibility

Whether an LLC is member-managed or manager-managed, its operating agreement may provide for the election or appointment of officers, agents or a management committee to which certain management responsibilities may be delegated by the members or the managers.[1] The requirements and restrictions imposed on officers and other agents by the operating agreement will bind the members (and managers, if the company is manager-managed and the managers are party thereto), but not third parties, unless they have notice of such restrictions.[2] The members' delegation of some responsibilities to officers may well affect whether membership interests will be considered "securities" for purposes of federal and state securities laws.[3]

§ 2.31 Limited Liability Companies—Management—Standard of Care

Managers, whether they are members of the LLC or not, and members performing management duties are required to perform such duties "in good faith and with that degree of care that an ordinarily prudent person in a like position would use under similar circumstances."[1] A member who is not a manager does not owe a duty to the LLC or its members, except to the extent he or it participates in the management of the LLC. In either case, in performing management duties, a manager or managing member may rely in good faith on information, opinions, reports and statements, including financial statements, prepared by LLC agents or employees, counsel and others, if believed within their professional competence, or produced by other

§ 2.29
1. NYLLCL § 402(e).
2. NYLLCL § 1002(c). It is unclear whether this provision requires the vote of a majority in interest as defined in the operating agreement or as defined in the NYLLCL.

§ 2.30
1. *See* NYLLCL §§ 408(a), 418(a), 419(a).
2. *See supra*, §§ 2.17, and *infra*, 2.32.
3. *See infra*, discussion at § 2.106.

§ 2.31
1. NYLLCL § 409(a).

classes of managers believed to be acting within their authority.[2] If he performs his duties in accordance with Section 409 of the NYLLCL, a manager or managing member "shall have no liability by reason of being or having been a manager" of the LLC.[3]

In a provision similar to Section 402(b) of the NYBCL, the operating agreement may limit a manager's personal liability to the company and/or its members for a breach of duty in such capacity unless the breach involved bad faith, intentional misconduct, a knowing violation of law or an unpermitted financial or other gain for the manager.[4] In addition, the operating agreement (and/or the Articles) may allow the company to indemnify its members, managers, employees and/or agents for damages, and to advance expenses, in connection with any claims not involving bad faith or an improper personal, financial or other gain.[5] Practically, the ability to limit liability and to indemnify managers for acts which may breach their obligation to serve with due care may undercut the standard set forth in Section 409(a) of the Act. The question remains, to what extent a manager's liability for damages (or for contribution claims in respect of damages) incurred by third parties resulting from acts in breach of the Section 409(a) standard may be limited. If a limitation of liability is included in the company's Articles, a manager's responsibility may well be reduced in all respects to the level set forth therein.

§ 2.32 Limited Liability Companies—Management—Agency Authority

As noted in Section 2.26, *supra*, unless an LLC's Articles provide for management by managers, every member is an agent of the LLC for the purpose of its business, and acts for apparently carrying on that business in the usual way will bind the LLC *vis-a-vis* third parties. Lack of authority is a defense to an LLC's obligation only if the member in fact had no authority to act for the LLC in the particular matter and the person with whom the member was dealing had knowledge of that fact.[1] Membership in a member-managed LLC thus confers upon members substantial authority to deal with third parties, but, unlike partners in general partnerships, not much liability for those dealings (either to the third parties or to the LLC or its other members). Accordingly, one's fellow members in a member-managed LLC should be selected with care. Even a passive investor of a member-managed LLC has agency authority to bind the LLC, but with limited personal risk for his actions.

Section 412(b) of the NYLLCL provides that, if the Articles of Organization indicate that management is vested in one or more manag-

2. NYLLCL § 409(b).
3. NYLLCL § 409(c).
4. NYLLCL § 417(a).
5. NYLLCL § 420.

§ 2.32
1. NYLLCL § 412(a).

ers, then no member (as a member) is an agent of the LLC for the purpose of its business unless authority is delegated to the member by the managers or by the operating agreement. Every manager, however, is an agent of the company for the purpose of its business, and his acts for apparently carrying on that business in the usual way bind the LLC, unless the manager did not in fact have authority to act for the LLC on that matter and the person with whom the manager dealt knew it.[2]

Because the NYLLCL expressly authorizes an LLC to grant management authority to "one or more managers or classes of managers," there will always be a question lurking whether an action is within the scope of a manager's authority. That question can be resolved only by reading the LLC's organizational documents, including the operating agreement.

§ 2.33 Limited Liability Companies—Assignment of Interests

All or any portion of an LLC membership interest, including either the financial rights pertaining thereto or only the voting or other management rights associated with it, may be assigned by a member to the extent permitted by the operating agreement.[1] Like management arrangements, the transferability of membership interests, or portions thereof, is limited not by the NYLLCL, but by business considerations.

§ 2.34 Limited Liability Companies—Assignment of Interests—Default Rules

Unless otherwise provided in the operating agreement, assignment of a membership interest does not entitle the assignee to participate in the management of the LLC or to become or exercise any rights or powers of a member.[1] Instead, the assignee obtains only the right to receive the same distributions and allocation of profits and losses as the assignor.[2] In other words, under the default provisions of the Act, an assignee obtains only the economic rights of the assignor to the extent assigned. The ability to strip out and sell economic rights in an LLC's operations—in fact, the default understanding that members have a right to do so—may constitute those rights securities for securities law purposes.[3]

A pledge of, or the granting of a security interest, lien or other encumbrance in or with respect to, a membership interest does not

---

2. NYLLCL § 412(b).

§ 2.33

1. NYLLCL § 603(a).

§ 2.34

1. NYLLCL § 603(a)(2). Note that § 603 would be inconsistent with NYLLCL § 608, which permits certain successors-in-interest in involuntary transfers to exercise the rights of members, unless § 603 is read to apply to voluntary transfers only.

2. NYLLCL § 603(a)(3). The term "distributions" is not defined in the Act, but presumably includes distributions of cash, property, notes or intangibles, as well as distributions upon liquidation.

3. See infra, § 2.106.

result in loss of a member's rights and powers unless otherwise stated in the operating agreement.[4] Once a member assigns his entire membership interest, however, he ceases to have the rights and powers of a member.[5] If an assignee of all of a member's economic rights does not thereafter become a member, this leads to a curious result: there is no one able to exercise the voting and management rights relating to the assigned interest.[6]

§ 2.35 Limited Liability Companies—Assignment of Interests—Vote Required to Admit Assignee as Member

Unless the operating agreement otherwise specifies, the assignee of a membership interest may not become a member without the approval of a majority in interest of the remaining members.[1] An assignee of a member has no liability as a member until such time as he becomes a member or otherwise assumes such liability by contract or in accordance with the operating agreement.[2]

Once an assignee has become a member, he is liable for the capital contributions of his assignor under Section 502 of the NYLLCL, unless either he had no knowledge of the obligation at the time he became a member and could not determine from the operating agreement that it existed, or the operating agreement otherwise absolves him.[3] An assignee is not liable for the obligations of his assignor relating to wrongful distributions under Section 508 of the NYLLCL or for wrongful withdrawal in violation of the operating agreement under Section 606 of the NYLLCL. An assignee is not liable for obligations of an assignor accrued prior to the date of the assignment, unless the assignee specifically assumes such liabilities.[4] A member who assigns his entire membership interest is not relieved from any liabilities under the NYLLCL other than liabilities arising from false statements in filed documents or wrongful distributions, in each case made after the date of the assignment.[5]

---

4. NYLLCL § 603(a)(4). This provision is also closely patterned after NYPL § 121–702(a)(4).

5. NYLLCL § 603(a)(4). This Section apparently refers to an assignment of 100% of the assignor's interest in the profits, losses and distributions of the LLC since, barring a special provision in the operating agreement, an assignor cannot assign his voting or management rights or rights to become a member, even though he may be forced to give them up.

6. **PRACTICE POINTER**: One possible solution would be to ignore the profit percentage of an assignee who does not become a member and distribute the assignor's voting rights among the remaining members *pro rata* based on their current profit sharing percentages. *See* NYLLCL § 402(a).

§ 2.35

1. NYLLCL § 604(a).
2. NYLLCL § 603(c).
3. NYLLCL § 604(b).
4. *Id.*
5. NYLLCL § 605.

§ 2.36 Limited Liability Companies—Dissolution

The NYLLCL sets forth a substantial list of events that can cause dissolution of an LLC, in addition to any other events specified by its members. In the alternative, an operating agreement may override the statutory defaults and opt for continuous life, apart from the fate of its members. The default dissolution provisions of the NYLLCL were intended to prevent an LLC from possessing continuity of life and, thereby, perhaps being classified as a corporation for federal income tax purposes under prior law.[1] Now, fortunately, an LLC enterprise can avoid the inconvenient possibility of dissolution, a characteristic that might otherwise hamper its ability to obtain capital or financing.

§ 2.37 Limited Liability Companies—Dissolution—Events

An LLC is dissolved, according to the NYLLCL, upon the earliest to occur of any one of the following events:

(1) the latest date (if any) specified in the Articles of Organization;

(2) upon the occurrence of any event specified in the operating agreement;[1]

(3) the vote of two-thirds in interest of the members, unless a greater or lesser percentage or the consent of a class or group of members is specified in the operating agreement; or

(4) judicial dissolution.[2]

Section 702 of the NYLLCL provides for judicial dissolution of an LLC when it is "not reasonably practical" to carry on business in conformity with the Articles of Organization or the operating agreement. If New York courts look to partnership precedent for guidance on when it is not reasonably practical to carry on business,[3] manager misconduct, breach of fiduciary duty by the managers,[4] transfer or sale of all the assets of the LLC[5] or the inability to conduct business except at a loss[6] may all constitute sufficient cause. If New York courts look to corporate law, grounds for judicial dissolution might include circumstances where

---

§ 2.36

1. *See supra*, § 2.7.

§ 2.37

1. Such events might include a change in the character of the LLC's business, a sale of all or substantially all the assets of the LLC or a sale or completion of a specified project.

2. NYLLCL § 701(a), (b), (c), (e).

3. *See* NYPL § 63 for similar language: a "court shall decree dissolution when a partner conducts himself in matters relating to the partnership business [such] that it is not reasonably practical to carry on the business in partnership with him."

4. *See* May v. Flowers, 106 A.D.2d 873, 483 N.Y.S.2d 551 (4th Dep't 1984), appeal dismissed 64 N.Y.2d 611, 491 N.Y.S.2d 1025, 480 N.E.2d 749 (1985).

5. *See* Mumford v. McKay, 8 Wend. 442 (N.Y.1832).

6. NYPL § 63(e).

acts of managers or members in control of the LLC are illegal, fraudulent or oppressive,[7] or the property or assets of the LLC are being wasted or diverted for non-business purposes.[8] It may also be likely that deadlock of members or managers makes it "not reasonably practical" to continue the business.[9]

The bankruptcy, death, dissolution, expulsion, incapacity or withdrawal of any member, combination of members, or class of members as specified in the operating agreement, or any other event that terminates the membership of any member, may also result in the dissolution of an LLC unless it is continued as described below.[10]

§ 2.38 Limited Liability Companies—Dissolution—Continuation of Business After Dissolution Event

Within 180 days (or any shorter period provided in the operating agreement) after a member's voluntary or involuntary withdrawal as set forth above, an LLC nevertheless may be continued (i) by the vote or written consent of the percentage of members specified in the operating agreement; or, if no percentage is specified, (ii) by the vote or written consent of a majority in interest of the remaining members, or (iii) in accordance with a right to continue stated in the operating agreement.[1] Continuation of the business avoids dissolution.[2] If it did not, the successor LLC might not inherit the contracts, licenses, trade names, and insurance policies in the prior LLC's name, not to mention the tax problems that might result from the termination of the LLC.

§ 2.39 Limited Liability Companies—Dissolution—Winding Up

Upon dissolution, an LLC is obligated to wind up its business. Winding up consists generally of marshalling assets, paying creditors, disposing of and conveying LLC property and distributing any remaining assets to the members. Winding up may be conducted by members without affecting their liability as members;[1] it may also be conducted by the Supreme Court in the judicial district where the office of the LLC is

7. NYBCL § 1104–a (a)(1).

8. NYBCL § 1104–a (a)(2).

9. See NYBCL § 1104(a).

10. NYLLCL § 701(d). The Act defines bankruptcy as bankruptcy under the United States Bankruptcy Code or insolvency under any state insolvency act. NYLLCL § 102(d). See also Chapter 9, "Bankruptcy," infra.

§ 2.38

1. NYLLCL § 701(d).

2. NYLLCL § 701(d).

§ 2.39

1. NYLLCL § 703(a), (b). Managers or members winding up an LLC have authority to bind the LLC only in transactions for that purpose. The other duties and standards of care applicable to managers continue to apply during the winding up period.

located by appointing a receiver or liquidating trustee.[2] The persons winding up the LLC (a liquidating member or members, manager or managers) may bring or defend civil, criminal or administrative suits in the LLC's name.[3]

Upon winding up, the proceeds of the liquidation of an LLC's assets, or the assets themselves, must be distributed first to the creditors of the LLC, including members who are creditors.[4] Thereafter, remaining assets go to satisfy interim distributions declared but not paid and liabilities to withdrawn members in respect of their interests, then to members to return their capital, and finally to members in the same proportion as they share distributions, although the operating agreement may alter these priorities.[5]

Within 90 days following the beginning of the winding up process, Articles of Dissolution must be filed with the Department of State to terminate the LLC's existence in New York and to give third parties notice of its status.[6] At the time of this filing, the LLC's Articles of Organization are deemed canceled and the LLC terminates.[7] Articles of Dissolution must contain the name of the LLC, the dates of the filing of its Articles of Organization and subsequent amendments, a statement of the event causing dissolution and any other relevant information.[8]

§ 2.40 Limited Liability Companies—Conversions/Mergers

The NYLLCL authorizes domestic LLCs to merge or consolidate with or into one or more domestic or foreign LLCs or other business entities.[1] It also contemplates the conversion of limited or general partnerships to LLCs, in a simple procedure without tax consequence if the ownership of the entity remains substantially the same before and

---

2. NYLLCL § 703(a). A member or his representative may apply to the Court to wind up the LLC.

3. NYLLCL § 703(b).

4. NYLLCL § 704(a).

PRACTICE POINTER: Actual payment is not required as long as adequate reserves for such payments are established. The operating agreement may not alter this priority, presumably because it affects the rights of third parties. However, members who are creditors may agree (by signing the operating agreement or otherwise) to subordinate their claims to those of unaffiliated creditors.

5. NYLLCL §§ 704(b), (c).

6. NYLLCL § 705(a).

7. NYLLCL § 705(b).

8. NYLLCL § 705(a)(1)-(4). There seems to be no penalty for not filing Articles of Dissolution other than the fact that the LLC may continue in existence.

§ 2.40

1. "Business entity" includes virtually any organization, but excludes natural persons. NYLLCL § 102(v), (w). NYLLCL § 1001(b) is based on a similar provision of the NYRLPA, but it is, in fact, broader than the limited partnership law, which permits limited partnerships to merge or consolidate with or into other limited partnerships or LLCs only. NYPL § 121–1101.

CAVEAT: If a domestic LLC intends to merge with or into a foreign entity, it would be wise to confirm that the law governing the foreign entity specifically permits such a transaction.

after the conversion.[2] The merger of a corporation with or into an LLC, with the LLC intended to survive, however, does not receive the same benign tax treatment. Whether accomplished by merger or other means (for example, by contributing stock to a newly-formed LLC and thereafter having the corporation liquidate), the conversion of a corporation into an LLC will be treated as a liquidation of the corporation for tax purposes, and both the corporation[3] and its shareholders[4] will recognize gain or loss.

§ 2.41 Limited Liability Companies—Conversions/Mergers—Procedures

Agreements to merge or consolidate, setting out the terms of the transaction and the consideration to be paid, must be adopted by each of the participating entities.[1] In the case of a domestic LLC, members are entitled to at least 20 days' notice of a vote on such an agreement, and, notwithstanding any provision in the operating agreement purporting to reduce the required vote, at least a majority in interest of the members entitled to vote thereon must approve the transaction.[2] If the operating agreement does not address the subject, approval requires the vote of two-thirds in interest (based on shares of current profits) of the members entitled to vote thereon.[3]

A merger or consolidation involving a domestic LLC is effected by filing a Certificate of Merger with the New York Department of State.[4] The Certificate of Merger puts the public on notice of the transaction, and must recite, among other things, the jurisdictions of formation of the entities involved, requisite approval of the plan, the name of the surviving entity and changes to existing Articles of Organization.[5] The transaction is effective upon filing, or on a future date specified in the Certificate of Merger not more than 30 days after filing.[6] After the transaction, all of the property, rights, powers and purposes of the constituent entities vest in the survivor or resulting entity, as do all of their respective obligations, debts, liabilities and suits.[7] Personal liabilities of

---

2. See Rev. Rul. 84–52, 1984–1 C.B. 157; I.R.C. § 721.

3. I.R.C. § 336(a). If the corporation is an S corporation, corporate level gain will be passed through to the shareholders, thereby increasing their basis in the stock and decreasing their gain upon liquidation. If the S corporation was a C corporation at any time ten years prior to the conversion, built-in gain under I.R.C. § 1374 could create an additional tax at the corporate level. Under certain limited circumstances, loss may not be recognized by the corporation. See I.R.C. §§ 336(d), 267.

4. I.R.C. § 331.

§ 2.41

1. NYLLCL § 1002(b), (c).

2. **CAVEAT**: This non-waivable provision of the NYLLCL may create problems for LLCs that define required votes on a different basis. For example, even two-thirds of all members on a *per capita* basis may not hold a "majority in interest" as defined by the NYLLCL for purposes of this approval, creating a trap for the unwary.

3. NYLLCL § 1002(c).
4. NYLLCL § 1003(a).
5. Id.
6. NYLLCL § 1003(b).
7. NYLLCL § 1004(a).

members or partners existing before the transaction will continue afterwards. A merger or consolidation does not require a non-surviving domestic LLC party thereto to comply with the NYLLCL's provisions relating to dissolution and winding up, but the Certificate of Merger does act as Articles of Dissolution for that LLC.[8]

As noted above, the conversion of partnerships to LLCs may be effected in a relatively simple transaction requiring a meeting and vote of the partners of the converting partnership.[9] An agreement of conversion must "set forth" the terms and conditions of conversion, but it is unclear whether such agreement is required to be in writing.[10]

Conversion becomes effective upon the filing of a certificate of conversion for the new LLC if the converting partnership is a general partnership; a converting limited partnership must file a certificate of conversion and cancel its certificate of limited partnership in order for its conversion to be effective.[11] As in a merger or consolidation, partners with personal liability prior to conversion remain personally liable for obligations incurred before the conversion takes effect. A converted partnership does not require a new Federal Employer Identification Number ("EIN"), but its contractual arrangements should be examined to see if conversion triggers any defaults thereunder.

§ 2.42 Limited Liability Companies—Conversions/Mergers—Dissenters' Rights

A member who dissents from a proposed merger or consolidation, or a limited partner who dissents from the conversion of a limited partnership into an LLC, does not become a member or other owner of the surviving entity, but is entitled to receive in cash the fair value of his interest in the LLC (or partnership, as applicable). Fair value is determined as of the day prior to the effective date of the transaction, but without giving effect to it.[1] If dissenters and the LLC cannot agree on the fair value of their interests, either the dissenters or the LLC may institute a court proceeding to make that determination in the same manner authorized by the NYBCL for dissenting shareholders of corpo-

---

8. NYLLCL § 1004(c), (d).

9. NYLLCL § 1006. Unless their partnership agreement provides otherwise, all partners of a general partnership must approve conversion; all general partners of a limited partnership must approve, as well as two-thirds in interest (based on shares of current profits) of the limited partners unless the partnership agreement specifies a different percentage in interest of the limited partners (but never less than a majority in interest—as defined in the NYLLCL). The conversion concept has no analogue in either corporate or partnership law.

10. NYLLCL § 1006(d).

PRACTICE POINTER: If the operating agreement of the converted LLC sets forth such terms, however, there is no reason it may not serve as the conversion agreement.

11. NYLLCL § 1006(f), (g). The new substance of the certificate of conversion must be published in accordance with the requirements of NYLLCL § 206(c).

§ 2.42

1. NYLLCL § 1002(f).

rations.[2] Unless the merger or consolidation was not properly authorized or otherwise violates the Act or the LLC's operating agreement, a dissenter has no right to attack the validity of the transaction.

The NYLLCL addresses mergers and consolidations, but not necessarily other means of achieving the same results (for example, an asset acquisition in consideration for membership interests and the subsequent dissolution of the company from which the assets were acquired).[3] It may be that the protective provisions of the statute will be applied to such other transactions. If not, it would seem easy to avoid certain of the potentially burdensome or inconvenient requirements of the NYLLCL, like dissenters' rights, the 20-day notice requirement and the requirement that at least a majority in interest of those entitled to vote approve the merger.

§ 2.43 Limited Liability Companies—PLLCs

PLLCs may be formed by licensed professionals, including individuals, professional service corporations, other PLLCs, LLPs, partnerships and their foreign counterparts, under Article XII of the NYLLCL. Generally, requirements of the statute applicable to LLCs are applicable to PLLCs, although PLLCs are subject to certain additional restrictions and requirements as well as the jurisdiction of state licensing authorities. In this and many other respects, the provisions of the NYLLCL governing PLLCs owe a great deal to the provisions of the NYBCL governing professional service corporations.

Unlike LLCs, a PLLC is required to be formed "for pecuniary profit."[1] Unless the professional members render medical, dental, engineering, architecture, landscape architecture or surveying services, the NYLLCL permits PLLCs, subject to other applicable law, to provide more than one type of professional service.[2] If the PLLC engages in multiple permitted professions, at least one member of the PLLC must be licensed to practice each such profession in New York.[3] All profession-

---

2. NYLLCL § 1005(b), incorporating NYBCL § 623(h), (i), (j), (k).

CAVEAT: Query, however, how inconsistencies between applicable laws as to valuation or payment terms will be resolved when, for example, a dissenter from a domestic LLC with rights under the NYLLCL must pursue a surviving corporation governed by the NYBCL for payment of fair market value.

3. NYLLCL § 1001(b) indicates that covered entities "*may* merge or consolidate ..." (emphasis added).

§ 2.43
1. NYLLCL § 1203(a).
2. *Id.*

CAVEAT: Of course, under Disciplinary Rules 3–103 and 5–107 of the Code of Professional Responsibility, an attorney may not practice law in partnership with a non-lawyer or otherwise in an organization in which a non-lawyer has an interest or serves as an officer.

3. NYLLCL § 1203(a).

CAVEAT: All members of medical, dental, engineering, architectural, architectural landscaping and land surveying PLLCs, however, must be licensed by State authorities to practice their profession in New York.

al services must be rendered by licensed individuals, and those rendered in New York must be performed by individuals so licensed in New York.[4]

In addition to its profession or professions, a PLLC may conduct any other business or activity for which an LLC may be formed under the Act.[5] PLLCs must file certified copies of their Articles and each amendment thereto with applicable licensing authorities within thirty days after filing them with the Department of State, and must publish their Articles, or the substance thereof, as required of LLCs.[6]

The voting and transfer restrictions imposed on PLLCs by the NYLLCL are consistent with New York's philosophy that only those licensed to practice a profession should have any say in how, and by whom, professional services are rendered. Section 1207(c) of the statute prohibits a member of a PLLC from entering into a voting trust, proxy or other voting arrangement that would give any voting authority to a professional ineligible to become a member of the PLLC. Members of PLLCs otherwise have the same default voting rights as do members of LLCs. Transfers of membership interests to other than professionals qualified to be members of the PLLC are prohibited by Section 1211 of the NYLLCL. Transferees may become members only if at least a majority in interest (based on shares of current profits) of the members other than the transferor approve their admission (although the operating agreement may increase this requirement).[7] Assignees by operation of law or court decree have the same rights as assignees of LLC interests under the default provisions of Section 603 of the NYLLCL.[8]

If a member of a PLLC loses the ability to practice his profession in New York, that member must immediately sever all employment and financial relations with the PLLC.[9] Within six months after (a) a member's disqualification or loss of license, (b) the appointment of the legal representative of his estate or (c) the member's dissolution (unless dissolution is followed by immediate reconstitution under applicable partnership or LLP law and at least a majority of the total interests of the successor partnership are held by partners of the predecessor), a PLLC must repurchase the member's membership interest.[10] Unless otherwise determined by the operating agreement, the price of the interest will be the book value thereof as of the end of the month before the month in which the death, disqualification or dissolution took place, based on the records of the PLLC and its regular accounting method.[11] If

---

4. NYLLCL § 1204(a).

5. *Id*. For the reasons described in note 2, *supra*, a legal PLLC is limited by authority other than the Act in the non-legal businesses and activities in which it may engage, as are medical and other PLLCs.

6. NYLLCL § 1203(c).

7. NYLLCL § 1211(c).

8. NYLLCL § 1213.

9. NYLLCL § 1209. Only interests as a creditor or vested interests under a *bona fide* retirement plan may be maintained.

10. NYLLCL § 1210(a).

PRACTICE POINTER: The operating agreement may shorten the six-month period.

11. *Id*.

the period of a member's disqualification is less than six months, or if the member desires to transfer his interest to another acceptable, qualified professional within that period, a PLLC may nevertheless, but is not required to, repurchase the disqualified member's interest as set forth in the Act or in the operating agreement.[12]

Section 1205(a) of the NYLLCL, like the comparable provision of the NYBCL, holds each member of a PLLC personally liable for his own negligent or wrongful acts or misconduct and for those of any person under his direct supervision and control. Members are not, however, personally liable for the negligence or misconduct of employees not under their direct supervision and control or that of other members, nor are they responsible personally for the contractual debts and obligations of the PLLC.[13]

Foreign PLLCs are permitted to render services in New York through individuals licensed to practice in the State, upon the filing of an Application of Authority and additional documents evidencing New York licensure with the Department of State.[14] Unlike foreign LLCs, foreign PLLCs do not receive a Certificate of Authority to practice in the State.[15] Foreign PLLCs are subject to limitations and requirements, including publication of their Applications or the substance thereof, similar to those imposed on domestic PLLCs.[16]

Professional service corporations generally may not be formed to render more than one type of professional service, nor may they engage in any business or activity other than their profession and activities incident thereto.[17] Moreover, only individuals may hold shares in professional service corporations.[18] For these reasons, among many other general advantages of LLCs over corporations, professionals may prefer to organize as PLLCs rather than professional service corporations. Compared to LLPs, however, PLLCs cost more to establish (because a written operating agreement is required) and are subject to the extensive default rules of the NYLLCL. As noted in this Section 2.43, *supra*, PLLCs are also required to repurchase the membership interests of former members or their estates, while LLPs have no such obligation.

§ 2.44 General Partnerships

The general partnership is perhaps the most venerable of business organizations, having been in existence for hundreds of years. Its time,

---

PRACTICE POINTER: Book value may be inappropriate in many circumstances. Drafters of the operating agreement should give careful thought to buy-out provisions in situations as diverse as the death of a member or disqualification for actionable misconduct.

12. NYLLCL § 1210.
13. NYLLCL §§ 1205(a), 1213, 609(a).
14. NYLLCL §§ 1302, 1306.
15. NYLLCL § 1306.
16. *See, e.g.*, NYLLCL §§ 1304, 1306(d).
17. NYBCL § 1503(a); the exceptions are professional engineering, architecture, landscape architecture and land surveying, any or all of which may be practiced by qualified professionals in one professional service corporation. *Id.*
18. NYBCL § 1503(a).

however, may have passed. With LLCs now available in all states and the District of Columbia, general partnerships may be anachronistic for all but professional groups in the limited number of states that do not yet recognize PLLCs or LLPs. Partnership organization is flexible, like that of LLCs, but the chief failing of a general partnership—the unlimited personal liability of its partners—probably outweighs the disadvantages inherent in the LLC's novelty and cost.

§ 2.45 General Partnerships—Governing Law

Unlike LLCs and limited partnerships, general partnerships are not creatures of statute: they may be formed by agreement between parties and require no state or other filing to come into existence. The elements of a partnership, and the relative rights and duties of partners, were originally articulated through case law and continue to be refined in the courts.[1] Early in the twentieth century, New York adopted the Uniform Partnership Act, which codified the common law. Other than the addition of the NYRLPA as Article 8A of the State's partnership law, effective July 1, 1991, the NYPL has not been amended significantly over the years.

The NYPL imposes few restrictions on agreements that create a partnership. Partners generally may implement any arrangements they wish with respect to the management and operation of their business.[2] In many respects, however, the statute is inflexible. For example, partners are, by law, jointly personally liable for the contractual obligations of the partnership[3] and jointly and severally personally liable for torts committed by partners in the course of partnership business or otherwise with the authority of the partners.[4] Such responsibility cannot be altered by agreement solely among the partners (although a contract party might agree to limit its recourse to partnership assets alone).[5] Moreover, every partner is an agent of the partnership for the purpose of its business, and each partner may bind the partnership *vis-a-vis* third parties under normal circumstances.[6] Unlike LLCs and limited partnerships, where a statutory election will eliminate the agency authority of certain members or partners,[7] a general partner's agency authority cannot be limited as to third parties without knowledge that the partner

---

§ 2.45

1. *See, e.g.*, Blaustein v. Lazar Borck and Mensch, 161 A.D.2d 507, 555 N.Y.S.2d 776 (1st Dep't 1990).

2. *See* Riviera Congress Associates v. Yassky, 18 N.Y.2d 540, 277 N.Y.S.2d 386, 223 N.E.2d 876 (1966).

3. NYPL § 26(a)(2).

4. NYPL § 26(a)(1); *see also*, NYPL §§ 24, 25.

5. NYPL § 26(a).

6. NYPL § 20. *See infra*, § 2.60.

7. The non-manager members of an LLC whose Articles of Organization reflect that it is manager-managed are not generally agents of the LLC for any purpose. NYLLCL § 412(b); *see also, supra*, § 2.23. Limited partners are not agents of a limited partnership; only general partners have statutory agency authority for limited partnerships. *See* NYPL § 121–403(a).

does not, in fact, have authority in the matter.[8] Accordingly, each partner has the power to put all of the other partners' personal assets at risk. As a result, the NYPL and case law thereunder impose upon each general partner a fiduciary duty to all his partners.[9]

Library References:
West's Key No. Digests, Partnership ⚖2.

§ 2.46 General Partnerships—Formation

A partnership does not arise by operation of law.[1] It is, rather, formed when two or more persons or entities associate "to carry on as co-owners a business for profit."[2] Other than this vague statutory formulation, the NYPL does not really provide further useful guidelines as to when a partnership is created.[3] However simplistic such a statement may seem, a partnership usually exists when parties intend to form one.[4] Further, if there is intent to share the profits (and losses) of an enterprise[5] and responsibility for its management,[6] as well as an investment in the business,[7] a partnership probably exists, even if the parties deny that they are partners.[8] A written agreement is not required.[9]

---

8. NYPL § 20.

9. NYPL § 43; Auld v. Estridge, 86 Misc.2d 895, 382 N.Y.S.2d 897 (Sup.Ct., N.Y. County, 1976), aff'd 58 A.D.2d 636, 395 N.Y.S.2d 969, appeal denied 43 N.Y.2d 641, 401 N.Y.S.2d 1025, 371 N.E.2d 830. Each partner has a duty of due care to his other partners. In addition, the NYPL imports the elements of agency law into the partnership law. NYPL § 4(3). Accordingly, partners also have the same duties to each other as do agents to principles: the duties of due care and loyalty. *See also, infra*, § 2.59; *but see* Riviera Congress Associates, *supra*, note 2 (self dealing contemplated by agreement is not *ipso facto* impermissible, since partners have wide latitude to address whatever they wish in their agreement).

§ 2.46

1. Rizika v. Potter, 72 N.Y.S.2d 372 (1947).

2. NYPL § 10(1). Some people distinguish between a partnership and a joint venture by defining the latter as "a special combination of two or more persons, where in some specific venture a profit is jointly sought." *See* Gramercy Equities Corp. v. Dumont, 72 N.Y.2d 560, 534 N.Y.S.2d 908, 531 N.E.2d 629 (1988). Accordingly, a joint venture is a partnership for a limited purpose.

3. *See* NYPL §§ 10, 11. The NYPL merely defines "partnership" as noted and sets out a short list of relationships that would otherwise smell like a partnership, but which are not: *i.e.*, joint tenancy, tenancy in common, *et al. See* NYPL § 11(2).

4. Beckerman v. Sands, 364 F.Supp. 1197 (S.D.N.Y.1973).

5. In re Wells' Will, 36 A.D.2d 471, 321 N.Y.S.2d 200 (4th Dep't 1971), aff'd 29 N.Y.2d 931, 329 N.Y.S.2d 322, 280 N.E.2d 95 (1972).

6. *See* Cohen v. Biernoff, 84 A.D.2d 802, 444 N.Y.S.2d 152 (2d Dep't 1981); Blaustein, *supra*, § 2.45, note 1. Shared management responsibility may often distinguish a putative partnership from a tenancy in common or other form of common ownership, where profits may be shared but an understanding about management may be lacking.

7. *See* ACLI Government Securities, Inc. v. Rhoades, 813 F.Supp. 255 (S.D.N.Y. 1993), aff'd 14 F.3d 591 (2d Cir.1993); Bereck v. Meyer, 222 A.D.2d 243, 635 N.Y.S.2d 15 (1st Dep't 1995); M.I.F. Securities v. R.C. Stamm & Co., 94 A.D.2d 211, 463 N.Y.S.2d 771 (1st Dep't 1983), aff'd 60 N.Y.2d 936, 471 N.Y.S.2d 84, 459 N.E.2d 193 (1st Dep't 1983).

8. **CAVEAT**: Conduct alone may imply a partnership relationship, even if the parties state that no partnership is intended. *See* Greenstone v. Klar, 69 N.Y.S.2d 548, mod. on other grounds 272 App.Div. 892, 71 N.Y.S.2d 201, app. and reagm't denied 272 App.Div. 1004, 74 N.Y.S.2d 405 (1st Dep't 1947).

9. *See* Missan v. Schoenfeld, 95 A.D.2d 198, 465 N.Y.S.2d 706 (1st Dep't 1983).

§ 2.46 GENERAL PARTNERSHIPS—FORMATION

In general, the party asserting a partnership relationship has the burden of establishing its existence.[10] A person's receipt of a share of the profits of a business is *prima facie* evidence that he is a partner, as long as such profits were not paid in respect of a debt (as interest or otherwise), as compensation for services, as an annuity to a surviving spouse or in consideration of the sale of the good will of a business.[11] The assignment of the right to receive a share of profits, without more, however, does not make the assignee a partner.[12] Filing a Business Certificate of Partners raises the presumption that the parties formed a partnership and became partners.[13] A general partnership must obtain an EIN.

The name of a partnership need not contain any particular words or abbreviations. Except in limited circumstances, including the death or retirement of a person who was involved in the business,[14] a partnership may not use the name of a person who does not have an interest in the firm.[15] Moreover, a sole proprietor may not use phrases like "and associates" or "and company," which imply a partnership although one does not exist.[16]

Provided that they meet any other applicable requirements,[17] partners may conduct any type of business for pecuniary profit as a partnership, except those businesses which, by law, are required to be conducted in another form.[18] There are no statutory limitations on the powers of a partnership; accordingly, a partnership may, among other things, sue or be sued, purchase, lease or sell real or personal property, maintain offices in other jurisdictions, borrow and guarantee the obligations of others, and otherwise exercise the powers necessary or convenient to conduct its business.

CAVEAT: Oral partnership agreements create partnerships at will and are not barred by the Statute of Frauds. See Green v. Le Beau, 281 App.Div. 836, 118 N.Y.S.2d 585 (2d Dep't 1953); Rella v. McMahon, 169 A.D.2d 555, 564 N.Y.S.2d 409 (1st Dep't 1991).

10. Blaustein, *supra*, § 2.45, note 1.

11. NYPL § 11. *See* Olson v. Smithtown Medical Specialists, P.C., 197 A.D.2d 564, 602 N.Y.S.2d 649 (2d Dep't 1993). Shares in profits need not be on an equal or proportionate basis to create the inference of a partnership. *See* Christal v. Petry, 275 App. Div. 550, 90 N.Y.S.2d 620 (1st Dep't 1949), aff'd 301 N.Y. 562, 93 N.E.2d 450 (1950).

12. NYPL § 53; *see* Whalen v. Gerzof, 154 A.D.2d 843, 847, 546 N.Y.S.2d 705, 708 (3d Dep't 1989).

13. *See* In re Palega's Estate, 208 Misc. 966, 145 N.Y.S.2d 271 (Surr.Ct., N.Y. County, 1955). *See also, infra*, § 2.50.

14. *See* NYPL § 80.

15. NYPL § 82.

16. *Id.*

CAVEAT: The use of a name implying a partnership where one does not exist is a misdemeanor. General Business Law § 132.

17. Including, for example, licensure, capital and other requirements of state agencies, other applicable laws and professional oversight bodies.

18. *See supra*, § 2.16, note 1.

Library References:

West's Key No. Digests, Partnership ⟐1–26.

§ 2.47 General Partnerships—Formation—Agreement

As noted above,[1] the formation and conduct of a general partnership does not require a written agreement. Nevertheless, partners are well-advised to commit to writing their arrangements as to management and their relative rights and duties. A partnership agreement may include practically any terms and conditions desired for the sharing of profits and losses, priorities of distribution and the winding up of its affairs, subject to limited statutory prohibitions, common law rules and public policy considerations.[2] To the extent an agreement, written or oral, does not address issues with respect to the partners' relationship or the conduct of their business, or where the law is not permitted to be altered, the NYPL and case law precedent will supply the terms thereof.[3] Otherwise, the terms of a partnership agreement may be proved by a writing, the conduct of the parties, circumstantial evidence or oral testimony.[4]

An oral partnership arrangement is subject to the Statute of Frauds,[5] but is not unenforceable; it merely creates a partnership at will under the NYPL.[6] A partnership agreement may bind only those who have expressly consented thereto.[7] Accordingly, if there is a written partnership agreement, every partner must execute it; those who do not sign may not be considered partners or have the rights thereof, although they may be liable to third persons as though they were partners "by estoppel."[8]

Library References:

West's Key No. Digests, Partnership ⟐21, 22.

§ 2.48 General Partnerships—Formation—Business Certificate

Rather than a centralized state filing like those required of an LLC or a limited partnership, a general partnership need file a Business Certificate of Partners with the County Clerk of each of the counties in which the partnership will conduct business.[1] A Business Certificate sets forth the name of the partnership and the names and residence address-

§ 2.47

1. See supra, § 2.46, note 9.

2. Lanier v. Bowdoin, 282 N.Y. 32, 24 N.E.2d 732 (1939); but see supra, Riviera Congress Associates, § 2.45, note 2.

3. See supra, Rizikia, § 2.46, note 2.

4. See supra, Cohen § 2.46, note 7; In re Wells' Will, supra, § 2.46, note 5; Hartford Accident & Indemnity Co. v. Oles, 152 Misc. 876, 274 N.Y.S. 349 (Sup.Ct., N.Y. County, 1934).

5. See supra, § 2.46, note 9.

6. Green, supra, § 2.46, note 9.

7. Beckerman, supra, § 2.46, note 4.

8. NYPL § 27; see infra, § 2.53.

§ 2.48

1. General Business Law § 130(1)(a).

es of each of the partners, and must be amended when the membership of the partnership changes.[2]

A partnership's failure to file a Business Certificate is a misdemeanor,[3] but does not affect the validity of the partnership's contracts with third parties or its partners' personal liability therefor under the NYPL.[4] Neither the partners nor the partnership may maintain an action or proceeding in New York State courts unless and until a Business Certificate is filed, although a partnership may maintain an action against a partner for breach of fiduciary duty even in the absence of such a filing.[5]

§ 2.49 General Partnerships—Formation—Publication

Publication of a partnership's Business Certificate, the contents of its agreement or other facts relating to its formation is not required, although the Business Certificate is a matter of public record. As a result, setting up a general partnership does not involve the up-front, out-of-pocket costs of publishing an LLC's Articles of Association or a limited partnership's Certificate of Limited Partnership.

§ 2.50 General Partnerships—Formation—Other Issues

Because a filing is not necessary to form a general partnership, and because conduct alone may create such a relationship,[1] parties may unknowingly establish a partnership even absent specific intent to share losses or otherwise to undertake the duties and responsibilities legally imposed upon partners.[2] It is essential, therefore, to establish the terms of a business relationship, and its form, before beginning an enterprise. Otherwise, parties may find themselves personally liable for all actions taken by any of their putative partners during the period before their formal arrangements become effective.[3] Even if they desire to form a partnership, parties should reduce the specifics of their arrangements to writing in order to avoid the imposition of terms and obligations implied by law, but that might not reflect their intentions.[4]

---

2. General Business Law § 130(1)(a) and (3). A certified copy of the Certificate, as amended, must be kept at all premises where the business is conducted. General Business Law § 130(4).

3. General Business Law § 130(9).

4. General Business Law § 130(8).

5. General Business Law § 130(9). Filing a Business Certificate in a county is not an admission that the partnership has conducted business there. General Business Law § 130(6).

§ 2.50

1. *See supra*, Greenstone, § 2.46, note 8.

2. *See* Fay v. Waldron, 3 N.Y.S. 894 (Sup.Ct., N.Y. County, 1889) ("It is not necessary, to constitute a valid partnership, that the parties should describe themselves as partners, or that they should agree to share the losses.")

3. *See, e.g., supra*, § 2.19, with respect to the adoption of an operating agreement by an LLC as of a date after the filing of its Articles of Organization.

4. For example, all partners have equal rights in management, NYPL § 40(5), and equal shares of a partnership's profits and losses, NYPL § 40(1), unless otherwise agreed.

After formation, partnership books, to which all partners may have access at all times, must be maintained.[5] In the absence of agreement otherwise, the books must be kept at the partnership's principal place of business.[6]

Library References:
West's Key No. Digests, Partnership ⚖1–26.

§ 2.51 General Partnerships—Partners

Any type of person or entity may become a partner of a partnership,[1] and may contribute any type of goods or services to the capital of a partnership. Subject to the arrangements adopted by the partners, a partner's rights include (a) his rights in specific partnership property, (b) his interest in the partnership and (c) his right to participate in its management.[2]

Partnership property comprises all property brought into the partnership by partners or which is subsequently acquired by the partnership.[3] Property acquired with partnership funds is presumed to be partnership property unless a contrary intention appears.[4] Under the NYPL, a partner's right in specific partnership property—not to be confused with his partnership interest—is as a tenant in partnership.[5] Subject to any agreement between partners, tenants in partnership have equal rights with their partners to possess specific property for partnership purposes, but no right to possess partnership property for other purposes without the consent of their partners.[6] A partner's rights in specific partnership property are not assignable unless all the partners are assigning the same property,[7] and such rights are not subject to attachment except in connection with a claim against the partnership.[8] Upon the death of a partner, his rights in partnership property vest in the surviving partners.[9]

5. NYPL § 41.
6. Id.

§ 2.51

1. See Gelder Medical Group v. Webber, 41 N.Y.2d 680, 394 N.Y.S.2d 867, 363 N.E.2d 573 (1977).
2. NYPL § 50.
3. NYPL § 12(1).
4. NYPL § 12(2).
5. NYPL § 51(1).
6. NYPL § 51(2).

PRACTICE POINTER: Because partners have an undivided interest in partnership property, a partner cannot be convicted of larceny for misappropriating partnership property. See People v. Zinke, 76 N.Y.2d 8, 555 N.E.2d 263, 556 N.Y.S.2d 11 (1990). A partner's misappropriation would, however, breach his fiduciary duties to the partnership and the other partners.

7. NYPL § 51(2)(b).
8. NYPL § 51(2)(c).
9. NYPL § 51(2)(d). On the death of the last surviving partner, his rights in specific partnership property vest in his legal representative. The last surviving partner (or his legal representative) may not possess such property for other than a partnership purpose, and it becomes the duty of the last surviving partner to settle the partnership affairs. See NYPL § 51(2)(d); see also, In re Lutz' Will, 202 Misc. 903, 112 N.Y.S.2d 640 (Surr.Ct., Bronx County, 1952), aff'd 281 App.Div. 809, 118 N.Y.S.2d 751 (1st Dep't

A partner's interest in the partnership is his share of its profits and surplus, which is intangible personal property.[10] Unless they otherwise agree, partners share equally in the partnership's profits.[11] Unlike his rights in partnership property, a partner's partnership interest may be attached by his creditors to satisfy the partner's obligations.[12] It may also be subject to a charging order after a judgment against the partner.[13] Except as otherwise agreed by the partners, a partner is also obligated to contribute toward the partnership's losses, according to his share in its profits.[14]

The last element of a partnership interest is the partner's right to participate in the management of the partnership.[15] Barring an agreement to the contrary, each partner has equal rights in the management and conduct of partnership business.[16] Even if a partner's management rights are curtailed in the partnership agreement, each partner remains an agent of the partnership for the purpose of its business *vis-a-vis* third parties. Any act of a partner for apparently carrying on that business in the usual way will therefore bind the partnership, unless the partner so acting has in fact no authority and the third person with whom he is dealing has knowledge of that fact.[17]

A partner has certain other rights with respect to the partnership, unless the agreement restricts them. For example, partners may transact business with the partnership, provided that they do not thereby violate their fiduciary duties to their partners. Subject to agreement, each partner has the right to be repaid his contribution after the liabilities of the partnership have been satisfied, and, if the agreement so specifies, to

1953). *See generally*, Chapter 24, "Estate Planning," and Chapter 25, "Probate and Estate Administration," *infra*.

10. NYPL § 52. *See also,* In re Finkelstein's Estate, 40 Misc.2d 910, 245 N.Y.S.2d 225 (Surr.Ct., Rockland County, 1963).

CAVEAT: Note that an assignment of a partnership interest under NYPL § 53 conveys the right to receive the assignor's share of profits only.

11. NYPL § 40(1).

12. Jones v. Palermo, 105 Misc.2d 405, 432 N.Y.S.2d 288 (Sup.Ct., N.Y. County, 1980).

13. NYPL § 54.

CAVEAT: A charging order under NYPL § 54(1), however, gives a creditor not only the right to a partner's share of profits and surplus, but to any other money due or to fall due to the partner in respect of the partnership—presumably including his capital contribution, repayment of loans, right to indemnification and other payments provided for under the partnership agreement.

14. NYPL § 40(1). As to third parties, however, partners are jointly liable for a partnership's contractual obligations and jointly and severally liable for its other debts and obligations. *See* NYPL § 26; *see infra*, § 2.53.

15. NYPL § 40(5). Presumably, this includes the right to vote and the right to certain partnership information. It may also include the right to compel dissolution of the partnership, although assignees of a partnership interest who are not partners and creditors who have obtained a charging order against a partnership interest do have the right, under certain circumstances, to petition the court for dissolution. NYPL § 63(2); *see infra*, § 2.65.

16. *Id.*

17. NYPL § 20(1). *See infra*, discussion of agency authority at § 2.60.

receive interest on that contribution from the date it was made.[18] A partner who advances funds in aid of the partnership over and above his capital contribution requirements is entitled to have such advance repaid, with interest.[19] Moreover, the partnership must indemnify each partner for expenses and liabilities incurred for the benefit of the partnership.[20]

A partner is no longer a partner when he ceases to share in the ongoing business of the partnership.[21] A partner's bankruptcy,[22] death,[23] expulsion (if the partnership agreement expressly so permits)[24] or voluntary withdrawal separates him from the partnership.[25] Voluntary withdrawal may be prohibited by agreement, rendering a partner who breaches that agreement liable for damages caused by his action.[26]

The dissociation of a partner from a partnership, whether as a result of withdrawal, expulsion, death or bankruptcy, will cause the technical dissolution of the partnership unless the parties agree otherwise.[27] The partners' fiduciary duties to each other terminate upon dissolution, although the partnership is not terminated at that point because its business must be wound up (if it does not continue).[28] Upon dissolution, each partner is entitled to have the partnership property applied to discharge partnership liabilities, with the surplus going to pay in cash the partners' interests,[29] or the remaining partners may continue the business.

---

18. NYPL § 40(1). Unless the agreement otherwise provides, however, a partner is entitled to receive interest on his capital contribution only from the date it was required to have been repaid. NYPL § 40(4).

19. NYPL § 40(3).

20. NYPL § 40(2); see infra, § 2.54.

21. See Estate of Quirk v. C.I.R., 928 F.2d 751 (6th Cir.1991).

22. NYPL § 62(5).

23. NYPL § 62(4).

24. NYPL § 62(1)(d).

25. NYPL §§ 62(1)(b), 62(2).

26. NYPL § 69(2)(a), (c); see Napoli v. Domnitch, 18 A.D.2d 707, 236 N.Y.S.2d 549 (2d Dep't 1962), aff'd 14 N.Y.2d 508, 248 N.Y.S.2d 228, 197 N.E.2d 623 (1964).

27. See Odette Realty Co. v. DiBianco, 170 A.D.2d 299, 565 N.Y.S.2d 815 (1st Dep't 1991); NYPL § 62; see also, infra, discussion at § 2.65.

PRACTICE POINTER: In most cases, a partnership agreement should specifically state that a partner's dissociation will not result in dissolution of the partnership.

28. See, e.g., Matter of Silverberg, 81 A.D.2d 640, 438 N.Y.S.2d 143 (2d Dep't 1981); NYPL § 61.

29. NYPL § 69(1), (2)(a). Under NYPL § 40(4), each partner is entitled to receive interest on the value of his contribution from the date repayment is required to be made, by agreement or otherwise. This obligation may be altered by the partnership agreement. Note that NYPL § 40(1) also entitles each partner (subject to agreement otherwise) to be repaid his contribution to partnership capital from surplus remaining after all liabilities, including those to partners from whom the partnership has borrowed, have been satisfied, but no reference is made to dissolution. Repayment in cash is not required under NYPL § 40(1).

§ 2.52 General Partnerships—Partners—Admission of New Partners

Those who initially agree to become partners of a partnership are its original partners. Thereafter, unless the partnership agreement otherwise provides, all of the partners must consent to the admission of a new partner, whether the assignee of an existing partner or the recipient of an interest issued directly by the partnership.[1] A new partner is liable for the debts and obligations of the partnership incurred before he became a partner, but only to the extent of his interest in the partnership's assets.[2] He is not personally liable for such obligations.[3]

Library References:
West's Key No. Digests, Partnership ⟲224–242(8).

§ 2.53 General Partnerships—Partners—Liability

All partners of a general partnership are jointly and severally liable for torts and for certain breaches of trust committed by their partners and employees.[1] A tortfeasor acting in the ordinary course of the partnership's business, or otherwise with the authority of his partners, exposes both the partnership and each of his partners to joint and several liability for third-party losses, whether or not the other partners participated in, or had any knowledge of, the wrongdoing.[2] What constitutes action in the ordinary course of the partnership's business is a question of fact.[3]

Likewise, the partnership and all of its partners are jointly and severally liable for a breach of trust if a partner, acting within the scope of his apparent authority, misapplies the property of a third party,

---

§ 2.52

1. NYPL § 40(7). See also, Rapoport v. 55 Perry Co., 50 A.D.2d 54, 376 N.Y.S.2d 147 (1st Dep't 1975).

2. NYPL § 28. This limitation of liability appears to apply equally to partners who obtain their partnership interest from an existing partner in compliance with the partnership agreement and those who come into the partnership otherwise. The terms and conditions of the partnership agreement or the assignment agreement, as applicable, may alter such a rule by creating contribution or indemnification obligations between old and new partner.

3. Id. See also, Barbro Realty Co. v. Newburger, 53 A.D.2d 34, 385 N.Y.S.2d 68 (1st Dep't 1976).

§ 2.53

1. NYPL § 26(a)(1); see NYPL §§ 24, 25. Partners of professional partnerships that register as a limited liability partnership are not, however, personally liable for the professional negligence of their partners. See infra, § 2.74. See also, Chapter 28 "Legal Malpractice," and Chapter 29, "Medical Malpractice," infra.

2. NYPL § 24; see Guild v. Herrick, 51 N.Y.S.2d 326 (1944); Pedersen v. Manitowoc Co., 25 N.Y.2d 412, 306 N.Y.S.2d 903, 255 N.E.2d 146 (1969).

3. See, e.g., Barnhard v. Barnhard, 179 A.D.2d 715, 578 N.Y.S.2d 615 (2d Dep't 1992) (copartners not liable for their partner's forged endorsement on check for proceeds of dissolution of partnership, as the forgery was neither within the ordinary course of the partnership's business nor authorized by the other partners); Metflex Corp. v. Klafter, 123 A.D.2d 845, 507 N.Y.S.2d 460 (2d Dep't 1986) (one partner's failure to comply with discovery request would render all partners jointly and severally liable).

whether the property is in the custody of the partnership or comes directly to the dishonest partner.[4]

Partners are jointly, but not severally, liable for the contractual debts and obligations of the partnership.[5] In the absence of agreement to the contrary, the assets of a partnership must be exhausted before an action for breach of contract will lie against its individual partners.[6]

Usually, only those who actually are partners of each other may be charged with partnership liabilities. Under certain circumstances, however, a person may be estopped from denying that a partnership exists and will be liable to a third person as though he were a partner. For example, if a person, by word or conduct, represents himself as a partner in an existing partnership, or otherwise as a partner with others (who are not actually partners), or if he consents to such a representation being made about him, he is liable as a "partner by estoppel" to creditors who relied on the representation in advancing credit to the actual or apparent partnership.[7] Moreover, if such a representation is made publicly, reliance is not required for a creditor to recover from the partner by estoppel.[8] If all of the partners of an existing partnership consent to a representation that a non-partner is indeed a partner, the putative partner's actions can bind the partnership. Otherwise, the individual making the misrepresentation is jointly liable with the other persons, if any, consenting to the obligation or to the representation that they are partners.[9] Partnership by estoppel cannot be asserted retroactively.

Library References:

West's Key No. Digests, Partnership ⟜165–175.

§ 2.54 General Partnerships—Partners—Indemnity and Contribution Issues

Unless its agreement otherwise provides, a partnership is required to indemnify every partner "for payments made and personal liabilities reasonably incurred ... in the ordinary and proper conduct" of the partnership business, or otherwise to preserve the partnership's property.[1] In addition, absent provision to the contrary in the agreement, each

---

4. NYPL §§ 26(a)(1) and 25. See also, Clients' Sec. Fund of State v. Grandeau, 72 N.Y.2d 62, 530 N.Y.S.2d 775, 526 N.E.2d 270 (1988).

5. NYPL § 26(a)(2).

6. See, e.g., Nate B. & Frances Spingold Foundation v. Wallin, Simon, Black & Co., 184 A.D.2d 464, 585 N.Y.S.2d 416 (1st Dep't 1992).

7. NYPL § 27(1). See Fleet Bank NH v. Royall, 218 A.D.2d 727, 630 N.Y.S.2d 559 (2d Dep't 1995) (signer of partnership note estopped from denying existence of partnership and was personally liable under note where he held himself out as being a partner in an existing partnership).

8. Id.

9. Id.

§ 2.54

1. NYPL § 40(2). On the other hand, unless it would be unfair under the circumstances or the agreement provides otherwise, no partner is entitled to remuneration

partner must contribute toward the losses of the partnership based on his share of its profits.[2] Accordingly, if one partner bears more than his share of the losses of the partnership, or if the partnership is unable to fulfill its obligation to indemnify a partner for payments made on behalf of the partnership, that partner may seek contribution from his partners.[3]

§ 2.55 General Partnerships—Management

As noted in Section 2.51, *supra,* each partner is presumed, in the absence of an agreement to the contrary, to have equal rights and responsibility in the management of a partnership.[1] Partners may, however, alter this presumption and allocate management rights based on shares of profits of the partnership, contributions, seniority, to those who are elected managers, or on any other basis they desire. Frequently, a partner's management rights vary during his tenure. Notwithstanding internal allocations of management rights and responsibilities, each partner, by statute, remains an agent of the partnership in dealing with third persons for purposes of the partnership's business.[2]

The NYPL does not contain default provisions requiring partners to meet periodically or otherwise relating to management procedures. Rather, its agreement and the nature of the partners' fiduciary duties to one another will inform a partnership's approach to dealing with management issues.[3]

Library References:
West's Key No. Digests, Partnership ⚖︎79.

§ 2.56 General Partnerships—Management—Voting

While partners may make any arrangements they desire as to relative voting rights, if they do not address voting in their agreement, the NYPL requires the vote or consent of a simple *per capita* majority of partners to act on "ordinary matters connected with the partnership business."[1] What is such an ordinary matter may be defined in the partnership agreement; otherwise, it appears to be a question of fact.

for his services in connection with the conduct of the partnership business. NYPL § 40(6).

2. NYPL § 40(1).

3. *See* Schuler v. Birnbaum, 62 A.D.2d 461, 405 N.Y.S.2d 351 (4th Dep't 1978) (partner who advanced funds to settle claim against partnership entitled to contribution, *pro rata*, from other partner when partnership assets were insufficient to satisfy the payor's claim for indemnity); Belgian Overseas Securities Corp. v. Howell Kessler Co., 88 A.D.2d 559, 450 N.Y.S.2d 493 (1st Dep't 1982).

§ 2.55

1. NYPL § 40(5). Compare this approach to the default rule of the NYLLCL, which presumes management rights commensurate with members' relative shares of the profits of an LLC if the operating agreement does not address the subject.

2. NYPL § 20(1). *See infra*, § 2.60

3. *See infra*, § 2.59.

§ 2.56

1. NYPL § 40(8).

Under the default provisions of the NYPL, acts that contravene the partnership agreement must be approved by all of the partners.[2] Unfortunately, the NYPL does not provide default guidance on the vote required to take action that is neither "ordinary" nor which contravenes the parties' agreement.

With no default rules as to voting procedures, the NYPL appears not to restrict partners' ability to take action either at a meeting or by written consent, or to give their partners their proxy. A partner may thus delegate his management rights and responsibilities to others in the partnership; the election of a management committee, if authorized by the agreement, can have the same effect on a collective basis. If a management committee is contemplated, the basis of its members' voting (or the means of determining voting rights), quorum requirements and the matters within the scope of its authority, should be expressly defined by the partners.

Library References:

West's Key No. Digests, Partnership ⚖︎79.

§ 2.57 General Partnerships—Management—Non-waivable Requirements

The few default provisions of the NYPL governing a partnership's internal operations generally may be altered by agreement. One exception is the obligation of each partner to render to another partner or his representative, on demand, true and complete information about anything affecting the partnership.[1] The other non-waivable requirements include each partner's obligation to account to the partnership for benefits and profits derived without the consent of his partners from any transaction connected with the partnership[2] and each partner's right, under certain circumstances, to an accounting of the partnership's affairs.[3]

On the other hand, statutory provisions affecting the rights of third parties *vis-a-vis* the partnership and its partners may not be waived or altered by agreement among the partners. Accordingly, an obligee's rights in respect of a partnership obligation will not be affected even if the authority of the partner who bound the partnership thereto was restricted by the partnership agreement (unless the obligee had knowledge of the restriction).[4] Similarly, partners may make arrangements *inter se* limiting their personal liability for certain injuries to third

---

2. Id.

§ 2.57
1. NYPL § 42.
2. NYPL § 43(1).
3. NYPL § 44.

4. The other partners will, however, have a claim for breach of the partnership agreement and, perhaps, breach of fiduciary duty.

§ 2.58 General Partnerships—Management—Delegation of Responsibility

Unlike corporations or LLCs, partnerships do not typically appoint officers to whom management responsibilities are delegated.[1] Although partners may delegate some or all of their responsibilities to one or more of their partners, delegation does not alter the presumption that all partners have agency authority to bind the partnership in its ordinary course.

Library References:

West's Key No. Digests, Partnership ⚜79.

§ 2.59 General Partnerships—Management—Standard of Care

In addition to certain duties specified in the NYPL,[1] a partner owes the utmost good faith, fairness and loyalty to the partnership and his fellow partners with respect to partnership business.[2] A partner bears a fiduciary relationship to his partners and is, accordingly, held to a higher standard of care in his dealings with them than would be an unrelated party.[3] This duty arises at the time the partnership is formed and continues until it dissolves (although its business still remains to be wound up).[4]

Every partner must account to the partnership for benefits, and hold as a trustee for the partnership all profits, derived without the consent of the other partners from the formation, conduct or liquidation of the partnership or from his use of any of the partnership property.[5] Hence, a partner may not retain for himself alone any profits from the use of partnership property or keep secret profits from sales to or

---

§ 2.58

1. Naming corporate-type officers is arguably inconsistent with the fundamental presumptions about the partnership relationship, including that all partners are actively involved in and responsible for the management and operation of their business and that all have authority to act for the partnership in the ordinary course thereof. Partnerships do, of course, hire employees to perform services for them, but employees would not, absent specific authorization, be able to bind the partnership to any obligation.

§ 2.59

1. See NYPL §§ 42, 43, 44.

2. See Newburger, Loeb & Co., Inc. v. Gross, 563 F.2d 1057 (2d Cir.1977); cert. denied 434 U.S. 1035, 98 S.Ct. 769, 54 L.Ed.2d 782; Auld, *supra*, § 2.45, note 9.

3. Auld, *supra*, § 2.45, note 9.

4. Matter of Silverberg, *supra*, § 2.51, note 28. The partners' fiduciary responsibilities continue as to a withdrawn partner if his capital remains at risk and he continues to share (directly or indirectly) in the firm's profits and losses. Bassett v. American Meter Co., 20 A.D.2d 956, 249 N.Y.S.2d 815 (4th Dep't 1964). Although the duty terminates upon dissolution, partners will still have to account for the proceeds of liquidation of partnership assets and the payment thereof.

5. NYPL § 43(1).

purchases from the partnership.[6] Self-dealing is a violation of the statutory requirement as well as of the fiduciary responsibility imposed upon partners generally.[7]

As noted in Section 2.57, *supra,* each partner has a statutory obligation, whenever asked, to disclose all information relevant to the partnership.[8] New York courts not only prohibit partners from making misrepresentations to each other, but also require partners to disclose, even without a demand, information about their dealings with partnership assets and information which could harm the partnership.[9]

A partnership agreement may not limit or eliminate the duties enumerated in NYPL §§ 42 or 43, or eliminate a partner's right to a formal accounting of partnership affairs, as preserved in NYPL § 44.[10]

§ 2.60 General Partnerships—Management—Agency Authority

As to third parties, every partner is an agent of the partnership for purposes of its business.[1] Accordingly, unless the person with whom he is dealing knows that a partner has no authority in a matter,[2] each partner may bind the partnership by acts for "apparently carrying on in the usual way" the partnership business.[3] A partner does not, however, bind the partnership to any transaction not apparently within the scope of the partnership's business, unless his partners have authorized or ratified that action.[4] A partner attempting to bind the partnership by an unauthorized act is at least personally liable to the third party thereto.

---

6. *See* Elmsmere Associates v. Gladstone, 153 A.D.2d 501, 545 N.Y.S.2d 136 (1st Dep't 1989), app. denied 78 N.Y.2d 864, 578 N.Y.S.2d 879, 586 N.E.2d 62 (1991).

7. *See* Miltland Raleigh–Durham v. Myers, 807 F.Supp. 1025 (S.D.N.Y.1992) (general partners breached fiduciary duties to limited partners by, among other things, converting partnership property for their own use and by failing to advise the limited partners of offers to buy those properties); Sandler v. Fishman, 157 A.D.2d 708, 549 N.Y.S.2d 808 (2d Dep't 1990) (secret formation of exclusive new partnership using original partnership funds breached fiduciary duty to fellow partners and deprived them of a partnership opportunity; constructive trust in favor of excluded partners imposed).

8. NYPL § 42.

9. *See, e.g., supra,* Auld, § 2.45, note 9; Schneider v. Brenner, 134 Misc. 449, 235 N.Y.S. 55 (Sup.Ct., N.Y. County, 1929).

CAVEAT: Whether or not information is actually disclosed, every partner is charged with knowledge of each fact known to any partner.

10. *But see supra,* Riviera Congress Associates, § 2.45, note 2.

§ 2.60

1. NYPL § 20(1).

2. NYPL § 20(4). In this case, knowledge means both actual knowledge and knowledge of such other facts as would make denial of knowledge bad faith. NYPL § 3(1).

3. NYPL § 20(1). Any partner may convey title to real property in the partnership name as well, assuming the conveyance is in the ordinary course of business of the partnership. Even if the conveyance is not authorized, the partnership may not recover from a later purchaser for value who had no knowledge that the signatory's authority had been exceeded. NYPL § 21(1). As any act arguably in the ordinary course may therefore put all of the partners' individual assets at risk, it is well to know and trust one's partners implicitly.

4. NYPL § 20(2).

PRACTICE POINTER: Persons dealing with a partnership in matters arguably out-

Ch. 2   ASSIGNMENT OF INTERESTS—DEFAULT RULES   § 2.62

Certain types of transactions require the signatures of all the partners, unless they have otherwise authorized one or more partners to bind the partnership.[5] Without such authority, whether set out in the partnership agreement or elsewhere, fewer than all of the partners may not assign partnership property in trust to creditors, dispose of the partnership's good will, take any action that would make it impossible to carry on the ordinary business of the partnership, confess a judgment against the partnership, or submit a partnership claim to arbitration.[6]

As noted in Section 2.59, *supra*, except in cases of fraud, a partnership is charged with each partner's knowledge relating to partnership affairs and the facts of which he has notice.[7] Likewise, a partner acting on behalf of the partnership is charged with the knowledge of his fellow partners, if they reasonably could or should have communicated such knowledge to the acting partner.[8]

Library References:
West's Key No. Digests, Partnership ⟐125.

§ 2.61   General Partnerships—Assignment of Interests

Because partnership is a consensual relationship, one cannot, by assigning his partnership interest or a portion thereof to another, force the partnership to accept the assignee as a partner.[1] Accordingly, while the NYPL permits partners to assign their interests or portions thereof, the assignee, like the transferee of a membership interest in an LLC, in the absence of agreement otherwise, obtains only certain financial, and no management or other, rights with respect to the partnership.[2]

§ 2.62   General Partnerships—Assignment of Interests—Default Rules

While the assignment of a partnership interest does not dissolve the partnership, neither does it entitle the assignee to participate in partnership management, to have access to its books, or, in general, to require an accounting of partnership affairs, unless the partners have agreed otherwise. The transfer of a partnership interest merely entitles the transferee to receive the profits to which the assigning partner would have been entitled, in accordance with the terms of the assignment.[1] Upon dissolution, an assignee is entitled to receive the assignor's inter-

side the ordinary course of the partnership's business (including those listed in NYPL § 20(3)) should obtain specific written evidence, if possible, that the partner acting on behalf of the partnership has been authorized to do so.

5. NYPL § 20(3).
6. *Id.*

7. NYPL § 23.
8. *Id.*

§ 2.61
1. NYPL § 53(1).
2. *Id.*

§ 2.62
1. NYPL § 53(1).

est in the partnership (presumably including the partner's share of the surplus and the return of his capital, together with interest thereon), and at that time has the right to an accounting only from the date of the last account agreed to by all the partners.[2]

§ 2.63 General Partnerships—Assignment of Interests—Vote Required to Admit New Partner

No one may become a partner in a partnership, whether as a result of the sale or assignment of an interest or otherwise, unless all of the partners consent thereto.[1] This requirement may, however, be altered by agreement among the partners.[2]

§ 2.64 General Partnerships—Dissolution

Dissolution of a partnership occurs when the existing partners' relationship changes because one or more of them cease to be associated with the partnership in the conduct of its business.[1] Accordingly, any number of events, including a partner's voluntary or involuntary withdrawal from the partnership, result in its dissolution, unless the partnership agreement otherwise provides.[2] Dissolution, however, does not cause a partnership to terminate; it remains in existence for the limited purpose of winding up its business, or the remaining partners may, even in the absence of a pre-existing agreement to do so, decide to continue the partnership and its business.[3]

Library References:

West's Key No. Digests, Partnership ⇨259–348.

§ 2.65 General Partnerships—Dissolution—Events

Dissolution of a partnership occurs, in the absence of an agreement otherwise, upon any of the following events:

(1) the termination of its term, or the conclusion of the specific undertaking for which it was formed;

(2) at the will of any partner;[1]

(3) at any time by agreement of all partners who have not assigned their interests or otherwise subjected their interests to a charge by their creditors;

2. NYPL § 53(2).

§ 2.63

1. NYPL § 40(7).
2. Id.

§ 2.64

1. NYPL § 60.
2. See NYPL §§ 62, 63.

3. NYPL § 61; see NYPL §§ 69(2)(b), 72.

§ 2.65

1. See McQuillan v. Kenyon & Kenyon, 220 A.D.2d 395, 631 N.Y.S.2d 884 (2d Dep't 1995); Carola v. Grogan, 102 A.D.2d 934, 477 N.Y.S.2d 525 (3d Dep't 1984).

(4) the expulsion of any partner, but only if the agreement specifically confers the power to expel a partner;

(5) whenever it becomes unlawful to carry on the business of the partnership, or to carry on such a business in partnership form;

(6) the death of any partner;

(7) the bankruptcy of any partner or of the partnership;[2] or

(8) by judicial decree.[3]

If a partner dissolves a partnership in contravention of the partnership agreement, he is liable to the partnership and its remaining partners for damages resulting from the dissolution, including lost profits, even if the partnership is thereafter continued.[4]

Technically, the admission of a new partner should not result in the dissolution of a partnership, even though the addition modifies the relationship between the existing partners: NYPL § 60 defines dissolution in terms of a change as a result of a partner *ceasing* to be involved in the partnership.[5]

Upon application by a partner, a court may dissolve a partnership if:

(a) any partner has been declared incompetent or is shown to be of unsound mind;[6]

(b) any partner becomes incapable of performing his duties under the partnership agreement;

(c) any partner is guilty of conduct that "tends to affect prejudicially" the business of the partnership;

(d) any partner breaches the partnership agreement, willfully or persistently;

(e) any partner's conduct in matters relating to the partnership makes it "not reasonably practicable" to continue in partnership with him;

(f) the partnership business can only be carried on at a loss; or

(g) under other circumstances where dissolution is equitable.[7]

In addition, the assignee of a partnership interest or portion thereof, or a creditor who has obtained a charging order against a partner's partnership interest, may apply for judicial dissolution after the partnership's

2. *See generally,* Chapter 9 "Bankruptcy," *infra.*
3. NYPL § 62.
4. NYPL § 69(2).
5. **CAVEAT**: *But see* NYPL § 72(1), which refers to a "first or dissolved" partnership and a separate partnership "continuing the business" in the context of admission of a new partner. It may be useful, then, to provide expressly in the agreement that the addition of new partners will not effect a dissolution of the partnership.
6. NYPL § 63(1)(a); note that incompetence does not automatically cause dissolution, but requires a court proceeding to dissolve a partnership.
7. NYPL § 63(1)(b)—(f).

term ends or, if the partnership was "at will" when the assignment occurred or when the charging order issued, at any time thereafter.[8] This can give the creditor of a partner considerable leverage against a partnership that wishes to continue its business.

After dissolution, a partner binds the partnership only by acts appropriate for winding up its affairs (unless the business continues), or otherwise *vis-a-vis* third parties without notice that dissolution has taken place.[9] In no event will the partnership be bound, after dissolution, by the act of a bankrupt partner, or by a partner without authority if the third party with whom he was dealing was aware of the lack of authority.[10]

The dissolution of a partnership does not of itself, in the absence of agreement with its creditors otherwise, discharge the existing liabilities of any partner.[11]

§ 2.66 General Partnerships—Dissolution—Continuation of Business After Dissolution Event

A partnership agreement may provide for the continuation of the partnership after an event of dissolution, either automatically or upon the vote of the remaining partners. In addition, even in the absence of such an agreement, the NYPL permits a partnership to continue after the death or retirement,[1] expulsion[2] or withdrawal of a partner in breach of the partners' arrangements.[3] In any case where the business of the partnership continues, the creditors of the dissolved partnership remain creditors of the partnership continuing the business.[4]

If a partnership continues in business after the end of its term or after its particular undertaking is concluded, without any express agreement, the rights and duties of the partners remain the same as they were at the time of such termination, to the extent they are consistent with a partnership at will.[5] A partnership is presumed to have continued under such circumstances if its partners, or those among them who previously acted in the conduct of the business, continue the business without any settlement or liquidation of partnership affairs.[6]

---

8. NYPL § 63(2).
9. NYPL § 66(1). Unless a person has extended credit to the partnership, publication of notice of the partnership's dissolution in newspapers in each place where it conducted business is sufficient to constitute constructive notice of dissolution. NYPL § 66(1)(b).
10. NYPL § 66(3)(b), (c).
11. NYPL § 67(1).

§ 2.66
1. NYPL § 72(1), (2), (3).

2. NYPL § 72(6).
3. NYPL §§ 69(2), 72(5).
4. NYPL § 72.
5. NYPL § 45(1). To the extent the prior agreement imposed restrictions on the partners' ability to withdraw from the partnership, for example, such duties would probably be inconsistent with a partnership at will.
6. NYPL § 45(2).

When the business of the partnership continues after a wrongful dissolution, the partner who caused such dissolution is entitled to receive the value of his interest therein at the time of the event, not including the value of the partnership's good will, and less damages suffered by the partnership as a result of his action.[7] The withdrawing partner is also entitled to be released from all existing liabilities of the partnership.[8] Unless otherwise agreed, a retiring, deceased or outgoing partner who has not breached the partnership agreement is entitled to receive the value of his interest at the time of dissolution, plus interest or, in lieu of interest at the withdrawn partner's option, the profits attributable to the use of his right in the partnership's property.[9] A retiring, deceased or other properly withdrawing partner remains liable for obligations incurred by the partnership while he was a partner thereof.

Library References:

West's Key No. Digests, Partnership ⚖︎277.

§ 2.67 General Partnerships—Dissolution—Winding Up

The right to an accounting accrues to each partner upon an event of dissolution, unless otherwise agreed.[1] A partnership generally can be wound up only through an accounting, over which the court has considerable discretion.[2] Unless the partners have otherwise agreed, all of the partners who have not wrongfully caused the dissolution of the partnership are entitled to wind up its affairs. Partnership assets are valued, marshaled and applied to the claims of the partnership's creditors, and then to the partners, in accordance with the requirements of NYPL § 71. If a partnership's assets are insufficient to satisfy its liabilities, individual partners must contribute to such assets (except as otherwise required by law) and cover their insolvent partners' obligations to contribute.[3]

Library References:

West's Key No. Digests, Partnership ⚖︎277.

§ 2.68 General Partnerships—Conversions/Mergers

The NYPL does not specifically address the conversion or merger of a partnership with another entity. The NYBCL contemplates only the merger of New York corporations with other New York corporations. The NYLLCL provides for the merger of LLCs and virtually every other

---

7. NYPL § 69(2)(c)(II). See also, supra, McQuillan, § 2.65, note 1 (there can be no action for wrongful dissolution of an at-will partnership; accounting is the sole remedy).

8. Id.

9. NYPL § 73.

§ 2.67

1. NYPL § 74.
2. See NYPL § 75.
3. NYPL § 71(d).

type of organizational entity, including partnerships, as well as for the conversion of a partnership, limited or general, into LLC form.[1]

Notwithstanding the lack of specific statutory procedures, other types of entities may, in effect, combine with a partnership by contributing their assets thereto and becoming partners thereof, or the partnership itself might contribute its assets in return for an ownership interest in another entity and then dissolve, distributing those interests to its partners.

§ 2.69 General Partnerships—Conversions/Mergers—Procedures

Unless the partnership agreement otherwise provides, all partners must consent to the conversion of a partnership into an LLC.[1] The conversion process requires the filing of a Certificate of Conversion with the Secretary of State, and, most likely, some adjustment of the existing partnership agreement (including committing it to writing if it is not already written) into the form of an operating agreement.[2] It is hard to imagine why an LLC might wish to convert to a general partnership, but presumably that could be accomplished by disolving the LLC, canceling its Articles of Organization and filing a Business Certificate.

Combinations of partnerships and other entities can be accomplished by agreement, as noted above. Unless the partners have agreed otherwise, the terms on which a partnership merges or otherwise combines with another entity must be approved by all of the partners.[3] If the combining entities include partnerships, they will each terminate for tax purposes if their respective members cease to own 51% of the combined entity.

§ 2.70 General Partnerships—Conversions/Mergers—Dissenters' Rights

The rights of partners who do not agree to combine with another entity will most likely be addressed by a specific arrangement. In the absence of such an agreement, a dissenting partner presumably would be treated as one who withdraws from the constituent partnership, and would be entitled to receive the value of his interest therein before giving effect to the transaction.[1]

§ 2.68

1. *See supra*, §§ 2.40, 2.41, for a discussion of mergers and conversion involving LLCs.

§ 2.69

1. NYLLCL § 1006(c).
2. *See supra*, § 2.41.
3. *See* NYPL § 40(7), (8). Merger or combination would appear not to be an ordinary matter, and ultimately involves the addition of partners to a partnership relation; accordingly, it should require the consent of all partners of the affected entities.

§ 2.70

1. It would not make sense to give a dissenter the value of what his interest in the combined entity would have been, since he opposed that combination. *See* Wolfson

§ 2.71 General Partnerships—Professional Organizations

Historically, professional groups have chosen to organize as general partnerships because of their flexibility, tax benefits, lack of restrictions on their membership (compared to Subchapter S corporations) and because professional oversight bodies permit practice in such form.[1] The informality of partnership organization and management can be an attractive characteristic, particularly for groups comprising sophisticated professionals who are presumed to be able to protect themselves in the course of making their business arrangements. Moreover, professionals in small group practices may be able to choose their partners carefully enough to reduce the risks of their joint and several liability for any member's malpractice.

The availability of both PLLCs and LLPs, however, may spell the end of New York professional general partnerships.[2] Larger groups in particular may seize the opportunity to limit personal liability where it has become more difficult to assess all members' professional competence and oversee their professional activities.

§ 2.72 Limited Liability Partnerships

Under amendments to the NYPL that became effective in October, 1994, New York professional general partnerships may register as LLPs, thereby relieving partners of their traditional unlimited liability for the contractual and most other debts, obligations and liabilities of the partnership.[1] Like a shareholder of a New York professional corporation,[2] a partner of an LLP is personally liable for his own professional negligence or misconduct and that committed by others under his direct supervision and control, but he is not liable for any of the debts or obligations of the partnership, in contract, tort or otherwise.[3]

Registration as an LLP is a simple, straightforward process without effect other than the resulting limitation of the partners' liability.[4] A partnership that elects LLP status is the same entity for tax and other purposes that it was before registration.[5] Nor does registration as an

---

v. Rosenthal, 210 A.D.2d 47, 619 N.Y.S.2d 43 (1st Dep't 1994) (dissenter received value of his interest in terminated partnership after acquisition by another partnership). It is unclear, however, whether any such dissent could ever be considered a wrongful withdrawal, subject to the valuation restrictions discussed in § 2.66, *supra*.

§ 2.71

1. For ethical reasons, such bodies have traditionally prohibited practice in certain forms (for example, neither physicians nor lawyers may practice in limited partnerships, as that structure would permit limited partner professionals to avoid personal responsibility for their own malpractice).

2. *See infra*, §§ 2.72–2.76.

§ 2.72

1. *See* NYPL §§ 26, 121–1500.

2. *See* NYBCL § 1505(a).

3. NYPL § 26(b), (c).

4. NYPL § 121–5000(d).

5. *Id.*

§ 2.72 NON-CORPORATE ENTITIES Ch. 2

LLP require the adoption of a new partnership agreement;[6] indeed, a partnership may elect LLP status without adopting a written partnership agreement at all.

Library References:

West's Key No. Digests, Partnership ⚖349–376.

§ 2.73 Limited Liability Partnerships—Governing Law

As noted in Section 2.72, *supra*, conversion to an LLP is accomplished by registering the existing partnership as an LLP, rather than by creating a different type of business organization.[1] Accordingly, an LLP remains subject to the NYPL, as expressly amended by its new LLP provisions, and must be formed with attention to the same issues that affect a general partnership.

Only partnerships comprising "professionals," as defined in Title VIII of the New York Education Law, may register as LLPs.[2] This restriction was imposed to avoid creating a vehicle that could be used to deprive unsophisticated investors of the rights they would otherwise have by default as members of LLCs.[3] Professional firms have traditionally been organized as general partnerships and their partners are presumed to require less protection than passive investors because of both their sophistication and active involvement in rendering professional services.

LLPs and their partners also are subject to all applicable rules and regulations of the State licensing agencies governing or regulating their profession.[4]

Library References:

West's Key No. Digests, Partnership ⚖350.

§ 2.74 Limited Liability Partnerships—Comparison With General Partnerships

As noted in Section 2.72, *supra*, an LLP is, by law, the same entity it

---

6. *Id.*

PRACTICE POINTER: The firm's existing agreement may have to be amended to deal with the changed relationship among the partners resulting from the limitation of their personal liability. See *infra*, § 2.76.

§ 2.73

1. NYPL § 121–1500(d).
2. NYPL §§ 2, 121–1500(a).
3. LLPs neither require a written agreement, through which investors would be assured of their rights, nor are they subject to the elaborate default provisions of the NYLLCL as to internal governance, economic rights and other matters. Accordingly, an LLP does not offer the same investor protections afforded by an LLC or corporate structure. Presumably, however, active professionals do not require such protections. For a further discussion of the LLP drafting committee's deliberations, *see* S.R. Breslow, Ch. 14, "Limited Liability Partnerships," in Walker, *Limited Liability Companies and Partnerships: A Guide to Law and Practice* (West 1995).

4. NYPL § 121–1500(m).

Ch. 2   COMPARISON WITH GENERAL PARTNERSHIPS   § 2.74

was prior to its registration as such and subject to the same law.[1] The parties continue to be "partners," both in name and for purposes of other applicable laws.

The main difference between an LLP and a general partnership is the statutory limitation of the liability of an LLP's partners. Section 26 of the NYPL, as amended, provides, in pertinent part:

> (b) Except as provided by subdivisions (c) and (d) of this section, no partner of a partnership which is a registered limited liability partnership is liable or accountable, directly or indirectly (including by way of indemnification, contribution or otherwise), for any debts, obligations or liabilities of, or chargeable to, the registered limited liability partnership or each other, whether arising in tort, contract or otherwise, which are incurred, created or assumed by such partnership, while such partnership is a registered liability partnership, solely by reason of being such a partner or acting (or omitting to act) in such capacity or rendering professional services or otherwise participating (as an employee, consultant, contractor or otherwise) in the conduct of the other business or activities of the registered limited liability partnership.
>
> (c) Notwithstanding the provisions of subdivision (b) of this section, (i) each partner, employee or agent of a partnership which is a registered limited liability partnership shall be personally and fully liable and accountable for any negligent or wrongful act or misconduct committed by him or her or by any person under his or her direct supervision and control while rendering professional services on behalf of such registered limited liability partnership and (ii) each shareholder, director, officer, member, manager, partner, employee and agent of a professional service corporation, foreign professional service corporation, professional service limited liability company, foreign professional service limited liability company, registered limited liability partnership, foreign limited liability partnership or professional partnership that is a partner, employee or agent of a partnership which is a registered limited liability partnership shall be personally and fully liable and accountable for any negligent or wrongful act or misconduct committed by him or her or by any person under his or her direct supervision and control while rendering professional services in his or her capacity as a partner, employee or agent of such registered limited liability partnership. The relationship of a professional to a registered limited liability partnership with which such professional is associated, whether as a part-

---

§ 2.74

[1]. NYPL § 121–1500(d). The federal tax identification number will remain the same, as well.

CAVEAT: Nevertheless, the contracts to which the partnership is party should be checked carefully to make sure that conversion, and the resulting limitation of its partners' liability, does not trigger "due on sale" or other default provisions.

ner, employee or agent, shall not modify or diminish the jurisdiction over such professional of the licensing authority and in the case of an attorney and counselor-at-law or a professional service corporation, professional service limited liability company, foreign professional service limited liability company, registered limited liability partnership, foreign registered limited liability partnership, foreign professional service corporation or professional partnership, engaged in the practice of law, the other courts of this state.

Accordingly, third parties may not sue the partners of an LLP individually for the obligations of the partnership, except to the extent they result from the partners' own negligent or wrongful acts or those of persons under their direct supervision and control.[2] Nor may partners sue their fellow partners for contribution to liabilities incurred as a result of their own negligence or misconduct.[3] This protection begins upon registration as an LLP and continues with respect to all liabilities arising from actions or events occurring while the registration is in effect.[4]

Section 26(d) of the NYPL permits specified partners of an LLP to retain personal liability for "all or specified debts, obligations and liabilities" of the partnership to the extent that at least a majority of the partners have agreed. (The majority requirement may be altered in the partnership agreement.) Except as otherwise provided in the partnership agreement, this expanded liability may be amended or revoked only by vote of at least a majority of the partners.[5]

Like general partners and members of PLLCs, partners of an LLP may be liable for wrongful distributions under applicable insolvency or fraudulent transfer laws.[6] To the extent that distributions actually constitute compensation for professional services, it might not be appropriate for courts to insist that partners repay distributions for the benefit of an LLP's creditors.

Like a PLLC, an LLP must pay an annual per-member fee of $50 (with a minimum $325 per year and $10,000 maximum) to the state, but only if the LLP has New York source income.[7] The City of New York is authorized to impose the same annual fee on LLPs with New York City source income.[8]

Library References:

West's Key No. Digests, Partnership ⚍349.

2. *See* NYPL § 26(b), (c).
3. NYPL § 26(b).
4. *See* NYPL § 26(b), (c). Note that registration is effective upon filing, not publication. *See infra*, § 2.75.
5. *See* NYPL § 26(d). No such amendment or revocation will affect a partner's liability for any obligations incurred, created or assumed prior thereto.
6. *See supra*, § 2.53.
7. *See* Tax Law § 658(c)(3).
8. *See* Tax Law § 1304–c.

§ 2.75 Limited Liability Partnerships—Formation/Registration

To register as an LLP, an entity must (a) be organized as a general partnership, (b) include only partners who are "professionals," at least one of whom[1] is authorized by law to render a professional service in New York, and (c) be engaged in the practice of such profession, or within 30 days after the effectiveness of registration, become so engaged.[2] The professionals permitted to utilize LLPs include attorneys, physicians, architects, chiropractors, dental hygienists, dentists, professional engineers, surveyors, masseurs, pharmacists, nurses, physical therapists, podiatrists, certified psychologists, certified public accountants and veterinarians, among others.[3] The term "professional" includes licensed individuals, professional corporations, PLLCs, LLPs and partnerships, foreign or domestic.

The decision to register as an LLP is an "ordinary matter" of partnership business, requiring a majority vote of the partners unless their agreement alters such vote.[4] The registration filed with the Department of State must contain the following:

(i) the name of the LLP;

(ii) the address of its principal office;

(iii) the profession or professions to be practiced by the LLP and a statement that it is eligible to register as an LLP;

(iv) a designation of the Department of State as the LLP's agent for service of process, and the address within or without New York to which a copy of any process against the LLP served upon the Department of State shall be mailed;

(v) if the LLP has a registered agent, its name and address in New York, and a statement that it is to be the agent upon whom process against the LLP may be served;

(vi) a statement that the partnership is filing a registration for status as a registered LLP;

(vii) if the registration is to be effective on a date later than the filing date, such date, not to exceed 60 days after filing;

(viii) if all or specified partners of the LLP are to be liable in their capacity as partners for all or specified debts, obligations or liabilities of the LLP, a statement to that effect; and

---

§ 2.75

1. NYPL § 121–1500(q) requires all partners (not just one) of an LLP rendering medical, dental, legal, professional engineering, land surveying, architectural and/or landscape architectural services to be licensed in that profession.

2. NYPL § 121–1500(a).

3. See NYPL § 2 and Title VIII of the New York Education Law. Note that this definition of "profession" is the same used in NYBCL § 1501(b) and in NYLLCL §§ 1201(b), 1301(c).

4. See NYPL §§ 121–1500(1), 40(8).

(ix) any other matters the partnership determines to include in the registration.[5]

The LLP's name must contain either the words "Registered Limited Liability Partnership" or "Limited Liability Partnership," or any of the abbreviations "R.L.L.P.," "RLLP," "L.L.P.," or "LLP."[6] The registration may be signed by a single partner,[7] and is effective upon filing and payment of a $200 filing fee.[8] In addition, the new LLP must publish a copy of its registration or a notice containing its substance in two newspapers in the county in which its principal office will be located, once a week over a period of six consecutive weeks, within 120 days following the effective date of the LLP registration, and must file an affidavit of such publication with the Secretary of State.[9] Failure to publish does not impair the validity of any contract or other act of the LLP, and would appear (although this is not explicitly stated) not to impair its valid registration or the effectiveness of the liability protection afforded to its partners.[10] Until the defect is cured, however, the LLP may not maintain, on its own behalf, any action or special proceeding in New York.[11]

Changes in the information set forth in the registration after its filing do not affect the LLP's status.[12] Nevertheless, NYPL § 121–1500(j) requires an amendment to be filed within 90 days after a change in the LLP's name, registered agent or address for service of process, or the date on which a partner becomes aware that any statement in an earlier registration or statement was or has become inaccurate in any material respect.[13]

If an LLP dissolves, any successor partnership to the LLP will have the benefit of the prior LLP election. A partnership is a successor if a majority of its total profits interests are held by partners of the predeces-

---

5. NYPL § 121–1500(a). *See infra*, § 2.113, for a form of LLP registration.

6. NYPL § 121–1501.

PRACTICE POINTER: Prudent practice and the ethical requirements of most professions will require stationery, business cards and other items carrying the name of the partnership to reflect the new name. Many firms converting to LLP status also send a notice to their clients and suppliers informing them of the change.

7. *See* NYPL § 121–1500(b).

8. *See* NYPL §§ 121–1500(c), (d), (e). Note that the Department of State will not review the registration for its legal sufficiency.

9. *See* NYPL § 121–1500(a).

PRACTICE POINTER: Note that, if the registration itself is not published, the notice containing its substance must include information not required to be included in the registration: the date of dissolution of the LLP, if any, and a statement of the character or purpose of the LLP's business.

10. NYPL § 121–1500(a).

11. *Id.*

12. NYPL § 121–1500(d).

13. **CAVEAT**: Although the NYPL does not address the issue, query whether an LLP election could be impaired if the registration contained information that was inaccurate at the time of filing, and/or a partner knew of a defect and failed timely to correct it. In any event, amendments to LLP registrations need not be published like the original registration.

sor partnership.[14]

Following registration, an LLP must file periodic statements with the Department of State, accompanied by a $20 filing fee, within 60 days prior to the second anniversary of the effective date of LLP registration and every two years thereafter.[15] If an LLP fails to make the required filing, the Department of State may initiate revocation of the LLP registration, by providing at least 60 days' prior notice to that effect to the LLP.[16] An LLP election also may be voluntarily withdrawn at any time by one or more partners filing a written withdrawal notice, as authorized by a majority of the partners (unless a different vote is specified in the partnership agreement).[17] The voluntary or involuntary revocation of an LLP election does not affect the limited liability of partners as to "any debt, obligation or liability incurred, created or assumed while the partnership was a registered limited liability partnership."[18]

LLPs and their partners are governed by the same professional regulatory and licensing authorities both before and after registration.[19] A certified copy of the LLP registration and any amendment thereto must be filed with the relevant licensing authority within 30 days after it is filed with the Department of State.[20]

Library References:
West's Key No. Digests, Partnership ⚖352.

§ 2.76 Limited Liability Partnerships—Other Issues

Until recently, one disadvantage of LLPs (as compared to PLLCs or professional corporations) was that LLPs did not have comparable national acceptance.[1] Requirements of full faith and credit and comity make it likely that New York LLP partners doing business elsewhere will nonetheless enjoy the same limited liability afforded them under the New York statute, whether or not the other state permits the creation of LLPs or offers domestic LLP partners less comprehensive protection than the New York law. However, it is possible that, if the New York LLP or its partners were sued in connection with business conducted in another state, that state might conclude that it has a compelling public

---

14. NYPL § 121–1500(d).

15. NYPL § 121–1500(g). These statements must be executed by at least one partner and must contain the LLP's name and address and a statement of its continued eligibility for LLP status.

16. NYPL § 121–1500(g). Revocation occurs upon publication of a notice following expiration of the 60–day cure period; the LLP nevertheless has the continuing option to cure its filing defect and receive retroactive reinstatement of its LLP election. *Id.*

17. NYPL § 121–1500(f).

18. NYPL § 121–1500(f).

19. NYPL § 121–1500(m).

20. NYPL § 121–1500(p).

§ 2.76

1. At the date of this writing, however, LLPs are recognized in most states and the District of Columbia, and legislation is pending in the remaining states.

policy against respecting its or their limited liability.[2] It is also possible that professional licensing authorities in other states might prohibit professional firms under their jurisdiction from operating within their borders in LLP form, or might impose additional restrictions not mandated by New York law.[3]

Questions may also arise about the impact of registration as an LLP on a professional firm's culture.[4] Unlike partners in a traditional general partnership, partners in an LLP do not share unlimited personal exposure for their partners' malpractice. Accordingly, it may not be appropriate for partners in high-risk practice areas that are typically a firm's most lucrative to bear that risk alone, rather than sharing it with partners in other practice areas who nevertheless benefit from the high-risk work. Partners who bear a disproportionate personal risk may also demand additional compensation therefor.

Moreover, what it means to be liable for the negligence of persons under one's "direct supervision and control" is unclear, although that phrase is also used in the NYBCL.[5] It may be that an LLP's partners will be more reluctant, among other things, to assume training responsibility for its employees in light of this uncertainty. In any event, it would be naive to assume that an LLP election would never adversely affect the spirit of cooperation and sense of common interest desired in a firm.

In most cases, however, the disruptive effect of a conversion to LLP status on firm culture will be minimal, for a variety of reasons. Although partners in an LLP are not obligated to contribute to losses arising from other partners' malpractice, firm assets will nevertheless be available to satisfy such claims, as well as other types of claims against the LLP, and to indemnify defendant partners. As a result, all partners will continue to have a common interest in protecting the value of their enterprise and its professional reputation. Moreover, professional firms generally carry substantial professional liability insurance. The chances of a claim consuming the assets of the firm, together with all available insurance, seem remote.[6]

2. **CAVEAT**: Many states that recognize LLPs require them to carry certain minimum levels of insurance and/or cash reserves. If a New York LLP did not meet these requirements and committed malpractice in another state, the other state might not give effect to the partners' limited liability.

3. **CAVEAT**: Although the NYPL expressly provides that it will govern New York LLPs conducting business in other states, it nevertheless prohibits non-professional LLPs formed in other states from qualifying to do business as LLPs in New York and/or receiving liability protection when they do business here.

4. For a more detailed discussion of these issues in the context of law firms, see Stephanie R. Breslow, Ch. 14, "Limited Liability Partnerships," in Walker, *Limited Liability Companies and Partnerships: A Guide to Law and Practice* (West 1995).

5. *See* NYBCL § 1505(a).

6. Judgments against law firms in excess of insurance and firm assets are extremely rare. In any event, claims that exhaust available insurance and then force partners into bankruptcy, thereby causing a going concern to dissolve, do not necessarily best serve plaintiffs' interests.

Finally, it is also possible, though not necessarily advised, for LLP partners to address some of the cultural issues by entering into formal contribution arrangements among themselves. Obviously, if such personal contribution obligations were unqualified, there would be little point in making an LLP election. However, in some circumstances, partners may wish to contribute towards judgments against another partner. The question is whether it is possible to create a contribution obligation that is enforceable by the defendant partner but not by his creditors[7] or whether such an obligation may be enforceable only if the enforcing partner is not insolvent. If it is not possible to limit a contribution obligation in these ways, it might also be capped.[8] Partners could, of course, rely on informal assurances that they will take care of each other in circumstances that warrant such assistance.

Library References:

West's Key No. Digests, Partnership ⚷349–376.

§ 2.77 Limited Partnerships

Until the enactment of the NYLLCL, enterprises seeking pass-through tax treatment, limited liability for their investors and contractual flexibility usually opted for a limited partnership structure. Although a limited partnership requires at least one general partner who is personally liable for all of the partnership's debts and obligations, that liability can effectively be limited by creating a corporate general partner. If the corporate general partner can elect Subchapter S status and, in any event, has a small interest in the partnership, the benefits of pass-through tax treatment can be largely, if not entirely, realized.[1]

Library References:

West's Key No. Digests, Partnership ⚷349–376.

---

7. The answer would seem to be no, at least if the defendant partner is a debtor in bankruptcy; in any event, because such an arrangement would probably be discoverable in litigation, the practical effect thereof would be to increase the amount of any settlement acceptable to a creditor.

8. CAVEAT: A contribution cap may, however, merely set a floor for negotiations with claimants.

§ 2.77

1. PRACTICE POINTER: Easy as it may therefore seem to preserve both pass-through tax treatment and virtual limited liability for all participants in a more familiar and possibly more predictable vehicle than the LLC, the costs of establishing and maintaining such a two-tiered structure may substantially exceed those associated with forming and operating an LLC. Both LLCs and limited partnerships must make centralized filings to come into existence, and both must publish certain information over six weeks in two newspapers. The LLC carries with it an additional per member annual fee not applicable to partners of a limited partnership, but the cost of maintaining a New York corporation, particularly in New York City, probably will exceed that. The cost of drafting an operating agreement should be equivalent to the cost of preparing a limited partnership agreement. Moreover, limited partners are not permitted to exercise "control" over a limited partnership without risking loss of their limited liability. *See* NYPL § 121–303(a) and § 2.86, *infra*.

§ 2.78 Limited Partnerships—Governing Law

New York adopted the Revised Uniform Limited Partnership Act (1985) effective July 1, 1991. The NYRLPA, incorporated as Article 8A of the NYPL, governs all New York limited partnerships formed after its effective date, all foreign limited partnerships doing business in New York, no matter when they were organized, and pre-existing New York limited partnerships formed under Article 8 of the NYPL that elect, or are required, to be subject to the newer law.[1] Article 8 of the NYPL continues to govern New York limited partnerships organized prior to July 1, 1991, which have not elected, and have not been required, to comply with new Article 8A.[2]

The NYRLPA improves upon old Article 8 of the NYPL in several important respects. For example, the Certificate of Limited Partnership, the public document filed with the Department of State to create a New York limited partnership, no longer must include the names and contributions of its limited partners (the names and addresses of the general partners only are required).[3] Moreover, unlike Article 8 of the NYPL, the NYRLPA does not require the Certificate to be amended when a new limited partner joins the partnership or when a partner's contribution changes.[4] Accordingly, like those of members of LLCs, the identities and investments of limited partners are not a matter of public record.

The NYRLPA tracks the language of old NYPL Article 8 imposing personal liability as general partners upon limited partners who "participate in the control of the business."[5] The NYRLPA, however, limits substantially the class to which a limited partner exercising such control will be liable: only those doing business with the partnership who reasonably believe, based on the limited partner's conduct, that he is a general partner may recover from him.[6] The NYRLPA further protects limited partners from unwitting exposure to personal liability by specifying safe harbor activities that do not rise to the level of participating in the control of the partnership.[7] In general, the rights and duties of partners of a limited partnership are more detailed under the NYRLPA than under prior statutory law, without sacrificing any of the parties' flexibility to tailor a limited partnership agreement to their particular arrangements.

Anyone familiar with the NYLLCL will have a good grasp of how the NYRLPA operates, and vice versa, since the NYRLPA was the foundation for the NYLLCL.[8] Most of the concepts and considerations that

---

§ 2.78
1. NYPL §§ 121–1201, 121–1202.
2. Id.
3. NYPL § 121–201.
4. NYPL § 121–202(a).
5. NYPL § 121–303(a).
6. Id.
7. NYPL § 121–303. See infra, § 2.86.
8. See supra, § 2.15.

shape an LLC operating agreement will apply to a limited partnership agreement as well.[9]

Library References:

West's Key No. Digests, Partnership ⚖=350.

§ 2.79 Limited Partnerships—Formation

To form a New York limited partnership, its general partners must execute and file with the Secretary of State a Certificate of Limited Partnership[1] and they must execute a written partnership agreement.[2] The partnership is formed upon filing of the Certificate or such later date, not more than 60 days thereafter, provided in the Certificate.[3]

Subject to other applicable law,[4] a New York limited partnership may be formed to conduct any business that a general partnership might conduct.[5] Accordingly, a limited partnership may conduct only for-profit enterprises.[6] Its powers incident to carrying on such businesses are not restricted by statute.

A limited partnership's name must be distinguishable from that of any other domestic or foreign limited partnership on file with the State.[7] It may not contain certain words or phrases, including any words that are prohibited in a corporate name under the NYBCL, and it must include a designation such as "limited partnership" or "L.P."[8] A limited partner's name may be included in the name of the partnership, but if that partner expressly consented to such use, he will be liable as a general partner to creditors who extend credit without actual knowledge that he was not a general partner.[9]

Under the NYRLPA, a limited partnership may reserve its name in advance of formation, in a manner similar to that available to New York LLCs and corporations.[10] A limited partnership may also use a fictitious

---

9. See infra, §§ 2.82, 2.83.

§ 2.79

1. NYPL § 121–201(a); see infra, § 2.80.

2. NYPL § 121–110(a), (b). Limited partners may, but need not, execute the agreement. NYPL § 121–110(a).

PRACTICE POINTER: If the limited partners do not execute the partnership agreement, they should certainly execute a subscription or other purchase agreement incorporating its terms and conditions to avoid problems with the Statute of Frauds. Presumably, the Certificate of Limited Partnership could serve as a limited partnership agreement, see NYPL § 121–101(*l*), but for the same reasons an LLC's Articles of Organization should not be used as its operating agreement, this is not advised. See supra, § 2.19, note 3.

3. NYPL § 121–201(b).

4. Including, for example, the laws governing the practice of certain professions in New York that prohibit the rendering of professional services in limited partnership form.

5. NYPL § 121–107.

6. See NYPL §§ 121–101(h), 10(1).

7. NYPL § 121–102(a)(2).

8. See NYBCL § 301; NYPL § 121–102(a).

9. NYPL § 121–303(d).

10. NYPL § 121–103(a); see NYLLCL § 205 and NYBCL § 303.

name.[11]

Foreign limited partnerships must file an Application for Authority and a certificate of their existence with the Department of State, and thereafter publish the Application (in the same manner required for the publication of a domestic limited partnership's Certificate of Limited Partnership—*see infra*, Section 2.82) to become qualified to do business in New York.[12] Failure to do so does not impair the foreign limited partnership's contracts, but would prevent it from initiating or maintaining an action in the State.[13]

Library References:

West's Key No. Digests, Partnership ⚖︎352.

§ 2.80 Limited Partnerships—Formation—Certificate of Limited Partnership

A New York limited partnership must file a Certificate of Limited Partnership with the Secretary of State, signed by all general partners,[1] containing the following:

(i) the name of the limited partnership;

(ii) the county within New York State in which its office is to be located;

(iii) a designation of the Secretary of State as agent of the limited partnership upon whom process against the limited partnership may be served, and the post office address within or without New York State to which a copy of any process served against the Secretary of State shall be mailed;

(iv) if the limited partnership is to have a registered agent, its name and address within New York State and a statement that the registered agent is to be the agent of the limited partnership upon whom process may be served;

(v) the name and business or residence street address of each general partner;

(vi) the latest date upon which the limited partnership is to dissolve; and

(vii) any other matters the general partners determine to include.[2]

---

11. NYPL § 121–102(b); *see* General Business Law § 130.
12. NYPL § 121–902(a).
13. NYPL § 121–907.

§ 2.80
1. NYPL § 121–204(a)(1).

2. NYPL § 121–201(a). Note that, unlike an LLC, a limited partnership is required to state in its Certificate the latest date on which it will dissolve.

§ 2.80 CERTIFICATE OF LIMITED PARTNERSHIP

Like an LLC's Articles of Organization, a limited partnership's Certificate of Limited Partnership is the only document necessarily a matter of public record. For this reason, and to avoid frequent amendment of the Certificate, partners are usually advised to include only the bare-bones requirements of the statute in their Certificate.[3] The fee for filing a Certificate of Limited Partnership with the Department of State is $200. A limited partnership must also obtain an EIN.[4]

A Certificate of Limited Partnership must be amended within 90 days after the admission or withdrawal of a general partner, the continuation of the limited partnership's business after a general partner's withdrawal under NYPL § 121–801, or a change in the limited partnership's name, address for service of process or registered agent.[5] It may also be amended for any other proper purpose, as the general partners may determine.[6] A Certificate of Amendment need be signed only by a single general partner,[7] and by each person designated therein as a new general partner.[8] A general partner who becomes aware that a statement in any filing was false in any material respect when made, or has otherwise become inaccurate, must amend the Certificate within 90 days of becoming so aware.[9]

Any person who executes a publicly-filed document for or on behalf of a limited partnership, or who causes another to execute it, and who knows a statement therein to be false in any material respect at the time, is liable in damages to anyone who suffers loss by reasonable reliance on that statement.[10] In addition, any general partner who knows of a filing, and who knows or should have known with the exercise of reasonable care and diligence that a statement therein was false in any material respect, is liable to persons reasonably relying on the false statement, whether or not the general partner signs the document.[11] A general partner is also liable if he fails to amend a certificate when required under NYPL § 121–202(c).[12]

If a person required to do so under NYPL § 121–204 fails or refuses to execute or file any document for the limited partnership, any partner, or an assignee of a partner adversely affected thereby, may petition the Supreme Court in the judicial district where the partnership's office is located to compel execution and filing.[13]

Library References:

West's Key No. Digests, Partnership ⚖︎354.

3. See supra, § 2.17.
4. Id.
5. NYPL § 121–202(b).
6. NYPL § 121–202(d).
7. NYPL §§ 121–207(a)(1), (2).
8. NYPL § 121–204(a)(2).
9. NYPL § 121–202(c).
10. NYPL § 121–207(a)(1).
11. Id.
12. NYPL § 121–207(a)(2).
13. NYPL § 121–205(a).

§ 2.81 Limited Partnerships—Formation—Publication

Like the Articles of Organization of an LLC,[1] a copy of the Certificate of Limited Partnership or a notice containing the substance thereof must, within 120 days after filing, be published once a week for six successive weeks in two newspapers in the county in which the partnership's office is located.[2] The newspapers are to be designated by the county clerk, and one of them must be in the town where the partnership's principal place of business will be located.[3]

If the Certificate itself is not published, the notice of its substance must contain all of the items identified in Section 2.81, *supra*, required for the Certificate, plus a statement of the character or purpose of the partnership's business.[4] Amendments to a Certificate of Limited partnership do not require publication.

Proof of publication by the printer's or publisher's affidavit must be filed with the Department of State, at a filing fee of $25.[5] Failure to file such proof within the 120–day period does not impair the validity of any contract to which the limited partnership is party, the right of any other party to maintain any action thereon, nor does it otherwise prevent the partnership from defending such an action.[6] A limited partnership may not, however, initiate or maintain any action or special proceeding in New York until the failure is rectified.[7]

Library References:
West's Key No. Digests, Partnership ⇔352.

§ 2.82 Limited Partnerships—Formation—Agreement

A domestic limited partnership must adopt a written partnership agreement as to the conduct of its business and the terms of its partners' relations.[1] To the extent the agreement does not specifically alter the default provisions of the NYRLPA (such as they are),[2] they will prevail. A limited partnership agreement should deal with the same issues that an LLC operating agreement should address,[3] but, in particular, should set out the partners' relative voting rights, the issues to be voted upon, and the mechanics thereof, as the NYRLPA does not contain guidance on

---

§ 2.81

1. *See supra*, § 2.18.
2. NYPL § 121–201(c).

PRACTICE POINTER: Under the New York Arts and Cultural Affairs Law § 23.03(4), theatrical syndications organized as limited partnerships are exempt from the publication requirement of the NYRLPA.

3. NYPL § 121–201(c).
4. *Id.*
5. *Id.*, NYPL § 121–1300(f).
6. NYPL § 121–201(c).
7. *Id.*

§ 2.82

1. NYPL § 121–110(b).
2. The default provisions of the NYPL with respect to general partners are applicable to general partners of a limited partnership, but the NYRLPA does not contain many other default provisions for the operation of a partnership formed thereunder.
3. *See supra*, § 2.19.

these matters.[4] Unless the partners disclose its contents, a limited partnership agreement is not a matter of public record.

Most of the substantive provisions of the NYRLPA may be altered by a limited partnership agreement, including financial arrangements among the partners,[5] general powers and liabilities of a general partner to the partnership and the other partners,[6] the ability to assign partnership interests and admit new partners,[7] and voting on mergers and consolidations.[8]

Although all of a limited partnership's general partners must sign the partnership agreement, its limited partners are not required to do so.[9] The better practice, however, is to require limited partners to execute the agreement, or otherwise to sign a document incorporating its terms by reference, to avoid both misunderstandings and Statute of Frauds problems. Only those who sign the agreement as general partners have the rights, and are subject to the liabilities, of a general partner.[10]

A partnership agreement may be amended as set forth therein, but unless otherwise provided in the agreement, certain amendments may not be made without the written consent of each partner adversely affected thereby.[11] These amendments include increases in a limited partner's obligation to make contributions to the partnership, changes in allocations of income, gain, loss, deduction or credit or the manner in which distributions are calculated, changes in the voting or other rights of a limited partner, reducing to less than unanimity the consent required to compromise an obligation to make a contribution and changes in the procedures for amending the agreement.[12]

If a limited partner refuses to execute a partnership agreement, or any amendment thereto, in breach of his obligation to do so, any partner or assignee of a partner may petition the Supreme Court in the judicial

---

4. NYPL § 121–302 permits the creation of different classes of limited partners and, if a vote is granted to limited partners on any issue, the inclusion of provisions as to notice, waiver, action by consent and other rights with respect to the vote. NYPL § 121–405 permits the same with respect to general partners. NYPL § 121–110(c) provides that a limited partnership agreement may be amended from time to time as set forth therein, and then prohibits certain amendments without the consent of partners who would be adversely affected thereby. Otherwise, the NYRLPA does not establish defaults for amendment.

5. NYPL §§ 121–503, 504.

6. NYPL § 121–403(a), (c).

CAVEAT: Note that NYPL § 121–403(b) does not permit a partnership agreement to limit the liability of a limited partnership's general partner to third parties.

7. NYPL § 121–702.

8. NYPL § 121–1102.

9. NYPL § 121–110(a).

10. NYPL § 121–110(b).

CAVEAT: This limitation would appear to apply only to obligations *vis-a-vis* the partnership and the other partners, not to liabilities to third parties. See NYPL §§ 121–303(a), 121–304(b).

11. NYPL § 121–110(c).

12. Id.

§ 2.82   NON-CORPORATE ENTITIES   Ch. 2

district where the partnership's office is located to direct such execution.[13]

Library References:

West's Key No. Digests, Partnership ⌹352.

§ 2.83   Limited Partnerships—Formation—Other Issues

A domestic limited partnership must maintain certain records, including the partners' names (in alphabetical order), mailing addresses, contributions and shares of profits and losses, or information from which such shares can be readily derived; copies of the Certificate of Limited Partnership, all amendments thereto and powers of attorney pursuant to which any certificate has been executed; a copy of the partnership agreement, as amended from time to time, and copies of the partnership's federal, state and local income tax information returns and reports, if any, for its three most recent fiscal years.[1] These records may, but need not, be maintained in New York.[2] Any partner may, subject to reasonable standards established in the partnership agreement or by the general partners, inspect such records, as well as financial statements and other information regarding the affairs of the partnership, for any purpose reasonably related to his partnership interest.[3]

Library References:

West's Key No. Digests, Partnership ⌹352.

§ 2.84   Limited Partnerships—Partners

A natural person, partnership, limited partnership, LLC, trust, estate, custodian, nominee, association, corporation or any other individual or entity, domestic or foreign, may be either a limited or general partner.[1] A partnership interest is personal property[2] and comprises the partner's share of the profits and losses of the limited partnership, and any right to receive distributions therefrom.[3] Other rights may be granted by the partnership agreement, but they are contractual in nature.

A general partner of a limited partnership has the same rights and liabilities as a partner of a general partnership, except to the extent the

---

13. NYPL § 121–205(b).

§ 2.83

1. NYPL § 121–106(a).
2. Id.
3. NYPL § 121–106(b).

PRACTICE POINTER: Although the NYRLPA does not require a limited partnership to furnish affirmatively any records to its partners, the partnership agreement probably should address the delivery of reports, including tax information, to them.

§ 2.84

1. See NYPL § 121–101(f), (g), (n).
2. NYPL § 121–701.
3. NYPL § 121–101(m).

limited partnership agreement modifies them.[4] In no event may the agreement limit a general partner's liability to third persons for the partnership's debts and obligations.[5] A limited partnership interest, like an LLC interest, may be a certificated or an uncertificated security under Section 8–102 of the UCC.[6] If the requirements of the UCC are not met, a limited partnership interest is a general intangible.

Contributions to a limited partnership may be made in cash, property, services rendered, or a binding obligation to contribute cash or property or to render services in the future.[7] A general partner must make a contribution to the limited partnership, and may contribute as a limited partner, too.[8] Unless the agreement otherwise provides, a partner is liable to make any contribution he has agreed to make, even if unable to perform because of death, disability or otherwise; at the option of the partnership, a partner or his estate must contribute cash equal to the value of the contribution he is not able to make.[9] If the agreement does not set a lower standard, an obligation to make a contribution may be compromised only by consent of all the partners.[10] A partner who fails to make a required contribution may suffer such penalties as are imposed by the agreement, including forfeiture, subordination or redemption of his interest.[11]

Partners share in the profits and losses of the limited partnership, and receive distributions, as set forth in the partnership agreement.[12] If the agreement does not specify the partners' shares or the method of determining them, profits and losses are allocated, and distributions are made, based on the relative value of the partners' contributions (including obligations to make contributions) to the partnership, except to the extent any such obligations are in default.[13] A limited partnership may not make distributions if, after giving effect thereto, all of its liabilities

---

4. NYPL § 121–403(a), (c). Accordingly, it would appear that, notwithstanding the NYRLPA's limited definition of "partnership interest," a general partner's partnership interest in a limited partnership also includes certain management and other rights. *See supra*, § 2.51.

CAVEAT: NYPL § 121–403 imports from the general partnership law (both statutory and common) default rights of which an advisor should be aware. They include, for example, a general partner's right to be indemnified by the partnership for costs incurred in the ordinary conduct of the business, the right to receive interest on advances to the partnership, and equal rights (if there is more than one general partner) in management. See NYPL § 40.

5. NYPL § 121–403(b).

6. NYPL § 121–702(b).

7. NYPL §§ 121–101(b), 501.

8. NYPL § 121–404.

9. NYPL § 121–502(a).

10. NYPL § 121–502(b).

CAVEAT: Even if such an obligation is compromised, a creditor of the partnership who extends credit based on the obligation may enforce the original obligation to the extent of his reliance. This right may not be altered in the partnership agreement. *Id.*

11. NYPL § 121–502(c).

12. NYPL §§ 121–503, 504.

13. *Id.*

PRACTICE POINTER: Partners of a limited partnership should insist that their agreement specifically address allocations of profits and losses and rights to distributions, as the application of the default provision may not be appropriate in many situations.

(other than liabilities in respect of partnership interests and liabilities for which recourse is limited to specific partnership property) exceed the fair market value of its assets.[14]

Unless the partnership agreement restricts such transactions, a partner may lend to, borrow from, act as a guarantor of, provide collateral for the obligations of, and otherwise transact any other business with, a limited partnership.[15]

A limited partner may withdraw from the partnership as permitted in the partnership agreement or with the consent of all the partners.[16] Otherwise, a limited partner may withdraw, unless prohibited by the agreement, upon not less than six months' notice.[17] If such withdrawal violates the agreement, a limited partnership may recover damages for breach from the limited partner in the amount, or calculated as set forth in the agreement.[18]

A general partner may withdraw from a limited partnership at any time upon written notice to the other partners, but if the withdrawal violates the partnership agreement, the withdrawing general partner will be liable for damages for its breach.[19] A general partner also ceases to be a general partner upon the assignment of all of his partnership interest;[20] upon his removal, if and as provided in the partnership agreement; unless otherwise set forth in the agreement, under certain circumstances upon his assignment for the benefit of creditors or the commencement of bankruptcy, insolvency or similar proceedings; upon his death or incompetency, or upon its termination or dissolution, if not a natural person.[21]

Upon withdrawal, a partner is entitled to receive any distribution to which he is entitled under the partnership agreement.[22] In addition, subject to the terms of the partnership agreement, a withdrawing partner is entitled to receive, within a reasonable time after withdrawal, the fair value of his interest as of the date of withdrawal, determined based on his right to share in distributions of the partnership.[23] All such amounts may be offset by damages incurred by the limited partnership as a result of a wrongful withdrawal.[24] The partnership agreement should address all such issues in detail to avoid disputes over valuation, the period over which payment shall be made, or even whether a

---

14. NYPL § 121–607(a).
15. NYPL § 121–108.
16. NYPL § 121–603.
17. *Id.*
18. *Id.*
19. NYPL § 121–602.
20. NYPL § 121–702.
21. NYPL § 121–402.
22. NYPL § 121–604.
23. *Id.*

CAVEAT: A partner's share of partnership distributions will not often be an appropriate measure of the value of an interest, particularly in situations where that share varies over time or where a partner has foregone distributions for the better of the partnership, having made significant contributions thereto.

24. NYPL §§ 121–602, 121–603.

payment is due.[25]

A partner's judgment creditor may charge the partner's interest, just as a creditor of an LLC may charge a member's membership interest.[26] The creditor has only the rights of an assignee of the interest; *i.e.*, rights to the partner's share of the partnership's profits, losses and distributions.[27] A creditor of a limited partnership may pursue its general partners for payment of any liability not satisfied from the partnership assets and, in addition, may have rights to recover wrongful distributions made to limited partners under the circumstances set forth in NYPL § 121–607.

Unless a limited partner is also a general partner, he is not usually a proper party to proceedings by or against a partnership.[28] The exceptions to this rule occur when the proceeding is meant to enforce a limited partner's rights against, or liability to, the limited partnership, or when the proceeding is a derivative action brought by a limited partner in right of the partnership.[29]

§ 2.85 Limited Partnerships—Partners—Admission of New Partners

A person becomes a partner of a limited partnership on the date its Certificate of Limited Partnership becomes effective or on the date specified in the partnership agreement, whichever is later.[1] After the Certificate becomes effective, a person may acquire a limited partnership interest directly from the partnership in accordance with the partnership agreement or, if the agreement does not address the subject, upon the written consent of all partners.[2] Admission of a limited partner who acquires his interest by assignment from a partner is discussed in Sections 2.95 and 2.96, *infra*.

Additional or new general partners may be admitted to a limited partnership as provided in the partnership agreement or, if the agreement does not make provision therefor, with the written consent of all partners.[3]

---

25. *See also, supra*, § 2.21, for a discussion of similar points in connection with a member's withdrawal from an LLC.

26. NYPL § 121–703; *see supra*, § 2.21.

27. NYPL § 121–703.

28. NYPL § 121–1001.

29. *Id*. NYPL § 121–1002 authorizes limited partnership derivative actions. Demand on the general partners is required before such an action may be brought, and it may not be settled without court approval. NYPL § 121–1002. Unless the limited partners bringing a derivative suit have contributed at least 5% of the total capital contributed by all limited partners, or their contributions exceed $50,000 in value, the partner plaintiffs must post security for the expenses of the action. NYPL § 121–1003. Moreover, general partners may not be indemnified for costs incurred in the defense of a derivative action unless certain prerequisites are met. *See* NYPL § 121–1004.

§ 2.85

1. NYPL § 121–301(a).

2. NYPL § 121–301(b)(1).

3. NYPL § 121–401.

§ 2.85 NON-CORPORATE ENTITIES Ch. 2

Library References:

West's Key No. Digests, Partnership ⚍363.

§ 2.86 Limited Partnerships—Partners—Liability

The general partner(s) of a limited partnership are personally liable for the debts and obligations of the partnership, as though they were partners of a general partnership.[1] They may also be liable for misstatements contained in the partnership's publicly-filed documents.[2] Except under certain circumstances, limited partners are not liable for the contractual and other liabilities of the partnership unless they are also general partners or they "participate in the control of the business."[3] Even if a limited partner participates in the control of the partnership, he will be personally liable only to those who transact business with the partnership reasonably believing, based on his conduct, that he is a general partner.[4]

Unlike its predecessor, Article 8 of the NYPL, the NYRLPA provides statutory safe harbors for a limited partner's involvement in the partnership's management and business.[5] Possession of the rights, and/or engaging in the activities, enumerated will not constitute "control" of the partnership.[6] Accordingly, a limited partner may, without risking treatment as a general partner, do any or all of the following:

(i) be an employee or agent of, or otherwise transact business with, the limited partnership, or be an officer, director or shareholder of a corporate general partner (or the equivalent of a non-corporate general partner);

(ii) consult with or render professional services to a general partner, including with respect to the limited partnership's business;

(iii) act as a guarantor or surety for, or otherwise assume one or more debts of, the limited partnership;

(iv) call, or participate in any way in, any meeting of partners;

(v) initiate or participate in any derivative action brought in the right of the limited partnership;

(vi) propose or vote on amendments to the partnership agreement or the Certificate of Limited Partnership, or other significant undertakings of the partnership, including its dissolution, the sale, lease, mortgage or other transfer or pledge of any of its assets, its merger or consolidation, action with respect to incurring or discharging partnership debt, the admission or removal of a partner, a

---

§ 2.86

1. NYPL § 121–403(b). *See also, supra*, § 2.53.
2. *See* NYPL § 121–207 and § 2.81, *supra*.
3. NYPL § 121–303(a).
4. *Id.*
5. NYPL § 121–303(b), (c).
6. *Id.*

change in the nature of the partnership's business, matters involving conflicts of interest and indemnification, among others;

(vii) consult for, or be associated with, any person in which the limited partnership has an interest;

(viii) wind up the partnership; or

(ix) exercise rights or powers otherwise permitted limited partners under the NYRLPA.[7]

In addition, limited partners may conduct other activities *vis-a-vis* the partnership without necessarily being deemed to participate in its control.[8] A limited partner may possess and/or exercise, any number of times, some or all of the rights and powers listed in NYPL § 121–303(b) without reaching the "control" threshold.[9]

As noted in Section 2.79, *supra*, a limited partner whose name is included in the partnership name with his express written consent is personally liable to creditors without actual knowledge that he is not a general partner thereof.[10] Moreover, unless compromised in accordance with the law,[11] all partners are liable to make their contributions to the partnership as promised.[12] A limited partner who receives a distribution knowing at the time that the distribution rendered the limited partnership insolvent (as set forth in NYPL § 121–607(a)) may be required to return that distribution to the partnership at any time within three years thereafter.[13]

A person who makes a contribution to a limited partnership, believing in good faith that he has become a limited partner, may nevertheless be personally liable to third parties who reasonably believed, based on his conduct, that he was a general partner and who reasonably relied on that belief.[14] Such a limited partner will not be deemed to be a general partner if he either corrects the Certificate of Limited Partnership or withdraws from the partnership by written notice and files an appropriate certificate reflecting the withdrawal, in either case upon learning of the mistake.[15] He will, however, be liable to third parties, as described,

---

7. *Id.*
8. NYPL § 121–303(c).
9. NYPL § 121–303(e).
10. NYPL § 121–303(d).
11. NYPL § 121–502(b); *see also, supra,* § 2.84.
12. NYPL § 121–502(b).
13. NYPL §§ 121–607(b), (c).
14. NYPL § 121–304. It is hard to imagine how a situation of this sort could arise. A third party could rely on the Certificate of Limited Partnership listing the names and addresses of the general partners, and signed by each thereof, but someone executing that Certificate as a general partner would be hard-pressed to claim that he did not realize he was a general partner.
15. NYPL § 121–304(a).

CAVEAT: The statute does not establish the period after discovery within which correction or withdrawal must take place to avoid being treated as a general partner for all purposes. It may be that "as soon as practicable" is sufficient.

§ 2.87 Limited Partnerships—Partners—Contribution Issues

To the extent there is more than one general partner of a limited partnership, each general partner will be entitled to contribution from the other general partners in accordance with law governing contribution by partners of general partnerships.[1] Limited partners are liable only to the extent of their contributions, or agreements to make contributions, to the partnership.

Library References:

West's Key No. Digests, Partnership ⚖=353, 371.

§ 2.88 Limited Partnerships—Management

Subject to provisions of the limited partnership agreement granting limited partners certain rights with respect thereto (which provisions should be drafted after consideration of NYPL § 121–303(b), discussed at Section 2.86, *supra*), the general partner(s) are responsible for the management of a limited partnership.[1]

Library References:

West's Key No. Digests, Partnership ⚖=366, 368, 369.

§ 2.89 Limited Partnerships—Management—Voting: General Partners

By default to the general partnership law,[1] the NYRLPA relegates management of a limited partnership to its general partner(s), and thereby also presumably incorporates the general partnership law's default provisions with respect thereto.[2] Otherwise, meetings, notice, quorum requirements and the mechanics of voting (whether by general or limited partners) are not addressed in the NYRLPA, except to permit partners broad flexibility to set their own rules.[3]

---

16. NYPL § 121–304(b).

§ 2.87

1. *See supra*, discussion at § 2.54.

§ 2.88

1. NYPL §§ 121–403(a), 40(5).

§ 2.89

1. NYPL §§ 121–403(a), 40(5).

2. *Id.*; *see also*, *supra*, discussion at §§ 2.55–2.60.

3. NYPL § 121–405.

For example, different classes of general partners, with such relative rights and powers as desired, may be established in the partnership agreement, which may also provide for the future creation of additional classes.[4] The agreement may also deny any class of general partners the right to vote on any or every matter.[5] The basis of the general partners' vote, whether *per capita*, class, initial contribution, share of profits or otherwise, can be fixed by the agreement as well.[6] To the extent that there is more than one general partner, or that limited partners are permitted to participate in certain decisions, the partnership agreement must address all these matters.[7]

Library References:

West's Key No. Digests, Partnership ⚷366.

§ 2.90 Limited Partnerships—Management—Voting: Limited Partners

Unless the partnership agreement gives them authority with respect to specific matters, limited partners generally have no rights to vote or otherwise act in connection with the management of a limited partnership.[1] The agreement may, however, provide for classes of limited partners with such relative rights and duties as may be desired, and may grant or withhold from such classes, or any of them, the right to vote on any or all enumerated issues.[2] As with general partners, the partnership agreement may reserve the right to create new classes of limited partners in the future, and may deal in any appropriate way with the issues of meetings, notice thereof, waivers, quorum requirements and the basis for determining limited partners' relative voting rights.[3]

Library References:

West's Key No. Digests, Partnership ⚷368.

4. NYPL § 121–405(a).

5. *Id.*

6. NYPL § 121–405(b).

CAVEAT: Query whether the inclusion of this permissive provision in the NYRLPA overrides the default provision of the general partnership law, NYPL § 40(5), that gives each general partner equal rights in the management of a partnership, regardless of share of profits, contribution, etc. If so, there is no default provision whatsoever to determine voting rights in limited partnerships with more than one general partner.

7. NYPL § 121–405(a).

PRACTICE POINTER: The same issues discussed with respect to voting in LLCs in §§ 2.27 and 2.28, *supra*, should be considered when drafting a limited partnership agreement. *See also*, the list of items to be addressed in § 2.109, *infra*.

§ 2.90

1. The default exceptions to this rule include the limited partners' rights, in the absence of provisions in the partnership agreement otherwise, to give, or withhold, written consent to the admission of new general or limited partners (NYPL §§ 121–401, 121–301(b)(1), 121–704(a)); to give consent to the withdrawal of a limited partner (NYPL § 121–603); and to consent to the compromise of an obligation to make a contribution (NYPL § 121–502(b)).

2. NYPL § 121–302(a).

3. NYPL § 121–302(b).

§ 2.91 Limited Partnerships—Management—Delegation of Responsibility

The NYRLPA does not restrict a limited partnership's ability to delegate to agents responsibilities in connection with the conduct of its business. Under the NYRLPA, a limited partner may be employed by the partnership or act as its agent without such activities constituting participation in the control of the partnership.[1] Delegation of responsibilities to an agent will not, however, relieve a general partner of its liability for the debts and obligations of the partnership,[2] nor may a general partner delegate responsibility for the performance of its fiduciary duties to another, unless the partnership agreement so provides.[3]

Library References:

West's Key No. Digests, Partnership ⊙=366, 368.

§ 2.92 Limited Partnerships—Management—Standard of Care

Subject to limitation, extension or other alteration in their partnership agreement, a general partner's duties to the limited partnership, its limited partners and the other general partners is the same as that imposed upon partners of general partnerships.[1] General partners therefore owe a fiduciary duty to the limited partnership, including the duties of utmost good faith, fairness and loyalty,[2] unless the partners otherwise agree. The duty may not, however, extend to assignees of partnership interests if they are not admitted as partners of the partnership.[3]

Limited partners do not owe a statutory duty of care to the partnership or their other partners, but the partnership agreement may impose such duties.

Library References:

West's Key No. Digests, Partnership ⊙=353, 371.

§ 2.93 Limited Partnerships—Management—Agency Authority

Every general partner of a limited partnership is an agent of the partnership for the purpose of its business, subject to the same condi-

---

§ 2.91

1. NYPL § 121–303(b)(1).
2. NYPL § 121–403(b).
3. NYPL § 121–403(c).

§ 2.92

1. NYPL § 121–403(c); see NYPL § 43; § 2.59, supra.
2. See supra, Newberger, Loeb & Co., Inc., § 2.59, note 2.
3. See Levine v. Murray Hill Manor Company, 143 A.D.2d 298, 532 N.Y.S.2d 130 (1st Dep't 1988) (assignee had no standing to bring derivative action, nor could it claim general partner's breach of fiduciary duties where agreement disclaimed their extension to non-partner assignees).

tions and restrictions imposed upon the agency authority of partners of a general partnership.[1] Absent express delegation of authority, a limited partner is not an agent of a limited partnership either generally or for any particular transaction.[2]

§ 2.94 Limited Partnerships—Assignment of Interests

Like members of both general partnerships and LLCs, partners of limited partnerships may establish by agreement the extent to which partnership interests may be assigned to others and the circumstances under which those assignees can become partners. If the partnership agreement does not address the transferability of interests, the NYRLPA supplies default rules with respect thereto.[1]

§ 2.95 Limited Partnerships—Assignment of Interests—Default Rules

Unless the partnership agreement otherwise provides, both general and limited partnership interests in a limited partnership are assignable, in whole or in part.[1] An assignee does not, however, automatically become a partner of the partnership by virtue of the assignment, but merely becomes entitled to the distributions and allocations of profits and losses to which the assignor would be entitled.[2] Except as set forth in the partnership agreement, no other rights or powers are thereby transferred.[3] A transfer does not, in the absence of agreement otherwise, dissolve a limited partnership,[4] nor does an assignee have any liability as a partner solely by reason of the assignment (although he may assume certain liabilities by contract with the assignor).[5]

If a partner assigns all of his partnership interest to another, whether or not the assignee becomes a partner, the assignor ceases to be a partner and loses a partner's rights and powers.[6] The pledge of, or grant of a security interest in, a partnership interest in a limited partnership does not constitute such an assignment.[7]

§ 2.93

1. *See* NYPL § 121–403, § 2.60, *supra*.
2. **CAVEAT**: It is unclear whether a limited partner, exercising general agency authority for the limited partnership in his capacity as a limited partner pursuant to powers delegated in the partnership agreement, risks liability as a general partner because of his "participation in the control" of the partnership. For this reason, the delegation of such power is not advised.

§ 2.94

1. *See* NYPL §§ 121–702, 121–704, 121–705; *see also, infra*, § 2.95.

§ 2.95

1. NYPL § 121–702(a)(1).
2. NYPL § 121–702(a)(3).
3. NYPL § 121–702(a)(2). *See supra*, § 2.62, with respect to the assignment of general partnership interests.
4. NYPL § 121–702(a)(2).
5. NYPL § 121–702(c).
6. NYPL § 121–702(a)(4).
7. *Id.*

§ 2.96 Limited Partnerships—Assignment of Interests— Vote Required to Admit New Partner

In the absence of agreement otherwise, all partners must consent to admit the assignee of a general partner as a general partner of the partnership.[1] An assignee of a partnership interest, including the assignee of a general partner, may become a limited partner if all of the partners consent thereto in writing, or under the other circumstances set forth in the partnership agreement.[2]

An assignee who becomes a limited partner has the rights, powers and responsibilities ascribed to limited partners under the partnership agreement.[3] Unless the agreement requires otherwise, a new limited partner is liable to make the contributions his assignor would have been obligated to make and of which the assignee had notice at the time he became a limited partner.[4] The new limited partner is not liable for damages caused by his assignor's wrongful withdrawal, or for distributions made by the partnership to his assignor in violation of NYPL § 121–607 (those that render the partnership insolvent).[5] An assignor remains liable for his obligations that arose before the assignment, as well as those that accrue afterward, but is not responsible for (a) false statements in documents filed after the assignment, (b) wrongful distributions made after the assignment, or (c) contributions for which the assignee is liable because he has become a limited partner.[6]

§ 2.97 Limited Partnerships—Dissolution

A limited partnership will dissolve upon the occurrence of any of a number of events, including the withdrawal of a general partner.[1] Unlike an LLC, however, a limited partnership may not trump the statutory requirements by incorporating in its agreement an automatic right to continue its business notwithstanding such a withdrawal. Accordingly, a limited partnership is unlikely in any circumstance to possess continuity of life (although, by clever drafting or affirmative action of its partners, it may effectively achieve the same result), and may therefore be a less attractive vehicle for investment or other financing than an LLC.

Library References:
West's Key No. Digests, Partnership ⚖︎276.

§ 2.98 Limited Partnerships—Dissolution—Events

A limited partnership will be dissolved, and its affairs must be wound up, upon the first to occur of:

§ 2.96
1. NYPL § 121–401.
2. NYPL § 121–704(a).
3. NYPL § 121–704(b).
4. Id.; see also, NYPL § 121–705(b).
5. NYPL § 121–705(b).
6. NYPL § 121–705(a).

§ 2.97
1. See NYPL § 121–801.

(a) the date specified in its Certificate of Limited Partnership;

(b) any event specified in the partnership agreement as causing dissolution;

(c) subject to alteration of the required vote in the partnership agreement, upon the vote of all of the partnership's general partners and two-thirds in interest of each class of its limited partners;

(d) the withdrawal of a general partner,[1] unless the business can be continued as set forth in Section 2.99, *infra*; or

(e) judicial dissolution.[2]

The withdrawal of a limited partner, for whatever reason, will not cause the dissolution of the partnership.

The supreme court in the judicial district where the limited partnership's office is located may dissolve a limited partnership upon application by or for a partner[3] when it is "not reasonably practicable to carry on its business in conformity with the partnership agreement."[4]

Library References:

West's Key No. Digests, Partnership ⟐376.

§ 2.99 Limited Partnerships—Dissolution—Continuation of Business After Dissolution Event

When a general partner withdraws from a limited partnership, its business can be continued and dissolution and winding up avoided under certain circumstances. If there is at least one other general partner at the time, and the agreement permits, and the remaining general partner agrees to carry on the partnership business, withdrawal will not result in dissolution.[1] In the alternative, if all the remaining partners agree in writing, within 90 days following a general partner's withdrawal, to continue the partnership and to the appointment of one or more new general partners as of the date of withdrawal, the partnership will not dissolve.[2]

Library References:

West's Key No. Digests, Partnership ⟐376.

§ 2.98

1. See *supra*, § 2.84.
2. NYPL § 121–801.
3. Unlike an assignee or certain creditors of a partner in a general partnership, an assignee or creditor of a partner of a limited partnership may not institute dissolution proceedings. See *supra*, § 2.65.
4. NYPL § 121–802. See *supra*, cases cited at § 2.37, notes 4–5, and NYPL § 63(e) for circumstances in which it may not be "reasonably practicable" to carry on business.

§ 2.99

1. NYPL § 121–801(d).
2. *Id.* Note that the NYRLPA does not permit a limited partnership to elect to continue business hereunder if fewer than all remaining partners so agree.

§ 2.100 Limited Partnerships—Dissolution—Winding Up

Upon dissolution, the affairs of a limited partnership must be wound up, its assets liquidated and provision for the satisfaction of its liabilities made. Typically, the general partners who have not wrongfully withdrawn are charged with winding up the partnership; if there are none, the limited partners may act as its liquidators.[1] Acting in a liquidating capacity will not affect the liability of a limited partner.[2]

The assets of a dissolved limited partnership, or the proceeds thereof, must first be distributed to, or reserved for, its creditors, not including partners to whom distributions, in respect of withdrawal or otherwise, are due and owing.[3] Barring provision otherwise in the partnership agreement, such obligations to partners and former partners must be satisfied next.[4] Then, except as provided by agreement, the partners' unpaid capital contributions are returned, and any excess thereafter distributed to the partners in accordance with their respective shares in distributions.[5]

Within 90 days following dissolution and the commencement of winding up, or whenever there are no limited partners remaining, a Certificate of Cancellation of the limited partnership must be filed in accordance with NYPL § 121–203.[6] The Certificate becomes effective upon filing, but does not affect the liability of the limited partners in connection with the winding up and termination of the partnership.[7]

Library References:

West's Key No. Digests, Partnership ⬉376.

§ 2.101 Limited Partnerships—Conversions/Mergers

The NYRLPA contemplates the merger or consolidation of domestic limited partnerships with or into one or more domestic or foreign limited partnerships or LLCs.[1] As noted in Section 2.40, *supra*, the NYLLCL also authorizes the conversion of existing partnerships, general and limited, into LLCs upon compliance with the requirements outlined in NYLLCL § 1006. Despite the lack of specific statutory authorization for combinations of limited partnerships with other types of entities, transactions

§ 2.100

1. NYPL § 121–803(a). Otherwise, upon application of any partner, the Supreme Court may appoint a receiver or liquidating trustee to wind up the business. *Id.*
2. NYPL § 121–803(b).
3. NYPL § 121–804(a).
4. NYPL § 121–804(b).
5. NYPL § 121–804(c).
6. The Certificate must contain, among other things, a statement of the event requiring its filing, but detail appears to be optional.
7. NYPL § 121–203(b), (c).

§ 2.101

1. *See* NYPL §§ 121–1101, 121–1106.

§ 2.102 Limited Partnerships—Conversions/Mergers—Procedures

Limited partnerships that are party to a merger or consolidation, whether foreign or domestic, must adopt a plan for the transaction, including the terms and conditions of conversion of partnership interests and the partnership agreement of the surviving entity.[1] All general partners must approve the plan, unless the partnership agreement otherwise provides, and two-thirds in interest of the limited partners must agree, subject to different requirements in the agreement (but in no event less than a majority in interest of the limited partners).[2] All partners of the constituent entities are entitled to at least 20 days' notice to consider the agreement before the meeting seeking such approval.[3]

The merger or consolidation is effected upon the filing of a Certificate of Merger with the Department of State (or on such future date specified therein, not more than 30 days thereafter).[4] The Certificate is similar in content to the certificate of merger filed to effect a merger or consolidation involving an LLC[5] and must recite, among other things, salient information about the constituent entities, the surviving entity, and the approval of the agreement of merger underlying the transaction. The surviving entity inherits all of the rights, powers, claims and property of the constituent organizations, as well as their suits, liabilities and obligations.[6] The general partners of an extinguished limited partnership remain liable for obligations incurred by that partnership before the combination.

§ 2.103 Limited Partnerships—Conversions/Mergers—Dissenters' Rights

A limited partner who does not approve of a proposed merger or consolidation must give written notice of his dissent before the meeting at which the transaction is to be considered.[1] If his dissent is not withdrawn, but the transaction is approved, he will not become a limited partner in the surviving entity, but will be entitled to receive from it, within a reasonable time after the transaction, in cash, the fair market value of his interest in the uncombined entity immediately prior to the

---

2. *See, e.g., supra*, discussion at §§ 2.41 and 2.68.

§ 2.102
1. NYPL § 121–1102(a).
2. *Id.* Note that the default approval requirements of the NYRLPA purportedly may be altered only by partnership agreement, not by the law governing the internal affairs of a foreign limited partnership. Query whether such default requirements would be enforced over a foreign limited partnership's domestic law requiring otherwise.
3. *Id.*
4. NYPL § 121–1103.
5. *See supra*, discussion at § 2.41.
6. NYPL § 121–1104.

§ 2.103
1. NYPL § 121–1102(b).

§ 2.104 Limited Partnerships—Professional Organizations

While the NYPL itself does not address the provision of professional services by limited partnerships, many professional regulatory bodies prohibit the practice of professions in such form. Legal, medical, dental or accounting firms may not be organized as limited partnerships because individual practitioners are not permitted to avoid responsibility for their own misconduct or malpractice, as would be the case if they could practice as limited partners.

§ 2.105 Due Diligence Considerations

Counsel to non-corporate entities and to third parties dealing with LLCs and partnerships must have a basic strategy for addressing due diligence issues, including the entity's formation, power and the authority of those acting for it.

An attorney can confirm the formation of a domestic LLC, LLP or limited partnership, as well as certain fundamentals of its organization, by obtaining a certified copy of its Articles of Organization, Certificate of Limited Partnership or Registration from the New York Department of State.[1] The filing of the Articles, the Certificate or the Registration by the Secretary of State is evidence that certain of the formal requirements of organization were met.[2] Evidence of publication should also be requested (although failure to publish will not, by law, impair any of an LLC's, LLP's or limited partnership's contractual obligations). Because New York LLCs and limited partnerships must also adopt written agreements, a copy of that agreement, certified by a manager or member, as the case may be, of an LLC, or a general partner of a limited partnership, should be produced and reviewed.[3] An attorney must bear

---

2. NYPL § 121-1102(c).

3. NYPL § 121-1102(d). *See also,* NYPL § 121-1105 for the procedure to be followed to determine and pay the dissenter's interest.

§ 2.105

1. The Articles will indicate whether an LLC is member-managed or manager-managed; the Certificate will identify a limited partnership's general partners, and a Registration will identify the LLP's partners and profession. Filing data will reveal when the organization was formed or, in the case of an LLP, when it elected LLP status.

2. CAVEAT: The Secretary of State is authorized to issue certificates of "good standing" for LLCs but such certificates evidence only the filing of an LLC's Articles, not its subsequent compliance with applicable tax and other laws. Consequently, it makes sense to obtain a certified copy of the full Articles, rather than such a certificate.

3. The consequences of failing to adopt a written operating or limited partnership agreement are unclear. It is possible that the LLC or limited partnership will be deemed to have never been formed.

CAVEAT: In any event, an attorney should bear in mind that his third-party

in mind that the default provisions of the NYLLCL and the NYPL govern issues not addressed in the Articles, Certificate or agreement, and review the provisions of the applicable law as well.

Neither a general partnership nor an LLP is required to adopt a written partnership agreement, nor is a general partnership required to make any centralized filing with the State evidencing its formation. If feasible, to establish the formation of a general partnership and the identity of its partners (and, accordingly, those who have the power to bind it), an attorney should request a copy of its Business Certificate and/or require a statement, executed by each of the partners, reciting the name of the partnership, identifying all of the partners, indicating whether a written partnership agreement exists and, if possible, authorizing the transaction in question. If there is a written partnership agreement, it, or relevant extracts thereof, should be reviewed.

A question may arise as to whether an LLC had at least one member at the time of formation, as required under Section 203(c) of the NYLLCL, particularly if the Articles were executed by a non-member organizer.[4] Before opining as to due formation and good standing, an attorney should obtain representations from an LLC's managers (or certain members—in each case, perhaps, with a personal guarantee of the accuracy of such statements) covering these and other compliance issues over which the attorney had no control and which cannot be confirmed by state officials.

Foreign LLCs and limited partnerships doing business here should be qualified to do business in New York, as evidenced by a Certificate of Authority.[5] They also should produce an affidavit or other evidence of compliance with publication requirements. Copies of organizational documents, certified by a state official in the company's home jurisdiction or by a manager, member or general partner, if not of public record, should be delivered and reviewed. The law of the foreign state, which governs the internal operation of a foreign LLC or limited partnership, must also be studied.[6]

Whether an LLC has the power to undertake a transaction should be determinable from a review of the NYLLCL, the LLC's Articles and its operating agreement. Under the NYLLCL, an LLC has broad authority to pursue any lawful business purpose that is not required to be conducted in another form. General and limited partnerships may con-

client may well be charged with actual knowledge of all information contained in the operating or partnership agreement if it is delivered to the attorney.

4. The name and capacity of anyone who executes each filed document and certificate on behalf of an LLC must be set forth therein. NYLLCL § 207(d). It is not clear what the effects of a failure to meet the member requirement may be, particularly in light of the Act's solipsistic statement that no one becomes a member of an LLC until its Articles are filed. NYLLCL § 602(a)(1). (If so, how can a member exist, or execute the Articles, before filing?)

5. NYLLCL § 802(a); NYPL §§ 121-902, 121-904.

6. NYLLCL § 802(a); NYPL § 121-901.

duct any business, but only for profit, unless restricted by other laws. PLLCs, of course, must be organized to perform, on a for-profit basis, professional services of the type authorized by the NYLLCL. Limitations on the type of business to be conducted may be contained in an LLC's Articles or its operating agreement, or in the partnership agreement.

The NYLLCL confers upon LLCs extensive powers to conduct their business, although there are some default restrictions on an LLC's ability to enter guarantee and suretyship contracts that are not "necessary or convenient" to a company's business.[7] An LLC's powers are subject to change in the LLC's Articles only. The NYPL does not restrict a partnership's powers.

Unless its Articles specifically provide for management by managers, a domestic LLC is deemed to be member-managed, and each member is presumed to have agency authority to bind the LLC to carry on business in the usual way. In a manager-managed LLC, each manager is presumed to have such authority. In both general and limited partnerships, general partners are presumed to have agency authority to bind the partnership to carry on business in the usual way. Limited partners have no such authority unless, perhaps, they are specifically so authorized. Presumptions of agency authority may be overridden if a member, manager or partner did not in fact have such authority and the third party dealing with the LLC or partnership knew it. If the operating or partnership agreement contains restrictions on authority, a third party will probably be deemed to have notice thereof if it requested and received a copy of the agreement.

At least three questions must be addressed in the context of determining a person's authority to bind an LLC or a partnership in a transaction. First, who are the members, and/or managers, of the LLC, or the partners, and/or limited partners, of the partnership? They should be identified in the company's records, and, in an LLC's records, each member's contribution and share of profits and losses, or information from which his share may be readily derived, must appear.[8] Second, what is the scope of the company's business, and what transactions are therefore in the ordinary course of that business, as opposed to outside the ordinary course (requiring a different level of authorization)? Even if a third person lacks knowledge that a transaction was not authorized, he may not have any defense if the transaction was not in the usual course of the partnership's business. Accordingly, an attorney should require evidence of specific authorization for any transaction arguably not in the ordinary course of a company's business. Third, by what vote, if any, must the transaction be approved? The required number (majority, two-thirds, etc.), as well as the basis (*i.e., per capita,* shares of current profits,

7. NYLLCL § 202(e).   8. NYLLCL § 1102(a)(2).

relative capital accounts) must be determined, and assent confirmed, perhaps by officers' or other certificates.[9]

Agents other than members, managers or partners may be empowered to bind an entity and to execute documents on its behalf. Evidence of specific authorization thereof should be obtained, whether from the operating or partnership agreement or otherwise. In addition, if a transaction with an LLC involves a manager or a party in which a manager has an interest, the NYLLCL imposes special approval requirements, compliance with which may need to be confirmed by the other managers or the members consenting to the transaction.[10] The agency authority of persons acting on behalf of a foreign LLC or partnership and the company's authorization of the transaction must be confirmed in similar fashion, based on a review of the applicable foreign law and the entity's organizational documents.

§ 2.106 Securities Laws Issues

The application of state and/or federal securities laws to the issuance of membership or partnership interests can increase substantially the effort and cost of organizing and thereafter maintaining LLCs or partnerships. If securities laws apply, the issuance (or the issuer) either will have to be registered or qualify for an exemption from registration. Generally, if a membership or partnership interest, general or limited, is classified as a "security," securities laws will apply.[1]

Section 2(1) of the Securities Act of 1933, as amended,[2] defines a security to include:

> ... any note, treasury stock, bond, debenture, evidence of indebtedness, certificate of interest or participation in any profit-sharing agreement, collateral-trust certificate, preorganization certificate or subscription, transferable share, investment contract, voting-trust certificate, certificate of deposit for a security, fractional undivided interest in oil, gas or other mineral rights ... or, in general, any interest or instrument commonly known as a 'security', or any certificate of interest or participation in, temporary or interim certificate for, receipt for, guarantee of, or warrant or right to subscribe to or purchase, any of the foregoing.

---

9. Attorneys should also be mindful that the NYLLCL imposes certain non-waivable minimum requirements on quorum and approvals; see, e.g., supra, § 2.29. These requirements are defined in terms of members' shares of current profits, and may not be permitted to be overridden by different definitions in the operating agreement.

10. See NYLLCL § 411.

§ 2.106

1. For a more detailed analysis of securities law issues, see S.R. Berger, Ch. 13, "Membership Interests as Securities," in Walker, *Limited Liability Companies and Partnerships: A Guide to Law and Practice* (West 1995).

2. 15 U.S.C.A. § 77b(1).

The Securities Exchange Act of 1934, as amended, defines "security" in a slightly different manner, but the courts have treated the two definitions as virtually identical.

The New York Blue Sky laws do not specifically define "security." Section 352 of the General Business Law, which addresses investigations by the Attorney General, refers to:

> stocks, bonds, notes, evidences of interest or indebtedness or other securities, including oil and mineral deeds or leases and any interest therein, sold or transferred in whole or in part to the purchaser where the same do not effect a transfer of the title in fee simple to the land, or negotiable documents of title, or foreign currency orders, calls or options therefor hereinafter called security or securities ...[3]

Section 352–e of the General Business Law, dealing with real estate syndication offerings, refers to "securities" as "participation interests or investments in real estate, mortgages or leases, including stocks, bonds, debentures, evidences of interest or indebtedness, limited partnership interests or other security or securities, as defined in [Section 352] of this article."[4]

Except for real estate limited partnership interests under General Business Law § 352–e, general partnership interests, membership interests and other limited partnership interests are not expressly included within the foregoing definitions. Accordingly, whether any of them may be deemed to be a security will depend upon whether it qualifies as an "investment contract."

In *SEC v. W.J. Howey Co.*,[5] the Supreme Court held that an "investment contract" exists if the following elements are present: (1) a person's[6] investment of money, (2) in a common enterprise, (3) where such person expects profits, and (4) such profits are to be derived solely from the efforts of others.[7] In *United Housing Foundation v. Forman*,[8] the Supreme Court defined an investment contract as "an investment in a common venture premised on a reasonable expectation of profits to be derived from the entrepreneurial or managerial efforts of others." In 1986, the New York Court of Appeals adopted as persuasive the decisions of the federal courts, particularly the *Howey* test, construing the definition of "security" under the federal statutes on the theory that, while the language of the New York and the federal laws differ, the remedial

---

3. General Business Law § 352–e(1).
4. General Business Law § 352–e(1)(a).
5. 328 U.S. 293, 66 S.Ct. 1100, 90 L.Ed. 1244 (1946).
6. "Person" includes any natural person, partnership, corporation, trust, or any other legal entity capable of making an investment.
7. 328 U.S. at 298–99, 66 S.Ct. at 1102–1103.
8. 421 U.S. 837, 852, 95 S.Ct. 2051, 2060, 44 L.Ed.2d 621 (1975).

purposes of both laws are the same.[9] Other courts have added a fifth factor to the *Howey* test: the person risks loss of his investment.[10]

Many investments in for-profit enterprises will involve the first four *Howey* elements. Because limited partners usually do not manage or operate their partnerships in their capacity as limited partners, and therefore rely solely on the efforts of others (the general partners) for their profits, limited partnership interests typically meet all the investment contract prerequisites and are therefore considered securities. General partnership interests (in both general partnerships and limited partnerships) typically include the right to vote and a right to participate in the management of the partnership. Such management rights are inconsistent with the *Howey* requirement that the holder of an investment contract rely solely on the "efforts of others" for the success of the enterprise. It therefore seems clear that general partnership interests are unlikely to be treated as investment contracts.

One cannot, however, conclude that the statutory right to participate in the management of an LLC automatically precludes a membership interest from being characterized as an investment contract. First, an LLC's Articles may provide for management solely by managers, effectively eliminating a non-manager-member's management rights, and accordingly, indicating that his interest is, in fact, a security. Second, although a member's right to participate in the management of a member-managed LLC is very extensive, it may be limited by provisions of the LLC's operating agreement, therefore qualifying such an interest as a security notwithstanding the statutory default.[11] Consequently, a membership interest is not automatically qualified or disqualified as a security based on the presumed management structure, and one must examine the economic reality of a membership interest to determine its nature.[12] It seems likely, however, that a membership interest in a truly member-managed LLC, like a general partnership interest, will not be an investment contract, or, therefore, a security. On the other hand, a non-managing member's interest in a manager-managed LLC will probably qualify as both, like a limited partnership interest.

One interesting point to note is that the sale of an economic interest stripped out from an LLC membership interest, as permitted by the NYLLCL, may well require registration under applicable federal and

---

9. All Seasons Resorts, Inc. v. Abrams, 68 N.Y.2d 81, 87, 506 N.Y.S.2d 10, 13, 497 N.E.2d 33 (1986); People v. First Meridian Planning Corporation, 201 A.D.2d 145, 614 N.Y.S.2d 811, 816 (3d Dep't 1994).

10. GBJ Corporation v. Sequa Corporation, 804 F.Supp. 564, 567 (S.D.N.Y.1992); Department of Economic Development v. Arthur Andersen & Co. (U.S.A.), 683 F.Supp. 1463, 1472 (S.D.N.Y.1988). *See* Marine Bank v. Weaver, 455 U.S. 551, 557–59, 102 S.Ct. 1220, 1224–25, 71 L.Ed.2d 409 (1982).

11. *See* NYLLCL §§ 401 *et seq.*

12. Howey, *supra*, at note 5, 328 U.S. at 301, 66 S.Ct. at 1104; Marine Bank, *supra* at note 10 (an instrument seemingly within the expansive definition of security contained in the 1934 Act is not so considered if the context otherwise requires); Seagrave Corporation v. Vista Resources, Inc., 696 F.2d 227, 230 (2d Cir.1982).

state securities laws. Because management rights do not accompany the transferred interest, it closely resembles corporate stock.[13] If an operating agreement, by omitting to address the issue or otherwise, permits unlimited separation and sale of the economic portion of a membership interest, it should also address the burden of compliance with securities laws affecting any such sale.[14]

§ 2.107 Summary

Non-corporate entities like LLCs and partnerships, limited or general, can provide significant tax and other advantages over corporations.[1] Since tax classification simplification became law, a non-corporate entity no longer need comply with the somewhat arcane requirements of the corporate characteristics test for its income to be taxed at only one level. In addition, non-corporate entities are far more flexible than corporations in their management alternatives and the ability to make special allocations among owners.[2] Accordingly, the up-front costs of establishing a non-corporate entity, including expenses incurred to comply with state law requirements and to tailor the entity's documents to its owners' specifications, may outweigh those associated with forming a corporation, unless the corporation requires a personalized shareholders' agreement.

Among the most popular non-corporate entities, the LLC, although new and somewhat untested, is potentially the most useful to new enterprises.[3] Any person or type of entity may be a partner of any general or limited partnership or a member of an LLC.[4] Profits and losses may be allocated among partners or members in any way, so long as the allocations have substantial economic effect.[5] Whether by default provisions of governing law or under their agreements, both LLCs and partnerships are likely to restrict the transferability of interests therein and to require dissolution of the entity upon an owner's withdrawal, unless those remaining vote to continue its business.[6] Unlike any type of partnership, however, none of an LLC's members is required to be personally liable for the debts and obligations of the LLC.[7] Moreover, a one-member LLC may exist, while a one-partner partnership may not.[8]

---

13. *Id.*

14. CAVEAT: It is also conceivable under the definition of "dealer" that a member selling the separated economic interest might be a dealer required to register under the Martin Act.

§ 2.107

1. *See supra*, §§ 2.2, 2.3.
2. *See supra*, § 2.2.
3. *See supra*, §§ 2.10–2.13, and discussion of LLCs at §§ 2.14–2.43, *supra*.

4. *See supra*, §§ 2.21, 2.51, 2.84.
5. *See supra*, §§ 2.2, 2.3.
6. *See supra*, §§ 2.33–2.35, 2.61–2.63, 2.94–2.99, with respect to transfers of interests and §§ 2.36–2.38, 2.64–2.66, 2.97–2.99, *supra*, with respect to dissolution.
7. *See supra*, § 2.23.
8. *See supra*, § 2.24.

In other respects, the formation, management and operation of manager-managed LLCs and limited partnerships are very similar.[9] For example, like the general partners of a limited partnership, only the managers of a manager-managed LLC are agents of the LLC for purposes of its business—neither limited partners nor non-manager members are presumed to have such authority merely by virtue of their ownership status.[10] The establishment of LLCs and limited partnerships requires a centralized filing with the State;[11] both types of organization must adopt written agreements.[12] The costs of forming and maintaining an LLC will probably be on a par with those for a limited partnership, as the expense of creating a corporate (Subchapter C or Subchapter S) general partner for a limited partnership will probably offset the $50 per member per year fee imposed on an LLC (but not on the partnership).

The management and operation of a member-managed LLC are like that of a general partnership, other than with respect to the members' insulation from personal liability for the entity's debts.[13] All members of a member-managed LLC have the power to bind the LLC in the usual course of the LLC's business, just as do partners.[14] A general partnership, however, requires neither a centralized filing to come into existence nor a written agreement among partners.[15] As a result, a general partnership may be cheaper to establish than an LLC or limited partnership, but parties may by their conduct alone form a partnership, with its attendant responsibilities, even though they did not mean to do so.[16]

Although conversion from corporate form to an LLC may often be disadvantageous from a tax perspective,[17] partnerships may easily convert to LLCs under New York law, usually with no adverse tax consequences.[18] In addition, existing professional general partnerships may register as LLPs merely by filing a registration with the Secretary of State and paying the required annual fee.[19]

As a rule, general partnership interests and membership interests in member-managed LLCs probably will not constitute "securities" for purposes of the application of state and federal securities laws.[20] On the other hand, non-managing membership interests in manager-managed LLCs and limited partnership interests probably will qualify as securities, as will transferable financial rights accruing to LLC membership interests.[21]

9. *See, e.g., supra*, §§ 2.16, 2.78.
10. *See supra*, §§ 2.32, 2.93.
11. *See supra*, §§ 2.17, 2.80.
12. *See supra*, §§ 2.19, 2.82.
13. *See, e.g., supra*, §§ 2.25–2.28, 2.55–2.56.
14. *See supra*, §§ 2.32, 2.60.
15. *See supra*, §§ 2.46–2.50.
16. *See supra*, § 2.46.
17. *See supra*, § 2.40.
18. *See supra*, §§ 2.40–2.42, 2.68–2.70, 2.101–2.103.
19. *See supra*, §§ 2.72–2.76, for discussion and § 2.113, *infra*, for a form of LLP registration.
20. *See supra*, § 2.106.
21. *Id.*

In any event, plain vanilla general partnerships may soon become historical anomalies as businesspeople use the LLC structure to limit their personal exposure to liability. Even professionals who balk at forming, or converting their partnerships to, LLCs are likely to register as LLPs to limit their personal liability for the partnership's contractual debts and obligations and for their partners' misconduct or malpractice. It does not make sense to subject a person's assets to the liabilities of a partnership if a vehicle like the LLC is available to avoid the result.

§ 2.108 Chart Comparing New York Entities

CHARACTERISTIC	LLC	LLP	"S" CORP	"C" CORP	LIMITED PARTNERSHIP	GENERAL PARTNERSHIP
Restrictions on nature/number of owners	No restrictions.	Partners must be licensed to practice a "profession"; must have at least two partners.	Only individuals who are U.S. citizens or resident aliens and certain trusts may be shareholders; no more than 75 total.	No restrictions on nature or number.	No restrictions, but must have at least one general and one limited partner.	No restrictions, but must have at least two partners
Restrictions on what the entity may own	No restrictions.	Unless practicing legal, medical, dental and certain other professions, can conduct other businesses (no restrictions).	Previously could not own 80% or more (voting and value) of a subsidiary corp., but now liberalized -- no restrictions.	No restrictions.	No restrictions.	No restrictions (unless imposed by other applicable law or authority (e.g., state professional licensing authorities -- see LLPs).
Liability of owners for obligations of entity	None, except PLLCs (same as LLPs), and to return certain wrongful distributions and/or make promised contributions under certain circumstances.	None for entity's contractual obligations, but liable for own negligence and misconduct and that of persons under direct supervision or control.	None, except in "veil piercing" situations and in certain circumstances for employee salaries, but professionals same as LLPs.	Same as S corp.	General partner personally liable for all obligations; limited partners liable only to extent of their contributions.	All partners jointly liable for contractual obligations of entity (after partnership assets exhausted) and all jointly and severally liable for tort obligations

CHARACTERISTIC	LLC	LLP	"S" CORP	"C" CORP	LIMITED PARTNERSHIP	GENERAL PARTNERSHIP
Federal taxation of entity	Pass-through to members unless they elect otherwise. Losses may be deducted to extent of adjusted basis in interest.	Same as LLC.	As long as valid "S" election in place, no entity-level tax — pass-through to shareholders. Losses may be deducted to extent of adjusted basis in stock.	Income tax at corporate level and on distributions to shareholders. Also subject to accumulated earnings tax and personal holding company tax. No pass-through of losses.	Same as LLC. Publicly-traded LPs treated as corps.	Same as LLC. (No publicly-traded GPs.)
Special allocations and rights of owners	Except for certain allocations re: contributed property, any allocations permitted if they have "substantial economic effect."	Same as LLC.	Except for differences based on voting rights, one class of stock only permitted.	Dividends and liquidating distributions on basis of class rights. Difficult to allocate different types of income to different classes.	Same as LLC.	Same as LLC.
Management restrictions	Any structure permitted. Managers may act by less than unanimous written consent and by proxy. Statutory default to member-management.	Same as GP.	Unless Certificate of Incorporation elects shareholder management alternative, single board of directors manages. Managers may act by unanimous written consent or at meeting only.	Same as S corp.	Rights of limited partners to manage usually restricted in certain ways.	All partners usually manage; delegation permitted.

Ch. 2 CHART COMPARING NEW YORK ENTITIES § 2.108

CHARACTERISTIC	LLC	LLP	"S" CORP	"C" CORP	LIMITED PARTNERSHIP	GENERAL PARTNERSHIP
Transferability of interests	Flexible. Statutory default requires consent of majority in interest to admit new members, but financial interests only freely tradable.	Same as GP.	Subject to practical restrictions imposed by Subchapter S.	Freely tradable unless shareholders agree otherwise.	Usually limited.	Usually, all partners must consent to admit new partners.
What can be contributed as consideration for interests	Cash, property, past services, future services.	Same as LLC.	Same as C corp.	Cash, property, past services -- no future obligations.	Same as LLC.	Same as LLC.
Tax treatment of contributions of property	No gain or loss recognized by either member or LLC; no "control" after transfer required.	Same as LLC.	Same as C Corp.	No gain or loss recognized by shareholders on contribution of property (including cash) in return for stock if those contributing own at least 80% of shares and voting power immediately after transfer. No gain or loss recognized by corporation.	Same as LLC.	Same as LLC.

365

CHARACTERISTIC	LLC	LLP	"S" CORP	"C" CORP	LIMITED PARTNERSHIP	GENERAL PARTNERSHIP
Continuity of life	Flexible. Statutory default requires dissolution upon "withdrawal events" with respect to each member, unless a majority in interest votes to continue business. LLC can override such default for continuity.	Same as GP.	Perpetual	Same as S corp.	Dissolution upon withdrawal events with respect to general partners; business may be continued by consent.	Dissolution upon withdrawal events with respect to each partner; business may be continued by consent.
Actions by written consent of owners in lieu of meeting	Permitted; statutory default requires consent of same number as would be necessary at a meeting of all members.	As per partnership agreement.	Same as C corp	Permitted; unanimous consent required.	Same as LLP.	Same as LLP.

Ch. 2   CHART COMPARING NEW YORK ENTITIES   § 2.108

CHARACTERISTIC	LLC	LLP	"S" CORP	"C" CORP	LIMITED PARTNERSHIP	GENERAL PARTNERSHIP
State income taxation	None at entity level if treated as a pass-through for federal tax purposes. Annual fee if NYS source income -- $50/member, $325 minimum, $10,000 maximum.	Same as LLC.	1.40625%, with surcharges.	9%, with surcharges.	None at entity level	None at entity level.
City income taxation	4% UBIT; same annual fee as State fee authorized if NYC source income.	Same as LLC.	8.85%, but where profits can be paid as compensation to owner-employees, effective rate can be 2.65%.	8.85%.	4% UBIT.	4% UBIT
Public documents	Articles of Organization.	Registration form.	Certificate of Incorporation.	Certificate of Incorporation; if publicly traded, other material agreements.	Certificate of Limited Partnership.	Business Certificate.

§ 2.108 NON-CORPORATE ENTITIES Ch. 2

CHARACTERISTIC	LLC	LLP	"S" CORP	"C" CORP	LIMITED PARTNERSHIP	GENERAL PARTNERSHIP
Compensation to shareholder-employees	Profits pass through as guaranteed payments or as distributive share; members may also be paid salaries as managers or employees to reduce UBIT.	Same as LLC.	Generally, salary and pass-through of excess profits. However, special allocation of pass-through items not permitted (see above). Reasonable compensation issues may arise	Generally, in closely-held corps, shareholders receive all net profits as salary to reduce corporate income/avoid double taxation. Reasonable compensation issues may arise.	Same as LLC	Same as LLC.
Deductibility of health insurance, disability premiums	Itemized deduction for 30% (to be increased) of amount. Generally, no cafeteria plans for owners.	Same as LLC.	Same as LLC.	Fully deductible.	Same as LLC	Same as LLC.
FICA and Medicare tax	Self-employment (FICA rate) tax may not apply to pass-throughs to non-manager members, but probably are applicable on earnings up to cap for managing members.	Self-employment (FICA rate) tax payable on earnings up to cap. Distributive shares defined as self-employment income.	Same as C corp. but FICA not imposed on pass-through amounts.	Payable on salary up to $61,200; Medicare portion (2.9%) not subject to cap.	Same as LLC	Same as LLP.

§ 2.109 Drafting Checklist

The following issues should be explored with clients who have determined to organize a non-corporate entity and, if appropriate, should be addressed in its governing documents. Parenthetical Section references are to Sections of the text, *supra*, which discuss issues in more detail.

Generally

1. When was the entity formed? (*See* §§ 2.16, 2.19, 2.46, 2.79, 2.80, 2.82)
2. Name? Does it include words or abbreviations prohibited or required by law? (*See* §§ 2.16, 2.17, 2.48, 2.79, 2.80)
3. Names and addresses, fax numbers and Employee Identification Numbers of initial partners/members or managers, if any.
4. If an LLC, what provisions are contained in the Articles (to avoid duplication and inconsistencies)? (*See* §§ 2.17, 2.18, 2.19)
5. If an LLC or LLP, will one or more members assume liability for all the company's debts and obligations? (*See* §§ 2.6, 2.17, 2.75)
6. Is the LLC intended to have continuity of life? (*See* § 2.7)
7. Are interests, or portions thereof, intended to be freely transferable? (*See* §§ 2.8, 2.33–2.35, 2.61–2.63, 2.94–2.96)

Formation and Business of Company

1. Who may change the name of the company? If a professional business, may the names of certain partners/members be used after their deaths or retirement? (*See* §§ 2.43, 2.71, 2.72–2.76)
2. What is the business purpose of the company? Who may change the business of the company? If a professional entity, is its ability to conduct other businesses limited? (*See* §§ 2.16, 2.32, 2.46, 2.53, 2.60, 2.72–2.76, 2.79, 2.93)
3. Where is the company's principal office? Who may change the location of the office?
4. Will the company have a registered agent in New York? Name and address? Who may change the registered agent? (*See* §§ 2.17, 2.75, 2.80)
5. Should the company have a latest specified date of dissolution? If so, what should it be? (*See* §§ 2.7, 2.17, 2.80)

Capital Contributions and Capital Accounts

1. What, and in what form will, capital contributions be made (cash, property or services)? What is the value of non-cash contributions? Do contributors of different types of capital have different rights, management or otherwise (should they be different classes of members)? (*See* §§ 2.21, 2.25–2.31, 2.51, 2.55–2.59, 2.84, 2.88–2.92)
2. Are any contributions services to be performed in the future? What is their value? (Check tax implications for contributor)

3. If a contribution is to be made over time, will the contributing member receive his entire interest, and all rights pertaining thereto, up front, or will it vest as the contribution is actually made?
4. Will additional capital contributions be required? If so, will there be a limit on the total amount that may be required? Should one or more partners/members be obligated to make additional contributions (as opposed to all)? Who determines the amount and/or purpose of additional contributions? Should partners/members be able to determine whether they wish to acquire greater interests by making additional contributions? Should there be pre-emptive rights?
5. If additional capital contributions may be required, what will be the consequences of default? May other partners/members make up the default? If so, on what basis? Should "cure" by other partners/members be treated as additional contributions by them, or as a loan to the defaulting member? If a loan, on what terms? Should there be a penalty for default? Should there be a lien on the defaulting partner's/member's interest to secure repayment?
6. How should percentage interests be recalculated if a defaulting member does not cure its default? Should default be considered a withdrawal event?
7. Will partners/members receive interest on their capital account balances? At what rate?
8. Will partners/members have any obligation to make up negative capital account balances?

Distributions and Allocations

1. On what basis will distributions be made among partners/members? What amounts must be distributed? Will all cash available for distribution be distributed to partners/members? How frequently? Who may determine when distributions are made? Will distributions of proceeds from extraordinary transactions be distributed on a different basis?
2. Will certain partners/members receive priority returns? On what basis? Under what circumstances (*i.e.*, upon certain performance achievements or otherwise)? Will it affect their interests (in profits or with respect to management rights) over the life of the company?
3. How will percentage interests in profits, losses and distributions be determined? Set at the beginning, or varying on a year-to-year basis and determined in arrears, or prospectively? Will percentage interests depend on capital contributions, capital account balances or otherwise as determined by the partners/members? Who will determine, and where will records thereof be maintained?
4. Who shall have responsibility for preparing tax returns?
5. Will mid-year transfers of interests be permitted?
6. Will distributions or allocations be made based on a formula, as compensation for services to the company (particularly in professional entities)?

Management (See § 2.9)

1. Who will manage? All partners/members (where permitted), certain classes or committees of partners/members or, in an LLC, managers (whether members or not)? One of two or more general partners? If outside managers will manage an LLC, what will the terms of their employment and compensation be? If an entity is managed by particular partners/members, will they receive additional compensation? (*See* §§ 2.9, 2.25–2.32, 2.55–2.60, 2.88–2.93)

2. How will managers of an LLC (or a managing general partner, if more than one) be elected or appointed? For what term? What qualifications must all or some of them have (residents? members? age? experience?)? Should there be different classes of managers, with different duties, areas of responsibility, qualifications, voting weight, compensation? Should different classes be elected by different classes of members? (*See* §§ 2.26, 2.28, 2.88, 2.89)

3. What specific powers and responsibilities shall the managers have, and in what decisions must members or limited partners be involved? (*See* §§ 2.27–2.30, 2.56–2.58, 2.89–2.91)

4. What are managers' duties to the company? Is statutory default provision for LLC management ("ordinarily prudent person in like position") sufficient? Or should there be a higher or lower standard, generally or based on the type of activity? Will liability be limited? (*See* §§ 2.31, 2.53, 2.59, 2.74, 2.86, 2.92)

5. Should general partners/managers be subject to non-competition covenants or other limitations on their activities during the time they serve the company?

6. Under what circumstances may general partners/managers be removed? How should "cause" be defined, if that is a prerequisite to removal? Who replaces general partners/managers/fills vacancies? Does removal constitute a withdrawal or dissolution event requiring other action to continue the business? (*See* §§ 2.36–2.37, 2.64–2.65, 2.97–2.98)

7. How often and where should general partners/managers meet? What notice should be given? Should there be a quorum requirement less than all? On what basis (*per capita*, other) should managers vote? What vote is necessary to take action? Should certain actions require greater or lesser votes? If classes of managers are established, what are their relative responsibilities and voting powers? Will a general partner/manager or class thereof have veto power over certain decisions? (*See* §§ 2.25–2.29, 2.55–2.57, 2.88–2.90)

8. Will managers or partners be permitted to take action by written consent, or should meetings be required? Should managers be permitted to vote by proxy? (*See* §§ 2.28, 2.56, 2.89–2.90)

9. Should transactions between the company and general partners/managers or their affiliates be permitted?

10. May managers delegate authority to officers? How will officers be elected or appointed (by managers or partners/members)? Term? Titles? Qualifications (*i.e.*, partners/members or not)? Responsibilities? Limitations on authority? How may officers by removed? (*See* §§ 2.30, 2.58, 2.91)

11. What reports should general partners/managers deliver to partners/members, and when? (*See* §§ 2.20, 2.50, 2.83)

12. Will general partners/managers be responsible for an annual budget? Should limited partners/members have approval rights? If so, by what vote? What happens if a budget is not timely approved?

Meetings

1. Should dealings between the company and any partners/members or their affiliates be permitted? Should competitive or other activities of partners/members be circumscribed during any given term? (*See* §§ 2.21, 2.51, 2.84)

2. How often and where should partners/members meet? What notice should be given? What should the quorum requirement be? On what basis (*per capita*, relative capital accounts, profits interests, initial contributions, other) should votes be made? Should different votes—and different bases—be required for different issues? Should those who assign their financial rights continue to have a full vote, or are their voting rights extinguished? What vote is necessary to take certain actions? Should certain transactions (sale or mortgage of assets, amendment of organizational documents, etc.) require supermajority approval? If there are general partners/managers, over what transactions should limited partners/members have veto or approval power? Will different classes of partners/members be defined; will their voting rights and powers differ? (*See* §§ 2.25, 2.27, 2.29, 2.55–2.57, 2.89–2.90)

3. Should proxies and other voting arrangements be permitted?

4. Should partners/members be permitted to take action by written consent, or should meetings be required? (*See* §§ 2.25–2.28, 2.55–2.56, 2.88–2.90)

5. Who may create different classes of interests and set their relative rights, preferences, duties, etc. (general partners, managers or limited partners/members, and by what vote)? Will future or present classes of members be distinguished by voting rights, veto powers, priority returns? Will their rights change over time, or based on returns? Will they have different priorities upon dissolution only?

Transferability (See § 2.8)

1. Should economic interests (as opposed to entire interests) be fully transferable? If so, how will records be kept? Should transferors of partial interests retain voting rights, or are such rights to be dispersed among non-transferring members? Or, will such transfers be permitted only by consent? Who must consent, and by what vote? Will economic transferees succeed to a member's obligation to make unpaid capital contributions? Should different members or classes of members (including member-managers) have different consent standards for the transfer of their interests? (See §§ 2.33–2.35, 2.61–2.63, 2.94–2.96, 2.106)

2. Are all transfers of interests prohibited without the members' consent to admit a transferee as a member? Are pledges of interests permitted? Are transfers to certain classes (family members, etc.) freely permitted? May a certain percentage of an interest (up to 79%) be transferred without consent, or with a lower consent requirement? (See § 2.8)

3. Will a right of first refusal or right of first offer be imposed on any transfers (including transfers of economic rights alone, or pledges) of interests? If so, what will be the timing and other mechanical requirements? Will both partners/members and the company have such rights? (See § 2.8)

4. Will there be conditions, other than consent, to permitted transfers? What happens if proposed transfers cause a breach of agreements to which the company is a party?

5. What consent will be necessary to admit new partners/members? (See §§ 2.8, 2.34, 2.62, 2.95)

Withdrawal

1. Will "voluntary" withdrawal be permitted? What should be considered a "voluntary" or an "involuntary" withdrawal (i.e., breach of agreement, bankruptcy, death, retirement, other events)? Will a breach of the agreement be considered a withdrawal? (See §§ 2.21, 2.37, 2.65, 2.98)

2. What will the effect of withdrawal be? Will it differ based on whether withdrawal is voluntary or involuntary? Will the withdrawn partner's/member's interest be required to be repurchased? When (upon liquidation of the company, or within a specified period after withdrawal)? Will the withdrawn partner/member be entitled to receive distributions and allocations until repurchase? Will voting or other percentages be recalculated upon a withdrawal? (See §§ 2.21, 2.51, 2.84)

3. If any type of withdrawal is prohibited or restricted, will the withdrawn partner/member be liable for damages caused by his withdrawal in violation of such restriction? Will the amount of damages be

§ 2.109   NON-CORPORATE ENTITIES   Ch. 2

liquidated? When will any such damages be paid or offset? (*See* §§ 2.21, 2.51, 2.84)

4. If a withdrawn partner's/member's interest is to be repurchased, how will the purchase price be determined? Over what period will it be paid? (*See* §§ 2.21, 2.51, 2.84)

Dissolution and Termination (See § 2.7)

1. Will any specified event result in termination of the company (*i.e.*, sale of a specific property, etc.)? For an LLC, will only certain specified events result in termination, or all types of withdrawal events with respect to specified members? (*See* §§ 2.37, 2.65, 2.98)

2. What vote, and of whom, shall be/is required to continue the business of the company after a dissolution event? Within what period must the vote be taken? (*See* §§ 2.38, 2.66, 2.99)

3. Upon liquidation, who shall act as liquidator of the company's assets? Will the liquidator have any special responsibilities in the liquidation process? Will any partner/member have priorities upon liquidation? (*See* §§ 2.39, 2.67, 2.100)

Indemnification

1. Will the company indemnify partners/members, managers, officers and/or agents? Will there be limits (in addition to statutory restrictions) on the situations in which the company will indemnify? Will the company advance expenses to an indemnitee? Will the company be required to purchase insurance or make other arrangements to fund indemnity obligations? (*See* §§ 2.51, 2.54)

Miscellaneous

1. How will notice to partners/members be required to be given?

2. What types of records must be maintained by the company? Where will they be kept? Will the record-keepers and others be bound to maintain the confidentiality of certain information, whether about the company, its business or partners/members, even to the exclusion of the partners/members?

3. By what vote may the agreement be amended? Will certain types of amendments be permitted to be made by a different vote, or in the discretion of the general partner/manager (*i.e.*, if the amendments do not adversely affect any partner's/member's rights)? Will certain types of amendments require a higher consent, or the consent of each affected partner/member?

§ 2.110   Forms

The following forms are for guidance only and should not be used without a careful review of the client's particular situation.

§ 2.111 Forms—LLC Articles of Organization

ARTICLES OF ORGANIZATION
OF
_____, L.L.C.

Under Section 203 of the Limited Liability Company Law

FIRST: The name of the limited liability company is: _____, L.L.C.

SECOND: The county within this state in which the principal office of the limited liability company is to be located is: _____.

THIRD: The Secretary of State of the State of New York is designated as agent of the limited liability company upon whom process against it may be served. The post office address within or without this state to which the Secretary of State shall mail a copy of any process against the limited liability company served upon him or her is:_____.

FOURTH: The limited liability company is to be managed by [its members] [a manager].

FIFTH: The limited liability company may, with the consent of the [members] [manager] as specified in the operating agreement, issue interests in the limited liability company in such classes, or in series of such classes, having such designations, preferences and rights as may be determined by the [members] [manager] in the manner described in the operating agreement.

IN WITNESS WHEREOF, this certificate has been subscribed this ___ day of _____, 199_ by the undersigned who affirms that the statements made herein are true under the penalties of perjury.

_____
(name and capacity of signer)
(signature)

§ 2.112 Forms—Operating Agreement: Member-Managed LLC

The following form is a relatively simple operating agreement for a member-managed LLC owned by two members with almost equal interests therein. It contains, among other things, a list of decisions as to which both members must agree, a push-pull provision that comes into play when open matters cannot be decided, and takes advantage of the change in tax law to create continuity of the entity's life.

OPERATING AGREEMENT
OF
_____, L.L.C.

OPERATING AGREEMENT, dated as of _____ __, 1997, by and between _____ ("Member 1"), and _____ ("Member 2"), as the initial members, and such other persons who may be admitted from time to time as members hereunder (collectively, the "Members").

W I T N E S S E T H :

WHEREAS, on and as of the date hereof, the parties formed _____, L.L.C. (the "Company") by filing Articles of Organization with the Secretary of State of the State of New York; and

WHEREAS, the Members wish to set forth their agreements as to their respective rights, duties and obligations and the operation and management of the Company for the purposes stated herein;

NOW, THEREFORE, it is mutually agreed that:

ARTICLE I
DEFINITIONS

As used herein, the following terms have the meaning set forth below:

"Act" shall mean the New York Limited Liability Company Law, as in effect on the date hereof and as it may be amended hereafter from time to time.

"Affiliate" of a Person shall mean any relative of such Person, or any other Person that controls, is controlled by or is under common control with, such Person, or an officer, director, partner or trustee of such Person or any such other Person. "Control" shall mean the right or ability to direct the management of a Person by voting membership interest, the election of a majority of its Board of Directors or otherwise.

"Agreement" shall mean this Operating Agreement.

"Business Plan" shall have the meaning set forth in Section 4.4.

"Capital Account" shall have the meaning set forth in Section 6.1.

"Capital Contribution" shall mean, with respect to a particular Member, the amount or value of capital contributed or deemed to have been contributed by such Member to the Company pursuant to Sections 5.1 and 5.3.

"Cause" shall mean, with respect to any employee or officer of the Company, (a) any action or omission to act which exceeds the scope of such person's authority, as determined pursuant to Article IV; (b) any material misuse or misappropriation of the property or assets of the Company; (c) any conviction of a felony; (d) the commission of a fraud or other similar conduct detrimental to the Company; or (e) any action or omission to act which would constitute a breach of a fiduciary duty owed by such officer to the Company.

"Code" shall mean the Internal Revenue Code of 1986, as amended.

"*Company*" shall have the meaning set forth in the preamble of this Agreement.

"*Confidential Information*" shall have the meaning set forth in Section 10.11.

"*Default Rate*" shall have the meaning set forth in Section 5.3.

"*Interest*" or "*Interests*" shall mean membership interests in the Company.

"*Losses*" shall have the meaning set forth in Section 3.8(b).

"*Members*" shall have the meaning set forth in the first paragraph of this Agreement.

"*Notice Period*" shall have the meaning set forth in Section 3.10(b).

"*Percentage Interest*" of a Member shall mean such Member's right to share in the distributions, profits and losses of the Company as set forth in Section 5.2, but subject to Section 6.3.

"*Person*" shall mean any individual, entity, firm, corporation, partnership, association, limited liability company, joint-stock company, trust, or unincorporated organization.

"*Tax Matters Partner*" shall have the meaning set forth in Section 7.2.

"*Transfer*" shall mean, with respect to any Interest, to sell, assign, transfer, convey, exchange, mortgage, pledge or grant a security interest in, or otherwise encumber or dispose of, including by gift, merger, consolidation, dividend or distribution, such Interest (or any portion thereof or right therein), in each case, whether made directly or indirectly, voluntarily or involuntarily, absolutely or conditionally, by operation of law or otherwise, provided that the pledge or hypothecation of its Interest by either Member to a financial institution as part of a general pledge of its assets shall not be considered a Transfer hereunder.

"*Withdrawal*" shall have the meaning set forth in Section 8.1(a).

ARTICLE II
FORMATION

2.1 *Formation; Filings.* On and as of the date hereof, the parties have formed a limited liability company pursuant to the Act. Each of the Members agrees hereafter to execute or cause to be executed all other instruments, certificates, notices and documents, and shall do or cause to be done all such filings, recordings, publications and other acts, in each case as may be necessary or appropriate from time to time, to comply with all applicable requirements of the Act and under the laws of all other jurisdictions in which the Company shall desire to conduct business.

2.2 *Name and Office.*

(a) The name of the Company is "_____, L.L.C." and its business shall be carried on in this name until changed by the Members.

(b) The Company shall maintain an office at _____, or such other location or locations as the Members may from time to time determine.

2.3 *Business Purposes.* The purposes of the Company shall be to conduct a _____ business, to expand such business as the Members may from time to time determine, and to conduct any other lawful business as the Members may from time to time determine.

2.4 *Term.* The term of the Company shall commence on and as of the date hereof and shall continue until dissolved and liquidated in accordance with Article IX.

2.5 *Fiscal Year.* The fiscal year of the Company shall end on December 31.

ARTICLE III
MEETINGS OF MEMBERS

3.1 *Meetings of Members.*

(a) An annual meeting of the Members shall be held on such date and at such time and place as the Members shall determine. At such annual meeting, the Members shall transact such business as may properly be brought before the meeting.

(b) Regular meetings of the Members may be held at such times and places as the Members shall determine. At such meetings, the Members shall take such action as may be required in connection with the operation and management of the Company.

(c) Special meetings of the Members may be called for any purpose or purposes by any Member entitled to vote at such a special meeting. Only business within the purpose or purposes described in the notice of the special meeting may be conducted at such special meeting.

3.2 *Notice of Meetings.* Notice of each annual or special meeting of Members, and of the first regular meeting of Members (or of any regular meeting, the time or venue of which has changed from that of the last such regular meeting), stating the date, time and place and, in the case of a special meeting, the purposes thereof, shall be given to each Member entitled to vote at any such meeting in writing or by telephone not less than two nor more than 30 days before the date of such meeting. If notice is given in writing, it shall be delivered as set forth in Section 10.2. A Member's presence in person at any such meeting shall constitute waiver of prior notice of such meeting.

3.3 *Quorum of Members.* Members holding at least a majority of the Percentage Interests of the Members entitled to vote on a matter or consent thereto at a meeting of Members, present in person, shall constitute a quorum at each such meeting, except as otherwise provided by the Act. The Members present at a meeting of Members at which a quorum is not present may adjourn the meeting until such time and place as may be determined by vote of the Members holding a majority of the Percentage Interests present. At any such adjourned meeting at which a quorum shall be present and acting throughout, any business may be transacted that might have been transacted at the meeting as originally convened.

3.4 *Voting by Members.* Except as otherwise required by law or this Agreement, the affirmative vote of the Members holding a majority of the Percentage Interests of the Members entitled to vote thereon, make such determination or consent thereto, shall be required for the Members to take action with respect to any matter at any meeting of Members, or otherwise to make any determination or consent required or permitted to be made by the Members under this Agreement.

3.5 *Action without a Meeting.* Any action required or permitted to be taken at any annual, regular or special meeting of Members, including determinations and consents under this Agreement, may be taken without a meeting, without prior notice and without a vote if a consent or consents in writing, setting forth the action so taken, shall be signed by all of the Members whose vote or consent would have been required hereunder or under the Act to take such action at a meeting at which all Members were present, provided that prompt written notice of such action shall be given to each Member that has not executed such consent.

3.6 *Telephonic Meetings.* Members may participate in and hold meetings by conference telephone or similar communications equipment, by means of which all persons participating in such meeting can hear each other, and participation in a meeting pursuant to this Section shall constitute presence in person at such meeting.

3.7 *Dealings with the Company; Other Business Activity.* Subject to the requirements of this Agreement and any other agreements entered by the Members or any of their respective Affiliates from time to time, any Member or any Affiliate of any Member may make loans to, borrow from and transact such other business with, the Company as may be approved by the Members as set forth in Section 3.9. Except as set forth in Section 10.11, nothing contained in this Agreement shall be deemed to restrict or limit in any way any right of any Member or any Affiliate of any Member to pursue, conduct or participate in, directly or indirectly, any other business or activity whatsoever, including, without limitation, any business that competes generally with the Company's business from time to time.

3.8 *Liability of Members; Indemnity.*

(a) No Member shall be personally liable for the debts, obligations or liabilities of the Company solely by reason of being a Member, except to the extent of its Capital Contribution and any obligation to make a Capital Contribution.

(b) Each Member shall indemnify and hold the other Members (and, where applicable, their respective heirs, personal representatives, assigns, officers, partners, members, directors and shareholders) harmless from and against all claims, demands, costs, losses and damages, including, without limitation, attorneys' fees and expenses (collectively, "Losses") incurred as a result of or in connection with the indemnifying party's breach (directly or by its agents or other representatives) of any provision of this Agreement or action outside the scope of this Agreement.

(c) Subject to Section 3.8(b), the Company shall indemnify and hold each Member (and, where applicable, his or its respective heirs, personal representatives, assigns, officers, partners, members, directors and shareholders) harmless from and against all Losses incurred as a result of or in connection with (i) any claim that such Member is liable for any debt, obligation or liability of the Company or is directly or indirectly required to make payments in respect thereof or in connection therewith, and (ii) any act or omission by such Member for or on behalf of the Company, unless such act or omission was unauthorized, contrary to this Agreement or constituted gross negligence, fraud or a knowing violation of the law or resulted in financial or other gain to which the Member was not entitled.

(d) Each party to be indemnified under Section 3.8(b) or (c) shall give each indemnifying party notice of any Losses subject to the indemnity within 30 days after the indemnified party has received actual notice thereof. The indemnifying party shall be entitled to participate in or direct the defense of any action in connection with the reported Loss, provided that he employs counsel reasonably satisfactory to the indemnified party. An indemnifying party shall not be liable to an indemnified party in respect of settlements effected by the indemnified party without the written consent of the indemnifying party, which consent shall not be unreasonably withheld or delayed.

3.9 *Actions Requiring Unanimous Consent of Members.* Notwithstanding anything contained in Section 3.4 to the contrary, the following actions or types of transactions shall not be taken or consummated without the unanimous approval of the Members:

(a) except as specifically approved in the then current Business Plan, entering into, amending or terminating any contract, agreement or understanding (i) which involves the acquisition or disposition of assets, including intellectual property, in a single transaction or a related series of transactions for an aggregate amount in excess of [$_____], (ii) which has a term of more than one year (exclusive of contracts entered into in the ordinary course of business and in accordance with policies previously approved by the Members) or (iii) with any Member or any

Affiliate of any Member, or in connection with which any Member or any Affiliate of a Member has a direct or indirect financial interest (other than pursuant to plans or policies previously adopted in accordance with this Section that relate to employees generally);

(b) discharging, other than for Cause, any officer of the Company;

(c) amending or canceling the Articles of Organization of the Company or amending or waiving any provision of this Agreement;

(d) setting the terms of any issuance, sale, purchase or redemption by the Company of any Interest other than as contemplated in this Agreement;

(e) merging, consolidating or restructuring the Company;

(f) filing any petition by or on behalf of the Company seeking relief under the federal bankruptcy act or similar relief under any law or statute of the United States or any state thereof;

(g) establishing the Business Plan for each fiscal year and adopting any material changes thereto; and

(h) requiring additional Capital Contributions.

3.10 *Open Matters.*

(a) If the Members are unable to reach agreement upon any particular matter required to be determined by the Members unanimously hereunder, a Member may request, by delivery of written notice to the other Members, that the Members hold one or more informal meetings in an effort to discuss and resolve such open matter. Such meetings shall be held promptly (but in any event within ten days) following delivery of such a notice. In the event an open matter relates to the adoption of a Business Plan, the Members agree that, while such open matter remains unresolved, the business of the Company shall be operated, to the extent practicable, in accordance with the previous fiscal year's Business Plan, and consistent with the projections and objectives therein for the succeeding period.

(b) If the procedure specified in Section 3.10(a) has not led to satisfactory resolution of an open matter within 30 days after the end of the ten-day period referred to therein, then, upon a finding in good faith that failure to resolve such open matter threatens the continued commercial viability of, or will result in material injury to, the Company, (i) Member 1 may, at any time during the 30–day period (the "Notice Period") following the end of such ten-day period, require Member 2, by written notice to Member 2 during the Notice Period, to purchase Member 1's Interest, or (ii) Member 2 may, at any time during the Notice Period (but not after a notice from Member 1 hereunder) require Member 1, by written notice to Member 1 during the Notice Period, to sell its Interest to Member 2, in each case at the price and otherwise as set forth in Section 8.1(b).

(c) If neither Member 1 nor Member 2 shall have delivered a timely notice of its election to sell its Interest to Member 2, in the case of Member 1, or to purchase Member 1's Interest, in the case of Member 2, as set forth in Section 3.10(b), the open matter shall be resolved by arbitration as set forth in Section 10.12.

ARTICLE IV
MANAGEMENT AND CONDUCT OF THE BUSINESS OF THE COMPANY

4.1 *Management of the Company.*

(a) Subject to the requirements of this Agreement, the property, business and affairs of the Company shall be managed by the Members.

(b) All reasonable direct costs and expenses incurred by the Members in connection with the management and conduct of the Company's business and affairs shall be reimbursed by the Company as a Company expense.

4.2 *Duties and Liabilities of Members in Their Capacity as Managers.*

(a) The Members shall perform their management duties hereunder in good faith and with that degree of care that an ordinarily prudent person in a like position would use under similar circumstances. The Members shall be entitled to rely, in the performance of such duties, on information, opinions, reports or statements, including financial statements, in each case prepared by one or more agents or employees, counsel, public accountants or other persons employed by the Company as to matters that the Members believe to be within such person's competence.

(b) The Members shall not be personally liable for the debts, obligations or liabilities of the Company solely by reason of the performance of management duties hereunder. The Company shall indemnify and hold each Member (and, where applicable, his or its respective heirs, personal representatives, assigns, officers, partners, members, directors and shareholders) harmless from and against all Losses incurred as a result of or in connection with any act or omission by the Member, for or on behalf of the Company, in the exercise of its management duties hereunder, provided that such act or omission was consistent with its duties set forth in Section 4.2(a).

4.3 *Officers.* Subject to the requirements of Sections 3.9 and 4.5:

(a) _____ is hereby appointed President of the Company, with responsibility for managing the day-to-day business operations and affairs of the Company and supervising its employees, subject in each case to the direction, supervision and control of the Members. In general, the President shall have such powers, and shall perform such duties, as usually pertain to such office, and as from time to time may be assigned to him by the Members.

(b) _____ is hereby appointed Vice President of the Company, with such responsibilities in connection with the operation of the business as the Members may from time to time determine. In general, the Vice President shall have such powers, and shall perform such duties, as usually pertain to such office, and as from time to time may be assigned to him by the Members.

(c) The Members may also appoint from time to time such other officers as they may determine, each of whom shall have such powers, and shall perform such duties, as usually pertain to such offices and as from time to time may be assigned to such persons by the Members. Such officers need not be Members or Affiliates of Members.

(d) Each officer, including the President and Vice President, shall serve at the pleasure of the Members and may be removed or discharged at any time, with or without Cause.

(e) The Company shall indemnify each officer of the Company appointed in accordance herewith, his heirs, personal representatives and assigns, against all Losses incurred as a result of or in connection with any action, suit or proceeding, whether civil or criminal, to which he is a party by reason of the fact that he, his testator or intestate is or was an officer of the Company, except in relation to matters as to which it shall be adjudged that such officer is liable for negligence or misconduct in the performance of his duties. The expenses referred to herein shall be deemed to include (i) if any such action, suit or proceeding shall proceed to judgment, any and all costs and other expenses imposed upon such person by reason of such judgment, except in relation to matters as to which it shall be adjudged that such officer is liable for negligence or misconduct in the performance of his duties; and (ii) in the event of any settlement of any such action, suit or proceeding, all reasonable costs and other expenses of such settlement (other than any payments made to the Company itself), provided that the Members determine, either before or after such settlement, that such costs and expenses do not substantially exceed the expenses which might reasonably be incurred in conducting such litigation to a final conclusion. The foregoing rights of indemnification shall not be exclusive of any other rights to which any such officer may be entitled under any present or future law, statute, by-law, agreement, vote of the Members or otherwise.

4.4 *Business Plans*. The President shall prepare and submit to the Members for their approval, in accordance with Section 3.9, a business plan for each fiscal year of the Company (each, a "Business Plan"), not less than 45 days prior to the beginning of each such fiscal year. The Business Plan shall set forth, among other things, the Company's product development and marketing plans, budgeted capital expenditures and expense budgets. Such Business Plan shall also include a statement of long-range strategy and of short-term goals, objectives and tactics over the upcoming fiscal-year period. Each Business Plan shall be in a format similar to the preceding year's Business Plan, and shall specify quantitative and qualitative goals for the Company and relate the attainment of those goals to the Company's strategic objectives.

4.5 *Required Approvals.* The President and the other officers of the Company shall have the power, acting individually or jointly, to represent and bind the Company in all matters, in accordance with the scope of their respective duties, except that the following actions or types of transactions shall not be taken or consummated without the approval of the Members:

(a) determining significant policies regarding the marketing or provision of services offered by the Company and any material changes to previously adopted policies;

(b) except as specifically approved in the then-current Business Plan, entering into any transaction in which the Company would incur material debt, or grant, or permit the creation of, any lien, encumbrance or other security interest on any asset of the Company in an amount in excess of [$_____], or lend any money to any party, except for extensions of credit granted to customers in the ordinary course of business or advances to employees for reimbursable expenses;

(c) drawing checks on, or effecting transfers from, the Company's accounts in an amount in excess of [$_____] per check or transfer;

(d) establishing guidelines, restrictions and limits for the investment of surplus funds;

(e) retaining or terminating the retention of the Company's accountants or attorneys or making any material change with respect to the accounting policies of the Company;

(f) subject to Section 3.9(a)(iii), hiring or discharging, other than for Cause, any non-Member officer, employee or consultant;

(g) determining and adopting arrangements regarding compensation and benefits, including retirement benefits, for officers or employees generally, or for former officers or employees, and any changes thereto;

(h) subject to Section 3.9(a), except as specifically approved in the then-current Business Plan, purchasing, leasing, selling or encumbering any real estate; and

(i) undertaking any action with respect to a matter that is material to the Company and is not in the ordinary course of the Company's business and is not otherwise subject to the requirements of Section 3.9.

ARTICLE V
INTERESTS AND CAPITAL CONTRIBUTIONS

5.1 *Initial Contributions.* The Members shall make the following initial contributions to the capital of the Company, and each Member's acquisition of an Interest shall be effective on and as of the date on which such contributions have been made in full:

Member	Initial Contribution
Member 1	
Member 2	

(a) No interest shall otherwise accrue on, or on the value of, any Capital Contribution. No Member shall have the right to withdraw or to be repaid any Capital Contribution except as otherwise provided herein or by the Act.

5.2 *Percentage Interest.* For all purposes of this Agreement, the Members' Percentage Interests shall be as set forth below:

Member	Percentage Interest
Member 1	51%
Member 2	49%

5.3 *Additional Capital Contributions.* Subject to Section 3.9(h), the Members may determine that additional Capital Contributions from the Members, in proportion to their Percentage Interests or otherwise, are necessary to enable the Company to conduct its business. Within 20 days following their receipt of notice of such a determination stating the total amount of additional capital sought, the Members' shares thereof and the purpose for which such capital will be used, each Member shall contribute its share of the total amount required to the Company. If a Member fails to pay any amount required hereunder, the amount in default shall bear interest from the date of default until payment in full at an annual rate equal to the prime rate established by a bank selected by the Members, plus 5% (the "Default Rate"). In addition, if a non-defaulting Member makes an additional Capital Contribution in respect of all or any portion of any amount in default, such additional amount shall be treated as a loan to the defaulting Member and shall bear interest from the date made until repayment in full at the Default Rate. In either case, any payments or distributions payable by the Company to a defaulting Member may be retained by the Company and applied toward the amount in default, plus accrued interest, or paid to the Member making a loan to a defaulting Member in accordance herewith, in respect of such loan.

5.4 *Additional Issuance of Interests; Additional Classes of Interests.*

(a) In order to raise additional capital, acquire assets, redeem or retire debt of the Company or for any other purpose, the Company may issue Interests in addition to those issued pursuant to Section 5.1 to any Member or any other Person and may admit any such other Person to the Company as a Member, for the consideration, and on the terms and conditions, determined by the Members in accordance with Section 3.10.

(b) Subject to Section 3.9(d), the Company may issue Interests from time to time in one or more classes, or one or more series of such classes, which classes or series shall have, subject to the provisions of applicable law, such designations, preferences and relative, participating, optional or other special rights as shall be fixed by the Members, including, without limitation, with respect to: (i) the allocation of items of profit or loss to each such class or series; (ii) the right of each such class or series to share in distributions; (iii) the rights of each such class or series upon dissolution and liquidation of the Company; (iv) the price at which, and the terms and conditions upon which, each such class or series may be redeemed by the Company, if any such class or series is so redeemable; (v) the rate at which, and the terms and conditions upon which, each such class or series may be converted into another class or series of Interests; and (vi) the right of each such class or series to vote on Company matters, including matters relating to the relative rights, preferences and privileges of such class or series, if any such class or series is granted any voting rights.

5.5 *Interests*. A Member's Interest shall be personal property for all purposes. All property owned by the Company shall be deemed to be owned by the Company as an entity, and no Member shall be deemed to own any such property or any portion thereof.

5.6 *No Preemptive Rights*. Except as otherwise required or permitted by this Agreement, no Member shall have any preemptive, preferential or other right with respect to (a) additional Capital Contributions; (b) the issuance or sale of Interests; (c) the issuance of any obligations, evidences of indebtedness or securities of the Company convertible into or exchangeable for, or carrying or accompanied by any rights to receive, purchase or subscribe to, any Interests; (d) the issuance of any right of, subscription to or right to receive, or any warrant or option for the purchase of, any of the foregoing; or (e) the issuance or sale of any other interests or securities that may be issued or sold by the Company.

ARTICLE VI
CAPITAL ACCOUNTS, ALLOCATIONS AND DISTRIBUTIONS

6.1 *Capital Accounts*. The Company shall establish and maintain a capital account for each Member (a "Capital Account"), which shall have an initial balance equal to the value of such Member's initial Capital Contribution, as set forth in the books and records of the Company. A Capital Account shall be increased by the amount of any additional Capital Contributions by, and the income and gain allocated to, such Member, and shall be decreased by any losses and deductions allocated, and distributions made, to such Member pursuant to the terms of this Agreement and the requirements of applicable law. It is the intention of the Members that the Capital Accounts be maintained in accordance with Treas. Reg. Section 1.704–1(b)(2)(iv).

6.2 *Allocations of Profits and Losses.* All profits and losses of the Company, after payment or provision for payment of all expenses of the Company, shall be allocated to the Members in proportion to their Percentage Interests.

6.3 *Distributions.*

(a) The Company shall distribute its funds and other assets to the Members in accordance with their Percentage Interests. Distributions to the Members shall be made quarterly during the fiscal year, or at such other time or times as may be determined by the Members, and in such amounts as the Members determine to be appropriate.

(b) All distributions of the Company's property in kind shall be valued at its fair market value as of the date of distribution and the amount of any gain or loss that would be realized by the Company if it were to sell such property at such fair market value shall be allocated to the Members in accordance with Section 6.2.

6.4 *Limitation on Distributions.* No distribution shall be declared and paid unless, after giving effect thereto, the fair market value of the assets of the Company exceeds the Company's liabilities.

6.5 *No Right of Withdrawal.* No Member shall have the right to withdraw any portion of such Member's Capital Contributions or Capital Account except as expressly provided herein.

6.6 *Account Balances.* Notwithstanding the foregoing, at any time any Member may have a positive, negative or zero balance in its Capital Account, but no Member shall be required to pay to any Member, to the Company or to any creditor of the Company on behalf of the Company the amount of any such negative balance.

ARTICLE VII
BANKING, ACCOUNTING, BOOKS AND RECORDS, REPORTS

7.1 *Banking.* All funds of the Company shall be deposited in such bank or money market accounts as shall be established by the President with the approval of the Members. Withdrawals from and checks drawn on any such account shall be made upon the signature or signatures of the President and/or such other officers as may be designated by the Members.

7.2 *Tax Matters Partner.*

(a) Member 1 is hereby designated as the "Tax Matters Partner" of the Company under Section 6231(a)(7) of the Code. Member 1 is specifically directed and authorized to take whatever steps it deems necessary or desirable to perfect such designation, including, without limitation, filing any forms or documents with the Internal Revenue Service, and taking such other action as may from time to time be required under regulations of the United States Department of the Treasury. The Tax Matters Partner shall, upon the reasonable request of any Member, make, or refrain from making, any income or other tax elections for the Company as such Member deems necessary or advisable, including an election pursuant to Section 754 of the Code.

(b) The Tax Matters Partner shall cause to be prepared and sent to each Member (a) not less than 30 days before the due date of the Company's federal income tax return (IRS Form 1065 or any successor form thereto) an estimate of the information necessary for such Member to complete its federal and state income tax returns, and (b) on or before such due date, a copy of the Company's federal, state and local income tax or information returns for the year, together with all Schedules K–1. The Tax Matters Partner shall cause to be prepared and timely filed all tax returns and reports required to be filed for the Company in the jurisdictions in which the Company conducts business. Nothing contained herein shall prevent the Tax Matters Partner from obtaining extensions of the time for filing required reports and returns, as may be appropriate.

7.3 *Books of Accounts and Records.*

(a) There shall be maintained at the Company's principal place of business records and accounts of all operations and expenditures of the Company, including, without limitation, the following:

(i) a current list in alphabetical order of the name and mailing address of each of the Members, their respective facsimile numbers and their respective shares of profits and losses or information from which such shares can be derived;

(ii) a copy of the Articles of Organization of the Company and all amendments thereto, together with executed copies of any powers of attorney pursuant to which any such amendment has been executed;

(iii) copies of the Company's federal, state and local income tax returns and reports, if any, for the three most recent fiscal years;

(iv) copies of this Agreement, as in effect from time to time;

(v) any writings or other information with respect to each Member's obligation to make any Capital Contribution including, without limitation, the amount so contributed;

(vi) any financial statements of the Company for the three most recent fiscal years;

(vii) minutes of every annual, regular, special and court-ordered meeting of the Members; and

(viii) any written consents obtained from the Members for actions taken by the Members without a meeting.

(b) Upon reasonable advance notice, during normal business hours, any Member may, at his or its expense, inspect and copy the records described in Section 7.4(a) for any purpose reasonably related to his Interest.

7.4 *Reports to Members.* Within 90 days after the end of each fiscal year and within 45 days after the end of each of the first three fiscal quarters thereof, the President of the Company shall cause to be prepared and mailed to each Member financial statements of the Company, prepared in accordance with generally acceptable accounting principles consistently applied, which in the case of the Company's annual financial statements shall be certified by the Company's independent auditors, setting forth as of the end of such fiscal year or quarter, and comparable prior year periods:

(a) the assets and liabilities of the Company;

(b) the results of operations of the Company for such fiscal year or quarter and year to date, stated in reasonable detail;

(c) statements of cash flow, in reasonable detail, of the Company for such fiscal year or quarter and year to date;

(d) changes in the Members' respective Capital Accounts for such fiscal year or quarter and year to date, and the balance of each Member's closing Capital Account; and

(e) a schedule detailing transactions with Affiliates of any Member or in which any such Affiliate or any Member or executive officer has a significant interest, and any other information that a Member may reasonably request.

ARTICLE VIII
WITHDRAWAL OF MEMBERS, TRANSFERS OF INTERESTS

8.1 *Withdrawal by Members.*

(a) No Member may voluntarily withdraw or resign from the Company or otherwise voluntarily dissolve (each such event being hereinafter referred to as a "Withdrawal") without the consent of the other Members, provided that Member 1 may withdraw without such consent as a result of a sale of its Interest to Member 2 as contemplated by Section 3.10(b).

(b) In the event of a Withdrawal as permitted by Section 8.1(a), or if a Member dies, becomes incapacitated, is adjudged bankrupt, incompetent or otherwise involuntarily dissolves, the Company shall redeem the Interest of the withdrawn Member at a price equal to its fair market value, determined as follows, and payable in full within [_____] after such price has been so determined. The Members shall meet promptly to negotiate the price of the Interest, based on the value of the Company as a going concern, including its goodwill. If the Members cannot agree on the price within 30 days after the Company receives notice of the Withdrawal or an event set forth in Section 8.1(b), the price of the withdrawn Member's Interest shall be the appraised value thereof, determined as of the date on which the Withdrawal or such other event occurred, by appraisers designated by each of the Company and the withdrawn Member or his or its successor-in-interest within ten days following the date on which the Company and the withdrawn Member or his or its successor-in-interest acknowledge that they cannot otherwise agree on the price. For the purpose of making the appraisal, the appraisers shall be given access to, and may review, subject to appropriate confidentiality arrangements, all books and records and information available to the Company, and shall take into account whether the interest to be valued is a minority or majority interest. The appraisers shall prepare and submit their written appraisals to the Company and to the withdrawn Member or his or its successor-in-interest. If the two appraisers agree upon the appraised value, they shall jointly render a written report thereof. If they have not so agreed, within 15 days following their appointment, they shall appoint a third appraiser, who shall appraise the Company's assets, determine the appraised value and render a written report thereof. The two appraisers' determination (or the determination of the third appraiser, if required hereunder) shall be conclusive and binding on the parties. Each party shall pay the fees and expenses of the appraiser designated by that party and shall bear one-half of the fees and expenses of the third appraiser.

8.2 *Transfers of Interests.*

(a) Except as provided in this Section 8.2, no Member may Transfer all or any portion of, or any financial or other rights in or to, its Interest without the prior written consent of the other Members.

(b) The restriction set forth in Section 8.2(a) shall not apply to (i) the Transfer of an Interest or any right therein to another Member; (ii) subject to approval by the Members as set forth in Section 3.9, the issuance of an Interest directly by the Company to a new Member; or (iii) the Transfer of an Interest of a bankrupt, dissolved or incompetent Member to his or its successor-in-interest.

8.3 *Admission of Members.* An assignee of an Interest or portion thereof as permitted by Section 8.2 shall become a Member only upon the fulfillment of all of the following conditions (except that the requirement set forth in Section 8.3(a) shall not apply to transfers pursuant to Section 8.2(b)):

(a) all of the Members, other than the Member seeking to assign the Interest, shall have consented in writing to the substitution of the assignee as a Member;

(b) the assignee shall have paid to the Company all costs and expenses incurred in connection with such assignee's substitution as a Member, including, without limitation, all costs and expenses incurred in amending this Agreement; and

(c) the assignee shall have executed a counterpart of this Agreement and such other documents as the Company shall reasonably request as necessary or desirable to effect the substitution or addition of the assignee as a Member and to assure compliance with all applicable state and federal laws, including, without limitation, securities laws.

ARTICLE IX
DISSOLUTION OF COMPANY

9.1 *Dissolution.* The Company will be dissolved only upon the unanimous agreement of the Members to do so.

9.2 *Distribution upon Dissolution.* Upon the dissolution of the Company as set forth in Section 9.1, the remaining Members, acting together, shall proceed to liquidate the Company and apply the proceeds of such liquidation in the following order of priority:

(a) first, to the payment of debts and liabilities of the Company and the expenses of liquidation;

(b) second, to the establishment of any reserve which the Members may deem reasonably necessary for any contingent or unforeseen liabilities or obligations of the Company, which reserve may be paid over to any acceptable party as escrow agent to be held for disbursement in payment of any of the aforementioned liabilities and, at the expiration of such period as shall be deemed advisable by the Members, for distribution of the balance, in the manner provided in this Section 9.2;

(c) third, to all Members with positive Capital Account balances (after giving effect to Section 9.3 hereof) in proportion to such Capital Account balances, until such balances are reduced to zero; and

(d) finally, any remaining proceeds shall be distributed to the Members in accordance with their respective Percentage Interests.

9.3 *Distributions in Cash or in Kind.* Upon dissolution, the Members may, in their sole discretion (a) liquidate all or a portion of the Company assets and apply the proceeds of such liquidation as set forth in Section 9.2, or (b) determine the value of any Company assets not sold or otherwise disposed of (including, if they so determine, hiring an appraiser, in which event the cost of such appraisal shall be considered a debt of the Company), allocate any unrealized gain or loss based on such value to the Members' accounts as though the properties in question had been sold on the date of distribution and, after giving effect to any such adjustment, distribute said assets in the proportions set forth in Section 9.2; provided that the Members will in good faith attempt to liquidate sufficient Company assets to satisfy in cash the debts and liabilities (foreseen, contingent or otherwise) set forth in Section 9.2. Notwithstanding anything contained herein to the contrary, upon dissolution, all right, title and interest in and to the name "_____" held by the Company at such time shall be distributed in kind to Member 1.

9.4 *Time for Liquidation.* A reasonable time period shall be allowed for the orderly liquidation of the assets of the Company and the discharge of liabilities to creditors so as to enable the Members to minimize the losses attendant upon such liquidation.

9.5 *Termination.* Upon compliance with the foregoing distribution plan, the Company shall cease to be such and the Members, their successors or other representatives shall execute, acknowledge and cause to be filed a certificate of cancellation of the Company.

9.6 *Members Not Personally Liable for Return of Capital Contributions.* No Member shall be personally liable for the return of the Capital Contributions of any Member and such return shall be made solely from available Company assets, if any, and each Member hereby waives any and all claims he or it may have against the other Members in this regard.

ARTICLE X

MISCELLANEOUS PROVISIONS

10.1 *Amendments.* The terms and provisions of this Agreement may be modified or amended at any time and from time to time only with the written consent of all the Members.

10.2 *Notices.* All notices, consents and other communications given under this Agreement shall be in writing and shall be deemed to have been duly given (a) when delivered by hand or by Federal Express or a similar overnight courier to, (b) five days after being deposited with the United States Post Office enclosed in postage prepaid registered or certified envelope addressed to, or (c) when successfully transmitted by facsimile (with a confirming copy of such communication to be sent as provided in (a) or (b) above) to, the party for whom intended, at the address or facsimile number for such party set forth below, or to such other address or facsimile number as may be furnished by such party by notice in the manner provided herein; provided, however, that any notice of change of address or facsimile number shall be effective only upon receipt.

If to Member 1:

Attention:

Facsimile No.:

With a copy to:

Attention:
Facsimile No.:
If to Member 2:

Attention:
Facsimile No.:
With a copy to:

Attention:
Facsimile No.:

10.3 *Amendment by Agreement of Merger.* Notwithstanding anything to the contrary contained in this Agreement, in accordance with Section 1004(e) of the Act, an agreement of merger or consolidation approved by the Members as required by this Agreement may effect (a) amendments to this Agreement contained in the agreement of merger or consolidation or necessitated thereby, or (b) the adoption of a new operating agreement for the Company if it is the surviving or resulting entity, in each case without further action by the Members.

10.4 *Counterparts.* This Agreement may be executed in any number of counterparts, each of which shall be considered an original.

10.5 *Construction.* Headings used in this Agreement are for convenience only and shall not be used in the interpretation of this Agreement. References herein to Articles and Sections are to the articles and sections of this Agreement, unless otherwise specified. As used herein, the singular includes the plural.

10.6 *Successors and Assigns.* This Agreement shall inure to the benefit of, and be binding upon, the parties and their respective heirs, executors, administrators, successors and permitted assigns.

10.7 *Severability.* Every provision of this Agreement is intended to be severable. If any term or provision hereof is illegal or invalid for any reason whatsoever such term or provision shall be enforced to the maximum extent permitted by law and, in any event, such illegality or invalidity shall not affect the validity of the remainder of the Agreement.

10.8 *Non-Waiver.* No provision of this Agreement shall be deemed to have been waived unless such waiver is in writing and delivered to the party claiming such waiver. No waiver shall be deemed to be a waiver of any other or further obligation or liability of the party or parties in whose favor the waiver was given.

10.9 *Applicable Law.* This Agreement and the rights and obligations of the parties hereto shall be interpreted and enforced in accordance with, and governed by, the laws of the State of New York applicable to agreements made and fully to be performed in that State, and specifically, the Act.

10.10 *Entirety of Agreement.* This Agreement sets forth the entire understanding of the parties with respect to its subject matter, and merges and supersedes all prior and contemporaneous understandings, representations and warranties with respect to its subject matter. Except as expressly set forth in this Agreement, neither of the parties hereto makes any representation or warranty to any other party.

10.11 *Confidentiality.* Each of the Members understands and acknowledges that (a) as a result of the commencement and operation of the Company's business and the transactions contemplated in this Agreement, each of them may become informed of, and have access to, confidential information regarding customers, business plans, inventions, designs, trade secrets, technical information, plans and other information respecting the Company's business (collectively, "Confidential Information") and (b) all such Confidential Information shall be held by him or it in trust and shall not be disclosed to anyone other than their respective directors, officers, agents, employees and representatives who have a need to know, and all of whom have been made aware of their obligations to maintain confidentiality hereunder, nor shall such Confidential Information be used for any purpose that is not consistent with the Company's benefit. The Members' obligations under this Section shall survive any Withdrawal or any other Withdrawal of a Member or any dissolution or termination of the Company.

10.12 *Arbitration.* Any controversy or claim arising out of or relating to this Agreement shall be finally resolved by arbitration pursuant to the Commercial Arbitration Rules of the American Arbitration Association. Any such arbitration shall take place in _____, New York, before a single arbitrator chosen in accordance with such Rules. The parties further agree that (a) the arbitrator shall be empowered to include arbitration costs and attorneys' fees in the award to the prevailing party in any such proceeding and (b) the award in such proceeding shall be final and binding on the parties. Judgment on the arbitrator's award may be entered in any court having the requisite jurisdiction. Nothing in this Agreement shall require the arbitration of disputes between the parties that arise from actions, suits or proceedings instituted by third parties.

IN WITNESS WHEREOF, the undersigned have duly executed this Agreement as of the day and year first above written.

Member 1 _____

Member 2 _____

§ 2.113 Forms—Registration as LLP

CERTIFICATE OF REGISTRATION
OF
_____

Under Section 121–1500(a) of the Partnership Law

FIRST: The name of the registered limited liability partnership is: _____.

SECOND: The address of the principal office of the partnership without limited partners is: _____.

THIRD: The profession to be practiced by such partnership without limited partners is: _____, and such partnership without limited partners is eligible to register as a "registered limited liability partnership" pursuant to 121–1500(a) of the Partnership Law.

FOURTH: The Secretary of State is designated as agent of the registered limited liability partnership upon whom process against it may be served. The post office address within or without this state to which the Secretary of State shall mail a copy of any process served against the registered limited liability partnership served upon him or her is: _____ .

FIFTH: The partnership without limited partners is filing a registration for status as a registered limited liability partnership.

_____   _____
(signature)   (name and capacity of signer)

Library References:

West's Key No. Digests, Partnership ⚖⇒352.

§ 2.114 Forms—Certificate of Limited Partnership

CERTIFICATE OF LIMITED PARTNERSHIP
OF
_____

Under Section 121–201 of the Revised Limited Partnership Act

1. The name of the limited partnership is _____ (the "Limited Partnership").

2. The office of the Limited Partnership is to be located in _____ County.

3. The Secretary of State is designated as agent of the Limited Partnership upon whom process against it may be served. The post office address to which the Secretary of State shall mail a copy of any process against the Limited Partnership served on him is _____.

4. [If the Limited Partnership is designating a registered agent in addition to the Secretary of State, add: _____, whose address is _____, is to be the registered agent of the Limited Partnership upon whom process against the Limited Partnership may be served.]

5. The name and the [business] [residence] street address of each general partner is:

Name   Address
_____   _____
_____   _____

6. The latest date upon which the Limited Partnership is to dissolve is _____, unless sooner terminated at a prior time in accordance with the Limited Partnership Agreement.

[7. Any other matters which the general partners determine to include.]

[8. If the Certificate is to become effective not more than 60 days after the filing, state: The effective date of the Limited Partnership shall be _____.]

IN WITNESS WHEREOF, the undersigned, constituting all of the general partners of the Limited Partnership, have executed this Certificate of Limited Partnership this ___ day of ___, 19__, and affirm the statements contained herein as true under penalties of perjury.

_____
(Names and Signatures of General Partners)

Library References:
West's Key No. Digests, Partnership ⊆352.

§ 2.115 Forms—Limited Partnership Agreement

The following form deals with a simple, two-partner limited partnership formed to acquire and operate real property.

PARTNERSHIP AGREEMENT
OF
_____, L.P.

THIS AGREEMENT, dated as of the _____ day of _____, 199_, is made by and between _____, as general partner (the "General Partner"), and _____, as limited partner (the "Limited Partner") (collectively the "Partners" and each individually a "Partner").

W I T N E S S E T H :

WHEREAS, the Partnership is being formed for the purpose of acquiring, holding, maintaining, operating, financing and otherwise dealing with real property located at _____ (the "Property"); and

WHEREAS, the Partners wish to form a partnership to accomplish the foregoing;

NOW, THEREFORE, in consideration of the mutual agreements herein contained and other good and valuable consideration, the Partners hereby agree as follows:

ARTICLE I
FORMATION, NAME, PURPOSE AND TERM

1.1 *Formation, Name and Office.*

(a) The Partners hereby establish a limited partnership (the "Partnership") to be conducted under the name of _____, L.P., pursuant to the Revised Limited Partnership Act of New York (as it may hereafter be amended from time to time, the "Act").

(b) A Partner's interest in the Partnership shall be personal property for all purposes. All real and other property owned by the Partnership shall be deemed owned by the Partnership as an entity, and no Partner shall be deemed to own any of such property.

(c) For the purposes of this Agreement only, the principal office of the Partnership shall be located at _____ .

1.2 *Purposes.* The purposes of the Partnership are to acquire, hold, maintain, operate, finance, refinance and, ultimately, dispose of, the Property. The Partnership shall not engage in any other business or activity without the prior written consent of both Partners.

1.3 *Term.* The term of the Partnership shall commence on the date hereof and shall continue until _____ , unless sooner terminated as hereinafter provided.

ARTICLE II
CAPITAL CONTRIBUTIONS

2.1 *Contributions.* All capital contributions shall be made in cash, as follows:

General Partner	$1
Limited Partner	99

2.2 *Capital Accounts.* The Partnership shall establish and maintain capital accounts for each Partner, which shall have initial balances equal to such Partner's capital contribution. A Partner's capital account shall be increased by the amount of any additional capital contributions by such Partner and by the income and gain allocated to such Partner and shall be decreased by any losses and deductions allocated to or distributions made to such Partner pursuant to the terms of this Agreement. It is the intention of the Partners that capital accounts be maintained strictly in accordance with Treas. Reg. § 1.704–1(b)(2)(iv).

ARTICLE III
DISTRIBUTIONS; PROFITS AND LOSSES

All distributions and all items of income, gain, loss and deduction shall be allocated 1% to the General Partner and 99% to the Limited Partner.

ARTICLE IV
MANAGEMENT

The General Partner shall be responsible for the management and conduct of the Partnership business.

ARTICLE V
TERMINATION

5.1 *Events of Termination.* The Partnership shall be dissolved and its affairs wound up in the event that:

(a) the term of the Partnership expires;

(b) [the Property is sold or otherwise disposed of in one or more transactions;]

(c) the Partners agree to terminate the Partnership; or

(d) either of the following events occurs:

(i) the General Partner makes an assignment for the benefit of creditors, admits in writing that it is unable to pay its debts as they become due, files a voluntary petition in bankruptcy or for an adjudication that it is a bankrupt or insolvent, files any petition or answer seeking for itself any reorganization, arrangement, composition, readjustment, liquidation, dissolution or similar relief under any present or future statute, law or regulation, files any answer admitting (or failing to contest) the material allegations of a petition filed against it in any such proceeding, seeks or consents to or acquiesces in the judicial appointment of any trustee, fiscal agent, receiver or liquidator of it or of all or any substantial part of its properties, or takes any other action looking to its dissolution or liquidation; or

(ii) within 45 days after the commencement of any action against the General Partner seeking any bankruptcy, reorganization, arrangement, composition, readjustment, liquidation, dissolution or similar relief under any present or future statute, law or regulation, such action is not dismissed, or all orders or proceedings thereunder affecting its operations are not stayed, provided the stay of any such order or proceeding thereafter is not set aside, or, within 45 days after the judicial appointment without the consent or acquiescence of the General Partner of any trustee, fiscal agent, receiver or liquidator of it or of all or any substantial part of its properties, such appointment is not vacated.

Notwithstanding the provisions of this Section 5.1(d), the voluntary liquidation or reorganization of a Partner, provided that such liquidation or reorganization is not entered into because of insolvency or bankruptcy, shall not require the termination and dissolution of the Partnership.

5.2 *Voluntary Withdrawal Prohibited.* No Partner shall have the right to withdraw from the Partnership, nor shall either Partner have the right to withdraw any part of its contributions to the capital of the Partnership, except in accordance with the provisions of this Agreement.

5.3 *Winding Up.* Upon dissolution of the Partnership, the Partnership shall wind up its affairs promptly and in accordance with the directions of the General Partner (or of such person as may be designated by the Limited Partner, if the event of termination is an event described in Section 5.1(d) with respect to the General Partner) (the person directing the winding up hereafter referred to as the "Liquidator"). The assets of the Partnership shall be sold within a reasonable period of time to the extent necessary to pay or provide for the debts and liabilities of the Partnership and the expenses of dissolution and liquidation, and may be sold to the extent deemed commercially feasible by the Liquidator and all assets of the Partnership shall be applied and distributed as provided in Section 5.4.

5.4 *Distributions.* The proceeds of any dissolution of the Partnership shall be distributed in the following order of priority (to the extent that such order of priority is consistent with the laws of the State of New York):

(a) first, to the payment of the debts and liabilities of the Partnership and the expenses of dissolution and liquidation;

(b) then, to the establishment of any reserves which the Liquidator shall deem reasonably necessary for the payment of such other debts and liabilities of the Partnership (contingent or otherwise) as are specified by the Liquidator, and such reserves shall be held by a bank or trust company selected by the Liquidator, as escrow holder, to be disbursed as directed by the Liquidator in payment of any such specified debts and liabilities or, at the expiration of such period as the Liquidator may deem advisable, to be distributed in the manner hereinafter provided; and

(c) then, to the Partners as set forth in Article III hereof.

5.5 *Statements on Winding Up.* Upon termination of the Partnership, a statement shall be prepared by the Partnership's independent public accountants, which shall set forth the assets and liabilities of the Partnership as of the date of termination.

ARTICLE VI
PARTITION

Unless the Partners agree as to the division of an asset, they shall have no right of partition with respect to any assets of the Partnership, now existing or hereafter acquired.

ARTICLE VII
BANK ACCOUNTS AND REPORTS

7.1 *Bank Accounts.* All Partnership accounts shall be maintained in a bank which shall be a member of the Federal Deposit Insurance Corporation. All income, receipts and amounts deposited by the Partnership in such accounts shall be and remain the property of the Partnership and shall be received, held and disbursed only for the purposes herein specified.

7.2 *Reports.* The General Partner shall have the authority, responsibility and obligation to cause to be prepared, with the assistance of the Partnership's accountants, any reports or returns required to be filed for and on behalf of the Partnership. The General Partner shall prepare, or cause to be prepared, quarterly statements of the Partnership's operations and shall deliver them to the Limited Partner within 30 days after the end of each calendar quarter. All charges of the Partnership's accountants shall be borne by the Partnership.

ARTICLE VIII
OTHER INTERESTS OF THE PARTNERS

Either Partner, as well as any of his or its respective affiliates and partners, may engage in and possess an interest in other business ventures of every nature and description, whether or not in competition with or of a similar nature to the business of the Partnership, independently or with others, and neither the Partnership nor the other Partner shall have any rights in and to such independent ventures or the profits, losses, income or distributions relating thereto. Each Partner shall promptly notify the other in writing should any conflict of interest arise.

ARTICLE IX
MISCELLANEOUS

9.1 *Liability.*

(a) The Partners agree that the Partnership extends, and is limited, to only the rights and obligations provided in this Agreement, and nothing herein shall be construed to constitute any Partner the agent or partner of the other Partner in the conduct of his or its respective businesses or activities.

(b) Neither Partner shall be liable to the Partnership or to the other Partner for any act or omission of such Partner, except to the extent that such act or omission results from his or its gross negligence or fraud.

9.2 *Indemnification.*

(a) Each Partner shall indemnify and hold the other Partner and, where applicable, its respective officers, directors and shareholders, harmless from and against all claims, demands, losses or damages, including, without limitation, reasonable attorneys' fees (collectively, "Losses") which shall or may arise by reason of the indemnifying party's breach (directly or by agents or other representatives) of a provision of this Agreement or of any action outside the scope of this Agreement.

(b) Each Partner shall be indemnified and held harmless by the Partnership from and against any Losses incurred by such Partner by reason of any act or omission performed or omitted by him or it, except to the extent that such act or omission is contrary to this Agreement or results from such Partner's gross negligence or fraud.

(c) Each party to be indemnified under Section 9.2(a) or 9.2(b) hereof shall give each indemnifying party notice of any claim, demand, loss or damage subject to indemnification within thirty (30) days after he or it has received actual notice thereof, and the indemnifying party shall be entitled to participate in or direct the defense of such action, provided that he or it employs counsel reasonably satisfactory to the indemnified party. An indemnifying party shall not be liable to an indemnified party in respect of settlements effected by the indemnified party without the written consent of the indemnifying party.

9.3 *Further Assurances.* The Partners agree to execute such further instruments and documents, and to take such further actions, as may be necessary in order to implement the intent and purposes of the provisions of this Agreement.

9.4 *Integration.* This Agreement constitutes the entire agreement between the parties with respect to the subject matter hereof, and no alteration or modification hereof shall be binding unless in writing and signed by both Partners.

9.5 *Benefits and Obligations.* Except as otherwise specifically provided herein, this Agreement shall be binding upon and shall inure to the benefit of each of the Partners and their respective successors and assigns, and no other person shall have any legal or equitable right, remedy or claim under or in respect of this Agreement.

9.6 *Severability.* If any provision of this Agreement or portion thereof, or the application thereof to any person or circumstance, is held to be invalid or unenforceable, then the remainder of this Agreement, or the application of the provision or portion thereof to other persons or circumstances, shall not be affected thereby, provided that if any provision or portion thereof, or its application, is held to be invalid or unenforceable, then a suitable or equitable provision shall be substituted therefor in order to carry out, so far as may be valid or enforceable, the intent and purpose of the invalid or unenforceable provision or portion thereof.

9.7 *Enforcement of Provisions.* The failure to enforce any provision of this Agreement or to require performance by a party of any provision hereof shall in no way be construed to be a waiver of such provision or to affect either the validity of this Agreement, or any part hereof, or the right of any party thereafter to enforce each and every provision in accordance with the terms of this Agreement.

9.8 *Applicable Law.* This Agreement shall be construed and enforced in accordance with the laws of the State of New York applicable to agreements made and fully to be performed therein by residents thereof, and specifically, the Act.

9.9 *Counterparts.* This Agreement may be executed in counterparts, each of which shall be an original, but all of which together shall constitute one instrument.

9.10 *Headings.* The headings in this Agreement are solely for convenience of reference and shall not affect its interpretation.

IN WITNESS WHEREOF, the parties have caused this Agreement to be executed as of the day and year first above written.

[General Partner]

By: _____
    Name:
    Title:

[Limited Partner]

By:_____
    Name:
    Title:

Chapter 3

MUNICIPAL LAW

by
Ralph W. Bandel

Table of Sections

3.1 Scope Note.
3.2 Strategy.
3.3 Municipal Corporations.
3.4 ____ Creation.
3.5 ____ Consolidation, Annexation and Dissolution.
3.6 ____ ____ Annexation Checklist.
3.7 Powers of Municipal Corporations.
3.8 ____ Governmental v. Proprietary Powers.
3.9 ____ Police Powers.
3.10 Legislative Enactments.
3.11 ____ Resolutions.
3.12 ____ Ordinances.
3.13 ____ Rules and Regulations.
3.14 ____ Local Laws.
3.15 ____ Referendum Requirements.
3.16 Acquisition and Disposition of Property.
3.17 Officers and Employees.
3.18 ____ Qualifications.
3.19 ____ Terms.
3.20 ____ Removal.
3.21 ____ Collective Bargaining.
3.22 ____ Conflicts of Interest.
3.23 ____ ____ Checklist.
3.24 Contracts.
3.25 ____ Competitive Bidding.
3.26 Municipal Finance.
3.27 ____ Municipal Borrowing.
3.28 Public Meetings.
3.29 Access to Records.
3.30 Tort Claims Against Municipalities.
3.31 ____ Checklist.
3.32 Challenges to Governmental Determinations.
3.33 Special Purpose Units of Government.
3.34 ____ Industrial Development Agencies.
3.35 ____ Public Authorities.
3.36 Forms.

3.37 ___ Notice of Claim.
3.38 ___ Verified Complaint in Tort Action.

WESTLAW Electronic Research

See WESTLAW Electronic Research Guide preceding the Summary of Contents.

§ 3.1 Scope Note

The practice of municipal law in the State of New York is complicated by a myriad of different governmental entities having overlapping geographical boundaries and overlapping responsibility for the performance of governmental functions. In addition to counties, cities and towns, which are the basic units of local government found most commonly in other states, municipal lawyers in New York must also deal with villages, various special purpose districts created to provide services ranging from ambulance protection to street lighting, industrial development agencies, public authorities and various other special purposes governmental entities.

This chapter concentrates on the basics of municipal law that any practitioner involved either as counsel for a municipality or counsel for a client in proceedings before or against a municipal board or agency should be familiar with. For the purposes of this chapter, the terms "municipality" and "municipal corporation" will be used to apply collectively to counties, cities, towns and villages.

First, the manner of creation, consolidation, annexation and dissolution of municipal corporations is discussed in Sections 3.4 through 3.6. The powers of municipalities, including separate discussions of the distinction between governmental and proprietary powers and police powers, are covered in Sections 3.7 through 3.9.

The chapter goes on to discuss the powers of municipal corporations, the manner in which municipalities exercise their powers with a review of the various types of legislative enactments, and the procedural requirements for those enactments in Sections 3.11 through 3.15. In Section 3.16 the acquisition and disposition of property is discussed.

The next area covered relates to public officers and employees. Qualifications, terms of office, removal procedures, conflicts of interest and collective bargaining are discussed in Sections 3.16 through 3.23.

Municipal contracts, with separate sections on general requirements for contracts and competitive bidding, are discussed in Sections 3.24 and 3.25. Section 3.26 covers municipal budget and tax levying procedures and Section 3.27 covers municipal borrowing.

So-called "open government issues" including public meetings and access to records are discussed in Sections 3.28 and 3.29. This is followed by a discussion of the procedures for bringing tort claims against municipalities in Sections 3.30 through 3.31. The procedures for challenging governmental determinations are covered in Section 3.32.

The final topic covered in Sections 3.33 through 3.35 is special purpose units of government including industrial development agencies and public authorities.

The chapter concludes with forms for notice of claim against a municipality and a complaint in a typical tort action for damages sustained as a result of a defective sidewalk or road in Sections 3.36 through 3.38.

§ 3.2 Strategy

Given the large number of municipalities and other governmental entities in New York State, most lawyers are likely at some point in their career to represent either a private client in a matter over which a municipality or agency[1] has jurisdiction or represent a municipality in some capacity. Because different types of municipalities are governed by different statutes, the first step in most representations involving a municipality is to determine the type of municipality with which you are dealing and to identify the applicable law.

While this may appear to be a fairly obvious and simple first step for an attorney handling any matter, in transactions involving municipalities it frequently is not as simple as it first appears. In the first instance, each type of municipality is governed by a specific consolidated law.[2] Generally, this is the first body of law that counsel must be familiar with once the type of municipality you are dealing with has been identified. There also are numerous statutes which apply generally to all municipalities, but which treat different types of municipalities differently.[3] In addition to state statutes, municipal corporations also have the power to adopt local laws—so-called home rule power.[4] Furthermore, many important matters such as a municipality's zoning and land use regulations are contained exclusively in local codes.[5]

The collective body of local laws adopted by a municipality is generally contained in a municipal code of laws, rules and regulations or, in the case of cities, a city charter. Municipal codes and city charters are on file and may be reviewed in the office of the municipal clerk. In

§ 3.2

1. *See also*, Chapter 4 "Administrative Law," *infra* for discussion of agency practice.

2. *See, e.g.*, County Law; General City Law; Second Class Cities Law; Town Law; and Village Law.

3. *See, e.g.*, General Municipal Law; Public Officers Law; Highway Law; Local Finance Law; and Environmental Conservation Law.

4. *See* Municipal Home Rule Law. *See infra*, § 3.14 for a detailed discussion of local laws.

5. *See* Chapter 16 "Land Use," *infra* for a more detailed discussion of zoning and land use regulations.

matters involving cities, review of the charter is especially important, because most of the applicable substantive and procedural law will be found in the charter rather than in any state statute.

In addition to being aware of applicable state and local legislation, as well as any relevant case law, many matters involving municipalities also require a sensitivity for local politics. At a minimum, attorneys should be familiar with the general political climate in the municipality. For example, is the municipality essentially controlled by one party or is there a close split between the parties on the governing board? Some governing boards may be more prone to respond to political considerations than others and the attorney should be conscious of such factors in order to represent his or her client most effectively.

Timing is another consideration to be aware of when representing a private client in a matter with a municipality. The axiom that the wheels of government grind slowly is very true in most instances. For example, where a particular action requires a resolution of the governing board or other board of a municipality, it is important to remember that the board may meet on a bi-weekly or, in some cases, only on a monthly basis. Many actions, such as approval of subdivisions, municipal borrowing and the granting of permits for various types of facilities, must be preceded by public hearings and/or mandatory or permissive referenda.[6] These procedural requirements can take a significant amount of time to complete and the attorney must be prepared to advise his client with regard to both the time and expense of completing any applicable municipal approval process.

§ 3.3 Municipal Corporations

Corporations in New York State are classified either as public, not for profit or for profit.[1] Public corporations include municipal corporations, district corporations or public benefit corporations.[2] Municipal corporations are defined to include a county, city, town, village and school district.[3] Municipal corporations have been distinguished from other public corporations by their dual purposes of (1) assisting in the government of the state as an agent or arm of the State and (2) regulating and administering the local affairs of the area for which they have been incorporated.[4]

The terms municipal corporation, political subdivision and local

---

6. See infra, § 3.15 relative to referendum requirements.

§ 3.3
1. General Construction Law § 65(a).
2. General Construction Law § 65(b).
3. General Construction Law § 66(2); cf. General Municipal Law § 2, which defines a municipal corporation to include only a county, town, city or village.

4. Vilas v. Manila, 220 U.S. 345, 31 S.Ct. 416, 55 L.Ed. 491 (1911); see also Rhyne, *The Law of Local Government Operations* § 1.3 (1980).

government are often used interchangeably to mean the same thing.[5] Indeed, the New York State Constitution refers to local governments rather than municipal corporations or political subdivisions and recognizes four units of local government: counties, cities, towns and villages.[6]

The New York State Constitution provides that the Legislature "shall provide for the creation and organization of local governments in such manner as shall secure to them the rights, powers, privileges and immunities granted to them by this Constitution."[7] Because they are created by the State, the State has the power to prescribe the manner and the method by which municipal corporations may be created, enlarged, contracted or dissolved.[8]

§ 3.4 Municipal Corporations—Creation

Historically, there has been a distinction between counties and towns, on the one hand, and cities and villages on the other. Towns and counties are involuntary subdivisions of the State created for the most part for convenience and more expeditious state administration, while cities and villages are corporations organized by voluntary action of local inhabitants and limited by statute or charter.[1]

Counties are made up of towns and, in some cases, also contain cities.[2] Villages are generally included within the boundaries of towns,[3] while cities are separate geographic entities. Thus, all individuals residing in the State have a county residence, and also either a city residence or a town residence. Town residents may also have a village residence.

New villages may be incorporated under the provisions of Article 2 of the Village Law. Basically, these provisions require a petition signed by the requisite number of residents or property owners,[4] a public hearing on the petition,[5] and an election on the proposed incorporation.[6]

---

5. CAVEAT: Because these terms are often used interchangeably, and because they are not always defined the same way, even within the same statute, it is vitally important to determine the definition of those terms as used in each particular statute in order to determine whether the entity in question is covered by that statute. For example, for purposes of the urban renewal provisions in Article 15 of the General Municipal Law, a municipality does *not* include a county. See General Municipal Law § 502(2).

6. New York State Constitution Art. IX, § 3(d)(2).

7. New York State Constitution Art. IX, § 2(a).

8. In re Village of Spring Valley, 189 Misc. 324, 71 N.Y.S.2d 848 (Sup.Ct., Rockland County, 1947), aff'd 273 App.Div. 789, 75 N.Y.S.2d 664 (2d Dep't 1947). *See infra*, § 3.7.

§ 3.4

1. Curtis v. Eide, 19 A.D.2d 507, 244 N.Y.S.2d 330 (1st Dep't 1963).

2. Except for the five counties of Kings, Queens, New York, Richmond and Bronx, which together compromise New York City. The discussions of and references to counties in this chapter apply only to counties outside of New York City.

3. There are also several villages, including Mount Kisco, East Rochester and Scarsdale, which embrace the entire area of a town. These coterminous town-villages may be created pursuant to Article 17 of the Village Law.

4. Village Law § 2–202(1).

5. Village Law § 2–204.

6. Village Law § 2–212.

There are no provisions of law authorizing the creation of additional counties, cities or towns. Of course, the State Legislature retains power to provide for such creation, either by general or special legislation.[7]

Library References:

West's Key No. Digests, Municipal Corporations ⚖3–14.

§ 3.5 Municipal Corporations—Consolidation, Annexation and Dissolution

There are specific statutory provisions governing the manner in which two or more towns, or two or more villages, may consolidate with one another.[1] Pursuant to these provisions, two or more towns, or two or more villages with adjoining boundary lines, may be consolidated to form a single town or village. In general, consolidation requires the submission of a proposition and the approval of the proposition by a majority of the registered voters in each of the towns or villages which are proposed to be consolidated.[2]

There are no provisions of law authorizing two or more counties or two or more cities to consolidate with one another to form a single county or city. However, there are provisions prescribing procedures by which territory in one or more municipalities adjoining one or more other municipalities may be annexed to one another.[3]

Annexation proceedings must be commenced by a properly authenticated petition for annexation which must: (1) describe the territory involved; (2) state the approximate number of inhabitants in the territory; and (3) be signed either by at least 20% of the qualified voters or by the owners of a majority in assessed value of the real property in the territory proposed to be annexed.[4] In addition, the signatures on the petition must be authenticated and a certificate of the assessor or board of elections, whichever is applicable, must be attached to the petition.[5]

The petition must be submitted to the governing board or boards of the affected municipal corporation or corporations in which the proposed territory being annexed is situated. A certified copy or copies of the

---

7. See In re Village of Spring Valley, 189 Misc. 324, 71 N.Y.S.2d 848 (Sup.Ct., Rockland County, 1947), aff'd 273 App.Div. 789, 75 N.Y.S.2d 664 (2d Dep't 1947).

§ 3.5

1. See Town Law Art. 5–B, §§ 79–b et seq.; Village Law § 18–1806.
2. Town Law § 79–d; Village Law § 18–1806.
3. See General Municipal Law Art. 17, §§ 700 et seq.

CAVEAT: The term annexation does not include creation or dissolution of a municipality or consolidation of two or more counties, two or more cities, two or more towns or two or more villages and, therefore, the provisions of Article 17 may not be used for these purposes. General Municipal Law § 701(1).

4. General Municipal Law § 703(1).
5. General Municipal Law § 703(2), (3).

petition must also be submitted to the governing board or boards of the municipality to which the territory is proposed to be annexed.[6]

Following submission of a petition, the affected governing board or boards are required to hold a joint public hearing on the petition. Notice of the hearing must be given within 20 days after receipt of the petition, stating that a petition for annexation has been received, naming the municipality to which the territory is proposed to be annexed; and describing the territory to be annexed.[7] It must also state the time and place of the hearing.

Notice of the hearing must be published in the official newspaper or paper designated for such purpose by the governing board of each affected municipality and mailed to both residents and property owners in the area proposed to be annexed.[8] The hearing must be held not less than 20 days nor more than 40 days after publication and mailing of the notice.[9] Failure to mail the notice or failure of any addressee to receive the notice however, does not affect the validity of the petition.[10]

Notice must also be mailed to school districts in which all or part of the territory proposed to be annexed is situated not less than 10 days prior to the hearing.[11] Where the territory is proposed to be annexed to a city, notice must also be given to school districts adjoining the proposed annexed territory as well as to school districts located wholly or partially in the city.[12] In addition, in appropriate cases, notice must also be given to affected fire districts or other district corporations, public benefit corporations and town improvement districts with separate boards of commissioners located wholly or partly in the territory to be annexed.[13]

If an affected local government fails to publish or give the required notice or if a town board fails to cause copies thereof to be mailed to the appropriate parties, the governing boards of any other affected local government may, if they deem desirable, amend and republish and mail their notice on behalf of the local government or town board during an additional 20 day period following the original 40 day period.[14]

The hearing must consider procedural matters relevant to the submission of the petition (*e.g.*, whether the petition was properly signed, etc.) and whether the annexation is in the overall public interest

6. *Id.*
7. General Municipal Law § 704(1).
8. *Id.*
9. *Id.*
10. *Id.*
11. *Id.*
12. *Id.*
13. General Municipal Law § 704(2). The statute provides: "In a case where it is proposed to annex territory in a town or towns to another local government or governments, the town board or boards in which such territory is situated shall cause a copy of such notice to be mailed not less than ten days prior to the date of such joint hearing to the board of commissioners or other governing body of each fire district or other district corporation, public benefit corporation, and town improvement district operated by a separate board of commissioners, situated wholly or partly in the territory to be annexed."

14. General Municipal Law § 704(3).

of: (1) the territory proposed to be annexed; (2) the municipality or municipalities to which the territory is proposed to be annexed; (3) the remaining area of the municipality or municipalities in which the territory being annexed is located; and (4) affected school districts, fire districts and other improvement district.[15]

Within 90 days of the public hearing, the governing board of each affected municipality must determine whether the petition was properly submitted and whether the proposed annexation is in the overall public interest.[16] In the event that the governing boards of all the affected municipalities determine either that the proposed annexation is or is not in the overall public interest, the determination is final.[17]

If any of the governing boards determine that it is not in the overall public interest to approve the proposed annexation, the governing board of the municipality or municipalities favoring annexation may apply to the appellate division for a judicial determination that the proposed annexation is in the overall public interest.[18] The appellate division by order of reference must designate three referees, one of whom must be a justice of the supreme court or any judge temporarily assigned to the court, to hear the case and report to the court after a trial. The trial is conducted in the same manner as a court trying an issue without a jury.[19] To facilitate the determination of issues as far in advance as is practicable and to encourage the parties to agree to stipulate on questions of law and fact which may not be in dispute, a pre-trial conference is mandated.[20] Prior to submission of the matter to the referees, the parties must be given an opportunity to submit requests for proposed findings of fact.[21]

The referees must file a report setting forth findings of fact and conclusions of law within 30 days after the matter is finally submitted.[22] Upon receipt of the report, the appellate division must, after hearing oral argument on the report, make its own adjudication and determination on the law and the facts on all questions presented to the referees and substitute its judgment for that of any of the governing boards of the municipalities. The court must enter its judgment on whether the annexation proceeding is in the overall public interest and on any question of procedural compliance where the question is before the court.[23]

The role of the appellate division in an annexation proceeding has been described as "an extraordinary one which does not fit neatly within the usual rubric of judicial activity ... more closely analogous to what is normally considered to be a quasi-legislative activity, for it involves the

15. General Municipal Law § 705(1).
16. General Municipal Law § 711(1).
17. General Municipal Law § 711(4).
18. General Municipal Law § 712(1).
19. General Municipal Law § 712(6).
20. General Municipal Law § 712(7).
21. General Municipal Law § 712(8).
22. General Municipal Law § 712(9).
23. General Municipal Law § 712(10).

resolution of conflicting policy determinations by two governmental entities."[24] The decision of the appellate division may be appealed, but it can not be overturned by the Court of Appeals if the appellate division acted according to law and there was any rational basis for its findings and conclusions.[25]

In the event that the governing boards of all the affected municipalities or the final order of a court approves a proposed annexation, the issue must then go to the voters in the area of the proposed annexation. Residents of such area who are registered voters may vote in the election.[26]

With respect to the dissolution of municipal corporations, state law contains no provision for the dissolution of counties or cities. Towns without any bonded indebtedness may be dissolved and may be annexed to and become part of an adjoining town in the same county upon submission and approval of a proposition in the manner provided by law.[27]

A village board of trustees may, in its discretion, and must upon submission of an appropriate petition, submit a proposition for dissolution of the village to the voters.[28] A proposition for dissolution can not be submitted to the voters until the board of trustees of the village has held a public hearing.[29]

Library References:

West's Key No. Digests, Municipal Corporations ⚖=26–37, 51.

§ 3.6 Municipal Corporations—Consolidation, Annexation and Dissolution—Annexation Checklist

The following checklist summarizes the general requirements for annexation and the procedural requirements for the petition and notice of hearing on the petition for a proposed annexation.

1. Do boundaries of the municipalities for which annexation is proposed adjoin one another? If not, annexation is not permitted.[1] (*See* § 3.5)

2. The Petition must include the following:

    • A brief description of the territory to be annexed.

    • State the approximate number of inhabitants of the territory to be annexed.

---

24. Mayor of Village of Mount Kisco v. Supervisor of Town of Bedford, 45 N.Y.2d 335, 341, 408 N.Y.S.2d 414, 416, 380 N.E.2d 243, 245 (1978).

25. City Council of City of Mechanicville v. Town Board of Halfmoon, 27 N.Y.2d 369, 318 N.Y.S.2d 307, 267 N.E.2d 96 (1971).

26. General Municipal Law § 713(1).

27. *See* Town Law § 79–a.

28. Village Law § 19–1900(1).

29. Village Law § 19–1902.

§ 3.6

1. General Municipal Law § 703(1).

§ 3.6

- Be signed either by at least 20% of the registered voters in the area to be annexed or the owners of a majority in assessed value of real property in the area to be annexed, taken from the last preceding assessment roll.
- Signatures must be properly authenticated.
- For property owner petition, certificate of assessor must be attached.
- For registered voter petition, board of elections certificate must be attached.[2] (See § 3.5)

3. A notice of public hearing must contain the following information:
   - State that petition for annexation has been received.
   - Name the municipality or municipalities to which territory is proposed to be annexed.
   - Briefly describe the territory to be annexed.
   - State the time and place of hearing which must be not less than 20 or more than 40 days from the date of notice.[3] (See § 3.5)

4. Notice of public hearing must be:
   - Given within 20 days from receipt of petition.
   - Published once in the official newspaper or paper designated for such purpose by the governing board of each affected municipality.
   - Be mailed to property owners and registered voters of the territory being annexed.
   - Mailed not less than 10 days prior to hearing to school authorities of any school district in which all or part of territory to be annexed is located.
   - Where it is proposed to annex territory to a city, to the school authorities of any school district adjoining the territory proposed to be annexed and located wholly or partly within the city.
   - Where it is proposed to annex territory or to annex territory in a town(s) to another municipality mailed to the board of commissioners or other governing body of each fire district or other district corporation, public benefit corporation, and town improvement district operated by a separate board of commissioners, situated wholly or partly in the territory to be annexed.[4] (See § 3.5)

---

2. General Municipal Law § 703.
3. General Municipal Law § 704(1).
4. General Municipal Law § 704.

§ 3.7 Powers of Municipal Corporations

The most often cited and well known interpretation of the powers of a municipal corporation, known as Dillon's Rule, is that a municipal corporation possesses and can exercise the following powers, and no others: first, those granted in express words; second, those necessarily or fairly implied in or incident to the powers expressly granted; and third, those essential to the accomplishment of the declared objects and purposes of the corporation.[1]

Dillon's rule is still generally followed in most states, including New York.[2] One of the early cases which is still regularly cited as authority for the source and extent of powers of municipal corporations states the rule as follows:

> [T]owns and other municipal corporations are organized for governmental purposes, and their powers are limited and defined by the statutes under which they are constituted. They possess only such powers as are expressly conferred or necessarily implied. * * * It is the general, if not the universal, law of this country, and of England, that municipalities are not empowered to borrow money for municipal purposes, unless expressly authorized to do so by statute, or in the absence of a statute, unless the power is necessarily implied from some special duty imposed, for the discharge of which the power to borrow is not only convenient, but necessary.[3]

The difficulty in attempting to spell out in a statute every single municipal power is obvious. In New York, the Legislature has attempted to spell out a long list of very specific powers of each municipal corporation.[4] With respect to implied powers, the rule has generally been stated that in addition to the powers expressly granted, municipalities also possess such powers "as are necessarily incident to, or may fairly be implied from, those powers, including all that are essential to the declared object of its existence."[5] Numerous cases challenging the power

Library References:

West's Key No. Digests, Municipal Corporations ⌕33(1).

---

§ 3.7

1. 1 Dillon, *Law of Municipal Corporations* § 237, p.448–49 (5th ed. 1911).

2. *But see* Hyman, *Home Rule in New York 1941–1965 Retrospect and Prospect*, 15 Buffalo Law Review 315, 354 (1965–66), stating Dillon's Rule much more narrowly as meaning only that powers delegated to municipalities are to be narrowly construed and indicating that this aspect of the rule has not been invoked by New York courts.

3. Wells v. Town of Salina, 119 N.Y. 280, 287, 23 N.E. 870 (1890).

4. *See* Village Law § 4–412(1) and (3); Town Law § 64; County Law §§ 200–235; and General City Law § 20.

5. New York Trap Rock Corp. v. Town of Clarkstown, 299 N.Y. 77, 86, 85 N.E.2d 873, 878 (1949).

of municipalities to undertake particular activities turn on the existence of, or lack of, implied power to act on the matter at issue.[6]

Inasmuch as municipalities are created by the Legislature for governmental purposes, it has been stated that the power of the Legislature over municipalities is supreme and transcendental.[7] Thus, any power delegated by the State to a municipality may subsequently be diminished, modified or taken away.[8]

Although the power of the State Legislature to control the affairs of municipalities is broad, the Constitution provides that the Legislature may act in relation to the property, affairs or government of municipalities only by general law, or by special law only (1) upon request of two-thirds of the membership of its legislative body or on request of the chief executive officer concurred in by a majority of the membership, or (2) upon a message of necessity from the Governor based upon facts which, in his judgment, give rise to an emergency requiring enactment of such law and with the concurrence of two-thirds of the members of each house of the Legislature.[9]

A "general law" is a law which in terms and effect applies alike to all counties, all counties other than those wholly included within a city, all cities, all towns or all villages.[10] A "special" law is a law which in terms and in effect applies to one or more, but not all, counties, counties other than those wholly included within a city, cities, towns or villages.[11]

In general, power delegated by the State Legislature to a municipal corporation must be executed in strict accordance with the grant of power from the State.[12] However, when the method of exercising a

6. PRACTICE POINTER: New York courts have been fairly liberal in finding implied powers of municipal corporations. For example, in Cahn v. Town of Huntington, 29 N.Y.2d 451, 328 N.Y.S.2d 672, 278 N.E.2d 908 (1972), in the absence of a specific statutory authority to employ an attorney, the Court of Appeals nonetheless found implied authority for a town planning board to employ and compensate an attorney where the town attorney could not represent the board.

7. Brown v. Board of Trustees of Hamptonburg, School Dist. No. 4, 303 N.Y. 484, 104 N.E.2d 866 (1952).

8. In re County of Cayuga v. McHugh, 4 N.Y.2d 609, 176 N.Y.S.2d 643, 152 N.E.2d 73 (1958).

9. New York State Constitution Art. IX, § 2(b)(2). See infra, § 3.14 for a discussion of the affirmative grant of power to municipalities to act with respect to their property, affairs and government.

10. New York State Constitution Art. IX, § 3(d)(1). See also, Farrington v. Pinckney, 1 N.Y.2d 74, 150 N.Y.S.2d 585, 133 N.E.2d 817 (1956) (the court holding that a State law applicable to a class of counties based upon population of the counties could be a general law if based upon reasonable grounds for distinguishing on the basis of population and not merely to designate a particular county).

11. New York State Constitution Art. IX, § 3(d)(4). See also Hotel Dorset Co. v. Trust for Cultural Resources, 46 N.Y.2d 358, 413 N.Y.S.2d 357, 385 N.E.2d 1284 (1978) (holding that a statute which, upon enactment, affected only one museum was not a special law where it could not be factually shown, or found as a matter of law, that other institutions would not, in time, be affected by the legislation).

12. Novak v. Town of Poughkeepsie, 63 Misc.2d 385, 311 N.Y.S.2d 393 (Sup.Ct., Dutchess County, 1970).

municipal power is not prescribed by statute or charter, the municipality has discretion as to the manner of exercising the power, provided that the method chosen is reasonable.[13]

Action taken by a municipality in excess of its statutory or implied powers is *ultra vires*. A municipality may not be estopped from claiming that an act was *ultra vires*.[14] A distinction is made between *ultra vires* acts taken without, or in excess of, a municipality's powers, and those acts for which there is underlying authority but in the exercise of which there is a technical or procedural defect. A municipal governing body may, in the exercise of its discretion, subsequently ratify prior action which was unauthorized and invalid when taken by express action or by acts or conduct showing assent.[15]

Library References:

West's Key No. Digests, Municipal Corporations ⚖︎57.

§ 3.8 Powers of Municipal Corporations—Governmental v. Proprietary Powers

Municipal corporations have long been recognized as possessing two classes of functions and powers which are commonly referred to as "governmental" and "proprietary."[1] New York courts have defined governmental powers and functions as those which are "essentially public and for the general good of all the inhabitants."[2] Proprietary functions are those "relating to the accomplishment of private corporate purposes in which the public is only indirectly concerned, and as to which the corporation is regarded as a legal individual."[3]

The distinction between governmental and proprietary functions and powers was initially created by the courts in order to alleviate the hardship which would result from the application of the doctrine of sovereign immunity in the field of torts.[4] In this context, municipalities were entitled to sovereign immunity when acting in the same capacity as a private individual, *i.e.*, in a proprietary capacity, and therefore not subject to liability for their tortious conduct.[5] However, the distinction has been applied to determine the power of a municipality to act in many

---

13. See Rhyne, The Law of Local Government Operations § 4.11 (1980).

14. Solow v. City of New York, 25 A.D.2d 442, 266 N.Y.S.2d 823 (2d Dep't 1966), aff'd 20 N.Y.2d 960, 286 N.Y.S.2d 852, 233 N.E.2d 855 (1967).

15. Seif v. City of Long Beach, 286 N.Y. 382, 36 N.E.2d 630 (1941).

§ 3.8

1. *See generally* 2 McQuillin, *Municipal Corporations* § 10.05, p.487 (3d ed. 1988).

2. County of Nassau v. South Farmingdale Water District, 62 A.D.2d 380, 385, 405 N.Y.S.2d 742, 744 (2d Dep't 1978), aff'd 46 N.Y.2d 794, 413 N.Y.S.2d 921, 386 N.E.2d 832 (1978).

3. *Id.* at 62 A.D.2d at 385, 405 N.Y.S.2d at 744.

4. *Id.* at 62 A.D.2d at 384, 405 N.Y.S.2d at 744.

5. *See, e.g.*, Layer v. City of Buffalo, 274 N.Y. 135, 8 N.E.2d 307 (1937).

other areas.[6]

It has long been recognized that the test for distinguishing between governmental and proprietary activities is not easy to apply, particularly in light of the changing views of the function and role of government.[7] Consequently, at least for purposes of determining whether one municipality is exempt from the zoning requirements of another municipality in the development of real property outside its corporate boundaries, the governmental-proprietary test has been abandoned and a "balancing of public interests" test has been adopted.[8] Under the balancing of public interests test, immunity is not presumed unless a contrary legislative intent has been expressed. In addition to legislative intent, other factors to be considered include: the nature and scope of the instrumentality seeking immunity; the kind of function or land use involved; the extent of the public interest to be served; the effect local land use regulation would have on the enterprise concerned; and the impact on legitimate local interests.[9]

Library References:

West's Key No. Digests, Municipal Corporations ⚖=57.

§ 3.9 Powers of Municipal Corporations—Police Powers

The police power is not easily defined, nor is it subject to clearly defined limitations.[1] In general, the police power is a power of government inherent in the sovereignty and is to be exercised in the public interest for the public good.[2] The residual police power resides in the State, not in its political subdivisions. A municipality can only exercise the police power when it has specifically or impliedly received a delegation of the power from the State.[3] Both the Constitution and statutes

---

6. *See, e.g.*, Nehrbas v. Village of Lloyd Harbor, 2 N.Y.2d 190, 159 N.Y.S.2d 145, 140 N.E.2d 241 (1957)(use of village buildings and collection and disposal of refuse was held to be governmental matters exempt from local zoning); Little Joseph Realty v. Town of Babylon, 41 N.Y.2d 738, 395 N.Y.S.2d 428, 363 N.E.2d 1163 (1977) (town operation of an asphalt plant was a proprietary matter and subject to local zoning); Morin v. Foster, 45 N.Y.2d 287, 408 N.Y.S.2d 387, 380 N.E.2d 217 (1978)(a governing board may bind successor governing boards in proprietary but not governmental matters).

7. *See* County of Nassau, *supra* note 2; Nehrbas, *supra* note 6.

8. Matter of City of Rochester, 72 N.Y.2d 338, 533 N.Y.S.2d 702, 530 N.E.2d 202 (1988).

9. *Id.* at 72 N.Y.2d at 343, 533 N.Y.S.2d at 704.

CAVEAT: Although clearly the trend is away from using the governmental-proprietary distinction as a litmus test, the County of Monroe case appears to be limited to its facts and the governmental-proprietary distinction remains viable in other areas.

§ 3.9

1. American Consumer Industries, Inc. v. City of New York, 28 A.D.2d 38, 281 N.Y.S.2d 467 (1st Dep't 1967).

2. Nebbia v. New York, 291 U.S. 502, 54 S.Ct. 505, 78 L.Ed. 940 (1934).

3. Bon–Air Estates, Inc. v. Building Inspector of Ramapo, 31 A.D.2d 502, 298 N.Y.S.2d 763 (2d Dep't 1969)(citing Wells v. Town of Salina, 119 N.Y. 280, 287, 23 N.E. 870 (1890)).

confer upon municipalities the power to adopt and amend local laws for the protection, safety, health and well-being of their inhabitants.[4]

The courts have consistently held that a municipal enactment based upon the police power must be reasonably, properly and substantially related to public health, safety and welfare in order to be upheld.[5] Further, the validity of a police power regulation must depend upon the circumstances of each case and the character of the regulation.[6]

If an ordinance adopted pursuant to the police power has no reasonable relation to the morals, health and safety of the inhabitants of the municipality, it is invalid as an unauthorized exercise of the police power.[7] Further, while municipalities may exercise the police power to preserve public health, safety, morals and welfare, they may not arbitrarily or unreasonably infringe on private rights.[8] To justify interference with private property rights, a municipality generally must show that it acted in response to a dire necessity, that its action is reasonably calculated to alleviate or prevent a crisis condition and that it is taking steps to rectify the problem.[9]

The types of activity potentially subject to municipal regulation under the guise of exercise of the police power is practically limitless.[10] The State Legislature however, has restricted the ability of municipalities to adopt local laws regulating certain areas.[11]

Library References:
West's Key No. Digests, Municipal Corporations ⚖=589–629.

§ 3.10 Legislative Enactments

Like business corporations, municipal corporations generally authorize the actions which they undertake by action of the governing board. However, unlike business corporations, which normally act only by

---

4. New York State Constitution Art. IX, § 2(c)(10); see also Village Law § 4–412(1).

5. See People v. Goodman, 31 N.Y.2d 262, 338 N.Y.S.2d 97, 290 N.E.2d 139 (1972); Wiggins v. Town of Somers, 4 N.Y.2d 215, 173 N.Y.S.2d 579, 149 N.E.2d 869, remittitur amended 4 N.Y.2d 1045, 177 N.Y.S.2d 704, 152 N.E.2d 663 (1958).

6. Wulfsohn v. Burden, 241 N.Y. 288, 150 N.E. 120 (1925).

7. Saidel v. Village of Tupper Lake, 254 App.Div. 22, 4 N.Y.S.2d 814 (3d Dep't 1938).

8. New York Telephone Co. v. Town of North Hempstead, 41 N.Y.2d 691, 395 N.Y.S.2d 143, 363 N.E.2d 694 (1977)(town could not, under the guise of exercise of its police power, appropriate use of the telephone company's poles).

9. Belle Harbor Realty Corp. v. Kerr, 35 N.Y.2d 507, 364 N.Y.S.2d 160, 323 N.E.2d 697 (1974).

PRACTICE POINTER: Police power legislation which affects private property rights should include a statement of findings or of legislative intent showing that the legislative body has considered the private interests, that those interests are outweighed by the public interest in enacting the legislation and that the legislation is the best way to address the problem. The lack of such findings or other evidence that the legislative body has weighed all alternatives can be used in attacking the reasonableness of such legislation.

10. See 6A McQuillin, *Municipal Corporations* §§ 24.01–24.197 (3d ed. 1988).

11. See infra, § 3.14.

resolutions of the governing board, municipal legislative bodies generally have the power to act by ordinances, rules and regulations and local laws, as well as by resolution.[1]

Unlike the state and federal legislatures, which are separate and independent from the executive branch, in towns, villages and non-charter counties the legislative body includes the chief executive officer.[2] Legislative bodies are generally required to hold regular meetings[3] and to determine their own rules of procedure.[4]

A majority of the entire membership of the governing board normally constitutes a quorum for the transaction of business.[5] As a general rule, in the absence of a statute providing otherwise, a majority vote of the total membership of the governing board without regard to vacancies or disqualifications from voting, is necessary to approve any matter which comes before a municipal governing board.[6]

Municipal legislative enactments enjoy the same presumption of constitutionality as is afforded to acts of the State Legislature.[7] The burden of proof in any challenge to the validity of a municipal legislative act is upon the person alleging invalidity.[8] The courts have no power to question the wisdom of municipal legislation and generally may overturn an act only where there is no reasonable relation between the evil sought to be remedied and the remedy proposed.[9]

The general rule with respect to the effective date of legislative enactments is that they become effective immediately unless otherwise provided.[10] As a rule of construction, statutes are presumed to operate prospectively and not retroactively.[11]

§ 3.10

1. *See, e.g.*, Village Law § 20–2000; Town Law § 130; Vehicle and Traffic Law § 1640; *Cf.* County Law § 215(11) authorizing a county board of supervisors, by resolution or local law, to adopt rules, regulations or ordinances.

2. *See* Town Law § 60; Village Law § 4–401(1)(a)(mayor may vote on all matters coming before the board of trustees and shall vote in the case of a tie); County Law § 150.

3. Town Law § 62; County Law § 152.

4. Town Law § 63; Village Law § 4–412(2); County Law § 153(8).

5. Town Law § 63; Village Law § 4–412(2); County Law § 153(2).

6. General Construction Law § 41.

CAVEAT: Where only a quorum of a municipal governing board is present at a meeting, the affirmative vote of *all* members present is necessary for the adoption of any measures. Certain actions require for their adoption approval by a super-majority of the entire voting strength of the board without regard to absences or vacancies and therefore may not be validly enacted if only a quorum of the legislative body is present. *See e.g.*, Local Finance Law § 33.00(a) relative to certain bond and capital note resolutions; General Municipal Law § 103(5) relative to standardizing on purchase contracts.

7. Lighthouse Shores v. Town of Islip, 41 N.Y.2d 7, 390 N.Y.S.2d 827, 359 N.E.2d 337 (1976); Wiggins v. Town of Somers, 4 N.Y.2d 215, 173 N.Y.S.2d 579, 149 N.E.2d 869, remittitur amended 4 N.Y.2d 1045, 177 N.Y.S.2d 704, 152 N.E.2d 663 (1958).

8. Charles v. Diamond, 41 N.Y.2d 318, 392 N.Y.S.2d 594, 360 N.E.2d 1295 (1977).

9. *See, e.g.*, Good Humor v. City of New York, 290 N.Y. 312, 49 N.E.2d 153 (1943).

10. 5 McQuillin, *Municipal Corporations* § 15.39, p.157 (3d ed. 1989).

11. Statutes § 51(c).

Ch. 3   LEGISLATIVE ENACTMENTS—ORDINANCES   § 3.12

Notwithstanding the effective date of any local law, local laws do not become effective until filed with the Secretary of State.[12] However, the courts have recognized a distinction between the effective date of a statute and its operative date and have held that a legislative body may prescribe that a law becomes operative at a date prior to its effective date.[13]

§ 3.11   Legislative Enactments—Resolutions

The most common form of municipal legislative enactment in New York State is the resolution. The general rule is that whenever a statute or ordinance gives a municipal governing body alone the power to undertake a particular activity and is silent as to the manner by which the action must be taken, the action may be authorized by resolution.[1]

Unlike ordinances, resolutions have been held not to constitute legislation in the strict sense of the word, but rather are a ministerial act declarative of the will of the municipality.[2] Thus, it has been stated that all acts that are done by a municipality in its ministerial capacity and for a temporary purpose may be put in the form of resolutions, while matters on which the municipality wishes to legislate must be put in the form of ordinances.[3]

No statute prescribes a particular form for resolutions,[4] and in the absence of any specific requirement, no set or particular form is required.[5] Because of its nature as a temporary, ministerial act, it has been held that a resolution adopted for a particular and temporary purpose continues in force for a reasonable period only, and that a formal repeal is not required to terminate its operation.[6]

Library References:

West's Key No. Digests, Municipal Corporations ⟸85.

§ 3.12   Legislative Enactments—Ordinances

An ordinance is distinguished from a resolution by the greater

---

12. Municipal Home Rule Law § 27(3).

13. *See* Hehl v. Gross, 35 A.D.2d 570, 313 N.Y.S.2d 422 (2d Dep't 1970), aff'd 30 N.Y.2d 828, 334 N.Y.S.2d 914, 286 N.E.2d 285 (1972).

§ 3.11

1. 5 McQuillin, *Municipal Corporations* § 15.06, p.72 (3d ed. 1989); *see also* Jewett v. Luau-Nyack Corp., 31 N.Y.2d 298, 338 N.Y.S.2d 874, 291 N.E.2d 123 (1972)(citing 5 McQuillin, *Municipal Corporations* § 15.02, pp. 46–47 (2d ed. 1969)).

2. Civil Service Employees Assoc. v. City of Troy, 36 A.D.2d 145, 319 N.Y.S.2d 106 (3d Dep't 1971), aff'd 30 N.Y.2d 549, 330 N.Y.S.2d 611, 281 N.E.2d 555 (1972).

3. 5 McQuillin, *Municipal Corporations*, § 15.02, p.55 (3d ed. 1989).

4. *Cf.* Municipal Home Rule Law § 20 which prescribes the form for local laws.

5. 5 McQuillin, *Municipal Corporations* § 15.02, p.55 (3d ed. 1989).

6. Quaglia v. Village of Munsey Park, 54 A.D.2d 434, 389 N.Y.S.2d 616 (2d Dep't 1976), aff'd 44 N.Y.2d 772, 406 N.E.2d 30, 377 N.E.2d 473 (1978).

formality that is required for enactment of an ordinance.[1] An ordinance provides a permanent rule of government or conduct which will affect matters arising subsequent to its adoption.[2] In general, municipal legislatures are required to act by ordinance only in those cases where the enabling statute pursuant to which they are acting so requires.[3]

Because ordinances are a more formal form of legislative enactment than resolutions, they have more stringent procedural requirements attendant to their adoption than do resolutions.[4] These requirements generally consist of a public hearing on notice prior to adoption of the ordinance, recording of the votes by the members of the governing board in the minutes, and publication of the text of the ordinance in the official newspaper of the municipality after its adoption.[5] In second class cities, all legislative acts are required to be undertaken by ordinance.[6] In towns, a wide variety of police power regulatory type acts may be undertaken by ordinance.[7] Counties have limited specific authority to act by ordinance.[8]

In villages, the power to adopt ordinances was specifically eliminated when that portion of § 20–2000 of the Village Law which granted that power was repealed.[9] The Attorney General, citing the sponsor's memorandum in support of that legislation, stated that the purpose of the repeal was to adopt a uniform and exclusive procedure for the enactment of local legislation by villages, that procedure being the adoption of local laws.[10]

Library References:

West's Key No. Digests, Municipal Corporations ⚖=105–122.1(4).

§ 3.13 Legislative Enactments—Rules and Regulations

Every type of municipality is authorized to adopt traffic regulations

---

§ 3.12

1. Jewett v. Luau–Nyack Corp., 31 N.Y.2d 298, 338 N.Y.S.2d 874, 291 N.E.2d 123 (1972).

2. *See* Quaglia v. Village of Munsey Park, 54 A.D.2d 434, 389 N.Y.S.2d 616 (2d Dep't 1976), aff'd 44 N.Y.2d 772, 406 N.Y.S.2d 30, 377 N.E.2d 473 (1978); Jewett, *supra* note 1.

3. 5 McQuillin, *Municipal Corporations* § 15.03, p.63 (3d ed. 1989).

4. PRACTICE POINTER: Because of the time and expense associated with complying with the procedural formalities for the adoption of ordinances (and also local laws which are discussed *infra* in § 3.14), it is generally advisable to use less formal enactments whenever an ordinance (or local law) is not specifically required.

5. *See* Town Law §§ 130, 133.

6. Second Class Cities Law § 35.

CAVEAT: In order to determine the authority to adopt ordinances and the applicable procedures for ordinances in other cities, individual city charters must be examined.

7. *See* Town Law § 130.

8. *See* County Law § 215(8).

9. Ch. 974, L.1973.

10. *See* 1983 Op.Atty.Gen.N.Y.(Inf.) 1110, 1983 WL 167414 (Aug. 26, 1993).

CAVEAT: The inability of one type of municipality (*e.g.*, villages) to use a legislative enactment available to every other type of municipality is one of the many inconsistencies which pervade the municipal law statutes in New York. Municipal attorneys who represent villages as well as other types of municipalities must be aware that they cannot always use the same type of legislative enactment in villages as they use in other types of municipalities.

by rule or regulation.[1] As a result, probably the most common usage of rules and regulations by municipalities in New York is in connection with the regulation of traffic and parking.

In addition, separate boards and administrative agencies within a municipality are often empowered to act by rule or regulation.[2] In villages, any rule or regulation adopted by a separate board, the violation of which results in a fine or imprisonment, must be approved by the board of trustees. In addition, notice of hearing and publication must be conducted in the same manner as for the adoption of a local law.[3] Similarly, in towns, the definition of an ordinance includes any rule or regulation for the violation of which a penalty is imposed. The same procedural requirements necessary prior to adoption of an ordinance, *e.g.*, notice and public hearing, must be followed for the adoption of such a rule or regulation.[4]

Except as noted above with respect to rules and regulations where a penalty is imposed for violation, there are no specific statutory requirements for the enactment of rules and regulations. Rules and regulations adopted by the governing board are subject to the general requirement that they be approved by a majority of the members of the governing board.[5]

§ 3.14 Legislative Enactments—Local Laws

The State Constitution provides a broad affirmative grant of power to every local government to adopt and amend local laws (1) not inconsistent with the provisions of the Constitution or any general law relating to its property, affairs or government, and (2) not inconsistent with the provisions of the Constitution or any general law relating to certain enumerated subjects. These subjects include, but are not limited to: the powers and duties of officers and employees; the transaction of business; the acquisition, care and management of property, regardless of whether they relate to the property affairs or government of such local government, except to the extent that the Legislature restricts the adoption of such a local law.[1] In addition to this affirmative grant of power to municipalities, the Constitution restricts the power of the State in regard to local matters by providing that the State Legislature may act in relation to the "property, affairs or government" of any local government only by general law or, in certain limited cases, by special

§ 3.13

1. Vehicle and Traffic Law §§ 1640, 1650 and 1660.
2. *See, e.g.*, Village Law § 10–1002 (fire department regulations), § 11–1116 (water commission regulations); County Law § 264 (county districts); Second Class Cities Law § 133 (commissioner of public works).
3. Village Law § 20–2000.
4. Town Law § 131.
5. *See supra*, § 3.10.

§ 3.14

1. New York State Constitution Art. IX, § 2(c).

§ 3.14 MUNICIPAL LAW Ch. 3

law.[2] These two provisions together comprise what is commonly referred to as the municipal "home rule" power.[3]

This seemingly broad grant of authority to municipalities to adopt local laws has been limited by interpretation of the phrase "property, affairs or government." In *Adler v. Deegan*,[4] the leading case dealing with the authority of the State Legislature to act in relation to the property, affairs or government of a municipality, the Court of Appeals held that where the subject matter of particular legislation included elements of both state and local concern, the State Legislature was not precluded from legislating if the subject was to a substantial degree a matter of state concern. The notion that there are matters of so-called "state concern" established by the *Adler* decision has served as the basis for upholding State legislation dealing with numerous seemingly local matters including compensation of local officials,[5] filling of vacancies in local offices,[6] and invalidating local legislation which was inconsistent with State law relative to residency requirements for city firefighters.[7] Under *Adler* and its progeny, the State Legislature may adopt legislation dealing with matters of state concern without a home rule request.

In addition to the judicially created proscription against local laws which deal with matters of state concern, local laws also are not permitted where they are inconsistent with the provisions of the Constitution or a general law, or where the State has evidenced an intent to pre-empt local regulation over a particular subject matter. While inconsistency and pre-emption are closely related to one another, each can serve independently as grounds for invalidating a local law.[8]

In general, inconsistency is not limited to cases of express conflict between State and local laws, but can also occur where local laws prohibit what would be permissible under State law or impose additional restrictions that inhibit the operation of the State law.[9] Pre-emption of a particular area by the State Legislature may be evidenced either by express statement or by implication such as the enactment of a compre-

2. New York State Constitution Art. IX, § 2(b)(2).

3. *See* Hyman, *Home Rule in New York 1941–1965 Retrospect and Prospect*, 15 Buffalo Law Review 315, 337–338 (1965–66).

4. 251 N.Y. 467, 167 N.E. 705 (1929) (Cardozo, C.J. concurring opinion).

5. *See* Kelley v. McGee, 57 N.Y.2d 522, 457 N.Y.S.2d 434, 443 N.E.2d 908 (1982).

6. *See* Carey v. Oswego County Legislature, 91 A.D.2d 62, 458 N.Y.S.2d 283 (3d Dep't 1983), aff'd 59 N.Y.2d 847, 466 N.Y.S.2d 312, 453 N.E.2d 541 (1983).

7. *See* Uniformed Firefighters Assoc. v. City of New York, 50 N.Y.2d 85, 428 N.Y.S.2d 197, 405 N.E.2d 679 (1980).

8. Consolidated Edison Co. of New York v. Town of Red Hook, 60 N.Y.2d 99, 468 N.Y.S.2d 596, 456 N.E.2d 487 (1983).

9. *Id.* at 60 N.Y.2d at 108, 468 N.Y.S.2d at 601.

PRACTICE POINTER: While local laws which are inconsistent with State law are normally invalid, towns and villages have express authority to adopt local laws amending or superseding certain provisions of the Town Law and Village Law, respectively, insofar as those provisions apply to the town or village adopting the local law. Municipal Home Rule Law §§ 10(1)(ii)(d)(3) and (e)(3).

hensive regulatory scheme in a particular area.[10] In addition, the Municipal Home Rule Law places certain restrictions on the adoption of local laws.[11]

Subject to these restrictions, the power of municipalities to adopt local laws is to be liberally construed and is in addition to all other powers granted to municipalities by other provisions of law.[12] Any action which a municipality may take by ordinance, resolution, rule or regulation may also be taken by local law.[13]

A local law may address only one subject.[14] A proposed local law must be introduced by a member of the legislative body of the municipality at a meeting of the legislative body or as otherwise prescribed by the legislative body's rules of procedure.[15] No local law can be passed until it is in its final form and is either (1) on the desks or table of the members of the legislative body at least seven calendar days, exclusive of Sunday, prior to its final passage, or (2) mailed to each member in postpaid properly addressed and securely enclosed envelopes in a local post office at least ten calendar days, exclusive of Sunday, prior to its final passage. These requirements do not have to be met if the elective or appointive chief executive officer certifies to the necessity for the immediate passage of a local law[16] and the law is passed by the affirmative vote of two-thirds of the total voting power of the legislative body.[17] A public hearing must be held on any proposed local law before the legislative body or, before the elective chief executive officer if the municipality has an elective chief executive officer with the power to veto local laws or ordinances.[18]

Library References:

West's Key No. Digests, Municipal Corporations ⟲65.

§ 3.15 Legislative Enactments—Referendum Requirements

The general rule in New York is that a municipality may not submit a proposition to a referendum in the absence of express statutory authority.[1] A referendum which is not required or authorized by statute is illegal. Therefore, so-called "advisory referenda," which are generally

---

10. *Id.* at 60 N.Y.2d at 105, 468 N.Y.S.2d at 599.
11. *See* Municipal Home Rule Law § 11.
12. Municipal Home Rule Law § 10(2).
13. Municipal Home Rule Law § 51.
14. Municipal Home Rule Law § 20(3).
15. Municipal Home Rule Law § 20(4).
16. Where there is no chief executive officer, the chairman of the board of supervisors of a county, the mayor of a city or village or the supervisor of a town may certify to the necessity. See Municipal Home Rule Law § 20(4).
17. Municipal Home Rule Law § 20(4).
18. Municipal Home Rule Law § 20(5).

§ 3.15

1. McCabe v. Voorhis, 243 N.Y. 401, 153 N.E. 849 (1926).

intended to enable elected officials to get a sense of voter feeling on particular issues, are illegal and the results are not binding.[2] A municipality does have the power, by local law or charter provision, to require or permit a referendum on issues other than those provided for by State law.[3]

In certain instances, the adoption of resolutions, ordinances or local laws may be subject to either a mandatory referendum or permissive referendum.[4] As the name implies, where a proposed legislative enactment is subject to mandatory referendum, the proposed legislation *must* be submitted to the voters of the municipality for their approval or disapproval prior to taking effect.[5] The failure to hold a referendum on a local law which is subject to mandatory referendum invalidates the local law.[6]

Proposed legislation which is subject to permissive referendum will not take effect until a statutorily prescribed number of days after its adoption, during which time a prescribed number of qualified voters may submit a petition protesting against the legislation and requesting that a referendum vote be held.[7] If a petition is submitted, the proposed legislation will not become effective unless approved by a majority vote at the referendum.[8] If no petition is submitted, the proposed legislation normally becomes effective upon the expiration of the period for submitting a petition, unless a later date is specified.[9]

In order to determine whether there is a referendum requirement that a particular proposed legislative enactment is subject to, care must be taken to examine the enabling statute authorizing the legislation. Town and village boards have specific statutory authority, on their own motion, to submit to the voters any proposed legislative enactment which is subject to permissive referendum and the proceedings are the same as if a petition had been filed.[10] Counties, however, do not have similar specific statutory authority.

In certain instances where a particular action is subject to mandatory or permissive referendum, the form of the proposition is mandated by

---

2. Mills v. Sweeney, 219 N.Y. 213, 114 N.E. 65 (1916); Greene v. Town Board of Warrensburg, 90 A.D.2d 916, 456 N.Y.S.2d 873 (3d Dep't 1982), motion for leave to appeal denied 58 N.Y.2d 604, 459 N.Y.S.2d 1027, 445 N.E.2d 654 (1983).

3. 1980 Op.Atty.Gen.N.Y.(Inf.) 221, 1980 WL 107282 (Sept. 18, 1980).

4. *See, e.g.*, Town Law § 64(2)(resolution of town board authorizing conveyance of real property subject to permissive referendum); Municipal Home Rule Law § 24(2)(providing that the adoption of certain local laws shall be subject to permissive referendum).

5. *See* County Law § 100; Municipal Home Rule Law § 23(1).

6. Coutant v. Town of Poughkeepsie, 69 A.D.2d 506, 419 N.Y.S.2d 148 (2d Dep't 1979).

7. *See, e.g.*, Town Law § 91; Village Law § 9–902(1); County Law § 101(2).

8. *Id.*

9. *Id.*

10. *See* County Law § 101; Town Law § 91; Village Law § 9–902.

statute.[11] Where no particular form for a proposition is specified by statute, it has been held that the form is sufficient if the wording is clear enough so that anyone who can read can understand it.[12]

Library References:

West's Key No. Digests, Municipal Corporations ⚖108.10.

§ 3.16 Acquisition and Disposition of Property

In general, municipal corporations are authorized to acquire real and personal property for municipal purposes by lease, purchase, gift or grant.[1] In addition, where a municipality is authorized by law to acquire real property for municipal purposes, the municipality may, if it is unable to agree with the owner for the purchase of the property, acquire title by eminent domain.[2]

In connection with the acquisition of property by purchase, financing must be in place before a purchase or lease agreement can be signed.[3] Subject to the rule on binding successor governing boards,[4] there is no limitation on the term for which a town or village may acquire real property by lease; however, counties generally may not lease real property for a term in excess of five (5) years.[5]

In towns, the acquisition of real property for town purposes is subject to permissive referendum unless the acquisition is financed entirely from surplus funds.[6] However, in other municipalities, legislative enactments authorizing the acquisition of real or personal property generally are not subject to referendum requirements.[7]

---

11. *See, e.g.*, Village Law § 18–1824 prescribing form of proposition for creation of a commission to prepare a local law establishing position of village manager; General Municipal Law § 713(1) providing form of proposition for proposed annexation of territory of one municipality by another.

12. *See* Knapp v. Fasbender, 109 N.Y.S.2d 294 (Sup.Ct., Suffolk County, 1951), aff'd 1 N.Y.2d 212, 151 N.Y.S.2d 668, 134 N.E.2d 482 (1956).

§ 3.16

1. *See* Town Law § 64(2), (2-a); Village Law § 1–102(1); County Law § 215(3); Second Class Cities Law § 3(1); *See also* Municipal Home Rule Law § 10(1)(i) authorizing the adoption of local laws relating to a municipality's property.

2. General Municipal Law § 74; *See also* Chapter 14 "Eminent Domain," *infra* for a more detailed discussion of eminent domain.

3. *See generally infra*, § 3.24.

4. *See* Morin v. Foster, 45 N.Y.2d 287, 408 N.Y.S.2d 387, 380 N.E.2d 217 (1978).

5. County Law § 215(3).

6. Town Law §§ 81(3), (4) and 220(3), (4).

7. *See supra* note 1.

CAVEAT: While the decision of a village to acquire property typically is not subject to referendum requirements, if the acquisition is to be financed by the issuance of obligations under the Local Finance Law, the bonding authorization will be subject to a permissive referendum if the obligations will have a maturity of more than five (5) years. Local Finance Law § 36.00(a). In towns, where the acquisition of real property is to be financed by the issuance of obligations with a maturity of more than five (5) years, only a single proposition on financing the proposed expenditure needs to be submitted to the voters. *See* Fishman v. Town of Islip, 20 Misc.2d 180, 189 N.Y.S.2d 979 (Spec.Term, Suffolk County,1959), aff'd 10 A.D.2d 984, 204 N.Y.S.2d 82 (2d Dep't 1960).

§ 3.16   MUNICIPAL LAW   Ch. 3

With respect to the conveyance of municipally owned property, it has long been the rule that a municipality, without specific legislative authority, may not permit property acquired or held for public use to be wholly or partly diverted to private use.[8] This rule applies to public streets, wharves, cemeteries, hospitals, court houses and other public buildings and is based upon the notion that the municipality holds title to this property in trust for the benefit of the public.[9] However, municipalities may grant revocable licenses or concessions to use public facilities to private individuals and groups.[10]

It follows that personal property and real property owned by a municipality and not held for public use, *e.g.*, held in a proprietary capacity, may be conveyed without specific legislative authority.[11] With respect to the procedures for conveying real and personal property, if no provision is made by statute regarding the procedure for disposing of property and the conditions of the conveyance, such matters are within the reasonable discretion of the governing body.[12] In counties, there is a requirement that the governing body must first determine that the property is no longer necessary for municipal purposes before making a conveyance of real property.[13]

The State Constitution prohibits gifts of money or property by a municipality to a private person or entity.[14] It has been held that municipalities have a fiduciary duty to secure the best possible price or otherwise obtain the most favorable terms possible, in their judgment, when selling or leasing property.[15] However, a municipality may convey property to another municipal or public corporation without consideration.[16]

In towns, the conveyance of real property is subject to permissive

8. Lake George Steamboat Co. v. Blais, 30 N.Y.2d 48, 330 N.Y.S.2d 336, 281 N.E.2d 147 (1972); People ex rel. Swan v. Doxsee, 136 App.Div. 400, 120 N.Y.S. 962 (2d Dep't 1910), aff'd 198 N.Y. 605, 92 N.E. 1098 (1910).

9. *See* Meriwether v. Garrett, 102 U.S. 472, 513, 26 L.Ed. 197 (1880); Brooklyn Park Comrs. v. Armstrong, 45 N.Y. 234 (1871)(municipal park property may not be alienated without express legislative authority).

10. *See* Miller v. City of New York, 15 N.Y.2d 34, 255 N.Y.S.2d 78, 203 N.E.2d 478 (1964).

11. *See supra*, § 3.8 for a discussion of the distinction between proprietary and governmental functions.

12. *See* 10 McQuillin, *Municipal Corporations* § 28.44, p.160 (3d ed. 1990).

13. County Law §§ 215(4), (5).

14. New York State Constitution Art. VIII, § 1.

15. *See* Ross v. Wilson, 308 N.Y. 605, 127 N.E.2d 697 (1955); Orelli v. Ambro, 41 N.Y.2d 952, 394 N.Y.S.2d 636, 363 N.E.2d 360 (1977) (citing 10 McQuillin, *Municipal Corporation* § 28.44, p.137 (2d ed. 1969)); *see also* County Law § 215(6) requiring a public auction for lease or sale of unneeded county real property.

PRACTICE POINTER: In order to ensure compliance with this requirement, municipalities are well advised to utilize some form of public auction when disposing of municipal property.

16. General Municipal Law § 72–g, specifically authorizing the sale, lease or exchange of real property between municipal corporations and fire districts without consideration.

referendum.[17] In counties, the conveyance of real property no longer necessary for county purposes must be authorized by two-thirds vote of the entire governing board, without regard to vacancies or absences.[18] The Village Law, however, contains no specific procedural requirements for sale or lease of municipally owned property leaving it entirely within the discretion of the Village Board. The foregoing general rules may not apply in the case of real property acquired under special circumstances such as through tax enforcement proceedings[19] and real property in an urban renewal project.[20]

Library References:

West's Key No. Digests, Municipal Corporations ⇨221–225(6).

§ 3.17 Officers and Employees

Municipal corporations are required by the State Constitution and statutes to have certain offices.[1] These are generally the chief executive officer, the legislative body, a municipal clerk, justices and the heads of certain necessary administrative units of government such as the assessor's office and the tax collector.[2] In addition, municipalities may create additional public offices by local law.[3]

Not all persons employed by or working for a municipal corporation are deemed to be public officers and the distinction between an officer and an employee is often an important one as it may bear on a person's right to hold the position, to compensation, to receive fringe benefits and other matters. As a general rule, a position is a public office when it (1) is created by law, with duties cast on the incumbent which involve the exercise of some portion of the sovereign power and in the performance of which the public is concerned and (2) is continuing in its nature and not occasional or intermittent.[4] Specific factors to be considered in distinguishing between a public officer and a public employee include whether the position is created by the Constitution or statute,[5] whether the duties of the office are exercised independently or under the supervision of another,[6] and whether an oath of office is required.[7]

17. Town Law § 64(2); *see supra*, § 3.15 for a discussion of a permissive referendum.
18. County Law § 215(5).
19. County Law § 215(8).
20. General Municipal Law § 507(2).

§ 3.17

1. *See* New York State Constitution Art. XIII, § 13.
2. *See, e.g.*, Town Law § 20; Village Law § 3–301; County Law § 400.
3. Municipal Home Rule Law § 10(1)(ii)(a)(1).

4. *See* Smith v. Jansen, 85 Misc.2d 81, 379 N.Y.S.2d 254 (Sup.Ct., Suffolk County, 1975).
5. *See* Thompson v. Hofstatter, 265 N.Y. 54, 191 N.E. 772 (1934)(the position of county attorney, required under the County Law, was a public office); *cf.* Fisher v. Mechanicville, 225 N.Y. 210, 121 N.E. 764 (1919)(the position of village attorney, not required under the Village Law, was an employee).
6. *See* People ex rel. Hoefle v. Cahill, 188 N.Y. 489, 81 N.E. 453 (1907).

A public officer's right to hold office derives from his or her appointment by the appointing authority pursuant to statute while an employee has contractual rights to his or her position.[8] Consequently, a public officer has no vested rights to hold the office and the term of the incumbent may be shortened by legislation eliminating the office without violating any rights of the incumbent.[9]

Salary of a public official has been held to be an incident of the office and, therefore, a public officer is entitled to receive the salary fixed for the office without regard to services rendered.[10] A public employee, on the other hand, cannot enforce a claim for compensation except for services actually rendered.[11]

Library References:

West's Key No. Digests, Municipal Corporations ⚖123–174.

§ 3.18 Officers and Employees—Qualifications

The only constitutional qualification for holding a local government office in New York State is that the officer take and subscribe an oath to support the State Constitution and faithfully discharge the duties of the office.[1] Additional qualifications for holding a local office are provided by statute and these provisions generally prohibit any person from holding public office unless the person is at least eighteen years of age, a resident of the municipality for which he or she is being chosen, and has not been convicted of avoiding the draft.[2]

Municipalities may prescribe additional qualifications for holding office by local law.[3] Any qualifications must be non-discriminatory and have a reasonable relationship to the purpose of the legislation imposing the qualification.[4]

In addition to taking and filing an oath of office, certain officers may also be required to file an official undertaking for the faithful discharge

---

7. People ex rel. Dawson v. Knox, 231 App.Div. 490, 247 N.Y.S. 731 (3d Dep't 1931), aff'd 267 N.Y. 565, 196 N.E. 582 (1935).

8. Id.

9. See Smith, supra note 4.

10. Matter of Bookhout v. Levitt, 43 N.Y.2d 612, 403 N.Y.S.2d 200, 374 N.E.2d 111 (1978); Fitzsimmons v. City of Brooklyn, 102 N.Y. 536, 7 N.E. 787 (1886).

11. Gutheil v. New York, 119 App.Div. 20, 103 N.Y.S. 972 (2d Dep't 1907).

§ 3.18

1. New York State Constitution Art. VIII, § 1; see also, Public Officers Law § 10.

2. Public Officers Law § 3(1); see also, Town Law § 23; Village Law, § 3–300.

PRACTICE POINTER: There are numerous exceptions to the residency requirement for specific officers including members of police forces and volunteer firefighters. See Public Officers Law §§ 10(2), (3) and other subdivisions.

3. Municipal Home Rule Law § 10(1)(ii)(a)(1); see also supra, § 3.14.

4. Landes v. North Hempstead, 20 N.Y.2d 417, 284 N.Y.S.2d 441, 231 N.E.2d 120 (1967).

of the duties of the office. Typically, an undertaking is required from those officers (or employees) responsible for handling public funds.[5]

As a general rule, in the absence of a constitutional or statutory provision against holding more than one public office, an individual may simultaneously hold two or more public offices unless the offices are incompatible.[6] Incompatibility occurs when one office is subordinate to another or where there is an inherent inconsistency between the two offices.[7]

The common law rule on incompatibility of offices has been extended to prohibit the simultaneous holding of an office and a public employment, and the holding of two positions of public employment which are incompatible.[8] Whenever an issue of possible incompatibility arises, the specific powers and duties of the positions involved must be examined to determine whether the positions are either subordinate or inherently inconsistent.[9]

Even though two positions may not be incompatible with one another, a person may not appoint himself to another position over which, either individually or as a member of a board, he has appointment power. The leading case holds that any such appointment would be contrary to public policy, regardless of whether the vote of the individual being appointed was necessary for the appointment.[10]

Library References:
West's Key No. Digests, Municipal Corporations ⌐137–145, 217.3(4).

§ 3.19 Officers and Employees—Terms

When the term of any public officer is not provided by the State Constitution, it may be provided by statute, including a local law. If the term is not prescribed, the office is held at the pleasure of the appointing body.[1] Terms for elected officers are generally prescribed by statute.[2]

---

5. *See, e.g.,* Town Law § 25; Village Law § 3–306; County Law § 403. *See also,* Public Officers Law § 11 regarding the form of an official undertaking.

6. *See* People ex rel. Ryan v. Green, 58 N.Y. 295 (1874).

CAVEAT: The doctrine of incompatibility of offices, which relates to the propriety of an individual simultaneously holding two or more public offices, is sometimes confused with conflicts of interest. Conflicts of interest relate only to contractual relationships between public officers and employees and the municipality which they serve. *See infra,* § 3.22.

7. *Id.*

8. *See* 1992 Op.Atty.Gen.N.Y.(Inf.)1098, 1992 WL 479120 (Sept. 2, 1992).

9. **PRACTICE POINTER**: The Attorney General's office has rendered numerous opinions regarding compatibility of offices. These opinions are an excellent starting point for researching any question on compatibility of offices.

10. Wood v. Town of Whitehall, 120 Misc. 124, 197 N.Y.S. 789 (Sup.Ct., Washington County, 1923), aff'd 206 App.Div. 786, 201 N.Y.S. 959 (3d Dep't 1923).

§ 3.19

1. New York State Constitution Art. VIII, § 2.

2. *See, e.g.,* Town Law § 24; Village Law § 3–302(3).

State statutes generally do not prescribe terms for appointed officers and, therefore, unless a term for an appointed office has been prescribed by local law, the appointee serves at the pleasure of the appointing authority.

The State Legislature has no power to extend the term of an incumbent public officer beyond the length of the term for which the officer was chosen; any attempt would constitute a usurpation of the right of local self-government.[3] The Legislature may, however, extend the term of an office on a prospective basis.[4] In addition, there is no prohibition against legislation which shortens the term of an existing office so long as the legislation is directed at the office and not the incumbent.[5]

Where an office has a prescribed term and the term has expired and a successor has not been chosen and/or duly qualified, the incumbent continues in office until a successor is chosen and qualified.[6] This so-called "holding over" of public officers allows municipalities to continue to carry out their responsibilities in the face of any contingency which may stand in the way of the orderly succession of public officials.

Library References:

West's Key No. Digests, Municipal Corporations ⚿149.

§ 3.20 Officers and Employees—Removal

The constitutional provision directing the State Legislature to provide for the removal of public officers appears by its terms not to extend to local officers.[1] However, there are statutory provisions which provide for the removal of various local officers.[2] Section 36 of the Public Officers Law has been held not to be an unconstitutional delegation of legislative power.[3]

Clearly municipalities have the power to prescribe removal procedures for their officers and employees.[4] When the term of a public officer or employee is not fixed by law and there is no statutory provision for removal, the general rule is that the power of removal is necessarily

3. People ex rel. Lovett v. Randall, 151 N.Y. 497, 45 N.E. 841 (1897); Loew v. McNeill, 170 Misc. 647, 10 N.Y.S.2d 658, aff'd 279 N.Y. 806, 19 N.E.2d 94 (1939).

4. People ex rel. Lovett, *supra* note 3.

5. Lanza v. Wagner, 11 N.Y.2d 317, 229 N.Y.S.2d 380, 183 N.E.2d 670 (1962); Smith v. Jansen, 85 Misc.2d 81, 379 N.Y.S.2d 254 (Sup.Ct., Suffolk County, 1975).

6. Public Officers Law § 5.

§ 3.20

1. New York State Constitution Art XIII, § 5. *But see* New York State Constitution Art XIII, § 13 providing for the removal of certain law enforcement and other local officials.

2. *See* Public Officers Law § 36; County Law § 400(4–a).

3. Application of Baker, 87 Misc.2d 592, 386 N.Y.S.2d 313 (Sup.Ct., Warren County, 1976).

4. Municipal Home Rule Law § 10(1)(ii)(a)(1).

incidental to the appointment power and, therefore, the appointing authority has the power to remove the appointee at will without notice or hearing.[5] However, the power to remove has been held not to include the power to suspend and, therefore, in the absence of specific statutory authority, a municipality can not suspend an employee even though it had power to terminate that employee.[6]

Under Public Officers Law § 36, town, village, improvement district and fire district officers, except justices of the peace, may be removed from office by the supreme court for any misconduct, maladministration, malfeasance or malversation in office. An application for removal may be made by any citizen who is a resident of the town, village, improvement district or fire district or by the district attorney of the county in which the town, village, improvement district or fire district is located. The application must be made to the appellate division of the supreme court held within the judicial department embracing the town, village, improvement district or fire district.[7] It has been held that the intent of the statute is not to punish the offender, but to improve public service. Courts therefore, have declined to remove officers where the charges are not based upon malicious or intentional corrupt acts, moral turpitude or a violation of the public trust.[8]

Library References:
West's Key No. Digests, Municipal Corporations ⚖153–160, 218(1)–218(11).

§ 3.21 Officers and Employees—Collective Bargaining

The right of public employees to form labor unions and to bargain collectively with their employers derives from the Public Employees Fair Employment Act, commonly known and referred to as the Taylor Law.[1] The purpose of the statute as expressed in its Statement of Policy is to promote harmonious and cooperative relationships between government and its employees by granting to public employees the right of organization and representation; requiring state and local governments to negotiate with and enter into written agreements with recognized employee organizations; encouraging public employers and public employee organizations to agree on procedures for resolving disputes; creating a public

---

5. Cathy v. Prober, 195 A.D.2d 999, 600 N.Y.S.2d 561 (4th Dep't 1993), appeal denied 82 N.Y.2d 660, 605 N.Y.S.2d 5, 625 N.E.2d 590 (1993); People ex rel. Seward v. President, Etc., of Village of Sing Sing, 54 App.Div. 555, 66 N.Y.S. 1094 (2d Dep't 1900); see also Town Law § 24.

CAVEAT: The general rule does not apply to employees covered under the Civil Service Law. A discussion of those provisions is beyond the scope of this chapter.

6. Whelan v. Pitts, 150 A.D.2d 380, 540 N.Y.S.2d 536 (2d Dep't 1989).

7. Public Officers Law § 36.

8. See In re Greco, 99 A.D.2d 810, 472 N.Y.S.2d 140 (2d Dep't 1984); Deats v. Carpenter, 61 A.D.2d 320, 403 N.Y.S.2d 128 (3d Dep't 1978).

PRACTICE POINTER: In light of these and similar cases, it seems clear that a public officer may not be removed for incompetence, neglect of duties or even violation of the law.

§ 3.21

1. Ch. 392, L.1967 (codified at Civil Service Law §§ 200–214).

employment relations board to assist in resolving disputes; and continuing the prohibition against strikes by public employees.[2]

The statute provides that public employees have the right to form, join and participate in, or refrain from forming, joining or participating in, any employee organization of their own choosing.[3] It has been held that a municipality may not deny its employees their right to form, join or participate in an employee organization.[4] The statute further provides that public employees have the right to be represented by employee organizations to negotiate collectively with their public employers in the determination of their terms and conditions of employment and the administration of grievances arising thereunder.[5]

Public employers may, in their discretion, recognize employee organizations.[6] Alternatively, an employee organization may be certified pursuant to the provisions of the statute.[7] Where an employee organization has been recognized or certified, the public employer is required to negotiate collectively with that organization and agree upon the terms and conditions of employment of the public employees.[8] In the absence of a recognized or certified employee organization, it appears that a municipal employer is not legally required to engage in collective bargaining negotiations with its employees.

If a proposed provision of a collective bargaining agreement constitutes a term or condition of employment, the municipal employer must negotiate that provision and, upon reaching agreement, incorporate it into the collective bargaining agreement.[9] The fact that the municipality may not have express statutory authority to provide for a particular term or condition of employment does not preclude it from bargaining since the Taylor Law imposes a broad obligation to bargain except in those cases where there is an explicit statutory prohibition against making an agreement for a particular term or condition of employment.[10] Further, even if a proposed provision does not relate to terms and conditions of employment, the municipal employer must bargain with respect to that provision in the absence of plain and clear statutory prohibition, controlling decisional law or restrictive public policy.[11]

2. Civil Service Law § 200.
3. Civil Service Law § 202.
4. City of Albany v. Helsby, 29 N.Y.2d 433, 328 N.Y.S.2d 658, 278 N.E.2d 898 (1972).
5. Civil Service Law § 203.
6. Civil Service Law § 204(1).
7. See Civil Service Law §§ 206, 207.
8. Civil Service Law § 204(2); see also Clay v. Helsby, 45 A.D.2d 292, 357 N.Y.S.2d 291 (4th Dep't 1974), appeal after remand 51 A.D.2d 200, 379 N.Y.S.2d 896 (1976).
9. Board of Educ. of Huntington v. Associated Teachers of Huntington, 30 N.Y.2d 122, 331 N.Y.S.2d 17, 282 N.E.2d 109 (1972).

10. Id.

11. Board of Educ. of Yonkers City School Dist. v. Yonkers Federation of Teachers, 40 N.Y.2d 268, 386 N.Y.S.2d 657, 353 N.E.2d 569 (1976)(citing Huntington, supra note 9); In the Susquehanna Valley Cent. School Dist. v. Susquehanna Valley Teachers' Assn., 37 N.Y.2d 614, 376 N.Y.S.2d 427, 339 N.E.2d 132 (1975).

PRACTICE POINTER: Clearly, municipalities may not use Dillon's Rule as a shield to justify refusal to bargain on partic-

Library References:
West's Key No. Digests, Labor Relations ⚯171–180.

§ 3.22 Officers and Employees—Conflicts of Interest

In 1964, New York State enacted a generic law governing conflicts of interest of municipal officers and employers.[1] This law codified the common law rules and has the threefold purposes of protecting the public from municipal contracts influenced by avaricious officers, protecting innocent public officers from unwarranted assaults on their integrity, and encouraging each community to adopt an appropriate code of ethics to supplement the State statutory law.[2]

The statutory provision against conflicts of interest is set forth in a single sentence which provides in substance that unless one of a number of specific statutory exceptions is applicable, a municipal officer or employee may not have an interest in a municipal contract where the officer or employee has the power or duty to (1) negotiate, prepare, authorize or approve the contract or authorize or approve payment under the contract; (2) audit bills or claims under the contract; or (3) appoint an officer or employer who has any of these powers or duties.[3] This provision also prohibits any chief fiscal officer, treasurer or his deputy or employee of the municipality from having an interest in a bank or trust company designated as a depository, paying agent, registration agent, or designated for the investment of funds of the municipality.[4]

The key terms contained in the statutory prohibition against conflicts are "contract" and "interest." "Contract" is defined as:

> [A]ny claim, account or demand against or agreement with a municipality, express or implied, and shall include the designation of a depository of funds and the designation of a newspaper, including, but not limited to, an official newspaper, for the publication of any notice, resolution, ordinance, or other proceeding where such publication is required or authorized by law.[5]

"Interest" is defined as "a direct or indirect pecuniary or material benefit accruing to a municipal officer or employee as the result of a contract with the municipality which such officer or employee serves."[6]

---

ular terms or conditions of employment. *See supra*, § 3.7. Indeed, collective bargaining negotiations can become a sword to provide the necessary authority for undertaking certain actions which are not expressly prohibited by statute but for which specific affirmative authority is lacking.

§ 3.22
1. Ch. 946, L.1964 (codified at General Municipal Law §§ 800–809).
2. Ch. 946, L.1964 § 1.
3. General Municipal Law § 801.
4. *Id.*
5. General Municipal Law § 800(2).
6. *Id.*

§ 3.22

The statute provides that municipal officers and employees are deemed to have an interest in the contracts of: (1) their spouse and minor and dependent children (except an employment contract); (2) a firm, partnership or association of which they are a member or employee; and (3) a corporation of which they are an employee, director or officer, or in which they directly or indirectly own stock.[7]

In order for there to be a conflict of interest under the statute, there must be both a contract between a municipal officer or employee and the municipality he or she serves and an interest in the contract on the part of the officer or employee. If the transaction at issue is not a contract or if the municipal officer or employee does not have an interest, there can be no conflict of interest.

If the transaction at issue does constitute a conflict of interest, it will not be a prohibited conflict if one of the statutory exceptions applies.[8] Regardless of whether a particular interest in a contract is prohibited or not, municipal officers and employees are required to publicly disclose in writing to the governing board of the municipality the nature of any interest they have, will have or later acquire in a contract with the municipality they serve as soon as they have knowledge of the actual or prospective interest.[9]

Any contract wilfully entered into in which there is an interest prohibited by Article 18 is null, void and wholly unenforceable.[10] Furthermore, any municipal officer or employee who willfully and knowingly violates the provisions of Article 18 is guilty of a misdemeanor.[11]

In addition to dealing with interests in contract with the municipality which an officer serves or is employed by, Article 18 also prohibits certain other actions by municipal officers and employees including: (1) soliciting or accepting gifts under circumstances where it could reasonably be inferred that the gift was intended to influence the performance of his official duties; (2) disclosing confidential information acquired in the course of performing official duties; (3) receiving or contracting to receive compensation for services to be rendered in relation to any matter before any agency of the municipality of which he is an officer, member or employee or over which he has jurisdiction or appointment power; and (4) receiving or contracting to receive compensation for services to be rendered in relation to any matter before any agency of his

---

7. *Id.*

8. *See* General Municipal Law § 802 which lists 15 specific transactions which are not prohibited, notwithstanding the existence of a conflict of interest under General Municipal Law § 801.

9. General Municipal Law § 803. The disclosure requirement does not apply where an interest in contract derives from a municipal officer's or employee's ownership of stock in a corporation and the officer or employee owns or controls less than five percent of the outstanding stock.

10. General Municipal Law § 804.

11. General Municipal Law § 805.

municipality which is contingent upon any action by the agency with respect to the matter.[12]

Municipalities are also authorized to adopt codes of ethics prescribing the standards of conduct reasonably expected of them.[13] Local codes of ethics may prohibit conduct not prohibited under Article 18, but may not authorize conduct prohibited under that statute.[14]

Library References:

West's Key No. Digests, Municipal Corporations ⚖ 231(1)–231(4).

§ 3.23 Officers and Employees—Conflicts of Interest—Checklist

The following checklist can be used to determine whether there is a prohibited conflict of interest in any proposed contract between a municipality and a municipal officer or employee, as defined in General Municipal Law §§ 800(4) and (5).

1. Is there a "contract" as defined in General Municipal Law § 800(2)? (See § 3.22) If not, there can be no conflict. If yes, ask Question 2.

2. Does the officer or employee have an "interest" in the contract as defined in General Municipal Law § 800(3); that is, a direct or indirect pecuniary or material benefit accruing to the officer or employee as a result of a contract with the municipality? Remember, the officer or employee is deemed to have an interest in the contract of a:

    • Spouse, minor children and dependents, except an employment contract.

    • Firm, partnership or association that the officer or employee is a member or employee of.

    • Corporation of which the officer or employee is an officer, director or employee.

    • Corporation in which stock is owned or controlled directly or indirectly by the officer employee. (See § 3.22) If not, there can be no conflict. If yes, ask Question 3.

3. Does the officer or employee have General Municipal Law § 801 powers to:

    • Negotiate, prepare, authorize or approve the contract or authorize or approve payment under the contract.

---

12. General Municipal Law § 805–a.
13. General Municipal Law § 806.
14. Id.

PRACTICE POINTER: Local codes of ethics are often more restrictive than General Municipal Law Article 18, particularly with respect to municipal officers or employers appearing before boards or agencies of their municipality, and the existence and possible applicability of a local code of ethics should be determined in such cases.

- Audit bills or claims under the contract.
- Appoint an officer or employee who has any of these powers or duties. (*See* § 3.22)

4. Do any of the exceptions provided in General Municipal Law § 802 apply to the contract? (*See* § 3.22)

If yes, there is no prohibited conflict but disclosure is required as in 3 above. If not, there is a prohibited conflict of interest and, if willfully and knowingly entered into the contract is null and void and the officer or employee is guilty of a misdemeanor.[1] (*See* § 3.22)

§ 3.24 Contracts

General rules relating to contracts apply to agreements to which a municipal corporation is a party. Thus, the basic elements of any contract, *e.g.*, offer and acceptance, materiality, consideration, must be present in any contract with a municipality.[1]

Nonetheless, there are certain matters which are unique to contracts with a municipality which practitioners must be aware of when representing private individuals or entities in contract negotiations involving a municipality. This is especially important because it has been held that contracts entered into by a municipality with respect to subject matter beyond its corporate powers or without following statutorily mandated procedures are not enforceable against the municipality.[2]

The municipality must have legal authority to enter into the contract. Generally, this means that the contract must be in furtherance of some proper municipal purpose or function. The authority can be either express or implied.[3]

In addition, the contract must be authorized and executed by the proper board or officer. For example, in towns and villages the town supervisor and mayor, respectively, are required to execute all contracts in the name of the town or village.[4] A contract executed by an officer who does not have legal authority to contract on behalf of a municipality is not enforceable.[5]

Any applicable procedural requirements must also be observed. For example, purchase and public works contracts must be entered into in

---

§ 3.23
1. General Municipal Law §§ 804, 805.

§ 3.24
1. 10 McQullin, *Municipal Corporations* § 29.02, p.245 (3d ed. 1990). *See generally,* Chapter 5 *"Commercial Sales Contracts," infra.*
2. *See, e.g.,* Lutzken v. City of Rochester, 7 A.D.2d 498, 184 N.Y.S.2d 483 (4th Dep't 1959).

3. *See supra,* § 3.7, for a discussion of the powers of municipal corporations.
4. Town Law § 64(6); Village Law § 4–400(1)(i).
5. *See* City of Zanesville v. Mohawk Data Sciences Corp., 97 A.D.2d 64, 468 N.Y.S.2d 271 (4th Dep't 1983).

compliance with applicable competitive bidding requirements.[6] Contracts for the acquisition or sale of real property may be subject to referendum requirements.[7] As a general rule, unless the power to enter into contracts has been properly delegated to another board or officer, the governing board of the municipality must authorize the contract, typically by resolution.[8]

The general rule regarding duration of municipal contracts has been stated as follows:

> [I]t appears reasonable that a municipal contract may cover any length of time, provided it does not cede away control or embarrass the legislative or governmental powers of the municipality or render it unable in the future to control any municipal matter over which it has jurisdiction.[9]

In New York, it is well established that any contract which has the effect of binding a successor governing board in its legislative or governmental, as distinguished from its proprietary capacity, is void.[10] Where there is no statutory limit on the term and the contract does not deal with a governmental power, the contract generally may be for a reasonable term under the circumstances.[11]

In certain cases, municipal corporations may ratify contracts made on their behalf which have initially been entered into without proper legal authority. Thus, a municipal corporation may ratify a contract and make it a binding obligation if the contract was within its general powers but was invalid because it was defectively or irregularly executed, or because the officer or agent who executed it on behalf of the municipality lacked the requisite authority.[12] Ratification may take place either by express action or by implication.[13] Of course, where there is no underlying authority to enter into a contract in the first instance, *e.g.*, where the contract is *ultra vires*, the contract can not subsequently be ratified by the governing board.[14]

---

6. *See* General Municipal Law § 103; *see also infra*, § 3.25.

7. *See supra*, § 3.16.

8. PRACTICE POINTER: When representing a client who is entering into a contract with a municipality, it is always advisable to obtain proof that a resolution of the governing board of the municipality authorizing the contract has been duly adopted. If the contract is signed on behalf of the municipality by an officer other than the chief executive officer, it is advisable to determine whether authority to bind the municipality by contract has been properly delegated to the officer.

9. *See* 10A McQuillin, *Municipal Corporations* § 29.100 (3d ed. 1990).

10. Morin v. Foster, 45 N.Y.2d 287, 408 N.Y.S.2d 387, 380 N.E.2d 217 (1978).

11. *See* 10A McQuillin, *Municipal Corporations* § 29.100, p.35 (3d ed. 1990).

12. *See* Seif v. City of Long Beach, 286 N.Y. 382, 36 N.E.2d 630 (1941).

13. Seif, *supra* note 12; Centereach Rentals, Inc. v. Town of Huntington, 150 Misc.2d 462, 574 N.Y.S.2d 636 (Dist.Ct., Suffolk County, 1991)(citing 27 N.Y.Jur.2d Counties, Towns and Municipal Corporations § 1219).

14. 10A McQuillin, *Municipal Corporations* § 29.104, p.60 (3d ed. 1990).

Municipalities have the same obligations and are subject to the same limitations as other parties to a contract.[15] It follows that a municipality may be sued for damages for its breach of a contract in the same manner as if the contract had been made with an individual, firm or private corporation. Likewise, if not in default, a municipality may sue to enforce its contracts.[16] There are no special requirements for bringing an action against a municipality for breach of contract.[17]

Library References:

West's Key No. Digests, Municipal Corporations ⟐226–255.5, 326–376.5.

§ 3.25 Contracts—Competitive Bidding

While competitive bidding of municipal contracts generally has been required in New York State since the mid-1800's, prior to 1953, there was no comprehensive, uniform bidding statute applicable to all municipalities. In 1953, Article 5–A of the General Municipal Law[1] was enacted with the intent of establishing consistent, uniform competitive bidding requirements for all municipalities. Currently, all contracts for public work involving an expenditure of more than $20,000 and all purchase contracts involving an expenditure of more than $10,000 must be awarded by the appropriate officer, board or agency of a political subdivision or of any district therein, to the lowest responsible bidder furnishing the required security after the advertisement for sealed bids in the manner provided by the statute.[2]

Neither the term "purchase" nor "public work" is defined for purposes of Section 103. However, it is generally agreed that the term "purchase" applies to purchases of materials, supplies, equipment or apparatus.[3] The term "public work" applies to contracts involving labor and construction.[4]

There are a number of statutory and common law exceptions to the competitive bidding requirements of Section 103. Statutory exceptions

---

15. Bingham v. Town of Greenburgh, 30 Misc.2d 64, 218 N.Y.S.2d 888 (Sup.Ct., Westchester County, 1961).

16. See 10A McQuillin, *Municipal Corporations* § 29.124, p.164 (3d ed. 1990).

17. See infra, § 3.30 for a discussion of special requirements applicable to the institution of tort actions against municipalities.

§ 3.25

1. General Municipal Law §§ 100—109-b.

2. General Municipal Law § 103(1). For purposes of Section 103, the definition of a political subdivision includes school districts and boards of cooperative educational services.

CAVEAT: Section 103 is the exclusive law of the state governing competitive bidding and school districts and other municipalities are powerless to change the applicability of the provisions of § 103 by local law or other similar local legislative enactment.

3. Albion Industrial Center v. Town of Albion, 62 A.D.2d 478, 405 N.Y.S.2d 521 (4th Dep't 1978).

4. See Long Meadow Associates v. City of Glen Cove, 171 A.D.2d 731, 567 N.Y.S.2d 287 (2d Dep't 1991).

PRACTICE POINTER: Where a contract involves both the purchase of equipment and the provision of services, as a general rule it is best to apply the monetary limit of that component of the contract which involves the larger portion of the cost of work.

Ch. 3   CONTRACTS—COMPETITIVE BIDDING   § 3.25

include: emergencies;[5] purchases of surplus and second-hand supplies, materials or equipment from the federal government, the State of New York or from any other political subdivision, district or public benefit corporation;[6] and purchases of materials, equipment and supplies through the New York State Office of General Services, Division of Standards and Purchase.[7]

The most common of the common law exceptions to the competitive bidding requirements is the so-called "professional services" exception. Under this exception, the requirements of § 103 have been found to be inapplicable to contracts for "services which require in their proper performance scientific knowledge or professional skill."[8]

Another long-standing common law exception to competitive bidding requirements exists in cases where the subject matter of a contract is controlled by a sole source so that there is no possibility of competition. This exception covers any circumstance where there is only a single potential bidder and is intended to enable political subdivisions to save the time and expense of seeking bids where there is no possibility of competition.[9] However, goods and services which are not required by law to be procured pursuant to the competitive bidding procedures of General Municipal Law § 103 must be procured in a manner that assures the prudent and economical use of public monies in the best interests of the taxpayers and guards against favoritism, extravagance, fraud and corruption.[10]

The procedural requirements for competitive bidding are set forth in General Municipal Law § 103. Generally, these requirements include published advertisement for bids in the official newspaper of the municipality or another newspaper designated by the municipality for such purpose.[11] The bid specifications may be included in the advertisement itself, or, as is typical in construction projects, in a separate document that is referred to in the advertisement and which advises bidders on how to obtain copies of the bid specifications. On all contracts for the construction, reconstruction or alteration of buildings where the entire cost exceeds $50,000.00, separate bid specifications must be prepared for:

---

5. General Municipal Law § 103(4).
6. General Municipal Law § 103(6).
7. General Municipal Law § 104.
8. People ex rel. Smith v. Flagg, 17 N.Y. 584 (1858).

PRACTICE POINTER: The State Comptroller's Office has rendered numerous opinions on the applicability of competitive bidding requirements to various types of contracts, as well as on many other competitive bidding issues, and these opinions are a good starting point in researching any bidding question. Among the types of services which the Comptroller has found to come within the ambit of the professional services exception to competitive bidding are engineering services; legal services; insurance coverage and/or services of an insurance broker; architectural services; installation of certain security systems; and computer data processing services.

9. See Harlem Gaslight Co. v. City of New York, 33 N.Y. 309 (1865).
10. See General Municipal Law § 104-b.
11. General Municipal Law § 103(1), (3).

(1) plumbing and gas fittings; (2) heating and air conditioning apparatus; and (3) electrical work.[12] Pursuant to General Municipal Law § 103(2) at least five days must elapse between the first publication of the advertisement and the date on which bids are to be publicly opened and read.

Following advertisement for sealed bids and passage of the required notice period, contracts must be awarded by the appropriate officer, board or agency "to the lowest responsible bidder furnishing the required security."[13] With respect to the issue of "responsibility" of a bidder, the elements which courts have recognized as being valid considerations by the awarding body in determining responsibility of bidders are financial condition, working organization, prior experience and criminal record.[14]

It is common practice for municipalities when advertising for bids to reserve the right to reject all bids. Reservation of the right to reject all bids gives the municipality the ability to avoid awarding a contract where the bids are all higher than anticipated or where other unforeseen occurrences make it undesirable to go ahead with the contract.[15]

The general rule is that a contract entered into in violation of competitive bidding requirements is void and unenforceable. Courts have held that once a contract is proven to have been awarded without the required bidding, a waste of public funds is presumed and the contract may be set aside.[16] Further, the contractor under a contract entered into in violation of applicable bidding requirements may not recover for the amount of the contract price or for the value of the services rendered and may be required to return any payments previously received.[17]

Library References:

West's Key No. Digests, Municipal Corporations ⟹234–242, 330–337.

§ 3.26 Municipal Finance

Unlike Article VII of the State Constitution dealing with State finances and containing various requirements relative to the adoption of an annual budget, Article VIII of the State Constitution contains no provisions regarding the adoption of an annual budget by municipal

---

12. General Municipal Law § 101.

13. General Municipal Law § 103(1).

14. *See, e.g.*, Abco Bus Co., Inc. v. Macchiarola, 52 N.Y.2d 938, 437 N.Y.S.2d 967, 419 N.E.2d 870 (1981); Ward La France Truck Corp. v. City of New York, 7 Misc.2d 739, 160 N.Y.S.2d 679 (Sup.Ct., N.Y. County, 1957).

15. **CAVEAT**: The right to reject all bids is not unqualified and when exercising this right, a municipality must act reasonably and in good faith and must avoid favoritism, abuse of discretion and corruption. *See* Carucci v. Dulan, 24 A.D.2d 529, 261 N.Y.S.2d 677 (4th Dep't 1965).

16. *See, e.g.*, Gerzof v. Sweeney, 16 N.Y.2d 206, 264 N.Y.S.2d 376, 211 N.E.2d 826 (1965); S.T. Grand, Inc. v. City of New York, 32 N.Y.2d 300, 344 N.Y.S.2d 938, 298 N.E.2d 105 (1973).

17. *Id.*

corporations. Budgeting provisions are found in the general statutes for counties, towns and villages[1] and in city charter provisions.

In general, following the submission of estimated revenues and expenditures by each administrative unit to the budget officer, preliminary or tentative municipal budgets are prepared containing proposed appropriations and an estimate of revenues for the ensuing fiscal year.[2] The preliminary or tentative budget is then subject to a public hearing. After the hearing the governing body may adopt the budget as submitted or with changes that the governing body deems appropriate.[3] If the governing board fails to finally adopt a budget by the date required by law, the preliminary or tentative budget will be deemed by law to be the final budget.[4]

No expenditure or contract involving an expenditure of money may be entered into by any public officer or employee unless an amount has been appropriated and is available for such purpose or has been authorized to be borrowed pursuant to the Local Finance Law.[5] Supplemental appropriations and transfers of funds between appropriations may be made during a fiscal year provided monies are available.[6]

Real property taxes are the primary source of revenue for financing the governmental expenses of municipal corporations in New York. The amount of the annual real property tax levy is determined by subtracting from the total amount of appropriations the amount of estimated revenues other than from property taxes and the difference is the amount needed to be raised by real property taxes. The only limitation on the amount which municipalities may raise by real property taxes is the applicable tax limit contained in the State Constitution.[7]

The deposit and investment of public funds prior to expenditure is strictly regulated by statute. In general, these statutes restrict deposits of public fund to banks or trust companies designated by the governing board and restrict investment of public funds to: (1) special time deposit accounts or certificates of deposit issued by a bank or trust company; (2) obligations issued or guaranteed by the United States of America; and (3) obligations of the State of New York or of a municipal corporation.[8] All deposits and investments in excess of the amount which may be

---

§ 3.26

1. *See* County Law Art. 7; Town Law Art. 8; and Village Law Art. 5, respectively.

2. *See* County Law §§ 355, 356; Town Law §§ 104, 107; Village Law §§ 5–502, 5–506.

3. County Law § 359; Town Law § 108; Village Law § 5–508(3).

4. County Law § 361; Town Law § 109 (3); Village Law § 5–508(4).

5. County Law § 362(1); Town Law § 117; Village Law § 520(2).

6. County Law § 363; Town Law § 112; Village Law § 5–520(4).

7. New York State Constitution Art. VIII, § 10 which limits the amount of taxes in counties, cities and villages to certain percentages of the average full valuation of taxable real property of such municipalities subject to certain exclusions. Towns do not have a constitutional tax limit.

8. *See* General Municipal Law §§ 10, 11.

§ 3.26   MUNICIPAL LAW   Ch. 3

covered under the provisions of the Federal Deposit Insurance Act must be secured in the manner provided by statute.[9]

Library References:

West's Key No. Digests, Municipal Corporations ⇔879.

§ 3.27   Municipal Finance—Municipal Borrowing

Municipal corporations are authorized to borrow money to finance the acquisition, construction or reconstruction of capital improvements, equipment purchases and to meet their operating expenses. In general, municipal debt may be evidenced only by bonds or notes.[1] In addition, municipalities may enter into installment purchase contracts for the purchase of equipment, machinery and apparatus.[2]

Bonds are the instruments normally used to evidence long-term debt. Bonds are used to provide permanent financing for capital improvements and equipment purchases and to finance certain non-capital purposes such as the payment of settled claims and judgments. Bonds are normally payable over a period of more than one year. A portion of the principal amount of a bond must be paid in annual installments.[3] As a matter of custom in the municipal finance industry, interest is typically paid in semi-annual installments.

Notes are the instruments generally used to evidence short-term debt. Notes are used to provide cash flow financing and temporary financing for capital purposes. Generally, notes are payable within one year or less from the date of issuance, and may be renewed annually or at shorter intervals subject to certain restrictions on the number of renewals. The interest rate on a note is subject to renegotiation each time the note is renewed while interest on a bond is fixed for the life of the bond.

As an alternative to the issuance of bonds or notes to finance the acquisition of machinery, apparatus and equipment purchases, municipalities are also authorized to enter into installment purchase contracts. Installment purchase contracts are defined to include a lease purchase agreement, installment sale agreement or other similar agreement providing for periodic payments to be made to finance the acquisition of equipment, machinery or apparatus.[4]

Bonds and notes must contain a pledge that they are backed by the faith and credit of the issuing municipality.[5] Installment purchase con-

---

9. General Municipal Law § 10(3).

§ 3.27

1. Local Finance Law § 20.00(a).
2. Local Finance Law § 20.00(d); General Municipal Law § 109–b.
3. New York State Constitution Art. VIII, § 2; Local Finance Law §§ 21.00(b), 22.10(c).
4. General Municipal Law § 109–b(1)(b).
5. New York State Constitution Art. VIII, § 2; Local Finance Law § 51.00 (8).

tracts, on the other hand, must contain a provision to the effect that the contract is *not* backed by the full faith and credit of the municipality, that annual installment payments are subject to annual appropriation by the municipality, and that there is no legal or moral obligation to appropriate monies for the contract.[6]

The issuance of obligations by a municipality is governed by federal as well as State law. Federal law requirements pertain to the ability of purchasers of the obligations to exclude interest payments on the obligations from gross income for federal income tax purposes.[7] The interest earned on obligations issued by municipalities is also exempt from New York State and local income taxation.[8] Because the interest paid on local government obligations is currently excluded from federal and state income taxes, municipalities are able to borrow at interest rates which are normally several percentage points below the rates for comparable commercial loans.

While this Section will focus on State law requirements pertinent to the issuance of bonds and notes, it is important to note, that in order for the interest on these obligations to be eligible for exclusion from gross income for federal income tax purposes, a number of federal tax law requirements must be met in connection with the issuance of the bonds and use of bond-financed property. These requirements relate to matters including, but not limited to, the extent to which the proceeds of the obligations are used for private business purposes, temporary investment of the proceeds prior to expenditure, use of the proceeds to reimburse prior expenditures, and registration of the obligations.[9]

Generally, bonds and/or notes may be issued for capital purposes, to meet unanticipated current expenses and to meet cash flow needs. Capital purposes may be financed through the issuance of bond anticipation notes,[10] capital notes,[11] bonds[12] or some combination thereof.

Unanticipated current expenses are those expenses for which insufficient or no provision has been made in the annual budget. The type of obligation authorized to be used to finance unanticipated current ex-

---

6. General Municipal Law § 109–b(2)(f).
PRACTICE POINTER: The full faith and credit pledge pursuant to which municipalities pledge their tax levying power for the payment of bonds and notes allows these obligations to bear interest at a lower rate than the rate on an installment purchase contract or other similar government obligations which are subject to annual appropriation.
7. See I.R.C. § 103.
8. Local Finance Law § 162.00.
9. See I.R.C. § 148.
PRACTICE POINTER: Special counsel concentrating their practice in municipal finance known as Bond Counsel are often retained to render an approving opinion in connection with the issuance of municipal obligations. The opinion typically states in substance that, in the opinion of Bond Counsel, (1) the obligations have been duly authorized and issued and are valid obligations of the issuer and (2) interest on the obligations may be excluded from federal income taxation and New York State and local income taxation.
10. Local Finance Law § 23.00.
11. Local Finance Law § 28.00.
12. Local Finance Law § 21.00.

penses is a budget note. Budget notes may be issued to finance unanticipated expenses in amounts up to five percent of the annual budget and also to finance public emergencies which threaten lives and property without limitation as to amount.[13]

Cash flow needs may be financed either through tax anticipation notes ("TANS") or revenue anticipation notes ("RANS"). TANS may be issued in anticipation of the collection of real property taxes or assessments,[14] and RANS may be issued in anticipation of the collection of certain defined revenues other than real property taxes, e.g., State aid payments, water rents and sewer rents.[15] Generally, the amount of TANS or RANS which may be issued during a fiscal year is limited to the amount of taxes and assessments or the amount of revenues anticipated during that year less the amount of taxes and assessments or revenues received as of the date of issue.[16]

The Local Finance Law provides a two part test which must be met as a pre-requisite to any borrowing.[17] First, the object or purpose for which borrowing is proposed must have a period of probable usefulness set forth in § 11.00 of the Local Finance Law. Second, the municipality must be authorized to expend money for the object or purpose for which borrowing is proposed; that is, it must be a proper county, city, town or village purpose. In addition, the amount of proposed borrowing must be within the municipality's debt limit.[18] Debt incurred in excess of the applicable debt limit is void.[19]

There are, however, some significant exclusions from municipal debt limits. The most important exclusions are for indebtedness contracted for water and sewer improvements[20] and indebtedness contracted for any public improvement to the extent that the improvement is self-supporting.[21]

The issuance of bonds or notes must be authorized by the adoption of a bond or note resolution, as appropriate.[22] Bond resolutions and capital note resolutions must be adopted by a two-thirds vote of the

---

13. Local Finance Law § 29.00.

14. Local Finance Law § 24.00(a)(1).

15. Local Finance Law § 25.00(b).

16. *See* Local Finance Law §§ 24.00(g) and 25.00(d).

17. Local Finance Law § 10.00.

18. New York State Constitution Art. VIII, § 4 limits the amount of indebtedness which may be incurred by municipalities to specified percentages of the municipality's average full value. Average full value is determined on the basis of the full values of taxable real property taken from the most recently completed and four preceding years' assessment rolls.

19. *Id.*

20. New York State Constitution Art. VIII, § 5(B), (E); Local Finance Law § 124.10.

21. New York State Constitution Art. viii, § 5(C); Local Finance Law § 123.00.

22. **CAVEAT**: Under the State Environmental Quality Review Act and its implementing regulations, the adoption of a bond resolution has been held to constitute an "action" which must be preceded by appropriate environmental review before the issuance of bonds may be authorized. *See* Matter of Tri–County Taxpayers Ass'n., Inc. v. Town Board of Queensbury, 55 N.Y.2d 41, 447 N.Y.S.2d 699, 432 N.E.2d 592 (1982). *See generally*, Chapter 15 "Environmental Law," *supra*.

voting strength of the finance board (*e.g.*, the governing board or, in some cities, a board of estimate or board of estimate and apportionment) of the municipality except that where the resolution is subject to mandatory referendum or where the finance board determines that a bond resolution shall be submitted to a referendum, three-fifths approval of the finance board is sufficient.[23] Other types of note resolutions may be adopted by simple majority vote of the finance board and are not subject to referendum requirements.

Library References:
West's Key No. Digests, Municipal Corporations ⊙⇒869.

§ 3.28 Public Meetings

Town boards and county boards of supervisors are required to hold an annual organizational meeting at the beginning of each year, and monthly or regular meetings thereafter.[1] Although the Village Law contains a reference to the annual meeting,[2] there is no provision prescribing the time for holding the meeting nor is there any specific statutory requirement that an annual meeting be held. Typically, as a matter of custom and practice villages hold their annual meetings at the commencement of the official year.[3] In cities, the city charter must be examined to determine the specific requirements, if any, for holding an organizational meeting of the governing board and regular meetings thereafter.

Pursuant to the mandate of the Open Meetings Law,[4] every meeting of a "public body" except an executive session, must be open to the general public.[5] The definition of a "public body" includes the governing board of every municipal corporation as well as every meeting of a municipal department, agency, bureau or commission.[6] A meeting is defined simply as the official convening of a public body for the purpose of conducting public business[7] and an "executive session" is defined as that portion of a meeting not open to the general public.[8] Advisory and other similar committees which provide purely advisory, non-binding guidance have been held not to constitute public bodies for purposes of the Open Meetings Law.[9]

23. Local Finance Law § 33.00(a).

§ 3.28

1. Town Law § 62; County Law § 152.

2. Village Law § 3-302(2).

3. *See* Village Law § 3-302(1) for time of commencement of the official year.

4. Public Officers Law §§ 100–111.

5. Public Officers Law § 103(a).

6. *See* Public Officers Law § 102(2).

7. Public Officers Law § 102(1).

8. Public Officers Law § 102(3).

9. Goodson Todman Enterprises, Ltd. v. Town Board of Milan, 151 A.D.2d 642, 542 N.Y.S.2d 373 (2d Dep't 1989), appeal denied 74 N.Y.2d 614, 547 N.Y.S.2d 848, 547 N.E.2d 103 (1989).

CAVEAT: When advisory bodies exercise governmental functions, they may be subject to the Open Meetings Law. *See* Syracuse United Neighbors v. City of Syracuse, 80 A.D.2d 984, 437 N.Y.S.2d 466 (4th Dep't 1981), appeal dismissed 55 N.Y.2d 995, 449 N.Y.S.2d 201, 434 N.E.2d 270 (1982).

§ 3.28 MUNICIPAL LAW Ch. 3

The term "meeting" as used in the Open Meetings Law has been construed broadly. The leading case held that any gathering of a public body for the purpose of conducting business constitutes a meeting, regardless of whether there is any intent to take any particular action, and therefore concluded that a so-called "work session" held solely for the purpose of discussing a particular matter was nonetheless a meeting subject to the law.[10]

Public notice of every meeting of a public body must be given in the manner required by the Public Officers Law. Notice of the time and place of a meeting which is scheduled at least one week in advance must be given to the news media and conspicuously posted in one or more designated public locations at least 72 hours before the meeting.[11] Notice of the time and place of a meeting scheduled less than one week in advance must be given, to the extent practicable, to the news media and be conspicuously posted in one or more designated public locations at a reasonable time prior the meeting.[12] Publication of the notice of meeting as a legal notice is not required.[13]

The Public Officers Law does not mandate any particular place where meetings must be held.[14] Absent unusual extenuating circumstances, meetings should generally be held within the geographic boundaries of the municipality of the public body convening the meeting.

Every meeting of a public body must be open to the general public except where the body meeting calls an executive session.[15] A public body may call an executive session by majority vote of its total membership taken in an open meeting pursuant to a motion identifying the general area or areas of the subject or subjects to be considered.[16] An executive session may be convened only for the purpose of discussing one or more of the matters enumerated in Public Officers Law § 105(1). No action by formal vote may be taken which involves the appropriation of public monies at an executive session.[17]

Minutes of all open meetings and executive sessions are required to be kept consisting, at a minimum, of a record or summary of all motions, proposals, resolutions and any other matters formally voted on and the vote thereon.[18] All minutes of open meetings are required to be made

---

10. Orange County Publications v. Council of Newburgh, 60 A.D.2d 409, 401 N.Y.S.2d 84 (2d Dep't 1978), aff'd 45 N.Y.2d 947, 411 N.Y.S.2d 564, 383 N.E.2d 1157 (1978).

11. Public Officers Law § 104(1).

12. Public Officers Law § 104(2).

PRACTICE POINTER: Where public bodies prepare a schedule of meetings in advance for the upcoming year, such as at the annual organizational meeting, the notice requirements can be met by sending the schedule to the media and continuously posting the schedule in one or more conspicuous locations. Thereafter, additional meeting notices would be required only for emergency, unscheduled meetings.

13. Public Officers Law § 104(3).

14. *Cf.* Town Law § 62.

15. Public Officers Law § 103(1).

16. Public Officers Law § 105(1).

17. *Id.*

18. Public Officers Law § 106(1), (2).

available to the public within two weeks from the date of the meeting in accordance with the provisions of the Freedom of Information Law.[19] All minutes of executive sessions must be made available within one week from the date of the executive session.[20] It has also been held that persons attending public meetings may tape the meetings, provided that it is done in an unobtrusive manner.[21]

Aggrieved persons are entitled to seek judicial relief to enforce the Open Meetings Law provisions either by an Article 78 proceeding and/or an action for declaratory judgment and injunctive relief.[22] Actions taken in violation of the law, upon good cause shown, may be voided, in whole or in part.[23] Costs and reasonable attorney fees may be awarded in the discretion of the court.[24]

A Committee on Open Government is required to be created under the provisions of the Freedom of Information Law.[25] The Committee is required to issue advisory opinions from time to time as, in its discretion, may be required to inform public bodies and persons of the interpretations of the Open Meetings Law.[26]

Library References:

West's Key No. Digests, Municipal Corporations ⚖86–92.

§ 3.29 Access to Records

Access to public records is provided for by statute under the Freedom of Information Law or FOIL. New York's original FOIL was enacted in 1974[1] and repealed and reenacted in 1977.[2]

In general, under the statute, all records of an agency are open and available to the public for inspection unless they fall within one of the statutory exceptions. An agency is defined in pertinent part to include any municipal department, board, bureau, division, commission, public authority, public corporation, council, office or other governmental entity performing a governmental or proprietary function for the state or any one or more municipalities, except the judiciary.[3] This definition

---

19. *See infra*, § 3.29.

20. Public Officers Law § 106(3).

21. *See* Mitchell v. Board of Education of Garden City Union Free School District, 113 A.D.2d 924, 493 N.Y.S.2d 826 (2d Dep't 1985); Peloquin v. Arsenault, 162 Misc.2d 306, 616 N.Y.S.2d 716 (Sup.Ct., Franklin County, 1994); Comm. on Open Gov't. FOIL–AO–4826.

22. Public Officers Law § 107(1).

23. *Id*.

24. Public Officers Law § 107 (2).

25. Public Officers Law § 89(1)(a).

PRACTICE POINTER: Counsel's office for the Committee on Open Government can generally provide immediate informal advice on any questions involving open meetings or access to records.

26. Public Officers Law § 109.

§ 3.29

1. Chs. 578, 579, 580, L.1974.

2. Ch. 933, L.1977 (codified at Public Officers Law §§ 84 *et seq.*).

3. Public Officers Law § 86(3).

PRACTICE POINTER: Although judicial records are not subject to access under FOIL, they are subject to statutory, common law and constitutional presumptions of access which may only be overcome on a

§ 3.29   MUNICIPAL LAW   Ch. 3

clearly includes municipalities as well as any units thereof.[4]

Records are defined to include any information kept, held, filed, produced or reproduced by, with or for an agency in any physical form whatsoever including, but not limited to, reports, statements, examinations, memoranda, opinions, folders, files, books, manuals, pamphlets, forms, papers, designs, drawings, maps, photos, letters, microfilms, computer tapes or discs, rules, regulations or codes.[5] In general, this means a record or document which is prepared by an agency in the normal conduct of its business since FOIL specifically provides, with limited exceptions, that the statute should not be construed to require any entity to prepare any record not possessed or maintained by the entity.[6]

It is noteworthy that although the FOIL statute pre-dates the age of computers, the definition of records "in any physical form whatsoever" appears to be broad enough to include computer discs, tapes and other types of electronic data storage devices. Several cases have recognized the increased use of computers and have held that access to this data should not be denied or restricted merely because it is not in printed form.[7]

As previously noted, FOIL contains a presumption of access to records. Agencies are required to adopt rules and regulations pertaining to the availability of records and procedures to be followed including but not limited to: (1) the times and places records are available; (2) the persons from whom records may be obtained; and (3) fees for copies.[8] Denial of access to records is permitted only when specifically authorized.[9]

---

proper showing. *See* People v. Burton, 189 A.D.2d 532, 597 N.Y.S.2d 488 (3d Dep't 1993); Judiciary Law § 4.

4. *See* Buffalo News v. Buffalo Enterprise Dev. Corp., 84 N.Y.2d 488, 619 N.Y.S.2d 695, 644 N.E.2d 277 (1994) (holding that the definition of "agency" subject to FOIL should be liberally construed and that the Buffalo Enterprise Dev. Corp., which channeled funds into the community and enjoyed many of the attributes of public entities was an agency of the city).

5. Public Officers Law § 86(4).

6. Public Officers Law § 89(3). The only pertinent exceptions are that agencies are required to keep (a) a record of the final vote of each member in every proceeding in which the agency member votes; (b) a record setting forth the name, public office, address, title and salary of every officer and employee of the agency; and (c) a reasonably detailed current list, by subject matter, of all records in the possession of the agency, whether or not available under FOIL. Public Officers Law § 87(3).

7. *See* Brownstone Publishers, Inc. v. New York City Dept. of Buildings, 166 A.D.2d 294, 560 N.Y.S.2d 642 (1st Dep't 1990); Babigian v. Evans, 104 Misc.2d 136, 427 N.Y.S.2d 688 (Sup.Ct., N.Y. County, 1980), aff'd 97 A.D.2d 992, 469 N.Y.S.2d 834 (1st Dep't 1983).

8. Public Officers Law § 87(1)(b).

PRACTICE POINTER: Exemptions to access under FOIL are to be narrowly construed and the agency has the burden of showing that the materials for which access is denied fit within the claimed exemption. *See* Matter of Fink v. Lefkowitz, 47 N.Y.2d 567, 419 N.Y.S.2d 467, 393 N.E.2d 463 (1979).

9. *See* Public Officers Law § 87(2) which specifically authorizes agencies to deny access to certain records, or portions thereof, including but not limited to records exempt from disclosure by State or federal statute, records which, if disclosed, would constitute an unwarranted invasion of privacy, impair contract awards or collective

Ch. 3 ACCESS TO RECORDS § 3.29

Under FOIL, any person is entitled to records which are accessible without regard to whether the person is a citizen, taxpayer of the municipality or otherwise interested in the record sought to be disclosed.[10] Agencies may, however, require that requests for records be made in writing.[11] No particular form of request is required by the statute, but the request must "reasonably describe" the records sought to be provided.[12]

All agencies are required to appoint one or more persons as a records access officer responsible for coordinating agency responses to requests for access to records.[13] Agencies are required within five business days of receipt of a request for a record reasonably described to make the record available, deny the request in writing or acknowledge receipt of the request in writing and state the approximate date the request will be granted or denied.[14] Any person denied access to a record may within 30 days appeal in writing the denial to the head, chief executive or governing body of the entity denying access or the person designated by the head, chief executive or governing body.[15] Within ten days of the appeal the grounds for denying access must be fully explained in writing or the record must be provided.[16] Any denial of access may be challenged by the applicant pursuant to Article 78 of the Civil Practice Law and Rules.[17] Reasonable attorney's fees and other litigation costs may be assessed against the agency denying access if the applicant substantially prevails upon appeal and the court finds that the record sought was of clearly significant interest to the general public and there was no reasonable basis for withholding the record.[18]

When an applicant merely wishes to review a record at the office where it is maintained, there is no authority for the agency to impose any fee for making the record available. Agencies may impose a charge not to exceed twenty-five cents per photocopy for copies nine inches by fourteen inches or smaller, or the actual cost of reproducing any other record, except where a different fee is prescribed by some other statute.[19]

Library References:

West's Key No. Digests, Records ⚖︎30–35.

bargaining negotiations, records containing trade secrets and certain other records.

PRACTICE POINTER: When a record contains both exempt and non-exempt material, the applicant may ask the agency to redact the exempt material from the record and produce the balance which is non-exempt, rather than simply denying access to the entire record. See Wilson v. Town of Islip, 179 A.D.2d 763, 578 N.Y.S.2d 642 (2d Dep't 1992); Buffalo Broadcasting v. N.Y.S. Dept. of Corr. Services, 174 A.D.2d 212, 578 N.Y.S.2d 928 (3d Dep't 1992).

10. Burke v. Yudelson, 81 Misc.2d 870, 368 N.Y.S.2d 779 (Sup.Ct., Monroe County, 1975), aff'd 51 A.D.2d 673, 378 N.Y.S.2d 165 (4th Dep't 1976).

11. Public Officers Law § 89(3).

12. Id.

13. 21B NYCRR § 4401.2(a).

14. Public Officers Law § 89(3).

15. Public Officers Law § 89(4)(a).

16. Id.

17. Public Officers Law § 89(4)(b).

18. Public Officers Law § 89(4)(c).

19. Public Officers Law § 87(1)(b)(iii).

§ 3.30 Tort Claims Against Municipalities

The State, as a sovereign body, is immune from suit unless it has consented thereto.[1] This immunity is extended to counties, cities, towns and villages when engaged in the discharge of governmental duties.[2]

By statute, the State has waived its immunity from liability and consented to have liability determined in accordance with the same rules of law as applied to actions in the supreme court against individuals or corporations, provided the claimant complies with the limitations of the statute consenting to suit.[3] Concomitant to the State's waiver of immunity, the immunity of its subdivisions, including counties, cities, towns and villages, was also lost.[4]

As in the case of individuals and corporations, a municipality's liability must be premised upon the existence and breach of a duty owed by the municipality to the plaintiff.[5] Moreover, to sustain liability against a municipality, the duty breached must be more than a duty owing to the general public—a special relationship between the municipality and the plaintiff must exist, resulting in a duty to use due care for the benefit of a particular person or persons.[6] Similarly, a municipality may be liable for negligent failure to perform an act where its prior conduct gives rise to such a condition that its omission constitutes an injury.[7]

In general, municipalities owe no duty to provide particular services such as police or fire protection to the general public.[8] However, once a municipality by its actions creates a special duty to provide a particular service to a particular person, like any private citizen, it must exercise due care under the circumstances.[9]

In addition, before liability may be imposed upon a municipality there must be a showing that the municipality's acts were the proximate cause of an injury.[10] While municipalities are liable for the negligent acts of their officers, employees and agents under the rule of *respondeat*

---

§ 3.30

1. Brown v. Board of Trustees, 303 N.Y. 484, 104 N.E.2d 866 (1952).

2. Murtha v. New York Homeopathic Medical College and Flower Hospital, 228 N.Y. 183, 126 N.E. 722 (1920).

3. Court of Claims Act § 8.

4. Bernardine v. City of New York, 294 N.Y. 361, 62 N.E.2d 604 (1945).

5. *See* Motyka v. City of Amsterdam, 15 N.Y.2d 134, 256 N.Y.S.2d 595, 204 N.E.2d 635 (1965).

6. *See* Florence v. Goldberg, 44 N.Y.2d 189, 404 N.Y.S.2d 583, 375 N.E.2d 763 (1978).

7. Schuster v. City of New York, 5 N.Y.2d 75, 180 N.Y.S.2d 265, 154 N.E.2d 534 (1958).

8. H. R. Moch Co. v. Rensselaer Water Co., 247 N.Y. 160, 159 N.E. 896 (1928).

9. Caldwell v. Island Park, 304 N.Y. 268, 107 N.E.2d 441 (1952).

10. *See* Raimon v. City of Ithaca, 157 A.D.2d 999, 550 N.Y.S.2d 479 (3d Dep't 1990).

PRACTICE POINTER: The doctrine of comparative negligence applies in negligence actions against the State and its political subdivisions. *See* Flynn v. City of New York, 103 A.D.2d 98, 478 N.Y.S.2d 666 (2d Dep't 1984).

superior,[11] they generally are not responsible where such acts are *ultra vires*.[12]

Certain statutory provisions provide that a municipality may not be held liable for injuries resulting from defective conditions in streets and sidewalks unless the municipality was given written notice of the defect, and there was a failure or neglect to repair the defect within a reasonable time after notice was given. Written notice is not required however, where the defective condition was in existence for such a period of time that in the exercise of reasonable care and diligence it should have been discovered and remedied by the municipality.[13] Municipalities may, by local law, enact more stringent notice provisions requiring actual written (not constructive) notice as a condition to bringing an action for damages based upon injuries resulting from any property of the municipality being defective.[14] Failure to provide the requisite notice is grounds for dismissal of a complaint.[15] However, notice of a defective condition is not a necessary condition precedent to bringing an action against a municipality where it can be shown that the municipality created the defective condition itself.[16]

In any case founded upon tort where a notice of claim is required by law as a condition precedent to the commencement of an action or special proceeding against a municipality, or an officer, appointee or employee of the municipality, a notice of claim must be served in the manner provided by statute within 90 days after the claim arises. In wrongful death actions the notice of claim must be filed within 90 days from the appointment of a representative of the decedent's estate.[17]

The notice of claim statute contains detailed provisions with respect to the form and content of the notice,[18] the manner of service,[19] conditions under which leave for late filing may be granted[20] and other

11. Becker v. City of New York, 2 N.Y.2d 226, 159 N.Y.S.2d 174, 140 N.E.2d 262 (1957).

12. Augustine v. Brant, 249 N.Y. 198, 163 N.E. 732 (1928).

13. *See, e.g.*, Town Law § 65–a; Village Law § 6–628.

14. *See* Klimek v. Town of Ghent, 71 A.D.2d 359, 423 N.Y.S.2d 517 (3d Dep't 1979).

CAVEAT: In certain instances where a municipality's local notice provision is more stringent than an applicable State statute and the local notice provision has not been complied with, the municipality must raise such failure as an affirmative defense. *See* Shepardson v. Town of Schodack, 83 N.Y.2d 894, 613 N.Y.S.2d 850, 636 N.E.2d 1383 (1994).

15. Poirier v. City of Schenectady, 85 N.Y.2d 310, 624 N.Y.S.2d 555, 648 N.E.2d 1318 (1995).

16. Kanopka v. Freeport, 121 A.D.2d 690, 503 N.Y.S.2d 1012 (2d Dep't 1986).

17. General Municipal Law § 50–e(1)(a).

PRACTICE POINTER: The statutory requirement for filing the notice of claim as a condition to bringing an action or special proceeding is found in the General Municipal Law as well as in the general laws governing each type of municipality, (the CPLR for villages) and in city charters. *See* General Municipal Law § 50–c(1); County Law § 52; Second Class Cities Law § 244; Town Law § 67; CPLR 9801(1).

18. General Municipal Law § 50–e(2).

19. General Municipal Law § 50–e(3).

20. General Municipal Law § 50–e(5).

matters. Generally, the notice of claim must name the claimant and his attorney, describe the nature of the claim, when and how it arose, and the nature of the plaintiff's injuries.[21]

The notice of claim must be served by personal delivery or registered or certified mail to one who could be served a summons on the defendant's account or to the defendant's "regularly engaged attorney."[22] A defect in service will be waived if (1) the notice is served on time and the defendant demands an examination of the plaintiff or (2) it is shown that the defendant actually received the notice within the required time, unless the notice is returned to the plaintiff with a statement specifying the defect within 30 days after being received.[23] Similarly, defects in the content of the notice that are not prejudicial to the defendant are also curable.[24]

In regard to late service, it is in the discretion of the court to allow late notice.[25] However, the time to extend the service of the notice of claim can not be longer than the applicable Statute of Limitations.[26] An application to serve a late notice of claim is made to the appropriate supreme or county court.

An action or special proceeding based in tort can not be prosecuted or maintained against a municipality unless: (1) a notice of claim has been made and served in compliance with General Municipal Law § 50-e; (2) the complaint or moving papers contains an allegation that at least 30 days have elapsed since the service of the notice and that adjustment or payment has been neglected or refused; and (3) the action or special proceeding is commenced within one year and 90 days after the happening of the event upon which the claim is based or, in the case of a wrongful death action, two years after death.[27] Timely service of the notice of claim is deemed an element of the substantive cause of action which must be pleaded in the complaint.[28]

---

21. General Municipal Law § 50–e(2).

22. General Municipal Law § 50–e(3)(a).

23. General Municipal Law § 50–e(3)(c).

PRACTICE POINTER: Where the notice of claim is returned to the plaintiff within 30 days after being received pursuant to the statute, the plaintiff has 10 days to serve a new notice curing the defect. See General Municipal Law § 50–e(3)(d).

24. General Municipal Law § 50–e(6).

25. General Municipal Law § 50–e(5). Factors the court will consider include: whether the defendant had actual knowledge of the facts constituting the claim within the 90–day period or within a reasonable time thereafter; physical or mental incapacity; plaintiff's death during the 90–day period; whether there was justifiable reliance on settlement negotiations.

CAVEAT: The late notice of claim provisions apply only to cases where the defendant is a municipal corporation or other entity governed by General Municipal Law § 50–e. It does not apply to a notice of claim involving the State or a State agency. See Luciano v. Fanberg Realty Co., 102 A.D.2d 94, 475 N.Y.S.2d 854 (1st Dep't 1984).

26. General Municipal Law § 50–e(5).

27. General Municipal Law § 50–e(1)(a).

28. Rogers v. Village of Port Chester, 234 N.Y. 182, 137 N.E. 19 (1922).

PRACTICE POINTER: While failure to plead timely service of the notice of claim may be grounds for dismissal, the plaintiff

Ch. 3 GOVERNMENTAL DETERMINATIONS § 3.32

Library References:

West's Key No. Digests, Municipal Corporations ⚖═723–743.

§ 3.31 Tort Claims Against Municipalities—Checklist

This checklist summarizes the issues that should be reviewed prior to commencing a tort action against a municipality.

1. If a negligence action is based upon a dangerous or defective condition:

    - Determine whether notice of the condition must be served upon the appropriate municipal official as a condition precedent to bringing an action.

        (i) Written notice may not required where the defect or condition was in existence for such a period of time that it should have been discovered and remedied by the municipality.

        (ii) Notice is not required where the municipality created the defective condition. (See § 3.30)

    - If such notice is required and has not been provided, it will normally be grounds for dismissing a complaint.

    - If notice is required and has been provided, a reasonable time to cure the defect must be allowed.[1] (See § 3.30)

2. If the action is based upon negligence, a notice of claim must be filed within 90 days after the claim arises.[2] (See § 3.30)

    - Actions not based upon tort need not comply with this requirement. Counsel is cautioned however, that other notice of claim requirements may apply and should check the statutes covering the various municipalities.

3. All tort actions must be commenced not less that 30 days after service of the notice of claim and not more than one year and 90 days after the happening of the event upon which the claim is based or two years in the case of wrongful death actions.[3] (See § 3.30)

§ 3.32 Challenges to Governmental Determinations

In addition to tort claims and claims for breach of contract, certain

should be permitted to amend his complaint. See Fichtner v. Town of Babylon, 24 Misc.2d 56, 203 N.Y.S.2d 533 (Sup.Ct., Spec. Term, Nassau County, 1960).

§ 3.31
1. Town Law § 65–a; Village Law § 6–628.
PRACTICE POINTER: Review local laws and city charters.
2. General Municipal Law § 50–e.
3. General Municipal Law § 50–i(1).

governmental determinations and actions may be challenged.[1] This Section provides a brief summary of the types of actions available to aggrieved persons to challenge governmental determinations.

Certain governmental determinations may be challenged pursuant to the provisions of Article 78 of the CPLR which provide relief to parties personally aggrieved by governmental action.[2] An Article 78 proceeding may be brought against a "body or officer." A "body or officer" is defined to include every court, tribunal, board, corporation, officer or other person, or aggregation of persons, whose action may be affected by a proceeding under Article 78.[3] Municipal officers and governing boards fall within this definition and are subject to suit pursuant to Article 78.[4]

The only issues which may be raised in an Article 78 proceeding are whether: (1) the body or officer failed to perform a duty enjoined upon it by law; (2) the body or officer proceeded, or is proceeding or is about to proceed without or in excess of jurisdiction; (3) a determination was made in violation of lawful procedure, was affected by an error of law or was arbitrary and capricious or constituted an abuse of discretion; or (4) a determination made as a result of a hearing at which evidence was taken pursuant to direction by law is, on the entire record, supported by substantial evidence.[5] Thus, the Article 78 proceeding provides the primary mechanism through which administrative, judicial and quasi-judicial acts of municipal officers and boards may be reviewed.

The constitutionality of legislative acts, such as the adoption of resolutions, ordinances and local laws, as distinguished from administrative and judicial acts, is not subject to review under Article 78; such proceedings should be brought as an action for declaratory judgment pursuant to CPLR 3001.[6] However, an Article 78 proceeding is the proper proceeding to determine whether a particular legislative action has been applied in an unconstitutional manner.[7] In addition, failure to comply with the procedural requirements for the adoption of legislation may be reviewed in an Article 78 proceeding.[8]

§ 3.32

1. Contract actions against municipalities are conducted in the same manner as against private corporations and, therefore, this chapter contains no separate discussion of these actions.

2. Dunne v. Harnett, 92 Misc.2d 48, 399 N.Y.S.2d 562 (Sup.Ct., N.Y. County, 1977), aff'd without opinion 59 A.D.2d 1065, 399 N.Y.S.2d 552 (1st Dep't 1977).

3. CPLR 7802(a).

4. See Troy v. Santry, 151 Misc. 791, 272 N.Y.S. 320 (Sup.Ct., Herkimer County, 1934).

5. CPLR 7803.

6. Kovarsky v. Housing Development Administration, 31 N.Y.2d 184, 335 N.Y.S.2d 383, 286 N.E.2d 882 (1972).

PRACTICE POINTER: Provided all proper parties have been served pursuant to CPLR 103(c), the court should simply convert an improperly instituted Article 78 proceeding into an action for declaratory judgment. However, if the petitioner has failed to obtain jurisdiction over all necessary parties in the Article 78 proceeding, the action can be dismissed. See Overhill Bldg. Co. v. Delany, 28 N.Y.2d 449, 322 N.Y.S.2d 696, 271 N.E.2d 537 (1971).

7. Overhill Bldg. Co., *supra* note 6.

8. Voelckers v. Guelli, 58 N.Y.2d 170, 460 N.Y.S.2d 8, 446 N.E.2d 764 (1983).

As a general rule, legislative actions in matters involving the exercise of discretion or judgment, such as the granting or denial of permits or licenses, are not subject to Article 78 review so long as the officer or board making the determination acted within its jurisdiction and complied with applicable procedural requirements.[9] However, an Article 78 proceeding may be instituted to challenge a determination alleged to be arbitrary, capricious and unreasonable.[10]

Except where otherwise provided by law, an Article 78 proceeding may be instituted to challenge only a final determination made by a body or officer.[11] As a general rule, "finality" requires that there be no further act or determination necessary in order to determine the rights of the parties.[12]

In addition to Article 78 proceedings to review governmental determinations and declaratory judgments to challenge the constitutionality of legislative enactments, residents of New York State are authorized to institute so-called taxpayers' actions in various instances. The majority of taxpayers' actions are instituted under the authority granted by General Municipal Law § 51 to maintain an action to prevent an illegal official act, to prevent waste of a municipality's property and to compel restitution of illegal payments and expenditures. An action may be maintained against officers, agents, commissioners and other persons, acting, or who have acted, for and on behalf of any county, town, village or municipal corporation, to prevent their illegal official acts, prevent waste or injury, or to restore and make good any property, funds, or estate of the political body. A taxpayers' action may be brought by any person or corporation or any number of persons or corporations who separately or jointly are assessed in the amount of $1,000 and are liable to pay taxes on the assessments in the county, town, village or municipal corporation whose property is threatened by waste or injury, or who have been assessed or have paid taxes upon any assessment amounting to $1,000 within one year prior to the commencement of the action.[13] This seemingly broad grant of power to institute taxpayers' actions has generally been limited to those cases where the acts are fraudulent or a

CAVEAT: Where either an Article 78 proceeding or declaratory judgment action may be used to challenge a legislative determination, counsel for petitioners must be cognizant of the four month Statute of Limitations applicable to Article 78 proceedings. See Solnick v. Whalen, 49 N.Y.2d 224, 425 N.Y.S.2d 68, 401 N.E.2d 190 (1980) where the court stated that if the rights of the parties sought to be determined through a declaratory judgment action were open to resolution through another proceeding with a specific statutory limitation, then the time period for that proceeding limits the time for instituting the declaratory judgment action.

9. See Gimprich v. Board of Education, 306 N.Y. 401, 118 N.E.2d 578 (1954); Polo Park Civic Ass'n v. Kiernan, 133 A.D.2d 116, 518 N.Y.S.2d 652 (2d Dep't 1987), appeal denied 70 N.Y.2d 614, 524 N.Y.S.2d 676, 519 N.E.2d 622 (1988).

10. See New York v. Schoeck, 294 N.Y. 559, 63 N.E.2d 104 (1945).

11. See CPLR 7801.

12. Weinstock v. Hammond, 270 N.Y. 64, 200 N.E. 581 (1936). See Chapter 4 "Administrative Law," infra for a more detailed discussion of Article 78 proceedings.

13. General Municipal Law § 51.

waste of public property in the sense that they represent a use of public property or funds for illegal purposes or in furtherance of fraud, collusion or bad faith.[14]

In order to have standing to institute a taxpayers' action, generally the individual or corporation bringing the action must be a taxpayer of the municipality.[15] In addition, the plaintiff, upon commencement of the action, must furnish a bond to the defendant, to be approved by a justice of the supreme court or a county court judge in the county where the action is brought, in the amount of at least two hundred fifty dollars and conditioned to pay all costs that may be awarded the defendant if the court finally determines the action in favor of the defendant.[16]

Section 51 of the General Municipal Law was designed to protect taxpayers against fraud on the part of public officers and to prevent usurpation by public bodies or agents of powers not granted to them, the exercise of which could imperil public interests.[17] It is not intended to authorize the courts to interfere with the judgment and discretion delegated by law to public officers, at least in the absence of bad faith, collusion, fraud or lack of authority.[18]

It is not necessary for the plaintiff in a taxpayers' action to show any special injury to himself; the injury need only be the same as that sustained by all other taxpayers resulting from the challenged action.[19] However, the prevailing view is that in order to prevent an illegal act on the part of a public officer, the act complained of must be one which would result in injury to the municipal corporation or waste of public funds.[20] Generally, the courts will not grant relief where the alleged illegal act is technical in nature and of little consequence.[21]

Library References:

West's Key No. Digests, Municipal Corporations ⚖︎104.

§ 3.33 Special Purpose Units of Government

In addition to the basic units of municipal government—counties, cities, towns and villages—New York State probably has more separate

---

14. See, e.g., Gaynor v. Rockefeller, 15 N.Y.2d 120, 256 N.Y.S.2d 584, 204 N.E.2d 627 (1965).

15. See Metropolitan Waste Management Corp. v. Town of Hempstead, 135 Misc.2d 548, 515 N.Y.S.2d 956 (Sup.Ct., Nassau County, 1987); Central School Dist. No.1 v. Rochester Gas & Electric Corp., 61 Misc.2d 846, 306 N.Y.S.2d 765 (Sup.Ct., Monroe County, 1970).

16. General Municipal Law § 51.

17. Rogers v. O'Brien, 153 N.Y. 357, 47 N.E. 456 (1897).

18. Gaynor, supra note 14; Campbell v. New York, 244 N.Y. 317, 155 N.E. 628 (1927).

19. Spadanuta v. Incorporated Village of Rockville Center, 20 A.D.2d 799, 248 N.Y.S.2d 405 (2d Dep't 1964), aff'd 15 N.Y.2d 755, 257 N.Y.S.2d 329, 205 N.E.2d 525 (1965).

20. See Korn v. Gulotta, 72 N.Y.2d 363, 534 N.Y.S.2d 108, 530 N.E.2d 816 (1988).

21. Fisher v. Biderman, 154 A.D.2d 155, 552 N.Y.S.2d 221 (1st Dep't 1990), appeal denied 76 N.Y.2d 702, 559 N.Y.S.2d 239, 558 N.E.2d 41 (1990).

purpose units of government than any other state in the country.[1] Typically, as the name implies, special purpose units of government are established to furnish or provide a specific service such as water supply or fire protection. This Section briefly summarizes the types of special purpose units of government found in New York State.

Probably the most common special purpose units of government are sewer and water districts. In cities and villages municipal sewer and water service is generally provided as a function of the city or village government. However, towns and counties lack specific statutory authority to provide these services to residents except through the creation of a district or improvement.[2]

In general, the provisions of law governing the creation of sewer and water districts authorize a prescribed number of property owners within the area of a proposed district or the municipal governing body itself to begin proceedings to establish a district.[3] Before a district can be finally established, the municipal governing board must make a determination which is generally to the effect that: (1) all of the property and property owners within the proposed district are benefitted by the improvement; (2) all of the property and property owners benefitted are included within the boundaries of the proposed district; and (3) it is in the public interest to establish the proposed district. The decision of a county governing board to establish a district is subject to permissive referendum.[4] The decision of a town board to establish a district is not subject to permissive referendum unless the district formation process was instituted by the town board.[5]

Counties are also authorized to establish drainage and refuse districts. In general the procedures for establishing these districts are similar to the procedures discussed above.[6] There are also specific provisions governing the creation of and operation of hurricane protection, flood and shoreline erosion control districts,[7] and watershed protection districts.[8] In towns, the procedures for creating and operating water and sewer districts may also be followed for a wide variety of other services including drainage control, refuse collection and/or disposal,

§ 3.33

1. The proliferation of public corporations led to the adoption of a constitutional amendment in 1938 prohibiting the creation of any public corporation possessing both the power to contract indebtedness and the power to collect user charges for services (other than counties, cities, towns, villages, school districts, fire districts or town improvement districts), except by special act of the State Legislature. See New York State Constitution Art. X, § 5.

2. See generally Town Law Arts. 12, 12-A and 12-C; County Law Art. 5-A. Article 12-C of the Town Law provides a special procedure for sewer, water and drainage "improvements."

3. See Town Law §§ 190, 209-b, 209-q; County Law § 253(1).

4. County Law § 256.

5. See Town Law § 209-e(3).

6. County Law § 250.

7. County Law Art. 5-B.

8. County Law Art. 5-D.

§ 3.33 MUNICIPAL LAW Ch. 3

lighting, snow removal and ambulance service.[9] These special districts are generally considered to be departments or agencies of the municipality which created them and not independent corporate entities.[10]

Fire protection outside of cities and villages is also provided by the creation of a special purpose unit of government—generally either a fire district or a fire protection district.[11] Fire districts are autonomous entities with their own separately elected governing boards while fire protection districts are merely a specific geographic area of the town on behalf of which the town board is authorized to contract for fire protection but lacking any independent corporate status.[12]

Towns are required to include the annual fire district budget as prepared and submitted by the Board of Fire Commissioners without change in the annual town budget and to levy the necessary amount together with other town taxes.[13] As a territorial division of the State possessing both the power to contract indebtedness and to require the levy of taxes or benefit assessments, fire districts are considered to be district corporations.[14]

Cities, towns and villages have the power to establish business improvement districts.[15] Such districts may be established for the purpose of providing certain specified improvements including, but not limited to installation of landscaping, planting and park areas; improvements to enhance security; and construction of pedestrian sidewalks, ramps and malls within the boundaries of the district.[16] Unlike other types of improvement districts, business improvement districts have their own special tax and debt limits.[17]

Any municipal corporation is authorized to establish an industrial development agency. In addition, many municipalities have had public authorities created for them by special act of the State Legislature to carry out a wide variety of specific projects. These entities are capable of carrying out projects which have been legislatively determined to be in

---

9. Town Law § 190.

10. *See* Belinson v. Sewer District No. 16 of Town of Amherst, 65 A.D.2d 912, 410 N.Y.S.2d 469 (4th Dep't 1978); Tom Sawyer Motor Inns, Inc. v. Chemung County Sewer Dist. No. 1, 33 A.D.2d 720, 305 N.Y.S.2d 408 (3d Dep't 1969), aff'd 32 N.Y.2d 775, 344 N.Y.S.2d 958, 298 N.E.2d 120 (1973).

PRACTICE POINTER: Because they are merely agencies of the municipality, actions against an improvement district must be brought against the municipality for which the district was established.

11. Town Law Art. 11, §§ 170 *et seq.*

PRACTICE POINTER: This Article also authorizes the creation of fire alarm districts but this type of district, possessing only the authority to install and maintain a fire alarm system within its boundaries, is rarely used.

12. *See* Town Law §§ 174, 184; 1981 Op.St.Compt.N.Y. 81-1, 1981 WL 16574 (Jan. 3, 1981).

PRACTICE POINTER: Unlike improvement districts, fire districts must be sued independently in their own name and not as agencies of a town.

13. Town Law § 104.

14. General Construction Law § 66(3).

15. General Municipal Law Art. 19-A.

16. General Municipal Law § 980-c.

17. General Municipal Law § 980-*l*.

the public interest without using the debt contracting or tax levying powers of the municipalities which they serve.[18]

§ 3.34 Special Purpose Units of Government—Industrial Development Agencies

Industrial development agencies, commonly referred to as "IDAs," are defined by statute as corporate governmental agencies constituting public benefit corporations.[1] Individual IDAs must be established by a special act of the State Legislature, generally upon application of the municipality for whose benefit the agency is being established.[2] Once established, the agency is governed by the provisions contained in Article 18–A of the General Municipal Law and has the powers and duties specified therein, as well as those contained in its specific enabling legislation.

An IDA must consist of not less than three nor more than seven members who are appointed by and serve at the pleasure of the governing board of the municipality for which the agency was created.[3] Any one or more of the members of an agency may be an officer or employee of the municipality.[4]

IDAs are established pursuant to a declared policy of the State, among other things, "to promote the economic welfare of its inhabitants, and to actively promote, attract, encourage and develop recreation, economically sound commerce and industry ... for the purpose of preventing unemployment and economic deterioration."[5] Because the constitutional prohibition against gifts or loans of public funds to private individuals or entities by municipalities would seem to prohibit municipalities from directly providing financial assistance to private industry to promote job development,[6] authorization for the establishment of IDAs, which are not subject to this prohibition, with express power to provide financial assistance was deemed necessary.

IDAs carry out their statutory purpose by providing financial assistance to private developers undertaking projects which further the general purposes of the industrial development agency legislation.[7] The primary form of financial assistance is through the issuance of industrial revenue bonds, commonly referred to as IRB's or IDB's, which are issued by the agency to provide financing for projects undertaken by private firms.[8]

18. See infra, §§ 3.34, 3.35.

§ 3.34
1. General Municipal Law § 856(2).
2. General Municipal Law § 856(1)(a).
3. General Municipal Law § 856(2).
4. General Municipal Law § 856(4).
5. General Municipal Law § 852.
6. New York State Constitution Art. VIII, § 1.
7. See General Municipal Law § 854(14).
8. General Municipal Law § 864.

§ 3.34 MUNICIPAL LAW Ch. 3

The interest paid to the holders of these bonds is exempt from New York State personal income taxes[9] and, in many cases, also excludable from gross income for federal income tax purposes. In order for the interest on bonds issued by an IDA to be excludable from gross income for federal income tax purposes, the requirements of the Internal Revenue Code of 1986, as amended, as well as the regulations of the United States Treasury Department promulgated under the applicable sections of the Code, must be satisfied.[10]

IDA financings are usually structured as a sale and leaseback or as an installment sale contract. Either of these structures allows the IDA to acquire title to the project facility and thereby provide various tax benefits to the project developer.[11]

Under either structure, the bonds are special obligations of the IDA and repayment of the debt is secured solely by the revenues to be derived from the project facility.[12] Unlike municipal bonds issued directly by a municipality or the State, neither the municipality on whose behalf the IDA was created nor the State are liable for payment of the bonds.[13]

IDAs are not required to pay taxes upon any of the property they acquire or which is under their jurisdiction, control or supervision or upon their activities.[14] In addition, governmental entities, such as IDA's

---

9. General Municipal Law § 874(2).

10. *See generally* I.R.C. §§ 103 and 141–150.

PRACTICE POINTER: Interest rates on tax-exempt bonds are lower than the rates on taxable bonds. This lower cost of money is passed on to the project developer in the form of lower financing costs for constructing or expanding a facility. The tax-exempt status of the interest on IRB's, as well as certain other tax benefits, makes them an attractive alternative to conventional commercial financing for consideration by developers contemplating projects which qualify for such benefits.

11. **PRACTICE POINTER**: Under a typical sale and leaseback structure, title to the project is conveyed by the project developer to the IDA at the time the bonds are issued and the developer agrees to acquire, construct and install the project as agent of the IDA. The IDA then leases the project back to the developer and the developer promises to make rental payments in an amount sufficient to pay the principal and interest on the bonds as it becomes due and payable. At the end of the lease term, which generally coincides with the term of the bonds, the developer has an obligation to purchase the project for nominal consideration.

Under the installment sale structure, title to the project is conveyed to the IDA at the time the bonds are issued and the developer agrees to acquire, construct and install the project as agent of the IDA. The IDA conveys title to the project back to the developer pursuant to an installment sale contract, with title normally passing either at completion of construction or at some later time. The installment sale contract will require the developer to make installment payments in an amount sufficient to pay principal and interest on the bonds.

12. General Municipal Law § 864(1).

13. General Municipal Law § 870.

PRACTICE POINTER: Because IDB's are not full faith and credit bonds of the issuer, lenders will often require the developer to provide a personal guarantee or some other form of credit enhancement as additional security for payment of the bonds.

14. General Municipal Law § 874(1).

PRACTICE POINTER: Notwithstanding this exemption, it is common practice in IDA projects for the IDA and the developer to enter into a payment in lieu of tax or PILOT agreement pursuant to which the developer makes payments equal to the amount or a portion of the amount of taxes

are exempt from state and local sales and use taxes for materials incorporated into buildings and other real property improvements which are owned by an IDA.[15] Finally, any mortgage recorded covering real property owned by the IDA is exempt from the State mortgage recording tax.[16]

In order to qualify for the benefits of an IDA financing, certain administrative requirements must be satisfied (*e.g.*, IDA meetings to adopt resolutions and public approval requirements imposed by State and federal law). Compliance with these requirements can be time consuming and may require follow-up after the project is complete.[17]

Library References:

West's Key No. Digests, Municipal Corporations ⊕460.

§ 3.35 Special Purpose Units of Government—Public Authorities

The historical background for the creation of public authorities in New York State is worth noting. The Constitution places various restrictions on the manner in which the State and its municipalities may incur indebtedness to be paid from future tax levies. These restrictions include, in certain cases, referendum requirements and super majority legislative body approval, as well as limitations on the total amount of debt which may be incurred.[1]

These constitutional limitations operate in many instances to prevent the use of full faith and credit debt of a municipality (or the State) to finance improvements that elected officials perceive a need for. Public authorities arose to fill a need to provide a method of financing public improvement projects which was not secured by the government's power

---

which would have been due if the real property were not exempt as a result of the IDA's involvement in the project. *See* General Municipal Law § 858(15).

15. Tax Law § 1116(a)(1); Wegmans Food Markets v. Department of Taxation and Finance, 126 Misc.2d 144, 481 N.Y.S.2d 298 (Sup.Ct., Monroe County, 1984), aff'd 115 A.D.2d 962, 497 N.Y.S.2d 790 (4th Dep't 1985), appeal denied 67 N.Y.2d 606, 501 N.Y.S.2d 1025, 492 N.E.2d 1233 (1986). For a discussion of mortgage recording tax, *see infra*, Chapter 12 "Purchase and Sale of Real Property."

16. 1982 Op.St.Compt.N.Y. 82–188, 1982 WL 20287 (June 2, 1982).

PRACTICE POINTER: The potential savings to a developer from these tax exemptions as well as the lower interest rate on financing for those projects for which bonds qualify for tax exemption make IDA financing an attractive alternative to conventional financing. These savings must be balanced against higher transactional costs associated with an IDA financing. These costs include the administrative fee typically charged by the IDA and attorneys' fees which, because of the number of parties involved and complexity of IDA financing transactions, are above the amounts charged for a typical conventional financing.

17. CAVEAT: If time is of the essence in a project, IDA financing may not be the best financing alternative. However, IDAs are created to promote business development so most IDAs are willing to work with developers to complete financing as expeditiously as possible.

§ 3.35

1. *See supra*, § 3.15.

to raise taxes and, therefore, was not subject to the restrictions applicable to such debt.[2] Public authority debt is typically secured solely by the revenues to be derived from the project being financed rather than by a municipality's tax levying power and has been held to be free from debt limits and referenda requirements.[3]

In general, public authorities are public corporations constituting public benefit corporations.[4] Although created by the State and subject to dissolution by the State, public authorities are independent and autonomous, deliberately designed to be able to function with freedom and flexibility not permitted to an ordinary State board, department or commission.[5] The creation of public authorities as independent corporate entities is intended both to insulate the state and municipal corporations on whose behalf the authority is created from liability and also to enable the carrying out of public projects free from the restrictions which would otherwise be applicable.[6]

Public authorities are established to finance, construct, own, and operate specific types of public improvements. Public authorities have been used for the construction and operation of improvements such as highway systems, bridges, tunnels, airports, sports authorities, parking lots and parks, as well as for financing and or operating traditional municipal improvements as sewer, water and solid waste systems. Public authorities have also been used to provide assistance to municipalities experiencing financial distress.

In general, the legislative body of the municipality on whose behalf a public authority is created is given power to appoint the governing board

---

2. See Quirk & Wein, *A Short Constitutional History of Entities Commonly Known as Authorities*, 56 Cornell L. Rev. 521 (1976).

3. Robertson v. Zimmermann, 268 N.Y. 52, 196 N.E. 740 (1935).

4. PRACTICE POINTER: There are hundreds of public authorities in New York State. The enabling legislation for the majority of these entities is found in the Public Authorities Law, although legislation for certain specific types of authorities may be found in other statutes (See, e.g., Public Housing Law). Like industrial development agencies, each individual public authority is created by a special act of the State Legislature. Unlike industrial development agencies, there is no "generic" body of statutory law governing all public authorities. Therefore, in dealing with any question involving a public authority it will always be necessary to examine the enabling legislation for that particular authority. While the legislation prescribing the purposes, constitution and manner of appointment of the governing board will typically differ between public authorities, provisions dealing with general powers of the authority, corporate status, bonds and notes of the authority, tax exemptions and reporting requirements in general are similar, particularly among public authorities established to carry out the same or similar purposes.

5. New York Post Corp. v. Moses, 10 N.Y.2d 199, 219 N.Y.S.2d 7, 176 N.E.2d 709 (1961) (the Triborough Bridge and Tunnel Authority is not subject to taxpayers' action under § 51 of the General Municipal Law because the Authority was not an agency of the City); Plumbing, Heating, Piping & Air Conditioning Contractors Ass'n, Inc. v. New York State Thruway Authority, 5 N.Y.2d 420, 185 N.Y.S.2d 534, 158 N.E.2d 238 (1959)(the Thruway Authority is not subject to contractual requirements applicable to the State).

6. *Id.*

of the public authority.[7] The members of the governing board of an authority typically serve for a fixed term of years.[8] Except for certain financial reporting requirements,[9] public authorities operate largely outside the control of the elected officials of the municipality for which the authority was created.[10]

§ 3.36 Forms

The following Sections contain forms for use in proceedings against a municipality based upon negligence. Section 3.37 contains a form for the Notice of Claim which must be filed prior to the commencement of any action against a municipality based on tort.[1] Section 3.38 contains a form for a complaint in a typical "slip and fall" action.

§ 3.37 Forms—Notice of Claim

SUPREME COURT OF THE STATE OF NEW YORK
COUNTY OF _____

In the Matter of the Claim of

[name of claimant],

                Plaintiff,

  -against-

[name of municipality],

                Defendant.

NOTICE OF CLAIM

TO:

    PLEASE TAKE NOTICE, that _____*[name of claimant]*, the undersigned Claimant, does hereby make the following claim against the _____*[name of municipality]*, New York (Respondent), its respective officers, agents, servants, employees, departments, agencies, staff and/or personnel, for substantial monetary damages for the severe, catastrophic and permanent injuries, pain and suffering associated therewith, ex-

---

7. *See, e.g.,* Public Authorities Law § 1123(1).
8. *Id.*
9. *See* Public Authorities Law §§ 2500 *et seq.*
10. PRACTICE POINTER: The autonomy given to public authorities can be a double edged sword. The same freedom from control which enables authorities to carry out projects which would be difficult or impossible for a municipality to carry out itself also allows authorities to act outside the control of the elected officials who created the authority and appointed its members.

§ 3.36
1. *See supra,* § 3.30

penses related thereto, and medical expenses and damages, and in support thereof the Claimant states:

1. The Claimant herein is _____[*name of claimant*]. The Claimant's address is _____ [*claimant's address*]. [At the time of the incident giving rise to the claim herein, the Claimant resided at _____ [*address at time of injury if different*]].

2. Claimant's attorneys are the law firm of _____ [*name of attorney*], whose address is _____ [*attorney's address*].

3. This claim is against the Respondent for the severe and permanent personal injuries, pain and suffering, mental pain and anguish, and medical expenses arising therefrom, sustained by the Claimant, _____ [*name of claimant*] [*insert cause of injury*].

4. The claim arose on or about _____, _____ [*date*], at approximately _____ [*time*], at _____ [*address of location where claim arose*].

5. The injuries and damages for which the claim is hereby made arose in the following manner: [*insert description how claim arose*]

6. The Claimant herein contends that the Respondent was negligent, careless and reckless in that [*insert description of basis of claim*].

7. By reason of the negligence, carelessness and recklessness of the Respondent, its officers, agents, servants, employees, departments, agencies, staff and/or personnel, Claimant (name of claimant), has sustained certain serious, catastrophic and permanent personal injuries including, but not limited to: [*insert description of injuries*].

8. The [*insert cause of injury*] and the injuries and damages described herein and resulting therefrom, were caused in whole or in part by the negligent acts, conduct, omissions and/or commissions on the part of the Respondent, by and through its officers, agents, servants, employees, departments, agencies, staff and/or personnel, without any negligence or fault on the part of the Claimant contributing thereto.

9. This claim has been brought within one year and 90 days after the claim made herein arose, as required by law. Moreover, an application to file this Notice of Claim is made simultaneously herewith pursuant to General Municipal Law Section 50–e(5).

PLEASE TAKE FURTHER NOTICE, that in the event the Respondent fails to pay the within claim within the time limits provided pursuant to law, said Claimant shall commence an action against the Respondent, its respective officers, agents, servants, employees, departments, agencies, staff and/or personnel, upon said claim for the injuries, damages and expenses sustained as a result of the aforesaid fire and circumstances leading thereto.

WHEREFORE, Claimant respectfully requests that the claim made herein be allowed and paid by the _____ [*name of municipality*], New York.

Ch. 3 VERIFIED COMPLAINT IN TORT ACTION § 3.38

DATED:

[Name of Attorneys]
Attorneys for Claimant
Office and P.O. Address

Tel. _____

[verification]

Library References:

West's Key No. Digests, Municipal Corporations ⚭741.50.

§ 3.38 Forms—Verified Complaint in Tort Action

SUPREME COURT OF THE STATE OF NEW YORK
COUNTY OF _____

[Name of Plaintiff],	)
Plaintiff,	)
	) VERIFIED
-against-	) COMPLAINT
	)
	) Index No._____
[Name of Municipality],	)
Defendant.	)

The Plaintiff, through his attorneys, _____ [name of attorney] submits the following as and for a Complaint and respectfully alleges as follows:

1. At all time relative herein, the Plaintiff,_____ [name of Plaintiff], was a resident of _____ [Plaintiff's residence], State of New York.

2. At all times herein relevant, the Defendant,_____ [name of municipality] was and is a governmental and political subdivision of the State of New York, whose powers and duties are set forth in Article IX of the New York State Constitution.

3. At all times herein relevant, the Defendant, was responsible for the proper design, construction, maintenance, of a certain portion of sidewalk located in front of _____ [location where injury occurred].

4. Upon information and belief, at all times herein relevant, the sidewalk of the above-mentioned property was in a defective, unsafe and

unreasonably dangerous condition in that, among other things, the sidewalk immediately in front of _____ [*location where injury occurred*], New York was depressed and not level with the surrounding sidewalk and ice and/or water had accumulated in this depressed area, thus creating a dangerous and unsafe condition.

5. Upon information and belief, the sidewalk was in common use by occupants of the premises at _____ [*location where injury occurred*], New York and by passersby, and such use was known to the Defendant.

6. [*Where written notice was given, add the following allegation:*] That before the injury hereinafter complained of, written notice of such defective, unsafe and dangerous condition of such sidewalk at _____ [*location where injury occurred*] was given to the Defendant on or about _____, ___ [*date notice of defective condition was served*] and the Defendant thereafter failed and neglected to repair or remove said defective unsafe and dangerous condition after the lapse of a reasonable time therefore.

[*or*]

Upon information and belief, at all times herein relevant, the Defendant was on notice prior to _____, 19___ [*date of injury*], that a dangerous condition existed at or near the place where the Plaintiff fell, and that Defendant was obligated to repair and maintain that section of the sidewalk which constituted a dangerous and unsafe condition.

7. On or about _____, ___ [*date of injury*] at approximately _____ [*time of injury*], Plaintiff was entering the premises located at _____ [*location where injury occurred*] when he was caused to slip on an icy patch on the sidewalk directly in front of the said premises.

8. As a result of the accident, Plaintiff suffered certain serious and permanent personal injuries, emotional and psychological trauma and substantial damages.

9. At all times herein relevant, the Defendant, was under a duty to maintain the said sidewalk in such a manner as to render it reasonably safe for travel and passage thereupon.

10. The Plaintiff has been damaged as a direct result of the negligence of the Defendant without any fault on his part in any way contributing thereto.

11. On or about _____, 19___ [*date notice of claim was served*], a duly Verified Notice of Claim was served upon _____ [*person(s) notice of claim served upon*]. The service and timing of the Notice of Claim complied in all respects with the applicable legal requirements and statutes. The said Notice of Claim and contents thereof complied in all respects with the applicable requirements and statutes and more than thirty (30) days have elapsed since the service thereof to the institution

of this action by service of a Summons and Complaint, and payment of said claim has been neglected or refused.

12. By reason of the above, the Plaintiff has been substantially damaged and demands judgment against the Defendant pursuant to CPLR 3017(c).

WHEREFORE, the Plaintiff demands judgment against the Defendant on the first cause of action, together with the costs and disbursements of this actions and such other and further relief as this Court deems just and proper.

DATED:

> [Name of Attorneys]
> Attorneys for Claimant
> Office and P.O. Address
> _____
> _____
> Tel._____

[Verification]

Library References:

West's Key No. Digests, Municipal Corporations ⌲742(4).

Chapter 4

ADMINISTRATIVE LAW

by
Patrick J. Borchers
David L. Markell

Table of Sections

4.1 Scope Note.
4.2 Strategy.
4.3 ___ Checklist.
4.4 Procedural Due Process.
4.5 ___ Individualized State Action.
4.6 ___ Protected Interests.
4.7 ___ The Process Due.
4.8 ___ Summary.
4.9 ___ Checklist.
4.10 Adjudicatory Proceedings.
4.11 ___ Definition of an Adjudicatory Proceeding.
4.12 ___ Notice.
4.13 ___ Discovery.
4.14 ___ Right to Counsel.
4.15 ___ Evidence.
4.16 ___ Cross-Examination and Witness Attendance.
4.17 ___ Official Notice.
4.18 ___ Statement of Decision and Decisional Record.
4.19 ___ Burden of Proof.
4.20 ___ Intervention.
4.21 ___ Unreasonable Agency Delay.
4.22 ___ Agency Duty to Decide Consistently.
4.23 ___ Intra-agency Review.
4.24 ___ Checking Agency Bias.
4.25 ___ *Res Judicata* and Collateral Estoppel Effect.
4.26 ___ Special Rules Applicable to Licensing Matters.
4.27 ___ Special Issues in Handling Licensing Matters.
4.28 ___ ___ Basic License Information.
4.29 ___ ___ The Role of SAPA and SEQRA in the Licensing Process.
4.30 ___ ___ Accuracy and Completeness in Applications.
4.31 ___ ___ Opportunities to Expedite the Process.
4.32 ___ ___ Opportunities for Variances from Standard Approaches.
4.33 ___ ___ Renewal, Suspension and Revocation Issues.
4.34 ___ Special Issues in Handling Enforcement Matters.
4.35 ___ ___ Strategies to Minimize Violations.

4.36	___ ___ Agency Fact–Finding in the Pre-enforcement Phase.
4.37	___ ___ Agency Enforcement Options.
4.38	___ ___ The Settlement Process.
4.39	___ ___ The Hearing Process.
4.40	___ ___ Post–Hearing Issues.
4.41	___ Summary.
4.42	___ Checklist.
4.43	Administrative Rulemaking.
4.44	___ Rulemaking Compared With Other Agency Action.
4.45	___ Rulemaking Notice.
4.46	___ Comments and Agency Assessment of Comments.
4.47	___ Agency Duty to Reveal Underlying Information.
4.48	___ Notice of Adoption and Effective Date of Rules.
4.49	___ Ancillary Documentation and the Role of GORR.
4.50	___ Rule Filing and Publication.
4.51	___ Declaratory Rulings Regarding Rules.
4.52	___ Overlapping State and Federal Rules.
4.53	___ Special Strategic Considerations in Handling Administrative Rulemaking Matters.
4.54	___ ___ Basic Sources of Information on Rulemaking.
4.55	___ ___ Participating in the Rulemaking Process.
4.56	___ ___ Special Issues in Negotiated Rulemakings.
4.57	___ ___ Special Issues in Emergency Rulemakings.
4.58	___ ___ Agency Guidance Documents.
4.59	___ Summary.
4.60	___ Checklist.
4.61	Agency Information–Gathering.
4.62	___ Administrative Searches.
4.63	___ Administrative Subpoenas.
4.64	___ Reporting and Recordkeeping Requirements.
4.65	___ Summary.
4.66	___ Checklist.
4.67	Judicial Review.
4.68	___ Delegation of Authority to Agencies.
4.69	___ Standing to Seek Judicial Review.
4.70	___ Ripeness.
4.71	___ Final Order and Relief in the Nature of Prohibition.
4.72	___ Exhaustion of Administrative Remedies.
4.73	___ Primary Jurisdiction.
4.74	___ Statutory Preclusion of Judicial Review.
4.75	___ Article 78 and the Consolidation of the Common Law Prerogative Writs.
4.76	___ Standards of Review.
4.77	___ ___ Review of Agency Determinations of Law.
4.78	___ ___ Review of Agency Determinations of Fact Under the Substantial Evidence Test.
4.79	___ ___ Review of Agency Determinations of Fact Under the Arbitrary and Capricious Test.
4.80	___ ___ Review of Administrative Rules.
4.81	___ ___ Review of Administrative Discretion.
4.82	___ Statutes of Limitation Applicable to Judicial Review of Agency Action.

4.83 ___ Venue in Article 78 Proceedings.
4.84 ___ Subject Matter Jurisdiction in Article 78 Proceedings.
4.85 ___ Summary.
4.86 ___ Checklist.
4.87 Forms.
4.88 ___ Notice of Appearance in Licensing or Permitting Matter.
4.89 ___ Notice for Discovery and Inspection in an Administrative Proceeding.
4.90 ___ Notice of Deposition in an Administrative Proceeding.
4.91 ___ Notice to Permit Entry Upon Real Property.

WESTLAW Electronic Research

See WESTLAW Electronic Research Guide preceding the Summary of Contents.

§ 4.1 Scope Note

This chapter covers the body of law that defines, and governs practice before, New York State administrative agencies. The body of law that defines agencies has two principal sources: constitutional and statutory. The major constitutional provision that applies to agencies is the procedural component of the Due Process Clause, and we cover the Due Process obligations of agencies in Sections 4.4 through 4.9. The Fourth Amendment protection against unreasonable searches and seizures and the Fifth Amendment privilege against self-incrimination also play a role in limiting agency investigative authority, and we touch upon those constitutional provisions in Sections 4.61 through 4.66.

The considerably more intricate and difficult aspect of state administrative law comes from statutory sources. The primary statute that defines agency behavior is the State Administrative Procedure Act—which we refer to by its common acronym "SAPA"—passed originally by the Legislature in 1975. SAPA, although it has become more complex with each passing legislative session, still divides agency action into two broad categories.

The first is administrative adjudication. Agencies are often under a statutory obligation to conduct hearings "on a record" for matters that affect the legal rights of persons. To take a common example, before the Department of Health can take disciplinary action against a medical professional it must conduct a record hearing.[1] SAPA calls these "record" hearings "adjudicatory proceedings,"[2] and sets minimum procedural obligations on the agency in the conduct of these hearings.[3] We cover in detail the obligations that SAPA places on agencies in Sections 4.10 through 4.42.

§ 4.1
1. Education Law § 6510.
2. State Administrative Procedure Act § 102(3)("SAPA").
3. SAPA §§ 301–307.

Administrative adjudication can be further broken down into two important types: enforcement actions and licensing (or permitting) matters. Enforcement actions are those in which an agency seeks to impose an administrative penalty on a regulated party for a statutory or regulatory violation within the agency's competence. Enforcement matters arise, for instance, when the Department of Environmental Conservation seeks to impose a penalty for an alleged violation of one of the environmental laws that it administers,[4] or the Department of Labor seeks to impose a penalty for an alleged violation of one of the State's labor regulations. We discuss some of the special features of handling enforcement matters in Sections 4.34 through 4.40. Permitting or licensing (SAPA uses the terms essentially interchangeably)[5] matters also present some separate problems. In addition to the statutory obligations imposed on agencies in the conduct of adjudicatory proceedings, SAPA also imposes some special obligations for licensing matters.[6] We discuss those, and the special problems of handling these matters, in Sections 4.26 through 4.33.

The second major category of administrative action is rulemaking. Unlike adjudicatory proceedings, which closely replicate judicial action, administrative rulemakings are forward-looking and simulate legislation.[7] Rulemaking can take various forms. Administrative rules can directly affect large numbers of persons, as for instance when the Department of Corrections issues regulations applicable to all state prisoners, or only one or a few entities, as for instance when rates are set for a regulated utility. But, of course, even in this latter example, the indirect impact on other persons—most obviously the utility's customers—can be enormous. SAPA devotes an entire article—Article 2—to rulemaking, and we cover it in Sections 4.43 through 4.60. Because rulemaking is forward-looking in nature, SAPA offers opportunities for the public to participate in advance in the rulemaking process, and we discuss how to handle administrative rulemaking matters in Sections 4.53 through 4.58.

Besides their two most important functions, conducting adjudicatory proceedings and making administrative rules, agencies can also impact the regulated public in other ways. One important mechanism is through their investigative authority. Among the investigative tools frequently given to agencies is the authority to conduct administrative searches (often called administrative inspections), to require regulated parties to make reports and keep records, and to issue subpoenas requiring a party to testify, produce records, or both. We cover the authority of agencies to employ these tools, and the limits on their authority, in Sections 4.61 through 4.66.

4. *See* Chapter 15 "Environmental Law," *infra*.
5. SAPA § 102(4).
6. SAPA § 401.
7. *See, e.g.*, People v. Cull, 10 N.Y.2d 123, 218 N.Y.S.2d 38, 176 N.E.2d 495 (1961).

If a lawyer representing a client before an agency is to prevail, the best chance is usually before that agency. A victory before the agency is invariably more efficient and cost-effective than one obtained later. However, sometimes challenging an agency action in court becomes a necessity. Article 78 of the Civil Practice Law and Rules—which we refer to by its common acronym "CPLR"—provides a unified mechanism for challenging agency action in court. In Sections 4.67 through 4.86 we cover judicial review of agency action and the limitations thereupon.

Library References:
West's Key No. Digests, Administrative Law and Procedure ⚖1–17, 101–133.

§ 4.2 Strategy

Administrative agencies are an important fact of modern life, and hence of modern law practice. Lawyers are apt to see State agencies regularly if they specialize in areas of the law in which administrative regulation is intense, and it is in the environmental, health care, labor and many other fields. Lawyers with a more general practice are also likely to see agencies on a frequent basis and are likely to encounter a larger variety of State agencies. A lawyer with a general business practice may, for instance, have a client who owns a restaurant whose liquor license is being challenged by the State Liquor Authority.[1] A lawyer with a general litigation practice handling, for instance, an employment discrimination matter may find that the first litigation step involves one of several agencies.

An initial consideration in handling a client's matter involving State regulation is determining whether the governmental entity involved is covered by SAPA. Agencies are commonly defined as those organs of government that are neither courts nor the Legislature, yet affect the legal rights and relations of persons.[2] SAPA, however, defines the term "agency" in a more specialized way.[3] Under SAPA, a governmental entity qualifies as an agency only if it derives its authority from the *State* (not a local[4]) government and it is headed by one or more gubernatorial appointees. Thus, one might think of the Departments of Law and Audit as "agencies" in the colloquial sense, but because the heads of those entities (the Attorney General and the Comptroller, respectively) are elected, they do not fit the SAPA definition of an agency. In order to qualify as an agency under SAPA, the entity must also be able to

---

§ 4.2

1. *See* Chapter 36 "Alcohol Beverage Control Law," *infra*.

2. Bonfield and Asimow, State and Federal Administrative Law (1989) p.1.

3. SAPA § 102(1).

4. *See, e.g.*, Incorporated Village of Great Neck Plaza v. Nassau County Rent Guidelines Bd., 69 A.D.2d 528, 418 N.Y.S.2d 796 (2d Dep't 1979)(county rent control board not a SAPA agency); Mount Vernon Housing Auth. v. Jordan, 120 Misc.2d 670, 466 N.Y.S.2d 546 (City Ct., Mount Vernon, 1982), aff'd 124 Misc.2d 886, 480 N.Y.S.2d 72 (1984)(municipal housing authority not a SAPA agency).

conduct one of the two major functions of agencies under SAPA: either adjudicatory proceedings or rulemakings. Thus, a governmental entity might fit the colloquial definition of an agency, but if it lacks the authority either to conduct hearings "on a record"[5] or to make administrative rules,[6] it does not qualify as an agency under SAPA.[7] Finally, some important entities that would otherwise meet the definition of an agency are excluded from SAPA's coverage—including, most notably, the Workers' Compensation Board and the Unemployment Insurance Appeals Board.[8] Others are covered only partially; the Department of Corrections falls under SAPA in its capacity as a maker of administrative rules, but not otherwise.[9]

If, therefore, a client's problem is of the State regulatory variety, and the governmental entity is covered by SAPA, that act and the Constitution provide two important sets of limitations on the governmental party. Legislation specific to an agency, along with the agency's own administrative regulations, also must be consulted, as they may give additional powers to an agency, or limit its powers in ways that SAPA and the Constitution do not.[10] For an entity not covered by SAPA, the Constitution, legislation specific to an agency, and any administrative regulations promulgated by it, become the pertinent reference points.[11]

Assuming that the client's matter involves a governmental entity covered by SAPA, a necessary next step is to determine in a broad sense the type of agency action that the client faces. Here there are three major possibilities. One is that the agency is proposing to make a determination of the legal rights of persons, in a manner similar to a court deciding a case. In this instance, the agency is engaging in administrative adjudication. A second is that the agency action is forward-looking and broadly applicable, in the mode of legislation, in which case the agency is engaged in administrative rulemaking. A third is that the agency is in an investigative posture, and is proposing to—or is—inspecting the client's premises, is demanding records or reports, or is

---

5. SAPA § 102(3).
6. SAPA § 102(2)(definition of a rule).
7. 1978 Op.Atty.Gen.N.Y. 63 (June 29, 1978) (New York Temporary State Commission of Regulation of Lobbying is not an agency under SAPA because it does not have the power either to make rules or conduct adjudicatory proceedings).
8. SAPA § 102(1).
9. SAPA § 102(1).
10. **PRACTICE POINTER:** It is vitally important to consult both legislation and regulations specific to an agency. Either of these can significantly alter the manner in which a particular type of matter is handled before an agency. Hearing regulations are published in the New York Compilation of Rules and Regulations—often abbreviated "NYCRR." Agencies also frequently publish less formal guidance, in the form of handbooks and the like. Consulting with agency staff before handling a matter can often consolidate research, and make practice much easier for the lawyer who is a novice before a particular agency.
11. **PRACTICE POINTER:** For agencies not covered by SAPA it is even more vital to contact the agency directly to learn of other guidance materials that may be pertinent to handling a particular matter before that agency.

attempting to subpoena testimony or documents. Each of the three major categories presents different challenges and strategies.

If a client's problem fits into the first category, administrative adjudication, a further inquiry is immediately necessary. A good deal of administrative adjudication by State agencies is covered by Article 3 of SAPA.[12] Those administrative adjudications that Article 3 covers are called "adjudicatory proceedings."[13] Adjudicatory proceedings are among the most formal of agency matters. They are usually conducted in a manner fairly similar to a civil bench trial before an agency employee who usually has the title of Administrative Law Judge ("ALJ"), hearing officer, hearing examiner, or something similar. Parties are then entitled to have the agency itself review the matter. But determining whether SAPA Article 3 applies, and hence whether the matter is an "adjudicatory proceeding," requires immediate reference to the statute entitling a party to a hearing—which is found not in SAPA, but in the legislation specifically applicable to the agency. If the relevant statute gives a person a right to a hearing "on a record" then Article 3 of SAPA is triggered; if, however, the statute merely gives a person a right to a "hearing" or an "opportunity to be heard," then SAPA Article 3 is inapplicable.[14]

There is an important exception here, however. Under SAPA, "licensing" gets special treatment. SAPA defines "license" as any agency "form of permission required by law," and thus includes what are commonly referred to as permits, certificates and the like.[15] "Licensing" is defined as any agency action relative to a license, including matters such as granting, suspending and revoking a license.[16] If a client matter fits the definition of licensing, then it is more likely that SAPA Article 3 will be triggered, because in licensing matters a statutory reference simply to a "hearing" or an "opportunity to be heard" is sufficient to qualify the matter as an adjudicatory proceeding.[17] In addition, a few other procedural rules—not generally applicable in adjudicatory proceedings—attach in licensing matters.[18]

If a client matter meets the definition of an adjudicatory proceeding, then SAPA Article 3 provides a substantial array of guarantees of procedural fairness. These include a right to notice of the proceeding, counsel, cross-examination, rules governing the taking of official notice, rules regarding the preparation of a record and a statement of decision, rules protecting against unreasonable agency delay, limitations on agency bias (including *ex parte* contacts by agency decisionmakers) and intra-

12. SAPA §§ 301–307.
13. SAPA § 102(3).
14. *See, e.g.*, Vector East Realty Corp. v. Abrams, 89 A.D.2d 453, 455 N.Y.S.2d 773 (1st Dep't 1982) (statute giving tenant a right to a "hearing" in a condominium conversion matter does not trigger a right to an "adjudicatory proceeding" under Article 3 of SAPA).
15. SAPA § 102(4).
16. SAPA § 102(5).
17. SAPA § 401(1).
18. SAPA § 401(2), (3), (4).

agency review of the decision reached.[19] If, however, the matter does not fit the definition of an adjudicatory proceeding, then whatever protections exist come from the Due Process Clause or other statutory sources.

Adjudicatory proceedings resemble litigation in court, but there are some different strategic considerations that may well be relevant at the outset. Discovery, for instance, which is broadly available in civil litigation, is much more truncated in administrative matters. In fact, the question of whether discovery is allowed at all is entirely up to the agency, because SAPA states that if discovery is to be allowed it must be provided for in the agency's hearing regulations.[20] The only exception is that in matters in which an agency is proposing to revoke a previously granted license, each party must—upon demand—"disclose the evidence that the party intends to introduce at the hearing" preserving recognized evidentiary privileges.[21] The rules of evidence are much relaxed in administrative matters as well. The only real evidentiary limitations are relevance and recognized privileges, such as attorney-client and self-incrimination.[22] As a result, therefore, administrative adjudication is generally less formal and conducted at a swifter pace than is civil litigation.

The second major possibility for a lawyer handling a state regulatory matter is that an agency is proposing to make an administrative rule that could affect a client's interest. Rulemaking under SAPA is of the "notice and comment" variety. Notice of proposed regulations must be published in the State Register, and the public is entitled to comment upon the proposed regulation.[23] Generally the right to "comment" means written comment, although sometimes agency enabling legislation requires it to hold "public hearings" prior to making a rule, in which case the public gets a chance to comment orally.[24] Because rulemaking closely resembles legislative activity, *ex parte* contacts between agency personnel and affected persons are not restricted,[25] as they are in adjudicatory proceedings.[26] Participating effectively in the rulemaking process requires timely and thoughtful comment, and—especially if the client will be profoundly affected by a rule—may require informal discussions with agency personnel to point out difficulties in the proposed rule.[27]

---

19. *See generally*, SAPA §§ 301–307.
20. SAPA § 305.
21. SAPA § 401(4).
22. SAPA § 305(1).
23. SAPA § 202(1).
24. SAPA § 202(1).
25. *See, e.g.*, Winthrop Gardens, Inc. v. Goodwin, 58 A.D.2d 764, 396 N.Y.S.2d 400 (1st Dep't 1977).
26. SAPA § 307(2).
27. **PRACTICE POINTER**: New York's Freedom of Information Law gives the public fairly broad access to public records. *See* Public Officers Law §§ 84 *et seq.* A full discussion of this statute is beyond the scope of this chapter, but for a discussion of many of its features, *see* Borchers & Markell, *New York State Administrative Procedure and Practice* (West 1998) §§ 5.10—5.12. If a lawyer's client is likely to be affected by a proposed rule, effectively commenting on that rule may require reviewing the underlying documentation that an agency used to formulate the proposed rule. This can usually be accomplished by a FOIL request, or even an informal request

§ 4.2　ADMINISTRATIVE LAW　Ch. 4

Agencies also have the power to make emergency rules that, unlike other administrative rules, are effective immediately upon publication.[28] Agencies may promulgate emergency rules only if they can demonstrate that "the immediate adoption of a rule is necessary for the preservation of the public health, safety or general welfare" and that waiting for comments would be "contrary to the public interest."[29] Notwithstanding this apparently demanding standard, emergency rulemakings account for about one third of all state rulemakings, resulting in a high probability that a lawyer's client could be profoundly and immediately impacted by an emergency rulemaking. Emergency rules have an initial life of only 90 days, however, and if the agency decides to extend the emergency rule, it may do so only in 60-day increments, and must publish an assessment of public comment.[30] Therefore, if a client is being harmed by an emergency rule, effective representation may demand that the lawyer swiftly attempt to make contact with agency personnel in an effort to point out defects in the rule.

A relatively new kind of rulemaking in New York is "negotiated" rulemaking. Although it has been employed only sparingly thus far, it may see increased use.[31] In negotiated rulemakings, affected parties meet before a rule is proposed in an effort to draft a rule that is satisfactory to all interests. If a client has regular dealings with an agency, determining whether the agency plans to use negotiated rulemaking, and ensuring that a client's interests are represented in any negotiations, may prove wise.

The third manner in which an agency's activities may profoundly affect a client is through the agency's investigative tools. Agencies have three main tools for investigating a client's activities: subpoenas, administrative searches (or inspections, as they are often called) and reporting and recordkeeping requirements. Subpoenas that call for production of documents and other tangible things—subpoenas *duces tecum*, as they are known—are fairly easy for agencies to obtain to aid in investigations of potential regulatory violations. The primary requirements under New York law are that the agency has statutory authority to issue such subpoenas and that the information that prompted the agency to issue the subpoena passes a minimal threshold for reliability.[32] Although often raised, the Fifth Amendment privilege against self-incrimination provides only a slight check on agency acquisition of information through

to agency staff. SAPA now requires an agency to disclose any study that forms the "basis" for a rule. SAPA § 202–a(2)(b). However, effective commenting on a rule often demands having access to such information early on. If, for instance, an agency's study is flawed, it may be much easier to persuade an agency of that fact *before* the rule becomes final.

28. SAPA § 202(6).
29. SAPA § 202(6).
30. SAPA § 202(6).
31. Borchers and Markell, *New York State Administrative Procedure and Practice* (West 1998) §§ 10.13—10.16. Recent legislative proposals would broaden its availability considerably.
32. *See, e.g.*, Levin v. Murawski, 59 N.Y.2d 35, 462 N.Y.S.2d 836, 449 N.E.2d 730 (1983).

subpoenas. A party cannot successfully object to the production of documents in response to a subpoena merely because *the documents contain incriminating information*, the actual *act* of producing the documents must itself be independently testimonial and incriminating.[33]

Administrative searches are, like their criminal counterpart, regulated by the Fourth Amendment prohibition against unreasonable searches and seizures and its state constitutional counterpart.[34] The usual rule is that an administrative search requires the issuance of a search warrant, although an administrative search does not require some specific suspicion of wrongdoing.[35] In many cases, even the slight protection offered by a warrant is unavailable; if the industry is "pervasively" regulated and the search is truly one to discover regulatory (not criminal) violations, a search without a warrant is constitutionally acceptable.[36]

The protections against the third type of agency investigative mechanism, reporting and recordkeeping requirements, are similarly slight. By either statute (or administrative rule made pursuant to statutory authorization) a regulated party is often required to file regular reports with an agency[37] or to maintain records and make them available to an agency upon demand.[38] The only significant check on agency authority to gather information in this way is that it must be authorized by statute. Although often raised, the Fifth Amendment privilege against self-incrimination is of little help to a party resisting an agency because of exception to its principles for the maintenance of "required records."[39]

Given the poor chances for success of resisting agency investigations, a lawyer advising a client who is the subject of agency information-gathering activities may face some important tactical choices. An unsuccessful attempt to block an agency investigation may make those agency personnel more suspicious about the existence of serious violations than had no resistance been offered. Even a successful challenge may provide only fleeting relief. A regulated entity that successfully resists an agency inspection on the grounds that a search warrant was required will, of course, prevent the inspection for the time being. But because the issuance of a warrant for an administrative search does not require the agency to show any individualized suspicion of wrongdoing, agency

---

33. Borchers and Markell, *New York State Administrative Procedure and Practice* (West 1998) § 6.3.

34. New York Constitution Art. I, § 12.

35. *See, e.g.*, See v. City of Seattle, 387 U.S. 541, 87 S.Ct. 1737, 18 L.Ed.2d 943 (1967).

36. *See* People v. Keta, 79 N.Y.2d 474, 583 N.Y.S.2d 920, 593 N.E.2d 1328 (1992), on remand 185 A.D.2d 994, 591 N.Y.S.2d 782 (1992)(statute authorizing searches of second-hand auto parts dealers are unconstitutional because they are really directed at finding criminal, not regulatory, violations).

37. *E.g.*, Banking Law § 125.

38. *E.g.*, Alcohol Beverage Control Law §§ 103(7), 104(10). *See also*, Chapter 36 "Alcohol Beverage Control Law," *infra*.

39. *See, e.g.*, In re Grand Jury Subpoena Dated December 14, 1984 v. Kuriansky, 69 N.Y.2d 232, 242, 513 N.Y.S.2d 359, 365, 505 N.E.2d 925, 930 (1987), cert. denied 482 U.S. 928, 107 S.Ct. 3211, 96 L.Ed.2d 698 (1987).

investigators will return promptly with a warrant in hand, and perhaps a less forgiving disposition.

Finally, successful client representation may require challenging agency action in court. New York has a unified mechanism for judicial review of agency action: Article 78 of the CPLR. Although we cover judicial review in much greater detail in later sections,[40] two important strategic concerns bear mention here. The first is the very dangerous area of Statutes of Limitation in judicial review. The most commonly employed Statute of Limitations in judicial review of administrative action is CPLR 217,[41] although many shorter Statutes of Limitation apply to specific types of administrative action.[42] Further, the statutory period can begin to run at a surprisingly early point in time. The general rule is that the limitations period begins to run when the agency decision is "final and binding"[43] and the affected party is so notified, but courts have sometimes interpreted the decision to be final even before its impact is felt.[44] It is thus equally vital that the lawyer determine early on when the statutory period began to run.[45]

The second important strategic consideration that must be addressed early on is the standard of review that a court will employ in reviewing an agency decision. In most cases, an agency determination need only be "rational" in order to survive judicial review—a standard

---

40. *See infra*, §§ 4.67—4.86.

41. CAVEAT: There are some older cases holding that some kinds of challenges to administrative action, most commonly constitutional challenges, are subject to the six-year catch-all Statute of Limitations. *See, e.g.*, Lutheran Church in America v. City of New York, 27 A.D.2d 237, 278 N.Y.S.2d 1 (1st Dep't 1967); Rock Hill Sewerage Disposal Corp. v. Town of Thompson, 27 A.D.2d 626, 276 N.Y.S.2d 188 (3d Dep't 1966); Chandler v. Coughlin, 131 Misc.2d 442, 500 N.Y.S.2d 628 (Sup.Ct., Albany County, 1986). These cases are almost surely not good law. In New York City Health and Hospitals Corp. v. McBarnette, 84 N.Y.2d 194, 616 N.Y.S.2d 1, 639 N.E.2d 740 (1994) and Press v. County of Monroe, 50 N.Y.2d 695, 431 N.Y.S.2d 394, 409 N.E.2d 870 (1980) the Court of Appeals appeared to leave no room for the application of the six year Statute of Limitations in challenges to *administrative* action. A lawyer should not, therefore, assume that the six year statute governs review of administrative action, even if the form of the action is something other than an Article 78 petition. In McBarnette, for instance, the Court of Appeals held that the fact that the action was styled as an action for declaratory relief was irrelevant, and that the four-month period in CPLR 217 still applied.

42. *See, e.g.*, Village Law § 7–712–c(1) (30–day period).

CAVEAT: By one count, there are 30 such statutes. J. McLaughlin, *Practice Commentaries*, to CPLR 217, C:217:1, p. 673. Some set extremely short time periods. If judicial review of an agency action becomes a necessity, immediate research on the question of whether there is a shorter Statute of Limitations should be a priority.

43. CPLR 217.

44. *See, e.g.*, Edmead v. McGuire, 114 A.D.2d 758, 494 N.Y.S.2d 712 (1st Dep't 1985), aff'd 67 N.Y.2d 714, 499 N.Y.S.2d 934, 490 N.E.2d 853 (1986) (police officer challenging agency determination that he was unfit to serve and must retire; four month limitation period began to run when he was notified of decision, even though actual separation from employment occurred six weeks later).

45. CAVEAT: When in doubt, the safest route is to choose the *earliest* date upon which the statutory period might have commenced, and calculate the four month period from that date.

that is, of course, highly favorable to the agency.[46] The best chance for upsetting an agency determination is if the issue is one of legal interpretation. Although agencies frequently get some deference in matters of legal interpretation, the leeway given them in this area is less than in others.[47] Therefore, successful representation on a petition for judicial review may involve attempting to package a challenge as one involving an issue of law. If the challenge cannot be so packaged—and even if it can—an important strategic consideration is whether the chances of success justify the cost of seeking review.

§ 4.3 Strategy—Checklist

1. Is the state regulatory entity covered by SAPA? If unsure, make the following determinations: (See § 4.2)

- Does the regulatory entity have the power to either make administrative rules or to decide adjudicatory proceedings? If it does not have the power to perform at least one of these two functions, then it is *not* covered by SAPA.

- Does the regulatory entity derive its power from the State, as opposed to a local or the federal government? An entity can only be subject to SAPA if it gets its power from the State.

- Is the entity headed by one or more gubernatorial appointees? Unless the entity is headed by one or more gubernatorial appointees, it is *not* covered by SAPA. Thus governmental entities that are headed by elected officials are not covered by SAPA.

- Is the entity specifically excluded from the definition of an "agency" by SAPA § 102(1)? Some entities (such as the Workers' Compensation Board and the Unemployment Insurance Appeals Board) that would otherwise qualify as "agencies" under SAPA are excluded by statute. Others, such as the Department of Corrections, are excluded for some purposes.

2. What is the nature of the administrative action that is affecting or could potentially affect your client? (See § 4.2) Administrative adjudication, administrative rulemaking, administrative investigation, or fact-gathering?

- If unsure, make the following determinations:

    (i) Is the agency activity in the nature of litigation in the sense that the outcome of the proceeding will adjudge the legal rights and relations of the parties before the agency? If so, then the agency action is administrative adjudication.

---

46. *See, e.g.,* Pell v. Board of Educ., 34 N.Y.2d 222, 356 N.Y.S.2d 833, 313 N.E.2d 321 (1974).

47. *See* Borchers and Markell, *New York State Administrative Procedure and Practice* (West 1998) § 8.3.

(ii) Is the agency activity forward-looking, either setting broad standards of conduct for the future in a manner similar to legislation, or making economic determinations for the future, as in the case of ratemaking? If so, then the agency action is administrative rulemaking.

(iii) Is the agency activity one that gathers information, either through recordkeeping or reporting requirements, agency subpoenas, or administrative inspections? If so, then the agency action is administrative investigation or fact-gathering.

3. If the agency action is administrative adjudication, make the following determinations:

- Is the agency action an "adjudicatory proceeding" as defined in SAPA § 102(3)? (See § 4.11) If the matter is an adjudicatory proceeding, then the parties have all of the rights set forth in SAPA §§ 301—307. (See §§ 4.10—4.28 for a discussion of the procedures employed in adjudicatory proceedings.) If the matter involves a license, permit or similar form of permission, then the parties also have the rights set forth in SAPA § 401. (See § 4.26 for a discussion of the special rules applicable in these proceedings.) If the matter is not an adjudicatory proceeding, the procedural rights of the parties will be determined by statutes other than SAPA and by the Due Process Clause. (See §§ 4.4—4.9 for an overview of the Due Process rights of parties in administrative forums)

- If unsure whether the matter is an "adjudicatory proceeding," make the following determinations:

    (i) If the entity is not an "agency" as defined by SAPA, the matter is not an "adjudicatory proceeding" under SAPA. (See § 4.2)

    (ii) If the entity is an "agency" as defined by SAPA, consult the enabling legislation specific to this agency and this kind proceeding. Does that legislation guarantee a hearing "on a record" or use very similar language? If the enabling legislation uses "on a record" or very similar language, then the matter is an adjudicatory proceeding. If the matter involves a license, permit or similar form of permission, then the matter is an adjudicatory proceeding even if the enabling legislation only refers to a right to a "hearing" or an "opportunity to be heard." (See § 4.2)

    (iii) If the enabling legislation simply refers to a right to a "hearing" or an "opportunity to be heard" (and the matter is *not* one involving a license, permit or similar form of permission) and does *not* refer to a hearing "on a record" then the matter is *not* an adjudicatory proceeding.

- Is the matter an administrative enforcement matter? If so, are there special tactical considerations? (*See* §§ 4.34—4.40)

- Is the matter a licensing matter? If so, are there special tactical considerations? (*See* §§ 4.26—4.33)

4. If the matter is an administrative rulemaking matter, make the following determinations:

- Is the entity that is proposing to make the rule covered by SAPA? If so, then all of the provisions of SAPA §§ 201–206 apply. (*See* §§ 4.43—4.52 for a discussion of these provisions in SAPA.) If the entity is not covered by SAPA, then the procedures for making rules come from other statutes.

- If the rulemaking is covered by SAPA, what procedure must be employed by the agency for accepting comments? Written comments only, written or oral comments? No comments prior to issuing the rule? (*See* §§ 4.53—4.57 for a discussion of how to employ these mechanisms to your client's advantage.)

- If unsure what kind of comments will be accepted, make the following determinations:

    (i) If the rulemaking is an ordinary rulemaking in which notice of the rulemaking has been published in the State Register, the agency is only obliged to accept written comments.

    (ii) If a statute specific to the agency requires it to hold a "public hearing" prior to making the rule, or the agency voluntarily agrees to do so, then oral and written comments will be accepted.

    (iii) If the rulemaking is stated in the State Register to be an emergency rulemaking, no comments are given prior to making the rule, but can be submitted after the rule takes effect.

- Is the agency considering negotiated rulemaking? If so, *see* § 4.56 for a discussion of the negotiated rulemaking process.

5. If the matter is one of agency-information gathering, make the following determinations:

- Are there any legal objections that can be raised successfully to the manner in which the agency is attempting to gather the information? (*See* §§ 4.61—4.66)

- If there are legal objections that can be raised successfully to the manner in which the agency is attempting to gather information can the agency cure them easily? If so, consider whether it is tactically wise to raise them. (*See* § 4.36 for a discussion of some of the tactical considerations.)

6. If the matter is one of seeking judicial review of an agency determination, make the following determinations:

- When must the petition for judicial review be filed in order to be timely? (*See* § 4.82)

- If unsure, make the following determinations:

    (i) Is there a special Statute of Limitations applicable in this case? If there is, that period is applicable. If there is not, then in all likelihood, the four-month period set forth in CPLR 217 applies, *regardless* of the form in which judicial review is sought.

    (ii) When did the statutory period start to run? Generally this is the date upon which the agency determination is "final and binding" and the parties are so notified, although this can occur even before the determination actually takes effect. Requests for reconsideration before the agency generally do not affect the time to seek judicial review. If still in doubt, calculate the statutory period from the *earliest* possible date.

- What standard of review will a court apply in reviewing the agency action? (*See* §§ 4.76—4.81)

- Given the standard of review applied, is seeking judicial review of the agency action cost-justified?

§ 4.4 Procedural Due Process

The Due Process Clause, particularly its procedural component, sets the backdrop for much of administrative law. The Fourteenth Amendment's Due Process Clause sets a minimum standard of fairness below which state-sponsored procedures cannot descend. The New York Constitution also contains its own Due Process Clause,[1] but with only one minor exception, New York courts have construed the State and the Federal Clauses identically.[2]

Procedural Due Process principles are of the most direct relevance to informal agency action. For instance, when an agency is conducting an "adjudicatory proceeding" as defined in Section 102(3) of SAPA, the wide variety of procedural protections mandated by Article 3 of SAPA

---

§ 4.4

1. New York Constitution Art. I, § 6.

2. *See, e.g.*, People v. Smith, 86 A.D.2d 251, 450 N.Y.S.2d 57 (3d Dep't 1982) (applying the same standards under State and Federal Clauses). The minor exception is Sharrock v. Dell Buick–Cadillac, 45 N.Y.2d 152, 408 N.Y.S.2d 39, 379 N.E.2d 1169 (1978) in which the Court of Appeals held the State Due Process Clause has a lower threshold of governmental involvement necessary to constitute "state action" and thereby trigger the Clause's operation. This is of essentially no relevance for our purposes, however, because any entity that meets the SAPA definition of an agency, SAPA § 102(1), is necessarily a state actor.

come into play.³ The procedural protections require, among other things, a detailed notice of the proceeding and extensive cross-examination.⁴ In the large majority of adjudicatory proceedings, therefore, the process actually given exceeds the process due. Serious Due Process objections are much more likely to arise in settings in which few or no statutory procedures are set forth, and the agency attempts to dispose of the matter much more informally.⁵

Library References:

West's Key No. Digests, Administrative Law and Procedure ⟠302; Constitutional Law ⟠318.

§ 4.5 Procedural Due Process—Individualized State Action

A fundamental prerequisite to engaging in an analysis of procedural Due Process principles is that the challenged activity must be individualized, governmental action. The requirement that the action be governmental is easily satisfied if the entity taking the action is an "agency" as defined by SAPA § 102(1), as well as in other cases in which the actor is an arm of the government.¹ The requirement that the governmental action be "individualized" is a bit trickier, though.

A governmental actor is under a constitutional obligation to provide Due Process if the action is individually directed at a person or entity, or a small group thereof.² On the other hand, governmental action that is broad, policy-making action (and therefore applies to a large group) does not trigger an obligation to provide procedural Due Process.³ To take a simple example, an agency decision to reduce a recipient's welfare benefits by 20% because of finding that he was earning more income than previously reported is individualized action, and triggers a governmental obligation to give a hearing.⁴ In such a case, the legitimacy of the governmental decision would depend upon the particular facts of the case, hence constitutional requirement of a hearing. On the other hand, a legislative decision to reduce welfare benefits to all recipients by 20%

---

3. SAPA §§ 301—307. See infra, §§ 4.10—4.26 for a discussion of the procedures in adjudicatory proceedings.

4. SAPA §§ 301(2), 306(3).

5. See, e.g., Valmonte v. Bane, 18 F.3d 992 (2d Cir.1994) (state procedure of listing parents on the Central Register of Child Abuse and Maltreatment based only upon an uncorroborated report of abuse violates Due Process Clause).

§ 4.5

1. Borchers and Markell, *New York State Administrative Procedure and Practice* (West 1998) § 2.2.

2. See, e.g., Londoner v. Denver, 210 U.S. 373, 28 S.Ct. 708, 52 L.Ed. 1103 (1908) (taxpayer whose parcel was individually reassessed is entitled to a hearing as a matter of due process).

3. See, e.g., Bi-Metallic Investment Co. v. State Board of Equalization, 239 U.S. 441, 36 S.Ct. 141, 60 L.Ed. 372 (1915) (landowner not entitled to a hearing on a governmental decision to increase assessments across-the-board by 40%).

4. See, e.g., Goldberg v. Kelly, 397 U.S. 254, 90 S.Ct. 1011, 25 L.Ed.2d 287 (1970) (hearing required before welfare termination decisions).

would not trigger a governmental obligation to give affected recipients a hearing; in this latter case, the political process is assumed to be sufficient protection.[5]

This division between individualized and "collective" or "generalized" governmental action is quite close to the line between administrative adjudication and administrative rulemaking. In the former, agencies simulate courts and determine the rights of named persons. Such action is by its very nature individualized. On the other hand, administrative rulemaking usually involves pronouncements of broad standards, and is thus usually generalized action immune from procedural Due Process scrutiny, just as most legislative action falls outside the boundaries of the procedural Due Process inquiry.[6] Some kinds of rulemaking are, however, individualized because they are directed at a very small number of entities. For instance, an agency ratemaking meets the definition of rulemaking under SAPA,[7] but often constitutes individualized action for Due Process purposes.[8]

§ 4.6 Procedural Due Process—Protected Interests

The Due Process Clause protects against deprivations of "life, liberty or property."[1] Agencies, quite obviously, have no authority to impose the death penalty. Thus, assuming that the agency action is "individualized,"[2] an agency falls under a duty to give Due Process if its actions work a violation of property or liberty. In some cases, the deprivation of property or liberty is readily apparent. If, for instance, an agency initiates an enforcement action that could result in a monetary penalty, the regulated party obviously has property at stake, and the agency is under an obligation to provide Due Process. Or, for example, an agency action that deprives a person of a liberty interest that the Supreme Court has recognized as "fundamental" also triggers an obligation to provide procedural Due Process.[3] These are a fairly narrow class of interests, however; even apparently severe deprivations—such as the transfer of a prisoner to solitary confinement—do not affect fundamental

---

5. *See, e.g.,* Atkins v. Parker, 472 U.S. 115, 105 S.Ct. 2520, 86 L.Ed.2d 81 (1985) (adjustment across the board in AFDC income rules does not trigger procedural due process obligation).

6. *See, e.g.,* Sheldon v. Town of Highlands, 73 N.Y.2d 304, 539 N.Y.S.2d 722, 536 N.E.2d 1141 (1989) (town decision to redraw boundaries of a sewer district is "legislative" in nature, and therefore does not trigger a procedural due process inquiry).

7. SAPA § 102(2).

8. *See, e.g.,* ICC v. Louisville & Nashville R. Co., 227 U.S. 88, 33 S.Ct. 185, 57 L.Ed. 431 (1913) (Due Process applies to ratemakings).

§ 4.6

1. U.S. Constitution Amend. XIV.

2. *See supra,* § 4.5.

3. *See, e.g.,* Santosky v. Kramer, 455 U.S. 745, 102 S.Ct. 1388, 71 L.Ed.2d 599 (1982) (New York statute allowing Department of Social Services to terminate parental rights upon a showing of neglect by only a "fair preponderance" of the evidence is unconstitutional; fundamental liberty interest exists in keeping family together and statute did not provide adequate guarantees of fairness in determination).

liberty.[4] Moreover, generalized interests, such as an interest in reputation, usually are insufficient to qualify as deprivations of fundamental liberty.[5]

Simply because a party cannot show an obvious loss of property or liberty does not mean that the governmental action does not amount to deprivation of liberty or property. The other important source of liberty and property interests is state law. If State law creates a definite entitlement to a benefit, the benefit cannot be taken away without a hearing.[6] Thus, interests as diverse as welfare benefits[7] and tenured public university positions[8] have been held to be protected by the Due Process Clause.[9]

4. *See, e.g.*, Sandin v. Conner, 515 U.S. 472, 115 S.Ct. 2293, 132 L.Ed.2d 418 (1995); Hewitt v. Helms, 459 U.S. 460, 103 S.Ct. 864, 74 L.Ed.2d 675 (1983).

5. *See, e.g.*, Paul v. Davis, 424 U.S. 693, 96 S.Ct. 1155, 47 L.Ed.2d 405 (1976). The test employed for determining whether a loss of reputation due to a governmental action amounts to a loss of fundamental liberty is commonly called the "stigma plus" test. See Borchers and Markell, *New York State Administrative Procedure and Practice* (West 1998) § 2.5. In general, a foreseeable effect on reputation will not qualify as a loss of fundamental liberty. *See, e.g.*, Siegert v. Gilley, 500 U.S. 226, 111 S.Ct. 1789, 114 L.Ed.2d 277 (1991)(negative letter of recommendation written by governmental employee not a liberty interest because loss of reputation only amounted to "stigma"; failure to get the job as a result of the letter does not qualify as a "plus" because result was foreseeable result of letter). However, unexpected negative collateral consequences coupled with a loss of reputation do qualify as losses of fundamental liberty. *See, e.g.*, Valmonte v. Bane, 18 F.3d 992 (2d Cir.1994)(listing a person on New York's Central Registry of Child Abuse and Maltreatment qualifies as a fundamental liberty loss because loss of reputation coupled with inability to get employment in child care field).

6. The leading case is Board of Regents v. Roth, 408 U.S. 564, 92 S.Ct. 2701, 33 L.Ed.2d 548 (1972), which held that an untenured university professor did not have a state-created property interest in his job because state law created an entitlement to continued employment only for tenured professors. The test articulated by the Supreme Court is that a person has a property interest only if he has "more than an abstract need or desire for it ... He must, instead, have a legitimate claim of entitlement to it ..." The Court then explained that such interests are not rooted in the Constitution, but "are created and their dimensions are defined by existing rules or understandings that stem from an independent source such as state law—rules or understandings that secure benefits and that support claims of entitlement to those benefits." *Id.* at 568, 92 S.Ct. at 2704, 33 L.Ed.2d at 555.

7. *See, e.g.*, Goldberg v. Kelly, 397 U.S. 254, 90 S.Ct. 1011, 25 L.Ed.2d 287 (1970).

8. *See, e.g.*, Perry v. Sindermann, 408 U.S. 593, 92 S.Ct. 2694, 33 L.Ed.2d 570 (1972)(understandings created by a faculty handbook akin to an implied-in-fact contract create a property interest). Some recent cases hold, however, that governmental contracts do not always create a property interest. *See, e.g.*, S & D Maintenance Co. v. Goldin, 844 F.2d 962 (2d Cir.1988) (ordinary commercial contract with government does not create a property interest); Henry Modell v. City of New York, 159 A.D.2d 354, 552 N.Y.S.2d 632 (1st Dep't 1990).

9. **PRACTICE POINTER**: It is important to collect all governmental publications of relevance in order to demonstrate the existence of a property or liberty interest. Although more formal sources such as statutes and regulations often demonstrate the existence of the "understandings" or "entitlements" critical to the constitutional analysis, less formal sources can also suffice. *See, e.g.*, Perry v. Sindermann, 408 U.S. 593, 92 S.Ct. 2694, 33 L.Ed.2d 570 (faculty handbook).

CAVEAT: In many cases, federal courts have found liberty interests created by prison regulations that are written in "mandatory" language. *See, e.g.*, Hewitt v. Helms, 459 U.S. 460, 103 S.Ct. 864, 74 L.Ed.2d 675

§ 4.7 Procedural Due Process—The Process Due

Assuming that a person can show that individualized governmental action[1] is or could deprive him of liberty or property,[2] the final step in the constitutional inquiry is to determine how much process is necessary to satisfy the Constitution. At one time, the Supreme Court followed a fairly rigid, absolutist approach by requiring a hearing—with many of the elements of a civil trial—*before* the deprivation of liberty or property in all but unusual cases.[3] Since then, however, the absolutist approach has been replaced with a much more flexible balancing test.[4]

Under the balancing approach, "some form of hearing is required before an individual is finally deprived of a property [or liberty] interest,"[5] but government has much more discretion on how to structure the hearing and when it is held. The balancing approach depends upon three variables.[6] The first is the seriousness of the deprivation. The more serious the deprivation, the more formal the hearing needed before a person is ultimately deprived of it. The second is the cost of the proposed additional procedure. The more costly the procedure, the less likely it is to be constitutionally necessary. The third, which correlates the other two, is the degree to which additional procedures will contribute to an accurate resolution of the matter. A procedure that significantly contributes to an accurate resolution is more likely to be constitutionally compelled than one that contributes only slightly.

The balancing test requires courts and lawyers to consider all three variables and their relationship to each other. For instance, reasonable notice of a hearing is a nearly absolute constitutional prerequisite because it costs very little and contributes greatly to a fair and accurate resolution of the matter. Thus, even under the flexible approach, reasonable notice is a constitutional necessity, even in matters in which the property or liberty interest is small. On the other hand, the full array of procedures that usually accompany a civil trial is not a necessity—because of their cost and relatively small marginal contribution to

---

(1983); Lowrance v. Achtyl, 20 F.3d 529 (2d Cir.1994)(New York prison regulations create a liberty interest in avoiding "administrative segregation"). The Supreme Court, however, has now rejected this approach in the prison context, holding that a prisoner has a liberty interest only if he can show an "atypical and significant hardship on [him] in relation to the ordinary incidents of prison life." *See* Sandin v. Conner, 515 U.S. 472, 115 S.Ct. 2293, 132 L.Ed.2d 418 (1995), on remand 61 F.3d 751 (9th Cir. 1995). In that case, the court specifically found that disciplinary segregation—solitary confinement—was not such a hardship. Sandin specifically rejects the "mandatory language" approach of Hewitt, and by implication appears to reject cases such as Lowrance. Thus, lawyers litigating prisoner due process matters should treat pre-Sandin authority with caution.

§ 4.7

1. *See supra*, § 4.5.

2. *See supra*, § 4.6.

3. *See* Goldberg v. Kelly, 397 U.S. 254, 90 S.Ct. 1011, 25 L.Ed.2d 287 (1970).

4. *See* Mathews v. Eldridge, 424 U.S. 319, 96 S.Ct. 893, 47 L.Ed.2d 18 (1976).

5. *Id.* at 333, 96 S.Ct. at 898, 47 L.Ed.2d at 32.

6. *See* Borchers and Markell, *New York State Administrative Procedure and Practice* (West 1998) § 2.8.

accuracy—except in circumstances in which the interest is very valuable.[7]

Library References:

West's Key No. Digests, Constitutional Law ⚖318.

§ 4.8 Procedural Due Process—Summary

Serious arguments concerning procedural Due Process present themselves most often in cases in which governmental entities, including agencies, take more informal action. In cases in which the action is more formal—as it is in adjudicatory proceedings under SAPA[1]—the statutory procedures are likely to exceed the constitutional minimum, making constitutional considerations practically irrelevant. Governmental entities, including agencies, are under a duty to provide procedural Due Process only if they take individualized action—action directed at one or a small group of persons.[2] Generalized action that sets across-the-board policy is not subject to the constraints of procedural Due Process. In order to trigger a procedural Due Process inquiry, this individualized action must deprive a person of either liberty or property.[3] Sometimes the loss of a property or liberty interest is clear, as it is in the case of a traditional property interest (such as money) or a recognized fundamental liberty interest. In other cases, however, the existence of a property or liberty interest will depend upon whether State law has created an entitlement or understanding.[4] Finally, assuming that the government is taking individualized action that deprives a person of liberty or property, the constitutionality of this action depends upon a flexible balancing test that weighs the value of the interest to the individual, the cost of the additional procedures to the government, and the marginal contribution of the additional procedure to accurate resolution of the matter.[5]

§ 4.9 Procedural Due Process—Checklist

1. Is the proposed agency action individualized action? (*See* § 4.5)

   - If unsure, make the following determinations:

     (i) If the action is directed at one or a small group of persons or entities, then it is individualized. On the other hand, action that sets policy across-the-board is not individualized, but generalized. Administrative adjudication is typically individualized, because it determines the rights of the named parties. Administrative rulemaking is often generalized as it sets broad standards of conduct for the future. However, rulemakings

---

7. *See* Chapter 16 "Land Use," *infra* for a discussion of Due Process issues in land use law ("Due Process").

§ 4.8

1. SAPA §§ 102(3), 301–307.

2. *See supra*, § 4.5.

3. *See supra*, § 4.6.

4. *See supra*, § 4.6.

5. *See supra*, § 4.7.

§ 4.9 ADMINISTRATIVE LAW Ch. 4

aimed at a small group—as is sometimes the case in ratemakings—are individualized. (*See* § 4.5)

2. If the proposed agency action is individualized, of what interest does or might it deprive a person? Liberty interest? Property interest? No recognized interest? If the individualized governmental action is or might deprive a person of a liberty or property interest, then some process is due. If no recognized interest is threatened, then no process is constitutionally due. (*See* § 4.6)

- If unsure what if any interest is at stake, make the following determinations:

    (i) Does the agency action threaten a commonly recognized property interest, as in the case of an enforcement action that could result in a monetary penalty? If so, then there is a property interest at stake. If not, consider the other possibilities.

    (ii) Does the agency action threaten a recognized fundamental liberty interest, such as speech, voting or family unity? If so, then there is a fundamental liberty interest at stake. If not, consider the other possibilities.

    (iii) Does the agency action threaten a person's reputation *plus* some other, negative collateral consequence beyond that which would normally be expected to accompany a loss of reputation? If so, then there is a fundamental liberty interest at stake. If not, consider the other possibilities.

    (iv) Does the agency action threaten to take away some entitlement or understanding conferred by state law? If so, then there is a state-created liberty or property interest at stake. If not, consider the other possibilities.

3. If the agency action is individualized and threatens a liberty or property interest, what additional procedure would contribute to an accurate resolution of the matter? (*See* § 4.7)

- Does the value of the interest at stake and the improved accuracy of the proceeding with the additional procedure outweigh the cost to the government in being required to provide it? If so, then the procedure is constitutionally required; if not, then the procedure is not constitutionally required. (*See* § 4.7)

§ 4.10 Adjudicatory Proceedings

As discussed above,[1] administrative action divides into three main categories: adjudication, rulemaking and agency information-gathering. SAPA provides for one kind of administrative adjudication, which it calls

---

§ 4.10

1. *See supra,* § 4.2.

Ch. 4   DEFINITION OF ADJUDICATORY PROCEEDING   § 4.11

"adjudicatory proceedings."[2] SAPA devotes an entire article—Article 3[3]—to the manner in which adjudicatory proceedings are conducted. Agencies, of course, make other individualized determinations that are less formal, and therefore do not qualify as adjudicatory proceedings,[4] but nevertheless fit into the broad category of administrative adjudication. Under the Federal APA these less formal individualized determinations are known as informal adjudications.[5] Under SAPA, however, these less formal individualized determinations rest in a kind of statutory limbo. Sometimes they are known by the confusing term "administrative" action,[6] but essentially they are unregulated by SAPA's provisions. Thus, in this chapter we concentrate on the more formal kind of administrative adjudication: adjudicatory proceedings. Less formal administrative activity is subject to other constraints, including the Due Process Clause[7] and statutes other than SAPA.[8]

Library References:

West's Key No. Digests, Administrative Law and Procedure ⬯441–513.

§ 4.11   Adjudicatory Proceedings—Definition of an Adjudicatory Proceeding

Under SAPA § 102(3), individual determinations of "legal rights, duties, or privileges" qualify as "adjudicatory proceedings" provided that they are "required by law to be made only on a record after an opportunity for hearing."[1] Adjudicatory proceedings therefore simulate court litigation in the sense that both involve individual determination of legal rights. SAPA's phrase "required by law" is intended as a reference to the enabling legislation specific to each agency. Thus, in order to

---

2. SAPA § 102(3).

3. SAPA §§ 301–307.

4. See infra, § 4.11.

5. See, e.g., City of West Chicago, Ill. v. United States Nuclear Regulatory Comm'n, 701 F.2d 632 (7th Cir.1983)(Section 189 of the Atomic Energy Act does not require NRC proceedings to be "on the record" and thus do not qualify as formal adjudication under the federal APA).

6. See, e.g., Gross v. Perales, 72 N.Y.2d 231, 236, 532 N.Y.S.2d 68, 71, 527 N.E.2d 1205, 1208 (1988). The term "administrative action" is confusing because it connotes the entire range of administrative activity, not the small subset to which it actually refers.

7. See supra, §§ 4.4—4.9.

8. **PRACTICE POINTER**: For administrative activity that is not regulated by SAPA, it is vitally important to consult statutes that are specifically applicable to an agency, as well as any administrative rules. This advice goes as well for administrative activity that is regulated by SAPA, as are adjudicatory proceedings. SAPA really sets minimum procedural norms that other statutes and regulations can build upon. For instance, agencies adopt their own hearing regulations which describe and limit the conduct of adjudicatory proceedings in more detail than does SAPA itself. See, e.g., 6 NYCRR §§ 624 et seq. (DEC permit hearing regulations); 9 NYCRR § 9977 et seq. (local government ethics hearings); 15 NYCRR §§ 124 et seq. (DMV traffic offense hearings). Agencies also publish less formal guidance in the form of handbooks and memoranda. A lawyer practicing before an agency should obtain all such agency-specific guidance as is available.

§ 4.11

1. SAPA § 102(3)

§ 4.11   ADMINISTRATIVE LAW   Ch. 4

determine whether an agency proceeding is an "adjudicatory proceeding" under SAPA, one must consult the legislation specific to that agency.

The crucial question when consulting the agency legislation is whether it refers to a hearing "on a record," or uses very similar language. If the agency legislation employs the crucial "on a record" language, then the matter is an adjudicatory proceeding. If, however, the agency legislation simply refers to a "hearing" or an "opportunity to be heard" *without* using the phrase "on a record," then courts have uniformly held that the matter does not qualify as an adjudicatory proceeding.[2]

An important exception to this structure is licensing matters. SAPA defines "license" as any "agency permit, certificate, approval, registration, charter, or similar form of permission required by law"[3] and "licensing" as essentially agency activity relative to a license, including granting, revoking or suspending.[4] SAPA provides that in cases of licensing a mere reference to a "hearing" or an "opportunity to be heard" is sufficient to qualify the matter as an adjudicatory proceeding.[5] Therefore, while in the non-licensing context a statutory reference merely to a hearing would not qualify the matter as an adjudicatory proceeding,[6] in the licensing context an identical statutory reference would so qualify the matter. Licensing matters also trigger some additional procedural rules that do not attach in other adjudicatory proceedings.[7]

Library References:

West's Key No. Digests, Administrative Law and Procedure ⚖442.

§ 4.12   Adjudicatory Proceedings—Notice

SAPA requires notification of named parties prior to the commencement of an adjudicatory proceeding.[1] Specifically, SAPA requires that the notice state the "time, place, and nature of the hearing,"[2] the agency's "legal authority and jurisdiction,"[3] "the particular sections of the statutes and rules involved, where possible,"[4] the "matters asserted" in "short and plain" fashion,[5] and that interpreter services are available to

---

2. *See, e.g.*, Mary M. v. Clark, 100 A.D.2d 41, 473 N.Y.S.2d 843 (3d Dep't 1984); Landesman v. Board of Regents, 94 A.D.2d 827, 463 N.Y.S.2d 118 (3d Dep't 1983); Vector East Realty v. Abrams, 89 A.D.2d 453, 455 N.Y.S.2d 773 (1st Dep't 1982).

3. SAPA § 102(4)
4. SAPA § 102(5).
5. SAPA § 401(1).
6. *See supra*, note 2.

7. SAPA § 401(2), (3), (4). *See infra*, § 4.26 for a discussion of those special procedural rules applicable in licensing matters.

§ 4.12
1. SAPA § 301(2).
2. SAPA § 301(2)(a).
3. SAPA § 301(2)(b).
4. SAPA § 301(2)(c).
5. SAPA § 301(2)(d).

the deaf at no charge.[6] SAPA § 301 also provides that agency denials of requests for more definite notice are not subject to judicial review, although courts do in fact review such denials to determine whether they are "purely arbitrary."[7]

Courts have been fairly generous to agencies in construing the notice requirements. Neither SAPA nor the Due Process Clauses require the notice to contain as much detail as a criminal indictment.[8] A notice may be sufficient if it, when read together with other documents, provides sufficient information.[9] Courts have also refused to vacate hearings based upon notices with only technical, non-prejudicial errors.[10] However, prejudicial errors require vacatur of the results on an adjudicatory proceeding, although the agency is allowed to proceed again upon an adequate notice.[11]

Library References:

West's Key No. Digests, Administrative Law and Procedure ⬤─452.

§ 4.13 Adjudicatory Proceedings—Discovery

One major factor in the relative informality and swiftness of administrative litigation is the general lack of pre-hearing discovery. SAPA § 305 leaves the matter of how much, if any, discovery to allow entirely to agencies.[1] Thus, the place to turn to learn whether discovery is allowed in a particular adjudicatory proceeding is that agency's hearing regulations.[2] Parties also turn to other sources to attempt to force agencies to allow discovery.[3] One argument occasionally raised is that the Due Process Clause requires discovery in a particular case. That conten-

---

6. SAPA § 301(2)(e).

7. *See, e.g.*, Eden Park Health Servs., Inc. v. Whalen, 73 A.D.2d 993, 424 N.Y.S.2d 33 (3d Dep't 1980).

8. *See, e.g.*, Block v. Ambach, 73 N.Y.2d 323, 540 N.Y.S.2d 6, 537 N.E.2d 181 (1989)(short and plain statement of facts of alleged sexual misconduct by a doctor sufficient both under SAPA § 301 and the Due Process Clause).

9. *See, e.g.*, Ritzel v. Blum, 81 A.D.2d 1029, 1030, 440 N.Y.S.2d 428, 430 (4th Dep't 1981); Eden Park Health Services Inc. v. Whalen, 73 A.D.2d at 993, 424 N.Y.S.2d at 34.

10. *See, e.g.*, S. & J. Pharmacies, Inc. v. Axelrod, 91 A.D.2d 1131, 1132-33, 458 N.Y.S.2d 728, 730 (3d Dep't 1983)(typographical inconsistency between notice and matters raised at hearing does not justify vacatur of proceeding).

11. *See, e.g.*, Alvarado v. State of New York, 110 A.D.2d 583, 584, 488 N.Y.S.2d 177, 178-79 (1st Dep't 1985)(cursory notice insufficient in boxing license revocation hearing).

§ 4.13

1. SAPA § 305.

2. *See, e.g.*, 6 NYCRR § 624.7 (DEC permit hearing regulations).

3. PRACTICE POINTER: One important source of information, that can sometimes substitute for conventional discovery, is the Freedom of Information Law, or "FOIL" as it is commonly known. *See* Public Officers Law §§ 84 *et seq.* FOIL allows for fairly broad public access, upon written demand, to documents being held or kept by most organs of the government, including local and state government. For a more complete discussion of some of FOIL's aspects, *see* Borchers and Markell, *New York State Administrative Procedure and Practice* (West 1998) §§ 5.10—5.12.

tion, however, has usually been rejected,[4] and the one reported case in which this argument prevailed was vacated by the Court of Appeals on procedural grounds.[5] In a return visit of that case to the Court of Appeals, however, the court ruled that disclosure of the specific information was required by a statute specifically applicable to that agency.[6] An important exception to the general rule is licensing revocation matters, in which SAPA § 401 requires each party, at least seven days prior to the hearing, to respond to a demand "to disclose the evidence that the party intends to introduce at the hearing . . . "[7]

Library References:

West's Key No. Digests, Administrative Law and Procedure ⚖466.

§ 4.14 Adjudicatory Proceedings—Right to Counsel

SAPA § 501 gives parties a right to counsel in "any agency proceeding," although the term "counsel" is limited to lawyers and an agency is not under a duty to permit non-lawyer representatives.[1] By its terms, this right to counsel applies to all agency proceedings, not just adjudicatory proceedings. Thus, it would appear from the face of the statute that a person involved in an agency that does not qualify as an adjudicatory proceeding ought also have a right to a lawyer. However, courts have taken a relatively narrow view of the matter, holding that in less formal agency proceedings neither SAPA nor the Due Process Clause forces an agency to permit representation by counsel.[2] Thus, while the right to counsel is absolute in adjudicatory proceedings, its status is less certain in other agency proceedings.

Library References:

West's Key No. Digests, Administrative Law and Procedure ⚖474.

§ 4.15 Adjudicatory Proceedings—Evidence

Another feature of administrative adjudication that contributes to its relative informality is the relaxed evidentiary rulings. SAPA provides that in adjudicatory proceedings "[i]rrelevant or unduly repetitious evidence or cross-examination may be excluded" and elaborates that

---

4. *See, e.g.*, Sinha v. Ambach, 91 A.D.2d 703, 457 N.Y.S.2d 603 (3d Dep't 1982).

5. Doe v. Axelrod, 123 A.D.2d 21, 510 N.Y.S.2d 92 (1st Dep't 1986), rev'd on other grounds 71 N.Y.2d 484, 527 N.Y.S.2d 368, 522 N.E.2d 444 (1988).

6. McBarnette v. Sobol, 83 N.Y.2d 333, 610 N.Y.S.2d 460, 632 N.E.2d 866 (1994).

7. SAPA § 401(4). For a further discussion, *see infra*, § 4.26.

§ 4.14

1. SAPA § 501

2. *See, e.g.*, Gruen v. Chase, 215 A.D.2d 481, 626 N.Y.S.2d 261 (2d Dep't 1995)(SAPA § 501 does not require a State University to permit lawyers to represent students in disciplinary matters); Mary M. v. Clark, 100 A.D.2d 41, 473 N.Y.S.2d 843 (3d Dep't 1984)(same); *see also* Walters v. National Ass'n of Radiation Survivors, 473 U.S. 305, 105 S.Ct. 3180, 87 L.Ed.2d 220 (1985), on remand 111 F.R.D. 595 (N.D.Cal. 1986)(Due Process Clause does not invalidate a statute preventing paid counsel in veterans benefit matters).

"agencies need not observe the rules of evidence observed by courts, but shall give effect to the rules of privilege recognized by law."[1] Therefore, evidence—such as hearsay—that would be excluded in a civil trial is fully admissible in adjudicatory proceedings,[2] although evidentiary privileges, such as attorney-client and self-incrimination, must be preserved.[3] At one time New York followed the so-called "legal residuum rule," which provided that although hearsay was admissible in administrative proceedings, critical facts had to be proved by at least one non-hearsay source. The Court of Appeals, however, has definitively abandoned the legal residuum rule,[4] meaning that a party's proof can rest entirely upon hearsay evidence in an adjudicatory proceeding.[5]

Library References:

West's Key No. Digests, Administrative Law and Procedure ⚖458.

§ 4.16 Adjudicatory Proceedings—Cross–Examination and Witness Attendance

A fundamental aspect of an adjudicatory proceeding is a right of cross-examination, although "unduly repetitious" examination may be precluded.[1] New York courts also consider reasonable cross-examination to be required by the Due Process Clause in formal administrative adjudications.[2] There is general agreement, however, that the right of cross-examination extends only to witnesses who appear in the case; to extend it to out-of-court declarants would convert it to a right of

---

§ 4.15

1. SAPA § 306(1).

2. *See, e.g.*, EJG Corp. v. New York State Liquor Auth., 213 A.D.2d 924, 624 N.Y.S.2d 68 (3d Dep't 1995); Swick v. New York State and Local Employees' Retirement System, 213 A.D.2d 934, 623 N.Y.S.2d 960 (3d Dep't 1995)(allegation that a piece of evidence was materially altered goes only to its weight).

PRACTICE POINTER: Although hearsay is admissible in administrative proceedings this does not, of course, mean that it is the most probative. In many cases it may be vastly preferable to obtain the presence of the declarant at the adjudicatory proceeding because his testimony will be far more persuasive than hearsay testimony as to his out-of-court statements.

3. *See, e.g.*, American Auto. Plan, Inc. v. Corcoran, 166 A.D.2d 215, 560 N.Y.S.2d 435 (1st Dep't 1990).

4. *See* 300 Gramatan Avenue Associates v. State Division of Human Rights, 45 N.Y.2d 176, 180 n. *, 408 N.Y.S.2d 54, 56 n. *, 379 N.E.2d 1183, 1185 n. * (1978).

5. *See, e.g.*, Grossman v. Kralik, 217 A.D.2d 625, 629 N.Y.S.2d 467 (2d Dep't 1995)(disciplinary action against employee sustained although based entirely upon hearsay evidence); Abdur–Raheem v. Mann, 85 N.Y.2d 113, 623 N.Y.S.2d 758, 647 N.E.2d 1266 (1995)(prison disciplinary decision appropriately based on hearsay evidence).

PRACTICE POINTER: Agency hearing regulations occasionally set limits on evidence beyond those in SAPA. Consult them carefully in connection with any evidentiary issue. *See, e.g.*, 15 NYCRR § 124.5(b)(3), (c) (in DMV hearings on traffic offenses those constitutional evidentiary objections that would be present in a court with concurrent criminal jurisdiction also apply in the administrative forum).

§ 4.16

1. SAPA § 306(1), (3).

2. *See, e.g.*, Hecht v. Monaghan, 307 N.Y. 461, 121 N.E.2d 421 (1954)(pre-SAPA case holding that cross-examination is a matter of constitutional necessity in a license revocation proceeding).

confrontation, and deny agencies their traditional freedom to admit hearsay evidence.[3] Limiting the right of cross-examination to witnesses who appear does not raise any significant fairness problems, because SAPA § 304(2) to request the ALJ or the agency to issue a subpoena to command the attendance of unwilling witnesses.[4]

Library References:

West's Key No. Digests, Administrative Law and Procedure ⚖︎463.

§ 4.17 Adjudicatory Proceedings—Official Notice

Another distinctive feature of agency adjudication is the broad official notice powers of agencies. Agencies are entitled to take official notice of everything of which courts could take judicial notice.[1] Agencies are also entitled to take official notice "of other facts within the specialized knowledge of the agency."[2] Agencies, must, however give notice and an opportunity to respond to all parties if they intend to take official notice of a matter within their expertise.[3] In many cases there is a fine line between the agency taking official notice and simply "evaluating" the evidence. But if it falls on the former side of the line, and the agency fails to inform the party of its intent to take official notice, this is a fatal defect in the proceedings.[4]

Library References:

West's Key No. Digests, Administrative Law and Procedure ⚖︎459.

§ 4.18 Adjudicatory Proceedings—Statement of Decision and Decisional Record

SAPA § 302 requires agencies conducting adjudicatory proceedings to prepare a decisional record. The record must contain "all notices,

---

3. See Borchers and Markell, *New York State Administrative Procedure and Practice* (West 1998) § 3.8.

4. SAPA § 304(2).

§ 4.17

1. SAPA § 306(4).
2. SAPA § 306(4).
3. SAPA § 306(4).

PRACTICE POINTER: It is probably wise in most circumstances not to trust an agency to remember that it is under a duty to do so. A lawyer representing a client has some options available in this regard, however. One is to make a Freedom of Information Law request for any reports or studies that an agency has on technical issues that might arise during the course of the adjudicatory proceeding. This approach has the advantage that the agency's technical information may be available to lawyer and client at a date much earlier than if one waits for the agency to indicate that it will take official notice of it. This may also alert the lawyer of the need to hire an expert witness or consultant to rebut or interpret the agency's technical information. Another step that can be taken to protect clients is to make a direct inquiry to the agency staff representing the agency in the adjudicatory proceeding whether they intend to have the agency take official notice of any specialized matters during the course of the adjudicatory proceeding.

4. *See, e.g.*, Cohen v. Ambach, 112 A.D.2d 497, 490 N.Y.S.2d 908 (3d Dep't 1985)(failure of agency to inform opposing party that it intended to take official notice of what kinds of advertising were in "the public interest" requires vacating license suspension for inappropriate advertising).

pleadings, motions, intermediate rulings,"[1] "evidence presented,"[2] "a statement of all matters officially noticed except matters so obvious that a statement of them would serve no useful purpose,"[3] "questions and offers of proof, objections thereto, and rulings thereupon,"[4] "proposed findings and exceptions, if any,"[5] "any findings of fact, conclusions of law or other recommendations made by" the ALJ,[6] and "any decision, determination, opinion, order or report rendered."[7] SAPA also requires a record of all testimony, although in contrast to the usual judicial practice of having a stenographic transcript generated, SAPA allows for tape recording.[8] Agency decisions must be based exclusively upon the record and all matters officially noticed.[9]

SAPA also requires that ultimate agency decisions adverse to a private party be in writing.[10] A recent amendment makes this requirement applicable to all final agency determinations, including those made in the course of proceedings *other* than adjudicatory proceedings.[11] The written decision either can take the form of enumerated findings of fact and conclusions of law, or may be a more general statement of "reasons," often in the style of a judicial opinion.[12] If the agency heads reverse a decision of an ALJ, they must explain in writing why their decision conflicts with the ALJ's.[13] The written decision must be sufficient to make the agency's reasoning process transparent.[14] In simple cases, relatively little written explanation is necessary.[15] But in more complicated ones, a more detailed written explanation becomes necessary.[16]

Library References:
West's Key No. Digests, Administrative Law and Procedure ⟐489, 506.

§ 4.19 Adjudicatory Proceedings—Burden of Proof

SAPA follows the traditional administrative law practice of placing

§ 4.18
1. SAPA § 302(1)(a).
2. SAPA § 302(1)(b).
3. SAPA § 302(1)(c).
4. SAPA § 302(1)(d).
5. SAPA § 302(1)(e).
6. SAPA § 302(1)(f).
7. SAPA § 302(1)(g).
8. SAPA § 302(2).
9. SAPA § 302(3). *See also* Simpson v. Wolansky, 38 N.Y.2d 391, 380 N.Y.S.2d 630, 343 N.E.2d 274 (1975)(setting aside as a Due Process violation administrative decision obviously based upon matters not contained in the evidentiary record).
10. SAPA § 307(1).
11. Ch. 648, L. 1995.
12. SAPA § 307(1).
13. N.Y. Exec. Order No. 131, 9 NYCRR § 4.131 (1989).
14. *See, e.g.*, Montauk Improvement v. Proccacino, 41 N.Y.2d 913, 394 N.Y.S.2d 619, 363 N.E.2d 344 (1977)(findings so conclusory as to amount only to a conclusion, and therefore inadequate).
15. *See, e.g.*, Shermack v. Board of Regents of State Univ. of New York, 64 A.D.2d 798, 407 N.Y.S.2d 926 (3d Dep't 1978)(sparse findings "minimally adequate" in case that turned essentially upon the credibility of one witness).
16. Koelbl v. Whalen, 63 A.D.2d 408, 406 N.Y.S.2d 621 (3d Dep't 1978)(conclusory findings accompanied by citations to transcript insufficient in complex case involving multiple alleged nursing home regulatory violations).

"the burden of proof ... on the party who initiated the proceeding."[1] For example, applicants for government aid have the burden of producing evidence and persuading the agency that they meet the criteria for eligibility.[2] But if the agency initiates the proceeding, as it does in enforcement matters, then it bears the burden of proof.[3] SAPA refers to the burden of proof as one of "substantial evidence,"[4] which is odd because the substantial evidence standard is the traditional standard for *judicial review* of an agency's factual findings in a formal proceeding. In practice, however, the standard of proof appears to operate very much like the preponderance of the evidence standard commonly applied in civil cases.[5]

Library References:
West's Key No. Digests, Administrative Law and Procedure ⚖=460.

§ 4.20 Adjudicatory Proceedings—Intervention

In most circumstances, the only parties who wish to participate in an adjudicatory proceeding are those most directly and obviously interested. In a license revocation matter, for instance, the holder whose license is in jeopardy and the agency itself obviously will be parties. Sometimes, however, persons with a less direct interest in the matter wish to participate. For instance, a business whose customer base might be eroded may wish to oppose an applicant for a license to operate a similar business nearby.[1] SAPA, however, does not address itself to the question of intervention. As a result, the question of intervention is left almost entirely to the agency to address either by administrative rule or case by case.[2] Thus, a less-directly affected party wishing to participate in an adjudicatory proceeding should consult the administrative hearing

§ 4.19

1. SAPA § 306(1)

2. *See, e.g.*, Martinez v. Blum, 624 F.2d 1 (2d Cir.1980) (AFDC applications have burden of proof); Arimento v. McCall, 211 A.D.2d 958, 621 N.Y.S.2d 409 (3d Dep't 1995)(petitioner has burden of proof to establish disability in claiming disability retirement).

PRACTICE POINTER: Some agency regulations have detailed standards for intervention, and also allow participation as an *amicus*. *See, e.g.*, 6 NYCRR § 625.5 (DEC permit hearing regulations).

3. *See, e.g.*, LaBounty v. Coughlin, 153 A.D.2d 981, 545 N.Y.S.2d 425 (3d Dep't 1989)(government failed to prove that the account of a prisoner who submitted spurious overtime slips was overcredited; therefore, government wrongfully deducted $1.42 from his account).

4. SAPA § 306(1).

5. *See* Borchers and Markell, *New York State Administrative Procedure and Practice* (West 1998) § 3.12.

§ 4.20

1. *See, e.g.*, Dairylea Co-op. Inc. v. Walkley, 38 N.Y.2d 6, 377 N.Y.S.2d 451, 339 N.E.2d 865 (1975)(economic competitor of a license applicant has standing to seek judicial review of agency decision granting license).

2. *See, e.g.*, Dairylea, 38 N.Y.2d at 10–11, 377 N.Y.S.2d at 455, 399 N.E.2d at 868; Campo Corp. v. Feinberg, 279 A.D. 302, 308–09, 110 N.Y.S.2d 250, 256–57 (3d Dep't), aff'd 303 N.Y. 995, 106 N.E.2d 70 (1952); *but see* Zimet v. New York State Liquor Auth., 27 A.D.2d 558, 276 N.Y.S.2d 79 (2d Dep't 1966) (agency ordered to allow economic competitor to participate in new license hearing).

regulations to see if there is any guidance, or hope for a favorable exercise of agency discretion. If neither route proves satisfactory, a party denied admission to the hearing may have to wait for the outcome, and then attempt to set the decision aside on judicial review.

Library References:
West's Key No. Digests, Administrative Law and Procedure ⚖=451.

§ 4.21 Adjudicatory Proceedings—Unreasonable Agency Delay

SAPA purports to ensure that "all parties shall be afforded an opportunity for hearing within a reasonable time."[1] The Court of Appeals, however, has interpreted this duty fairly narrowly. The time period between the incident giving rise to the hearing and agency notification of the hearing is *not* relevant to determining whether SAPA's "reasonable time" requirement has been fulfilled. Rather, the relevant time period is the interval between any request for the hearing and its occurrence.[2] Even assuming that there is a substantial delay in the relevant period, a party attempting to obtain dismissal under SAPA's "reasonable time" requirement must do so in the context of a four-factor test. These factors are: 1) "the private interest allegedly compromised by the delay," 2) "actual prejudice to the private party," 3) "the causal connection between the conduct of the parties and the delay," and 4) "the underlying public policy advanced by the governmental regulation."[3]

As a practical matter, this test makes it difficult for parties to obtain a dismissal. One significant obstacle is that the period between the incident and the notification of the hearing is not included in the calculation. Another is that courts have repeatedly held that the mere passage of time itself does not constitute prejudice; the complaining party must point to some concrete disadvantage wrought by the delay.[4] Although SAPA, as interpreted by the Court of Appeals, does not take into account the interval between the incident and the notice of hearing in its "reasonable time" computation, an extremely long delay of this

---

§ 4.21

1. SAPA § 301(1).

2. *See* Cortlandt Nursing Home v. Axelrod, 66 N.Y.2d 169, 179, 495 N.Y.S.2d 927, 933, 486 N.E.2d 785, 791 (1985)(delay did not violate SAPA § 301(1)); *but see* Sharma v. Sobol, 188 A.D.2d 833, 835, 591 N.Y.S.2d 572, 574 (3d Dep't 1992)(passage of four years between incident and hearing deprived a key witness of "the ability to testify with reasonable certainty" therefore requiring dismissal). *See generally* Borchers and Markell, *New York State Administrative Procedure and Practice* (West 1998) § 3.14 (criticizing Sharma as being inconsistent with Court of Appeals' decision in Cortlandt).

3. *Id.* at 178, 495 N.Y.S.2d at 932, 486 N.E.2d at 790.

4. *See, e.g.*, Louis Harris & Assoc. v. deLeon, 84 N.Y.2d 698, 622 N.Y.S.2d 217, 646 N.E.2d 438 (1994)(10–year delay in conducting hearing on whether blind job applicant could have been accommodated does not require dismissal); Reid v. Axelrod, 164 A.D.2d 973, 559 N.Y.S.2d 417 (4th Dep't 1990)(mere passage of time does not by itself constitute prejudice).

§ 4.22 Adjudicatory Proceedings—Agency Duty to Decide Consistently

Agencies have a fundamental obligation to decide like cases alike, or to offer a reasoned explanation for departure from precedent. Thus, if an agency decides apparently identical cases inconsistently without any explanation, New York courts have not hesitated to set aside the decisions as inherently arbitrary.[1] This duty is sufficiently fundamental that it applies with equal force to adjudications that are not covered by SAPA.[2] This duty to decide cases consistently does not, however, prevent agencies from resolving cases on close factual points or from knowingly departing from agency precedent, as long as a reasonable explanation is offered.[3]

Library References:

West's Key No. Digests, Administrative Law and Procedure ⚖502.

§ 4.23 Adjudicatory Proceedings—Intra-agency Review

As discussed above,[1] administrative adjudication is usually initially conducted before an agency employee, who may have one of several titles—the most common being Administrative Law Judge, hearing officer and hearing examiner—for which we use the generic term "ALJ."

---

5. *See, e.g.*, Heller v. Chu, 111 A.D.2d 1007, 1009, 490 N.Y.S.2d 326, 327 (3d Dep't 1985), appeal dismissed 66 N.Y.2d 696, 496 N.Y.S.2d 424, 487 N.E.2d 281 (1985)(16-year delay in tax assessment proceeding is "contrary to fundamental notions of fairness and is unacceptable").

§ 4.22

1. *See, e.g.*, Matter of Charles A. Field Delivery Service, 66 N.Y.2d 516, 498 N.Y.S.2d 111, 488 N.E.2d 1223 (1985)(inconsistent agency adjudications as to whether delivery drivers are employees or independent contractors renders agency decisions inherently arbitrary).

2. *See, e.g.*, *id* (applying duty to agency not covered by SAPA).

3. *See, e.g.*, Deem v. Bane, 159 Misc.2d 461, 605 N.Y.S.2d 191 (Sup.Ct., Nassau County, 1993)(agency explanation that prior decisions were based upon erroneous interpretation of law complies with duty to decide cases consistently or offer a reasoned explanation).

PRACTICE POINTER: Sometimes demonstrating that an agency decision is inconsistent with prior cases is not a simple matter. SAPA § 307(3) requires each agency that conducts adjudicatory proceeding to "maintain an index by name and subject matter of all written final decisions, determinations and orders rendered by the agency in adjudicatory proceedings," and to make it available for inspection and copying. In practice, however, some agency indices are difficult to use because of poor subject matter indexing, or are not up to date. A Freedom of Information Request for the final written decisions in similar cases may prove useful.

§ 4.23

1. *See supra*, § 4.2.

The decisions of ALJs are then subject to review by the agency head or heads, a process that often called "intra-agency review." There is no legal obstacle to an agency head actually conducting adjudicatory proceedings in the first instance, but workload usually requires the delegation of the initial responsibilities to ALJs.

It is tempting to think of this review process of ALJ decisions by the agency heads as analogous to review of trial court decisions by appellate courts. To be sure, there are some similarities. As a practical matter, how an ALJ resolves the case is likely to carry great weight with the agency head or heads. Precise statistics are difficult to locate, but probably the large majority of ALJ decisions are either wholly or substantially confirmed by the agency heads.

The analogy to an appeal in a civil case is imperfect, however, because it ignores a central feature of agency adjudication. Agencies are unitary entities; in administrative adjudication, agencies operate essentially as judge, jury and prosecutor. The ALJ is still ultimately an agency employee, and the agency head or heads reviewing the decision are his supervisors. Therefore, agencies retain essentially unfettered authority to modify the decisions of their ALJs. The only real limitation on this power is a 1989 executive order that requires agency heads to explain in writing why they have modified the ALJ's decision, but the executive order does not purport to limit traditional agency freedom to alter the decisions of the ALJs.[2]

In contrast, trial courts have much more structural independence from appellate courts. Trial courts, for instance, have nearly the final say in factual matters; their factual determinations cannot be upset unless "clearly erroneous."[3] An ALJ's factual determinations are not, however, insulated from modification by the full agency. It is important to remember, therefore, that while prevailing before the ALJ is an important—often, as a practical matter, essential—step on the road to victory, preserving the result before the agency itself is just as crucial.

§ 4.24 Adjudicatory Proceedings—Checking Agency Bias

Administrative agencies occupy a slightly uneasy place in American jurisprudence because in administrative adjudication—including, of course, adjudicatory proceedings under SAPA—the agency plays the role of judge, jury and prosecutor. It is well established, however, that this combination of functions does not by itself violate the Due Process Clause.[1] Instead, the fundamental fairness of administrative adjudication

---

2. N.Y. Exec. Order No. 131, 9 NYCRR § 4.131 (1989).

3. *See, e.g.*, People v. Raja, 77 A.D.2d 322, 433 N.Y.S.2d 200 (2d Dep't 1980).

§ 4.24

1. *See, e.g.*, Withrow v. Larkin, 421 U.S. 35, 95 S.Ct. 1456, 43 L.Ed.2d 712 (1975).

is regulated by several overlapping sources of which the administrative law practitioner must be aware.

SAPA allows a party in an adjudicatory proceeding to challenge the "presiding officer"—meaning either the ALJ or an agency head hearing the case—by "filing in good faith a timely and sufficient affidavit of personal bias ...."[2] If such an affidavit is filed, the agency is required to "determine the matter as part of the record in the case, and its determination shall be a matter subject to judicial review at the conclusion of the adjudicatory proceeding."[3] While SAPA is quite clear on the procedures for challenging an agency decisionmaker for bias, it provides no hint as to what standards are to be applied to determine what amounts to "personal bias."

The task of determining what constitutes personal bias has thus fallen to the courts, which have fleshed out the standards as a matter of both common and constitutional law. It is clear that the mere fact that the ALJ works for an agency does not by itself constitute "personal bias"; if it did, the whole of agency adjudication would be unconstitutional.[4] Other closer relationships, however, have been found to constitute bias, as in the case in which an agency employee serves as a "prosecutor" in a case, and—after being promoted to the head of the agency—sits in review of one of the cases she prosecuted.[5]

A related manner in which an agency decisionmaker can be challenged for personal bias is if there is some individual factor that indicates an unacceptable risk that the decisionmaker has prejudged the case. For instance, an agency head who has expressed specific views about the appropriate disposition of an adjudicatory proceeding cannot then sit in review of an ALJ's disposition of that matter.[6] Similarly, an agency decisionmaker who stands to personally benefit or has a personal reason to believe or disbelieve crucial evidence is constitutionally unacceptable.[7]

---

2. SAPA § 303.

3. SAPA § 303.

4. *See, e.g.*, Whalen v. Slocum, 84 A.D.2d 956, 956–57, 446 N.Y.S.2d 727, 727–28 (4th Dep't 1981)(employment relationship between agency and ALJ does not by itself constitute illegal bias).

5. *See* General Motors Corp. v. Rosa, 82 N.Y.2d 183, 604 N.Y.S.2d 14, 624 N.E.2d 142 (1993)(General Counsel later promoted to agency head cannot sit in judgment on review of an ALJ's decision in a case prosecuted by one of her subordinates while she was General Counsel).

6. *See, e.g.*, 1616 Second Avenue Restaurant, Inc. v. New York State Liquor Auth., 75 N.Y.2d 158, 163, 551 N.Y.S.2d 461, 464, 550 N.E.2d 910, 913 (1990)(agency head who testified before a legislative committee with regard to a particular case that "what I am trying to do ... is to bring to bear on these kinds of charges some innovative ways of establishing guilt by substantial evidence ..." must be recused from voting on whether to confirm ALJ decision on administrative penalty).

7. *See, e.g.*, New York Public Interest Research Group, Inc. v. Williams, 127 A.D.2d 512, 511 N.Y.S.2d 864 (1st Dep't 1987)(temporary ALJ whose firm stood to gain consulting contracts if license issued must be recused from matter); Cafaro v. Pedersen, 123 A.D.2d 860, 507 N.Y.S.2d 645 (2d Dep't 1986)(ALJ could not sit in matter in which spouse was a material witness).

Another important guarantee of fundamental fairness in agency adjudication is limitation on *ex parte* contacts. In general, both SAPA and a 1989 executive order prohibit ALJs from having *ex parte* discussions on issues of fact.[8] On issues of law, ALJs generally are allowed to consult with other agency personnel, as long as they are not the very personnel performing the prosecuting function in that or a factually related case.[9] The more relaxed rules concerning *ex parte* contacts on issues of law bow to the fact that agencies, unlike courts, are unitary entities expected to take a unitary stance on matters of policy.[10]

Library References:
West's Key No. Digests, Administrative Law and Procedure ⚖︎314.

§ 4.25 Adjudicatory Proceedings—Res Judicata and Collateral Estoppel Effect

New York courts are fairly generous in according *res judicata* and collateral estoppel effect to administrative adjudications. As a general matter, prior adjudications preclude parties and their privies from relitigating issues and claims decided adversely to them in a prior proceeding. Administrative determinations have this effect if they are "quasi-judicial."[1] Adjudicatory proceedings obviously qualify as "quasi-judicial" under this test, but less formal administrative determinations can also be accorded preclusive effect as long as they entail individualized determinations of fact and law.[2]

---

8. SAPA § 307(2); N.Y. Exec. Order No. 131, 9 NYCRR § 4.131 (1989).

9. SAPA § 307(2); N.Y. Exec. Order No. 131, 9 NYCRR § 4.131 (1989).

10. **PRACTICE POINTER**: Some agency hearing regulations contain special rules on limiting *ex parte* contacts that are more detailed than SAPA or Executive Order 131. *See, e.g.*, 6 NYCRR § 624.10 (DEC permit regulations). Others contain nothing on the subject. Consult the agency hearing regulations carefully.

CAVEAT: Before challenging an agency decision on the grounds that there were illegal *ex parte* contacts, be sure to review both SAPA § 307 and Executive Order 131 with care. Both contain an important exception for initial license determinations for public utilities and carriers. They also list ratemaking as an exception, which is redundant, because both SAPA § 307 and Executive Order 131 apply only to adjudicatory proceedings, and ratemakings are specifically defined by SAPA § as rulemakings. *See* SAPA § 102(2)(a)(ii). SAPA § 307 appears to apply to all agency decisionmakers, including agency heads, while Executive Order 131 (in Section I(B)) specifically excludes agency heads from its coverage. The Executive Order also contains (in Section I(A)) a slightly longer list of agencies that are specifically exempted from its reach than does SAPA. *See* SAPA § 102(1).

§ 4.25

1. *See, e.g.*, Allied Chemical v. Niagara Mohawk Power Corp., 72 N.Y.2d 271, 274, 532 N.Y.S.2d 230, 231, 528 N.E.2d 153, 154 (1988), cert. denied 488 U.S. 1005, 109 S.Ct. 785, 102 L.Ed.2d 777 (1989).

2. *See, e.g.*, Allied Chemical v. Niagara Mohawk Power Corp., 72 N.Y.2d 271, 532 N.Y.S.2d 230, 528 N.E.2d 153, cert. denied 488 U.S. 1005, 109 S.Ct. 785, 102 L.Ed.2d 777 (1989) (Public Service Commission ratemaking); Ryan v. New York Telephone Co., 62 N.Y.2d 494, 478 N.Y.S.2d 823, 467 N.E.2d 487 (1984)(unemployment insurance determination); Freddolino v. Village of Warwick Board of Zoning Appeals, 192 A.D.2d 839, 596 N.Y.S.2d 490 (3d Dep't 1993)(municipal zoning determination); *but see* Staatsburg Water Co. v. Staatsburg Fire Dist., 72 N.Y.2d 147, 531 N.Y.S.2d 876, 527 N.E.2d 754 (1988)(party who enters pro-

§ 4.26 Adjudicatory Proceedings—Special Rules Applicable to Licensing Matters

As noted above,[1] licensing matters get different treatment in determining whether they qualify as "adjudicatory proceedings." Normally, before a matter is treated as an adjudicatory proceeding, the agency enabling legislation must specifically refer to the need for a hearing "on a record," but in the case of licensing matters, a mere reference to the need for a "hearing" or an "opportunity to be heard" suffices.[2] Assuming that a licensing matter qualifies as an adjudicatory proceeding, it is treated for the most part as is any other adjudicatory proceeding. There are, however, some special rules applicable only in licensing cases.

First, if a license holder has a valid license in effect, and makes a "timely and sufficient application for the renewal of a license or a new license with reference to any activity of a continuing nature" then the old license remains in effect "until the application has been finally determined by the agency."[3] Even if the renewal is denied or restricted, the old license remains in effect until the time to seek review of the agency decision passes.[4] This rule sensibly recognizes that a licensee who makes a prompt application for renewal should not be punished if the agency does not or cannot respond in a timely fashion.

Second, SAPA allows for temporary suspension of a license if "the agency finds that the public health, safety or welfare imperatively requires emergency action, and incorporates a finding to this effect in its order."[5] The suspension takes effect no earlier than service of a certified copy of the order on the licensee.[6] A suspended licensee is entitled to a hearing "promptly" after the suspension.[7]

Third, SAPA also provides for discovery in licensing revocation matters in a form not mandated in other adjudicatory proceedings.[8] In license revocation hearings, either party is entitled to force the other to "disclose the evidence that the party intends to introduce at the hearing, including documentary evidence and identification of witnesses."[9] Upon such a demand, the party must make the disclosure at least seven days

---

ceeding with reasonable expectation that issue will not be resolved can avoid preclusive effect of attempted resolution by agency).

§ 4.26

1. See supra, § 4.2.
2. SAPA § 401(1).
3. SAPA § 401(2).
4. SAPA § 401(2).
5. SAPA § 401(3).
6. SAPA § 401(3).

7. SAPA § 401(3). See also Saumell v. New York State Racing Ass'n, 58 N.Y.2d 231, 460 N.Y.S.2d 763, 447 N.E.2d 706 (1983)(holding that such a post-deprivation hearing is constitutional only if there is a true emergency, and that requiring a pre-suspension hearing would interfere with an important regulatory objective).

8. SAPA § 401(4).
9. SAPA § 401(4).

before the hearing, and if the party decides after the disclosure to rely on evidence not disclosed, must supplement the disclosure.[10]

The Office for Regulatory Management and Assistance ("ORMA") is designed in part to assist businesses in the licensing process.[11] Among other things, ORMA is to "provide comprehensive information" on licenses, "assist applicants in obtaining timely and efficient [license] review," "consolidate hearings" and offer "official opinion[s] as to the general acceptability of ... undertakings requiring" a license.[12] Lawyers with clients engaged in activities that might or do require a license may well find that a discussion with ORMA personnel is a resource-saving first step. ORMA's activities in this regard have been taken over by a new entity called the Governor's Office for Regulatory Reform ("GORR").[13]

Library References:
West's Key No. Digests, Licenses ⚖=22.

§ 4.27 Adjudicatory Proceedings—Special Issues in Handling Licensing Matters

Just as licensing matters raise some specialized legal issues,[1] so too do they raise specialized strategic considerations. Almost every business in New York State requires a permit or license[2] from one or more state agencies.[3] Because of the variation between and among agencies, generalized pronouncements concerning the licensing process must be made with care. For example, while most licenses are issued within one month of application,[4] a 1994 report on state license activity published by the State's Office for Regulatory and Management Assistance indicates that twenty types of licenses took longer than six months to be issued.[5] Certain licenses issued by the Departments of Health, Environmental Conservation, Alcoholism and Substance Abuse, Education, Agriculture and Markets, and Motor Vehicles, and by the Public Service Commission, fall into this latter category.[6] Most licenses are issued by an agency without a hearing. But, in those circumstances in which there are

---

10. SAPA § 401(4).
11. Executive Law § 878.
12. Executive Law § 878(1), (4), (6).
13. N.Y. Exec. Order 20.

§ 4.27
1. See supra, § 4.26.
2. SAPA uses the terms "license" and "permit" interchangeably, see SAPA § 102(4), but refers to the topic as one of "licensing." SAPA § 401. Many agencies, including the Department of Environmental Conservation, commonly use the term "permit." See Chapter 15 "Environmental Law," infra. We will use the SAPA preferred term "license," although our discussion is arguably applicable to permits.

3. Report of Action Unit No. 5 of the New York State Bar Association, New York State Regulatory Reform 2 (1979).

4. State of New York Office for Regulatory and Management Assistance, Rep. of Ann. Bus. Permit Issuing Activity by New York State Agencies For Fiscal Year 1992–1993 1 (1994).

5. Id. at 13. ORMA was created by Article 39 of the Executive Law.

6. Id.

§ 4.27 ADMINISTRATIVE LAW Ch. 4

disputed questions as to whether the license should issue, the applicant is often entitled to a hearing, thereby triggering procedures applicable to an adjudicatory proceeding.[7]

Library References:

West's Key No. Digests, Licenses ⛞22.

§ 4.28 Adjudicatory Proceedings—Special Issues in Handling Licensing Matters—Basic License Information

A first step in obtaining necessary licenses is to determine which agencies have jurisdiction over the proposed activity, and what licenses they require. ORMA's Official Directory of New York State Business Permits, published by the New York State Bar Association, lists all of the business licenses issued by the various New York State agencies. It also provides details concerning each type. Consequently, this reference is a good starting point to determine the answers to these questions.

Another place to start is with the issuing agencies themselves. There appears to be a heightened emphasis on the part of these agencies to be responsive to requests for information of this sort. For example, the State Department of Environmental Conservation has opened several toll-free numbers for information on different DEG activities.[1] ORMA, discussed in more detail below,[2] views itself as an ombudsman for applicants and therefore institutionally is well suited to responding to requests for information as well. ORMA's activities in this respect have been taken over by a new entity called the Governor's Office for Regulatory Reform.[3] GORR has essentially replaced ORMA, and also wields a large number of powers that ORMA did not have.

§ 4.29 Adjudicatory Proceedings—Special Issues in Handling Licensing Matters—The Role of SAPA and SEQRA in the Licensing Process

SAPA guarantees licensees certain rights as against the government and others. It ensures, for example, that agency delay in processing a licensee's application to renew cannot terminate the licensee's authority to operate if the license expires before the agency renews it. Instead, SAPA provides that a licensee that has filed a "timely and sufficient" renewal application may continue to operate after its term expires.[1]

7. See supra, § 4.26.

§ 4.28

1. Author's telephone interview with Sue Cumo, September 25, 1997.

2. See infra, at § 4.31.

3. N.Y. Exec. Order 20.

§ 4.29

1. SAPA § 401(2).

Further, in an apparent effort to provide fair process, SAPA requires agencies seeking to revoke a party's authority to operate under a license to provide the party with the relevant evidence in advance of the hearing.[2] Again, however, the licensee is not automatically assured this protection. The agency need not unilaterally provide this information.[3] Instead, the licensee must affirmatively request it to trigger the agency's obligation to furnish the information.

A third overarching SAPA requirement in this context is its empowerment of agencies to summarily suspend licenses.[4] SAPA's only condition on such authority is that the agency must incorporate into the summary order a finding that "public health, safety, or welfare imperatively require[ ] emergency action."[5]

In contrast to SAPA's relatively modest impact on the license process the State Environmental Quality Review Act (SEQRA) impacts significant numbers of license proceedings each year, particularly those involving new or expanded operations or developments.[6] Even though SEQRA is an environmental law, it affects far more than just the State Department of Environmental Conservation. SEQRA requires each State agency to consider environmental impacts associated with its activities.[7] And, SEQRA's edict is clear, as expressed in its implementing regulations: "[n]o agency involved in an action shall carry out, fund or approve the action until it has complied with the provisions of SEQR."[8]

SEQRA applies to a wide variety of State agency actions, although it does not apply to every State agency action of any sort. For example, it does not apply to agency decisions involving issuance of a building permit if issuance of the permit is a ministerial action. In essence, SEQRA applies to *discretionary* agency actions that *may affect the environment*, whether the action be one that the agency is undertaking itself, or an action that the agency must approve or fund.[9]

Under SEQRA, the agency in the lead in connection with a particular license application reviews the proposed action to determine whether it may have a significant impact on the environment.[10] If the agency

2. SAPA § 401(4).

3. SAPA § 401(4).

4. SAPA § 401(3).

5. SAPA § 401(3).

6. SEQRA is found in Environmental Conservation Law Article 8. ECL §§ 8–0101 to 8–0117. For comprehensive discussions of SEQRA, see infra, §§ 15.2–15.4 and M.B. Gerrard et al., Environmental Impact Review in New York (1994). For a discussion of SEQRA in local land use decisions, see § 15.3 et seq. (discussing local environmental review under SEQRA).

7. ECL § 8–0109.

8. 6 NYCRR § 617.3(a).

9. ECL § 8–0105. By its terms, SEQRA exempts certain types of actions from coverage even if they may affect the environment. These are known as "exempt," "excluded," "and" "Type II" actions. See 6 NYCRR § 617.3.

10. Under SEQRA, one agency maintains "lead agency" status for the pendency of the SEQRA process. 6 NYCRR § 617.6. As the phrase suggests, in essence this agency oversees the permit application through the SEQRA process. See generally Chapter 15 "Environmental Law," *infra* §§ 15.3–15.4 (discussing local environmental review).

resolves this issue in the negative, it issues a "negative declaration."[11] If the agency determines that the proposed action may have a significant impact on the environment, it issues a "positive declaration."[12] For proposed actions that receive a "positive declaration," the applicant must prepare a draft Environmental Impact Statement ("EIS").[13] The draft EIS must contain the following types of information, among others:

1. A concise description of the proposed action, including a description of its purpose and benefits;
2. A concise description of the environmental setting of the areas to be affected;
3. An evaluation of the environmental impacts of the proposed action, including an evaluation of any adverse environmental impacts that cannot be avoided or adequately mitigated; and
4. A description and evaluation of a range of reasonable alternatives to the action which are feasible, considering the objectives and capabilities of the applicant.[14]

Submittal of an adequate draft EIS moves the SEQRA process forward to the next stage, which is the public comment period. Following the public comment period, the EIS is finalized; in its final form, the EIS must include a summary of the substantive comments provided by the public. The lead agency issues a Notice of Completion of the Final EIS when the EIS is complete.[15] Each involved agency then prepares a SEQRA findings statement. A positive findings statement certifies the approvability of the project under SEQRA; it reflects both that the activity approved will minimize or avoid environmental impacts to the extent possible, and that the agency balanced the need for the project against its impacts.[16]

A final point is that compliance with SEQRA is necessary, but not necessarily sufficient, to obtain a license. An applicant that successfully navigates the SEQRA process must also meet the substantive and other requirements relevant to the activity at issue.

§ 4.30 Adjudicatory Proceedings—Special Issues in Handling Licensing Matters—Accuracy and Completeness in Applications

In many cases, licensees maintain a long term relationship with the issuing agency. Developing a complete and accurate application is an

---

11. See 6 NYCRR §§ 617.2(y), 617.6(g). Appendix F of the SEQRA regulations contain a model negative declaration. 6 NYCRR § 617.21.

12. 6 NYCRR §§ 617.10(b), 617.2(cc).

13. 6 NYCRR § 617.8.

14. 6 NYCRR § 617.14(f).

15. 6 NYCRR § 617.10(f); The New York State Dep't of Environmental Conservation, The SEQR Cookbook: A Step-by Step Discussion of the SEQR Process 15 (1992).

16. 6 NYCRR § 617.9; New York Dep't of Environmental Conservation, The SEQR Handbook 81 (1992).

important first step in getting this long term relationship off on the right foot. Further, agencies often have considerable flexibility to set license conditions; demonstrating one's seriousness and competence by filing an accurate and complete application should help to convince the agency to set conditions accordingly.

Candor is a virtue in completing license applications because, under some circumstances, agencies may pursue criminal prosecutions for filing an inaccurate application. The Penal Law makes it a crime to submit false information to the government.[1] In some cases, agencies have prosecuted filers of such false information.[2]

Completeness in filing an application may also be of enormous importance to the applicant because it makes it clear that the agency made its decision with all of the relevant information in its possession. Collateral attacks on the licensed activity are therefore less likely to succeed. This is probably the case regardless of whether such collateral attacks are founded on common law theories or are based on statutory causes of action. A 1993 Second Circuit decision is an example of the latter. In *Atlantic States Legal Found., Inc. v. Eastman Kodak Co.*,[3] the court held that a citizen suit did not lie under the Clean Water Act in connection with Kodak's discharges of a number of water pollutants, because Kodak, in its license application, had notified DEC of the company's discharges of these pollutants and DEC had issued the license while declining to impose limits on these discharges.[4]

§ 4.30

1. *See generally* Penal Law Art. 175. *See, e.g.*, Penal Law § 175.30 (offering a false instrument for filing in the second degree, a Class A misdemeanor). This section provides as follows:

> A person is guilty of offering a false instrument for filing in the second degree when, knowing that a written instrument contains a false statement or false information, he offers or presents it to a public office or public servant with the knowledge or belief that it will be filed with, registered or recorded in or otherwise become a part of the records of such public office or public servant.
>
> Offering a false instrument for filing in the second degree is a class A misdemeanor.

Section 175.35, offering a false instrument for filing in the first degree, is a Class E felony. Penal Law § 175.35. This section provides as follows:

> A person is guilty of offering a false instrument for filing in the first degree when, knowing that a written instrument contains a false statement or false information, and with intent to defraud the state or any political subdivision thereof, he offers or presents it to a public office or public servant with the knowledge or belief that it will be filed with, registered or recorded in or otherwise become a part of the records of such public office or public servant.
>
> Offering a false instrument for filing in the first degree is a class E felony.

2. People v. Kase, 76 A.D.2d 532, 431 N.Y.S.2d 531 (1st Dep't 1980), aff'd 53 N.Y.2d 989, 441 N.Y.S.2d 671, 424 N.E.2d 558 (1981)(liquor license application); People v. Abedi, 156 Misc.2d 904, 595 N.Y.S.2d 1011 (Sup.Ct., N.Y. County, 1993)(filings with the New York State Banking Department).

3. 12 F.3d 353 (2d Cir.1993).

4. *Id.* at 354.

§ 4.31 Adjudicatory Proceedings—Special Issues in Handling Licensing Matters—Opportunities to Expedite the Process

Recourse to the Governor's Office for Regulatory Reform—acting as ORMA's successor—is a possible strategy to expedite issuance of a license, regardless of the identity of the agency responsible for actual issuance. GORR has the potential to be particularly helpful with respect to license applications in economic development zones. At the applicant's request, GORR will "red stamp" the license application; through an informal agreement with other agencies, such red stamped applications receive priority attention for processing.[1]

GORR—again, as ORMA's successor—has developed a second, more generic approach to expedite license processing known as the master application procedure.[2] This procedure is designed to "coordinate and expedite the delivery of governmental services to business locating or expanding in New York State."[3] The applicant submits a completed master application project information form to GORR, which then distributes the form to every state agency that GORR "believes to have a possible interest in the business undertaking."[4] With some limited exceptions, agencies that fail to respond, or that respond that no licenses are required, are barred from thereafter requiring a license.[5]

The master application process, in short, offers two significant potential benefits to applicants. It enables them to learn early on which licenses apply to a particular activity, with the government doing the work of developing and providing this information to the applicant. In addition, it minimizes the likelihood that a state agency will ambush an applicant with new demands late in the process. Use of this process is likely to be especially worthwhile for applicants with projects falling under the jurisdiction of multiple agencies.

In addition to GORR's tools for expediting the process, an applicant also needs to review the issuing agency's procedures to determine whether that agency offers other opportunities to accelerate matters. With the renewed focus on "regulatory reform"[6] agencies increasingly are likely to direct their energies toward customer-friendly approaches.[7]

---

§ 4.31

1. Telephone Interview with Judith Wolfe Sampson, ORMA Senior Project Manager (Jan. 4, 1995).

2. 9 NYCRR Part 8600. *See also* N.Y. Exec. Order 20.

3. 9 NYCRR § 8600.1(a).

4. 9 NYCRR § 8600.4(c).

5. 9 NYCRR § 8600.4(f). For a discussion of these exceptions, *see* Borchers and Markell, *New York State Administrative Procedure and Practice* (West 1998) § 9.12.

6. Governor George Pataki, State of the State Message (Jan. 4, 1995).

7. For a discussion of DEC approaches of this sort, *see* Borchers and Markell, *New York State Administrative Procedure and Practice* (West 1998) § 9.12.

Library References:
West's Key No. Digests, Licenses ⚖︎22.

§ 4.32 Adjudicatory Proceedings—Special Issues in Handling Licensing Matters—Opportunities for Variances From Standard Approaches

License applicants should always explore opportunities for special, favorable treatment in terms of both substantive and procedural requirements. Small businesses may well qualify for such special treatment. SAPA's requirement that agencies focus specifically on a regulation's impact on small businesses has led agencies to relax requirements for such businesses in some cases. For example, DEC's regulations waive fees for municipal permit applicants with populations of less than 3,500 people.[1]

Other types of special treatment to explore include technical and financial assistance associated with the permitted activity. Agencies ranging from the Department of Health to the Department of Environmental Conservation offer such assistance under certain circumstances. Because of the increased attention given to "regulatory reform" alluded to above, provision of these and other types of assistance is likely to expand in future years. Accordingly, it behooves the practitioner to stay current on the types of assistance an agency offers.

§ 4.33 Adjudicatory Proceedings—Special Issues in Handling Licensing Matters—Renewal, Suspension and Revocation Issues

Because many licenses terminate after a fixed term, the licensee must renew its permission to operate when the original authorization expires. It is difficult to overstate the importance of timely seeking such renewal. SAPA § 401(2) provides that a licensee continues its ability to operate by filing a "timely and sufficient" application for renewal.[1] This provision ensures that agency delay in processing the renewal application, resulting in apparent expiration of the old license prior to finalization of the new one, will not harm the licensee. Instead, as suggested above, filing a timely and sufficient renewal application guarantees a licensee's right to continuity in operation, at least until the agency acts on the renewal application. Failure to file a timely and sufficient renewal application leaves the licensee susceptible to a termination of its authorization to do business pending consideration of the renewed permit.[2]

---

§ 4.32
1. 6 NYCRR § 621.3(b)(2).

§ 4.33
1. SAPA § 401(2).

2. *See e.g.*, In the Matter of the Town of Haverstraw (Rockland County), No. 3-1754/8908 (Oct. 20, 1993), aff'd Town of Haverstraw v. Jorling, 213 A.D.2d 654, 624 N.Y.S.2d 941 (2d Dep't 1995).

The sanctions of suspension and revocation of licenses typically are encountered by licensees that have engaged in behavior unacceptable to the issuing agency. Revocation is the more extreme sanction of the two. While agencies tend to be circumspect in invoking their revocation authority, the case law is replete with instances of agencies instituting revocation proceedings against licensees who had engaged in behavior deemed unacceptable by the agency.[3] The practitioner concerned about the possibility of an agency instituting such a proceeding should review previous revocation cases to obtain hints as to the types of conduct that the agency deems sufficiently egregious to warrant revocation. If an agency initiates such a proceeding, at a minimum the practitioner needs to consider invoking SAPA § 401, which guarantees that parties to a revocation proceeding may obtain the evidence the other side intends to introduce at the hearing.[4]

As a sanction, suspension falls somewhat short of revocation in terms of severity, largely because suspension is temporary but revocation is permanent. Because suspension is intended for emergency situations, a licensee has few procedural rights in connection with a suspension. SAPA § 401(3) authorizes agencies to summarily suspend a license upon a finding that "public health, safety, or welfare imperatively requires emergency action."[5] SAPA is silent concerning the nature and timing of process an agency is required to afford a licensee in suspension situations.

Library References:
West's Key No. Digests, Licenses ⟺22, 38.

§ 4.34 Adjudicatory Proceedings—Special Issues in Handling Enforcement Matters

Besides licensing matters, the other large category of administrative adjudication is enforcement matters, which raises its own special strategic concerns. One of an administrative agency's responsibilities is to monitor compliance with the laws it is charged with administering, and to pursue strategies designed to maximize such compliance. One such

---

3. *See, e.g.*, Beer Garden, Inc. v. New York State Liquor Auth., 79 N.Y.2d 266, 582 N.Y.S.2d 65, 590 N.E.2d 1193 (1992)(SLA unsuccessfully sought revocation for violation of regulation against premises becoming the focus of police attention); Hodes v. Axelrod, 70 N.Y.2d 364, 520 N.Y.S.2d 933, 515 N.E.2d 612 (1987)(Commissioner of Health sought revocation of nursing home operating certificate for industry related felony convictions); Perrotta v. City of New York, 66 N.Y.2d 859, 498 N.Y.S.2d 368, 489 N.E.2d 255 (1985)(Department of Buildings sought revocation of building permit because structure built did not conform to the plans for a single family home); Harris v. Codd, 44 N.Y.2d 978, 408 N.Y.S.2d 501, 380 N.E.2d 327 (1978)(Police Commissioner revoked pistol permit for indiscriminate use of the pistol); Rembert v. Perales, 187 A.D.2d 784, 589 N.Y.S.2d 649 (3d Dep't 1992)(Department of Social Services revoked home day care center certification for violation of state regulations). See Chapter 36 "Alcohol Beverage Control Law," *infra* for a discussion of license revocation.

4. SAPA § 401(4).

5. SAPA § 401(3).

Ch. 4   STRATEGIES TO MINIMIZE VIOLATIONS   § 4.35

strategy involves taking enforcement actions against violators. An agency typically will seek to design its enforcement actions to produce both general and specific deterrence.[1] The former involves convincing members of the regulated community generally that they will be better off by complying with legal requirements than committing violations. The latter entails sending a message to the individual violator that it will be better off in the future if it complies with its obligations. Administrative agencies may have a broad range of enforcement options, including filing a civil complaint, pursuing a criminal prosecution, or initiating a case before an ALJ.

Library References:

West's Key No. Digests, Administrative Law and Procedure ⇐901–938.

§ 4.35 Adjudicatory Proceedings—Special Issues in Handling Enforcement Matters—Strategies to Minimize Violations

Violating agency legal requirements has the potential to subject the violator to significant sanctions. Sufficiently egregious behavior may lead the agency to revoke or significantly circumscribe the violator's authority to operate. Additionally, or alternatively, substantial violations may lead to criminal prosecution (which may include the possibility of jail time), or to civil or administrative actions that include significant penalties. Such sanctions, combined with the importance that many regulated parties attach to a positive public image, suggest that the best policy is to comply fully with legal requirements.

Tickler systems, which list regulatory obligations, including due dates, are one relatively simple strategy to minimize non-compliance. A complementary strategy is to ensure that employees receive adequate training in regulatory obligations. A third strategy, which many companies have adopted in the environmental arena, is periodically to conduct self-audits of compliance with regulatory obligations. While few would dispute that this third strategy is effective in uncovering violations, the practitioner needs to be mindful that companies performing such audits that discover violations effectively hand the government an enforcement case on a silver platter, especially if the audit findings are reduced to writing and accessible to government officials. Accordingly, a debate is currently ongoing, at both the national and state levels, concerning how best to encourage such self-audits without undermining governmental regulatory authority. While this debate rages, some private practitioners urge that companies exercise caution before undertaking self-auditing

§ 4.34
1. New York State Dep't of Environ-   mental Conservation, Enforcement Di-

activities.[1] These practitioners recommend that, among other measures, companies should structure the self-audits—using the Attorney-Client privilege and other possible tools—to minimize the likelihood that the results will be disclosable.

A separate strategy for the likelihood of an enforcement action is to determine the agency's priorities, and to make those the licensee's compliance priorities as well. Thus, if the Department of Health makes it a priority to take enforcement action against violators of certain requirements, a regulated party should allocate its resources accordingly, with the goal of complying fully with the requirements the agency has placed at the top of its list. Identifying agency priorities is not necessarily a simple task. Review of past agency enforcement actions, or agency guidance documents, may be worthwhile. Both are available under the Freedom of Information Law ("FOIL").[2] One former government official captures this issue succinctly as follows: "aside from trying to avoid all violations, facilities should avoid high-priority violations altogether or do what they can to reduce violations that may cause them to be classified as high-priority violators in order that they be considered lower level violators."[3]

§ 4.36 Adjudicatory Proceedings—Special Issues in Handling Enforcement Matters—Agency Fact-Finding in the Pre-enforcement Phase

Regulatory agencies generally enjoy considerable latitude in monitoring operations of parties they regulate. Sending out agency inspectors to evaluate site conditions is one frequently employed strategy. The practitioner should determine whether regulatory agency staff generally arrive unannounced or, in contrast, provide advance notice of their plan

---

rectives: Civil Penalty Policy (June 20, 1990).

§ 4.35

1. See, e.g., J. Moore, *A Response to "The Case Against an Environmental Audit Privilege,"* Nat'l Envt'l Enforcement J., Dec. 1994/Jan. 1995, at 3, 7. One possible downside to conducting self-audits, particularly in situations in which the audit discloses violations that the company fails to correct immediately, is that the audit may elevate the situation to a knowing violation, increasing the risk of criminal prosecution. Bennett et al., *Internal Investigations of Potential Criminal Misconduct Under Environmental Laws*, Envt'l R. 1887, 1893 (Feb. 3, 1995). For an introduction to some of the issues associated with the self-audit concept, see Borchers and Markell, *New York State Administrative Procedure and Practice* (West 1998) § 11.2.

2. Public Officer's Law §§ 84 *et seq.*

3. See Barry, *A Practical Guide to Surviving Multimedia Inspections*, 24 Envt'l L. Rep. 10305, 10309 (June 1994). A tactical question the regulated party should consider in situations in which the regulatory requirements are complex, time-consuming, and expensive to achieve is whether to ask the regulatory agency to approve a staggered compliance schedule, thereby effectively providing the company with additional time to address low priority issues. This option is not likely to be available when the violations are relatively simple and inexpensive to fix. Attorneys, in discussing anything less than full compliance, need to be mindful of their obligations under the Code of Professional Responsibility. *See, e.g.*, DR § 1–102(a)(5), (a)(7).

to inspect. Practitioners need to be prepared for agency inspections, regardless of which approach an agency follows. In the latter case, the regulated party should review in advance any information it has provided to the government, recognizing that government staffs are likely to target areas of concern and, in many cases, the primary source of information on such concerns is the regulated party itself. To prevent being caught unprepared, parties that are subject to unannounced inspections should periodically review such reports, and at a minimum be prepared to address any deficiencies noted therein. In either case, the ideal response to materials submitted to the government that disclose violations is to correct them quickly and unilaterally.

The practitioner should give careful thought to the issue of how best to structure actual interaction with government officials during an inspection. A few practical recommendations may be of value:

> How company officials interact with government personnel may affect the nature of the inspection and the government's attitude. A few common sense points are appropriate here. First, try to help to formulate the scope and duration of the inspection. The goal of the regulated party should be to structure the inspection to put the operation in its best light. This includes influencing its scope and length and ensuring that it does not become a fishing expedition. It also includes considering carefully who should serve as the company's liaison with the inspectors.
>
> A company should, if possible, 'immediately correct any violations found during the site inspection.' At the same time, company officials should be careful not to admit the existence of violations or agree with inspectors that violations exist. Remember that as pleasant and cooperative as an inspector appears, he or she has the goal of documenting non-compliance.[1]

In conducting inspections, inspectors may directly observe conditions, take photographs, secure samples, review records, and conduct interviews of personnel. The regulated party needs to determine how it will prepare its staff for inspectors' use of such techniques. Further, the party should decide how to respond to an inspector's use of each of these approaches. For example, the party should consider tape recording or videotaping the inspection or parts thereof, having its own camera available for photographs, splitting samples with the government, and maintaining records of any documents copied by the government.

At the conclusion of the inspection, officials of the regulated party should seek the government's reaction. Officials should generally correct identified violations immediately, or commit to take such action in a

---

§ 4.36

1. Borchers and Markell, *New York State Administrative Procedure and Practice* (West 1998) § 11.3 (citing Barry, A *Practical Guide to Surviving Multimedia Inspections*, 24 Envt'l L.Rev. 10305, 10315 (June 1994)).

timely way. As suggested above, confessions of error do not need to be part of this give and take with government officials.

Observations concerning inspections that we have offered elsewhere hold equal relevance here:

> Agency inspections of a regulated party's operations pose significant challenges, as well as opportunities, for the regulated party. Learning as much as possible as early as possible about the likely focus of such inspections, ensuring that one maintains the proper tone or relationship in one's dealing with agency officials, ensuring that one is prepared to participate in an inspection in a manner that maximizes protection of one's rights, and being prepared to pursue post-inspection follow up with the inspectors, are important ingredients in handling an inspection effectively. Through such preparation, a regulated party should be able to minimize the possibility that the inspection will serve as a basis for subsequent formal enforcement action, and maximize the likelihood that the inspection will serve to promote future compliance and strengthen the relationship with the regulatory agency.[2]

§ 4.37 Adjudicatory Proceedings—Special Issues in Handling Enforcement Matters—Agency Enforcement Options

Administrative law is largely statutory in nature. Accordingly, a practitioner faced with violations and likely government enforcement action should review the statutes that authorize agency enforcement action to determine its enforcement options. Two points are salient here. First, an agency may have several enforcement options available to it, including criminal enforcement, institution of a civil action in the New York court system, or commencement of an administrative enforcement action. Second, depending on the circumstances, these options may not be mutually exclusive. That is, an agency may have the ability to proceed on parallel or sequential tracks. For example, some violations of the environmental laws are actionable civilly as well as criminally.[1] It obviously is of critical importance for the practitioner to determine the universe of an agency's enforcement options, and which of its options the agency is likely to use in a particular case.

§ 4.38 Adjudicatory Proceedings—Special Issues in Handling Enforcement Matters—The Settlement Process

As is the case in the court system, the vast majority of administrative enforcement matters are resolved long before reaching trial. To

---

2. Borchers and Markell, *New York State Administrative Procedure and Practice* (West 1998) § 11.3.

§ 4.37

1. *See, e.g.*, ECL § 71–0307.

maximize prospects for engaging in successful negotiations with agency officials, the practitioner needs to do considerable leg work to develop an understanding of relevant process issues as well as substantive matters. A threshold process question involves determining which parts of the agency will participate in the negotiations, and will need to sign off on any final settlement. A related question is who within the agency has authority to enter into a settlement. Some agencies require the agency head to approve settlements, while others delegate this authority to various agency staff. In some cases, agencies may handle different matters differently—the Commissioner of the Department of Environmental Conservation, for example, has delegated authority for different types of settlements to different officials within the Department.[1] Discussions with agency staff, and review of relevant agency guidance documents, should produce answers to these questions.

The substance of settlement discussions is likely to focus on issues of liability and relief. The agency's eagerness to litigate will obviously depend on its perception of the strength of its case. Consequently, a first step is to evaluate the government's liability case. For example, some cases are of the "open and shut" variety, for example cases based on reports filed by the alleged violator that establish violations on their face.[2] Other cases are far more tenuous. For example, a case may be founded upon alleged violations of subjective standards, based on conflicting testimony from non-agency witnesses. The agency will obviously be much more willing to compromise during settlement discussions in a case involving facts closer to the latter scenario than to the former.

In preparing for negotiations, it is especially important that the regulated party determine the scope of the agency's authority to impose sanctions. This inquiry includes researching a series of issues, including the following:

1. What types of injunctive authority does the agency have? What elements of proof must the agency establish to obtain injunctive

---

§ 4.38

1. New York State Dep't of Environmental Conservation, Enforcement Directives: Order on Consent Enforcement Policy 2 (1990) (Commissioner of the Department of Environmental Conservation delegated authority to execute routine consent orders to Regional Directors). The Commissioner of the Department of Health has similarly delegated authority to execute consent orders to several executive staff members. Letter from Peter Millock, former counsel to the Department of Health (March 4, 1995).

2. *See, e.g.,* Sierra Club v. Simkins Indus., 847 F.2d 1109, 1115 n. 8 (4th Cir. 1988), cert. denied 491 U.S. 904, 109 S.Ct. 3185, 105 L.Ed.2d 694 (1989)(court held that reports required under the Clean Water Act may be used as admissions in court to establish a defendant's liability); Public Interest Research Group of New Jersey, Inc. v. Rice, 774 F.Supp. 317, 324 (D.N.J.1991)(stating that reports or records required to be submitted by law can be used as admissions in establishing civil liability); United States v. Ward, 448 U.S. 242, 100 S.Ct. 2636, 65 L.Ed.2d 742 (1980)(court used reports the defendant was required to submit under the Clean Water Act to establish liability); United States v. Aluminum Co. of America, 824 F.Supp. 640, 648 (E.D.Tx.1993)(holding self-reported violations "conclusive evidence of violations").

relief? What types of injunctive relief has the agency sought and obtained in similar cases?

2. What penalty authority does the agency possess? What is the maximum penalty the agency legally may impose based on the facts of the case? What level of penalties has the agency sought and obtained in similar cases? What criteria, if any, has the agency established to guide it in assessing penalties?

3. What other enforcement authority is available to the agency? Does it have authority to pursue criminal prosecution? If so, do the circumstances for doing so exist in the case at hand?

4. Is the agency likely to seek to modify, or even revoke, the regulated party's permit to operate in response to the alleged violations? What types of modifications to the permit to operate is the agency likely to seek?

Several sources of information are available to help to answer these questions. The starting point for such research should generally be the agency's enabling legislation. This legislation will delimit the scope of the agency's enforcement authorities. A follow up step is to review the agency's regulations, to determine whether, *inter alia*, the agency has elaborated in its regulations on when it is likely to impose specific sanctions made available to it by the Legislature. A third source is agency guidance documents.[3] Agency settlement documents are a valuable form of precedent. Agency adjudicatory decisions are a second form of precedent. A regulated party has the right to obtain all three of these types of documents—guidance documents, settlement precedent, and adjudicatory decisions—under the Freedom of Information Law (FOIL).[4] Some of the electronic data bases are also beginning to carry these decisions.[5] Other sources of information may be helpful as well. For instance, the relevant Bar Association section may be a helpful resource,[6] and both agency-sponsored and private newsletters may contain useful information.[7]

---

3. For example, DEC has issued a general guidance document explaining its approach to enforcement matters. *See* New York State Dep't of Environmental Conservation, Enforcement Directives: Civil Penalty Policy (June 20, 1990).

4. Public Officer's Law §§ 84 *et seq.*

5. For example, WESTLAW carries the decisions of the following agencies: Department of Environmental Conservation, Workers Compensation Board, Department of Public Service and Department of Taxation and Finance, among others.

6. The Bar Association's Environmental Law Section has compiled a comprehensive index of DEC guidance documents, which it makes available on either hard copy or computer disk.

7. The DEC, for example, publishes the Environmental Notice Bulletin, which provides timely information on developments in that agency. A number of private newsletters also track agency developments. *See, e.g.,* New York Business Environment (Clarence D. Bassett, Publisher, Clifton Park, N.Y.) (focusing almost exclusively on New York State Department of Environmental Conservation-related activities); Environmental Law in New York (Matthew Bender, Conklin, N.Y.) (covering significant federal and local actions, as well as DEC activities).

§ 4.39 Adjudicatory Proceedings—Special Issues in Handling Enforcement Matters—The Hearing Process

Many alleged violations do not result in a settlement, but instead proceed through the administrative adjudicatory process. The practitioner involved in such a hearing needs to consider a host of issues.

An agency typically needs to follow prescribed procedures; it is always worthwhile to review whether the agency has done so or whether a misstep has occurred. A second issue involves determining the tools available to obtain information concerning the agency's case—what types of discovery does the agency allow? A related matter is what types of information gathering an agency will be likely to pursue once it has charted its course to be that of administrative litigation.

Pre-hearing Practice. A separate set of issues involves other features of pre-hearing administrative practice. It is important to determine the types of motions an agency authorizes to be filed before the hearing commences. For example, does the agency allow parties to file the administrative counterpart of motions for summary judgment?[1] It is also important to review other customary features of pre-hearing practice before the agency. For instance, does the agency require, or authorize, pre-hearing conferences as a tool to promote settlement? If so, does the agency create incentives to participate in such conferences? The DEC, for example, in its 1994 revisions to its enforcement hearing regulations, provides that parties that fail to attend a pre-hearing conference are subject to a default judgment.[2] This is strong encouragement for going through the motions of pursuing settlement, or at least narrowing the issues, prior to commencement of the hearing itself. Related to all of these questions are other issues, such as the nature and role of the administrative judiciary. Thus, it is important to learn what role the ALJ plays in pre-hearing conferences and whether pre-hearing motions are considered initially by the ALJ and, if so, whether the agency provides for interlocutory appeals of adverse decisions. As to all of these issues, it obviously is critically important to research the agency's enabling legislation and implementing regulations to determine the legal framework that governs this pre-hearing phase.

Attorney Preparation. Preparing for the hearing itself involves two fundamental tasks: determining the substantive issues to be adjudicated, marshaling the evidence in connection with these issues and "scouting the forum," as one expert has put it, to understand the format of the hearing.[3] The experienced civil litigator will likely have little trouble completing this first task. It is similar in significant respects to

---

§ 4.39
1. CPLR 3212.
2. 6 NYCRR § 622.8(c).

3. McElhaney, *Advocacy in Other Forums: Litigators Must Adapt to New Dispute Resolution Settings*, ABA J. 76, 76 (Feb. 1995).

preparing for civil litigation. One significant point worth emphasis is that the causes of action are statutory in nature. Thus, the dispositive legal principles, and the elements of proof that must be addressed, lie in the statute books and in the New York Compilation of Rules and Regulations sections the agency has promulgated to implement these statutes.

These substantive issues are likely to divide into two significant subcategories—liability and relief. It is important to determine what elements of proof the government needs to establish to prove the regulated party's liability, and the proof available to counter the government's affirmative case on this issue. It is also important to determine the types of relief the government may obtain. Typically, as discussed above,[4] the government may obtain penalties and injunctive relief. It is critical to assess the maximum exposure a regulated party faces, to ascertain the factors or criteria the agency uses in determining specific penalties in particular cases and to prepare one's case accordingly. Likewise, the practitioner needs to assess the facts of the case in light of agency injunctive authority as set out in its governing legislation and regulations, and develop strategy suitably. Again, the civil litigator will have a wealth of experience in conducting this type of research and in developing an appropriate litigation strategy based on the substantive principles at issue.

Hearing Format. Newcomers to administrative practice before a particular agency are likely to be somewhat apprehensive about the format of the hearing. These apprehensions have some basis in reality. For example, the qualifications and expertise of the person hearing the case, and the rules governing the proceeding, may well differ significantly from the legal environment in which the civil litigator is accustomed to operating.

It is worthwhile to determine the background and role of the ALJ. Even the appellations of the ALJ vary by agency.[5] While some judges are attorneys, others are not. Similarly, some judges may simply preside over the taking of evidence and then turn the record over to another agency official for consideration and decision, while others may also make decisions or, at a minimum, prepare recommended decisions for the agency's ultimate decision maker. The role the ALJ plays may well affect the practitioner's strategy in developing the case.

---

4. *See supra,* § 4.37.

5. For example, administrative hearings at the Public Service Commission and the Department of Health are presided over by Administrative Law Judges (ALJs). Letter from Peter Millock, former Counsel to the Department of Health (March 4, 1995). In contrast, the Department of Social Services uses the term "Hearing Officer." In yet another variation, the Department of Motor Vehicles refers to its equivalent of an ALJ as a Motor Vehicle Referee. The Department of Labor uses Assistant Commissioners to hear cases. Telephone Conversation with Kim Greene, former Deputy Counsel to the Department of Labor (Feb. 27, 1995).

A second format question involves the taking of evidence. For example, the practitioner needs to determine whether all testimony is provided orally, or whether the ALJ may allow direct testimony to be provided in written form. Another issue is whether the judge will follow the rules of evidence. SAPA is clear that agencies do not need to adhere to the civil rules of evidence.[6] It is important to ascertain the standard the agency uses to admit evidence into the administrative record.[7] A telling observation that should bring the significance of this issue home to civil litigators is that an agency's factual findings in a case may rest solely upon evidence that would not be admissible in a civil proceeding.[8]

To conclude, it behooves the practitioner to become familiar with these format issues and to plan the case accordingly. Otherwise, as one expert puts it, frustration levels are likely to mount as the practitioner sees his best laid plans go awry due to the different rules that apply in the administrative forum.[9]

§ 4.40 Adjudicatory Proceedings—Special Issues in Handling Enforcement Matters—Post–Hearing Issues

The practitioner needs to review post-hearing issues in at least two contexts. First, it is important to determine the post-hearing process within the agency itself. For example, does the agency allow appeals from adverse agency decisions? If so, at what stage of the proceeding are appeals allowed (or required)? Similarly, at what stage(s) of the proceeding is briefing of the case anticipated?

The practitioner also needs to be alert to issues relating to judicial review of adverse agency decisions, discussed in detail below.[1] Perhaps the fundamental point is the notion that, with rare exceptions, cases are won or lost before the agency.[2]

§ 4.41 Adjudicatory Proceedings—Summary

Adjudicatory proceedings are the type of administrative adjudication for which SAPA provides. Normally, a matter does not qualify as an adjudicatory proceeding unless it purports to determine the legal rights of parties and the agency's enabling legislation mandates a hearing "on a record," although in licensing matters a statutory provision for simply

6. SAPA § 306(1).

7. *See supra,* § 4.15 for a discussion of agency evidence rules.

8. *See* Borchers and Markell, *New York State Administrative Procedure and Practice* (West 1998) §§ 3.7, 11.19.

9. McElhaney, *Advocacy in Other Forums: Litigators Must Adapt to New Dispute Resolution Settings,* ABA J. 76, 76 (Feb. 1995).

§ 4.40

1. *See supra,* §§ 4.67—4.86.

2. *See, e.g.,* Pell v. Board of Education, 34 N.Y.2d 222, 356 N.Y.S.2d 833, 313 N.E.2d 321 (1974)(holding that a penalty assessed by the agency must be beyond any reasonable proportion to the violation to warrant adjustment by the judiciary).

a "hearing" or an "opportunity to be heard" will qualify the matter as an adjudicatory proceeding.[1]

Article 3 of SAPA provides fairly detailed standards for the conduct of adjudicatory proceedings. These include a right to a detailed notice, of cross-examination of witnesses who appear, to request issuance of a subpoena to command the attendance of witnesses, to a statement of decision, to a compilation of a decisional record, of placement of the burden of proof on the initiating party, of avoidance of unreasonable delay in scheduling the hearing once one is requested, of consistency in agency decisionmaking, and to limitations on agency bias including limitations on *ex parte* contacts with agency decisionmakers on issues of fact.[2] Agency hearing regulations often expand upon these fundamental rights, and should be consulted carefully prior to pursuing an adjudicatory proceeding before any agency. Other matters, such as discovery of information before the hearing and intervention in the hearing, are regulated entirely by an agency's hearing regulations, or on a case by case basis.[3] Agency determinations that are "quasi-judicial" have *res judicata* and collateral estoppel effect in the same manner as court judgments.[4] "Quasi judicial" agency determinations include adjudicatory proceedings, but also include less formal agency determinations, as long as they represent an individualized determination of fact and law.[5]

SAPA provides additional procedural rules in the case of licensing matters.[6] These include the right to have the license continued during consideration of a timely application for a renewal, fairly extensive pre-hearing discovery in license revocation matters, and the ability of an agency to suspend a license in emergencies, provided a prompt post-suspension hearing is given. Additionally, licensing matters implicate special strategic issues.[7] There may be, for instance, ways to obtain variances from the standard licensing procedures, or there may be ways to expedite the process. The other large category of administrative adjudication, enforcement matters, raises its own strategic concerns. Regulated parties need to consider how to minimize the risk of enforcement actions and how to effectively handle enforcement hearings if they occur.

§ 4.42 Adjudicatory Proceedings—Checklist

1. Is the state regulatory entity covered by SAPA? (*See* § 4.2)
    - If unsure, make the following determinations:
        (i) Does the regulatory entity have the power to either make administrative rules or to decide adjudicatory proceed-

§ 4.41
1. See supra, § 4.11.
2. See supra, §§ 4.12–4.24.
3. See supra, § 4.13.
4. See supra, § 4.25.
5. See supra, § 4.25.
6. See supra, § 4.26.
7. See supra, §§ 4.27–4.33.

ings? If it does not have the power to perform at least one of these two functions, then it is *not* covered by SAPA.

(ii) Does the regulatory entity derive its power from the State, as opposed to a local or the federal government? An entity can only be subject to SAPA if it gets its power from the state.

(iii) Is the entity headed by one or more gubernatorial appointees? Unless the entity is headed by one or more gubernatorial appointees, it may not be covered by SAPA. Thus governmental entities that are headed by elected officials are not covered by SAPA.

(iv) Is the entity specifically excluded from the definition of an "agency" by SAPA § 102(1)? Some entities (such as the Workers' Compensation Board and the Unemployment Insurance Appeals Board) that would otherwise qualify as "agencies" under SAPA are excluded by statute. Others, such as the Department of Corrections, are excluded for some purposes.

2. Is the matter an adjudicatory proceeding as defined in SAPA § 102(3)? (*See* § 4.11) If so, then all of the provisions of SAPA article 3 will apply. If not, consult the agency's enabling legislation, any hearing regulations, and any informal sources of guidance.

- If unsure whether the matter is an "adjudicatory proceeding," make the following determinations:

    (i) If the entity is not an "agency" as defined by SAPA, the matter is not an "adjudicatory proceeding" under SAPA.

    (ii) If the entity is an "agency" as defined by SAPA, consult the enabling legislation specific to this agency and this kind proceeding. Does that legislation guarantee a hearing "on a record" or use very similar language? If the enabling legislation uses "on a record" or very similar language, then the matter is an adjudicatory proceeding. If the matter involves a license, permit or similar form of permission, then the matter is an adjudicatory proceeding even if the enabling legislation only refers to a right to a "hearing" or an "opportunity to be heard."

    (iii) If the enabling legislation simply refers to a right to a "hearing" or an "opportunity to be heard" (and the matter is *not* one involving a license, permit or similar form of permission) and does *not* refer to a hearing "on a record" then the matter is *not* an adjudicatory proceeding.

3. Have the agency's hearing regulations been located? (*See* § 4.54) If not, consult the index to the New York Official Compilation of Rules and Regulations. Check the State Register for recent amendments, and double check with agency personnel.

4. Have other sources of guidance published by the agency been located? (*See* § 4.58) If not, consult the agency to determine whether such information is available. Some agencies, including the Department of Environmental Conservation, have special telephone numbers for this purpose. If this is unsuccessful, either consider a Freedom of Information Law request for such information, or consulting the State Law Library to see if the agency is listed as having any such publications.

5. If the matter is an adjudicatory proceeding, consider the following matters:

- Is the notice issued in the matter sufficient? (*See* § 4.12) If unsure, consult SAPA § 301(2), and consider whether the notice, read in conjunction with other agency documents provides all of the following:

    (i) The time place and nature of the hearing.

    (ii) The agency's legal authority and justification

    (iii) The particular sections of statutes and rules involved, where possible.

    (iv) The matters asserted in short and plain fashion.

    (v) That interpreter services for the deaf are available at no charge.

- What methods of discovery are allowed beyond obtaining documents under the Freedom of Information Law? (*See* § 4.13)

    (i) If unsure, consult the agency's hearing regulations. In rare circumstances, the Due Process Clause or a special statute (other than the Freedom of Information Law) may require that a party be allowed some discovery. If the matter is a licensing revocation matter, a pre-hearing exchange of evidence is required upon the demand of either party.[1] (*See* § 4.23)

- Is a right to counsel being given? (*See* § 4.14) In adjudicatory proceedings, and perhaps other agency proceedings, SAPA § 501 requires that a party be allowed to hire his own lawyer to represent him at any stage of the proceedings.

- Are there any limitations on evidence that can be presented at a hearing beyond recognized privileges such as attorney-client? (*See* § 4.15)

- If unsure, consult the agency's hearing regulations. Some provide special evidentiary rules.

- Is a right to reasonable cross-examination being given? (*See* § 4.16) In adjudicatory proceedings, reasonable cross-examination of attending witnesses is a matter of right.[2] Subpoenas for the

§ 4.42
1. SAPA § 401(4).
2. SAPA § 306(3).

Ch. 4   ADJUDICATORY PROCEEDINGS—CHECKLIST   § 4.42

attendance of unwilling witnesses can be requested under SAPA § 304(2).

- Is it possible that the agency will take official notice of matters within its expertise? (*See* § 4.17) If so, the agency will come under a duty to give the opposing party notice and an opportunity to rebut. If so, consider whether the following steps have been taken.
- Has a Freedom of Information Law request been made for any agency studies or reports that might represent the agency's expert understanding on the subject?
- Has an expert witness been consulted to review the information, and possibly give testimony on the subject?
- Has the agency been formally asked whether it plans to take official notice on any matter within its expertise?
- Is the burden of proof being placed on the party who initiated the proceeding? (*See* § 4.19)
- Has there been a substantial delay between the time in which a hearing was requested and the hearing itself? (*See* § 4.21) If so, the following factors bear on whether the private party can dismiss the matter under SAPA § 301:

    (i) The private interest allegedly compromised by the delay.

    (ii) The actual prejudice to the private party.

    (iii) The causal connection between the conduct of the parties and the delay.

    (iv) The underlying public policy advanced by the governmental regulation.

- Has there been an extremely long delay between the incident giving rise to the hearing and the hearing itself? If so, in rare cases of extremely long delays (16 years in one reported case) proceeding with the hearing may violate the private party's rights under the Due Process Clause.
- Is the result in the adjudicatory proceeding actually or potentially inconsistent with the outcome in similar proceedings, and has the agency actually or potentially failed to explain any inconsistency? (*See* § 4.22) If so, the agency decision is inherently arbitrary and can be successfully challenged on judicial review.

    (i) If unsure about consistency with earlier decision, consult the index of final opinions in adjudicatory and other proceedings required of each agency by SAPA § 307(3) and if this proves unsuccessful consider a Freedom of Information Law request for pertinent opinions.

- Are there potential grounds for challenging the agency decisionmaker on bias grounds through a timely affidavit under SAPA

§ 303? (*See* § 4.23) If unsure, make the following determinations, a positive response to any of which will provide a good ground for challenge:

    (i) Is the agency decisionmaker one who has participated directly or through an immediate subordinate in the prosecution of the case?

    (ii) Has the agency decisionmaker expressed an opinion previously as to the appropriate outcome in the case?

    (iii) Does the agency decisionmaker stand to benefit or suffer personally depending upon on the outcome of the matter?

    (iv) Does the agency decisionmaker have a special reason to believe or disbelieve a material witness; for instance, a witness is a family member of the decisionmaker?

- Is the adjudicatory proceeding one that could affect (through granting, suspending, revoking etc.) a permit, license, or similar form of agency permission? (*See* § 4.26) If so, SAPA § 401 applies, and adds the following procedural considerations:

    (i) A party with a valid license, permit or similar form of permission who makes a timely application for renewal, or a new license for a continuous activity, is entitled to have the old license remain in effect during consideration of the new one, including through the period for review of any denial.

    (ii) Either party is entitled to demand an exchange of evidence seven days prior to the hearing if license revocation is sought. A party who intends to rely on evidence not exchanged must supplement its response.

    (iii) An agency is entitled to suspend a license for valid emergency reasons upon serving the suspension order on the licensee, provided that a prompt hearing is held after the suspension order.

- If the matter is in the license application stage, have the following been considered:

    (i) Is the relevant SEQRA documentation complete? (*See* § 4.29)

    (ii) Is the application complete and accurate? (*See* § 4.30)

    (iii) Has GORR been consulted, or are there other means to expedite the process? (*See* § 4.31)

    (iv) Are there opportunities for variances from the standard process? (*See* § 4.32)

    (v) Is the matter a potential or actual enforcement proceeding? (*See* § 4.34)

- If so, consider the following:

Ch. 4   ADJUDICATORY PROCEEDINGS—CHECKLIST   § 4.42

(i) What strategies are being employed to minimize or eliminate violations? (*See* §§ 4.35, 4.36)

(ii) What enforcement options are available to the agency? (*See* § 4.37)

(iii) If a hearing has been commenced, are there optional or mandatory settlement procedures? (*See* § 4.38)

(iv) Have the features of the hearing process peculiar to that agency been identified? (*See* § 4.39)

(v) Has the agency's post-hearing process, such as when intra-agency appeals are allowed, been identified? (*See* §§ 4.23, 4.40.)

6. If the adjudicatory proceeding has been completed, consider the following:

- If the decision was adverse to a private party, is the agency's statement of decision sufficiently detailed to make the agency's reasoning process transparent? (*See* § 4.18) If not, the decision is vulnerable to attack on judicial review.

- Does the decisional record contain all of the following: (*See* § 4.18)

    (i) All notices, pleadings, motions and intermediate rulings.

    (ii) All evidence presented.

    (iii) A statement of all matters officially noticed except matters so obvious that a statement of them would serve no useful purpose.

    (iv) Questions and offers of proof, objections thereto, and rulings thereupon.

    (v) Proposed findings and exceptions, if any.

    (vi) Any findings of fact, conclusions of law or other recommendations made by the ALJ.

    (vii) Any decision, determination, opinion, order or report rendered.

    (viii) A record of all testimony, either by tape recording or stenographically.

- Has the decision been based on any material not included in the decisional record? (*See* § 4.16) If so, the decision may be vulnerable to attack on judicial review.

- Are there any potential *res judicata* or collateral estoppel effects to the final decision in the adjudicatory proceeding? (*See* § 4.25)

§ 4.43 Administrative Rulemaking

Another large category of administrative action is rulemaking. In contrast to administrative adjudication, in which agencies simulate courts, agencies simulate the Legislature when they make rules or regulations.[1] As a practical matter, the impact on a client of a valid administrative rule is every bit as direct as that of a statute. The number of agencies with rulemaking authority is large, and a quick glance at *The State Register* (the official publication that tracks agency rulemakings) reveals that at any given time, hundreds of rulemakings are under way. Apparently because of the fairly large volume of rules that agencies make, the rulemaking process in New York has become more controversial.[2] Despite the substantial changes made to the rulemaking process in recent years, rulemaking in New York is basically of the so-called "notice and comment" variety. Agencies must give notice (in *The State Register*) of the proposed rule under consideration, and must accept comments on the proposed rule before finally adopting it. In spite of its simple structure, the rulemaking process is of immense significance to the administrative law practitioner because of the enormous impact that agency rules and regulations can have on clients, and for that reason we give it substantial attention in the following sections.

Library References:

West's Key No. Digests, Administrative Law and Procedure ⚖=381–427.

§ 4.44 Administrative Rulemaking—Rulemaking Compared With Other Agency Action

As we have seen,[1] administrative adjudication has its own article in SAPA: Article 3. Similarly, administrative rulemaking gets its own article: Article 2.[2] There are also some statutes in the Executive Law that govern rulemaking, but for the most part they track the fundamental procedures set forth in SAPA.[3]

SAPA also contains a definition of a rule, which is as follows:

"Rule" means (i) the whole or part of each agency statement, regulation or code of general applicability that implements or applies law, or prescribes a fee charged by or paid to any agency or the procedure or practice requirements of any agency, including the amendment, suspension or repeal thereof and (ii) the amendment, suspension, repeal, approval or prescription for the future of rates,

---

§ 4.43

1. The terms "rule" and "regulation" mean the same thing in this context, and we use them interchangeably.

2. One of Governor Pataki's first actions as governor was to temporarily suspend the rulemaking authority for all agencies whose head or heads serve at the pleasure of the Governor. See N.Y. Exec. Order No. 2, 9 NYCRR § 5.2.

§ 4.44

1. *See supra,* §§ 4.10—4.43.

2. SAPA § 201–206.

3. Executive Law §§ 101-a, 102.

wages, security authorizations, corporate or financial structures or reorganization thereof, prices, facilities, appliances, services or allowances therefor or of valuations, costs or accounting, or practices bearing on any of the foregoing whether of general or particular applicability.[4]

SAPA therefore divides rules into two broad categories. There are those—provided for in subdivision (i)—that are "general" rules that set standards of conduct much in the mode of legislation. And there are those—provided for in subdivision (ii)—that are "economic" rules that make rate and similar determinations for regulated entities.

The fundamental distinction between administrative adjudication and rulemaking is generally one of timing. Administrative adjudication looks back to a past transaction, and assesses the legal consequences of it. Just as court adjudication is essentially retrospective, so too is administrative adjudication.[5] Because of its retrospective nature, administrative adjudication names specific parties, and binds them directly. In contrast to administrative adjudication's fundamentally retrospective nature, administrative rulemaking is essentially prospective. Although interpreting the State Constitution's provision for filing of administrative rules,[6] in a leading case the Court of Appeals referred explicitly to this prospective aspect when it defined a rule as a pronouncement that "embraces any kind of legislative or quasi-legislative norm or procedure which establishes a pattern or course of conduct for the future."[7] Because of its prospective nature, rules do not bind specific parties in the same manner as adjudications; instead, rules are general in the sense that they apply to all whose activities fall within their scope.

Library References:

West's Key No. Digests, Administrative Law and Procedure ⚖ 381.

§ 4.45 Administrative Rulemaking—Rulemaking Notice

The most fundamental prerequisites for an agency making a valid rule are that the agencies have statutory authority to do so[1] and that it

---

4. SAPA § 102(2). The Executive Law also has a definition of a rule, which tracks the portion of the SAPA definition that follows subdivision (i) in SAPA § 102(2). See Executive Law § 101–a(1)(b).

5. See Borchers and Markell, *New York State Administrative Procedure and Practice* (West 1998) § 4.1.

6. See infra, § 4.50.

7. See People v. Cull, 10 N.Y.2d 123, 126, 218 N.Y.S.2d 38, 40, 176 N.E.2d 495, 497 (1961). Retroactive rulemaking is not a logical impossibility, but because of the heavy presumption that rules operate prospectively only, it requires special statutory authorization. See, e.g., Jewish Home and Infirmary of Rochester, New York, Inc. v. Commissioner of the Department of Health, 84 N.Y.2d 252, 616 N.Y.S.2d 458, 640 N.E.2d 125 (1994)(retroactive ratemaking not authorized); Jewish Memorial Hospital v. Whalen, 47 N.Y.2d 331, 418 N.Y.S.2d 318, 391 N.E.2d 1296 (1979)(retroactive rate adjustments specifically authorized by statute).

§ 4.45

1. See, e.g., Gross v. New York City Alcoholic Beverage Control Bd., 7 N.Y.2d 531, 200 N.Y.S.2d 12, 166 N.E.2d 818

promulgates the rule in a manner consistent with Article 2 of SAPA.[2] Rulemaking in New York is of the "notice and comment" variety, implying (correctly) that the primary components of such a system are notice and comment.

Most rulemaking procedure is contained in SAPA § 202 (although the Secretary of State has promulgated rules that contain some additional requirements[3]) and we cover its major features here.[4] SAPA requires any agency that wishes to make a rule to submit a "notice of proposed rulemaking" to the Secretary of State for publication in *The State Register*.[5] The notice must precede by 45 days any agency action to adopt the rule.[6] If an agency is required by statute to hold a "public hearing" before adopting a rule, then the notice must precede by 45 days the first public hearing.[7] SAPA also requires that the rulemaking notice be submitted to various high-ranking State political officials as well as persons who make standing requests for an agency's rulemaking notices.[8]

The required contents of a rulemaking notice are spelled out in some detail in SAPA § 202(1)(f) and amplified in the Secretary of State's regulations.[9] Generally, the notice must contain the statutory authority for the rule, the date and place of any public hearings, the text of the proposed rule (a summary if the rule exceeds 2000 words), the text (or a summary) of various ancillary documents,[10] contact information for a "knowledgeable" agency official, and the last date for comments.[11] A rule is invalid if founded on a notice not in "substantial" compliance with these requirements.[12]

(1960)(lack of statutory authority voids rule).

2. *See, e.g.*, Cordero v. Corbisiero, 80 N.Y.2d 771, 587 N.Y.S.2d 266, 599 N.E.2d 670 (1992)(attempt to announce de facto rule in the context of an adjudication makes "rule" void).

3. 19 NYCRR §§ 260.1, 260.2. Additionally, the Secretary of State's office publishes and updates a pamphlet containing basic rulemaking forms and information on the rulemaking process. New York Department of State, New York State Register Procedure Manual (1994).

4. A complete description of all aspects of rulemaking procedure would be beyond the scope of this chapter. For a discussion of the rulemaking process in more depth, see Borchers and Markell, *New York State Administrative Procedure and Practice* (1998) Ch. 4 and 10.

5. SAPA § 202(1)(a)(i).

6. SAPA § 202(1)(a)(i).

7. SAPA § 202(1)(a)(ii).

8. SAPA §§ 202(1)(c), 202(6–a)(c).

PRACTICE POINTER: If a client has regular dealings with an agency, a standing request of this nature is a good idea because it ensures that notices of proposed rules will come immediately to the client's or the lawyer's attention. These requests expire annually and must be renewed.

9. 19 NYCRR § 260.3.

10. These are regulatory flexibility analyses, regulatory impact statements, and rural area flexibility analyses. These are discussed *infra*, § 4.49. If they exceed 2000 words, a summary is to be included.

11. *See generally* SAPA § 202.

12. SAPA § 202(8). The basic requirement appears to be that deviations from the statutory requirements be sufficiently minor that they not impugn the agency's essential good faith in attempting to comply. *See, e.g.*, United States v. Gehl, 852 F.Supp. 1150, 1168, n. 37 (N.D.N.Y.1994). Time requirements are apparently construed strictly. *See, e.g.*, People v. Harris Corp., 104

Rulemaking notices for general (non-economic) rulemakings have an initial life of 180 days.[13] The clock on the 180 days starts to run from the date that the notice appears in *The State Register*, or the last public hearing mentioned in the notice, whichever is later.[14] An agency can, however, obtain up to 185-day extension of this period by filing a notice of continuation some time in the last 60 days of the lifetime of the original notice.[15]

If during the rulemaking, the agency decides to make a "substantial revision" to the proposed rule, the agency must submit a notice of revised rulemaking to the Secretary of State for publication in *The State Register*.[16] Essentially the contents of a notice of a revised rulemaking mirror those for rulemakings generally,[17] although SAPA requires that the notice of revised rulemaking indicate the last date for making comments, and the revised notice also acts as a notice of continuation, giving the agency the extra 185 days mentioned above.[18] Thus, if the revision is "insubstantial" then the agency may adopt the rule upon the original notice; but if the revision is "substantial" then the agency must proceed upon a revised notice. The cases interpreting this provision indicate that a revision is "insubstantial" as long as it represents a "logical outgrowth" of the original rulemaking notice, meaning essentially that the rule ultimately adopted must cover the same subjects as the proposed rule that was the basis for the original notice.[19]

Library References:

West's Key No. Digests, Administrative Law and Procedure ⚖︎394, 395.

A.D.2d 130, 483 N.Y.S.2d 442 (3d Dep't 1984)(failure to file within 180 day period invalidates rule).

13. SAPA § 202(2).

14. SAPA § 202(2)(a)(ii).

15. SAPA § 202(3)(b). An agency can sometimes get yet another 90 days beyond the original 180 days and the extension of 185 days. If an agency submits a notice of a *revised* rulemaking in the last 90 days of an already-continued rulemaking another 90 days can be tacked on. *See generally* Borchers and Markell, *New York State Administrative Procedure and Practice* (West 1998) § 4.3.

16. SAPA § 202(4–a).

17. There are some slight differences, notably that the minimum comment period shrinks from 45 to 30 days with a revised notice, and the revised notice must identify the revisions to the rule. *See generally* SAPA § 202(4–a).

18. SAPA § 202(4–a).

19. SAPA § 102(9) defines "substantial revision" as a change that "materially alters" the "purpose, meaning or effect" of a rule. The cases on the subject have interpreted this in accordance with the federal "logical outgrowth" test. *See, e.g.*, Motor Vehicle Mfg. Ass'n v. Jorling, 152 Misc.2d 405, 408–09, 577 N.Y.S.2d 346, 349 (Sup. Ct., Albany County, 1991).

PRACTICE POINTER: From the standpoint of agencies, if the question is close as to whether the revised rule is a "logical outgrowth," the safer course is to issue a notice of revised rulemaking. The costs of doing this will surely be less than defending the rule's validity in court.

CAVEAT: SAPA has special truncated rulemaking procedures for what it defines as "minor," "obsolete" and "invalid" rules. Essentially, rulemakings of this type are to make very small alterations in rules, or to repeal rules that are not, or cannot be, enforced. Because these are of relatively little consequence in practice, we do not cover them here. For a discussion of these special rulemaking procedures, *see* Borchers and Markell, *New York State Administrative Procedure and Practice* (West 1998) § 4.4.

§ 4.46 Administrative Rulemaking—Comments and Agency Assessment of Comments

SAPA provides that an agency "shall afford the public an opportunity to submit comments on [a] proposed rule."[1] "Comments," however, means only written comments,[2] although nothing prevents an agency from soliciting oral comments in a public hearing if it so desires. In some circumstances, a statute other than SAPA places on agencies the duty to hold "public hearings,"[3] although the term means simply a chance to express views orally to an agency, not a "trial-type" hearing with cross-examination of witnesses.[4] If no public hearing is required, the minimum comment period is 45 days, beginning with publication of the rulemaking notice.[5] If a public hearing is mandatory, the 45 days run from the date of the first public hearing.[6] For general (non-economic) rulemakings, an agency is required to publish an assessment of the comments with the notice of adoption, and must specifically address cost estimates at odds with those generated by the agency in preparing its regulatory flexibility and impact documentation.[7]

Library References:

West's Key No. Digests, Administrative Law and Procedure ⚖︎392.

§ 4.47 Administrative Rulemaking—Agency Duty to Reveal Underlying Information

The Court of Appeals has ruled that an agency is not under any common law duty to reveal underlying studies and data in the rulemaking process.[1] This decision has, however, been partially overturned by statute. SAPA now provides that, in the regulatory impact statement,[2] the agency must include a "citation to each [scientific or statistical] study, report or analysis" that "served as the basis for the rule . . . "[3] Additionally, the agency must explain how the study "was used to

§ 4.46

1. SAPA § 202(1)(a).

2. *See, e.g.*, Gasda Ltd. v. Adduci, 179 A.D.2d 173, 176, 582 N.Y.S.2d 525, 527–28 (3d Dep't 1992).

3. *See, e.g.*, ECL § 3–0301(2)(a).

4. *See* Gifford, *The New York State Administrative Procedure Act: Some Reflections Upon its Structure and Legislative History*, 26 Buff.L.Rev. 589, 604 (1977).

5. SAPA § 202(1)(a)(i).

6. SAPA § 202(1)(a)(ii).

7. SAPA § 202(5). For a discussion of regulatory flexibility and impact documentation, *see infra*, § 4.49.

PRACTICE POINTER: For proposed rules that will have a significant economic impact on a client, it may be wise to submit a formal study of the economic impact as part of the comments. This may have the effect of convincing that agency to revise the rule in a manner favorable to the client, or—if the agency's response to the economic study is inadequate—may make the rule vulnerable to attack on judicial review.

§ 4.47

1. *See* Industrial Liaison Comm. of the Niagara Falls Area Chamber of Commerce v. Williams, 72 N.Y.2d 137, 145, 531 N.Y.S.2d 791, 795, 527 N.E.2d 274, 278 (1988).

2. *See infra*, § 4.49 for a discussion of regulatory impact statements and other ancillary documentation.

3. SAPA § 202–a(3)(b).

determine the necessity for or the benefits to be derived from the rule.'"[4] Thus, an agency comes under a duty to ultimately reveal scientific or statistical studies that were central to developing the rule.

Library References:
West's Key No. Digests, Administrative Law and Procedure ⚖︎392, 404.

§ 4.48 Administrative Rulemaking—Notice of Adoption and Effective Date of Rules

The final step on the road to legal effectiveness for an administrative rule is adoption. Under SAPA, this is accomplished by filing the rule with the Secretary of State and submitting a "notice of adoption" for publication in *The State Register*.[1] The notice of adoption must include a citation to the statutory authority for the rule, the complete text of the rule (or a summary if it exceeds 2000 words), a notation of any changes between the final rule and the most recently proposed version of the rule, state the effective date of the rule, any revised versions of ancillary documents,[2] an assessment of public comment,[3] the name of an agency contact who can supply the full text of the rule, and a statement as to whether any rulemakings are underway to revise the rule.[4] Unlike its federal counterpart,[5] SAPA does not mandate a delayed effective date for rules. SAPA § 202 requires only that the notice of adoption state the effective date of a rule, and SAPA § 203 and the Executive Law[6] require only that the effective date not precede the date of publication in *The State Register*.[7]

Library References:
West's Key No. Digests, Administrative Law and Procedure ⚖︎407, 418.

---

4. SAPA § 202–a(3)(b).

PRACTICE POINTER: There can, of course, be some extremely close questions as to whether a study or report formed the "basis" for a rule, or whether it was simply consulted by the agency. A more effective route is to make a Freedom of Information Law request for any studies or reports that the agency consulted in formulating the proposed rule. If made quickly enough, such a request should allow access to such information in time to allow comments on the rule to incorporate comments on any underlying study or report.

§ 4.48

1. SAPA § 202(5)(a). On the constitutional duty of filing and publication, see infra, § 4.50.

2. On ancillary documentation for rules, see infra, § 4.49.

3. See supra, § 4.46.

4. SAPA § 202(5)(c). The notice of adoption in emergency rulemakings serves a slightly different purpose. While the notice must include substantially the same information as the notice of adoption of a non-emergency rule, it must also include findings as to the necessity of proceeding by the emergency route and state whether the notice is also intended as a notice of a proposed rulemaking on a non-emergency basis. See SAPA § 202(6)(d). On emergency rulemakings generally, see infra, § 4.57.

5. 5 U.S.C.A. § 553(d)(rules generally cannot take effect until 30 days after publication in *The Federal Register*).

6. Executive Law § 102.

7. **CAVEAT:** Emergency rules, see infra, § 4.57, and economic rules (such as rates) are excluded from the requirement that a rule not take effect until publication in *The State Register*. SAPA § 203(1); Executive Law § 102(1)(a).

§ 4.49 Administrative Rulemaking—Ancillary Documentation and the Role of GORR

One of the ways in which rulemaking in New York has changed most significantly in recent years has been the addition of ancillary documentation that must be prepared during the course of most rulemakings. One is a "regulatory impact statement." The substantive goal of requiring agencies to prepare regulatory impact statements is to force them to consider less economically restrictive goals for accomplishing their regulatory objectives.[1] To accomplish this goal, SAPA requires that agencies, when proposing a rule, prepare a regulatory impact statement that includes the statutory authority for the rule, the needs and benefits of the rule, the costs (or the agency's best estimate), the existence of any local government mandates created, a discussion of any overlap with existing law, a discussion of significant alternatives and why they were not adopted, a discussion of relevant federal standards, and a compliance schedule.[2] Economic[3] rulemakings are exempt.[4]

A second piece of required ancillary documentation is a "regulatory flexibility analysis."[5] Unlike the regulatory impact statement, which is targeted at the general economic impact of the rule, the regulatory flexibility analysis is targeted at the effects of rules on small businesses.[6] To accomplish this end, SAPA requires agencies proposing rules to consider how to reduce the impact of their rules on small businesses through use of "differing reporting, recordkeeping or other compliance requirements," "use of performance rather than design standards," and exemptions from the rule for small businesses.[7] As is the case for regulatory impact statements, economic rulemakings are exempt from the requirement of a regulatory flexibility analysis, as are rules that the agency specifically finds not to have any significantly adverse impacts on small businesses.[8] If a regulatory flexibility analysis is required, it must include a description of the types and estimated numbers of small

---

§ 4.49

1. SAPA § 202–a(1).
2. SAPA § 202–a(3).
3. SAPA § 102(2)(a)(ii). Included in these are ratemakings.
4. SAPA § 202–a(5). So-called "obsolete" and "invalid" rulemakings are exempt. SAPA § 202–a(5)(b). So-called "minor" rules require only a truncated version of the statement. SAPA § 202–a(5)(d). A merely "technical" amendment to a rule is exempted as well. SAPA § 202–a(5)(a). A series of closely connected rulemakings may be handled by a single statement. SAPA § 202–a(4)(a). Emergency rulemakings, see infra, § 4.57, get different treatment. The regulatory impact statement is due at the time of the promulgation of the rule, or within 30 days if a statement to that effect is filed with the emergency rule. SAPA § 202–a(2). Substantial revisions in rules require revised statements if the revisions to the rule would alter the content of the statement. SAPA § 202–a(6)(ii).

5. SAPA § 202–b.
6. SAPA § 202–b(1).
7. SAPA § 202–b(1).
8. SAPA § 202–b(3). The treatment for minor, obsolete, invalid, emergency and closely-related rulemakings is roughly the same in the context of regulatory flexibility analyses as it is in the context of regulatory impact statements. SAPA § 202–b(3), (4). In a manner that also parallels regulatory impact statements, revised flexibility analyses are required in some circumstances. SAPA § 202–b(7). See supra, note 4.

businesses affected, a description of additional duties imposed and the need for professional assistance, an indication of any mitigation measures made on behalf of small businesses, and a statement as to what effort was made to include small businesses in the development of the rule.[9] If a regulatory flexibility analysis is required, SAPA also details special efforts that must be made to obtain the participation of the small business community in the development of the rule.[10]

A new addition to the collection of ancillary documents is the rural area flexibility analysis.[11] The rural area flexibility analysis requirement is clearly modeled upon the regulatory flexibility analysis, and contains many of the same important exemptions, including the one for economic rulemakings.[12] Paralleling the regulatory flexibility analysis exemption for rules that do not adversely impact small businesses, proposed rules that do not adversely impact rural areas—defined as any county with less than 200,000 in population and any town with a population density of less than 15 persons per square mile[13]—are exempted from the rural area flexibility analysis requirement.[14] The substantive goal of this requirement is to force agencies to "consider utilizing approaches that will accomplish the objectives of the applicable statutes while minimizing any adverse impact of the rule on public and private sector interests in rural areas."[15] Mirroring the regulatory flexibility analysis, this provision requires agencies to consider differing reporting and compliance standards, as well as increased performance or outcome standards.[16] If such an analysis is required, its contents parallel those for a regulatory flexibility analysis, adapted to consider impacts on rural areas (instead of small businesses.)[17] Special efforts must be made to notify the rural community of the proposed rule if a rural area flexibility analysis is required.[18] An even newer addition is the requirement of a "job impact" analysis for certain rules.[19] Similar in structure to the other three ancillary documents, this analysis requires an assessment on employment opportunities in some cases.

From a practical standpoint, one of the more significant aspects of these ancillary documentation requirements is the role played by the Office for Regulatory and Management Assistance ("ORMA").[20] The bulk of ORMA's responsibilities with regard to the ancillary documents is set

9. SAPA § 202–b(2).
10. SAPA § 202–b(6).
11. SAPA § 202–bb.
12. SAPA § 202–bb(4).
13. Executive Law § 481(7).
14. SAPA § 202–bb(4). The same basic exemptions that apply to the other two ancillary documents apply here as well. SAPA § 202–bb(4). See supra, notes 4 and 8.
15. SAPA § 202–bb(2)(b).
16. SAPA § 202–bb(2).
17. SAPA § 202–bb(3).
18. SAPA § 202–bb(7).
19. SAPA § 201–a.
20. ORMA is created by Article 39 of the Executive Law, and has gone through many name changes. See Borchers and Markell, *New York State Administrative Procedure and Practice* (West 1998) § 4.13. Its functions have been essentially assumed by GORR as a result of Governor Pataki's Executive Order 20.

out in SAPA § 202–c. Once the various ancillary documents are prepared, they must be submitted to ORMA, at which time ORMA reviews both those documents and the rule itself.[21] Although ORMA has no formal veto power over rules, it can require agencies to explain what ORMA perceives to be specified deficiencies in the rule or the ancillary documentation.[22] If the agency's responses eventually fail to satisfy ORMA, it has the power ultimately to extend the comment period and force the agency to hold a public hearing on the rule.[23] If it chooses to, therefore, ORMA can make life extremely difficult for agencies attempting to promulgate rules or submit ancillary documents that ORMA believes to be deficient.

ORMA's role, and the general matter of requiring ancillary documents, is of great practical significance in two respects for the administrative law practitioner. First, the fairly complicated nature of the required ancillary documents make inviting targets for attempted judicial invalidation of rules that harm a client's interests. Although courts generally have been deferential to agencies on these matters, courts have indicated that they stand ready to invalidate rules in which the ancillary document requirements were not substantially followed.[24] Second is the substantial role of ORMA. ORMA is a generally "business friendly" organ of government. Attempts to persuade the agency that a proposed regulation is overly burdensome may receive a more sympathetic hearing with ORMA, which could conceivably result in indirect pressure being placed on the agency to modify the proposed regulation.

ORMA's authority to operate expired, however, on the last day of 1995.[25] At about the time that ORMA's authority was expiring, Governor Pataki promulgated Executive Order 20 creating the Governor's Office for Regulatory Reform ("GORR"). GORR is intended in many ways to be the successor to ORMA. However, the Director of Regulatory Reform—GORR's head—in conjunction with four other senior advisors to the Governor have the power to veto proposed regulations, a power well beyond that exercised by ORMA.[26]

§ 4.50 Administrative Rulemaking—Rule Filing and Publication

SAPA excludes from the definition of a "rule" various agency pronouncements that would otherwise qualify as rules.[1] Some of these

---

21. SAPA § 202–c(4), (10).

22. SAPA § 202–c(5), (6).

23. SAPA § 202–c(6), (7), (8).

24. *See, e.g.*, Pacific Salmon Unlimited v. New York State Dep't of Envt'l Conserv., 208 A.D.2d 241, 622 N.Y.S.2d 820 (3d Dep't 1995)(rule upheld because ancillary documentation in substantial compliance with statutes).

25. *See* SAPA § 202–c (expired Dec. 31, 1995).

26. N.Y. Exec. Order 20.

§ 4.50

1. SAPA § 102(2)(b). For an extensive discussion of these exceptions, *see* Borchers and Markell, *New York State Administrative Procedure and Practice* (West 1998) §§ 4.14—4.18.

exclusions are quite significant. For instance, SAPA excludes "interpretive statements and statements of general policy which in themselves have no legal effect but are merely explanatory."[2] Thus, if an agency pronouncement merely restates existing law, or is only general in nature, it need not undergo the notice and comment process.[3] Agencies may not, however, disguise truly substantive rules as interpretive or general policy statements.[4] Another important exception from SAPA's definition of a rule is "rules concerning the internal management of the agency which do not directly and significantly affect the rights of or procedures or practices available to the public."[5] This has been interpreted fairly narrowly, so that agency pronouncements that have some significant impact on the public cannot be recast as internal.[6] Besides these significant exceptions to the definition of a rule, SAPA contains various other narrow exceptions, many of which would not appear to fit the definition of a rule in the first instance.[7]

As discussed above, the final step on the road to legal effectiveness of a substantive rule under SAPA is filing with the Secretary of State and then publication in *The State Register*.[8] This process of filing and publication of substantive rules is not, however, merely a function of SAPA, it is also mandated by the State Constitution.[9] The relevant provision of the State Constitution provides that "[n]o rule or regulation made by any state department, board, bureau, officer, authority or commission, except as relates to the organization or internal management of a state department, board, bureau, authority of commission shall be effective until it is filed in the office of the department of state."[10] This same Article of the Constitution also requires the Legislature to enact appropriate laws for the "speedy publication of such rules,"

---

2. SAPA § 102(2)(b)(iv).

3. *See, e.g.*, Henn v. Perales, 186 A.D.2d 740, 588 N.Y.S.2d 653 (2d Dep't 1992)(agency pronouncement merely interpretive).

4. *See, e.g.*, Yaretsky v. Blum, 456 F.Supp. 653 (S.D.N.Y.1978)(Department of Health "point system" for assigning patients to appropriate health facility is a substantive rule, not an interpretive statement, and is invalid unless preceded by notice and comment as required by SAPA); Schwartfigure v. Hartnett, 83 N.Y.2d 296, 610 N.Y.S.2d 125, 632 N.E.2d 434 (1994) (Department of Labor policy offsetting half of current unemployment benefits to repay past overpayments is a substantive rule, not an interpretive or general policy statement, and must be preceded by notice and comment under SAPA).

5. SAPA § 102(2)(b)(ii).

6. *See, e.g.*, Schwartfigure v. Hartnett, 83 N.Y.2d 296, 610 N.Y.S.2d 125, 632 N.E.2d 434 (1994)(Department of Labor policy offsetting half of current unemployment benefits to repay past overpayments is a substantive rule, not an internal rule, and must be preceded by notice and comment under SAPA); Jones v. Smith, 64 N.Y.2d 1003, 1005, 489 N.Y.S.2d 50, 51, 478 N.E.2d 191, 192 (1985)(Department of Corrections rules concerning prisoners are not internal because they are directed at "that segment of the 'general public' over which the [agency] exercises direct authority ...").

7. For a complete listing of them, *see* SAPA § 102(2)(b). For a discussion, *see* Borchers and Markell, *New York State Administrative Procedure and Practice* (West 1998) § 4.18.

8. *See supra*, § 4.48.

9. New York Constitution Art. IV, § 8.

10. *Id.*

a mission that the Legislature has carried out by passing The State Register Act.[11]

This constitutional provision has prompted a fair amount of litigation as to what types of agency pronouncements need to be filed with the Secretary of State and then published in *The State Register*. The courts have generally tended to assume that those agency pronouncements that are excluded from the definition of a rule under SAPA are also excluded from the term "rule or regulation" as used in the State Constitution.[12] The boundaries of the constitutional duty of publication are marked primarily by two Court of Appeals cases. In the first, *People v. Cull*,[13] the court held that administrative "orders" setting speed limits on streets were rules that had to be filed with the Secretary of State because they set a "pattern or course of conduct for the future."[14] In *Roman Catholic Diocese of Albany v. New York State Department of Health*,[15] the Court of Appeals—adopting the dissenting Appellate Division opinion—held that the Constitution did not require filing and publication of a Department of Health pronouncement calling for the approval of new abortion clinics if less than 50% of the abortion services within the county were available on an out-of-hospital basis. The court held that this so-called "50% rule" was not a "rule or regulation" within the meaning of the State Constitution because it operated only as a "guideline," and the agency considered other factors in deciding whether to grant the license application for a new clinic.[16] The reconciliation of these cases thus turns on the effect of the agency pronouncement. If, as in *Cull*, the agency pronouncement conclusively determines how an agency will exercise its discretion, then it is a rule that falls within the constitutional duty of filing and publication. If, however, as in *Roman Catholic*, the agency pronouncement is only one of several factors indicating how an agency will exercise its discretion, it is not subject to the constitutional duty of filing and publication.

11. Executive Law §§ 145—149.

12. *See, e.g.*, Henn v. Perales, 186 A.D.2d 740, 588 N.Y.S.2d 653 (2d Dep't 1992)(assuming that exclusion from definition of a rule under SAPA also excludes from definition of rule or regulation for publication under the State Constitution); Leichter v. Barber, 120 A.D.2d 776, 777, 501 N.Y.S.2d 925, 927 (3d Dep't 1986) (same). As discussed in Borchers and Markell, *New York State Administrative Procedure and Practice* (West 1998) § 4.20, it is far from clear that this is the way things should be. Some kinds of agency pronouncements, such as interpretive statements, are reasonably excluded from the notice and comment process, but clearly should be published in a central publication such as The State Register. Federal agencies are required to publish interpretive and general policy statements, *see* 5 U.S.C.A. § 552(a)(1)(D), although such pronouncements are excluded from the federal notice and comment process. See 5 U.S.C.A. § 553.

13. 10 N.Y.2d 123, 218 N.Y.S.2d 38, 176 N.E.2d 495 (1961).

14. *Id.* at 126, 218 N.Y.S.2d at 40, 176 N.E.2d at 497. When the Legislature passed SAPA it was apparently aware of *Cull*, as it excluded from the SAPA definition of a "rule" traffic regulations communicated to the public by means of street signs. SAPA § 102(2)(b)(xi).

15. 109 A.D.2d 140, 490 N.Y.S.2d 636 (3d Dep't), rev'd on dissenting opn. below 66 N.Y.2d 948, 498 N.Y.S.2d 780, 489 N.E.2d 749 (1985).

16. 109 A.D.2d at 146–47, 490 N.Y.S.2d at 641–42 (Levine, J., dissenting).

All of this has at least two important ramifications for the administrative law practitioner. First, even though agency pronouncements such as the "50% rule" excluded from publication in *Roman Catholic* are not conclusive of the outcome of an adjudication, they clearly are important documents—and competent representation requires obtaining access to them. Thus, one cannot assume that all of an agency's policy on a particular subject can be learned simply by looking in *The State Register* and the New York Compiled Code of Rules and Regulations. Less formal sources of guidance, whether in the form of handbooks, agency memoranda or guidance documents, can be extremely informative. Second, the boundary between what are "rules or regulations" that must be published, and "guidelines" that need not, is far from clear.

Library References:

West's Key No. Digests, Administrative Law and Procedure ⊘407, 410.

§ 4.51 Administrative Rulemaking—Declaratory Rulings Regarding Rules

SAPA gives parties a fairly broad right to seek from agencies declaratory rulings regarding rules.[1] A party may petition an agency for a declaration as to the applicability of a rule to it, and "whether any action by [the party] should be taken pursuant to the rule."[2] Any declaratory ruling issued is binding on the agency unless it is set aside by a court on judicial review, and thus any declaratory ruling must be modified prospectively only.[3] If a party is seeking a declaratory ruling on whether or not to take some action pursuant to a rule, the agency has 30 days to either issue the ruling or decline to do so.[4] A declaratory ruling may be based entirely upon hypothetical facts,[5] although if the facts ultimately are determined to be materially different from those presented to the agency, the agency clearly would not be bound by its earlier ruling. SAPA's declaratory ruling provisions are stated to be voluntary, and not a precondition to seeking judicial review.[6]

SAPA gives a substantial role to ORMA—now, apparently GORR as ORMA's successor—in the declaratory rulings process. If, in the case of a

---

§ 4.51

1. SAPA § 204.
2. SAPA § 204(1).
3. SAPA § 204(1). *See also* Allied Chemical v. Niagara Mohawk Power Corp., 72 N.Y.2d 271, 532 N.Y.S.2d 230, 528 N.E.2d 153 (1988), cert. denied 488 U.S. 1005, 109 S.Ct. 785, 102 L.Ed.2d 777 (1989)(agency declaratory ruling binding in subsequent proceeding involving petitioner).
4. SAPA § 204(2)(a). The agency can by rule set a longer time period, but not to exceed 60 days.
5. *See, e.g.*, City of New York v. New York State Dep't of Health, 164 Misc.2d 247, 623 N.Y.S.2d 491 (Sup.Ct., Albany County, 1995).
6. SAPA § 204(2)(c). This appears to be partially contradicted by the Secretary of State's regulations on seeking declaratory rulings from that agency, *see* 19 NYCRR § 264.1, although it is possible that these provisions can be reconciled. *See* Borchers and Markell, *New York State Administrative Procedure and Practice* (West 1998) § 4.21.

party seeking a declaratory ruling on whether or not to take an action pursuant to a rule, the agency refuses to issue one, GORR must issue an "advisory ruling" on the question within 60 days.[7] This is, of course, consistent with GORR's general mission to ease the regulatory burden on businesses by encouraging agencies to issue such rulings, and in the absence of such ruling offer some guidance.

The declaratory rulings process offers an attractive option for parties who are genuinely unsure as to whether an activity is proscribed by an administrative rule. As a general proposition, informal agency statements and pronouncements have no estoppel value, and therefore one cannot safely rely upon them.[8] But, by statute, a properly issued declaratory ruling has this effect. In some circumstances, therefore, the route of seeking such a ruling is clearly safer and more cost-efficient than hoping to successfully advance the same position in litigation.

§ 4.52 Administrative Rulemaking—Overlapping State and Federal Rules

SAPA addresses the fairly-frequently occurring problem of similar state and federal regulations on the same subject.[1] If a regulated party is subject to similar state and federal regulations, that entity may petition the agency for a declaratory ruling that compliance with the federal regulations satisfies their state counterparts.[2] An agency that receives a request for such a ruling must submit a copy of it to GORR.[3]

An agency in receipt of such a request has three options. First, it can rule that compliance with the federal regulations does not serve the purposes of the relevant state *statute*, in which case the agency must provide a statement of reasons for so ruling to the party, and must also submit the statement to GORR.[4] Second, an agency can rule that compliance with the federal standards *would* satisfy the purposes of the relevant state *statute*, but *would not* satisfy the relevant state *administrative rules*.[5] Such a statement must also be submitted to GORR, but SAPA provides that if this is an agency's ruling, the agency "may initiate a rulemaking proceeding ... to consider revising its rule to accept compliance with such federal requirement,"[6] which is a broad hint to agencies to avoid pointless "double" regulation. Third, agencies can

---

7. SAPA § 204(2)(b). ORMA has adopted regulations implementing its duties under SAPA § 204, which are presumably followed by GORR. *See* 9 NYCRR Pt. 8800.

8. *See, e.g.*, New York State Medical Transporters Ass'n v. Perales, 77 N.Y.2d 126, 564 N.Y.S.2d 1007, 566 N.E.2d 134 (1990)(common law doctrines of estoppel and ratification do not bind agency to continuing its practice of giving "retroactive" prior approval to requests for non-emergency medical transport).

§ 4.52

1. SAPA § 206.
2. SAPA § 206(2).
3. SAPA § 206(2).
4. SAPA § 206(3).
5. SAPA § 206(4).
6. SAPA § 206(4).

rule that compliance with federal regulations is sufficient, in which case the agency is required to issue a binding declaratory ruling so indicating along with the "terms and conditions under which it intends to" accept federal compliance, and again must provide GORR with such a statement.[7]

This provision in SAPA may prove useful in circumstances in which a regulated party is involved in a complicated endeavor requiring multiple and overlapping licenses, permits and similar approvals. Seeking a ruling under this provision may provide the best of outcomes, which is that compliance with state regulations is unnecessary. At the very least, it may well alert GORR to the potential for unnecessary regulation, which may pay dividends in terms of placing informal pressure on the agency to relax its requirements. Additionally, a recent amendment to SAPA requires agencies that promulgate regulations which overlap or conflict with federal rules to address this matter in a regulatory impact statement, and to identify measures taken to minimize the impact on regulated parties.[8]

§ 4.53 Administrative Rulemaking—Special Strategic Considerations in Handling Administrative Rulemaking Matters

Agency regulations are the engines that drive a great deal of administrative practice. It is a customary practice of agencies charged with administering a new statute to develop regulations to fill in the interstitial gaps of the enabling legislation.[1] Consequently, conducting an activity regulated by a state statute often also subjects the actor to administratively promulgated regulations as well. The importance of participating actively in rulemaking proceedings in an effort to shape the agency's final rule therefore should be self-evident.

§ 4.54 Administrative Rulemaking—Special Strategic Considerations in Handling Administrative Rulemaking Matters—Basic Sources of Information on Rulemaking

The New York Code of Rules and Regulations ("NYCRR") is the official repository for New York administrative regulations.[1] The NYCRR is organized as follows:

---

7. SAPA § 206(5).
8. Ch. 628, L. 1995.

§ 4.53

1. *See e.g.*, Nicholas v. Kahn, 47 N.Y.2d 24, 416 N.Y.S.2d 565, 389 N.E.2d 1086 (1979)(regulations implementing conflict of interest statute).

§ 4.54

1. The NYCRR also is referred to as the Official Compilation of Codes, Rules and Regulations of the State of New York. Subscriptions to the NYCRR cost $1,895, with supplements available at a cost of $565 per year. Subscriptions are available from West Group, Aqueduct Building, Rochester, NY 14694; telephone number: 800-527-0430.

Title	Name
1	Agriculture and Markets
2	Audit and Control
3	Banking
4	Civil Service
5	Economic Development
6	Conservation
7	Correctional Services
8	Education
9	Executive
10	Health
11	Insurance
12	Labor
13	Law
14	Mental Hygiene
15	Motor Vehicles
16	Public Service
17	Transportation
18	Social Services
19	State
20	Taxation and Finance
21	Miscellaneous
22	Judiciary

A weekly publication of the Department of State, *The State Register*, is the other primary source of information on New York agency rulemaking activity.[2] *The State Register* contains all of the significant documents relating to a regulation, or, at a minimum, summaries of such documents. Thus, *The State Register* contains the notice of proposed rulemaking, which is the document that initiates the rulemaking process, and it contains the notice of adoption of a rule, which memorializes an agency's adoption of a rule. Practitioners with a need to monitor rulemaking developments therefore need to monitor both the NYCRR and *The State Register*.

SAPA § 202(6–a)(c) provides an alternative vehicle to keep abreast of an agency's rulemaking activity. It authorizes interested parties to submit "standing requests" to be notified of rulemaking activity directly

---

In addition, in November 1994, West Group (then Lawyers Cooperative Publishing) announced that it is making the NYCRR available on CD–ROM. For this version of the NYCRR, the cost for a single user license is $720 annually, including quarterly updates. The announcement provides a contact telephone number of 800–307–8143. The NYCRR is also available online through LRS, the New York State Bill Drafting Commission's data base. For information on how to access this data base, contact LRS, State of New York Legislative Bill Drafting Commission, 55 Elk Street, Albany, NY 12210; telephone number: 800–356–6566.

2. The State Register is published by the Department of State, Office of Information Services. The address is 41 State Street, Albany, NY 12231. The telephone number is (518) 474–1785.

with particular agencies.[3] These requests remain in effect for one year, and obligate the receiving agency to provide the requesting party with copies of all notices of proposed rulemaking during that time.[4] Parties that interact extensively with a particular agency may find it worthwhile annually to file such a request.

Library References:

West's Key No. Digests, Administrative Law and Procedure ⚖381–427.

§ 4.55 Administrative Rulemaking—Special Strategic Considerations in Handling Administrative Rulemaking Matters—Participating in the Rulemaking Process

The notice of proposed rulemaking that initiates the rulemaking process identifies opportunities for participating formally in the process. At a minimum, agencies must provide an opportunity to submit written comments on proposed regulations.[1] If their enabling legislation requires it, agencies must hold public hearings at which they take oral testimony as well.[2] Of course, an agency may hold hearings voluntarily even if they are not legally obligated to do so.

To aid the commenter in understanding the substance of a proposed rule, and the agency's rationale in developing it, the initial notice of proposed rulemaking must contain four major parts. The most obvious is the text of the proposed rule itself. One might think that the entire proposed rule would be published in *The State Register* to facilitate meaningful public involvement, as is the case in the federal system, which requires federal agencies to publish the entire text of proposed rules in *The Federal Register*, which is the counterpart to *The State Register* in New York. That is not the case, however. SAPA merely requires that agencies publish summaries of proposed rules in *The State Register*, if the proposed text exceeds 2000 words.[3] It then is necessary for the interested member of the public to contact the agency to obtain a complete copy of the proposed text.[4]

The notice of proposed rulemaking generally also must include three other documents, a Regulatory Impact Statement ("RIS"), a Regulatory Flexibility Analysis ("RFA"), and a Rural Area Flexibility Analysis ("RAFA").[5] The RIS is intended to "describe the effect the proposal will have on state and local government and on regulated parties."[6] The RFA

---

3. SAPA § 202(6–a)(c).
4. SAPA § 202(6–a)(c).

§ 4.55
1. SAPA § 202(1)(a).
2. For example, ECL § 3–0301 requires DEC to hold public hearings.
3. SAPA § 202(1)(f)(v).

4. The notice is required to include the name and telephone number of an agency contact person. SAPA § 202(1)(f)(viii).
5. SAPA § 202(1)(f)(vi), (vii).
6. SAPA §§ 202(1)(f)(vi), 202–a.

focuses on the impact of the proposed regulation on small businesses.[7] Finally, the RAFA covers the proposed regulation's effect on rural areas.[8] SAPA now also requires a job impact analysis for certain rulemakings.[9] We discuss these ancillary documents in detail elsewhere.[10]

Formal participation. Formal participation in a rulemaking process represents an important opportunity to influence the agency's thinking concerning the rule while the agency's mind is open on the rule's final content. While cynical readers may be skeptical concerning the openness of the agency to changing its position from that articulated in the proposed rule, SAPA's requirement that an agency include in its final regulatory package an "assessment of public comment" and a "statement of reasons" why it determined not to adopt significant alternative regulatory approaches helps to ensure that agencies give comments serious consideration.[11]

Formal participation in the rulemaking process also enhances prospects for success if recourse to the courts to challenge the rule proves necessary. Courts will look largely to the administrative record before the agency in reviewing the legal validity of rules. It is incumbent upon a party interested in a particular rule, therefore, to ensure that the record contains information and analyses that support its position and challenge the rationality of the agency's approach.

Informal participation. Parties interested in rulemakings also should consider interaction with the proposing agency on a parallel, less formal track in an effort to shape the content of the final rule. Individual contacts with the agency should be considered. A party also should determine whether the agency has already established a mechanism to promote a dialogue with interested parties. The advisory groups that the Department of Environmental Conservation has created to deal with Clean Air Act implementation, enforcement, and other issues are examples of such vehicles.

Parties interested in meaningfully influencing a rulemaking proceeding should adopt a strategy that contains the following prongs, among others. First, develop an understanding of the agency's objectives. Second, determine why the government has adopted its proposed strategy to achieve these objectives; and to the extent that it has rejected other strategies, why it has done so. Third, review the extent to which you endorse the means and ends the agency has adopted. Finally, to the

---

7. SAPA §§ 202(1)(f)(vii), 202–b; New York Dep't of State, State Register Procedure Manual 10–11 (1994). An agency need not submit an RFA if the proposed rule "will not impose any adverse impact, reporting, record keeping or other compliance costs on small businesses." New York Dep't of State, State Register Procedure Manual 10 (1994).

8. SAPA § 202–bb(2)(b).

9. SAPA § 201–a.

10. *See supra,* § 4.49.

11. SAPA § 202(5)(b).

extent that the regulated party disagrees with either or both, focus on educating the agency as to why, from a policy, legal, or technical perspective, its proposed approach is deficient, and why the approach you endorse is preferable.

The common sense point that honesty and accuracy should characterize one's dealings with the proposed agency is worth reinforcing. This is so not only because such an approach maximizes one's credibility and influence with the agency; it also stems from the need to maintain a long-term view of one's relationship with an agency. A relationship with an agency rarely begins and ends with a rulemaking proceeding.

Other entities in State government sometimes influence the shape of regulations and, accordingly, a party interested in a proposed regulation needs to consider contacting these entities as well as the sponsoring agency. ORMA is in the strongest position to influence agency regulations. ORMA reviews every proposed regulation.[12] While ORMA lacks veto power over such regulations, its formal notification to the sponsoring agency of deficiencies in the proposed regulation obligates the agency to provide a formal response. A second ORMA notice of deficiency obligates the sponsoring agency to conduct a public hearing on the rulemaking and prepare a brief report responding to ORMA's criticisms.[13] Thus, ORMA has the ability to require an agency to provide its positions on issues on the record, thereby reducing the likelihood of post hoc reasoning in the event the final regulation is subject to judicial review. ORMA's role has now been taken over by GORR pursuant to Executive Order 20, which gives the Director of Regulator Reform—the head of GORR—and four other senior advisors to the Governor the authority to veto proposed regulations.

In the Legislature, the Administrative Regulations Review Commission ("ARRC") "exercises continuous oversight of the process of rule making."[14] While ARRC lacks GORR's authority to require agencies to address certain issues on the record and to veto regulations, ARRC is a frequent commenter on regulations and, at least in ARRC's own view, agencies often "recognize[ ] the merits of these [ARRC's] comments and conform[ ] [their] actions to the recommendations."[15]

Library References:

West's Key No. Digests, Administrative Law and Procedure ⌾392.

12. SAPA § 202–c(4)(now expired).
13. SAPA § 202–c(7)(now expired).
14. Legislative Law § 87(1).
15. The New York State Administrative Regulations Review Comm'n, 1993 Report 2 (1994). In its 1990 Annual Report, the ARRC's then Assembly Chair similarly noted that "[i]n many instances, ARRC challenged agencies on the statutory basis for rules and regulations.... In general, I have found agencies to be cooperative and responsive to ARRC's role." The New York State Administrative Regulations Review Comm'n, 1990 Report, Cover Letter from Assembly Chair (undated).

§ 4.56 Administrative Rulemaking—Special Strategic Considerations in Handling Administrative Rulemaking Matters—Special Issues in Negotiated Rulemakings

New York State has limited experience with using a negotiated rulemaking process to develop regulations. In 1992, then Governor Cuomo issued Executive Order 156, directing the Department of Environmental Conservation to experiment with a negotiated rulemaking approach in two rulemakings.[1] While the Department has done so, these experiments merely represent initial pilot projects. No single definition of negotiated rulemaking has yet been adopted in the state; similarly, no final decision has yet been made as to the future of negotiated rulemaking in agencies' development of regulations.

With these qualifications, it is possible to make a number of observations, and draw several conclusions, from the negotiated rulemaking activity that has occurred in the state to date. Negotiated rulemaking essentially involves opening up the rulemaking process to non-agency participants *prior to* development of the proposed regulation. In other words, instead of the normal practice, which involves the agency's development of a proposed regulation internally and then providing notice thereof in *The State Register*, triggering public comment, negotiated rulemaking contemplates outside involvement in development of the initial rulemaking proposal.

A state agency interested in using a negotiated rulemaking process to develop a regulation typically will identify likely participants based on its knowledge of the regulated community and other interested parties. The agency also will formally solicit public involvement at this early stage by publishing a "Notice of Proposed Negotiated Rule Making" in *The State Register*.[2] The Department of State's Procedure Manual provides that each such notice should contain the following five parts:

1. A description of the subject and scope of the rule to be developed and the issues to be considered;

2. A list of the interests which are likely to be significantly affected by the rule;

3. A proposed agenda and schedule for completing the work of the committee, including a target date for publication by the agency of a proposed rule for notice and comment;

4. The proposed membership of the negotiated rulemaking committee, including, to the extent feasible, an identification of the persons proposed to represent the agency and outside interests; and

§ 4.56
1. Exec. Order No. 156, 9 NYCRR § 4.156.

2. New York Dep't of State, State Register Procedure Manual 5 (1994).

5. An explanation of how a person may apply for membership on the committee.[3]

A negotiated rulemaking is likely to include an impartial facilitator, whose role will be to manage the discussions.[4] Participants will likely include representatives of the disparate interests concerned about the proposed rule. The participants will probably find it useful to develop a protocol to govern the negotiating process. This protocol will define key concepts, such as whether unanimous agreement is required on issues, or whether a super-majority or some other approach will be used.[5]

Use of a negotiated rulemaking process in no way curtails other components of the rulemaking process. Development of a proposed rule through a negotiated process is followed by initiation of the traditional rulemaking process. The sponsoring agency provides full public notice and an opportunity to comment on the proposed rule. As two commentators have noted, use of negotiated rulemaking is likely to raise a host of issues:

> Two issues concerning this process are unresolved at this point. First, to what extent may the agency proceed to adopt a final rule that differs from the proposed rule? To the extent that the process follows that of an ordinary rulemaking, a negotiated, proposed rule may be revised after proposal. But, as a practical matter, having invested its efforts in the negotiation process, the agency may be reluctant to tinker with the results. Second, and perhaps related, is the question of under what circumstances parties may challenge the validity of the rule, either facially or as applied. As the DEC facilitator for the dry cleaning negotiations pointed out, one of the benefits to an agency of spending the resources to conduct a negotiation is that a successful effort presumably should make real the notion that "an ounce of prevention is worth a pound of cure" by discouraging or even precluding legal challenges to the agreed-upon regulation. The agency therefore is likely to push for agreement in the Organizational Protocols that the participants commit not to bring suit if the negotiated rule becomes law.[6]

---

3. New York Dep't of State, State Register Procedure Manual 5 (1994).

4. In one of the two negotiated rulemakings DEC has conducted to date the Department used an in-house person as the facilitator, while in the other an outside person served in this capacity. *See* Ira B. Lobel, *Negotiated Rulemaking in New York*, Part II, Vol. 2, No. 1 New York State Forum on Conflict & Consensus Newsletter 1 (1995); Lenore R. Kuwik, *Using the Negotiated Rule-Making Process in New York—Lessons Learned and A View to the Future*, Vol. 1, No. 2 New York State Forum on Conflict & Consensus Newsletter 4 (1994).

5. Unanimous agreement was required in the dry cleaning negotiated rulemaking. Lenore R. Kuwik, *Using the Negotiated Rule-Making Process in New York—Lessons Learned and A View to the Future*, Vol. 1, No. 2 New York State Forum on Conflict & Consensus Newsletter 4 (1994).

6. Borchers and Markell, *New York State Administrative Procedure and Practice* (West 1998) § 10.14.

§ 4.56 ADMINISTRATIVE LAW Ch. 4

In short, negotiated rulemaking offers a window into the rulemaking process at its earliest stages. It remains to be seen whether New York State agencies will embrace this approach or continue to use traditional rulemaking procedures.

§ 4.57 Administrative Rulemaking—Special Strategic Considerations in Handling Administrative Rulemaking Matters—Special Issues in Emergency Rulemakings

Another special kind of rulemaking is emergency rulemaking. Emergency rulemakings are of great practical import. Currently, they represent about one-third of all administrative rulemakings in New York. Unlike traditional notice and comment rulemakings, emergency rulemakings proceed without any necessary advance commentary on the rule. As a result, emergency rules can affect a client's interest with little or no advance warning.

SAPA § 202(6) provides that if "immediate adoption of a rule is necessary for the preservation of the public health, safety and welfare" then agencies may adopt a rule and dispense with all of the usual notice requirements.[1] In the case of emergency rules, the notice of adoption of the rule plays some of the role normally fulfilled by the notice of a proposed rule,[2] such as identifying the statutory basis for the rule.[3] Surprisingly, there is little law on when the "public health, safety and welfare" standard is met, although agency clearly must make a meaningful effort to detail the alleged emergency.[4]

Emergency rules are limited in their duration. SAPA limits their original effective period to 90 days.[5] A 60–day renewal is permissible if the agency has noticed proposed adoption of the emergency rule as a permanent rule.[6] Subsequent renewals are allowed only if the agency submits an assessment of public comment along with the renewal.[7] If a

---

§ 4.57
1. SAPA § 202(6).
2. See supra, § 4.45 for a discussion of how agencies must give notice of a proposed rule.
3. SAPA § 202(6)(d)(i).
4. In a recent case, the Supreme Court in Albany County struck down a Department of Environmental Conservation "emergency" rulemaking to allow the marketing of 100% DEET insect repellants in New York, a sharp change of policy from a DEC rule (adopted very shortly before) limiting the DEET content of insect repellants to 30%. The court held that the failure of the agency to make anything more than conclusory findings of the nature of the emergency rendered the rule invalid. See Brodsky v. Zagata, 165 Misc.2d 510, 629 N.Y.S.2d 373 (Sup.Ct., Albany County, 1995).

5. SAPA § 202(6)(a)(i).
6. SAPA § 202(6)(e).
7. SAPA § 202(6)(e).

PRACTICE POINTER: Because emergency rules can strike a client's interests immediately, and the time for formal comment may not follow for a significant period, effective representation may mean contacting immediately the agency personnel responsible for the rule's drafting. Informal, *ex parte* contacts—which are closely regulated in adjudicatory proceedings, see SAPA § 306—are legally permissible in rulemakings. See, e.g., Winthrop Gardens, Inc. v.

client is affected by an emergency rule, immediate action may be required, either through informal contacts with the agency, or immediate judicial relief.

§ 4.58 Administrative Rulemaking—Special Strategic Considerations in Handling Administrative Rulemaking Matters—Agency Guidance Documents

Agencies sometimes use "guidance documents" instead of, or in addition to, formal regulations, to administer their enabling legislation. Consequently, practitioners with a matter before particular agencies must determine not only whether a regulation is relevant to the matter; the practitioner also must determine whether the agency has developed an informal policy or guidance document that bears on the matter as well.

Three issues are particularly salient with respect to agency guidance documents. The first involves strategies for learning about their existence. Agencies are not required to follow prescribed procedures in developing guidance documents. Formal public notice is not required either. Consequently, the practitioner should determine whether the agency has developed mechanisms for publicizing the existence of such documents. For example, in the case of DEC, the agency provides notice of both draft and final guidance documents in its Environmental Notice Bulletin.[1] The New York State Bar Association's Environmental Law Section has developed, and maintains, a comprehensive index of such documents as well. Finally, a number of private newsletter vendors monitor developments, including issuance of guidance documents, and report such information.[2]

Second is the issue of the relevance of guidance documents to individual matters. Unlike statutes or regulations, guidance documents are not binding or enforceable as a matter of law. Nevertheless, as a practical matter, these documents are likely to carry considerable weight in particular proceedings. Agency staff generally will try to follow agency guidance documents in handling individual matters. Reviewing courts are likely to be influenced by such documents as well in ruling on the legal defensibility of agency action in a particular case.[3]

Goodwin, 58 A.D.2d 764, 396 N.Y.S.2d 400 (1st Dep't 1977).

§ 4.58

1. See, e.g., Department of Environmental Conservation, Improving Our Environment, Improving Our Economy: Regulatory Reform of the Department of Environmental Conservation 22 (1994).

2. See, e.g., New York Business Environment phone 518-383-1471; Environmental Law in New York, phone 800-833-9844; New York Environmental Compliance Update, phone 800-274-6774.

3. Borchers and Markell, New York State Administrative Procedure and Practice (West 1998) § 12.5.

§ 4.58 ADMINISTRATIVE LAW Ch. 4

Finally, existence of a guidance document, particularly if it suggests an outcome that is unfavorable in connection with the matter at hand, should cause the practitioner to evaluate whether the document should have been promulgated as a regulation. The line between rules and non-rules may be difficult to draw in individual cases. The various legal tests for doing so are discussed in detail above.[4] In evaluating whether to challenge agency guidance documents, the practitioner needs to consider whether it is preferable to have an adverse informal guidance document, rather than an adverse formally promulgated regulation.

§ 4.59 Administrative Rulemaking—Summary

Administrative rulemaking is the kind of agency action that simulates legislation. It is prospective, as opposed to the retrospective character of adjudication.[1] SAPA divides rules into two large groups: "general" rules that set broad standards of conduct for the future, and "economic" rulemakings such as ratemakings and price authorizations.[2]

Rulemaking under SAPA commences with the rulemaking notice, which must be published in *The State Register* and contains certain basic information about the proposed rule. With the exception of certain specialized kinds of rulemakings—such as emergency rulemakings—agencies proposing rules under SAPA must allow a minimum of 45 days for written comment on the proposed rule. In cases in which the agency is required by statute to hold a "public hearing" on a proposed rule, the minimum 45 days for comment begins from the first public hearing. Rulemaking notices have a life of 180 days, but can be extended by the agency for up to another 185 days, and certain shorter extensions are available in certain circumstances.[3] For general rulemakings agencies are required to publish an assessment of comments, and when an agency publishes a regulatory impact statement it must cite any scientific or statistical studies that formed the "basis" for the rule.[4]

For many general rulemakings, SAPA now requires that the agency prepare three ancillary documents when proposing the rule. These documents are a regulatory impact statement, which is designed to assess the rule's economic impact, and a regulatory flexibility and a rural area flexibility analysis, which are designed to determine and mitigate the impact of a rule on small businesses and sparsely-populated regions, respectively.[5] The statutes requiring preparation of these documents give a significant role to ORMA—and now to GORR by executive order, as ORMA's successor—in reviewing them and the rule itself, all of which

4. See supra, § 4.50.

§ 4.59
1. See supra, § 4.44.
2. See supra, § 4.44.
3. See supra, § 4.45.
4. See supra, § 4.46.
5. See supra, § 4.49.

can give GORR tremendous leverage to work modifications in rules that do not meet with GORR's approval.[6]

The final step on the road to a rule taking legal effect is the notice of adoption.[7] The notice of adoption provides certain basic information about the rule, including its effective date. The rule ultimately adopted cannot be a "substantial revision" of the one proposed; if an agency decides to substantially revise a rule it must proceed upon a new proposed rule. Substantial revisions in rules also require revisions in the ancillary documents if the revisions would change the contents of those ancillary documents.[8]

SAPA excludes some kinds of agency pronouncements, which would otherwise qualify as rules, from the definition of a rule.[9] Prominent among these are interpretive and general policy statements, and rules of internal agency management. Essentially these are pronouncements that, unlike substantive rules, have no or a limited impact on the public. Filing (with the Secretary of State) and publication (in *The State Register*) of administrative rules are required by the State Constitution. As construed by the Court of Appeals, this constitutional duty extends to agency pronouncements with a definite and firm impact, as opposed to pronouncements that merely influence how an agency exercises it discretion.[10]

SAPA allows a party unsure about a rule's impact on it to seek a binding declaratory ruling on the question from the agency.[11] In cases of potentially overlapping state and federal regulations, SAPA allows a more specialized kind of declaratory ruling. In both cases, ORMA has some involvement in the process, and seeking such a ruling can become a way in which to bring informal pressure on the agency through ORMA.[12]

Two important special kinds of rulemakings are negotiated and emergency rulemakings. The former, used only sparingly thus far, involves interested parties negotiating over the contents of an agency's court proposed rule. The latter involve rules that take effect immediately because of a danger to the public health, safety and welfare.

§ 4.60 Administrative Rulemaking—Checklist

1. Is the state regulatory entity covered by SAPA? (*See* § 4.2)

    • If unsure, make the following determinations:

    (i) Does the regulatory entity have the power to either make administrative rules or to decide adjudicatory proceedings? If it does not have the power to perform at least one of these two functions, then it is *not* covered by SAPA.

6. *See supra,* § 4.49.
7. *See supra,* § 4.48.
8. *See supra,* § 4.48.
9. *See supra,* § 4.50.
10. *See supra,* § 4.50.
11. *See supra,* § 4.51.
12. *See supra,* §§ 4.56–4.57.

(ii) Does the regulatory entity derive its power from the state, as opposed to a local or the federal government? An entity can only be subject to SAPA if it gets its power from the state.

(iii) Is the entity headed by one or more gubernatorial appointees? Unless the entity is headed by one or more gubernatorial appointees, it is *not* covered by SAPA. Thus governmental entities that are headed by elected officials are not covered by SAPA.

(iv) Is the entity specifically excluded from the definition of an "agency" by SAPA § 102(1)? Some entities (such as the Workers' Compensation Board and the Unemployment Insurance Appeals Board) that would otherwise qualify as "agencies" under SAPA are excluded by statute. Others, such as the Department of Corrections, are excluded for some purposes.

2. Does the rulemaking notice contain all of the required information? (*See* § 4.45) If not, failure to substantially comply with the elements stated in SAPA § 202(1)(f) invalidates the rule, including the following elements:

- Statutory authority for the rule, including particular subsections and subdivisions.
- Date, time and place of any public hearings, whether they are accessible to persons with mobility impairments, and informing those with hearing impairments that interpreter services will be made available free of charge.
- The text of the rule if 2000 words or less; a summary if over 2000 words.
- The text of any regulatory impact statement, regulatory flexibility analysis, and rural area flexibility analysis; summaries for any that exceed 2000 words.
- The name, office address and office phone number of a knowledgeable agency contact person.

3. If the proposed rule is a general (non-economic) rule, has more than 180 days passed since the notice of proposed rulemaking appeared in *The State Register* or the last public hearing announced in the notice (whichever is later) without the adoption of a final rule? (*See* § 4.45)

- If so, has the agency published in *The State Register* a 185–day notice of continuation of the rulemaking notice (or a notice of revised rulemaking) at some point in the last 60 days of the life of the original notice? If no, the rulemaking has expired. If yes, the rulemaking notice continues in effect through the extra 185–day period, and can be further briefly extended if ORMA intervenes and under other circumstances. *See* SAPA § 202(3)(d) for a complete description of the circumstances under which the rulemaking notice's life can be further extended.

4. Has the proposed rule undergone a "substantial revision" as defined in SAPA § 102(9)? (*See* § 4.45) If so, the agency must proceed upon a notice of revised rulemaking, and must prepare new regulatory impact, flexibility and rural area flexibility documentation if the revision in the rule impacts those ancillary documents.[1] If not, the agency may proceed upon the original notice with the original ancillary documentation.

5. Is a regulatory impact statement required to be prepared with the proposed rule? (*See* § 4.49)

- If so, does it contain the information required by SAPA § 202–a? (*See* § 4.49)

6. Is a regulatory flexibility analysis required to be prepared with the proposed rule? (*See* § 4.49)

- If so, does it contain the information required by SAPA § 202–b? (*See* § 4.49)

7. Is a rural area flexibility analysis required to be prepared with the proposed rule? (*See* § 4.49)

- If so, does it contain the information required by SAPA § 202–bb? (*See* § 4.49)

8. Has the agency provided a minimum 45–day comment period, measured from the publication of the notice of proposed rule or the first mandatory public hearing (if any)? (*See* § 4.46) If not, consider whether the rule is exempt from pre-adoption comments as an emergency rule (*see* § 4.57) or for some other reason. (*See* § 4.46).

9. If the rule is a general (non-economic) rule for which comments were required, has the agency published with the notice of adoption the mandatory assessment of public comments, including addressing any cost estimates at odds with the agency's? (*See* § 4.46)

10. If the rule is one for which a regulatory impact statement has been prepared, has the agency cited to any statistical or scientific studies that have formed the "basis" for the proposed rule? (*See* § 4.47)

11. Has a Freedom of Information Law request, or other means, been employed to discover any other studies that may have been relevant during the agency's preparation of the proposed rule? (*See* § 4.47)

12. If a notice of adoption of a rule has been filed, what is the effective date of the rule? (*See* § 4.48)

13. Is the agency pronouncement exempt from the notice and comment process under any of the exceptions to the definition of the term "rule" in SAPA § 102(2)(b)? (*See* § 4.50)

---

§ 4.60   1. *See* SAPA § 202(4–a).

14. Is the agency pronouncement exempt from the constitutional mandate of filing with the Secretary of State and publication in *The State Register*? (*See* § 4.50)

15. Does the client wish to engage in activity for which it is doubtful as to a rule's coverage? (*See* § 4.51) If so, consider obtaining a declaratory ruling from the agency under SAPA § 204.

16. Is the client subject to potentially overlapping state and federal regulations. (*See* § 4.52) If so, consider obtaining a declaratory ruling under SAPA § 206.

17. Is the agency considering negotiated rulemaking on any subject of import to the client? (*See* § 4.56)

§ 4.61 Agency Information–Gathering

The two primary functions of administrative agencies are adjudication and rulemaking. In the former agencies simulate courts; in the latter they simulate legislatures. Agencies, however, also need access to information upon which to base their other activities. In order for an agency to know whether to bring an enforcement proceeding against a regulated party, it must have some mechanism for discovering whether violations of the law have taken place. In order to promulgate sensible rules the agency must have access to fundamental information about the regulated industry. In opposition to agencies' need for access to governmental information stands our political and constitutional tradition of a government of limited authority. It is perhaps thus not surprising that in this area practitioners of state administrative law often confront constitutional principles directly.

Library References:
West's Key No. Digests, Administrative Law and Procedure ⚖=341–370.

§ 4.62 Agency Information–Gathering—Administrative Searches

An important mechanism for agency gathering of information is through administrative searches—or, as they are commonly known, administrative inspections. In order to conduct inspections, agencies need statutory authorization to do so.[1] Such statutes are fairly common.[2]

Administrative inspections also need to comply with the constitutional proscriptions against unreasonable searches and seizures: the Fourth Amendment to the United States Constitution, and Article I, Section 12 of the New York Constitution. Although the relevant wording

§ 4.62
1. *See, e.g.*, People v. Rizzo, 40 N.Y.2d 425, 428, 386 N.Y.S.2d 878, 880, 353 N.E.2d 841, 843–45 (1976).

2. *See, e.g.*, Public Health Law § 1350(1).

of the two provisions is identical, the New York Constitution has been interpreted in a manner more restrictive of governmental authority than its federal counterpart.[3]

Federal and state constitutional law are identical, however, in several respects. Generally, administrative inspections require a search warrant.[4] However, in contrast to the usual rule that a search warrant can issue only upon a showing of individualized suspicion amounting to probable cause,[5] a warrant for an administrative search can issue if the agency applying for the warrant can show a neutral reason for the search such as the passage of time or a random program of inspections.[6] Thus, for instance, an agency inspector for Labor Code violations could obtain a warrant by showing that the inspection was being conducted because the target of the search was chosen by a random drawing.

Many administrative searches can be conducted without even obtaining a warrant, although this is an area in which the State Constitution more heavily restricts the government than does the Federal Constitution. Under federal law, an agency may conduct a warrantless search only if there is a statute authorizing the search that sets forth a neutral scheme,[7] the industry that is the target of the search is one that is "pervasively" regulated,[8] and the search has the legitimate administrative purpose of uncovering regulatory violations.[9] The Court of Appeals follows the same three-pronged test, but is more demanding in its application of the "pervasive regulation" and "administrative purpose" prongs. In *People v. Keta*,[10] the Court of Appeals held unconstitutional as a matter of *state* constitutional law a statute that the United States Supreme Court had *upheld* as a matter of *federal* constitutional law.[11] The statute in question authorized warrantless searches of auto junkyards. The Court of Appeals held that dealers of second hand auto parts were not part of a pervasively regulated industry (because the industry had no extensive history of regulation) and the high likelihood that the

---

3. *See, e.g.*, People v. Keta, 79 N.Y.2d 474, 583 N.Y.S.2d 920, 593 N.E.2d 1328 (1992), on remand 185 A.D.2d 994, 591 N.Y.S.2d 782 (1992).

4. *See, e.g.*, Camara v. Municipal Court of San Francisco, 387 U.S. 523, 87 S.Ct. 1727, 18 L.Ed.2d 930 (1967); See v. City of Seattle, 387 U.S. 541, 87 S.Ct. 1737, 18 L.Ed.2d 943 (1967).

5. *See, e.g.*, B.T. Productions v. Barr, 44 N.Y.2d 226, 236, 405 N.Y.S.2d 9, 14–15, 376 N.E.2d 171, 176 (1978).

6. *See, e.g.*, Camara v. Municipal Court of San Francisco, 387 U.S. at 538, 87 S.Ct. at 1735, 18 L.Ed.2d 943.

7. *See, e.g.*, Donovan v. Dewey, 452 U.S. 594, 101 S.Ct. 2534, 69 L.Ed.2d 262 (1981).

8. *See, e.g.*, Marshall v. Barlow's, Inc., 436 U.S. 307, 313, 98 S.Ct. 1816, 1820–21, 56 L.Ed.2d 305 (1978)(pervasively regulated industries include at least those such as alcohol and firearms, which have a long history of governmental regulation).

9. *See, e.g.*, New York v. Burger, 482 U.S. 691, 107 S.Ct. 2636, 96 L.Ed.2d 601 (1987)(search has a legitimate administrative purpose even if it might have the effect of frequently disclosing violations of the criminal law).

10. 79 N.Y.2d 474, 583 N.Y.S.2d 920, 593 N.E.2d 1328 (1992), on remand 185 A.D.2d 994, 591 N.Y.S.2d 782 (1992).

11. *See* New York v. Burger, 482 U.S. 691, 107 S.Ct. 2636, 96 L.Ed.2d 601 (1987)(upholding New York Vehicle and Traffic Law § 415–a(5)(a)).

search could uncover criminal violations (for example, sale of stolen auto parts) rendered the statute violative of Article I, Section 12 of the State Constitution. Attacks on administrative searches are therefore best couched in state constitutional terms.[12]

Assuming that one can demonstrate that the search was unconstitutional, the question of the remedy for the violation is a difficult one. At one time the Court of Appeals' position appeared to be that evidence gathered in an unconstitutional search was subject to the exclusionary rule, and should be suppressed in administrative hearings.[13] More recently, however, the Court of Appeals has held that exclusion of the evidence is the appropriate remedy only if the utility of exclusion (deterrence of illegal searches) outweighs the harm in hampering the government in its pursuit of its legitimate regulatory objectives.[14] Under this test, there clearly will be circumstances in which evidence is excluded in administrative proceedings. For instance, if the illegal search were conducted by agency employees, and the evidence seized is the foundation of the case against the target of the search, then the deterrent value would probably be high enough to justify exclusion.[15] But the administrative law practitioner should not automatically assume that illegally gathered evidence will be excluded, and if exclusion is sought must be able to demonstrate the deterrent value of doing so.

§ 4.63 Agency Information–Gathering—Administrative Subpoenas

Statutes commonly grant agencies the power to issue two kinds of subpoenas: *ad testificandum* and *duces tecum*. The first requires a witness to attend and testify, and presents little opportunity for advance challenge because objections to the testimony usually must be raised during questioning, not upon issuance of the subpoena.[1] The second type

12. **PRACTICE POINTER:** Whether to resist the administrative inspection at all can be a difficult tactical question. Even if agency inspectors show up without a warrant in a circumstance in which one is required, refusing to allow entry and requiring them to obtain a warrant may do more harm than good. Because warrants for administrative inspections are so easy to obtain, agency inspectors will surely return shortly with a warrant in hand, and perhaps a less forgiving disposition. The target of the search may buy enough time to address easily-remedied violations, but the suspicions of the inspectors will surely be heightened.

13. *See, e.g.*, Finn's Liquor Shop v. State Liquor Auth., 24 N.Y.2d 647, 301 N.Y.S.2d 584, 249 N.E.2d 440 (1969) (evidence excluded in administrative proceeding against license holder).

14. *See* Boyd v. Constantine, 81 N.Y.2d 189, 597 N.Y.S.2d 605, 613 N.E.2d 511 (1993) (evidence not excluded in misconduct action against State Police Officer because evidence not gathered by agency officials, therefore no deterrent value in exclusion).

15. *See, e.g.*, People ex rel. Piccarillo v. New York State Board of Parole, 48 N.Y.2d 76, 421 N.Y.S.2d 842, 397 N.E.2d 354 (1979)(evidence excluded in parole revocation hearing where evidence gathered formed basis for action against parolee).

§ 4.63

1. *See, e.g.*, New York State Comm'n on Gov't Integrity v. Congel, 142 Misc.2d 9, 21–22, 535 N.Y.S.2d 880, 889 (Sup.Ct., N.Y. County, 1988) (objections must be raised during testimony, not on issuance).

CAVEAT: It is conceivable that in some circumstances an objection could be raised

of subpoena, subpoenas *duces tecum*, require the recipient to turn over material evidence, usually in the form of writings. Because it is extremely likely that private parties in administrative proceedings possess writings of central relevance, agencies frequently employ subpoenas *duces tecum* in the context of adjudicatory proceedings, particularly enforcement actions against parties for alleged regulatory violations.

New York law sets up a three-part test for determining whether an agency can employ subpoenas *duces tecum*. An agency needs to have (1) statutory authority, (2) an "authentic factual basis to warrant the investigation," and (3) the ability to demonstrate "that the evidence sought is reasonably related to the subject of the inquiry."[2] None of the three prongs is particularly difficult to satisfy. Statutes giving agencies subpoena power are extremely common, although they are construed narrowly and literally.[3] As for the second prong requiring an "authentic basis," the Court of Appeals has made clear that barebones affidavits to the effect that the agency is investigating a "complaint" about a regulated party will not suffice.[4] At a minimum an agency is required to provide supporting affidavits that make a "threshold" showing of the reliability of the information leading to the complaint, although agencies have had little trouble clearing this hurdle simply by providing a modest amount of detail as to the reason for their investigation.[5] The third prong of the test—requiring a reasonable relationship—requires only a modest connection between the information sought and the investigation,[6] although this requirement is enforced more vigorously later in the investigation, at which point the agency is presumably in a better position to make a

at the time of issuance of the subpoena if the only relevant testimony that a witness could give would be objectionable. If, for example, an agency issued a subpoena *ad testificandum* to a party's attorney, an objection on issuance might be possible. Such circumstances, however, if they exist at all are extremely rare.

2. *See* Abrams v. Thruway Food Market & Shopping Center, Inc., 147 A.D.2d 143, 146, 541 N.Y.S.2d 856, 858 (2d Dep't 1989) (summarizing Levin v. Murawski, 59 N.Y.2d 35, 39, 462 N.Y.S.2d 836, 838, 449 N.E.2d 730, 732 (1983)).

3. *See, e.g.*, Moon v. New York State Dep't of Social Services, 207 A.D.2d 103, 621 N.Y.S.2d 164 (3d Dep't 1995) (statutory grant of authority to issue subpoenas to agency, coupled with regulation delegating this authority to hearing offices, means that attorneys for the agency cannot issue subpoenas without first applying to hearing officers).

4. *See, e.g.*, Levin v. Murawski, 59 N.Y.2d 35, 39, 462 N.Y.S.2d 836, 838, 449 N.E.2d 730, 732 (1983).

5. *See, e.g.*, Chassin v. Helaire Nursing Agency, 211 A.D.2d 581, 621 N.Y.S.2d 611 (1st Dep't 1995) (affidavits sufficient to allow production of nursing home records during investigation); Atkins v. Guest, 201 A.D.2d 411, 607 N.Y.S.2d 655 (1st Dep't 1994)(affidavits sufficient to allow production of documents regarding medical treatment of patient); Abrams v. Thruway Food Market & Shopping Center, Inc., 147 A.D.2d 143, 541 N.Y.S.2d 856 (2d Dep't 1989)(affidavit from agency employee regarding two observed violations sufficient to force production of four years of business records).

6. *See, e.g.*, New York State Comm'n on Judicial Conduct v. Doe, 61 N.Y.2d 56, 471 N.Y.S.2d 557, 459 N.E.2d 850 (1984) (most financial records of a sitting judge must be produced in an investigation into alleged unethical transactions).

more focused inquiry.[7]

Constitutional and evidentiary principles operate as a modest check on agency subpoena power. Ordinary evidentiary privileges apply to subpoenas; so, for instance, a party could resist that portion of a subpoena *duces tecum* directed at correspondence between an attorney and client.[8] Parties frequently assert the Fifth Amendment privilege against self-incrimination in attempting to resist agency subpoenas, but usually with little success. The difficulty of raising the self-incrimination privilege has several contributing factors. First, the fact that the *document* requested is incriminating does not by itself raise a Fifth Amendment issue. In order to raise the privilege successfully, the *act* of producing the document must be implicitly testimonial, and the testimonial aspect of production must implicate the producer in a way that the document itself does not. The act of producing documents can, in some circumstances, have a substantial testimonial component; it might admit that the documents exist or that they are in possession of the target of the subpoena, or it might implicitly authenticate the documents. But only if that testimonial component is substantial and incriminating can the Fifth Amendment privilege be raised successfully.[9]

Obstacles stand in the way of successfully raising the Fifth Amendment privilege besides its inherently narrow scope. The government can obtain criminal immunity. The privilege also does not apply to corporations, even corporations with a single shareholder. Thus, even if turning over the documents might incriminate the custodian of the corporate records, this presents no obstacle to production.[10]

Challenges to administrative subpoenas are properly presented to the agency in the first instance. If this provides no relief, the matter may then be presented to the supreme court in a county that would have venue in an Article 78 proceeding to review agency determinations.[11]

Library References:

West's Key No. Digests, Administrative Law and Procedure ⚖=357, 358, 399, 464, 465.

§ 4.64 Agency Information–Gathering—Reporting and Recordkeeping Requirements

Another way in which agencies gather information is through reporting and recordkeeping requirements imposed upon the regulated

---

7. *See, e.g.*, New York State Comm'n on Gov't Integrity v. Congel, 142 Misc.2d 9, 20–21, 535 N.Y.S.2d 880, 889–90 (Sup.Ct., N.Y. County, 1988).

8. *See* Stern v. Morgenthau, 62 N.Y.2d 331, 336, 476 N.Y.S.2d 810, 812, 465 N.E.2d 349, 351 (1984) (ordinary evidentiary privileges limit subpoenas *duces tecum*).

9. *See generally* Melilli, *Act of Production Immunity*, 52 Ohio St.L.J. 223, 225 (1991).

10. *See, e.g.*, Braswell v. United States, 487 U.S. 99, 109–110, 108 S.Ct. 2284, 2290–91, 101 L.Ed.2d 98 (1988).

11. CPLR 2304; CPLR 2304, cmt. 6 (venue of challenge governed by CPLR 506(b)).

industry. New York courts treat recordkeeping and reporting requirements as "an analogue of the power conferred upon the agency to issue a subpoena *duces tecum*."[1] As a practical matter, therefore, the only real requirement is that the agency have statutory authorization to require reporting or recordkeeping, or that it has imposed the requirement by rule pursuant to statutory authorization. The other requirements for a subpoena *duces tecum*, relevance to the inquiry and authentic basis,[2] are mooted by the existence of legislative consensus that the requirement is essential to the agency's mission.[3] Constitutional and other evidentiary challenges to such requirements are extremely difficult to raise successfully. As it is in the case of subpoenas,[4] the Fifth Amendment privilege against self-incrimination is a tempting basis for a challenge. The Fifth Amendment comes into play if the record or the report would, if completed accurately, contain incriminating information. However, in all but very limited circumstances, the so-called "required records" doctrine acts an exception to the self-incrimination privilege, making the Fifth Amendment extremely difficult to raise successfully in this context.[5]

§ 4.65 Agency Information–Gathering—Summary

An important function of agencies is to gather information upon which to base their decisions. Agencies can gather information in several ways: administrative inspections and searches, subpoenas and reporting and recordkeeping requirements. Each method presents slightly different legal issues.

Administrative searches and inspections require statutory authori-

---

§ 4.64

1. *See* Glenwood T.V., Inc. v. Ratner, 103 A.D.2d 322, 329, 480 N.Y.S.2d 98, 103 (2d Dep't 1984)(Titone, J.), aff'd 65 N.Y.2d 642, 491 N.Y.S.2d 620, 481 N.E.2d 252 (1985), appeal dismissed 474 U.S. 916, 106 S.Ct. 241, 88 L.Ed.2d 250 (1985).

2. *See supra*, § 4.63.

3. *See* Borchers and Markell, *New York State Administrative Procedure and Practice* (West 1998) § 6.4.

4. *See supra*, § 4.63.

5. *See, e.g.*, Shapiro v. United States, 335 U.S. 1, 68 S.Ct. 1375, 92 L.Ed. 1787 (1948)(creating exception); In re Grand Jury Subpoena Date December 14, 1984 v. Kuriansky, 69 N.Y.2d 232, 513 N.Y.S.2d 359, 505 N.E.2d 925 (1987)(referring to the required records doctrine as nearly absolute); Glenwood T.V., Inc. v. Ratner, 103 A.D.2d 322, 329, 480 N.Y.S.2d 98, 103 (2d Dep't 1984), aff'd 65 N.Y.2d 642, 491 N.Y.S.2d 620, 481 N.E.2d 252 (1985), appeal dismissed 474 U.S. 916, 106 S.Ct. 241, 88 L.Ed. 2d 250 (1985)(rejecting Fourth and Fifth Amendment challenges to New York City ordinance requiring repair shops to keep records).

PRACTICE POINTER: The only circumstance in which the Fifth Amendment can be raised successfully are in those situations in which the reporting or recordkeeping requirement requires a regulated party to report criminal activity that occurred before the reporting or recordkeeping requirement existed. In such a circumstance, a party would have no opportunity to avoid incriminating himself. In this usual circumstance, however, a party can avoid criminal liability by keeping accurate records or completing accurate reports, and avoiding criminal activity for the relevant period. *See, e.g.*, Marchetti v. United States, 390 U.S. 39, 88 S.Ct. 697, 19 L.Ed.2d 889 (1968) (striking down requirement that gamblers self-report and pay an excise tax).

ty.[1] They are also regulated by the constitutional prohibition against unreasonable searches and seizures. Although state and federal constitutional law parallel on many points regarding administrative searches, the State Constitution is more restrictive of governmental authority than its Federal counterpart.[2] Administrative searches generally require a warrant, but unlike ordinary criminal searches, a warrant may issue for a criminal search merely upon a showing that the search is taking place pursuant to some neutral scheme, such as a program of random inspections. In some circumstances, an administrative search is permissible even without a warrant, although it is in this respect that the State Constitution is palpably more demanding than the Federal.[3] Under the State Constitution, a warrantless administrative search is permissible only if the statute authorizing the search takes place pursuant to a neutral scheme, the industry is pervasively regulated, and the search is genuinely directed at uncovering administrative (not criminal) violations. Exclusion of evidence in administrative hearings is the appropriate remedy for illegal searches only if the utility of exclusion outweighs the disutility of frustrating the government's legitimate regulatory objectives.[4]

Agencies commonly have authority to issue two kinds of subpoenas: *ad testificandum* and *duces tecum*.[5] Both require statutory authority, but the first issues essentially as of right. Objections to witness testimony are almost always presented only when the witness testifies, not upon issuance of the subpoena. The latter type of subpoena requires production of material things—most commonly written records—and requires not only statutory authority, but an "authentic factual basis to warrant the investigation" and a showing that the "evidence sought is reasonably related to the subject of the inquiry." Ordinary evidentiary privileges, such as the attorney-client, apply, but Fifth Amendment self-incrimination objections are extremely difficult to raise successfully.[6]

Reporting and recordkeeping requirements must be imposed pursuant to statutory authority, or a rule made pursuant to a statutory delegation of authority.[7] Objections to requirements of this sort are extremely difficult to raise successfully. Although the Fifth Amendment privilege against self-incrimination is often raised, assertions of the privilege almost always fail because of the so-called "required records" doctrine.[8]

The following checklist summarizes some of the considerations that a lawyer faces in advising a client on issues of this kind.

§ 4.65
1. See supra, § 4.62.
2. See supra, § 4.62.
3. See supra, § 4.62.
4. See supra, § 4.62.
5. See supra, § 4.63.
6. See supra, § 4.63.
7. See supra, § 4.64.
8. See supra, § 4.64.

§ 4.66 Agency Information–Gathering—Checklist

1. How is the agency attempting to gather information from the client? Administrative inspection or search? Agency subpoena *ad testificandum*? Agency subpoena *duces tecum*? Reporting requirement? Recordkeeping requirement?

2. If the mechanism is an administrative inspection or search, make the following determinations: (*See* § 4.62)

- Do the agency inspectors have a search warrant reasonably describing the premises and the object of the inspection?

- If so, then the search is legal if there is statutory authority for inspections of this type and a neutral scheme for obtaining warrants, such as the passage of time or a program of random inspections.

- If not, the search is legal only if all three of the following requirements are met:

    (i) The search is pursuant to a statute authorizing the search upon a neutral scheme.

    (ii) The regulated industry is "pervasively" regulated, meaning generally (under New York State Constitutional law) that it is an industry with a long history of active governmental supervision, such as alcohol or firearms.

    (iii) The object of the search is genuinely one of uncovering regulatory, as opposed to criminal, violations. Under New York State Constitutional Law, "administrative" searches with a very high probability of discovering criminal violations are likely to be viewed as a pretext for criminal searches requiring a warrant.

- If the search is illegal, is exclusion of the evidence the remedy sought? If so, exclusion is the appropriate remedy only if the utility of exclusion (deterrence of illegal searches) outweighs the disutility of frustrating the government's pursuit of its legitimate regulatory objectives.

- If the administrative search has not yet taken place, is the objection to the search one that could be met easily, for example by obtaining a warrant or a more particular warrant? If so, consider whether it is tactically wise to make the objection. (*See* § 4.36)

2. If the mechanism is an administrative subpoena *ad testificandum*, does the agency have statutory authority to issue such subpoenas? If so, then the subpoena issues as of right; any evidentiary objections must be made during the testimony. If not, the subpoena may be quashed. (*See* § 4.63)

3. If the mechanism is an administrative subpoena *duces tecum*, does the agency have statutory authority to issue such subpoenas? If not, the subpoena may be quashed. If so, the subpoena is properly issued only if both of the following additional conditions are met: (*See* § 4.63)

- There is an "authentic factual basis" for the investigation, that the agency has demonstrated with more than conclusory affidavits.

- The information sought is "reasonably related" to the subject of the inquiry.

- Are there potential evidentiary objections that can be made to the evidence sought? If unsure, make the following determinations:

    (i) Ordinary evidentiary objections (such as the attorney-client privilege) apply in the usual fashion.

    (ii) The Fifth Amendment privilege against self-incrimination can be raised successfully only by individuals and only if the *act* of producing the evidence is implicitly testimonial (by admitting possession of, existence of, or authenticating the documents) and that testimonial component is independently incriminating.

4. If the mechanism is a reporting or recordkeeping requirement, is there statutory authorization for such a requirement? (*See* § 4.64) If not, the requirement can be resisted. If so, the requirement generally cannot be admitted. The Fifth Amendment privilege against self-incrimination can be raised successfully only on rare occasions because of the so-called "required records" doctrine.

§ 4.67 Judicial Review

Judicial review is an important facet of administrative law. Yet, either as a legal or practical matter, it may not be available. It may be legally unavailable if, for instance, the party seeking review lacks standing or the matter is not yet ripe for judicial review. Judicial review may not be available for practical reasons because the client cannot afford to pursue the matter past the agency level, or judicial intervention may be impossible until a point at which it is of little practical use. Further, pursuing judicial review unsuccessfully (or even successfully) can have negative collateral consequences for future dealings with the agency. Judicial review of administrative action is thus nothing to be undertaken lightly, although in many circumstances it becomes the only realistic route to relief.

Library References:

West's Key No. Digests, Administrative Law and Procedure ⚖═651–821.

§ 4.68 Judicial Review—Delegation of Authority to Agencies

Agencies derive their authority from the political branches of government. Thus, an agency can take action in either of its primary forms—administrative adjudication or rulemaking—only if it has statutory authorization to do so. Beyond the requirement of statutory authorization lie considerations of separation of powers. The three major branches of government cannot give away too much of their authority without violating the State Constitution. The constitutional boundaries are seldom crossed, however.

With regard to delegation of legislative authority, the State Constitution only requires that the statute give the agency some "intelligible principle" to guide it in the exercise of its rulemaking authority.[1] Thus, the Court of Appeals has upheld some extremely vague delegations of authority to agencies.[2] However, the constitutional considerations do occasionally enter the picture. In the important case of *Boreali v. Axelrod*[3] the Court of Appeals invalidated some extremely far-reaching regulations promulgated by the Public Health Council purporting to regulate secondhand tobacco smoke in New York. Although refusing to invalidate the statutory delegation of authority to the Council, the court held that the enormous breadth of the regulations persuaded it "that the difficult-to-define line between administrative rule-making and legislative policy-making [had] been transgressed."[4]

Just as the Court of Appeals has been relatively tolerant of delegations of legislative authority, so too has it been tolerant of delegations of judicial authority.[5] Thus, the Court of Appeals has stated that it would not approve delegating to agencies "core" judicial functions such as placing criminal defendants in jail or awarding consequential damages, such as compensation for pain and suffering. But the court has been willing to approve of nearly any delegation short of this. Thus, in *Rosenthal v. Hartnett*[6] the Court of Appeals upheld a statute granting an agency authority to impose penalties in traffic offenses not requiring imprisonment as a punishment, and in *Motor Vehicle Manufacturers*

---

§ 4.68

1. *See, e.g.*, Nicholas v. Kahn, 47 N.Y.2d 24, 416 N.Y.S.2d 565, 389 N.E.2d 1086 (1979).

2. *See, e.g. id.*, (upholding delegation to agency to regulate "substantial" conflicts of interest); Levine v. Whalen, 39 N.Y.2d 510, 516, 384 N.Y.S.2d 721, 724, 349 N.E.2d 820, 823 (1976) (upholding delegation to Commissioner of Department of Health to make rules to "provide for the protection and promotion of the health of the inhabitants of this state").

3. 71 N.Y.2d 1, 11, 523 N.Y.S.2d 464, 469, 517 N.E.2d 1350, 1355 (1987).

4. *Id.*

5. *See, e.g.*, Mount St. Mary's Hospital v. Catherwood, 26 N.Y.2d 493, 505, 311 N.Y.S.2d 863, 871, 260 N.E.2d 508, 514 (1970)("there is no doubt that a legislature may establish a tribunal, other than a court, to hear and determine disputes even where substantial property rights are involved.").

6. 36 N.Y.2d 269, 367 N.Y.S.2d 247, 326 N.E.2d 811 (1975).

§ 4.68　　　　　ADMINISTRATIVE LAW　　　　　Ch. 4

Association of the United States v. State of New York[7] the court approved private arbitrators determining automobile "Lemon Law" cases in which one of the possible remedies was restitution of the purchase price of the automobile.[8] In most circumstances, therefore, the delegation of authority to an agency is unimpeachable, although occasionally in cases involving novel statutory schemes the issue presents itself.

Library References:
West's Key No. Digests, Constitutional Law ⚖︎62.

§ 4.69　Judicial Review—Standing to Seek Judicial Review

An important precondition to a party seeking judicial review is that the party have standing. In many cases this presents no difficulty. A private party ordered to pay a penalty in an enforcement action, or denied a license, obviously has standing to pursue judicial recourse because that party has the most direct and obvious interest possible. But more marginal cases, such as an economic competitor who wishes to challenge the grant of a license to a neighboring business,[1] present much more difficult issues.

The Court of Appeals employs a two-step test for determining whether a party has standing to challenge an administrative action. First, the party must have suffered an "injury in fact." The injury may be economic or non-economic, but it is crucial that the party challenging the decision be able to demonstrate some non-speculative harmful effect that flows from the administrative action.[2] Second, the party must be able to show that the injury is "arguably within the zone of interest to be protected by the statute" under which the agency acted.[3] Although at times the Court of Appeals has made this "zone of interest" test only a weak check on standing,[4] more recently the court has applied it much more stringently. Under the more stringent version of the zone of interest test, the party must be able to demonstrate some injury palpably distinct from the public at large and must be the "type" of party at which the legislation is apparently directed.[5]

---

7. 75 N.Y.2d 175, 551 N.Y.S.2d 470, 550 N.E.2d 919 (1990).

8. For further discussion of the Lemon Law *see* Chapter 7 "Consumer Law," *infra*.

§ 4.69

1. *See, e.g.*, Dairylea Cooperative, Inc. v. Walkley, 38 N.Y.2d 6, 377 N.Y.S.2d 451, 339 N.E.2d 865 (1975) (economic competitor has standing to challenge grant of a license to sell dairy products in vicinity).

2. Dairylea Cooperative, Inc. v. Walkley, 38 N.Y.2d at 10–11, 377 N.Y.S.2d at 454–55, 339 N.E.2d at 867–68.

3. *Id.* at 9, 377 N.Y.S.2d at 454, 339 N.E.2d at 867.

4. *See, e.g.*, Dental Society of New York v. Carey, 61 N.Y.2d 330, 474 N.Y.S.2d 262, 462 N.E.2d 362 (1984) (society of dentists has standing to challenge allegedly inadequate reimbursement schedule for Medicaid patients for dental coverage).

5. *See, e.g.*, Society of the Plastics Industry, Inc. v. County of Suffolk, 77 N.Y.2d 761, 570 N.Y.S.2d 778, 573 N.E.2d 1034 (1991) (plastics manufacturers trade group lacks standing to challenge county ordinance for alleged non-compliance with State

In some circumstances, associations have standing to pursue judicial review on behalf of their members. Associational standing is possible if at least one member of the association would have standing on its own, and the purposes of the suit are "germane" to the association's purpose.[6] Like the notion of what kind of injury falls within a statute's "zone of interest," the notion of what constitutes litigation that is "germane" to an association's purpose has proved to be flexible. While in the past the Court of Appeals was quite generous in construing an association's purpose,[7] in recent times the Court has been more skeptical of claims that the litigation relates in a reasonable fashion to the association's purposes.[8]

In some circumstances, the Court of Appeals has allowed challenges to agency decisions based upon status as a New York taxpayer.[9] However, taxpayer standing is allowed only in circumstances in which the agency decision has a direct and palpable fiscal impact. Thus, for instance, courts have refused to allow taxpayer standing to challenge regulations that are allegedly illegal for failure to prepare an accompanying environmental impact report, even though the petitioners alleged that the cost of printing and mailing the regulations thereby amounted to an "illegal" disbursement of state funds.[10] More direct fiscal effects have, however, allowed for taxpayer standing.[11]

Environmental Quality Review Act because of non-differentiated harm and lack of perceived "environmental" purpose behind the litigation).

PRACTICE POINTER: In cases of doubtful standing, it is sometimes advisable to name several different parties as petitioning for judicial review. If at least one party represented by counsel has standing, courts will often bypass the standing issue, and proceed directly to the merits of the matter. See, e.g., Brodsky v. Zagata, 165 Misc.2d 510, 629 N.Y.S.2d 373 (Sup.Ct., Albany County, 1995) (because at least one petitioner has standing no need to address standing issue in detail). Similarly, allegations of alternative grounds for standing (perhaps taxpayer standing) may provide a safety net in cases in which standing is a difficult question.

6. See, e.g., Dental Society of New York v. Carey, 61 N.Y.2d 330, 334, 474 N.Y.S.2d 262, 263, 462 N.E.2d 362, 363 (1984) (society of dentists has standing to challenge allegedly inadequate reimbursement schedule for Medicaid patients for dental coverage because issue germane to society's purpose).

7. See, e.g., id.

8. See, e.g., Society of the Plastics Industry, Inc. v. County of Suffolk, 77 N.Y.2d 761, 570 N.Y.S.2d 778, 573 N.E.2d 1034 (1991) (environmental suit not "germane" to purposes of plastics trade association despite declaration from president of association to the contrary).

9. See, e.g., Boryszewski v. Brydges, 37 N.Y.2d 361, 372 N.Y.S.2d 623, 334 N.E.2d 579 (1975) (taxpayer standing allowed to challenge constitutionality of state statutes regarding expenditures of state funds). Applying analogous reasoning, the Court of Appeals recently adopted the notion of "voter" standing for state governmental decisions that deny a voter the right to vote in an election. See Schulz v. State of New York, 81 N.Y.2d 336, 599 N.Y.S.2d 469, 615 N.E.2d 953 (1993) (allegedly disguised state loans should have been subject to voter approval; petitioner has voter standing). Thus, if an agency decision actually had the effect of denying a voter the right to vote, standing would be allowed on this theory.

10. New York State Builders Ass'n v. State, 98 Misc.2d 1045, 414 N.Y.S.2d 956 (Sup.Ct., Albany County, 1979).

11. See, e.g., Chester Civic Improvement Ass'n v. New York City Transit Auth., 122 A.D.2d 715, 505 N.Y.S.2d 638 (1st Dep't 1986) (taxpayer standing to challenge agency decision to dispose of property).

Library References:

West's Key No. Digests, Administrative Law and Procedure ⟐665.

§ 4.70 Judicial Review—Ripeness

An agency action needs to be "ripe" for review before judicial intervention can be sought successfully. In the large majority of cases this presents no great difficulty. A party who, for instance, has been subjected to a final agency determination imposing a penalty in an enforcement matter obviously has a matter that is ripe for judicial review because no further agency action is contemplated.

The issue of ripeness comes up frequently, however, in rulemaking matters. If an agency promulgates a rule that will impact on a private party, and that party wishes to challenge the legality of that rule, parties often desire to challenge the rule before an agency makes any effort to enforce it. Such a challenge is commonly called "pre-enforcement review," and can raise significant ripeness concerns, because in such a circumstance further agency action is contemplated.[1] A party wishing to challenge the legality of such a rule has the option of waiting until the agency asserts that the party has violated the rule, thus allowing the party to challenge the legality of the rule in the context of an enforcement action. At one time, federal courts routinely denied pre-enforcement review on ripeness grounds, but that trend was reversed by a trilogy of famous United States Supreme Court cases holding that pre-enforcement review is available if waiting for the enforcement action would serve no purpose other than to delay the challenge.[2] The Court of Appeals follows this federal case law as a matter of state law.[3] Thus, in cases in which an enforcement action would not contribute any factual development germane to the challenge, then rules may be challenged before they are enforced.[4] But, if further factual development in the

---

§ 4.70

1. Borchers and Markell, *New York State Administrative Procedure and Practice* (West 1998) § 7.6.

2. *See* Abbott Laboratories v. Gardner, 387 U.S. 136, 87 S.Ct. 1507, 18 L.Ed.2d 681 (1967) (pre-enforcement review allowed because challenge to legality of rule did not depend upon any factual matter that might be developed in an enforcement proceeding); Toilet Goods Ass'n v. Gardner, 387 U.S. 158, 87 S.Ct. 1520, 18 L.Ed.2d 697 (1967) (pre-enforcement review denied on ripeness grounds because enforcement action could help explain how agency planned to exercise its discretion under rule; how agency exercised discretion under rule relevant to challenge); Gardner v. Toilet Goods Ass'n, 387 U.S. 167, 87 S.Ct. 1526, 18 L.Ed.2d 704 (1967) (following Abbott Labs and Toilet Goods).

3. *See, e.g.*, Church of St. Paul and St. Andrew v. Barwick, 67 N.Y.2d 510, 505 N.Y.S.2d 24, 496 N.E.2d 183 (1986), cert. denied 479 U.S. 985, 107 S.Ct. 574, 93 L.Ed.2d 578 (1986).

4. *See, e.g.*, Community Housing Improvement Program, Inc. v. New York State Division of Housing and Community Renewal, 175 A.D.2d 905, 573 N.Y.S.2d 522 (2d Dep't 1991) (pre-enforcement review allowed because attack on rule purely facial; enforcement proceeding would not contribute to understanding basis for challenge).

CAVEAT: As discussed *infra*, § 4.82, challenges to rules are governed usually by the four month Statute of Limitations applicable to Article 78 proceedings generally. If pre-enforcement review of a rule is possible because the matter is ripe as of the effective date of the rule, it is probably wise

context of an enforcement matter would be relevant to understanding the basis for the challenge, then review must await enforcement.[5]

Library References:

West's Key No. Digests, Administrative Law and Procedure ⚖︎704.

§ 4.71 Judicial Review—Final Order and Relief in the Nature of Prohibition

Generally, a private party must await a final order before challenging an agency determination. Although frequently confused with the doctrine of exhaustion of administrative remedies,[1] the requirement of a final order is distinct. The final order requirement mandates that a party not challenge an interlocutory determination of an agency, such as an agency's denial of discovery.[2]

The final order requirement is the flip side of the common law limitations that existed on the availability of the writ of prohibition. When the three common law prerogative writs available to challenge agency action—prohibition, *certiorari* and *mandamus*—were consolidated, the common law limitations on them were retained.[3] The writ that was available to interrupt agency proceedings was prohibition, but prohibition was an extraordinary remedy at the common law, available only in limited circumstances.[4] Thus if a party wishes to challenge an agency action without a final order and thus in an interlocutory posture, the only writ that would have been available to do this was prohibition, and thus Article 78 relief is not available unless prohibition would have been available at the common law.[5]

---

to undertake such review if there is a basis for challenging the rule. It is possible that the Statute of Limitations for a challenge to the rule that can be challenged in a pre-enforcement context would begin to run from the rule's effective date. On the theory of "better safe than sorry," an attempted pre-enforcement challenge is better than a later Statute of Limitations dismissal.

5. *See, e.g.*, Church of St. Paul and St. Andrew v. Barwick, 67 N.Y.2d 510, 505 N.Y.S.2d 24, 496 N.E.2d 183 (1986), cert. denied 479 U.S. 985, 107 S.Ct. 574, 93 L.Ed.2d 578 (1986)(pre-enforcement challenge not allowed because designation of church as a landmark did not necessarily forbid structural changes desired by owners); Hospital Ass'n of New York State v. Axelrod, 164 A.D.2d 518, 565 N.Y.S.2d 243 (3d Dep't 1990) (pre-enforcement review denied because enforcement action relevant to showing of "hardship" exemption from rule).

§ 4.71

1. On the difference between the two, *see* Borchers and Markell, *New York State Administrative Procedure and Practice* (West 1998) § 7.7.

2. *See, e.g.*, Doe v. Axelrod, 71 N.Y.2d 484, 527 N.Y.S.2d 368, 522 N.E.2d 444 (1988) (relief in the nature of prohibition not available to challenge interlocutory order of agency denying private party access to patient records during the course of a license revocation matter).

3. *See generally* Borchers and Markell, *New York State Administrative Procedure and Practice* (West 1998) § 8.2 (discussing consolidation and retention of common law limitations).

4. *See, e.g.*, La Rocca v. Lane, 37 N.Y.2d 575, 376 N.Y.S.2d 93, 338 N.E.2d 606 (1975).

5. *See, e.g.*, Doe v. Axelrod, 71 N.Y.2d 484, 527 N.Y.S.2d 368, 522 N.E.2d 444 (1988) (relief in the nature of prohibition

§ 4.71 ADMINISTRATIVE LAW Ch. 4

The most common formulation of the test for the circumstances under which prohibitory relief is available is that it will lie only to challenge "jurisdictional errors."[6] "Jurisdiction" is not meant in a technical sense; it is a shorthand expression for serious and obvious errors that would be effectively unreviewable if the agency proceedings were allowed to run their course.[7] In determining whether relief of this sort is available, the Court of Appeals has identified the "gravity of the harm," the availability of "ordinary proceedings" (meaning review once a final order is entered) and the completeness and efficacy of prohibitory relief as the relevant variables.[8] Thus, if waiting for a final order would impose no hardship other than requiring the petitioner to await the end of the administrative matter, relief in the nature of prohibition is not available.[9] In the unusual circumstance in which the mere fact of proceeding with the hearing would do substantial and irreparable harm to the petitioner, and the right to relief is clear, relief in the nature of prohibition is allowed.[10]

Library References:

West's Key No. Digests, Administrative Law and Procedure ⚖︎229, 704.

§ 4.72 Judicial Review—Exhaustion of Administrative Remedies

The most important, and probably most litigated, precondition to judicial review is the requirement that the petitioner have exhausted the available administrative remedies. At its most basic, the exhaustion requirement demands that persons wishing to pursue judicial remedies first attempt to obtain whatever administrative relief might be available. Thus, for instance, a party challenging a tax assessment must attempt to obtain abatement of the bill before the taxing authority before challenging the assessment in court.[1] Or, to take another common example, a

not available to challenge interlocutory order of agency denying private party access to patient records during the course of a license revocation matter).

6. *See, e.g.,* Holtzman v. Goldman, 71 N.Y.2d 564, 528 N.Y.S.2d 21, 523 N.E.2d 297 (1988).

7. *See* Borchers and Markell, *New York State Administrative Procedure and Practice* (West 1998) §§ 7.7, 8.2.

8. *See, e.g.,* Dondi v. Jones, 40 N.Y.2d 8, 14, 386 N.Y.S.2d 4, 9, 351 N.E.2d 650, 655 (1976) (criminal case, but mirroring test as applied in administrative proceedings).

9. *See, e.g.,* Town of Huntington v. New York State Division of Human Rights, 82 N.Y.2d 783, 786, 604 N.Y.S.2d 541, 542–43, 624 N.E.2d 678, 679–80 (1993)(relief in the nature of prohibition not available for challenge to agency action on collateral estoppel grounds); Doe v. Axelrod, 71 N.Y.2d 484, 527 N.Y.S.2d 368, 522 N.E.2d 444 (1988)(relief in the nature of prohibition not available to challenge interlocutory order of agency denying private party access to patient records during the course of a license revocation matter).

10. *See, e.g.,* Nicholson v. State Comm'n on Judicial Conduct, 50 N.Y.2d 597, 431 N.Y.S.2d 340, 409 N.E.2d 818 (1980) (relief in the nature of prohibition allowed because allowing agency investigation into judge's campaign conduct to continue would jeopardize First Amendment freedoms).

§ 4.72

1. *See, e.g.,* Young Men's Christian Ass'n v. Rochester Pure Waters Dist., 37 N.Y.2d 371, 372 N.Y.S.2d 633, 334 N.E.2d 586 (1975).

party who suffers an adverse decision before the ALJ must present the matter to the agency itself before attempting to obtain judicial correction.[2]

Although most applications of the exhaustion concept are straightforward, its relatively expansive and poorly-defined exceptions lead to fairly frequent litigation regarding the issue. One important exception is for allegedly unconstitutional agency actions. Although potentially sweeping in its scope, this exception has been limited to constitutional challenges to agency action that do not require further factual development—usually so-called "facial" challenges.[3]

Another exception applies when the agency is acting "wholly beyond its grant of power."[4] Essentially this is a restatement of the availability of relief in the nature of prohibition for so-called "jurisdictional" errors.[5] But, as usually is the case for relief of this sort, it depends upon showing a clear right to relief and that extraordinary harm will come from having to pursue the matter through the agency process.[6]

The two other commonly invoked exceptions are futility and irreparable harm. Futility is premised on the idea that a litigant should not be required to invoke administrative remedies where doing so would be nothing more than a pointless exercise.[7] Irreparable harm addresses circumstances in which a litigant cannot wait for the agency process to come to its conclusion and must seek immediate judicial intervention.[8] Often these exceptions are considered together, and represent different

---

2. *See, e.g.*, Patchogue Nursing Ctr. v. New York State Dep't of Health, 189 A.D.2d 1054, 592 N.Y.S.2d 900 (3d Dep't 1993).

3. *See, e.g.*, Watergate II Apartments v. Buffalo Sewer Auth., 46 N.Y.2d 52, 412 N.Y.S.2d 821, 385 N.E.2d 560 (1978) (exhaustion excused for facial constitutional challenges to agency action, but not for challenges regarding alleged miscomputation of taxes); Honey Dippers Septic Tank Servs., Inc. v. Landi, 198 A.D.2d 402, 604 N.Y.S.2d 128 (2d Dep't 1993) (constitutional challenges not barred by exhaustion); Pyramid Co. v. Chu, 177 A.D.2d 970, 970, 577 N.Y.S.2d 1015, 1016 (4th Dep't 1991) (facial constitutional challenges not barred).

CAVEAT: It is not quite accurate to say that only facial challenges are excused from exhaustion. Occasionally "as applied" challenges are excused, as long as no further factual development is required, as in a case in which the relevant facts are essentially undisputed but the constitutional challenge is properly conceived of as an "as applied" challenge. *See, e.g.*, Mindel v. Village of Thomaston, 150 A.D.2d 653, 541 N.Y.S.2d 526 (2d Dep't 1989) (as applied challenge to zoning ordinance not barred by failure to exhaust remedies by seeking a special use permit; challenge would not depend upon resolution of any disputed factual matters).

4. *See* Watergate II Apartments v. Buffalo Sewer Auth., 46 N.Y.2d 52, 57, 412 N.Y.S.2d 821, 824, 385 N.E.2d 560, 563 (1978).

5. *See supra*, § 4.71.

6. *See, e.g.*, Levine v. Board of Educ. of New York, 173 A.D.2d 619, 570 N.Y.S.2d 200 (2d Dep't 1991).

7. *See, e.g.*, Amsterdam Nursing Home Corp. v. Commissioner of New York State Dep't of Health, 192 A.D.2d 945, 596 N.Y.S.2d 877 (3d Dep't 1993).

8. *See, e.g.*, Uzwij v. Robins, 133 A.D.2d 695, 519 N.Y.S.2d 866 (2d Dep't 1987) (woman faced with immediate eviction from home because of loss of public assistance payments need not seek relief from agency).

expressions of the same concern.[9] Exhaustion is not an absolute rule; it is a principle tempered by fairness considerations. In circumstances in which a petitioner can demonstrate some substantial unfairness in being forced to pursue administrative redress to its end, exhaustion will be excused.

§ 4.73 Judicial Review—Primary Jurisdiction

The notion that agencies have "primary jurisdiction" over some issues, requiring that the matter first be referred to them, is often confused with the doctrine of exhaustion of administrative remedies. To be sure, there are some similarities between exhaustion and primary jurisdiction doctrine. The difference is often explained that exhaustion is applicable if the agency has exclusive original jurisdiction over the matter, and primary jurisdiction is the relevant doctrine if the agency and the court have concurrent jurisdiction.[1] The question of whether an agency has exclusive or original jurisdiction often can be answered by looking to the relief available in the administrative forum. If the relief sought in court is available in the administrative forum, then the relevant doctrine is exhaustion.[2] If on the other hand, the relief sought in court is not available before the agency, then the question is one of primary jurisdiction.[3] Instead, primary jurisdiction allows a court to stay the case while the agency is consulted on some issue relevant to the case on which the agency has expertise—if indeed it is an issue on which the agency is expert.[4] Unlike exhaustion (which acts as a bar where it applies) primary jurisdiction is an abstention doctrine, merely requiring that the litigation temporarily abate while an agency is consulted on the matter.

Library References:

West's Key No. Digests, Administrative Law and Procedure ⚖︎228.1.

§ 4.74 Judicial Review—Statutory Preclusion of Judicial Review

In some circumstances, statutes purport to prevent judicial review of

---

9. See Borchers and Markell, *New York State Administrative Procedure and Practice* (West 1998) § 7.9.

§ 4.73

1. See, e.g., Staatsburg Water Co. v. Staatsburg Fire Dist., 72 N.Y.2d 147, 156, 531 N.Y.S.2d 876, 880, 527 N.E.2d 754, 758 (1988).

2. See, e.g., Sohn v. Calderon, 78 N.Y.2d 755, 579 N.Y.S.2d 940, 587 N.E.2d 807 (1991) (in matter involving attempted demolition of rent controlled building, question is one of exhaustion because exact relief sought in court would be available if agency issued favorable determination).

3. See, e.g., Capital Telephone Co. v. Pattersonville Telephone Co., 56 N.Y.2d 11, 451 N.Y.S.2d 11, 436 N.E.2d 461 (1982) (discussing—though rejecting application of—primary jurisdiction in antitrust matter because enforcement of antitrust laws not within the agency's competence).

4. *Id.* at 22–23, 451 N.Y.S.2d at 16, 436 N.E.2d at 466.

agency decisions.[1] The Court of Appeals, however, has long held that some minimal judicial review is a constitutional requirement under the Due Process Clause.[2] Thus, while a statute purporting to preclude review clearly narrows the scope of the judicial inquiry, the Court of Appeals' view continues to be "that no matter how explicit the statutory language, judicial review cannot be completely precluded."[3] Judicial review is always available for an aggrieved party to attempt to demonstrate that the agency has acted "illegally, unconstitutionality, or in excess of its jurisdiction."[4] Although the court's formulation of the test for the minimum amount of judicial review required is certainly flexible, in practice it appears to require an aggrieved party to demonstrate a clear and serious error on the part of the agency.[5] Thus, a party attempting to seek—in the face of a "no review" statute—judicial correction of an alleged agency error faces a severely uphill climb.

Library References:

West's Key No. Digests, Administrative Law and Procedure ⊕651, 701.

§ 4.75 Judicial Review—Article 78 and the Consolidation of the Common Law Prerogative Writs

Article 78 of the Civil Practice Law and Rules provides a unified mechanism for judicial review of administrative action by collecting the substance of the three common law prerogative writs: *mandamus*, prohibition and *certiorari*. Article 78 was not intended to make any substantive change in the law of judicial review.[1] The modern consequences of Article 78 having not made any substantive changes in the common law are several.

Probably most importantly, Article 78 is not available as a mechanism for relief unless one of the common law writs would have been available. Consequently, it is common to see judicial opinions referring to Article 78 petitions as "in the nature of" *certiorari*, prohibition or *mandamus* as way of ensuring that at least one of the common law writs

---

§ 4.74

1. *See, e.g.*, Civil Service Law § 76 (providing that in some circumstances agency decisions are "final and conclusive, and not subject to further review in any court"); SAPA § 301(2) (agency decision not to give more detailed notice of adjudicatory proceeding "not subject to judicial review").

2. *See, e.g.*, Mount St. Mary's Hospital v. Catherwood, 26 N.Y.2d 493, 503–04, 311 N.Y.S.2d 863, 870–71, 260 N.E.2d 508, 513–14 (1970); Guardian Life Ins. Co. v. Bohlinger, 308 N.Y. 174, 183, 124 N.E.2d 110, 114 (1954).

3. *See* New York City Dep't of Envt'l Protection v. New York City Civil Serv. Comm'n, 78 N.Y.2d 318, 323, 574 N.Y.S.2d 664, 666, 579 N.E.2d 1385, 1387 (1991).

4. *Id.*

5. *See* Borchers and Markell, *New York Administrative Practice and Procedure* (1998) § 7.10.

§ 4.75

1. *See, e.g.*, Newbrand v. City of Yonkers, 285 N.Y. 164, 33 N.E.2d 75 (1941).

would have been available.[2] Understanding Article 78 requires at least a basic understanding of each of the common law prerogative writs.

The writ of *mandamus* had both a discretionary and non-discretionary face. In its non-discretionary capacity, *mandamus* was called "*mandamus* to compel."[3] *mandamus* to compel was available to force agencies to perform so-called "ministerial duties," that is, duties about which there could be no "reasonable doubt or controversy."[4] To take a straightforward example, if an agency were under a statutory duty to hold a "hearing on a record," and refused to hold such a hearing, the judicial mechanism to force the agency to do so was a writ of *mandamus* to compel. The discretionary face of *mandamus* was *mandamus* to review. *Mandamus* to review was the writ available to review individualized agency action (in the sense of affecting one or a few persons) that did not involve a formal hearing—so-called "administrative actions."[5] Courts employing the writ of *mandamus* to review set aside agency action only if the petitioner could demonstrate that the action was "arbitrary and capricious."[6]

Closely related to the writ of *mandamus* to review was the writ of *certiorari*. *Certiorari* reviewed formal administrative adjudications.[7] In the modern terminology employed by SAPA, the line between *certiorari* and *mandamus* to review essentially tracks the line between "adjudicatory proceedings"[8] and other, less formal, agency determinations. The former are required to be determined on a record with extensive procedural guarantees, while the latter are not limited to the record and far fewer procedures are required.[9] From the standpoint of modern Article 78 practice, the line between *certiorari* and *mandamus* to review continues to carry some significance. If the Article 78 review is in the nature of *mandamus* to review, then the standard of review—as indicated immediately above—is "arbitrary and capricious," and review is not limited to the administrative record.[10] Review in the nature of *certiorari* requires the reviewing court to employ the "substantial evidence" standard to

---

2. *See, e.g.*, Town of Huntington v. New York State Div. of Human Rights, 82 N.Y.2d 783, 604 N.Y.S.2d 541, 624 N.E.2d 678 (1993) (relief under Article 78 not available because relief would not have been available by writ of prohibition).

3. *See, e.g.*, Legal Aid Society v. Scheinman, 53 N.Y.2d 12, 439 N.Y.S.2d 882, 422 N.E.2d 542 (1981).

4. *See* Association of Surrogate and Supreme Court Reporters Within the City of New York v. Bartlett, 40 N.Y.2d 571, 574, 388 N.Y.S.2d 882, 884, 357 N.E.2d 353, 355 (1976).

5. For a case using the term "administrative actions" to refer to these informal individualized agency determinations, *see* New York City Health and Hospitals Corp. v. McBarnette, 84 N.Y.2d 194, 203, n. 2, 616 N.Y.S.2d 1, 5, n. 2, 639 N.E.2d 740, 744, n. 2 (1994).

6. *See, e.g., id.*; DeMilio v. Borghard, 55 N.Y.2d 216, 448 N.Y.S.2d 441, 433 N.E.2d 506 (1982).

7. *See, e.g.*, Stork Restaurant v. Boland, 282 N.Y. 256, 26 N.E.2d 247 (1940).

8. SAPA § 102(3).

9. *See supra*, § 4.11.

10. *See* Borchers and Markell, *New York State Administrative Procedure and Practice* (West 1998) § 8.6.

any factual determinations made by the agency, and review is confined to the administrative record.[11]

The final writ, prohibition, was in some sense the converse of *mandamus* to compel. While *mandamus* to compel was available to force ("compel") agencies to take ministerial action, prohibition was available to restrain ("prohibit") agencies from taking actions that they had a ministerial obligation to avoid.[12] The distinction between "taking action" and "refraining" from taking action is almost always a matter of semantics, but prohibition also had the special character of being available in an interlocutory posture.[13] Thus, if a petitioner wanted to obtain relief before the agency has issued a final order, the only writ that was available was the writ of prohibition, which in turn was available only for very serious, clear errors by the agency—so-called "jurisdictional errors."[14]

The carryover from the distinctions between the three writs is clearly visible in the text of Article 78. CPLR 7803 sets the parameters of "the only questions that may be raised in a proceeding" under Article 78.[15] The first is "whether the body or officer failed to perform a duty enjoined upon it by law,"[16] a codification of the writ of *mandamus* to compel. The second is "whether the body or officer proceeded, is proceeding or is about to proceeding without or in excess of jurisdiction,"[17] a codification of the writ of prohibition. The third is "whether a determination was made in violation of lawful procedure, was affected by an error of law or was arbitrary and capricious or an abuse of discretion, including abuse of discretion as to the measure or mode of penalty or discipline imposed,"[18] a codification of the writ of *mandamus* to review. The final question is "whether a determination made as a result of a hearing held, and at which evidence was taken, pursuant to direction by law is, on the entire record, supported by substantial evidence,"[19] a codification of the writ of *certiorari*. As a result, the classification that the action would have had at common law is significant both in determining whether Article 78 is available at all, and—if so—what standard of review will be employed.[20]

---

11. *See, e.g.*, Simpson v. Wolansky, 38 N.Y.2d 391, 380 N.Y.S.2d 630, 343 N.E.2d 274 (1975) (agency decision set aside under substantial evidence standard because manifestly based on non-record information).

12. Borchers and Markell, *New York State Administrative Practice and Procedure* (West 1998) § 8.6.

13. *See supra*, § 4.72.

14. *See* Doe v. Axelrod, 71 N.Y.2d 484, 527 N.Y.S.2d 368, 522 N.E.2d 444 (1988) (relief in the nature of prohibition not available to force agency to honor petitioner's discovery request prior to agency issuing final order); *see also supra,* § 4.72 for a discussion of the limits on prohibition.

15. CPLR 7803.

16. CPLR 7803(1).

17. CPLR 7803(2).

18. CPLR 7803(3).

19. CPLR 7803(4).

20. Whether the Article 78 petition is initially passed on by the supreme court, or the appellate division, also depends on the writ that would have covered the matter at common law. *See infra*, § 4.84.

§ 4.76 Judicial Review—Standards of Review

A crucial question in any Article 78 proceeding is the standard of judicial review to be applied to each issue. Essentially, asking what standard of review will be applied is to ask how much deference the reviewing court will give the agency. In some situations, courts give the agency's determination no presumption of correctness—so-called *"de novo"* review. In other circumstances, courts treat the agency determination as nearly conclusive, reversible for only the most extreme of errors.

Essentially, agencies make four different kinds of determinations, and the standard of review varies between—and sometimes within—each category. First, agencies make determinations of law. Questions of law can appear in almost any kind of agency determination, and they range from the momentous to the mundane. Agencies make such momentous determinations as deciding the constitutional boundaries of the authority,[1] and such mundane determinations as resolving tiny statutory ambiguities.[2] Second, agencies make determinations of historical facts, as in an adjudicatory proceeding in which the agency fact finders are required to determine whose testimony to believe.[3] Third, agencies make purely discretionary determinations, as in the case of deciding what measure of penalty is appropriate to punish a regulatory offense.[4] And fourth, agencies make policy or political judgments, as for instance in determining whether a new or revised administrative rule will prove politically desirable.[5]

Library References:

West's Key No. Digests, Administrative Law and Procedure ⚚741–800.

§ 4.77 Judicial Review—Standards of Review—Review of Agency Determinations of Law

Agency determinations of law come in all kinds and in all procedural vessels. Whether the agency action is a rulemaking, an adjudicatory proceeding, an inspection or some other matter, the agency must constantly judge the legal boundaries of its authority. For this reason, Article 78 thrice mentions errors of law as a ground for attack of an

---

§ 4.76

1. See, e.g., Boreali v. Axelrod, 71 N.Y.2d 1, 523 N.Y.S.2d 464, 517 N.E.2d 1350 (1987).

2. See, e.g., Allen v. Howe, 84 N.Y.2d 665, 621 N.Y.S.2d 287, 645 N.E.2d 720 (1994) (upholding Civil Service regulation interpreting statutory requirement of one year's disability to mean one continuous year).

3. See, e.g., Berenhaus v. Ward, 70 N.Y.2d 436, 522 N.Y.S.2d 478, 517 N.E.2d 193 (1987) (refusing to disturb agency credibility determination).

4. See, e.g., Pell v. Board of Educ., 34 N.Y.2d 222, 356 N.Y.S.2d 833, 313 N.E.2d 321 (1974) (refusing to disturb agency penalty determinations unless irrational).

5. See, e.g., Unimax Corp. v. Tax Appeals Tribunal, 79 N.Y.2d 139, 581 N.Y.S.2d 135, 589 N.E.2d 358 (1992) (refusing to disturb agency rule regarding deductions).

agency decision.[1] In fact, errors of law remain as a kind of catch all category. If the challenge to the agency action does not fit into one of the other categories—fact, policy or discretion—it must be a challenge on legal grounds.

No matter what the context, however, the principles for evaluating the correctness of an agency determination of law remain essentially constant. Some agency determinations of law receive no presumption of correctness; in other words, they are subject to *de novo* review. Those that are subject to *de novo* review are matters of "pure law," *i.e.*, subjects on which the agency has no special competence.[2] For issues of legal interpretation that involve the agency's specialized competence, the agency's interpretation is presumptively correct, and can be disturbed only if unreasonable.[3] It is not, of course, impossible to demonstrate that an agency's legal interpretation is unreasonable, but the petitioner clearly has an uphill climb in persuading a court to set aside an administrative legal interpretation on a matter within the agency's special competence.[4]

Library References:

West's Key No. Digests, Administrative Law and Procedure ⟿796.

§ 4.77

1. *See* CPLR 7803(1)("duty enjoined on it by law"); CPLR 7803(2)(agency acting "in excess of jurisdiction"); CPLR 7803(3)(agency action "in violation of lawful procedure, [or] affected by error of law"). For a discussion of the standards of review applied to local land use decisions, *see* § 4.76 ("Standards for Judicial Review").

2. *See, e.g.*, Teachers Insurance and Annuity Ass'n of America v. City of New York, 82 N.Y.2d 35, 41–42, 603 N.Y.S.2d 399, 401–02, 623 N.E.2d 526, 528–29 (1993) (determination as to whether an area was "customarily open or accessible" not an issue of interpretation upon which the agency had any special expertise, therefore subject to de novo review); Industrial Liaison Committee v. Williams, 72 N.Y.2d 137, 144, 531 N.Y.S.2d 791, 794, 527 N.E.2d 274, 277 (1988) (agency interpretation of SAPA's rulemaking procedure not a subject on which agencies have any special expertise, therefore subject to *de novo* review).

3. *See, e.g.*, Teachers Insurance and Annuity Ass'n of America v. City of New York, 82 N.Y.2d 35, 41–42, 603 N.Y.S.2d 399, 401–02, 623 N.E.2d 526, 528–29 (1993) (determination of whether an area is one of "special historical or aesthetic interest" is a question calling for the agency's specialized knowledge; therefore, agency determination can only be disturbed in the petitioner can demonstrate its unreasonableness); Medical Malpractice Ins. Ass'n v. Superintendent of Ins. of New York, 72 N.Y.2d 753, 757, 537 N.Y.S.2d 1, 2, 533 N.E.2d 1030, 1031 (1988), cert. denied 490 U.S. 1080, 109 S.Ct. 2100, 104 L.Ed.2d 661 (1989)(agency determinations on specialized issues of law to be disturbed only if unreasonable).

4. *See* Borchers and Markell, *New York State Administrative Procedure and Practice* (West 1998) § 8.3 (discussing cases).

PRACTICE POINTER: From the standpoint of a private petitioner attempting to set aside an agency determination, it is desirable to attempt to characterize the error as one of law. It is considerably easier to persuade courts to reverse agencies on issues of law than on issues of policy, fact or discretion. Within the category of legal errors, the desirable classification from the petitioner's standpoint is one of "pure law," because the agency's determination is entitled to no presumption of correctness. Thus, from the advocate's standpoint, it is desirable to attempt to analogize the question to one of those that appellate courts have characterized as matters of "pure law."

§ 4.78 Judicial Review—Standards of Review—Review of Agency Determinations of Fact Under the Substantial Evidence Test

In circumstances in which agencies make individualized determinations they must make determinations of historical fact. Before an agency can determine, for instance, whether to suspend a tavern's liquor license for serving underage patrons it must determine whether the patrons were, in fact, underage and served alcohol. Agencies must make such determinations in a huge variety of circumstances ranging from the very informal to the relatively formal setting of an adjudicatory proceeding.[1]

Of course, parties unhappy with an agency determination will often dispute the agency's determination of the historical facts, and an important question is what standard of review will a court apply to such factual determinations. An agency's factual determination is clearly entitled to some deference, as the agency has the benefit of seeing the witnesses for itself and having direct access to the relevant evidence. The prerogative writ that was available to challenge agency determinations in formal adjudications—called "adjudicatory proceedings" by SAPA[2]—was the writ of certiorari.[3] The standard of review employed by the writ of *certiorari* was the "substantial evidence" standard, and this standard is carried forward in Article 78.[4]

In practice, the substantial evidence standard is highly deferential to agencies, making it fairly difficult for a petitioner to prevail in its argument that an agency factual finding lacked sufficient evidentiary support. The leading Court of Appeals case on the substantial evidence test is still its 1940 decision *Stork Restaurant v. Boland*.[5] In that case the court held that the substantial evidence test requires only that agency's factual findings be "reasonable."[6] A reviewing court may not set aside an agency's factual findings under this test simply because it would have reached a different result on its own; rather, the agency's determination must be so implausible that the contrary conclusion was the only reasonable one. As a result, courts have held that agency determinations on matters such as witness credibility, motive, intent and other mental states are nearly unassailable.[7]

Although it is relatively difficult for a petitioner to prevail under the substantial evidence standard, it is not impossible. First, if a petitioner can demonstrate a crucial gap in the record—a point upon which the agency failed to develop any probative evidence—the agency's determina-

---

§ 4.78

1. *See* Chapter 36 "Alcohol Beverage Control Law," *infra*.
2. *See* SAPA § 102(3).
3. *See supra*, § 4.75.
4. *See* CPLR 7803(4).
5. 282 N.Y. 256, 26 N.E.2d 247 (1940).
6. *Id.* at 267, 26 N.E.2d at 252.
7. *See, e.g.*, Berenhaus v. Ward, 70 N.Y.2d 436, 443, 522 N.Y.S.2d 478, 481, 517 N.E.2d 193, 196 (1987) (agency credibility determinations effectively unreviewable).

tion can be attacked successfully.[8] Second, if an agency makes a factual determination in the face of overwhelmingly contrary evidence, the determination can be set aside. The substantial evidence test requires a reviewing court to evaluate the "whole record," not just the portion that supports the agency's findings.[9] Third, if an agency reverses its own ALJ on a factual point this tends to make the agency determination vulnerable to attack on judicial review. Although it is the *agency's* (not the ALJ's) factual determination that is subject to substantial evidence review, as a practical matter disagreement between the agency and the ALJ on a factual point may raise serious questions as to the soundness of the agency's conclusions.[10] Finally, because in adjudicatory proceedings agencies are confined to making their determinations "on a record,"[11] an agency determination manifestly based on evidence or considerations not contained in the record is vulnerable to attack on review.[12]

Library References:

West's Key No. Digests, Administrative Law and Procedure ⚖︎791.

§ 4.79 Judicial Review—Standards of Review—Review of Agency Determinations of Fact Under the Arbitrary and Capricious Test

As discussed above, the common law writ that reviewed informal agency determinations was *mandamus* to review, which required the petitioner to demonstrate that the agency's action was "arbitrary and capricious," a standard carried forward into Article 78.[1] Many informal agency actions—often referred to as "administrative actions"[2]—closely resemble adjudicatory proceedings in the sense that both make individualized determinations of the rights and duties of particular persons. The difference is that adjudicatory proceedings, which are reviewed on factual grounds under the substantial evidence test, are more formal, "on a record"[3] determinations, while "administrative actions" are less formal and not subject to the detailed procedures of SAPA. The factual determinations of agencies in these informal matters are reviewed under the "arbitrary and capricious" test.

---

8. *See, e.g.*, New York City Trans. Auth. v. New York State Dep't of Labor, 211 A.D.2d 432, 621 N.Y.S.2d 312 (1st Dep't 1995) (failure of agency to adduce any probative evidence on crucial point as to whether employer failed to list hazardous chemicals means agency's determination must be set aside for lack of substantial evidence).

9. *See, e.g.*, Acosta v. Wollett, 55 N.Y.2d 761, 763, 447 N.Y.S.2d 241, 241, 431 N.E.2d 966, 966 (1981) (review requires examination of whole record).

10. *See, e.g.*, Simpson v. Wolansky, 38 N.Y.2d 391, 380 N.Y.S.2d 630, 343 N.E.2d 274 (1975); Henry v. Wilson, 85 A.D.2d 885, 446 N.Y.S.2d 730 (4th Dep't 1981).

11. *See* SAPA § 102(3).

12. *See, e.g.*, Simpson v. Wolansky, 38 N.Y.2d 391, 380 N.Y.S.2d 630, 343 N.E.2d 274 (1975).

§ 4.79

1. CPLR 7803(3).

2. *See, e.g.*, Gross v. Perales, 72 N.Y.2d 231, 236, 532 N.Y.S.2d 68, 71, 527 N.E.2d 1205, 1208 (1988).

3. SAPA § 102(3).

§ 4.79　　　　　　　ADMINISTRATIVE LAW　　　　　　　Ch. 4

From the verbal difference between the substantial evidence and arbitrary and capricious tests, one might expect there to be significant difference in the way the two are applied, but in fact there is not. In *Pell v. Board of Education*,[4] the Court of Appeals offered an extended restatement of the principles of judicial review of administrative action. The court defined arbitrary action as being "without sound basis in reason and ... without regard to the facts."[5] The court also linked the two standards by stating that "rationality is what is reviewed both under the substantial evidence rule and the arbitrary and capricious standard."[6]

Ultimately, therefore, both the arbitrary and capricious and substantial evidence tests exist to set aside unreasonable factual findings and to validate reasonable ones. Courts applying the arbitrary and capricious test must uphold "rational" or "reasonable" factual determinations,[7] and must not "substitute" their judgment for that of the agency.[8] Thus, as is the case under the substantial evidence test, credibility findings and other purely factual determinations are extremely difficult to assail under the arbitrary and capricious test.[9] The arbitrary and capricious test differs from the substantial evidence test, however, in that in the former the agency is not confined to the administrative record in drawing factual inferences, while under the latter it is.[10] The reason is that in adjudicatory proceedings the agency is required to conduct the hearing "on a record" and to prepare an extensive record, thus providing a reason to confine agency fact finding to that record. In less formal matters, however, an agency is entitled to rely on information in its files and available to it from other sources, as long as the information passes a basic threshold for reliability and trustworthiness.[11]

---

4. 34 N.Y.2d 222, 356 N.Y.S.2d 833, 313 N.E.2d 321 (1974).

5. *Id.* at 231, 356 N.Y.S.2d at 839, 313 N.E.2d at 325.

6. *Id.*

7. *See, e.g.*, Morley v. Arricale, 66 N.Y.2d 665, 495 N.Y.S.2d 966, 486 N.E.2d 824 (1985).

8. *See, e.g.*, Board of Visitors–Marcy Psychiatric Center v. Coughlin, 60 N.Y.2d 14, 20, 466 N.Y.S.2d 668, 671, 453 N.E.2d 1085, 1088 (1983).

9. *See, e.g.*, Heintz v. Brown, 80 N.Y.2d 998, 1001, 592 N.Y.S.2d 652, 654, 607 N.E.2d 799, 801 (1992)(denial of disability benefits to police officer not arbitrary because "evidence to support" finding that officer ignored an obvious hazard); Asen Bros. & Brook v. Leventhal, 54 N.Y.2d 839, 840, 444 N.Y.S.2d 58, 59, 428 N.E.2d 390, 391 (1981)(applying "evidence to support" test).

10. *See, e.g.*, Department of Envt'l Protection of the City of New York v. Department of Envt'l Conservation of the State of New York, 120 A.D.2d 166, 508 N.Y.S.2d 643 (3d Dep't 1986).

11. *See, e.g.*, Fink v. Cole, 1 N.Y.2d 48, 52, 150 N.Y.S.2d 175, 177, 133 N.E.2d 691, 693 (1956).

PRACTICE POINTER: A consequence of the fact that in less formal agency proceedings the agency is not confined to the administrative record, is that on judicial review a trial may be necessary to determine whether the agency really did have an adequate factual basis for making the determination that it did. A trial could be necessary if the parties genuinely dispute the nature of the information available to the agency at the time it decided. *Cf.* York v. McGuire, 99 A.D.2d 1023, 473 N.Y.S.2d 815 (1st Dep't 1984), aff'd 63 N.Y.2d 760, 480 N.Y.S.2d 320, 469 N.E.2d 838 (1984)(trial not necessary because petitioner failed to

The ability to journey outside the administrative record does not mean, however, that the agency is free to invent *post hoc* rationalizations. An agency determination justified on one basis before the agency, but defended on another ground on judicial review, is inherently arbitrary.[12]

Library References:

West's Key No. Digests, Administrative Law and Procedure ⟐763.

§ 4.80 Judicial Review—Standards of Review—Review of Administrative Rules

Review of administrative rules presents some challenging conceptual issues. Administrative rules can be invalidated for purely legal reasons, such as the agency failing to comply with SAPA in promulgating the rule or exceeding the bounds of its statutory delegation of authority.[1] But in the course of deciding whether to promulgate a rule, an agency is required to make policy judgments about the utility and political wisdom of its action. Agency policy judgments of this sort are reviewed under the "arbitrary and capricious" test.[2]

The basis requirement under this test is that the agency has made a "rational" policy decision based upon the information reasonably known to it.[3] Although this standard is deferential to agencies, and most administrative rules are upheld, New York courts are not a rubber stamp for administrative policy judgments. In an important decision, *New York State Association of Counties v. Axelrod*,[4] the Court of Appeals struck down a Department of Health rule readjusting downward the reimbursement rates for nursing homes. A majority of the Court of Appeals held that the agency's explanation for the need for the readjustment—that the nursing homes were completing their paperwork more carefully—had not been justified empirically, and thus could not form the basis for

---

show existence of a triable issue of fact). Perhaps for this reason, jurisdiction in Article 78 matters under the arbitrary and capricious standard is vested in the supreme court, while under the substantial evidence standard the appellate division is the first to pass on the matter. See *infra*, § 4.84.

12. See, e.g., Scherbyn v. Wayne–Finger Lakes Board of Cooperative Educ. Services, 77 N.Y.2d 753, 758, 570 N.Y.S.2d 474, 478, 573 N.E.2d 562, 565 (1991).

§ 4.80

1. See, e.g., Boreali v. Axelrod, 71 N.Y.2d 1, 523 N.Y.S.2d 464, 517 N.E.2d 1350 (1987).

2. PRACTICE POINTER: This test operates as kind of a catch-all in administrative law. As discussed *supra*, § 4.79 this test applies to factual determinations in informal agency action. Because it comes into play in several different areas, this test operates differently from context to context. Thus, in the course of doing research, one should not assume that cases applying the arbitrary and capricious test are necessarily of any precedential value in another context. Instead, one should look for cases applying the test in closely analogous situations.

3. See, e.g., Unimax Corp. v. Tax Appeals Tribunal, 79 N.Y.2d 139, 581 N.Y.S.2d 135, 589 N.E.2d 358 (1992)(controversial tax deduction upheld as a rational exercise of policy judgment).

4. 78 N.Y.2d 158, 573 N.Y.S.2d 25, 577 N.E.2d 16 (1991).

rational agency action.[5] Although the Court later made clear that the *NYSAC* decision does not announce a strict rule that agencies must always justify their rules empirically,[6] and the Court has upheld controversial rules,[7] these recent decisions are a strong message that agencies cannot promulgate rules based on unadorned speculation.

Library References:

West's Key No. Digests, Administrative Law and Procedure ⚖797.

§ 4.81 Judicial Review—Standards of Review—Review of Administrative Discretion

Agencies make determinations that are neither obviously legal nor obviously factual, yet involve discretion and fall within an agency's specialized competence. The best example of this kind of determination is one fixing the penalty after finding a regulatory violation.[1] Article 78 provides that such a determination may be set aside only if "arbitrary and capricious, or an abuse of discretion, including an abuse of discretion as to the measure or mode of penalty or discipline imposed . . ."[2] The most significant case on judicial review of discretionary decisions is *Pell v. Board of Education*,[3] which made clear that agencies are to be given a great deal of deference in such matters, and their determinations are to be upset only in extraordinary circumstances. *Pell* dealt specifically with the problem of administrative penalties, and held that a reviewing court may adjust the agency's determination only if "such punishment is so disproportionate to the offense, in light of all the circumstances, as to be shocking to one's sense of fairness."[4] After *Pell*, most administrative penalties have been upheld, even in cases in which the punishments were quite severe.[5] A petitioner can prevail on an argument that a punishment is excessive by mustering specific arguments that the penalty is disproportionate, such as by showing that persons in similar

---

5. *Id.* at 168, 573 N.Y.S.2d at 31, 577 N.E.2d at 22.

6. *See* Consolation Nursing Home, Inc. v. Commissioner of the New York State Dep't of Health, 85 N.Y.2d 326, 624 N.Y.S.2d 563, 648 N.E.2d 1326 (1995)(rule upheld; documented studies not necessary to justify rule).

7. *See, e.g.*, Chemical Specialties Mfg. Ass'n v. Jorling, 85 N.Y.2d 382, 626 N.Y.S.2d 1, 649 N.E.2d 1145 (1995)(upholding DEC rule limiting DEET concentration in insect repellents to 30%).

§ 4.81

1. *See, e.g.*, Pell v. Board of Educ., 34 N.Y.2d 222, 356 N.Y.S.2d 833, 313 N.E.2d 321 (1974). There are other examples of discretionary determinations, however. *See, e.g.*, Morrissey v. Sobol, 176 A.D.2d 1147, 1150, 575 N.Y.S.2d 960, 963 (3d Dep't 1991)(agency decision on whether to allow supplementation of record within agency's discretion).

2. CPLR 7803(3).

3. 34 N.Y.2d 222, 356 N.Y.S.2d 833, 313 N.E.2d 321 (1974).

4. *Id.* at 233, 356 N.Y.S.2d at 841, 313 N.E.2d at 327 (citations and internal quotations omitted).

5. *See, e.g.*, Berenhaus v. Ward, 70 N.Y.2d 436, 522 N.Y.S.2d 478, 517 N.E.2d 193 (1987)(upholding dismissal of police officers with otherwise exemplary records).

circumstances received less severe treatment from the agency.[6]

Library References:
West's Key No. Digests, Administrative Law and Procedure ☞754.

§ 4.82 Judicial Review—Statutes of Limitation Applicable to Judicial Review of Agency Action

An extremely dangerous area for administrative law practitioners is the question of the Statute of Limitation applicable to seeking judicial review. The law is in flux on such questions, and thus one should always be on guard for statutory changes and new decisions. And the conventional wisdom that a petition should always be filed early enough to avoid creating any doubtful questions is well worth heeding.[1]

The most important statute in judicial review of administrative actions is CPLR 217, which provides generally that "unless a shorter time is provided ... a proceeding against a body or officer must be commenced within four months after the determination to be reviewed becomes final and binding ..."[2] The "shorter time" clause in CPLR 217 is an important reminder that there are special Statutes of Limitation applicable to certain kinds of proceedings that would be otherwise covered by CPLR 217; in fact, by one count there are 30 such statutes lurking in the codes, each one an invitation to malpractice.[3]

Different kinds of administrative actions present different difficulties in determining when the clock on the statutory period begins to run. One of the most problematic areas is calculating the statutory time period for challenging the validity of an administrative rule. For a considerable period of time there was confusion as to whether challenges to administrative rules were even cognizable under Article 78,[4] which in turn raised the question of whether the four-month period of CPLR 217

---

6. *See, e.g.*, Slominski v. Codd, 83 Misc.2d 260, 261, 372 N.Y.S.2d 294, 295 (Sup.Ct., N.Y. County, 1975)(dismissal penalty overturned upon a showing that fellow employee committing same offense received only minor punishment).

PRACTICE POINTER: Making such a showing obviously requires having access to information about penalties imposed in similar circumstances. A good place to begin this search may be by making a Freedom of Information Law request. An advantage to such a request is that it is available even when other forms of discovery are not. If arguments for lenient treatment are to be made, it is obviously desirable to present them to the agency in the first instance. It is far less expensive and stressful on a client to prevail before the agency than on an Article 78 petition, and failure to present the information to the agency may foreclose presenting it on judicial review.

§ 4.82

1. *See* Siegel, *New York Practice* (2d ed. 1991) § 566.

2. CPLR 217.

3. *See* McLaughlin, *Practice Commentaries*, to CPLR 217 C217:1. For a discussion of the 30–day period in Eminent Domain proceedings, *see* Chapter 14 "Eminent Domain Proceedings," *infra* § 14.37 ("30–day Statute of Limitations").

4. *See, e.g.*, Lakeland Water Dist. v. Onondaga County Water Auth., 24 N.Y.2d 400, 301 N.Y.S.2d 1, 248 N.E.2d 855 (1969) (suggesting that "quasi-legislative" administrative action not cognizable under Article 78).

§ 4.82 ADMINISTRATIVE LAW Ch. 4

was indeed the appropriate limitation to apply.[5] But in *New York City Health and Hospitals Corp. v. McBarnette*,[6] the Court of Appeals held that the four-month Statute of Limitations is, indeed, applicable to challenges to administrative rules on the grounds that they are either "arbitrary and capricious" or affected by an "error of law."[7]

Another difficult question in challenging rules is determining when the statutory period begins to run. Some decisions hold that the period begins to run from the date of adoption of the rule.[8] The date of adoption test works well enough when an affected party can determine the impact of the rule on it from the rule's face, but is unfair if only later events determine the rule's impact and whether a party will have a basis for a challenge. In these circumstances, courts have waited to start the four-month clock until the regulated party can determine the rule's impact.[9]

---

5. CAVEAT: There are some older cases holding that some kinds of challenges to administrative action, most commonly constitutional challenges, are subject to the six-year catch-all Statute of Limitations. *See, e.g.*, Lutheran Church in America v. City of New York, 27 A.D.2d 237, 278 N.Y.S.2d 1 (1st Dep't 1967); Rock Hill Sewerage Disposal Corp. v. Town of Thompson, 27 A.D.2d 626, 276 N.Y.S.2d 188 (3d Dep't 1966); Chandler v. Coughlin, 131 Misc.2d 442, 500 N.Y.S.2d 628 (Sup.Ct., Albany County, 1986), rev'd 126 A.D.2d 886, 511 N.Y.S.2d 176 (1987). As discussed in the text of this section, these cases are almost surely not good law. In New York City Health and Hospitals Corp. v. McBarnette, 84 N.Y.2d 194, 616 N.Y.S.2d 1, 639 N.E.2d 740 (1994) and Press v. County of Monroe, 50 N.Y.2d 695, 431 N.Y.S.2d 394, 409 N.E.2d 870 (1980) the Court of Appeals appeared to leave no room for the application of the six-year Statute of Limitations in challenges to *administrative* action. A lawyer should not, therefore, assume that the six year statute governs review of administrative action, even if the form of the action is something other than an Article 78 petition. In McBarnette, for instance, the Court of Appeals held that the fact that the action was styled as an action for declaratory relief was irrelevant, and that the four-month period in CPLR 217 still applied.

6. 84 N.Y.2d 194, 616 N.Y.S.2d 1, 639 N.E.2d 740 (1994).

7. In an earlier case, the Court of Appeals held that CPLR 217 was applicable to a constitutional challenge to a local government's administrative action. *See* Press v. County of Monroe, 50 N.Y.2d 695, 431 N.Y.S.2d 394, 409 N.E.2d 870 (1980). McBarnette and Press seem to cover the entire universe of challenges to administrative rules, leaving no room for the application of the six-year catch-all Statute of Limitations that had been applied by some courts, even if petition for review is styled as a declaratory relief action. *See supra*, note 5. Thus, one should not rely on the earlier cases employing the six-year statute.

8. *See, e.g., id.* at 205, 616 N.Y.S.2d at 6, 639 N.E.2d at 745 (period began from the date of letter memorializing rule); Allstate Ins. Co. v. Stewart, 29 N.Y.2d 925, 329 N.Y.S.2d 102, 279 N.E.2d 858 (1972)("date of adoption" test).

9. *See, e.g.*, New York State Ass'n of Counties v. Axelrod, 78 N.Y.2d 158, 573 N.Y.S.2d 25, 577 N.E.2d 16 (1991)(clock started to run on challenge to rate when affected party received notice of computation of rate as applied to that party). An extremely difficult question is whether a party subject to an enforcement proceeding on the basis of a rule can challenge the validity of an underlying rule, even if the rule is more than four months old. In United States v. Gehl, 852 F.Supp. 1150, 1161–62 (N.D.N.Y.1994), a federal court held that a defendant in a criminal case could challenge the validity of a state regulation that was more than four months old, where a violation of the regulation is an element of the crime. The court's reasoning strongly implied that the same rule would attend in a non-criminal enforcement action, which would appear to be consistent with the philosophy that the clock does not start to run until a party has a reason to know the rule's impact. Authority on this point is difficult to locate, however, and one should probably not rely upon the rule in this case, and should file a challenge to a rule at the earliest possible date.

In doubtful cases, the statutory period should be calculated from the earliest of the alternative dates.

The question of the applicable limitation period for challenging the outcome of adjudicatory proceedings and informal, so-called "administrative" actions, presents different problems. It is clear, absent a special statute, that the four-month statute applies. But the question of when that statutory period starts to run is—as it is in the case of challenges to administrative rules—fraught with some uncertainty. CPLR 217 provides that the period begins to run when the determination is "final and binding," and it is clear that requests for reconsideration of the agency decision do nothing to toll the limitation period—the period starts when the petitioner is notified of the agency's final decision.[10] A difficult question arises, however, when the petitioner is notified of the final decision, but the decision does not take effect until later, as in the case of a decision to discharge a public employee but in which the actual separation from employment occurs some weeks after the final decision. Unfortunately, there is authority on both sides of this question, but the better reasoned and more recent cases hold that the period begins from the *earlier* of the two dates.[11]

The calculus changes once again if the Article 78 proceeding is one in the nature of *mandamus* to compel, that is, to attempt to force an agency to perform a ministerial legal duty.[12] CPLR 217 provides that in such cases the period begins to run "after the [agency's] refusal upon demand to perform its duty . . . "The triggering point, therefore, is the petitioner's notification of the agency's refusal on clear demand.[13] In an important case, however, the Court of Appeals held that an apparently ambiguous refusal by an agency can start the period if the petitioner should know from the surrounding circumstances that the communication is, in fact, a refusal.[14] A petitioner cannot toll the period *ad infinitum* by simply delaying making the demand, because the common law doctrine of laches will bar such actions if the delay prejudices the

---

10. See De Milio v. Borghard, 55 N.Y.2d 216, 220, 448 N.Y.S.2d 441, 442, 433 N.E.2d 506, 507 (1982). On the question of what it means to be "notified," see Borchers and Markell, *New York State Administrative Law* (West 1998) § 8.13.

11. See Edmead v. McGuire, 114 A.D.2d 758, 494 N.Y.S.2d 712 (1st Dep't 1985), aff'd 67 N.Y.2d 714, 499 N.Y.S.2d 934, 490 N.E.2d 853 (1986)(period starts from notification of decision; actual separation from employment irrelevant); *cf.* De Milio v. Borghard, 55 N.Y.2d at 218, 448 N.Y.S.2d at 441, 433 N.E.2d at 506 (stating in a dictum that period begins to run from date of separation from employment, "if later").

CAVEAT: Relying on the "if later" language in De Milio is extremely dangerous in light of Edmead. Again, in any doubt, assume that the period will run from the earliest possible date.

12. See supra, § 4.75 for a discussion of such Article 78 petitions.

13. *See, e.g.*, Austin v. Board of Higher Educ., 5 N.Y.2d 430, 186 N.Y.S.2d 1, 158 N.E.2d 681 (1959).

14. *See* Waterside Assocs. v. New York State Dep't of Envt'l Conservation, 72 N.Y.2d 1009, 534 N.Y.S.2d 915, 531 N.E.2d 636 (1988).

§ 4.82   ADMINISTRATIVE LAW   Ch. 4

agency's position.[15]

If the Article 78 petitioner is in the nature of prohibition, and thus attempting to interrupt an ongoing agency proceeding,[16] there is no formal Statute of Limitations. The reason is that the petitioner always would have the option of waiting until the agency issued a final order, which would then on notification trigger the four-month period to bring a challenge. Thus, the only limitation on an Article 78 petition in the nature of prohibition is the common law doctrine of laches, which again requires the agency to demonstrate that its position has been prejudiced.[17]

Library References:

West's Key No. Digests, Administrative Law and Procedure ⚖️722.

§ 4.83   Judicial Review—Venue in Article 78 Proceedings

Venue in Article 78 proceedings is governed by CPLR 506. In most circumstances venue is allowed

> "[I]n any county within the judicial district where the respondent made the determination complained of or refused to perform the duty specifically enjoined upon him by law, or where the proceedings were brought or taken in the course of which the matter sought to be restrained originated, or where the material events otherwise took place, or the principal office of the respondent is located ... "[1]

Most of the terms in CPLR 506 are relatively free from constructional difficulty. The phrase that probably causes the most consternation is "where the material events otherwise took place." Clearly this term must mean something more than "where the determination was made," because otherwise it is purely redundant.[2] In many circumstances, however, this phrase does not confer any additional venues. But, in circumstances in which events of some significance to the administrative determination occur in another county, this portion of the venue statute broadens the range of venue choices.[3] Even if the venue chosen by the petitioner is one allowed by the statute, courts have fairly broad discretion to transfer matters to serve "the convenience of the material

---

15. See Steinberg, *The Statute of Limitations in Article 78 Practice*, N.Y.St.B.J., Oct. 1990, at 34.

16. See supra, § 4.75.

17. See, e.g., Town of Fenton v. New York State Dep't of Envt'l Conservation, 117 A.D.2d 920, 922, 498 N.Y.S.2d 923, 924 (3d Dep't 1986).

§ 4.83

1. CPLR 506(b).

2. See Weinstein et al., 8 New York Civil Practice ¶ 7804.3 (1992).

3. See, e.g., Hecht v. New York State Teachers' Retirement System, 138 Misc.2d 198, 523 N.Y.S.2d 742 (Sup.Ct., Suffolk County, 1987) (decedent's last domicile confers additional venue in dispute concerning death benefits).

witnesses and the ends of justice ... "[4] Because of a 1992 amendment to CPLR 506, some actions against important state agencies must be venued in Albany County Supreme Court.[5]

Library References:
West's Key No. Digests, Administrative Law and Procedure ⚖664.

§ 4.84 Judicial Review—Subject Matter Jurisdiction in Article 78 Proceedings

Article 78 contains some fairly intricate mechanisms for dividing subject matter jurisdiction between the supreme court and the appellate division.[1] Article 78 petitions naming a state agency are filed, as an original matter, in the supreme court in a county where there is venue.[2] Article 78 petitions that do not raise any substantial evidence question are passed upon in their entirety by the supreme court, leaving—of course—the appellate divisions with appellate jurisdiction over the supreme court's disposition of the matter.[3] If, however, the petition raises a substantial evidence question it must be transferred—with or without a request from either party[4]—to the appellate division embracing the supreme court, so that the appellate division may then dispose of the petition in the first instance.[5]

There is an exception, however, to this "immediate transfer" rule for petitions raising a question of substantial evidence. In cases of "mixed" petitions—those raising a substantial evidence issue along with other issues—the supreme court "shall first dispose of such other objections as could terminate the proceeding, including but not limited to lack of jurisdiction, Statute of Limitations and *res judicata*."[6] The meaning of the term "such other objections as could terminate the proceeding" is not free from doubt. Clearly it covers classic affirmative defenses, including those mentioned in the statute such as *res judicata*,

---

4. CPLR 510(2), (3).

5. CPLR 506(b)(2).

PRACTICE POINTER: In cases in which the venue is not set by special statute, the venue statute allows a range of choices. At a minimum, every county within some judicial district is available. If, for instance, a client needs a quick resolution, it makes sense to choose the venue with the smallest backlog.

§ 4.84

1. *See also* Chapter 37 "Civil Appellate Practice Before the Appellate Division and Other Intermediate Appellate Courts," and Chapter 38 "Criminal Appellate Practice Before the Appellate Division and Other Intermediate Appellate Courts," *infra*.

2. *See* CPLR 506(b).

3. *See* CPLR 7804(g).

4. *See, e.g.,* Tipon v. Appeals Bd. of Administrative Adjudication Bureau, 52 A.D.2d 1065, 384 N.Y.S.2d 324 (4th Dep't 1976) (transfer mandatory even without request from either party).

5. CPLR 7804(g). *See* Chapter 37 "Civil Appellate Practice Before the Appellate Division and Other Intermediate Appellate Courts," and Chapter 38 "Criminal Appellate Practice Before the Appellate Division and Other Intermediate Appellate Courts," *infra*.

6. CPLR 7804(g)(second sentence).

but there is case law interpreting it to mean essentially any dispositive legal or factual point other than the question of substantial evidence.[7]

Fortunately, the problems of subject matter jurisdiction really are more of internal judicial administration than litigation strategy. The petition must be filed in the supreme court. If the supreme court mistakenly decides issues that should have first been resolved by the appellate division, the appellate division is always free to ignore the supreme court's ruling and take the matter up itself on appeal.[8] Conversely, if the supreme court mistakenly transfers a petition to the appellate division, the appellate division is not required to remand to the supreme court, it may take the matter up itself without benefit of the supreme court's views.[9]

Library References:
West's Key No. Digests, Administrative Law and Procedure ⛭663.

§ 4.85 Judicial Review—Summary

Judicial review is an important topic in administrative law, and in some circumstances is the only practical route to relief. A petitioner seeking judicial review of administrative action faces several preliminary considerations. One is whether the agency has been lawfully delegated the power that it purports to be exercising, and has exercised it consistently with that delegation.[1] In the case of rulemaking, agencies are prohibited by separation of powers considerations from making policy wholesale, and in the case of adjudication, are generally prohibited from invading "core" judicial functions such as awarding consequential damages or imprisoning persons. Short of these boundaries, however, agencies have authority to operate.

A party seeking judicial relief faces several important threshold requirements. First, the petitioner must have standing to seek judicial review.[2] Second, the matter must be ripe for review.[3] And third, the petitioner must have exhausted available administrative remedies, or an exception to exhaustion must apply.[4] Judicial review is also generally only available from final agency orders; relief from non-final orders is in

---

7. See Shapiro v. New York City Police Dep't, 157 Misc.2d 28, 595 N.Y.S.2d 864 (Sup.Ct., N.Y. County, 1993), aff'd 201 A.D.2d 333, 607 N.Y.S.2d 320 (1994)(claim of hearing officer bias is an "objection as could terminate the proceeding"); but see G & G Shops, Inc. v. New York City Loft Bd., 193 A.D.2d 405, 597 N.Y.S.2d 65 (1st Dep't 1993) (constitutional objection to agency action not an "objection as could terminate the proceeding").

8. See, e.g., G & G Shops, Inc. v. New York City Loft Bd., 193 A.D.2d 405, 597 N.Y.S.2d 65 (1st Dep't 1993).

9. See, e.g., City School Dist. of City of Elmira v. New York State Public Employment Relations Bd., 144 A.D.2d 35, 536 N.Y.S.2d 214 (3d Dep't 1988), aff'd 74 N.Y.2d 395, 547 N.Y.S.2d 820, 547 N.E.2d 75 (1989).

§ 4.85

1. See supra, § 4.68.
2. See supra, § 4.69.
3. See supra, § 4.70.
4. See supra, § 4.72.

the nature of a writ of prohibition, which requires the petitioner to demonstrate that the agency has acted in excess of its "jurisdiction."[5] In cases in which agencies and courts have concurrent jurisdiction over a matter, the doctrine of primary jurisdiction may require that a court refer an issue to an agency for its disposition, if the agency is expert on that issue.[6] In some circumstances judicial review may be apparently precluded by statute, although the Court of Appeals has consistently held that some minimal amount of judicial review is a constitutional necessity.[7]

Assuming that judicial review is available to the petitioner, the question then becomes the standard under which a court will review the agency action. Article 78 of the CPLR provides a unified mechanism for review of all agency action, including rulemaking—previously thought to be at least partially outside the scope of Article 78. Article 78 consolidates the common law prerogative writs of *certiorari*, *mandamus* and prohibition, and relief is not available unless one of the common law writs would have been available. Moreover, CPLR 7803 carries forward the standards of review that were applied at common law.

Judicial review can be broken down into review of four different kinds of agency determinations. The first is agency determinations of law. These can occur in any administrative setting, as the agency must constantly judge the legal boundaries of its authority, in actions ranging from rulemakings to inspections. Agency determinations of law are reviewed under the non-deferential *de novo* standard if they are questions of "pure law," that is, questions of ordinary legal interpretation on subjects on which the agency is not expert. On legal questions about which the agency has expertise, the agency's determinations of legal issues are reviewed only for reasonableness.[8]

The second is agency determinations of historical fact, such as witness credibility. This occurs when an agency makes an individualized determination, as it does when it decides an adjudicatory proceeding, or makes an informal individualized decision—often called "administrative action." If the agency makes the factual determination in the course of an adjudicatory proceeding, then relief under Article 78 is in the nature of certiorari, and the review is conducted under the substantial evidence test.[9] The substantial evidence test invalidates only those factual conclusions that are irrational in light of the whole administrative record. If the agency makes the factual determination in the course of "administrative action," then relief under Article 78 is in the nature of *mandamus* to review, and the review is conducted under the arbitrary and capricious test.[10] Like the substantial evidence test, this test checks

5. *See supra,* § 4.71.
6. *See supra,* § 4.73.
7. *See supra,* § 4.74.
8. *See supra,* § 4.77.
9. *See supra,* § 4.78.
10. *See supra,* § 4.79.

§ 4.85   ADMINISTRATIVE LAW   Ch. 4

agency determinations for rationality, although the informality of the agency action allows the agency to justify its conclusions with information not contained in the administrative record, as long as it passes a threshold of basic reliability.

Third, agencies make determinations of policy. This occurs in rule-makings in which agencies are required to evaluate the utility and political wisdom of varying courses of action. These policy choices are reviewed under the arbitrary and capricious test, which demands that the policy choices be rational.[11] Recent Court of Appeals decisions have made clear that this review is much more than a rubber stamp of the agency's choice, and that the agency must be able to justify its choices with non-speculative rationales, often backed up by documented studies or evidence.

Fourth, agencies make purely discretionary decisions. Most often these are the penalties to be imposed for regulatory violations. These are reviewed under the "arbitrary and capricious, abuse of discretion" test. Under this test, an agency's penalty must be upheld unless it "shocks" the reviewing court's sense of fairness.[12] As a practical matter, agency penalties are difficult to set aside unless the petitioner can demonstrate that the agency's penalty is substantially disproportionate to penalties assessed in similar cases.

Petitioners must be cognizant of the relevant Statute of Limitations in seeking judicial review. Usually the period is four months, although there are many special statutes setting even shorter periods.[13] Moreover, in some cases the clock on the four-month time period starts to run at surprisingly early juncture, making caution a high virtue. As to choosing the court in which to file a petition, venue is governed by CPLR 506, which in many circumstances gives a fairly broad range of venue choices. Petitions are filed in supreme court, although the appellate division makes the initial determination on substantial evidence questions.

§ 4.86 Judicial Review—Checklist

1. Has the agency been delegated authority to act in the area in which it is acting? (*See* § 4.68)

- Is the agency acting outside the scope of its delegation? (*See* § 4.68)
- If unsure, agencies are generally prohibited from making policy wholesale through exercise of the rulemaking authority. Agencies are generally prohibited from invading core judicial functions, such as awarding consequential damages or imprisoning persons, but may make other significant determinations of the legal rights and duties of persons.

11. *See supra*, § 4.80.
12. *See supra*, § 4.81.
13. *See supra*, § 4.82.

2. Does the petitioner have standing to seek judicial review? (*See* § 4.69)
   - If unsure, an affirmative answer to any of the following will provide standing:
      (i) Has the petitioner suffered an injury (either pecuniary or non-pecuniary) as a result of the agency action, and is the injury within the "zone of interests" protected by the statute (usually defined to mean an injury distinct from the public at large and that the petitioner is the "type" of party meant to be protected by the statute)?

      (ii) Is the petitioner an association with one or more members who would have standing individually, and the suit is "germane" to the association's interests?

      (iii) Is the petitioner a New York taxpayer, and the agency action has a substantial, direct effect on State expenditures or revenues?

3. Is the matter ripe for judicial review? (*See* § 4.70)
   - If unsure, questions of ripeness usually arise if a petitioner is seeking to challenge an administrative rule before the rule has been enforced against the petitioner. The matter is ripe for judicial review pre-enforcement if the enforcement proceeding would not contribute any factual development necessary to resolve the challenge to the rule. Otherwise, the matter is not ripe for judicial review.

4. Has the agency arrived at a final order? (*See* § 4.71)
   - If not, relief must be had in the nature of a writ of prohibition, which requires the petitioner to demonstrate that the agency is acting in excess of its "jurisdiction."

5. Has the petitioner exhausted available administrative remedies? (*See* § 4.72)
   - If not, judicial review is not available unless one or more of the following exceptions apply:
      (i) The challenge to the agency action is a constitutional challenge not requiring resolution of significant factual matters.

      (ii) The agency action is "wholly beyond" the agency's authority.

      (iii) Exhausting administrative remedies would be futile.

      (iv) Exhausting administrative remedies would cause the petitioner irreparable harm.

6. If the matter is one over which the agency and a court have concurrent jurisdiction, does the doctrine of primary jurisdiction require reference of one or more issues to the agency? (*See* § 4.73)

§ 4.86

7. Is there a statute purporting to preclude judicial review? (*See* § 4.74) If not, the ordinary standard of judicial review applies. If so, judicial review is narrowed, but not completely precluded.

8. What standard of review will a court apply in reviewing the agency action? (*See* §§ 4.75—4.81)

- Given the standard of review applied, is seeking judicial review of the agency action cost-justified?

9. When must the petition for judicial review be filed in order to be timely? (*See* § 4.82)

- If unsure, make the following determinations:

    (i) Is there a special Statute of Limitations applicable in this case? If there is, that period is applicable. If there is not, then in all likelihood, the four-month period set forth in CPLR 217 applies, *regardless* of the form in which judicial review is sought.

    (ii) When did the statutory period start to run? Generally this is the date upon which the agency determination is "final and binding" and the parties are so notified, although this can occur even before the determination actually takes effect. Requests for reconsideration before the agency generally do not affect the time to seek judicial review. If still in doubt, calculate the statutory period from the *earliest* possible date.

10. In which counties can the Article 78 petition be venued? (*See* § 4.83)

11. Is the petition one upon which the appellate division will make the initial determination? (*See* § 4.84)

§ 4.87 Forms

What follows are generic forms that can be modified to a particular agency matter. They are general, but would usually be suitable in adjudicatory proceedings under Article 3 of SAPA.

§ 4.88 Forms—Notice of Appearance in Licensing or Permitting Matter

State of New York: Department of _____

_____

In the matter of the application of   )
_____, for a permit to   )
operate a _____ pursuant to   ) NOTICE OF
[*insert*] Article ____, Title ____;   ) APPEARANCE
and also pursuant to Title _____   )
of the Official Compilation of   ) ____ [*agency*] Project
Codes, Rules and Regulations of the   ) No. _____
State of New York.   ) [*insert project number*]
)

_____

Ch. 4 FORMS—NOTICE FOR DISCOVERY § 4.89

PLEASE TAKE NOTICE, that the undersigned attorneys, shall be representing _____ [insert name of party], and hereby appear as the attorneys of record for said [applicant or intervenor] in the above-captioned matter.

Dated: _____, 19___.
_____ [location]

          Yours, etc.

          _____

          Attorney for
          Applicant [or Intervenor]
          P.O. Address
          Tel. No.

To: _____
ALJ's Name
Administrative Law Judge
Agency
P.O. Address
Tel. No.

_____
Agency Attorney's Name
Agency
P.O. Address
Tel. No.

_____
[Other Attorneys]
P.O. Address
Tel. No.

§ 4.89 Forms—Notice for Discovery and Inspection in an Administrative Proceeding

State of New York: Department of _____

In the matter of	)
	) NOTICE FOR DISCOVERY
	) AND INSPECTION
	)
[summarize matter]	)
	) ___ [agency]
	) No. _____
	) [insert matter number]
_____	)

§ 4.89 ADMINISTRATIVE LAW Ch. 4

REQUEST OF ____ [NAME OF PARTY] FOR THE PRODUCTION OF DOCUMENTS

PLEASE TAKE NOTICE, that pursuant to __ NYCRR __ and New York Civil Practice Law and Rules § 3120(a)(1)(i), _____ [name of party], by and through their attorneys hereby request that _____ [name of party from whom discovery is sought] produce for inspection and copying the documents requested below, at the offices of [specify name, address, and time when documents should be produced].

DEFINITIONS

1. "Document" or "documents" includes without limitation all written, printed, typed, recorded, graphic, charted, photographic, electronic, or taped matter, however produced or reproduced, no matter by whom prepared, and all drafts prepared in connection with such documents, whether used or not, and any other tangible object.

DOCUMENT REQUESTS

3. All documents recording, referring, or relating to _____ [specify documents to be produced].

Dated: _____, 19__.
_____ [location]

                                       Yours, etc.

                                       Attorney for
                                       Applicant [or *Intervenor*]
                                       P.O. Address
                                       Tel. No.

To: _____
ALJ's Name
Administrative Law Judge
Agency
P.O. Address
Tel. No.

Agency Attorney's Name
Agency
P.O. Address
Tel. No.

[*Other Attorneys*]
P.O. Address
Tel. No.

§ 4.90 Forms—Notice of Deposition in an Administrative Proceeding

State of New York: Department of _____

In the matter of the application of)
_____, for a permit to _____)
[complete details] pursuant to [insert] Article) NOTICE OF
____, Title ____; and also pursuant to) DEPOSITION
Title ___ of the Official Compilation of) _____ [agency]
Codes, Rules and Regulations of the) Project
State of New York.) No. _____
) [insert project
) number]
_____)

PLEASE TAKE NOTICE, that pursuant to __ NYCRR __ and Article 31 of the Civil Practice Law and Rules the testimony, upon oral examination, of _____ [specify the name and affiliation of proposed deponent], will be taken before a Notary Public who is not an attorney, or employee of an attorney, for any party or prospective party herein, at _____ [insert time, date, and location], with respect to evidence material and necessary in connection with this action:

[Specify name of person] is required to produce at such examination the following:

1. [Specify records and documents] not already included in its submission to the Department of _____ [specify name of agency].

Dated: _____, 19__.
_____ [location]

                                            Yours, etc.

                                            Attorney for
                                            Applicant [or *Intervenor*]
                                            P.O. Address
                                            Tel. No.

To: _____
    ALJ's Name
    Administrative Law Judge
    Agency
    P.O. Address
    Tel. No.

§ 4.90   ADMINISTRATIVE LAW   Ch. 4

Agency Attorney's Name
Agency
P.O. Address
Tel. No.

[*Other Attorneys*]
P.O. Address
Tel. No.

§ 4.91   Forms—Notice to Permit Entry Upon Real Property

State of New York: Department of _____

In the matter of   )
)   NOTICE TO PERMIT ENTRY
)   UPON REAL PROPERTY
)
[*summarize matter*]   )
) ___ [*agency*]
) No. ___
) [*insert matter number*]
)

_____ [*name of party*] REQUEST FOR PERMISSION
TO ENTER UPON REAL PROPERTY

PLEASE TAKE NOTICE, that pursuant to ___ NYCRR ___ and New York Civil Practice Law and Rules § 3120, you are hereby requested to permit [*party seeking permission*], their attorneys, or consultants acting on their behalf to enter upon _____ [*specify type of project and location*], for the purpose of inspecting, measuring, surveying, sampling, testing, photographing or otherwise recording _____ [*specify details to be addressed*].

The entry for the foregoing purpose will be made at _____ [*specify time and date*], or such later date as may be agreed upon by the parties, and will continue from day to day thereafter until the activities described above are complete.

Dated: _____, 19___.
_____ [*location*]

                                             Yours, etc.

                                             Attorney for
                                             Applicant [or *Intervenor*]
                                             P.O. Address
                                             Tel. No.

Ch. 4   PERMIT ENTRY UPON REAL PROPERTY   § 4.91

To: _____
    ALJ's Name
    Administrative Law Judge
    Agency
    P.O. Address
    Tel. No.

Agency Attorney's Name	*[Other Attorney]*
Agency	P.O. Address
P.O. Address	Tel. No.
Tel. No.	

Chapter 5

COMMERCIAL SALES CONTRACTS

by
Lawrence Kaplan

Table of Sections

5.1 Scope Note.
5.2 Strategy.
5.3 Transactional Checklist—Breach of Contract.
5.4 Defining a Contract.
5.5 Governing Law.
5.6 ___ Freedom to Contract—Generally.
5.7 ___ ___ Presumption of Legality.
5.8 ___ ___ ___ Burden of Proof.
5.9 ___ ___ ___ Determining the Contract's Validity.
5.10 ___ ___ ___ Not All Illegal Contracts Are Unenforceable.
5.11 ___ Public Policy Issues.
5.12 ___ Unconscionability.
5.13 ___ ___ Elements.
5.14 ___ ___ Codification in UCC.
5.15 ___ Duty of Good Faith—Generally.
5.16 ___ ___ Codification in UCC.
5.17 The Written Contract—Statute of Frauds.
5.18 ___ ___ General Rules.
5.19 ___ ___ Formal Requirements.
5.20 ___ ___ Nature of the Writing.
5.21 ___ Parol or Extrinsic Evidence.
5.22 ___ Offer.
5.23 ___ Acceptance.
5.24 ___ ___ Additional Terms.
5.25 ___ Indefiniteness.
5.26 ___ Use of Open Terms.
5.27 Warranties.
5.28 ___ Warranty of Title Against Infringement.
5.29 ___ Express Warranty.
5.30 ___ Implied Warranty of Merchantability.
5.31 ___ Implied Warranty of Fitness for a Particular Purpose.
5.32 Assumption of the Risk of Loss.
5.33 ___ In the Absence of Breach.
5.34 ___ In the Event of a Breach.
5.35 Performance.
5.36 ___ Buyer's Response to Tender of Delivery.

Ch. 5   COMMERCIAL SALES CONTRACTS

5.37 __ __ Acceptance.
5.38 __ __ Rejection.
5.39 __ __ Revocation of Acceptance.
5.40 Breach of Contract.
5.41 __ Seller's Remedies.
5.42 __ __ Action for the Price.
5.43 __ __ Withholding the Goods and Stopping Delivery.
5.44 __ __ Recovery of Goods Delivered.
5.45 __ __ Resale.
5.46 __ __ Damages for Non-acceptance or Repudiation.
5.47 __ Buyer's Remedies.
5.48 __ __ Cover.
5.49 __ __ Damages for Non-delivery.
5.50 __ __ Damages for Breach Regarding Accepted Goods.
5.51 __ __ Specific Performance or Replevin.
5.52 __ Liquidated Damages.
5.53 __ Mitigation of Damages.
5.54 Third-Party Interests.
5.55 __ Subsequent Buyers.
5.56 __ Other Creditors.
5.57 Drafting Checklists—Order of Goods for Resale by Buyer.
5.58 __ Verified Complaint On Account Stated for Goods, Services and Wares Delivered.
5.59 __ Plaintiff's Notice of Motion for Summary Judgment in Contract Action.
5.60 __ Affidavit of Officer of Plaintiff Company in Support of Summary Judgment Motion in Contract Action.
5.61 __ Notice of Petition for Order Staying Arbitration in Dispute Over Contract for Sale of Goods.
5.62 __ Petition for Order Staying Arbitration in Dispute Over Contract for Sale of Goods.
5.63 __ Affidavit in Opposition to Petition for Order Staying Arbitration in Dispute Over Contract for Sale of Goods.
5.64 __ Answer to Petition for Order Staying Arbitration in Dispute Over Contract for Sale of Goods.
5.65 Forms—Order of Goods for Resale by Buyer.
5.66 __ Verified Complaint On Account Stated for Goods, Services and Wares Delivered.
5.67 __ Plaintiff's Notice of Motion for Summary Judgment in Contract Action.
5.68 __ Affidavit of Vice President of Plaintiff Purchaser in Support of Summary Judgment Motion in Contract Action.
5.69 __ Notice of Petition for Order Staying Arbitration in Dispute Over Contract for Sale of Goods.
5.70 __ Petition for Order Staying Arbitration in Dispute Over Contract for Sale of Goods.
5.71 __ Affidavit in Opposition to Petition for Order Staying Arbitration in Dispute Over Contract for Sale of Goods.
5.72 __ Answer to Petition for Order Staying Arbitration in Dispute Over Contract for Sale of Goods.

§ 5.1 Scope Note

This chapter provides an overview of basic contract law, with a focus on commercial sales contracts including the distinctive elements of the buyer/seller relationship under Article 2 of the Uniform Commercial Code.

After defining a contract[1] and examining the differences between basic contract law and the law of commercial sales,[2] the chapter moves to a discussion of freedom to contract,[3] including an examination of unconscionability and the duty of good faith under the UCC.[4] Next is an analysis of the need for a written contract,[5] the essential elements of the writing in a commercial context under the Statute of Frauds,[6] parol evidence,[7] offer and acceptance,[8] and how trade usage and course of dealing are used to fill "gaps" in a commercial contract setting.[9] The discussion then moves to treatment of sales warranties[10] and assumption of the risk in the event or absence of a breach.[11] Also covered are performance issues, including acceptance,[12] rejection,[13] and revocation of acceptance.[14] Breach of contract is next covered,[15] including seller's[16] and buyer's remedies,[17] liquidated damages[18] and mitigation of damages.[19]

The chapter concludes with an analysis of third-party interests,[20] drafting checklists,[21] and transactional and litigation forms.[22] Forms include: an order of goods for resale;[23] a complaint on an account stated;[24] a motion for summary judgment in a breach of contract action;[25] and

§ 5.1

1. See infra, § 5.4.
2. See infra, § 5.5.
3. See infra, §§ 5.6–5.10.
4. See infra, §§ 5.11–5.16. For further discussion of commercial sales agreements see Haig, et al., *Commercial Litigation in New York State Courts* (West 1995) Ch. 60 "Sale of Goods."
5. See infra, §§ 5.17–5.18.
6. See infra, §§ 5.19–5.20.
7. See infra, § 5.21.
8. See infra §§ 5.22–5.24.
9. See infra, §§ 5.25–5.26.
10. See infra, §§ 5.27–5.31.
11. See infra, §§ 5.32—5.34.
12. See infra, § 5.37.
13. See infra, § 5.38.
14. See infra, § 5.39.
15. See infra, § 5.40.
16. See infra, §§ 5.41—5.46.
17. See infra, §§ 5.47—5.51.
18. See infra, § 5.52.
19. See infra, § 5.53. See also, Chapter 30 "Damages," *infra*.
20. See infra, §§ 5.54—5.56.
21. See infra, §§ 5.57—5.64.
22. See infra, §§ 5.65–5.72.
23. See infra, § 5.65.
24. See infra, § 5.66.
25. See infra, §§ 5.67, 5.68.

papers pursuant to a petition for a stay of commercial arbitration.[26]

Library References:

West's Key No. Digests, Sales ⚖1–53(3).

§ 5.2 Strategy

Unless a transaction is of unusual scope and size, practitioners will usually not be retained until the contract is in breach. For that reason, this section is focused on those instances in which either buyer or seller is charged with breach of contract, rather than focusing on strategies for drafting instruments. Likewise, the chapter itself is focused on enforceability of the instrument, performance, breach and remedies, rather than contract drafting.

Should a breach occur, there are a number of remedies available, and there is much that can be done to maximize recovery, minimize exposure, and ensure that a party is in a legally defensible position.[1] Additionally, the buyer and seller each have certain legal obligations to mitigate damages when the other party defaults.[2] The practitioner should be thoroughly familiar with these and be ready to provide sound advice where necessary to protect a client's interests.

When interviewing the commercial client, it is important to obtain not only all relevant original documents and detailed information pertinent to the dispute, but also a factual history of dealings between the parties. This history may be useful in resolving the current dispute. The practitioner should request the names of all witnesses and individuals involved in the transaction(s), as well as their addresses, phone numbers and their respective roles in the transactions. Counsel should also advise the client to avoid discussing the case with anyone and to refer all questions regarding the dispute to counsel.

It is advisable to prepare a letter with detailed instructions to the client as to the course of business with the adversary party. Each such letter of instruction depends, of course, upon the facts and circumstances of the case. The practitioner should not provide the client with a boilerplate letter used in all cases. Standardized letters should be customized at least in part, with instructions that are unique to the circumstances.

A buyer who has rejected a delivery of non-conforming goods should be advised to notify the seller of the rejection within a reasonable time.[3] Although the term "reasonable" is open to interpretation, it is obvious that sooner is better than later.

26. See infra, §§ 5.69—5.72.

§ 5.2

1. See infra, §§ 5.40 et seq.

2. See infra, § 5.53.

3. See infra, § 5.38.

Counsel must also make sure that the buyer will be able to establish proof that the seller received notice of the rejection. The buyer should be advised that any exercise of ownership after rejection is wrongful. Also, a buyer who has taken physical possession of goods prior to rejecting them must be advised to retain them, using reasonable care, and must permit the seller to remove them.[4]

Counsel should also inform the buyer of its obligation to follow the seller's reasonable instructions about the goods after rejection, and that absent such instructions, the buyer must make an effort to sell perishable goods. The buyer is entitled to reimbursement for its reasonable expenses and should be advised to document such expenditures.

If no instructions are provided, the buyer may be instructed by counsel to store the goods for the seller's account, reship them, or sell them for the seller's account. In all its actions with regard to rejected goods, however, the buyer must at all times be advised to act in good faith.

If the buyer has revoked its acceptance of goods because its discovery of non-conformity occurred after acceptance, or because the seller has reneged on a promise to cure, counsel should advise the buyer to provide notice of the rejection within a reasonable time.

Counsel representing the seller will likewise be called upon to give advice in the event of breach. If the buyer has breached by revoking acceptance, failing to make payment, or repudiating the contract in whole or part, counsel should advise the seller of the alternative courses of action that may be available to it: Depending upon the circumstances, it may withhold delivery; stop delivery by a bailee; resell undelivered goods and seek recovery of damages; use its judgment about completing the manufacture of unfinished goods; seek recovery of damages for non-acceptance or for the price; and/or cancel the contract.[5]

Counsel should pay particular attention to the requirements of a complaint for breach of contract. There are many different types of breach, each with its own elements that are required to be alleged in a complaint.[6]

§ 5.3 Transactional Checklist—Breach of Contract

It is important to carefully consider the range of remedies available to a buyer or seller in the event of a breach of contract. The checklist below should be reviewed to determine available remedies.

1. If the seller breaches the contract by shipment of non-conforming goods, the buyer:

---

4. *See infra,* § 5.38.

5. *See infra,* § 5.41.

6. *See infra,* §§ 5.3, 5.41, 5.47, 5.58 for allegations of breach of contract in particular areas, and *see infra,* §§ 5.66–5.72 for illustrative forms to be used in litigation.

- May accept the whole;[1]
- May reject the whole;[2]
- May accept part and reject part;[3]
- must provide timely notice of rejection of whole or part.[4] (*See* §§ 5.36—5.39)

2. A buyer may revoke prior acceptance on the grounds that:
   - The seller promised to cure a non-conforming delivery of goods and failed to do so;[5] or
   - The non-conformity of goods was not discovered until after acceptance based on the difficulty of discovery or the seller's assurances as to the quality of the goods.[6] (*See* § 5.39)

3. A buyer who is in possession of rejected goods should:
   - Retain them, using reasonable care to preserve them;[7]
   - Follow the seller's reasonable instructions;[8]
   - In the absence of instructions, make efforts to sell perishable goods;[9]
   - If no instructions have been provided, the buyer may reship the goods, store the goods for the seller's account, or sell them for the seller's account.[10] (*See* § 5.38)

4. A buyer's remedies for a seller's breach include the following options:
   - Cancel the contract;[11]
   - Recover so much of the price as has been paid;[12]
   - Cover, by purchasing goods in substitution;[13]
   - Recover damages for non-delivery;[14]
   - Recover goods that have been identified to the contract;[15]
   - In a proper case, obtain specific performance or replevy the goods.[16] (*See* §§ 5.47 *et seq.*)

5. A buyer may breach a contract by:

§ 5.3

1. UCC § 2–601(b).
2. UCC § 2–601(a).
3. UCC § 2–601(c).
4. UCC § 2–602.
5. UCC § 2–608(1)(a).
6. UCC § 2–608(1)(b).
7. UCC § 2–602(2)(b).
8. UCC § 2–603(1).
9. *Id.*
10. UCC § 2–604.
11. UCC § 2–711(1).
12. *Id.*
13. UCC §§ 2–711(1)(a), 2–712(1).
14. UCC §§ 2–711(1)(b), 2–713.
15. UCC §§ 2–502, 2–711(2)(a).
16. UCC §§ 2–711(2)(b), 2–716.

- Wrongful rejection of delivery;[17]
- Wrongful revocation of acceptance;[18]
- Failure to make payment;[19] or
- Repudiation of the contract in whole or in part.[20]

6. If a buyer breaches the contract, the seller may:
   - Withhold delivery;[21]
   - Stop delivery by a bailee;[22]
   - Resell undelivered goods and recover damages;[23]
   - Use reasonable judgment and good faith about completing manufacture of unfinished goods;[24]
   - Recover damages for non-acceptance,[25] or in a proper case recover the price;[26]
   - Cancel the contract.[27] (*See* §§ 5.41 *et seq.*)

§ 5.4 Defining a Contract

The most oft-used definition of a contract is a promise or set of promises for the breach of which the law provides a remedy, or the performance of which the law recognizes as a duty.[1] This is a rather static definition, for it fails to consider the wide range of agreements that are fully executed. A more helpful (although not perfect) definition is that provided by the Uniform Commercial Code, *i.e.*, that a contract is the total legal obligation that results from the bargain of the parties as found in their language or by implication from other circumstances, including course of dealing, usage of trade and course of performance, as affected by the rules of law.[2] While this is a useful definition, it is not, and cannot be, the final word on the subject because "transactions are continually escaping from old forms and patterns ... [while] new classifications are continually required, and old generalizations must be limited or replaced."[3]

Library References:

West's Key No. Digests, Contracts ⋘1–142; Sales ⋘1–53(3).

17. UCC § 2–703.
18. UCC §§ 2–703, 2–607.
19. UCC § 2–703.
20. *Id.*
21. UCC § 2–703(a).
22. UCC §§ 2–703(b), 2–705.
23. UCC §§ 2–703(d), 2–706.
24. UCC § 2–704(2).
25. UCC §§ 2–703(e), 2–708.
26. UCC §§ 2–703(e), 2–709.
27. UCC § 2–703(f).

§ 5.4

1. *Corbin on Contracts*, § 1.3 (West 1993). *See also Restatement (Second) Contracts* § 1.
2. *Id.* at p.13. *See* UCC § 1–201(3), (11).
3. *Id.* at p.13.

§ 5.5 Governing Law

UCC § 1-103 provides that unless displaced by a particular provision of the UCC, the principles of law and equity, including the law merchant and the law relative to capacity to contract, principal and agent, estoppel, fraud, misrepresentation, duress, coercion, mistake, bankruptcy, or other validating or invalidating cause shall supplement its provisions. Essentially this Section provides that unless explicitly displaced by statutory provision, basic common law principles of contract law are applicable to the sales of goods.

Some areas of divergence between common law and Article 2 include unconscionable contract terms;[1] transfer of the risk of loss to the holder of goods;[2] rights of *bona fide* purchasers;[3] and limitations on the buyer's right of rejection in case of a breach.[4]

§ 5.6 Governing Law—Freedom to Contract, Generally

Fully competent individuals may freely enter into enforceable contracts with other parties.[1] Absent some violation of law or transgression of a strong public policy, the parties to a contract are basically free to make whatever agreement they wish.[2] The power to contract, however, is not unlimited, as there are restrictions imposed by legislation, public policy, and the "nature of things."[3] Parties cannot enter into an enforceable contract in violation of law or of public policy, nor can they by agreement " ...change the laws of nature, or of logic, or create relations, physical, legal, or moral, which can not be created."[4]

Library References:

West's Key No. Digests, Contracts ⇒1-142.

§ 5.7 Governing Law—Freedom to Contract—Presumption of Legality

It is a generally accepted rule that when a contract requires something to be done which cannot be performed without violating the law,

§ 5.5

1. *See infra,* §§ 5.12 *et seq.*
2. *See infra,* §§ 5.32-5.34.
3. *See infra,* § 5.38. *See infra,* § 5.55.
4. **PRACTICE POINTER:** Since Article 2 of the UCC supersedes basic contract law, in the event of a breach of a sales contract, the search for a remedy must begin with a review of the applicable provisions of the Code before resort is made to the common law.

§ 5.6

1. 379 Madison Avenue, Inc. v. Stuyvesant Co., 242 A.D. 567, 570, 275 N.Y.S. 953, 956 (1st Dep't 1934), aff'd 268 N.Y. 576, 198 N.E. 412 (1935).
2. Rowe v. Great Atlantic & Pacific Tea Co., Inc., 46 N.Y.2d 62, 412 N.Y.S.2d 827, 385 N.E.2d 566 (1978).
3. Sternaman v. Metropolitan Life Insurance Co., 170 N.Y. 13, 19, 62 N.E. 763, 764 (1902).
4. *Id.*

the contract is void and unenforceable.[1] When a contract, however, is to do something which is capable of lawful performance, as well as performance in violation of the law, the contract is presumed valid so long as there is no proof that both parties intended to violate the law.[2] Even knowledge on the part of a seller that the buyer intends to use the property unlawfully is not necessarily a good defense to an action, by the seller for the price of the property.[3] Thus, whenever possible, contracts are construed in favor of their legality[4] and are presumed legal until it appears upon their face or by pleading that they are illegal.[5]

However, no court will allow itself to be made the instrument of enforcing obligations arising out of an illegal agreement or transaction.[6] A party to an illegal contract may not ask a court to help carry out the illegal object; nor may a party plead or prove a case in which, as a basis for the claim, they must show an illegal purpose.[7] Nevertheless, under principles of equity, a person may not be unjustly enriched at the expense of another. Thus, although a contract is tainted with illegality, and recovery may not be had on the basis of express contract, relief may be granted upon an implied contract " ...founded upon the moral obligation resting upon the defendant to account for the value of the money or property or services received."[8]

§ 5.7

1. Lloyd Capital Corp. v. Pat Henchar, Inc., 80 N.Y.2d 124, 589 N.Y.S.2d 396, 603 N.E.2d 246 (1992); New York State Medical Transporters Ass'n v. Perales, 77 N.Y.2d 126, 564 N.Y.S.2d 1007, 566 N.E.2d 134 (1990); Dodge v. Richmond, 10 A.D.2d 4, 196 N.Y.S.2d 477 (1st Dep't 1960), aff'd 8 N.Y.2d 829, 203 N.Y.S.2d 90, 168 N.E.2d 531(1960); Village of Upper Nyack v. Christian & Missionary Alliance, 143 Misc.2d 414, 540 N.Y.S.2d 125 (Sup.Ct., Rockland County, 1988), aff'd 155 A.D.2d 530, 547 N.Y.S.2d 388 (2d Dep't 1989).

2. Telemark Constr. v. Greenberg, 205 A.D.2d 438, 613 N.Y.S.2d 900 (1st Dep't 1994); Lee v. Caric, 125 A.D.2d 453, 509 N.Y.S.2d 383 (2d Dep't 1986).

3. Dodge v. Richmond, 10 A.D.2d 4, 14, 196, N.Y.S.2d 477, 486 (1st Dep't 1960), aff'd 8 N.Y.2d 829, 203 N.Y.S.2d 90, 168 N.E.2d 531 (1960).

4. Shedlinsky v. Budweiser Brewing Co., 163 N.Y. 437, 439, 57 N.E. 620 (1900); Brum v. Niagara Falls, 145 A.D.2d 928, 535 N.Y.S.2d 856 (4th Dep't 1988), app. denied 74 N.Y.2d 608, 545 N.Y.S.2d 104, 543 N.E.2d 747.

5. Brearton v. DeWitt, 252 N.Y. 495, 500, 170 N.E. 119, 120 (1930); Posner v. United States Fidelity & Guaranty Co., 33 Misc.2d 653, 226 N.Y.S.2d 1011, aff'd 16 A.D.2d 1013, 229 N.Y.S.2d 160 (3d Dep't 1962).

6. Carmine v. Murphy, 285 N.Y. 413, 35 N.E.2d 19 (1941).

7. Stone v. Freeman, 298 N.Y. 268, 271, 82 N.E.2d 571, 572 (1948); United Calendar Mfg. Corp. v. Huang, 94 A.D.2d 176, 463 N.Y.S.2d 497 (2d Dep't 1983); Braunstein v. Jason Tarantella, Inc., 87 A.D.2d 203, 450 N.Y.S.2d 862 (2d Dep't 1982).

8. Katz v. Zuckermann, 126 Misc.2d 135, 138, 481 N.Y.S.2d 271, 274 (Sup.Ct., Queens County, 1984), aff'd 119 A.D.2d 732, 501 N.Y.S. 2d 144 (1986).

PRACTICE POINTER: Where a client discloses that its contract is tainted with illegality, counsel should consider advising the client to mitigate damages and to act in good faith. For example, if the client is a wholesaler in a sale of goods between the manufacturer and the ultimate purchaser, and the client discovers that the goods sold are illegal (*e.g.*, unsterilized gloves sold as sterilized to a hospital), counsel should advise the client to immediately inform the purchaser of the problem at the earliest possible time and negotiate from there. Hiding the fact of the illegality will only inure to the client's detriment in any subsequent litigation.

Furthermore, a contract will not be rendered void unless an intention to violate the law clearly appears.[9] Thus, the mere possibility that a party in performing a contract might break the law is not sufficient to render the contract void.[10]

Library References:

West's Key No. Digests, Contracts ⚖141(1).

§ 5.8 Governing Law—Freedom to Contract—Presumption of Legality—Burden of Proof

Unless the illegality of a contract appears on the face of the complaint, it must be pleaded as an affirmative defense.[1] Although the courts will not enforce an illegal bargain, the defendant must show that plaintiff's cause of action arose out of, or in connection with, the illegality asserted.[2] Connection, however, is a matter of degree. If the illegalities are incidental to the contract sued on, they will not insulate a party from liability for work done or goods furnished.[3] Since a contract is presumed to be valid and enforceable, once a plaintiff has established a *prima facie* case, the burden is on the defendant to prove that the contract is illegal.[4]

Where a contract is alleged to be void by statute, facts must be pleaded showing the nature of the illegality, and that the contract was made within the jurisdiction where the prohibitive statute is effective.[5]

Library References:

West's Key No. Digests, Contracts ⚖141(1).

9. I. Tanenbaum Son & Co. v. Brooklyn Furniture Co., 229 A.D. 469, 470, 242 N.Y.S. 381, 382 (1st Dep't 1930), aff'd 255 N.Y. 579, 175 N.E. 321 (1930).

10. Hizington v. Eldred Refining Co. of New York, 235 A.D. 486, 488, 257 N.Y.S. 464, 467 (4th Dep't 1932).

§ 5.8

1. CPLR 3018(b). *See* Brearton v. DeWitt, 252 N.Y. 495, 500, 170 N.E. 119, 120 (1930); *see also* National Recovery Systems v. Mazzei, 123 Misc.2d 780, 475 N.Y.S.2d 208 (Sup.Ct., Suffolk County, 1984); Vrooman v. Village of Middleville, 106 Misc.2d 945, 436 N.Y.S.2d 662 (Sup.Ct., Herkimer County, 1981).

PRACTICE POINTER: Where it appears that the contract is illegal, counsel drafting any complaint based on the contract would be well advised to add actions resting in equitable remedies such as unjust enrichment, *quantum meruit* or quasi contract. This will permit recovery even though the contract is not enforceable.

2. Bunge Corporation v. Manufacturers Hanover Trust, 65 Misc.2d 829, 845, 318 N.Y.S.2d 819, 838 (Sup.Ct., N.Y. County, 1971), mod. on other grounds 37 A.D.2d 409, 325 N.Y.S.2d 983 (1st Dep't 1971), aff'd 31 N.Y.2d 223, 335 N.Y.S.2d 412, 286 N.E.2d 903 (1972).

3. McConnell v. Commonwealth Pictures Corp., 7 N.Y.2d 465, 471, 199 N.Y.S.2d 483, 487, 166 N.E.2d 494, 497 (1960).

4. Liss v. Manuel, 58 Misc.2d 614, 616, 296 N.Y.S.2d 627, 630 (Civ.Ct., N.Y. County, 1968) citing Springs v. James, 137 A.D. 110, 121 N.Y.S. 1054 (1st Dep't 1910), aff'd 202 N.Y. 603, 96 N.E. 1131 (1910); *see also* Murray v. Narwood, 192 N.Y. 172, 177, 84 N.E. 958, 959 (1908).

5. Donnelly v. Bauder, 217 A.D. 59, 61, 216 N.Y.S. 437, 438 (4th Dep't 1926).

§ 5.9 Governing Law—Freedom to Contract—Presumption of Legality—Determining the Contract's Validity

A contract's validity is determined as of the time the contract was entered into,[1] except that it may be affected by subsequent legislation in the exercise of the police power or by a subsequent statute announcing a new public policy or by repeal of a prohibitory act.[2] There is no distinction in principle between a contract rendered void due to its unlawfulness at the time of its execution and a contract rendered void because a subsequent change in the law has made its further performance unlawful.[3]

As a general rule, a contract's validity is determined by the law of the jurisdiction where the contract was made.[4] A well-established exception to this rule provides that the courts will not enforce a contract, despite its being valid where made, if its enforcement would contravene the state's public policy.[5]

Library References:
West's Key No. Digests, Contracts ⚖101–142.

§ 5.10 Governing Law—Freedom to Contract—Presumption of Legality—Not All Illegal Contracts Are Unenforceable

Although illegal contracts are generally unenforceable,[1] the violation of a statute that is merely *malum prohibitum* (*i.e.*, an act which would not be prohibited but for the statute) will not necessarily render a contract unenforceable.[2] Relief in such cases will not be denied if the statute which had been violated does not expressly provide that its violation would result in the deprivation of the parties' right to sue on the contract, and if the *denial* of relief is entirely out of proportion to the

§ 5.9

1. Goldfarb v. Goldfarb, 86 A.D.2d 459, 450 N.Y.S.2d 212 (2d Dep't 1982).

2. In re Guccione, 41 B.R. 289 (Bank. S.D.N.Y.1984).

3. Commoss v. Pearson, 190 A.D. 699, 180 N.Y.S. 482, 485 (1st Dep't 1920).

4. Russell v. Societe Anonyme Des Etablissements Aeroxon, 268 N.Y. 173, 181, 197 N.E. 185, 188 (1935).

5. People v. Martin, 175 N.Y. 315, 320–321, 67 N.E. 589, 591 (1903); *see* Fox v. Ashland Oil, Inc., 134 A.D.2d 850, 521 N.Y.S.2d 594 (4th Dep't 1987) (court refused to enforce contract which as a result of its being excessively broad, was counter to New York's public policy despite the fact that the contract provided that its terms should be interpreted under Kentucky law where the language would be enforceable); Clifton Steel Corp. v. General Electric Co., 80 A.D.2d 714, 437 N.Y.S.2d 734 (3d Dep't 1981) (waiver of right to file mechanic's lien was valid under the law of Connecticut, where the contract was made, but will not be enforced in New York, as against public policy).

§ 5.10

1. John E. Rosasco Creameries v. Cohen, 276 N.Y. 274, 278, 11 N.E.2d 908, 909 (1937); *see also* Lloyd Capital Corp. v. Pat Henchar, Inc. 80 N.Y.2d 124, 127, 589 N.Y.S.2d 396, 397, 603 N.E.2d 246 (1992).

2. *Id.*

requirements of public policy or appropriate individual punishment.[3] Nevertheless, the Court of Appeals has refused, on public policy grounds, to enforce agreements entered into in violation of statutes that were enacted to protect public health and safety.[4]

Library References:
West's Key No. Digests, Contracts ⟜138(1).

§ 5.11 Governing Law—Public Policy Issues

The refusal of courts to enforce contracts which are against public policy is based upon the theory that such an agreement is injurious to the interests of society in general, and that the only way to stop the making of such contracts is to refuse to enforce them,[1] leaving the parties without a remedy for their breach.[2] Public policy essentially refers to the law of the state, whether based on the Constitution, the statutes, or judicial decisions.[3] However, because public policy is continually evolving, controversies involving questions of public policy can rarely, if ever, be resolved by the blind application of sedentary legal principles.[4] Contracts are illegal at common law, as being against public policy, when they are such as to injuriously affect or subvert the public interests. As a matter of public policy, courts will never recognize or uphold any transaction which in its object, operation, or tendency, is calculated to be prejudicial to the public welfare.[5] It is not necessary to plead the illegality of a contract which is contrary to public policy; the court on its own motion, will intervene and deny the right to any relief under the contract, regardless of the pleadings, whenever it becomes apparent that the agreement is antagonistic to the interests of the public.[6]

3. Id.

4. Lloyd Capital Corp. v. Pat Henchar, Inc. 80 N.Y.2d 124, 128, 589 N.Y.S.2d 396, 398, 603 N.E.2d 246 (1992); see Charlebois v. J.M. Weller Associates, Inc., 72 N.Y.2d 587, 535 N.Y.S.2d 356, 531 N.E.2d 1288 (1988). As to public policy issues see infra, § 5.11.

§ 5.11

1. Attridge v. Pembroke, 235 A.D. 101, 102, 256 N.Y.S. 257, 260 (4th Dep't 1932).

2. See Hartman v. Bell, 137 A.D.2d 585, 524 N.Y.S.2d 477 (2d Dep't 1988); United Calendar Mfg. Corp. v. Huang, 94 A.D.2d 176, 463 N.Y.S.2d 497 (2d Dep't 1983).

3. F.A. Straus and Co. v. Canadian Pacific Railway Co., 254 N.Y. 407, 413, 173 N.E. 564, 566 (1930); Walters v. Fullwood, 675 F.Supp. 155 (S.D.N.Y.1987).

4. Matter of Sprinzen, 46 N.Y.2d 623, 415 N.Y.S.2d 974, 389 N.E.2d 456 (1979).

In its discussion on the evolving nature of public policy, the Court of Appeals wrote: "The very nature of the concept of public policy militates against any attempt to define its ingredients in a manner which would allow one to become complacent in the thought that those precepts which society steadfastly embraces today will continue to serve as the foundation upon which society will function tomorrow." Id. at 628.

5. Johnston v. Fargo, 184 N.Y. 379, 384, 77 N.E. 388, 390 (1906); Village of Upper Nyack v. Christian & Missionary Alliance, 143 Misc.2d 414, 540 N.Y.S.2d 125 (Sup.Ct., Rockland County, 1988), aff'd 155 A.D.2d 530, 547 N.Y.S.2d 388 (2d Dep't 1989).

6. Attridge v. Pembroke, 235 A.D. 101, 102, 256 N.Y.S. 257, 260 (4th Dep't 1932); National Recovery Systems v. Mazzei, 123 Misc.2d 780, 475 N.Y.S.2d 208 (Sup.Ct., Suffolk County, 1984).

§ 5.11 COMMERCIAL SALES CONTRACTS Ch. 5

A contract is not void as against public policy unless it attempts to contravene a statute or a well-grounded principle of the common law or its operation has a tendency injurious to and against the public, and it conflicts with the morals of the time or contravenes some well-established interest of society.[7]

As a matter of public policy, the law generally looks with disfavor upon contracts intended to absolve individuals from the consequences of their own negligence, and to the extent such agreements bar suits against willful or gross negligence, they are void.[8] However, where a claim sought to be foreclosed is one grounded in ordinary negligence, the contract may be enforced, but only after the agreement has been subjected to intense judicial scrutiny whereby the agreement will be strictly construed against its draftsman.[9] Parties will not be presumed to have intended to exempt themselves from the consequences of their own negligence in the absence of express and unmistakable language to that effect.[10] For an exculpatory clause to be given legal effect, it must precisely provide that the limitation of liability " ...extends to [the] negligence or other fault of the party attempting to shed his ordinary responsibility."[11] As the Court of Appeals held in *Gross v. Sweet*:[12]

> By and large, if [it] is the intention of the parties to [exclude liability for negligence], the fairest course is to provide explicitly that claims based on negligence are included [in the exculpatory language].... That does not mean that the word 'negligence' must be employed for courts to give effect to an exculpatory agreement; however, words conveying a similar import must appear.[13]

Library References:

West's Key No. Digests, Contracts ⚛︎108.

---

7. F. F. Proctor Troy Properties Co. v. Dugan Store, 191 A.D. 685, 688, 181 N.Y.S. 786, 789 (3d Dep't 1920); *see also* Birger v. Tuner, 104 Misc.2d 63, 427 N.Y.S.2d 904 (Civ.Ct., Queens County, 1980).

8. Gross v. Sweet, 49 N.Y.2d 102, 106, 424 N.Y.S.2d 365, 367, 400 N.E.2d 306, 308 (1979); *see also* Willard Van Dyke Prods v. Eastman Kodak Co., 12 N.Y.2d 301, 304, 239 N.Y.S.2d 337, 340, 189 N.E.2d 693 (1963); Ciofalo v. Vic Tanney Gyms, 10 N.Y.2d 294, 220 N.Y.S.2d 962, 177 N.E.2d 925 (1961); Abramowitz v. New York University Dental Center, College of Dentistry, 110 A.D.2d 343, 494 N.Y.S.2d 721 (2d Dep't 1985).

9. Abramowitz v. New York University Dental Center, College of Dentistry, 110 A.D.2d 343, 494 N.Y.S.2d 721, 723 (2d Dep't 1985); *see also* Gross v. Sweet, 49 N.Y.2d 102, 106, 424 N.Y.S.2d 365, 367, 400 N.E.2d 306, 308 (1979).

10. *See* Willard Van Dyke Productions, Inc. v. Eastman Kodak Co., 12 N.Y.2d 301, 304, 239 N.Y.S.2d 337, 340, 189 N.E.2d 693 (1963) (language which is "absolutely clear"); Ciofalo v. Vic Tanney Gyms, 10 N.Y.2d 294, 297, 220 N.Y.S.2d 962, 965, 177 N.E.2d 925 (1961) (language which is "sufficiently clear and unequivocal"); Boll v. Sharp & Dohme, 281 A.D. 568, 121 N.Y.S.2d 20 (1st Dep't 1953), aff'd 307 N.Y. 646, 120 N.E.2d 836 (1954) (language which is "clear and explicit").

11. Howard v. Handler Bros. & Winell, Inc., 279 A.D. 72, 76, 107 N.Y.S.2d 749, 753 (1st Dep't 1951), aff'd 303 N.Y. 990, 106 N.E.2d 67 (1952); *see* Rappaport v. Phil Gottlieb–Sattler, Inc., 280 A.D. 424, 114 N.Y.S.2d 221 (1st Dep't 1952), aff'd 305 N.Y. 594, 111 N.E.2d 647 (1953).

12. Gross v. Sweet, 49 N.Y.2d 102, 424 N.Y.S.2d 365, 400 N.E.2d 306 (1979).

13. *Id.* at 107–108, 424 N.Y.S.2d at 368, 400 N.E.2d at 309.

§ 5.12 Governing Law—Unconscionability

An unconscionable contract has been defined by the Court of Appeals as one which is " ...so grossly unreasonable ... in light of the mores and business practices of the time and place as to be unenforceable according to its literal terms."[1] Unconscionability is a flexible doctrine, rooted in equitable principles, and intended " ...to be sensitive to the realities and nuances of the bargaining process."[2] The concept has been employed primarily in the area of consumer protection in an attempt to deal with " ...[the] never ending stream of consumer gypsters and fraudulent operators, whose principal victims are the poor."[3] The doctrine is primarily a means by which to protect " ...[the] commercially illiterate consumer beguiled into a grossly unfair bargain by a deceptive vendor or finance company."[4] The doctrine has little applicability in the commercial setting because it is presumed that business people deal at arm's length with relative equality of bargaining power.[5] Commercial transactions by business people in a commercial setting, under terms that are standard in the trade, give rise to a presumption of lack of unconscionability.[6]

Library References:
West's Key No. Digests, Contracts ⟐1.

§ 5.13 Governing Law—Unconscionability—Elements

An agreement will not be set aside as unconscionable simply because it was improvident.[1] A determination of unconscionability generally

§ 5.12

1. Gillman v. Chase Manhattan Bank, N.A., 73 N.Y.2d 1, 10, 537 N.Y.S.2d 787, 791, 534 N.E.2d 824 (1988), quoting Mandel v. Liebman, 303 N.Y. 88, 94, 100 N.E.2d 149, 154 (1951).

PRACTICE POINTER: As a practical matter, the concept of unconscionability will not often be successfully applied in the context of commercial sales. Generally courts will take a dim view of a business person's allegations that a business deal he entered into in the ordinary course of business was unconscionable, since most judges assume the parties were well aware of what they were doing when they entered into the agreement.

2. State of New York v. Avco Fin. Serv., 50 N.Y.2d 383, 389, 429 N.Y.S.2d 181, 184, 406 N.E.2d 1075, 1078 (1980).

3. Hertz Corp. v. Attorney General of the State of New York, 136 Misc.2d 420, 424, 518 N.Y.S.2d 704, 708 (Sup.Ct., N.Y. County, 1987). *See generally*, Chapter 7 "Consumer Law," *infra*.

4. Equitable Lumber Corp. v. I.P.A. Land Development Corp., 38 N.Y.2d 516, 523, 381 N.Y.S.2d 459, 464, 344 N.E.2d 391, 396 (1976). *See* Chapter 7 "Consumer Law," *infra*.

5. Equitable Lumber Corp. v. I.P.A. Land Development Corp., 38 N.Y.2d 516, 523, 381 N.Y.S.2d 459, 464, 344 N.E.2d 391, 396 (1976); *see also* Morris v. Snappy Car Rental, 84 N.Y.2d 21, 614 N.Y.S.2d 362, 637 N.E.2d 253 (1994).

6. Equitable Lumber Corp. v. I.P.A. Land Development Corp., 38 N.Y.2d 516, 523, 381 N.Y.S.2d 459, 464, 344 N.E.2d 391, 396 (1976); *see also* Morris v. Snappy Car Rental, 84 N.Y.2d 21, 614 N.Y.S.2d 362, 637 N.E.2d 253 (1994).

§ 5.13

1. Clermont v. Clermont, 198 A.D.2d 631, 603 N.Y.S.2d 923, 924 (3d Dep't 1993); State v. Wolowitz, 96 A.D.2d 47, 468 N.Y.S.2d 131 (2d Dep't 1983).

requires a showing that the contract was both procedurally and substantively unconscionable when made.[2] To support a claim of unconscionability, a party must make some showing of an absence of meaningful choice on its part, together with terms that are unreasonably favorable to the other party.[3]

The procedural element of unconscionability requires an examination of the contract process and the alleged lack of meaningful choice.[4] An examination of the contract formation process focuses on matters such as the size and commercial setting of the transaction; whether deceptive or high pressured tactics were employed; the use of fine print in the contract; the experience and education of the party claiming unconscionability; and whether there was disparity in bargaining power.[5]

The substantive element of unconscionability requires an analysis of the substance of the bargain to determine whether the terms are unreasonably favorable to the party against whom unconscionability is alleged.[6] Substantive analysis focuses on the content of the terms of the contract *per se*, such as inflated prices, unfair disclaimers or termination clauses.[7]

Although determinations of unconscionability ordinarily require the presence of both procedural and substantive aspects, there have been exceptional cases where a provision of the contract was so outrageous as to warrant a finding of unconscionability based on the substantive aspect alone.[8] Similarly, where the disparity in the consideration exchanged by the parties is overwhelming, that factor alone may sustain a finding that the contract is unconscionable since such disparity itself leads inevitably to the conclusion that knowing advantage was taken of one party.[9]

Library References:
West's Key No. Digests, Contracts ⊂⇒1.

§ 5.14 Governing Law—Unconscionability—Codification in UCC

The doctrine of unconscionability has been codified in the Uniform

2. Gillman v. Chase Manhattan Bank, N.A., 73 N.Y.2d 1, 10, 537 N.Y.S.2d 787, 791, 534 N.E.2d 824, 827 (1988); Rosiny v. Schmidt, 185 A.D.2d 727, 587 N.Y.S.2d 929 (1st Dep't 1992), app. denied 80 N.Y.2d 762, 592 N.Y.S.2d 671, 607 N.E.2d 818 (1992).

3. Gillman v. Chase Manhattan Bank, N.A., 73 N.Y.2d 1, 10, 537 N.Y.S.2d 787, 791, 534 N.E.2d 824, 827 (1988).

4. State v. Avco Financial Service, Inc., 50 N.Y.2d 383, 429 N.Y.S.2d 181, 406 N.E.2d 1075 (1980).

5. Gillman v. Chase Manhattan Bank, N.A., 73 N.Y.2d 1, 10, 537 N.Y.S.2d 787, 791, 534 N.E.2d 824, 827 (1988).

6. Sablosky v. Edward S. Gordon Co., 73 N.Y.2d 133, 538 N.Y.S.2d 513, 535 N.E.2d 643 (1989).

7. Industralease Automated & Scientific Equipment Corp. v. R.M.E. Enterprises, Inc., 58 A.D.2d 482, 489, 396 N.Y.S.2d 427, 431, note 4 (2d Dep't 1977).

8. *See, e.g.*, State of New York v. Wolowitz, 96 A.D.2d 47, 67, 468 N.Y.S.2d 131, 150 (2d Dep't 1983).

9. Matter of Friedman, 64 A.D.2d 70, 85, 407 N.Y.S.2d 999, 1008 (2d Dep't 1978).

Commercial Code.[1] UCC § 2–302(1) provides that, if the court finds a contract or any clause of a contract to have been unconscionable at the time it was made, it may refuse to enforce the contract, or it may enforce the remainder of the contract without the unconscionable clause, or it may so limit the application of an unconscionable clause as to avoid any unconscionable result.[2] The concept, as defined in the UCC, is not aimed at "disturbance of allocation of risks because of superior bargaining power" but, instead, at the "prevention of oppression and unfair surprise."[3] UCC § 2–302(2) provides that, in order to aid the court in making a determination as to the unconscionability of a contract or any clause thereof, the parties shall be afforded a reasonable opportunity to present evidence as to its commercial setting, purpose and effect.[4] In light of the dependency upon the particular circumstances surrounding a transaction, courts and commentators have consistently construed UCC § 2–302(2) to mandate at least the opportunity for an evidentiary hearing.[5]

UCC § 2–302 is intended to allow the court to pass directly on the unconscionability of the contract or particular clause therein and to make a conclusion of law as to its unconscionability. The basic test is whether, in the light of the general commercial background and the commercial needs of the particular trade or case, the clauses involved are so one-sided as to be unconscionable under the circumstances existing at the time of the making of the contract.[6]

Library References:

West's Key No. Digests, Sales ⟸1(1).

§ 5.15 Governing Law—Duty of Good Faith—Generally

Implicit in all contracts is an implied covenant of fair dealing and good faith between the parties.[1] The courts may thus take into consideration the fact that one construction would make a contract unreasonable, and endeavor to construe the contract equitably to both parties rather than in a manner that would give one of the parties an unfair or unreasonable advantage over another.[2]

§ 5.14

1. UCC § 2–302.
2. UCC § 2–302(1).
3. UCC § 2–302, Official Comment 1; State v. Avco Financial Service, Inc., 50 N.Y.2d 383, 429 N.Y.S.2d 181, 406 N.E.2d 1075 (1980).
4. UCC § 2–302(2).
5. State of New York v. Avco Financial Service, Inc., 50 N.Y.2d 383, 390, 429 N.Y.S.2d 181, 185, 406 N.E.2d 1075, 1078 (1980); State v. Wolowitz, 96 A.D.2d 47, 468 N.Y.S.2d 131 (2d Dep't 1983).
6. UCC § 2–302, Official Comment 1.

§ 5.15

1. UCC § 1–203; Kalisch–Jarcho, Inc. v. New York, 58 N.Y.2d 377, 461 N.Y.S.2d 746, 448 N.E.2d 413 (1983); Gelder Medical Group v. Webber, 41 N.Y.2d 680, 394 N.Y.S.2d 867, 363 N.E.2d 573 (1977); Safe Flight Instrument Corp. v. Atlantic Aviation Corp., 205 A.D.2d 747, 613 N.Y.S.2d 681 (2d Dep't 1994).
2. Matter of Friedman, 64 A.D.2d 70, 82, 407 N.Y.S.2d 999, 1006 (2d Dep't 1978).

§ 5.16 Governing Law—Duty of Good Faith—Codification in UCC

UCC § 1-203 sets forth a basic principle running throughout the entire UCC and governing all commercial transactions:[1] Good faith is required in the performance and enforcement of all agreements or duties.[2] UCC § 2-103 defines "good faith" in the case of a merchant as meaning honesty in fact and the observance of reasonable commercial standards of fair dealing in the trade.[3]

UCC § 1-203 does not support an independent cause of action for failure to perform or enforce in good faith.[4] Rather, the section means that a failure to perform or enforce in good faith a specific duty or obligation under the terms of a contract constitutes a breach of that contract or makes unavailable, under the particular circumstances, a remedial right or power.[5] Thus, the doctrine of good faith merely requires a court to interpret a contract within the commercial context in which it has been created, performed and enforced; it does not create a separate duty of fairness and reasonableness which can be independently breached.[6]

Library References:
West's Key No. Digests, Contracts ⚖168; Sales ⚖54.

§ 5.17 The Written Contract—Statute of Frauds

UCC § 2-204 provides that a contract for the sale of goods may be made in any manner that is sufficient to show an agreement to have been made. This includes conduct by both parties that recognizes the existence of the contract.[1]

Section 2-204 continues New York's basic policy of recognizing any manner of expression giving rise to an agreement, whether written or

---

§ 5.16

1. UCC § 1-203.
2. UCC § 1-203, Official Comment.

PRACTICE POINTER: If the client informs counsel that there is a possibility of a failure of good faith, counsel should immediately take steps to document each and every allegation and act of bad faith. Documentary evidence of bad faith is powerful in contract litigation and may precipitate a successful summary judgment motion by the plaintiff, or defeat summary judgment by a plaintiff who has acted in bad faith.

3. UCC § 2-103(b).
4. UCC § 1-203, Official Comment.
5. UCC § 1-203, Official Comment.
6. UCC § 1-203, Official Comment.

§ 5.17

1. UCC § 2-204(1). Pursuant to UCC § 2-105(1), the term "goods," as used in the statute, means all things, including specially manufactured goods, that are movable at the time of identification to the contract for sale. The definition is based on the concept of movability. "It is not intended to deal with things which are not fairly identifiable as movables before the contract is performed." UCC § 2-105, Official Comment 1.

oral. The legal effect of the agreement, however, is qualified by other provisions of UCC Article 2. Specifically, UCC § 2–201(1) provides that a commercial contract for the sale of goods for the price of $500 or more requires a "writing sufficient to indicate that a contract for sale has been made between the parties...."[2] The contract must be signed " ...by the party against whom enforcement is sought."[3] However, a party may be bound by the signature of its authorized agent or broker.[4]

The Official Comment to UCC § 2–201 provides:

The required writing need not contain all the material terms of the contract and such material terms as are stated need not be precisely stated. All that is required is that the writing afford a basis for believing that the offered oral evidence rests on a real transaction. It may be written in lead pencil on a scratch pad. It need not indicate which party is the buyer and which the seller. The only term which must appear is the quantity term which need not be accurately stated but recovery is limited to the amount stated.[5]

Thus, an oral agreement between sellers and buyers is unenforceable if it involves a purchase for $500 or more and if it is not in writing as required by UCC § 2–201.[6]

Library References:

West's Key No. Digests, Frauds, Statute of ⊜81–96.

§ 5.18 The Written Contract—Statute of Frauds—General Rules

A contract that is not drawn within the Statute of Frauds is not automatically void, only voidable or unenforceable, subject to the interposition of UCC § 2–201 as a defense.[1]

UCC § 2–201(3)(a) provides that a non-conforming contract will nevertheless be valid if the goods are to be specially manufactured for the buyer, are not suitable for sale to others in the ordinary course of business, and the seller has substantially begun their manufacture or has made commitments for their procurement. Under Subdivision (3)(b), a non-conforming contract becomes valid if the party against whom enforcement is sought admits the making of the contract in pleadings or in court. The contract is enforceable to the extent of the admission.

---

2. UCC § 2–201(1).
3. UCC § 2–201(1).
4. UCC § 2–201(1).
5. UCC § 2–201, Official Comment 1.
6. *See, e.g.,* Modu Craft, Inc. v. Liberatore, 89 A.D.2d 776, 453 N.Y.S.2d 488 (4th Dep't 1982).

§ 5.18

1. *See* CPLR 3018(b). *See also* Felicie, Inc. v. Leibovitz, 67 A.D.2d 656, 412 N.Y.S.2d 625 (1st Dep't 1979); In re Exeter Mfg. Co., 254 A.D. 496, 5 N.Y.S.2d 438 (1st Dep't 1938).

§ 5.18   COMMERCIAL SALES CONTRACTS   Ch. 5

Furthermore, the Statute of Frauds is not to be applied to contracts which have been fully carried out by the parties, *i.e.*, it is applicable to executory, not executed contracts.[2]

Finally, the Statute does not apply to qualified financial contracts, as defined in Section 5–701 of the General Obligations Law, if there is a written agreement to be bound by the non-conforming contract, or other evidence as required by the General Obligations Law. Qualified financial contracts involve the purchase and sale of securities, commodities and currencies.

Library References:

West's Key No. Digests, Frauds, Statute of ⚖︎81–96.

§ 5.19 The Written Contract—Statute of Frauds—Formal Requirements

UCC § 2–201, the Statute of Frauds, states that "A writing is not insufficient because it omits or incorrectly states a term agreed upon but the contract is not enforceable ... beyond the quantity of goods shown in such writing."[1]

It is not necessary for the writing to identify which party is the buyer and which is the seller. The only term that must appear in the writing is the quantity, and that need not be accurately stated. However, recovery will be limited to the amount stated in the contract. "The price, time and place of payment or delivery, the general quality of the goods, or any particular warranties may all be omitted."[2]

For example, an oral agreement of the parties can be confirmed on a dated invoice that contains the names and addresses of the parties, the price and description of the goods, and the amount to be sold.[3]

Between merchants, a confirmation of a contract that is sent within a reasonable time to another party who has reason to know its contents satisfies the formal requirements of the Statute of Frauds; provided,

---

2. UCC § 2–201(3)(c); L. Fatato, Inc. v. Decrescente Distributing Co., Inc., 86 A.D.2d 600, 446 N.Y.S.2d 120 (2d Dep't 1982); *see* Brown v. Farmers. Loan & Trust Co., 117 N.Y. 266, 22 N.E. 952 (1889). In Fatato, a case involving an oral contract for the sale of beer, plaintiff paid for the shipment of beer but claimed that he had been overcharged. Since the contract had been fully executed, it did not come within the Statute of Frauds.

§ 5.19

1. UCC § 2–201(1).

2. UCC § 2–201, Official Comment 1.

3. B & R Textile Corp. v. Domino Textiles, Inc., 77 A.D.2d 539, 430 N.Y.S.2d 89 (1980). *See* Franklin Research & Dev. Corp. v. Swift Elec. Supply Co., 236 F.Supp. 992 (S.D.N.Y.1964), aff'd 340 F.2d 439 (2d Cir. 1964) (buyer's letter to seller asking for delay in delivery of lighting fixtures and letter seeking cancellation of order sufficient to establish contract); *but see* Oswald v. Allen, 417 F.2d 43 (2d Cir.1969) (letter of coin collection owner to prospective buyer did not delineate parties' understanding but merely referred to delivery arrangement and did not state quantity of coins to be sold; no contract formed).

however, that no objection is raised within ten days by the party to be charged.[4]

Failure to object in writing within ten days to a writing confirming an oral contract has been held not to signify assent to the contract. It merely deprived the party charged of the opportunity to raise the Statute of Frauds as a defense.[5]

Library References:

West's Key No. Digests, Frauds, Statute of ⌾97–118(5).

§ 5.20 The Written Contract—Statute of Frauds—Nature of the Writing

The Official Comment to UCC § 2–201 states that there are only three requirements with regard to a writing to satisfy the Statute of Frauds: "First, it must evidence a contract for the sale of goods; second, it must be 'signed,' a word which includes any authentication which identifies the party to be charged; and third, it must specify a quantity."[1]

An invoice on a seller's letterhead containing the names and addresses of the buyer and seller, the date, the description, amount and price of goods, has been held to satisfy the formal requirements of the Statute of Frauds.[2]

A buyer's letter confirming an order for the shipment of coal was sufficient to satisfy the Statute of Frauds in the absence of the seller's timely objection.[3]

Similarly, a memorandum of goods purchased on an order blank,[4] and a telex transmission stating quantity, price, and delivery terms[5] have been held to satisfy the Statute of Frauds.

A printed signature is sufficient to satisfy the Statute[6] and an authorized agent or broker may sign, thereby binding a buyer or seller to the contract.[7]

---

4. UCC § 2–201(2).

5. Whitemarsh Industries Inc. v. Sears Roebuck and Co., 192 A.D.2d 331, 595 N.Y.S.2d 763 (1st Dep't 1993).

§ 5.20

1. UCC 2–201, Official Comment 1. Note that UCC § 2–203 provides that "The affixing of a seal to a writing evidencing a contract for sale or an offer to buy or sell goods does not constitute the writing of a sealed instrument and the law with respect to sealed instruments does not apply to such a contract or offer."

2. B & R Textile Corp. v. Domino Textiles, Inc., 77 A.D.2d 539, 430 N.Y.S.2d 89 (1st Dep't 1980).

3. East Europe Domestic Intern. Sales Corp. v. Island Creek Coal Sales Co., 572 F.Supp. 702 (S.D.N.Y.1983).

4. Bazak Intern. Corp. v. Mast Industries, Inc., 73 N.Y.2d 113, 538 N.Y.S.2d 503, 535 N.E.2d 633 (1989).

5. Apex Oil Co. v. Vanguard Oil & Service Co., Inc., 760 F.2d 417 (2d Cir.1985).

6. Goldowitz v. Kupfer, 80 Misc. 487, 141 N.Y.S. 531 (Sup.Ct., N.Y. County, 1913).

7. UCC § 2–201.

§ 5.21 The Written Contract—Requirement of a Writing—Parol or Extrinsic Evidence

The terms of a writing intended by the parties as a final expression of their agreement with respect to such terms may not be contradicted by a prior agreement or a contemporaneous oral agreement; however, the contract may be explained or supplemented by: (1) a course of dealing or usage of trade; (2) a course of performance; and (3) evidence of consistent additional terms.[1]

UCC § 1–205 defines a course of dealing as " ... a sequence of previous conduct between the parties to a particular transaction which is fairly to be regarded as establishing a common basis of understanding for interpreting their expressions and other conduct."[2] In *Sternheim v. Silver Bell of Roslyn*,[3] the 12–year relationship of jeweler to jewelry carrier, during which time the carrier limited its liability to $200 per delivery, was sufficient to establish a course of dealing that supplemented the terms of the contract. Although five rings never reached their intended destination and their gross value was substantially more than the carrier's $200 limited liability, the court limited the defendant's liability to the stated amount.

In *Schubtex, Inc. v. Allen Snyder, Inc.*,[4] the New York Court of Appeals acknowledged that trade usage or a prior course of dealing may be used to supplement the express terms of a contract for the sale of goods.[5] However, on the facts of this case, the court would not rely on a prior course of dealing to enforce an arbitration clause in the contract. The court held that the agreement to arbitrate, printed on the confirmation of order, was a change to a material term of the contract that could not be enforced over a party's objection.

Under UCC § 2–208, a course of performance is always relevant to determine the meaning of an agreement.[6] However, where it is not reasonable to construe the course of performance or custom or usage in a trade as being consistent with the express terms of the contract, the express terms are controlling over the course of performance.[7]

§ 5.21

1. UCC § 2–202.

2. New York Annotation (1) to UCC § 1–205 provides: "The subsection seems consistent with Sinkwich v. E. F. Drew & Co., 9 A.D.2d 42, 189 N.Y.S.2d 630 (1959), where a continued interpretation of the contract bound the parties." UCC § 1–205, N.Y. Anno. (1).

3. 66 Misc.2d 726, 321 N.Y.S.2d 965 (Civ.Ct., N.Y. County, 1971) (carrier stamped on plaintiff's memorandum a receipt which specifically limited liability to $200; large sign over area where carrier received packages indicated the same).

4. 49 N.Y.2d 1, 424 N.Y.S.2d 133, 399 N.E.2d 1154, reargument denied 49 N.Y.2d 801, 426 N.Y.S.2d 1029, 403 N.E.2d 466 (1980).

5. *See* Kamakazi Music Corp. v. Robbins Music Corp., 534 F.Supp. 57 (S.D.N.Y. 1981).

6. UCC § 2–208, Official Comment 2.

7. UCC § 2–208. *See also* Division of Triple T Service, Inc. v. Mobil Oil Corp., 60 Misc.2d 720, 304 N.Y.S.2d 191 (Sup.Ct., N.Y. County, 1969), aff'd 34 A.D.2d 618, 311 N.Y.S.2d 961 (2d Dep't 1970).

Ch. 5   THE WRITTEN CONTRACT—ACCEPTANCE   § 5.23

Under UCC § 2–202, the admission into evidence of "consistent additional terms" is permitted where the writing does not appear to state the complete contract.[8]

Library References:

West's Key No. Digests, Frauds, Statute of ⟐158.

§ 5.22 The Written Contract—Offer

In a commercial contract, an offer to make a contract invites acceptance in any manner and by any medium reasonable under the circumstances.[1] UCC § 2–206 provides that an offer to buy goods invites acceptance by the prompt or current shipment of conforming or nonconforming goods or the prompt promise to ship,[2] except that shipment of non-conforming goods does not constitute acceptance if the seller seasonably notifies the buyer that the shipment is being offered only as an accommodation. An offeror who is not notified of acceptance within a reasonable period of time may treat the offer as having lapsed.[3]

Library References:

West's Key No. Digests, Frauds, Statute of ⟐97–118(5).

§ 5.23 The Written Contract—Acceptance

Any reasonable manner of acceptance may be made unless the offeror has made it quite clear that it will not be acceptable.[1] "Former technical rules as to acceptance, such as requiring that telegraphic offers be accepted by telegraphed acceptance, etc., are rejected...."[2] The question of whether there has been an acceptance is determined by the meaning of the terms of the offer.[3]

---

8. UCC § 2–202, N.Y. Anno. (3), citing Mitchill v. Lath, 247 N.Y. 377, 160 N.E. 646 (1928).

PRACTICE POINTER: Under the UCC, it is very common and thoroughly acceptable that terms will be added to a contract. Unless (1) the contract clearly states that it is a final expression of the agreement's terms or (2) the addition of terms materially changes the agreement, a court may be disposed to find that the additional terms are enforceable. A client who objects to the addition of terms should be advised to promptly notify the other party of the objection.

§ 5.22
1. UCC § 2–206(1)(a).
2. UCC § 2–206(1)(b).

3. UCC § 2–206(2). See UCC § 2–205 "Firm Offers," providing: "An offer by a merchant to buy or sell goods in a signed writing which by its terms gives assurance that it will be held open is not revocable, for lack of consideration, during the time stated or if no time is stated for a reasonable time, but in no event may such period of irrevocability exceed three months; but any such term of assurance on a form supplied by the offeree must be separately signed by the offeror."

§ 5.23
1. UCC § 2–206.
2. UCC § 2–206, Official Comment 1.
3. Petterson v. Pattberg, 248 N.Y. 86, 161 N.E. 428 (1928).

§ 5.23   COMMERCIAL SALES CONTRACTS   Ch. 5

In one case, a purchaser's letter that was an unqualified, timely expression of acceptance created a valid contract although both offer and acceptance omitted the price term.[4]

Library References:
West's Key No. Digests, Frauds, Statute of ⟶97–118(5).

§ 5.24   The Written Contract—Acceptance—Additional Terms

UCC § 2–207 provides:

A definite and seasonable expression of acceptance or a written confirmation which is sent within a reasonable time operates as an acceptance even though it states terms additional to or different from those offered or agreed upon, unless acceptance is expressly made conditional on assent to the additional or different terms.[1]

The additional terms are treated as proposals for additions to the contract. However, between merchants, the additional terms become part of the contract unless: (1) the offer limits acceptance to its terms, or (2) the additional terms materially alter the contract, or (3) they are expressly rejected.[2]

New York takes an objective approach to the question of contract formation, *i.e.*, the court will look to the terms of the parties' agreement rather than to their subjective intent.[3]

However, where the writings do not establish the existence of a contract, conduct of the parties evidencing recognition of its existence is sufficient to establish the contract.[4]

Library References:
West's Key No. Digests, Frauds, Statute of ⟶97–118(5).

§ 5.25   The Written Contract—Indefiniteness

UCC § 2–204(1) provides that a contract for the sale of goods may be made in any manner sufficient to show agreement. Conduct by both

---

4. Matter of McManus, 83 A.D.2d 553, 440 N.Y.S.2d 954 (2d Dep't), aff'd 55 N.Y.2d 855, 447 N.Y.S.2d 708, 432 N.E.2d 601, appeal dismissed 55 N.Y.2d 605, 447 N.Y.S.2d 1029, 432 N.E.2d 604 (1982). The Statute of Frauds, UCC § 2–201, provides that only the quantity, not the price, must be specified in the writing.

§ 5.24

1. UCC § 2–207(1).

2. Official Comment 1 to UCC § 2–207 provides that mere suggestions, such as "rush," "ship by Tuesday" or "ship draft against bill of lading inspection allowed" are to be treated as additions to the contract and do not materially alter it. UCC § 2–207, Official Comment 1.

3. *See* J. Baranello & Sons v. Hausmann Industries, Inc., 571 F.Supp. 333 (E.D.N.Y. 1983).

4. UCC § 2–207(3). *See* Thomaier v. Hoffman Chevrolet, Inc., 64 A.D.2d 492, 410 N.Y.S.2d 645 (2d Dep't 1978) (although car dealer did not sign purchase agreement, where he accepted $1,000 deposit and placed order with manufacturer for identical vehicle, dealer's conduct evidenced contract).

Ch. 5 WRITTEN CONTRACT—USE OF OPEN TERMS § 5.26

parties recognizing the existence of the contract is sufficient. A contract may be found to exist even though the moment of its making is undetermined.[1]

UCC § 2-204(3) states: "Even though one or more terms are left open a contract for sale does not fail for indefiniteness if the parties have intended to make a contract and there is a reasonably certain basis for giving an appropriate remedy."[2] Under this section of the Code, if the parties intend to enter into an agreement, a valid agreement is formed despite the absence of terms, provided there is a reasonable basis for granting a remedy.[3]

For example, a contract for the manufacture of wardrobes has been held enforceable despite the fact that the parties had not reached agreement on the work to be done by a third-party who was to contribute an essential component of the contract.[4]

Library References:
West's Key No. Digests, Frauds, Statute of ⚖97–118(5).

§ 5.26 The Written Contract—Use of Open Terms

UCC § 2-305(1) provides that the parties, if they intend, " ...can conclude a contract for sale even though the price is not settled." The dominant intention of the parties to be bound is controlling. Since there is usually a reasonably certain basis for granting an appropriate remedy for breach, the contract need not fail for indefiniteness.[1]

When a price fails to be fixed through the fault of one party, the other party may treat the contract as canceled or fix a reasonable price.[2] However, when the parties do not intend to be bound absent the fixing of a price, there is no contract.[3]

Where the contract fails to specify a place for delivery, then delivery is at the seller's place of business, or, if he has none, at his residence.[4] When the identified goods contracted for are "... known to both parties to be in some location other than the seller's place of business or

§ 5.25

1. UCC § 2-204(2). The New York Annotation to this section provides: "No New York authority has been found which indicates that a finding of the exact time of the formation of the contract is essential to a determination that a contract has been formed...." UCC § 2-204(2), N.Y. Anno. (2).

2. **PRACTICE POINTER**: The drafter should clearly determine what the parties want the contract to state, and should include terms with particularity and not rely on the default provisions of the UCC.

3. UCC § 2-204, Official Comment 1.

4. J. Baranello & Sons v. Hausmann Industries, Inc., 571 F.Supp. 333 (E.D.N.Y. 1983). See City University of New York v. Finalco, Inc., 93 A.D.2d 792, 461 N.Y.S.2d 830 (1st Dep't 1983), appeal after remand 129 A.D.2d 494, 514 N.Y.S.2d 244 (1987)(contract did not fail despite dispute as to a material term).

§ 5.26

1. UCC § 2-305, Official Comment 1.
2. UCC § 2-305(3).
3. UCC § 2-305(4).
4. UCC § 2-308(a).

residence, the parties are presumed to have intended that place to be the place of delivery."[5]

Where the time for the delivery of goods is not specified, the proper time for delivery is deemed to be a reasonable time.[6] A contract providing for successive performances that is indefinite in duration is valid for a reasonable time but may be terminated at any time by either party unless the parties have a contrary agreement.[7] UCC § 2-309 also provides that notification of termination of a going contract must be reasonable; an agreement dispensing with notification is invalid if its operation would be unconscionable.[8]

UCC § 2-311 also provides that a contract for sale is not invalid because it leaves the particulars of performance to be specified by one of the parties. "The party to whom the agreement gives power to specify the missing details is required to exercise good faith and to act in accordance with commercial standards so that there is no surprise and the range of permissible variations is limited by what is commercially reasonable."[9]

As a general rule, if the parties intended to enter into an agreement, a valid agreement will be found despite the absence of terms, provided there is a reasonable basis for granting a remedy.[10]

When terms are missing in a contract, the UCC provides rules to determine price,[11] place for delivery,[12] time for shipment,[13] and for particulars of performance that are to be specified by one of the parties.[14]

Library References:

West's Key No. Digests, Frauds, Statute of ⇔97–118(5).

§ 5.27 Warranties

UCC Article 2 provides for a warranty of title against infringement;[1] an express warranty by affirmation, description or sample;[2] an implied warranty of merchantability;[3] and an implied warranty of fitness for a particular purpose.[4]

5. UCC § 2-308, Official Comment 2.

6. UCC § 2-309(1). See Timme v. Steinfeld, 214 A.D. 611, 213 N.Y.S. 110 (1st Dep't), aff'd 244 N.Y. 536, 155 N.E. 887 (1925) (indefinite extension of time to tender delivery of goods deemed to have expired after 18 months; contract unenforceable).

7. UCC § 2-309(2).

8. UCC § 2-309(3).

9. UCC § 2-311, Official Comment 1.

10. UCC § 2-204.

11. See UCC § 2-311.

12. See UCC § 2-305.

13. See UCC § 2-308.

14. See UCC § 2-311.

§ 5.27

1. UCC § 2-312. For a more detailed discussion of warranties see Chapter 27, "Products Liability," infra.

2. UCC § 2-313.

3. UCC § 2-314.

4. UCC § 2-315. See also, Kreindler, Rodriguez, et al., New York Law of Torts (West 1997) §§ 16.2–16.9.

§ 5.28 Warranties—Warranty of Title Against Infringement

UCC § 2-312 provides that a seller warrants both good title to the goods sold, and that the goods are delivered free of any security interest or other lien or encumbrance of which the buyer at the time of contracting has no knowledge. Thus, a corporation breached its warranty under this section where it sold an aircraft encumbered by a chattel mortgage.[1] Such warranty may only be excluded or modified by specific language or by circumstances informing the buyer that the seller does not claim title in himself, or only purports to sell such title as he or a third person may have.[2]

A merchant regularly dealing in the goods sold also warrants freedom from claims of infringement, unless otherwise agreed, or unless the infringement arises out of the seller's compliance with the buyer's specifications.[3]

Library References:

West's Key No. Digests, Sales ⟐263.

§ 5.29 Warranties—Express Warranty

Under UCC § 2-313(1), an express warranty may be made by affirmation, promise, description, or sample, provided, however, that such offering is made part of the basis of the bargain.[1] It has been held that a necessary element in the creation of an express warranty is the buyer's reliance upon the seller's affirmation or promise.[2]

Library References:

West's Key No. Digests, Sales ⟐259.

§ 5.28

1. Marine Midland Trust Co. of Western New York v. Halik, 28 A.D.2d 1077, 285 N.Y.S.2d 136 (4th Dep't 1967), aff'd 23 N.Y.2d 789, 297 N.Y.S.2d 297, 244 N.E.2d 868 (1968).

2. UCC § 2-312(2). The Official Comment for this subsection states: "Subsection (2) recognizes that sales by sheriffs, executors, foreclosing lienors and persons similarly situated are so out of the ordinary commercial course that their peculiar character is immediately apparent to the buyer and therefore no personal obligation is imposed on the seller...." UCC § 2-312, Official Comment 5.

3. UCC § 2-312(3).

§ 5.29

1. UCC § 2-313(1).

2. Scaringe v. Holstein, 103 A.D.2d 880, 477 N.Y.S.2d 903 (3d Dep't 1984); Friedman v. Medtronic, Inc., 42 A.D.2d 185, 345 N.Y.S.2d 637 (2d Dep't 1973).

§ 5.30 Warranties—Implied Warranty of Merchantability

The implied warranty of merchantability[1] means that the goods: (1) must pass without objection in the trade under the contract description; (2) in the case of fungible goods, are of fair, average quality; (3) are fit for the ordinary purposes for which such goods are used; (4) are of even kind, quality and quantity within and among all units, within the ranges of variation permitted by the agreement; (5) are adequately contained, packaged and labeled; and (6) conform to the promises or affirmations made on the label.[2]

Library References:
West's Key No. Digests, Sales ⟐272.

§ 5.31 Warranties—Implied Warranty of Fitness for a Particular Purpose

The implied warranty of fitness for a particular purpose[1] arises where the seller at the time of contracting is aware of any particular purpose for which the goods are required and that the buyer is relying on the seller's skill or judgment to select or furnish suitable goods.

For example, an implied warranty of fitness for a particular purpose has been held to exist where silk was sold with the knowledge that it was to be used for the manufacture of neckties,[2] or where a paint manufacturer knew that a contractor's bid specifications required paint over sealer and recommended that certain paint be used over sealer, although the sealer was unfit for use and/or paint.[3]

UCC § 2–316 provides that, "Words or conduct relevant to the creation of an express warranty and words or conduct tending to negate or limit warranty shall be construed wherever reasonable as consistent with each other...."[4] Nonetheless, unless circumstances dictate otherwise, all implied warranties are excluded by expressions like "as is,"[5] "with all faults" or similar language that draws the buyer's attention to

---

§ 5.30

1. See UCC § 2–314.
2. See UCC § 2–316(2), which provides that "to exclude or modify the implied warranty of merchantability or any part of it the language must mention merchantability and in case of a writing must be conspicuous...."

§ 5.31

1. UCC § 2–315.
2. In re A. W. Cowen & Bros., 11 F.2d 692 (2d Cir.1926).
3. Emerald Painting, Inc. v. PPG Industries, Inc., 99 A.D.2d 891, 472 N.Y.S.2d 485 (3d Dep't 1984). See also Village of Chatham v. Board of Fire Com'rs of Delmar Fire Dist., 90 A.D.2d 860, 456 N.Y.S.2d 494 (3d Dep't 1982) (seller of pumper truck knew well the purpose for which the vehicle was being purchased).

4. UCC § 2–316.

5. **CAVEAT:** The buyer should be advised to be on guard against the use of such terms as "as is" in the fine print of the contract. If the seller intends the sale "as is," this term should be printed boldly and prominently on the contract.

Ch. 5   IN THE ABSENCE OF BREACH   § 5.33

the exclusion of warranties.[6] Thus, for example, mobile home sellers were found not to be liable for breach of warranty for a particular purpose where the contract excluded such warranties and the mobile home was purchased "as is."[7] However, an "as is" clause may not be used to counter a claim for damages under an express warranty.[8]

Library References:

West's Key No. Digests, Sales ⚖=265.

§ 5.32 Assumption of the Risk of Loss

Prior to the enactment of the Uniform Commercial Code, New York law placed the risk of loss by reference to objective facts such as delivery to the carrier, and tender and receipt of goods.[1] The emphasis under prior law was on the passage of title; specifically, the party to whom title had passed bore the risk of loss.[2] The modern approach, however, is contractual in nature, *i.e.*, the controlling factor is what the parties intended when they entered their agreement.

UCC § 2–401, concerning the passing of title, states that, "Each provision of this Article with regard to the rights, obligations and remedies of the seller, the buyer, purchasers or other third parties applies irrespective of title to the goods except where the provision refers to such title."[3]

As provided in the Official Comment to UCC § 2–401: "This Article deals with the issues between seller and buyer in terms of step by step performance or non-performance under the contract for sale and not in terms of whether or not 'title' to the goods has passed."

In the absence of specific contractual provisions to the contrary, risk of loss in the absence of breach is covered by UCC § 2–509, and the effect of breach on the risk of loss is covered by UCC § 2–510.

§ 5.33 Assumption of the Risk of Loss—In the Absence of Breach

Under UCC § 2–509, where the contract authorizes the seller to ship the goods by carrier, if it does not require him to deliver them at a

---

6. UCC § 2–316(3). *See* Sky Acres Aviation Services, Inc. v. Styles Aviation, Inc., 210 A.D.2d 393, 620 N.Y.S.2d 442 (2d Dep't 1994) (implied warranties of merchantability and fitness excluded where disclaimer in bold print indicated product sold in "as is" condition).

7. Christman v. Filer, 167 A.D.2d 819, 562 N.Y.S.2d 311 (4th Dep't 1990).

8. Barrientos v. Sulit, 133 Misc.2d 1061, 509 N.Y.S.2d 288 (City Ct., Long Beach, 1986).

§ 5.32

1. UCC § 2–509, N.Y. Anno.

2. *See* American Aniline Products, Inc. v. D. Nagase & Co., 187 A.D. 555, 176 N.Y.S. 114 (1st Dep't 1919) (under Uniform Sales Act, seller could not maintain action for price of goods until title in the goods had passed to buyer).

3. UCC § 2–401.

particular destination, risk of loss passes to the buyer when the goods are delivered to the carrier. This is the case even though the shipment is under reservation.[1] If the goods are required to be delivered to a particular destination, the risk of loss passes to the buyer when the goods are there tendered, so that the buyer may take delivery. A clear expression of this rule was found in one case where it was determined that risk of loss passed to the buyer when the goods were delivered to the carrier. Although the contract did not require shipment by carrier, such shipment was authorized.[2]

The underlying theory of this rule is that a merchant who is to make physical delivery at his or her own place of business continues to control the goods and can be expected to insure his or her interest in them. Also, it is unlikely that the buyer will retain insurance on goods not in his or her possession.[3]

UCC § 2–509(2) provides that where the goods are held by a bailee to be delivered without being moved, risk of loss passes to the buyer (1) on the buyer's receipt of a negotiable document of title, or (2) on acknowledgment by the bailee of the buyer's right to possession, or (3) after the bailee's receipt of a non-negotiable document of title or other written directive.[4]

The Official Comment to UCC 2–509 recites that,

> Where the agreement provides for delivery of the goods as between the buyer and seller without removal from the physical possession of a bailee, the provisions on manner of tender of delivery apply on the point of transfer of risk. Due delivery of a negotiable document of title covering the goods or acknowledgment by the bailee that he holds for the buyer completes the 'delivery' and passes the risk.[5]

In any other case, risk of loss passes to the buyer on receipt of goods if the seller is a merchant; otherwise, the risk passes to the buyer on tender of delivery.[6]

The above provisions are subject to change by agreement of the parties, and are also subject to the provisions of UCC Article 2 on sale on approval,[7] and on the effect of breach on risk of loss.[8]

---

§ 5.33

1. *See* UCC § 2–505 "Seller's Shipment Under Reservation." Where the seller has identified goods to the contract by or before shipment, his procurement of a negotiable bill of lading to his own order or otherwise reserves in him a security interest in the goods.

2. A.M. Knitwear Corp. v. All America Export–Import Corp., 41 N.Y.2d 14, 390 N.Y.S.2d 832, 359 N.E.2d 342 (1976).

3. UCC § 2–509, Official Comment 3.

4. *See also* UCC § 2–503(4)(b).

5. UCC § 2–509, Official Comment 4.

6. UCC § 2–509(3).

7. UCC § 2–509(4). UCC § 2–327, concerning "sale on approval," provides that unless otherwise agreed, "the risk of loss and the title do not pass to the buyer until acceptance."

8. UCC § 2–510.

§ 5.34 Assumption of the Risk of Loss—In the Event of a Breach

Where delivery of goods so fails to conform to the contract's term as to provide the buyer a right of rejection, the risk of loss remains on the seller until cure or acceptance.[1] Pursuant to UCC § 2–508(1), where the buyer rejects non-conforming goods and the time for performance has not yet expired, the seller may " ... seasonably notify the buyer of his or her intention to cure ... " and then make a conforming delivery within the contract time.[2] Section 2–508(2) provides that where the seller has reasonable grounds to believe that the buyer will accept delivery, the seller may seasonably notify the buyer and have further reasonable time to substitute a conforming delivery.[3]

Where the buyer rightfully revokes acceptance, " ... he may to the extent of any deficiency in his effective insurance coverage treat the risk of loss as having rested on the seller from the beginning."[4] Similarly, where the buyer as to conforming goods already identified to the contract of sale repudiates or is otherwise in breach before the risk of loss has passed to him or her, " ... the seller may to the extent of any deficiency in his effective insurance coverage treat the risk of loss as resting on the buyer for a commercially reasonable time."[5]

With regard to the provisions of Subsections 2 and 3 of this Section, the Official Comment provides "[I]f the one in control of the goods is the aggrieved party, whatever loss or damage may prove to be uncovered by his insurance falls upon the contract breaker ... rather than upon him."

§ 5.35 Performance

Section 2–301, concerning the general obligations of the parties, provides: "The obligation of the seller is to transfer and deliver and that of the buyer is to accept and pay in accordance with the contract."

Tender of delivery is a condition to the buyer's duty to accept goods. Tender entitles the seller to acceptance of the goods by the buyer and to payment under the contract.[1]

Section 2–503, "Manner of Seller's Tender of Delivery," requires the seller to "put and hold" conforming goods at the buyer's disposal and to give the buyer any notice reasonably necessary to enable him to take delivery.[2] In addition to the above requirements, where delivery is

---

§ 5.34
1. UCC § 2–510.
2. UCC § 2–508(1).
3. UCC § 2–508(2).
4. UCC § 2–510(2).
5. UCC § 2–510(3).

§ 5.35
1. UCC § 2–507(1).
2. UCC § 2–503(1). See First Coinvestors, Inc. v. Coppola, 88 Misc.2d 495, 388 N.Y.S.2d 833 (Dist.Ct., Suffolk County, 1976).

§ 5.35   COMMERCIAL SALES CONTRACTS   Ch. 5

required at a particular destination, the seller must comply with that provision.[3]

Where goods are in the possession of a bailee and are to be delivered without being moved, tender of delivery requires the seller (1) to " ... either tender a negotiable document of title ... or procure acknowledgment by the bailee of the buyer's right to possession of the goods ...," or (2) absent objection by the buyer, to provide to the buyer a non-negotiable document of title or a written direction to the bailee to deliver.[4] Where the contract requires the seller to deliver documents, he or she must tender the documents in correct form; tender through banking channels is also sufficient, although dishonor of a draft constitutes non-acceptance or rejection.[5]

Where a seller is required or authorized under a contract to send goods to the buyer he must (1) give them to a carrier for delivery, making such contract for their delivery as is reasonably necessary; (2) obtain and tender any documents necessary to enable the buyer to obtain possession; and (3) promptly notify the buyer of the shipment.[6] The general principles embodied in Section 2–504 cover the special cases of F.O.B. point of shipment contracts and C.I.F. (cost of goods, insurance, freight) and C.F. (cost of goods and freight) contracts.[7]

UCC § 2–319(1)(a) provides that "[W]hen the term is F.O.B. [free on board] the place of shipment, the seller must at that place ship the goods in the manner provided in this Article (Section 2–504) and bear the expense and risk of putting them into the possession of the carrier...." The terms C.I.F. and C.F. impose those costs on the seller unless otherwise agreed.[8]

Library References:
West's Key No. Digests, Sales ⊜135–196.

§ 5.36   Performance—Buyer's Response to Tender of Delivery

Upon the seller's tender of delivery, the buyer's obligation is to accept and pay in accordance with the contract.[1] However, if the goods or tender of delivery fail to conform to the contract in any respect, the buyer may (1) reject the whole; (2) accept the whole; or (3) accept any commercial unit or units and reject the rest.[2]

3. UCC § 2–503(2), (3).
4. UCC § 2–503(4). See Cundill v. Lewis, 245 N.Y. 383, 157 N.E. 502 (1927).
5. UCC § 2–503(5).
6. UCC § 2–504.
7. UCC § 2–504, Official Comment 1.
8. UCC § 2–320.

§ 5.36
1. UCC § 2–301.
2. UCC § 2–601.

PRACTICE POINTER: Where a buyer rejects a shipment of goods in whole or part, the practitioner should advise the buyer that his or her communications to the seller should be clear, unequivocal, and

For instance, where a delivery provided less than the quantity required under the contract, the buyer was entitled to refuse such tender.[3]

The Official Comment to Section 2–601 states:

A buyer accepting a nonconforming tender is not penalized by the loss of any remedy otherwise open to him. This policy extends to cover and regulate the acceptance of a part of any lot improperly tendered in any case where the price can reasonably be apportioned. Partial acceptance is permitted whether the part of the goods accepted conforms or not. The only limitation on partial acceptance is that good faith and commercial reasonableness must be used to avoid undue impairment of the value of the remaining portion of the goods.[4]

A major exception to the rules framed in Section 2–601 concerns installment contracts, which require or authorize the delivery of goods " . . . in separate lots to be separately accepted, even though the contract contains a clause 'each delivery is a separate contract' or its equivalent."[5]

Section 2–612 provides that the buyer may reject a non-conforming installment if the non-conformity impairs the value of the installment and cannot be cured.[6] However, if the seller gives adequate assurance that he or she will cure, the buyer must accept the installment, subject, however, to Section 2–612(3), which provides:

Whenever non-conformity or default with respect to one of more installments substantially impairs the value of the whole contract there is a breach of the whole. But the aggrieved party reinstates the contract if he accepts a non-conforming installment without seasonably notifying of cancellation or if he brings an action with respect only to past installments or demands performance as to future installments.[7]

Subsection (3) is intended to further the continuance of the contract in the absence of an outright cancellation.[8]

A buyer may also limit his or her remedies under § UCC 2–601 by agreement as to liquidation or limitation of damages,[9] or by contractual modification of remedies.[10]

---

timely to ensure that the buyer is subsequently in a legally defensible position.

3. Robert R. Scott Corp. v. D. Kwitman & Son, Inc., 3 Misc.2d 812, 146 N.Y.S.2d 518 (App. Term, 1st Dep't 1955) (contract called for 3000 yards; 1972 delivered); Hind v. Willich, 127 Misc. 355, 216 N.Y.S. 155 (Sup.Ct., N.Y. County, 1926), aff'd 221 A.D. 857, 224 N.Y.S. 819 (1st Dep't 1927), motion denied 221 A.D. 857, 224 N.Y.S. 819 (1st Dep't 1926) (quantity short and certification concerning quality lacking).

4. UCC § 2–601, Official Comment 1.
5. UCC § 2–612.
6. UCC § 2–612(2).
7. UCC § 2–612(3).
8. UCC § 2–612, Official Comment 6.
9. UCC § 2–718.
10. UCC § 2–719.

§ 5.37 Performance—Buyer's Response to Tender of Delivery—Acceptance

A buyer accepts goods in the following ways: when, after a reasonable opportunity to inspect them, the buyer signifies that the goods are conforming or that he or she will accept them in spite of non-conformity; when the buyer fails to make an effective rejection, provided such acceptance does not occur until after the buyer has had a reasonable opportunity to inspect the goods; or, the buyer does any act inconsistent with the seller's ownership, but if such act is wrongful against the seller, acceptance is only valid if ratified by the seller.[1] Section 2-606(2) further provides that, "Acceptance of a part of any commercial unit is acceptance of that entire unit."[2]

Payment made after tender is one circumstance tending to signify that goods have been accepted.[3] However, it is not conclusive.[4] The duration of retention of goods may be a factor in determining that goods have been accepted.[5] Use of goods[6] or resale of goods[7] may constitute acceptance.

Library References:
West's Key No. Digests, Sales ⊱178, 179.

§ 5.38 Performance—Buyer's Response to Tender of Delivery—Rejection

Rejection of goods must be made within a reasonable time after their delivery or tender. It will be considered ineffective unless seasonable notice is provided to the seller.[1]

Subject to the provisions of Sections 2-603 (Merchant Buyer's Duties as to Rightfully Rejected Goods) and 2-604 (Buyer's Options as to

---

§ 5.37

1. UCC § 2-606(1).

2. PRACTICE POINTER: It is important for a purchaser to effect a timely inspection to identify any non-conforming goods as soon as is reasonable under the circumstances. A buyer's rejection of delivery must be made within a reasonable time.

3. *See, e.g.*, Robert Hunt Co. v. S & R Coachworks, Inc., 215 A.D.2d 361, 625 N.Y.S.2d 662 (2d Dep't 1995).

4. UCC § 2-606, Official Comment 3.

5. Sears, Roebuck & Co. v. Galloway, 195 A.D.2d 825, 600 N.Y.S.2d 773 (3d Dep't 1993) (continued retention and use of boiler, covering several heating seasons); Frankel v. Foreman, 33 F.2d 83 (2d Cir. 1929) (four month retention constituted acceptance); DiDomenico Packaging Corp. v. Nails Again, Inc., 139 Misc.2d 525, 527 N.Y.S.2d 676 (Civ.Ct., N.Y. County, 1988) (buyer could not revoke goods four to six months after delivery).

6. *See* V. Zappala & Co., Inc. v. Pyramid Co. of Glens Falls, 81 A.D.2d 983, 439 N.Y.S.2d 765 (3d Dep't 1981), app. denied 55 N.Y.2d 603, 447 N.Y.S.2d 1025, 431 N.E.2d 643 (1981) (buyer used non-conforming blocks in construction).

7. Sunkyong America, Inc. v. Beta Sound of Music Corp., 199 A.D.2d 100, 605 N.Y.S.2d 62 (1st Dep't 1993).

§ 5.38

1. UCC § 2-602(1).

Salvage of Rightfully Rejected Goods), Section 2–602(2) provides that any exercise of ownership by the buyer after rejection of the goods is wrongful against the seller. If the buyer has, before rejection, taken physical possession of goods in which he does not have a security interest under Section 2–711(3), the buyer must retain them, using reasonable care, for a time sufficient to permit the seller to remove them. The buyer has no further obligations with regard to goods rightfully rejected.

Even though a buyer's rejection is of wholly non-conforming goods, he or she must inform the seller of the rejection.[2] A rejection of non-conforming goods within one month of delivery was held to have been timely where the time period was within the industry standard.[3]

Section 2–603 requires the buyer in possession or control of rejected goods to follow any reasonable instructions from the seller with respect to the goods. In the absence of instructions, the buyer must make reasonable efforts to sell the goods if they are perishable.[4] If a buyer's demand for indemnity for expenses is not forthcoming, then the seller's instructions are deemed not to be reasonable.[5] The buyer is entitled to reimbursement for his or her reasonable expenses.[6] In complying with this section, the buyer is held only to good faith, and conduct under this section is neither acceptance nor conversion.[7]

Section 2–604 provides:

Subject to the provisions of the immediately preceding section on perishables if the seller gives no instructions within a reasonable time after notification of rejection the buyer may store the rejected goods for the seller's account or reship them to him or resell them for the seller's account with reimbursement as provided in the preceding section. Such action is not acceptance or conversion.

This section is intended to accord a great deal of leeway to a rightfully rejecting buyer who is acting in good faith. The listing of what the buyer may do in the absence of instructions from the seller is intended to be illustrative rather than exhaustive.[8]

Library References:

West's Key No. Digests, Sales ⚖135–196.

§ 5.39 Performance—Buyer's Response to Tender of Delivery—Revocation of Acceptance

The buyer may revoke his or her acceptance of a lot or commercial unit whose non-conformity substantially impairs its useful value where

2. DeJesus v. Cat Auto Tech Corp., 161 Misc.2d 723, 615 N.Y.S.2d 236 (Civ.Ct., Bronx County, 1994).

3. D.C. Leathers, Inc. v. Gelmart Industries, Inc., 125 A.D.2d 738, 509 N.Y.S.2d 161 (3d Dep't 1986).

4. UCC § 2–603(1).

5. UCC § 2–603(1).

6. UCC § 2–603(2).

7. UCC § 2–603(3).

8. UCC § 2–604, Official Comment.

he accepts the lot or unit on the reasonable assumption that its nonconformity will be cured and it has not been seasonably cured, or where the buyer accepts it without discovery of such non-conformity if acceptance was reasonably induced by the seller's assurances or by the difficulty of discovery.[1] The buyer must provide notice of his revocation of acceptance within a reasonable time and before any substantial change in the condition of the goods; revocation is not effective until the buyer notifies the seller.[2]

Under this section, the buyer is no longer required to elect between revocation of acceptance and recovery of damages for breach. Both are now available.[3] The Official Comment provides: "The section no longer speaks of 'rescission,' a term capable of ambiguous application either to transfer of title to the goods or to the contract of sale and susceptible also to confusion with cancellation for cause of an executed or executory portion of the contract." Partial revocation of acceptance is also permissible.[4]

Library References:

West's Key No. Digests, Sales ⚖︎112–134.

§ 5.40 Breach of Contract

A failure in the performance of an agreement for a sale of goods, with concomitant damages to one or more parties, will often result in an action for breach of contract.

In this regard, the buyer must pay at the contract rate for any goods accepted[1] and thus a breach of contract action may ensue from the buyer's failure to do so.

Once the buyer accepts a delivery of goods, the seller acquires a right to his price on the contract terms. In cases of partial acceptance, payment may be apportioned at the contract rate, " ... which is the rate determined from the bargain in fact (the agreement) after the rules and policies of this Article have been brought to bear."[2]

Section 2–607(2) provides that acceptance of goods precludes their rejection. Further, if acceptance is made with knowledge of a non-conformity, acceptance cannot be revoked because of such non-conformi-

§ 5.39

1. UCC § 2–608(1).

2. UCC § 2–608(2). See White Devon Farm v. Stahl, 88 Misc.2d 961, 389 N.Y.S.2d 724 (Sup.Ct., N.Y. County, 1976) (where facts are not in dispute, question of what is reasonable time to inspect and reject goods is to be decided by the court). Section 2–608(3) provides that, "A buyer who so revokes has the same rights and duties with regard to the goods involved as if he had rejected them."

3. UCC § 2–608, Official Comment 1.

4. UCC § 2–608, N.Y. Anno. See Portfolio v. Rubin, 233 N.Y. 439, 135 N.E. 843 (1922); Display Printers, Inc. v. Globe Albums, Inc., 24 Misc.2d 331, 200 N.Y.S.2d 453 (Mun.Ct., Bronx County, 1959).

§ 5.40

1. UCC § 2–607(1).

2. UCC § 2–607, Official Comment 1.

ty unless the acceptance was based on the reasonable assumption that the non-conformity would be cured. Acceptance, however, does not impair any other remedy provided by Article 2 for non-conformity.[3]

Where the buyer has accepted goods, he or she must notify the seller of any breach within a reasonable time after discovery or be forever barred from any remedy.[4] Where goods have been accepted, the burden is on the buyer to establish any breach.[5]

Where the buyer is sued by third parties for breach of warranty or other obligation for which the seller is answerable, the buyer must give the seller written notice of the litigation. If the notice states that the seller must come in and defend or be bound by any action, the seller will be so bound if he does not come in and defend.[6] If the claim is one for infringement of title, the original seller may demand that the buyer turn over control of the litigation to him, including settlement, or else be barred from any remedy. If the seller agrees to bear all expense and to satisfy any adverse judgment, the buyer, after receipt of the notice, is barred from any remedy.[7]

§ 5.41 Breach of Contract—Seller's Remedies

Section 2–703, "Seller's Remedies in General," provides a convenient catalog of remedies available to the seller upon the buyer's breach of a contract of sale. The section provides that where the buyer wrongfully rejects or revokes acceptance, or fails to make a payment due on or before delivery, or repudiates with respect to any part or the whole, the seller may, with respect to goods already delivered, or if the breach is of the whole contract, then with respect to the undelivered balance: (1) withhold delivery; (2) stop delivery by a bailee; (3) proceed pursuant to UCC § 2–704;[1] (4) resell and recover damages;[2] (5) recover damages for

---

3. See UCC § 2–608, "Revocation of Acceptance in Whole or in Part;" Walbern Press, Inc. v. C.V. Communications, Inc., 212 A.D.2d 460, 622 N.Y.S.2d 951 (1st Dep't 1995) (buyer's inspection of goods before receipt and failure to provide seasonable notice to sell non-conforming goods precluded claim); Lenkay Sani Products Corp. v. Benitez, 47 A.D.2d 524, 362 N.Y.S.2d 572 (2d Dep't 1975).

4. UCC § 2–607(3). See Rajala v. Allied Corp., 919 F.2d 610 (10th Cir.1990), cert. denied 500 U.S. 905, 111 S.Ct. 1685, 114 L.Ed.2d 80 (1991) (buyer's failure to provide 30 days written notice precluded buyer from asserting claim). Pursuant to Section 2–607(3)(b), if seller has failed to provide good, clean title and buyer is sued as a result, buyer must notify the seller within a reasonable time after he receives notice of the litigation "... or be barred from any remedy over for liability established by the litigation."

5. UCC § 2–607(4).

6. UCC § 2–607(5)(a).

7. UCC § 2–607(5)(b).

§ 5.41

1. The Official Comment to UCC § 2–704 states: "This section gives an aggrieved seller the right at the time of breach to identify to the contract any conforming finished goods, regardless of their resalability, and to use reasonable judgment as to completing unfinished goods. It thus makes the goods available for resale ... and in the special case in which resale is not practicable, allows the action for the price ..."

2. UCC § 2–706 provides that the only condition precedent to the seller's right to resell goods is a breach by the buyer. Where

§ 5.41   COMMERCIAL SALES CONTRACTS   Ch. 5

non-acceptance[3] or, in a proper case, for the price;[4] (6) cancel.

Library References:

West's Key No. Digests, Sales ⚖=289–389.

§ 5.42 Breach of Contract—Seller's Remedies—Action for the Price

The most effective remedy from the seller's point of view is an action for the price. It is, in effect, the equivalent of specific performance,[1] and it avoids loss of volume sales and minimizes the seller's obligation to safeguard the goods after breach. UCC § 2–709 limits recovery of the price to three situations.

The first is where the buyer accepts a timely tender of conforming goods but fails to pay the price as it becomes due.[2] Unlike wrongful rejection, which would entitle the seller to damages and other remedies,[3] acceptance by the buyer entitles the seller to recover the price.

In the second situation, the goods are lost or damaged within a commercially reasonable time after the risk of loss has passed to the buyer. This might occur where the seller tenders conforming goods to a public carrier under a shipment contract,[4] and the goods are lost or damaged in transit. Risk of loss passes to the buyer upon their due delivery to the carrier,[5] and the buyer becomes liable to the seller for the price, even though the buyer has not accepted the goods and they are non-conforming when they are tendered to him.[6]

The third circumstance under which the seller may recover the price occurs when the buyer wrongfully rejects conforming goods or repudiates the contract, and the goods are identified to the contract and are such that they cannot be resold at a reasonable price after a reasonable

---

the resale must be made in good faith and in a commercially reasonable manner, the seller may recover the difference between the resale price and the contract price together with any incidental damages allowed under UCC § 2–710.

3. Under UCC § 2–708, the measure of damages for non-acceptance is the difference between the market price at the time and place for delivery and the unpaid contract price, together with any incidental damages as permitted by Section 2–710. Section 2–708(2) provides that if this remedy is inadequate to put the seller in as good a position as performance would have done, then the measure of damages is based on the profit (including reasonable overhead) that the buyer would have made from full performance together with incidental damages.

4. The Official Comment to UCC § 2–709 states: "The action for the price is now generally limited to those cases where resale of the goods is impracticable except where the buyer has accepted the goods or where they have been destroyed after risk of loss has passed to the buyer." UCC § 2–709, Official Comment 2.

§ 5.42

1. *See* Karen v. Cane, 152 Misc.2d 639, 578 N.Y.S.2d 85 (N.Y.C.Civ.Ct.1991).

2. UCC § 2–709(1)(a).

3. UCC §§ 2–708, 2–709(3).

4. UCC § 2–504.

5. UCC § 2–509(1)(a).

6. UCC § 2–709(1)(a).

effort.[7] This might take place where goods are specially manufactured for a buyer's needs and there is no market for them. Under such circumstances, the seller is obliged to hold the goods for the buyer, and if resale becomes possible, he may sell them prior to collection of the judgment for the price. Upon payment of the judgment, the buyer becomes entitled to the proceeds of such a sale, and to any goods not resold.[8]

Library References:

West's Key No. Digests, Sales ⚖︎340–368.

§ 5.43 Breach of Contract—Seller's Remedies—Withholding the Goods and Stopping Delivery

Where the buyer's ability to pay is in doubt, the seller may wish to retain or regain possession of the identified goods, rather than attempt to recover the price. When the buyer wrongfully rejects or revokes acceptance, or fails to make payment when due on or before delivery, or repudiates the contract, the seller may withhold delivery of the goods affected. If the breach affects the whole contract, then the whole undelivered balance may be withheld.[1]

When the seller discovers the buyer to be insolvent, he may " ... refuse delivery except for cash including payment for all goods theretofore delivered under the contract, and stop delivery under this Article (Section 2–705)."[2] If the goods have been shipped by public carrier or are in possession of a warehouseman to be delivered without being moved when the fact of insolvency is discovered, the seller may stop delivery upon such discovery.[3] Notice from the seller to the bailee must be such as to enable the bailee by reasonable diligence to prevent delivery.[4] Such notice is effective against the buyer until receipt of the goods by the buyer, or a warehouseman's acknowledgment to the buyer that the goods are held for him, or negotiation to the buyer of a negotiable document passing title to him.[5]

---

7. UCC § 2–709(1)(b). It has been held that even where a carpet has been cut to order, the seller is obliged to make an effort to resell as a remnant before bringing an action for the price. Karen v. Cane, 152 Misc.2d 639, 578 N.Y.S.2d 85 (N.Y.C.Civ.Ct. 1991). On the other hand, a publisher of study aids was not obligated to attempt to resell an outline it had created for a bar review course organizer after the buyer's wrongful repudiation of the contract. Other bar reviews already had outlines, and the material had no value to other buyers. Emanuel Law Outlines, Inc. v. Multi-State Legal Studies, Inc., 899 F.Supp. 1081 (S.D.N.Y.1995).

8. UCC § 2–709(2).

§ 5.43

1. UCC § 2–703.

2. UCC § 2–502(1). UCC § 1–201(23) provides that a person is "insolvent" who " ...either has ceased to pay his debts in the ordinary course of business or cannot pay his debts as they become due or is insolvent within the meaning of the federal bankruptcy law."

3. UCC § 2–705(1).

4. UCC § 2–705(3)(a).

5. UCC § 2–705(2). See Siderpali, S.P.A. v. Judal Industries, Inc., 833 F.Supp. 1023 (S.D.N.Y.1993) (seller has no right to stop delivery to buyer after a bill of lading is negotiated).

If the buyer is solvent, but repudiates the contract or fails to make a payment when due, the same stop-delivery provisions apply to goods that are warehoused. However, when goods are in transit, the seller may stop delivery only of "carload, truckload, planeload or larger shipments of express or freight" upon such repudiation or default. The expense and inconvenience to the carrier of stopping smaller shipments outweighs the risk to the seller when the buyer is solvent.[6]

Short of breach or insolvency, if reasonable grounds for insecurity arise with regard to the buyer's performance, the seller may, if commercially reasonable, suspend performance until receipt of adequate assurance of due performance is obtained from the buyer.[7]

Library References:

West's Key No. Digests, Sales ⚖︎289–299.

§ 5.44 Breach of Contract—Seller's Remedies—Recovery of Goods Delivered

Normally, unless a security interest has been perfected under Article 9 of the UCC,[1] the seller will have no right to possession upon breach by the buyer. However, pursuant to the provisions of UCC § 2-702(2), a seller who discovers that the buyer has received goods on credit while insolvent may reclaim the goods upon demand made within ten days after receipt of the goods.[2] The ten-day limitation is inapplicable if written misrepresentation of the solvency was made to the seller within three months before delivery.[3] Successful reclamation excludes all other remedies with respect to the goods reclaimed.[4]

The seller's right of reclamation is made subject to the rights of good faith purchasers. Thus, if the seller delivers goods to a buyer who is in fact insolvent, but has misrepresented his solvency, and the buyer then sells and delivers to a good faith purchaser for value, title is passed to that purchaser, and the seller may not reclaim the goods.[5]

Library References:

West's Key No. Digests, Sales ⚖︎316–331.

6. See Hunter v. Payne, 113 Misc. 385, 184 N.Y.S. 433 (1920), aff'd 197 A.D. 919, 188 N.Y.S. 926 (1920).

7. UCC § 2–609(1).

§ 5.44

1. See UCC § 9–503, as to the secured party's right to take possession after default.

2. See e.g., In re Koreag, Controle et Revision S.A., 961 F.2d 341 (2d Cir.1992), cert. denied sub nom. Koreag, Controle et Revision S.A. v. Refco F/X Associates, Inc., 506 U.S. 865, 113 S.Ct. 188, 121 L.Ed.2d 132 (1992).

3. UCC § 2–702(2).

4. UCC § 2–702(3).

5. UCC §§ 2–403(1), 2–702(3). See In re Blinn Wholesale Drug Co., Inc., 164 B.R. 440 (Bankr.E.D.N.Y.1994) (seller's right to reclaim pharmaceuticals sold to an insolvent dealer was subject to the rights of a company providing financing to the dealer and holding a security interest in the dealer's inventory; the company qualified as a good faith purchaser for value).

§ 5.45 Breach of Contract—Seller's Remedies—Resale

Where the buyer wrongfully rejects or revokes acceptance, or fails to make payment when due on or before delivery, or repudiates the contract, and the seller has possession, or is able to regain possession from the buyer or a bailee, the seller may resell the goods concerned, or the undelivered balance thereof, and may recover from the buyer the difference between the resale price and the contract price, together with incidental damages, but less the expenses saved in consequence of the buyer's breach.[1]

The resale may be at public or private sale, and must be conducted in the manner prescribed by UCC § 2-706, including the requirements as to notice. However, a good faith purchaser at a resale takes the goods free of the rights of the original buyer even though the seller fails to comply with one or more of the requirements of Section 2-706.[2]

While the seller may recover the difference between the resale price and the contract price, the seller is not accountable to the breaching buyer for any profit made on any resale.[3]

Resale is not mandatory. The seller may choose to retain the goods and seek general damages for breach.[4] If the seller does choose to resell goods identified to the contract, and is unable to do so at a reasonable price after reasonable efforts, an action for the price will lie against the buyer.[5]

If, at the time of the breach, the goods have not been identified to the contract, a seller in possession or control of conforming goods may identify them to the contract and then proceed with a resale under UCC § 2-706.[6] Where the goods are unfinished, the seller may, in the exercise of reasonable commercial judgment, complete manufacture and then identify the goods to the contract and resell, or the seller may cease manufacture and resell for scrap or salvage value, or proceed in any other reasonable manner.[7] It is not necessary that the goods be in existence or be identified to the contract before the breach in order for the resale to be authorized under Section 2-706.[8]

The seller may not choose the option of completing manufacture if "the exercise of reasonable commercial judgment as to the facts as they

---

§ 5.45

1. UCC § 2-706(1). Incidental damages, under UCC § 2-710, include any commercially reasonable charges, expenses or commissions incurred in stopping delivery, in the transportation, care and custody of goods after the buyer's breach, in connection with the return or resale of the goods or otherwise resulting from the breach.

2. UCC § 2-706(5).

3. UCC § 2-706(6). The theory is that the seller is entitled to the benefit of both bargains, since it would have made both sales if the buyer had not breached its contract. In re 375 Park Avenue Assocs., Inc., 182 B.R. 690 (Bankr.S.D.N.Y.1995).

4. UCC § 2-708.

5. UCC § 2-709(1)(b).

6. UCC § 2-704(1)(a).

7. UCC § 2-704(2).

8. UCC § 2-706(2).

appear at the time he learns of the breach makes it clear that such action will result in a material increase in damages. The burden is on the buyer to show the commercially unreasonable nature of the seller's action in completing manufacture."[9]

Library References:

West's Key No. Digests, Sales ☞332–339.

§ 5.46 Breach of Contract—Seller's Remedies—Damages for Non-acceptance or Repudiation

Rather than resell and recover the difference, or sue for the price, where that form of relief is available, the seller may choose to retain the goods and sue for damages. The measure of damages is generally the difference between the market price[1] at the time and place for tender and the unpaid contract price, together with any incidental damages,[2] less expenses saved in consequence of the breach.[3]

If the difference between market price and contract price is inadequate to put the seller in as good a position as performance would have done, then the measure of damages is the profit (including reasonable overhead) which the seller would have made from full performance by the buyer together with any incidental damages, due allowance for costs reasonably incurred, and due credit for payments or proceeds of resale.[4]

Library References:

West's Key No. Digests, Sales ☞369–389.

§ 5.47 Breach of Contract—Buyer's Remedies

Section 2–711 provides that where the seller fails to make delivery or repudiates, or where the buyer rightfully rejects or justifiably revokes acceptance, then with respect to any goods involved, and, if appropriate, with respect to the whole contract, in addition to recovering so much of the price as has been paid, the buyer may: (1) cover by purchasing goods

---

9. UCC § 2–704, Official Comment 2.

§ 5.46

1. As to proof of market price, see UCC § 2–723.

2. As to incidental damages, see UCC § 2–710. See, e.g., Harry Kolomick Contractors, Inc. v. Shelter Rock Estates, Inc., 172 A.D.2d 492, 567 N.Y.S.2d 845 (2d Dep't 1991), in which the seller was entitled to recover expenses incurred in performing its part of the contract where the buyer wrongfully rejected delivery of landfill.

3. UCC § 2–708(1). The awarding of the full contract price of a telephone system to the seller was deemed excessive when the system had been returned to the seller. The proper measure of recovery required deduction of the value of the returned system. Bell–Tronics Communications, Inc. v. Winkler, 178 A.D.2d 455, 577 N.Y.S.2d 126 (2d Dep't 1991).

4. UCC § 2–708(2). Consequential damages may include the buyer's lost profits, where the seller had reason to know of the buyer's plans to resell the goods. National Microsales Corp. v. Chase Manhattan Bank, N.A., 761 F.Supp. 304 (S.D.N.Y.1991).

in substitution;[1] or (2) recover damages for non-delivery.[2] Where the seller fails to deliver or repudiates, the buyer may also (1) recover goods that have been identified or (2) in a proper case, obtain specific performance or replevy the goods.[3] The buyer may also resell rejected goods if he or she has paid part of the price or incurred expenses in the inspection, receipt, transportation, care and custody of the goods.

Library References:
West's Key No. Digests, Sales ⟿390–448.

§ 5.48 Breach of Contract—Buyer's Remedies—Cover

Where the seller repudiates the contract or fails to deliver the goods, or the buyer justifiably rejects or revokes acceptance, the buyer may cancel the contract and "cover" by making, in good faith and without unreasonable delay, any reasonable purchase of, or contract to purchase, goods in substitution for those due from the seller.[1] The buyer is then entitled to recover the difference between the cost of cover and the contract price, together with any incidental or consequential damages, less any expenses saved in consequence of the breach.[2]

Incidental damages include expenses reasonably incurred in inspection, receipt, transportation, and care and custody of goods rightfully rejected, any commercially reasonable charges, expenses or commissions incurred in effecting cover, and any other reasonable expense incident to the breach.[3] Consequential damages include any loss resulting from the buyer's requirements which the seller had reason to know of at the time of contracting, and which could not reasonably be prevented by cover or otherwise.[4] Consequential damages also include injury to person or property proximately resulting from any breach of warranty.[5]

Like the seller's remedy of resale, the buyer's remedy of cover is optional. Failure to effect cover does not bar the buyer from any other

§ 5.47

1. The Official Comment to UCC § 2–712, concerning cover, states that this section is directed at providing the buyer "...with a remedy aimed at enabling him to obtain the goods he needs thus meeting his essential need...." UCC § 2–712, Official Comment 1. Under this Section, the buyer may recover as damages the difference between the cost of cover and the contract price, together with incidental or consequential damages as allowed by Section 2–715. UCC § 2–712, Official Comment 3.

2. Section 2–713 states that the measure for damages for non-delivery or repudiation is the difference between the market price at the time the buyer learned of the breach and the contract price, together with incidental damages under UCC § 2–715. UCC § 2–713(1).

3. See UCC § 2–716 on buyer's right to specific performance or replevin.

§ 5.48

1. UCC § 2–712(1).

2. UCC § 2–712(2). Where the cost of replacement is less than the contract price, and the buyer recovers any payments under the contract, the buyer sustains no damage in covering. Allied Semi–Conductors Intern., Ltd. v. Pulsar Components Intern., Inc., 907 F.Supp. 618 (E.D.N.Y.1995).

3. UCC § 2–715(1).

4. UCC § 2–715(2)(a).

5. UCC § 2–715(2)(b).

§ 5.48   COMMERCIAL SALES CONTRACTS

available remedy.[6] However, the right to replevy identified goods in the seller's possession may be unavailable if reasonable efforts to effect cover have not been made,[7] and the buyer may be limited to recovery of damages under Section 2–713.

Library References:

West's Key No. Digests, Sales ⇌418(7).

§ 5.49   Breach of Contract—Buyer's Remedies—Damages for Non-delivery

Failure to make delivery or repudiation by the seller, or justifiable rejection or revocation of acceptance by the buyer entitles the buyer to recover damages under Section 2–713.[1] Damages under this Section are completely alternative to cover, and apply only to the extent that the buyer has not covered.[2]

Subject to the provisions of Section 2–723, regarding proof of market price,[3] the measure of damages for non-delivery or repudiation is the difference between contract price and market price at the time the buyer learned of the breach, together with incidental and consequential damages,[4] less expenses saved in consequence of the breach.[5]

Market price is determined at the place of tender, or in cases of rejection after arrival or revocation after acceptance, at the place of arrival.[6]

Library References:

West's Key No. Digests, Sales ⇌404–423.

§ 5.50   Breach of Contract—Buyer's Remedies—Damages for Breach Regarding Accepted Goods

Acceptance of non-conforming goods, with knowledge of the non-conformity, and with no reasonable assumption that the defect will be cured, precludes revocation of the acceptance, but does not of itself

---

6. UCC § 2–712(3). *See* Jewell–Rung Agency, Inc. v. Haddad Org., Ltd., 814 F.Supp. 337 (S.D.N.Y.1993).

7. UCC § 2–716(3).

§ 5.49

1. UCC § 2–711(1)(b).

2. UCC § 2–713, Official Comment 5.

3. UCC § 2–723(1) provides that if an action based on anticipatory repudiation comes to trial before the date of performance, the market price shall be measured as of the time the aggrieved party learned of the repudiation. Subdivision (2) provides that if the market price at the designated time and place is unavailable, the price at a reasonable time before or after, or at a place which would serve as a reasonable substitute may be used, with allowance made for transport. Subdivision (3) provides that a substituted time or place is only admissible in evidence if the other party has been given sufficient notice to prevent surprise. *See also* UCC § 2–724 as to admissibility of market quotations.

4. *See* UCC § 2–715.

5. UCC § 2–713(1).

6. UCC § 2–713(2). *See also* UCC § 2–723(2), (3) as to reasonable substitute if the prevailing price at the place described is unavailable.

impair any other remedy provided by Article 2 for non-conformity.[1] If the buyer seasonably notifies the seller of the breach,[2] and sustains its burden of establishing a breach with regard to the goods accepted,[3] the buyer is entitled to damages under Section 2–714.

The buyer may recover as damages for the non-conforming tender the loss resulting in the ordinary course of events from the seller's breach, as determined in any reasonable manner.[4] Where there is a breach of warranty, the measure of damages is the difference, at the time and place of acceptance, between the value of the goods accepted and the value as warranted, unless special circumstances show proximate damages of a different amount.[5] Incidental[6] and consequential[7] damages are also available in a proper case.[8]

Thus, acceptance by the buyer of non-conforming goods entitles the seller to the contract price, as adjusted for the damage caused by the non-conformity.[9] A buyer, on notice to the seller of its intention to do so, may deduct all or part of any of the damages resulting from any breach of the contract from any part of the price still due under the same contract.[10]

Library References:

West's Key No. Digests, Sales ⟶404–423.

§ 5.51 Breach of Contract—Buyer's Remedies—Specific Performance or Replevin

Section 2–716 affords the buyer the remedies of specific performance and replevin, each of which entitles the buyer to possession of identified goods retained by the seller. Specific performance may be decreed where

§ 5.50

1. UCC § 2–607(2).
2. UCC § 2–607(3)(a).
3. UCC § 2–607(4).
4. UCC § 2–714(1). *See, e.g.*, B. Milligan Contracting Inc. v. Andrew R. Mancini Assocs., Inc., 174 A.D.2d 136, 578 N.Y.S.2d 931 (3d Dep't 1992).
5. UCC § 2–714(2).
6. It has been held that interest paid or incurred in connection with the purchase of defective goods may be recovered. Fedmet Trading Corp. v. Ekco Intern. Trade Corp., 151 Misc.2d 927, 574 N.Y.S.2d 122 (Sup.Ct., N.Y. County, 1991).
7. Lost profits have been deemed recoverable as consequential damages where such damages were foreseeable. Delchi Carrier SpA v. Rotorex Corp., 71 F.3d 1024 (2d Cir.1995); Model Imperial Supply Co., Inc. v. Westwind Cosmetics, Inc., 829 F.Supp. 35 (E.D.N.Y.1993).
8. UCC § 2–714(3). *See* UCC § 2–715 as to buyer's incidental and consequential damages.
9. The buyer may interpose a counterclaim for breach of the sales agreement to defeat or diminish a seller's action for the price. *See, e.g.*, Flick Lumber Co., Inc. v. Breton Industries, Inc., 223 A.D.2d 779, 636 N.Y.S.2d 169 (3d Dep't 1996). The damages offset the balance due under the contract. Carcone v. Gordon Heating & Air Conditioning Co., Inc., 212 A.D.2d 1017, 623 N.Y.S.2d 679 (4th Dep't 1995). However, a buyer may not offset losses from one contract against the price owed to the same seller on another contract. *See* Cliffstar Corp. v. Riverbend Products, Inc., 750 F.Supp. 81 (W.D.N.Y.1990).
10. UCC § 2–717.

§ 5.51 COMMERCIAL SALES CONTRACTS Ch. 5

the goods are unique, or in other proper circumstances.[1] The decree may contain such terms and conditions as the court may deem just with regard to payment of the price, damages or other relief.[2]

The Official Comment to the Section states:

The test of uniqueness under this section must be made in terms of the total situation which characterizes the contract. Output and requirements contracts involving a particular or peculiarly available source or market present today the typical commercial specific performance situation, as contrasted with contracts for the sale of heirlooms or priceless works of art which were usually involved in the older cases. However, uniqueness is not the sole basis of the remedy under this section for the relief may also be granted "in other proper circumstances" and inability to cover is strong evidence of "other proper circumstances."[3]

A buyer has a right of replevin as to goods identified to the contract if after reasonable effort cover cannot be effected, or if such an effort would be unavailing, or if the goods are shipped under reservation and satisfaction of the security interest in them has been made or tendered.[4]

Library References:

West's Key No. Digests, Replevin ⟲1–16; Specific Performance ⟲67.

§ 5.52 Breach of Contract—Liquidated Damages

Section 2–718 provides for the agreement between the parties for the liquidation or limitation of damages. The amount agreed upon, however, must be reasonable in light of the anticipated or actual harm caused by the breach, the difficulties of proof of loss, and the difficulty of otherwise obtaining an adequate remedy.[1]

Where the seller justifiably withholds delivery of goods because of the buyer's breach, Section 2–718(2) provides that the buyer is entitled to restitution of any amount by which the sum of his payment exceeds: " ... (a) the amount to which the seller is entitled by virtue of terms liquidating the seller's damages in accordance with subsection (1), or (b) in the absence of such terms, twenty per cent of the value of the total performance for which the buyer is obligated under the contract or $500, whichever is smaller."[2] The Official Comment to Subsection (2) states that the statute refuses to recognize a forfeiture unless the amount

---

§ 5.51

1. UCC § 2–716(1).
2. UCC § 2–716(2).
3. UCC § 2–716, Official Comment 2.
4. UCC § 2–716(3).

§ 5.52

1. *See* Brecher v. Laikin, 430 F.Supp. 103 (S.D.N.Y.1977) (where court sustained liquidated damages clause, measure of damages will be no more or less than sum specified in clause).
2. UCC § 2–718(2).

represents a reasonable liquidation.[3] The buyer's right to restitution under UCC § 2–718(2) is subject to offset to the extent that the seller establishes (1) a right to recover damages under Article 2 other than in UCC § 2–718(1) and (2) the value of the benefits received by the buyer under the contract.[4]

Where the seller has received payment in goods, their reasonable value or their resale must be treated as payments for purposes of Section 2–718(2).[5] However, if the seller has notice of the buyer's breach before reselling, the resale is subject to the conditions laid down in Section 2–706.[6]

Subject to the limitations in UCC § 2–718, Section 2–719 provides that the contract may provide for remedies in addition to or in substitution of those provided in Article 2.[7] Where circumstances cause an exclusive or limited remedy to fail, it must give way to the general remedy provisions of Article 2.[8] Consequential damages may be limited or excluded. However, their limitation or exclusion must not be unconscionable.[9]

Library References:

West's Key No. Digests, Damages ⚖︎74–86.

§ 5.53 Breach of Contract—Mitigation of Damages

Section 2–603 requires a merchant buyer in possession or control of rejected goods to follow any reasonable instructions from the seller with respect to the goods if the seller has no agent at the market of rejection. In the absence of instructions, the buyer must make reasonable efforts to sell the goods if they are perishable or threaten to speedily decline in value.[1] If a buyer's demand for indemnity for expenses is not forthcoming, then the instructions are deemed not to be reasonable.[2] The buyer is entitled to reimbursement for his reasonable expenses.[3] In complying with this section, the buyer is held only to good faith and conduct under this Section is neither acceptance nor conversion.[4]

---

3. UCC § 2–718, Official Comment 2. See Fifty States Management Corp. v. Pioneer Auto Parks, Inc., 46 N.Y.2d 573, 415 N.Y.S.2d 800, 389 N.E.2d 113 (1979) (equity abhors forfeiture; court will look closely at terms of liquidated damages agreement).

4. UCC § 2–718(3).

5. UCC § 2–718(4).

6. UCC § 2–718(4).

7. The Official Comment to UCC § 2–719 states that the parties are left free to shape their remedies to their particular requirements, and reasonable agreements are to be given effect. "However, it is of the very essence of a sale contract that at least minimum adequate remedies be available." UCC § 2–719, Official Comment 1.

8. UCC § 2–719(2). See also, Chapter 30 "Damages," infra.

9. UCC § 2–719(3).

§ 5.53

1. UCC § 2–603(1).
2. UCC § 2–603(1).
3. UCC § 2–603(2).
4. UCC § 2–603(3).

Section 2–604 provides:

Subject to the provisions of the immediately preceding section on perishables if the seller gives no instructions within a reasonable time after notification of rejection the buyer may store the rejected goods for the seller's account or reship them to him or resell them for the seller's account with reimbursement as provided in the preceding section. Such action is not acceptance or conversion.[5]

Section 2–604 is intended to accord a great deal of leeway to a rightfully rejecting buyer who is acting in good faith. The listing of what the buyer may do in the absence of instructions from the seller is intended to be illustrative rather than exhaustive.[6]

Section 2–704, concerning the seller's right to identify goods to the contract and to salvage unfinished goods, allows the seller to resell the goods intended for the contract. Under this Section, "... the seller is given express power to complete manufacture or procurement of goods for the contract unless the exercise of reasonable commercial judgment as to the facts as they appear at the time he learns of the breach makes it clear such action will result in a material increase in damages."[7] In this situation, the burden is on the buyer to show the commercially unreasonable nature of the seller's action.

Library References:
West's Key No. Digests, Sales ⟲418.

§ 5.54 Third–Party Interests

The rights of creditors and secured parties are covered by Section 2–402. Essentially, the rights of unsecured creditors of the seller with respect to goods identified to the contract are subject to the buyer's right to recover the goods under UCC Article 2.[1] However, nothing in Article 2 should be deemed to affect the rights of a secured creditor under UCC Article 9 on Secured Transactions.[2] Section 2–403 provides that a *bona fide* purchaser is given title to all that his transferor had power to give.

Library References:
West's Key No. Digests, Sales ⟲219–245.5.

§ 5.55 Third–Party Interests—Subsequent Buyers

Section 2–403(1) provides that a person with voidable title has the power to transfer good title to a good faith purchaser. When goods are delivered under a purchase transaction, the purchaser has such power even though:

- The transferor was deceived as to the identify of the purchaser; or

---

5. UCC § 5–604.
6. UCC § 2–604, Official Comment.
7. UCC § 2–704, Official Comment 2.

§ 5.54
1. UCC § 2–402(1).
2. UCC § 2–402(3)(a).

- The delivery was in exchange for a check which is later dishonored; or
- It was agreed that the transaction was to be a "cash sale"; or
- The delivery was procured through fraud punishable as larcenous under the criminal law.

Section 2–403(2) provides that any entrusting of goods to a merchant who deals in goods of that kind gives him the right to transfer the entruster's rights in the goods to a buyer in the ordinary course of business. Under this provision " ... protection is afforded to one who purchases in the ordinary course of business from a merchant, to whom the goods have been entrusted, even though the merchant was given no authority to deal with the goods by the entruster."[1]

Library References:

West's Key No. Digests, Sales ⬦234–245.5.

§ 5.56 Third–Party Interests—Other Creditors

The rights of unsecured creditors of the seller with respect to goods identified to a contract are subject to the buyer's right to recover the goods.[1]

A creditor of the seller may treat a sale or an identification of goods to a contract for sale as void if, as against the creditor a retention by the seller is fraudulent under any rule of law.[2] However, retention or possession by a merchant-seller in good faith and current course of trade for a commercially reasonable period of time after a sale or identification is not fraudulent.[3]

Nothing in Article 2 is intended to impair the rights of a creditor under Article 9 on Secured Transactions.[4]

§ 5.57 Drafting Checklists—Order of Goods for Resale by Buyer

This checklist highlights the clauses necessary in a basic order form agreement for the purchase of manufactured goods. The actual form is found at § 5.65.

1. Specify when the order is accepted and the limitations of acceptance to the terms of the agreement.[1] (See § 5.23)
2. Insert a clause referring to the buyer's right to cancel prior to receipt of acceptance.

§ 5.55
1. UCC § 2–403, N.Y. Anno. (2).

§ 5.56
1. UCC § 2–402(1).
2. UCC § 2–402(2).
3. UCC § 2–402(2).
4. UCC § 2–402(3).

§ 5.57
1. UCC § 2–206.

§ 5.57 COMMERCIAL SALES CONTRACTS Ch. 5

3. Include a "time of the essence" clause to provide an escape for the buyer if the goods or services are not timely delivered.
4. A warranty clause must identify the specific warranties required of the seller in addition to warranties express or implied in law.[2] (See § 5.27)
5. Expressly note that the goods are purchased for resale, including a clause providing for damages to the buyer in lost profits.
6. Specify the seller's obligations to comply with all pertinent laws or regulations.
7. Insert a clause limiting the price to the "lawful" contract price permitted by law where relevant.
8. Incorporate an indemnification clause running from seller to buyer.
9. Identify the seller's obligations with regard to the marking and shipment of each package, including responsibility for shipping costs.
10. Include a clause that upon cancellation of the order the buyer is absolved of obligations under the order.
11. Expressly state the conditions under which the seller will avoid liability for shipment delays, such as fire, strikes, lockouts, machinery breakdown, or governmental action.
12. Include clause that the contract expresses the entire agreement between the parties.

§ 5.58 Drafting Checklists—Verified Complaint on Account Stated for Goods, Services and Wares Delivered

To properly allege a cause of action sounding in an account stated, the verified complaint must include, at a minimum, the following allegations:

1. That a specific sum was owed by the defendant to the plaintiff;
2. That demands by the plaintiff for payment of this sum were ignored by the defendant and the amount is still due and owing; and
3. That the defendant has not objected to the fact that the amount is due and owing.[1]

Library References:
West's Key No. Digests, Account Stated ⚖18.

2. UCC §§ 2–312—2–315.

§ 5.58
1. See infra, § 5.66 for a sample Complaint alleging an account stated for goods and services.

§ 5.59 Drafting Checklists—Plaintiff's Notice of Motion for Summary Judgment in Contract Action

A motion for summary judgment dismissing a breach of contract complaint under CPLR 3212 must:

1. Only be made after issue is joined;
2. Be supported by affidavit by a person having knowledge of the facts, copies of the pleadings and any other available proof such as depositions or written admissions; and
3. Set forth the grounds upon which the motion is made which would warrant the court as a matter of law to direct judgment in the plaintiff's favor.[1]

Library References:

West's Key No. Digests, Judgment ⚖︎182.

§ 5.60 Drafting Checklists—Affidavit of Officer of Plaintiff Company in Support of Summary Judgment Motion in Contract Action

An affidavit in support of a motion to dismiss a breach of contract complaint under CPLR 3212 must:

1. Be by a person having knowledge of the facts;
2. Recite all material facts; and
3. Show that there is no defense to the cause of action, or that the defense has no merit.[1]

Library References:

West's Key No. Digests, Judgment ⚖︎182.

§ 5.61 Drafting Checklists—Notice of Petition for Order Staying Arbitration in Dispute Over Contract for Sale of Goods

A petition to stay an arbitration proceeding must be brought by notice of petition in the court and county in which the arbitration is sought to be heard.

1. An application to stay arbitration must be made within 20 days after service of a notice or demand to arbitrate.[1]

---

§ 5.59

1. *See infra,* § 5.67 for an illustrative Notice of Motion for Summary Judgment in a contract action.

§ 5.60

1. *See infra,* § 5.68 for an illustrative Affidavit in Support of a Motion for Summary Judgment in a contract action.

§ 5.61

1. CPLR 7503(c).

§ 5.61 COMMERCIAL SALES CONTRACTS Ch. 5

2. Notice of an application to stay arbitration must be served in the same manner as a summons or by registered or certified mail, return receipt requested.[2]
3. Service of an application for stay of arbitration must be made on the adverse party, or upon counsel for the adverse party if counsel's name appears on the demand for arbitration or notice of intention to arbitrate.[3]
4. Any provisions in the arbitration agreement waiving the right to apply for a stay are null and void;[4]
5. In addition to the notice of petition, annexed petition and necessary affidavits from individuals familiar with the facts, as well as an attorney affidavit with legal argument.[5]

Library References:

West's Key No. Digests, Arbitration ⇔23.5.

§ 5.62 Drafting Checklists—Petition for Order Staying Arbitration in Dispute Over Contract for Sale of Goods

1. Set forth sufficient facts and documentary evidence to show that the dispute is not subject to arbitration.
2. Append sales agreements to the petition.
3. Set forth the nature of dispute.
4. Show (if true) that no prior disputes had been resolved by arbitration between parties.
5. Verify petition.[1]

Library References:

West's Key No. Digests, Arbitration ⇔23.5.

§ 5.63 Drafting Checklists—Affidavit in Opposition to Petition for Order Staying Arbitration in Dispute Over Contract for Sale of Goods

1. Append the agreement between the parties containing the arbitration clause.
2. State that industry custom is to arbitrate disputes between parties.

2. CPLR 7503(c).
3. CPLR 7503(c).
4. CPLR 7503(c).
5. See infra, § 5.69 for form of Notice of Petition.

§ 5.62

1. See infra, § 5.70 for form of Petition.

644

Ch. 5 ORDER OF GOODS FOR RESALE BY BUYER **§ 5.65**

3. State that it is the regular course of business between the parties to resolve their disputes in arbitration—that the parties have always done business in this manner.

4. If service has not been effected within 20 days of notice of or demand for arbitration set forth, sufficient facts supporting service.[1]

Library References:

West's Key No. Digests, Arbitration ⟺23.5.

§ 5.64 Drafting Checklists—Answer to Petition for Order Staying Arbitration in Dispute Over Contract for Sale of Goods

1. Deny all allegations in Petition supporting a claim that a stay of arbitration should be granted.

2. Set forth affirmative defenses.

3. Set forth ordinary defenses.[1]

Library References:

West's Key No. Digests, Arbitration ⟺23.5.

§ 5.65 Forms—Order of Goods for Resale by Buyer

This is a standard order for goods for resale by the buyer, generally a wholesaler. It is drafted to protect the interests of the buyer.

THE WITHIN ORDER IS SUBJECT TO THE FOLLOWING ADDITIONAL TERMS AND CONDITIONS.

1. This order, when accepted by Seller, is the entire contract of the parties. ACCEPTANCE IS LIMITED TO THE TERMS OF THIS ORDER and no variation, modification, or addition to this order, or the contract resulting from this order, or the terms and conditions of either, and no waiver of any provision of either, shall be effective without Buyer's written consent. Despite the provisions of the acceptance, only this order is the contract of the parties. Prior dealings or trade usage shall not change, add to or detract from the provisions of this order.

2. Buyer reserves the right to cancel this order at any time before actual receipt of Seller's written acceptance of all terms of this order, and also if such acceptance is not received within fifteen (15) days from the date of this order, and also if delivery is not made as specified.

3. Time is of the essence in this contract. If delivery of conforming goods or rendering of services is not complete by the time(s) specified, or

---

§ 5.63

1. *See infra,* § 5.71 for form of Affidavit in Support of Petition.

§ 5.64

1. *See infra,* § 5.72 for form of Answer to Petition.

645

if Seller breaches any terms of this order, Buyer reserves the right, without liability and in addition to its other rights and remedies, to cancel this contract and to reject in whole or in part those goods not yet delivered or services not yet rendered, and to purchase substitute goods or services elsewhere, and to charge Seller and hold Seller liable for any loss incurred. Any provision herein for delivery of goods or for rendering services by installments shall not be construed as making Seller's obligations severable.

4. In addition to all express and implied warranties, Seller warrants: that all goods and services covered by this order shall comply with the terms of this order and with all specifications, drawings, samples or other descriptions furnished or adopted by Buyer; that same shall be in accord with all representations made by Seller to Buyer; that same shall be merchantable, fit for the purpose intended, of the best quality and workmanship, free from all defects, latent or patent, and safe for consumer use. If Buyer determines that the goods are defective or nonconforming or that Seller has otherwise breached this contract, Buyer reserves the right, without liability and in addition to its other rights and remedies, to reject and return the goods at Seller's expense (including transportation and handling costs), and, in addition thereto, Buyer shall have the right to cancel any undelivered portion of this order and to cancel any other order placed with Seller.

5. Seller is aware that the goods covered by this contract are purchased by Buyer for resale pursuant to actual or prospective contracts and that any breach by Seller of this contract, whether by failure to make timely delivery or otherwise, may cause Buyer to sustain loss, and Seller shall not be liable to Buyer for any such loss, including special damages, loss of profits and loss of anticipated profits.

6. This order is confidential. Seller shall not make disclosure to any third person of this order, or of any details thereof, or of any technical data furnished by the Buyer incident to the order. Anything furnished to Seller by Buyer, including but not limited to samples, drawings, patents and materials, shall be kept confidential and remain the property of Buyer, held at Seller's risk, to be used exclusively by Seller for performance of this contract, and all of same shall be returned to Buyer on demand.

7. Seller represents that the goods covered by this order have been manufactured in accordance with the requirements of the Fair Labor Standards Act and all other applicable federal, state and municipal laws, rules and regulations. All goods, wrappers and containers must bear markings and labels required by applicable federal, state, and municipal laws and regulations. If any of the goods covered by this order are subject to the Federal Food, Drug & Cosmetic Act, the Wool Products Labeling Act, the Fur Products Labeling Act, the Textile Fiber Products Identification Act, the Flammable Fabrics Act, the Federal Hazardous

Substances Labeling Act, or any other legislation, Seller's invoice shall bear the separate guarantees provided for under such acts, or shall contain an appropriate statement that a continuing guaranty has been filed in accordance with such Acts and applicable rules and regulations of the Federal Trade Commission.

8. Seller represents that the contract price does not exceed that permitted by law. If the price charged is in excess of the lawful price, Seller agrees to refund such excess. Unless otherwise specified, payment shall be made subject to the terms of this order in U.S. dollars, net sixty (60) days after receipt of conforming goods or services. Credit terms shall bind Seller and Seller has no right to demand cash on delivery pursuant to the Uniform Commercial Code § 2–702(1), or upon any other cause or pretext whatever.

9. Seller shall indemnify Buyer, its customers, users of its goods and products, and its and their successors and assigns, from any loss or damage, including all costs, expenses and counsel fees incident to any claim or action for infringement or otherwise of any patent, copyright, trademark, label, name, design or stamp used by Seller, or incident to any claim of unfair competition arising from Seller's activities. Seller, at its sole expense and upon reasonable notice, shall defend and care for any such claim, suit or action.

10. Buyer shall have the right of inspection and approval. All warranties, remedies and undertakings by Seller shall survive delivery, inspection, acceptance and payment. All warranties, representations and undertakings of Seller shall be for the benefit of Buyer, its customers and users of the goods, and no waiver by Buyer of a breach of any provision of this contract shall constitute a waiver of any other breach or of any of the provisions of this contract.

11. Seller shall clearly mark each package and shipment with the destination address and Buyer's purchase order number unless Buyer otherwise directs in writing. Unless specifically agreed to by Buyer in writing, no charge of any kind, including but not limited to charges for boxing, packaging, storage and cartage, shall be allowed. The Buyer's purchase order number shall be shown on packing slips, bills of lading and invoices.

12. Buyer, upon canceling this order, shall be released of and from any obligation under this order.

13. Seller shall not delegate any duties hereunder, nor assign this contract in whole or in part, without the prior written consent of Buyer.

14. This contract shall be governed and construed by New York State law. It is the entire agreement of the parties. It inures to the benefit of the Buyer, its customers, and their respective successors and assigns, and it obligates Seller and its successors and assigns. It may not be changed or discharged orally. Any dispute, action, controversy or

§ 5.65   COMMERCIAL SALES CONTRACTS   Ch. 5

claim incident to this contract shall be submitted to a New York State court pursuant to the Simplified Procedure for Court Determination of Disputes.

TERMS:

REMARKS:

CONDITIONS (Imposed by seller):

Seller is not responsible for delay or inability to deliver due either directly or indirectly to fire, strikes, lockouts, breakdown of machinery, failure of crop, of raw material or accident of any kind, or due to interference with or inability to obtain transportation, suitable insurance or any license or permit now or hereafter required, or due to municipal, state, federal or other governmental action, regulation or prohibition affecting the production, transportation, sale or delivery of the goods affected by this contract, or due to any current or future war conditions or the development thereof, or due to the loss, destruction, embargo or detention of shipping, or for any reason whatever due to the failure of sub-contractors, carriers, or manufacturers in Seller's control. Any unforeseen increases or new export or import taxes, and/or duties, transportation and insurance fees imposed upon Seller shall be for Buyer's account.

All terms, provisions or conditions contained in Buyer's order that are in addition to or inconsistent with the terms stated herein shall be a nullity unless expressly accepted in writing by the Seller. This contract constitutes the entire agreement between the parties hereto, and there are no understandings, representations or warranties of any kind not expressly set forth herein.

The Seller assumes no responsibility or liability for infringement of any patent and/or trademark held by a third party with respect to any product supplied on order of Customer. All such liability shall be assumed by Customer and Seller shall be held harmless by Customer for all expenses and losses incurred by Seller as a result of any such infringement.

In the event shipment or delivery of all or any part of the above merchandise is delayed for any of the reasons specified in the preceding paragraph hereof, (1) Buyer nevertheless agrees to accept delivery of all or the parts of the merchandise of which delivery has been delayed at the times when same becomes available, and the time for Seller to make delivery shall be deemed extended accordingly; or (2) Seller may at any time before delivery, at its option, and upon written notice to Buyer, cancel this agreement in whole or as to any unfilled portion thereof without recourse by either party against the other, except that the Buyer remains liable for any previous unpaid shipments. Any controversies or claims between the parties hereunder shall be submitted to arbitration in New York City under the auspices and rules then obtaining of the American Arbitration Association.

ACCEPTED:

_____   _____
           Buyer   Seller

Please return duplicate duly signed.

§ 5.66 Forms—Verified Complaint on Account Stated for Goods, Services and Wares Delivered

This is a complaint brought on an account stated. This form is to be used where a sum certain is due the plaintiff on a sale of goods, and there has been no objection to the account stated by the defendant.

SUPREME COURT OF THE STATE OF NEW YORK
COUNTY OF _____

_____,   )
) VERIFIED
                  Plaintiff,   ) COMPLAINT
)
     -against-   )
) Index No. _____
)
_____,   )
)
                 Defendants.   )
)

Plaintiff, appearing by its attorneys, _____, _____, _____ & _____, P.C., and complaining of the defendants herein, respectfully shows to the Court as follows:

1. That the plaintiff is and was at all times material to this cause of action a corporation organized and existing pursuant to the laws of the State of New York with offices to do business in the County of _____ and State of New York.

§ 5.66   COMMERCIAL SALES CONTRACTS   Ch. 5

2. That upon information and belief, and at all times material to this cause of action, plaintiff had its principal place of business at _____ Avenue, _____, New York in the State of New York.

3. That prior hereto, the plaintiff delivered to the defendants, at their the special instance and request, certain goods, wares and services for an agreed price and upon an open account.

4. That at various times during the delivery of such goods, wares and services, and on numerous occasions thereafter, accounts were stated between the plaintiff and the defendants; that there is presently due and owing from the defendants to the plaintiff for such goods, wares and services delivered, after the deduction of all amounts paid by the defendants to the plaintiff in partial satisfaction thereof, the sum of _____ Dollars ($_____), with interest thereon from _____, 19__, representing the agreed price and reasonable value of such services delivered by the plaintiff.

5. That an account was stated between the plaintiff and the defendants in the amount of _____ Dollars ($_____), with interest thereon from _____, 19__, as to which defendant has rendered no objections.

WHEREFORE the plaintiff demands judgment against the defendants in the amount of _____ Dollars ($_____), with interest thereon from _____, 19__, together with the costs and disbursements of this action.

_____ [insert attorney's
name, address and
telephone number]

[Verification]

Library References:

West's Key No. Digests, Account Stated ⚖=18.

§ 5.67 Forms—Plaintiff's Notice of Motion for Summary Judgment in Contract Action 💾

This is a standard form for use in making a plaintiff's summary judgment motion. The notice itself does not contain reference to the nature of the underlying action, which is a dispute over a sale of goods. Such facts are more appropriately inserted in an accompanying affidavit. (See § 5.68)

Ch. 5   AFFIDAVIT: SUMMARY JUDGMENT MOTION   § 5.68

SUPREME COURT OF THE STATE OF NEW YORK
COUNTY OF _____

```
_____,              )
                              ) NOTICE OF MOTION
              Plaintiff,      )
                              )
    -against-                 ) Index No. _____
                              )
_____,              )
                              ) ORAL ARGUMENT IS
              Defendants.     ) REQUESTED
                              )
```

PLEASE TAKE NOTICE, that upon the annexed affidavit of _____, sworn to on the _____, 19__, and the attached exhibits, and upon all of the pleadings and proceedings heretofore had in this action, the undersigned attorneys for the plaintiff will move this Court at IAS Part _____, Room _____, before the Honorable _____, to be held at the Courthouse, located at _____ Avenue, _____, New York on the _____, 19__ at _____ a.m./p.m. or as soon thereafter as counsel can be heard, for an order pursuant to CPLR 3212 granting the plaintiff summary judgment on its complaint herein, and against the defendant on its defenses and counterclaims upon the ground that there are no genuine material issues of fact requiring trial.

PLEASE TAKE FURTHER NOTICE that pursuant to CPLR 2214(b), answering papers, if any, must be served upon the undersigned at least seven (7) days before the return date of this motion.

Dated: _____

                                              YOURS, ETC.

                                              _____ *[insert attorney's name, address and telephone number]*

TO: _____ *[insert attorney's name, address and telephone number]*

Library References:
    West's Key No. Digests, Judgment ⚖182.

§ 5.68 Forms—Affidavit of Vice President of Plaintiff Purchaser in Support of Summary Judgment Motion in Contract Action

This is an affidavit supporting the notice of motion in § 5.67. Note the factual nature of its allegations intertwined with advocacy and

§ 5.68   COMMERCIAL SALES CONTRACTS   Ch. 5

argument. The object in the preparation of supporting affidavits is thoroughness and an understanding of the factual predicates necessary to obtain a successful ruling on the motion. This motion also serves the purpose of seeking dismissal of the defendant's defenses and counterclaims against plaintiff.

SUPREME COURT OF THE STATE OF NEW YORK
COUNTY OF _____

```
_____,           )
                                   )  AFFIDAVIT IN SUPPORT
                        Plaintiff, )  OF SUMMARY JUDGMENT
                                   )
          -against-                )
                                   )  Index No. _____
                                   )
_____,           )
                                   )
                        Defendants.)
_____            )
```

STATE OF _____)
) ss:
COUNTY OF _____)

_____, being duly sworn, deposes and says:

1. I was Vice President of plaintiff _____, Inc., from 19__ to 19__. I am fully familiar with the facts and circumstances of this matter.

2. I submit this affidavit in support of plaintiff's motion for summary judgment on its complaint against defendant _____, Inc., and against defendant on its defenses and counterclaims in the above-captioned action.

3. In this action, plaintiff seeks payment of $710,000 plus interest, costs and disbursements for 1000 metric tons of high density polyethylene delivered to defendant. Summary judgment is appropriate on plaintiff's claim because there is no genuine dispute as to the following facts:

   a) that the plaintiff agreed to sell, and defendant agreed to buy, the 1000 MT of polyethylene;

   b) that the plaintiff delivered 1000 MT of Polyethylene to defendant;

   c) that the defendant accepted delivery and resold the Polyethylene;

   d) that the defendant never paid for the Polyethylene.

4. Defendant's defenses and counterclaims are all based on its claim that plaintiff wrongly refused or was unable to deliver a second 1000 MT shipment which was non-severable from the first.

Ch. 5   AFFIDAVIT: SUMMARY JUDGMENT MOTION   § 5.68

5. However, plaintiff was fully justified in refusing shipment of the second lot because defendant breached a material term of the contract by failing to open appropriate letters of credit to pay for either lot.

6. Moreover, the delivery of the lots was severable because the contract provided, and defendant specifically requested, that the shipments be made in separate lots. Significantly, defendant thereafter submitted a letter of credit which expressly permitted partial shipments.

7. Defendant's reliance on an alleged purchase order which purports to contain boilerplate severability provisions is misplaced, as that order, by its terms, applies only to the first 1000 MT lot, which was fully delivered. Moreover, that order was expressly repudiated by defendant two months before the controlling contract was executed.

8. Furthermore, as defendant did not reject, but fully accepted and subsequently resold the first 1000 MT, its claim does not excuse its failure to pay for the goods received.

PROCEDURAL HISTORY

9. Plaintiff commenced this action by filing a summons and complaint on _____, 19__. Issue was joined on _____, 19__, when the parties submitted a joint statement pursuant to CPLR 3031 under the New York Simplified Procedure for Court Determination of Disputes. A copy of the joint statement (exhibits omitted) is annexed hereto as Exhibit __. A Note of Issue was filed in _____, 19__.

10. Extensive document production was conducted and is now substantially complete. Depositions of both parties have been completed, including those of _____, President of plaintiff; _____, President of defendant; and _____, Vice President of defendant. I was deposed in my capacity as Vice President of plaintiff. Additionally, the depositions of _____ and _____, former employees of plaintiff, were taken.

11. Accordingly, as discovery is substantially complete, the parties have agreed that the matter is ripe for summary judgment.

THE FACTS

12. Plaintiff is a New York corporation engaged, among other things, in the resale of chemical compounds. Defendant is a Texas corporation engaged in the resale of chemical compounds.

13. On _____, 19__, the parties entered into a contract of sale whereby plaintiff agreed to sell and defendant agreed to buy 1000 MT of high density polyethylene at $510 USD per net MT, CNF Calcutta, or $500 USD per net MT, CNF Bombay (Buyer's option) for delivery in late _____, 19__.

14. Plaintiff confirmed the purchase and sale agreement by written sales contract confirmation No. _____ dated _____, 19__. The contract required that defendant make payment by opening a confirmed,

653

irrevocable letter of credit in an amount covering the entire shipment. A copy of the contract is annexed hereto as Exhibit ___.

15. Plaintiff also sent a telex confirming the order on the same date, reciting the identical terms, including the letter of credit. That telex also offered for sale a second 1000 MT lot. A copy of that telex is annexed hereto as Exhibit ___.

16. The parties subsequently amended the contract to include the second 1000 MT lot, and to move the delivery date to _____, 19__. A copy of that contract, plaintiff's Sales Confirmation No. _____ dated _____, 19__, is annexed hereto as Exhibit ___.

17. Except for the amount of product and delivery date, the amended contract was identical to the original and did not vary with respect to the price or payment terms. Plaintiff further confirmed this by sending a telex the same day indicating that "all other terms and conditions remain unchanged." A copy of that telex, dated _____, 19__, is annexed hereto as Exhibit ___.

18. Thus, the amended contract expressly retained the requirement that payment for the entire 2000 MT be made by "confirmed, irrevocable letter of credit." Accordingly, on _____, 19__, I sent the following telex to the defendant's comptroller and credit manager:

> As you might have learned, we have a possibility to ship above parcel early February. However, in order to make proper arrangements, it is imperative that you will open L/C immediately. It would be appreciated when you advise us L/C No.—amount and opening bank by [telex] return.

A copy of that telex is annexed hereto as Exhibit ___.

19. Defendant confirmed this understanding by a telex dated _____, 19__. That telex stated:

> We hereby give you release for [shipment] of 2000 on [vessel] around _____, 19__. Exact quantities for each port will be informed to [you] upon [receipt] of clean L/C for each port.

A copy of that telex from _____ to _____, is annexed hereto as Exhibit ___.

20. By telex dated _____, 19__, I notified defendant that we had yet to receive evidence that it had opened a letter of credit for the first lot. A copy of that telex is annexed hereto as Exhibit ___.

21. By telex dated _____, 19__, I again notified defendant that plaintiff was still missing the letter of credit. A copy of that telex is annexed hereto as Exhibit ___.

22. By telex dated _____, 19__, defendant notified plaintiff of its regret that the letter had not been opened, blaming the delay on the bank. Defendant advised that the letter would be opened that day. A

Ch. 5   AFFIDAVIT: SUMMARY JUDGMENT MOTION   § 5.68

copy of that telex, from _____, of defendant, to myself is annexed hereto as Exhibit __.

23. Plaintiff did not receive the letter of credit until_____, 19__. That letter of credit provided for payment covering 1,000 MT/CNF Bombay. A copy of that letter, dated _____, 19__, is annexed hereto as Exhibit __.

24. However, the letter of credit was partially illegible. I notified defendant that plaintiff would deny liability in the event that a nonconformance in presentment for payment should arise as a result of said illegibility. A copy of that telex, dated _____, 19__ to _____, is annexed hereto as Exhibit __.

25. Nevertheless, on _____, 19__, plaintiff fulfilled its contractual obligations by commencing shipment of the first 1000 MT of polyethylene. A copy of the Certificate of Quality and Quantity certifying the shipment is annexed hereto as Exhibit __.

26. By telex dated _____, 19__, plaintiff advised defendant that the estimated time of arrival for the first lot would be on or about _____, 19__, Bombay, on the vessel Holstein Racer. A copy of that telex from _____ to _____, is annexed hereto as Exhibit __.

27. By telex dated _____, 19__, defendant requested that plaintiff hold the product at the transshipment point for an additional two weeks because it had not completely negotiated its required letter of credit. A copy of that telex is annexed hereto as Exhibit __.

28. On _____, 19__, I informed defendant that despite plaintiff's best efforts, it was not possible to delay product at the transshipment point. A copy of my telex to _____ is annexed hereto as Exhibit __.

29. On or about _____, 19__, I notified defendant that plaintiff would not be liable for any demurrage or losses as a result of defendant's failure to present a clean letter of credit. A copy of that telex to _____, is annexed hereto as Exhibit __.

30. In late _____, 19__, I spoke to defendant's Comptroller, _____, who agreed that defendant would notify its confirming bank that the parties had agreed to allow the product to be delivered with a transshipment and that a late shipment would be acceptable.

31. In addition, Mr. _____ assured me that defendant would instruct its confirming bank to waive strict compliance with the letter of credit terms.

32. On _____, 19__, plaintiff completed the delivery of 1,000 MT of high density polyethylene at $500 USD per net MT/CNF Bombay. As conceded by defendant's Vice President, _____, the goods were received and accepted by defendant's customers. (See Exhibit __)

§ 5.68   COMMERCIAL SALES CONTRACTS   Ch. 5

33. The same day, plaintiff made a presentment to defendant's confirming bank, _____ Bank, New York, New York, for payment under the terms of the letter of credit.

34. Despite the assurances of Mr. _____, however, defendant did not waive compliance with the literal terms of the letter, and the bank refused to honor it.

35. Accordingly, by telex dated _____, 19__, I informed defendant the second shipment would not be made until defendant fulfilled its agreement to waive discrepancies in the letter of credit. A copy of that telex is annexed hereto as Exhibit __.

36. By telex dated _____, 19__, I again notified defendant that plaintiff had no evidence that the letter of credit would be honored. I reiterated that arrangement for the shipment of the second lot would not be made until the letter was honored and defendant had provided the required letter of credit for the second lot. A copy of my telex to Ms. _____, of defendant, is annexed hereto as Exhibit __.

37. Defendant did not respond until _____, 19__. Ignoring its contractual obligation to make payment for the first lot or open a letter of credit for the second, defendant insisted that plaintiff ship out the second 1000 MT without any assurance of payment. A copy of defendant's telex from _____ to me, dated _____, 19__, is annexed hereto as Exhibit __.

38. By telex dated _____, 19__, I repeated plaintiff's demand for payment for the first lot and informed defendant that the second lot would be ready by mid-_____, 19__. A copy of that telex to _____ is annexed hereto as Exhibit __.

39. By telex dated _____, 19__, I informed defendant that plaintiff had just been advised that defendant had specifically instructed the bank to refuse to honor plaintiff's presentment for the letter of credit. A copy of that telex to _____, is annexed hereto as Exhibit __.

40. At his deposition, _____ confirmed that defendant had given the bank such instructions (_____'s deposition at _____, annexed hereto as Exhibit __).

41. By letter dated _____, 19__, _____ Bank advised plaintiff that its presentment was rejected. The letter stated that at the advice of defendant, payment would be handled "outside of the L/C terms." A copy of the Bank's written rejection is annexed hereto as Exhibit __.

42. Accordingly, by telex dated _____, 19__ I notified defendant that plaintiff had fully complied with the letter of credit terms and expected direct payment for the goods by _____, 19__. A copy of that telex to _____ is annexed hereto as Exhibit __.

43. Defendant never arranged for payment outside of the L/C terms or through any means. Instead, by telex dated _____, 19__,

Ch. 5   AFFIDAVIT: SUMMARY JUDGMENT MOTION   § 5.68

defendant repeated its demand for shipment of the second lot, again refusing to make any arrangements for payment of either lot. A copy of that telex from _____ to me is annexed hereto as Exhibit __.

44. By telex dated _____, 19__, plaintiff's President, _____, informed defendant that in view of its failure to pay for the first shipment, plaintiff held it in default of its obligations and would not make the second shipment. A copy of Mr. _____'s telex to _____ is annexed hereto as Exhibit __.

45. Thus, there is simply no issue of fact concerning defendant's default under the contract. Defendant agreed to buy, accepted delivery of, and resold 1000 MT of polyethylene without ever paying or making proper arrangements to pay for it.

DEFENDANT'S DEFENSES AND COUNTERCLAIMS

46. Defendant attempts to justify its failure to pay for the goods which it admittedly received, accepted and resold by claiming that plaintiff unreasonably demanded a letter of credit which was not required by the contract, and thereafter refused to deliver the second 1000 MT which was allegedly non-severable from the first.

47. However, both of these claims are contradicted by the terms of the _____, 19__ contract and the documented course of dealing between the parties.

48. Plaintiff was fully justified in refusing shipment of the second lot upon defendant's refusal to provide a letter of credit or otherwise pay for the first lot. As noted above, the _____, 19__ contract specifically required a "confirmed, irrevocable letter of credit." (See Exhibit __).

49. Defendant made no objection to plaintiff's subsequent, repeated demands for the letter, openly acknowledged its obligation to provide one, and in fact submitted a proposed letter on _____, 19__ (see above paragraphs 18–22 and accompanying Exhibits).

50. Defendant did not dispute its obligation to pay by letter of credit until after its default. It was not until _____, 19__, that defendant first asserted that the contract required no letter of credit. A copy of that telex is annexed hereto as Exhibit __.

51. Although defendant annexed to the Joint Statement a copy of what it purported to be the original copy of the _____, 19__ contract with the letter of credit term crossed out, and the term "net 30," (i.e., requiring no letter of credit) written in by hand, it was established during the course of discovery that the document was no more than a transparent, post-litigation attempt by defendant to manufacture evidence.

52. Defendant's President, _____, admitted that he, and not anyone at plaintiff corporation, had crossed out the letter of credit term. (See _____'s deposition at _____, annexed hereto as Exhibit __.)

53. Although Mr. _____ alleged that he returned the original copy of the contract to plaintiff after making this alteration, he conceded that he could produce no cover letter establishing that the original was actually sent. (See _____'s deposition at _____, annexed hereto as Exhibit __.)

54. In fact, the original copy of the contract (with the alterations in blue ink) was produced by Mr. _____ at his deposition. (See _____'s deposition at _____, annexed hereto as Exhibit __.) Thus, the original could not have been sent to plaintiff, as it was produced from the files of defendant. As I testified at my deposition, the altered contract was never received by plaintiff.

55. Additionally, Mr. _____'s testimony raised grave doubts as to whether the alterations were made upon receipt of the sales confirmation in Houston on _____, 19__, or at some other time during the course of the litigation. Mr. _____ "couldn't remember" whether he was in the United States on _____, 19__ (See _____'s deposition at _____, annexed hereto as Exhibit __), but later recalled that he, _____, left the country "sometime in January of '87'" and did not return until March (_____'s dep. at 282).

56. Similarly, defendant's reliance on its _____, 19__ purchase order indicating that the sale was on a "net 30" basis is wholly improper. That order indicated a sale of only 1000 MT, and thus did not reflect the final agreement of the parties for a 2000 MT sale as embodied in the final, binding, _____, 19__ contract. A copy of that order is annexed hereto as Exhibit __.

57. Indeed, by telex dated _____, 19__, defendant expressly repudiated any reliance on the _____, 19__ purchase order by purporting to cancel it. A copy of that telex from _____ to _____ is annexed hereto as Exhibit __.

58. The defendant's President, _____, also admitted that there were no discussions of the terms of the _____, 19__ purchase order, stating that defendant in fact shortly thereafter canceled that order (see _____'s deposition at _____, annexed hereto as Exhibit __).

59. Although Mr. _____ subsequently alleged that defendant had an oral agreement with Mr. _____ to the effect that payment would be made on open terms, he admitted that he had no records or written confirmation of such an agreement. (See _____'s deposition at _____, annexed as Exhibit __.)

60. Plaintiff's president, _____, testified that no such agreement was ever made with or negotiated by plaintiff. (See _____'s deposition at _____, annexed hereto as Exhibit __.)

61. Moreover, Mr. _____ testified that he would not have put the letter of credit term in the contract had Mr. _____ not agreed to it. (See _____'s deposition at _____, annexed as Exhibit __.)

Ch. 5   AFFIDAVIT: SUMMARY JUDGMENT MOTION   § 5.68

62. Accordingly, the fact that the contract between the parties required a letter of credit cannot be seriously disputed. Defendant's reliance on fabricated or canceled contracts does not raise an issue of fact. Nor does defendant's wholly undocumented, post-litigation assertion of an "oral agreement" to change that material term merit a trial in view of the unambiguous language of the contract and defendant's repeated, documented acknowledgments of its obligation to open the letter.

63. Nor is there any serious dispute over the severability of the two lots. The contract expressly provides for delivery in "_____, 19__ and _____, 19__," indicating two separate shipments, one in each month.

64. Furthermore, although by amendment the second lot was included in the same contract as the first, each lot was negotiated separately. As noted, the original contract between the parties covered only the first lot.

65. In fact, separate shipment of the first lot was arranged before defendant accepted the second lot. By telex dated _____, 19__, plaintiff confirmed that shipment of the first 1000 MT would be rescheduled for the first half of January and requested that defendant confirm its intention to purchase the second 1000 MT. A copy of that telex from _____ to _____ is annexed hereto as Exhibit __.

66. Thereafter, by telex dated _____, 19__, defendant confirmed that the first 1000 MT was scheduled for mid-January and promised to confirm its order for the second 1000 MT within the week. A copy of that telex from _____ to _____ is annexed hereto as Exhibit __.

67. By telex dated _____, 19__, plaintiff informed defendant that the first 1000 MT was scheduled for shipment on _____, 19__, and requested letter of credit details for that shipment. Plaintiff further notified defendant that the second 1000 MT shipment had been rescheduled for _____, 19__. A copy of that telex from _____ to _____ is annexed hereto as Exhibit __.

68. By telex dated _____, 19__, defendant requested that the first 1000 MT lot be shipped in varying amounts to Bombay and Calcutta, and noted that it would "try" to accept the additional 1000 MT to be shipped in February. A copy of that telex from _____ to _____ is annexed hereto as Exhibit __.

69. The parties continued to anticipate separate shipments after the two lots were combined in the same contract. Thus, paragraph 9 of the letter of credit provided by defendant expressly stated that partial shipment was permitted (See Exhibit __).

70. Although plaintiff shipped the first lot on _____, 19__, it was not until _____, 19__, that defendant sent plaintiff a telex stating that "we hereby give you a release for second 1000 MT". A copy of that telex from defendant to me is annexed hereto as Exhibit __.

§ 5.68 COMMERCIAL SALES CONTRACTS Ch. 5

71. Thus, defendant specifically requested that the lots be delivered in separate shipments and did not give clearance to ship the second installment until over a week after the first installment had been shipped by plaintiff.

72. Defendant again relies exclusively on the preprinted, boilerplate clauses on the reverse of its _____, 19__ purchase order in arguing that delivery of the lots was non-severable. However, as noted above, that order was expressly repudiated by defendant (see above paragraphs 57–58 and accompanying exhibits).

73. Furthermore, even if controlling, that order by its terms applies only to the first 1000 MT. Defendant does not allege that plaintiff made a partial shipment of that lot.

74. Finally, defendant's allegation that plaintiff failed to deliver the second lot because that lot had been diverted by its former employee, _____, is both irrelevant and untrue.

75. Significantly, this spurious charge was first raised by defendant on _____, 19__, only after plaintiff's repeated demands for payment on the first lot which had been shipped out nearly two months before. As defendant never paid or even arranged to make payment on that lot, plaintiff's alleged inability to make the second, severable delivery is irrelevant to this action.

76. Furthermore, the contract did not give defendant specific rights to any particular lot of polyethylene. Mr. _____ testified that an additional 7,000–8,000 tons were available to plaintiff from its supplier (See _____'s deposition at _____, annexed as Exhibit __). Plaintiff President, _____, testified that had defendant provided the appropriate letters of credit, plaintiff would have definitely shipped a second 1000 MT lot (See _____'s deposition at _____, annexed as Exhibit __.)

77. Thus, defendant's charges of a conspiracy to defraud it are frivolous, especially in view of defendant's subsequent business relationship with Mr. _____ and his new company.

78. For example, Mr. _____ testified that after he left plaintiff, he formed his own company, _____, Inc. (See _____'s deposition at _____, annexed hereto as Exhibit __.)

79. Defendant's President, _____, testified that defendant continued to trade with Mr. _____ through _____ Inc. immediately after Mr. _____ left plaintiff in 19__ (See _____'s deposition at _____, annexed hereto as Exhibit __.)

80. Although Mr. _____ testified that _____ has transacted no business with plaintiff since it was formed, he stated that _____, Inc., has transacted sales and purchases with defendant totaling between $1,000,000–$1,500,000 since 1987. (_____'s Dep. at 116, annexed hereto as Exhibit __.)

Ch. 5   PETITION: STAY OF ARBITRATION   § 5.69

81. Indeed, defendant's own computer records indicate that defendant purchased 115 MT of high density polyethylene from _____, Inc., on _____, 19__, less than a month after defendant defaulted on its contract with plaintiff. A copy of defendant's computer printout listing transactions with _____, Inc., in 19__ is annexed hereto as Exhibit __.

82. In view of defendant's continuous and continuing business relationship with Mr. _____, and its purchase from his company of over a hundred tons of the very product it accuses him of diverting from plaintiff, its counterclaim for fraud cannot be accorded any credibility.

83. Accordingly, plaintiff is entitled to full payment for the 1000 tons of polyethylene it delivered to defendant. The delivery was made to defendant in good faith and in reliance upon defendant's repeated promises that it would make proper arrangement for payment. Having fully accepted and resold the first lot, defendant's insistence on the delivery of a separately negotiated second lot without any assurance of payment for either lot was unreasonable and in violation of the written contract and documented course of dealing between the parties.

84. Defendant's reliance upon alleged contracts which it has unilaterally altered or expressly repudiated cannot form the basis for a denial of summary judgment. Nor can defendant's last-minute allegations of an "oral amendment" or its spurious, undocumented claims of fraud defeat plaintiff's right to payment for over half a million dollars worth of polyethylene which was undeniably delivered, accepted and resold by defendant.

WHEREFORE, plaintiff _____, Inc., demands judgment against defendant, _____, in the amount of $710,000.00, plus interest, costs and disbursements, and the dismissal of defendant's counterclaims in their entirety.

[*Jurat*]

Library References:

West's Key No. Digests, Judgment ⚖=182.

§ 5.69   Forms—Notice of Petition for Order Staying Arbitration in Dispute Over Contract for Sale of Goods

This Notice of Petition alleges that there was no valid agreement to arbitrate disputes between the parties. The Notice is supported by a Petition. (*See* § 5.70 for form of Petition).

§ 5.69   COMMERCIAL SALES CONTRACTS   Ch. 5

SUPREME COURT OF THE STATE OF NEW YORK
COUNTY OF _____

_____
_____,)
) NOTICE OF PETITION
                 Petitioner,)
)
     -against-   )
) Index No. _____
)
_____,)
)
                 Respondent.)
_____)

     Upon the annexed petition of _____, Inc., sworn to by _____ the _____ day of _____, 19__, and the exhibits annexed thereto, the undersigned will make an application to this Court at the Motion Support Office at the _____ County Courthouse, _____ Avenue, _____, New York, on the _____ day of _____, 19__, at _____A.M or as soon thereafter as counsel can be heard, for an order pursuant to CPLR 7503(b) staying the arbitration instituted by the respondent against the petitioner before the American Arbitration Association, and for other relief, upon the ground that there is no valid agreement between the petitioner and the respondent requiring that disputes between them be submitted to arbitration, and for such other and further relief as to this Court shall appear to be just and proper.

     Please take further notice that pursuant to CPLR 403(b), an answer, answering affidavits and all other papers, if any, are to be served at least seven days before the return date of this application.

     Pursuant to CPLR 7502(a), _____ County is designated as the place of trial since the respondent's principal place of business is located in _____ County and the proposed arbitration proceeding is to be held at the offices of the American Arbitration Association in _____ County.

     Dated: _____

                                             YOURS, ETC.

                                             _____ [*insert attorney's name, address and telephone number*]

TO: _____ [*insert attorney's name, address and telephone number*]

     Library References:
         West's Key No. Digests, Arbitration ⚖=23.5.

Ch. 5   PETITION: STAY OF ARBITRATION   § 5.70

§ 5.70 Forms—Petition for Order Staying Arbitration in Dispute Over Contract for Sale of Goods

This Petition provides factual support for the Notice of Petition found at § 5.69. It provides sufficient facts on its face to support a ruling that the dispute was not arbitrable, including the pertinent sales agreements which, although containing arbitration clauses, were unsigned.

SUPREME COURT OF THE STATE OF NEW YORK
COUNTY OF _____

_____,) VERIFIED
) PETITION
            Petitioner,)
)
   -against-   )
) Index No. _____
)
_____,)
)
            Respondent.)

Petitioner, by its attorneys, _____, _____, _____ & _____, P.C., respectfully alleges:

1. The petitioner is a corporation duly organized and existing under the laws of the State of _____, having its principal place of business at _____ Avenue, _____, New York. At all times material herein, the petitioner has been a manufacturer of _____.

2. Upon information and belief, the respondent is a corporation duly organized and existing under the laws of the State of New York, having its principal place of business at _____ Avenue, _____, New York. At all times material herein, the respondent was an importer and converter of textiles.

3. Under date of _____, 19__, the petitioner issued to the respondent four purchase orders, bearing numbers __, __, __ and __, wherein the petitioner ordered from the respondent quantities of products offered for sale by the respondent. Copies of each of the purchase orders are annexed as joint Exhibit __. Each of the said purchase orders was printed on one side of the paper only, and none contained an arbitration clause.

4. Under date of _____, 19__, the respondent issued to the petitioner a sales contract with respect to each of the purchase orders, as follows:

§ 5.70   COMMERCIAL SALES CONTRACTS   Ch. 5

Purchase Order No.   Sales Contract No.

————   ————
————   ————
————   ————
————   ————

A copy of each of the said sales contracts is annexed as joint Exhibit __. Each sales contract was issued with reference to a preexisting purchase order. Each of the sales contracts is printed on two sides with a purported arbitration clause, in small print, on the reverse side (Exhibit __).

5. Although the sales contract forms provide for signature by both the seller (the respondent) and the purchaser (the petitioner), they were signed by neither.

6. At no time has the petitioner ever agreed to the arbitration of any disputes which might arise between the petitioner and the respondent.

7. Because of late delivery and defects in the goods, a dispute has arisen between the petitioner and the respondent relating to the goods described in the petitioner's purchase orders, Exhibit __.

8. Respondent has sent to petitioner a Demand for Arbitration under the Commercial Arbitration Rules of the American Arbitration Association, a copy of which is annexed as Exhibit __.

9. The provisions of the petitioner's purchase orders were not superseded by any subsequent sales confirmation form issued by the respondent which purported to provide new and different terms or conditions. Accordingly, at no time has the petitioner ever entered into any agreement with the respondent to arbitrate disputes which may arise between them with respect to the goods specified in the purchase orders, and the petitioner is not bound to arbitrate any of the disputes presently existing between the petitioner and the respondent.

10. Petitioner has not participated in any arbitration proceedings between the parties, nor has petitioner been served with any notice or application to compel arbitration.

WHEREFORE, the petitioner respectfully requests that an order be entered:

(a) Staying the arbitration instituted by the respondent against the petitioner before the American Arbitration Association;

(b) Restraining the American Arbitration Association and any arbitrators which it might appoint from proceeding with arbitration or rendering any award in respect thereto;

(c) Providing to the petitioner such other and further relief in this matter as to the Court may appear to be just and proper under the circumstances; and

Ch. 5 AFFIDAVIT OPPOSING STAY § 5.71

(d) Awarding to the petitioner its costs and disbursements in this proceeding.

Dated: _____

YOURS, ETC.

_____ [insert attorney's name, address and telephone number]

TO: _____ [insert attorney's name, address and telephone number]

[Verification]

Library References:
West's Key No. Digests, Arbitration ⇌23.5.

§ 5.71 Forms—Affidavit in Opposition to Petition for Order Staying Arbitration in Dispute Over Contract for Sale of Goods

This affidavit in opposition to a stay of arbitration simply points out the arbitration language in the contract between the parties, as well as the fact that in the industry implicated by this action (textiles), the usual method of settling disputes is arbitration.

SUPREME COURT OF THE STATE OF NEW YORK
COUNTY OF _____

_____,
               Petitioner,

-against-

_____,
               Respondent.

AFFIDAVIT

Index No. _____

STATE OF NEW YORK   )
) ss.
COUNTY OF _____   )

_____, being duly sworn, deposes and says:

1. I am the Controller of Respondent, _____, and have knowledge of the facts set forth in this affidavit opposing the Petition of _____, to stay arbitration.

§ 5.71   COMMERCIAL SALES CONTRACTS   Ch. 5

2. The annexed affidavit of _____ evidences that the petition to Stay Arbitration was not commenced within the time required by CPLR 7503(c) and must be dismissed as untimely.

3. Both parties are in the textile business and arbitration in this industry is the usual method of settling disputes. _____ has had numerous contracts for the sale of goods with the petitioner, _____, prior to the ones now in dispute. All of these prior sales were confirmed by Respondent _____ with the identical sales contract which provides on its face that "This contract is subject to the terms and conditions on this and the reverse side hereof, including the provision providing for ARBITRATION ..." Paragraph __ on the reverse side of the sales contract provides for arbitration in New York City in accordance with the rules of the American Arbitration Association or the General Arbitration Council of Textile and Apparel Industries as follows:

"9. (a) Any controversy arising out of or relating to this contract or any modification or extension thereof, including any claim for damages and/or rescission, shall be settled by arbitration before a panel of three arbitrators in New York City in accordance with the rules then obtaining of the American Arbitration Association or the General Arbitration Council of the Textile & Apparel Industries as the party instituting arbitration proceedings shall elect."

4. Since the sales contract containing the terms does not duplicate well and the copies are not that clear, a blank form of the sales contract is attached as Ex. __.

5. On its face, the sales contract provides:

"This contract shall become binding for the entire quantity of merchandise specified herein upon its acceptance by Seller, such acceptance being complete when the contract is signed by Seller or when Seller delivers or bills all or any part of the merchandise specified herein, and upon the occurrence of one or more of the following events: (1) Upon Buyer's returning a signed copy of this contract to Seller; (2) Upon Buyer's retaining this contract for ten (10) days without making written objection thereto; (3) Upon Buyer's giving instructions to Seller respecting assortment and/or delivery (including instructions to bill and hold); (4) upon Buyer's accepting delivery of all or any part of the merchandise specified herein; (5) Upon Buyer's paying for all or any part of the merchandise specified herein; (6) Upon Buyer's indicating in some other manner its acceptance of this contract."

6. The Buyer did retain the sales contracts without written objection; Respondent _____ did deliver and bill Petitioner _____ for the goods; Buyer did accept and pay for part of the goods. On all prior sales, Petitioner _____ received these standard sales contracts from Respondent _____ containing the same provision for arbitration and never made any written objection to these terms.

WHEREFORE, the motion to stay arbitration should be denied.

[*Jurat*]

Library References:

West's Key No. Digests, Arbitration ⚖➪23.5.

§ 5.72 Forms—Answer to Petition for Order Staying Arbitration in Dispute Over Contract for Sale of Goods

In this answer, respondent admits the existence of a dispute and denies the facts which, if accepted, could lead to a stay of arbitration. Moreover, the answer provides both substantive and procedural defenses to the motion for a stay.

The substantive defense is that the parties had always used the same form of agreement which always contained an arbitration clause. The respondent then asserts that no prior objection to the existence of the clause in the agreements had ever been made by the petitioner. Here, the sales agreements had not been signed, and the respondent must show that in spite of the lack of signatures, the intent of the parties was always to arbitrate disputes. It is further alleged in the answer that the buyer accepted the contract without objection for ten days, as well as some of the goods. Respondent asserts that this is sufficient to overcome a failure of execution of the sales agreement.

The procedural defense is couched in the failure to timely serve the Notice of Petition for a stay of arbitration.

SUPREME COURT OF THE STATE OF NEW YORK
COUNTY OF _____

_____,

    Petitioner,

-against-

_____,

    Respondent.

) ANSWER TO PETITION

) Index No. _____

Respondent herein, by its attorney, _____, for its answer to the Petition herein:

§ 5.72 COMMERCIAL SALES CONTRACTS Ch. 5

FIRST: Denies each and every allegation of paragraphs 6 and 9 of the petition.

SECOND: Admits that a dispute has arisen, but except as so admitted, denies the remaining allegations of paragraph 7 of the Petition.

AS A FIRST AFFIRMATIVE DEFENSE TO THE PETITION RESPECTFULLY ALLEGES:

THIRD: Upon information and belief, that petitioner is a California corporation duly authorized to do business in the State of New York and has duly filed a certificate with the New York State Secretary of State.

FOURTH: That the Demand for Arbitration, dated _____, 19__, sent by Respondent to Petitioner under the Commercial Arbitration Rules of the American Arbitration Association was mailed to Petitioner, _____, INC., on _____, 19__, by certified mail, return receipt requested.

FIFTH: That Petitioner, _____, INC., duly signed the domestic return receipt, PS Form 3811, on _____, 19__, attesting to receipt of the Demand for Arbitration on that date.

SIXTH: That the Notice of Petition, Petition and verification of Petition, all dated _____, 19__, were served on _____, 19__.

SEVENTH: That the application to stay arbitration was not commenced within the _____ day period from the service of the Demand for Arbitration, as provided by CPLR 7503(c).

EIGHTH: That the motion is not timely.

AS A SECOND DEFENSE RESPECTFULLY ALLEGES:

NINTH: That the face of the sales contracts of the Respondent, ABC PRODUCTS & TEXTILES, INC., requiring arbitration, inter alia, provided that the sales contracts become binding when the contract is signed, or when Seller delivers or bills for any part of the merchandise, or upon Buyer retaining the sales contract without written objection for ten (10) days, or upon Buyer accepting delivery, or upon Buyer paying for any part of the goods.

TENTH: That Buyer did retain the contract without written objection; that Buyer did accept delivery and Buyer did pay for part of the goods.

AS A THIRD DEFENSE RESPECTFULLY ALLEGES:

ELEVENTH: That the parties had several prior sales transactions.

TWELFTH: That Petitioner received several prior sales contracts in the past from Respondent on the previous transactions, all of which had the same provisions, including the arbitration clause.

Ch. 5   ANSWER TO PETITION FOR STAY   § 5.72

WHEREFORE, Respondent respectfully requests that the petition be dismissed and that Respondent be awarded its costs and disbursements of this proceeding.

Dated: _____

                              YOURS, ETC.

                              _____ [*insert attorney's name, address and telephone number*]

TO: _____ [*insert attorney's name, address and telephone number*]

[*Verification*]

Library References:

West's Key No. Digests, Arbitration ⚖23.5.

Chapter 6

BUYING AND SELLING A SMALL BUSINESS

by
Mark S. Pelersi
Michele A. Santucci

Table of Sections

6.1	Scope Note.
6.2	Strategy: Representing the Buyer—Introduction.
6.3	—— The Attorney's Role.
6.4	—— Different Considerations Depending on the Type of Transaction.
6.5	—— General Stages of the Transaction.
6.6	Representing the Buyer—Investigating the Business.
6.7	—— Nature and Operation of Business.
6.8	—— Geographic Location.
6.9	—— The Negotiating Team.
6.10	—— The Letter of Intent.
6.11	—— Confidentiality Agreements.
6.12	—— Drafting the Agreement.
6.13	Due Diligence Investigation.
6.14	—— Legal Issues.
6.15	—— —— Organizational Documents.
6.16	—— —— Ownership Documents.
6.17	—— —— Existing Contracts.
6.18	—— —— Liens and Security Interests.
6.19	—— —— Corporate and Trade Names.
6.20	—— —— Real Estate.
6.21	—— —— Compliance With Law.
6.22	—— —— Litigation Investigation.
6.23	—— Financial Issues—General Considerations.
6.24	—— —— Seller's Records From the Buyer's Position.
6.25	—— —— Buyer's Records From the Seller's Position.
6.26	—— —— Public Records.
6.27	—— —— Financial Statements.
6.28	—— —— The Need for Other Professionals.
6.29	—— —— Valuation of the Business.
6.30	—— —— Tax Returns.
6.31	Tax Issues for Buyer.
6.32	—— Asset Purchase.
6.33	—— —— Allocation of Purchase Price.
6.34	—— —— Depreciation of Assets.

Ch. 6   BUYING & SELLING A SMALL BUSINESS

6.35 __ __ Land.
6.36 __ __ Good Will and Covenants Not to Compete.
6.37 __ __ Inventory.
6.38 __ __ Cash.
6.39 __ __ Supplies.
6.40 __ __ Patents, Franchises, Trademarks, Trade Names.
6.41 __ Stock Purchase.
6.42 __ __ Basis of Stock.
6.43 __ __ Basis of Corporate Assets.
6.44 __ __ Election to Treat Stock Purchase as Asset Purchase.
6.45 __ Mergers, Consolidations, and Exchanges.
6.46 Structuring the Buyer's Transaction.
6.47 __ Type of Payment.
6.48 __ Assumption of Seller's Liabilities.
6.49 __ Security to Seller.
6.50 __ Notes.
6.51 __ Escrow Arrangements and Agreements.
6.52 Drafting the Buyer's Asset Purchase Agreement.
6.53 __ Identification of the Parties.
6.54 __ Recitals.
6.55 __ Assets and Property to Be Conveyed.
6.56 __ Retained Assets of Seller.
6.57 __ Purchase Price and Method of Payment.
6.58 __ Closing.
6.59 __ Representations, Warranties and Covenants of Seller.
6.60 __ Representations, Warranties and Covenants of Buyer.
6.61 __ Conduct of Business Prior to Closing.
6.62 __ Indemnifications.
6.63 __ Corporate or Other Name.
6.64 __ __ Notice to Customers and Suppliers.
6.65 __ __ UCC Bulk Sale Notices or Escrow Agreement in Lieu of UCC Bulk Sale Notice.
6.66 __ __ NYS Sales Tax and Bulk Sale Notification.
6.67 __ __ Covenant Not to Compete.
6.68 __ Matters Respecting Real Property.
6.69 __ Conditions Precedent to Purchaser's Obligations.
6.70 __ Conditions Precedent to Seller's Obligations.
6.71 __ Nature and Survival of Representations and Warranties.
6.72 __ Non-disclosure Provisions.
6.73 __ Miscellaneous Agreements Between Buyer and Seller.
6.74 __ Documents to Be Delivered to Purchaser at Closing.
6.75 __ Documents to Be Delivered to Seller at Closing.
6.76 __ Notices, Severability and Other General Provisions.
6.77 __ Documents to Be Prepared or Reviewed Prior to Closing.
6.78 Drafting the Buyer's Stock Purchase Agreement.
6.79 __ Identification of the Parties.
6.80 __ Recitals.
6.81 __ Sale of Shares.
6.82 __ Purchase Price and Method of Payment.
6.83 __ Closing.
6.84 __ Representations, Warranties and Covenants of Seller.

6.85	___ Representations, Warranties and Covenants of Buyer.
6.86	___ Conduct of Business Prior to Closing.
6.87	___ Indemnifications.
6.88	___ Covenant Not to Compete.
6.89	___ Matters Respecting Real Property.
6.90	___ Nondisclosure Provisions.
6.91	___ Conditions Precedent to Purchaser's Obligations.
6.92	___ Conditions Precedent to Seller's Obligations.
6.93	___ Nature and Survival of Representations and Warranties.
6.94	___ Documents to Be Delivered to Purchaser at Closing.
6.95	___ Documents to Be Delivered to Seller at Closing.
6.96	___ Notices, Severability and Other General Provisions.
6.97	___ Documents to Be Prepared or Reviewed Prior to Closing.
6.98	Post–Contract and Pre-closing.
6.99	___ Bulk Sales Act—UCC Article 6.
6.100	___ NYS Sales Tax and Bulk Sale Notification.
6.101	___ Plant Closing Notice.
6.102	___ Environmental Searches and Testing.
6.103	___ Certificate of Good Standing.
6.104	___ Real Property Transfer Gains Tax.
6.105	Closing and Post–Closing.
6.106	Strategy: Representing the Seller—Introduction.
6.107	___ The Attorney's Role.
6.108	___ Different Considerations Depending on the Type of Transaction.
6.109	___ General Stages of the Transaction.
6.110	Representing the Seller—General Investigation.
6.111	___ Investigating the Buyer.
6.112	___ The Negotiating Team.
6.113	___ The Letter of Intent.
6.114	___ Confidentiality Agreements.
6.115	___ Drafting the Agreement.
6.116	Tax Issues for the Seller—General Overview.
6.117	___ Asset Sale.
6.118	___ ___ Allocation of Purchase Price.
6.119	___ ___ Depreciation Recapture.
6.120	___ ___ Capital Gains or Losses.
6.121	___ ___ Ordinary Income.
6.122	___ ___ Income to Corporation.
6.123	___ ___ Real Property Transfer Gains Tax.
6.124	___ ___ Covenant Not to Compete and Consulting Agreements.
6.125	___ Stock Sale—General Advantages.
6.126	___ ___ Capital Gain or Loss.
6.127	___ ___ No Concern for Income to a Corporate Entity.
6.128	___ ___ Real Property Transfer Gains Tax.
6.129	___ ___ Consulting and Non-compete Agreements.
6.130	___ ___ I.R.C. § 1244 Stock and Qualified Small Business Stock.
6.131	___ ___ Stock Transfer Tax.
6.132	___ ___ Collapsible Corporation.
6.133	___ ___ Mergers, Consolidations and Exchanges.
6.134	Structuring the Seller's Transaction—General Overview.
6.135	___ Purchase Price and Payment Terms.

Ch. 6 BUYING & SELLING A SMALL BUSINESS

6.136 ____ Security to Seller.
6.137 ____ Notes.
6.138 ____ Escrow Arrangements.
6.139 Drafting the Seller's Asset Sale Agreement.
6.140 ____ Identification of the Parties.
6.141 ____ Recitals.
6.142 ____ Assets and Property to Be Conveyed.
6.143 ____ Assets Retained by Seller.
6.144 ____ Sale Price and Method of Payment.
6.145 ____ Closing.
6.146 ____ Representations, Warranties and Covenants of Buyer.
6.147 ____ Representations, Warranties and Covenants of Seller.
6.148 ____ Conduct of Business Prior to Closing.
6.149 ____ Indemnifications.
6.150 ____ Matters Respecting Real Property.
6.151 ____ Notice to Customers and Suppliers.
6.152 ____ Covenant Not to Compete and Consulting Agreements.
6.153 ____ UCC Bulk Sale Notices or Escrow Agreements in Lieu of UCC Bulk Sale Notice.
6.154 ____ New York State Sales Tax and Bulk Sale Notification.
6.155 ____ Nature and Survival of Representations and Warranties.
6.156 ____ Non-disclosure Provisions.
6.157 ____ Conditions Precedent to Seller's Obligations.
6.158 ____ Conditions Precedent to Buyer's Obligations.
6.159 ____ Documents to Be Delivered to Seller at Closing.
6.160 ____ Documents to Be Delivered to Buyer at Closing.
6.161 ____ Notices, Severability and Other General Provisions.
6.162 ____ Documents to Be Prepared or Reviewed Prior to Closing.
6.163 Drafting the Seller's Stock Sale Agreement.
6.164 ____ Identification of the Parties.
6.165 ____ Recitals.
6.166 ____ Sale of Shares.
6.167 ____ Sale Price and Method of Payment.
6.168 ____ Closing.
6.169 ____ Representations, Warranties and Covenants of Buyer.
6.170 ____ Representations, Warranties and Covenants of Seller.
6.171 ____ Conduct of Business Prior to Closing.
6.172 ____ Indemnifications.
6.173 ____ Matters Respecting Real Property.
6.174 ____ Non-disclosure Provisions.
6.175 ____ Covenants Not to Compete and Consulting Agreements.
6.176 ____ Notice to Customers and Suppliers.
6.177 ____ Conditions Precedent to Seller's Obligations.
6.178 ____ Conditions Precedent to Buyer's Obligations.
6.179 ____ Nature and Survival of Representations and Warranties.
6.180 ____ Documents to Be Delivered to Seller at Closing.
6.181 ____ Documents to Be Delivered to Buyer at Closing.
6.182 ____ Notices, Severability and Other General Provisions.
6.183 ____ Documents to Be Prepared or Reviewed Prior to Closing.
6.184 Post–contract and Pre-closing.
6.185 Closing and Post–Closing.

§ 6.1   BUYING & SELLING A SMALL BUSINESS   Ch. 6

6.186   Forms.
6.187   ____ Asset Purchase and Sale Agreement.
6.188   ____ Agreement of Purchase and Sale of Stock.

WESTLAW Electronic Research

See WESTLAW Electronic Research Guide preceding the Summary of Contents.

---

§ 6.1 Scope Note

This chapter presents a comprehensive overview of the legal and practical issues involved in representing a client who is either buying or selling a business in New York. The information contained in the following sections is designed to assist the attorney in counseling his or her client from the first meeting up to and after the closing of the business transaction.

The legal and practical skills required of the attorney in this type of transaction are many and diverse, and range from counsel's ability to assist the client in his or her business plan, to the development of strategy, the performance of the due diligence investigation (if applicable), and the negotiation, preparation, and closing of the deal. The following sections contain carefully developed procedures, strategies and pointers designed to guide the attorney through every step of his or her representation of the client.

The information contained in this chapter is divided into two major areas, the first, dealing with the representation of the buyer in a transaction,[1] and the second, dealing with representing the seller.[2] These areas are further separated as to whether the transaction involved is an asset purchase or sale, or a stock purchase or sale. Sections 6.2 through 6.12 discuss the attorney's role in representing the buyer; the preliminary steps involved in investigating the business; and the various legal and technical aspects of a business acquisition. Sections 6.13 through 6.30 contain an in-depth discussion of the various elements of one of the most important stages of the process—the due diligence investigation. Tax considerations for the buyer are discussed in Sections 6.31 through 6.44 and methods of structuring the manner of payment for the business to the buyer's advantage are explored in Sections 6.46 through 6.51. The practitioner is provided with the tools necessary for the drafting of buyer's acquisition agreement in Sections 6.52 through 6.97, which sections discuss with particularity the elements of both the asset purchase agreement[3] and the buyer's stock purchase agreement.[4] There follows in Sections 6.98 through 6.105 important information for the

§ 6.1
1. See infra, §§ 6.2–6.105.
2. See infra, §§ 6.106–6.185.
3. See infra, §§ 6.53–6.57.
4. See infra, §§ 6.59–6.97.

buyer's attorney concerning the pre-closing, closing and post-closing stages of the buyer's transaction.

Sections 6.106 through 6.133 discuss the role of the practitioner when representing the seller, and provide an in-depth view of the monetary, tax and legal issues to be considered by the seller during the course of the sale of his or her business. Structuring the transaction to the seller's advantage is discussed in Sections 6.134 through 6.133; and in Sections 6.139 through 6.183, the practitioner is provided with the tools necessary to prepare the seller's contract of sale. Sections 6.184 through 6.185 explore in detail the pre-closing, closing and post-closing stages of the seller's transaction.

At the end of the chapter, in Sections 6.186 through 6.188, the authors have included a sample Asset Purchase and Sale Agreement and a sample Stock Purchase and Sale Agreement.

§ 6.2 Strategy: Representing the Buyer—Introduction

An attorney embarking on the representation of a small business buyer is in a unique position to perform a very valuable service for his or her client.

The Buyer's Strategy. At the outset, counsel should review with his or her client the client's business plan. This plan should outline the client's business objectives, the financial needs of the business and how these needs and objectives will be attained. The business plan is the foundation of the transaction and will dictate much of the buyer's strategy and plan of action. The strategy and plan of action, which should be prepared by counsel and client together, must be flexible to allow change as the transaction evolves, and should be memorialized in outline or notation form.

It is essential that this strategy be discussed with and clearly understood by the buyer and the buyer's team. The strategy should identify, at a minimum, the following:

1. Who will make up the negotiating team and what their respective duties will be;[1]

2. The legal structure of the transaction (either a purchase of assets,[2] purchase of stock,[3] or a combination of entities);[4]

3. The most advantageous method of dealing with the seller;

4. The timing of the transaction;

5. Whether to initially use a letter of intent[5] or a full purchase agreement;

---

§ 6.2
1. See infra, § 6.9.
2. See infra, §§ 6.32–6.40, 6.52–6.77.
3. See infra, §§ 6.41–6.44, 6.78–6.97.
4. See infra, § 6.45.
5. See infra, § 6.10.

6. The amount and makeup of the purchase offer;[6]

7. The security, if any, to be supplied to the seller;

8. The legal structure of the purchasing entity;[7] and

9. The willingness of the buyer to provide personal financial information and personal guarantees.

In some transactions, such as a cash payment for a small business, many of these strategies will have little importance. In other transactions they may be of utmost importance.

The information contained in Sections 6.3 through 6.105 is intended to provide the attorney with the practical skills necessary to assist the client in his or her endeavor to plan, investigate, negotiate and close on what will hopefully be a successful business venture.

§ 6.3 Strategy: Representing the Buyer—The Attorney's Role

Many times the attorney must be a counselor to the client as well as a competent legal advisor. Often the client is extremely optimistic and has not thoroughly and objectively considered all aspects of the transaction. It is very important that counsel understand what the motivations, goals, and interests of the client are in reference to acquiring the new business. More often than not, the client will rely upon the attorney for practical as well as legal advice. Counsel may want to find out from the client why it is this particular business that the client wants to acquire and whether the client has any experience or knowledge of this business. One of the most important questions an attorney can ask the client is: Why is the seller selling the business?

During his or her initial interview with the client, counsel should assess the client's level of sophistication, willingness to take risks and, most important of all, the client's financial concerns.

The purchase of a business very often involves a lengthy process throughout which much information is gathered, obligations and liabilities are weighed and risks are assessed. It is normally at the end of the process that the client must decide whether or not to go forward with the deal. The attorney should be prepared to assist the client in investigating the business being purchased, to inform the client as to the possible risks involved, and to negotiate the best possible deal for the client.[1]

---

6. *See infra*, §§ 6.29, 6.47.

7. *See* Chapter 1 "Business Organizations: Corporations," *supra*, and Chapter 2 "Non-corporate Entities: Limited Liability Companies and Partnerships," *supra*.

§ 6.3

1. **PRACTICE POINTER:** The attorney should set forth in a written retainer agreement the scope of the attorney's activities and the fee arrangement. If at any time the scope of the attorney's work

Library References:
West's Key No. Digests, Attorney and Client ⊕105–129.5.

§ 6.4 Strategy: Representing the Buyer—Different Considerations Depending on the Type of Transaction

The information contained in this chapter is separated into four sections depending upon whether you, as the attorney, are representing the buyer, or the seller, and whether the business transaction contemplated involves the purchase or sale of the assets of a business, or whether it involves the purchase or sale of the stock, or other ownership interests in a business.

When representing the seller of a business, counsel will be concerned primarily with making sure that full payment is received for the business being transferred, that the seller is protected from liabilities which may arise after the business has been transferred and that the seller is afforded the most advantageous tax treatment possible.

The buyer's attorney's role is somewhat more involved, and ranges from helping the client determine whether the transaction he is entering into is the right one for him, to negotiating an advantageous deal, to making sure ownership is properly conveyed and that all laws and regulations applicable to the running of the business are complied with.

Sections 6.6 to 6.51, below, discuss how to structure a transaction to the buyer's advantage from both the legal and tax point of view.

For the seller, it is often more advantageous to structure the transaction as a sale of stock of the business, generally because a stock sale is less complicated than an asset sale. With the sale of stock, the seller may transfer all of the property of the business to the buyer. In an asset sale, seller could be left with unwanted assets which he may not be able to sell to another buyer. In addition, a transfer of stock will obviate the necessity of the seller's complying with cumbersome UCC Bulk Sales[1] provisions, and will assure seller of the tax advantage of capital gains treatment on the proceeds of the sale.

In the case of a buyer, the purchase of the assets of the business is generally more advantageous. The purchase of assets will enable the buyer to avoid the assumption of undisclosed, unknown or contingent liabilities usually inherent in a stock purchase. The buyer can also avoid pre-acquisition business liabilities of seller which he does not expressly assume, so long as the parties comply with the Bulk Sales laws.[2] There

changes, this should also be indicated in writing to the client.

§ 6.4
1. See infra, § 6.65, regarding UCC Bulk Sales provisions.

2. **CAVEAT:** Compliance with Bulk Sales Laws will not protect a buyer from the rights of secured creditors, or from other types of liabilities (e.g., transferee tax

are also numerous tax advantages to a buyer in an asset purchase transaction which include, among others, the ability of the buyer to avoid the built-in gains or loss problems of the seller and the ability to obtain favorable basis step-ups upon allocation of the purchase price.

Sections 6.31 through 6.44 discuss in detail the advantages, disadvantages and tax aspects of both asset purchase and stock purchase transactions from the point of view of the buyer.

Section 6.45 discusses the transfer of a small business by means of merger or consolidation. A properly constructed merger or consolidation will enable the seller to exchange its stock for the stock of the buyer, without tax consequences. Section 6.45 also provides information concerning "like-kind" exchanges under Section 1031 of the Internal Revenue Code ("I.R.C.").

§ 6.5 Strategy: Representing the Buyer—General Stages of the Transaction

In addition to assisting the client in his or her business review and developing strategy as discussed in Section 6.2 above, counsel's representation of a client who is purchasing a business will consist of the following:

Investigating the business (§§ 6.6–6.8);

Performing the due diligence investigation (§§ 6.13–6.30);

Evaluating the tax implications of the transaction (§§ 6.31–6.45);

Structuring the purchase of the business (§§ 6.46–6.51);

Negotiating and drafting the agreement (§§ 6.9–6.12, and §§ 6.52–6.97);

Performing the post-contract and pre-closing steps of the transaction (§§ 6.98–6.104); and

Closing the transaction (§§ 6.105–6.109).

§ 6.6 Representing the Buyer—Investigating the Business

Assuming a targeted business has been found, the attorney and the client must consider if the business is a good fit. Is the business the right business for the client considering the client's aptitudes and desires? Does the client have experience in the same or a similar line of business either as an owner, manager, or employee? Is the client entering into the transaction with little or no knowledge of the business? What are the sellers motives for selling the business? If the client has other business interests, does the target business complement or conflict with the other interests?

liability) other than those associated with
the rights of unsecured creditors.

§ 6.7 Representing the Buyer—Nature and Operation of Business

The client, or the client in conjunction with his attorney and other experts,[1] should explore all aspects of the business as an economic venture. He or she should review the nature of the industry and the general trends in the industry as well as the average financial ratios for similar sized businesses. If the target business' ratios diverge significantly from the financial ratios of similar businesses, investigation of the differences should be undertaken. An analysis of the industry trends and future projections for the industry should indicate if the business is in a growing, stable or declining industry. If there are any unique features of the target business, these must be carefully evaluated to determine if they are the reason for any substantial divergence from the general trends.[2]

A comparison of the financial ratios of the target business to the industry should provide insight into the efficiencies of the operation of the target business and other potential abnormalities. Abnormalities may range from generous executive salaries and perks to the non-reporting of sales. The under-reporting of sales must always be considered when dealing with a cash business.[3]

Certain businesses also require permits (*e.g.,* cigarette sale permits), licenses (*e.g.,* liquor licenses),[4] or have privileges, such as operating privileges at various hospitals, associated with them. Investigation must be made into the transferability and/or availability of these items.[5]

The client or the attorney should also attempt to determine the compensation paid by the business to the seller to determine if the target business can support the buyer's financial requirements[6] (*e.g.,* expected cash flow, return on investment, etc.) Since this information is not

---

§ 6.7

1. Such as accountants, business brokers and business consultants, among others.

2. **PRACTICE POINTER:** Depending upon the type of business, a divergence from the trends could be caused by many factors, such as the introduction of a new product in the geographic location of the business, the expansion of the geographic area serviced by the business, weak competition, or a rapidly expanding economy in the geographic area of the business.

3. **PRACTICE POINTER:** In the area of industry trends and financial ratios, a business consultant or accountant familiar with the industry can provide valuable assistance. In addition, attending an industry trade show can be very helpful.

4. **PRACTICE POINTER:** *See* Chapter 36 "Alcoholic Beverage Control Law," *infra.*

5. **PRACTICE POINTER:** Other permits or licenses such as liquor licenses, cigarette sale permits, food processing permits, sale permits and professional service licenses may also be involved.

6. **PRACTICE POINTER:** Usually by this point in the transaction a price for the business has been discussed or is anticipated. If the business purchase is only palatable to your client with a large price reduction, it is suggested that the seller be approached to ascertain the acceptability of the proposed offer before substantial additional time and effort is invested in the transaction. A letter of intent may be useful here. *See infra,* § 6.10.

§ 6.7   BUYING & SELLING A SMALL BUSINESS   Ch. 6

always easy to obtain, a confidentiality agreement[7] may need to be entered into. Entering into a confidentiality agreement is a small price to pay to obtain this information.

In exploring the specific nature and operation of the target business, there are many aspects to consider, such as:

Personnel

1. Quality of the existing personnel;
2. Pending labor issues;
3. Number of employees needed to run the business;
4. Number of hours currently worked by the owner; if excessive, will additional employees be needed?
5. Continued employment of current employees after the business is purchased, especially key employees (seller) or family members;
6. Current compensation of key family members; is it above or below market rates?
7. Number of needed management personnel;

Transition

8. Training or special expertise required for the buyer;
9. Continued employment of employees with special expertise;

Market Factors

10. Current and future demand for the service or product; is a market survey required to determine this demand?[8]
11. Availability of needed services or suppliers;
12. Contractual agreements with suppliers or service providers;
13. Seasonal or cyclical nature of the business;
14. Product mix of the business; does the business rely heavily on one product, service or customer and if so, how secure is this relationship for the future?
15. Adequacy of the existing production facilities and equipment for current and future operations;
16. Buyer's financial ability to purchase and operate the business; and

---

7. *See infra,* § 6.11.

8. **PRACTICE POINTER:** A marketing survey can be expensive and is of little help unless properly done. Advise the client to consult a marketing expert, preferably with experience in the particular business area, and also ascertain the cost before embarking upon a marketing survey. Most existing businesses have marketing information and a marketing track record.

17. Nature and extent of competition now and in the future.[9]

§ 6.8 Representing the Buyer—Geographic Location

The proposed or existing geographic location of the business is important not only from the general marketing and competitor perspective, but also for site-specific problems. A site inspection by the client is always necessary and it is often helpful if the client and the attorney visit the site. Aspects of the site that should be evaluated include, but are not limited to:

1. Traffic flow considerations;

2. Current and future road expansion;

3. Availability of adequate parking;

4. Room for anticipated future expansion;

5. Ability to comply with local, state and federal laws and regulations for handicap access requirements,[1] fire codes, materials safety, etc.

In addition, depending upon the roadway abutting the site, permission for access to the roadway or for a new access may have to be obtained from local or state authorities.

If expansion of the business is contemplated, do the public utilities (*e.g.*, water, sewer, electric) support the expansion or would they need to be enhanced?

Finally, if the business is moving to a new location or if the operation of the business is going to change, will there be significant neighborhood opposition to the business or other impediments?[2]

§ 6.9 Representing the Buyer—The Negotiating Team

In selecting the negotiating team, personalities of the individuals and their expertise must be taken into account to ensure that team members can work together as an effective team among themselves and

---

9. PRACTICE POINTER: A physical investigation of the immediate geographic area may reveal existing or future competitors. Also, a review of local general circulation and business newspapers may reveal future competition. WESTLAW maintains many general circulation and business newspapers in its data bases. A subject matter search may reveal information about future competition, especially if the competition may come from a large publicly traded company.

§ 6.8

1. Americans With Disabilities Act, 42 U.S.C.A. §§ 12101 *et seq.*

2. PRACTICE POINTER: In some jurisdictions, certain businesses may not be located within close proximity to other community activities (*e.g.*, there are restrictions in the New York State Alcohol Beverage Control Law regarding the proximity of businesses selling alcohol to places of worship.) Alcoholic Beverage Control Law § 105. *See generally* Chapter 36 "Alcoholic Beverage Control Law," *infra.*

with the seller and/or the seller's negotiating team. Individuals who may make up the buyer's negotiating team are the buyer's accountant, the buyer's business broker and the business consultant or appraiser if one is used.

Also, one must consider past relationships among the buyer, the seller, and the members of the respective negotiating teams. However, many times the attorney in a small business transaction does much of the negotiating on behalf of his client. To effectively negotiate, the attorney must have knowledge of the business, the risk and financial tolerances of his client, and usually the impact of the tax law.

§ 6.10 Representing the Buyer—The Letter of Intent

The letter of intent is usually a non-binding agreement to agree.[1] It should clearly state the extent to which it will be enforceable, if at all. Although the use of the letter of intent varies widely among attorneys (some of whom argue that it is a waste of time), it is often helpful, early in the deal, to have an outline of the major points of the transaction agreed upon by all parties. The letter of intent will generally define the essential terms of the contract such as price, payment terms, legal structure of the transaction, and a timetable for consummating the transaction. The letter of intent is usually informal in format and relatively short. Sophisticated clients may have a letter of intent when they first consult with their attorney.

It often provides for a deposit by the purchaser as a demonstration of his seriousness with respect to the transaction. The deposit is usually held in escrow by an escrow agent. The disposition of any deposit, if the parties fail to agree, should be clearly set forth in the letter of intent.

§ 6.11 Representing the Buyer—Confidentiality Agreements

Understandably, the seller is often hesitant to disclose information needed by the buyer. Confidentiality and non-disclosure agreements provide some measure of protection for the disclosing party. Before any information is exchanged, the receiving party must agree (a) to keep all information strictly confidential; (b) to use the information only for the purposes of the contemplated transaction; and (c) to return all original documents and copies upon request of the party providing them. Some confidentiality and non-disclosure agreements include penalties in the form of liquidated damages for any disclosure.

---

§ 6.10
1. **PRACTICE POINTER:** One must be careful when using a letter of intent. Even though it is not legally binding it may be difficult to change the terms and still save the transaction.

§ 6.12 Representing the Buyer—Drafting the Agreement

The usual advice is to draft the agreement for your client. The custom and usage is that the buyer drafts the purchase offer documents and presents them to the seller. Sometimes it is advantageous to deviate from these practices.

At times, the economics of the transaction may cause the seller's attorney to take a more active role in drafting the agreement. Other times a more active role is motivated by a desire to "move the transaction along," to obtain the "drafting advantage," or just to split the drafting burden. How much assistance is allowed or accepted is part of the buyer's strategy. Depending on the buyer's bargaining position, the buyer's attorney may be able to allow the other side to prepare the initial draft and then, with little or no concern, strike all objectionable provisions. Allowing the other party to do the initial drafting can be beneficial if the initial draft either omits items unfavorable to your client, but which would otherwise be expected, or contains ambiguities that would be construed against their drafts-person.

If the buyer's attorney is drafting the agreement, should the first draft be "stacked" in the buyer's favor, "fair" or "in between"? Consideration must be given to the advantages, disadvantages and economics.[1]

§ 6.13 Due Diligence Investigation

The due diligence investigation constitutes one of the most important aspects of the buyer's acquisition transaction. It is the due diligence investigation which will enable the buyer to evaluate the positive and negative aspects of the contemplated transaction and ultimately, whether or not to go forward with the purchase.

The due diligence investigation of the seller's business is generally comprised of two separate forms of analysis: the legal review and the financial assessment.

§ 6.14 Due Diligence Investigation—Legal Issues

The "legal review" aspect of the due diligence investigation will consist of a thorough and in-depth review of the organizational, legal and contractual matters pertaining to the seller's business.

Because the "legal" due diligence investigation may require that the buyer's attorney be versed in numerous areas of the law (such as

---

§ 6.12

1. **PRACTICE POINTER:** Be mindful of the objectives of the client. Most small business clients are not impressed with high legal expenses caused by numerous drafts or revisions relating to insubstantial matters. Small business clients usually are more impressed with a realistic and reasonable document that protects their interests rather then a document full of burdensome and overreaching provisions which drive up the cost of the transaction and may even threaten the transaction itself.

corporate and business law, real estate law, tax law, pension and benefits law, labor law, securities law and anti-trust law to name a few), counsel should be prepared from time to time to seek the advice of other attorneys or individuals with expertise in such areas.

Library References:

West's Key No. Digests, Attorney and Client ⚖︎105.

§ 6.15 Due Diligence Investigation—Legal Issues—Organizational Documents

In the course of the due diligence investigation, it is crucial for the buyer's attorney to review the organizational and other documents related to the formation and operation of the seller's business.

Counsel should determine at the outset whether the seller's business has been properly organized and whether it has been operating in compliance with law. Investigation into the seller's organizational and related documents will not only disclose to the buyer important information as to the structure and operation of the seller's business, but will also enable the buyer to determine whether the business has been experiencing any problems, whether there are any pending or threatened claims against the business, whether the business is in good standing, and whether there may exist any impediments to the sale of the assets of the business.

In the case of a transfer of assets (as opposed to a sale of stock), the buyer's attorney should determine whether appropriate corporate or other action has been taken to authorize such transfer. Section 909 of the Business Corporation Law provides that a sale of all or substantially all of the assets of a corporation must be authorized by the seller's Board of Directors. In addition, such proposal must be submitted to a vote of shareholders. Each shareholder of record, whether or not entitled to vote, must be given notice of the meeting, which notice must disclose appraisal rights.[1] The shareholders must then approve the sale and fix, or authorize the board to fix, the terms, conditions and consideration of the sale by a two-thirds vote. Under § 910 of the Business Corporation Law, dissenting shareholders will have appraisal rights[2] unless: (1) the sale is entirely for cash and (2) shareholder approval is conditioned upon: (a) the dissolution of the corporation, and (b) the distribution of net assets to shareholders within one year of the transaction.

"Appraisal Rights" refer generally to the right of a shareholder who opposes a sale of corporate assets to have his or her shares appraised for their fair value and to receive payment therefor.[3]

§ 6.15

1. NYBCL § 605.

2. NYBCL § 623 (procedures concerning appraisal rights).

3. NYBCL § 910.

The buyer's investigation, in the case of a corporation, should consist of a review of the seller's Certificate of Incorporation, and all amendments, as well as the seller's bylaws, stock records, shareholder agreements and the corporate minutes. The seller's organizational documents (the Certificate of Incorporation and Bylaws) should be reviewed to determine whether it is duly organized and whether it is properly authorized to engage in the business it is in. Any limitations on corporate duration should be noted. The buyer should verify that all corporate minutes are up to date, that all directors and officers have been duly elected and that all material actions taken by the Corporation were authorized or ratified by the directors and/or shareholders, as the case may be. The buyer should also determine whether all stock certificates are accounted for. If the buyer is purchasing shares, as opposed to assets, counsel must verify that the holders of all outstanding shares are willing to sell.

At this stage in the due diligence investigation, the buyer's attorney should either contact the Secretary of State to determine that the seller is in good standing[4] in the State of New York or request that the seller provide a Certificate of Good Standing.

If the seller is a partnership or Limited Liability Company, the buyer's attorney should investigate the partnership agreement or the Articles of Organization and Operating agreement, as the case may be, as well as any other documentation the seller might have pertaining to the operation of its business.

In the case of a partnership, the buyer should verify whether Certificates of Conducting Business have been filed in each county in which business is transacted.[5] It is also important at this point for the buyer's counsel to determine if the seller was doing business outside of New York and if so, whether there was proper authorization to conduct business under the laws of other states.[6]

§ 6.16 Due Diligence Investigation—Legal Issues—Ownership Documents

One of the most important concerns of a buyer is that he acquire good title to the assets he is purchasing. The buyer's attorney should examine all documents of title or other instruments evidencing the seller's ownership of its tangible assets (such as deeds, leases, licenses, title to motor vehicles and the like) in order to determine whether the

---

4. *See infra,* § 6.103 note 1 (obtaining Certificate of Good Standing from Secretary of State).

5. General Business Law § 130(1)(a).

6. **PRACTICE POINTER:** The acquisition agreement should contain a provision requiring seller to indemnify buyer from any claims, loss or damage to buyer arising out of seller's having failed to qualify to transact business and/or to remain in good standing in any foreign jurisdiction.

seller has good and marketable title to, or valid leasehold interests in, such assets.

If other parties hold security interests in the seller's assets, the buyer must determine the nature and extent of those interests. At this stage of the due diligence investigation, the buyer's attorney will normally run UCC searches in the Office of the Secretary of State[1] (if seller is a corporation) and in the office of the clerk of the county where the seller's assets are located. The buyer's counsel is also advised at this time to run judgment lien searches in the County Clerk's offices, in order to determine whether there are any outstanding judgment, tax or other liens on the assets of the seller. The buyer's inquiries and a careful review of all of seller's books and records should disclose whether there are any unsecured liabilities, such as those of general trade creditors.

When reviewing the seller's leasehold interests, the buyer should verify whether seller has complied with all material provisions of such leases. Counsel should determine whether all rents and fees have been paid, whether the required insurance has been maintained, whether licenses and permits required under the leases are in effect, and the like. Counsel should also pay special attention to the duration provisions of such leases to verify that they have not expired. It is also important for the buyer's attorney to determine whether the seller's leases are assignable to the buyer, and if so, whether any provisions contained in the leases are negotiable.

During this stage of the due diligence investigation, counsel should also find out whether the seller is covered under any title insurance policies or extended warranties or service contracts on the assets being transferred, and whether such coverage may be transferred to or obtained by buyer. It is also important that counsel request and review copies of any appraisals of machinery, vehicles and equipment which the seller may have.

§ 6.17 Due Diligence Investigation—Legal Issues—Existing Contracts

One of the most important aspects of the due diligence investigation is the review by counsel of all contracts related to the conduct and operations of seller's business.

The types of contracts which should be reviewed include the following:

---

§ 6.16

1. The Uniform Commercial Code Offices of the Secretary of State are located at 41 State St. 2nd Floor, Albany, New York 12231. The mailing address for this office is: Department of State, UCC Bureau, 41 State St., Albany, New York 12231. Fees vary as to type of search requested. The Secretary of State may be contacted at (518) 474–4763.

PRACTICE POINTER: When running the UCC search, it is important to pay careful attention as to whether any of the security interests have expired and also whether such interests attach to after-acquired property or proceeds.

Employment agreements, such as Collective Bargaining agreements, Employee Handbooks, Confidentiality, Trade Secret and Non Competition agreements, and Salesperson's agreements;

Pension and Benefits Contracts, including pension plans, deferred compensation arrangements, stock option plans, cafeteria plans and other fringe benefit obligations, including salary increases, bonus programs and severance plans;

Supplier agreements, advertisement and promotion agreements, software and computer agreements and other agreements related to the purchase of goods and services which enable the seller to conduct its business;

Customer Lists and Customer agreements, unfilled purchase orders, sales contracts, and the seller's agreements to service or warrant its products;

Franchise agreements, dealer and consignment agreements, consulting agreements, research and development contracts;

Lines of credit, letters of credit, financing arrangements, security interests owned by the seller; and

Intellectual property rights, including patents, trademarks and copyrights.

All of the agreements should be reviewed to determine how they will be affected by the transfer of the seller's business to the buyer. The buyer should determine the assignability of the seller's contracts and should also determine whether any customers or suppliers are likely to be lost in the transfer.

When reviewing employment and related agreements, the buyer should determine whether any of the seller's employees should be retained. In the event that the buyer intends to terminate certain employment agreements, such agreements should be reviewed as to length of term and termination provisions. At the time of closing, the buyer should require the seller to deliver written assurances from the seller's employees that they will not compete with the buyer or disclose confidential information concerning the business being transferred.[1] It is also important at this stage to determine whether the contractual obligations of the seller, such as employment agreements and benefits plans, will result in the buyer's assuming expensive and perhaps unwanted liabilities. The buyer's attorney should consider engaging special counsel or other benefits professionals to review existing retirement plans and determine whether they should be continued, modified or terminated. At a minimum, counsel should determine whether all re-

---

§ 6.17

1. *See infra,* §§ 6.67 (concerning covenants not to compete), 6.114 (concerning confidentiality agreements).

quired pension contributions have been made by the seller prior to transfer in order to avoid liability therefor.[2]

If the seller's business is subject to collective bargaining agreements, the buyer's lawyer should take care to determine if any unfair labor practices have been asserted against the seller. Notwithstanding the fact that the buyer is purchasing only the assets of seller's business, buyer may be obliged to correct such practices.[3]

§ 6.18 Due Diligence—Legal Issues—Liens and Security Interests

Prior to the commencement of the legal due diligence investigation, the buyer's counsel should have in its possession a complete list of all assets which are to be transferred.

Counsel must determine as to each asset or category of assets whether there are any outstanding liens or judgments against, or any security interests in, such assets. It is important at this stage of the investigation that counsel obtain UCC searches in the office of the clerk of the county where the seller's assets are located, and in the event that the seller is a corporation, in the Office of the Secretary of State.[1] The buyer should also perform judgment and lien searches in County Clerks' offices where assets of the seller are located.[2]

§ 6.19 Due Diligence Investigation—Legal Issues—Corporate and Trade Names

When the corporate or other trade name is to be transferred to the buyer under the terms of the acquisition agreement, it is important that the buyer determine whether such names have been properly used and registered by seller and whether any impediment to the use of such name by buyer exists by virtue of any claims which might be asserted by third parties.

2. *See* Upholsterers' International Union Pension Fund v. Artistic Furniture of Pontiac, 920 F.2d 1323 (7th Cir.1990) (purchaser of assets of a corporation was held liable for unpaid pension contributions).

3. *See* Golden State Bottling Co. v. NLRB, 414 U.S. 168, 94 S.Ct. 414, 38 L.Ed.2d 388 (1973) (employer who assumed predecessor's assets, continued predecessor's operations, and had notice of unfair labor practice charge at time of acquisition, was required to remedy the unfair labor practice).

§ 6.18

1. The Uniform Commercial Code Offices of the Secretary of State are located at 41 State St., 2nd Floor, Albany, New York 12231. The mailing address for this office is Department of State, UCC Bureau, 41 State St., Albany, New York 12231. Fees vary as to type of search requested. The Secretary of State may be contacted at (518) 474-4763.

2. PRACTICE POINTER: UCC, judgment, tax and other searches can be done by most title insurance companies or by legal search firms such as Nationwide Information Services, Inc. located in Albany, or Prentice Hall Legal and Financial Services, located in both Albany and New York City.

Assumed Names. If the seller has used an assumed or trade name, buyer's counsel should make sure that the seller has filed Certificates of Conducting Business under an Assumed Name in each county in which the seller has transacted business.[1] In the case of a corporation, buyer's attorney should verify that a Certificate of Assumed Name was filed with the Secretary of State.[2] It is also important for the buyer's attorney to make sure that upon transfer of the seller's name to the buyer, the seller formally withdraws its rights to use the trade name by filing Certificates of Discontinuance in all places in which the Assumed Name Certificates were filed.

Trade Names. Under New York law, a "trade name" means any name lawfully adopted and used by any person engaged in any business to identify or distinguish it from the businesses or trade of others, whether or not such trade name has been filed, registered or recorded under any law.[3] The fact that the use of the corporate name of the seller was authorized by the Secretary of State when the seller filed (or amended) its Certificate of Incorporation may afford the seller little protection from a claim or challenge by someone else using the same or similar name.[4] Under New York law applicable to trademarks and trade names, numerous rights and remedies, including injunctive relief and damages, exist where an infringement of trade name or mark is found.[5] It may be advisable for the buyer's counsel to determine, prior to the purchase of the seller's name by the buyer, that the same or a similar name is not being used by another person or entity.[6]

§ 6.20 Due Diligence Investigation—Legal Issues—Real Estate

Review of Title. As discussed in Section 6.16 above, all deeds and documents of title should be carefully reviewed by the buyer's counsel. It is important when purchasing real property to determine whether the seller's title to such property is good and marketable, whether it is free of all liens and encumbrances and whether there are any restrictions as to the ownership, use or transfer of such property to the buyer. All of this information will be disclosed in the buyer's title search. When to order the title search is an issue left to the judgment of counsel, depending upon the circumstances of the transaction. If expense is not an issue for the buyer, or if it appears to counsel that the transaction more likely than not will close, counsel may elect to order title insurance during the due diligence investigative process. Otherwise, counsel may

---

§ 6.19

1. General Business Law § 130(1)(a).

2. General Business Law § 130(1)(b).

3. General Business Law § 360(a-iii).

4. *See* 13 N.Y.Jur.2d, *Business Relationships* § 130.

5. *See* 13 N.Y.Jur.2d, *Business Relationships* §§ 132–139.

6. For fees which may run from $50.00 to approximately $300.00, buyer's attorney may engage a Legal Service Organization, such as Prentice Hall in Albany, to conduct a federal, state and/or common law search for this information.

defer the matter until such time as the asset purchase agreement is signed.[1]

Environmental Issues. One of buyer's major concerns in the purchase of real property as part of a going business is that the use of the real property in the conduct of the business is in compliance with all federal, state and local environmental laws. Environmental concerns, of course, will vary depending upon the nature and use of the real property. During the due diligence investigation, if the nature of the property is such as to cause the buyer concern in this area, the buyer will want to elicit from the seller information concerning past use and current site conditions of the property. The Comprehensive Environmental Response, Compensation and Liability Act of 1980 ("CERCLA") as amended by The Superfund Amendments and Reauthorization Act of 1986,[2] which imposes Federal Superfund liability, provides that an "innocent landowner" will not incur such liability if at the time of purchase he did not know, and had no reason to know, that the property purchased was contaminated.[3] To avail himself of such a defense, a buyer must demonstrate that he undertook a reasonable investigation of the property consistent with current practices in the real estate industry.[4] Many times, a seller will conduct its own site assessment, prior to offering his property for sale. The buyer's attorney should ascertain whether such an assessment has been conducted. If so, the buyer should have his consultant review this assessment. If no assessment was previously conducted, the buyer should consider conducting his own assessment. As the costs associated with such assessments can be burdensome, the allocation of costs should be discussed with the seller.

Occupancy and Use Restrictions. In its due diligence investigation, counsel should determine whether the seller has complied with all zoning regulations, building restrictions and other local ordinances, including fire and health codes. Counsel should also determine whether any such rules or regulations will prevent the buyer from using the subject real property in its business or whether any licenses or permits affecting the use of the real property will be required.

Site Inspection. It is advisable for counsel to inspect the real property with the buyer during the due diligence investigation with the intention of identifying issues which may arise and pose problems for the buyer. Counsel should note, among other things, the access to and from the real property, whether there are any obvious encroachments, the

---

§ 6.20

1. *See infra,* § 6.68 for an in-depth discussion of post-contract/pre-closing matters relating to Real Property. Counsel should be mindful of the issues described in § 6.68, (title searches, surveys, real gains tax and other related taxes), while conducting his or her due diligence investigation.

2. 42 U.S.C.A. § 9620(h).

3. Karlsson, *The Impact of Environmental Liabilities on Real Estate Contract Negotiations,* 8 Pace Envtl. L. Rev. 37 (1990) (WESTLAW: NY–JLR database, ci(8 PA-CENVLR 37)).

4. *Id.*

general condition of the improvements to the real property, whether there is debris which should be removed by the seller, and whether any hazardous conditions might exist which would affect the real property. At the time of inspection, the buyer should note any recent repairs or improvements to the real property which may indicate the possibility of a mechanics or materialmen lien problem.[5]

Broker's Fees. The New York General Obligations Law requires all business brokerage contracts to be in writing.[6] The buyer should obtain from the seller copies of all such agreements entered into by the seller. The purpose of this procedure is to obviate any confusion which might arise at a later date as to whom the broker was representing and as to who should bear the responsibility for the broker's fees or commissions. Unless the broker was retained and authorized to act by the buyer, counsel will want to make sure that the seller is going to pay such broker's fees.

§ 6.21 Due Diligence Investigation—Legal Issues—Compliance With Law

Many businesses such as restaurants, pharmaceutical companies, food manufacturers, insurance companies and the like are subject to or dependent upon government regulation for their existence. During the due diligence investigation, the buyer's counsel should ascertain whether the seller is subject to licensure or regulation by any governmental entity.[1] If so, the buyer's counsel should review all applicable statutes and regulations to determine not only whether the seller has complied in the past with such requirements or regulations, but also whether there are any actions pending against the seller by such agencies due to noncompliance. The buyer's attorney should specifically ascertain at this stage of the investigation whether the buyer will qualify and meet the standards of all such laws and regulations in order to be granted any required licenses or permits. Finally, the buyer's counsel should determine what, if any, consents, actions, or approvals might be required in order to effect the transfer of the seller's business to the buyer.

Library References:

West's Key No. Digests, Attorney and Client ⚖112.50.

---

5. For a comprehensive discussion of mechanics and materialmen liens, see Chapter 10 "Mechanic's Liens," *infra*.

6. General Obligations Law § 5-701(10).

§ 6.21

1. PRACTICE POINTER: The five-volume "Official Directory of New York State Business Permits" published by the New York State Office of Business Permits and Regulatory Assistance ("OBPRA") lists all State-required licenses and permits. Included is information about the issuing agencies, persons to contact, length of determination process and fee requirements. The telephone number of OBPRA is 1–800–342–3464.

§ 6.22 Due Diligence Investigation—Legal Issues—Litigation Investigation

One of the most important aspects of the buyer's due diligence investigation is establishing whether there are any claims, pending or threatened, against the seller or the seller's business. In investigating legal claims, the buyer's attorney should determine the nature of such claims (*e.g.*, regulatory, tort, contract, employment, environmental, etc.), the status of such claims, and whether or not the seller is insured against such claims. If counsel determines that there are pending or threatened claims, the seller's insurance policies should be carefully reviewed to determine not only whether there is coverage, but what the limits of insurance are. Where litigation is pending, the buyer should seek litigations reports, counsel reports and estimates of liability from the seller's attorneys.

§ 6.23 Due Diligence Investigation—Financial Issues—General Considerations

There is an old saying in the negotiation of a business transaction which goes: "It's not the money, but it's the money." In business transactions, it all comes down to the money. Unless the buyer has special knowledge or information regarding the target business, it is essential that the buyer become educated in the financial ratios of the industry and the usual methods for valuing a business in the industry. Some businesses are purchased based upon a capitalization of earnings, a percentage of sales, or a value per unit sold, among other valuation methods. A business consultant or accountant familiar with the industry may provide valuable assistance with financial issues.

After becoming knowledgeable about the industry and the methods employed in establishing a purchase price, the buyer must obtain financial information from the seller to continue the buyer's investigation.

The buyer should also consider obtaining an appraisal of the business.[1]

An analysis of the financial information (and the appraisal if available) should provide the client with a clear economic picture of the business and the ability to determine trends specific to the business.[2]

§ 6.24 Due Diligence Investigation—Financial Issues—Seller's Records From the Buyer's Position

The attorney should advise the buyer to obtain all the available information on the business and the business owner(s) in as much detail as possible. Of particular interest are the following:

§ 6.23
1. See infra, § 6.29.

2. See also, supra, § 6.7.

Ch. 6 BUYER'S RECORDS FROM SELLER'S POSITION § 6.25

1. Income statements;
2. Balance sheets;
3. Cash flow statements;
4. Sales records;
5. Other income sources;
6. Accounts receivable and accounts receivable written off;
7. A listing of expenses;
8. Inventory records, especially a recent physical inventory count;
9. Marketing information and records;
10. Customer list with purchase and payment history;
11. Suppliers lists and their required payment terms;
12. List of liabilities of the seller;
13. Volume of each product line sold (if appropriate to the business);
14. Copies of the business's tax returns;
15. A listing of physical assets and their location;
16. Prior appraisals of the business as a whole, its real property, or its business assets; and
17. Copies of the accountant's work papers in preparing financial statements and/or tax returns (if they can be obtained).

For all of these items, obtain copies at least for the prior three years. For the core items such as financial statements, tax returns and unit sales information, obtain copies for at least the prior five years.[1]

§ 6.25 Due Diligence Investigation—Financial Issues—Buyer's Records From the Seller's Position

Unless the transaction is a cash purchase, the seller may want records and information regarding the financial stability of the buyer. Usually, this information is requested to provide comfort to the seller that any short or long term financing involved in the transaction will be paid.

Some of the items which may be requested are as follows:

1. The buyer's comprehensive business plan for the business being purchased;
2. Documentation of the buyer's business experience;

---

§ 6.24
1. **PRACTICE POINTER:** Historical information will allow the buyer to check for trends in the business. *See also, supra,* § 6.7.

3. Financial statements including a net worth statement of the buyer; and

4. Appraisals or other certifications of the value attributed to assets on the buyers net worth statement.

§ 6.26 Due Diligence Investigation—Financial Issues— Public Records

In addition to searching public records in the course of performing his legal due diligence, the buyer may wish to obtain information on the business from such sources as Dun and Bradstreet, Standard and Poor's Register of Corporations, TRW Business Credit Profile, or any other of a number of business data bases.[1] In addition, if the business is publicly traded, information may be obtained from the Securities and Exchange Commission.

§ 6.27 Due Diligence Investigation—Financial Issues— Financial Statements

Financial statements come in several sizes, shapes and formats; however, if the financial statements are prepared by an accountant employed outside of the business being purchased, they generally fall into one of three categories. (1) Audited Statement (sometimes called Certified Statement); (2) Review Statements; and (3) A Compilation Statement.

Audited Statements are the most reliable and Compilation Statements are the least reliable. An Audited Statement contains the opinion of an independent certified public accountant ("CPA") and states the following:

1. the financial statements fairly represent the financial condition of the business;

2. the financial affairs of the business are stated in accordance with generally accepted accounting principles ("GAAP"); and

3. the undersigned accountant performed the necessary tests in the course of the audit to enable him to render said opinion.

A Compilation Statement, on the other hand, while it is prepared and presented in accordance with generally accepted accounting principles, only reflects the financial information provided by the business, with no independent verification or examination by the accounting firm. Review Statements generally fall somewhere in between the Audited Statement and the Compilation Statement, meaning that certain inde-

§ 6.26

1. WESTLAW from West Group also provides many business data bases, including those mentioned.

pendent testing and verification has been done by the accountant, but not to the extent performed for Audited Statements.[1]

§ 6.28 Due Diligence Investigation—Financial Issues— The Need for Other Professionals

If the complexity of the transaction and/or the dollar value involved warrant it, other professionals may be needed. Business consultants and accountants familiar with the business, as well as tax experts and business appraisers, are not uncommon. In addition, depending upon the nature of the business, the services of other professionals, such as engineers, geologists, computer hardware and software experts and experts in intellectual property and other intangible property may be required.[1]

Library References:
West's Key No. Digests, Attorney and Client ⚖112.50.

§ 6.29 Due Diligence Investigation—Financial Issues— Valuation of the Business

Business valuation is not a science, it is an art. Although the seller may have some idea of the "value" of the business, it may be clouded by subjective feelings or skewed by the mechanical application of an industry formula or reference to the company's financial statements (*e.g.*, book value, net book value, or some multiple of either). Book value, which is often assumed to be some indication of asset value, is a misnomer. It is not a standard of value, but represents the historical cost of the company's assets less depreciation and other adjustments. Net book value is book value minus the liabilities. It is not likely that either of these will provide an accurate indication of value.

The value of a business usually encompasses more than the dollar amounts shown in the financial statements. Intangible items, such as goodwill, business reputation in the community, business location and the amount of competition can substantially affect the value of a business.

A proper valuation requires the aid of a qualified business appraiser with special education, experience and training. Although some accountants may regularly perform business valuations, many do not. Any business appraiser's credentials, whether an accountant or otherwise,

---

§ 6.27
[1] For example, review statements do not confirm information with banks.

§ 6.28
[1] **PRACTICE POINTER:** In small transactions, other experts are often too expensive. After you have advised your client regarding the risks and benefits of proceeding with or with the use of other experts, let the client make the decision. However, be sure to memorialize your communications regarding your advice and the client's decision.

should be reviewed to determine that he or she has the required education, experience, skill and training, preferably with similar businesses.

Although there are many factors to be considered in valuing a business, the valuation methods generally fall into five broad areas.

1. ***Asset Value Factor.*** This method is also referred to as the "cost method" or the "net asset value analysis method." With the cost method the value of a business is based on the cost of replacing its assets less an amount for depreciation due to physical deterioration or functional and economic obsolescence. When using the net asset value method, debts are also subtracted to determine the value of the business. The asset value factor valuation, which approaches liquidation value, is most appropriate for investment or holding companies where the actual assets of the business, such as real estate, are most indicative of the value of the business.

2. ***Capitalized Earnings Method.*** When earnings generated by the business are the main value factor of the business, such as in the case of businesses involving services, distribution or manufacturing, the capitalized earnings method may be the best indication of value. Both the courts and the IRS agree that, in the absence of comparable sales of similar businesses, primary emphasis should be placed on a business's anticipated future earnings in determining its fair market value.[1] In general, the appraiser will accord primary consideration to earnings when valuing stock of companies which sell products or services to the public. Using the earnings factor, value is established by (1) projecting the future earnings of the business and then (2) capitalizing the earnings, *i.e.*, dividing the earnings by a rate that reflects both the nature of the business and its risks. The capitalization rate is usually stated as a percentage. For example, to determine the value of a company with a 10% capitalization rate and $10,000 in earnings it would be computed by dividing $10,000 by .10; the value of the business is $100,000. Generally, the more stable and established a business, the lower the capitalization rate. The lower the capitalization rate, the higher the value of the business.

Another method applying the capitalized earnings method, is to determine the rate of return an investor demands from an investment. If the required rate of return is 10% and the business

---

§ 6.29

1. Internal Revenue Service Revenue Ruling 59–60 states that: "Earnings may be the most important criteria of value in some cases whereas asset value will receive primary consideration in others." Revenue Ruling 59–60 also provides other guidance on valuations. Revenue Ruling 59–60, 1959–1 C.B. 237.

produces $10,000 in profits, an investor should expect to pay $100,000 for the business.

3. *Cash Flow Method.* This method is similar to the capitalized earnings method except that the discounted cash flow of the business, rather than its earnings, is capitalized to arrive at the business value.

4. *Market Value Method.* The market value method compares the business to similar businesses which have been sold or which are publicly traded. This method can be particularly difficult in the case of a small business. Often, there are no comparable sales in the area and publicly traded companies are often substantially larger than the target business. If actual market sales of similar businesses can be found, this is often the most reliable indication of the fair market value of the business.

5. *Other Methods.* In addition to the general methods, other approaches include industry formulas, book value formulas, excess earnings approaches and methods based on units of product sold.

Other factors that an appraiser may also consider to arrive at a value for the company are lack of marketability, control, management, earnings (which are "normalized" for significant non-recurring items), access to capital markets, the nature and history of the business, the existence or lack of goodwill or other intangible value, the tax impact on earnings, estimated taxes, and estimated expenses.

In addition, when only a portion of the business is being purchased, ownership control discounts or premiums for ownership control may be applied.

The appraiser may also make adjustments for potentially uncollectible accounts receivable, obsolescence of equipment, expected future costs, contingent liabilities, and any other items which are reasonably expected to result from continued operations and may impact the value of the company.[2]

§ 6.30 Due Diligence Investigation—Financial Issues—Tax Returns

Depending upon the type of business being purchased, the federal tax return will be filed using one of the following:

1. Schedule C for individuals doing business as sole proprietorships;

2. Form 1065 for businesses operating as partnerships;

2. PRACTICE POINTER: Unless you, the attorney, have the skill, training and experience in valuing businesses, you should refrain from expressing any opinion of value. The attorney's role should be to identify the need for a business appraiser and assist the client in making the selection.

3. Form 1120 for businesses operating as C Corporations;
4. Form 1120S for businesses operating as S Corporations;
5. A Limited Liability Company (LLC) taxed as a corporation;
6. Form 1065 for Limited Liability Companies ("LLC") taxed as partnerships.[1]

Corporation returns generally provide the most information with the Schedule C providing the least.[2]

Library References:

West's Key No. Digests, Internal Revenue ⟶4470–4483.

§ 6.31 Tax Issues for Buyer

Depending upon the transaction (*e.g.*, an asset purchase, a stock purchase or a merger or consolidation), the tax implications and consequences will vary significantly. If the attorney is not familiar with these areas, a tax expert should be consulted.

With an asset purchase, the buyer receives a basket of items, many of which can be depreciated or expensed. With a stock purchase, the buyer generally receives the seller's basis in the business assets received. With a merger, consolidation or exchange, if they are properly executed, the buyer will receive the seller's basis in the assets received, but the seller will not incur any tax liability due to the transaction.

Generally the seller prefers to sell stock and the buyer prefers to purchase assets. Some advantages and disadvantages to the buyer and seller of the respective types of transactions are as follows:

1. Asset Sale Advantages.

   a. The parties may be selective in the assets sold or purchased, with the seller retaining certain items and the purchaser refusing to purchase certain items.

   b. The buyer may purchase the assets and conduct the business with an S Corporation, C Corporation, Limited Liability Company, Partnership, Sole Proprietorship, or a combination of these.

   c. The buyer avoids the problems of built-in gains or losses and other tax attributes of the seller.

   d. The allocation of a portion of the purchase price to specific assets gives the buyer a step-up in basis for depreciation.

---

§ 6.30

1. *See also,* Chapter 35 "Income Tax," *infra.*

2. **PRACTICE POINTER:** Although expenses may be questionable, the stated income may often be viewed as a minimum since few taxpayers are willing to pay tax on income they have not received. *See also,* Chapter 1 "Business Organizations: Corporations," and Chapter 2 "Non-corporate Entities: Limited Liability Companies and Partnerships," *supra.*

§ 6.31

2. Asset Sale Disadvantages.
    a. Sales tax on some assets.
    b. Licenses, contracts, or financing may need to be assigned and may require third-party approvals.
    c. Additional documents in the form of bills of sale, deeds, contract assignments, etc., may be needed.
    d. The transaction may result in double tax if the liquidation of a C Corporation is involved.
    e. The seller will be taxed when appreciated assets are sold at a gain.
    f. The seller may have depreciation recapture.
    g. The parties must consider bulk sales compliance for purpose of both New York State sales tax and Uniform Commercial Code, Article 6.
    h. The seller needs two-thirds shareholder authorization for a sale of all or substantially all assets.[1]

3. Stock Sale Advantages.
    a. The mechanics of transfer are simpler for both parties.
    b. The seller has no continuing problems or entanglements with the business.
    c. It avoids the need to assign leases or contracts.
    d. It avoids compliance with bulk sale statutes.
    e. It may avoid triggering acceleration provisions in mortgages and other financing of the seller.
    f. There is no sales tax on assets purchased.
    g. The buyer does not need to form a new business entity.
    h. Corporate and shareholder approvals are not required.
    i. The seller may avoid tax recapture costs such as depreciation recapture.
    j. The buyer may be able to utilize net operating losses of the seller.
    k. There is one level of tax for the seller, usually capital gain, which may be at a lower tax rate than ordinary income.[2]
    l. The seller transfers all assets, liabilities and obligations of the business.

§ 6.31
[1] NYBCL § 909.
[2] **PRACTICE POINTER:** Capital gains rates are often more favorable than ordinary income tax rates. The tax brackets and circumstances of the parties must be reviewed to know whether capital gains or ordinary income is best. *See also,* Chapter 35 "Income Tax," *infra.*

§ 6.31 BUYING & SELLING A SMALL BUSINESS Ch. 6

4. Stock Sale Disadvantages.
   a. The buyer may acquire unknown, undisclosed, or potential future liabilities.
   b. The buyer may acquire unwanted assets.
   c. The buyer may want to do business using a different business entity.
   d. There may be problems if the buyer cannot acquire all of the shares.
   e. The purchase contract may become complex, especially the provisions relating to the seller's representations and indemnification and set-off clauses.

§ 6.32 Tax Issues for Buyer—Asset Purchase

In the basket of assets purchased, the buyer may receive the following types of assets:

1. Depreciable assets such as equipment and buildings;
2. Amortizable assets such as goodwill and covenants not to compete;
3. Expense items such as supplies; and
4. Land which cannot be expensed, amortized or depreciated.

The buyer usually prefers to purchase assets because he or she will obtain a tax basis in the asset equal to what he or she has paid without regard to the seller's old tax basis. This amount, the tax basis, can be written off against business income as an expense or through depreciation or amortization.

§ 6.33 Tax Issues for Buyer—Asset Purchase—Allocation of Purchase Price

In the body of the contract, general allocations of the purchase price should be set forth for items such as covenants not to compete, goodwill and going concern value, inventory, and assets. The inventory and assets should be further detailed on attached schedules. The contract should state the method for valuing the inventory to be purchased, the mechanics for taking a physical inventory and who is to be responsible for the costs of taking the physical inventory.[1] The contract should also provide that neither party will take a position on any income tax return or in any judicial proceeding that is inconsistent with the allocation in the contract.

§ 6.33
1. **PRACTICE POINTER:** Schedules attached to the contract are an easy method to identify assets and are more easily revised during the course of negotiations. The schedule should also specify the location of the assets and who will bear the cost of delivery, if appropriate.

Since the Tax Reform Act of 1986, I.R.C. § 1060 has controlled the allocation of the purchase price. This section seeks to insure proper allocation to goodwill. To determine the allocation to goodwill, the "residual method" must be used. The purchase price must first be allocated to cash, accounts receivable and other identifiable tangible and intangible assets based on their fair market value. Any remaining purchase price amount should then be allocated to goodwill or going concern value.[2]

Although the contract allocation of the purchase price is not binding on the Internal Revenue Service, if reasonable and in accordance with I.R.C. § 1060, it generally is not challenged by the IRS.

Library References:

West's Key No. Digests, Internal Revenue ⚖3710, 3715.

§ 6.34 Tax Issues for Buyer—Asset Purchase—Depreciation of Assets

The law permits the deduction against business income of a reasonable allowance for the exhaustion and wear and tear of property used in a trade or business.[1] This deduction is called depreciation or amortization.

Depreciation applies to tangible assets (*e.g.*, equipment, buildings, etc.). Amortization applies to intangible assets (*e.g.*, start up costs, goodwill, etc.).

Longer lasting assets, such as buildings, have a longer depreciation period (depreciable life) than assets that wear out faster such as equipment. Items such as land, inventory, cash, and supplies are not depreciable, though some are expensed.[2]

Depreciation and amortization result in a deduction against the ordinary income of the business. Generally, the purchaser desires to allocate as much of the purchase price as possible to assets with the shortest depreciation or amortization period because this will reduce taxable income.[3]

The I.R.C. identifies the methods of depreciation and their respective depreciation periods. For example, business real property, meaning

---

2. Internal Revenue Code Regulation § 1.1060–1T(h). *See also,* Internal Revenue Code § 338(b)(5) and I.R.C. Reg. § 1.1060–1T. Internal Revenue Service Form 8594 "Asset Acquisition Statement" must be filed with each party's income tax return for the year of acquisition.

§ 6.34

1. I.R.C. § 167 and I.R.C. Reg. § 1.167(a)–1.

2. *See infra,* §§ 6.36, 6.38, 6.39, 6.40.

3. PRACTICE POINTER: I.R.C. § 1060 allows an allocation of the purchase price *up to* the asset's fair market value. Depending on the asset mix, it may be possible to allocate purchase price first to items with a shorter depreciable (or amortizable) life, such as equipment or covenants not to compete, with the residual value being allocated to buildings and finally to goodwill and going concern value.

§ 6.34   BUYING & SELLING A SMALL BUSINESS   Ch. 6

buildings, placed in service after May 12, 1993, must be depreciated over 39 years. For buildings placed in service after 1986 and before May 13, 1993, depreciation is computed over 31.5 years.[4] On the other hand, equipment used in a business may be depreciated over periods ranging from 3 to 20 years with most items being depreciated over 5 or 7 years. One can also immediately expense (write off) up to $17,500 of equipment in the first year and each year thereafter subject to certain restrictions; this is referred to as Section 179 expense, after the section of the I.R.C. which allows it.[5]

Library References:

West's Key No. Digests, Internal Revenue ⇔3470–3505.

§ 6.35   Tax Issues for Buyer—Asset Purchase—Land

Real property (*i.e.*, unimproved land) is not depreciable. As a result, buyers usually seek to allocate the smallest value possible to land because a smaller allocation to land, and to buildings which are depreciable over a long period of time, may be beneficial to all parties, because it allows a greater value to be assigned to assets with a shorter depreciable life. This will enhance the depreciation for the buyer, the seller's income taxes may be unchanged and the seller may have a lower real property transfer gains tax.[1]

Library References:

West's Key No. Digests, Taxation ⇔348.

§ 6.36   Tax Issues for Buyer—Asset Purchase—Good Will and Covenants Not to Compete

Prior to August 10, 1993, good will was not depreciable; however, covenants not to compete were amortizable (*i.e.*, they could be written off) over the life of the covenant. Accordingly, in certain instances, substantial write-offs were obtained over a relatively short 3–5 year period of time for the non-compete covenant, but no longer. Business acquisitions after August 10, 1993, can amortize the cost of goodwill,[1] and must amortize the purchase price allocated to covenants not to compete, over a 15 year period beginning in the month of acquisition.[2]

---

4. PRACTICE POINTER: Prior to 1986 the depreciation periods were even more favorable. If a building is a substantial portion of the assets to be purchased, an entity purchase (stock purchase) with a carry-over of the seller's basis and depreciation schedule may be more advantageous than an asset purchase. *See* I.R.C. §§ 167–168 and I.R.C. Regs. §§ 1.167–1.168.

5. I.R.C. § 179.

§ 6.35

1. Tax Law §§ 1440 *et seq. See infra,* § 6.104.

§ 6.36

1. Prior to August 10, 1993, goodwill could not be amortized or depreciated.

2. I.R.C. § 197.

The intangible items included under I.R.C. § 197 must be amortized on a straight line basis over 15 years regardless of the term of the covenant not to compete or the alleged life of the intangible asset.

Library References:

West's Key No. Digests, Internal Revenue ⚖3181.

§ 6.37 Tax Issues for Buyer—Asset Purchase—Inventory

Inventory comprises the items to be sold to the business customers or used in the manufacture of a final product.

Inventory is usually purchased at the seller's cost or the fair market value of the inventory, whichever is less. The inventory amounts are usually determined by a physical count and inspection of the inventory.

Inventory is not depreciable. As the inventory is sold, it is deducted by the business as a cost of goods sold.

Library References:

West's Key No. Digests, Internal Revenue ⚖3701.

§ 6.38 Tax Issues for Buyer—Asset Purchase—Cash

In an asset purchase transaction for a small business, there is usually no cash being purchased. If cash is purchased, it must be valued at its face value and it is not depreciable.

Library References:

West's Key No. Digests, Internal Revenue ⚖3714.

§ 6.39 Tax Issues for Buyer—Asset Purchase—Supplies

Supplies are items used in the daily operation of the business, not items (inventory) held for use in the production process or for sale to customers. Supplies are usually valued at the seller's cost or fair market value, whichever is less. Unless an exceptional situation arises, supplies are consumed by the business in a short period of time. Hence, supplies are usually a business operating expense deduction.

Library References:

West's Key No. Digests, Internal Revenue ⚖3712.1.

§ 6.40 Tax Issues for Buyer—Asset Purchase—Patents, Franchises, Trademarks, Trade Names

Patents, franchises, trademarks, trade names and the like are usually considered to be intangibles and amortized over 15 years under I.R.C.

§ 197. However, the costs associated with certain franchises and patents may be amortizable over shorter periods of time.[1]

Patents have a 17 year life. Copyrights, which are also I.R.C. § 179 intangibles, are legally protected for the life of the author plus 50 years.[2]

§ 6.41 Tax Issues for Buyer—Stock Purchase

When a buyer purchases the stock of a corporation, the buyer, for better or for worse, inherits the tax aspects of the corporation. Unless an election is made under I.R.C. § 338,[1] the buyer inherits all of the tax aspects attributable to the assets of the entity. That is, the buyer must follow elections previously made by the seller and does not get a step-up in basis to the purchase price paid for depreciable assets. (I.R.C. § 338 only applies to corporations. The same concept also applies to the purchase of a partnership interest or a membership interest in a limited liability company. An election similar to, but not exactly the same as, an I.R.C. § 338 election can be made under I.R.C. §§ 743 and 754 for partnerships and LLCs taxed as partnerships.[2])

§ 6.42 Tax Issues for Buyer—Stock Purchase—Basis of Stock

The buyer's basis in the stock of the corporation acquired is the amount paid for the stock. Unless the entity acquired is an S Corporation,[1] the basis for the stock purchased will remain the same. Partnerships and limited liability companies taxed as partnerships allow for basis changes[2] since they are "flow-through" tax entities.

§ 6.43 Tax Issues for Buyer—Stock Purchase—Basis of Corporate Assets

When a business is acquired by purchasing the stock of a corporation, the buyer receives the same basis and depreciation schedules as were used by the seller. There is no step-up in basis to the amount paid for individual assets as may happen with an asset purchase transaction. For example, in a stock purchase, the buyer of a piece of equipment with a current tax basis of $1,000, but a fair market value of $5,000, inherits the $1,000 stock basis (even though the stock purchase price reflects a $5,000 value). In an asset purchase transaction, the buyer could pay up to $5,000 for this asset and depreciate the whole $5,000.

§ 6.40
1. See I.R.C. Reg. § 1.167(a)–6 (patents) and I.R.C. § 1253(d)(1) (franchises).
2. 7 U.S.C.A. §§ 302–304.

§ 6.41
1. See infra, § 6.44.

2. See I.R.C. §§ 743, 754. See also, Chapter 2 "Non-corporate Entities: Limited Liability Companies and Partnerships," supra.

§ 6.42
1. See I.R.C. §§ 1361 et seq.
2. See I.R.C. § 701 et seq.

§ 6.44 Tax Issues for Buyer—Stock Purchase—Election to Treat Stock Purchase as Asset Purchase

If the seller insists on a stock sale, a step-up in basis of the assets may be acquired by the purchaser in certain situations. The purchaser, which must be a corporation, must make an election to treat the purchase price of the stock as the purchase price of the assets of the acquired corporation.[1] In other words, the tax basis of the assets in the acquired business are increased to the amount paid for the stock.[2]

The provisions of I.R.C. § 338 are complex and they may come with a price. With the repeal of the General Utilities Rule by the Tax Reform Act of 1986, a corporate level tax may be payable by the target (purchased) corporation because the assets of the target corporation are "deemed" to be sold by the target corporation to the new corporation at the stepped-up basis amounts. The elected stepped-up basis in most cases will exceed the tax basis of the assets, resulting in taxable gain.

§ 6.45 Tax Issues for Buyer—Mergers, Consolidations and Exchanges

Corporate mergers and consolidations involve swapping the securities of one corporation, the buyer, for the securities of the other corporation, the seller. If properly structured, the gain which would otherwise be recognized by the seller's shareholders, is deferred until such time as they sell the securities.[1] A tax deferred exchange works in a similar manner except that actual assets are exchanged.[2]

If properly structured, no gain or loss is recognized by either the stockholders[3] or the corporation[4] upon an exchange of stock or assets in a qualified reorganization. The consideration received by a stockholder in the restructured corporation is restricted to stock or securities of a corporation which is part of the reorganization.

I.R.C. § 368(a) lists seven qualifying reorganizations. The reorganization must fall within one of the seven categories (often referenced by their designating capital letter) which may be summarized as follows:

A. a statutory merger or consolidation;[5]

B. the acquisition by one corporation, in exchange solely for all or part of its voting stock, of the controlling stock of another corporation;

§ 6.44
1. I.R.C. § 338.
2. The purchasing corporation must make a Statement of Election under I.R.C. § 338(g) on Form 8023.

§ 6.45
1. I.R.C. §§ 354, 355, 361, 368.
2. I.R.C. § 1031.
3. I.R.C. § 354.
4. I.R.C. § 361.
5. In accordance with the NYBCL.

§ 6.45 BUYING & SELLING A SMALL BUSINESS Ch. 6

C. the acquisition by one corporation, in exchange solely for all or part of its voting stock or that of a corporation which controls it, of substantially all of the properties of another corporation;

D. a transfer by a corporation of all or part of its assets to another corporation if immediately after the transfer the transferor or one or more of its shareholders or any combination thereof is in control of the corporation to which the assets are transferred;

E. a recapitalization;

F. a mere change in identity, form or place of organization, however effected; and

G. a bankruptcy reorganization.

In addition to the reorganization provisions of I.R.C. § 368, a tax deferred exchange of assets may be available. The assets must be held for productive use in a trade or business or for investment and they must be exchanged solely for property of like-kind, either for productive use in a trade or business or for investment.[6]

The "like-kind" definition is liberal for real property.[7] Hence, a farm can be exchanged for a rental apartment, a condominium for vacant land, a co-op interest for a condominium.[8] But real estate located in the United States cannot be exchanged for foreign real estate.[9]

The rules under I.R.C. § 1031 applicable to personal property are more stringent. The assets exchanged must all come under the same Internal Revenue Service General Business Asset Classification to avoid taxation.[10]

Most businesses have inventory and a combination of personal property and real property. Because inventory does not qualify for an I.R.C. § 1031 exchange,[11] and due to the more stringent requirements imposed on the exchange of personal property, like-kind exchanges are seldom used in business transactions.

Library References:

West's Key No. Digests, Internal Revenue ⚙︎3660–3686.

§ 6.46 Structuring the Buyer's Transaction

Except for the legal due diligence considerations and any special needs or risks of the particular transaction, the structuring of the buyer's transaction is usually driven by three main issues:

---

6. I.R.C. § 1031.
7. I.R.C. Reg. § 1.1031(a)–1(a)(2), (b).
8. *Id.*
9. I.R.C. Reg. § 1.1031(a)–2(b)(2).
10. *See* Revenue Procedure 87–56, 1987–2 C.B. 674, for General Business Asset Classifications.
11. I.R.C. § 1031(a)(2)(A).

Ch. 6   ASSUMPTION OF SELLER'S LIABILITIES   § 6.48

1. business considerations and economics;
2. protection for the buyer; and
3. income taxes.

Business considerations will often dictate if the transaction will be a sale and the type of sale, an asset purchase, a stock purchase, or any exchange. Economics, besides influencing the purchase price, will also dictate the type and method of payment.

Protection for the buyer may be provided by covenants not to compete,[1] set-off clauses and escrow arrangements, among others.[2]

Tax considerations are interlaced throughout the structure of the transaction,[3] but they are usually not a deal breaker if both parties want the transaction.

§ 6.47 Structuring the Buyer's Transaction—Type of Payment

The usual type of payment is cash. Sometimes in small business purchases there is an exchange of stock or securities of the buyer, but this is not common. Although payment in securities of the buyer can have certain tax advantages, such forms of payment are usually reserved for larger transactions where the buyer's stock is traded on an established securities exchange.

Installment payments are usually preferred by purchasers rather than lump sum payments. This benefits the purchaser in a number of ways. It may allow the purchaser to consummate the transaction without the expense and entanglements of bank financing, buyers are usually able to negotiate with the seller for an interest rate somewhat lower than banks, and it will provide a measure of security to the buyers, as a fund for set-off, if representations or other obligations of the seller are not met.

In certain transactions, payment may be made in kind (product) or in the providing of services. This is especially true when the buyer is a supplier or service provider who purchases part, but not all, of the seller's business and continues doing business with the seller.[1]

§ 6.48 Structuring the Buyer's Transaction—Assumption of Seller's Liabilities

Although not the rule, the buyer may provide part or all of the

§ 6.46
1. *See infra*, § 6.66.
2. *See infra*, § 6.51.
3. *See supra*, §§ 6.31–6.45.

§ 6.47
1. **PRACTICE POINTER:** All products or services received by the seller are taxable.

purchase price by assuming some or all of the seller's liabilities.[1] Such an assumption may be advantageous to the buyer, for it may save the buyer the expense and burden of obtaining additional financing and provide the opportunity to keep a favorable pre-existing interest rate.[2]

§ 6.49 Structuring the Buyer's Transaction—Security to Seller

If a seller provides part of the financing for the transaction, unless it involves a distress sale, the seller will likely require security in the form of a first security interest in all of the assets of the business and a mortgage against any business real property. In addition, it is not uncommon for the seller to request personal guarantees from the buyer, and the buyer's spouse as well, as additional collateral over and above the business assets. The additional collateral may take the form of pledged bank accounts, securities, or mortgages against other real property of the purchaser. The purchaser may also be required to maintain a certain net worth (with a formula dictating how net worth is defined) and provide an opinion from his independent certified public accountant that the net worth statement provided by the buyer is accurate. This provides an additional measure of comfort to the seller because the seller may have recourse against the buyer's accountant as well as against the buyer if the net worth is misstated.

Library References:

West's Key No. Digests, Secured Transactions ⊱41–51.

§ 6.50 Structuring the Buyer's Transaction—Notes

If the seller is financing all or a portion of the transaction, the amount owed will normally be evidenced by promissory notes secured by a security agreement, mortgage(s), pledge agreement(s) or any other form or combination of collateral the seller can obtain. The promissory note will usually provide that any default under the purchase and sale agreement will also constitute a default under the terms of the promissory note. If there are any set-offs provided for in the purchase and sale agreement, they should also be provided for in the promissory note.[1] The

§ 6.48

1. PRACTICE POINTER: With an entity (stock) purchase, liabilities are assumed in practice and by definition.

2. PRACTICE POINTER: With any assumption of liabilities, the buyer should obtain written verification from the creditor of the balance due on the liability and confirmation that the seller is not in default. The terms of some debt instruments also require the consent of the lender.

§ 6.50

1. PRACTICE POINTER: In addition to stating any set-off or indemnification provisions of the purchase and sale agreement in the promissory note, it is good practice to make the promissory note subject to all of the terms and conditions of the purchase agreement and attach it as an exhibit to the promissory note. Another technique to protect the buyer is to make the note(s) non-negotiable, at least for the

Ch. 6 ESCROW ARRANGEMENTS AND AGREEMENTS § 6.51

promissory notes will also typically have an acceleration in the event of default. The buyer can negotiate for a period of time to cure any event of default, and if reasonable, it is usually granted by the seller.

Library References:

West's Key No. Digests, Bills and Notes ⚖︎1–115.

§ 6.51 Structuring the Buyer's Transaction—Escrow Arrangements and Agreements

The agreement usually contains numerous representations and warranties by the seller. In addition, the contracts often contain specific goals or quotas for sales, accounts receivable, number of customers etc., and returned merchandise by customers based on the seller's representations, history and experience in the business.

These provisions are often applicable both before and after the closing of the transaction. In addition, escrow arrangements are commonly used to protect the buyer from the seller's non-payment of existing or contingent liabilities. Escrow arrangements provide a financial remedy to the buyer if these seller liabilities are not paid or the quotes and representation provisions are not met. An escrow arrangement is especially important with a lump sum cash purchase.

Similar protection may be obtained by using a set-off clause allowing the buyer to deduct these amounts from payments due to the seller.[1] The escrow arrangement should state when and how payment by the escrow agent from the escrow fund is to be made, as well as when the escrow agent is to be released from liability of the escrow arrangement.[2] It should also provide a substitute escrow agent.

The escrow agent should always be an independent person and many times is one of the law firms involved in the transaction.[3] Escrow arrangements are useful when the buyer and seller desire to waive the bulk sale requirements imposed by the Uniform Commercial Code and the Sales Tax Law.[4]

duration of any seller obligations, such as covenants not to compete.

§ 6.51

1. See supra, § 6.46.
2. **PRACTICE POINTER:** Depending on the significance of the amount and the duration of time, the escrow funds should be placed in an interest bearing investment. It is suggested that the account be titled in the name of the escrow agent as agent for (usually) the seller using the seller's tax identification number. Use the tax identification number of the party to whom it is expected the funds and interest income will be paid. The signatory on the account should be the escrow agent and all statements should be mailed to the escrow agent.

3. **PRACTICE POINTER:** Being an escrow agent may cause a conflict of interest for the escrow agent law firm if the buyer and seller later engage in litigation.

4. See infra, §§ 6.65–6.66.

PRACTICE POINTER: When an escrow arrangement is used, an estimate of the maximum liability is often made to avoid escrowing excessive amounts.

§ 6.52 Drafting the Buyer's Asset Purchase Agreement

As discussed in Section 6.12 above, counsel must weigh the advantages and disadvantages associated with taking it upon himself to draft the buyer's asset purchase agreement.

Sections 6.53 to 6.76 below contain discussions of the various provisions found in a typical asset purchase agreement. A sample agreement appears at the end of the chapter.[1]

Library References:

West's Key No. Digests, Sales ⚖1–53(3).

§ 6.53 Drafting the Buyer's Asset Purchase Agreement—Identification of the Parties

The initial paragraph of the asset purchase agreement which identifies the parties to the agreement should establish the following:

- The name and address of each of the parties;
- The business or legal description of each entity, such as "a New York Business Corporation" or "a Vermont Corporation authorized to do business in New York" or "a Partnership";
- The position of each party and the term to which such party is referred in the agreement, such as "Buyer," "Seller," "Escrow Agent," "Guarantor," "Sole Shareholder";[1]
- If a party is a business entity, the location of the main office of such entity.

Library References:

West's Key No. Digests, Sales ⚖15, 28.

§ 6.54 Drafting the Buyer's Asset Purchase Agreement—Recitals

The "Recitals" section of the asset purchase agreement will establish the background of the transaction and the intent of the parties as to the transaction. The recitals may also set forth important information which may not otherwise appear in the text of the agreement, such as the fact that a party conducts business under another name, or that a certain relationship exists between the parties to the agreement, or that there is a specific purpose underlying the business transaction being entered into. While the recitals are not technically part of the operative

---

§ 6.52

1. *See infra,* § 6.187.

§ 6.53

1. **PRACTICE POINTER:** When the buyer and/or seller are corporations, the shareholders should be made parties to the agreement, so that the obligations to be undertaken by the corporations become binding upon and guaranteed by the individual shareholders.

agreement, the information contained in the recitals can be critical in case of a later contract dispute.[1]

Library References:

West's Key No. Digests, Sales ⬯28.

§ 6.55 Drafting the Buyer's Asset Purchase Agreement—Assets and Property to Be Conveyed

The asset purchase agreement must contain the covenant of the seller to sell and the covenant of the buyer to purchase the assets of the business as well as a description of the assets being sold. The description may be a general description contained in the body of the contract such as:

> "all of the inventory, furniture, fixtures and equipment contained in the premises and identified and agreed to in writing by the parties as of the close of business on (date),"

or the assets may be specifically identified in a schedule or schedules attached to and made a part of the agreement. Classes of assets generally include the following:

- Land, buildings and improvements;
- Machinery, furniture, fixtures and equipment;
- Inventory;[1]
- Transportation equipment, vehicles;
- Raw materials, works in process, supplies;
- Corporate and trade names;
- Formulas, trade secrets, patents, patent applications, copyrights;
- Manuals, catalogues, sales and advertising materials;
- Customer lists, supplier lists;
- Purchase orders, sales agreements and commitments;
- Rights of seller under any licensing, franchise or other agreements;
- Goodwill.

If the assets to be transferred are subject to liabilities, then the liabilities to be assumed by the purchaser as well as the liens associated with them should be specifically identified. In any event, there should be an accurate and complete description of all assets to be transferred, and of the liabilities to be assumed and not assumed.

§ 6.54

1. Recitals may be incorporated into and made a part of the operative agreement, if the drafter so chooses.

§ 6.55

1. *See supra,* § 6.37 for suggested contract provisions relating to inventory.

§ 6.55　BUYING & SELLING A SMALL BUSINESS　Ch. 6

This section of the agreement should further specify when and where the assets are to be delivered and the legal documents which will be required to effect the transfer of title, such as bills of sale, deeds, assignments of leases and similar instruments.[2] It is advisable to include in schedules attached to the agreement copies of all assignments of leases and assumption agreements which will be executed and delivered at closing.

If there will be any costs involved relative to the transfer of assets, such as fees for the taking of inventory, delivery charges or filing or recording fees, they should be identified and appropriated to the proper parties in this section of the agreement.

Library References:
West's Key No. Digests, Sales ⚷28, 67.

§ 6.56 Drafting the Buyer's Asset Purchase Agreement—Retained Assets of Seller

There should be an accurate and complete description of assets to be retained by the seller so that no controversy as to this issue arises at closing or at a later date. Generally, the seller will retain all cash, bids or other deposits paid by the seller for services or contract awards, advances paid to employees, prepaid expenses and most importantly, the seller's corporate minute books, corporate seal, tax returns and insurance contracts. Often, the seller will also choose to retain accounts receivable arising prior to closing.[1]

Library References:
West's Key No. Digests, Sales ⚷67.

§ 6.57 Drafting the Buyer's Asset Purchase Agreement—Purchase Price and Method of Payment

This section of the asset purchase agreement will describe the purchase price and its method of allocation, how the purchase price will be paid and such other matters as debt assumption and securitization, if applicable.

Purchase Price. The purchase price need not be an identified dollar amount, especially where there may be contingencies as to the price to be paid. In such event the agreement will provide for part of the purchase price to be ascertained at a later date, based on a fixed formula or other identified method to be used which has been agreed upon by the

---

2. In the alternative, a provision for the delivery of assets and legal documents effecting transfer of title to seller may be included in the "Closing" section of the agreement. *See infra,* § 6.58.

§ 6.56

1. For suggested language from a sample agreement, *see infra,* § 6.187, Section 2.

parties at the time of negotiation of the purchase price. Any provisions for adjustments[1] to the purchase price to which the parties have agreed will also appear in this section of the asset purchase agreement.

Allocation of Purchase Price. It is generally advisable for the parties to agree as to allocation for IRS purposes and to state the allocations in the asset purchase agreement. The allocations are important to the buyer because they determine the buyer's basis for depreciation and for gain or loss on sale. The buyer will generally seek a higher allocation to items that can be expensed,[2] depreciable property and amortizable intangibles,[3] whereas the seller will want a higher allocation to capital assets.[4] The agreement should contain a provision stating that neither the buyer nor the seller will take a position in any income tax return or in any judicial proceeding that is inconsistent with the allocations in the agreement.[5]

Manner of Payment. The manner of payment of the purchase price should be described with specificity in this section of the agreement. If the whole of the purchase price is to be paid in cash, as opposed to installments, the buyer should require part of such payment to be placed in escrow against any default of the seller under the terms of the agreement.[6]

Security for Payment of Purchase Price. If the purchase price in whole or part is to be paid by the buyer in installments, the seller may require the buyer to furnish security in the form of mortgages or other liens on the transferred assets, or in the form of letters of credit, pledges of stock or personal guaranties of the buyer.[7] Whatever the form of security required, it should also be described with specificity in this section of the agreement. In addition, copies of all such security agreements, financing statements, notes, mortgages, and other security instruments should be attached to, and be made a part of, the agreement.

Promissory Notes of Buyer. Copies of any promissory notes to be endorsed by the buyer at closing should be appended to the asset purchase agreement. The agreement should describe the type of note to be signed by the buyer, as well as the material provisions of such note,

§ 6.57

1. Adjustments are normally made for items such as insurance premiums, rents, deposits with utility companies, payroll, payroll taxes, etc.

2. *See* I.R.C. § 179.

3. *See supra,* § 6.34 for a more comprehensive discussion of favorable tax allocations for buyer.

4. *See supra,* § 6.120 for a more comprehensive discussion of favorable capital gains tax treatment for seller.

5. **PRACTICE POINTER:** Buyer should consider adding to this part of the agreement a provision requiring seller to indemnify buyer for any costs assessed against buyer by the IRS, in the event that seller fails to abide by the agreed upon allocations. While the IRS is not bound to the parties' allocations, it will generally follow them, unless the parties are in conflict.

6. For a more comprehensive discussion of this issue, *see supra,* § 6.51.

7. *See infra,* § 6.136 for a more comprehensive discussion of security interests retained by seller.

including the amount of the note, whether it is to be negotiable or non-negotiable,[8] the term and interest rate of the note and other important considerations such as acceleration, pre-payment, securitization, presentment (or waiver thereof), and default provisions. As discussed earlier, the promissory note should contain a provision stating that any default under the terms of the agreement shall constitute a default under the note.[9] In addition, if the buyer has retained any rights to set-off under the terms of the agreement, such provisions should also be set forth in the promissory note.

Library References:

West's Key No. Digests, Sales ⚖︎74.

§ 6.58 Drafting the Buyer's Asset Purchase Agreement—Closing

The acquisition agreement should identify the date, place and time of closing. The date need not be a fixed date but may be conditioned on the happening of certain events, for example:

"Closing shall occur six weeks from the date of the last to occur of the contingencies identified in sections _____ of the agreement."

This section of the agreement may also contain provisions as to the manner of payment of the purchase price, the property, documents and other instruments to be delivered at closing, and such other events as may be expected to occur at closing.

Library References:

West's Key No. Digests, Sales ⚖︎135–196.

§ 6.59 Drafting the Buyer's Asset Purchase Agreement—Representations, Warranties and Covenants of Seller

The representations and warranties of the seller constitute one of the most important sections of the asset purchase agreement from the point of view of the buyer. The seller's representations must be carefully drafted, as it is these representations which will disclose to the buyer important information about every aspect of the seller's business. A material misstatement of any of the seller's representations, or a breach

---

8. PRACTICE POINTER: Buyer should consider issuing promissory notes which are non-negotiable in form, at least for any period in which buyer may have a right of set-off against seller, or for any period in which buyer's performance may be contingent upon any representation or covenant of seller. For example, if seller has agreed not to compete with buyer for a period of three years, buyer's note for such three-year period should be non-negotiable. If under the terms of the agreement, buyer's note is to be for a ten-year period, buyer can issue two notes: the first, a non-negotiable note for the first three years, and the second, a negotiable instrument for the remaining seven years of the term.

9. See supra, § 6.50.

Ch. 6   WARRANTIES & COVENANTS OF SELLER   § 6.59

by the seller of any of the warranties or covenants contained in this section, will provide a basis for the buyer to avoid or rescind the agreement, or to seek indemnification from the seller in the event that the buyer suffers any loss or injury as a result of such misstatement or breach.

The representations and warranties generally mirror the due diligence investigation performed by the buyer, and in addition, should cover any issue which the buyer was unable to discover during its investigations. The asset purchase agreement should contain a provision requiring verification by the seller that the warranties, representations and covenants made as of signing are true as of closing,[1] and in addition, a provision stating that the warranties, representations and covenants will survive for a stated period subsequent to closing.[2]

The buyer's attorney will generally require the representations to be drafted in the absolute, that is, without qualification. For example, the buyer might request that the seller warrant that the equipment is in excellent condition and working order, capable of meeting highest industry standards. The seller, on the other hand, may deem it to be in his best interest to represent that the equipment is, to the best of his knowledge, in good working order and sufficient for the operations of the business in its current state.

The representations, warranties and covenants of the seller will usually include the following:[3]

- That the seller is duly incorporated, validly existing, in good standing and qualified to do business;
- That the seller has no affiliations, subsidiaries or other business interests;
- That the seller possesses the requisite authority to enter into the asset purchase agreement and to perform in accordance with its terms;
- That there are no conflicts between the asset purchase agreement and other agreements of the seller;
- That there are no conflicts of interests between the seller and any third party;
- That the seller possesses the corporate power necessary to own the assets and property and to carry on business;

§ 6.59

1. For suggested language from a sample agreement, see infra, § 6.187, Section 16(a).

2. For suggested language from a sample agreement, see infra, § 6.187, Section 18.

3. CAVEAT: The representations and warranties which appear in this Section are for illustrative purposes only and are not comprehensive in scope. Counsel is advised to carefully draft each representation in accordance with the circumstances of the transaction.

§ 6.59   BUYING & SELLING A SMALL BUSINESS   Ch. 6

- That the seller has good and marketable title to the assets and the right to transfer assets free and clear of encumbrances;
- That there exist no service agreements, maintenance agreements, warranties or other obligations outstanding on the seller's products, except as set forth;
- That the assets are in compliance with all federal, state and local laws, rules and regulations;
- That there are no licenses or leases in effect concerning the assets except those specified;
- That the seller has good and marketable title to the real estate;
- That there are no mechanics or materialmen liens or bases for such liens on the real estate transferred;
- That the seller has delivered to the buyer the following financial statements, which are true and complete, and which accurately represent the financial condition of the seller: (a) balance sheets; (b) a statement of profits and losses; and (c) tax returns;
- That except to the extent reflected in the balance sheet, dated ___, there are no liabilities of any nature, and the seller represents that it does not know, or have reason to know, of any liability of any nature not fully reflected in the balance sheet;
- That since the dates of the balance sheet and tax returns provided to the buyer, there has not been: (a) any change in assets, liabilities, or the financial condition of the seller's business; (b) any damage, loss, or destruction to the assets of the business that are not covered by insurance; (c) any sales other than in the regular course of business; (d) any pending litigation, and none is pending; (e) any labor union organizing activity or actual or threatened employee strikes; (f) any institution or settlement of any litigation related to the seller or its business; (g) any failure to replace inventory and supplies; or (h) any failure to pay any debt when it has become due;
- That the seller has delivered to the buyer a true and complete list of all accounts receivable as of ___, as reflected in the balance sheet, and that if, following closing, any such accounts remaining unpaid are not paid in full upon demand when due, then the seller shall pay the same upon demand of the buyer (against delivery by the buyer of an assignment of such defaulted accounts);[4]
- That the seller has filed all required tax returns;
- That inventory is merchantable and in good condition and that, as of the date of closing, it will consist of current, readily saleable goods and merchandise;

4. Not applicable if seller is retaining Accounts Receivable.

Ch. 6 WARRANTIES & COVENANTS OF SELLER § 6.59

- That the seller has no notice or knowledge of its violation of any federal, state and local laws, rules and regulations;
- That the seller possesses all necessary licenses, permits and consents required to carry on business;
- That the seller has delivered to the buyer an accurate list of all contracts, oral and written, to which the seller is a party; such contracts being as follows: (a) employment contracts; (b) contracts with salespersons and distributors; (c) pension, benefit and related agreements; (d) agreements with suppliers, consultants, support services, providers and the like; (e) customer agreements, unfilled purchase orders, sales contracts; (f) customer lists; (g) franchise agreements, dealer and consignment agreements, research and development contracts; (h) lines of credit and loans; and (i) contracts with labor organizations; all of which have been entered into in the ordinary course of business;
- That the seller has complied with material provisions of all contracts, leases, licenses, other agreements, and that they are valid and in good standing;
- That all contracts, leases, licenses and other agreements are assignable, except as indicated, and that the seller will provide the buyer with consents to such assignment at closing;
- That there are no collective bargaining agreements in effect and that the seller has no knowledge of any labor union organizing activity or any strikes or threatened strikes;
- That the seller has delivered to the buyer an accurate list of all insurance policies, including any pending claims;
- That the seller will maintain all such insurance until closing or until such time as the assets are transferred to the buyer;
- That there are no environmental hazards or conditions affecting the assets;
- That there is no litigation pending or threatened against or relating to the seller, its properties or business;
- That the seller has delivered to the buyer an accurate list of all patents, patent applications, trademarks, trade names, and copyrights, presently held by the seller, all of which are valid and in good standing;
- That from the date of execution of the asset purchase agreement until the time of closing, there will be no new leases, tenancies or contracts affecting the assets without the prior written approval of the buyer;
- That the seller will perform all necessary repairs and maintenance on the assets and real property prior to closing;

§ 6.59   BUYING & SELLING A SMALL BUSINESS

- That the seller will pay vacation time and other employee benefits which have accrued up to and including closing date;
- That no broker brought about this transaction (or, in the alternative: that the seller will indemnify and hold the buyer harmless from any claim for brokerage commissions);
- That no representation, warranty or covenant of the seller in the agreement or in any writing furnished to the buyer contains any untrue statement of fact or failure to state any material fact;
- That the seller has disclosed all material adverse facts known to it; and
- That the representations, warranties and covenants of the seller shall be true at the time of closing as though such representations and warranties were made at such time.

In certain circumstances, the asset purchase agreement may not be executed by the parties until the time of closing. In the event that closing is to occur after the date of the execution of the asset purchase agreement by the parties, the buyer must make sure that the seller will continue to operate the business in the ordinary course. To that end, the buyer should obtain "Pre-closing" covenants from the seller. Pre-closing covenants of the seller normally include the following:

- That since the date of execution of the asset purchase agreement, the seller has operated the business only in the ordinary course and there has not been:
- any change in assets, liabilities, or the financial condition of the seller's business since the date of such financial statements, tax returns or other documents;
- any damage, loss or destruction to the seller's assets that are not covered by insurance;
- any sale other than in the regular course of business;
- any pending or threatened litigation;
- any labor union organizing activity or actual or threatened employee strike;
- any litigation instituted or settled relating to the seller or its assets;
- any failure to replace inventory and supplies; and
- any chemical spill or other environmental condition affecting the assets.

Library References:
West's Key No. Digests, Sales ⊛246–288.5.

§ 6.60 Drafting the Buyer's Asset Purchase Agreement—Representations, Warranties and Covenants of Buyer

In the asset purchase agreement, the representations, warranties and covenants of the buyer will not be as comprehensive as the representations of the seller.

The buyer's representations will generally include the following:

- That the buyer is duly incorporated, validly existing, in good standing and qualified to do business;
- That the buyer possesses the corporate power necessary to own the assets and property and to carry on the business;
- That the buyer possesses the requisite authority to enter into the asset purchase agreement and to perform in accordance with its terms; and
- That no broker brought about this transaction (or, in the alternative: that the buyer will indemnify and hold the seller harmless from any claim for brokerage commissions).

In the event that the purchase price is to be paid by the buyer in installments, the seller will normally require additional representations and warranties as to the financial condition of the buyer and of the guarantors of the buyer's obligations.[1]

§ 6.61 Drafting the Buyer's Asset Purchase Agreement—Conduct of Business Prior to Closing

In the event that closing is to occur after the date of the execution of the asset purchase agreement by the parties, the agreement should contain a provision for the conduct of business by the seller up to the time of closing. The purpose for such a provision is twofold: First, it will assure the buyer that the seller will continue to conduct its business without interruption, and secondly, it will provide the buyer with the affirmation of the seller that during this period the seller will not transfer assets or do anything outside of the ordinary course of business. In this section of the agreement, the buyer will require the seller to operate in a manner consistent with prior operations. In addition, the buyer will require assurance that the seller will continue to maintain insurance on its assets, that the seller will continue to replace inventory and that the seller will allow the buyer access to the books, records and operations of the seller during this period.

This section may also provide that the seller, while in continued possession of the business, is to pay for all materials and services

---

§ 6.60

1. See infra, § 6.146 for buyer's representations as to financial condition.

§ 6.61   BUYING & SELLING A SMALL BUSINESS

pertaining to the operations of the business which have been delivered to the seller prior to closing, and that the buyer is to pay for all such materials and services delivered after closing. Additionally, there should be a provision for accounts receivable to the effect that receivables derived from goods or other business products shipped after closing will become the property of the buyer, and receivables from goods shipped prior to closing are to be paid to the seller.[1]

Library References:

West's Key No. Digests, Sales ⚖54–88.

§ 6.62   Drafting the Buyer's Asset Purchase Agreement—Indemnifications

As discussed above, the seller's representations and warranties comprise one of the most important elements of the asset purchase agreement in that the buyer relies heavily upon them in deciding to purchase the assets of the seller's business.[1] The failure or falsity of any of the material representations or warranties of the seller could cause the buyer serious injury in the form of excessive costs, losses or exposure to legal action.

The purpose of the seller's indemnifications of the buyer is to protect the buyer from such injury.

In drafting the indemnification provisions, the buyer's attorney is advised to require broad indemnification from the seller (as seller's attorney would be advised to limit and restrict the seller's indemnifications as much as possible).

The buyer's asset purchase agreement should be drafted[2] to provide that the seller will indemnify and hold the buyer harmless from all liabilities, losses, costs and expenses (including legal fees) relative to or arising from:

- Liabilities, obligations and claims against the seller not expressly assumed by the buyer—including any claims for warranty, product liability, or the repair or replacement of products sold by the seller prior to closing; and

- Any claims or costs resulting from a misrepresentation or breach by the seller of its covenants and warranties contained in the asset purchase agreement or other documents delivered to the buyer pursuant to the asset purchase agreement.

§ 6.61

1. For suggested language from a sample agreement, see § 6.187, Section 8(b).

§ 6.62

1. See supra, § 6.59.
2. For suggested language from a sample agreement, see infra, § 6.187, Section 9.

Library References:

West's Key No. Digests, Indemnity ⚖=8(3).

§ 6.63 Drafting the Buyer's Asset Purchase Agreement—Corporate or Other Name

It is important for the buyer that the terms of the asset purchase agreement contain the seller's covenant that the seller is transferring its name (including assumed names) to the buyer and that the seller agrees that it will no longer use such name or names for any purpose. In addition, the buyer should also require the seller to warrant that the seller has filed, or will file, Certificates of Discontinuance in each appropriate venue prior to the transfer of the seller's name to the buyer.[1]

§ 6.64 Drafting the Buyer's Asset Purchase Agreement—Corporate or Other Name—Notice to Customer and Suppliers

Over time, a business develops relationships with its suppliers and customers. To avoid confusion and minimize the disruption of an ownership change, the purchase and sale contract should provide for a notice to the business's customers and suppliers introducing the buyer.[1] Appropriately worded, this can be very positive for the buyer.

§ 6.65 Drafting the Buyer's Asset Purchase Agreement—Corporate or Other Name—UCC Bulk Sale Notices or Escrow Agreement in Lieu of UCC Bulk Sale Notice

A Uniform Commercial Code ("UCC") Bulk Transfer is any transfer in bulk of a major part of the materials, supplies, merchandise or other inventory not in the ordinary course of the transferor's business. The bulk transfer provision of the UCC generally applies to businesses engaged in the sale of merchandise and not services, but it does specifically cover restaurants. The intention of this provision is to protect creditors who rely on the merchandise as security for payment of credit extended to the business.[1] To comply with the UCC Article 6 Bulk Transfer provisions the following must occur:

§ 6.63

1. *See supra,* § 6.19 (corporate and trade names).

§ 6.64

1. PRACTICE POINTER: The notice is usually prepared for the seller's signature and at a minimum introduces the buyer and informs the customers and suppliers of the change of ownership. Where appropriate, the notice should also indicate that the same quality service or product will be provided by the buyer and that the past relationships and practices between the business and its suppliers and customers will continue.

§ 6.65

1. UCC § 6–102.

1. The buyer must obtain a list of the seller's existing creditors and the property to be transferred. The buyer must preserve this list and allow inspection and copying by creditors for a period of six (6) months following the transfer.[2]

2. The list must be signed and sworn to, or affirmed, by the seller.[3]

3. A notice must be provided to creditors which states a bulk sale is about to be made, the names and business addresses of the seller and buyer, whether or not all the debts of the seller are to be paid in full as they fall due, and the address where creditors should send their bills.

4. If the debts of the seller are not to be paid in full, or if the purchaser is uncertain, the notice must also state the location and general description of the property to be transferred, the estimated total of the seller's debt, the address where the schedule of property and list of creditors may be inspected, whether the transfer is to pay existing debts, and if so, the amount of such debts and to whom, and whether the transfer is for new consideration, and if so, the amount, and the time and place of payment.[4]

5. The notice must be delivered personally or sent by registered or certified mail to all creditors on the creditor's list.[5]

6. The notice must be sent to the creditors at least ten (10) days before the buyer takes possession of the goods or pays for them, whichever is sooner.[6]

Since the UCC bulk sale provisions are, at times, misinterpreted by the public as a "going out of business" notice, both parties often choose to waive them and protect the buyer with an escrow agreement,[7] or a set-off against the seller.[8]

The agreement should simply state that the UCC bulk sale statute will be complied with or waived.

Library References:

West's Key No. Digests, Fraudulent Conveyances ⚿47.

2. UCC § 6-104.
3. Id.
4. UCC § 6-107.
5. Id.
6. **CAVEAT:** Failure to comply makes the transfer ineffective against the creditor. That is, the creditor can disregard the transfer and levy on the goods as if they still belonged to the seller, or a receiver representing the creditors can take the goods by whatever procedure local law provides. The New York State Personal Property Law provides that, "upon application of any of the creditors," the buyer "shall become a receiver and be held accountable to such creditors" for the transferred property. See UCC § 6-105. Unless the purchase and sale transaction is concealed, creditors must take action within six (6) months of the date of the transaction. See UCC § 6-111.

7. See supra, § 6.51.

8. **PRACTICE POINTER:** If the agreement provides for non-negotiable installment notes to the seller, the buyer has a virtually unlimited right of set-off via counterclaim in any enforcement action by the seller.

§ 6.66 Drafting the Buyer's Asset Purchase Agreement—Corporate or Other Name—NYS Sales Tax and Bulk Sale Notification

In an asset purchase transaction, New York State sales tax usually must be paid on at least a portion of the assets.[1] There are many exceptions and exclusions from the sales tax such as the purchase of manufacturing and production equipment and the purchase of assets for resale (inventory);

The parties must also comply with the New York State Sales Tax Law's bulk sales provisions.[2] Care must be exercised because the applied definition of a bulk sale under the sales tax law is broader than under the Uniform Commercial Code[3] and covers any transfer outside the ordinary course of business.[4] If the parties do not comply with the provisions of the Tax Law regarding sales tax, the buyer becomes liable for any past unpaid sales tax of the seller up to the amount of the purchase price, and[5] is held personally responsible for the payment of the tax.[6]

Library References:

West's Key No. Digests, Fraudulent Conveyances ⇌47.

§ 6.66

1. **PRACTICE POINTER**: The sales tax collected on the sale of assets should be reported on the seller's final sales tax return. If the seller is not obligated to collect sales tax in the course of his business, a sales tax return is nonetheless due on the sale of assets. The seller should file a casual sales tax return to report and pay the sales tax for the assets sold on Form ST 131. Tax Law § 1105.

2. Tax Law § 1141

3. **CAVEAT**: The UCC bulk sale requirements and the NYS Sales Tax bulk sale requirements are two separate and distinct requirements. *Both* laws must be complied with if applicable to the transaction.

4. **PRACTICE POINTER**: The Tax Law does not define bulk sale per se. Tax Law § 1141(c) and 20 NYCRR § 537.1(a)(1) describe a bulk sale as the transfer or assignment in Bulk of any portion or the whole of business assets. One cannot rely on the UCC definition of "major portion" in determining if a bulk sale has occurred under the New York Tax Law. The New York State Department of Taxation and Finance takes an aggressive position. If in doubt, assume a bulk sale has occurred.

5. **PRACTICE POINTER**: The bulk sale provisions are found in Tax Law § 1141(c) and 20 NYCRR Part 537. In essence, notice of the sale and its terms must be given to the Tax Department at least ten days before taking possession or paying for the business assets. Form AU–196.10 is generally used. If within five days after filing the notice of bulk sale with the Department, the Department notifies the buyer of a possible claim for taxes due, the buyer is prohibited from transferring money or other consideration to the seller (except amounts in excess of the Department's claim). The Department then has ninety days to determine the amount of the tax obligation, if any, during which period the seller cannot be paid. These provisions only apply to bulk sales by businesses required to collect sales tax. The statute of limitations for a sales tax assessment is three years from the date the sales tax return is filed. Tax Law § 1147(b).

6. Tax Law § 1447(3)(a).

§ 6.67 Drafting the Buyer's Asset Purchase Agreement—Corporate or Other Name—Covenant Not to Compete

The buyer of a business normally wants assurances from the seller and his key personnel (particularly those not retained in the buyer's employ), that they will not compete with the buyer. The covenant not to compete may be part of the purchase and sale agreement or may be a separate agreement.[1] The restrictions in the covenant not to compete must be reasonable regarding duration of time and geographic location; and the restrictions should be only so broad as to protect the legitimate business interests of the buyer in the geographical area of the business and that of the seller's goodwill.

Restrictive covenants to protect the goodwill of a purchased business do not violate the anti-trust laws. Reasonable restrictive covenants are enforceable (even though they curtail competition) because they are conducive to the overall freedom of trade and the sellers right to sell his business. They will be enforceable as long as they are not injurious to the public. In addition, restrictive covenants must be ancillary to the sale of a business, otherwise they are a restriction of trade and unenforceable.

The covenant not to compete agreement should describe the need to protect the business, its goodwill, customer lists, confidential information, and trade secrets and the consideration furnished. It must also describe the nature and kinds of business activities prohibited in the protected area, and should provide that the seller cannot engage in these activities as agent for, or in concert with, others. A severability clause should be included. Then, if any portion of the agreement is deemed unenforceable, the remaining portions will nonetheless be effective.[2] In addition, the agreement should specifically grant a Court the power to amend any restrictions it finds to be too broad without rendering the agreement unenforceable.

§ 6.67

1. **PRACTICE POINTER:** If a business owner (other than a sole proprietor) is one of the parties to the covenant not to compete, drafting separate covenants (or agreements) providing for direct payments to the owner can be beneficial from a tax standpoint. Although the payments to the individual are ordinary income, if they are separately allocated to and paid to the individual rather than his corporation, the seller can avoid double taxation. The buyer can amortize these payments over 15 years, as well as payments made to the business entity. *See supra*, § 6.36.

2. **CAVEAT:** The legal area has its own set of rules. Cohen v. Lord, Day & Lord, 75 N.Y.2d 95, 551 N.Y.S.2d 157, 550 N.E.2d 410 (1989); Denburg v. Parker Chapin Flattau & Klimpl, 82 N.Y.2d 375, 604 N.Y.S.2d 900, 624 N.E.2d 995 (1993), appeal after remand 213 A.D.2d 297, 624 N.Y.S.2d 151 (1st Dep't 1995). *But see* Graubard Mollen Dannett & Horowitz v. Moskovitz, 86 N.Y.2d 112, 629 N.Y.S.2d 1009, 653 N.E.2d 1179 (1995); Keogh v. Breed, Abbott & Morgan, 224 A.D.2d 180, 637 N.Y.S.2d 124 (1st Dep't 1996). Do not be misled by this confusion. Restrictive covenants in other areas are still enforceable.

The duration of most covenants not to compete is relatively short, usually 3–5 years, but longer covenants are appropriate if the circumstances justify it. Where the protected geographic area is large, skillful drafting which carefully defines the prohibited activities within the protected area will help preserve the enforceability of the covenant.

The measure of damages for a breach of the covenant not to compete is lost profits. This is often difficult to prove. There may also be other intervening factors, such as a general decline in the economy, which can further complicate any litigation. For these reasons, the buyer should seek to include a liquidated damages provision.

Liquidated damages, as opposed to general lost profits, will also limit the buyer's damages. For this reason, the buyer should include clauses in the agreement providing for "other damages" as well as liquidated damages.

If a covenant not to compete agreement with liquidated damages is part of the transaction, liquidated damages are often computed by reference to a mathematical formula such as the prior twelve month's sales by the business to a customer. Liquidated damages must also be reasonable, or they may be held to be a penalty and hence enforceable.[3]

The buyer usually desires that the payments for the covenant not to compete be paid in installments over a number of years. As part of the liquidated damages clause these payments may stop.[4]

Library References:

West's Key No. Digests, Contracts ⇒115.

§ 6.68 Drafting the Buyer's Asset Purchase Agreement—Matters Respecting Real Property

If real estate is one of the assets purchased, there are additional considerations to be provided for in the asset purchase agreement. Generally, the old rule *"Caveat Emptor"* (buyer beware) applies. Some of the usual provisions that should be included are as follows:

1. That the seller has good, marketable and insurable title to the real property;

2. A description sufficient to identify the real property purchased (preferably a legal description). It may be stated in the operative agreement or included in an attached schedule.[1]

---

3. PRACTICE POINTER: Upon the breach of a covenant not to compete, typically the buyer suspends installment payments to the seller until such time as the dispute is resolved.

4. Weiss v. Weiss, 206 A.D.2d 741, 615 N.Y.S.2d 468 (3d Dep't 1994); Parante v. Drozd, 171 A.D.2d 847, 567 N.Y.S.2d 534 (2d Dep't 1991). *See* Chapter 30 "Damages," *infra*.

§ 6.68

1. PRACTICE POINTER: Often, a copy of the deed(s) is attached as a schedule.

3. That the property is free from environmental contamination, and that the buyer may perform environmental assessments. (Seller representations and warranties regarding environmental matters may also be inserted here.)

4. That the seller will convey the real property to the buyer on the closing date, subject only to specifically referenced items such as:

a) Real property taxes, water charges and sewer rents, if any, which are liens on the real property at the closing date, subject to adjustment between the buyer and seller;

b) Any state of facts a current survey may show, provided that it does not render the title unmarketable, and provided further that all buildings, structures and all other improvements are located totally within the boundaries of the real property;

c) Zoning laws, regulations, building restrictions and ordinances of the local municipality and/or other governmental authorities, agencies, boards, departments or instrumentalities having jurisdiction over the real property, provided that none of the regulations, restrictions or ordinances prohibit or prevent (after the closing date) the present or intended use of the property or require special permission, permits or licenses;

d) Other continuing liens or encumbrances which are disclosed and part of the negotiations;

5. That the seller is required to cure any defects or objections to title that come to the buyer's attention which the buyer is unwilling to waive. (This clause should provide the seller with a reasonable period of time to cure the defect or objection; it should further provide that if the seller fails to do so within the time provided, the buyer has the option of waiving the defect and accepting title with an allowance for the cost of removing the defeats (including, without limitation, attorneys fees), or of rejecting the title and terminating the agreement.);[2]

6. That the seller is obligated to pay and discharge all liens, defects or objections to title on the closing date and allow the seller to use the cash portion of the purchase price to do so;

7. That the seller is required to deliver at closing all instruments to convey title, in recordable form, and resolve all objections and liens to the satisfaction of the title insurance company insuring title, and that the seller must deposit sufficient funds, acceptable to, and as required by the title company, to assure that any lien or defect not

---

2. PRACTICE POINTER: By allowing the buyer to terminate the agreement, this clause provides the buyer an opportunity to renegotiate the purchase price if the defect cannot be cured (if the defect is not so serious as to substantially impede the buyer's use of the property).

satisfied or cured at closing will be removed or paid and/or that any missing documentation will be obtained;[3]

8. That the buyer make payment of all amounts by certified check;

9. That the buyer (or the seller) pay the costs for title abstracting, title insurance fees, fees to record documents and the documentary stamps (deed stamps);[4]

10. That the items to be apportioned between the seller and the buyer, as set forth in the agreement be apportioned as of midnight of the day immediately preceding the closing. The usual items apportioned are real property and school taxes, water and sewer charges, heating fuel, and at times, electricity, gas, propane, and telephone services among others;[5]

11. That the seller (or the buyer) assumes the risk for loss or damage to the premises after execution of the contract, but prior to the transfer of title at closing. This clause should state the following:

a. Whether insurance proceeds will be paid to the buyer or seller;

b. Whether the buyer is to receive a credit against the price if the insurance proceeds are insufficient to restore the damaged property;

c. Whether the buyer can terminate the agreement in the event of substantial damage; and

d. The application of Section 5-1311 of the New York State General Obligations Law,[6] which controls unless waived;

---

3. PRACTICE POINTER: The buyer should require the title company to insure or omit the defect or lien. This protects the buyer's title, and leaves the resolution of the item to the title company and the seller.

4. PRACTICE POINTER: The usual practice is that the documentary stamps are paid by the seller, as well as the fee to record the real property transfer gains tax affidavit. The recording fees for the deed and other documents, as well as the mortgage tax, if any, abstracting costs, title insurance costs and the fee to record the equalization and assessment form are usually paid by the purchaser. *See* Chapter 12 "Purchase and Sale of Real Estate," *infra*.

5. PRACTICE POINTER: Except for the apportionment of property and school taxes, many of the other items are metered or can be measured by the service provider. Meter readings and measurements should be taken on the date of closing or as close thereto as practicable.

6. General Obligations Law § 5-1311 (Uniform Vender and Purchaser Risk Act). This statute provides at § 5-1311(1)(a):

"[w]hen neither the legal title nor the possession of the subject matter of the contract has been transferred to the purchaser: (1) if all or a material part thereof is destroyed without fault of the purchaser or is taken by eminent domain, the vendor cannot enforce the contract, and the purchaser is entitled to recover any portion of the price that he has paid; but nothing herein contained shall be deemed to deprive the vendor of any right to recover damages against the purchaser for any breach of contract by the purchaser prior to the destruction or taking; (2) if an immaterial part thereof is destroyed without fault of the purchaser or is taken by eminent domain, neither the vendor nor the purchaser is thereby deprived of the right to enforce the contract; but there shall be, to the extent of the destruction or taking, an abatement of the purchase price."

§ 6.68   BUYING & SELLING A SMALL BUSINESS   Ch. 6

12. (If the real estate being acquired has separate legal descriptions) that all parcels (as appropriate) be contiguous, and without any gores (gaps) between the boundary lines;

13. That access to the parcel via private easements, rights-of-way and public highways are accurately represented.[7]

§ 6.69   Drafting the Buyer's Asset Purchase Agreement—Conditions Precedent to Purchaser's Obligations

In preparing the buyer's asset purchase agreement, counsel will normally condition the buyer's performance upon the happening of certain events and the performance by the seller of certain material terms of the agreement at or prior to closing. Such conditions should include:

- Performance by the seller of all obligations specified in the asset purchase agreement;
- Accuracy of the covenants, representations and warranties made by the seller;
- Absence of adverse change in the financial and other condition of the seller as well as in the business, properties, assets or prospects of the seller;
- Delivery to the buyer of a certificate executed by the seller or by its officers and shareholders certifying the fulfillment of the above conditions;
- Delivery to the buyer by the seller of all documents required to be delivered under the terms of the asset purchase agreement;
- The buyer's acquiring regulatory approval;
- The buyer's obtaining financing;
- Tax rulings, if applicable; and
- Required consents to transfers and assignments.

It is also advisable when representing the buyer to condition its performance on the results of a cost-study, or other formal investigation into profitability of the seller's business. In the event that the results of such study indicate a profit margin less than that expected by the buyer, the buyer should have the right to terminate the asset purchase agreement.

If either legal title or possession passes to the buyer, these provisions do not apply and the buyer is subject to these risks.

7. PRACTICE POINTER: Rather than burden the operative agreement with numerous real estate provisions, it may be advantageous to use a separate agreement for the real property provisions which is attached to the operative agreement as an exhibit. *See also,* Chapter 12 "Purchase and Sale of Real Estate," *infra.*

Ch. 6   NATURE & SURVIVAL OF REPRESENTATIONS   § 6.71

The buyer may also want to condition its performance on such other issues as entering into other contracts or agreements without which it could not profitably operate the business, such as the license of a particular patent from a third party.

Library References:

West's Key No. Digests, Sales ⚖︎85.

§ 6.70 Drafting the Buyer's Asset Purchase Agreement—Conditions Precedent to Seller's Obligations

In the asset purchase agreement, the seller's performance is generally conditioned upon the following:[1]

- Performance by the buyer of all obligations specified in the asset purchase agreement;

- Accuracy of the covenants, representations and warranties made by the buyer;

- Absence of adverse change in the buyer's financial condition;[2]

- Delivery to the seller of a certificate executed by the buyer or by its officers and shareholders certifying the fulfillment of the above conditions; and

- Delivery to the seller by the buyer of all documents required to be delivered under the terms of the asset purchase agreement.

Library References:

West's Key No. Digests, Sales ⚖︎85.

§ 6.71 Drafting the Buyer's Asset Purchase Agreement—Nature and Survival of Representations and Warranties

Every asset purchase agreement should contain a provision requiring that all representations, warranties, indemnities, covenants and agreements made by the parties survive the closing. The purpose of this provision is to ensure that the material provisions of the purchase agreement remain enforceable after the transfer of assets has taken place, so that each party may have remedies in the event of breach.[1]

§ 6.70

1. For suggested language from a sample agreement, *see infra*, § 6.187, Section 17.

2. Applicable if seller is financing all or part of the purchase price or if payment is being made by buyer in installments.

§ 6.71

1. For suggested language from a sample agreement, *see infra*, § 6.187, Section 18.

§ 6.72 Drafting the Buyer's Asset Purchase Agreement—Non-disclosure Provisions

It is in the non-disclosure provisions of the asset purchase agreement that the parties covenant to keep confidential all information about each other acquired during the course of the transaction. This representation is especially important to the seller in the event the transaction is not consummated.

Library References:
West's Key No. Digests, Contracts ⚖118.

§ 6.73 Drafting the Buyer's Asset Purchase Agreement—Miscellaneous Agreements Between Buyer and Seller

The asset purchase agreement should refer to all other agreements between the buyer and the seller not included under the provisions of the present agreement or subject to its terms. These might include agreements as to the employment of the seller as a consultant for a fixed period after closing or perhaps the commitment of the seller to supply other goods and services to the buyer after closing.

Library References:
West's Key No. Digests, Sales ⚖54–88.

§ 6.74 Drafting the Buyer's Asset Purchase Agreement—Documents to Be Delivered to Purchaser at Closing

The Documents to be delivered by the seller to the buyer at closing normally include the following:

- All documents effecting transfer of title;
- The opinion of the seller's counsel that the seller is duly organized, validly existing and in good standing; that seller has the corporate power and authority to enter into and perform the asset purchase agreement; that the asset purchase agreement is a valid and binding obligation of the seller; and that the execution and delivery of the asset purchase agreement and performance by the seller do not conflict with the seller's organizing instruments or other contracts or obligations, or violate any law, rule or regulation;
- Certified copies of minutes and the consents of the shareholders and directors of the seller approving the asset purchase agreement and the consummation of the sale transaction;
- The certificate of the seller affirming the performance of all conditions precedent to the buyer's obligations;

Ch. 6 DOCUMENTS DELIVERED TO SELLER **§ 6.75**

- Executed non-competition and continuity of business dealings agreements;
- All contracts, licenses, leases and permits pertaining to the assets, including plans and specifications for buildings located on the real property;
- All customer lists and supplier lists;
- A list of accounts receivable;
- All keys to buildings, vehicles, and file cabinets;
- Confidentiality agreements and covenants not to compete from departing employees of the seller;
- Written assurances from the seller's broker respecting confidentiality;
- Other documents to be delivered to the buyer under the terms of the agreement; and
- Such further instruments of transfer or other documents as may reasonably be required by the buyer to effect the provisions contained in the agreement.

Library References:

West's Key No. Digests, Sales ⚖=135–196.

§ 6.75 Drafting the Buyer's Asset Purchase Agreement—Documents to Be Delivered to Seller at Closing

The Documents to be delivered by the buyer to the seller at closing normally include the following:

- Documents effecting payment of the purchase price;
- Certified copies of minutes and the consents of the Shareholders and Directors of the buyer approving the asset purchase agreement and the consummation of the purchase transaction;
- Executed mortgages and other security documents;
- The opinion of the buyer's counsel that the buyer is duly organized, validly existing and in good standing; that the buyer has the corporate power and authority to enter into and perform the asset purchase agreement; that the asset purchase agreement is a valid and binding obligation of the buyer; and that the execution and delivery of the asset purchase agreement and performance by the buyer do not conflict with the buyer's organizing instruments or other contracts or obligations, or violate any law, rule or regulation;
- Other documents to be delivered to seller under the terms of the agreement; and

§ 6.75 BUYING & SELLING A SMALL BUSINESS Ch. 6

- Such further instruments of transfer or other documents as may reasonably be required by the seller to effect the provisions contained in the agreement.

Library References:

West's Key No. Digests, Sales ⚖︎135–196.

§ 6.76 Drafting the Buyer's Asset Purchase Agreement—Notices, Severability and Other General Provisions

Notices and other provisions usually included at the end of an agreement are referred to as the "Boilerplate." These provisions generally consist of the following:[1]

- Notice procedures;
- Severability clause;
- Governing law;
- Non-waiver provision;
- Savings clause;
- Provisions concerning modifications and changes to the agreement;
- Disclaimer as to captions and headings;
- Provisions acknowledging the "binding effect" of the agreement;
- Provisions acknowledging that the agreement constitutes the "entire agreement" of the parties;
- Agreement to execute additional documents and counterparts;
- "Time is of the essence" provisions, and
- Arbitration provisions.

Library References:

West's Key No. Digests, Sales ⚖︎54–88.

§ 6.77 Drafting the Buyer's Asset Purchase Agreement—Documents to Be Prepared or Reviewed Prior to Closing

After the asset purchase agreement has been executed, buyer's counsel must either prepare, or review, as the case may be, all documents or instruments referred to in the agreement or required under its

---

§ 6.76

1. For suggested language as to some of these provisions, from a sample agreement, see *infra*, § 6.187, Section 21.

provisions. Such documents, known as the "collateral documents" may include the following:

- Bills of sale;
- Deeds and related real estate documents;
- Security agreements, promissory notes, and mortgages;
- Escrow agreements;
- Corporate resolutions;
- Assignments of contracts, leases and other interests;
- Motor vehicle, boat and other registrations;
- Equipment lists;
- Inventory descriptions, including count and valuation;
- Lists of other assets;
- Legal opinions of counsel;
- New contracts (novations);
- Employment and collective bargaining agreements;
- Lists of all seller's other contracts and agreements;
- Certificates respecting name change;
- Certificates of Dissolution and/or Discontinuance;
- Assumed Name Certificates;
- Sales tax returns;
- Lists of all insurance policies and pending claims;
- Lists of all patents, patent applications, trademarks, trade names, and copyrights;
- Covenants not to compete; and
- Confidentiality agreements.

Copies of all such collateral documents should be attached to the asset purchase agreement and made a part of such agreement.

Library References:

West's Key No. Digests, Sales ⚖135–196.

§ 6.78 Drafting the Buyer's Stock Purchase Agreement

As discussed earlier, counsel must weigh the advantages and disadvantages associated with taking it upon himself to draft the buyer's stock purchase agreement.[1]

§ 6.78

1. See supra, § 6.15.

§ 6.78   BUYING & SELLING A SMALL BUSINESS   Ch. 6

Sections 6.79–6.96 contain discussions of the various provisions found in a typical stock purchase agreement. A sample agreement appears at the end of the chapter.[2]

§ 6.79   Drafting the Buyer's Stock Purchase Agreement—Identification of the Parties

The initial paragraph of the stock purchase agreement which identifies the parties to the agreement should establish the following:

- The name and address of each of the parties;

- The business or legal description of each entity, such as "a New York Business Corporation," or "a Vermont Corporation, authorized to do business in New York," or "a Partnership";

- The position of each party and the term to which such party is referred in the agreement, such as "Buyer," "Seller," "Escrow Agent," "Guarantor," "Sole Shareholder";

- If a party is a business entity, the location of the main office of such entity.

In a stock purchase transaction, the seller(s) of the stock will be either the corporation or the individual shareholders, depending upon how the transaction is structured.

In the stock purchase agreement, if the seller of the shares is the corporation, the shareholders should be made parties to the agreement and should be identified in the agreement as the individuals responsible for the obligations, representations, warranties and covenants and all other performance requirements of the seller. This may be done in one of two ways: In each undertaking by the seller, the terms of the agreement should refer to "the seller and the shareholders, jointly and severally"[1] or, in the alternative, a separate section of the agreement should be drafted to provide that all performance requirements of seller are jointly and severally guaranteed by the shareholders.

NOTE: In the sample agreement at the end of the chapter,[2] the seller of the shares is the individual shareholder. The corporation has been made a party to the agreement for the purpose of assuring cooperation by the corporation's agents as required under the terms of the agreement.

Library References:

West's Key No. Digests, Corporations ⇔116.

2. *See infra,* § 6.188.

§ 6.79
1. For example, "The Seller and each individual shareholder jointly and severally acknowledge and agree that . . . ," or "The Seller and the sole shareholder, jointly and severally, represent and warrant that . . ."

2. *See infra,* § 6.187.

734

§ 6.80 Drafting the Buyer's Stock Purchase Agreement—Recitals

The "Recitals" section of the stock purchase agreement will establish the background of the transaction and the intent of the parties as to the transaction. The recitals might also set forth important information which may not otherwise appear in the text of the agreement, such as the fact that a party conducts business under another name, or that a specific relationship exists between the parties to the agreement, or that there is a specific purpose underlying the business transaction being entered into. While the recitals are not technically part of the operative agreement, the information contained in the recitals can be critical in case of a later contract dispute.[1]

Library References:

West's Key No. Digests, Corporations ⟐116.

§ 6.81 Drafting the Buyer's Stock Purchase Agreement—Sale of Shares

Every stock purchase agreement will contain the covenant of the seller to sell and the covenant of the buyer to purchase shares.

This section of the agreement will generally specify the number, class and type of shares being transferred and indicate the name of each shareholder and the number of shares owned. The buyer should require that at the time of transfer, the shares be free of all liens and encumbrances and that they have the required stock transfer stamps affixed.[1] This section of the agreement should also contain a provision stating that the buyer will have no obligation to purchase unless all of the shares of the seller are delivered to him at closing in proper form for transfer.

Transfer of Shares. The procedure for the transfer of shares is generally as follows: (a) the shares to be transferred are endorsed to the buyer; (b) the shares are then surrendered to the corporation, with the transfer to the buyer noted in the books of the corporation; and finally (c) new share certificates are issued in the name of the buyer.

Library References:

West's Key No. Digests, Corporations ⟐116.

§ 6.80

1. Recitals may be incorporated into and made a part of the operative agreement, if the drafter so chooses.

§ 6.81

1. *See infra,* § 6.131, concerning New York Stock Transfer Tax and Stock Transfer Stamps.

§ 6.82 Drafting the Buyer's Stock Purchase Agreement—Purchase Price and Method of Payment

This section of the stock purchase agreement will describe the purchase price, how the purchase price will be paid and such other matters as securitization, if applicable.

Purchase Price. The purchase price need not be an identified dollar amount, especially where there may be contingencies as to the price to be paid. In such event the agreement will provide for part of the purchase price to be ascertained at a later date based on a fixed formula or other identified method to be used which has been agreed upon by the parties at the time of negotiation of the purchase price. Any provisions for adjustments[1] to the purchase price to which the parties have agreed will also appear in this section of the stock purchase agreement.

Manner of Payment. The manner of payment of the purchase price should be described with specificity. If the purchase price in whole or in part is to be paid by the buyer in installments,[2] the seller may require that the transferred shares be placed in escrow until full payment is made. In the alternative, the seller may deliver a portion of the shares as each payment is made by the buyer.

Shares Placed in Escrow. In the event that the transferred shares are to be placed in escrow, the agreement will normally provide that: (a) upon delivery of the buyer's note to the seller, share certificates issued in the name of the buyer will be delivered to the buyer;[3] (b) that the buyer will deliver the share certificates, endorsed in blank to the Escrow Agent; and (c) that the Escrow Agent will hold such shares until the purchase price is paid in full or until the event of the buyer's default.

Other Security. In addition to the escrow of shares as security for the payment of the purchase price, the seller may require the buyer to furnish security in the form of mortgages or other liens on the transferred assets, or in the form of letters of credit, pledges of stock, or insurance on the assets of the business or on the life of the buyer. The seller may also require that payment be guaranteed by the shareholders of the purchaser. Copies of such security agreements, financing statements, notes, mortgages, and other security instruments to be signed by the buyer (and its guarantors) are usually attached to, and made a part of, the agreement.

§ 6.82

1. Adjustments are normally made for items such as insurance premiums, rents, deposits with utility companies, payroll, payroll taxes, etc.

2. **PRACTICE POINTER:** If the whole of the purchase price is to be paid in cash, as opposed to installments, buyer should require part of such payment to be placed in escrow against any default of seller under the terms of the agreement. For a more comprehensive discussion of this issue, *See supra,* § 6.51.

3. The certificates should be delivered to buyer to assure that buyer gets title prior to the delivery of the shares in escrow. Section 8–301(1) of the UCC states that title to securities passes upon delivery of the securities.

Ch. 6   WARRANTIES & COVENANTS OF SELLER   § 6.84

Promissory Notes of Buyer. Copies of any promissory notes to be endorsed by the buyer at closing should be attached to the stock purchase agreement. The agreement should describe the type of note to be signed by the buyer as well as material provisions of such note, including the amount of the note, whether it is to be negotiable or non-negotiable,[4] the term and interest rate of the note and other important considerations such as pre-payment, acceleration, securitization, presentment (or waiver thereof), and default provisions. As discussed earlier, the promissory note should contain a provision stating that any default under the terms of the agreement shall constitute a default under the note.[5] In addition, if the buyer has retained any rights to set-off under the terms of the agreement, such provisions should also be set forth in the promissory note.

Library References:

West's Key No. Digests, Corporations ⚖︎116.

§ 6.83 Drafting the Buyer's Stock Purchase Agreement—Closing

The stock purchase agreement should identify the date, place and time of closing. The date need not be a fixed date but may be conditioned on the happening of certain events, for example:

"Closing shall occur six weeks from the date of the last to occur of the contingencies identified in sections _____ of the agreement."

This section of the agreement may also contain provisions as to the manner of payment of the purchase price, the shares and other items to be delivered by the seller at closing, and such other events as may be expected to occur at closing.

Library References:

West's Key No. Digests, Corporations ⚖︎116.

§ 6.84 Drafting the Buyer's Stock Purchase Agreement—Representations, Warranties and Covenants of Seller

The representations and warranties of the seller constitute one of the most important sections of the stock purchase agreement from the

---

4. PRACTICE POINTER: Buyer should consider issuing promissory notes which are non-negotiable in form, at least for any period in which buyer may have a right of set-off against seller, or for any period in which buyer's performance may be contingent upon any representation or covenant of seller. For example, if seller has agreed not to compete with buyer for a period of three years, buyer's note for such three-year period should be non-negotiable. If under the terms of the agreement, buyer's note is to be for a ten-year period, buyer can issue two notes: the first, a non-negotiable note for the first three years, and the second, a negotiable instrument for the remaining seven years of the term.

5. *See supra,* § 6.50.

§ 6.84 BUYING & SELLING A SMALL BUSINESS Ch. 6

point of view of the buyer. When the buyer is purchasing the stock of the seller's business, as opposed to the assets, the buyer is also purchasing all of the liabilities of the seller's business, whether disclosed or not disclosed to the buyer and whether or not they are known or unknown to the seller.

The seller's representations must be carefully drafted, as it is these representations which will disclose to the buyer important information about every aspect of the seller's business. A material misstatement of any of the seller's representations, or a breach by the seller of any of the warranties or covenants contained in this section, will provide a basis for the buyer to avoid or rescind the agreement, or to seek indemnification from the seller in the event that the buyer suffers any loss or injury as a result of such misstatement or breach.

The representations and warranties generally mirror the due diligence investigation performed by the buyer and in addition should cover any issue which the buyer was unable to discover during its investigations. The stock purchase agreement should contain a provision requiring verification by the seller that the warranties, representations and covenants made as of signing are true as of closing,[1] and in addition a provision stating that the warranties, representations and covenants will survive for a stated period subsequent to closing.[2] The buyer's attorney is advised to draft the seller's representations in the absolute, that is, without qualification. For example, the buyer might request that the seller warrant that the seller's equipment is in excellent condition and working order, capable of meeting highest industry standards. The seller, on the other hand, will seek to represent that the equipment is, to the best of the seller's knowledge, in good working order and sufficient for the operations of the business in its current state.

The representations, warranties and covenants of the seller will usually include the following:[3]

- That the seller is duly incorporated, validly existing, in good standing and qualified to do business;
- That the aggregate number of shares the corporation is authorized to issue is ___, of which ___ are issued and outstanding;
- That all shares are validly issued and fully paid and that there are no outstanding subscriptions, options, warrants;
- That the seller has delivered to the buyer a true and complete list of: (a) the names of all shareholders of the corporation; (b) the

---

§ 6.84

1. For suggested language from a sample agreement, see infra, § 6.187, Section 16(a).

2. For suggested language from a sample agreement, see infra, § 6.188, Section 15.01.

3. The representations and warranties which appear in this section are for illustrative purposes only and are not comprehensive in scope. Counsel is advised to carefully draft each representation in accordance with the circumstances of the transaction.

names of all of the corporation's officers and directors; (c) the names of all individuals who receive compensation from the corporation, and a statement of compensation as to each; (d) the names of all persons holding powers of attorney for the corporation; and (e) a list of each bank in which the corporation has an account, as well as a list of all persons authorized to draw on such accounts;

- That each shareholder represents he is the owner of ___ shares and that he has full right and authority to transfer the same to the buyer;

- That the seller has no affiliations, subsidiaries or other business interests;

- That there are no conflicts between the stock purchase agreement and other agreements of the seller;

- That there exist no service agreements, maintenance agreements, warranties or other obligations outstanding on the seller's products, except as set forth;

- That the seller is in compliance with all federal, state and local laws, rules and regulations;

- That there are no licenses or leases in effect concerning the assets and property of the business, except those specified;

- That the seller has good and marketable title to the real estate;

- That there are no mechanics or materialmen liens or bases for such liens on the real estate transferred;

- That the seller has delivered to the buyer the following financial statements, which are true and complete and accurately represent the financial condition of the seller: (a) balance sheets; (b) statement of profits and losses; and (c) tax returns;

- That, except to the extent reflected in the balance sheet, dated ___, there are no liabilities of any nature and the seller represents that it does not know or have reason to know of any liability of any nature not fully reflected in the balance sheet;

- That since the dates of the balance sheet and tax returns provided to the buyer, there has not been: (a) any change in assets, liabilities or the financial condition of the seller's business; (b) any damage, loss, or destruction to the assets of the business that are not covered by insurance; (c) any sale other than in the regular course of business; (d) any pending or threatened litigation; (e) any labor union organizing activity or actual or threatened employee strike; (f) any litigation relating to the seller or its business that has been instituted or settled; (g) any failure to replace inventory and supplies; (h) any failure to pay any debt when it has come due; (i) any declaration, or setting aside or payment of a

dividend; or (j) any increase in compensation, or any bonus, payable to any officer, director, employee or agent of the seller;
- That the seller has filed all required tax returns;
- That the seller has delivered to the buyer a true and complete list of all accounts receivable as of ___, as reflected in the balance sheet, and that if, following closing, any such accounts remaining unpaid are not paid in full on demand when due, then the seller shall pay the same upon demand of the buyer (against delivery by the buyer of an assignment of such defaulted accounts);
- That inventory is merchantable and in good condition, and that as of the date of closing, it will consist of current, readily saleable goods and merchandise;
- That the seller has no notice or knowledge of violation by the seller of any federal, state and local laws, rules and regulations;
- That the seller possesses all necessary licenses, permits and consents required to carry on the business;
- That the seller has delivered to the buyer an accurate list of all contracts, oral and written, to which the seller is a party; such contracts being as follows: (a) employment contracts; (b) contracts with salespersons and distributors; (c) pension, benefit and related agreements; (d) agreements with suppliers, consultants, support services, providers and the like; (e) customer agreements, unfilled purchase orders, sales contracts; (f) customer lists; (g) franchise agreements, dealer and consignment agreements, research and development contracts; (h) lines of credit and loans; and (i) contracts with labor organizations; all of which have been entered into in the ordinary course of business;
- That the seller has complied with material provisions of all the above contracts, leases, licenses, and other agreements, and that the same are valid and in good standing;
- That the transfer of shares will not constitute a prohibited assignment of any of the contracts, leases, licenses and other agreements and that the same will remain in full force and effect;
- That there are no collective bargaining agreements in effect and that the seller has no knowledge of any labor union organizing activity or any strikes or threatened strikes;
- That the seller has delivered to the buyer an accurate list of all insurance policies including any pending claims;
- That the seller will maintain all such insurance until closing or until such time as the shares are transferred to the buyer;
- That there are no environmental hazards or conditions affecting the assets, property or business of the seller;

- That there is no litigation pending or threatened against or relating to the seller, its properties or business;
- That the seller has delivered to the buyer an accurate list of all patents, patent applications, trademarks, trade names, and copyrights, presently held by the seller all of which are valid and in good standing;
- That from the date of execution of the stock purchase agreement until the time of closing, there will be no new leases, tenancies or contracts affecting the assets or properties of the business without prior written approval of the buyer;
- That the seller will perform all necessary repairs and maintenance on its assets and real property prior to closing;
- That the seller will pay vacation time and other employee benefits which have accrued up to and including the closing date;
- That no broker brought about this transaction (or, in the alternative: that the seller will indemnify and hold the buyer harmless from any claim for brokerage commissions);
- That no representation, warranty or covenant of the seller in the agreement or in any writing furnished to the buyer contains any untrue statement of fact or failure to state any material fact;
- That the seller has disclosed all material adverse facts known to the seller; and
- That the representations, warranties and covenants of the seller shall be true at the time of closing as though such representations and warranties were made at such time.

In the event that closing is to occur after the date of the execution of the stock purchase agreement by the parties, the buyer will want to make sure that the seller will continue to operate the business in the ordinary course. To that end, the buyer should obtain "Pre–Closing" covenants from the seller. Pre-closing covenants of the seller normally include the following:

- That since the date of (execution of the stock purchase agreement), the seller has operated the business only in the ordinary course and there has not been:
    a. any change in assets, liabilities, financial condition of the seller's business since the date of such financial statements, tax returns or other documents;
    b. any change in the corporation's certificate of incorporation or bylaws;
    c. any change in the corporation's authorized or issued shares;
    d. any dividend or other distribution declared or paid;

§ 6.84   BUYING & SELLING A SMALL BUSINESS   Ch. 6

    e. any increase in compensation payable to any employee, officer or director;

    f. any change affecting personnel;

    g. any damage, loss, or destruction to the assets or properties of the business, not covered by insurance;

    h. any sales other than in the regular course of business;

    i. any pending or threatened litigation;

    j. any labor union organizing activity or actual or threatened employee strikes;

    k. any institution or settlement of any litigation relating to the seller or its business;

    l. any failure to replace inventory and supplies;

    m. any failure to pay any debt as it has become due; and

    n. any chemical spills or other environmental conditions affecting the assets or properties of the business.

Library References:

West's Key No. Digests, Corporations ⚖116, 120.

§ 6.85 Drafting the Buyer's Stock Purchase Agreement—Representations, Warranties and Covenants of Buyer

In the stock purchase agreement, the representations, warranties and covenants of the buyer will not be as comprehensive as the representations of the seller.

The buyer's representations will generally include the following:

- That the buyer is duly incorporated, validly existing, in good standing and qualified to do business;

- That the buyer possesses the requisite authority to enter into the stock purchase agreement and to perform in accordance with its terms;

- That no broker brought about this transaction (or, in the alternative: that the buyer will indemnify and hold the seller harmless from any claim for brokerage commissions).

In the event that the purchase price is to be paid by the buyer in installments, the seller will normally require additional representations and warranties as to the financial condition of the buyer and of the guarantors of the buyer's obligations.[1]

---

§ 6.85

1. See infra, § 6.169 for buyer's representations as to financial condition.

Library References:

West's Key No. Digests, Corporations ⚖116, 120.

§ 6.86 Drafting the Buyer's Stock Purchase Agreement—Conduct of Business Prior to Closing

In the event that closing is to occur after the date of the execution of the stock purchase agreement by the parties, the agreement should contain a provision for the conduct of business by the seller up to the time of closing. The purpose for such a provision is twofold: First, it will assure the buyer that the seller will continue to conduct its business without interruption, and secondly, it will provide the buyer with the affirmation of the seller that during this period the seller will not transfer assets or do anything outside of the ordinary course of business. In this section of the agreement, the buyer will require the seller to operate in a manner consistent with prior operations. In addition, the buyer will want to make sure that the seller will continue to maintain insurance on its assets, that the seller will continue to replace inventory, and that the seller will allow the buyer access to the books, records and operations of the seller during this period.

This section should also provide that the seller, while in continued possession of the business, is to pay for all materials and services pertaining to the operations of the business which have been delivered to the seller prior to closing, and that the buyer is to pay for all such materials and services delivered after closing. Additionally, there should be included a provision concerning accounts receivable to the effect that receivables derived from goods or other business products shipped after closing are to become the property of the buyer, and receivables from goods shipped prior to closing are to be paid to the seller.[1]

Library References:

West's Key No. Digests, Corporations ⚖116.

§ 6.87 Drafting the Buyer's Stock Purchase Agreement—Indemnifications

As discussed earlier, the seller's representations and warranties comprise one of the most important elements of the stock purchase agreement in that the buyer relies heavily upon them in deciding to purchase the seller's business.[1] The failure or falsity of any of the material representations or warranties of the seller could cause the buyer serious injury in the form of excessive costs, losses or exposure to legal action.

---

§ 6.86

[1] For suggested language from a sample agreement, *see infra*, § 6.187, Section 8(b).

§ 6.87

[1] *See supra*, § 6.84.

The purpose of the seller's indemnifications of the buyer is to protect the buyer from such injury.

In drafting the indemnification provisions, the buyer's attorney is advised to require broad indemnification from the seller (as the seller's attorney would be advised to limit and restrict the seller's indemnifications as much as possible).

The buyer's stock purchase agreement should be drafted to provide that the seller will indemnify and hold the buyer harmless from all liabilities, losses, costs and expenses, (including legal fees) relative to or arising from:

- Liabilities, obligations and claims against the seller not expressly assumed by the buyer—including any claims for warranty, product liability, or the repair or replacement of products sold by the seller prior to closing;
- Any claims or costs resulting from a misrepresentation or breach by the seller of its covenants and warranties contained in the stock purchase agreement or other documents delivered to the buyer pursuant to the stock purchase agreement; and
- Any nonpayment on demand when due of accounts receivable following closing.

Library References:

West's Key No. Digests, Corporations ⌲116.

§ 6.88 Drafting the Buyer's Asset Purchase Agreement—Covenant Not to Compete

The buyer of a business normally wants assurances from the seller and his key personnel (particularly those not retained in the buyer's employ) that they will not compete with the buyer. The covenant not to compete may be part of the purchase and sale agreement or may be a separate agreement.[1] The restrictions in the covenant not to compete must be reasonable regarding duration of time and geographic location; and the restrictions should be only so broad as to protect the legitimate business interests of the buyer in the geographical area of the business and that of the seller's goodwill.

Restrictive covenants to protect the goodwill of a purchased business do not violate the anti-trust laws. Reasonable restrictive covenants are

---

§ 6.88

1. **PRACTICE POINTER:** If a business owner (other than a sole proprietor) is one of the parties to the covenant not to compete, drafting separate covenants (or agreements) providing for direct payments to the owner can be beneficial from a tax standpoint. Although the payments to the individual are ordinary income, if they are separately allocated and paid to the individual rather than his corporation, the seller can avoid double taxation. The buyer can amortize these payments over 15 years as well as payments made to the business entity. *See supra*, § 6.36.

enforceable (even though they curtail competition) because they are conducive to the overall freedom of trade and the sellers right to sell his business. They will be enforceable as long as they are not injurious to the public. In addition, restrictive covenants must be ancillary to the sale of a business, otherwise they are a restriction of trade and unenforceable.

The covenant not to compete agreement should describe the need to protect the business, its goodwill, customer lists, confidential information, trade secrets and the consideration furnished. It must also describe the nature and kinds of business activities prohibited in the protected area, and recite that the seller cannot engage in these activities as agent for, or in concert with, others. A severability clause should be included. Then, if any portion of the agreement is deemed unenforceable, the remaining portions will nonetheless be effective.[2] In addition, the agreement should specifically grant a court the power to amend any restrictions it finds to be too broad without rendering the agreement unenforceable.

The duration of most covenants not to compete is relatively short, usually three to five years, but longer covenants are appropriate if the circumstances justify it. Where the protected geographic area is large, skillful drafting which carefully defines the prohibited activities within the protected area will help preserve the enforceability of the covenant.

The measure of damages for a breach of the covenant not to compete is lost profits. This is often difficult to prove. There may also be other intervening factors, such as a general decline in the economy, which can further complicate any litigation. For these reasons, the buyer should seek to include a liquidated damages provision.

Liquidated damages, as opposed to general lost profits, will also limit the buyer's damages. For this reason, the buyer should include clauses in the agreement providing for "other damages" as well as liquidated damages.

If a covenant not to compete agreement with liquidated damages is part of the transaction, liquidated damages are often computed by reference to a mathematical formula such as the prior 12 month's sales by the business to a customer. Liquidated damages must also be reasonable, or they may be held to be a penalty and hence enforceable.

---

2. CAVEAT: The legal area has its own set of rules. Cohen v. Lord, Day & Lord, 75 N.Y.2d 95, 551 N.Y.S.2d 157, 550 N.E.2d 410 (1989); Denburg v. Parker Chapin Flattau & Klimpl, 82 N.Y.2d 375, 604 N.Y.S.2d 900, 624 N.E.2d 995 (1993), appeal after remand 213 A.D.2d 297, 624 N.Y.S.2d 151 (1995). *But see* Graubard Mollen Dannett & Horowitz v. Moskovitz, 86 N.Y.2d 112, 629 N.Y.S.2d 1009, 653 N.E.2d 1179 (1995); Keogh v. Breed, Abbott & Morgan, 224 A.D.2d 180, 637 N.Y.S.2d 124 (1st Dep't 1996). Do not be misled by this confusion. Restrictive covenants in other areas are still enforceable.

The buyer usually desires that the payments for the covenant not to compete be paid in installment payments over a number of years. As part of the liquidated damages clause these payments may stop.[3]

Library References:

West's Key No. Digests, Corporations ⚛116.

§ 6.89 Drafting the Buyer's Stock Purchase Agreement—Matters Respecting Real Property

With a stock purchase transaction, the buyer is purchasing the business entity as a whole, which may include real estate. The agreement should specifically identify the real estate owned by the business entity. It should also include legal descriptions for all real estate owned. By reference in schedules attached to the agreement, often a copy of the deed is attached to the agreement as a schedule.

The provisions set forth in Section 6.68 also apply to stock purchases except that the liabilities of the business entity (which may be a lien against the real property) and adjustments for property and school taxes, fuel, etc., may be referenced in the liabilities assumed section of the agreement rather than the real estate section.

Library References:

West's Key No. Digests, Corporations ⚛116.

§ 6.90 Drafting the Buyer's Stock Purchase Agreement—Nondisclosure Provisions

It is in the non-disclosure provisions of the stock purchase agreement that the parties covenant to keep confidential all information about each other acquired during the course of the transaction. This representation is especially important to the seller in the event that the transaction is not consummated.

Library References:

West's Key No. Digests, Corporations ⚛116.

§ 6.91 Drafting the Buyer's Stock Purchase Agreement—Conditions Precedent to Purchaser's Obligations

In preparing the buyer's stock purchase agreement, counsel should condition the buyer's performance upon the happening of certain events and the performance by the seller of certain material terms of the agreement at or prior to closing. Such conditions should include:

---

3. PRACTICE POINTER: Upon the breach of a covenant not to compete, typically the buyer suspends installment payments to the seller until such time as the dispute is resolved.

- Performance by the seller of all obligations specified in the stock purchase agreement;
- Accuracy of the covenants, representations and warranties made by the seller;
- Absence of adverse change in the financial and other condition of the seller as well as in the business, properties, assets or prospects of the seller;
- Delivery to the buyer of a certificate executed by the seller or its officers and shareholders certifying the fulfillment of the above conditions;
- Delivery to the buyer by the seller of all documents required to be delivered under the terms of the stock purchase agreement;
- Delivery to the buyer of all of the shares of the corporation at closing in proper form for transfer;
- The buyer's acquiring regulatory approval;
- The buyer's obtaining financing; and
- Tax rulings, if applicable.

It is also advisable when representing the buyer to condition its performance on the results of a cost-study or other formal investigation into the profitability of the seller's business. In the event that the results of such study indicate a profit margin less than that expected by the buyer, the buyer should have the right to terminate the stock purchase agreement.[1]

The buyer may also want to condition its performance on such other issues as entering into other contracts or agreements without which the buyer could not profitably operate the business, such as the license of a particular patent from a third party.

Library References:

West's Key No. Digests, Corporations ⚖︎116.

§ 6.92 Drafting the Buyer's Stock Purchase Agreement—Conditions Precedent to Seller's Obligations

In the stock purchase agreement, the seller's performance is generally conditioned upon the following:[1]

- Performance by the buyer of all obligations specified in the stock purchase agreement;

§ 6.91
1. For suggested language from a sample agreement, *see infra,* § 6.187, Section 16(e).

§ 6.92
1. For illustrative language from a sample agreement, *see infra,* § 6.188, Article 6.

§ 6.92   BUYING & SELLING A SMALL BUSINESS   Ch. 6

- Accuracy of the covenants, representations and warranties made by the buyer;
- Absence of adverse change in the buyer's financial condition;[2]
- Delivery to the seller of a certificate executed by the buyer or its officers and shareholders certifying the fulfillment of the above conditions; and
- Delivery to the seller by the buyer of all documents required to be delivered under the terms of the stock purchase agreement.

Library References:

West's Key No. Digests, Corporations ⬗116.

§ 6.93   Drafting the Buyer's Stock Purchase Agreement—Nature and Survival of Representations and Warranties

Every stock purchase agreement should contain a provision requiring that all representations, warranties, indemnities, covenants and agreements made by the parties survive the closing. The purpose of this provision is to ensure that the material provisions of the purchase agreement remain enforceable after the transfer of shares has taken place, so that each party may have remedies in the event of breach.[1]

Library References:

West's Key No. Digests, Corporations ⬗116, 120.

§ 6.94   Drafting the Buyer's Stock Purchase Agreement—Documents to Be Delivered to Purchaser at Closing

The documents to be delivered by the seller to the buyer at closing normally include the following:

- Certificates for all shares of the corporation, duly endorsed with all transfer stamps affixed;
- The opinion of the seller's counsel that the seller is duly organized, validly existing and in good standing; that the seller has the corporate power and authority to enter into and perform the stock purchase agreement; that the stock purchase agreement is a valid and binding obligation of the seller; and that the execution and delivery of the stock purchase agreement and performance by the seller do not conflict with the seller's organizing instruments or

---

2. Applicable if seller is financing all or part of the purchase price or if payment is being made by buyer in installments.

§ 6.93

1. For suggested language from a sample agreement, see *infra*, § 6.188, Article Fifteen.

other contracts or obligations, or is not in violation of any law, rule or regulation;

- Certified copies of minutes and the consents of the shareholders and directors of the seller approving the stock purchase agreement and the consummation of the sale transaction;
- The certificate of the seller and individual shareholders affirming the performance of all conditions precedent to the buyer's obligations;
- Executed non-competition and continuity of business dealings agreements;
- All corporate records, reports, files, contracts, books, licenses, leases and permits, and all other corporate papers and instruments of every kind, including plans and specifications for buildings located on the real property;
- The share certificate book, minute book, corporate seal, auditors' reports and copies of tax returns and tax reports covering all years since incorporation;
- Resignations of all officers and directors, releases of all claims they may have against the corporation and cancellations of any contacts between the corporation and such individuals;
- All customer lists and supplier lists;
- A list of accounts receivable;
- All keys to buildings, vehicles, and file cabinets;
- Confidentiality agreements and covenants not to compete from departing employees of the seller;
- Written assurances from the seller's broker respecting confidentiality;
- Other documents to be delivered to the buyer under the terms of the agreement; and
- Such further instruments of transfer or other documents as reasonably may be required by the buyer to effect the provisions contained in the agreement.

Library References:

West's Key No. Digests, Corporations ⚖116.

§ 6.95 Drafting the Buyer's Stock Purchase Agreement—Documents to Be Delivered to Seller at Closing

The documents to be delivered by the buyer to the seller at closing normally include the following:

- Documents effecting payment of the purchase price;

§ 6.95   BUYING & SELLING A SMALL BUSINESS   Ch. 6

- Certified copies of minutes and the consents of the shareholders and directors of the buyer approving the stock purchase agreement and the consummation of the purchase transaction;
- Executed mortgages and other security documents;
- The opinion of the buyer's counsel that the buyer is duly organized, validly existing and in good standing; that the buyer has the corporate power and authority to enter into and perform the stock purchase agreement; that the stock purchase agreement is a valid and binding obligation of the buyer; and that the execution and delivery of the stock purchase agreement and performance by the buyer do not conflict with the buyer's organizing instruments or other contracts or obligations, and are not in violation of any law, rule or regulation;
- Other documents to be delivered to the seller under the terms of the agreement; and
- Such further instruments of transfer or other documents as reasonably may be required by the seller to effect the provisions contained in the agreement.

Library References:

West's Key No. Digests, Corporations ⚖=116.

§ 6.96 Drafting the Buyer's Stock Purchase Agreement—Notices, Severability and Other General Provisions

Notices and other provisions usually included at the end of an agreement are referred to as the "boilerplate." These provisions generally consist of the following:[1]

- Notice procedures;
- A severability clause;
- Governing law;
- A non-waiver provision;
- A savings clause;
- Provisions concerning modifications and changes to the agreement;
- A disclaimer as to captions and headings;
- Provisions acknowledging the "binding effect" of the agreement;

---

§ 6.96
1. For suggested language from a sample agreement as to some of these provisions, see infra, § 6.187, Section 21.

Ch. 6   DOCUMENTS PREPARED PRIOR TO CLOSING   § 6.97

- Provisions acknowledging that the agreement constitutes the "entire agreement" of the parties;
- An agreement to execute additional documents and counter parts;
- "Time is of the essence" provisions; and
- Arbitration provisions.

Library References:

West's Key No. Digests, Corporations ⚖116.

§ 6.97 Drafting the Buyer's Stock Purchase Agreement—Documents to Be Prepared or Reviewed Prior to Closing

After the stock purchase agreement has been executed, the buyer's counsel must either prepare, or review, as the case may be, all documents or instruments referred to in the agreement or required under its provisions. Such documents, known as the "collateral documents" may include the following:

- Proposed share certificates, stock powers, cancellation of the seller's shares, stock transfer records, stock transfer taxes and stamps;
- Security agreements, promissory notes, and mortgages;
- Escrow agreements;
- Corporate resolutions;
- Assignments of contracts, leases and other interests;
- Equipment lists;
- Inventory descriptions including count and valuation;
- Lists of other assets;
- Legal opinions of counsel;
- Employment and collective bargaining agreements;
- Lists of all of seller's other contracts and agreements;
- Certificates respecting name change;
- Certificates of Dissolution and/or Discontinuance;
- Assumed Name Certificates;
- Lists of all insurance policies and pending claims;
- Lists of all patents, patent applications, trademarks, trade names, and copyrights;
- Covenants not to compete; and
- Confidentiality agreements.

§ 6.97   BUYING & SELLING A SMALL BUSINESS   Ch. 6

Copies of all such collateral documents should be attached to the stock sale agreement and made a part of such agreement.

Library References:

West's Key No. Digests, Corporations ⚖116.

§ 6.98   Post-contract and Pre-closing

At this stage of the transaction the attorney must undertake all the necessary tasks to implement the now executed agreement, provide required information and documents to the seller, and prepare himself and his client for closing.

A good place to begin this process is with a review of the signed agreement. A competently drafted agreement will, through its many clauses, address the many issues of the transaction and thereby provide an outline of many of the items which must be reviewed or repaired for closing. It is good practice to prioritize items chronologically, using either the date contained in the agreement or an estimate of the time needed to obtain or prepare items for closing, with the more time consuming items being undertaken first.

Some, but not all of the items which must be undertaken at this stage, many of which are described in greater detail in other sections of this chapter, are as follows:

1. Prepare a list of all items to be obtained or prepared by the buyer and delivered to the seller;
2. Prepare a list of all items to be obtained from or be prepared by the seller and delivered to the buyer;
3. If appropriate, order environmental inspections;
4. Make application for financing;
5. Prepare plant closing or layoff notices, if appropriate;
6. Prepare bulk sales tax notices, if required;
7. Prepare UCC bulk sale notices, if required;
8. Negotiate and prepare new contracts (novations), as appropriate, with suppliers, customers, and lessors, among others;
9. Order searches such as title searches, tax searches, judgment searches and UCC searches;
10. Review collective bargaining agreements and comply with any notification provisions therein;
11. Prepare corporate resolutions or other business entity authorizations approving the transaction;
12. Prepare notices to suppliers and customers;
13. Draft and/or obtain counsel opinion letters;

14. Prepare and/or obtain assignments of contracts;
15. If appropriate, order and obtain structural inspections;
16. Prepare, as appropriate, doing business as (DBA) certificates or corporate name change certificates to be filed with county clerk's offices and the New York State Secretary of State;
17. Prepare the closing adjustments or termination notices for such things as telephone, power and light, insurance policies, real property and school tax adjustments, and inventory adjustments among others; and
18. Prepare a closing memorandum.

The closing memorandum should list all of the documents to be delivered or received at the time of closing; all the documents to be signed at the time of closing and by whom, provide the method of payment and how payment is to be made; provide a list of all adjustments and calculations in arriving at the final purchase price and the funds to be exchanged; and other necessary items, such as, the exchange of keys to business premises.

Prior to the date of closing, the attorneys for the buyer and seller should resolve all adjustments and other pre-closing matters to enable the closing the proceed smoothly.[1] All negotiations should be done and all material items agreed to by the parties prior to the closing.

§ 6.99 Post-contract and Pre-closing—Bulk Sales Act—UCC Article 6

When the buyer is purchasing the stock of a corporation or other ownership interest in a business entity (such as membership interests of a limited liability company, or partnership interests), UCC Article 6 does not apply. UCC Article 6 only applies to the transfer of a major portion of assets (*e.g.*, the materials, supplies, merchandise or other inventory).[1]

If the UCC bulk sale provisions apply and are not waived, the buyer's attorney must obtain the seller's creditor list and assure that timely notices are provided to the seller's creditors.[2] The notices should be given after the contract has been signed, but before the closing.

§ 6.98

1. **PRACTICE POINTER:** If the documents are available and time allows, the attorney should review all documents and adjustments with his client before the closing.

§ 6.99

1. **CAVEAT:** Since the legal requirements of UCC Article 6 do not apply, the protection afforded the buyer by these procedures is lost. Hence, the purchase agreement must contain provisions to protect the buyer from the seller's liabilities, as well as require an affidavit identifying the seller's creditors and the amount each creditor is owned. In addition, the mere reference, contained in many purchase agreements, that the parties will comply with the bulk sales statutes or some other similar language must be replaced by affirmative provisions protecting the buyer. With an entity purchase, unless stated otherwise, the buyer assumes all of the liabilities of the seller.

2. *See supra*, § 6.65, § 6.65 notes 1–6.

§ 6.99   BUYING & SELLING A SMALL BUSINESS   Ch. 6

If the UCC bulk sale provisions have been waived, the buyer's attorney, either before or at closing, must assure compliance with any protective provisions in the agreement for the benefit of the buyer, such as escrow arrangements.[3]

Library References:

West's Key No. Digests, Fraudulent Conveyances ⚌47.

§ 6.100 Post-contract and Pre-closing—NYS Sales Tax and Bulk Sale Notification

The bulk sales provisions of the New York State Tax Law apply only to a sale of business assets. These provisions do not apply to stock (entity) purchases.[1]

With an entity purchase, the buyer is at risk for prior sales tax and other liabilities of the seller.

Accordingly, the buyer should carefully consider the potential for pre-sale sales tax liability of the seller.[2]

The New York States Sales Tax law, including its bulk sale provisions, does apply to an asset purchase. Sales tax on the assets bought must be paid by the buyer to the seller who then reports and remits the tax to New York State, with his final or next regular sales tax return, or with a casual sales tax return.[3] If the bulk sale provisions are not waived, the attorney must assure that his client complies with the notices to be given to the New York State Department of Taxation and Finance to avoid liability to his client. These notices should be given as soon as practicable after the agreement is signed.[4]

Library References:

West's Key No. Digests, Taxation ⚌1311.

§ 6.101 Post-contract and Pre-closing—Plant Closing Notice

The Worker Adjustment and Retraining Notification Act (WARN ACT) requires employers to provide employees and local governments

---

3. See supra, § 6.65, § 6.66 notes 7–8. See also, supra, § 6.51.

§ 6.100

1. Tax Law § 1141.
2. **PRACTICE POINTER:** A recent "no change" audit by the Tax Department would be very assuring, but is seldom available. An escrow arrangement, and set-off in the event an audit of past sales tax returns, result in tax liability. See supra, § 6.51. The seller and his accountant (especially if the accountant prepared the sales tax returns) should represent that all sales tax returns and all sales tax payments have been paid and filed on time, and that there are no open sales tax audits (or disclose the details regarding any on-going audit). The statute of limitation for assessment of sales taxes is three years from the date the sales tax return was filed. Tax Law § 1147(b).

3. See supra, § 6.66.
4. See supra, § 6.66, § 6.66 notes 5–6.

Ch. 6 ENVIRONMENTAL SEARCHES & TESTING **§ 6.102**

with a 60 day notice prior to a plant closing or a mass lay-off. The employer must also notify the employee representatives (union), if any.

WARN only applies to employers with 100 or more employees, excluding part-time employees, or 100 or more employees who work, in the aggregate, at least 4,000 hours per week, excluding overtime.[1]

For a violation of the WARN Act, the employer can be held liable for employees' wages and pension benefits until the 60 day notice requirement is fulfilled. A fine of up to $500 per day for each day of noncompliance may also be imposed.[2]

The WARN Act is usually a concern of the seller, but if the buyer anticipates lay-offs or plant closings, the buyer may want to provide the required notice prior to closing.

§ 6.102 Post-contract and Pre-closing—Environmental Searches and Testing

Whether the client is purchasing or leasing commercial property, environmental searches and inspections (a Phase I Assessment) should be done if there is any sign of environmental contamination. If contamination exists or further environmental concerns are disclosed by the Phase I Assessment, a Phase II Environmental Assessment should be done.

Potential liability exists for the purchaser of contaminated real property under both federal and New York State environmental statutes.[1]

When acquiring the stock of a corporation (or the ownership interest of another entity), the continuing business entity will be responsible for prior contamination caused by the business entity. Therefore, an investigation of the real property will be acquired, and any leased or previously owned property must be conducted.[2]

If the business entity leases its premises and is not responsible for contamination, the buyer, before assuming the lease, should obtain representations and indemnifications[3] from the seller and the landlord

---

§ 6.101

1. 29 U.S.C.A. §§ 2101 *et seq.*

2. **CAVEAT:** This statute and the federal regulations have many exceptions. If there is any question if the WARN Act applies, the statute must be carefully reviewed.

§ 6.102

1. *See* Chapter 15 "Environmental Law," *infra*. *See also*, *supra*, § 6.21.

2. **PRACTICE POINTER:** In investigating previously owned or leased real property, the buyer will likely be limited to the representations of the seller, the limited physical observations of the buyer's environmental experts, and the information disclosed in a Phase I Environmental Assessment. The seller is usually unwilling to allow a more detailed investigation as the mere suspicion of potential contamination may cause problems for the seller.

3. **PRACTICE POINTER:** Representations, warranties, and remedies via "set-offs" or other provisions will provide important protection to the buyer.

§ 6.102 BUYING & SELLING A SMALL BUSINESS Ch. 6

regarding environmental matters.[4] The clean-up or remediation of contamination may be very disruptive and damaging to a business even if the prior business was responsible for the contamination.

Library References:
West's Key No. Digests, Health and Environment ⛛25.5.

§ 6.103 Post-contract and Pre-closing—Certificate of Good Standing

Whenever a limited liability company or corporation is purchased, a Certificate of Good Standing should be obtained from the New York State Secretary of State indicating that the entity was properly formed and exists, and is in good standing under the laws of the State of New York.[1]

A certificate should also be obtained for asset purchases to assure the entity has not been dissolved or does not suffer from other legal defects which may affect its ability to consummate the transaction.

§ 6.104 Post-contract and Pre-closing—Real Property Transfer Gains Tax

The New York State Real Property Transfer Gains Tax was repealed effective for transfers occurring on or after June 15, 1996, but there may still be tax liability imposed on sellers and buyers relating to transactions before June 15, 1996. This section analyzes the tax as it applies to transfers before that date.

Under the New York State Real Property Transfer Gains Tax Law,[1] a 10% tax was imposed on the seller's gain if the sale price of the real property exceeded $1 million. Transactions for less than $1 million were exempt from the tax. A taxable transfer of real property included the transfer or acquisition of a controlling interest in any entity which owned real property.[2] Transactions exceeding $1 million and involving the purchase of a controlling interest in a business entity owning real property in New York State could have been subject to tax.[3] In determin-

---

4. **CAVEAT:** Contamination at food processing, packaging or manufacturing sites could affect the client's product, or be so perceived by the public.

§ 6.103

1. **PRACTICE POINTER:** The New York State Secretary of State requires that the request for a Certificate of Good Standing be in writing and accompanied by a $25 payment. The Certificate will be forwarded in 5–10 business days. If the Certificate is needed sooner, expedited next day service may be obtained for an additional fee of $25. The address for requesting Certificates from the Department of State is: New York State Department of State, Corporations and State Records Division, 162 Washington Avenue, Albany, New York 12231.

§ 6.104

1. Tax Law §§ 1440 et seq.
2. Tax Law § 440(7).
3. **CAVEAT:** In determining the gain, and hence the tax, the fair market value of the real property, without any offset for liens is used. The statute has its own formula for the computation of gain which is

ing the tax, the fair market value of the real property, without any offset for liens, was used. If the buyer purchased 100% of the stock in a corporation owning real property in New York State worth $1.2 million, the transaction was subject to the real property transfer gains tax provisions. (Tax was paid only on the gain). Controlling interest is defined in the tax law[4] as 50% or more of the total combined voting power, or 50% or more of the capital profits or beneficial interest in the business entity. If less than 100% of the business entity was acquired, the apportionment of the fair market value to the interest acquired was made before the $1 million exemption was applied (*e.g.* if the business real property was worth $1.2 million and a 70% interest was acquired, the 70% controlling interest was worth $840,000 and the transaction was not subject to gains tax). The tax also applied to transfers of options, contracts of sale coupled with the use and occupancy of the real property and certain leases[5] (*e.g.*, if the buyer obtained a lease with an option to purchase, and the present value of the net rental payments, plus the amount paid for the option, and the purchase price to be paid upon exercise of the option, exceeded $1 million, the transaction was subject to gains tax).[6]

To comply with the Real Property Transfer Gains Tax, notices were filed with the New York State Department of Taxation and Finance by both the transferor and the transferee.[7] If notice was not given to the Tax Department the transferee may be held personally responsible for payment of the seller's gains tax.

Library References:
West's Key No. Digests, Taxation ⚖105.5.

§ 6.105 Closing and Post-Closing

By the time of closing, all negotiations and agreements between the parties will have been finalized, all documents in form ready for signing will have been prepared, and all pre-closing filings will have been made.

At closing, the consideration will be paid and all documents and instruments will be signed by the parties. Guarantors and obligors who are not parties to the transaction need not appear at closing, as long as their duly executed and acknowledged instruments are available for delivery to the proper parties.

The buyer's attorney should have a list of all documents to be signed and delivered by both the buyer and the seller at closing, and should

---

different than the amount of gain for income tax purposes.

4. Tax Law § 1440(2).

5. Tax Law § 1440(7).

6. PRACTICE POINTER: For a reference in this area, see Comeau, Heckelman, and Helm, *New York Tax Analysis*, Vol 3, Part VII, Real Property Gains Tax.

7. Form TP–580, New York State Real Property Transfer Gains Tax Questionnaire, Transferor; and form TP–581, New York State Real Property Transfer Gains Tax Questionnaire, Transferee.

§ 6.105   BUYING & SELLING A SMALL BUSINESS   Ch. 6

prepare a "Closing Memorandum." The closing memorandum will normally identify the place, date and time of closing, name the individuals who attended the closing, list the documents and instruments signed and delivered, identify the further steps to be taken by each party, and record other important information concerning the transaction.

After closing, counsel should deliver to his or her client the originals of all pertinent documents, making sure to retain copies of all such documents for counsel's records. It is advisable to include in this delivery a letter to the client summarizing the actions taken by counsel, such as filings made or returns prepared, as well as instructions for further actions to be taken by the client. If any documents or instruments will require re-filing at later dates, counsel should instruct the client as to these matters.

It is important that after closing, counsel take the opportunity to discuss with his or her client other legal matters which might arise. The client should be advised as to the legal issues involved in the continued operation of the business, such as recordkeeping, succession planning, employment matters, pension and benefit issues, and the like.

Owners of small businesses many times neglect keeping corporate records and minutes because most of their time is spent attending to day to day business activities. It is important that owners keep proper corporate records, not only for operational purposes, but to avoid losing the limited liability protection afforded corporations under law. Counsel should advise his or her client of this necessity.[1]

§ 6.106   Strategy: Representing the Seller—Introduction

An attorney embarking on the representation of a client who is selling a business will be called upon to perform a number of services for the client. These services range from advising the client as to the legal aspects of the sale to counseling the client as to the practical and other issues which might arise. A client who has operated a business for a number of years and has developed valuable and long-standing relationships with employees, customers and suppliers will many times be concerned as to what will happen when a new owner takes over. These issues will no doubt continue to surface and counsel should be prepared to deal with these matters at the outset and during the course of negotiations with the purchaser.

§ 6.105
1. **PRACTICE POINTER:** Many law firms provide their clients with minutes of annual meetings for a small yearly fee. Such minutes, at a minimum, should indicate that the shareholders have had an annual meeting, that the indicated directors were elected and have met, that the indicated officers were elected, and that all actions taken by the directors and officers of the corporation during the past year have been approved and ratified.

The Seller's Strategy. At the initial interview, counsel should review with his or her client the client's reasons for selling the business as well as the client's objectives and financial requirements.

Counsel should prepare, with the client, a strategy and plan of action, outlining the client's goals and how these goals will be met. This strategy must be flexible to allow change as the transaction evolves, and should be reduced to writing.

Depending on the nature and size of the transaction, the client may require the services of other professionals in addition to her or her attorney.[1] If the seller's team is to consist of other individuals, it is important that the strategy be discussed with and understood by each member of the team. The strategy should identify, at a minimum, the following:

1. The legal structure of the transaction (either a sale of the assets or a sale of the stock of the business, or a combination of entities);
2. The most advantageous method of dealing with the buyer;
3. The timing of the transaction;
4. Whether to initially use a letter of intent or a full purchase agreement;
5. The sale price of the business;
6. If the purchase is for other than cash, the willingness and ability of seller to finance the sale;[2]
7. The security for payment of the purchase price;
8. The willingness of the seller to train the buyer both before and after closing;
9. How the business is to be marketed; and
10. Whether the seller and other key members of the business will be willing to continue with the business either as employees or consultants, and for what length of time.

The information contained in Sections 6.107 through 6.185, *infra*, is intended to provide the attorney with the practical skills necessary to assist the client in his or her endeavor to plan, investigate, negotiate and close on what will hopefully be a successful sale of the business.

§ 6.107 Strategy: Representing the Seller—The Attorney's Role

Many times the attorney must be a counselor to the client as well as a competent legal advisor. The attorney may sometimes find that the

---

§ 6.106

1. See *infra*, § 6.112 for a comprehensive discussion concerning seller's negotiating team.

2. See *infra*, § 6.111 (concerning investigation of the buyer's ability to purchase and finance the business).

client has not thoroughly or objectively considered all aspects of the transaction, and that the client will rely on counsel for practical as well as legal advice. It is very important that the attorney understand what the motivations, goals, and interests of the client are in reference to selling his or her business.

During his or her initial interview with the client, counsel should assess the client's level of sophistication, willingness to take risks and, most important of all, the client's financial concerns.

The sale of a business very often involves a lengthy process during which the buyer will spend much time gathering information about the seller's business, assessing the possible liabilities of the business, and weighing the risk of whether or not to purchase. Counsel will sometimes find that his or her client will become annoyed with the depth of the buyer's investigation or the length of time being taken. The attorney should be prepared to advise his or her client as to the legal issues involved in the process, including the probable concerns of the buyer.[1] In addition counsel must be prepared to assist the client in protecting the confidentiality of its business during the course of the buyer's investigations. Counsel will also be called upon to assist the seller in his own investigation of the buyer and the buyer's ability to acquire, own and operate the business. Finally, the attorney should be prepared to inform the client as to the tax issues involved in the sale of a business, and to negotiate the best possible deal for the client.

It is advisable at the outset that the attorney set forth in a written retainer agreement the scope of the attorney's activities and fee arrangement. If, at any time, the scope of the attorney's work changes, this should also be indicated in writing to the client.

Library References:
West's Key No. Digests, Attorney and Client ⚖=105–129.5.

§ 6.108 Strategy: Representing the Seller—Different Considerations Depending on the Type of Transaction

When representing the seller of a business, counsel will be concerned primarily with making sure that full payment is received for the business being transferred, that the seller is protected from liabilities which may arise after the business has been transferred, and that the seller is afforded the most advantageous tax treatment possible.

Sections 6.116 to 6.139 discuss how to structure a transaction to the seller's advantage from both the legal and tax point of view. As indicated

---

§ 6.107

1. *See supra,* §§ 6.13–6.30 for an in-depth discussion of the buyer's due diligence investigation of the seller's business.

below, it is often more advantageous for the seller to structure the transaction as a sale of stock of the business, generally because a stock sale is less complicated than an asset sale. With the sale of stock, the seller may transfer all of the property of the business to the buyer. In an asset sale, seller could be left with unwanted assets which he may not be able to sell to another buyer. In addition, a transfer of stock will obviate the necessity of the seller's complying with cumbersome UCC Bulk Sales[1] provisions, and will assure the seller of the tax advantage of capital gains treatment on the proceeds of the sale.

Sections 6.116 to 6.132, *infra*, discuss in detail the advantages, disadvantages and tax aspects of both asset purchase and stock purchase transactions from the point of view of the seller.

Section 6.133 discusses the transfer of a small business by means of merger or consolidation. A properly constructed merger or consolidation will enable the seller to exchange its stock for the stock of the buyer without tax consequences.

§ 6.109 Strategy: Representing the Seller—General Stages of the Transaction

In addition to developing the strategy of the transaction with the client as discussed earlier,[1] counsel's representation of a client who is selling a business will consist of the following:

Investigating the buyer's ability to purchase, own and operate the business, and protecting the confidentiality of the seller (§§ 6.110–6.115);

Evaluating the tax implications of the transaction (§§ 6.116–6.133);

Structuring the sale (§§ 6.134–6.138);

Negotiating and drafting the sale agreement (§§ 6.139–6.183);

Performing the post-contract and pre-closing steps of the transaction (§ 6.184); and

Closing the transaction (§ 6.185).

§ 6.110 Representing the Seller—General Investigation

An attorney embarking on the representation of a small business seller is in a unique position to perform a very valuable service for his client. Many times, the attorney must be a counselor as well as a competent legal advisor.

Often the seller has given little thought to a sale of his business other than the fact that he has decided to sell. Usually the seller is overly

§ 6.108
1. *See infra,* § 6.153 regarding UCC Bulk Sales provisions.

§ 6.109
1. *See supra,* § 6.106.

optimistic, and one of the first things the attorney must do is to help the seller determine a realistic price.

This can be done in a number of ways. An appraisal of the business is one of the best ways, but also expensive.[1]

Another approach for setting the price is to retain the services of a business broker familiar with the industry and businesses in the area. The broker may also provide guidance to the seller regarding price and financing. The seller may need to finance all or a portion of the sale. Brokers charge a brokerage or finders fee, usually in the range of 10% of the selling price.

Lacking an appraisal or a business broker, local accountants, trade groups and an industry consultant may be helpful in determining a price range.

§ 6.111 Representing the Seller—Investigating the Buyer

Selling a business and negotiating the closing of the transaction is a time consuming endeavor that can be expensive as well as emotionally taxing for the seller.

A business broker will screen all interested parties and only present serious buyers. If a business broker is not used, the seller and his attorney must quickly separate the "browsers" and "tire kickers" from the serious buyers. Attempt to learn as much as possible about the buyer by contacting other professionals who may be familiar with the buyer and by searching business data bases such as Dun and Bradstreet, Standard and Poors Register of Corporations, TRW Business Credit Profile and others.[1] If early negotiations involve seller financing, a resume, credit report, and a net worth statement from the buyer should be requested to ascertain the buyer's ability to purchase and operate the business.

§ 6.112 Representing the Seller—The Negotiating Team

The members of the negotiating team are usually the seller's attorney, accountant and business broker. The team may also be joined by business consultants and other experts, as needed.[1]

§ 6.110

1. See supra, § 6.29.

§ 6.111

1. WESTLAW from West Group also provides many business data bases, including those mentioned.

§ 6.112

1. Such as marketing experts in the industry or profession.

In selecting the negotiating team, personalities of the individuals and their expertise must be taken into account to ensure that team members can work together as an effective team among themselves and with the buyer and/or the buyer's negotiating team. Also, one must consider past relationships among the buyer, the seller, and the members of the respective negotiating teams. However, many times the attorney in a small business transaction does much of the negotiating on behalf of his client. To effectively negotiate, the attorney must have knowledge of the business, the risk to, and the financial tolerances of his client, and usually, the impact of the tax law.

§ 6.113 Representing the Seller—The Letter of Intent

The letter of intent is usually a non-binding agreement to agree. It should clearly state the extent to which it is enforceable, if at all. Although the use of a letter of intent varies widely among attorneys (some of whom argue that it is a waste of time), it is often helpful, early in the deal, to have an outline of the major points of the transaction agreed upon by all parties. The letter of intent will generally define the essential terms of the contract such as price, payment terms, and a timetable for consummating the transaction. The letter is usually informal in format and relatively short. Sophisticated clients may have a letter of intent when they first consult with their attorney.

The letter of intent often provides for a deposit by the purchaser as a demonstration of his seriousness with respect to the transaction. The deposit is usually held in escrow by an escrow agent. The disposition of any deposit, if the parties fail to agree, should be clearly set forth in the letter of intent.

§ 6.114 Representing the Seller—Confidentiality Agreements

Business clients are often hesitant to disclose information about their businesses. They understandably fear that their business may fall into the hands of competitors and be used against them. Confidentiality and non-disclosure agreements provide some measure of protection for the disclosing party. Before any information is exchanged, the receiving party must agree (a) to keep all information strictly confidential; (b) to use the information only for the purposes of the contemplated transaction; and (c) to return all original documents and copies upon request to the party providing them. Some confidentiality and disclosure agreements include penalties in the form of liquidated damages for any disclosure.

§ 6.115 Representing the Seller—Drafting the Agreement

The custom and usage is that the buyer drafts the purchase offer documents and presents them to the seller. Sometimes it is advantageous to deviate from this practice.

§ 6.115   BUYING & SELLING A SMALL BUSINESS   Ch. 6

At times, the economics of a small business transaction may cause the seller's attorney to take a more active role in drafting the agreement. Other times, a more active role is motivated by a desire to "move the transaction along," to obtain the "drafting advantage," or just to split the drafting burden. How much assistance is offered is part of the seller's strategy. Allowing the buyer to do the initial drafting can be beneficial if the initial draft either omits items unfavorable to the seller, but which would otherwise be expected, or contains ambiguities that would be construed against the draftsman.

If the seller's attorney is drafting the agreement, should the first draft be "stacked" in the seller's favor, "fair," or "in between?" In deciding the seller's strategy, the advantages, disadvantages and economics of the transaction must be considered.[1]

§ 6.116   Tax Issues for the Seller—General Overview

Generally, a seller prefers to receive income classified as long term capital gains. Historically, long term capital gains have received favorable tax treatment.

Starting July 29, 1997 to be treated as a long term capital gain, the asset must be held by the taxpayer for more than 18 months. This is usually not a problem for the seller of a business. Gains from assets held less than 18 months are short term capital gains, that produce ordinary income.[1]

§ 6.115

1. PRACTICE POINTER: Be mindful of the objectives of the client. Most small business clients are not impressed with high legal expenses caused by numerous drafts or revisions relating to insubstantial matters. Small business clients usually are more impressed with a realistic and reasonable document that protects their interest rather than a document full of burdensome and overreaching provisions that drive up the cost of the transaction and may even threaten the transaction itself.

§ 6.116

1. For asset sales on or before July 18, 1997, the holding period for long-term capital gain treatment is more than 12 months. In addition to changing the holding period, the new law has complicated the calculation of tax. Sales *on or before* May 6, 1997 are taxed at a maximum rate of 28% or the taxpayer's marginal bracket if lower (*i.e.*, 15%).

For sales *on or after* May 7, 1997 through July 28, 1997, the holding period remains more than 12 months but the long-term capital gains tax rate is reduced to 20% if the taxpayer is in the 28%, 31%, 36% or 39% marginal tax bracket. The rate is reduced to 10% if the taxpayer is in the 15% marginal tax bracket.

For sales on or after July 29, 1997, the holding period for long-term capital gain treatment increases to more than 18 months but, if an asset is sold on or after July 19, 1997 which has been held by the taxpayer for more than 12 months but not more than 18 months, the gain is taxed using the rules for sales on or before May 6, 1997. Although a taxpayer in this position will not receive the benefits of the change in the law, he will not be penalized by the increased holding period.

In addition, a new lower rate for long-term capital gain treatment of 18% (8% for individuals in the 15% tax bracket) will apply to sales after December 31, 2000 for assets held more than five years. The 10% and 20% rates will still apply to assets held more than 18 months but not more than five years.

For taxpayers in marginal brackets above 15%, the five year holding period only applies to assets acquired after December 31,

Generally, a stock sale, (rather than an asset sale), is more favorable to the seller from a tax standpoint, because the gain is treated as a long term capital gain. However, if a seller has a flow-through business entity (*e.g.*, an S Corporation, an LLC or a Partnership), owning assets which have dropped in value, an asset sale may be more beneficial because it may generate losses which can be deducted on the seller's individual income tax return.

§ 6.117 Tax Issues for the Seller—Asset Sale

As a general rule, an asset sale is usually not favorable to the seller. In an asset sale the seller recognizes gain or loss on the sale of each asset. Unless the business is conducted as a sole proprietorship, the gain or loss is recognized by the business entity. If the business entity is a C corporation (rather than a flow-through entity) which is to be dissolved, there may be double taxation to the seller (*i.e.* the business entity recognizes the gain on the sale of an asset and the business owner recognizes income upon the distribution of the sale proceeds to him from the C corporation).

§ 6.118 Tax Issues for the Seller—Asset Sale—Allocation of Purchase Price

The operative portion of the agreement usually provides allocations of purchase price to items such as covenant not to compete, goodwill and going concern value, inventory, equipment and other assets.[1]

The agreement should also provide that neither party will take a position on any income tax return or in any judicial proceeding which is inconsistent with the purchase price allocation.

Allocation of the purchase price among the business assets determines the tax treatment for the seller and buyer. Since the Tax Reform Act of 1986, I.R.C. § 1060 has controlled the allocation of the purchase price. This section seeks to insure proper allocation to goodwill and going concern value and provides that the "residual method" must be used. The residual method requires that the purchase price first be allocated to cash, accounts receivable and other identifiable tangible and intangible assets based on the asset's fair market value. Any remaining purchase price is allocated to goodwill or going concern value.

Within these guidelines the parties are free to determine the allocation of purchase price to assets.[2] Although the allocation chosen by the

---

2000. Taxpayer Relief Act of 1997 § 311(a), (e); I.R.C. § 1(h).

§ 6.118

1. PRACTICE POINTER: The inventory, equipment and other assets should be further detailed on attached schedules. Schedules are an easy way to specifically identify the assets and are easily revised during the course of negotiations. *See infra,* §§ 6.142–6.143.

2. I.R.C. § 1060, I.R.C. Reg. § 1.1060–1T(h). *See also,*, I.R.C. § 338(b)(5), I.R.C. Reg. § 1.1060–1T. IRS Form 8594 "Asset

§ 6.118 BUYING & SELLING A SMALL BUSINESS   Ch. 6

parties is not binding on the IRS, if the allocation is reasonable and in accordance with I.R.C. § 1060, the allocation generally will not be challenged by the IRS.

Library References:
West's Key No. Digests, Internal Revenue ⇐3200, 3715.

§ 6.119 Tax Issues for the Seller—Asset Sale—Depreciation Recapture

The law permits a deduction (against business income) of a reasonable allowance for the exhaustion and wear and tear of property used in a trade or business.[1] This is called depreciation or amortization.

Depreciation applies to tangible assets (*e.g.*, equipment, buildings, etc.) Amortization applies to intangible assets (*e.g.*, start-up costs, goodwill, etc.)

Depreciation and amortization allow the business owner to deduct (write off) the cost of the asset against business income over a period of time. This period of time is based upon an estimate of the useful life of the asset and is often referred to as the asset's depreciable life.

To prevent a taxpayer from deducting depreciation expense against ordinary income and then selling the asset to obtain favorable long term capital gain tax treatment, the I.R.C. provides for depreciation recapture.[2] The depreciation recapture provisions require that the proceeds from the sale of a depreciated asset be allocated first to the recapture of the previously taken depreciation expense; the remainder is recognized as capital gain. As a result, the previously deducted depreciation (and amortization) expense is recognized as ordinary income on the sale of the asset. Only the amount over and above the depreciation recapture receives favorable capital gain treatment.[3]

Library References:
West's Key No. Digests, Internal Revenue ⇐3703.

§ 6.120 Tax Issues for the Seller—Asset Sale—Capital Gains and Losses

In order to receive favorable capital gains tax treatment, the gain must result from the sale of a capital asset. A "capital asset" means all

Acquisition Statement" must be filed with each party's income tax return for the year of the transaction.

§ 6.119
1. I.R.C. § 167 and I.R.C. Reg. 1.167(a)–1.
2. I.R.C. §§ 1245, 1250.
3. **PRACTICE POINTER:** If a seller is receiving installment payments, the capital gain portion can be deferred until the payment is received by using the installment sales provisions of the I.R.C. (*See* I.R.C. § 453). The ordinary income generated by depreciation recapture must be reported in the year of the sale; it cannot be deferred. If the seller receives a small amount of sale proceeds in the year of the sale, and has a large amount of depreciation recapture, the seller may have to use other funds to pay the tax liability.

property (whether or not connected with a trade or business) except the following:

1. Inventory;
2. Property held primarily for sale to customers in the ordinary course of a taxpayer's trade or business (even though not classified technically as inventory);
3. Accounts receivable or notes receivable acquired in the ordinary course of a trade or business;
4. Depreciable business property;
5. Real property used in a taxpayers trade or business;
6. A copyright, a literary, musical or artistic composition, a letter or memorandum, or similar property (but not a patent or invention) held by the taxpayer who created it; or a U.S. Government publication held by a taxpayer who received it other than by purchase at the price at which the publication is offered to the public.[1]

Generally, business real estate and depreciable business property is excluded from the definition of "capital assets." However, when the business property qualifies as I.R.C. § 1231 property, and gains from the sale of such property exceed losses, then each gain or loss is treated as though it were derived from the sale of a long term capital asset.[2] Due to this exception, it is possible to obtain long term capital gain treatment for the sale of business assets, but a portion of the sale proceeds will likely require depreciation recapture which is treated as ordinary income.[3]

Capital gains and losses are further classified as short term capital gains and losses, and long term capital gains and losses. Long term capital gains and losses are generated by the sale of capital assets held by the seller for more than 18 months.[4] All other capital asset sales generate short term capital gains or losses.

Only long term capital gains receive favorable tax treatment; short term capital gains generate ordinary income treatment. The seller is required to offset long and short term capital gains and losses against each other on his tax return. This may result in a long term capital loss offsetting the ordinary income of a short term capital gain.

Library References:

West's Key No. Digests, Internal Revenue ⚖3225–3261.

§ 6.120

1. **PRACTICE POINTER:** Since Congress frequently changes the tax laws, one must consult the tax law to determine the current tax treatment of long term capital gains. There are also special provisions relating to capital losses. See I.R.C. §§ 1201 et seq. and Chapter 35 "Income Tax," infra.

2. I.R.C. § 1231.
3. I.R.C. § 1221.
4. See supra, § 6.116 note 1.

§ 6.121 Tax Issues for the Seller—Asset Sale—Ordinary Income

A sale of business assets, other than those qualifying as capital assets, generates ordinary income or loss to the business entity. The sale of items, such as inventory and supplies, generates ordinary income. Ordinary income receives no favorable tax treatment. Accordingly, within the parameters allowed by I.R.C. § 1060, the seller usually prefers to allocate the purchase price to capital assets.

Library References:

West's Key No. Digests, Internal Revenue ⌾3225–3261.

§ 6.122 Tax Issues for Seller—Asset Sale—Income to Corporation

If the seller is an entity, other than an individual doing business as a sole proprietorship, the income or loss generated by a sale of business asset is reported by the business entity.

If the business entity is a flow-through tax entity such as a corporation which has elected I.R.C. Subchapter S status or a limited liability company taxed as a partnership, the gain recognized by the entity will flow through to and be reported on the entity owner's tax return, and any tax will be paid by the owner, not the entity. This produces a result similar to a sole proprietorship. On the other hand, if the selling entity is a C corporation, the corporation must recognize the income (or loss) and the corporation must pay a tax on any gain. The income or loss will not flow through to the owner's tax return. Later, when the owner receives a distribution of the sale proceeds from the corporation, the distribution will be taxed again.[1]

§ 6.123 Tax Issues for Seller—Asset Sale—Real Property Transfer Gains Tax

The New York State Real Property Transfer Gains Tax was repealed effective for transfers occurring on or after June 15, 1996, but there may still be tax liability imposed on sellers and buyers relating to transactions before June 15, 1996. This section analyzes the tax as it applies to transfers before that date.

---

§ 6.122

1. **PRACTICE POINTER:** The double tax may be mitigated by electing S corporation status, but one must consider the impact of the built-in gains tax. *See* I.R.C. § 1374. If there is only one or a small number of owners, another approach is to provide for payment directly to the owners (rather than the corporation), for covenants not to compete and for consulting services. Economic reality must be maintained in

Ch. 6 REAL PROPERTY TRANSFER GAINS TAX § 6.123

Under the New York State Real Property Transfer Gains Tax Law,[1] a 10% tax was imposed on the seller's gain when the sale price of real property exceeded $1 million. Transactions for less than $1 million were exempt from the tax. A taxable transfer of real property included the transfer or acquisition of a controlling interest in an entity which owned real property.[2] Transactions which exceeded $1 million and involved the purchase of a controlling interest in a business entity owning real property in New York State could have been subject to tax.[3] In determining the tax, the fair market value of the real property, without any offset for liens, was used. If the seller sold 100% of the stock in a corporation owning real property in New York State worth $1.2 million, the transaction was subject to the real property transfer gains tax provisions. (Tax is paid only on the gain). Controlling interest is defined in the tax law[4] as 50% or more of the total combined voting power, or 50% or more of the capital profits or beneficial interest in the business entity. If less than 100% of the business entity was acquired, the apportionment of the fair market value to the interest acquired was made before the $1 million exemption was applied (*e.g.* if the business real property was worth $1.2 million and a 70% interest was acquired, the 70% controlling interest was worth $840,000 and the transaction was not subject to gains tax). The tax also applied to transfers of options or contracts of sale coupled with the use and occupancy of the real property and to certain leases[5] (*e.g.* if the buyer obtained a lease with an option to purchase and the present value of the net rental payments plus the amount paid for the option, and the purchase price to be paid upon exercise of the option, exceeded $1 million, the transaction was subject to gains tax).[6]

To comply with the Real Property Transfer Gains Tax, notices had to be filed with the New York State Department of Taxation and Finance by the transferor and the transferee.[7] If notice was not given to the Tax Department, the transferee could be held personally responsible for payment of the seller's gains tax.

Library References:

West's Key No. Digests, Taxation ⚖︎105.5.

these allocations or they may successfully be challenged by the IRS.

§ 6.123
1. Tax Law §§ 1440 *et seq.*
2. Tax Law § 440(7).
3. **CAVEAT:** The statute has its own formula for the computation gain which is different than the amount of gain for income tax purposes.
4. Tax Law § 1440(2).
5. Tax Law § 1440(7).
6. **PRACTICE POINTER:** For a reference in this area, *see* Comeau, Heckelman, and Helm, *New York Tax Analysis*, Vol 3, Part VII, Real Property Gains Tax.
7. Form TP–580, New York State Real Property Transfer Gains Tax Questionnaire, Transferor; and form TP–581, New York State Real Property Transfer Gains Tax Questionnaire, Transferee.

§ 6.124 Tax Issues for Seller—Asset Sale—Covenant Not to Compete and Consulting Agreements

Payments for both covenants not to compete and consulting agreements are ordinary income to the seller.[1] Payments for consulting services rendered by an individual are also subject to social security and medicare tax.

§ 6.125 Tax Issues for the Seller—Stock Sale—General Advantages

The primary advantage of a stock sale is that stock of a corporation is usually a capital asset to the individual and is not subject to depreciation recapture.[1] If the seller has a gain, he may receive favorable long term capital gains tax treatment. This also applies to other business interests such as partnerships and LLC interests, but not to sole proprietorships. Another advantage to the seller is the avoidance of double taxation when the business entity sold is a C corporation.

§ 6.126 Tax Issues for Seller—Stock Sale—Capital Gain or Loss

Capital gains and losses only apply to capital assets.[1] Stock and other business ownership interests (*i.e.* LLCs and partnerships) are usually capital assets. Their sale generates capital gains or losses.

Capital gains and losses are further segregated into short term gains and losses and long term gains and losses. Capital assets held for more than 18 months generate long term capital gains or losses. Most other capital asset sales generate short term capital gains or losses.[2]

Only long term capital gains receive favorable tax treatment. Short term capital gains are treated as ordinary income. The seller is required to offset long and short term capital gains and losses against each other on his tax return. This may result in a long term capital loss offsetting the ordinary income of a short term capital gain.

§ 6.124

1. PRACTICE POINTER: As previously discussed, covenants not to compete and consulting agreements may be an avenue to provide payments directly to a business owner rather than a business entity. *See supra,* § 6.122 note 1. If the payments must be made to a business entity (even a C corporation), and if the owner continues to render services to the business entity, the income from the covenant not to compete and consulting agreements can be offset by wages paid to the owner. The business entity will be required to pay its portion of social security and medicare taxes, and may be required to pay unemployment insurance, disability insurance and workers' compensation depending on the number of employees and the ownership structure of the entity.

§ 6.125

1. *See supra,* § 6.120.

§ 6.126

1. *See supra,* § 6.120 for a definition of capital assets.

2. *See supra,* § 6.116 note 1.

Library References:

West's Key No. Digests, Internal Revenue ⊱3225–3261.

§ 6.127 Tax Issues for Seller—Stock Sale—No Concern for Income to a Corporate Entity

In a stock or entity ownership sale, the proceeds of the sale go directly to the owners of the business rather than to the corporate or other business entity (as happens with an asset sale). Accordingly, the business entity neither receives nor recognizes any income. This avoids double taxation.[1]

§ 6.128 Tax Issues for Seller—Stock Sale—Real Property Transfer Gains Tax

The New York State Real Property Transfer Gains Tax was repealed effective for transfers occurring on or after June 15, 1996, but there may still be tax liability imposed on sellers and buyers relating to transactions before June 15, 1996. This section analyzes the tax as it applies to transfers before that date.

Under the New York State Real Property Transfer Gains Tax Law [1], a 10% tax was imposed on the seller's gain when the sale price of real property exceeded $1 million. Transactions for less than $1 million were exempt from the tax. A taxable transfer of real property included the transfer or acquisition of a controlling interest in an entity which owned real property.[2] Transactions exceeding $1 million and involving the sale of a controlling interest in a business entity owning real property in New York State could have been subject to tax.[3] In determining the tax, the fair market value of the real property, without any offset for liens, was used. If the seller sold 100% of the stock in a corporation owning real property in New York State worth $1.2 million, the transaction was subject to the real property transfer gains tax provisions. (Tax was paid only on the gain). Controlling interest is defined in the tax law[4], as 50% or more of the total combined voting power, or 50% or more of the capital profits or beneficial interest in the business entity. If less than 100% of the business entity was acquired, the apportionment of the fair market value to the interest acquired was made before the $1 million exemption was applied (*e.g.* if the business real property was worth $1.2 million and a 70% interest was acquired, the 70% controlling interest was worth $840,000 and the transaction was not subject to gains tax). The tax also applied to transfers of options, contracts of sale coupled

§ 6.127

1. *See supra,* § 6.122.

§ 6.128

1. Tax Law §§ 1440 *et seq.*
2. Tax Law § 440(7).

3. **CAVEAT:** The statute has its own formula for the computation of gain which is different than the amount of gain for income tax purposes.

4. Tax Law § 1440(2).

§ 6.128 BUYING & SELLING A SMALL BUSINESS Ch. 6

with the use and occupancy of the real property and certain leases[5] (*e.g.* if the buyer obtained a lease with an option to purchase, and the present value of the net rental payments plus the amount paid for the option, and the purchase price to be paid upon exercise of the option, exceeded $1 million, the transaction was subject to gains tax).[6]

Library References:
West's Key No. Digests, Taxation ⚍105.5.

§ 6.129 Tax Issues for Seller—Stock Sale—Consulting and Non-compete Agreements

Payments for consulting services and non-compete covenants are ordinary income to the seller, therefore separate allocations for consulting and non-compete payments are not advantageous to the seller from a tax standpoint. However, payments for stock usually result in favorable long term capital gain tax treatment.[1]

§ 6.130 Tax Issues for the Seller—Stock Sale—I.R.C. § 1244 Stock and Qualified Small Business Stock

A loss from the sale or exchange, or from the worthlessness, of corporate stock usually results in a capital loss. Capital losses are treated less favorably than ordinary losses for income tax purposes.[1] Upon the sale at a loss, or upon the worthlessness, of "small business stock" issued by a qualifying small business corporation, an individual may deduct the loss as an ordinary loss.[2] This is commonly call "Code Sec. 1244 Stock."[3] To qualify as small business stock, the corporation's capitalization (assets contributed to capital for the stock and as paid in surplus) must not exceed $1 million. This determination is made at the time the stock is issued. There are many statutory requirements, such as, the corporation must be an operating company (not an investment company), the stock must have been issued to the individual taxpayer or to the individual taxpayer's partnership and the maximum amount

---

5. Tax Law § 1440(7).

6. **PRACTICE POINTER:** For a reference in this area *see* Comeau, Heckelman, and Helm, *New York Tax Analysis*, Vol 3, Part VII, Real Property Gains Tax.

§ 6.129

1. *See generally supra,* §§ 6.120, 6.125, 6.126.

§ 6.130

1. I.R.C. § 1211 and I.R.C. Reg. § 1.1211 require that capital gains offset capital losses. Any remaining capital losses may be deducted on the individual's tax return, but this amount is limited to a maximum of $3,000 per year. Ordinary losses, as opposed to capital losses, are not limited to $3,000 per year.

2. I.R.C. § 1244.

3. **PRACTICE POINTER:** Previously, in order to qualify as I.R.C. § 1244 stock the corporation, upon the issuance of the stock, had to adopt a corporate resolution indicating that it intended the stock to be Section 1244 stock. Although it is still a good practice, if the resolution is not adopted, the seller will still be afforded ordinary loss treatment if the other requirements are met.

deductible as an ordinary loss in one year is $50,000 (or $100,000 on a joint, husband and wife, return).

For stock issued after August 10, 1993 a non-corporate taxpayer can exclude 50% of the gain from a sale or exchange of qualified small business stock held for more than five years.[4] A qualified small business is a domestic C corporation with aggregate gross assets that do not exceed $50 million before or immediately after the date of the stock issuance. The gain eligible for the 50% exclusion may not exceed the greater of $10 million or ten times the taxpayer's basis in the stock. Any excess gain is taxed as long term capital gain, without any 50% exclusion.

There are other statutory requirements, such as, 80% of the corporation's assets must be used in the active conduct of one or more qualified trades or businesses. Many professional activities, such as services in the field of health, law, engineering and architecture, are not qualified trades or businesses.

Library References:
West's Key No. Digests, Internal Revenue ⚖3243.

§ 6.131 Tax Issues for Seller—Stock Sale—Stock Transfer Tax

The New York State Tax Law imposes a transfer tax on the transfer of shares (stock) in corporations, but the tax does not apply to the original issuance of stock.[1] For small share transactions this tax is usually not significant. The amount of the tax depends upon the sale price of the stock. The maximum tax for share prices of $20 or more is $.05 per share.[2] The tax law also provides for a refund of the stock transfer tax paid.[3] The tax cost may ultimately be $0, but under the tax law, failure to pay the tax is a misdemeanor.[4]

Library References:
West's Key No. Digests, Taxation ⚖105.5.

§ 6.132 Tax Issue for the Seller—Stock Sale—Collapsible Corporation

The term "collapsible corporation" is applied by the I.R.C. and the IRS to a corporation which is formed for the purpose of converting ordinary income into long term capital gain.[1] Accordingly, a "collapsible corporation" is not a type of corporation, but a use of the corporate form

4. I.R.C. § 1202.

§ 6.131
1. Tax Law § 270; 20 NYCRR § 440.1(h).
2. Tax Law § 270.2.

3. Tax Law § 280–a.
4. Tax Law § 272.1.

§ 6.132
1. I.R.C. § 341.

773

by taxpayers to convert ordinary income items (or the gain from ordinary income items) into gain from the sale of stock. The sale of stock is a capital asset and in these cases the sale is structured to receive long term capital gain treatment.[2]

> **EXAMPLE:** A corporation is organized to construct a satellite. Upon completion of the satellite, the satellite becomes inventory to the corporation and the sale of the satellite generates ordinary income to the corporation. If the proceeds are distributed as dividends to the stockholders, the dividends are ordinary income to the stockholders. On the other hand, upon completion of the satellite, but prior to its sale, the stockholders sell their stock in the corporation to the buyer of the satellite and the stockholders claim long term capital gain treatment. I.R.C. § 341 will classify this corporation as a collapsible corporation and deny long term capital gain treatment to the stockholders.

I.R.C. § 341 applies not only to inventory assets, but also to unrealized receivables, fees, and other property.

§ 6.133 Tax Issues for the Seller—Stock Sale—Mergers, Consolidations and Exchanges

Because a seller will usually have an income tax gain upon the sale of his business, a merger, consolidation or exchange, if acceptable to the parties, is normally beneficial to the seller from a tax standpoint. Generally, in a merger, consolidation or exchange, the seller receives asset or securities (usually stock) of the buyer in exchange for the seller's business or business assets. Under the I.R.C., the seller's gain (and loss) from the transaction is deferred[1] until the securities are later sold by the seller.[2]

Mergers, consolidations and exchanges are generally referred to as reorganizations. I.R.C. § 368(a) lists seven qualifying categories of reorganizations. The reorganization, to assure tax deferred treatment, must fall within one of the seven categories. The seven categories (often referenced by their designating capital letter) can be summarized as follows:

- A. A statutory merger or consolidation (in accordance with the New York State Business Corporation Law);

- B. An acquisition by one corporation, in exchange solely for all or part of its voting stock, of controlling stock of another corporation;

---

2. PRACTICE POINTER: The taxpayer's goal is to receive favorable long term capital gain treatment.

2. CAVEAT: An exchange also defers recognition of a loss. For this reason it is not desirable if the seller is selling at a loss.

§ 6.133
1. I.R.C. §§ 354, 355, 361, 368.

C. An acquisition by one corporation, in exchange solely for all or part of its voting stock or that of a corporation which controls it, of substantially all of the properties of another corporation;

D. The transfer by a corporation of all or part of its assets to another corporation if immediately after the transfer the transferor, or one or more of its shareholders or any combination thereof, is in control of the corporation to which the assets are transferred;

E. A recapitalization (change of stock structure);

F. A mere change in identity, form, or place of organization, however effected; and

G. A bankruptcy reorganization.

In addition to the reorganization provisions of I.R.C. § 368, a tax deferred exchange of assets may be available. The assets must be held for productive use in a trade or business or for investment, and they must be exchanged solely for property of like-kind either for productive use in a trade or business or for investment.

The "like-kind" definition is liberal for real property. Hence, a farm can be exchanged for a rental apartment, a condominium for vacant land, or a co-op interest for a condominium. One cannot exchange real estate located in the United States for foreign real estate.

The rules under I.R.C. § 1031 applicable to personal property are more stringent. The assets exchanged must all come under the same Internal Revenue Service General Business Asset Classification to defer taxation.

Most businesses have a combination of personal property and real property. Due to the more stringent requirements imposed on the exchange of personal property, like-kind exchanges are seldom used in business transactions.

Library References:

West's Key No. Digests, Internal Revenue ⇐3660–3686.

§ 6.134 Structuring the Seller's Transaction—General Overview

Unless the seller has special needs or considerations, the structure of the transaction is usually driven by three main issues:

1. Business considerations and economics;
2. Protection for the seller; and
3. Taxes.

Business considerations (and negotiations with the buyer) will often dictate if the transaction is structured as a sale, the type of sale (*e.g.*, an asset purchase, a stock purchase), or an exchange. Economics will also dictate the type and method of payment.

Payment protection for the seller is provided by security agreements, mortgages, stock pledges and seats on the buyer's board of directors along with affirmative and negative covenants in the seller's favor.[1]

Tax considerations are important to both parties, but especially the seller. Depending on the seller's gain or loss, and the structure of the transaction, the seller may have a large tax liability payable in the near future.

The seller prefers to receive long term capital gain tax treatment, which is generally associated with a stock or entity sale.[2]

§ 6.135 Structuring the Seller's Transaction—Purchase Price and Payment Terms

Sellers seldom give much thought to the value of their businesses. One of the most important, if not the most important items in any transaction is the price. The seller should retain the services of a business appraiser, a business broker or a consultant in the industry familiar with the value of similar business. There are many methods of valuation.[1] The type of business will dictate the appropriate valuation method.

Cash is king, hence the preferred method of payment is a lump sum payment in cash; but financing is often provided by the seller.[2] An exchange of stock or securities in small business purchases is not common.

If the seller is receiving part of the purchase price in installments over two or more years, he may elect installment sale tax treatment.[3]

In some transactions, payment of the purchase price is made in the form of product or services. This is especially so when the buyer is a supplier or service provider of the seller and only a portion of the seller's business is sold.

§ 6.136 Structuring the Seller's Transaction—Security to Seller

If the seller is not receiving the full sale price in a lump sum payment of cash, the seller should require protection to assure that

§ 6.134

1. Affirmation covenants require the buyer to act (*e.g.*, the buyer must supply financial information to the seller at regular intervals). Negative covenants prohibit certain actions (*e.g.*, the compensation of buyer's officers and owners may be capped).

2. See *supra*, §§ 6.117, 6.120, 6.125, 6.126.

§ 6.135

1. See *supra*, § 6.29.

2. **PRACTICE POINTER:** Installment sale tax treatment allows the seller to receive purchase payments over a period of years and report the gain on the sale as the payments are received. See I.R.C. § 453.

3. See *supra*, note 2.

future payments are made by the buyer. This protection typically takes the form of a security agreement with perfected security interests in all of the personal assets of the business (and the proceeds therefrom), and a first mortgage lien against all real estate owned by the business. In addition, it is common for the seller to request personal guarantees from the buyer and the buyer's spouse, and at times, the posting of additional collateral over and above the business assets. The additional collateral may take the form of pledged bank accounts or securities, or mortgages against other real property of the buyer. The buyer may also be required to maintain a specified net worth[1] and provide an opinion from his independent certified public accountant that the net worth statement is accurate and complete. Although the net worth statement may indirectly limit the indebtedness and activities of the business, the seller (especially in a stock purchase transaction) may desire to limit the amount of indebtedness incurred by the business entity, limit investments, dividends, or distributions to shareholders and the compensation and perks for officers and owners. In addition, the seller may demand as part of his security a seat on the board of directors of the buyer's corporation. As further security, the seller often requires the buyer to pledge the stock or other ownership certificates of the business entity to the seller.[2]

In a small business, protection against the loss of assets and key personnel may be vital to securing the seller's payments. To protect the collateral, the seller, and the assets of the business, casualty and liability insurance coverage is often required. To protect the seller if a key management person should die, key man insurance may also be obtained.[3]

Library References:

West's Key No. Digests, Secured Transactions ⚖︎41–51.

§ 6.137 Structuring the Seller's Transaction—Notes

If the seller is financing all or a portion of the purchase price, the amount owed is normally evidenced by promissory notes. The promissory notes should be secured by all of the business assets and any other

---

§ 6.136

1. CAVEAT: The agreement should define how net worth is to be calculated and the seller should ensure that the net worth calculation includes all items for which the buyer may be contingently liable, such as guarantees.

2. PRACTICE POINTER: Unless there is a default, the buyer usually retains all voting and other rights pertaining to the stock or other ownership interests, except the right to sell or incumber the interests.

3. CAVEAT: Unless the seller has an insurable interest in the life of the insured (key man *e.g.*, financing for a sole proprietorship), the key man insurance must be purchased and owned by the business entity. The seller can be named as the beneficiary of the policy and it should be assigned to the seller. Lapse of the policy should be

security provided by the buyer.[1] Any default under the purchase and sale agreement or security agreement is usually a default under the promissory note (this is referred to as cross defaults).

In addition, the note usually contains an acceleration clause in the event of a default. The promissory notes should also be negotiable (that is, not tied to the agreement or any set-off provisions which would impair the negotiability) and, at times, issued in series.[2] The notes may also be guaranteed by the buyer or his corporation as well as the buyer's spouse or other parties to add strength to the Promissory Note.[3]

Library References:
West's Key No. Digests, Bills and Notes ⚯1–115.

§ 6.138 Structuring the Seller's Transaction—Escrow Arrangements

Escrow arrangements are usually for the protection of the buyer, not the seller. They are often used to provide a fund for adjustments if expectations are not met or representations by the seller prove to be inaccurate. If the escrow arrangement is used properly and reasonably funded, it is difficult for the seller to oppose it without losing credibility.

To the fullest extent possible, the seller's attorney should seek to specifically limit the escrow arrangement to the specific contract provision in issue. The maximum potential monetary adjustment should also be estimated and the seller should oppose amounts in excess of the estimate.

An escrow arrangement may be advantageous when the seller is only selling a portion of his business and is concerned about negative inferences from complying with the Uniform Commercial Code bulk sale provisions. The public often perceives these notices as a "going out of business" announcement which may be detrimental to a seller. When the buyer is protected with an escrow arrangement, he is often willing to waive the Uniform Commercial Code bulk sale notices.[1] Also, to avoid delaying the transaction in order to comply with the New York State Sales Tax bulk sale requirements[2] escrow arrangements are often used.

an event of default in the purchase and sale agreement and the promissory note.

§ 6.137
1. See supra, § 6.136.
2. PRACTICE POINTER: If the amount financed is evidenced by a series of relatively small denomination promissory notes, some maturing each month, but each accelerated in the event of a default, the seller is enabled to sell (i.e. discount) some of the notes without selling the entire amount.

3. PRACTICE POINTER: The guarantee should be one of payment and not just collection. This allows the seller to seek payment from the buyer and/or the guarantors, without first pursuing the buyer.

§ 6.138
1. PRACTICE POINTER: The seller often wishes to waive compliance with the notice requirements of the Uniform Commercial Code bulk sale provision. See supra, § 6.65.
2. Tax Law § 1141.

Ch. 6 **IDENTIFICATION OF THE PARTIES** **§ 6.140**

The seller should strive to limit the escrow arrangement only to the sales tax liability of the seller and fund it with an amount not exceeding a realistic estimate of the liability.[3]

The escrow agreement should clearly state when and how payment of these escrow funds by the escrow agent will be made. It should also release the escrow agent upon fulfillment of his duties or at the end of a stated time period.[4] The escrow agent should always be an independent person, and many times is a law firm involved in the transaction.[5]

§ 6.139 Drafting the Seller's Asset Sale Agreement

Sections 6.140 to 6.162, *infra*, contain discussions of the various provisions found in a standard Asset Purchase and Sale Agreement. Included in the discussions are pointers and guidelines as to positions normally taken by seller. References in the following sections are to the sample Asset Purchase and Sale Agreement which appears at the end of the chapter.[1]

Library References:

West's Key No. Digests, Sales ⚖1–53(3).

§ 6.140 Drafting the Seller's Asset Sale Agreement— Identification of the Parties

The initial paragraph of the asset sale agreement which identifies the parties to the agreement should establish the following:

- The name and address of each of the parties;
- The business or legal description of each entity, such as "a New York Business Corporation" or "a Vermont Corporation authorized to do business in New York" or "a Partnership;"
- The position of each party and the term to which such party is referred in the agreement, such as "Seller," "Buyer," "Escrow

---

3. PRACTICE POINTER: Here the seller is at a negotiating disadvantage because the bulk sale provisions prohibit the buyer from transferring any funds or any other consideration to the seller if the New York State Department of Taxation and Finance notifies the buyer of a possible claim for taxes due. The Department then has 90 days to determine the amount of tax due, if any. *See supra*, § 6.100.

4. PRACTICE POINTER: If the amount is significant or the period of time lengthy, an interest bearing investment should be used. Any escrow fund should be titled in the name of the escrow agent as agent for (usually) the seller, using the seller's tax identification number. The signatory on the account should be the escrow agent and all statements should be mailed to the escrow agent.

5. CAVEAT: If an attorney is acting as escrow agent and a dispute arises between the parties involving the escrow arrangement, the attorney and his firm may have a conflict in representing their client. At the very least, the escrow agent must step down. The escrow arrangement should always name an alternate escrow agent.

§ 6.139

1. *See infra*, § 6.187.

§ 6.140 BUYING & SELLING A SMALL BUSINESS Ch. 6

Agent," "Guarantor," "Sole Shareholder";[1] and

- If a party is a business entity, the location of the main office of such entity.

Library References:

West's Key No. Digests, Sales ⚖15, 28.

§ 6.141 Drafting the Seller's Asset Sale Agreement—Recitals

The "Recitals" section of the asset sale agreement will establish the background of the transaction and the intent of the parties as to the transaction. The recitals may also set forth important information which may not otherwise appear in the text of the agreement, such as the fact that a party conducts business under another name, or that a specific relationship exists between the parties to the agreement, or that there is a specific purpose underlying the business transaction being entered into. While the recitals are not technically part of the operative agreement, the information contained in the recitals can be critical in case of a later contract dispute.[1]

Library References:

West's Key No. Digests, Sales ⚖28.

§ 6.142 Drafting the Seller's Asset Sale Agreement—Assets and Property to Be Conveyed

Every asset sale agreement must contain the covenant of the seller to sell and the covenant of the buyer to purchase the assets of the business as well as a description of the assets being sold. The description may be a general description contained in the body of the contract such as:

"all of the inventory, furniture, fixtures and equipment contained in the premises and identified and agreed to in writing by the parties as of the close of business on (date),"

or, the assets may be specifically identified in a schedule or schedules attached to and made a part of the agreement. Classes of assets generally include the following:

- Land, buildings and improvements;
- Machinery, furniture, fixtures and equipment;

---

§ 6.140

1. **PRACTICE POINTER:** When the buyer and/or seller are corporations, the shareholders themselves should be made parties to the agreement, so that the obligations to be undertaken by the corporations become binding on and guaranteed by the individual shareholders.

§ 6.141

1. Recitals may be incorporated into and made a part of the operative agreement, if the drafter so chooses.

780

- Inventory;[1]
- Transportation equipment, vehicles;
- Raw materials, works in process, supplies;
- Corporate and trade names;
- Formulas, trade secrets, patents, patent applications, copyrights;
- Manuals, catalogues, sales and advertising materials;
- Customer lists, supplier lists;
- Purchase orders, sales agreements and commitments;
- Rights of seller under any licensing, franchise or other agreements; and
- Goodwill.

If the assets to be transferred are subject to liabilities, then the liabilities to be assumed by the buyer as well as the liens associated with them should be specifically identified. In any event, there should be an accurate and complete description of all assets to be transferred, and of the liabilities to be assumed and not assumed.

This section of the agreement should further specify when and where the assets are to be delivered and the legal documents which will be required to effect the transfer of title, such as bills of sale, deeds, assignments of leases and similar instruments.[2] It is advisable to append to the agreement copies of all assignments of leases and assumption agreements which will be executed and delivered at closing.

If there will be any costs involved relative to the transfer of assets, such as fees for the taking of inventory, delivery charges or filing or recording fees, the same should be identified and appropriated to the proper parties in this section of the agreement.

Library References:
West's Key No. Digests, Sales ⚖=28, 67.

§ 6.143 Drafting the Seller's Asset Sale Agreement—Assets Retained by Seller

There should be an accurate and complete description of assets to be retained by seller so that no controversy as to this issue arises at closing or at a later date. Generally, seller will retain all cash, bids or other deposits paid by seller for services or contract awards, advances paid to employees, prepaid expenses and most importantly, seller's corporate minute books, seal, tax returns and insurance contracts. Many times

§ 6.142

1. *See supra,* § 6.33 for suggested contract provisions relating to inventory.
2. In the alternative, a provision for the delivery of assets and legal documents effecting transfer of title to seller may be included in the "Closing" section of the agreement. *See infra,* § 6.145.

seller will also choose to retain accounts receivable arising prior to closing.[1]

Library References:

West's Key No. Digests, Sales ⚖67.

§ 6.144 Drafting the Seller's Asset Sale Agreement—Sale Price and Method of Payment

This section of the asset sale agreement will describe the sale price and its method of allocation, how the sale price will be paid and such other matters as debt assumption and securitization, if applicable.

Sale Price. The sale price need not be an identified dollar amount, especially where there may be contingencies as to the price to be paid. In such event the agreement will provide for part of the sale price to be ascertained at a later date based on a fixed formula or other identified method to be used which has been agreed upon by the parties at the time of negotiation of the sale price. Any provisions for adjustments[1] to the sale price to which the parties have agreed will also appear in this section of the asset sale agreement.

It is generally advisable for the parties to agree as to allocation for IRS purposes and to state the allocations in the agreement. The allocations are important to the seller because the higher the allocation to capital assets, the greater the tax advantage to the seller.[2] While the seller will seek a higher allocation to capital assets, the buyer will want to have a higher allocation to items that can be expensed, depreciable property and amortizable intangibles. The agreement should contain a provision stating that neither the buyer nor the seller will take a position in any income tax return or in any judicial proceeding that is inconsistent with the allocation in the agreement.[3]

Manner of Payment. The manner of payment of the sale price should be described with specificity. If the sale price in whole or in part is to be paid by the buyer in installments, the seller should require the buyer to furnish security in the form of mortgages or other liens on the transferred assets, or in the form of letters of credit, pledges of stock, or insurance on the assets transferred or on the life of the buyer. In

---

§ 6.143

1. For suggested language from a sample agreement, *see infra*, § 6.187, Section 2.

§ 6.144

1. Adjustments are normally made for items such as insurance premiums, rents, deposits with utility companies, payroll, payroll taxes, inventory, etc.

2. Gain on the sale of capital assets is taxed at capital gains tax rates.

3. While the IRS is not bound to the parties' allocations, it will generally follow them unless the parties are in conflict.

PRACTICE POINTER: Seller should add to this part of the Agreement a provision requiring buyer to indemnify seller for any costs assessed against seller by the IRS in the event that buyer fails to abide by the agreed upon allocations.

Ch. 6   WARRANTIES AND COVENANTS OF BUYER   § 6.146

addition, the seller should require that the buyer personally guarantee the payment of the sale price.[4]

Whatever the form of security required, it should also be described with specificity in this section of the agreement, and copies of all such security agreements, financing statements, notes, mortgages, and other security instruments to be signed by the buyer (and its guarantors) should be attached to, and made a part of, the agreement.

Promissory Notes of Buyer. Copies of any promissory notes to be endorsed by the buyer at closing should be appended to the asset sale agreement. The agreement should describe the type of note to be signed by the buyer as well as material provisions of such note, including the amount of the note, whether it is to be negotiable or non-negotiable, the term and interest rate of the note and other important considerations such as acceleration,[5] pre-payment and presentment (or waiver thereof).

Library References:
West's Key No. Digests, Sales ⟐74.

§ 6.145   Drafting the Seller's Asset Sale Agreement—Closing

The asset sale agreement should identify the date, place and time of closing. The date need not be a fixed date but may be conditioned on the happening of certain events, for example:

"Closing shall occur six weeks from the date of the last to occur of the contingencies identified in sections _____ of the agreement."

This section of the agreement may also contain provisions as to the manner of payment of the sale price, the property, documents and other instruments to be delivered at closing, and such other events as may be expected to occur at closing.

Library References:
West's Key No. Digests, Sales ⟐135–196.

§ 6.146   Drafting the Seller's Asset Sale Agreement—Representations, Warranties and Covenants of Buyer

In the asset sale agreement, the representations, warranties and covenants of the buyer will not be as comprehensive as the representations of the seller.

---

4. PRACTICE POINTER: If the buyer is a corporation, seller should require that all shareholders jointly and severally guarantee payment of the purchase price.

5. PRACTICE POINTER: As discussed earlier, the promissory note of buyer should contain a provision for acceleration in the event of any default under the terms of the agreement. *See supra,* § 6.137. Seller should also make sure that the note contains a provision for the payment of attorney's fees in the event that buyer defaults.

§ 6.146 BUYING & SELLING A SMALL BUSINESS Ch. 6

The seller will generally require that the buyer's representations include the following:

- That the buyer is duly incorporated, validly existing, in good standing and qualified to do business;
- That the buyer possesses the corporate power necessary to own the assets and property and to carry on business;
- That the buyer possesses the requisite authority to enter into the asset sale agreement and to perform in accordance with its terms; and
- That no broker brought about this transaction (or, in the alternative, that the buyer will indemnify and hold the seller harmless from any claim for brokerage commissions).

In the event that the sale price is to be paid by the buyer in installments, whether or not evidenced by the buyer's promissory note, the seller should require the following representations and warranties as to the financial condition of the buyer and of the guarantors of the buyer's obligations:

- That the buyer has delivered to the seller the following financial statements, which are true and complete and accurately represent the financial condition of the buyer: (a) balance sheets; (b) statement of profits and losses; and (c) tax returns;
- That except to the extent reflected in the balance sheet, dated ___, there are no liabilities of any nature and the buyer represents that it does not know or have reason to know of any liability of any nature not fully reflected in the balance sheet;
- That since the dates of the balance sheet and tax returns provided to the buyer, there has not been any material change in the buyer's assets, liabilities or financial condition;
- That the buyer has no absolute or contingent liabilities which are not shown in its financial statements;
- That the amounts set up as provision for payment of taxes on the buyer's financial statements are sufficient for payment of all accrued and unpaid taxes of the buyer;
- That the buyer will maintain its net worth of $___ during the period that any notes or other obligations to the seller are outstanding;
- That the buyer will acquire insurance policies on the business and assets transferred to the buyer in an amount equal to ___ of the outstanding balance of the notes or obligations payable to seller and that such policies shall name seller as a co-insured or named insured until such obligations are paid, and that buyer will submit proof of such coverage from time to time upon seller's request; or

Ch. 6 WARRANTIES AND COVENANTS OF SELLER § 6.147

- That the buyer will assign to the seller the policy of insurance on the buyer's life owned by him in the amount of $___, and that the buyer will pay all premiums when due; and
- That there is no litigation pending or threatened against the buyer that its insurance will not cover.

In addition, in the event that the buyer has assumed some or all of the liabilities of the seller in the transaction, the seller should require that the buyer represent and warrant that it will pay all such liabilities and that it will remain solvent until such liabilities are paid.

Another representation which the seller might wish to obtain from the buyer may be the following:

- That the buyer acknowledges that the seller has made no representation to the buyer as to the gross income or profitability of the seller's business.

§ 6.147 Drafting the Seller's Asset Sale Agreement—Representations, Warranties and Covenants of Seller

The representations and warranties of the seller constitute one of the most important sections of the asset sale agreement from the point of view of the buyer. The seller's representations must be carefully drafted by counsel. A material misstatement of any of the seller's representations, or a breach by the seller of any of the warranties or covenants contained in this section, will provide cause for the buyer to avoid or rescind the agreement, or to seek indemnification from the seller in the event that the buyer suffers any loss or injury as a result of such misstatement or breach.

The representations and warranties generally mirror the due diligence investigation performed by the buyer. When negotiating the terms of the Agreement, the buyer's counsel will normally attempt to have the seller's representations drafted in such a way as to cover issues which the buyer was unable to discover during its investigations. The buyer will also draft the seller's representations in the absolute, that is, without qualification. For example, the buyer might request that the seller warrant:

"That all equipment transferred hereunder is in excellent condition and working order, capable of meeting highest industry standards."

The seller, on the other hand, would normally prefer to qualify,[1] or otherwise limit, its representations. The seller might represent:

---

§ 6.147

1. The seller qualifies a representation by stating that it is "to the best of seller's knowledge."

"That the equipment transferred hereunder is, to the best of seller's knowledge, in reasonable working order and sufficient for the operations of the business in its current state."

or

"That buyer has inspected the equipment to be transferred hereunder by seller and that buyer agrees to accept transfer of the same in its present condition ("as is") subject to normal wear and tear to the date of closing."

The representations, warranties and covenants of the seller will usually include the following:[2]

- That the seller is duly incorporated, validly existing, in good standing and qualified to do business;
- That the seller has no affiliations, subsidiaries or other business interests;
- That the seller possesses the requisite authority to enter into the asset sale agreement and to perform in accordance with its terms;
- That, to the best of the seller's knowledge, there are no conflicts between the asset sale agreement and other agreements of the seller;
- That, to the best of the seller's knowledge, there are no conflicts of interests between the seller and any third party;
- That the seller possesses the corporate power necessary to own the assets and property and to carry on business;
- That, to the best of the seller's knowledge, the seller has good and marketable title to the assets and the right to transfer assets free and clear of encumbrances;
- That, to the best of the seller's knowledge, there exist no service agreements, maintenance agreements, warranties or other obligations outstanding on the seller's products, except as set forth;
- That, to the best of the seller's knowledge, the assets are in compliance with all federal, state and local laws, rules and regulations;
- That there are no licenses or leases in effect concerning the assets except those specified;
- That, to the best of the seller's knowledge, the seller has good and marketable title to the real estate;

---

2. The representations and warranties which appear in this section are for illustrative purposes only and are not comprehensive in scope. Counsel is advised to carefully draft each representation in accordance with the circumstances of the transaction.

- That, to the best of the seller's knowledge, there are no mechanics or materialmen liens or bases for such liens on the real estate transferred;
- That the seller has delivered to the buyer the following financial statements, which, to the best of the seller's knowledge, are true and complete and accurately represent the financial condition of the seller: (a) balance sheets; (b) statement of profits and losses; and (c) tax returns;
- That except to the extent reflected in the balance sheet, dated ___, there are no liabilities of any nature and the seller represents that it does not know or have reason to know of any liability of any nature not fully reflected in the balance sheet;
- That since the dates of the balance sheet and tax returns provided to the buyer, to the best of the seller's knowledge, there has not been: (a) any change in assets, liabilities, financial condition of the seller's business; (b) any damage, loss, or destruction to the assets of the business not covered by insurance; (c) any sales other than in the regular course of business; (d) any pending or threatened litigation; (e) any labor union organizing activity or actual or threatened employee strikes; (f) any institution or settlement of any litigation related to the seller or its business; (g) any failure to replace inventory and supplies; or (h) any failure to pay any debt when it has come due;
- That, to the best of the seller's knowledge, the seller has filed all required tax returns;
- That the seller has delivered to the buyer a true and complete list of all accounts receivable as of ___, as reflected in the balance sheet, and that if, following closing, any such accounts remaining unpaid are not paid in full on demand when due, then the seller shall pay the same upon demand of the buyer (against delivery by the buyer of an assignment of such defaulted accounts);
- That the inventory is merchantable and in good condition;
- That the seller has no notice or knowledge of violation by the seller of any federal, state and local laws, rules and regulations;
- That, to the best of the seller's knowledge, the seller possesses all necessary licenses, permits and consents required to carry on business;
- That the seller has delivered to the buyer an accurate list of all contracts, oral and written, to which the seller is a party, such contracts being as follows: (a) employment contracts; (b) contracts with salespersons and distributors; (c) pension, benefit and related agreements; (d) agreements with suppliers, consultants, support services, providers and the like; (e) customer agreements, unfilled purchase orders, sales contracts; (f) customer lists; (g) franchise

§ 6.147 BUYING & SELLING A SMALL BUSINESS Ch. 6

agreements, dealer and consignment agreements, research and development contracts; (h) lines of credit and loans; and (i) contracts with labor organizations, all of which have been entered into in the ordinary course of business;

- That, to the best of the seller's knowledge, the seller has complied with material provisions of all contracts, leases, licenses and other agreements, and that the same are valid and in good standing;
- That all contracts, leases, licenses and other agreements are assignable, except as indicated, and that the seller will utilize its best efforts to provide the buyer with consents to such assignments at closing;
- That there are no collective bargaining agreements in effect and that the seller has no knowledge of any labor union organizing activity or any strikes or threatened strikes;
- That, to the best of the seller's knowledge, the seller has delivered to the buyer an accurate list of all insurance policies including any pending claims;
- That the seller will maintain all such insurance until closing or until such time as the assets are transferred to the buyer;
- That, to the best of the seller's knowledge, there are no environmental hazards or conditions affecting the assets;
- That there is no litigation pending, and to the best of the seller's knowledge, there is no litigation threatened against or relating to the seller, its properties or business;
- That the seller has delivered to the buyer an accurate list of all patents, patent applications, trademarks, trade names, and copyrights, presently held by the seller, all of which are, to the best of the seller's knowledge, valid and in good standing;
- That from the date of execution of the asset sale agreement until the time of closing there will be no new leases, tenancies or contracts affecting the assets without prior written approval of the buyer;
- That the seller will perform such repairs as may be agreed upon between the buyer and seller on the assets and real property prior to closing;
- That the seller will pay vacation time and other employee benefits which have accrued up to and including closing date;
- That no broker hired by the seller brought about this transaction (or, in the alternative: that the agreement entered into between the seller and its broker has been provided to the buyer and that the seller will indemnify and hold the buyer harmless from any claim for commissions by such broker to the extent that the broker did not perform services for the buyer);

- That, to the best of the seller's knowledge, and except for facts unable to be discovered by the seller, no representation, warranty or covenant of the seller in the agreement, or in any writing furnished to the buyer, contains any untrue statement of fact or failure to state any material fact;
- That the seller has disclosed all material adverse facts known to the seller; and
- That the representations, warranties and covenants of the seller shall be true at the time of closing as though such representations and warranties were made at such time.

In the event that closing is to occur after the date of the execution of the asset sale agreement by the parties, the buyer will normally request that the seller continue to operate the business in the ordinary course. To that end, the buyer will probably require "pre-closing" covenants from the seller. Pre-closing covenants of the seller normally include the following:

- That, since the date of (execution of the asset sale agreement), the seller has operated the business only in the ordinary course and, to the best of the seller's knowledge, there has not been:
    a. any change in assets, liabilities, or financial condition of the seller's business since the date of such financial statements, tax returns or other documents;
    b. any damage, loss, or destruction to the assets not covered by insurance;
    c. any sales other than in the regular course of business;
    d. any pending or threatened litigation;
    e. any labor union organizing activity or actual or threatened employee strikes;
    f. any institution or settlement of litigation related to the seller or its assets;
    g. any failure to replace inventory and supplies;
    h. any failure to pay any debt which has become due; and
    i. any chemical spills or other environmental conditions affecting the assets.

Library References:
West's Key No. Digests, Sales ⇒246–288.5.

§ 6.148 Drafting the Seller's Asset Sale Agreement—Conduct of Business Prior to Closing

In the event that closing is to occur after the date of the execution of the asset sale agreement by the parties, the agreement will normally contain a provision for the conduct of business by the seller up to the time of closing. The purpose for such a provision is twofold: First, it will assure the buyer that the seller will continue to conduct its business without interruption, and secondly, it will provide the buyer with the affirmation of the seller that during this period, the seller will not transfer assets or do anything outside of the ordinary course of business. In this section of the agreement, the buyer will require the seller to operate in a manner consistent with prior operations. In addition, the buyer will request assurances that the seller will continue to maintain insurance on its assets, that the seller will continue to replace inventory, and that the seller will allow the buyer access to the books, records and operations of the seller during this period.

This section may also provide that the seller, while in continued possession of the business, is to pay for all materials and services pertaining to the operations of the business which have been delivered to the seller prior to closing, and that the buyer is to pay for all such materials and services delivered after closing. Additionally, there may be included a provision concerning accounts receivable to the effect that receivables derived from goods or other business products shipped after closing are to become the property of the buyer, and receivables from goods shipped prior to closing are to be paid to the seller.[1]

Library References:
West's Key No. Digests, Sales ⚖=54–88.

§ 6.149 Drafting the Seller's Asset Sale Agreement—Indemnifications

As discussed earlier, the seller's representations and warranties comprise one of the most important elements of the asset sale agreement.[1] The buyer relies heavily upon these representations in deciding to purchase the assets of the seller's business. The failure or falsity of any of the material representations or warranties of the seller could expose the seller to excessive costs, possible legal action or the termination of the agreement by the buyer.

The buyer's counsel will normally seek broad indemnification from the seller. The indemnifications of the seller usually provide that the seller will indemnify and hold the buyer harmless from all liabilities, losses, costs and expenses, (including legal fees) relative to or arising from:

- Liabilities, obligations and claims against the seller not expressly assumed by the buyer—including any claims for warranty, prod-

§ 6.148

1. For suggested language from a sample agreement, *see infra*, § 6.187, Section 8(b).

§ 6.149

1. *See supra*, § 6.147.

uct liability, or the repair or replacement of products sold by the seller prior to closing; and

- Any claims or costs resulting from a misrepresentation or breach by the seller of the seller's covenants and warranties contained in the asset sale agreement or other documents delivered to the buyer pursuant to the asset sale agreement.

The seller's attorney, in drafting or negotiating such provisions, is advised to limit and restrict the seller's indemnifications as much as possible. Generally, such limitations or restrictions appear in the form of monetary thresholds and/or baskets placed in such provisions. A "threshold" refers generally to a set amount used to cap the liability. For example, the seller might indemnify and hold the buyer harmless from any claims against or costs incurred by the buyer in an amount of up to $10,000.[2] Or, using a basket, which is usually an amount below which no indemnification will be made, the seller will indemnify and hold the buyer harmless from and against any claims, costs or losses, but only if such claims, costs or losses exceed a certain amount. For example:

"The indemnifications hereunder shall be effective only after and to the extent that valid and enforceable claims for indemnification exceed $25,000."

The seller should also consider putting a limit on the period of validity of its representations and warranties, such as:

"The indemnifications hereunder shall expire and be of no further force and effect unless written claim is made by the buyer on or before (a date which is two years from the date of closing)."[3]

As to indemnification from the buyer, the seller will want such coverage to be as broad as possible. The seller will generally require the buyer to indemnify and hold the seller harmless from all liabilities, losses costs and expenses (including legal fees) relative to or arising from:

- Liabilities, obligations and claims against the buyer—including any claims for warranty, product liability, or the repair or replacement of products sold by the buyer subsequent to closing;

- Liabilities, obligations and claims against the seller arising under any leases, contracts, agreements, licenses, permits, etc., which were initiated by the seller but which were assumed by, taken over, or continued by the buyer, or arising in relation to any claims of creditors relative to liabilities expressly assumed by the buyer under the terms of the agreement; and

- Any claims or costs resulting from a misrepresentation or breach by the buyer of its covenants and warranties contained in the

---

2. For suggested language from a sample agreement, see infra, § 6.188, Section 9.01.

3. For suggested language from a sample agreement, see infra, § 6.188, Section 9.01.

§ 6.149   BUYING & SELLING A SMALL BUSINESS   Ch. 6

asset sale agreement or other documents delivered to the seller pursuant to the asset sale agreement.

Library References:

West's Key No. Digests, Indemnity ⚖=8(3).

§ 6.150 Drafting the Seller's Asset Sale Agreement—Matters Respecting Real Property

If real estate is one of the assets sold, there are additional considerations.[1] Some of the usual considerations for the seller are as follows:

1. A description sufficient to identify the real property sold (preferably a legal description) must be part of the agreement. The legal description may be stated in the operative agreement or included in an attached schedule.[2]

2. The agreement should state that the seller will convey the real property to the buyer on the closing date to specifically referenced items such as:

   a) Real property taxes, water charges and sewer rents, if any, which are a lien on the real property at the closing date subject to adjustment between the buyer and seller on the closing date;

   b) Any state of facts a current survey may show, provided that it does not render title unmarketable, and provided further that all buildings, structures and other improvements are located totally within the boundaries of real property;

   c) Zoning laws, regulations, building restrictions and ordinances of the local municipality and/or other governmental authorities, agencies, boards, departments or instrumentalities having jurisdiction over the real property, provided that none of the regulations, restrictions or ordinances renders the title unmarketable;

   d) Other continuing liens or encumbrances disclosed in the agreement.

3. A clause allowing the seller to cure any defects or objections to title that come to the buyer's attention which he is unwilling to waive. This clause should provide the seller with a reasonable period of time to cure the defect or objection; and it should further provide that if the seller fails to do so within the time provided (or cannot do so), the buyer has the option of waiving the defect, and accepting title with a deduction from the purchase price to be agreed upon by the parties. If the parties cannot agree upon the amount of the price reduction, or if this is unacceptable to the buyer, the agreement should allow either party to cancel the agreement without further liability to the other, except for the return of any deposits.

§ 6.150

1. For more discussion of these issues see Chapter 12, "Purchase and Sale of Real Estate," supra.

2. **PRACTICE POINTER:** Often, a copy of the deed is attached as a schedule.

4. The agreement should provide that the seller may pay and discharge all liens, defects or objections to title on the closing date and allow the seller to use the cash portion of the purchase price to do so.

5. The agreement should allow the seller to request the buyer to make payment of all funds by certified check, and it should designate who will pay the cost for title abstracting, title insurance fees, fees to record documents and the documentary stamps that must be affixed to the deed.[3]

6. All items to be apportioned between the seller and the buyer should be set forth in the agreement and apportioned as of midnight of the day immediately preceding the closing. The usual items apportioned are real property and school taxes, water and sewer charges, heating fuel and, if appropriate, electricity, gas, propane and telephone services, among others.[4]

7. The risk of loss for damage to the premises after execution of the contract, but prior to the closing date, should be specifically set forth. This clause should state the following:

    a. Whether insurance proceeds will be paid to the buyer or seller;

    b. Whether the buyer is to receive a credit against the price if the insurance proceeds are insufficient to restore the damaged property;

    c. Whether the buyer can terminate the agreement in the event of substantial damage; and

    d. The controlling effect, unless waived, of New York State General Obligations Law Section 5–1311.[5]

§ 6.151 Drafting the Seller's Asset Sale Agreement—Notice to Customers and Suppliers

Over time, a seller develops relationships with customers and suppliers. To avoid confusion and minimize the disruption of an ownership

---

3. PRACTICE POINTER: The usual practice (which can be changed by agreement) is that the documentary stamps are paid by the seller, as well as the fee to record the real property transfer gains tax affidavit. The recording fees for the deed and other documents, as well as the mortgage tax, if any, abstracting costs, title insurance costs and the fee to record the equalization and assessment form are usually paid by the purchaser. *See* Chapter 12 "Purchase and Sale of Real Estate," *infra*.

4. PRACTICE POINTER: Except for the apportionment of property and school taxes, many of the other items are metered or can be measured by the service provider. Meter readings and measurements should be taken on the date of closing or as close thereto as practicable.

5. General Obligations Law § 5–1311 (Uniform Vender and Purchaser Risk Act). This statute is applicable "[w]hen neither the legal title nor the possession of the subject matter of the contract has been transferred to the purchaser." General Obligations Law § 5–1311(1)(a).

change, the agreement should require a notice to be sent to the business's customers and suppliers announcing the change in ownership.[1] Appropriately worded, this can be a very positive introduction for the buyer. The notice should be prepared prior to the closing and, ideally, it should be sent to coincide with the takeover of the business by the buyer. Although this notice is usually viewed as a benefit to the buyer, it can also be advantageous to the seller.[2]

Library References:

West's Key No. Digests, Sales ⚖219–233.

§ 6.152 Drafting the Seller's Asset Sale Agreement—Covenant Not to Compete and Consulting Agreements

The buyer of a business normally wants assurances from the seller and his key personnel (particularly those not retained in the buyer's employ) that they will not compete with the buyer. The covenant not to compete may be part of the purchase and sale agreement, or it may be a separate agreement. The restrictions in the covenant not to compete must be reasonable regarding duration of time and geographic location, and the restrictions should be only so broad as to protect the legitimate business interests of the buyer in the geographical area of the business and that of the seller's goodwill.

Restrictive covenants to protect the goodwill of a purchased business do not violate the anti-trust laws. Reasonable restrictive covenants are enforceable (even though they curtail competition) because they are conducive to the overall freedom of trade and the seller's right to sell his business. They will be enforceable as long as they are not injurious to the public. In addition, restrictive covenants must be ancillary to the sale of a business, otherwise they are a restriction of trade and unenforceable.

The duration of most covenants not to compete is relatively short, usually 3–5 years, but longer covenants are appropriate if the circumstances justify it. Where the protected geographic area is large, skillful drafting can limit the prohibited activities within the protected area and thereby reduce the impact of the covenant to the seller.

§ 6.151

1. PRACTICE POINTER: The Notice is usually prepared for the seller's signature, and at a minimum introduces the buyer and informs the customers and suppliers of the change of ownership. Where appropriate, the notice should also indicate that the same quality service or product will be provided by the buyer and that the past relationships and practices with the suppliers and customers will continue.

2. PRACTICE POINTER: If the seller is providing financing to the buyer, it is in the seller's interest to assure a smooth transition of the business. A notice also helps avoid confusion and the inconvenience of forwarding invoices and payments sent to the wrong parties.

The measure of damages for a breach of the covenant not to compete is lost profits. This is often difficult to prove and there may also be many other intervening factors, such as a general decline in the economy, which can further complicate any litigation. For these reasons, the buyer often seeks to include a liquidated damages provision.

Counsel for the seller should ideally try to eliminate the covenant not to compete, arguing that only the implied-in-law non-compete provisions should apply. If this argument is unsuccessful, the attorney should either draft provisions limiting liquidated damages or propose a specific formula favorable to the seller. Liquidated damages, as opposed to general lost profits, will also limit the buyer's damages. For this reason, the seller should strike any clauses in the agreement providing "other damages" unless this language is specifically defined and limited. Liquidated damages are often computed by reference to a mathematical formula such as the prior 12 month's sales by the business to a customer. They must also be reasonable or they may be held to be a penalty, and hence unenforceable.

Payments for a covenant not to compete may provide tax advantages to the seller. The advantages and disadvantages must be weighed before deleting these provisions.[1]

Some sale transactions provide for the continuing services of the seller after the sale. In such cases, the seller is usually compensated via a consulting agreement.[2]

The consulting agreement must define the type of services to be rendered, the expected number of hours, the location(s) where services will be rendered and the compensation to be paid. It should also allow the seller to provide consulting services to other businesses. However, the non-compete agreement will usually prohibit consulting services to similar businesses in the buyer's protected territory.

Library References:

West's Key No. Digests, Contracts ⚖115.

§ 6.153 Drafting the Seller's Asset Sale Agreement—UCC Bulk Sale Notices or Escrow Agreements in Lieu of UCC Bulk Sale Notices

A Uniform Commercial Code bulk transfer is any transfer in bulk of a major part of the materials, supplies, merchandise or other inventory not in the ordinary course of the transferor's business. The bulk transfer provisions of the UCC generally apply to businesses engaged in the sale

---

§ 6.152

1. *See supra,* § 6.124.
2. **PRACTICE POINTER:** Being paid as a consultant allows the seller to set up his own Schedule C business. In addition to the general business deductions, this may also allow the seller to maintain and deduct the expense of an office in his home.

of merchandise and not services, but it does specifically cover restaurants. The intention of this provision is to protect creditors who rely on the merchandise as security for payment of credit extended to the business.[1] To comply with the UCC Article 6 Bulk Transfer provisions, the following must occur:

1. The buyer must obtain a list of the seller's existing creditors and the property to be transferred. The buyer must preserve this list and allow inspection and copying by creditors for a period of six months following the transfer.[2]

2. The list must be signed and sworn to or affirmed by the seller.[3]

3. A notice must be given to creditors which states that a bulk sale is about to be made, the names and business addresses of the seller and buyer, if all debts of the seller are to be paid in full as they fall due and the address where creditors should send their bills.

4. If the debts of the seller are not to be paid in full, or if the purchaser is uncertain, the notice must also state the following:

   a. The location and general description of the property to be transferred;

   b. An estimate of the seller's debt;

   c. The address where the schedule of property and list of creditors may be inspected;

   d. If the transferee is to pay existing debts, the amount of such debts and to whom owed; and

   e. If the transfer is for new consideration, the amount, time and place of payment.[4]

5. The notice must be delivered personally or sent by registered or certified mail to all creditors on the creditor's list.[5]

6. The notice must be sent to the creditors at least ten days before the buyer takes possession of the goods or pays for them, whichever is sooner.[6]

Since UCC bulk sale notices, at times, are misinterpreted by the public as a "going out of business" announcement, both parties often choose to waive them.[7] When waiving these provisions, most contracts[8]

---

§ 6.153

1. UCC § 6–102.
2. UCC § 6–104.
3. Id.
4. UCC § 6–107.
5. Id.
6. See UCC § 6–111.
7. **PRACTICE POINTER**: If the seller is only selling a portion of the business, it is extremely important that suppliers understand the seller is not "going out of business." The notice should specifically inform the suppliers that the seller is only transferring a portion of the business, that their bills will be paid in full according to the usual billing cycle and that the seller looks forward to continuing his relationship with the suppliers. The UCC bulk sale provisions provide notices to suppliers only, but word of the transaction often filters out to the

protect the buyer with an escrow agreement or a set-off against indebtedness owed to the seller.

The agreement should simply state that the UCC bulk sale statute will be complied with or waived. The set-off and escrow provisions should be restricted to the bulk sale areas of the agreement.[9]

Library References:

West's Key No. Digests, Fraudulent Conveyances ⟐47.

§ 6.154 Drafting the Seller's Asset Sale Agreement—New York State Sales Tax and Bulk Sale Notification

The bulk sale provisions of the New York State Sales Tax Law [1] apply to a sale of business assets. These provisions do not apply to stock (entity) sales. A bulk sale under the sales tax law covers any transfer in bulk outside the ordinary course of business.[2] If the parties do not comply with the provisions of the Tax Law regarding sales tax, the buyer becomes liable for any past unpaid sales tax of the seller up to the amount of the purchase price.[3]

Although the bulk sale provisions mostly impact the buyer, the seller is primarily responsible for collecting sales tax on the sale of assets.[4]

---

general public and to the seller's customers. For this reason, if the seller is only selling a portion of the business, it is usually advantageous for the seller to provide an escrow agreement or some other security to the buyer in lieu of sending out bulk sale notices.

8. *See infra,* § 6.51.

9. CAVEAT: If the transaction includes non-negotiable installment notes, the buyer has a virtually unlimited right of set-off via counterclaim in any enforcement action by the seller.

§ 6.154

1. Tax Law § 1141.

2. PRACTICE POINTER: The Tax Law does not define bulk sale per se. Tax Law § 1141(c) and 20 NYCRR § 537.1(a)(1) describe a bulk sale as the transfer or assignment in bulk of any portion or the whole of business assets. One cannot rely on the UCC definition of "major portion" in determining if a bulk sale has occurred under the Tax Law. The New York State Department of Taxation and Finance takes an aggressive position. If in doubt, assume a bulk sale has occurred. The sales tax bulk sale provisions are separate and distinct from the UCC bulk sale provisions. Where both apply *both* must be complied with.

3. PRACTICE POINTER: The bulk sale provisions are found in Tax Law § 1141(c) and 20 NYCRR Part 537. In essence, notice of the sale and its terms must be given to the Tax Department at least ten days before taking possession or paying for the business assets. Form AU–196.10 is generally used. If, within five days after filing the notice of bulk sale with the Department, the Department notifies the buyer of a possible claim for taxes due, the buyer is prohibited from transferring money or any other consideration to the seller (except amounts in excess of the Department's claim). The Department then has ninety days to determine the amount of the tax obligation, if any, during which period the seller cannot be paid. These provisions only apply to bulk sales by businesses required to collect sales tax. The statute of limitations for a sales tax assessment is three years from the date the sales tax return was filed. Tax Law § 1147(b).

4. PRACTICE POINTER: The sales tax collected on the sale of assets should be reported on the seller's final sales tax re-

797

§ 6.155 Drafting the Seller's Asset Sale Agreement— Nature and Survival of Representations and Warranties

Every asset sale agreement should contain a provision requiring that all representations, warranties, indemnities, covenants and agreements made by the parties survive the closing. The purpose of this provision is to ensure that the material provisions of the asset sale agreement remain enforceable after the transfer of assets has taken place, so that each party may have remedies in the event of breach.[1]

§ 6.156 Drafting the Seller's Asset Sale Agreement— Non-disclosure Provisions

It is in the non-disclosure provisions of the asset sale agreement that the parties covenant to keep confidential all information about each other acquired during the course of the transaction. This representation is especially important to the seller in the event that the transaction is not consummated.[1]

Library References:
West's Key No. Digests, Contracts ⚖118.

§ 6.157 Drafting the Seller's Asset Sale Agreement— Conditions Precedent to Seller's Obligations

In preparing the seller's asset sale agreement, counsel will normally condition the seller's performance upon the happening of certain events and the performance by the buyer of certain material terms of the agreement at or prior to closing. Such conditions should include:[1]

- Performance by the buyer of all obligations specified in the asset sale agreement;
- Accuracy of the covenants, representations and warranties made by the buyer;

turn. If the seller is not obligated to collect sales tax in the course of his business, a sales tax return is nonetheless due on the sale of assets. The seller should file a casual sales tax return to report and pay the sales tax due for the assets sold on Form ST 131.

§ 6.155
1. For suggested language from a sample agreement, *see infra*, 6.187, Section 18.

§ 6.156
1. **PRACTICE POINTER:** Seller should require that buyer take reasonable steps to insure that the confidential information obtained about seller not be disclosed to outside sources and should specifically define the "confidential information" to include such things as customer lists, supplier lists, trade secrets, pricing policy and other information as may be designated by seller.

§ 6.157
1. For suggested language from a sample agreement, *see infra*, § 6.187, Section 17.

- Absence of adverse change in the buyer's financial condition;[2]
- Delivery to the seller of a certificate executed by the buyer or its officers and shareholders certifying the fulfillment of the above conditions; and
- Delivery to the seller by the buyer of all documents required to be delivered under the terms of the asset sale agreement.

Library References:

West's Key No. Digests, Sales ⚖=85.

§ 6.158 Drafting the Seller's Asset Sale Agreement—Conditions Precedent to Buyer's Obligations

Generally, the conditions precedent to the buyer's obligations under the agreement include the following:

- Performance by the seller of all obligations specified in the asset sale agreement;
- Accuracy of the covenants, representations and warranties made by the seller;
- Absence of adverse changes in the financial and other condition of the seller as well as in the business, properties, assets or prospects of the seller;
- Delivery to the buyer of a certificate executed by the seller, or by its officers and shareholders, certifying the fulfillment of the above conditions;
- Delivery to the buyer by the seller of all documents required to be delivered under the terms of the asset sale agreement;
- The buyer's acquisition of regulatory approval;
- The buyer's acquisition of financing;
- Tax rulings, if applicable; and
- Required consents to transfers and assignments.

Library References:

West's Key No. Digests, Sales ⚖=85.

§ 6.159 Drafting the Seller's Asset Sale Agreement—Documents to Be Delivered to Seller at Closing

The documents to be delivered by the buyer to the seller at closing normally include the following:

---

2. Applicable if seller is financing all or part of the purchase price or if payment is being made by buyer in installments.

§ 6.159 BUYING & SELLING A SMALL BUSINESS

- Documents effecting payment of the sale price;
- Certified copies of minutes and the consents of the shareholders and directors of the buyer approving the asset sale agreement and the consummation of the purchase transaction;
- Security agreements, executed mortgages and other security instruments;
- The opinion of the buyer's counsel that the buyer is duly organized, validly existing and in good standing; that the buyer has the corporate power and authority to enter into and perform the asset sale agreement; that the asset sale agreement is a valid and binding obligation of the buyer; and that the execution and delivery of the asset sale agreement and performance by the buyer do not conflict with the buyer's organizing instruments or other contracts or obligations, and are not in violation of any law, rule or regulation;
- Other documents to be delivered to the seller under the terms of the agreement; and
- Such further instruments or documents as may reasonably be required by the seller to effect the provisions contained in the agreement.

Library References:

West's Key No. Digests, Sales ⚖︎135–196.

§ 6.160 Drafting the Seller's Asset Sale Agreement—Documents to Be Delivered to Buyer at Closing

The documents to be delivered by the seller to the buyer at closing normally include the following:

- All documents effecting transfer of title;
- The opinion of the seller's counsel that the seller is duly organized, validly existing and in good standing; that the seller has the corporate power and authority to enter into and perform the asset sale agreement; that the asset sale agreement is a valid and binding obligation of the seller; and that the execution and delivery of the asset sale agreement and performance by the seller do not conflict with the seller's organizing instruments or other contracts or obligations, and are not in violation of any law, rule or regulation;
- Certified copies of minutes and the consents of the shareholders and directors of the seller approving the asset sale agreement and the consummation of the sale transaction;

Ch. 6   GENERAL PROVISIONS   § 6.161

- The certificate of the seller affirming the performance of all conditions precedent to the buyer's obligations;
- Executed non-competition and continuity of business dealings agreements;
- All contracts, licenses, leases and permits pertaining to the seller's assets, including plans and specifications for buildings located on the real property;
- All customer lists and supplier lists;
- A list of accounts receivable;
- All keys to buildings, vehicles and file cabinets;
- Confidentiality agreements and covenants not to compete from departing employees of the seller;
- Written assurances from the seller's broker respecting confidentiality;
- Other documents to be delivered to the buyer under the terms of the agreement; and
- Such further instruments of transfer or other documents as may reasonably be required by the buyer to effect the provisions contained in the agreement.

Library References:

West's Key No. Digests, Sales ⚖︎135–196.

§ 6.161 Drafting the Seller's Asset Sale Agreement—Notices, Severability and Other General Provisions

Notices and other provisions usually included at the end of an agreement are referred to as the "boilerplate." These provisions generally consist of the following:[1]

- Notice procedures,
- A severability clause,
- Governing law,
- A non-waiver provision,
- A savings clause,
- Provisions concerning modifications and changes to the agreement,
- A disclaimer as to captions and headings,

---

§ 6.161

1. For suggested language from a sample agreement as to some of these provisions, see infra, § 6.187, Section 21.

§ 6.161 BUYING & SELLING A SMALL BUSINESS   Ch. 6

- Provisions acknowledging the "binding effect" of the agreement,
- Provisions acknowledging that the agreement constitutes the "entire agreement" of the parties,
- Agreement to execute additional documents and counter parts,
- "Time is of the essence" provisions, and
- Arbitration provisions.

Library References:

West's Key No. Digests, Sales ⚖54–88.

§ 6.162 Drafting the Seller's Asset Sale Agreement—Documents to Be Prepared or Reviewed Prior to Closing

After the asset sale agreement has been executed, the buyer's counsel must either prepare or review, as the case may be, all documents or instruments referred to in the agreement or required under its provisions. Such documents, known as the "collateral documents" may include the following:

- Bills of sale,
- Deeds and related real estate documents,
- Security agreements, promissory notes, and mortgages,
- Escrow agreements,
- Corporate resolutions,
- Assignments of contracts, leases and other interests,
- Motor vehicle, boat and other registrations,
- Equipment lists,
- Inventory descriptions including count and valuation,
- Lists of other assets,
- Legal opinions of counsel,
- New contracts (novations),
- Employment and collective bargaining agreements,
- Lists of all of the seller's other contracts and agreements,
- Certificates respecting name change,
- Certificates of dissolution and/or discontinuance,
- Assumed name certificates,
- Sales tax returns,
- Lists of all insurance policies and pending claims,

- Lists of all patents, patent applications, trademarks, trade names, and copyrights,
- Covenants not to compete, and
- Confidentiality agreements.

Copies of all such collateral documents should be attached to the asset sale agreement and made a part of such agreement.

Library References:

West's Key No. Digests, Sales ⚖135–196.

§ 6.163 Drafting the Seller's Stock Sale Agreement

Sections 6.164 through 6.182, *infra,* contain discussions of the various provisions found in a standard Stock Purchase and Sale Agreement. Included in the discussions are pointers and guidelines as to positions normally taken by the seller. References in the following sections are to the sample Stock Purchase and Sale Agreement at the end of the chapter.[1]

§ 6.164 Drafting the Seller's Stock Sale Agreement— Identification of the Parties

The initial paragraph of the stock sale agreement which identifies the parties to the agreement should recite the following:

- The name and address of each of the parties;
- The business or legal description of each entity, such as "a New York Business Corporation" or "a Vermont Corporation, authorized to do business in New York," or "a Partnership;"
- The position of each party and the term to which such party is referred in the agreement, such as "Seller," "Buyer," "Escrow Agent," "Guarantor," "Sole Shareholder;" and
- If a party is a business entity, the location of the main office of such entity.

In a stock sale transaction, the buyer of the stock will be either a corporation or its individual shareholders, depending upon how the transaction is structured.

In the stock purchase agreement, if the buyer of the shares is the corporation, the shareholders should be made parties to the agreement and should be identified in the agreement as the individuals responsible for the obligations, representations, warranties and covenants and all other performance of the buyer. This may be done in one of two ways: In each undertaking by the buyer, the terms of the agreement should refer

§ 6.163   1. *See infra,* § 6.187.

§ 6.164 BUYING & SELLING A SMALL BUSINESS Ch. 6

to "the buyer and its shareholders, jointly and severally"[1] or, in the alternative, a separate section of the agreement should be drafted to provide that all performance of the buyer is jointly and severally guaranteed by its shareholders.

Library References:
West's Key No. Digests, Corporations ⇌116.

§ 6.165 Drafting the Seller's Stock Sale Agreement—Recitals

The "Recitals" section of the stock sale agreement will establish the background of the transaction and the intent of the parties as to the transaction. The recitals may also set forth important information which may not otherwise appear in the text of the agreement, such as the fact that a party conducts business under another name, or that a specific relationship exists between the parties to the agreement, or that there is a specific purpose underlying the business transaction being entered into. While the recitals are not technically part of the operative agreement, the information contained in the recitals can be critical in case of a later contract dispute.[1]

Library References:
West's Key No. Digests, Corporations ⇌116.

§ 6.166 Drafting the Seller's Stock Sale Agreement—Sale of Shares

Every stock sale agreement will contain the covenant of the seller to sell and the covenant of the buyer to purchase shares.

This section of the agreement will generally specify the number, class and type of shares being transferred and indicate the name of each shareholder and the number of shares owned. The buyer will normally require that at the time of transfer, the shares be free of all liens and encumbrances and that they have the required stock transfer stamps affixed.[1] The buyer will probably also condition its performance on the delivery of all shares of the selling corporation at closing. The seller's attorney should verify that all shareholders of the corporation have

---

§ 6.164

1. For example, "The buyer and each individual shareholder, jointly and severally acknowledge and agree that . . . ," or "The buyer and the sole shareholder, jointly and severally, represent and warrant that . . ."

§ 6.165

1. Recitals may be incorporated into and made a part of the operative agreement if the drafter so chooses.

§ 6.166

1. See supra, § 6.131 concerning New York Stock Transfer Tax and Stock Transfer Stamps.

Ch. 6   SALE PRICE AND METHOD OF PAYMENT   § 6.167

authorized or ratified the sale of shares and that all shareholders are prepared to deliver their shares for transfer.

The procedure for the transfer of shares is generally as follows: (a) the shares to be transferred are endorsed to the buyer; (b) the shares are then surrendered to the corporation, with the transfer to the buyer noted in the books of the corporation; and finally (c) new share certificates are issued in the name of the buyer.

Library References:

West's Key No. Digests, Corporations ⚷116.

§ 6.167   Drafting the Seller's Stock Sale Agreement— Sale Price and Method of Payment

This section of the stock sale agreement will describe the sale price for the shares, how the sale price will be paid and such other matters as securitization, if applicable.

Sale Price. The sale price need not be an identified dollar amount, especially where there may be contingencies as to the price to be paid. In such event, the agreement will provide for part of the sale price to be ascertained at a later date based on a fixed formula or other identified method to be used which has been agreed upon by the parties at the time of negotiation of the sale price. Any provisions for adjustments[1] to the sale price to which the parties have agreed will also appear in this section of the stock sale agreement.

Manner of Payment. The manner of payment of the sale price should be described with specificity. If the sale price in whole or part is to be paid by the buyer in installments, the seller should require that the transferred shares be placed in escrow until full payment is made. In the alternative, the seller may deliver a portion of the shares as each payment is made by the buyer.

Shares Placed in Escrow. In the event that the transferred shares are to be placed in escrow, the agreement should provide that: (a) upon delivery of the buyer's note to the seller, share certificates issued in the name of the buyer will be delivered to the buyer;[2] (b) that the buyer will deliver the share certificates, endorsed in blank, to the escrow agent; and (c) that the escrow agent will hold such shares until the sale price is paid in full or until the event of the buyer's default.

§ 6.167

1. Adjustments are normally made for items such as insurance premiums, rents, deposits with utility companies, payroll, payroll taxes, inventory, etc.

2. The certificates should be delivered to buyer to assure that buyer gets title prior to the delivery of the shares in escrow. Title to securities passes upon delivery of the securities. UCC § 8–301(1). In order for seller to have a valid security interest in the stock, the buyer must have ownership rights in the collateral. See UCC § 9–203(1).

§ 6.167   BUYING & SELLING A SMALL BUSINESS   Ch. 6

Other Security. In addition to the escrow of shares as security for the payment of the sale price, the seller should also require the buyer to furnish security in the form of mortgages or other liens on the transferred assets, or in the form of letters of credit, pledges of stock, or insurance on the assets of the business or on the life of the buyer. The seller should also require that payment be guaranteed by the shareholders of the purchaser. Copies of such security agreements, financing statements, notes, mortgages, and other security instruments to be signed by the buyer (and its guarantors) should be attached to, and made a part of, the agreement.

Promissory Notes of Buyer. Copies of any promissory notes to be endorsed by the buyer at closing should be appended to the stock sale agreement. The agreement should describe the type of note to be signed by the buyer, as well as the material provisions of such note, including the amount of the note, whether it is to be negotiable or non-negotiable, the term and interest rate of the note, and other important considerations such as acceleration,[3] pre-payment and presentment (or waiver thereof).

Library References:
West's Key No. Digests, Corporations ⚖116.

§ 6.168   Drafting the Seller's Stock Sale Agreement—Closing

The stock sale agreement should identify the date, place and time of closing. The date need not be a fixed date but may be conditioned on the happening of certain events, for example:

"Closing shall occur six weeks from the date of the last to occur of the contingencies identified in sections _____ of the agreement."

This section of the agreement may also contain provisions as to the manner of payment of the sale price, the shares and other items to be delivered by the seller at closing, and such other events as may be expected to occur at closing.

Library References:
West's Key No. Digests, Corporations ⚖116.

§ 6.169   Drafting the Seller's Stock Sale Agreement—Representations, Warranties and Covenants of Buyer

In the stock sale agreement, the representations, warranties and covenants of the buyer will not be as comprehensive as the representations of the seller.

---

3. **PRACTICE POINTER:** As discussed earlier, the promissory note of buyer should contain a provision for acceleration in the event of any default under the terms of the agreement. *See supra,* § 6.50. Seller should also make sure that the note contains a provision for the payment of attorney's fees in the event that buyer defaults.

§ 6.169

The seller will generally require that the buyer's representations include the following:

- That the buyer is duly incorporated, validly existing, in good standing and qualified to do business;
- That the buyer possesses the requisite authority to enter into the stock sale agreement and to perform in accordance with its terms; and
- That no broker brought about this transaction (or, in the alternative: that the buyer will indemnify and hold the seller harmless from any claim for brokerage commissions).

In the event that the sale price is to be paid by the buyer in installments, whether or not evidenced by the buyer's promissory note, the seller should require the following representations and warranties as to the financial condition of the buyer and of the guarantors of the buyer's obligations:

- That the buyer has delivered to the seller the following financial statements, which are true and complete and accurately represent the financial condition of the buyer: (a) balance sheets; (b) statement of profits and losses; and (c) tax returns;
- That except to the extent reflected in the balance sheet, dated ___, there are no liabilities of any nature and the buyer represents that it does not know or have reason to know of any liability of any nature not fully reflected in the balance sheet;
- That since the dates of the balance sheet and tax returns provided to the buyer, there has not been any material change in the buyer's assets, liabilities or financial condition;
- That the buyer has no absolute or contingent liabilities which are not shown in its financial statements;
- That the amounts set up as provision for payment of taxes on the buyer's financial statements are sufficient for payment of all accrued and unpaid taxes of the buyer;
- That the buyer will maintain its net worth of $_____ during the period that any notes or other obligations to the seller are outstanding;
- That the buyer will acquire insurance policies on the business and assets of the corporation in an amount equal to ___% of the outstanding balance of the notes or obligations payable to the seller, and that such policies shall name the seller as a co-insured or named insured until such obligations are paid, and that the buyer will submit proof of such coverage from time to time upon the seller's request, until such obligation to the seller is paid; or
- That the buyer will assign to the seller the policy of insurance on the buyer's life owned by him in the amount of $_____, and that

the buyer will pay all premiums when due until the buyer's obligation to the seller is paid;

- That there is no litigation pending or threatened against the buyer that its insurance will not cover; and
- That the buyer acknowledges that the seller has made no representation to the buyer as to the gross income or profitability of the seller's business.

Library References:

West's Key No. Digests, Corporations ⟐116, 120.

§ 6.170 Drafting the Seller's Stock Sale Agreement—Representations, Warranties and Covenants of Seller

The representations and warranties of the seller constitute one of the most important sections of the stock sale agreement from the point of view of the buyer. The seller's representations must be carefully drafted by counsel. A material misstatement of any of the seller's representations or a breach by the seller of any of the warranties or covenants contained in this section will provide a basis for the buyer to avoid or rescind the agreement, or to seek indemnification from the seller in the event that the buyer suffers any loss or injury as a result of such misstatement or breach.

The representations and warranties generally mirror the due diligence investigation performed by the buyer. When negotiating the terms of the agreement, the buyer's counsel will normally attempt to have the seller's representations drafted in such a way as to cover issues which the buyer was unable to discover during its investigations. The buyer will also want the seller's representations to be drafted in the absolute, that is, without qualification. For example, the buyer might request that the seller warrant:

> "That all equipment owned by seller is in excellent condition and working order, capable of meeting highest industry standards."

The seller, on the other hand would normally prefer to qualify,[1] or otherwise limit, its representations. The seller might represent:

> "That the equipment owned by seller is, to the best of seller's knowledge, in reasonable working order and sufficient for the operations of the business in its current state."

---

§ 6.170

1. The seller qualifies a representation by stating that it is "to the best of seller's knowledge."

Ch. 6 COVENANTS OF SELLER § 6.170

or

"That buyer has inspected the equipment of seller and that buyer agrees to accept transfer of the same in its present condition ("as is") subject to normal wear and tear to the date of closing."

The representations, warranties and covenants of the seller will usually include the following:[2]

- That the seller is duly incorporated, validly existing, in good standing and qualified to do business;
- That the aggregate number of shares the corporation is authorized to issue is ___, of which ___ are issued and outstanding;
- That all shares are validly issued and fully paid and that there are no outstanding subscriptions, options or warrants;
- That the seller has delivered to the buyer a true and complete list of: (a) the names of all shareholders of the corporation; (b) the names of all of the corporation's officers and directors; (c) the names of all individuals who receive compensation from the corporation, and a statement of compensation as to each; (d) the names of all persons holding powers of attorney for the corporation; and (e) a list of each bank in which the corporation has an account as well as a list of all persons authorized to draw on such accounts;
- Each shareholder represents that he is the owner of ___ shares and that he has full right and authority to transfer the same to the buyer;
- That the seller has no affiliations, subsidiaries or other business interests;
- That, to the best of the seller's knowledge, there are no conflicts between the stock sale agreement and other agreements of the seller;
- That, to the best of the seller's knowledge, there exist no service agreements, maintenance agreements, warranties or other obligations outstanding on the seller's products, except as set forth;
- That, to the best of the seller's knowledge, it is in compliance with all federal, state and local laws, rules and regulations;
- That there are no licenses or leases in effect concerning the business and property of the seller except those specified;
- That, to the best of the seller's knowledge, it has good and marketable title to the assets, property and real estate;

---

2. The representations and warranties which appear in this Section are for illustrative purposes only and are not comprehensive in scope. Counsel is advised to carefully draft each representation in accordance with the circumstances of the transaction.

809

- That, to the best of the seller's knowledge, there are no mechanics or materialmen liens or bases for such liens on the real estate transferred;
- That the seller has delivered to the buyer the following financial statements, which, to the best of the seller's knowledge, are true and complete and accurately represent the financial condition of the seller: (a) balance sheets; (b) statement of profits and losses; and (c) tax returns;
- That except to the extent reflected in the balance sheet, dated ___, there are no liabilities of any nature and the seller represents that it does not know or have reason to know of any liability of any nature not fully reflected in the balance sheet;
- That since the dates of the balance sheet and tax returns provided to the buyer, to the best of the seller's knowledge, there has not been: (a) any change in assets, liabilities or the financial condition of the seller's business; (b) any damage, loss, or destruction to the assets of the business that are not covered by insurance; (c) any sales other than in the regular course of business; (d) any pending or threatened litigation; (e) any labor union organizing activity or actual or threatened employee strikes; (f) any institution or settlement of any litigation related to the seller or its business; (g) any failure to replace inventory and supplies; (h) any failure to pay any debt when it has come due; (i) any declaration, or setting aside, or payment of a dividend; or (j) any increase in compensation, or any bonus, payable to any officer, director, employee or agent of the seller;
- That, to the best of the seller's knowledge, it has filed all required tax returns;
- That the seller has delivered to the buyer a true and complete list of all accounts receivable as of ___, as reflected in the balance sheet, and that if, following closing, any such accounts remaining unpaid are not paid in full on demand when due, then the seller shall pay the same upon demand of the buyer (against delivery by the buyer of an assignment of such defaulted accounts);
- That the inventory is merchantable and in good condition;
- That the seller has no notice or knowledge of its violation of any federal, state or local laws, rules or regulations;
- That, to the best of the seller's knowledge, it possesses all necessary licenses, permits and consents required to carry on business;
- That the seller has delivered to the buyer an accurate list of all contracts, oral and written, to which the seller is a party, such contracts being as follows: (a) employment contracts; (b) contracts with salespersons and distributors; (c) pension benefit and related agreements; (d) agreements with suppliers, consultants, support

services, providers and the like; (e) customer agreements, unfilled purchase orders, sales contracts; (f) customer lists; (g) franchise agreements, dealer and consignment agreements, research and development contracts; (h) lines of credit and loans; and (i) contracts with labor organizations, all of which have been entered into in the ordinary course of business;

- That, to the best of the seller's knowledge, it has complied with all material provisions of all contracts, leases, licenses, other agreements, and that the same are valid and in good standing;
- That the transfer of shares will not constitute a prohibited assignment of any of the contracts, leases, licenses and other agreements, and that the same will remain in full force and effect;
- That there are no collective bargaining agreements in effect and that the seller has no knowledge of any labor union organizing activity or any strikes or threatened strikes;
- That, to the best of the seller's knowledge, it has delivered to the buyer an accurate list of all insurance policies, including any pending claims;
- That the seller will maintain all such insurance until closing;
- That, to the best of the seller's knowledge, there are no environmental hazards or conditions affecting the assets, property or business of the seller;
- That there is no litigation pending, and to the best of the seller's knowledge, there is no litigation threatened against or relating to the seller, its properties or business;
- That the seller has delivered to the buyer an accurate list of all patents, patent applications, trademarks, trade names, and copyrights, presently held by the seller, all of which are, to the best of the seller's knowledge, valid and in good standing;
- That from the date of execution of the stock sale agreement until the time of closing, there will be no new leases, tenancies or contracts affecting the assets or properties of the business without prior written approval of the buyer;
- That the seller will perform such repairs as may be agreed upon between the buyer and seller on the assets and properties of the business prior to closing;
- That the seller will pay vacation time and other employee benefits which have accrued up to and including the closing date;
- That no broker hired by the seller brought about this transaction (or, in the alternative: that the agreement entered into between the seller and its broker has been provided to the buyer and that the seller will indemnify and hold the buyer harmless from any

§ 6.170   BUYING & SELLING A SMALL BUSINESS   Ch. 6

claim for commissions by such broker to the extent that broker did not perform services for the buyer);

- That, to the best of the seller's knowledge, and except for facts unable to be discovered by the seller, no representation, warranty or covenant of the seller in the agreement, or in any writing furnished to the buyer, contains any untrue statement of fact or failure to state any material fact;
- That the seller has disclosed all material adverse facts known to it; and
- That the representations, warranties and covenants of the seller shall be true at the time of closing as though such representations and warranties were made at such time.

In the event that the closing is to occur after the date of the execution of the stock sale agreement by the parties, the buyer will normally request that the seller continue to operate the business in the ordinary course. To that end, the buyer will probably require "pre-closing" covenants from the seller. Pre-closing covenants of the seller normally include the following:

- That, since the date of (execution of the stock sale agreement), the seller has operated the business only in the ordinary course and, to the best of the seller's knowledge, there has not been:
    a. any change in assets, liabilities or financial condition of the seller's business since the date of such financial statements, tax returns or other documents;
    b. any change in the corporation's certificate of incorporation or bylaws;
    c. any change in the corporation's authorized or issued shares;
    d. any dividend or other distribution declared or paid;
    e. any increase in compensation payable to any employee, officer or director;
    f. any change affecting personnel;
    g. any damage, loss, or destruction to the assets or properties of the business that is not covered by insurance;
    h. any sales other than in the regular course of business;
    i. any pending or threatened litigation;
    j. any labor union organizing activity or actual or threatened employee strikes;
    k. any institution or settlement of litigation related to the seller or its business;
    l. any failure to replace inventory and supplies;

m. any failure to pay a debt which has become due; and

n. any chemical spills or other environmental conditions affecting the business or property of the seller.

Library References:

West's Key No. Digests, Corporations ⚭116, 120.

§ 6.171 Drafting the Seller's Stock Sale Agreement—Conduct of Business Prior to Closing

In the event that closing is to occur after the date of the execution of the stock sale agreement by the parties, the agreement will normally contain a provision for the conduct of business by the seller up to the time of closing. The purpose for such a provision is twofold: First, it will assure the buyer that the seller will continue to conduct its business without interruption and, secondly, it will provide the buyer with the affirmation of the seller that during this period, the seller will not transfer assets or do anything outside of the ordinary course of business. In this section of the agreement, the buyer will require the seller to operate in a manner consistent with prior operations. In addition, the buyer will want to make sure that the seller continues to maintain insurance on its business and properties, that the seller will continue to replace inventory, and that the seller will allow the buyer access to the books, records and operations of the seller during this period.

This section may also provide that the seller, while in continued possession of the business, is to pay for all materials and services pertaining to the operations of the business which have been delivered to the seller prior to closing, and that the buyer is to pay for all such materials and services delivered after closing. Additionally, there may be included a provision concerning accounts receivable to the effect that receivables derived from goods or other business products shipped after closing are to become the property of the buyer, and receivables from goods shipped prior to closing are to be paid to the seller.[1]

Library References:

West's Key No. Digests, Corporations ⚭116.

§ 6.172 Drafting the Seller's Stock Sale Agreement—Indemnifications

As discussed earlier, the seller's representations and warranties comprise one of the most important elements of the stock sale agree-

§ 6.171

1. For suggested language from a sample agreement, *see infra*, § 6.187, Section 8(b).

ment.[1] The buyer relies heavily upon these representations in deciding to purchase the seller's business. The failure or falsity of any of the material representations or warranties of the seller could expose the seller to excessive costs, possible legal action or the termination of the agreement by the buyer.

The buyer's counsel will normally seek broad indemnification from the seller. The indemnification of the seller usually provides that the seller will indemnify and hold the buyer harmless from all liabilities, losses, costs and expenses (including legal fees) relative to or arising from:

- Liabilities, obligations and claims against the seller not expressly assumed by the buyer—including any claims for warranty, product liability, or the repair or replacement of products sold by the seller prior to closing; and

- Any claims or costs resulting from a misrepresentation or breach by the seller of its covenants and warranties contained in the stock sale agreement or other documents delivered to the buyer pursuant to the stock sale agreement.

The seller's attorney, in drafting or negotiating such a provision, is advised to limit and restrict the seller's indemnification as much as possible. Generally, such limitations or restrictions appear in the form of monetary thresholds and/or baskets placed in such provisions. A "threshold" refers generally to a set amount used to cap the liability. For example, the seller might indemnify and hold the buyer harmless from any claims against or costs incurred by the buyer in an amount of up to $10,000.[2] Or, using a basket, which is usually an amount below which no indemnification will be made, the seller will indemnify and hold the buyer harmless from and against any claims, costs, or losses, but only if such claims, costs or losses exceed a certain amount. For example:

"The indemnifications hereunder shall be effective only after and to the extent that valid and enforceable claims for indemnification exceed $25,000."

The seller should also consider putting a limit on the period of validity of its representations and warranties, such as:

"The indemnifications hereunder shall expire and be of no further force and effect unless written claim is made by buyer on or before (a date which is two years from the date of closing)."[3]

§ 6.172
1. See supra, § 6.170.
2. For suggested language from a sample agreement, see infra, § 6.188, Section 9.01.
3. For suggested language from a sample agreement, see infra, § 6.188, Section 9.01.

As to indemnification from the buyer, the seller will want such coverage to be as broad as possible. The seller will generally require the buyer to indemnify and hold the seller harmless from all liabilities, losses, costs and expenses (including legal fees) relative to or arising from:

- Liabilities, obligations and claims against the buyer—including any claims for warranty, product liability, or the repair or replacement of products sold by the buyer subsequent to closing;
- Liabilities, obligations and claims against the seller arising under any leases, contracts, agreements, licenses, permits, etc., after closing or arising in relation to any claims of creditors relative to liabilities after closing; and
- Any claims or costs resulting from a misrepresentation or breach by the buyer of its covenants and warranties contained in the stock sale agreement or other documents delivered to the seller pursuant to the stock sale agreement.

Library References:
West's Key No. Digests, Corporations ⟜116.

§ 6.173 Drafting the Seller's Stock Sale Agreement—Matters Respecting Real Property

In a stock sale transaction the seller is selling the business entity as a whole, which may include real estate. Although nothing need be specifically stated in the agreement, the buyer will, at a minimum, want assurances from the seller regarding the real estate, such as representations that the business entity has good title to its real property, among others.[1] The agreement should also specifically identify the real estate owned by the business entity. It should include legal descriptions for all of the real estate owned or incorporate them by reference in schedules attached to the agreement. Often a copy of the deed is attached to the agreement as a schedule.

The buyer's other concerns may be addressed in the agreement section other than the real estate section, such as, the seller representations section or the section on liabilities and encumbrances.

Library References:
West's Key No. Digests, Corporations ⟜116.

§ 6.174 Drafting the Seller's Stock Sale Agreement—Non-disclosure Provisions

It is in the non-disclosure provisions of the stock sale agreement that the parties covenant to keep confidential all information about each

---

§ 6.173
1. See supra, § 6.68 for a discussion of real estate provisions usually required.

§ 6.174 BUYING & SELLING A SMALL BUSINESS Ch. 6

other acquired during the course of the transaction. This representation is especially important to the seller in the event that the transaction is not consummated.[1]

Library References:
West's Key No. Digests, Corporations ⊙=116.

§ 6.175 Drafting the Seller's Asset Sale Agreement—Covenants Not to Compete and Consulting Agreements

The buyer of a business normally wants assurances from the seller and his key personnel (particularly those not retained in the buyer's employ) that they will not compete with the buyer. The covenant not to compete may be part of the purchase and sale agreement or it may be a separate agreement. The restrictions in the covenant not to compete must be reasonable in duration of time and geographic location; and the restrictions should be only so broad as to protect the legitimate business interests of the buyer in the geographical area of the business and that of the seller's goodwill.

Restrictive covenants to protect the goodwill of a purchased business do not violate the anti-trust laws. Reasonable restrictive covenants are enforceable (even though they curtail competition) because they are conducive to the overall freedom of trade and the seller's right to sell his business. They will be enforceable as long as they are not injurious to the public. In addition, the restrictive covenants must be ancillary to the sale of a business, otherwise they are a restriction of trade and unenforceable.

The duration of most covenants not to compete is relatively short, usually 3–5 years, but longer covenants are appropriate if the circumstances justify it. Where the protected geographic area is large, skillful drafting can limit the prohibited activities within the protected area and thereby reduce the impact of the covenant to the seller.

The measure of damages for a breach of the covenant is lost profits. This is often difficult to prove and there may be other intervening factors, such as a general decline in the economy, which can further complicate any litigation. For these reasons, the buyer often seeks to include a liquidated damages provision. The attorney for the seller should try to eliminate the covenant not to compete completely and should argue that only the implied-in-law non-compete provisions should apply. If this argument is unsuccessful, the attorney should draft provi-

---

§ 6.174

1. **PRACTICE POINTER:** Seller should require that buyer take reasonable steps to insure that the confidential information obtained about seller not be disclosed to outside sources and should specifically define the "confidential information" to include such things as customer lists, supplier lists, trade secrets, pricing policy and other information, as may be designated by seller.

Ch. 6   NOTICE TO CUSTOMERS AND SUPPLIERS   **§ 6.176**

sions limiting liquidated damages or propose a specific formula favorable to the seller. Liquidated damages, as opposed to general lost profits, will also limit the buyer's damages. For this reason, the seller should strike any clauses in the agreement providing "other damages" unless this language is specifically defined and limited. Liquidated damages are often computed by reference to a mathematical formula, such as the prior 12 month's sales by the business to a customer. The formula must also be reasonable or the liquidated damages amount may be held to be a penalty and hence unenforceable.[1]

Payments for a covenant not to compete may also provide tax advantages to the seller.

All advantages and disadvantages must be weighed before deleting these provisions.

Some sale transactions provide for the continuing services of the seller after the sale. In such cases, the seller is usually compensated via a consulting agreement.[2]

The consulting agreement must define the type of services to be rendered, the expected number of hours, the location(s) where services will be rendered and the compensation to be paid. It should also allow the seller to provide consulting services to other businesses. However, the non-compete agreement usually prohibits consulting services to similar business in the buyer's protected territory.

Library References:

West's Key No. Digests, Corporations ⚖116.

§ 6.176 Drafting the Seller's Stock Sale Agreement— Notice to Customers and Suppliers

Over time, a seller develops relationships with his customers and suppliers. To avoid confusion and minimize the disruption of an ownership change, the agreement should require a notice be sent to the business' customers and suppliers announcing the change in ownership.[1] Appropriately worded, this can be a very positive introduction for the buyer and helpful to the seller. The notice should be prepared prior to

---

§ 6.175

1. *See supra,* § 6.124.
2. **PRACTICE POINTER:** Being paid as a consultant allows the seller to set up his own sole proprietorship or business entity. In addition to the general business deductions, this may also allow the seller to maintain and deduct the expense of an office in his home.

§ 6.176

1. **PRACTICE POINTER:** The notice is usually prepared for the seller's signature, and at a minimum introduces the buyer and informs the customers and suppliers of the change of ownership. Where appropriate, the notice should also indicate that the same quality service or product will be provided by the buyer and that the past relationships and practices which the suppliers and customers will continue.

817

§ 6.176 BUYING & SELLING A SMALL BUSINESS Ch. 6

the closing and, ideally, sent to coincide with the take over of the business by the buyer.[2]

Library References:

West's Key No. Digests, Corporations ⚖116.

§ 6.177 Drafting the Seller's Stock Sale Agreement—Conditions Precedent to Seller's Obligations

In preparing the seller's stock sale agreement, counsel will normally condition the seller's performance upon the happening of certain events and the performance by the buyer of certain material terms of the agreement at or prior to closing. Such conditions should include:[1]

- Performance by the buyer of all obligations specified in the stock sale agreement;
- Accuracy of the covenants, representations and warranties made by the buyer;
- Absence of adverse change in the buyer's financial condition;
- Delivery to the seller of a certificate executed by the buyer and its officers and shareholders certifying the fulfillment of the above conditions; and
- Delivery to the seller by the buyer of all documents required to be delivered under the terms of the stock sale agreement.

Library References:

West's Key No. Digests, Corporations ⚖116.

§ 6.178 Drafting the Seller's Stock Sale Agreement—Conditions Precedent to Buyer's Obligations

Generally, the conditions precedent to the buyer's obligations under the agreement include the following:

- Performance by the seller of all obligations specified in the stock sale agreement;
- Accuracy of the covenants, representations and warranties made by the seller;

---

2. **PRACTICE POINTER:** If the seller is providing financing to the buyer, it is in the seller's interest to assure a smooth transition of the business. A notice may also help avoid the inconvenience of bills and payments being sent to the wrong party.

§ 6.177

1. For illustrative language from a sample agreement, see infra, § 6.188, Article Six.

- Absence of adverse change in the financial and other condition of the seller as well as in the business, properties, assets or prospects of the seller;
- Delivery to the buyer of a certificate executed by the seller, or by its officers and shareholders, certifying the fulfillment of the above conditions;
- Delivery to the buyer by the seller of all documents required to be delivered under the terms of the stock sale agreement;
- The buyer's acquiring regulatory approval;
- The buyer's obtaining financing; and
- Tax rulings, if applicable.

Library References:

West's Key No. Digests, Corporations ⚖116.

§ 6.179 Drafting the Seller's Stock Sale Agreement—Nature and Survival of Representations and Warranties

Every stock sale agreement should contain a provision requiring that all representations, warranties, indemnities, covenants and agreements made by the parties survive the closing. The purpose of this provision is to ensure that the material provisions of the stock sale agreement remain enforceable after the transfer of stock has taken place, so that each party may have remedies in the event of a breach.[1]

Library References:

West's Key No. Digests, Corporations ⚖116, 120.

§ 6.180 Drafting the Seller's Stock Sale Agreement—Documents to Be Delivered to Seller at Closing

The documents to be delivered by the buyer to the seller at closing normally include the following:

- Documents effecting payment of the sale price;
- Certified copies of minutes and the consents of the shareholders and directors of the buyer approving the stock sale agreement and the consummation of the purchase transaction;
- Security agreements, executed mortgages and other security instruments;

§ 6.179

1. For suggested language from a sample agreement, *see infra,* § 6.188, Article Fifteen.

§ 6.180 BUYING & SELLING A SMALL BUSINESS — Ch. 6

- The opinion of the buyer's counsel that the buyer is duly organized, validly existing and in good standing; that the buyer has the corporate power and authority to enter into and perform the stock sale agreement; that the stock sale agreement is a valid and binding obligation of the buyer; and that the execution and delivery of the stock sale agreement and performance by the buyer do not conflict with the buyer's organizing instruments or other contracts or obligations, and are not in violation of any law, rule or regulation;
- Other documents to be delivered to the seller under the terms of the agreement; and
- Such further instruments or documents as may reasonably be required by seller to effect the provisions contained in the agreement.

Library References:
West's Key No. Digests, Corporations ⚖116.

§ 6.181 Drafting the Seller's Stock Sale Agreement—Documents to Be Delivered to Buyer at Closing

The documents to be delivered by the seller to the buyer at closing normally include the following:

- Certificates for all shares of the corporation, duly endorsed, with all transfer stamps affixed;
- The opinion of the seller's counsel that the seller is duly organized, validly existing and in good standing; that the seller has the corporate power and authority to enter into and perform the stock sale agreement; that the stock sale agreement is a valid and binding obligation of the seller; and that the execution and delivery of the stock sale agreement and performance by the seller do not conflict with the seller's organizing instruments or other contracts or obligations, and are not in violation of any law, rule or regulation;
- Certified copies of minutes and the consents of the shareholders and directors of the seller approving the stock sale agreement and the consummation of the sale transaction;
- The certificate of the seller and individual shareholders affirming the performance of all conditions precedent to the buyer's obligations;
- Executed non-competition and continuity of business dealings agreements;
- All corporate records, reports, files, contracts, books, licenses, leases and permits and all other corporate papers and instruments

of every kind, including plans and specifications for buildings located on the real property;

- The share certificate book, minute book, corporate seal, auditors' reports and copies of tax returns and tax reports covering all years since incorporation;
- The resignations of all officers and directors, releases of all claims they may have against the corporation, and cancellations of any contacts between the corporation and such individuals;
- All customer lists and supplier lists;
- A list of accounts receivable;
- All keys to buildings, vehicles, file cabinets;
- Confidentiality agreements and covenants not to compete from departing employees of the seller;
- Written assurances from the seller's broker respecting confidentiality;
- Other documents to be delivered to the buyer under the terms of the agreement; and
- Such further instruments of transfer or other documents as may reasonably be required by the buyer to effect the provisions contained in the agreement.

Library References:

West's Key No. Digests, Corporations ⬳116.

§ 6.182 Drafting the Seller's Stock Sale Agreement— Notices, Severability and Other General Provisions

Notices and other provisions usually included at the end of an agreement are referred to as the "boilerplate." These provisions generally consist of the following:[1]

- Notice procedures;
- A severability clause;
- Governing law;
- A non–waiver provision;
- A savings clause;
- Provisions concerning modifications and changes to the agreement;

§ 6.182

1. For suggested language as to some of these provisions from a sample agreement, see *infra*, § 6.187, Section 21.

§ 6.182 BUYING & SELLING A SMALL BUSINESS Ch. 6

- A disclaimer as to captions and headings;
- Provisions acknowledging the "binding effect" of the agreement;
- Provisions acknowledging that the agreement constitutes the "entire agreement" of the parties; and
- An agreement to execute additional documents and counter parts.

Library References:
West's Key No. Digests, Corporations ⚖116.

§ 6.183 Drafting the Seller's Stock Sale Agreement—Documents to Be Prepared or Reviewed Prior to Closing

After the stock sale agreement has been executed, the seller's counsel must either prepare or review, as the case may be, all documents or instruments referred to in the agreement or required under its provisions. Such documents, known as the "collateral documents" may include the following:

- Proposed share certificates, stock powers, cancellation of the seller's shares, stock transfer records, stock transfer taxes and stamps;
- Security agreements, promissory notes, and mortgages;
- Escrow agreements;
- Corporate resolutions;
- Assignments of contracts, leases and other interests;
- Equipment lists;
- Inventory descriptions including count and valuation;
- Lists of other assets;
- Legal opinions of counsel;
- Employment and collective bargaining agreements;
- Lists of all of seller's other contracts and agreements;
- Certificates respecting name change;
- Certificates of dissolution and/or discontinuance;
- Assumed name certificates;
- Lists of all insurance policies and pending claims;
- Lists of all patents, patent applications, trademarks, trade names, and copyrights;
- Covenants not to compete;
- Confidentiality agreements.

Copies of all such collateral documents should be attached to the stock sale agreement and made a part of such agreement.

Library References:
West's Key No. Digests, Corporations ⟐116.

§ 6.184 Post-contract and Pre-closing

At this stage of the transaction the attorney must undertake all the necessary tasks to implement the agreement, provide required information and documents to the buyer, and prepare himself and his client for closing.

A good place to begin this process is with a review of the signed agreement. A competently drafted agreement will, through its many clauses, address the individual issues of the transaction and provide an outline of many of the items which must be reviewed or repaired for closing. It is good practice to prioritize items chronologically, using either the date contained in the agreement or an estimate of the time needed to retain or prepare items for closing, with the more time consuming items being undertaken first.

A list of some, but not all, of the items which must be undertaken at this stage, many of which are described in greater detail in other sections of this chapter, are as follows:

1. Prepare a list of all items to be obtained by or prepared by the seller and delivered to the buyer;

2. Prepare a list of all items to be obtained or prepared by the buyer and delivered to the seller;

3. Prepare a list of contingency and default dates contained in the agreement along with a short description of the consequences for failure to comply with the agreement requirements;

4. If appropriate, order environmental inspections;

5. Obtain a list of back title information and surveys and deliver it to the buyer;

6. If required, prepare the bulk sales tax notifications for the New York Sales tax (*see* further discussion below);

7. If required, prepare a UCC creditor list for UCC bulk sales notifications (*see* further discussion below);

8. If required, prepare plant closing notices (*see* further discussion below);

9. Assist the buyer with any new contract, novations, or amendments to existing contracts with suppliers, lessors, and customers;

§ 6.184 BUYING & SELLING A SMALL BUSINESS Ch. 6

10. Prepare and obtain corporate resolutions or other authorizations from the business entity, as necessary;
11. Prepare contracts to be assigned to the buyer;
12. Review and comply with any requirements in collective bargaining agreements;
13. If required by the agreement, arrange for a physical inventory to be taken;
14. Prepare notices to be sent to suppliers and customers regarding the change in ownership and where to forward future payments and invoices;
15. Coordinate with the buyer and the buyer's attorney to transfer services such as telephone service, power and light service and insurance coverages, among others;
16. Prepare and obtain opinions of counsel as required;
17. Coordinate with the buyer regarding the preparation of doing business as ("DBA") and the preparation of corporate name change certificates;
18. Cooperate with the buyer regarding structural inspections;
19. Review the title search, tax search and judgment and lien searches obtained by the buyer and undertake the necessary actions to satisfy or obtain releases for liens, and to cure any defects in title;
20. Prepare closing adjustments such as real estate tax adjustments;
21. Prepare a closing memo.

The closing memorandum should list all of the documents to be delivered or received at the time of closing; all documents to be signed at the time of closing and by whom; provide the method of payment and how payment is to be made; provide a list of all adjustments and calculations in arriving at the final purchase price and the funds to be exchanged; and the necessary items, such as the exchange of keys to business premises.

Prior to the date of closing, the attorneys for the buyer and seller should resolve all adjustments and other pre-closing matters to enable the closing to proceed smoothly.[1]

Plant Closing Notice. The Worker Adjustment and Retraining Notification Act[2] (WARN Act) requires employers to provide employees and local governments with a 60 day notice prior to a plant closing or

§ 6.184
1. **PRACTICE POINTER:** If the documents are available and time allows, the attorney should review all documents and adjustments with his client before the closing.

2. 29 U.S.C.A. §§ 2101 *et seq.*

mass lay-off. The employer must also notify the employee representatives (union), if any.

WARN only applies to employers with 100 or more employees, excluding part-time employees, or 100 or more employees who work, in the aggregate, at least 4,000 hours per week, excluding overtime.

For a violation of the WARN Act, the employer can be held liable for employees' wages and pension benefits until the 60 day notice requirement is fulfilled. A fine of up to $500 per day for each day of non-compliance may also be imposed.[3]

New York State Sales Tax and Bulk Sale Notification. The bulk sale provisions of the New York State Sales Tax Law[4] apply to a sale of business assets. These provisions do not apply to stock (entity) sales. A bulk sale under the sales tax law covers any transfer in bulk outside the ordinary course of business.[5] If the parties do not comply with the provisions of the Tax Law regarding sales tax, the buyer becomes liable for any past unpaid sales tax of the seller up to the amount of the purchase price.[6] Although the bulk sale provisions mostly impact the buyer, the seller is primarily responsible for collecting sales tax on the sale of assets.[7]

UCC Bulk Sale Notices or Escrow Agreements in Lieu of UCC Bulk Sale Notices. A Uniform Commercial Code bulk transfer is any transfer in bulk of a major part of the materials, supplies, merchandise or other inventory not in the ordinary course of the transferor's busi-

---

3. PRACTICE POINTER: This statute and the federal regulations have many exceptions and interpretations. If there is any question whether the WARN Act applies or not, the statute should be carefully reviewed.

4. Tax Law § 1141.

5. PRACTICE POINTER: The Tax Law does not define bulk sale per se. Tax Law § 1141(c) and 20 NYCRR § 537.1(a)(1) describe a bulk sale as the transfer or assignment in bulk of any portion or the whole of business assets. One cannot rely on the UCC definition of "major portion" in determining if a bulk sale has occurred under the Tax Law. The New York State Department of Taxation and Finance takes an aggressive position. If in doubt, assume a bulk sale has occurred. The sales tax bulk sale provisions are separate and distinct from the UCC bulk sale provisions. Where both apply *both* must be complied with. *See also, supra,* § 6.154.

6. PRACTICE POINTER: The bulk sale provisions are found in Tax Law § 1141(c) and 20 NYCRR Part 537. In essence, notice of the sale and its terms must be given to the Tax Department at least ten days before taking possession or paying for the business assets. Form AU–196.10 is generally used. If within five days after filing the notice of bulk sale with the Department, the Department notifies the buyer of a possible claim for taxes due, the buyer is prohibited from transferring money or any other consideration to the seller (except amounts in excess of the Department's claim). The Department then has ninety days to determine the amount of the tax obligation, if any, during which period the seller cannot be paid. These provisions only apply to bulk sales by businesses required to collect sales tax. The statute of limitations for a sales tax assessment is three years from the date the sales tax return was filed. Tax Law § 1147(b).

7. PRACTICE POINTER: The sales tax collected on the sale of assets should be reported on the seller's final sales tax return. If the seller is not obligated to collect sales tax in the course of his business, a sales tax return is nonetheless due on the sale of assets. The seller should file a casual sales tax return to report and pay the sales tax due on Form ST 131.

§ 6.184   BUYING & SELLING A SMALL BUSINESS   Ch. 6

ness. The bulk transfer provisions of the UCC generally apply to businesses engaged in the sale of merchandise and not services, but it specifically covers restaurants. The intention of this provision is to protect creditors who rely on the merchandise as security for payment of credit extended to the business.[8] To comply with the UCC Article 6 Bulk Transfer provisions the following must occur:

1. The buyer must obtain a list of the seller's creditors and the property to be transferred. The buyer must preserve this list and allow inspection and copying by creditors for a period of six months following the transfer;[9]

2. The list must be signed and sworn to or affirmed by the seller;[10]

3. A notice must be given to creditors which states that a bulk sale is about to be made, the names and business addresses of the seller and buyer, if all debts of the seller are to be paid in full as they fall due and the address where creditors should send their bills;

4. If the debts of the seller are not to be paid in full, or if the purchaser is uncertain, the notice must also state the following:

   a. The location and general description of the property to be transferred;

   b. An estimate of the seller's debt;

   c. The address where the schedule of property and list of creditors may be inspected;

   d. If the transferor is to pay existing debts, the amount of such debts and to whom owed; and

   e. If the transfer is for new consideration, the amount, time and place of payment.[11]

5. The notice must be delivered personally or be sent by registered or certified mail to all creditors on the creditor's list;[12]

6. The notice must be sent to the creditors at least ten days before the buyer takes possession of the goods or pays for them, whichever is sooner.[13]

Since the UCC bulk sale notices, at times, are misinterpreted by the public as a "going out of business" announcement, both parties often choose to waive them.[14] When waiving these provisions, most

8. UCC § 6–102.
9. UCC § 6–104.
10. See supra, note 2.
11. UCC § 6–107.
12. See supra, note 4.
13. See UCC § 6–111.

14. **PRACTICE POINTER**: If the seller is only selling a portion of the business it is extremely important that suppliers and customers understand the seller is not "going out of business." The notice should specifically inform the suppliers that the seller is only transferring a portion of the business, that their bills will be paid in full

contracts[15] protect the buyer with an escrow agreement or a set-off against indebtedness owed to the seller.

The agreement should simply state that the UCC bulk sale statute will be complied with or waived. The set-off and escrow provisions should be restricted to the bulk sale areas of the agreement.[16]

§ 6.185 Closing and Post-closing

By the time of closing, all negotiations and agreements between the parties will have been finalized, all documents in form ready for signing will have been prepared, and all pre-closing filings will have been made.

At closing, the consideration will be paid and all documents and instruments will be signed by the parties. Guarantors and obligors who are not parties to the transaction need not appear at closing as long as their duly executed and acknowledged instruments are available for delivery to the proper parties.

The seller's attorney should have a list of all documents to be signed and delivered by both the seller and the buyer at closing, and should prepare a "Closing Memorandum." The closing memorandum will normally identify the place, date and time of closing, name the individuals who attended the closing, list the documents and instruments signed and delivered, identify the further steps to be taken by each party, and record other important information concerning the transaction.

After closing, counsel should deliver to his or her client the originals of all pertinent documents. Counsel should make sure to retain copies of all such documents for his or her records. It is advisable to include in this delivery a letter to the client summarizing the actions taken by counsel, such as filings made or returns prepared, as well as instructions for further actions to be taken by the client. If any documents or instruments will require re-filing at later dates, counsel should instruct the client as to these matters, and should set up a tickler file with this information.

§ 6.186 Forms

What follows are an asset purchase and sale agreement and an agreement of purchase and sale of stock. The practitioner is advised to

according to the usual billing cycle and that the seller looks forward to continuing his relationship with the suppliers. The UCC bulk sale provisions provide notices to suppliers only, but word of the transaction often filters out to the general public and to the seller's customers. For this reason, if the seller is only selling a portion of the business it is usually advantageous for the seller to provide an escrow agreement or some other security to the buyer in lieu of sending out bulk sale notices.

15. *See infra,* § 6.51.

16. CAVEAT: If the transaction includes non-negotiable installment notes, the buyer has a virtually unlimited right of set-off as well as counterclaim in any enforcement action by the seller.

carefully review the acts underlying the transaction and adapt these forms accordingly.

§ 6.187 Forms—Asset Purchase and Sale Agreement[1]

ASSET PURCHASE AND SALE AGREEMENT

THIS ASSET PURCHASE AND SALE AGREEMENT ("Agreement") is made and entered into this ___ day of ___, 199__, by and between ABC, Inc., a New York corporation, with offices located at 115 Random Street, Troy, New York ("Seller"), and John Smith and Mary Smith, both residing at 101 Warren Street, Troy, New York ("Shareholders"), and XYZ, Inc., a New York corporation, with offices located at 345 Down Street, Albany, New York ("Buyer") and Robert Jones, the Sole Shareholder of Buyer, residing at 75 Grant Street, Albany, New York ("Jones").

WITNESSETH:

WHEREAS, Seller is engaged in the business of manufacturing and selling widgets (the "Business") from its facility located at 115 Random Street, Troy, New York (the "Facility"); and

WHEREAS, Buyer desires to buy and Seller desires to sell certain assets of Seller used in connection with the Business on the terms and subject to the conditions hereinafter set forth;

NOW, THEREFORE, in consideration of the covenants, agreements, representations and warranties herein set forth, the parties hereto mutually covenant and agree as follow:

1. *Assets and Property to be Conveyed to Buyer.*

On the terms and subject to the conditions set forth in this Agreement, Seller agrees to sell, convey, assign, transfer and deliver to Buyer at the Closing all of Seller's right, title and interest in and to the following assets (collectively, but excluding those assets specifically defined as Retained Assets in Section 2 hereof, the "Assets"):

(a) Land, building and improvements located at 112 Random Street, Troy, New York, consisting of twelve (12) + acres, more particularly described in "Exhibit A", annexed hereto (hereinafter sometimes referred to as the "Real Property"), together with all of Seller's right, title and interest in and to any land lying in the bed of any street or avenue in front of or adjoining the Real Property, it being the intention of the parties that Buyer shall have free, permanent and unrestricted access to 115 Random Street over the driveways now located on Real Property;

§ 6.187   1. *See supra,* §§ 6.52 and 6.139.

(b) All machinery and equipment, related fixtures, replacement parts and supplies, tools, office furniture, furnishings, equipment and supplies used or useful in the conduct of the Business, said items being more particularly described on "Exhibit B", annexed hereto and made a part hereof;

(c) All transportation equipment and vehicles used or useful in the conduct of the Business, together with related spare parts, said vehicles being more particularly described on "Exhibit C", annexed hereto and made a part hereof;

(d) Raw materials, work-in-progress, supplies and finished goods inventories at the Facility or in any off-site storage facilities and in transit to customers at the date of Closing including scrap newspaper, chemicals, packaging supplies, testing supplies and all other items held for resale (all such property being hereinafter referred to collectively as "Inventories");

(e) All of Seller's right, title to and interest in the names "ABC, Inc.," and "ABC Widgets", and federal or state tradenames or marks, business logos and designs employed by the Seller in its operation of the Business;

(f) All formulas, trade secrets, patents and patent applications, know-how and process procedures for manufacture of the Seller's product lines, and all manuals, catalogs, sales and advertising material pertaining to Seller's product lines;

(g) All customer lists, including names, addresses, phone numbers, pricing terms, rebate terms, quantities purchased and dollar and unit purchases in each of the last three years for all installer-dealer retail accounts and others;

(h) All supplier lists, including names, addresses, phone numbers, purchase terms and dollar and unit purchases in each of the last three years;

(i) All purchase orders, sales commitments, licenses, permits, agreements, security interests, and post office boxes pertaining to Seller's ordinary operation of the Business;

(j) All rights of Seller under any licensing, franchise or other agreements whereby Seller has exclusive rights in any machinery or other Assets to be transferred to Buyer; and

(k) The goodwill of the Business as a going concern.

2. *Retained Assets of Seller.*

Anything herein to the contrary notwithstanding, Seller is retaining, and is not selling, conveying, assigning, transferring or delivering to Buyer any of its interest of any kind or nature whatsoever in the following property of Seller (collectively the "Retained Assets"):

(a) any cash or cash equivalents whether on hand, in banks or in transit, whether or not relating to the Business;

(b) any and all accounts and notes receivable of the Business arising prior to the Closing Date;

(c) Seller's $10,000 bid deposit which was paid to Nifty Construction Company located at Schodack Center, New York, advances to employees and prepaid insurance; and

(d) Seller's corporate minute books, corporate seal, tax returns and insurance contracts.

3. *Purchase Price.*

(a) The purchase price for all of the Assets referred to in Section 3 shall be NINE HUNDRED AND FIFTY THOUSAND DOLLARS ($950,000.00), which shall be paid at Closing as follows:

(i) $100,000.00 to be paid to Seller in cash, cashier's check or bank check; and

(ii) $850,000.00 to be paid to Seller in the form of the Promissory Note (hereinafter "Note") attached hereto as "Exhibit D".

(b) Buyer agrees to maintain at all times so long as the Note is unpaid the following:

(i) Working Capital of at least $2,000,000;

(ii) Current ratio (as that term is defined by generally accepted accounting principles) of at least 1.25:1; and

(iii) Debt to Worth (Fund Balance) not to exceed 1:1.

(c) Buyer agrees to present to Seller Audited Financial Statements by May 1 of each year during the term of the Note. In the event that Buyer fails to maintain the Working Capital, Current Ratio or Debt to Worth as above set forth, Seller's sole remedy shall be to accelerate the payment of the Note in accordance with the provisions contained in the Note. The preceding sentence will not limit or impair Seller's right to demand immediate payment in full of the Note following payment of the 84th Monthly Payment, as provided in paragraph 4 of Schedule A–1 of the Note.

(d) Buyer's Promissory Note shall be secured by a first purchase money mortgage, in the form attached hereto as "Exhibit E", covering the real property described in "Exhibit A" hereto attached, for the full amount of the Note, and by a first lien security interest evidenced by a security agreement in the form attached hereto as "Exhibit F", covering all of the Assets conveyed hereunder, excluding only real estate and inventory. Both the mortgage and security agreement shall contain after-acquired property clauses.

(e) The parties hereto agree that the purchase price described in paragraph (a) above shall be allocated as follows:

Furniture, fixtures, equipment	$
Motor Vehicles	$
Inventory	$
Land	$
Buildings	$
Intellectual Property	$
Restrictive Covenant	$
Name	$
Customer Lists	$
Good Will	$

4. *Assumption of Liabilities.*

Buyer shall assume liability for all costs of operation of the business which arise out of activities commencing upon Closing, with any prepaid costs by Seller prior to Closing prorated and refunded to Seller. Except as set forth in Section 6(h), below, it is expressly understood and agreed that Buyer does not assume any liabilities or obligations of Seller, including but not limited to, claims for breach of contract, products liability, negligence, accounts payable, or any obligations or liability thereunder, or any obligation to administer or terminate any pension, profit sharing, or any other retirement plan or benefit plan of Seller, or otherwise and Seller agrees to indemnify and hold Buyer harmless for all costs, expenses and losses arising therefrom including, but not limited to, reasonable attorney's fees.

5. *Closing.*

(a) At the time of Closing, Seller shall execute and deliver to Buyer such bills of sale and other instruments as may be necessary to transfer to Buyer the Assets referred to in Section 1, and shall deliver possession thereof to Buyer. All such bills of sale and other instruments will contain full warranties and affidavits of title and will effectively transfer to Buyer full title to the Assets referred to in Section 1, free and clear of all liens, security interests and encumbrances. The Seller shall also deliver any releases, subordinations, waivers of security interest, liens, encumbrances, or other claims against the Assets as Buyer may reasonably require except for the security interests to be granted to Seller by Buyer by the Security Agreement which is to be executed pursuant to this agreement.

(b) Closing shall occur at the offices of Pattison, Sampson, Ginsberg & Griffin, P.C., Troy, New York, on December 31, 1996 at 10:00 a.m.

6. *Representations, Warranties and Covenants of Seller.*

Seller and each of the Shareholders, jointly and severally, hereby represent, warrant and covenant as follows:

(a) That Seller is a corporation duly incorporated, validly existing and in good standing under the laws of the State of New York, and has the corporate power necessary to own the Assets and to carry on the Business as presently conducted by it, and to enter into and perform this Agreement and the transactions contemplated hereunder. To the best of Seller's knowledge, Seller is duly qualified to transact business and is in good standing as a foreign corporation in any jurisdiction in which such qualification is required.

(b) That Seller has taken all requisite corporate action to authorize and approve the execution and delivery of this Agreement and the consummation of the transactions contemplated hereunder.

(c) That the execution and delivery of this Agreement does not, and the consummation of the transactions contemplated hereby will not, violate any provision of, result in the acceleration of any obligation under, or give any person, firm or corporation any right to terminate any mortgage, lien, lease, contract or other agreement of any kind to which Seller is a party or by which Seller is bound; or violate or conflict with any other restriction of any kind or character to which Seller is subject, including, without limitation, any regulation, order or directive of any court, agency or other authority.

(d) That Seller has good and marketable title to and the unqualified right to convey, transfer, assign and deliver the Assets free and clear of all liens and encumbrances, and that there are no leases or licenses in effect with respect to any of the Assets, except as otherwise set forth in this Agreement or in any Exhibit annexed hereto.

(e) That the Assets are now, and on the Closing Date shall be, in full compliance with all laws and regulations of applicable federal, state, town, village or other governmental authorities having jurisdiction over or concerning any of the uses of the property being sold to Buyer hereunder, including, without limitation, all laws and regulations with respect to land, housing, buildings, fire and health codes. Seller has received no notice of, and has no knowledge of any violations of any federal, state or local rule, regulation, order or ordinance, applicable to the Assets, and Seller has received no notice of, and has no knowledge of, any condition which may give rise to any violation of any law, rule, regulation, order or ordinance applicable to the Assets.

(f) That the inventories are of merchantable quality and quantity and are usable or saleable as first quality goods in the ordinary course of Seller's business, and that to the best of Seller's knowledge, all of the Seller's machinery, equipment, tools and other tangible personal property to be transferred to Buyer are in good operating condition and repair and are adequate and sufficient for operation of the Business.

(g) That prior to the Closing, Seller shall perform, or cause to be performed, all ordinary and necessary repairs and maintenance (including preventive maintenance and overhauls) with respect to the Assets.

(h) That there are no service, maintenance, utility, warranty or other contracts or agreements (collectively the "Contracts") affecting the Assets, oral or written, except as set forth on "Exhibit G", annexed hereto and made a part hereof. Seller and Buyer hereby acknowledge and agree that (i) Seller shall assign to Buyer at the Closing, and Buyer shall then assume, Seller's obligations under any such Contracts as Buyer may select; (ii) Seller at its expense, if any, shall cancel all Contracts, not assigned to Buyer, with such cancellation to be effective no later than the Closing Date and (iii) Buyer shall have no liability or obligation under any of said Contracts not assigned to Buyer and shall not be bound by them.

(i) That Seller has good, marketable and insurable title to the Real Property, and Seller will convey the Real Property to Buyer on the Closing Date, subject only to the following matters, being herein collectively referred to as the "Permitted Encumbrances":

(i) any state of facts a current survey may show, provided that such state of facts does not render title unmarketable, and provided further that all buildings, structures and all other improvements are to be located totally within the boundaries of the Real Property;

(ii) real property taxes and water charges and sewer rents, if any, which are a lien on the Real Property or any portion thereof on the Closing Date, subject to adjustment as herein provided; and

(iii) zoning regulations and building restrictions and ordinances of the City of Troy and the State of New York and/or any other governmental authority, agency, board, department or instrumentality having or claiming jurisdiction over or with respect to, or affecting the Real Property now or prior to the Closing Date in force, provided that none of the regulations, restrictions or ordinances prohibit or prevent after the Closing Date the present uses of, or require after the Closing Date special permission or special permits or licenses (other than any of the Permits described in Section 6(v), below) for, the present uses of any of the Real Property.

(j) That Seller knows of no malfunction or inadequacy of any portion of the roof, plumbing, heating, air-conditioning, ventilating, mechanical or other systems of the Real Property.

(k) That all payments required to be made to contractors, subcontractors, mechanics, materialmen and all other persons in connection with work done or services performed with respect to Real Property have been made, and there is no basis for the filing of any lien against the Real Property.

(*l*) That to the best of Seller's knowledge, no part of the Real Property has been utilized for the generation, manufacture, refining, transportation, treatment, storage, handling or disposal of hazardous or toxic substances or chemicals, wastes or pollutants, whether above or below ground, and the Real Property and the use thereof are in full compliance with all environmental laws and regulations of applicable federal, state, town, village, and other governmental authorities.

(m) That the financial statements of Seller consisting of Balance Sheets, Statements of Profits and Losses and Tax Returns, copies of which are annexed hereto as "Exhibit H", represent fairly the financial position, income and expenses of the Seller as of the dates thereof and the results of the operations of the Seller and of the Business for the periods therein indicated, and were prepared in accordance with generally accepted accounting principles except as otherwise noted, as historically applied by Seller in accounting for the Business.

(n) That except to the extent reflected in the Balance Sheet dated _____, 19__, there are no liabilities of any nature, and Seller represents that it does not know or have reason to know of any liability of any nature not reflected in the said Balance Sheet.

(o) That Seller has filed all federal, state and local tax returns required to be filed by reason of the conduct of its business and has paid all income, franchise, real property, sales, and use and all other taxes due and payable which are applicable thereto, and shall file all tax returns and pay all taxes of whatever nature arising out of Seller's conduct of Business prior to the Closing Date.

(p) That since on or about _____, 199__, Seller has operated the Business only in the ordinary course and there has not been or occurred:

    (i) any change in the assets, liabilities or condition of Seller or the Business except changes in the ordinary course of business, which changes have not been, in the aggregate, materially adverse to the Seller or the Business;

    (ii) any damage, destruction or loss, whether covered by insurance or not, materially adversely affecting the Seller or the Business;

    (iii) any sales made or services rendered by the Seller other than sales made or services rendered in the regular course of business upon usual terms;

    (iv) any labor union organizing activity or any actual or threatened employee strikes, work stoppages, slow-downs or lockouts;

    (v) the institution or settlement of, or agreement to settle, any litigation, action or proceeding before any Court or governmental body relating to Seller or its property which would affect Buyer or encumber the Assets or the Business in any way;

    (vi) any failure to replenish Seller's inventories and supplies in a normal and customary manner consistent with its prior practice and prudent business practices prevailing in the industry, nor the making of any purchase commitment in excess of the normal, ordinary and usual requirements of the Seller's business or at any price in excess of the then current market price, or upon terms and conditions more onerous than those that are usual and customary in the industry, nor any change in Seller's selling pricing, promotion programs, advertising or personnel practices inconsistent with its prior practice and prudent business practices prevailing in the industry; or

(vii) any failure to pay any debt as it has become due.

(q) That Seller has complied with the material provisions of all of the contracts, licenses, agreements, leases, commitments and instruments of every kind entered into and pertaining to the ordinary course of the operation of Business.

(r) That attached hereto as "Exhibit I" is an accurate list of all patents, patent applications, trademarks, tradenames and copyrights presently held by Seller, all of which are valid and in good standing; and that Seller knows of no violation by others of the patents, trademarks, tradenames and other items to be transferred to Buyer or of the assertion of any claim adverse to any such rights.

(s) That except as otherwise noted herein, the services of a broker or finder have not been used by Seller in connection with any of the matters pertaining to this transaction. No broker's or finder's fee will become payable by Buyer by reason of the execution and delivery of this Agreement or the consummation of the transactions contemplated hereunder and arising out of the acts or omissions of Seller. Seller shall be responsible for payment of any and all brokerage commissions and fees of _____. Seller shall hold harmless and indemnify Buyer from and against any claim for broker's or finder's fees, including any cost or expense incurred in connection with the defense of any suit claiming such fees, or in any other manner pertaining to claims for such fees, which may become payable by reason of the acts or omissions of Seller.

(t) That Seller shall not, between the date hereof and the Closing Date, enter into any lease, tenancy or new contract affecting any of the Assets without prior written consent of the Buyer.

(u) That there are no actions, suits or proceedings, governmental or otherwise, pending or, to the best of the knowledge of the Seller, threatened against or affecting the Seller or any of the Assets (including, without limitation, condemnation or environmental proceedings), and there are no actions, suits or proceedings pending, contemplated or threatened by the Seller in connection with the Assets (including, without limitation, tax reduction proceedings) or by others protesting taxes affecting the Assets; and from and after the date hereof, the Seller shall not commence or allow to be commenced on its behalf any action, suit or proceeding with respect to the Assets without the prior written consent of the Buyer, which consent shall not be unreasonably withheld or delayed.

(v) That Seller holds all necessary licenses, permits and consents as are required to carry on the Business; that the schedule annexed hereto as "Exhibit J" is a true, correct and complete statement of all permits and licenses (collectively, the "Permits") issued by federal, state, municipal or other governmental departments or boards having authority as to lands, housing, vehicles, buildings, fire, health, labor or any other entity having jurisdiction over the Assets and the uses thereof; that no other permits or licenses are required in connection with the ownership or operation of the Assets or the Business; that at the Closing, Seller shall assign to Buyer all Permits which are assignable, and prior to and after the Closing, Seller shall cooperate with and assist Buyer in Buyer's obtaining in Buyer's own name any such Permits which are not assignable.

(w) That the only insurance policies maintained by the Seller with respect to the Assets (collectively, the "Insurance Policies") were obtained through _____ in Albany, New York, and Seller grants Buyer full authority to ascertain all information relating to such Insurance Policies and related matters directly from _____; that Seller shall maintain the Insurance Policies from the date hereof and through the Closing or the earlier termination of this Agreement; and that at or before the Closing, Seller shall advise Buyer in writing of any cancellation (or notice thereof) of any of the Insurance Policies.

(x) That attached as "Exhibit K" is a list and brief description of any oral or written agreement or arrangement to which Seller is a party, other than those described on other Exhibits to sections of this Agreement, of the following types:

(i) contracts for the employment of any officer, employee or agent which are not terminable on 30 days (or less) notice;

(ii) consulting agreements or distributor, dealer, manufacturer's representative, sales agency, licensing or royalty agreements, or advertising contracts which are not terminable on 30 days (or less) notice;

(iii) contracts with any labor organization;

(iv) holiday or other bonus, salary increase or gift programs for employees, distributors and/or customers of Seller;

(v) remuneration, profit sharing, bonus, stock option, stock purchase, severance pay, insurance, hospitalization, pension, retirement of similar contracts, plans or agreements providing employee benefits;

(vi) contracts or commitment for Seller's servicing or warranting of its products;

(vii) contracts or agreements with any prior owners of or parties who have had an interest in the Business, any or all of which, at Buyer's option, shall be assigned to Buyer at the Closing; and

(viii) agreements whereby Seller has a security interest in any assets owned by others.

and that all such agreements, arrangements or commitments to which Seller is a party and which are described in this subsection (none of which are to be assumed by Buyer except as otherwise expressly provided herein) have been entered into in the ordinary course of business.

(y) That following the Closing, Seller shall promptly pay (and provide Buyer with written confirmation of payment) any amounts of accrued or accruable up to the Closing Date on account of vacation time or vacation pay attributable to services performed by its employees prior to Closing Date.

(z) That no representation or warranty by Seller contained in this Agreement, or in any writing to be furnished pursuant hereto or previously furnished to Buyer, contains, or will to the best of Seller's knowledge contain, any untrue statement of fact, or omits, or will omit to state, any material fact required to make the statements herein or therein contained not misleading.

(aa) That Seller has disclosed to Buyer all material adverse facts known to it relating to the Assets or Business to Seller.

(bb) That the representations, warranties and covenants of Seller shall be true at the time of closing as though such representations and warranties were made at such time.

7. *Representation, Warranties and Covenants of Buyer.*

Buyer and Robert Jones, jointly and severally hereby represent, warrant, and covenant as follows:

(a) That Buyer is a corporation duly incorporated, validly existing and in good standing under the laws of the State of New York, is duly qualified and has the corporate power and authority to own its properties and to carry on its businesses as presently owned and conducted by it and as contemplated hereunder and to enter into and perform its obligations under this Agreement and the transactions contemplated hereunder.

(b) That Buyer has taken all requisite corporate action to authorize and approve the execution and delivery of this agreement and the consummation of the transactions contemplated hereunder.

(c) That this Agreement has been duly executed and delivered by Buyer and constitutes a valid and binding obligation of Buyer, enforceable against Buyer in accordance with its terms.

(d) That the execution and delivery of this Agreement and the performance of the agreements and covenants herein contemplated do not result in any breach of any of the terms, conditions or provisions of, or constitute a default under, any indenture, agreement or other instrument to which Buyer is a party or by which Buyer is bound or affected; nor shall it result in the violation of any law, or of any regulation, order or directive of any court, agency or other authority.

(e) That the financial statements of Buyer consisting of Balance Sheets, Statements of Profits and Losses and Tax Returns, copies of which are annexed hereto as "Exhibit N", represent fairly the financial position, income and expenses of the Buyer as of the dates thereof and the results of the operations of the Buyer and of the business of Buyer for the periods therein indicated, and that they were prepared in accordance with generally accepted accounting principles except as otherwise noted, as historically applied by Buyer in accounting for its business.

(f) That except to the extent reflected in the Balance Sheet dated _____, 19 __, there are no liabilities of any nature, and Buyer represents that it does not know or have reason to know of any liability of any nature not reflected in the said Balance Sheet.

(g) That Buyer will maintain the Working Capital, Current Ratio and Debt to Worth as described in Section 3(b) above during the period that any notes or other obligations to Seller are outstanding;

(h) That the services of a broker, finder or financial advisor have not been used by Buyer in connection with any of the matters pertaining to this transaction and no broker's, finder's or financial advisor's fee will become payable by Seller by reason of the execution and delivery of this Agreement or the consummation of the transactions contemplated hereunder and arising out of the acts or omissions of Buyer; and that Buyer shall hold Seller harmless and indemnify it from and against any claim for broker's, finder's or financial advisor's fees, including any cost or expense incurred in connection with the defense of any suit claiming such fees, or in any manner pertaining to claims for such fees, which may become payable by reason of the acts or omissions of Buyer.

8. *Conduct of Business Prior to Closing.*

(a) From the date hereof to the Closing Date, Seller covenants and agrees:

(i) to conduct the Business only in the ordinary course;

(ii) to maintain all insurance policies applicable to the Business in full force and effect and to maintain normal insurance coverage on the Business and the Assets;

(iii) unless the prior written consent of Buyer has been obtained, not to pay or agree to pay any special bonuses or special remuneration to any of its employees or establish or make any special contribution under or to any incentive or other compensation plan, or increase the salary or wage rate or other remuneration of any of its employees (except those regularly scheduled during such period and the amounts of which are in accordance with existing policy), or enter into any written employment contract, or put into effect any general compensation increase;

(iv) except as otherwise requested by Buyer, to use its best efforts to preserve the Business intact, to maintain the services of its present employees, and to preserve the goodwill of those having relations with Seller;

(v) to comply with all laws, regulations, ordinances, orders, injunctions and decrees applicable to Seller and the Business;

(vi) to afford to the officers and authorized representatives of Buyer (including, but not limited to, the attorneys and accountants of Buyer), full access to all of the Assets and properties, books, contracts, documents and records of Seller applicable to the Business, and to furnish to Buyer such information, including copies of pertinent records and documents, as Buyer reasonably may require to enable it to make a full and complete investigation of the affairs of Seller and the Business;

(vii) to the extent Seller has control, not to perform, take any action to incur or permit to exist any of the acts, transactions or occurrences of the type described in Section 6(p) hereof;

(viii) to maintain all services in connection with the Assets as presently maintained until the Closing Date, and from and after the date hereof, and until the Closing Date or the earlier termination of this Agreement, to keep and maintain the assets in the same manner in which they are currently being maintained and not to cause or permit any waste or nuisance to or against the Assets, and to the maintenance and operation of the Assets between the date hereof and the Closing Date so that the Assets shall be of the same quality and condition on the Closing Date as they are on date hereof;

(ix) unless the prior written consent of Buyer has been obtained, not to enter into any lease or license with respect to any of the Assets;

(x) not to disclose to its employees, customers or suppliers or others having business relations with Seller the details of the consideration to be paid by Buyer for the Assets.

(b) Buyer will take possession of the Assets and management of the Business being sold hereunder immediately after the Closing. In the regular course of business, purchase orders for materials and service have been placed by Seller with third parties and purchase orders from customers have been accepted. Payment for all materials and/or services received before the Closing Date will be made by Seller. Responsibility for payment for all services and materials received and accepted by Buyer, if any, after the Closing Date shall be borne by Buyer. Buyer shall have the option to fulfill all commitments to customers to furnish materials in accordance with the terms of such commitments as the same exists at the Closing Date. Accounts receivable for all merchandise shipped in the ordinary course of business prior to the Closing Date, whether billed or not, are to be the property of Seller. Accounts receivable for all merchandise shipped after the Closing, whether manufactured before or after that time, will be the property of Buyer.

Seller will deliver to Buyer at the Closing a true and correct list of all accounts receivable of the Business as of that date. The list shall also include any potential refunds owed by Seller. Seller shall be entitled to all payments on or in settlement of these accounts receivable and, to the extent Buyer shall receive any of these payments, Buyer shall promptly transfer or transmit same to Seller; provided, however, that Buyer may deduct from any of these payments any refunds due to the account of the debtor. All payments from customers listed on this list as delivered at the Closing shall first be presumed to be payments toward, or in satisfaction of, these accounts receivable in the order of the oldest invoice first and, after satisfaction of these accounts receivable, any remaining funds from these payments or any additional payments shall be presumed to be payments to the account of Buyer for materials sold by Buyer. All other payments on accounts receivable received by Buyer from and after the date of Closing under this Agreement, regardless of from whom and when accrued, shall be the property of Buyer. To the extent that Seller receives any payments from customers which are the property of Buyer, Seller shall promptly transfer or transmit same to Buyer

9. *Indemnification of Buyer.*

(a) Seller and Shareholders jointly and severally agree to defend, indemnify and hold Buyer harmless from any and all claims, injuries, damages, costs and expenses of any nature whatsoever, including attorneys' fees, arising from or connected with the following:

(i) any and all liabilities and obligations of and claims against Seller and/or Shareholders not expressly assumed by Buyer hereunder (including, but not by way of limitation, any claims for warranty and/or product liability, product correction or replacement arising out of products of the Business sold prior to the Closing Date, none of which claims or liabilities are being assumed by the Buyer);

(ii) any damages or loss incurred by Buyer in the event it elects to waive compliance with the Bulk Sales law set forth in Section 15 hereof; and

(iii) any and all claims, losses, damages and deficiencies resulting from a misrepresentation or a representation or breach of warranty of Seller contained in this Agreement, or any breach of any obligations of Seller or the Shareholders under any agreement delivered pursuant hereto including, without limitation, the agreements referred to in Section 11(e) and 11(f) hereof.

(b) Upon obtaining knowledge thereof, Buyer shall promptly notify Seller of any claim or demand pursuant to this Section 9 which Buyer has determined has given or could give rise to a right of indemnification under this Agreement, and Seller shall have a reasonable time to contest any such claim. If such claim or demand relates to a claim or demand asserted by a third party against Buyer, Seller shall have a reasonable time to contest any such claim and shall have the right to employ counsel to defend any such claim or demand asserted against Buyer, and Buyer shall have the right to cooperate in the defense of any such claim. So long as Seller is defending such claim, Buyer will not settle such claim. Buyer shall make available to Seller and its representatives all relevant records and materials required by it for its use in contesting any such claims hereunder.

10. *Insurance.*

For so long as the Promissory Note of Buyer remains unpaid, Buyer covenants, acknowledges and agrees that it shall purchase and maintain insurance on the Real Property described in "Exhibit A", including insurance on the buildings and all improvements located thereon, against loss or damage by fire and against loss or damage by such other risks as Seller shall require with such carrier and in such form as to be satisfactory to Seller. In no way limiting the foregoing, such insurance shall include a so-called "broad extended coverage endorsement" in amounts at all times sufficient to prevent Buyer or Seller from becoming co-insurer under the terms of applicable policies, but in any event no less than 100% of the then full insurable value of the building. The term "full insurable value" shall mean actual replacement value (exclusive of costs of excavations, foundations and footings). Said policy shall have endorsements for boiler insurance and for elevator insurance in such amount as shall be determined and approved by Seller. Seller shall be named as an additional insured on said policies of insurance, and the proceeds of such insurance shall be payable to Seller as its interest may appear.

Copies of the policies required hereunder or certificates evidencing such insurance shall be provided to Seller within 10 days of delivery to Seller of the Promissory Note described in Section 3 above. Buyer shall deliver to Seller certificates of endorsement naming Seller as additional insured in all the above policies of insurance. Notwithstanding the foregoing, such policies shall provide that any named insured may sue another named insured and the carrier shall in such event, defend and indemnify the named insured under the policy, and shall further provide that the carrier expressly waive the right of subrogation, if any, that it may have against any named insured.

§ 6.187   BUYING & SELLING A SMALL BUSINESS   Ch. 6

Buyer shall pay or cause to be paid premiums for all of the insurance policies which Buyer is obligated to carry hereunder and will deliver to Seller evidence of such payment before the payment of such premiums come into default. Such policies shall provide that Seller shall be entitled to 30 days written notice of cancellation. Buyer shall cause renewals of expiring policies to be written and the policies or copies thereof to be delivered to Seller at least ten days before the expiration date of such expiring policies.

11. *Seller's Deliveries to Buyer at Closing.*

At the Closing, Seller shall deliver or cause to be delivered to Buyer, as appropriate, the following:

(a) All such deeds (including without limitation, a warranty deed with lien covenants in proper form for recording, conveying the Real Property described in "Exhibit A" hereof), bills of sale, contract assignments, patent and trademark assignments and other assignments, in form reasonably acceptable to Buyer's counsel, which are reasonably required to convey, transfer and assign the Assets to Buyer in accordance with the terms of this Agreement;

(b) The opinion of _____, counsel for Seller, dated the Closing Date, to the effect that:

(i) Seller is a corporation duly organized, validly existing and in good standing under the laws of the State of New York;

(ii) Seller has the corporate power and authority to enter into and perform this Agreement, and that the execution, delivery and performance of this Agreement, and the transactions contemplated hereunder, have been duly authorized on the part of, and the Agreement has been duly executed and delivered by, Seller;

(iii) This Agreement is a valid and binding obligation of Seller and is enforceable against Seller in accordance with its terms, except as may be limited by any bankruptcy, insolvency or other similar laws affecting the enforcement of creditors' rights in general or general principles of equity; and

(iv) The execution and delivery of this Agreement and the performance by Seller of the terms herein do not conflict with or result in a violation of the Certificate of Incorporation or By-laws of Seller or, to the knowledge of such counsel, result in a breach of any material terms, conditions or provisions of, or constitute a material default under, any material indenture, agreement or other instrument to which Seller is a party or by which Seller is bound or affected or the violation of any law, or of any regulation, order or directive of any court, agency or other authority;

(c) Certified copies of minutes or unanimous written consents of the Shareholders and Board of Directors of Seller approving the execution of this Agreement and the consummation of the transactions contemplated hereunder in accordance with Section 909 of the Business Corporation Law of the State of New York and other applicable law;

(d) The certificate referred to in Section 16(d) hereof;

(e) Executed Non–Competition, confidentiality, and Continuity of Business Dealings Agreement in the form annexed hereto as "Exhibit L";

(f) All contracts, licenses, permits, files and documents pertaining to the Assets being sold hereunder, including all plans and specifications, if any, for the buildings and improvements located on the Real Property, and all customer lists, suppliers' names and similar data utilized by Seller in its conduct of the Business from _____, 19 __ through the Closing Date (and Buyer and Seller shall have full access after Closing to such records held by the other party for the purpose of completing their bookkeeping and accounting procedures and for other purposes for which such access is reasonably necessary or proper);

(g) The list of accounts receivable referred to in Section 8(b) hereof;

(h) All keys to the buildings and improvements, file cabinets, vehicles and other Assets;

(i) Written assurance from _____, Brokers, respecting the confidentiality of the within transaction in the form annexed hereto as "Exhibit M".

(j) All other documents required to be delivered to Buyer under the provisions of this Agreement which are mentioned herein, and such further instruments of conveyance, transfer and assignment or other documents as may reasonably be required by the Buyer or its counsel in order to effectuate the provisions of this Agreement and the transactions contemplated herein.

12. *Buyer's Deliveries to Seller at Closing.*

At the Closing, Buyer, as appropriate, shall deliver or cause to be delivered to Seller:

(a) Payment of the Purchase Price of the Assets pursuant to Section 3;

(b) Certified copies of minutes or unanimous written consents of the Board of Directors of Buyer and, if required, the Stockholders of Buyer, approving the execution of this Agreement and the consummation of the transactions contemplated hereunder;

(c) The mortgage and security agreement referred to in Section 3(d) hereof;

(d) The opinion of Pattison, Sampson, Ginsberg and Griffin, P.C., counsel for Buyer, dated the Closing Date, stating that:

(i) Buyer is a corporation duly organized and is validly existing and in good standing under the laws of the State of New York;

(ii) Buyer has the corporate power and authority to enter into and perform this Agreement and the transactions contemplated hereunder, and that the execution, delivery and performance of this Agreement, and the transactions contemplated hereunder, have been duly authorized by all requisite corporate action on the part of, and this Agreement has been duly executed and delivered by, Buyer;

(iii) This Agreement is a valid and binding obligation of Buyer and is enforceable against Buyer in accordance with its terms, except as may be limited by any bankruptcy, insolvency or other similar laws affecting the enforcement of creditors' rights in general or general principles of equity; and

(iv) The execution and delivery of this Agreement and the performance by Buyer of the terms herein do not conflict with or result in a violation of its Certificate of Incorporation or By-laws or, to the knowledge of such counsel, result in a breach of any of the terms, conditions or provisions of, or constitute a default under, any indenture, agreement or other instrument to which Buyer is a party or by which Buyer is bound or affected; nor shall it result in the violation of any law or of any regulation, order or directive of any court, agency or other authority;

(e) All other documents required to be delivered to Seller under the provisions of this Agreement which are mentioned herein, and such further documents as may reasonably be required by the Seller or its counsel in order to effectuate the provisions of this Agreement and the transactions contemplated herein.

13. *Matters Respecting the Real Property*.

(a) If, at or prior to the Closing Date, defects or objections to title come to Buyer's notice, and if Buyer shall be unwilling to waive the same, Buyer shall notify Seller and Seller shall take such action as shall be necessary to cure or dispose of such defects. Seller shall be entitled to a reasonable adjournment of the Closing Date, not to exceed forty-five days (but in no event shall the period of adjournment exceed the date of expiration of any financing commitment from any lending institution providing Buyer with financing for acquisition of the Assets) to cure any such defects. If Seller shall fail to cure any such defects, Buyer shall have the option of accepting such title as Seller is able to convey with an allowance equal to all costs of removing such defects (including, without limitation, attorneys' fees) or of rejecting such title and terminating this Agreement.

(b) If on the Closing Date there are any other defects or objections to title to the Real Property which Seller is obligated to pay and discharge, Seller may use any portion of the cash balance of the purchase price payable to it to satisfy the same, provided Seller shall simultaneously either (i) deliver to Buyer at the Closing instruments, in recordable form, sufficient to satisfy or record such objections to title, together with the identity of the title insurance company issuing a policy, or (ii) deposit with the title company sufficient monies, acceptable to and required by the title company, to insure the obtaining and recording of such satisfaction and the issuance of title insurance to Buyer free of any such objections to title. Buyer, if request is made within a reasonable time prior to the Closing Date, agrees to provide at the Closing separate certified checks as requested, aggregating the amount of the cash balance of the purchase price, to facilitate the satisfaction of any such defects or objections to title. The existence of any such defects or objections to title shall not be deemed objections to title if Seller shall comply with the foregoing requirements.

(c) Seller has no knowledge of any special or other assessments now affecting, planned or contemplated to affect, the Real Property or any part thereof, and Seller shall advise Buyer forthwith of any such assessment, existing or threatened, of which Seller becomes aware on or prior to the Closing Date. If on the Closing Date the Real Property, or any part thereof, shall be or shall have been affected by one or more assessments which are or may become payable in installments, Seller shall cause to be paid at the Closing any installment then due but unpaid, and the next installment coming due after the Closing shall be prorated as of the Closing Date, and Seller shall then pay its proportionate share to Buyer.

(d) Seller agrees to execute and deliver to the title company at Closing such documentation, if any, as the title company shall reasonably require to evidence that the execution and delivery of this Agreement and the consummation of the transactions contemplated hereby have been duly authorized.

(e) The cost of abstracting title and the fees for title insurance shall be borne by Buyer.

(f) At the Closing, Seller shall deliver to Buyer (i) a check payable to the order of the recording office of Rensselaer County for the amount of the documentary stamps to be affixed to the deeds to the Real Property in accordance with Article 31 of the New York Tax Law, and (ii) a check payable to the order of the appropriate officer for any real property gains tax, if any, payable by reason of delivery of said deeds.

(g) At the Closing, the following items shall be apportioned between Seller and Buyer as of midnight of the day immediately preceding the Closing Date, except as otherwise specifically provided for herein:

(i) real property taxes and water charges and sewer rents, if any, on the basis of the fiscal year for which assessed;

(ii) to the extent Seller is billed for electricity, gas or telephone services, charges therefor, provided, however, that Seller shall notify the utility companies furnishing such services that the billing thereof to Seller shall be discontinued on the day immediately preceding the Closing Date, in which event Buyer shall make arrangements to have such billing charged to Buyer commencing with the Closing Date and Seller shall pay all charges with respect to such utilities for the period prior to the Closing Date promptly after receipt of such bills; and

(iii) fuel, if any.

(h) *Risk of Loss.* If, prior to the Closing Date, the building or any other improvements constituting a portion of the Real Property, or any machinery and equipment utilized in the Business, are materially damaged by fire or other casualty, or if any portion of the Real Property shall be taken by eminent domain, or there shall be a material obstruction of access to any of the buildings or other improvements by virtue of a taking by eminent domain, Seller shall, within ten (10) days of such damage or taking (but in any event prior to the Closing Date if the Closing Date falls within the 10–day notice period), notify Buyer thereof and Buyer shall have the option to terminate this Agreement upon notice to Seller; provided further, however, that Buyer's rights under this Agreement to consummate the transactions contemplated hereby shall be extended, if necessary, so that the Closing Date shall not be prior to the termination of said 10–day notice period. In the event that Buyer shall so elect to terminate this Agreement, both parties shall, except as otherwise provided herein, be relieved and released from any further liability hereunder. In the event that Buyer shall not elect to terminate this Agreement upon any such taking or material damage (or in the event that the damage shall not be deemed material as hereinafter provided) the following provisions shall apply: (a) Seller shall not have the right to terminate this Agreement, (b) Seller shall receive all proceeds of insurance and all condemnation awards in trust for Buyer unless Seller shall elect to restore such damage, (c) Seller, if it elects to restore such damage so that it will not be deemed "material", or if requested by Buyer, shall commence all repairs and restoration necessitated by such damage or taking, (d) the adjustment of losses with the insurance carrier, to the extent effected prior to the Closing Date, shall be done by Buyer, and the same shall apply in the case of negotiations with any condemning authority (provided that Seller has not elected to restore such damage), (e) the purchase price shall not be affected by such damage or taking, (f) Seller, at the Closing and upon receipt of the purchase price, shall pay to Buyer any sums of money collected by Seller under the Insurance Policies or as condemnation awards and shall assign, transfer and set over to Buyer all Seller's right, title and interest in, to and under the Insurance Policies and awards (except to the extent that such may be on account of personal property not included in this sale) and any further sums payable thereupon or by reason thereof unless Seller shall elect to restore such damage, and (g) Buyer shall have the right to accelerate the Closing Date upon at least ten (10) days prior written notice to Seller unless Seller shall elect to restore such damage, wherein Buyer shall designate a substitute date for the Closing.

Any damage by fire or other casualty shall be deemed "material" (i) if the cost to repair or restore such damage, as estimated by a reputable and experienced contractor designated by Buyer and approved by Seller (which approval shall not be unreasonably withheld or delayed), shall be more than $50,000.00 and Seller shall elect not to restore such damage. The parties expressly waive the provisions of Section 5–1311 of the New York General Obligations Law and agree that their respective rights in the case of fire or casualty or condemnation shall be governed by the provisions in this Section 12(i). In the event that Seller shall incur expenses in performing repairs or restoration authorized by Buyer (providing that Seller has not elected to restore such damage) and Seller has not been reimbursed from the proceeds of insurance or condemnation awards on or prior to the Closing Date, Buyer shall pay to Seller at the Closing the amount of such reasonable expenses as certified by Seller against delivery of the assignment referred to above of Seller's right, title and interest in and to the insurance proceeds and awards, as the case may be.

14. *Change of Corporate Name.*

At the Closing, Seller will deliver to Buyer a duly executed and acknowledged certificate of amendment to Seller's certificate of incorporation or other appropriate document which is required to change Seller's corporate name to a new name bearing no resemblance to its present name so as to make Seller's present name available to Buyer. Buyer is hereby authorized to file such certificate or other document in order to effectuate such change of name on or after the Closing Date as Buyer shall elect.

15. *Bulk Sales Compliance.*

At least fifteen (15) days prior to Closing, Seller shall furnish Buyer with (a) a true and accurate schedule of Seller's assets, (b) a list of the names and addresses of all of Seller's creditors, including all creditors which to Seller's knowledge have disputed or contingent claims against Seller as of such date, (c) a long form of notice addressed to each such creditor, and (d) any other documents or information necessary to effect compliance in all respects with all applicable Bulk Sales Laws so as to render Buyer free of any of Seller's liabilities not assumed by Buyer hereunder, all of which unassumed liabilities Seller agrees promptly to pay or cause to be paid when due. Buyer may at Seller's request, but shall not be required to, waive compliance with the Bulk Sales Laws as aforesaid, in which event Seller shall indemnify Buyer for any damages incurred by Buyer resulting from such waiver or from Buyer's reliance upon the completeness and accuracy of any information provided to Buyer by Seller under this Section 15.

16. *Conditions Precedent to Buyer's Obligations.*

All obligations of Buyer hereunder are subject to the fulfillment of each of the following conditions at or prior to the Closing, and Seller shall exert its best efforts to insure that each such condition is fulfilled:

(a) All representations and warranties of Seller contained herein, and in any document delivered pursuant hereto, shall be true and correct when made and at, and as of, the Closing;

(b) All obligations required by the terms of this Agreement to be performed by Seller at or before the Closing shall have been duly and properly performed;

(c) Since the date of this Agreement, there shall not have occurred any material adverse change in the condition (financial or otherwise), business, properties, assets or prospects of Seller;

(d) There shall be delivered to Buyer a certificate executed by the President and Secretary of Seller, and by its Shareholders, individually, dated the date of the Closing, certifying to the fulfillment of the conditions set forth in paragraphs (a), (b) and (c) of this Section 16;

(e) At Buyer's option, the obligations of Seller to sell and of Buyer to buy the Assets are further conditioned upon Buyer's review and acceptance of the results of a cost study of the Business to be undertaken by Buyer's certified public accountants, such study to be performed within ten (10) days of the date of the execution of this Agreement. If Buyer concludes, based upon such cost study, that the gross profits percentages are not in line with its anticipated results, it may cancel this Agreement by giving written notice to Seller within five (5) days of receipt of such study, and no party shall then have any claim against the others. This condition is waived if Seller has not received a Notice of Cancellation within twenty (20) days of the date of this Agreement; and

(f) All documents required to be delivered to Buyer by Seller at or prior to the Closing shall have been so delivered.

17. *Conditions Precedent to Seller's Obligations.*

All obligations of Seller at the Closing are subject to the fulfillment of each of the following conditions at or prior to the Closing:

(a) All representations and warranties of Buyer contained herein, and in any document delivered pursuant hereto, shall be true and correct when made and at, and as of, the Closing;

(b) All obligations required by the terms of this Agreement to be performed by Buyer at or before the Closing shall have been duly and properly performed;

(c) There shall be delivered to Seller a certificate executed by the President and Secretary of Buyer, dated the date of the Closing, certifying to the fulfillment of the conditions set forth in paragraphs (a) and (b) of this Section 17; and

(d) All documents required to be delivered to Seller by Buyer at or prior to the Closing shall have been so delivered.

18. *Nature and Survival of Representations and Warranties.*

(a) All statements made by Seller in this Agreement or in any certificate or other instrument delivered by or on behalf of Seller pursuant to this Agreement shall be deemed joint and several representations and warranties of Seller and each of the Shareholders who are made parties to this Agreement for purposes of making such statements.

(b) All representations, warranties, indemnities, covenants and agreements made by Buyer, Seller and the Shareholders hereunder shall survive the Closing.

19. *Restrictive Covenant.*

Seller's Shareholders jointly and severally covenant and agree that for a period of five (5) years commencing on the Closing date, they will not, (i) directly or indirectly, whether as principal or agent, officer, director, employee, consultant or otherwise, alone or in association with any other person, firm, corporation or other business organization, carry on or be engaged, concerned or take part in or render services to, or own, share in the earnings of, or invest in the stocks, bonds or other securities of any person, firm, corporation or other business organization (other than Buyer or its affiliates) engaged in the business of Seller or Buyer as presently conducted within _____ miles of any operating office of the business. Seller's Shareholders further covenant and agree that they shall not, whether for their own account or for the account of any other person, firm, corporation or other business entity, interfere with the Buyer's relationship with, or endeavor to entice away from the Buyer any person, firm, corporation or other business entity who is or has been an employee, consultant, distributor, distributing agent or subagent, production contractor, supplier, source of material and/or product, or a customer of, or in the habit of dealing with Seller. Seller's Shareholders further agree not to divulge, communicate, use to the detriment of Buyer or for the benefit of themselves or any other persons, or misuse in any way, any confidential information, trade secrets of Seller or Buyer, including personnel, information, secret processes, know-how, customer lists, formulas or other technical data for so long as such information, data or trade secrets shall remain confidential. The Shareholders acknowledge and agree that any information or data which they have acquired concerning any of these matters or items was received in confidence and as fiduciaries of Seller or Buyer.

In the event of a breach or threatened breach of the provisions of this Section 19, Buyer shall be entitled to a temporary restraining order and preliminary and permanent injunction enjoining such breach or threatened breach, and in either case, no bond or other security shall be required in connection therewith. Nothing herein shall be construed as prohibiting Buyer from pursuing any other remedies available at equity or in law for such breach or threatened breach, including but not limited to the recovery of damages.

In the event that any court having jurisdiction should find any part of this Section 19 to be unenforceable in any respect, it is the intention of the parties that such finding shall not serve to invalidate the remainder of this Section 19, or of this Agreement, and that this Agreement, and particularly this Section, shall be deemed automatically modified to a scope of application which makes it valid and enforceable as the same may be determined by such court, and the remainder of this Agreement shall remain in full force and effect.

20. *Additional Agreements.*

Seller and Buyer covenant and agree as follows:

(a) Seller and Buyer will cooperate with one another in making available to each other records, personnel and other assistance which may be necessary or convenient in connection with defending any claim or claims made by any third party against any of the other parties relating to the Business.

(b) Seller shall retain title to all books and records pertaining to the Assets and/or the Business unless otherwise provided for herein; but notwithstanding the foregoing, Buyer shall have the right to have such books and records physically located at the Facility for a period of two (2) months following Closing, and shall have the unrestricted right to photocopy any or all such books and records as it may desire.

(c) For a period of seven (7) years from the Closing, Buyer will not destroy or otherwise dispose of any books and records of the Business acquired by Buyer hereunder, and Seller for a like period agrees that it will not destroy or otherwise dispose of any books and records in its possession pertaining to the Business. Seller and Buyer shall exercise due care and diligence in preserving and maintaining all such books and records pertaining to the Business and shall make the same available to each other and their representatives upon reasonable prior notice and during normal business hours for the purpose of inspection and making copies of extracts therefrom. In the event Buyer shall at any time after the aforementioned period determine that it has no further use for any of said books and records, it shall then have the right, upon twenty (20) days' notice to Seller, to return the same to Seller, and, unless Seller advises Buyer that it will accept such return, Buyer shall have the right to destroy same.

(d) Seller and Buyer agree that with respect to any agreements or other instruments requiring the consent of a third party for a valid conveyance, transfer, assignment or delivery, each party will continue to use its best efforts to obtain any third party consents required but not obtained by the Closing Date.

(e) Seller and Buyer agree to make no independent announcement of this Agreement to customers or suppliers of the Business and not to disclose to such parties at any time on or after the Closing Date any details of the consideration paid by Buyer for the Business or any details of the royalties provided for herein.

(f) At the closing, Seller shall collect and Buyer shall pay the New York State sales tax due by reason of the sale of the Assets to Buyer. Notwithstanding the foregoing, it is agreed that Buyer shall not be responsible for any sales tax due on any sales made by Seller in the course of its operation of the Business.

(g) From and after the time of Closing, Buyer shall be responsible for all insurance with respect to the Assets and the Business, it being understood and agreed that all insurance coverage carried by Seller will terminate with respect to the Assets and the Business upon the Closing.

(h) Seller and Buyer agree to cooperate and to take such action as is possible in order to enable Buyer to constitute a "successor employer" with respect to Buyer's employees for the calendar year 19 __ for purposes of FICA and the withholding of federal and state income taxes, this to be at no cost to Seller.

21. *General Provisions.*

(a) Except as otherwise expressly and specifically provided herein, each party shall pay its own expenses incident to the preparation and consummation of this Agreement and the transactions contemplated hereunder including, without limitation, all fees of its counsel and accountants.

(b) Waiver by any party of any breach of or failure to comply with any provision of this Agreement by another party shall not be construed as, or constitute a continuing waiver of, or a waiver of any other breach of, or failure to comply with, any other provision of this Agreement.

(c) All notices and other communications with respect to this Agreement and the transactions contemplated hereunder shall be given by an instrument or instruments in writing; and no notice or other communication with respect to this Agreement or any of the transactions contemplated hereunder shall be effective unless and until given by such an instrument or instruments in writing.

(d) Unless otherwise notified in writing to the contrary, all notices and other communications (including, without limitation, copies of process) with respect to this Agreement and the transactions contemplated

§ 6.187   BUYING & SELLING A SMALL BUSINESS   Ch. 6

hereunder, (i) if directed to Seller shall be addressed to it at _____, New York, Attention: _____; with a copy thereof directed to _____, New York, (ii) if directed to _____ shall be addressed to him C/O _____; (iv) if directed to Buyer shall be addressed to it at _____, New York, Attention: _____, with a copy thereof directed to Pattison, Sampson, Ginsberg & Griffin, P.C., 22 First Street, Troy, New York 12180, Attention: _____, Esq.

(e) All notices and other communications with respect to this Agreement and the transactions contemplated hereunder which are directed as provided in Section 20(d) hereof, if delivered personally, shall be effective and deemed to have been given upon delivery; if delivered by telegraph, shall be effective and deemed to have been given upon delivery to the telegraph office; if delivered by telex, shall be effective and deemed to have been given upon transmission, and, if delivered by mail, shall be effective and deemed to have been given three business days after deposit in the United States mail, registered or certified, postage prepaid.

(f) This Agreement shall be construed and interpreted in accordance with and governed by the laws of the State of New York, excluding the "conflict of laws" rules of that state.

(g) The captions as to the contents of particular sections herein are inserted only for the convenience of the parties and are in no way to be construed as part of this Agreement or as a limitation or expansion of the scope of the particular sections to which they refer.

(h) In the event any provision of this Agreement or portion thereof is found to be wholly or partially invalid, illegal or unenforceable in any judicial proceeding, then such provision shall be deemed to be modified or restricted to the extent and in the manner necessary to render the same valid and enforceable, or shall be deemed excised from this Agreement, as the case may require, and this Agreement shall be construed and enforced to the maximum extent permitted by law as if such provision had been originally incorporated herein, as so modified or restricted, or as if such provision had not been originally incorporated herein, as the case may be.

(i) The rights, remedies, powers and privileges provided in this Agreement are cumulative and not exclusive and shall be in addition to any and all other rights, remedies, powers and privileges granted by law, rule, regulation or instrument.

(j) This writing constitutes the entire agreement of the parties with respect to the subject matter hereof and may not be modified, amended or terminated except by a written agreement specifically referring to this Agreement signed by all of the parties hereto.

(k) This Agreement shall be binding upon and inure to the benefit of the parties, their successors and assigns.

(*l*) Each party hereto shall cooperate, shall take such further action and shall execute and deliver such further documents as may be reasonably requested by any other party in order to carry out the provisions and purposes of this Agreement.

(m) This Agreement may be executed in one or more counterparts, all of which, taken together, shall be deemed one original.

IN WITNESS WHEREOF, the parties have duly executed this Agreement on the day and year first above written.

Exhibit D
NOTE
THIS NOTE IS NON-NEGOTIABLE

$850,000.00

Dated: Troy, New York
November ___, 1996

FOR VALUE RECEIVED, the undersigned, XYZ, Inc., and ROBERT JONES (the "Makers") promise to pay to the order of JOHN SMITH AND MARY SMITH, residing at 101 Warren Street, Troy, New York (the "Payees"), at said address of Payees or at such other place as may be designated in writing from time to time by the Payees of this Note, the principal sum of EIGHT HUNDRED FIFTY THOUSAND and no/100 DOLLARS ($850,000.00), lawful money of the United States, together with interest thereon at the rates determined from time to time in accordance with the provisions set forth in the Schedule A–1 annexed hereto and made a part hereof, said principal sum and such interest to be paid in the manner set forth in said Schedule A–1.

Each of the following shall be an "Event of Default": (1) if any installment or payment of principal and/or interest is not paid within ten (10) days of its due date and any Maker fails to pay such installment or payment in full within ten (10) days after receipt by Makers of written Notice from Payees that such installment or payment is ten (10) days past due, or (2) if any Maker files a petition in bankruptcy, or (3) if a petition in bankruptcy is filed against any Maker and such Maker fails to have the same discharged within ninety (90) days, or (4) if XYZ, Inc., is dissolved as a corporate entity, or (5) if XYZ, Inc., fails to maintain, during the term of this Note, the following:

(a) Working Capital of at least $2,000,000;

(b) Current ratio (as that term is defined by generally accepted accounting principles) of at least 1.25:1; and

(c) Debt to Worth (Fund Balance) not to exceed 1:1

and if Payees, within 10 days of such failure by such Maker gives written notice thereof, specifying such failure to such Maker and if any Maker fails to cure the same within 10 days of receipt of said notice; or (6) if XYZ, Inc., or a Maker breaches any material term of an agreement dated October 7, 1996 (hereinafter "Agreement") and if Payees, within 10 days of such breach, give written notice thereof, specifying such breach and if such Maker fails to cure the same within 10 days of receipt of said notice; or (7) if any Maker sells all or substantially all of the assets, not in the ordinary course of business, purchased from ABC, Inc., under the said Agreement dated October 7, 1996.

In the event of the occurrence of any Event of Default and the failure of any Maker to cure the same within the grace period (if any) applicable thereto, the entire unpaid principal balance and all accrued but unpaid interest shall, at the option of Payees, become immediately due and payable in full. Payees shall give Makers written notice of any such election by Payees to declare this Note to be immediately due and payable, and in the event that Payees exercises their option to accelerate the unpaid principal balance and all accrued but unpaid interest of this Note in accordance with the terms and provisions above set forth, the Makers hereby authorize any attorney to appear for them in the Supreme Court, Rensselaer County, New York, and waive the issuance and service of process and confess a judgment against them in favor of Payees for the unpaid principal balance and all accrued but unpaid interest of this Note.

No waiver or extension of time granted by Payees with respect to any Event of Default shall be construed as a waiver or extension of time with respect to any subsequent Event of Default.

This Note is secured by, inter alia, a Mortgage made by Makers to Payees bearing even date herewith and intended to be recorded in the _____ County Clerk's Office and a Security Agreement by and between Makers and Payees bearing even date herewith and intended to be recorded in the _____ County Clerk's Office. The entire unpaid principal balance of this Note shall, at the option of the Payees, become immediately due and payable in full upon the occurrence of any default or event which, under the terms of said Mortgage and/or Security Agreement, and/or of any other document incidental to this Note, and/or said Mortgage or Security Agreement, gives the Payees the right to declare the whole of said principal sum to become immediately due and payable in full. The terms and provisions of said Mortgage and Security Agreement are hereby made a part of this Note, and are incorporated herein by reference.

Each Maker hereby represents that it has full power, authority and legal right and capacity to execute this Note, and XYZ, Inc., hereby represents that such execution and delivery were duly authorized by its Board of Directors.

The obligations of the Makers hereunder are joint and several.

Any Maker may prepay all or any part of this Note at any time, without penalty.

This Note may not be changed or terminated orally. Any such change to this Note must be in writing and signed by the parties.

This Note may not be assigned by the Makers without the prior written consent of Payees.

This Note shall be governed by the laws of the State of New York.

This Note shall be binding upon the Makers and their successors and assigns and shall inure to the benefit of Payees and their heirs and personal representatives (provided, however, this Note is not negotiable, and except for such transfer of this Note as may result from the death of either or both Payees, neither any Payee nor any heir, personal representative, successor or assign of any Payee may assign, transfer, pledge, hypothecate, grant security interests in or otherwise dispose of this Note or any interest in this Note without the prior written consent of the Makers).

IN WITNESS WHEREOF the Makers have duly executed this Note as of the date first written above.

XYZ, Inc.

By:_____
ROBERT JONES, President

_____
ROBERT JONES

STATE OF NEW YORK)
) ss.:
COUNTY OF)

On this _____ day of _____, 19__, before me personally came ROBERT JONES, to me known, who, being by me duly sworn, did depose and say that he resides at 75 Grant Street, Albany, New York; that he is the President of XYZ, Inc., the corporation described in and which executed the within instrument; that the foregoing instrument was executed by order of the Board of Directors of said corporation and that he signed his name thereto by like order.

_____
Notary Public

STATE OF NEW YORK)
) ss.:
COUNTY OF)

§ 6.187   BUYING & SELLING A SMALL BUSINESS   Ch. 6

On this _____ day of _____, 19__, before me personally came ROBERT JONES, to me personally known and known to me to be the individual described in and who executed the foregoing instrument, and he acknowledged to me that he executed the same.

_____
Notary Public

Schedule A-1

Payment Provisions

1. (a) The unpaid principal balance of this Note shall bear interest computed from the date hereof at the rates determined from time to time in accordance with the following provisions: The interest rate shall be eight and three quarters per cent (8.75%) per annum from the date hereof to September 30, 1997, inclusive. Thereafter, the interest rate shall be adjusted on the first day of October of each year, starting with the first day of October, 1997, and continuing to and including the first day of October, 2005 (each date on which the interest rate is to be adjusted being hereinafter referred to as an "Interest Rate Change Date"). On each such Interest Rate Change Date, the interest rate shall become equal to the sum of (x) the "Prime Rate" (as hereinafter defined) as published most recently prior to such Interest Rate Change Date plus (y) one percent (1.0%) per annum; provided, however, that if the interest rate as so computed on any Interest Rate Change Date would exceed the maximum rate permitted by any Usury Law applicable to this obligation, the interest rate becoming effective on such Interest Rate Change Date shall be equal to such maximum rate. The interest rate becoming effective on each Interest Rate Change Date shall remain in effect from such Interest Rate Change Date to and including the day before the next Interest Rate Change Date; provided, however, that the interest rate becoming effective on the final Interest Rate Change Date (October 1, 2005) shall remain in effect from October 1, 2005, through the date on which this Note shall have been repaid in full.

(b) The "Prime Rate" shall be the prime rate of interest, in per cent per annum, as published from time to time in The Wall Street Journal, or its successor. If said "Prime Rate" shall cease to be published in The Wall Street Journal, Payee shall designate a reasonably comparable interest rate index which shall thereafter be used as the "Prime Rate" hereunder.

2. (a) A payment of interest only shall be due on the first day of November, 1996. Thereafter, payments of principal and interest (hereinafter referred to as "Monthly Payments") shall be due and payable on the first day of each month, starting with the first day of December, 1996, and continuing to and including the first day of November, 2006.

Ch. 6   **ASSET PURCHASE**   **§ 6.187**

The amount of the Monthly Payments shall be adjusted from time to time in accordance with the provisions hereinafter set forth.

(b) Each such Monthly Payment falling due between December 1, 1996, and October 1, 1997, inclusive, shall be in the amount of $_____ , and each such Monthly Payment shall be applied first toward interest computed at the rate of 8.75% per annum and then toward reduction of the unpaid principal balance.

(c) Each Monthly Payment falling due between November 1, 1997, and October 1, 1998, inclusive, shall be in the amount of the monthly installment necessary to amortize in full the principal balance remaining unpaid after application of the Monthly Payment due on October 1, 1997, together with interest thereon computed at the rate becoming effective on October 1, 1997, in 109 equal monthly installments, and each such Monthly Payment shall be applied first toward interest computed at the rate becoming effective on October 1, 1997, and then toward reduction of the principal balance.

(d) Each Monthly Payment falling due between November 1, 1998, and October 1, 1999, inclusive, shall be in the amount of the monthly installment necessary to amortize in full the principal balance remaining unpaid after application of the Monthly Payment due on October 1, 1998, together with interest thereon computed at the rate becoming effective on October 1, 1998, in 97 equal monthly installments, and each such Monthly Payment shall be applied first toward interest computed at the rate becoming effective on October 1, 1998, and then toward reduction of the principal balance.

(e) Each Monthly Payment falling due between November 1, 1999, and October 1, 2000, inclusive, shall be in the amount of the monthly installment necessary to amortize in full the principal balance remaining unpaid after application of the Monthly Payment due on October 1, 1999, together with interest thereon computed at the rate becoming effective on October 1, 1999, in 85 equal monthly installments, and each such Monthly Payment shall be applied first toward interest computed at the rate becoming effective on October 1, 1999, and then toward reduction of the principal balance.

(f) Each Monthly Payment falling due between November 1, 2000, and October 1, 2001, inclusive, shall be in the amount of the monthly installment necessary to amortize in full the principal balance remaining unpaid after application of the Monthly Payment due on October 1, 2000, together with interest thereon computed at the rate becoming effective on October 1, 2000, in 73 equal monthly installments, and each such Monthly Payment shall be applied first toward interest computed at the rate becoming effective on October 1, 2000, and then toward reduction of the principal balance.

(g) Each Monthly Payment falling due between November 1, 2001, and October 1, 2002, inclusive, shall be in the amount of the monthly

§ 6.187   BUYING & SELLING A SMALL BUSINESS   Ch. 6

installment necessary to amortize in full the principal balance remaining unpaid after application of the Monthly Payment due on October 1, 2001, together with interest thereon computed at the rate becoming effective on October 1, 2001, in 61 equal monthly installments, and each such Monthly Payment shall be applied first toward interest computed at the rate becoming effective on October 1, 2001, and then toward reduction of the principal balance.

(h) Each Monthly Payment falling due between November 1, 2002, and October 1, 2003, inclusive, shall be in the amount of the monthly installment necessary to amortize in full the principal balance remaining unpaid after application of the Monthly Payment due on October 1, 2002, together with interest thereon computed at the rate becoming effective on October 1, 2002, in 49 equal monthly installments, and each such Monthly Payment shall be applied first toward interest computed at the rate becoming effective on October 1, 2002, and then toward reduction of the principal balance.

(i) Each Monthly Payment falling due between November 1, 2003, and October 1, 2004, inclusive, shall be in the amount of the monthly installment necessary to amortize in full the principal balance remaining unpaid after application of the Monthly Payment due on October 1, 2003, together with interest thereon computed at the rate becoming effective on October 1, 2003, in 37 equal monthly installments, and each such Monthly Payment shall be applied first toward interest computed at the rate becoming effective on October 1, 2003, and then toward reduction of the principal balance.

(j) Each Monthly Payment falling due between November 1, 2004, and October 1, 2005, inclusive, shall be in the amount of the monthly installment necessary to amortize in full the principal balance remaining unpaid after application of the Monthly Payment due on October 1, 2004, together with interest thereon computed at the rate becoming effective on October 1, 2004, in 25 equal monthly installments, and each such Monthly Payment shall be applied first toward interest computed at the rate becoming effective on October 1, 2004, and then toward reduction of the principal balance.

(k) Each Monthly Payment falling due between November 1, 2005, and November 1, 2006, inclusive, shall be in the amount of the monthly installment necessary to amortize in full the principal balance remaining unpaid after application of the Monthly Payment due on October 1, 2005, together with interest thereon computed at the rate becoming effective on October 1, 2005, in 13 equal monthly installments, and each such Monthly Payment shall be applied first toward interest computed at the rate becoming effective on October 1, 2005, and then toward reduction of the principal balance.

3. November 1, 2006, shall be the "Date of Maturity". The entire principal balance, if any, outstanding on the Date of Maturity, together with any and all interest then accrued but unpaid, shall be due and payable in full on said Date of Maturity.

4. Notwithstanding the provisions of paragraph 3 above, at any time following payment of the 84th Monthly Payment (i.e., at any time following payment of the Monthly Payment due on November 1, 2003), Payees may give Makers, or either of them, written demand for payment in full of the entire principal balance then outstanding under this Note, which demand shall specify the date, which shall be not less than ninety (90) days after such demand is given, on which such payment in full is required, and if such written demand is given, such date specified in such demand (which date shall be not less than ninety (90) days after such demand is given) shall be the "Accelerated Date of Maturity", and the entire principal balance, if any, outstanding on such Accelerated Date of Maturity, together with any and all interest then accrued but unpaid, shall be due and payable in full on such Accelerated Date of Maturity. It is understood and agreed that interest, computed at the rates determined from time to time in accordance with the provisions set forth in paragraph 1 above, shall accrue through the date of such payment, but that no interest shall accrue and/or become payable after the date of such payment.

5. Notwithstanding any other provision of this Note or of any other document incidental to this Note to the contrary, it is understood and agreed that Makers, or either of them, shall have the right to prepay, at any time, all of any part of the principal balance outstanding under this Note, without penalty. Any principal sum prepaid by any Maker shall bear interest, computed at the rates determined from time to time in accordance with the provisions set forth in paragraph 1 above, through the date of such prepayment, but no interest shall accrue and/or become payable on such prepaid principal sum after the date of such prepayment.

6. Notwithstanding any other provision of this Note or of any other document incidental to this Note to the contrary, it is understood and agreed that in the event that Payees shall elect to declare the entire principal balance of this Note to be immediately due and payable in full by reason of the occurrence of any Event of Default and the failure of any Maker to cure such Event of Default within the grace period (if any) applicable thereto, such principal balance shall bear interest, computed at the rates determined from time to time in accordance with the provisions set forth in paragraph 1 above, through the date of payment of such principal balance, but no interest shall accrue and/or become payable on such principal balance after the date of such payment.

§ 6.188 BUYING & SELLING A SMALL BUSINESS   Ch. 6

§ 6.188 Forms—Agreement of Purchase and Sale of Stock[1]

AGREEMENT OF PURCHASE AND SALE OF STOCK
TABLE OF CONTENTS

PAGE

ARTICLE ONE; PURCHASE AND SALE OF SHARES ....
- Section 1.01 Sale and Transfer of Shares ....
- Section 1.02 Closing and Closing Date.................
- Section 1.03 Purchase Price ....

ARTICLE TWO; REPRESENTATIONS AND WARRANTIES OF THE CORPORATION AND THE SHAREHOLDERS ....
- Section 2.01 Organization, Standing and Qualification of the Corporation ....
- Section 2.02 Capital Structure........................
- Section 2.03 Shareholders...........................
- Section 2.04 Subsidiaries and Affiliates.................
- Section 2.05 Financial Statements ....
- Section 2.06 Absence of Specified Changes.............
- Section 2.07 Absence of Undisclosed Liabilities ....
- Section 2.08 Tax Returns and Audits..................
- Section 2.09 Real Property ....
- Section 2.10 Zoning ....
- Section 2.11 Inventory..............................
- Section 2.12 Other Tangible Personal Property ....
- Section 2.13 Accounts Receivable ....
- Section 2.14 Trade Names and Trademarks ....
- Section 2.15 Patents and Patent Rights ....
- Section 2.16 Title to Assets ....
- Section 2.17 Customers and Sales ....
- Section 2.18 Existing Employment Contracts ....
- Section 2.19 Insurance Policies......................
- Section 2.20 Other Contracts........................
- Section 2.21 Compliance with Laws ....
- Section 2.22 Litigation.............................
- Section 2.23 Agreement Will Not Cause Breach or Violation..
- Section 2.24 Authority and Consents..................
- Section 2.25 Interest in Customers, Suppliers and Competitors....................................
- Section 2.26 Corporate Documents...................
- Section 2.27 Identification and Compensation of Employees..
- Section 2.28 Employee Benefit Plans ....
- Section 2.29 Powers of Attorney and Authority ....
- Section 2.30 Working Relationships..................
- Section 2.31 Business Complete ....
- Section 2.32 No Adverse Event ....

§ 6.188   1. See supra, §§ 6.78 and 6.163.

		PAGE
Section 2.33	Brokerage	
Section 2.34	Disclosure	

ARTICLE THREE; REPRESENTATIONS AND WARRANTIES OF THE BUYER ....

Section 3.01	Organization and Standing of the Buyer	
Section 3.02	Authority	
Section 3.03	Brokerage	

ARTICLE FOUR; OBLIGATIONS OF THE CORPORATION AND THE SHAREHOLDERS BEFORE CLOSING ....

Section 4.01	Buyer's Access to Premises and Information	
Section 4.02	Conduct of Business in Normal Course	
Section 4.03	Preservation of Business and Relationships	
Section 4.04	Corporate Matters	
Section 4.05	Maintenance of Insurance	
Section 4.06	Employees and Compensation	
Section 4.07	New Transactions	
Section 4.08	Dividends, Distributions and Acquisitions of Stock	
Section 4.09	Payment of Liabilities and Waiver of Claims	
Section 4.10	Existing Agreements	
Section 4.11	Representations and Warranties True at Closing	

ARTICLE FIVE; CONDITIONS PRECEDENT TO BUYER'S PERFORMANCE ....

Section 5.01	Accuracy of Representations and Warranties by the Corporation and the Shareholders	
Section 5.02	Performance by the Corporation and the Shareholders	
Section 5.03	No Adverse Change	
Section 5.04	Certification by the Corporation and the Shareholders	
Section 5.05	Opinion of Counsel	
Section 5.06	Absence of Governmental or Other Proceedings or Litigation	
Section 5.07	Approvals and Consents	
Section 5.08	Corporate Documents	
Section 5.09	Corporate Approval	
Section 5.10	Good Standing Certificate	
Section 5.11	Employment Agreements	
Section 5.12	Agreement with Minority Shareholders	
Section 5.13	General Release	
Section 5.14	Escrow Agreement	
Section 5.15	Approval of Documentation	
Section 5.16	Consent of Bank	
Section 5.17	Resignations	
Section 5.18	Other Documents and Action	

§ 6.188   BUYING & SELLING A SMALL BUSINESS   Ch. 6

PAGE

ARTICLE SIX; CONDITIONS PRECEDENT TO SHAREHOLDERS' PERFORMANCE ....
- Section 6.01   Accuracy of Representations and Warranties ....
- Section 6.02   Performance by the Buyer ....
- Section 6.03   Certification by the Buyer ....
- Section 6.04   Opinion of Counsel for the Buyer ....
- Section 6.05   Certification from the Buyer ....
- Section 6.06   Approvals and Consents ....
- Section 6.07   Corporate Documents ....
- Section 6.08   Corporate Approval ....
- Section 6.09   Good Standing Certificate ....
- Section 6.10   Employment Agreements ....
- Section 6.11   General Releases ....
- Section 6.12   Approval of Documentation ....
- Section 6.13   Consent and Release of Bank ....
- Section 6.14   Other Documents and Action ....

ARTICLE SEVEN; CERTAIN OCCURRENCES ....
- Section 7.01   Material Damage or Casualty Loss ....
- Section 7.02   Repair or Replacement ....
- Section 7.03   Notices ....

ARTICLE EIGHT; THE CLOSING ....
- Section 8.01   Obligations of the Corporation and the Shareholders at Closing ....
- Section 8.02   Buyer's Obligations at Closing ....

ARTICLE NINE; OTHER OBLIGATIONS ....
- Section 9.01   Shareholder's Indemnity ....
- Section 9.02   Competition by the Shareholders ....
- Section 9.03   Further Assurances ....

ARTICLE TEN; PUBLICITY ....
- Section 10.01   Publicity ....

ARTICLE ELEVEN; COST ....
- Section 11.01   Expenses ....

ARTICLE TWELVE; FORM OF AGREEMENT ....
- Section 12.01   Effect of Headings ....
- Section 12.02   Entire Agreement; Modification; Waiver .....
- Section 12.03   Counterparts ....

ARTICLE THIRTEEN; PARTIES ....
- Section 13.02   Assignment ....

ARTICLE FOURTEEN; REMEDIES ....
- Section 14.01   Arbitration ....

Ch. 6 **AGREEMENT OF PURCHASE** **§ 6.188**

PAGE

Section 14.02 Specific Performance ....
Section 14.03 Conditions Permitting Termination ....

ARTICLE FIFTEEN; NATURE AND SURVIVAL OF REPRESENTATIONS ....
Section 15.01 Shareholders ....
Section 15.02 Corporation ....

ARTICLE SIXTEEN; NOTICES ....
Section 16.01 Notices...................................

ARTICLE SEVENTEEN; GOVERNING LAW..................
Section 17.01 Governing Law ....

AGREEMENT OF PURCHASE AND SALE OF STOCK

This Agreement, dated _____, is made among _____ _____ a corporation organized and existing under the laws of the State of _____ (the "Buyer") with main offices at _____, a corporation with mail offices at _____ (the "Corporation"), JOHN Q. PUBLIC ("Public"), residing at _____, Albany, New York 11111, JANE A DOE ("Doe"), residing at _____ Avenue, _____, NY 11111, A. REASONABLE MAN ("MAN"), residing at _____, Albany, New York 11111, and _____ (Public, Doe and Man, each being sometimes hereinafter referred to as a "Shareholder" and collectively being sometimes hereinafter referred to as the "Shareholders"). [use a shareholder schedule if the shareholders are numerous]

WHEREAS, the Shareholders are the owners, beneficially and of record, of the following shares of capital stock of the Corporation:

Name	Common Stock Class A	Common Stock Class B	Preferred Stock
Public			
Doe			
Man			

(such shares being hereinafter collectively referred to as the "_____" Shares); and

WHEREAS, the Buyer desires to purchase from the Shareholders and the Shareholders desire to sell to the Buyer the Capital Shares; and

WHEREAS, being delivered concurrently herewith and incorporated herein by reference as a part of this Agreement is a schedule (the "Disclosure Schedule") intended to set forth all information required by this Agreement to be included therein; and

WHEREAS, the Corporation desires that this transaction be consummated;

§ 6.188   BUYING & SELLING A SMALL BUSINESS   Ch. 6

NOW THEREFORE, in consideration of the mutual covenants, agreement, representations and warranties contained in this Agreement, and intending to be bound thereby, the parties hereto agree as follows:

ARTICLE ONE
PURCHASE AND SALE OF SHARES

Section 1.01. *Sale and Transfer of Shares.* On the basis of the representations and warranties herein contained and subject to the terms and conditions set forth in this Agreement, on the Closing Date (as defined in Section 1.02), the Shareholders will transfer and convey the Shares to the Buyer, and the Buyer will acquire the Shares from the Shareholders.

Section 1.02. *Closing and Closing Date.* The transfer and delivery of the Shares by the Shareholders to the Buyer and payment of the purchase price therefor as set forth in Section 1.03 (the "Closing"), shall take place at the offices of _____, Albany, New York, at 10:00 a.m. local time, on _____, 19__, or at such other time and place as the parties may agree in writing (the "Closing Date").

Section 1.03. *Purchase Price.* As full payment for the transfer of the Shares by Shareholders to the Buyer, the Buyer agrees to pay to Shareholders the aggregate amount of Twenty Million Dollars (the "Purchase Price") representing a purchase price of Twenty-Thousand Dollars ($20,000.00) for each share of Class A Common Stock, and Ten Thousand Dollars ($10,000.00) for each share of Class B Common Stock (as hereinafter defined), and One Thousand Dollars ($1,000.00) for each share of Preferred Stock (as hereinafter defined),

(i) of which the sum of ____ Million Dollars ($__,000,000), shall be paid, as follows:

(a) to Public, _____ Dollars ($_____) by certified funds [wire transfer to (named account)];

b) to Doe, _____ Dollars ($_____) by certified funds [wire transfer to (named account)];

c) to Man, _____ Dollars ($_____) by certified funds [wire transfer to (named account)]; and

(ii) of which the sum of Two Hundred Thousand Dollars ($200,000) shall be delivered to an escrow agent (the "Escrow Agent") at the Closing, together with directions to retain, hold and dispose of such funds in accordance with the terms of an escrow agreement which shall be in the form set forth in Exhibit A to this Agreement (the "Escrow Agreement"); and

(iii) of which the sum of _____ Dollars ($_____) representing the amount of New York State Real Property Transfer Gains Tax due on the real property of the Corporation located in _____, New York, known as _____ Avenue, shall be delivered to the Escrow Agent at the Closing,

864

together with directions to pay such funds when due to the New York State Department of Taxation and Finance. (The parties agree that a portion of the Purchase Price in the amount _____ Dollars ($_____) has been allocated to the aforementioned real property.)

(Those Shareholders listed in Exhibit B hereto shall pay to the Corporation simultaneously with the payment to such Shareholders of the amounts payable to them pursuant to clause (i) above, an amount equal to their respective unpaid loans referred to in Exhibit B.)

ARTICLE TWO
REPRESENTATIONS AND WARRANTIES OF THE CORPORATION AND THE SHAREHOLDERS

Except as set forth in the Disclosure Schedule (with explicit reference to the appropriate representation and warranty), the Corporation and each of the Shareholders, jointly and severally, represent, warrant and covenant as follows:

Section 2.01. *Organization, Standing and Qualification of the Corporation.* The Corporation is a corporation duly organized, validly existing and in good standing under the laws of New York, has all necessary corporation powers to own its properties and to carry on its business as now owned and operated by it, and is not qualified to do business in any other state. New York State is the only jurisdiction in which the nature of the Corporation's business or of its properties makes such qualification necessary.

Section 2.02. *Capital Structure.* The authorized stock of the Corporation consists of shares of Class A Voting Common Stock with no par value (the "Class A Common Stock"), of which 700 shares are issued and outstanding on the date hereof, shares of Class B Non–Voting Common Stock with no par value (the "Class B Common Stock"), of which _____ shares are issued and outstanding on the date hereof, and shares of preferred stock, par value $1000 per share (the "Preferred Stock"), of which _____ shares are issued and outstanding on the date hereof.

Section 2.03. *Shareholders.* Exhibit C hereto sets forth a correct and complete list of all shareholders of the Corporation, together with the number of shares of Class A Common Stock, Class B Common Stock and Preferred Stock, respectively, owned by each shareholder. Except as set forth in Exhibit B hereto, the Corporation has received full payment for, and has been reimbursed for the full amount loaned to any shareholders for the purchase of, the shares of capital stock of the Corporation. All of the outstanding shares of capital stock of the Corporation are validly issued, fully paid and nonassessable and have not been issued in violation of federal securities laws or the securities laws of any other jurisdiction. There are no outstanding subscriptions, options, rights, warrants, convertible securities or other agreements or commitments obligating the Corporation to issue, reissue, acquire or otherwise transfer any additional shares of its capital stock. Except as set forth in the Disclosure Schedule (i) the shareholders set forth in Exhibit C hereto are the respective owners, beneficially and of record, of all the shares of capital stock of the Corporation free and clear of all liens, encumbrances, security agreements, equities, options, claims, charges, restrictions and adverse interests of any kind and (ii) the Shareholders have full and complete power to transfer the Capital Shares to the Buyer without obtaining the consent or approval of any other person or governmental authority. This Agreement constitutes a legal, valid and binding obligation of the Corporation and each of the Shareholders, enforceable in accordance with its terms, subject only to obtaining the consent of _____ Bank of _____ ("_____ Bank") to the transactions contemplated under this Agreement.

Section 2.04. *Subsidiaries and Affiliates.* The Corporation owns all of the outstanding capital stock of _____ Incorporated, a New York corporation. [Recite business interest and other particulars of the subsidiary.]

Except as set forth above, the Corporation does not own (and, since _____, 19__, has not owned), directly or indirectly, any interest or investment (whether equity or debt) in any corporation, partnership, business, trust or other entity, and, except as set forth in the Disclosure Schedule, is not a participant in any joint venture, partnership or other entity. Each of the Corporation's and _____ presently owned subsidiaries and affiliates identified above is a corporation duly organized, validly existing and in good standing under the laws of the state or country of its incorporation, has full power to own all of its properties and to carry on its business as it is now being conducted, is duly qualified to do business as it is now being conducted, and is duly qualified to do business as a foreign corporation in the jurisdictions listed opposite its name in Exhibit D, which are the only jurisdictions in which the ownership of property or the conduct of its business makes such qualification necessary. All the issued and outstanding shares of capital stock of each of the subsidiaries and affiliates identified above that are owned by the Corporation are validly issued, fully paid and non-assessable and have not been issued in violation of federal securities laws or the securities laws of any other jurisdiction, and are owned by the Corporation, free and clear of all liens, encumbrances, security agreements, equities, options, claims, charges and restrictions of any kind, except as set forth in the Disclosure Schedule. There are no outstanding subscriptions, options, rights, warrants, convertible securities or other agreements or commitments obligating the Corporation, any of the subsidiaries or affiliates identified above and presently owned by the Corporation or any of the Shareholders to issue, reissue, or transfer, or cause to be issued, reissued or transferred, any shares of capital stock of any of such subsidiaries or affiliates, except as set forth in the Disclosure Schedule. The Corporation has full power to transfer these shares without obtaining the consent or approval of any other person or governmental authority, except as set forth in the Disclosure Schedule.

Section 2.05. *Financial Statements*. Exhibit E to this Agreement sets forth the audited consolidated and consolidating balance sheets of the Corporation at December 31, 19__, and December 31, 19__, and the related statements of income and retained earnings for each of the two years ended on those dates, prepared by _____, the Corporation's independent certified public accountant, whose report with respect to such audited financial statements (the "Audited Statements") is set forth in Exhibit E to this Agreement. The Audited Statements are in accordance with the books and records of the Corporation and have been prepared in accordance with generally accepted accounting principles consistently followed by the Corporation throughout the periods indicated and on a basis consistent with that of prior years, are correct and complete and fairly present the financial position of the Corporation as of their respective dates, including the results of its operations for the respective periods indicated, and the Audited Statements contain no untrue statement of any material fact nor omit to state any material fact required to be stated to make the Audited Statements not misleading.

Exhibit F sets forth the internally prepared unaudited consolidated and consolidating balance sheet of the Corporation at _____, 19__, together with related unaudited statements of income and retained earnings for the one-month and nine-month periods ended on such date (the "Interim Financial Statements"). To the best knowledge of the Shareholders and the Corporation, the Interim Financial Statements are in accordance with the books and records of the Corporation and have been prepared in accordance with generally accepted accounting principles applicable to such unaudited interim statements consistently followed by the Corporation throughout the periods indicated and on a basis consistent with that of prior periods, and fairly present the financial position of the Corporation as of _____, 19__, including the results of its operations for the period indicated.

Section 2.06. *Absence of Specified Changes*. Except as set forth in the Disclosure Schedule, since _____, 19__, there has not been any:

(a) material transaction by the Corporation other than in the ordinary course of business as conducted on that date;

(b) incurrence by the Corporation of, nor has the Corporation become subject to, any material obligation or liability (absolute or contingent) except (i) current or long-term liabilities incurred in the ordinary course of business as conducted on that date, and (ii) obligations under contracts entered into in the ordinary course of business as conducted on that date;

(c) payment of any obligation in discharge or satisfaction by the Corporation of any lien or encumbrance not disclosed by the Audited Statements, or payment by the Corporation of any obligation or liability (absolute or contingent), other than current or long-term liabilities reflected in the Audited Statements or incurred since _____, 19__, in the ordinary course of business as conducted on that date;

(d) single capital expenditure by the Corporation exceeding [$100,000];

(e) material adverse change in the financial condition, liabilities, assets, earnings or business of the Corporation;

(f) destruction of, damage to, or loss of any asset of the Corporation (whether or not covered by insurance) that materially and adversely affects the financial condition or business of the Corporation;

(g) labor trouble or other event or condition involving the Corporation and their employees or others working on behalf of it adversely affecting, or which could adversely affect, the financial condition, business or assets of the Corporation in any material respect;

(h) making of any commitment or incurrence of any liability by or on behalf of the Corporation to any labor organization through negotiation or otherwise;

(i) change in accounting methods or practices (including, without limitation, any change in depreciation or amortization policies or rates) by the Corporation;

(j) revaluation by the Corporation of any of its respective assets;

(k) declaration, setting aside or payment of a dividend or other distribution with respect to the capital stock of the Corporation, or any direct or indirect redemption, purchase or other acquisition by the Corporation of any of its shares of capital stock;

(*l*) increase in the salary or other compensation or payment payable to or to become payable by the Corporation to any of its officers or directors, or any declaration, payment, commitment or obligation of any kind for the payment by the Corporation of a bonus or other additional salary, compensation or moneys to any such person;

(m) increase in the salary or other compensation payable, or to become payable, by the Corporation to any of its employees (other than officers) or any declaration, payment, commitment or obligation of any kind for the payment by the Corporation of a bonus or other additional salary or compensation to any such person, except for increases in the ordinary course of business and consistent with prior practice;

(n) sale or transfer of any asset of the Corporation except in the ordinary course of business;

(*o*) amendment or termination of any contract, agreement or license to which the Corporation is a party, except in the ordinary course of business or as necessary to effect the transactions contemplated hereby;

(p) loan by the Corporation to any person or entity, or guaranty by the Corporation;

(q) mortgage, pledge, assignment, hypothecation or other encumbrance of any asset, tangible or intangible, or the Corporation;

(r) waiver or release of any right or claim of the Corporation, except for the full consideration thereof or in the ordinary course of business;

(s) other event or condition of any character that had, has or would have a material adverse effect on the financial condition, business or assets of the Corporation;

(t) issuance, sale or reclassification by the Corporation of any shares of capital stock of any class, or bonds or of any other of their corporate securities; or

(u) agreement by the Corporation to do any of the things described in the preceding clauses (a) through (t).

Section 2.07. *Absence of Undisclosed Liabilities.* Except as set forth in the Audited Statements and in the Interim Financial Statements or in the Disclosure Schedule, the Corporation does not have any material obligation or liability (whether accrued, absolute, contingent, unliquidated, or otherwise, whether due or to become due) arising out of or due to transactions entered into at or prior to the Closing Date, or any action or inaction at or prior to the Closing Date, or any state of facts existing at or prior to the Closing Date.

Section 2.08 *Tax Returns and Audits.* Within the times and in the manner prescribed by law, the Corporation has filed all federal, state and local tax returns required by law and all such returns are, in all respects, complete, accurate and in accordance with all legal requirements applicable thereto. The Corporation has paid all taxes, assessments and penalties due and payable. [The federal income tax returns of the Corporation were last audited by the Internal Revenue Service for the fiscal year ended December 31, 19__.] Except as set forth in the Disclosure Schedule, no claim of deficiency or other adjustment is pending or, to the best knowledge of the Shareholders, likely with respect to the Corporation and there are no present or, to the best knowledge of the Shareholders, likely disputes as to federal, state, county or local taxes of any nature payable by the Corporation. The provisions for taxes reflected in the Corporation's consolidated balance sheet at December 31, 19__, are adequate for any and all liabilities for federal, state, county and local taxes for the period ended on the date of such balance sheet and for all prior periods, whether or not disputed.

Section 2.09. *Real Property.* Exhibit G sets forth a correct and complete description of each parcel of real property owned by or leased to the Corporation. Exhibit G contains a description of all buildings, fixtures and other improvements located on these real properties and a list of the policies of title insurance issued to the Corporation for these properties.

With respect to all the leases listed in Exhibit G, (i) the Corporation is the current lessee thereunder; (ii) a true and complete copy of each such lease has been furnished to the Buyer and said copies have been initialed by the Corporation and the Shareholders; (iii) each lease is in full force and effect and has not been amended or modified; (iv) there exists no default (or other fact or circumstance, including the consummation of the transactions contemplated hereby, which, with the passage of time or the giving of notice, or both, would constitute a default) by landlord or tenant under any of the leases, no notices of default have been received from any of the landlords under the leases, and no notices of violations have been received from governmental agencies or insurance companies; (v) the Corporation is legally in possession of all space presently occupied by it, and shall have the right to remain in such possession for the full term of such lease, and has not sublet nor assigned same nor granted any rights therein to any other party, nor does the Corporation share any of the leased space with any other party; (vi) adequate means of ingress and egress exist to and from the premises demised pursuant to each lease; (vii) the fixed rent due under each lease has been paid through the current months; and (ix) all charges for gas, electricity, light, heat, power, sewage, garbage and telephone and/or other utility services used, rented or supplied upon or in connection with the premises demised pursuant to a lease have been paid through the current billing.

[Exhibit G also sets forth the base rent due for 19___ under each lease listed therein and the estimated amounts due under each lease for 19___ with respect to (i) real estate and/or any other taxes, (ii) common area maintenance charges, including utility charges, (iii) any other maintenance charges, and (iv) any insurance charges, as well as whether any of the foregoing amounts have been paid.]

Section 2.10. *Zoning.* To the best knowledge of the Shareholders, the zoning of each parcel of property described in Exhibit G permits the presently existing improvements and the continuation of the business presently being conducted on such parcel.

Section 2.11. *Inventory.* The inventories of raw materials, work in process and finished goods (collectively called "inventories") shown on the consolidated balance sheet of the Corporation at _____, 19__, included in the Interim Financial Statements, as well as the inventory ("Closing Inventory") which was taken on or about _____, 19__ (the "Inventory Date"), consists of items of a quality and quantity useable and saleable in the ordinary course of business by the Corporation, except for obsolete and slow-moving items and items below standard quality, determined in accordance with past business practice consistently followed by the Corporation, which in the aggregate are not greater than _____ Dollars ($). All items included in the inventories are the property of the Corporation, except for items sold in the ordinary course of business since the date of such balance sheet or the Inventory Date, as the case may be; for each of these sales either the purchaser has made full payment or the purchaser's liability to make full payment is reflected on the books of the Corporation and is fully collectible, subject to an allowance for bad debts consistent with other accounts receivable of the Corporation.

Except as set forth in the Disclosure Schedule, no items included in the inventories have been pledged as collateral or are held by the Corporation on consignment from others. The inventories shown on all the balance sheets included in the Audited Statements and the Closing Inventory are based on quantities determined by physical count or measurement, taken on or about the end of the periods covered by such balance sheets (or, with respect to the Closing Inventory, on the Inventory Date), and, in the Audited Statements, are valued at the lower of cost (determined on a first-in, first-out basis) or market value and on a basis consistent with that of prior years. The Corporation shall deliver a copy of the Closing Inventory to the Buyer's representative prior to the Closing Date.

Section 2.12. *Other Tangible Personal Property.* Prior to the Closing Date, the Corporation shall deliver to the Buyer's representative a complete and correct schedule describing, and specifying the location of, substantially all depreciable personal property owned by, in the possession of, or used by the Corporation. Such personal property constitutes substantially all such depreciable tangible personal property reasonably necessary for the conduct by the Corporation of its business as now conducted.

Except as set forth in the Disclosure Schedule, no personal property used by the Corporation in connection with its business is held under any lease, security agreement, conditional sales contract, or other title retention or security arrangement, or is located other than in the possession of the Corporation. All personal property reasonably necessary for the manufacture of the Corporation's products, the maintenance of their respective records and the communications with their respective customers and suppliers is in good operating condition and repair, ordinary wear and tear excepted, and has been serviced routinely. Prior to the Closing Date, the Corporation shall deliver to the Buyer's representative a copy of all service and repair records as may exist involving [$500] or more (for service performed by persons other than employees of the Corporation) for a period commencing January 1, 19__, to the date of delivery of such records for such personal property having an original purchase cost of $100,000.00 or more. All other personal property of the Corporation is in reasonably good operating condition and repair, ordinary wear and tear excepted. [Insert Inspection by Buyer language if desired]

Section 2.13. *Accounts Receivable.* Prior to the Closing Date, the Corporation shall deliver to the Buyer's representative a complete and correct list of the accounts receivable of the Corporation as of December __, 19__. All such accounts receivable, and all accounts receivable of the Corporation created after the date up to and including the Closing Date, shall have arisen from valid sales in the ordinary course of business. Such accounts shall have been collected, or will be collectible, at their full amounts, except to the extent that a reserve for bad debts has been established on the books of the Corporation for such accounts. It is the policy of the Corporation to credit payments received by either of them to the oldest accounts receivable for the particular customer, and such policy will be continued in the future for determining the extent to which accounts receivable shall have been collected.

Section 2.14. *Trade Names, Trademarks and Copy-rights.* Exhibit H sets forth a complete and correct list of all trade names, trademarks, trademark applications, service marks and copyrights and their registrations, whether domestic or foreign, owned by the Corporation or in which either of them has any rights or licenses, together with a brief description of each, and except as otherwise clearly specified in the Disclosure Schedule, the Corporation has full and exclusive ownership to the same and right to use the same. To the best knowledge of the Shareholders, the Corporation has not infringed, and is not now infringing, on any trade name, trademark, service mark or copyright belonging to any other person, firm or corporation. Neither the Corporation, nor any of the Shareholders is in receipt of any notice or complaint of conflict with, or infringement of, the asserted rights of others in any trade name, trademark, service mark or copyright used or owned by the Corporation. Except as set forth in the Disclosure Schedule, the Corporation is a not party to any license, agreement or arrangement, whether as licensor, licensee, or otherwise, with respect to any trademarks, service marks, trade names, or applications for them, or any copyrights. The Corporation owns, or holds adequate licenses or other rights to use, all trademarks, service marks, trade names and copyrights as presently used in the conduct of all phases of its business in the manner presently conducted by it, and, to the best knowledge of Shareholders, such ownership or use does not, and will not, conflict with, infringe on, or otherwise violate any rights of others. Prior to the Closing Date, the Corporation shall deliver to the Buyer's representative a true and correct copy of all registrations and applications for registration of the trade names, trademarks, service marks and copyrights contained in Exhibit H.

Section 2.15. *Patents and Patent Rights.*

(a) Exhibit I is a complete schedule of all patents and applications for patents owned by the Corporation or in which it has any rights, licenses or immunities. The patents and applications for patents listed in Exhibit I are, to the best knowledge of the Shareholders, valid and in full force and effect. Except as set forth in the Disclosure Schedule, there have not been any interference actions or other judicial, arbitration or other adversary proceedings to which the Corporation was a party nor, to the best knowledge of the Shareholders, any other such actions or proceedings concerning the patents or applications for patents listed in Exhibit I.

Each patent application is awaiting action by its respective patent office except as otherwise indicated in Exhibit I. To the best knowledge of the Shareholders, the manufacture, use or sale of the inventions, models, designs and systems covered by the patents and applications for patents listed in Exhibit I do not violate or infringe on any patent or any proprietary or personal right of any person, firm or corporation; and, to the best knowledge of the Shareholders, the Corporation has not infringed, and is not infringing, on any patent or other right belonging to any person, firm or corporation. Except as set forth in the Disclosure Schedule, the Corporation is not a party to any license, agreement or arrangement, whether as licensee, licensor, or otherwise, with respect to any patent, application for patent, invention, design, model, process, trade secret or formula. To the best knowledge of the Shareholders, except as set forth in the Disclosure Schedule, the Corporation has the right and authority to use such inventions, trade secrets, processes, models, designs and formulas as are necessary to enable them to conduct and to continue to conduct all phases of their businesses in the manner presently conducted by them, and, to the best knowledge of the Shareholders, that use does not, and will not, conflict with, infringe on or violate any patent or other rights of others. [Supplementation with respect to specific patents or patent rights.]

Section 2.16. *Title to Assets.* Except as set forth in the Disclosure Schedule, the Corporation has good and marketable title to all the respective assets and interests in assets, whether personal, real, mixed, tangible or intangible, owned by them, which constitute all the assets and interests in assets that are used in the businesses of the Corporation, and all these assets are free and clear of restrictions on or conditions to transfer or assignment and are free and clear of mortgages, liens, pledges, charges, encumbrances, equities, claims, easements, rights of way, covenants, conditions or restrictions. Prior to the Closing Date, the Corporation shall deliver to the Buyer's representative a true, correct and complete copy of whatever files as may exist (including, without limitation, all manufacturing specifications and financial and other records) concerning or relating to all operating machinery and computers of the Corporation having an original purchase cost of $100,000 or more. Following the consummation of the transactions contemplated by this Agreement, the Corporation shall retain all files of any nature which may exist with respect to any other asset of the Corporation.

Neither any Shareholder, nor any officer of director of the Corporation, nor any spouse, child or other relative of any of these persons, nor any employee of the Corporation, nor any spouse, child or other relative of any such employee, owns, or has any interest, directly or indirectly, in any of the personal property owned or used by or leased to the Corporation or any patents, trademarks, service marks, trade names, or applications for any of them, or trade secrets or copyrights owned, used or licensed by the Corporation.

Section 2.17. *Customers and Sales*. Prior to the Closing Date, the Corporation shall deliver to the Buyer's representative a complete and correct list of all customers of the Corporation as of December ___, 1986, to whom sales during 19__ have exceeded $50,000. To the best knowledge of the Shareholders, none of such customers has ceased or intends, or has threatened to cease, doing business with the Corporation, as the case may be.

All purchase orders, as of the Closing Date, of the Corporation's customers for goods not delivered on or prior to the Closing Date shall have arisen in the ordinary course of business and shall be valid, and the cancellation of any of them shall not have been threatened.

Section 2.18. *Existing Employment Contracts*. Set forth in Exhibit J is a complete and correct list of all employment contracts and collective bargaining agreements, and all pension, bonus, profit-sharing, stock option or other agreements or arrangements providing for employee remuneration or benefits to which the Corporation is a party or by which the Corporation is bound, which are not otherwise disclosed in Exhibit O. Prior to the Closing Date, the Corporation shall deliver to the Buyer's representative true, correct and complete copies of all such agreements. All contracts and arrangements set forth in Exhibit J are in full force and effect in accordance with their terms, and the Corporation, nor any other party, is in default under them. There have been no claims of defaults and there are no facts or conditions which, if continued, or on notice, would result in a default under these contracts or arrangements. There is no pending or threatened labor dispute, strike or work stoppage or labor organizing effort affecting the Corporation's business.

Section 2.19. *Insurance Policies*. Exhibit K contains a complete and correct description of all policies of casualty, extended coverage, theft, fire, errors and omissions, liability, life and other forms of insurance owned or held by the Corporation in which the Corporation or any officer or director of either of them in such capacity is a named payee or beneficiary, concerning its businesses and properties. Prior to the Closing Date, the Corporation shall deliver to the Buyer's representative true and correct and complete copies of the policies set forth in Exhibit K. All such policies are in the principal amounts set forth in Exhibit 11, which amount, to the best knowledge of the Shareholders, are consistent with generally accepted industry practice for comparable companies of similar size and situation. Such policies in such amounts are outstanding and duly in force on the date hereof. Exhibit K contains a list of all claims, whether or not insured against, made against the Corporation in the past five years for an amount exceeding $5,000. To the best knowledge of the Shareholders, after reasonable investigation, there is not now pending any claim against the Corporation in excess of applicable insurance. Within the past five years there has not been any insurable claim asserted against the Corporation which was for an amount in excess of the insurance coverage then or now maintained by the Corporation against such claim.

Section 2.20. *Other Contracts.* Except as set forth in the Disclosure Schedule, the Corporation is not a party to, nor is its property bound by, any distributor's or manufacturer's representative or agency agreement, output or requirements agreement, indenture, mortgage or deed of trust, or any lease or other agreement which was entered into not in the ordinary course of business. All distributor's or manufacturer's representative or agency agreements, output or requirement agreements, indentures, mortgages, deeds of trust, leases, outstanding letters of credit, service contracts, warranty agreements or other agreements or contracts of any nature not heretofore listed and described, and to which the Corporation is a party, or by which its property is bound, and which involve a stated payment or commitment greater than $25,000 and a stated period of performance greater than one (1) year, are listed and described in Exhibit M. Prior to the Closing Date, the Corporation shall deliver to the Buyer's representative true, correct and complete copies of all such agreements and contracts. Whether pursuant to transactions contemplated by this Agreement or (to the best knowledge of Shareholders) otherwise, there is no default or event that, with notice or lapse of time, or both, would constitute a default by the Corporation or any of the Shareholders under any of these agreements or contracts, nor any default or event that, with notice or lapse of time, or both, would constitute a default by any other party to any of these agreements or contracts. The Corporation has not received notice that any party to any of these agreements or contracts intends to cancel or terminate any of these agreements or contracts or to exercise or not exercise any options under any of these agreements or contracts, which cancellations, terminations, exercises, or non-exercises of options would have a material adverse effect on the financial position or business of the Corporation. Neither the Corporation, nor any of the Shareholders, is a party to, nor is any of them or their property bound by, any agreement or contract that, to the best knowledge of the Shareholders, is materially adverse to the business, properties or financial condition of the Corporation.

Section 2.21. *Compliance with Laws.* Except as set forth in the Disclosure Schedule, the Corporation has not received any notice of violation of, and, to the best knowledge of the Shareholders, the Corporation has complied with, and is not in violation of, applicable federal, state or local statutes, laws regulations and rules affecting its properties or the operation of its businesses.

Section 2.22. *Litigation.* (a) Except as set forth in the Disclosure Schedule, there is no suit, action, arbitration or legal, administration or other proceeding, or governmental investigation pending or, to the best knowledge of the Shareholders, threatened against or affecting the Corporation, any of the Shareholders or any of the officers or employees of the Corporation, which may, individually or in the aggregate, materially adversely affect the business, assets or financial condition of the Corporation. Neither the Corporation, nor any of the Shareholders, is in default with respect to any judgment, order, writ, injunction or decree of any federal, state, local or foreign court, department, agency or instrumentality which may, individually or in the aggregate, materially adversely affect the business assets or financial condition of the Corporation. The Corporation is not presently engaged in any legal action to recover moneys due to it or damages sustained by it.

(b) There has not been, within the last five years, any product liability suit, action, arbitration or proceeding to which the Corporation, or any of the Shareholders was or is a party nor any product liability claim against any of these parties.

(c) Except as set forth in the Disclosure Schedule, there have been no suits, actions, arbitrations or legal, administrative or other proceedings or governmental investigations against or materially affecting the Corporation during the past five years.

(d) Except as set forth in the Disclosure Schedule, neither the Corporation nor any of the Shareholders is subject to any judgment, order, writ, injunction or decree.

Section 2.23. *Agreement Will Not Cause Breach or Violation.* Except as set forth in the Disclosure Schedule, the execution and delivery of this Agreement and the other agreements contemplated hereby, and the consummation of the transactions contemplated by this Agreement, will not result in or constitute any of the following: (a) a breach or violation of the certificate of incorporation or by-laws of the Corporation; (b) a default or event that, with notice or lapse of time or both, would constitute a default, breach or violation of any judgment, order, decree, lease, license, promissory note, conditional sales contract, commitment, indenture, mortgage, deed of trust, insurance policy or other agreement, instrument or arrangement to which the Corporation, or any of the Shareholders is a party, or by which any of them, or the property of any of them, is bound; (c) an event that would permit any party to terminate any agreement or to accelerate the maturity of indebtedness or other obligation of the Corporation or any of the Shareholders; or (d) the creation or imposition of any lien, charge or encumbrance on any of the properties of the Corporation.

Section 2.24. *Authority and Consents.* Subject to obtaining the consent of _____ Bank to the transactions contemplated hereunder, the Corporation and each of the Shareholders have the right, power, legal capacity and authority to enter into, and perform their respective obligations under, this Agreement, and no approvals or consents of any persons other than the Corporation and the Shareholders are necessary in connection with the execution and delivery of this Agreement and the consummation of the transactions contemplated hereby. The execution and delivery of this Agreement by the Corporation have been duly authorized by its board of directors and the Shareholders.

Section 2.25. *Interest in Customers, Suppliers and Competitors.* Except as set forth in the Disclosure Schedule, neither the Shareholders, nor any officer or director of the Corporation, nor any spouse or child of any of them, nor any employee of the Corporation, nor any spouse, child or other relative of any such employee, has any direct or indirect interest in any competitor, supplier or customer of the Corporation or in any person from whom or to whom the Corporation leases any real or personal property, or in any other person with whom the Corporation is doing business.

Section 2.26. *Corporate Documents.* The Corporation and the Shareholders have furnished or made available to the Buyer for its examination (a) true, correct and complete copies of the certificate of incorporation, as amended to date, and by-laws, as amended to date, of the Corporation; (b) the minute books of the Corporation containing all records required to be set forth of all proceedings, consents, actions and meetings of the Shareholders and board of directors of the Corporation; (c) the stock transfer book of the Corporation setting forth all transfers of any capital stock of the Corporation; and (d) all documents identified in the Disclosure Statement.

Section 2.27. *Identification and Compensation of Employees.* Exhibit N sets forth a correct and complete list of the names and addresses of all officers and directors of the Corporation as of the date hereof, stating the number of years of service of each and the terms of compensation payable to each. Prior to the Closing Date, the Corporation shall deliver to the Buyer's representative a correct and complete list of all employees of the Corporation as of the date of delivery of such list setting forth comparable information.

Section 2.28. *Employee Benefit Plans.* The term "Employee Plan" shall mean any pension, retirement, profit-sharing, deferred compensation, bonus or other incentive plan, any other employee program, arrangement, agreement or understanding, any medical, vision, dental or other health plan, any life insurance plan, or any other employee benefit plan, including, without limitation, any "employee benefit plan" as defined in Section 3(3) of the Employee Retirement Income Security Act of 1974, as amended ("ERISA"), to which the Corporation contributes or

§ **6.188** BUYING & SELLING A SMALL BUSINESS Ch. 6

is a party or is bound or under which it may have a liability and under which employees of the Corporation (or their beneficiaries) are eligible to participate or derive a benefit.

Immediately prior to the Closing Date, the only Employee Plan which is a pension plan (as defined in Section 3(2) of ERISA) is the _____ Profit Sharing Plan (hereinafter referred to as the "Plan"). No Employee Plan is a multi-employer plan within the meaning of Section 3(37) of ERISA. Set forth in Exhibit O hereto is a true and complete list of all Employee Plans in existence immediately prior to the Closing Date. Prior to the Closing Date the Corporation shall provide the Buyer with true, correct and complete copies (incorporating all amendments) of the Plan and of any Employee Plan which is an employee welfare benefit plan (within the meaning of Section 3(1) of ERISA); in the case of any unwritten Employee Plans, descriptions thereof; with respect to the Plan, all trust agreements or other funding agreements, including insurance contracts, all amendments thereto and, with respect to any Employee Plan or any plan amendments thereto, all determination letters issued by the Internal Revenue Service after September 1, 1974, all notices of intent to terminate, all notices of reportable events, all administrative forms and any other communications required by law including, without limitation, employee notices, memoranda, worksheets and election forms and the most recent of the following; actuarial valuations, annual reports, summary plan descriptions, summaries of material modification and summary annual reports.

Each Employee Plan complies in all material respects with all applicable laws (including, without limitation, ERISA, the Internal Revenue Code of 1986, as amended ("Code")), and any applicable collective bargaining agreements to which the Corporation may be subject. As of the Closing Date, other than claims for benefits submitted by participants or beneficiaries in the normal course, there is no litigation, legal action, suit, investigation, claim, counterclaim or proceeding pending or threatened against or affecting any Employee Plan which would have a material adverse impact on the Corporation or the Buyer or on any such Employee Plan. Neither the Corporation nor any Administrator or fiduciary of any Employee Plan (or any agent of the foregoing) has engaged in any transaction or acted or failed to act in a manner which could subject the Corporation or the Buyer to any liability for a breach of fiduciary duty under ERISA or any other applicable law.

With respect to any Employee Plan, no prohibited transaction (within the meaning of Section 406 of ERISA and Section 4975 of the Code) which has not been exempted exists which could subject the Corporation or the Buyer to any liability or civil penalty pursuant to Section 502(i) of ERISA or a tax imposed by Section 4975 of the Code. No representations or communications with respect to participation, eligibility for benefits, vesting, benefit accrual or coverage under Employee Plans have been made prior to the Closing Date to employees of the Corporation who shall become employees of the Buyer as of the Closing Date, other than those which are in accordance with the terms and provisions of such Employee Plans as in effect immediately prior to the Closing Date.

The assets of the Plan on the Closing Date will at least equal the sum of the vested accrued benefits of all beneficiaries of the Plan as of such date, calculating such vested accrued benefits as if all participants in the Plan were 100% vested on that date.

Section 2.29. *Powers of Attorney and Authority.* Exhibit P sets forth a correct and complete list of (i) the names and addresses of all persons holding a power of attorney on behalf of the Corporation; and (ii) the names and addresses of all banks or other financial institutions in which the Corporation has an account (including any other account over which the Corporation has payment or withdrawal authority), deposit or safe-deposit box, with an identification of such accounts, deposits, or boxes, and with the names of all persons authorized to draw thereon or who have access thereto.

Section 2.30. *Working Relationships.* Except as set forth in the Disclosure Schedule, no employees of the Corporation are union employees or have any collective bargaining agreements, and none of such employees have petitioned for a representation election, and, to the best knowledge of the Shareholders, no union is presently attempting to organize any of such employees. The Corporation has not experienced any labor disputes or any work stoppage due to labor disagreements and there is no situation, and the Shareholders and the Corporation are not aware of any situation, which might involve the Corporation in any labor dispute or disagreement.

Section 2.31. *Business Complete.* To the best knowledge of the Shareholders, there is no existing condition, occurrence or thing of any kind, including the transactions covered by this Agreement, which will, after the consummation of the transactions contemplated by this Agreement, cause less than the total business of the Corporation to be owed by the Buyer.

Section 2.32. *No Adverse Event.* To the best knowledge of the Shareholders, there is no present event, condition or thing of any kind or character pertaining to the business, assets or prospects of the Corporation that will materially adversely affect their respective businesses, assets or prospects.

Section 2.33. *Brokerage.* Neither the Corporation nor any of the Shareholders has contacted any broker, agent or finder or paid or agreed to pay any brokerage or commission or any finder's fee to any broker, agent or finder on account of this Agreement or the matters contemplated hereby.

Section 2.34. *Disclosure.* To the best knowledge of the Shareholders, none of the representations and warranties made herein by the Corporation or any of the Shareholders, or made in any certificate or memorandum furnished or to be furnished by any of them, or on their behalf, contains or will contain any untrue statement of a material fact, or omits to state any material fact necessary to make the statements of fact contained therein not misleading. The Corporation and the Shareholders acknowledge and understand that the Buyer, in purchasing the Capital Shares pursuant hereto, is relying upon the representations, warranties, covenants and statements contained herein regardless of any independent investigation made by or on behalf of the Buyer concerning such representations, warranties, covenants and statements, and agree that Buyer is justified in so doing.

ARTICLE THREE
REPRESENTATIONS AND WARRANTIES OF THE BUYER

The Buyer represents, warrants and covenants as follows:

Section 3.01. *Organization and Standing of the Buyer.* The Buyer is a corporation duly organized, validly existing and in good standing under the laws of the State of New York, and has all necessary corporate powers to own its properties and to carry on its business as now owned and operated by it.

Section 3.02. *Authority.* The execution and delivery of this Agreement by the Buyer has been duly authorized, and the Buyer has the right, power, legal capacity and authority to enter into this Agreement. This Agreement represents a legal, valid and binding obligation of the Buyer, enforceable in accordance with its terms.

Section 3.03. *Brokerage.* The Buyer has not contacted any broker, agent or finder or paid or agreed to pay any brokerage or commission or any finder's fee to any broker, agent or finder on account of this Agreement or the matters contemplated hereby.

ARTICLE FOUR
OBLIGATIONS OF THE CORPORATION AND THE SHAREHOLDERS BEFORE CLOSING

The Corporation and each of the Shareholders covenant that from the date of this Agreement up to an including the Closing Date:

Section 4.01. *Buyer's Access to Premises and Information.* The Buyer and its counsel, accountants and other representatives shall have full access during normal business hours to all properties, books, accounts, records, contracts and documents of or relating to the Corporation. The Corporation and the shareholders shall furnish or cause to be furnished to the Buyer and its representatives all data and information concerning the business, finances, machinery and properties of the Corporation that may reasonably be requested, including but not limited to the schedules, lists and copies of records required to be delivered to the Buyer's representative prior to the Closing Date pursuant to Article 2 hereof.

Section 4.02. *Conduct of Business in Normal Course.* The Corporation will carry on its business and activity diligently and in substantially the same manner as it previously has been carried out and shall not make or institute any unusual or novel methods of manufacture, purchase, sale, lease, management, accounting or operation that will vary from those methods used by the Corporation as of _____ __, 19__.

Section 4.03 *Preservation of Business and Relationships.* The Corporation will use its best efforts (i) to preserve its business intact, (ii) to keep available to it its present officers and employees and (iii) to preserve its present relationships with suppliers, customers and others having business dealings with them consistent with past practices.

Section 4.04. *Corporate Matters.* Except as set forth in the Disclosure Schedule, the Corporation will not, (i) amend its certificate of incorporation or by-laws; (ii) issue, sell or deliver any stock, bonds or other corporate securities (whether authorized and unissued or held in treasury); (iii) issue or create any warrants, obligations, subscriptions, options, convertible securities or other commitments under which any additional stock, or bonds or other corporate securities, might be directly or indirectly authorized, issued or transferred; (iv) liquidate or dissolve; (v) solicit any tender offers or merger or consolidation inquiries or agreements from any person or business entity; (vi) merge or consolidate with any corporation, acquire control of any corporation or business entity, or take any steps incident to or in furtherance of any such actions; or (vii) agree to do any of the acts listed above.

Section 4.05. *Maintenance of Insurance.* The Corporation will continue to carry its existing insurance.

Section 4.06. *Employees and Compensation.* Except as set forth in the Disclosure Schedule, the Corporation will not do or agree to do any of the following acts:

(a) elect, employ, engage or contract with any officer, employee, sales agent or representative not heretofore elected, employed, engaged or contracted with;

(b) grant any increase in salaries payable by it, or to become payable by it, to any officer, employee, sales agent or representative;

(c) increase benefits payable or otherwise accruing to any officer, employee, sales agent or representative under any profit-sharing, bonus, deferred compensation, insurance, pension or retirement plan or other contract or commitment;

(d) lend any moneys to any officer, employee, sales agent or representative; or

(e) enter into any collective bargaining agreement to which it would be a party or by which it would be bound.

Section 4.07. *New Transactions.* Except as set forth in the Disclosure Schedule, the Corporation will not, without the Buyer's written consent, do, or agree to do, any of the following acts:

(a) enter into any contract, commitment or other transaction not in the usual and ordinary course of its business;

(b) borrow any funds or voluntarily incur, or assume or become subject to, whether directly or by way of guarantee or otherwise, any borrowing, obligation or liability (absolute or contingent) except obligations and liabilities incurred in the ordinary course of its business;

(c) mortgage or pledge any part of its assets or property, tangible or intangible;

(d) sell or transfer any part of its assets, property or rights used in the conduct of its business;

(e) enter into any agreement or arrangement granting any preferential rights to purchase any of its assets, property or rights used in the conduct of its business or requiring the consent of any party to the transfer and assignment of any such assets, property or rights;

(f) enter into any contract, agreement or course of action which may increase its liabilities, except in the ordinary course of business;

(g) make any capital expenditures in excess of $10,000 for any single item or $50,000 in the aggregate, or enter into any leases of capital equipment or property under which the annual lease charge is in excess of $10,000; or

(h) sell or dispose of any assets with a net book value in excess of $10,000, individually, or $50,000 in the aggregate.

Section 4.08. *Dividends, Distributions and Acquisitions of Stock.* Except as set forth in the Disclosure Schedule, the Corporation will not:

(a) declare, set aside or pay any dividend or make any distribution of assets to the holders of its capital stock;

(b) directly or indirectly purchase, redeem or otherwise acquire any shares of its stock; or

(c) enter into any agreement obligating it to do any of the foregoing prohibited acts.

Section 4.09. *Payment of Liabilities and Waiver of Claims.* The Corporation will not do or agree to do any of the following acts, other than in the ordinary course of business:

(a) pay any obligation or liability, fixed or contingent, other than current liabilities;

(b) waive or compromise any right or claim; or

(c) cancel, without full payment, any note, loan or other obligation owing to the Corporation.

Section 4.10. *Existing Agreements.* The Corporation will not modify, amend, cancel or terminate, other than in the ordinary course of business, any of the existing contracts, agreements or licenses to which it is a party, or agree to do any of those acts without the prior written consent of the Buyer.

Section 4.11. *Representations and Warranties True at Closing.* All representations and warranties of the Corporation and the Shareholders set forth in this Agreement and in any written statements delivered to the Buyer by the Corporation and the Shareholders or on their behalf under this Agreement will remain true and correct.

ARTICLE FIVE
CONDITIONS PRECEDENT TO BUYER'S PERFORMANCE

The obligations of the Buyer to purchase the Shares under this Agreement are subject to the satisfaction, on or before the Closing Date, of all the conditions set out below in this Article Five which conditions, if not satisfied, will serve to excuse performance by the Buyer at the Closing. The Buyer may, by a written instrument, waive any or all of these conditions in whole or in part without prior notice, provided, however, that no such waiver of a condition shall constitute a waiver by the Buyer of any of its other rights or remedies, at law or in equity, if the Corporation or any of its Shareholders shall be in default with respect to any of the representations, warranties or covenants under this Agreement, except as may be specifically provided in such waiver.

Section 5.01. *Accuracy of Representations and Warranties by the Corporation and the Shareholders.* Except as otherwise permitted by this Agreement, all representations and warranties by the Corporation or any of the Shareholders in this Agreement, or in any written statement that shall be delivered to the Buyer by any of them, or on their behalf, under this Agreement shall be true from the date of this Closing Date as if made on each such date.

Section 5.02. *Performance by the Corporation and the Shareholders.* The Corporation and all Shareholders shall have materially performed, satisfied and complied with all material covenants, agreements and conditions required by this Agreement to be performed or complied with by them, or any of them, on or before the Closing Date.

Section 5.03. *No Adverse Change.* During the period from December __, 19__, up to and including the Closing Date, there shall not be any material adverse change in the financial condition or the results of the operations of the Corporation, and the Corporation shall not sustain any material loss or damage of its assets, whether or not insured, that affects its ability to conduct its business.

Section 5.04. *Certification by the Corporation and the Shareholders.* Buyer shall have received a certificate, dated the Closing Date, signed by the Shareholders and by the Corporation's president, certifying, in form and substance satisfactory to the Buyer, that the conditions specified in Sections 5.01 and 5.02 have been fulfilled, that the Corporation has not sustained any loss or damage specified in Section 5.03, and that there has been no material adverse change in the financial condition or results of operations of the Corporation since December 31, 19__.

Section 5.05. *Opinion of Counsel for the Corporation and the Shareholders.* The Buyer shall have received from counsel for the Corporation and the Shareholders, an opinion, dated the Closing Date, in the form annexed hereto as Exhibit Q.

Section 5.06. *Absence of Governmental or Other Proceedings or Litigation.* The Buyer shall have received a certificate, dated the Closing Date and executed by the Shareholders and by the Corporation's president, in form and substance satisfactory to the Buyer, to the effect that, no order of any court or administrative agency shall be in effect which restrains or prohibits the transactions contemplated hereby, and no suit, action, investigation, inquiry or proceedings by any governmental body or other person or entity or legal or administrative proceeding shall have been instituted or threatened or received, on or before the Closing Date, which questions the validity or legality of the transactions contemplated hereby.

Section 5.07. *Approvals and Consents.* All approvals of United States or foreign public authorities, including federal, state and local authorities, if any, and all approvals and consents of any private person, the granting of which are material for the consummation of the transactions, including, but not limited to, those specifically referred to in Section 5.16, shall have been obtained and delivered to the Buyer, and all waiting periods, if any, specified by law shall have passed, on or before the Closing Date.

Section 5.08. *Corporate Documents.* The Buyer shall have received a copy of the certificate of incorporation of the Corporation as amended to date, certified by the Secretary of State of New York as of a recent date, and a copy of the by-laws of the Corporation, as amended to date, certified by their respective corporate secretaries and dated the Closing Date, and a certificate of their respective corporate secretaries, dated the Closing Date, certifying as to the incumbency of the officers of the Corporation and as to changes in the Buyer's certificate of incorporation of the Corporation since the date of the Secretary of State's certificates referred to above.

Section 5.9. *Corporate Approval.* The execution and delivery of this Agreement by the Corporation, and the performance of its covenants and obligations under it, shall have been duly authorized by all necessary corporate action, and the Buyer shall have received copies of all resolutions of the board of directors and Shareholders of the Corporation, in a form satisfactory to the Buyer, pertaining to such authorization, certified by the secretary of the Corporation.

Section 5.10. *Good Standing Certificate.* The Buyer shall have received appropriate certificates or other documents acceptable to the Buyer to the effect that the Corporation is an existing corporation and is in good standing and has paid all taxes due and payable in the State of New York.

Section 5.11 *Employment Agreements.* Employment agreements, dated the Closing Date, satisfactory in form and substance to the Buyer, providing for the employment of _____ by the Corporation, shall have been executed by the employee and delivered to the Corporation.

Section 5.12. *Agreement with Minority Shareholders.* An Agreement, dated the date hereof, in substantially the form of Exhibit R0, between and among the Buyer and _____, providing for the purchase by the Buyer of the shares of capital stock of the Corporation beneficially owned by such individuals shall have been executed and delivered by all the parties thereto, and such shares shall have been tendered on the Closing Date in accordance with the terms thereof.

Section 5.13. *General Release.* The Shareholders and the Buyer shall have executed and delivered a mutual general release in the form set forth in Exhibit S to this Agreement.

Section 5.14. *Escrow Agreement.* The Shareholders shall have executed and delivered the Escrow Agreement.

Section 5.15. *Approval of Documentation.* The form and substance of all certificates, instruments, opinions and other documents delivered to the Buyer under this Agreement, including the exhibits and the Disclosure Schedule, shall be satisfactory in all respects to the Buyer.

Section 5.16. *Consent of Bank.* The consent of _____ Bank to the transfer of all the Shares from the Shareholders to the Buyer shall have been delivered to the Buyer, together with appropriate termination statements executed by _____ Bank respecting its security interests in the property and rights of the Corporation serving as collateral under the financing and security agreements referred to in the Disclosure Schedule.

Section 5.17. *Resignations.* The Corporation and the Shareholders shall have delivered to the Buyer the written resignations of all the officers and directors of the Corporation that the Buyer may request, and will cause any other action to be taken with respect to these resignations that the Buyer may request.

Section 5.18. *Other Documents and Action.* The Corporation and the Shareholders shall have furnished to the Buyer such other certificates, instruments or other documents in form and substance satisfactory to the Buyer, and shall have taken such other action, as the Buyer may reasonably request.

ARTICLE SIX
CONDITIONS PRECEDENT TO SHAREHOLDERS' PERFORMANCE

The obligations of the Shareholders to sell the Shares under this Agreement are subject to the satisfaction, on or before the Closing Date, of all the conditions set out below in this Article Six, which conditions, if not satisfied, will serve to excuse performance by the Shareholders at the Closing. The Shareholders may, by a written instrument, waive any or all of these conditions in whole or in part without prior notice, provided, however, that no such waiver of a condition shall constitute a waiver by the Shareholders of any of their other rights or remedies, at law or in equity, if the Buyer shall be in default with respect to any of its representations, warranties or covenants under this Agreement, except as may be specifically provided in such waiver.

Section 6.01. *Accuracy of Representations and Warranties by the Buyer.* Except as otherwise permitted by this Agreement, all representations and warranties by the Buyer in this Agreement, or in any written statement that shall be delivered to the Shareholders by the Buyer or on its behalf under this Agreement, shall be true from the date of this Agreement and on each day through and as of the Closing Date as if made on each such date.

Section 6.02. *Performance by the Buyer.* The Buyer shall have materially performed, satisfied and complied with all material covenants, agreements and conditions required by this Agreement to be performed or complied with on or before the Closing Date.

Section 6.03. *Certification by the Buyer.* The Shareholders shall have received a certificate, dated the Closing Date, signed by the Buyer certifying, in form and substance satisfactory to the Shareholders, that the conditions specified in Sections 6.01 and 6.02 have been fulfilled.

Section 6.04. *Opinion of Counsel for the Buyer.* The Shareholders shall have received from counsel for the Buyer an opinion, dated the Closing Date, in the form annexed hereto as Exhibit T.

Section 6.05. *Certification from the Buyer.* The Shareholders shall have received a certificate, dated the Closing Date and executed by the Buyer, in form and substance satisfactory to the Shareholders, to the effect that no order of any court or administrative agency shall be in effect which restrains or prohibits the transactions contemplated hereby, and no suit, action, investigation, inquiry or proceedings by any governmental body or other person or entity or legal or administrative proceeding shall have been instituted or threatened or received, on or before the Closing Date, which questions the validity or legality of the transactions contemplated hereby.

Section 6.06. *Approvals and Consents.* All approvals of United States or foreign public authorities, including federal, state and local authorities, if any, and all approvals and consents of any private persons, the granting of which are material for the consummation of this transaction, including but not limited to those specifically referred to in Section 6.13, shall have been obtained and delivered to the Shareholders, and all waiting periods, if any, specified by law shall have passed, on or before the Closing Date.

Section 6.07. *Corporate Documents.* The Shareholders shall have received a copy of the certificate of incorporation of the Buyer, as amended to date, certified by the Secretary of State of New York as of a recent date, and a copy of the by-laws of the Buyer, as amended to date, certified by its corporate secretary and dated the Closing Date, certifying as to the incumbency of the officers of the Buyer and as to changes in the Buyer's certificate of incorporation since the date of the Secretary of State's certificate referred to above.

Section 6.08. *Corporate Approval.* The execution and delivery of this Agreement by the Buyer, and the performance of its covenants and obligations under it, shall have been duly authorized by all necessary corporate action, and the Shareholders shall have received copies of all resolutions of the board of directors and Shareholders of the Buyer, in a form satisfactory to the Shareholders, pertaining to such authorization, certified by the secretary of the Buyer.

Section 6.09. *Good Standing Certificate.* The Shareholder shall have received appropriate certificates or other documents acceptable to them to the effect that the Buyer is an existing corporation and is in good standing and has paid all taxes due and payable in the States of New York.

Section 6.10. *Employment Agreements.* Employment agreements, dated the Closing Date, satisfactory in form and substance to the Shareholders, providing for the employment of _____ by the Corporation, shall have been executed and delivered to the Corporation.

Section 6.11. *General Release.* The Shareholders and Buyer shall have executed and delivered a mutual general release in the form set forth in Exhibit S to this Agreement.

Section 6.12. *Approval of Documentation.* The form and substance of all certificates, instruments, opinions and other documents delivered to the Shareholders under this Agreement shall be satisfactory in all respects to the Shareholders.

Section 6.13. *Consent and Release of Bank.* The consent of _____ Bank to the transfer of all the Shares from the Shareholders to the Buyer and the release of the Shareholders of all obligations of the Corporation guaranteed by the Shareholders to said _____ Bank shall have been executed and delivered.

Section 6.14. *Other Documents and Action.* The Buyer shall have furnished to the Shareholders such other certificates, instruments or other documents in form and substance satisfactory to the Shareholders, and shall have taken such other action, as the Shareholders may reasonably request.

ARTICLE SEVEN
CERTAIN OCCURRENCES

Section 7.01. *Material Damage or Casualty Loss.* The Corporation shall promptly notify the Buyer of any material damage or casualty loss from any cause whatsoever to any of the significant assets of the Corporation. Any such notice shall include the Corporation's best estimate of the cost of repair or replacement of such assets and the time necessary to complete such repair or replacement. The term Significant Assets shall mean any asset, without regard to its value or the cost of its repair or replacement, which, in the reasonable opinion of the Corporation is essential to the Corporation's business.

Section 7.02. *Repair or Replacement.* If such significant assets can be repaired or replaced for an aggregate cost of less than Fifty Thousand Dollars ($50,000) prior to the closing date, the Corporation shall complete such repairs or replacements as promptly as possible.

If such Significant Assets cannot be repaired or replaced for less than Fifty Thousand Dollars ($50,000) or prior to the Closing Date, the Buyer may, at its option, elect to (i) terminate this Agreement, (ii) consummate this transaction on the Closing Date, in which case the estimated cost of repair or replacement shall be deducted from the purchase price payable pursuant to Section 1.03(i) (and, upon completion of such repair or replacement, an adjustment shall be made for the actual cost therefor so that either monies deducted in excess of the actual cost of repair or replacement shall be paid to the Shareholders or monies shall be paid to the Buyer from the escrow account), (iii) consummate this transaction at the purchase price, reduced by such amount as the parties may agree to, or (iv) postpone the Closing until the Corporation has completed such repair or replacement to the reasonable satisfaction of the Buyer, in which case the actual cost of such repair or replacement shall be deducted from the purchase price payable pursuant to Section 1.03(i). If the Buyer makes the election provided in (iii), the parties shall use their best efforts to agree upon the amount of the reduction. If the parties cannot agree upon the reduction within 120 days of the Buyer's election, the Buyer shall have the right to reelect, in which case it promptly shall choose any of the remaining options provided for in this paragraph. In the event that the purchase price shall be reduced as provided in (ii), (iii) or (iv) and the Corporation subsequently is reimbursed by insurance for such repair or replacement, the Shareholders shall be entitled to receive the proceeds of such insurance coverage to the extent (but only to the extent) of the reduction in purchase price.

Section 7.03. *Notices.* Any election the Buyer may have under Section 7.02 (with the exception of any reelection provided for in such Section) shall be made by giving notice to the Corporation within 30 days after receipt by the Buyer of a notice from the Corporation, and in the event the Closing Date is scheduled for a day prior to the end of such 30 day period, the Closing Date shall automatically be postponed until the last day of such period, or _____ __, 19__, whichever is earlier.

ARTICLE EIGHT
THE CLOSING

Section 8.01. *Obligations of the Corporation and the Shareholders at Closing.* At the Closing, the Shareholders shall deliver to Buyer:

(a) certificates representing the Shares, registered in the name of the respective Shareholders, duly endorsed by each respective Shareholder for transfer, or accompanied by an assignment of the Shares duly executed by each respective Shareholder, and with all required documentary stock transfer stamps affixed or accompanied by the respective Shareholder's certified personal check for the amount of these stamps; and

(b) Such other certificates, instruments or documents as contemplated by Article Five hereof or as the Buyer may reasonably request.

Section 8.02. *Buyer's Obligations at Closing.* On the Closing Date, the Buyer, upon delivery of the items specified in Section 8.01, shall comply with the obligations imposed upon it by Section 1.03 hereof.

ARTICLE NINE
OTHER OBLIGATIONS

Section 9.01. *Shareholder's Indemnity.* The Shareholders shall jointly and severally indemnify, defend and hold harmless the Buyer and the Corporation from and against and in respect of any and all claims, demands, losses, costs, expenses, obligations, liabilities, damages, recoveries or deficiencies, joint or several, to which the Buyer or the Corporation may become subject by virtue of any breach of, or failure by the Corporation or any of the Shareholders to perform any of their representations, warranties, covenants or agreements in this Agreement or any schedule, certificate, exhibit or other instrument furnished or to be furnished by them under this Agreement ("Liabilities"), and the Shareholders shall promptly reimburse the Buyer and the Corporation for any legal or other expenses (including reasonable counsel fees of counsel selected by the Buyer) incurred by them in connection with defending any actions relating to such Liabilities.

The Buyer shall notify the Shareholders in writing of any Liabilities. Upon receipt of such notice, the Shareholders shall have, at the Shareholders' election, the right to compromise or defend any matters involving any third party claim asserted against the Shareholders, or the Corporation through counsel of the Shareholders' choosing, at the expense of the Shareholders. The Buyer shall have the right, but not the obligation, to participate in any such defense. With respect to any third party claim, the giving to the Shareholders of such notice and opportunity to compromise or defend shall constitute a condition precedent to any liability of the Shareholders under the indemnity contained in this Section 9. In the event the Shareholders undertake to compromise or to defend any such Liability, they shall notify the Buyer in writing promptly (in any event no later than thirty (30) days after receipt of notice from the Buyer or such shorter time as is required to protect the Corporation or the Buyer from default, entry of judgment or other adverse action) of their intention to do so and the proposed terms thereof, and the Buyer agrees to reasonably cooperate with the Shareholders and with their counsel in compromising or defending against such Liability. The Shareholders shall not compromise or settle any such Liability if, in the opinion of the Buyer, such compromise or settlement could adversely affect the Corporation or the Buyer; provided, however, that, if, by virtue of this clause, the Shareholders shall not be so entitled to compromise or settle any such Liability, the defense (and the cost thereof) and ability to compromise with respect to any such Liability shall be assumed by the Buyer and the obligation of the Shareholders to so indemnify the Buyer or the Corporation shall be limited to the terms of the compromise or settlement which the Shareholders had so proposed if such compromise or settlement could have been achieved. In the event that the Shareholders shall fail to exercise their right to compromise or defend any claim asserted by a third party against the Buyer, the Corporation or the Shareholders after having been afforded the opportunity to do so pursuant to this Section 9, the Shareholders shall be estopped from attacking the terms of any agreement and compromise or judgment of a court of competent jurisdiction resulting in final disposition thereof. The Shareholders shall reasonably cooperate with the Buyer in the defense of any matter as to which indemnification may be sought. The Shareholders agree to pay the Buyer on demand the full amount of any Liability which the Buyer pays, or to which the Buyer shall become obligated to pay. With respect to the preceding sentence and to any third party claim, the Shareholders shall be obligated to pay the Buyer for any Liability only after the opportunity shall have been tendered to the Shareholders to defend and/or compromise said claim as provided herein and either (a) the Shareholders shall have rejected the opportunity to settle or defend or, (b) having undertaken to settle or defend, the Shareholders shall have permitted entry of judgment without staying or paying same within thirty (30) days of entry of judgment; provided, however, that if the Buyer shall be compelled to make any payment for the Corporation hereunder prior to the time otherwise specified herein in order to prevent imposition of lien or loss of property, and for which the Shareholders are obligated to indemnify the Buyer, then the Shareholders shall, notwithstanding such specified time, promptly fulfill their indemnification obligations, but if the Shareholders shall choose to seek refund or reimbursement of any such payment made by the Buyer, the Shareholders shall have the right to do so at the Shareholders' sole expense, in the name of the Corporation if the use of said name is reasonably required to prosecute such claim. The Buyer shall make available, and cause the Corporation to make available at the Shareholders' expense, all information and assistance that the Shareholders may reasonably request in connection with the defense against any Liability. The remedy provided in this Section 9.01 shall not be the sole and exclusive remedy of the Buyer (and shall not affect the ability of the Buyer to seek equitable or any other relief available to the Buyer, including relief in the form of an injunction or of specific performance of the obligation of the Corporation and the Shareholders to close) against the Shareholders with respect to any breach or failure of the Corporation and the Shareholders with respect to any of their representations, warranties, covenants or agreements under this Agreement or in any schedule, exhibit or certificate.

The Shareholders shall be liable only with respect to those Liabilities as to which the Buyer shall give the Shareholders notice in writing on or before the expiration of two (2) years from and after the Closing Date; provided, that there shall be no time limit with respect to Liabilities arising by virtue of a breach of the representations, warranties and covenants contained in Sections 2.02 and 2.03 hereof. If the Buyer or the Corporation shall receive a tax benefit from any payment made by the Buyer or the Corporation and reimbursed by the Shareholders, or made by the Shareholders on behalf of the Buyer or the Corporation, the Shareholders shall be reimbursed for any such benefit within 60 days after the filing of a tax return reflecting such benefit; provided, however, that the Shareholders shall reimburse the Buyer or the Corporation for any such benefit which is subsequently disallowed, such reimbursement, together with interest and penalties, to be within 60 days of such disallowance and such reimbursement obligation to survive beyond the two-year period referred to in Section 15.01 hereof.

NOTWITHSTANDING ANYTHING TO THE CONTRARY HEREIN CONTAINED:

(i) the maximum liability of each Shareholder by reason of any and all breaches of the warranties or representations contained in Article Two of this Agreement shall be limited to such Shareholder's allocable portion of the purchase price (before deduction of taxes);

(ii) the maximum liability of each of the Shareholders by reason of any and all breaches of any warranties or representations made in

Article Two shall be limited to the respective percentage interest (of the amount of any such liability) of each of the Shareholders in all of the shares of the Corporation being sold by the Shareholders under this Agreement, provided that no such limitation shall be applicable to any liability of any Shareholder which arises under Sections 2.02 or 2.03 hereof;

(iii) the liability of the Shareholders, if any, for indemnification hereunder shall, except with respect to claims arising under Sections 2.02, 2.03, 2.21 and 2.22 hereof, be limited to the amount by which such liability for any and all claims exceeds on a cumulative basis the sum of One Hundred Thousand Dollars ($100,000.00) (the "Threshold Amount"), and provided further that the amount of indemnification in excess of said Threshold Amount owing to the Buyer by the Shareholders shall in all events be limited to the aggregate amount of liabilities, losses and expenses in excess of said Threshold Amount computed in accordance with generally accepted accounting principles in respect of which indemnification has not theretofore been made, less net income tax savings to the Buyer, and/or the Corporation actually received by the Buyer and/or the Corporation, or reasonably estimated by the Shareholders to be received by the Buyer or the Corporation, arising from the state of facts giving rise to such indemnification. With respect to claims arising under Section 2.21 hereof, the indemnification shall apply only to individual claims exceeding $10,000.

Section 9.02. *Competition by the Shareholders.* The Shareholders agree and covenant that for a period of five (5) years commencing on the Closing Date, they will not, (i) directly or indirectly, and whether as principal or agent, officer, director, employee, consultant, or otherwise, alone or in association with any other person, firm, corporation, or other business organization, carry on, or be engaged, concerned, or take part in, or render services to, or own, share in the earnings of, or invest in the stocks, bonds, or other securities of any person, firm, corporation, or other business organization (other than the Corporation or its affiliates) engaged in the business of the Corporation as presently conducted (a "Similar Business") in the United States and Canada; provided that this restriction shall not apply to the areas identified in Exhibit U as the licensed territory; and provided, further, that the Shareholders may invest in stocks, bonds, or other securities of any Similar Business (but without otherwise participating in the activities of such Similar Business) if (A) such stocks, bonds, or other securities are listed on any national or regional securities exchange or have been registered under Section 12(g) of the Securities Exchange Act of 1934; and (B) their investment does not exceed, in the case of any class of the capital stock of any one issuer, 2% of the issued and outstanding shares, or in the case of bonds or other securities, 2% of the aggregate principal amount thereof issued and outstanding; or (ii) whether for their own account or for the account of any other person, firm, corporation or other business organization, interfere with the Corporation's relationship with, or endeavor to entice away from the Corporation, any person, firm, corporation or other business organization who is or has been an employee, consultant, distributor, distributing agent or subagent, production contractor, supplier, source of material and/or product or a customer of, or in the habit of dealing with, the Corporation. The period of time during which any Shareholder is prohibited from engaging in certain activities pursuant to the terms of this Section 9.02 shall be extended by the length of time during which such Shareholder is in breach of the terms of this Section 9.02. [The Shareholders further agree not to divulge, communicate, use to the detriment of the Corporation or for the benefit of any other person or persons, or misuse in any way, any confidential information or trade secrets of the Corporation, including personnel information, secret processes, know-how, customer lists, formulas or other technical data for so long as such information, data or trade secrets shall remain confidential. The Shareholders acknowledge and agree that any information or data they have acquired on any of these matters or items was received in confidence and as a fiduciary of the Corporation.]

The Shareholders acknowledge that the provisions of this Section 9.02 are reasonable and necessary for the protection of the Corporation, and that each provision, and the period or periods of time, geographic areas and types and scope of restrictions on the activities specified herein are reasonable and are, and are intended to be, divisible. In the event that any provision of this Section 9.02, including any sentence, clause or part hereof, shall be deemed contrary to law or public policy or for any reason invalid or unenforceable, the remaining provisions shall not be affected, but shall remain in full force and effect and any invalid or unenforceable provisions shall be deemed, without further action on the part of the parties, modified, amended and limited to the extent necessary to render the same valid and enforceable.

Section 9.03. *Further Assurances.* Each of the parties agrees to use all reasonable efforts to take, or cause to be taken, all action and to do, or cause to be done, all things necessary, proper or advisable to consummate and make effective, and to afford to the parties the full benefit of, the transactions contemplated by this Agreement.

ARTICLE TEN
PUBLICITY

Section 10.01. *Publicity.* Except as may be necessary to fulfill obligations under this Agreement, all notices to third parties and all other publicity concerning the transactions contemplated by this Agreement shall be planned and coordinated by and between the Buyer and the Corporation and the Shareholders. None of the parties shall act unilaterally in this regard without the prior written approval of the others.

ARTICLE ELEVEN
COST

Section 11.01. *Expenses*. Each of the parties shall pay all costs and expenses incurred or to be incurred by it in negotiating and preparing this Agreement and in closing and carrying out the transactions contemplated by this Agreement.

ARTICLE TWELVE
FORM OF AGREEMENT

Section 12.01. *Effect of Headings*. The subject headings of the sections and subsections of this Agreement are included for purposes of convenience only and shall not affect the construction or interpretation of any of its provisions.

Section 12.02. *Entire Agreement; Modification; Waiver*. This Agreement constitutes the entire agreement among the parties pertaining to the subject matter contained in it and supersedes all prior and contemporaneous agreements, representations and understandings of the parties. No supplement, modification or amendment of this Agreement shall be binding unless executed in writing by the party against whom enforcement is sought. No waiver of any of the provisions of this Agreement shall be deemed, or shall constitute, a waiver of any other provision, whether or not similar, nor shall any waiver constitute a continuing waiver. No waiver shall be binding unless executed in writing by the party making the waiver.

Section 12.03. *Counterparts*. This Agreement may be executed simultaneously in one or more counterparts, each of which shall be deemed an original, but all of which together shall constitute one and the same instrument.

ARTICLE THIRTEEN
PARTIES

Section 13.01. *Parties in Interest*. Nothing in this Agreement, whether express or implied, is intended to confer any rights or remedies under or by reason of this Agreement on any persons other than the parties to it and their respective successors and assigns, nor is anything in this Agreement intended to relieve or discharge the obligation or liability of any third persons to any party to this Agreement, nor shall any provision give any third persons any right of subrogation or action over against any party to this Agreement.

Section 13.02. *Assignment*. This Agreement shall be binding on, and shall inure to the benefit of, the parties to it and their respective heirs, legal representatives, successors and assigns. The obligations of any of the Shareholders may not be assigned without the prior written consent of the Buyer. The obligations of the Buyer may be assigned to an affiliate of the Buyer, in which case, however, the Buyer shall continue to remain liable for such assigned obligations.

ARTICLE FOURTEEN
REMEDIES

Section 14.01. *Arbitration.* Any controversy or claim arising out of, or relating to, this Agreement, or the making, performance or interpretation thereof (other than any issues relating to payment of the Purchase Price), shall be settled by arbitration by a single arbitrator in Albany, New York, in accordance with the rules of the American Arbitration Association then existing, and judgment on the arbitration award may be entered in any court having jurisdiction over the subject matter of the controversy.

Section 14.02. *Specific Performance.* Certain of the obligations of the parties under this Agreement are unique. If any party should default in such obligations (e.g., duties not to compete or to keep matters confidential) under this Agreement, the parties each acknowledge that it would be extremely impracticable to measure the resulting damages; accordingly, the non-defaulting party, in addition to any other available rights or remedies, may sue in equity for specific performance, and the parties each expressly waive in such instances the defense that a remedy in damages will be adequate.

[Section 14.03. *Conditions Permitting Termination.* The Buyer may on or prior to the Closing Date terminate this Agreement without any party having any liability to any other party;

(a) if any bona fide action or proceeding shall be pending against either party on the Closing Date that could result in an unfavorable judgment, decree or order that would prevent or make unlawful the carrying out of this Agreement, or if any agency of the federal or of any state government shall have objected at or before the Closing Date to this acquisition or to any other action required by or in connection with this Agreement; or

(b) if the legality and sufficiency of all steps taken and to be taken by the parties and their shareholders in carrying out this Agreement, including the fulfillment of any condition contained herein, shall not have been approved by the Buyer as required by this Agreement; or

(c) if the Corporation or any of the Shareholders default in the due and timely performance of any of their warranties, covenants or agreements under this Agreement.]

ARTICLE FIFTEEN
NATURE AND SURVIVAL OF REPRESENTATIONS

Section 15.01. *Shareholders.* Subject to the last paragraph of Section 9.01 hereof, all representations, warranties, covenants and agreements of the Shareholders contained in this Agreement, or in any instrument, certificate, opinion or other writing provided for herein, shall survive for a period of two years after the Closing. The representations, warranties and covenants included in Sections 2.02 and 2.03 hereof shall survive the Closing without limitation.

Section 15.02. *Corporation.* All representations, warranties, covenants and agreements of the Corporation contained in this Agreement, or in any instrument, certificate, opinion or other writing provided for herein, shall not survive the Closing.

ARTICLE SIXTEEN
NOTICES

Section 16.01. *Notices.* All notices, requests, demands and other communications under this Agreement shall be in writing and shall be deemed to have been duly given on the date of service if served personally on the party to whom notice is to be given, or on the fifth day after mailing if mailed to the party to whom notice is to be given, by first class mail, registered or certified, postage prepaid, and properly addressed as follows:

Any party may change its address for purposes of this Section 16.01 by giving the other parties written notice of the new address in the manner set forth above.

ARTICLE SEVENTEEN
GOVERNING LAW

Section 17.01. *Governing Law.* This Agreement shall be construed in accordance with, and governed by, the laws of the State of New York.

IN WITNESS WHEREOF, the parties to this Agreement have duly executed it on the day and year first above written.

†

GENERAL PRACTICE IN NEW YORK

Volume 20

By

ROBERT L. OSTERTAG
HON. JAMES D. BENSON

Sections 1.1 to 6.188

1999 Pocket Part

Insert this Pocket Part in back of Volume

ST. PAUL, MINN.
WEST GROUP
1999

GENERAL PRACTICE IN NEW YORK FORMS ON DISK™

The **Forms on Disk**™ which accompany these volumes provide instant access to WordPerfect 5.1/5.2 versions of the forms included in *General Practice in New York*. These electronic forms will save you hours of time drafting legal documents. The electronic forms can be loaded into your word processing software and formatted to match the document style of your law firm. These electronic forms become templates for you to use over and over without having to retype them each time.

The forms in Volumes 20, 21, 22, 23, 24 and 25 that are included on the accompanying disks are marked with the following disk icon for easy identification.

COPYRIGHT © 1999
By
WEST GROUP

This is the 1999 Pocket Part to Volume

20

of

WEST'S NEW YORK PRACTICE SERIES

West's New York Practice Series

Vol. 1	Walker, et al., New York Limited Liability Companies and Partnerships: A Guide to Law and Practice
Vols. 2-4	Haig, et al., Commercial Litigation in New York State Courts
Vol. 5	Barker and Alexander, Evidence in New York State and Federal Courts
Vol. 6	Greenberg, Marcus, et al., New York Criminal Law
Vol. 7	Marks, et al., New York Pretrial Criminal Procedure
Vol. 8	Davies, Stecich, Gold, et al., New York Civil Appellate Practice
Vol. 9	Ginsberg, Weinberg, et al., Environmental Law and Regulation in New York
Vol. 10	Sobie, et al., New York Family Court Practice
Vols. 11-12	Scheinkman, et al., New York Law of Domestic Relation

Vol. 13	Taber, et al., Employment Litigation in New York
Vols. 14-16	Kreindler, Rodriguez, et al., New York Law of Torts
Vols. 17-19	Field, Moskin, et al., New York and Delaware Business Organizations: Choice, Formation, Operation, Financing and Acquisitions
Vols. 20-25	Ostertag, Benson, et al., General Practice in New York
Vol. 26	Borchers, Markell, et al., New York State Administrative Procedure and Practice
Vol. A	Borges, et al., Enforcing Judgments and Collecting Debts in New York
Vols. B-C	Bensel, Frank, McKeon, et al., Personal Injury Practice in New York
Vols. D-E	Preminger, et al., Trusts and Estates Practice in New York
Vols. F-G	Finkelstein and Ferrara, Landlord and Tenant Practice in New York

FOREWORD

Here is the first update to *General Practice in New York*, volume 20 of the New York Practice Series. The pocket part covers the significant changes in the applicable law from publication of the original volume until 1999. Many of the updates were prepared by one or more of the original chapter authors; others were editorially prepared in-house by West and are so indicated. With respect to chapters of the book not updated at all, West makes no representations with respect to the current status of ther material therein.

December 1999

COORDINATED RESEARCH IN NEW YORK FROM WEST

New York Practice 2d
David D. Siegel

Handling the DWI Case in New York
Peter Gerstenzang

New York Elder Law Practice
Vincent J. Russo and Marvin Rachlin

WEST'S McKINNEY'S FORMS
Civil Practice Law and Rules

Uniform Commercial Code

Business Corporation Law

Matrimonial and Family Law

Real Property Practice

Estates and Surrogate Practice

Criminal Procedure Law

Not-For-Profit Corporation Law

Tax Practice and Procedure

Local Government Forms

Selected Consolidated Law Forms

McKinney's Consolidated Laws of New York Annotated

West's New York Legal Update

New York Digest

New York Law Finder

PAMPHLETS
New York Civil Practice Law and Rules

New York Sentence Charts

Westlaw®

COORDINATED RESEARCH FROM WEST GROUP

WEST*Check*® and WESTMATE®

West CD–ROM Libraries™

To order any of these New York practice tools, call your West Group Representative or 1–800–328–9352.

NEED RESEARCH HELP?

If you have research questions concerning Westlaw or West Group Publications, call West Group's Reference Attorneys at 1-800–733–2889.

WESTLAW® ELECTRONIC RESEARCH GUIDE

Coordinating Legal Research with Westlaw

The *New York Practice Series* is an essential aid to legal research. Westlaw provides a vast, online library of over 8000 collections of documents and services that can supplement research begun in this publication, encompassing:

- Federal and state primary law (statutes, regulations, rules, and case law), including West's editorial enhancements, such as headnotes, Key Number classifications, annotations

- Secondary law resources (texts and treatises published by West Group and by other publishers, as well as law reviews)

- Legal news

- Directories of attorneys and experts

- Court records and filings

- Citators

Specialized topical subsets of these resources have been created for more than thirty areas of practice.

In addition to legal information, there are general news and reference databases and a broad array of specialized materials frequently useful in connection with legal matters, covering accounting, business, environment, ethics, finance, medicine, social and physical sciences.

This guide will focus on a few aspects of Westlaw use to supplement research begun in this publication, and will direct you to additional sources of assistance.

Databases

A database is a collection of documents with some features in common. It may contain statutes, court decisions, administrative materials, commentaries, news or other information. Each database has a unique identifier, used in many Westlaw commands to select a database of interest. For example, the database containing New York cases has the identifier NY-CS.

The Westlaw Directory is a comprehensive list of databases with information about each database, including the types of documents each contains. The first page of a standard or customized Westlaw Directory is displayed upon signing on to Westlaw, except when prior, saved research is resumed. To access the Westlaw Directory at any time, enter DB.

Databases of potential interest in connection with your research include:

NY-AG	New York Attorney General Opinions
NYETH-EO	New York Ethics Opinions
NYETH-CS	Legal Ethics & Professional Responsibility - New York Cases
WLD-NY	West's Legal Directory - New York
LAWPRAC	The Legal Practice Database

For information as to currentness and search tips regarding any Westlaw database, enter the SCOPE command SC followed by the database identifier (e.g., SC NY-CS). It is not necessary to include the identifier to obtain scope information about the currently selected database.

Westlaw Highlights

Use of this publication may be supplemented through the Westlaw Bulletin (WLB), the Westlaw New York State Bulletin (WSB-NY) and various Topical Highlights. Highlights databases contain summaries of significant judicial, legislative and administrative developments and are updated daily; they are searchable both from an automatic list of recent documents and using general Westlaw search methods for documents accumulated over time. The full text of any judicial decision may be retrieved by entering FIND.

Consult the Westlaw Directory (enter DB) for a complete, current listing of highlights databases.

Retrieving a Specific Case

The FIND command can be used to quickly retrieve a case whose citation is known. For example:

FI 616 A.2d 1336

Updating Case Law Research

There are a variety of citator services on Westlaw for use in updating research.

KeyCite[SM] is an enhanced citator service that integrates all the case law on Westlaw. KeyCite provides direct and negative indirect history for any case within the scope of its coverage, citations to other decisions and secondary materials on Westlaw that have mentioned or discussed the cited case, and a complete integration with West Group's Key Number System so that you can track a legal issue explored in a case. KeyCite is as current as Westlaw and includes all cases on Westlaw, including unpublished opinions. To view the KeyCite history of a displayed

WESTLAW ELECTRONIC RESEARCH GUIDE

case, enter the command KC. To view the KeyCite information for a selected case, simply enter a command in the following form:

KC 113 SCT 2786

To see a complete list of publications covered by KeyCite, enter the command KC PUBS. To ascertain the scope of coverage, enter the command SC KC. For the complete list of commands available enter KC CMDS.

Retrieving Statutes, Court Rules and Regulations

Annotated and unannotated versions of the New York statutes are searchable on Westlaw (identifiers NY-ST-ANN and NY-ST), as are New York court rules (NY-RULES) and New York Administrative Code (NY-ADC).

The United States Code and United States Code - Annotated are searchable databases on Westlaw (identifiers USC and USCA, respectively), as are federal court rules (US-RULES) and regulations (CFR).

In addition, the FIND command may be used to retrieve specific provisions by citation, obviating the need for database selection or search. To FIND a desired document, enter FI, followed by the citation of the desired document, using the full name of the publication, or one of the abbreviated styles recognized by Westlaw.

If Westlaw does not recognize the style you enter, you may enter one of the following, using US, NY, or any other state code in place of XX:

FI XX-ST	Displays templates for codified statutes
FI XX-LEGIS	Displays templates for legislation
FI XX-RULES	Displays templates for rules
FI XX-ORDERS	Displays templates for court orders

Alternatively, entering FI followed by the publication's full name or an accepted abbreviation will normally display templates, useful jump possibilities, or helpful information necessary to complete the FIND process. For example:

FI USCA	Displays templates for United States Code - Annotated
FI FRAP	Displays templates for Federal Rules of Appellate Procedure
FI FRCP	Displays templates for Federal Rules of Civil Procedure
FI FRCRP	Displays templates for Federal Rules of Criminal Procedure
FI FRE	Displays templates for Federal Rules of Evidence
FI CFR	Displays templates for Code of Federal Regulations
FI FR	Displays templates for Federal Register

To view the complete list of FINDable documents and associated prescribed forms, enter FI PUBS.

WESTLAW ELECTRONIC RESEARCH GUIDE
Updating Research in re Statutes, Rules and Regulations

When viewing a statute, rule or regulation on Westlaw after a search or FIND command, it is easy to update your research. A message will appear on the screen if relevant amendments, repeals or other new material are available through the UPDATE feature. Entering the UPDATE command will display such material.

Documents used to update New York statutes are also searchable in New York Legislative Service (NY-LEGIS). Those used to update rules are searchable in New York Orders (NY-ORDERS).

Documents used to update federal statutes, rules, and regulations are searchable in the United States Public Laws (US-PL), Federal Orders (US-ORDERS) and Federal Register (FR) databases, respectively.

When documents citing a statute, rule or regulation are of interest, Shepard's Citations on Westlaw may be of assistance. That service covers federal constitutional provisions, statutes and administrative provisions, and corresponding materials from many states. The command SH PUBS displays a directory of publications which may be Shepardized on Westlaw. Consult the Westlaw manual for more information about citator services.

Using Westlaw as a Citator

For research beyond the coverage of any citator service, go directly to the databases (cases, for example) containing citing documents and use standard Westlaw search techniques to retrieve documents citing specific constitutional provisions, statutes, standard jury instructions or other authorities.

Fortunately, the specific portion of a citation is often reasonably distinctive, such as 22:636.1, 301.65, 401(k), 12-21-5, 12052. When it is, a search on that specific portion alone may retrieve applicable documents without any substantial number of inapplicable ones (unless the number happens to be coincidentally popular in another context).

Similarly, if the citation involves more than one number, such as 42 U.S.C.A. §1201, a search containing both numbers (e.g., 42 +5 1201) is likely to produce mostly desired information, even though the component numbers are common.

If necessary, the search may be limited in several ways:

A. Switch from a general database to one containing mostly cases within the subject area of the cite being researched;

WESTLAW ELECTRONIC RESEARCH GUIDE

B. Use a connector (&, /S, /P, etc.) to narrow the search to documents including terms which are highly likely to accompany the correct citation in the context of the issue being researched;

C. Include other citation information in the query. Because of the variety of citation formats used in documents, this option should be used primarily where other options prove insufficient. Below are illustrative queries for any database containing New York cases:

> N.Y.Const.I Const.I Constitution /s 6 VI +3 3

will retrieve cases citing the New York State Constitution, Art. 6, §3; and

> "Criminal Procedure Law" CPL /s 30.30

will retrieve cases citing Criminal Procedure Law §30.30.

Alternative Retrieval Methods

WIN® (Westlaw Is Natural™) allows you to frame your issue in plain English to retrieve documents:

> Does new trial motion extend (toll) the time for filing (taking) appeal?

Alternatively, retrieval may be focused by use of the Terms and Connectors method:

> TO(30) /P DI(NEW +1 TRIAL /P EXTEND!
> EXTENSION TOLL! /P APPEAL)

In databases with Key Numbers, either of the above examples will identify Appeal and Error ⌐345.1 as a Key Number collecting headnotes relevant to this issue if there are pertinent cases.

Since the Key Numbers are affixed to points of law by trained specialists based on conceptual understanding of the case, relevant cases that were not retrieved by either of the language-dependent methods will often be found at a Key Number.

Similarly, citations in retrieved documents (to cases, statutes, rules, etc.) may suggest additional, fruitful research using other Westlaw databases (e.g., annotated statutes, rules) or services (e.g., citator services).

Key Number Search

Frequently, case law research rapidly converges on a few topics, headings and Key Numbers within West's Key Number System that are likely to contain relevant cases. These may be discovered from known, relevant reported cases from any jurisdiction; Library References in West publications; browsing in a digest; or browsing the Key Number System on Westlaw using the JUMP feature or the KEY command.

WESTLAW ELECTRONIC RESEARCH GUIDE

Once discovered, topics, subheadings or Key Numbers are useful as search terms (in databases containing reported cases) alone or with other search terms, to focus the search within a narrow range of potentially relevant material.

For example, to retrieve cases with at least one headnote classified to Appeal and Error ⇨345.1, sign on to a caselaw database and enter

30k345.1   [use with other search terms, if desired]

The topic name (Appeal and Error) is replaced by its numerical equivalent (30) and the ⇨ by the letter k. A list of topics and their numerical equivalents is in the Westlaw Reference Manual and is displayed in Westlaw when the KEY command is entered.

Using JUMP

Westlaw's JUMP feature allows you to move from one document to another or from one part of a document to another, then easily return to your original place, without losing your original result. Opportunities to move in this manner are marked in the text with a JUMP symbol (▶). Whenever you see the JUMP symbol, you may move to the place designated by the adjacent reference by using the Tab, arrow keys or mouse click to position the cursor on the JUMP symbol, then pressing Enter or clicking again with the mouse.

Within the text of a court opinion, JUMP arrows are adjacent to case cites and federal statute cites, and adjacent to parenthesized numbers marking discussions corresponding to headnotes.

On a screen containing the text of a headnote, the JUMP arrows allow movement to the corresponding discussion in the text of the opinion,

▶ (3)

and allow browsing West's Key Number System beginning at various heading levels:

- ▶ 30   APPEAL AND ERROR
- ▶ 30VII   Transfer of Cause
- ▶ 30VII(A)   Time of Taking Proceedings
- ▶ 30k343   Commencement of Period of Limitation
- ▶ 30k345.1 k. Motion for new trial.

To return from a JUMP, enter GB (except for JUMPs between a headnote and the corresponding discussion in opinion, for which there is a matching number in parenthesis in both headnote and opinion). Returns from successive JUMPs (e.g., from case to cited case to case cited by cited case) without intervening returns may be accomplished by repeated entry of GB or by using the MAP command.

WESTLAW ELECTRONIC RESEARCH GUIDE

General Information

The information provided above illustrates some of the ways Westlaw can complement research using this publication. However, this brief overview illustrates only some of the power of Westlaw. The full range of Westlaw search techniques is available to support your research.

Please consult the Westlaw Reference Manual for additional information or assistance or call West's Reference Attorneys at 1-800-REF-ATTY (1-800-733-2889).

For information about subscribing to Westlaw, please call 1-800-328-9352.

SUMMARY OF CONTENTS

Page

Volume 20

Chapter
1. Business Organizations: Corporations 2
2. Non-corporate Entities 16
3. Municipal Law 19
4. Municipal Law 21
6. Buying and Selling a Small Business 25

Volume 21

7. Consumer Law 2
8. Enforcement of Money Judgments 4
9. Bankruptcy 5
11. Mortgage Foreclosure 11
12. Purchase and Sale of Real Estate 25

Volume 22

14. Eminent Domain 2
15. Environmental Law 5
16. Land Use Law 8
17. Employment Law 14
18. Civil Rights Law 16
19. Immigration and Nationality Law Permanent Residence Applications 39
20. Adoptions 52

Volume 23

21. Domestic Relations 2
22. Guardianship 9
23. Elder Law 21
24. Estate Planning 30
25. Probate and Estate Administration 37
26. Personal Injury 51

Volume 24

28. Legal Malpractice 2
29. Medical Malpractice 20
30. Damages 21

XVII

SUMMARY OF CONTENTS

Chapter	**Page**
31. Insurance	31
32. Workers' Compensation	34
33. Local Criminal Court Practice	39
34. Social Security Disability Cases	50
35. Income Tax	55
37. Civil Appellate Practice Before the Appellate Division and Other Intermediate Appellate Courts	58

Volume 25

38. Criminal Appellate Practice Before the Appellate Division and Other Intermediate Appellate Courts | 2
39. Civil and Criminal Appeals to the Court of Appeals | 4

Table of Statutes | 5
Table of Rules and Regulations | 15
Table of Cases | 17
Index | 31

WEST'S NEW YORK PRACTICE SERIES

General Practice in New York

Volume 20

Chapter 1

BUSINESS ORGANIZATIONS: CORPORATIONS

by
Ronald David Greenberg

Table of Sections

Sec.	
1.1	Scope Note
1.5	Definitions
1.7	Formation of Corporations—Certificates; Notices
1.18	____ Registered Agent for Service of Process
1.21	____ Certificate of Incorporation
1.22	____ Bylaws
1.23	____ Organization Meeting; Biennial Statement; Franchise Taxes
1.30	Capital Structure—Consideration and Payment for Shares
1.34	____ Federal Income Taxation Aspects
1.38	Distributions—Dividends; Share Distributions and Changes
1.39	____ Purchase or Redemption of Shares
1.43	Shareholders' Meetings and Agreements—Generally
1.44	____ Notice Requirements
1.45	____ Voting
1.46	____ Quorum Requirements
1.47	____ Agreements; Voting Trusts
1.52	Shareholders' Rights—Preemptive Rights
1.63	Directors—Meetings—Quorum and Voting Requirements
1.65	____ Fiduciary Duties
1.69	Officers
1.73	Amendment of Certificate of Incorporation—Procedure
1.75	____ Certificate of Amendment
1.77	____ Restated Certificate of Incorporation
1.83	Business Combinations—Mergers and Consolidations—Procedures
1.84	____ Mergers and Consolidations—Effect
1.88	____ Share Exchanges
1.97	Dissolution—Non-judicial Dissolution—Certificate of Dissolution
1.103	____ Judicial Dissolution—Petition Upon Deadlock Among Directors or Shareholders and in Other Circumstances
1.114	Foreign Corporations
1.116	____ Application for Authority
1.117	____ Application for Authority—Effect of Filing
1.118	____ Surrender of Authority
1.119	____ Termination of Existence
1.125	Foreign Professional Service Corporations

Westlaw Electronic Research

See Westlaw Electronic Research Guide preceding the Summary of Contents.

§ 1.1 Scope Note

PAGE 5:

[*Add the following to the end of note 1.*]

1. For a useful reference on federal income tax issues discussed in this chapter, see, e.g., 1999 CCH U.S. Master Tax Guide (82nd ed. 1998) ("Master Tax Guide").

§ 1.5 Definitions

PAGE 13:

[*Add the following as new subparagraph (1) and renumber old subparagraphs (1) through (12) as subparagraphs (2) through (13).*]

(1) "Authorized person" means a person, whether or not a shareholder, officer, or director, authorized to act on behalf of a corporation or foreign corporation.

§ 1.7 Formation of Corporations—Certificates; Notices

PAGE 16:

[*Replace the text accompanying notes 5 and 6 with the following.*]

Except as otherwise specified in the NYBCL, certificate must be signed by an officer, director, attorney-in-fact, or duly authorized person[5] and must include the name and capacity in which such person signs the certificate.[6]

5. NYBCL § 104(d).
6. *Id.*

PRACTICE POINTER: This requirement is important not only in signing certificates but is a good practice to follow on contracts and other documents signed on behalf of the corporation to avoid any question that the signer is acting in his or her own behalf rather than that of the corporation. *See infra*, § 1.10.

CAVEAT: Whenever an instrument is required to set forth the date of filing of the certificate of incorporation, the original certificate of incorporation is meant. NYBCL § 104(c). This requirement is satisfied, in the case of a corporation created by special act, by setting forth the chapter number and year of passage of the act. *Id. See supra*, 1.21, note 1. *See also*, NYBCL §§ 104(a) and (e) (English language, addresses, consent of public official attached).

§ 1.18 Formation of Corporations—Registered Agent for Service of Process

PAGE 29:

[*Replace the sentence accompanying note 9 with the following.*]

If the agent resigns, a certificate entitled "Certificate of resignation of registered agent of [name of designating corporation] under section

§ 1.18 BUSINESS ORGANIZATIONS: CORPORATIONS   Ch. 1

305 of the Business Corporation Law" must be signed by the registered agent and delivered to the Department of State.[9]

§ 1.21 Formation of Corporations—Certificate of Incorporation

PAGES 32–33:

[*Replace the sentence accompanying note 1 with the following.*]

The certificate must be entitled "Certificate of incorporation of [name of corporation] under section 402 of the Business Corporation Law" and must be signed by the incorporators (with their names and addresses included in the certificate) and delivered to the Department of State.[1]

§ 1.22 Formation of Corporations—Bylaws

PAGE 36:

[*Replace the sentence accompanying note 2 with the following.*]

Thereafter, subject to limitations on the right to vote under NYBCL § 613, bylaws may be adopted, amended, or repealed by a majority of the votes of shares entitled to vote for the election of directors.[2]

§ 1.23 Formation of Corporations—Organization Meeting; Biennial Statement; Franchise Taxes

PAGE 38:

[*In the text accompanying note 11, replace clause (a) with the following.*]

(a) the name and business address of its chief executive officer,

§ 1.30 Capital Structure—Consideration and Payment for Shares

PAGE 47:

[*Replace the sentence accompanying note 3 with the following.*]

The obligation of the subscriber for future services may constitute payment or part payment for shares of a corporation.[3]

[*In note 3 delete "NYBCL § 504(b)." and replace the first sentence after the deleted cite with the following.*]

3. They are permitted to constitute consideration for interests in limited liability companies (LLCs).

Ch. 1   BUSINESS ORGANIZATIONS: CORPORATIONS   § 1.39

§ 1.34   Capital Structure—Federal Income Taxation Aspects

PAGE 54:

[*Add the following to the end of note 1.*]

1. *See, also*, 1999 CCH U.S. Master Tax Guide (82nd ed. 1998) ("Master Tax Guide").

PAGE 58:

[*Add the following to the end of the CAVEAT at the end of note 28.*]

1. The general rule of I.R.C. § 351(a) does not apply, and gain or loss is recognized, where property is transferred to an investment company or pursuant to a plan while the corporation is under the jurisdiction of a court in a title 11 (bankruptcy) or similar case. I.R.C. § 351(e). A transfer of property is considered to be a transfer to an investment company if (i) the transfer results, directly or indirectly, in diversification of the transferors' interests and (ii) the transferee is (a) a regulated investment company, (b) a real estate investment trust, or (c) a corporation more than 80 percent of the value of whose assets (excluding cash and nonconvertible debt obligations from consideration) are held for investment and are readily marketable stocks or securities or are interests in regulated investment companies or real estate investment trusts. Treas. Reg. § 1.351–1(c)(2). *See, also, e.g.*, B. Bittker and J. Eustice, Federal Income Taxation of Corporations and Shareholders ¶ 3.15 (6th ed. 1994). A similar, but not identical, exception applies to transfers to partnerships. The general rule of I.R.C. § 721(a) (nonrecognition of gain or loss on contribution to a partnership) does not apply to *gain* realized on a transfer of property to a partnership that would be treated as an investment company (within the meaning of I.R.C. § 351) if the partnership were incorporated. I.R.C. § 721(b). *See, also, e.g.*, 2 A. Willis, J. Pennell, P. Postlewaite, Partnership Taxation ¶ 4.02[8] (1997 student ed.); W. McKee, W. Nelson, R. Whitmire, Fed. Taxation of Partnerships and Partners ¶ 4.08 (3rd ed. 1996). This exception would appear to apply to limited liability companies. *See, e.g.*, Master Tax Guide ¶ ¶ 402, 402A, and 402B.

§ 1.38   Distributions—Dividends; Share Distributions and Changes

PAGE 70:

[*Replace note 16 with the following.*]

16. NYBCL § 511(a)(1) and (a)(2).

§ 1.39   Distributions—Purchase or Redemption of Shares

PAGES 74–75:

[*Replace the text accompanying note 13 with the following.*]

Unless the purchase or agreement to purchase is approved by the board of directors and by a majority of the votes of all outstanding shares entitled to vote (unless the certificate of incorporation requires a greater percentage of the votes of the outstanding shares for approval).[13]

§ 1.43 Shareholders' Meetings and Agreements—Generally

PAGE 82:

[*Replace the sentence accompanying note 14 with the following.*]

The record date may not be more than 60 nor fewer than ten days before the date of the meeting, nor more than 60 days prior to any other action.[14]

§ 1.44 Shareholders' Meetings and Agreements—Notice Requirements

PAGE 84:

[*Replace the text accompanying notes 5 and 6 with the following.*]

A copy of the notice of any meeting must be given, personally or by first class mail, no fewer than ten nor more than 60 days before the date of the meeting, to each shareholder entitled to vote at the meeting.[5] A copy of the notice may be given by third class mail no fewer than 24 nor more than 60 days before the date of the meeting.[6]

[*Add the following sentence after the third sentence of the first full paragraph.*]

If transmitted electronically, the notice is given when directed to the shareholder's electronic mail address as supplied by the shareholder to the secretary of the corporation or as otherwise directed pursuant to the shareholder's authorizations or instructions.[7.1]

7.1 *Id.*

[*Add the following text after the first sentence of the third full paragraph.*]

Waiver of notice may be written or electronic.[12.1] If the waiver is written, it must be executed by the shareholder (or the shareholder's authorized officer, director, employee, or agent) by signing the waiver or causing the shareholder's signature to be affixed to the waiver by any reasonable means, including, but not limited to, facsimile signature.[12.2] If the waiver is electronically transmitted, it must set forth (or be submitted with information permitting a reasonable determination) that it was authorized by the shareholder.[12.3]

12.1 *Id.* 12.3 *Id.*
12.2 *Id.*

§ 1.45 Shareholders' Meetings and Agreements—Voting

PAGE 87:

[*Replace note 18 with the following.*]

18. NYBCL § 609(a). Without limiting the manner in which a shareholder may authorize another person or persons to act as proxy pursuant to NYBCL § 609(a), valid means by which a shareholder may grant such authority are specified in NYBCL § 609(i). A shareholder may execute a writing authorizing another person or per-

sons to act as the shareholder's proxy. NYBCL § 609(i)(1). Execution may be accomplished by the shareholder or the shareholder's authorized officer, director, employee, or agent signing such writing or causing his or her signature to be affixed to such writing by any reasonable means including, but not limited to, by facsimile signature. *Id.* A shareholder may authorize another person or persons to act for the shareholder as proxy by transmitting or authorizing the transmission of a telegram, cablegram, or other means of electronic transmission to the person who will be the holder of the proxy or to a proxy solicitation firm, proxy support service organization, or like agent duly authorized by the person who will be the holder of the proxy to receive such transmission, provided that any such telegram, cablegram, or other means of electronic transmission must set forth (or be submitted with information permitting a reasonably determination) that the telegram, cablegram, or other electronic transmission was authorized by the shareholder. NYBCL § 609(i)(2). If such telegrams, cablegrams, or other electronic transmissions are determined to be valid, the inspectors (or, if none, such other persons making that determination) must specify the nature of the information upon which they relied. *Id.* Any copy, facsimile telecommunication, or other reliable reproduction of the writing or transmission created pursuant to NYBCL § 609(i) may be substituted or used in lieu of the original writing or transmission for any and all purposes for which the original writing or transmission could be used, provided that such reproduction is a complete reproduction of the entire original writing or transmission. NYBCL § 609(j).

[*Replace the sentence accompanying note 19 with the following.*]

No proxy is valid after the expiration of eleven months from the date of the proxy, unless otherwise provided therein.[19]

[*Add the following at the end of note 23.*]

23. This limitation does not apply to votes, proxies, or consents given by holders of preferred shares in connection with a proxy or consent solicitation made available on identical terms to all holders of shares of the same class or series and remaining open for acceptance for at least 20 business days. *Id.*

§ 1.46 Shareholders' Meetings and Agreements—Quorum Requirements

PAGE 92:

[*Replace the sentence accompanying note 1 with the following.*]

The holders of a majority of the shares entitled to vote constitute a quorum at a meeting of shareholders for the transaction of any business, provided that when a specified item of business is required to be voted on by a particular class or series, voting as a class, the holders of a majority of the shares of the class or series constitute a quorum for that purpose.[1]

§ 1.46 BUSINESS ORGANIZATIONS: CORPORATIONS Ch. 1

[*Substitute "the shares entitled to vote," for "all outstanding shares entitled to vote," in the second sentence of note 3.*]

§ 1.47 Shareholders' Meetings and Agreements—Agreements; Voting Trusts

PAGES 93–94:

[*Substitute "the shares entitled" for "all outstanding shares entitled" at two places in the first sentence of note 5.*]

PAGE 94:

[*Substitute "the shares" for "outstanding shares" and "particular class or series" for "class or series" in the last sentence of note 5.*]

§ 1.52 Shareholders' Rights—Preemptive Rights

PAGE 108:

[*Substitute "NYBCL § 622(a) and (b)" for "NYBCL § 620(a) and (b)" at the beginning of note 3 before the CAVEAT.*]

[*Substitute "NYBCL § 622(b)(1) and (c)" for "NYBCL § 622(b)(2) and (c)" at the end of the first sentence of the CAVEAT in note 3.*]

§ 1.63 Directors—Meetings—Quorum and Voting Requirements

PAGES 122–123:

[*Substitute "a specified proportion of the votes of the shares, or particular class" for "vote of a specified proportion of the holders of outstanding shares, or class" in the last sentence of note 5.*]

§ 1.65 Directors—Fiduciary Duties

PAGE 125:

[*Substitute "NYBCL § 713(b)" for "Id." in note 12.*]

PAGE 126:

[*Substitute "NYBCL § 714(a)(2)" for "BCL § 714(a)(2)" in the last sentence of note 15.*]

§ 1.69 Officers

PAGE 137:

[*In note 1 replace "NYBCL § 715(a)." with the following to precede the PRACTICE POINTER.*]

NYBCL § 715(a). For an inspection list of directors and officers, *see* NYBCL § 718. *See, also, supra,* § 1.59 (subheading *Inspection List of Directors and Officers*).

§ 1.73 Amendment of Certificate of Incorporation—Procedure

PAGE 142:

[*Delete "of the holders of" preceding "a majority" in the second line of the first sentence.*]

§ 1.75 Amendment of Certificate of Incorporation—Certificate of Amendment

PAGE 143:

[*In note 1 replace the first sentence and citation in the Procedure with the following.*]

1. To accomplish any amendment, a certificate of amendment, entitled "Certificate of amendment of the certificate of incorporation of _____ (name of corporation) under section 805 of the Business Corporation Law," must be signed and delivered to the Department of State. *Id.*

§ 1.77 Amendment of Certificate of Incorporation—Restated Certificate of Incorporation

PAGE 145:

[*In note 1 replace the first sentence of the Procedure with the following.*]

1. A restated certificate of incorporation, entitled "Restated certificate of incorporation of _____ (name of corporation) under section 807 of the Business Corporation Law," must be signed and delivered to the Department of State.

§ 1.83 Business Combinations—Mergers and Consolidations—Procedures

PAGE 151:

[*Add the following to the end of the first paragraph of note 1.*]

1. ; "constituent entity" means a domestic or foreign corporation or other business entity that is participating in the merger or consolidation with one or more domestic or foreign corporations (NYBCL § 901(b)(6)); "other business entity" means any person other than a natural person, general partnership (including any registered limited liability partnership or registered foreign limited liability partnership), or a domestic or foreign business corporation (NYBCL § 901(b)(7)).

[*Delete "NYBCL § 901(b)." at the end of the first paragraph of note 1.*]

PAGE 152:

[*Add the following to the end of note 2.*]

2. One or more domestic corporations and one or more other business entities, or one or more foreign corporations and one or more other business entities, may merge into a single domestic or foreign corporation or other business entity or consolidate into a single domestic or foreign corporation or other business entity. NYBCL § 901(c). *See, also, infra,* § 1.83 (subheading *Combination of Corporations and Other Business Entities*).

§ 1.83 BUSINESS ORGANIZATIONS: CORPORATIONS   Ch. 1

[Replace the first enumerated clause of the text accompanying note 3 with the following.]

(1) the name of each constituent entity (and, if the name of any of them has been changed, the name under which it was formed) and the name of the surviving, or consolidated, corporation;

[Replace the sentence accompanying note 6 with the following.]

The plan must be adopted by a majority of the votes of the shares entitled to vote.[6]

PAGE 153:

[Insert "NYBCL § 903(a)(2)." between the sentence ending with "NYBCL § 804 (class voting on amendment)." and the beginning of the next sentence in note 6.]

[Replace the sentence accompanying note 8 with the following.]

In that case, in addition to the authorization by the requisite number of votes of all outstanding shares entitled to vote thereon, the merger or consolidation must be authorized by a majority of the votes of all outstanding shares of each such class or series.

[Delete "and verified" in the first sentence of note 10.]

PAGE 154:

[Replace the first sentence of the Procedure in note 12 with the following.]

12. The certificate must be signed and delivered to the Department of State by the surviving corporation.

PAGE 155:

[Replace "verified," with "verified [sic]," in the first sentence of the Procedure in note 17.]

[Delete "and verified" in the first sentence of the Procedure in note 18.]

[Add the following at the end of § 1.83.]

Combination of Corporations and Other Business Entities. One or more domestic corporations and one or more other business entities (or one or more foreign corporations and one or more other business entities) may as provided by the NYBCL and the NYLLCL[18.1] merge into a single domestic or foreign corporation or other business entity (which must be one of the constituent entities) or consolidate into a single domestic or foreign corporation or other business entity (which must be a new domestic or foreign corporation or other business entity to be formed pursuant to the consolidation).[18.2]

18.1 NYLLCL § 1001. See, also, Chapter 2 "Non-Corporate Entities: Limited Liability Companies and Partnerships," *infra*. See *supra*, § 1.83, note 1.

18.2 NYBCL § 901(c). *Procedure.* After adoption of the agreement of merger or consolidation by the board and shareholders of each corporation participating in the merger or consolidation (unless the merger or consolidation is abandoned in accordance with NYBCL § 903(b), NYLLCL § 1002(d), or other applicable statute), a certificate of merger or consolidation, entitled "Certificate of merger (or consolidation) of.... and.... into.... (names of constituent entities) under section nine hundred four-a of the business corporation law," must be signed on behalf of each constituent entity and delivered to the Department of State. NYBCL § 904–a(a). It must set forth: (1) the name of each constituent entity and, if the name of any of them has been changed, the name under which it was formed; (2) the date when the certificate of incorporation or articles of organization of each domestic constituent entity was filed by the Department of State; (3) if a constituent entity is a foreign business corporation or foreign other business entity, the jurisdiction and date of filing of its initial certificate of incorporation or formation document, if any, and the date when its application for authority was filed by the Department of State, or if no such application has been filed, a statement to such effect and (if the constituent foreign corporation is the surviving entity) that it is not to do business in New York until an application for such authority has been filed with the Department of State; (4) a statement that an agreement of merger or consolidation has been approved and executed by each constituent entity; (5) the name of the surviving or consolidated corporation; (6) if the surviving or resulting entity is a domestic corporation, in case of a merger, a statement of any amendments or changes in the certificate of incorporation of the surviving corporation to be effected by such merger; in case of consolidation, all statements required to be included in a certificate of incorporation for a corporation formed under the NYBCL; (7) if the surviving or resulting entity is a foreign corporation, an agreement that the surviving or consolidated foreign corporation may be served with process in New York in any action or special proceeding for the enforcement of any liability or obligation of any domestic or foreign entity, previously amenable to suit in New York, that is a constituent entity in such merger or consolidation, and for the enforcement, as provided in the NYBCL, of the right of shareholders or members of any constituent domestic entity to receive payment for their interests against the surviving or consolidated corporation; (8) if the surviving or resulting entity is a foreign corporation, a designation of the Secretary of State as its agent upon whom process against it may be served in the manner set forth in NYBCL § 306(b) in any action or special proceeding, and a post office address, within or without this state, to which the Secretary of State is to mail a copy of any process against it served upon the Secretary; (9) if the surviving or resulting entity is a foreign corporation, an agreement that, subject to the provisions of NYBCL § 623, NYLLCL § 1005, and any other applicable statute, the surviving or consolidated foreign corporation will promptly pay to the shareholders of each constituent domestic corporation and owners of any constituent other business entity the amount, if any, to which they shall be entitled under the provisions of the NYBCL and the NYLLCL, or any other applicable statute relating to the right of shareholders, owners, and members to receive payment for their interests; (10) the effective date of the merger or consolidation if other than the date of filing of the certificate of merger or consolidation by the Department of State; (11) for each foreign corporation, foreign limited liability company, or other business entity, a statement that such merger or consolidation is permitted by its jurisdiction of incorporation or organization and is in compliance therewith; (12) that the agreement of merger or consolidation is on file at a place of business of the surviving or resulting domestic or foreign corporation and states the address thereof. *Id.* The post office address designated in NYBCL § 904–a(a)(8) supersedes any prior address designated as the address to which process is to be mailed. *Id.* The surviving or consolidated domestic or foreign corporation must file a copy of such certificate, certified by the Department of State, in the office of the clerk of each county in which each office of a participating domestic or foreign corporation, other than the surviving corporation, is located, and in the office of the official who is the recording officer of each county in New York in which real property of a participating domestic or foreign corporation, other than the surviving corporation, is situated. NYBCL § 904–a(b).

§ 1.83 BUSINESS ORGANIZATIONS: CORPORATIONS Ch. 1

PAGES 155–156:

[*Replace the citation at the end of note 18 with "NYBCL § 907(g)."*]

§ 1.84 Business Combinations—Mergers and Consolidations—Effect

PAGE 156:

[*Substitute "90" for "ninety" in note 1.*]

[*Replace the text accompanying note 4 with the following.*]

(2) all the property, real and personal, including subscriptions to shares, causes of action, and every other asset of each of the constituent entities, vests in the surviving or consolidated corporation without further act or deed;[4]

[*Replace the text accompanying note 5 with the following.*]

(3) the surviving or consolidated corporation assumes, and is liable for, all the liabilities, obligations, and penalties of each of the constituent entities;[5]

PAGES 156–157:

[*Revise note 5 to read as follows.*]

5. NYBCL § 906(b)(3). No obligations of, or claims against, any constituent entity, or any of its shareholders, members, officers, or directors, are released or impaired by the merger or consolidation. *Id.* No action, or proceeding, whether civil or criminal, then pending by or against any constituent entity, or any of its shareholders, members, officers, or directors, abates or is discontinued by the merger or consolidation and may be enforced, prosecuted, settled, or compromised as if such merger or consolidation had not occurred, or the surviving or consolidated corporation may be substituted in such action or special proceeding in place of any constituent entity. *Id.*

§ 1.88 Business Combinations—Share Exchanges

PAGE 160:

[*In the second paragraph of note 3 add "NYBCL § 913(c)(2)(A)" between the end of the first sentence and the beginning of the last sentence.*]

[*Substitute "NYBCL § 913(c)(2)(A)" for "NYBCL § 913(c)(2)(A)(ii)" in the last sentence of the second paragraph of note 3.*]

[*Delete "and verified" from the sentence accompanying note 4.*]

§ 1.97 Dissolution—Non-judicial Dissolution—Certificate of Dissolution

PAGE 175:

[*In note 1 replace the first sentence of the Procedure with the following.*]

1. A certificate of dissolution entitled "Certificate of dissolution of . . . (name of corporation) under section 1003 of the Business Corporation Law" must be signed and delivered to the Department of State.

Ch. 1   BUSINESS ORGANIZATIONS: CORPORATIONS § 1.114

§ 1.103   Dissolution—Judicial Dissolution—Petition Upon Deadlock Among Directors or Shareholders and in Other Circumstances

PAGE 180:

[Add "shares representing" between "holders of" and "at least one-half of all outstanding shares" in the second line of the first paragraph.]

[Add "shares representing" between "holders of" and "more than one-third of the votes" in note 2.]

[Add "shares representing" between "holders of" and "twenty percent or more" in the text accompanying note 5 and replace "twenty" with "20" in that text.]

PAGE 181:

[Replace "ninety" with "90" in the text accompanying note 11.]

§ 1.114   Foreign Corporations

PAGE 192:

[Replace the first sentence of the second paragraph (and accompanying note) with the following.]

A foreign corporation doing business in New York must produce a record of its shareholders upon at least five days' written demand of any New York resident who has been a shareholder of record of the corporation.[8]

8. NYBCL § 1315(a). The record must set forth the names and addresses of all shareholders, the number and class of shares held by each, and the dates when they respectively became the owners of record. *Id.* The shareholder making the demand has the right (1) to examine in person or by agent or attorney at the New York office of the foreign corporation (or at the office of its transfer agent or registrar in New York or at such other place in the county in New York in which the foreign corporation is doing business as may be designated by the foreign corporation) during the usual business hours, the record of shareholders or an exact copy thereof certified as correct by the corporate officer or agent responsible for keeping or producing such record and (2) to make extracts therefrom. *Id.* Any such agent must be authorized in a writing that satisfies the requirements of a writing under NYBCL § 609(b) (proxies). *Id.* The corporation must make the record available in the format in which it is maintained by the corporation and is not required to provide it in any other format. *Id.* If the demand includes a request to furnish information regarding beneficial owners, the corporation must make available such information in its possession regarding beneficial owners as is provided to the corporation by a registered broker or dealer, or a bank, association, or other entity that exercises fiduciary powers in connection with the forwarding of information to such owners. *Id.* The corporation is not be required to obtain information about beneficial owners not in its possession. *Id.* Resident holders of voting trust certificates representing shares of the foreign corporation are regarded as shareholders. *Id.* See also, NYBCL §§ 1315(b) (denial of examination for refusal to furnish affidavit on purpose of examination and prior sale of record of shareholders) and 1315(c) (application to Supreme Court, upon denial of examination, to permit examination of record of shareholders).

[Replace note 11 with the following.]

11. NYBCL § 1318. See *supra*, § 1.38.

§ 1.116 Foreign Corporations—Application for Authority

PAGE 194:

[*In note 1 replace the first sentence of the Procedure with the following.*]

1. The application, entitled "Application for authority of _____ (name of corporation) under section 1304 of the Business Corporation Law," must be signed and delivered to the Department of State.

§ 1.117 Foreign Corporations—Application for Authority—Effect of Filing

PAGE 196:

[*In note 8 replace the first sentence of the Procedure with the following.*]

8. A certificate entitled "Certificate of amendment of application for authority of _____ (name of corporation) under section 1309 of the Business Corporation Law" must be signed and delivered to the Department of State. NYBCL § 1309(a).

[*Replace "NYBCL § 1309(a)." with "Id." in note 8 at the end of the second sentence.*]

PAGE 197:

[*In note 9 replace the first sentence of the Procedure with the following.*]

9. A certificate entitled "Certificate of change of application for authority of _____ (name of corporation) under section 1309-A of the Business Corporation Law" must be signed and delivered to the Department of State. NYBCL § 1309-A(b).

[*Replace "NYBCL § 1309-A(b)." with "Id." at the end of note 9.*]

§ 1.118 Foreign Corporations—Surrender of Authority

PAGE 197:

[*In note 1 replace the first sentence of the Procedure with the following.*]

1. A certificate entitled "Certificate of surrender of authority of _____ (name of corporation) under section 1310 of the Business Corporation Law" must be signed and delivered to the Department of State.

§ 1.119 Foreign Corporations—Termination of Existence

PAGE 198:

[*In note 1 replace the last sentence and citation of the Procedure with the following.*]

1. The post office address may be changed by signing and delivering to the Department of State a certificate of change setting forth the statements required under NYBCL § 1309-A to effect a change in the post office address under NYBCL § 1308(a)(7). *Id.*

§ 1.125 Foreign Professional Service Corporations
PAGE 210:

[*In note 12 replace the second sentence of the Procedure with the following.*]

12. It must be signed and delivered to the Department of State. *Id.*

Chapter 2

NON-CORPORATE ENTITIES

(update prepared in-house)

Table of Sections

2.16	Limited Liability Companies—Formation
2.17	___ Formation—Articles of Organization
2.18	___ ___ Publication
2.21	___ Members
2.23	___ ___ Liability
2.26	___ Management—Members vs. Managers
2.37	___ Dissolution—Events
2.43	___ PLLCs
2.53	General Partnerships—Partners—Liability
2.75	Limited Liability Partnerships—Formation/Registration
2.106	Securities Laws Issues

Westlaw Electronic Research

See Westlaw Electronic Research Guide preceding the Summary of Contents.

---

§ 2.16 Limited Liability Companies—Formation

PAGE 277:

5. NYLLCL § 202.

§ 2.17 Limited Liability Companies—Formation—Articles of Organization

PAGE 280:

8. NYLLCL § 211(a) (referring to § 207).

§ 2.18 Limited Liability Companies—Formation—Publication

PAGE 281:

[*All references to § 206(c) in the footnotes 1–5 should be changed to § 206. There is no 206(c).*]

§ 2.21 Limited Liability Companies—Members

PAGE 284:

[*Replace note 18 with the following.*]

18. Id.

§ 2.23 Limited Liability Companies—Members—Liability

PAGE 287:

6. NYLLCL § 212. Both corporate law and limited partnership law produce the same result.

8. NYLLCL § 508(c). An agreement to the contrary could extend or shorten this statute of limitations.

§ 2.26 Limited Liability Companies—Management—Members vs. Managers

PAGE 289:

[*Delete note 3 and replace with the following.*]

3. NYLLCL §§ 401(a), 408(a).

§ 2.37 Limited Liability Companies—Dissolution—Events

PAGE 297:

[*Change the introductory sentence to read as follows.*]

An LLC is dissolved, according to the NYLLCL § 701, upon the earliest to occur of any one of the following events: ...

[*Replace note 3 with the following.*]

3. See NYPL § for similar language: "The court shall decree a dissolution when _ (d) A partner _ so conducts himself in matters relating to the partnership business that it is not reasonably practicable to carry on the business in partnership with him."

§ 2.43 Limited Liability Companies—PLLCs

PAGE 304:

[*Excise the following sentence from the 7th paragraph of the section.*]

Unlike foreign LLCs, foreign PLLCs do not receive a Certificate of Authority to practice in the State.

§ 2.43

[Also remove the corresponding footnote, fn. 15.]

§ 2.53 General Partnerships—Partners—Liability

PAGE 314:

[Replace note 8 with the following.]

8. NYPL § 27.

§ 2.75 Limited Liability Partnerships—Formation/Registration

PAGE 329:

[In note 1, add "veterinary" between "medical" and "dental".]

PAGE 331:

[Change the first sentence of the first full paragraph to read as follows.]

Following registration, an LLP must file periodic statements with the department of state, accompanied by a $20 filing fee, within 60 days and every two years thereafter.

§ 2.106 Securities Laws Issues

PAGE 359:

[Replace note 10 with the following.]

10. GBJ Corporation v. Sequa Corporation, 804 F.Supp. 564, 567 (S.D.N.Y.1992); Marine Bank v. Weaver, 455 U.S. 551, 557–59, 102 S.Ct. 1220, 1224–25, 71 L.Ed.2d 409 (1982).

Chapter 3

MUNICIPAL LAW

By
Ralph W. Bandel

Table of Sections

3.12 Legislative Enactments—Ordinances
3.22 Officers and Employees—Conflicts of Interest
3.24 Contracts

Westlaw Electronic Research

See Westlaw Electronic Research Guide preceding the Summary of Contents.

§ 3.12 Legislative Enactments—Ordinances

PAGE 420:

[*Delete note 8 and replace with the following.*]

8. *See* County Law § 215(11).

CAVEAT: Counties may adopt ordinances only when they have previously adopted a local law or resolution authorizing the adoption of ordinances. In addition, the power to adopt ordinances is further limited to certain traffic matters making county ordinances, in effect, akin to rules or regulations. *See infra*, § 3.13.

§ 3.22 Officers and Employees—Conflicts of Interest

PAGE 435:

13. Note that the authorization to adopt local codes of ethics is mandatory for cities, counties, towns, villages and school districts but permissive for other types of "municipalities" as that term is defined in Article 18 of the General Municipal Law. While the authorization to adopt a code of ethics is mandatory, the establishment of a local board of ethics is permissive. *See also* 30 Opn. St. Compt. 30, 1976.

§ 3.24 Contracts

PAGE 438:

[*Add to end of section.*]

However, in the case of towns, rather than the six-year statute of limitations generally applicable to actions based upon breach of contract, such an action must be commenced within eighteen months after the cause of action accrued. In addition, a written verified claim must be filed with the town clerk within six months of the date the cause of action accrued.[18]

§ 3.24

[Add corresponding note 18.]

18. *See* Town Law § 65(3).

Chapter 4

MUNICIPAL LAW

By
Patrick J. Borchers
and David L. Markell

Table of Sections

4.6 Procedural Due Process—Protected Interests
4.7 ⎯⎯ The Process Due
4.11 Adjudicatory Proceedings—Definition of an Adjudicatory Proceeding
4.15 ⎯⎯ Evidence
4.19 ⎯⎯ Burden of Proof
4.21 ⎯⎯ Unreasonable Agency Delay
4.22 ⎯⎯ Agency Duty to Decide Consistently
4.49 Administrative Rulemaking—Ancillary Documentation and the Role of GORR
4.50 ⎯⎯ Rule Filing and Publication
4.57 ⎯⎯ Special Strategic Considerations in Handling Administrative Rulemaking Matters—Special Issues in Emergency Rulemakings
4.71 Judicial Review—Final Order and Relief in the Nature of Prohibition
4.77 ⎯⎯ Standards of Review—Review of Agency Determinations of Law
4.78 ⎯⎯ ⎯⎯ Review of Agency Determinations of Fact Under the Substantial Evidence Test
4.81 ⎯⎯ ⎯⎯ Review of Administrative Discretion
4.82 ⎯⎯ Statutes of Limitation Applicable to Judicial Review of Agency Action

Westlaw Electronic Research

See Westlaw Electronic Research Guide preceding the Summary of Contents.

§ 4.6 Procedural Due Process—Protected Interests

PAGE 484:

3. Miller v. DeBuono, 90 N.Y.2d 783, 666 N.Y.S.2d 548, 689 N.E.2d 518 (1997)(allowing the entry of a nurse's aide's name in registry of patient abusers upon a showing of less than a preponderance of the evidence is unconstitutional because of liberty interest held by aide in avoiding stigma plus other negative consequences).

§ 4.7 Procedural Due Process—The Process Due

PAGE 487:

7. But compare Miller v. DeBuono, 90 N.Y.2d 783, 666 N.Y.S.2d 548, 689 N.E.2d 518 (1997)(requiring the burden of proof of a civil trial because of the serious nature of the liberty interest involved in the case).

§ 4.11 Adjudicatory Proceedings—Definition of an Adjudicatory Proceeding

PAGE 490:

2. Loyal Tire and Auto Center, Inc. v. New York State Thruway Auth., 227 A.D.2d 82, 652 N.Y.S.2d 804 (3d Dep't 1997)(no statute requiring an on-the-record hearing and thus SAPA Article 3 not applicable).

§ 4.15 Adjudicatory Proceedings—Evidence

PAGE 493:

1. *See also* Aria Contracting Corp. v. McGowan, 256 A.D.2d 1204, 684 N.Y.S.2d 93 (4th Dep't 1998)(ALJ within rights to exclude two witnesses from testifying on the grounds that their testimony would have been irrelevant); Kinlock v. New York State Local and Employees' Retirement System, 237 A.D.2d 810, 655 N.Y.S.2d 457 (3d Dep't 1997)(agency need not follow formal rules of evidence and may accept written medical reports in lieu of live testimony).

§ 4.19 Adjudicatory Proceedings—Burden of Proof

PAGE 496:

[*Add to the end of this section.*]

In fact, this approach appears to be constitutionally required in some cases. In Miller v. DeBuono[3] the Court of Appeals held that allowing a nurse's aide's name to be placed upon a registry of patient abusers on less than a showing of preponderance of the evidence violated the aide's due process rights. The Court distinguished the substantial evidence standard as involving a lesser threshold, but held that such an application of a lower standard would be unconstitutional in this circumstance because of the severe consequences to the aide.

3. 90 N.Y.2d 783, 666 N.Y.S.2d 548, 689 N.E.2d 518 (1997).

§ 4.21 Adjudicatory Proceedings—Unreasonable Agency Delay

PAGE 497:

4. Goldsmith v. DeBuono, 245 A.D.2d 627, 665 N.Y.S.2d 727 (3d Dep't 1997)(petitioner's generalized assertions of memory loss about incidents in question not sufficient to show actual prejudice).

§ 4.22 Adjudicatory Proceedings—Agency Duty to Decide Consistently

PAGE 498:

1. Brusco v. State, Division of Housing and Community Renewal, 239 A.D.2d 210, 657 N.Y.S.2d 180 (1st Dep't 1997)(agency failure to explain departure from practice of giving landlords opportunity to cure defects violated agency's duty under *Field*).

§ 4.49 Administrative Rulemaking—Ancillary Documentation and the Role of GORR

PAGE 534:

[*Add to the end of the section.*]

A separation-of-powers challenge to GORR's authority to veto rules was dismissed for lack of standing.

§ 4.50 Administrative Rulemaking—Rule Filing and Publication

PAGE 535:

4. Alca Indus. Inc. v. Delaney, 92 N.Y.2d 775, 686 N.Y.S.2d 356, 709 N.E.2d 97 (1999)(criteria for withdraw of a particular bid included in bid documents are not rules because criteria are ad hoc depending upon contract and do not set a general pattern for future conduct); Pallette Stone Corp. v. State of New York Office of General Services, 245 A.D.2d 756, 665 N.Y.S.2d 457 (3d Dep't 1997)(procedure for post-bid reductions in price need not have been formulated by rule); but see Matter of 10 Apartment Assoc., Inc. v. New York State Division of Housing and Community Renewal, 240 A.D.2d 585, 658 N.Y.S.2d 674 (2d Dep't 1997)(requirement of two years of ownership of rental property before seeking rental increase is a rule that must be promulgated in accordance with Article 2 of SAPA).

§ 4.57 Administrative Rulemaking—Special Strategic Considerations in Handling Administrative Rulemaking Matters—Special Issues in Emergency Rulemakings

PAGE 546:

4. *See also* United Water New York, Inc. v. Public Service Comm'n, 252 A.D.2d 810, 676 N.Y.S.2d 709 (3d Dep't 1998)(agency rationally concluded that regulated party's delay in filing application did not create an emergency requiring expedited consideration of application).

§ 4.71 Judicial Review—Final Order and Relief in the Nature of Prohibition

PAGE 566:

9. Adelphi Univ. v. Board of Regents, 229 A.D.2d 36, 652 N.Y.S.2d 837 (3d Dep't 1997)(question of SAPA's applicability to regent removal proceedings can be successfully raised at conclusion of proceedings and thus Article 78 relief in the nature of prohibition does not lie).

§ 4.77 Judicial Review—Standards of Review—Review of Agency Determinations of Law

PAGE 573:

2. Dawn Joy Fashions, Inc. v. Commissioner of Labor, 90 N.Y.2d 102, 659 N.Y.S.2d 196, 681 N.E.2d 363 (1997)(agency's attempt to impose a "strict liability" for certain regulatory violations runs contrary to ordinary interpretation of statute and thus not entitled to deference and not upheld)

3. Ellis Center for Long Term Care v. DeBuono, 175 Misc.2d 443, 669 N.Y.S.2d 782 (3d Dep't 1998)(agency's method of calculating statewide average of reimburse-

§ 4.77 MUNICIPAL LAW Ch. 4

ment rates involves agency expertise and agency method upheld under reasonableness standard)

§ 4.78 Judicial Review—Standards of Review—Review of Agency Determinations of Fact Under the Substantial Evidence Test

PAGE 574:

7. Aria Contracting Corp. v. McGowan, 256 A.D.2d 1204, 684 N.Y.S.2d 93 (4th Dep't 1998)(agency credibility determinations essentially unassailable under substantial evidence standard); Ciotoli v. Goord, 256 A.D.2d 1192, 683 N.Y.S.2d 683 (4th Dep't 1998)(same); Goldsmith v. DeBuono, 245 A.D.2d 627, 665 N.Y.S.2d 727 (3d Dep't 1997)(testimony of two witnesses who observed patient abuse constitutes substantial evidence upon which agency properly based finding of patient abuse).

§ 4.81 Judicial Review—Standards of Review—Review of Administrative Discretion

PAGE 578:

5. Aria Contracting Corp. v. McGowan, 256 A.D.2d 1204, 684 N.Y.S.2d 93 (4th Dep't 1998)(upholding $34,000 fine and two-year suspension of license for asbestos removal in light of seriousness of violation and previous violation).

§ 4.82 Judicial Review—Statutes of Limitation Applicable to Judicial Review of Agency Action

PAGE 580:

9. AT & T Communications of New York, Inc. v. Public Service Comm'n, 231 A.D.2d 155, 659 N.Y.S.2d 362 (3d Dep't 1997)(regulated party could challenge tariff filed more than four months earlier because tariff only recently applied to regulated party).

10. *See also* MCI Telecommunications Corp. v. Public Service Comm'n, 231 A.D.2d 284, 659 N.Y.S.2d 563 (3d Dep't 1997)(request for agency reconsideration does not toll statute of limitations because decision to grant reconsideration is completely with agency's discretion and thus decision was "final and binding" for more than four months before petition filed).

Chapter 6

BUYING AND SELLING A SMALL BUSINESS

by
Mark S. Pelersi
Michele A. Santucci

Table of Sections

6.27	Due Diligence Investigation—Financial Issues—Financial Statements
6.30	___ ___ Tax Returns
6.34	Tax Issues for Buyer—Asset Purchase—Depreciation of Assets
6.40	___ ___ Patents, Franchises, Trademarks, Trade Names
6.66	Drafting the Buyer's Asset Purchase Agreement—Corporate or Other Name—New York State Sales Tax and Bulk Sale Notification
6.88	___ Covenant Not to Compete
6.102	Post Contract and Pre-closing—Environmental Searches and Testing
6.103	___ Certificate of Good Standing
6.114	Representing the Seller—Confidentiality Agreements
6.116	Tax Issues for the Seller—General Overview
6.117	___ Asset Sale
6.119	___ ___ Depreciation Recapture
6.120	___ ___ Capital Gains and Losses
6.122	___ ___ Income to Corporation
6.126	___ Stock Sale—Capital Gain or Loss
6.130	___ ___ I.R.C. 1244 Stock and Qualified Small Business Stock
6.150	Drafting the Seller's Asset Sale Agreement—Matters Respecting Real Property
6.153	___ UCC Bulk Sale Notices or Escrow Agreements in Lieu of UCC Bulk Sale Notices
6.154	___ New York State Sales Tax and Bulk Sale Notification
6.175	___ Covenants Not to Compete and Consulting Agreements
6.176	___ Notice to Customers and Suppliers
6.184	Post-contract and Pre-closing
6.188	Forms—Agreement of Purchase and Sale of Stock

Westlaw Electronic Research

See Westlaw Electronic Research Guide preceding the Summary of Contents.

§ 6.27   BUYING AND SELLING A SMALL BUSINESS   Ch. 6

§ 6.27   Due Diligence Investigation—Financial Issues—Financial Statements

PAGE 694:

2. PRACTICE POINTER: Unless required by an outside party, such as a lending institution or bonding company, most small businesses only have a Compilation Statement if any. Buyers often must rely on other investigative tools such as tax returns (income and sales tax), bank records and industry financial ratios.

§ 6.30   Due Diligence Investigation—Financial Issues—Tax Returns

PAGE 698:

[*Replace current text with the following.*]

    4. A Limited Liability Company ("LLC") taxed as a corporation files Form 1120.

[*Add to end of text.*]

The New York State Real Property Transfer Gains Tax was repealed effective for transfers occurring on or after June 15, 1996. Tax liability may be encountered for prior transactions. For a more detailed discussion see § 6.104.

§ 6.34   Tax Issues for Buyer—Asset Purchase—Depreciation of Assets

PAGE 702:

[*Add to end of section.*]

    I.R.C. § 179 expensing limits are:

        1998 ... $18,500
        1999 ... $19,000
        2000 ... $20,000
        2001 ... $24,000
        2003 ... $25,000.

§ 179 expense and the depreciation of assets also have further limitations and complications.[6]

    6. *See also*, Chapter 35 "Income Tax", infra.

§ 6.40   Tax Issues for Buyer—Asset Purchase—Patents, Franchises, Trademarks, Trade Names

PAGE 704:

[*Replace last paragraph with the following.*]

    Patents generally have a 20 year life.[1.1] Copyrights, which are also I.R.C. § 197 intangibles, are legally protected for the life of the author plus 70 years.[2]

Ch. 6   BUYING AND SELLING A SMALL BUSINESS   § 6.116

1.1   17 U.S.C.A. §§ 302–304.
2.   *Id.*

§ 6.66   Drafting the Buyer's Asset Purchase Agreement—Corporate or Other Name—New York State Sales Tax and Bulk Sale Notification

PAGE 723:

[*Replace note 6 with the following.*]

6.   Tax Law § 1147(c).

PAGE 744:

[*Replace section heading with the following.*]

§ 6.88   Drafting the Buyer's Stock Purchase Agreement—Covenant Not to Compete

§ 6.102   Post Contract and Pre-closing—Environmental Searches and Testing

PAGE 755:

[*Replace the third paragraph's last sentence with the following.*]

Therefore, an investigation of the real property to be acquired and any leased or previously owned property must be conducted.

§ 6.103   Post-contract and Pre-closing—Certificate of Good Standing

PAGE 756:

[*Replace the last sentence of **Practice Pointer** with the following.*]

The address for requesting Certificates from the Department of State is: New York State Department of State, Corporations and State Records Division, 41 State Street, Albany, New York 12231.

§ 6.114   Representing the Seller—Confidentiality Agreements

PAGE 763:

[*Replace the second sentence with the following.*]

They understandably fear that their business information may fall into the hands of competitors and be used against them.

§ 6.116   Tax Issues for the Seller—General Overview

PAGE 766:

1.   For taxpayers in marginal brackets above 15% (most business sellers), the long term capital gains tax rate for **purchases** made before January 1, 2000 is 20% even if the property is held more than five years.

27

§ 6.116 BUYING AND SELLING A SMALL BUSINESS   Ch. 6

For sales after December 31, 1997, assets held for more than 12 months qualify for long term capital gains tax treatment.

§ 6.117 Tax Issues for the Seller—Asset Sale

PAGE 765:

[*Add at end of section.*]

If the Seller is an S Corporation for tax purposes and sells property that had appreciated when the corporation was a C Corporation the corporation may be subject to built in gains tax on the sale even though the seller is a flow through entity (S Corporation), *see* I.R.C. § 1374.

§ 6.119 Tax Issues for the Seller—Asset Sale—Depreciation Recapture

PAGE 766:

[*Add to end of section.*]

To clarify, only the sale proceeds of a depreciated asset <u>in excess</u> of the asset's depreciated basis are allocated first to depreciation recapture.

When selling I.R.C. § 1250 property (generally depreciable buildings used in a trade or business) held more than 12 months for more than the property's tax basis special rules apply.

If an accelerated depreciation method (one resulting in depreciation deductions greater than if the straight line method were chosen) was used the depreciation taken in excess of what would have been allowed by the straight line method (accelerated depreciation) must be recognized as ordinary income, the balance of the gain up to the amount of straight-line depreciation taken is taxed at a 25% rate and any remaining gain is taxed at the regular long term capital gains tax rates.[4]

4. I.R.C.§ 1(h)

§ 6.120 Tax Issues for the Seller—Asset Sale—Capital Gains and Losses

PAGE 767:

[*Replace note 3 with the following.*]

3. I.R.C. §§ 1245 and 1250.

[*Add to end of section.*]

For sales after December 31, 1997 assets held for more than 12 months qualify for long term capital gains tax treatment.

§ 6.122 Tax Issues for Seller—Asset Sale—Income to Corporation

PAGE 768:

[*Add to end of section.*]

See I.R.C. § 1372 and Supplement § 6.117 regarding built in gains tax which may be imposed on S Corporations.

Note that a partnership is also a flow through entity.

§ 6.126 Tax Issues for Seller—Stock Sale—Capital Gain or Loss

PAGE 770:

[*Add to end of section.*]

For sales after December 31, 1997 the holding period for long term capital gain treatment is 12 months.

§ 6.130 Tax Issues for the Seller—Stock Sale—I.R.C. § 1244 Stock and Qualified Small Business Stock

PAGE 773:

[*Add to end of section.*]

The Tax Reform Act of 1997 allows a rollover option for Qualified Small Business (I.R.C. § 1202) stock sales. For sales after August 5, 1997 gain from the sale of Section 1202 stock may be rolled over, within 60 days of the sale, into the stock of another Section 1202 small business, including partnerships and S Corporations. The stock rolled over must have been held at least 6 months to qualify for the deferral, and Corporate taxpayers can not use this deferral section. To defer all gain, the cost of the new § 1202 stock must equal the sale proceeds of the old § 1202 stock. For the rollover provisions see I.R.C. § 1045.

There are many restrictions relating to I.R.C. § 1244 and § 1202 stock and the § 1045 rollover provisions. The I.R.C. Regulations and Revenue Ruling must be consulted.

§ 6.150 Drafting the Seller's Asset Sale Agreement—Matters Respecting Real Property

PAGE 792:

[*Replace current text with the following.*]

2. The agreement should state that the seller will convey the real property to the buyer on the closing date subject to specifically referenced items such as: ...

3. A clause allowing the seller to cure any defects or objections to title that come to the buyer's attention which buyer is unwilling to waive...

§ 6.153 Drafting the Seller's Asset Sale Agreement—UCC Bulk Sale Notices or Escrow Agreements in Lieu of UCC Bulk Sale Notices

PAGE 796:

[*Replace note 6 with the following.*]

6. *See* UCC § 6-105.

§ 6.154 Drafting the Seller's Asset Sale Agreement—New York State Sales Tax and Bulk Sale Notification

PAGE 797:

[*Replace fourth sentence of note 3 with the following.*]

If, within five business days after filing the notice of bulk sale with the Department, the Department notifies the buyer of a possible claim for taxes due, the buyer is prohibited from transferring money or any other consideration to the seller (except amounts in excess of the Department's claim).

§ 6.175 Drafting the Seller's Stock Sale Agreement—Covenants Not to Compete and Consulting Agreements

PAGE 816:

[*In the heading in the Main Volume replace the word "Asset" with the word "Stock".*]

§ 6.176 Drafting the Seller's Stock Sale Agreement—Notice to Customers and Suppliers

PAGE 817:

[*Replace the last sentence of note 1 with the following.*]

1. Where appropriate, the notice should also indicate that the same quality service or product will be provided by the buyer and that the past relationships and practices with the suppliers and customers will continue.

§ 6.184 Post-contract and Pre-closing

PAGE 823:

[*Replace second sentence of second paragraph with the following.*]

A competently drafted agreement will, through its many clauses, address the individual issues of the transaction and provide an outline of many of the items which must be reviewed or prepared for closing.

PAGE 825:

[*Replace fourth sentence of note 6 with the following.*]

6. If, within five business days after filing the notice of bulk sale with the Department, the Department notifies the buyer of

a possible claim for taxes due, the buyer is prohibited from transferring money or any other consideration to the seller (except amounts in excess of the Department's claim).

PAGE 826:

[*Replace note 10 with the following.*]

   10. *Id.*

[*Replace note 12 with the following.*]

   12. *Id.*

[*Replace note 13 with the following.*]

   13. *See* UCC § 6–105.

§ 6.188 Forms—Agreement of Purchase and Sale of Stock

PAGE 863:

[*Add at beginning of section.*]

It is suggested that a table of schedules, exhibits and attachments be added as the first attachment, with the name and a short description of each item.

PAGE 864:

[*Section 1.03, sub-section (iii) should be deleted.*]

PAGE 874:

[*At third-to-last line on page, replace "Exhibit 11" with*]

   Exhibit K

PAGE 875:

[*Add right before Section 2.20.*]

   NOTE: The agreement should note that there is no Exhibit L (or a new exhibit appropriate to your agreement should be inserted at Exhibit L).

PAGE 885:

[*In section 5.12, replace "Exhibit R0" with*]

   Exhibit R